Complete
Psychology

Editor: GRAHAM DAVEY

Complete Psychology

I. ALBERY

C. CHANDLER

A. FIELD

D. JONES

D. MESSER

S. MOORE

C. STERLING

Hodder Arnold

A MEMBER OF THE HODDER HEADLINE GROUP

Orders: please contact Bookpoint Ltd, 130 Milton Park, Abingdon, Oxon OX14 4SB. Telephone: (44) 01235 827720. Fax: (44) 01235 400454. Lines are open from 9.00-5.00, Monday to Saturday, with a 24-hour message answering service. You can also order through our website www.hoddereducation.co.uk.

British Library Cataloguing in Publication Data
A catalogue record for this title is available from the British Library

ISBN-10: 0 340 81568 X
ISBN-13: 978 0 340 81568 7

First Published 2004
Impression number   10 9 8 7 6 5 4 3
Year   2007 2006

Typeset by Fakenham Photosetting Limited, Fakenham, Norfolk
Printed in Dubai for Hodder Arnold, an imprint of Hodder Education, a member of the Hodder Headline Group, 338 Euston Road, London NW1 3BH.

Acknowledgements

Graham Davey:
Helping to produce this text book was one of the most intense — yet rewarding — experiences of my career, and it shows what can be achieved with the dedication, good-will and expertise of a excellent mixture of psychologists and publishers! I would especially like to apologise to all the contributors, whom I either pestered or bullied during the course of the writing of this text — but I also want to thank each one of them for their thoughtful and highly relevant contributions. Also in need of thanks are those many academic psychologists who took the time to review various aspects of this text before publication, and to advise on the contents. They are all listed on p. vii. I must thank my close family, friends and colleagues for having to put up with me talking about this book non-stop throughout the summer of 2003! They include my partner Benie, who helped put together much of the material in the Health Psychology chapter, and my daughters Kate and Lizzie, who found time to soundly criticise every cover design. Andy Field bought me copious pints of Stella Artois when I needed it, and tried manfully to prevent me singing *You've Lost That Loving Feeling* at the top of my voice after I had drunk them. Finally, a bucketload of thanks should go to Emma Woolf, the commissioning editor for this text. She had the vision to fully commit to a text of this kind when the UK market was crying out for such a book and when other publishers were procrastinating. She has been an excellent colleague and friend over the past year.

Ian P. Albery:
I'd like to thank everyone involved in the inception and production of this project at Hodder, but most especially Emma Woolf for her tireless work and, for me, essential motivation. Also, Henry, Beth and Will for being a source of necessary distraction, mum and dad for not showing any signs of boredom when bombarded with details of the Hodder project, and finally the CAR I adore.

Chris Chandler:
For Max, Guy and Diane.
And also for Moira and Nick.
And in memory of Kate and Cliff.

Andy Field:
To Graham, because:
'You never close your eyes anymore when I kiss your lips,
And there's no tenderness like before in your fingertips,
You're trying hard not to show it (baby),
But baby, baby I know it. . .
You've lost that lovin' feeling,

Whoa, that lovin' feeling,
You've lost that lovin' feeling,
Now it's gone, gone, gone etc.'
And to Leonora because her lips are much nicer to kiss than Graham's (not that I've kissed his lips
obviously. . .).

Dai Jones:
My deepest thanks and love go to Sara, for putting up with me during the writing, and Poppy, for making me
laugh. Thanks also to Emma Woolf, for her guidance and leadership, and Graham Davey, for his careful and
constructive suggestions.

David Messer:
Many thanks to family and friends for tolerance and support.

Simon Moore:
My thanks to Chris and Richard for their foresight and sacrifice in terms of my academic opportunities. My
thanks to Hannah for her encouragement and support; to Matthew for providing valuable feedback and
suggestions; lastly to Pablo who kept me company whilst I was chained to my computer during this project.

Christopher Sterling:
For Candan and Alexander.

List of Advisors

The authors wish to thank the following for their advice and assistance during the writing of this text. Most advised on relevant content issues, while some advised on style and presentation:

Professor Martyn Barrett (University of Surrey)
Professor Pam Briggs (Northumbria University)
Dr Peter Clifton (University of Sussex)
Professor Martin Conway (University of Durham)
D. Charles Crook (Loughborough University)
Professor Ian Deary (University of Edinburgh)
Professor Hugh Foot (Strathclyde University
Professor Adrian Furnham (University College, London)
Professor Vicky Lewis (The Open University)
Dr Jeremy Miles (University of York)
Professor Karin Mogg (University of Southampton)
Dr Philip Quinlan (University of York)
Dr Martin Rosier (Thames Valley University)
Professor Elizabeth Valentine (Royal Holloway)
Professor Margie Wetherall (The Open University)
Dr Dan Wright (University of Sussex)
Dr Peter Wright (University of Edinburgh)

Picture Credits

The authors and publishers would like to thank the following for permission to reproduce material in this book:

Page 3, © Reuters/CORBIS; page 4, © Shai Ginott/CORBIS; page 5, © David Turnley/CORBIS; page 11, © CORBIS; page 12, © Hulton-Deutsch Collection/CORBIS; page 20, © CORBIS; page 22, British Psychological Society; page 25, Sue Wilkinson; page 31, Fremantle Media Stills Library; page 43 (left), © Bill Miles/CORBIS; page 43 (right), © CORBIS; page 45, © Strauss/Curtis/CORBIS; page 55, Camerapress; page 60, © CORBIS; page 73, © Rune Hellestad/CORBIS; page 122, © Bettman/CORBIS; page 128, Oxford Scientific Films Ltd; page 184, © Phil Schermeister/CORBIS; page 185, © Jorn Tomter/CORBIS; page 187, © David Muench/CORBIS; page 188 (top), © Hulton-Deutsch Collection/CORBIS; page 188 (left), © Jorn Tomter/CORBIS; page 188 (right), © Lester Lefkowitz/CORBIS; page 195, Associated Press; page 226, © Dmitri Lindt, TempSport/CORBIS; page 233, Endel Tulving; page 234, © Bettman/CORBIS; page 237, © Siner Jeff/CORBIS SYGMA; page 239, © Ralf-Finn Hestoft/CORBIS; page 256, Hulton Archive/Spy; page 273, Associated Press; page 278, Rex Features; page 285 (left), Albert Bandura, Stanford University; page 285 (top), Associated Press; page 285 (middle), © Farrell Grehan/CORBIS; page 285 (bottom), © Rick Friedman/CORBIS; page 286, © Bernard Bisson/CORBIS SYGMA; page 289, Leonard Lessin/FBPA/Science Photo Library; page 290 (a), Dr Yorgos Nikas/Science Photo Library; page 290 (b), Edelmann/Science Photo Library; page 290 (c), Neil Bromhall/Science Photo Library; page 290 (d), © Owen Franken/CORBIS; page 293, © Jose Luis Pelaez, Inc./CORBIS; page 294 (left), David Montford/Photofusion; page 294 (right), Ron Gregory/Life File Photo Library; page 299 (top left), Judy Harrison/Photofusion; page 299 (top right), B. Apicella/Photofusion; page 299 (middle), Judy Harrison/Photofusion; page 299 (bottom right), Judy Harrison/Photofusion; page 299 (bottom right), B. Apicella/Photofusion; page 305, Nicola Sutton/Life Photo Library; page 318© Annie Griffiths Belt/CORBIS; page 324, Angela Mayard/Life File Photo Library; page 343 (left), © David Turnley/CORBIS; page 343 (right), © Norbert Schaefer/CORBIS; page 349, Nicola Sutton/Life File Photo Library; page 358 (top), © Richard Olivier/CORBIS; page 358 (middle), © Helen King/CORBIS; page 358 (bottom), © Adam Woolfitt/CORBIS; page 363, Akg-images; page 368, Bob Battersby; page 374, from *Psychology & Life* by Philip Zimbardo © P.G. Zimbardo, Stanford University; page 376, PA Photos; page 388, provided by TV Licensing, March 2004; page 391, Bob Battersby; page 399, Rex Features; page 403, © Jennie Woodcock; Reflections Photolibrary/CORBIS; page 417 (left), Alex Freund/Getty Images; page 417 (right), © Tom & Dee Ann McCarthy/CORBIS; page 425, © Patrick Ward/CORBIS; page 426, © LWA-Dann Tardif/CORBIS; page 434, © Museum of London; page 442, PA Photos; page 443, Actionplus; page 444 (left), © Neema Frederic/CORBIS SYGMA; page 444 (right), © Wu Xiaoling/Xinhua Photo/Corbis; page 454, © Jennie Woodcock; Reflections Photolibrary/CORBIS; page 456, Ronald Grant Archive; page 459, Andrew Ward/Life File Photo Library; page 462, Richard T. Nowitz/Science Photo Library; page 464, Actionplus; page 467 (top), Actionplus; page 467 (bottom), Actionplus; page 468, Anthony Redpath/CORBIS; page 474, Actionplus; page 485, Jeremy Hoare/Life File Photo Library; page 487, Granada Visual; page 507, Actionplus; page 509, Ronald Grant Archive; page 511 (left), Matilda and Emily Pearce; page 511 (right), Hank Morgan/Science Photo Library; page 512, Ronald Grant Archive; page 517 (a), © Gianni Dagli Orti/CORBIS; page 517 (b), © Archivo Iconografico, S.A./CORBIS; page 517 (c and d), © Bettmann/CORBIS; page 518 (b), © Bettmann/CORBIS; page 518 (c)© Bettmann/CORBIS; page 518 (d), © Bettmann/CORBIS; page 522, © Langevin Jacques/CORBIS SYGMA; page 531, © Bryn Colton/Assignments Photographers/CORBIS; page 534, BBC; page 549 (left), Rex Features; page 549 (right), © Tom Bean/CORBIS; page 559, Bob Battersby; page 561, Actionplus; page 563, British Psychological Society; page 578, Redferns Music Picture Library Ltd; page 598, Ronald Grant Archive; page 605, Ronald Grant Archive; page 619 (top), Staying Alive/Viacom/KFF/NAT; page 619 (middle), Department of Health; page 619 (bottom), Department of Transport; page 627, Sealand Aerial Photography Ltd; page 637, © Rune Hellestad/CORBIS; page 641, Actionplus; page 649, A. Barrington Brown/Science Photo Library; page 699, Science Photo Library; page 712, British Psychological Society; page 714, Peter de Trey-White/Photofusion; page 715, Jacky Chapman/Photofusion; page 717, Department for Transport; page 719, BBC; page 736, © Patrick Ward/CORBIS; page 737, Photofusion/Jacky Chapman. Cartoons pages 205, 249, 274, 552 and 600 courtesy of www.CartoonStock.com.

Every effort has been made to obtain necessary permission with reference to copyright material. The publishers apologise if inadvertently any sources remain unacknowledged and will be glad to make the necessary arrangements at the earliest opportunity.

Contents

1 Introduction 1

Section 1 Conceptual and historical issues 9
2 Approaches to psychology 10
3 Psychology as science 28
4 Bias in psychology 42
5 Issues and debates in psychology 53

Section 2 Psychobiology 65
6 Introduction to psychobiology 66
7 Basic foundations of psychobiology 86
8 Animal learning and cognition 120
9 Motivation, brain reward mechanisms and behaviour 138
10 Emotion and sleep 150
11 Perceptual systems and motor control 161

Section 3 Cognitive psychology 179
12 Perception 180
13 Attention 204
14 Memory 220
15 Language 246
16 Thinking and reasoning 263

Section 4 Developmental psychology 281
17 An introduction to developmental psychology 282
18 Cognitive development: thinking, information and representations 299
19 Communication, language and literacy 321
20 The self, others and social relationships 340

Section 5 Social psychology 361
21 Issues and themes in social psychology 362
22 Attitudes, persuasion and attitude change 376

Complete
Psychology

23 Attribution	395
24 Impression formation and social interaction	409
25 Social influence and group processes	429
Section 6 Personality and intelligence	**451**
26 The psychology of emotion	452
27 Motivation	464
28 The self and social identity	477
29 Personality	487
30 Intelligence	514
31 Psychometric testing	530
Section 7 Abnormal, clinical and health psychology	**543**
32 Basic issues in psychopathology	544
33 Psychological disorders	558
34 Treating psychological disorders	595
35 Health psychology	618
Section 8 Research methods and statistics	**635**
36 Why do we need research methods?	636
37 Collecting data	652
38 Summarising data	671
39 Going beyond your sample	692
Appendix 1 Careers and study skills	**711**
i Being a psychologist	712
ii Study skills in psychology	723
Appendix 2 *Probability values of z-scores from the normal distribution*	**751**
References	**759**
Name Index	**809**
Subject Index	**823**

Introduction

What is psychology?

Psychology is about *people*. In particular, it is about why people do the things they do. It is also about *groups of people*. Why do people in the same group behave differently? Why are some people leaders and other people followers? Psychology is also about *helping people*. It enables us to develop treatments for psychological problems, put together effective health campaigns, facilitate education, help catch criminal offenders, and increase productivity and health in the workplace. Psychology is also about the very *basis of our biology*. These are the things we take for granted and never even have to think about: our response to pain, riding a bicycle, experiencing a visual illusion or learning to speak. Psychology is also about *science*, and the scientific investigation of our human nature and the social and biological contexts in which we live.

But in addition to all this – and unlike most other disciplines – psychology is about *you*. When you learn about psychology, you don't just learn about why other people do the things they do, you also learn about yourself – both as a social being and a biological organism. It is very rarely that a student of psychology completes a course without encountering an unexpected insight into their own psychology, or acquiring some knowledge that contributes to their personal growth as an individual. That's quite a lot! But that is why psychology is one of the most popular undergraduate degrees around the world, and why psychology at secondary level in the UK has expanded rapidly since the mid-1990s. It is difficult to think of any other discipline that gives the student a broader and more rounded education than

psychology. The psychology graduate doesn't just learn about people's behaviour, their personality and intelligence (the kinds of knowledge you might think useful in many areas of applied psychology, such as occupational psychology, clinical psychology, educational psychology and so on), they will inevitably acquire knowledge of the practical skills necessary to interact with people in a variety of occupations and careers. In understanding and comparing psychological theories, they will also acquire skills of critical thinking and analysis. In addition, the need to construct and analyse psychological studies will provide them with valuable methodology and statistical skills that will be prized by many employers. Finally, psychology graduates will also take with them a knowledge of computing and presentational skills, which are now part and parcel of an undergraduate degree in the social and biological sciences.

You will encounter a lot of people unfamiliar with psychology who claim it is all 'just common sense'. Well, much of it *is* common sense – we all have to use a bit of psychology to negotiate our lives, regardless of whether or not we have studied it. However, much of what seems like common sense in psychology is often so only with hindsight. For example, one of the simplest rules of behaviour is that if you reward someone for doing something, they are more likely to do it again (the principle of reinforcement – see Chapter 8, page 130). Yet how many of us actually verbalise that rule and use it consistently? Certainly not the mother who responds to her child's tired tantrum in the street by buying them a toy or magazine, nor the person who showers his/her

Introduction
Graham Davey

partner with attention and affection when they are having a jealous sulk at a party. So while some psychology is common sense, much of what we learn about people when we study them closely is counterintuitive – and some of it is downright strange! Focus Point 1.1 gives you the flavour of some of the unusual facts you will come across during the course of your reading of this book.

FOCUS POINT 1.1

Is psychology just common sense?

- Individuals who have reported being abducted by space aliens are prone to exhibiting false memory effects – that is, in laboratory tests of memory they claim to recall and recognise items they have never previously been shown (see Chapter 33, page 575).
- People who are shown a film of a car crash and then asked how quickly the cars were going when they 'smashed into' each other estimate the speed up to 30 per cent faster than people asked the same question, but with the words 'hit' or 'collided with' used instead of 'smashed into' (see Chapter 14, page 237).
- Most people have an optimistic bias. If asked to respond to the statement 'Compared with others your age, are your chances of developing cancer greater than them/same as them/less than them', most people will judge themselves as being *less* at risk than their contemporaries. This is why it is often so difficult to get people to switch from unhealthy behaviours (such as smoking) to healthy ones (such as exercising regularly) (see Chapter 35, page 621).
- People tend to accept vague and general personality descriptions as being uniquely applicable to them without realising that the same descriptions can be applied to just about anyone! If you give a group of people a personality test, then ignore their answers and give everyone the same general positive feedback, they will each believe the description is true of them! This is what makes some people so gullible when they read the vaguely worded predictions in horoscopes (see Chapter 28, page 482).
- Your spouse or partner is probably the person you think you would find it easiest to recognise. However, an individual with the disorder *apperceptive agnosia* cannot recognise familiar objects (such as tables, chairs, books etc.) because they have a perceptual impairment. Sufferers often cannot point out a shape in a busy picture or recognise an object from an unusual angle. One sufferer couldn't recognise his wife when she was standing in front of him, but could recognise her when she moved or when she spoke (see Chapter 12, page 190).
- Would you raise the alarm if smoke suddenly started billowing into the room you were in? In one study, students attended an interview to discuss life at their university. While they were filling in a preliminary questionnaire, smoke was pumped into the room. Participants were either by themselves, with two confederates who completely ignored the smoke, or with two other people (non-confederates) who were strangers to them. About 75 per cent of people who were alone reported the smoke, although only about 38 per cent of those in the other two groups did so (see Chapter 24, page 423).

The potential of psychology

The largest proportion of students who apply to psychology degree programmes in the UK do so because they claim to have an interest in becoming an 'applied' psychologist. That is, they want to apply their knowledge of psychology in some way – perhaps as a clinical psychologist, an occupational psychologist or maybe as one of the increasing numbers of sports psychologists. The British Psychological Society (BPS) has an increasing number of Divisions and Special Groups whose purpose is to develop and regulate the application of psychology to ever more specific, and important, areas of daily life. The BPS has Divisions of Clinical Psychology, Educational and Child Psychology, Occupational Psychology, Forensic Psychology, Counselling Psychology, Teachers and Researchers in Psychology, Health Psychology, and Neuropsychology (see http://www.bps.org.uk/ sub-syst/subsystems_div1.cfm).

However, psychology is not just about generating professionals and practitioners who apply their practical skills in specific settings, it is also about personal understanding and personal growth, and to this extent the discipline has a duty to ensure that psychological knowledge informs daily life. One of

the mission objectives of the BPS is, in its broadest sense, to 'take psychology to the people'. This means finding ways not only of helping people to understand themselves and why they do the things they do, but also making people aware of the range of activities that psychology can be applied to – with positive effects.

To get an idea of the range of activities psychologists have been involved in during the past few years – some more extraordinary than others – have a look at Table 1.1. It draws on some items taken from the BBC news website (http://news.bbc.co.uk).

TABLE 1.1

SOME HEADLINES FROM THE BBC NEWS WEBSITE, TO GIVE AN IDEA OF THE RANGE OF ACTIVITIES TO WHICH PSYCHOLOGISTS APPLY THEIR SKILLS AND EXPERTISE

Date	Headline and Summary	Expertise
10 October 2003	**Profiler aids murder inquiry** Detectives hunting the killer of Margaret Irvine will consult a behavioural psychologist in an effort to establish a profile of the person responsible.	Offender profiling
6 September 2003	**Psychologists aid football policing** UK psychologists are to advise the Portuguese police on how best to handle England's football fans during Euro 2004.	Understanding the dynamics of crowd behaviour

TABLE 1.1	CONTINUED	
SOME HEADLINES FROM THE BBC NEWS WEBSITE, TO GIVE AN IDEA OF THE RANGE OF ACTIVITIES TO WHICH PSYCHOLOGISTS APPLY THEIR SKILLS AND EXPERTISE		
Date	**Headline and Summary**	**Expertise**
3 February 2003	**Interview style helps child witnesses** Psychologists are encouraging police to use a special interview technique to get more accurate and reliable evidence from child witnesses. Research published in the *Journal of Criminal Psychology* shows that when a technique known as cognitive interviewing is used, children recall more details and are less likely to be influenced by leading questions.	Eye-witness testimony: providing procedures to ensure that children can act as reliable witnesses
21 January 2003	**Tories' psychologist to tempt women** The Conservatives have brought in a psychologist to sort out the party's problems recruiting women candidates.	Skills training for potential MPs (including public speaking, social skills and listening skills)
22 May 2002	**Evolution of supercats** Anyone who has ever owned a cat will know that there is no limit to feline charm. Now a US psychologist has come up with evidence that nature is giving a helping hand. Nicholas Nicastro, of Cornell University, believes moggies are evolving into supercats that are better able to exploit humans.	Applying evolutionary theory to the behaviour of pets

TABLE 1.1 CONTINUED

SOME HEADLINES FROM THE BBC NEWS WEBSITE, TO GIVE AN IDEA OF THE RANGE OF ACTIVITIES TO WHICH PSYCHOLOGISTS APPLY THEIR SKILLS AND EXPERTISE

Date	Headline and Summary	Expertise
10 January 2003	**Rhinos turn to mind power** They say that success is all in the mind – and Super League outfit Leeds Rhinos hope to prove it. The club has just become the first in Rugby League to appoint a sports psychologist. 'I'm here to help with the mental side. In the first instance I'll work to bring the squad together. Second, I want to build self-confidence.'	Sports psychology
26 July 2002	**Building golf courses using environmental psychology** The study of environmental psychology has built a substantial amount of information on how surrounding environments affect humans. Almost every golf course architecture book ever written mentions the importance of aesthetics and how they can subconsciously influence the golfer. Studies appear to have recurrent features that would help improve the experience of golf. Environmental psychology is a relatively new field of study that examines the interrelationship between environments and human behaviour. It has a lot to offer in creating landscapes (e.g. golf courses) that are responsive to the requirements of humans who will be taking part in the setting (e.g. the golfers). Cognitive informational factors such as coherence, legibility, complexity and mystery all help to create *experience*, whether it be unpleasant or pleasurable. These elements can benefit golf course architects when creating golf holes that impart feelings of grandeur, intimidation or possibly confidence within the golfer.	Environmental psychology

Introduction
Graham Davey

The psychology curriculum

This book has been written with the UK psychology undergraduate in mind. However, it assumes no prior knowledge of psychology and so should be quite accessible to the interested lay person, as well as to those studying psychology at a range of different educational levels, including Access courses, GCSE, A and AS level, college evening courses, diploma courses, and to those studying disciplines related to psychology (such as medicine, nursing, speech therapy and counselling).

The book's curriculum is based on the most recent revision of the BPS's Qualifying Examination syllabus (October 2001). This syllabus sets the criteria for the accreditation of undergraduate psychology degrees in the United Kingdom, and only those students who take BPS-accredited degree programmes will be eligible on completing their degree to register as a full graduate member of the BPS. Such membership is essential if the student wishes to pursue a career as a practising psychologist (e.g. as a clinical or educational psychologist), or become a Chartered Psychologist once they have acquired the appropriate training and experience (see Appendix 1i).

This book acts as a comprehensive foundation for the full undergraduate syllabus, and offers a detailed introduction to all the main areas of psychology required for BPS accreditation. It covers eight major areas of psychology. The seven core areas are:

- the conceptual and historical issues on which psychology is based
- psychobiology (formerly the biological foundations of behaviour)
- cognitive psychology (covering the areas of perception, attention, memory, language and thinking)
- developmental psychology
- social psychology
- personality and intelligence, and
- an introduction to research methods and statistics.

In addition to these, this book includes an eighth section, which deals with abnormal, clinical and health psychology. Abnormal and clinical psychology is already an established topic of study in many undergraduate degree programmes, and health psychology is a rapidly developing area that is beginning to find its way on to undergraduate curricula as a precursor to postgraduate vocational courses in this area.

The eight core areas in this book are supported by a comprehensive chapter on study skills, designed specifically for psychology undergraduates, which covers basic study principles, tips on lecture note-taking, writing essays and laboratory reports, and revision and exam skills. A separate chapter on careers gives the reader an in-depth understanding of how psychologists are employed, and this is illustrated with professionals' own insights into their specialised areas of psychology.

Apart from ensuring full coverage of the most recent psychology curriculum, we have aimed to present this material in an accessible and structured way. The full-colour presentation of this book, with plentiful illustrative material, is designed to make your reading and learning experience as pleasant as possible. All chapters contain highlighted Focus Points to draw your attention to interesting or important facts and concepts. Chapters also contain Applications and Research Methods boxes, which are designed to provide you with examples of practical applications of psychological knowledge and familiarise you with the different types of research methodologies used across the differing areas of psychology. Finally, each chapter provides suggestions for activities that will facilitate learning and understanding; further support and information are available on the book's website at www.completepsychology.co.uk

Finally, despite being geared to the syllabus designed by the BPS for UK higher education institutions, the curriculum presented in this book is an eclectic one that will map very closely on to contemporary psychology curricula in Europe, Asia and the USA, so feel free to use it wherever you may live or study.

Section one

Dai Jones

Conceptual and Historical Issues

2	Approaches to psychology	10
3	Psychology as science	28
4	Bias in psychology	42
5	Issues and debates in psychology	53

2

Approaches to psychology

Route map of the chapter

In this chapter we will look at the ways in which psychologists go about understanding human behaviour. We'll do this in two ways. First, we will look at where psychology came from and how it developed. This will help us to understand how our ideas of what psychology is, and should be, have changed. We will then look at how psychology is approached today, and see that there are six main theoretical approaches. We will cover each of these individually, discuss their main assumptions, and evaluate the strengths and weaknesses of each.

Introduction

How do psychologists go about trying to understand human behaviour? You've probably heard a range of different theories that explain human behaviour. For example, that 'it's all in the unconscious', or 'it's all in the genes', or 'it's the result of learning'. Are these all part of psychology? Why are there so many different kinds of explanation? We'll answer these questions in this chapter. We'll see that there are indeed several different approaches to psychology, and these give different kinds of explanations of human behaviour. The different approaches work together to give a fuller picture of behaviour than one approach alone can provide. We'll start, though, by looking at where psychology came from and how it developed. If we understand the history of psychology we should be able to get a better grasp of what psychology is like today.

A brief history of psychology

It has been said that 'psychology has a long past, but its real history is short' (Ebbinghaus, 1908: 3). The standard view of psychology's history is that it stretches back to Ancient Greek philosophers, but only became independent when Wilhelm Wundt founded a psychology laboratory at Leipzig in 1879. However, in the last 30 years, approaches to its history have changed from giving a list of events to understanding the contexts within which the discipline developed (Benjamin, 1997). We'll try to give a flavour of this approach in outlining a brief history of psychology.

Before psychology

The idea that psychology can be traced back to the Ancient Greeks comes about because of the kinds of questions philosophers like Plato and Aristotle asked. The Greeks tried to answer questions about personality types and the association between the mind and the body. Such questions are part of psychology today but, as we shall see, psychology uses rather different methods to answer questions.

The way psychology is today has been shaped by the work of philosophers since the Greeks. The Greeks started a tradition of rational thought, trying to explain things using logical reasoning. This was developed by seventeenth-century philosophers like Descartes, Locke and Hobbes. Descartes claimed there was a separation between the mechanical body, which could be investigated through science, and the spiritual soul, which was a gift of God (the principle of Cartesian Dualism). Locke and Hobbes, by contrast, claimed that only matter existed, that the mind was the result of the operation of nerves and the brain, and that ideas were acquired from the environment. This led to a concentration on physical explanations of phenomena, and a belief that the mind is a side-effect of the material brain. This inhibited the development of a science of mind during the seventeenth and eighteenth centuries because the mind was viewed as not worth investigating (Leahey, 2001).

Philosophers were not the only ones asking questions about human nature. Theologians, doctors and teachers all tried to understand human nature. What makes people good or bad? How can we explain madness? How do children learn? Again, these are all questions that are part of psychology. Of course, philosophy, theology, medicine and education are still around today, and still asking the same kinds of questions. So why do we have psychology? All of these disciplines are doing what Richards (2002) calls *reflexive discourse* – talking about human nature. They differ in the methods they use to answer questions, and the kinds of answers that are looked for (theology, for example, tries to find answers in religious doctrine). Psychology came about as a new kind of reflexive discourse because people began to want a way of using *science* to explain human nature.

The emergence of psychology

The usual story about the birth of psychology (as mentioned above) is that Wilhelm Wundt opened a psychology laboratory in Leipzig in 1879 and started a new discipline. However, psychology actually developed gradually over the course of the nineteenth century, and a range of forms of psychology existed before Wundt's lab opened. The idea that Wundt was the founder of psychology is now seen as an origin myth, with Wundt being chosen because he was the first to do experiments in psychology (Jones and Elcock, 2001). Modern histories describe the emergence of psychology as a logical progression from how people were describing human nature. So, let's look at how psychology emerged.

Forerunners of psychology

The late eighteenth and early nineteenth centuries saw an increasing interest in the range of mental faculties humans possessed, in where these faculties

came from, and in how people differed in their capabilities. The discipline of phrenology claimed that faculties were performed by organs in the brain, and tried to map the locations of these organs on phrenology busts (such as that in the accompanying photo). The discipline of faculty psychology, taught in Church-based universities in the USA, tried to identify faculties that could be improved, with the appropriate moral guidance. Neither approach used scientific methods to investigate these faculties, but they had the effect of preparing people for the idea of a scientific psychology (Richards, 2002).

A more scientific approach to understanding human nature came from physiology. During the nineteenth century, physiologists developed better understandings of how nerves and sense organs worked, and started to investigate mental processes in perception. Science was getting closer to investigating mental life, but was inhibited by the dominance of the Church. Human nature was still widely seen as a gift from God and outside the scope of natural science. For a science of mind to become possible, human nature had to be made natural. This happened with the development of evolutionary thought.

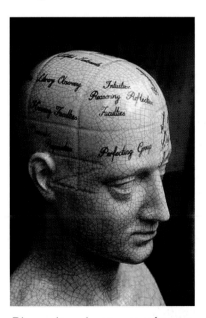

Phrenology busts are often used to represent psychology, but actually date back to before the development of the discipline.

The theory of evolution

Evolutionary thought suggests that species change over time. Evolutionary theories started appearing in the late eighteenth century, but few people were convinced. This changed with Charles Darwin's formulation of a theory of evolution by natural selection (1859/1959). This quickly became accepted, and firmly located humans in the animal kingdom, opening the possibility of psychology as part of natural science.

A major advocate of the evolutionary approach was Herbert Spencer. He developed an adaptational psychology (1855/1897) that investigated how individuals acquire and pass on psychological characteristics. The most notable example of this is Spencer's formulation of Social Darwinism – the view that natural selection should be allowed to run its course in the way it affected the human species. For Spencer, individuals differed in their fitness to thrive in society, and passed on their degree of fitness to their offspring. Spencer argued that governments should not intervene to help the poor and weak because this would allow them to survive in the face of evolutionary pressure, overturning the process of evolution. Instead, Spencer argued, the poor and weak should be weeded out by natural selection. This view continues to influence some attempts to explain differences between groups in society (Gould, 1997). More generally, Spencer's work laid the foundations for comparative psychology, which compared human behaviours to those of other animals, and for Francis Galton's work on individual differences and the inheritance of psychological traits. This approach was to have a fundamental influence on the development of psychology.

The early schools of psychology

Psychology grew quickly from the 1880s onwards, but it soon became apparent that people had different views of what psychology should be about. Some wanted to explain universal aspects of consciousness, some wanted to apply psychology to social problems, and still others wanted to develop therapeutic techniques. These different purposes needed different kinds of theories and different

Herbert Spencer (1820–1903), the father of British adaptational psychology.

methods. Soon different groups of psychologists emerged, divided in terms of their views of the appropriate subject matter and methods of psychology. These groups became known as the early 'schools of psychology', and included those described below.

Structuralism

A development of Wundt's work that emphasised the search for the structure of consciousness through introspection.

Functionalism

Functionalism attempted to explain how mental functions enabled humans to behave in ways that were effective for survival. It introduced a focus on application, but it became necessary to focus on behaviour rather than consciousness as the subject matter of psychology.

Behaviourism

Behaviourism was the logical consequence of the shift to studying behaviour. Behaviourism emphasised the role of the environment in guiding behaviour.

Gestalt

Gestalt was a German school of psychology, which rejected the reductionism of other approaches, and emphasised instead holistic aspects of mental processes. Its major insights were in the areas of perception and problem-solving, but it also influenced social psychology.

Psychoanalysis

While American psychology focused on behaviour and German psychology on consciousness, Sigmund Freud developed a psychology of the unconscious. Freud concentrated on investigating the causes of mental disorders, explaining them with a theory based on the idea of conflict in components of the unconscious.

TABLE 2.1

NOTABLE DATES IN THE HISTORY OF PSYCHOLOGY

1650	René Descartes proposes the separation of mind and body (Cartesian dualism)
1651	Hobbes suggests mental life is composed of ideas
1690	Locke proposes that the newborn mind is a blank slate (*tabula rasa*)
1855	Spencer publishes *Principles of Psychology*
1859	Darwin publishes *The Origin of Species*
1860	Fechner publishes *Elements of Psychophysics*
1861	Broca identifies speech areas in the brain through autopsy
1869	Galton publishes *Hereditary Genius*
1872	Darwin publishes *The Expression of the Emotions in Man and Animals*
1873	Wundt publishes *Principles of Physiological Psychology*
1875	The Psychological Society of Great Britain formed; ends in 1879
1876	First issue of *Mind: a quarterly journal of psychology and philosophy* published
1879	Wundt opens experimental psychology laboratory at Leipzig
1880	Galton introduces use of questionnaires
1884	Hall sets up first experimental psychology laboratory in the USA
1885	Ebbinghaus publishes *Memory*

TABLE 2.1   CONTINUED

NOTABLE DATES IN THE HISTORY OF PSYCHOLOGY

1890	James publishes *Principles of Psychology*
1892	Hall founds American Psychological Association
1898	First experimental psychology laboratories established in Britain, by W. H. R. Rivers
1899	Thorndike publishes *Animal Intelligence*
1900	Freud publishes *The Interpretation of Dreams*
1901	British Psychological Society founded
1904	Spearman proposes concept of general intelligence
1905	Binet and Simon develop first intelligence tests
1906	Pavlov publishes findings on classical conditioning
1912	Wertheimer describes the phi phenomenon, the first account of Gestalt psychology
1913	Watson publishes 'Psychology as the behaviourist views it'
1916	Stanford–Binet IQ test developed
1929	Boring publishes *A History of Experimental Psychology*
1932	Bartlett publishes *Remembering*
1938	Skinner publishes *The Behaviour of Organisms*
1951	Rogers publishes *Client-Centred Therapy*
1952	Translation into English of Piaget's *The Origin of Intelligence in the Child*
1953	Skinner publishes *Science and Human Behaviour*
1956	Miller publishes work on the 'magic number' 7±2; Bruner, Goodnow and Austin publish *A Study of Thinking*; beginnings of cognitive psychology
1967	Neisser publishes *Cognitive Psychology*
1970	*Journal of Cross-cultural Psychology* first published
1974	American Psychological Association decides, by vote, that homosexuality is not a disorder

Theoretical approaches to psychology

Up until the 1950s it was common to characterise psychology in terms of the different schools that psychologists adhered to. For most psychologists their favoured school was behaviourism. However, after the Second World War the discipline of psychology diversified considerably, and a range of fields of study began to be identified – for example, social psychology, child development and learning theory. At the same time, psychologists started to use different ways to investigate phenomena. Two psychologists studying the same field might approach a topic using quite different approaches to investigation and to theory development, and produce different kinds of explanation (see Focus Point 2.1). It's now usual to characterise psychology in terms of fields of study and the theoretical approaches used in those fields. This book is organised according to the different fields of study in contemporary psychology and this section provides an overview of the different approaches that are used in the various fields.

FOCUS POINT 2.1

Ways of explaining

Different approaches to psychology exist because a given psychological phenomenon, such as emotion, can be explained in a range of different ways. For example, emotions can be explained as a set of cognitive thought processes, or as a set of physiological brain processes. The classic illustration is of explaining a handshake. A handshake can be explained from a range of different approaches, as follows.

- To the behaviourist, the handshake could be the result of previous conditioning, having been associated with some reward.
- To the psychoanalyst, the handshake could be the result of a desire for physical contact.
- To the cognitive psychologist, the handshake would be the result of purposive mental processes – for example, the result of consciously deciding to show friendship.
- To the humanist, the handshake may be the result of a need for acceptance.

- To the physiologist, the handshake might be the result of particular sets of neural and muscular processes; alternatively, it might be due to a gene for sociability.
- To the social constructionist, a person might shake hands because it's been constructed within society as the right thing to do.

No one form of explanation is necessarily the right one to use; all offer some insights into human behaviour. The approaches usually complement each other, and often psychologists will consider a phenomenon from a range of approaches, or work in teams with other psychologists with different perspectives.

Psychologists differ in their preferred form of explanation. They adopt a particular approach for a range of reasons, some of which we'll look at in Chapters 4 and 5. As you learn more about psychology and the approaches it uses you'll find that you develop a preferred approach too.

Behaviourist

Behaviourism was the dominant school in English-speaking psychology until the end of the 1950s. It had a rigorous scientific method, promised to explain all aspects of behaviour and lent itself to application in areas as diverse as behavioural therapy and education. It is no longer dominant, but remains an important approach in some areas of psychology, particularly in the study of learning and in therapeutic applications (see Chapters 8 and 34 respectively).

Key features

Behaviourism is often presented as a revolution in psychology stirred up by John Watson's paper

'Psychology as the behaviourist views it' (1913). However, it is more realistic to say that behaviourism was the inevitable result of a move in American psychology from investigating mental events to investigating behaviour (Leahey, 2001). Certainly, though, Watson led the move to behaviourism and outlined the initial scope of the approach. He suggested that psychology should discard the notion of mind and other mentalistic concepts, since these could not be observed objectively. For psychology to meet the assumptions of science (see Chapter 3), Watson argued that psychologists should investigate only observable behaviour.

Behaviourism changed the subject of psychology from mind to behaviour, but also changed the terms in which psychology explained human nature. Previous approaches explained behaviour in terms of evolutionary adaptation or mental processes. In contrast, behaviourism emphasised the importance of the environment in shaping behaviour. Behaviourism explained behaviour in terms of associations made between stimuli (S) and responses (R) through interaction with the environment. For example, you might smell food (the stimulus) and feel hungry (the response).

There are two main theories of learning: classical conditioning and operant conditioning. The theory of classical conditioning is based on the work of Pavlov. Pavlov noted that dogs salivate when they see food, and attempted to provoke salivation with an alternative stimulus. To achieve this, Pavlov sounded a bell whenever food was presented. Over time, the bell became a trigger for salivation, even when no food was present (see Chapter 8 for a fuller description).

The theory of operant conditioning comes from the work of B.F. Skinner. In operant conditioning the consequences of a response affect learning. Skinner investigated this by training rats to press a lever in exchange for food, and found that rewarding an action increased the likelihood of that action being performed. This is called positive reinforcement. Its opposite is negative reinforcement, whereby punishment (such as electrical shock) reduces the likelihood of an action occurring.

Evaluation

Behaviourism had, from its beginnings, a practical focus. A significant part of behaviourism's early appeal was that it promised to provide a means of social control. If behaviour is the result of experiential learning, then we can change behaviours by changing people's experiences. If we can change behaviours, then we can change society.

Applications of behaviourist theories are used frequently today. These include behavioural therapies such as desensitisation therapy and aversion therapy – based on the view that 'abnormal' behaviour arises through conditioning (see Chapter 34 for more on these therapies) – and teaching techniques such as programmed instruction, where tests are used to provide positive reinforcement to successful learning.

Behaviourism has had a significant effect on theory development in psychology. Current theories of learning rely on behaviourist principles, as does Bandura's (1977b) social learning theory. Behaviourism's greatest effect, however, has been on methodology. Behaviourism emphasised the principles of hypothesis testing and controlled experimentation that underpin scientific methodology in psychology (see Chapter 3).

Despite the influence of the behaviourist approach, a number of criticisms have been levelled at it (Barker, 2003). It is said that it is mechanistic, in that it ignores mental processes. It is overly environmentally deterministic, in that it overlooks the importance of biological factors in behaviour. It overlooks the finding that there are biological constraints on what behaviours a species can perform (for example, you can't teach rats to fly, no matter how much learning occurs). Finally, it has problems in accounting for a range of behaviours, particularly those that are complex, like driving, and those that are spontaneous, like language.

Psychodynamic

The term psychodynamic covers Freud's original theory and later theories based on Freud's work, such as those of Adler (1927), Erikson (1950) and Jung (1964). These theories argue that behaviour is shaped by the dynamic interaction of drives and forces within the individual, particularly in the unconscious mind. We'll concentrate on Freud's theory of *psychoanalysis* (Freud, 1949) as one example of the psychodynamic approach.

Key features

Freud claimed that the mind is made up of three parts: the *conscious*, the *preconscious* and the *unconscious*. The conscious mind contains thoughts and perceptions, but is only a small part of the total, usually described as the tip of an iceberg (see Figure 2.1). The preconscious contains material available to consciousness, including memories and stored knowledge. The unconscious is the largest part of mind, and contains wishes and desires formed during early childhood, and biological instincts and drives. Most of our behaviour is determined by the unconscious mind.

Personality is made up of three parts – the *id*, the *ego* and the *superego*. The id, located in the unconscious, contains sexual and aggressive instincts that demand instant gratification. The ego, located in the conscious and preconscious, develops in early life as a rational mechanism to decide between the id and the outside world. The superego is the conscience, which develops by the age of five under the influence of authority figures. The superego places constraints on behaviours, and uses feelings of pride and guilt to achieve compliance.

Psychological development is claimed to take place in a series of fixed psychosexual stages. Each stage represents the concentration of libido (pleasure derived from organs) on a different part of the body. Fixating on (sticking at) one stage may cause neuroses in later life. The stages are:

- oral (0–18 months)
- anal (18–36 months)
- phallic (3–6 years)
- latent (6 years–puberty)
- genital (puberty onwards).

The most important of these is the phallic stage, when the child becomes aware of his or her gender. It is at this stage that the Oedipus complex occurs. This is when an unconscious rivalry develops in the child

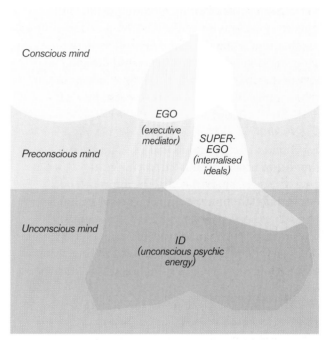

Figure 2.1 *Freud's 'mental iceberg' view of the mind*

between themselves and the same-sex parent for the affection of the opposite-sex parent. Boys experience castration anxiety, resolved through identification with the father, while girls experience penis envy, which becomes sublimated into a wish to have a baby.

The id, ego and superego are in constant conflict between their competing demands. The ego resolves conflict using defence mechanisms, including:

- repression, pushing unwanted ideas into the unconscious
- displacement, diverting energy into other activities
- denial, refusing to accept the existence of a threat
- reaction formation, when someone takes an attitude opposite to their real feelings.

The most important of these is repression, which is responsible for most of the contents of the unconscious. Once in the unconscious, threatening ideas continue to exert an influence and may lead to psychological problems.

Psychoanalysis emphasises the effect of early experiences in shaping adult personality. It attempts to treat neuroses by bringing thoughts from the unconscious into the conscious. Methods include free association, when the client says whatever comes into their mind in response to a cue, and dream analysis, where the analyst identifies unconscious material that is represented in dreams (see Chapter 34).

Evaluation

Psychoanalytic theory has had a significant impact. Freud's original work has led to a range of psychodynamic theories, and the approach has contributed to a range of topics within psychology, including those of personality, development and abnormality. The main impact of psychodynamics has been on therapeutic techniques within clinical and counselling psychology. Psychoanalysis has also had a significant cultural impact. Many people's everyday understanding of psychology is shaped by psychoanalysis, and psychoanalytic insights are used in analysing literature, film and art (see Focus Point 2.2). Richards (2002) claims that psychoanalysis has provided meaning to people's lives in a more accessible way than other approaches to psychology. Most theoretical approaches to psychology provide complex descriptions of the causes of behaviour that are difficult to understand without a wide knowledge of psychology, and that seem divorced from our everyday experiences. Psychoanalytic explanations, on the other hand, are easier to understand for the lay person and seem more directly related to our experiences. For example, most of us can understand how the nature of our relationship with our parents might affect our personalities.

FOCUS POINT 2.2

Psychoanalysis and film criticism

Psychoanalysis has proved influential in the field of film criticism. Let's look at an example. The extracts below are taken from a review of the 1999 film *Fight Club*, starring Brad Pitt and Ed Norton (Redd, 2000). The reviewer is clearly using psychoanalytic insights to interpret representations in the film.

In a twist that will catch most viewers by surprise, Tyler Durden turns out to be a fragment of Jack's personality, but this is merely a device to have this mysterious and powerful character (and manifestation of wish fulfilment) appear in Jack's life. (An analysis of Tyler Durden's name reveals that in antiquated English, 'Tyler' means gatekeeper or house builder. 'Durden' has the word root dour meaning hard (as in 'durable'). His initials, T.D., invoke Todd or death in German or perhaps D.T. (delirium tremens), since Tyler is a hallucination of Jack, the waking person.) Although a second viewing shows that the first understanding of the film meshes successfully with subsequent viewings, the narrative device of the alternate personality is just that and does little to tap into what is understood about multiple personalities. One of few consistencies with psychological literature is that Jack, the waking self, is depleted and becomes less powerful as Tyler becomes more dominant. . . .

The film, though violent and brutally blunt, is remarkably nonsexual. The love in the film is not love between Tyler (or Jack) and Marla, nor is it homoerotic (the idea that heterosexual men need to integrate their feminine side or embrace some of the sensitivity of gay men is completely avoided). There is not a single gay character. There only is the goal of self-love, both in the sense of a well-integrated self and in the sense of the central male character, Jack Tyler, loving his penis. . . .

There are also nagging fears of castration and mutilation that pervade the film. The first support meeting that Jack attends is a testicular cancer group where the members have had their testicles removed and commiserate, saying, 'We're still men.' One of the survivors of testicular cancer, Bob (Meatloaf), has grown huge breasts because of subsequent hormone imbalances, but there is no sense of his being effeminate. His breasts are almost incidental and (consistent with the rest of the film's dismissal of women) referred to as 'bitch tits.'

It has been suggested that psychoanalysis has had a limited impact on scientific psychology (Jones and Elcock, 2001). This is because psychoanalysis is widely seen as being unscientific, and hence as having little to contribute to scientific psychology. In addition, Freud's research is seen as being methodologically poor (Eysenck, 1985), being based on a small number of individual cases; as subjective, because therapy relies on the interpretation of analysts; and biased, because Freud's subjects were largely middle-class Viennese women. Many of Freud's concepts are said to be unfalsifiable (this means that they can't be tested). For example, the concept of reaction formation can be used to explain any unexpected results. A psychoanalyst might believe that a male client is fixated at the phallic stage and has not formed a strong identification with his father. If the client protests that they in fact have a very close identification with their father, then the analyst can explain this in terms of reaction formation: the client believes they have a close identification with the father as a defence against the castration anxiety that they unconsciously experience. In this way the analyst is always right.

In response to these criticisms, supporters of Freud have argued that complex theories are often untestable (Zeldow, 1995), and that the theory consists of many parts, some of which are more easily tested than others (Kline, 1989). In addition, recent studies have provided support for some aspects of Freud's theories (see Jarvis and Russell, 2002, for a review).

Humanistic

After the Second World War some psychologists became uncomfortable with the mechanistic view of human nature suggested by behaviourism. An approach known as *humanism* developed in response to these concerns. It is mainly applied in therapy within clinical and counselling psychology, and has had a relatively limited impact on academic psychology.

Key features

The humanistic approach rejects determinism and emphasises free will, believing that people act purposely to achieve psychological growth. There is a commitment to treating individuals as fully human, as only the individual can fully explain their own behaviour and experience. While scientific psychology adopts a detached perspective, humanism investigates phenomena from the subjective perspective of the individual. Humanistic psychologists also emphasise the need to study the whole person.

The leading humanists are Carl Rogers and Abraham Maslow. Both emphasise psychological health, in contrast to psychoanalysis's concentration on psychological distress. A fundamental concept for both is that of actualisation. Rogers (1951) suggested that people are born with an actualising tendency, driving them to achieve psychological health. A person's sense of self is an organised whole that is constantly being reformed, in contrast to most theories of self that see it as a fixed aspect of personality. Rogers identified two components of this self-concept: the perceived self (how we see ourselves) and the ideal self (how we would like to be). Psychological health is achieved when the two components match, while distress occurs when we feel we don't match up to the ideal.

Maslow (1954) suggested that humans are born with a hierarchy of needs (see Chapter 29), claiming that we need to satisfy lower needs before we can reach higher levels and achieve psychological growth. The goal of psychological growth is to achieve self-actualisation, where we find personal fulfilment.

Evaluation

The humanistic approach has had a considerable influence on the practice of counselling. Rogers' person-centred therapy is used extensively in clinical and counselling psychology, and humanistic psychology's emphasis on the counsellor helped develop the profession of counselling. Rogers also developed a range of techniques for evaluating the effectiveness of therapy, providing a research basis for clinical practice (see Chapter 34).

As with psychoanalysis, humanistic psychology has been criticised for being unscientific, which may explain its limited impact on academic psychology.

There's limited evidence for humanistic concepts – largely because these are not clearly defined. In addition, therapeutic intervention depends on the client being committed and capable of responding, and Maslow's work in particular has been criticised for having a western cultural bias (Jarvis, 2000).

Cognitive

From the 1950s onwards it became increasingly apparent that behaviourism couldn't account for complex behaviours like language use, and that it was necessary to consider mental processes to explain some psychological phenomena. The cognitive approach developed from the mid-1950s, based on the idea that the mind is like a computer. It has become the dominant approach to experimental psychology, replacing behaviourism.

Key features

The cognitive approach emphasises the importance of active mental processing. Behaviour is seen as being the result of information processing in the brain, just as computer outputs are the result of information processing in the machine. The task of cognitive psychologists is to develop models of mental processes, in terms of discrete processing modules with specific functions, and the flow of information between these modules. The approach is commonly used to explain the cognitive processes of perception, memory and problem-solving, but is also used to explain social behaviour and child development. Because of this, the approach is sometimes termed *cognitivism* (Jones and Elcock,

In May 1997 the IBM chess computer, Deep Blue, beat the world chess champion Garry Kasparov. The ability of computers to perform apparently intelligent behaviours, like playing chess, suggested that the human mind might operate like a computer. This idea formed the basis for cognitive psychology.

2001) to emphasise its independence of any one field of study.

The main method of investigation used by cognitive psychology is the controlled experiment, a methodology carried over from the behaviourists. Other methods include computer modelling, where psychologists write programs to attempt to make computers behave like humans (see Focus Point 2.3), and cognitive neuropsychology, where psychologists investigate patients with impairments following brain injury, to learn how intact brains function.

Eliza, the listening computer program

Since the development of the electronic computer in the 1940s, people have tried to get computers to behave intelligently (in pursuit of what is known as Artificial Intelligence). Examples include chess-playing computers, seeing robots and decision-making systems. These attempts to model intelligent behaviour strongly influenced the development of cognitive

psychology, the view being that if computers could behave intelligently then it must be the case that humans – who are intelligent – are like computers. Attempts to model intelligence have continued, and are seen by some as a way of modelling human cognition to produce theories in cognitive psychology (Strube, 2000).

This has been particularly true in the case of language processing. Human language is seen as

FOCUS POINT 2.3 (CONT.)

logical and rule based, and that's how computers work, so it seems quite plausible to believe that we can make computers understand language. As it turns out, it has proved rather more difficult than expected to understand language, and we're still some way from the situation portrayed in *Star Trek*, of talking naturally to computers and being understood. However, there are some interesting examples of computer models of language. In this Focus Point we'll look at an early, very simple, model of language understanding called Eliza (Weizenbaum, 1966).

Eliza emulates a Rogerian psychotherapist. Users type messages into the computer using a keyboard, and Eliza responds in a similar way to a therapist. Over time, a form of conversation develops. Eliza can be quite convincing, and people have been known to become quite attached to the program. However, the Eliza software is actually pretty stupid, relying on a small number of devices to give the appearance of understanding. These include substituting strings of words, using stock phrases and turning around what is typed in. Eliza has no real understanding of what is typed, and no knowledge of the world. This stupidity is a major reason why the software emulates a Rogerian psychotherapist. The Rogerian technique includes acting as an empty well, listening to what people say but not contributing knowledge to the conversation. This technique is designed to guide the client towards their own understandings of their situation.

As stated above, the Eliza software can be quite convincing. Let's look at some examples of conversations with Eliza.

> Hello, I am Eliza.
* Hello Eliza.
> How are you today? What would you like to discuss?
* I'm unhappy.
> Did you come to me because you are unhappy?

So far so good. There's some variation in the responses Eliza gives to keep up the illusion.

> Hello, I am Eliza.
* Hello Eliza.
> How are you today? What would you like to discuss?
* I'm unhappy.
> Do you believe it is normal to be unhappy?

The conversation continues in quite a convincing way, drawing information out of you.

> Do you believe it is normal to be unhappy?
* No I don't.
> Does that trouble you?
* Yes it does.
> I understand.

However, Eliza isn't actually that helpful.

* Can you help me?
> You want me to be able to help you?
* Yes, very much.
> I see.
* Will you help me?
> We were discussing you, not me.
* I want help.
> Why do you want help?

She also has a limited repertoire, and often uses the same stock phrases.

> We were discussing you, not me.
* I want help.
> Why do you want help?
* Because I'm unhappy.
> Do you believe it is normal to be unhappy?

Which brings us back to where we started. It turns out that even in this limited domain the system isn't very good at understanding language. As we heard earlier, though, Eliza was an early

FOCUS POINT 2.3 (CONT.)

attempt and is widely recognised to be stupid. Systems have improved since, but they are still a long way from real understanding. Perhaps the most important lesson of such models for psychology is that language understanding is more difficult than we first thought. In particular, it has become clear that language understanding relies on extensive background information, and can't always be characterised in terms of rules.

If you'd like to try Eliza for yourself, an online version can be found at http://www.manifestation.com/neurotoys/eliza.php3.

Evaluation

The cognitive approach has had a significant impact in the field of cognitive psychology, but also in social psychology and developmental psychology. The approach has led to theories of social cognition and of cognitive development in children. It has also led to applications, particularly in cognitive therapy, that involve the replacement of faulty thought patterns with more effective ones (see Chapter 34).

A particular strength of the cognitive approach is that it uses a range of rigorous research methods (Eysenck and Keane, 2000). This means that if findings from different methods give the same results we can have more faith in their validity.

Professor Alan Baddeley CBE, originator of the working memory model, is a leading British cognitive psychologist.

Despite the success of the cognitive approach it has still attracted a number of criticisms (Jones and Elcock, 2001). Cognitive research takes place in artificial settings, and may not reflect our cognition in the 'real world'. There's no integrating theoretical framework for cognitive psychology. Instead, there are several separate cognitive theories that don't relate well to each other. There is also some dispute as to whether the brain is best seen as being like a computer. Computers, after all, have no emotions, morals or unconscious, all of which might be expected to influence human behaviour.

Physiological

The *physiological* approach studies psychological functioning by examining biological processes – for example, brain structure and the operation of genetics.

Key features

There are three main areas of work within the physiological approach: brain function, biochemistry and heredity. These share the assumptions that biological factors underlie behaviour, and that behaviour is best explained in biological terms. The physiological approach is reductionist, in that psychological functions are explained in more basic biological terms. It is also deterministic, behaviour being seen as directly determined by biological factors.

Psychologists study brain function using techniques such as fMRI scanning (Carlson, 2004) in order to identify the brain areas involved in particular tasks (see Chapter 6). They also identify patterns of impaired and spared functioning in brain-damaged patients (Parkin, 1999).

Psychologists also study biochemistry in order to understand how brain chemistry affects behaviour (Carlson, 2004). The brain uses chemicals, called neurotransmitters, to communicate between cells, but imbalances in the levels of these chemicals cause problems. For example, the neurotransmitter serotonin is involved in regulating mood. Sufferers of depression have low levels of serotonin. Drugs like Prozac are effective because they increase the effectiveness of serotonin in the brain.

The study of heredity involves attempting to find a basis in our genetic inheritance for psychological phenomena. Psychologists study heredity because they believe that genes influence behaviour, and determine differences and similarities between people (Plomin, DeFries *et al.*, 1997). Behavioural geneticists attempt to identify genes that may underpin psychological phenomena such as personality and intelligence (see Chapters 29 and 30).

Evaluation

The physiological approach has provided explanations of behaviour across a wide range of areas of psychology, and has led to treatments for disorders such as depression and schizophrenia. It has also captured the popular imagination, with genetic explanations in particular providing a framework for understanding the behaviour of others and ourselves.

The main criticism of the physiological approach is that it is overly reductionist. It is suggested (Rose, 1998) that psychological phenomena should be explained in psychological rather than physiological terms. In addition, a range of criticisms has been levelled at evolutionary explanations. These include the view that evolutionary explanations ignore the influence of the environment, and that there is limited evidence for some evolutionary claims (Jarvis, 2000). A further concern is that evolutionary explanations may make anti-social behaviours, such as male aggression, seem natural and hence unavoidable, and may be used to excuse injustice (Byrne, 1994; see also Chapter 4).

Social constructionist

The social constructionist approach developed from the 1970s as a challenge to 'mainstream' psychology

(Fox and Prilleltensky, 1997). This challenge came in response to concerns about gender and sexuality bias in psychology leading to the misrepresentation of women, gays and lesbians (see Chapter 4).

Key features

Social constructionism is a diverse approach. However, social constructionists share a number of assumptions (Burr, 1995). The first is that our perceptions of the world don't necessarily correspond with natural categories. The second is that knowledge is culturally specific, so how we understand the world depends on a particular culture at a particular time. The third is that we construct our perception of the world through social interaction, particularly through language. The final assumption is that our constructions are associated with possible actions. So, for example, our construction of what it is to be female will affect our view of how women should behave.

Social constructionism rejects the positivist view of scientific psychology, that individuals can be studied objectively in isolation. Instead, social constructionists try to identify how knowledge is constructed through interactions. Social constructionists analyse people's language use through the techniques of conversation analysis and discourse analysis, to identify the ways in which people construct the world (see Research Methods 2.1).

RESEARCH METHODS BOX 2.1

Discourse analysis

Social constructionists use a range of techniques to investigate the ways in which people construct their social world. The most common of these is discourse analysis, which involves analysing transcripts of spoken interaction to identify what people are doing and seeking to achieve in communicating (Stainton Rogers, 2003). The focus is on identifying the kind of *discursive practices* that people use. For example, someone may focus on the worst case scenario when describing a situation – the practice of *extreme case formulation* ('They're all the same . . .'). Alternatively, people may use the practice of *disclaiming*, when they pre-emptively deny holding a particular view before expressing that view ('I'm not a racist but . . .').

As an example of discourse analysis in practice, consider the transcript presented below. This is taken from an interview conducted by researchers (Adair and Elcock, 1995) with four police officers, one a superintendent (labelled D), one a sergeant (labelled B), and two constables (labelled T and J). One of the constables (T) has been working undercover at illegal raves, and the interview is about the police officers' views of rave culture. The interview went on for some time, and only a brief section is given here. However, we shall see that we can learn important things from even a brief section of text.

D: And I think you're talking about a different culture really, the afro-Caribbean as opposed to the white person and I know you get you know a lot of white people down there but the sort of blues parties are all about relaxed atmospheres, it's not the heavy beat sort of music. I think it, it's a place to go and okay maybe have a drink but relax and enjoy it 'cause that's the way of life that the afro-Caribbean is. Totally different to what the white person is. The white person seems to you know has got this tremendous energy and as you say the, the tremendous aggression. I don't think the afro-Caribbean culture is like that. Course I'm not . . .
T: No they're definitely more mellow than us they don't . . .
B: How, I mean what was the proportion then down at the, the rave at [name of illegal rave that T attended]. I perceive raves . . .
T: Ninety five per cent white . . .
B: Yeah . . .
D: Mmm . . .
B: I mean every rave I've been to . . .

T: In fact the only afro-Caribbeans I saw there were selling drugs [B and D laugh, T continues] . . .
T: To be quite honest
D: If you had a better start there'd be a prime minister wouldn't there [laughs]
B: They were (**** 'em) [starts laughing more heartily again]
T: If, no but this is at that rave in [name] [D starts laughing, then both B and D stop]
T: That was the only afro-Caribbeans I saw there, there was three and they were all about twenty five and were all selling

There's a lot going on in this section of the interview. For example, careful analysis shows that power relationships between the officers of different rank are maintained through language, with the superintendent dominating the conversation. The researchers, though, focus on evidence of racism in the language and discursive practices used by the officers. First, the researcher notes how D draws a distinction between what he calls different cultures, between what are in D's words 'the afro-Caribbeans' and 'the white person'. At the end of D's passage it would appear that he is just about to disclaim racism, but T interrupts him, possibly in her eagerness to agree. The particular racist representation deployed by D, lack of energy, serves the pragmatic purposes of this interaction, explaining why black people don't rave. Second, the researcher notes the way that D refers to white persons or people, while in his references to 'the afro-Caribbeans' there is no personhood granted. The third piece of evidence is the way that D generalises from a particular instance (the blues party) to a group of people.

Evaluation

Social constructionism provides detailed analyses of particular phenomena, and draws on links with other disciplines, particularly sociology. It has been used to challenge sources of bias within psychology (see

Chapter 4). In addition, in challenging mainstream research methods (see Chapter 3) it has encouraged scientific psychologists to reflect on the methods they use.

A fundamental criticism of social constructionism is that it is anti-scientific, and that its findings are overly subjective (Stainton Rogers, 2003). This goes against mainstream views of what psychology should be. The problem in social constructionism is that the theories produced may be more a reflection of the views of the psychologist than of the phenomenon being investigated. In addition, most psychologists believe that there is a real social world external to individuals, and reject the social constructionist view that the world is constructed by people through interaction. The social constructionist view involves a radical re-conception of what the subject matter of

psychology is, and hence is incommensurable with mainstream approaches (Stainton Rogers, 2003). This difference is illustrated in Table 2.2.

Sue Wilkinson, a leading British feminist psychologist.

TABLE 2.2

MAINSTREAM AND SOCIAL CONSTRUCTIONIST VIEWS OF ATTITUDES

This table, derived from Stainton Rogers (2003), contrasts mainstream and social constructionist views of attitudes.

Mainstream	Social constructionist
Attitudes are evaluations of objects operating at personal, interpersonal and intergroup levels. They are believed to be discrete from other attitudes, and isolated from other factors such as social norms and value judgements.	Attitudes are interconnected, and related to other evaluations such as values.
Attitudes have cognitive, emotional and behavioural components. They are developed by individuals through experience and through external sources of information.	Attitudes are intersubjective – that is, they are based upon shared understandings rather than being the products of individual minds.
Attitudes are relatively fixed, and can be measured using attitude scales such as the Likert scale.	Attitudes are variable with context. Attitudes change over time and in different situations, and individuals may hold contradictory views of the same object.
Attitudes have four main functions: categorising knowledge, guiding behaviour, communicating with others, and building self-esteem.	Attitudes serve particular functions, and need to be investigated in terms of what attitudes are meant to achieve. For example, attitudes may be used to justify certain behaviours.

Section 1
Conceptual and historical issues

ACTIVITY BOX 2.1

Evaluating approaches

The range of theoretical approaches in psychology can be quite dizzying. One helpful way of understanding them all is to summarise the main features of each approach in a table.

Draw up a table like the one below, allotting a column to each approach. Each row of the table corresponds to a particular aspect of the approach. Use the aspects given here, but feel free to add your own too.

On the basis of your reading in this chapter, and also from the rest of the book, fill in the table. It will be helpful to keep a copy of the table and add to it as you learn more about each approach.

Approach	Behaviourist	Psycho-dynamic	Humanist	Cognitivist	Physiological	Social constructionist
Basic assumptions about human nature						
Methods of study						
Applications						
Main contributions						
Main criticisms						

Don't worry too much if you can't fill in everything straight away. It will come to you as you learn more about psychology. Similar tables are included in Barker (2003) and Malim and Birch (1998).

In Chapter 5, we look at a number of debates in psychology. After reading that chapter, add a row to the table saying where each approach stands on those debates.

Learning outcomes

When you have completed this chapter you should be able to:

- explain how and why psychology emerged as an independent discipline
- describe the early schools of psychology
- outline the key features of a range of theoretical approaches to psychology
- evaluate theoretical approaches to psychology
- explain how different approaches provide different kinds of explanation of psychological phenomena.

Key Terms

Behaviourism
Cognitivism
Conscious
Ego
Humanism
Id
Physiological
Preconscious
Psychoanalysis
Reflexive discourse
Social constructionism
Superego
Unconscious

Further reading

Ashworth, P. (2000) *Psychology and 'Human Nature'*. Hove: Psychology Press.

Jarvis, M. (2000) *Theoretical Approaches in Psychology*. London: Routledge.

Jones, D. and Elcock, J. (2001) *History and Theories of Psychology: A Critical Perspective*. London: Arnold.

Leahey, T. H. (2001) *A History of Modern Psychology*. Upper Saddle River, NJ: Prentice-Hall.

Richards, G. (2002) *Putting Psychology in its Place*. Hove: Psychology Press.

3

Psychology as science

Route map of the chapter

In this chapter we look at scientific psychology. We start by thinking about the ways in which we come to know things, and consider science to be a 'way of knowing' with particular strengths. We look at how views of science developed over time, and what the principles and assumptions underlying scientific psychology are. We then look at how psychology can be carried out scientifically, and evaluate whether it can be seen as a science. Following this, we consider a range of issues in scientific psychology, including threats to the validity of psychology research and ethical issues. We conclude by thinking about some alternatives to scientific psychology.

Introduction

'Is psychology a science?' This is probably the most common assessment question facing the new student of psychology. It might seem a strange question to ask, given that psychology is usually described as the science of mind and behaviour. The fact the question is asked at all might suggest that some psychologists have concerns about the status of scientific psychology.

It's not giving too much away to say that a short answer to the question is 'Yes, but . . .'. In this chapter, we examine the reasons for the 'Yes' answer, by looking at the features of science and how psychology corresponds to these. We also look at reasons for the 'but . . .', by considering some issues to be borne in mind when doing scientific psychology. We conclude by looking at some alternatives to scientific psychology.

Science as a way of knowing

We saw in Chapter 2 that psychology developed as an attempt to be scientific in answering questions about mind and behaviour. Here we look at why its early pioneers wanted to adopt a scientific approach, and at how the scientific approach developed.

Ways of knowing

People have used a range of different approaches to investigate human nature. Any approach, such as philosophy, has a common way of finding things out. In the case of philosophy, people try to understand human nature through logical reasoning. Any way of knowing is based on beliefs about what kinds of things exist (*ontology*), what we can know about these things (*epistemology*) and how we can find out about these things (methodology). These three areas are linked. Deciding what we think exists will affect what we think we can find out. For example, if we think the mind is linked to the brain (ontology), then we'll believe we can find the link (epistemology). We might further believe that we can find the link by using brain scans (methodology), but not by using questionnaires.

Most psychologists favour the scientific method to answer questions about mind and behaviour. What this means is that most psychologists adopt a certain view of the world, which says that psychological phenomena are real and that these real phenomena can be investigated through science.

The appeal of science

Science involves observing how things are, making informed predictions about the effects of different actions, and testing these predictions with evidence. For example, we might observe that short words are easier to remember than long ones. We then predict that if we give people lists of long and short words to remember they'll remember more short words. We test this by getting people to remember words and see if we were right. Of course, anyone else could test our idea in the same way. This means that others can independently verify our prediction. A major appeal of science is that findings can be tested, allowing us to be confident that what we know is actually true.

Another appeal of science is that it seems to have improved people's lives. It was science that led to the development of technologies like electric lighting and the telegraph. With the development of scientific psychology, there was a promise of explanations of mind and behaviour that could lead to practical interventions to help people (Jones and Elcock, 2001).

The development of science

Science developed over several hundred years, driven by the work of philosophers of science. In the early nineteenth century, Comte said science should concentrate on observed facts, so that we could find positive, rather than theological or philosophical, truths. This philosophy – known as positivism – emphasised the use of *induction*. Induction is the process of deriving general truths from observed facts, so if we observe that a number of people remember more short words than long words, we might derive the general truth that short words are easier to remember than long words. Wundt's first scientific psychology was positivist.

The 'Viennese Circle' of philosophers extended positivism in the 1920s to emphasise the development of logical theories (logical positivism). Logical positivism says that scientists should use *deduction* to make specific predictions on the basis of general principles. First, we develop theories to explain observations. We might theorise that we can remember words for a fixed period of time, say two seconds, and that we can fit more short words than long words into the two seconds. We then use this theory to make specific claims that we can test, so we might make the specific claim that if we give people

long and short words to remember, they'll remember more short words. If the prediction comes true, our theory has been verified, so if people do indeed remember more short words, we'll assume our theory was correct. If the prediction doesn't come true, if people remember more long words, our theory is wrong. This approach was adopted by behaviourism, and came to dominate experimental psychology. It has become the standard scientific methodology in psychology (McGhee, 2001).

Logical positivism has attracted some criticism. A major source of this was Sir Karl Popper. He argued that we should test theories, rather than try to verify them. This is because the same results can verify more than one theory, but only one theory can be true. Popper suggested that scientists should try to *disprove* their theories. For Popper, the mark of a good scientific theory is *falsifiability* (this means that the theory can be found to be false). This idea has been adopted in psychology, and is used to evaluate whether or not theories are scientific. For example, psychoanalysis is often criticised for being unscientific because many of its theories can't be disproved.

The logical positivists and Popper described how science *should* be done. However, Kuhn showed that science is *actually* done somewhat differently. He observed that scientists tend to stick to their theories even when they're not supported. Instead of modifying theories, scientists tend to dismiss contradictory results as false. Kuhn said there are periods of 'normal science', when scientists share a particular approach (a paradigm). Then, over time, more and more contradictory results are found and it becomes increasingly hard to dismiss them as false. Eventually, some scientists suggest a radically different approach that explains the results better than the standard paradigm. The new paradigm gradually becomes accepted and eventually replaces the previous paradigm in a 'scientific revolution'. The change from behaviourism to cognitive psychology is often described as a revolution in this sense.

Psychology as science

The nature of science

Science has certain assumptions, aims and methods. If psychology is a science, then we'd expect it to share these. In this section, we'll outline the nature of science. We'll then consider the extent to which psychology can be considered a science.

Assumptions of science

Science makes certain assumptions about how the world works. These include the following.

Order

The world has order, which means that events don't happen haphazardly. We should be able to identify regular patterns in events.

Determinism

If the world has order, then events have identifiable causes. Scientific psychology tries to find the causes of human behaviour.

Empiricism

Theories must be based on publicly available evidence, gathered through observation.

Parsimony

Explanations of events should not go beyond the available evidence, and should explain as much of an event as possible in the simplest way possible.

Aims of science

Science has aims of description, prediction, understanding and control, as described below.

Description

Science provides objective descriptions of phenomena, which are free of personal bias.

Prediction

Descriptions allow scientists to identify regular patterns in phenomena. This allows scientists to make testable predictions about how things are.

Understanding

Finding regular patterns, and testing predictions, allows scientists to identify causes and effects. This gives us a better understanding of the nature of events.

Control

If we have an accurate understanding of the causes of events, then we can control those events.

The scientific method

The scientific method is an approach to gathering data and developing theories. Data is collected objectively, in a way that is controlled, that is precisely defined and that can be replicated by others. Theories are developed on the basis of evidence, using a combination of induction and deduction. There are a number of stages in the scientific method, as follows.

Observe regularities

For example, television is getting more violent, and there's more violence in society.

Develop a theory

People imitate what they see on television, so watching violent programmes increases aggression.

Develop a prediction

Participants shown violent TV programmes will exhibit more aggression than those shown non-violent TV programmes.

Test the prediction

Run an experiment that shows one group of participants violent TV programmes and another group non-violent ones. Measure their aggression afterwards and see if there's a difference.

Evaluate the theory

If the prediction is supported, then assume that the theory is correct. If the prediction isn't supported, then change the theory.

This process is also known as the *hypothetico-deductive method* (see Figure 3.1).

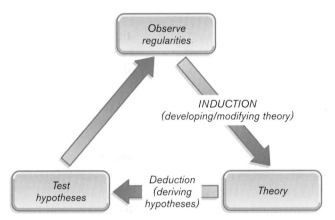

Figure 3.1 *The hypothetico-deductive method*
Source: adapted from Barker, 2003

Observe
regularities

INDUCTION
(developing/modifying theory)

Test
hypotheses

Deduction
(deriving
hypotheses)

Theory

ACTIVITY BOX 3.1

Thinking about experiments

We've used the example of an experiment studying the effect on levels of aggression of watching violent television programmes. The experiment involved:

- forming two groups of people
- showing one group of people violent television programmes and the other group non-violent television programmes
- measuring levels of aggression in our two groups of people, and checking to see if there is a difference between the two groups.

We believe that if we find that levels of aggression differ between the two groups, this is caused by showing the groups different television programmes. That is, violent television caused an increase in levels of aggression.

Think about the following questions.

1 If we find a difference between the groups, what other reasons might there be for the difference, apart from the kind of television programme watched?
2 How might we measure aggression in this study?

3 What does this study teach us about the causes of aggression in real life?

You might find these questions a bit strange at first. Read through the following section entitled 'Doing psychology scientifically' and try answering the questions again.

Doing psychology scientifically

Psychology uses the hypothetico-deductive method to generate and test predictions, and to develop theories. The standard approach to testing predictions is to conduct experiments. The logic of an experiment is that, all other things being equal, if we make a change in a situation and then observe an effect on some measurement, we can assume that the change caused the effect. In investigating whether watching violent television leads to an increase in aggression, then, we change the situation by varying the type of television programme (the independent variable). We gauge the effect of the type of programme by measuring aggression (the dependent variable). There are two main considerations in doing psychology experiments: the need for control, and defining measurements. We will look at these now.

The need for control

If we find that those watching violent television show more aggression than those watching non-violent television, then we assume that the type of television watched affects the level of aggression shown. In other words, we ascribe a cause and effect relationship. However, this conclusion is only valid if nothing else differs in the experiment. Alternatively, the people to whom we show violent programmes may be more aggressive than those shown non-violent programmes, so when we measure aggression later we're just finding a difference that already existed. Similarly, the violent programme and the non-violent programme might differ in other ways. One might be more emotional than the other, and that (rather than the violence) may have had an effect on aggression.

When we do experiments in psychology, it's important to use *experimental control* to ensure that the only things that differ in the experiment are those we want to differ. It can be difficult to control all the different things that affect human behaviour. When we do control everything possible, we may find that the study loses *validity*, because we end up with a very artificial situation.

When we, as experimenters, are responsible for changing the situation (for example, the type of programme) then we have a pure experiment. If we have adequate control, we can be confident that any effect we find was caused by the change we made. However, it's not always possible for us to change the situation. For example, if we're interested in gender differences in intelligence, we can't change the gender of our participants. In this case, we're looking for differences between groups that already exist. This kind of experiment is called a quasi-experiment. It has the same form as a pure experiment but we're not responsible for the differences. In this case, we can't ascribe cause and effect because there may be other causes of any differences we find. For example, we may find that girls score higher on intelligence than boys, but we can't guarantee that there are biological reasons for this. It may be that girls receive a better education than boys or are socialised to try harder. A fuller account of the use of the experimental method in psychology can be found in Chapter 37.

Defining measurements

The things that natural sciences investigate tend to be tangible, so people can agree what they are and how they should be measured. A physicist might investigate whether objects stretch when moving quickly by measuring them at rest and again when they are moving. The findings from such a study would be uncontroversial. However, the things psychology investigates are often unobservable, which positivist science can't discuss (Jones and Elcock, 2001). For example, we can't measure extroversion with a ruler. Instead, psychologists have to develop indirect measures of concepts using *operationism*. Operationism says that unobservable factors produce observable consequences. So, we can investigate them if we define the factors in terms of measures of their consequences. Extroversion leads people to behave in certain ways, so we can investigate extroversion by defining it in terms of these behaviours.

Operationism involves identifying an unobservable *hypothetical construct*. This is something that is claimed to exist, but that cannot be directly measured, like extroversion. We can give a *theoretical*

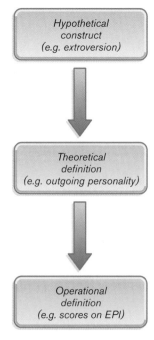

Figure 3.2 Operationism

FOCUS POINT 3.1

Operationism and the measurement of extroversion

As an illustration of operationism in action, let's focus on the measurement of extroversion. We start with a hypothetical construct. We might say that extroversion is a fixed personality characteristic that contributes, together with other traits such as neuroticism and psychoticism, to the totality of an individual's personality.

We need to specify what we think extroversion is, so we give a theoretical definition. We can define extroversion as an outward-directed and sociable personality trait that leads people to be impulsive and risk-taking. The theoretical definition is part of the hypothetical construct – we couldn't really say that there's this thing called extroversion without saying what we think it is.

Having developed a theoretical definition of the construct, we can then start to think about how we might measure it. We can't observe extroversion directly, so instead we need to use an operational definition of the construct to say, on the basis of the theoretical definition, how we can measure extroversion. Given that we've defined extroversion in terms of being sociable, risk-taking and impulsive, we might measure extroversion by counting how many of these behaviours people engage in. We can do this by observing their behaviour, but this may not be convenient. It's easier to ask people about their behaviour, so we can give an operational definition of extroversion in terms of people's reports of how often they engage in behaviours that we think are extroverted.

A good example of this is the Eysenck Personality Inventory (EPI) (Eysenck and Eysenck, 1964). This consists of a set of statements that ask people about their behaviour, including behaviour that is extroverted or introverted. Respondents are asked to indicate whether or not each statement applies to them. Some sample statements related to extroversion include 'Generally, do you prefer reading to meeting people?' and 'Are you fairly talkative when with a group of people?' A respondent's score for extroversion is based on how many extrovert behaviours they routinely engage in.

The process of operationism is illustrated in Figure 3.2.

definition of extroversion, as an outward-directed personality trait. This tells us what it is, but not how it can be measured, so we can't investigate extroversion scientifically. For that, we develop an operational definition that specifies how the construct is measured – for example, as a score on a questionnaire. Using this definition we can investigate extroversion scientifically (see Focus Point 3.1).

Evaluating scientific psychology

We've seen that science relies on the assumptions of order, determinism and empiricism. As you read through this book, you'll see that most theories in psychology reflect these assumptions. Psychologists use empirical data to develop ordered theories of how behaviour is caused. We saw that science has the aims of description, prediction, understanding and control. We'll see many examples of psychology's success in meeting these aims. Being a science also involves using the scientific method to investigate human behaviour. We've seen how psychology uses measurement, experimental control and the hypothetico-deductive method. It's clear that psychology can be done scientifically.

At the start of the chapter we said the short answer to the question 'Is psychology a science?' was 'Yes, but …'. We've already seen the reasons for the 'Yes'. There are two reasons for the 'but …'. First, there is a range of issues we need to consider to ensure that psychology is a good science. We will look at these in the next section. Second, there is an ongoing argument about whether psychology *should* be done scientifically, even though it can be. We consider this argument in the section below entitled 'Alternatives to scientific psychology'.

Issues in scientific psychology

Psychology differs from other sciences because its subject matter is often intangible, and also because people *react* to being studied. In addition, the things psychology investigates may change over time. If you watch a film or television programme from the 1950s you'll see that people seem to be very reserved. What counted as extroverted behaviour in the 1950s may seem very tame in modern society. For this reason, we need to be careful when doing scientific psychology.

Validity

Validity refers to the extent to which a study produces accurate results (*internal* validity) and produces results that are widely applicable (*external* validity). In our study of TV programmes and aggression, we need to know that the study does test the effects of watching TV, and that our results apply in other situations as well as our own study.

Internal validity

Internal validity refers to the extent to which an experiment actually tests the hypothesis it claims to test. This is independent of the results – a valid study may not support the hypothesis, while an invalid study may do so. Internal validity depends on the logic of the study's design, the appropriateness of the measurements used, and especially the adequacy of the experimental control (Rosnow and Rosenthal, 2003).

In the example of television and aggression, we may find that the group watching a violent programme does show more aggression. However, if that group was already more aggressive than the other group then the study doesn't have validity – the results aren't a test of the hypothesis but a reflection of a pre-existing difference. Similarly, asking people to say how aggressive they feel on a scale of 1 to 5 probably isn't adequate as a measurement.

External validity

External validity refers to the extent to which the results of an experiment can be applied to other situations. We may find that watching a violent programme leads to an increase in aggression in the laboratory, but would the same results be found in the real world? We usually want studies to allow generalisation, enabling us to make claims about the world in general on the basis of our findings. Studies that lack external validity only tell us about behaviour in the specific experimental setting.

There are two main threats to external validity. One results from a trade-off between internal and external validity (McGhee, 2001). The more we try to control every unwanted factor in an experiment, to improve internal validity, the more artificial we make the experimental setting. For example, to investigate immediate memory we might ask people to learn made-up words, to control for familiarity with real words. However, in the real world people seldom have to remember lists of invented words. Our study may have excellent internal validity but limited applicability to the real world.

The second threat to external validity comes from the people we study. If we want to explain human behaviour we can't test everyone, so we test a subset or sample instead. We hope that the sample is typical of the people we want to describe. We can only generalise our results if the sample is indeed typical or representative. If we're looking at gender differences in school achievement, we want to make claims about all girls and boys in the school system. We can't test all girls and boys, so we use a small group of children instead and we hope they are representative. If, however, all the children selected are educated at home, then they are not representative of children in the school system and our study loses validity. Most psychology studies rely on using undergraduate students as participants, but make claims about people in general. However, studies show that students differ from the wider population, typically being young, intelligent, introspective and male (Valentine, 1992). These differences may have a distorting effect on the validity of studies as explanations of general human behaviour. (See also Chapter 39 for a fuller discussion of the use of samples.)

Experiments and artefacts

Scientific psychology is based on objective observation. However, it is increasingly recognised that psychology experiments are social situations and that this affects people's behaviour. Such unwanted effects are called *artefacts*. Artefacts threaten the objectivity of observations and the internal validity of experiments. They may come from subjects or experimenters.

FOCUS POINT 3.2

Artefacts in experimental research

At the start of the twentieth century Europeans were amazed by a horse known as Clever Hans who seemed to be able to do maths. People would ask Hans questions (for example, what's 2 + 2) and Hans would reply by tapping his foot (four times in this case). Careful study showed that Hans was picking up cues from the questioner. When someone questioned Hans they would make a slight forward motion, and when Hans gave the right response they would move back again. Hans would then stop tapping (Thorne and Henley, 2001). Hans's abilities showed that participants pick up on cues from investigators.

More research on participants' behaviour came from Orne, who was interested in the social psychology of psychology experiments. Orne found that participants agree to ridiculous requests in experiments. In one study (Orne, 1962) participants were asked to do additions on sheets of random numbers, 224 additions on each of 2000 sheets. After five and a half hours Orne stopped the study, with his participants still adding up numbers. Orne's studies seemed to show that participants want to please the investigator, and so do as they're told.

A final example is a study by Rosenthal (described in Gross, 2003). Rosenthal asked experimenters to train rats to learn their way around a maze. Some experimenters were told their rats had been bred for brightness, and some were told their rats were bred for dullness, despite the fact that the rats had been allocated randomly to experimenters. Rosenthal found that the rats that were believed to be bright learned the maze faster than the rats believed to be dull. The difference was created by the expectations of the experimenters!

Participant artefacts

Participant artefacts come about because participants actively try to work out the nature of the study they're involved in. Orne (1962) suggested that there are cues in an experiment, called *demand characteristics*, that give away the nature of the study. These include, for example, the instructions used in the study. Orne believed that participants try to be good participants (the *good subject effect*) and so behave as they think the experimenter wants them to.

Why might people want to be good participants? Rosenthal and Rosnow (1991) suggest that people are motivated by altruism (a desire to be helpful), evaluation apprehension (a fear of being thought badly of) and obedience (see Figure 3.3). Participants may try to be good, they may try to be neutral or they may try to go against what the experimenter expects. However, only certain circumstances lead to participant artefacts:

- participants have to want and be able to spot demand characteristics
- participants have to be motivated to respond to them, either to be compliant or anti-compliant
- participants have to be able to respond to the demand characteristics.

It's not important whether participants are accurate in guessing what a study is about. If they guess wrongly, but alter their behaviour accordingly, then participant artefacts will still arise.

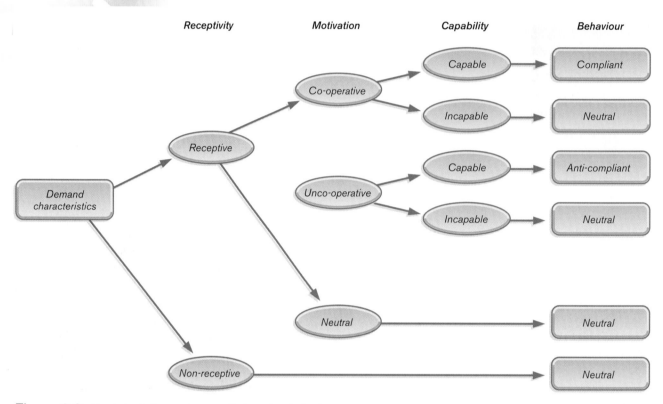

Figure 3.3 Factors influencing participant artefacts
Source: Rosenthal and Rosnow, 1991

Experimenter artefacts

Experimenter artefacts are when features of the experimenter influence the results of a study. They threaten the internal validity of studies and pose questions about whether experimenters can be truly objective. There are several kinds of experimenter artefact, including the following (Rosenthal and Rosnow, 1991).

Observer

These are errors of observation. Different people observe things in different ways, meaning that different investigators of the same phenomenon may produce different findings.

Interpreter

These are errors in the interpretation of data. For example, researchers may interpret findings only in the light of their preferred theory.

Intentional

Intentional effects arise from dishonesty or

sloppiness by the researcher. The classic example of an intentional interpreter effect is the work of Cyril Burt, which is described in Focus Point 3.3.

Expectancy

Expectancy effects occur when experimenters alter their behaviour to achieve the response they expect from a group. This changes the demand characteristics for different groups, leading to a difference in performance. For example, in a classic study (Rosenthal and Jacobson, 1968) teachers were told that a certain group of students were particularly bright, even though the students were chosen at random. The teachers' positive expectations of these students meant they behaved differently towards them, with the result that the students performed better, showing greater gains in IQ performance than the otherwise equivalent students. This particular form of expectancy effect is known as the Pygmalion effect, after the George Bernard Shaw play *Pygmalion* (on which the popular musical *My Fair Lady* was based).

FOCUS POINT 3.3

The case of Sir Cyril Burt

Sir Cyril Burt (1883–1971) is renowned for committing one of the most significant alleged frauds in the history of psychology. His case is an alleged example of intentional experimenter effects, but also indicates the problem of bias in psychology (which is covered in depth in Chapter 4).

Burt was one of the most influential psychologists of his time, and became Chair of the Psychology Department at University College in 1932. He was noted for his work on intelligence, including giftedness and backwardness, and more particularly the heritable basis of intelligence. Based on studies of identical twins raised apart, Burt found that the heritability of intelligence was 0.77, suggesting that intelligence was largely genetically determined. This research led to Burt's involvement in the establishment of a new British school system in the 1940s, which segregated children into grammar or secondary modern schools at the age of 11, based on their performance on a test of intellectual ability (the '11 plus'). It was thought that some children were innately fitted to academic education and should be educated separately from other children.

Doubts began to surface about Burt's research with the work of Kamin (1974). Hearnshaw's (1979) biography of Burt suggested that Burt had been engaged in a large-scale fraud. The number of children tested by Burt had apparently risen from 15 pairs of twins in 1943 to 53 pairs in 1966, yet the correlation between their IQ scores remained the same to three decimal places. This was highly improbable, and Kamin suggested that the data had been forged. This seemed to be supported when the co-investigators listed as co-authors of Burt's reports couldn't be found to confirm their validity. In 1980 the British Psychological Society endorsed Hearnshaw's conclusion that Burt had conducted a systematic fraud, and a number of academics admitted they had harboured doubts about Burt's findings.

Since the end of the 1980s there have been a number of attempts to rehabilitate Burt (for example, MacKintosh, 1995). It is claimed that Burt's co-workers have been identified, and other studies of identical twins reared apart have shown results similar to Burt's. A vigorous debate has emerged within psychology over the status of Burt's work. However, his work was destroyed shortly after his death, making the facts hard to determine. Most defenders of Burt contend that the case against him is unproven, and that at worst Burt was guilty of carelessness in conducting and reporting research. (This would also constitute an intentional experimenter artefact, according to Rosenthal and Rosnow's definition.)

The most interesting aspect of the Burt controversy is that people's views on the Burt case seem to correspond with their views on the heredity and environment debate, and more widely with their political persuasion. It seems that people's views are influenced by their pre-existing beliefs. We shall see more examples of this trend in Chapter 4. The irony of the case is that Burt is often demonised as pursuing an elitist social agenda, when his writings suggest that he was motivated by egalitarian concerns. He believed strongly that IQ was determined by heredity, but emphasised that all children, regardless of gender, ethnicity or class, were entitled to the best education they could benefit from.

Measurement

We have already seen that scientific psychology relies on creating measures of hypothetical constructs. For example, we might say that intelligence is measured by the number of correct responses on an intelligence test. However, there are a number of issues surrounding measurement.

The hypothetical constructs that psychologists try to measure are the creations of psychologists. We may develop measures for these constructs, but that doesn't mean they are meaningful. Richards (2002) gives the example of 'sanctity'. We might hypothesise a personality trait of sanctity, and develop a questionnaire that measures how holy people are by asking about their church-going behaviour, donations to charity, and so on. That doesn't mean sanctity exists as a stable personality trait!

It is said that everything that exists can be measured. However, it's not true that everything that can be measured exists. Developing a measure that seems to be successful leads people to believe that the construct exists (a process called *reification*), but this is never proven.

Another problem is that someone has to decide what counts as part of the measure. In measuring intelligence, we might count language skills as intelligent, but not interpersonal skills. Others may disagree. Measurements are also culturally and historically specific. Eysenck's (1957) Social Attitude Inventory included the item 'It would be best to keep coloured people in their own districts'. Those who disagreed with this were seen as 'tender minded'. However, few today would agree with the statement, and few psychologists would include the statement in an inventory. Measurements are devised in a specific context, and may not reflect a universal truth.

It is possible to have multiple measures for the same construct. For example, there are a number of IQ tests available for psychologists to use. They all measure the same hypothetical construct, but not necessarily in the same way. The results we get from different measures may not be directly comparable.

Before moving on to the next section, try Activity Box 3.2 to think more about doing psychology scientifically.

ACTIVITY BOX 3.2

Experimental control and measurement

In Activity Box 3.1 we answered questions about a study investigating the effects of watching violent television on levels of aggression.

The first question asked what other explanations there might be if we found a difference in aggression. Some possible explanations are as follows.

- The people in the two groups differed in their 'natural' levels of aggression. It so happened that those watching violent television were more aggressive than those watching non-violent television. The type of television made no difference.
- The two programmes didn't differ only in the level of violence they showed. The violent programmes were also emotionally upsetting, and it was because people got upset that they became more aggressive.
- The experimenters gave the game away to their participants by inadvertently giving clues. The people in the violent group picked up on the fact that they were supposed to show more violence, and behaved compliantly.

For each of these possible explanations, try to think of ways in which we could use experimental control to stop these possibilities from happening, so that we can have more confidence that our results are accurate.

Activity Box 3.1 also asked how we might measure aggression. Some possibilities include:

- observing people's behaviour, to record how often they behave aggressively
- taking physiological measures of people's arousal – for example, measuring heart rate or respiration rate
- asking people to fill in a questionnaire, which requires them to rate their level of aggression.

Think about how good each method is. How practical is it to use? Does it really measure aggression, or does it measure something else? Does it give us an accurate measure?

Ethics

Psychology is largely the study of human behaviour, so we must conduct research on humans. In the last 30 years there has been increasing awareness of the potential of psychological research to cause harm to participants. This has led to a commitment to *research ethics*.

Research ethics covers a number of concerns. These include considering the welfare of research participants, maintaining honesty in conducting and reporting research, giving appropriate credit to others and considering how knowledge should be used. The British Psychological Society (2000) has developed ethical principles that British psychologists must adhere to.

FOCUS POINT 3.4

Ethics in research

Two psychology studies are commonly used to demonstrate unethical research in psychology. These are the Milgram experiment and the Zimbardo experiment.

Milgram (1963) investigated obedience to authority. Participants were told they were acting as teachers in a study on the effects of punishment on learning. Participants were shown another participant – the learner – in a cubicle, wired up to an electric shock machine. They were then taken to another room, in hearing distance but out of sight, and told to ask the learner questions. Each time the learner got the question wrong the 'teacher' was to give the learner a shock, increasing the shock by 15 volts for each wrong answer. Milgram was interested in how long participants would go on giving shocks if told to do so by the experimenter. He found that most administered potentially lethal shocks, despite hearing screams from the learner.

After the study, participants were told that the screams had been faked and that no electric shocks had been administered. The study has been widely condemned as unethical, because of the use of deception and the potential distress caused to participants in finding that they were capable of administering the shocks.

Zimbardo's study (Haney, Banks *et al.*, 1973) may be familiar to you as the basis for the BBC TV programme *The Experiment*. Zimbardo and his colleagues simulated a prison environment, getting students to role-play the parts of either prisoners or guards. The study was scheduled to run for 14 days. However, the guards quickly became brutal and the prisoners began to show pronounced distress, so Zimbardo cancelled the study after just six days. Again, this study was condemned for the potential psychological harm caused to participants. There is good coverage of the original study, the BBC's follow-up and the ethical issues involved at http://www.bbc.co.uk/science/theexperiment/.

It is essential that psychologists are ethical in their research and practice. Besides the moral responsibility on psychologists not to cause harm, the viability of psychological research depends on participants being able to trust researchers to protect them. This doesn't mean that we shouldn't conduct research. Psychological research has the potential to increase our understanding of behaviour and leads to valuable therapeutic techniques. However, we should always ensure the welfare of those who participate in research.

A fuller discussion of the ethical issues important to the design of good psychological research can be found in Chapter 37.

Alternatives to scientific psychology

In asking whether psychology is a science, one answer is to assess whether psychology meets the assumptions of science. However, the question can also mean '*Should* psychology be a science?' In other words, is the scientific way of knowing the right one for psychology? Science searches for regularities in behaviour, but some believe that discovering such regularities doesn't give us a deep understanding of the behaviour and experience of individuals (Hepburn, 2003).

We saw in Chapter 2 that there is a range of approaches to psychology. Not all of these approaches use the scientific method. Humanism rejects the scientific method because it prefers to concentrate on the richness of an individual's experience. More recently, the social constructionist approach has led to the development of *new paradigm research*, which uses qualitative rather than quantitative methods.

New paradigm research rejects the principles of science, and instead (Barker 2003):

- studies people in real life settings
- uses open-ended methods, like diaries and interviews, to gather information
- tries to incorporate the views and biases of the researcher in the research
- sees participants as collaborators in the research.

An advantage of new paradigm research is that it has good external validity, because it emphasises research in the real world. However, its lack of control means it has poor internal validity and reliability, and it is less successful in identifying the causes of behaviour. Because it concentrates on studying individuals it has difficulty explaining the behaviour of people in general, which for many is the goal of psychology.

There is an ongoing argument within psychology about the relative value of scientific and new paradigm approaches. There are four schools of thought (Stevenson and Cooper 1997):

1   Psychology is and should be a science. Scientific methods are appropriate, although there may be room for improvement in how they are used.

2   We should reject the idea of psychology as a science and use new paradigm methods.

3   We should use different methods for different areas of psychology. For example, cognitive psychology should be scientific, but social psychology should not be.

4   We should use a mix of methods to get a richer view of human behaviour (epistemological pluralism). For example, we could use qualitative methods to get initial ideas about a phenomenon (the induction stage), but use quantitative methods to test the theories we have about the phenomenon (the deduction stage).

Learning outcomes

When you have completed this chapter you should be able to:

- explain the principles and assumptions of science
- discuss how psychology can be seen as a science, and how psychology's methods relate to this
- evaluate issues around control, measurement, validity and artefacts, and recognise the threats these pose to scientific psychology
- assess the importance of ethical research
- evaluate the scientific approach in psychology and alternatives to scientific psychology.

Key terms

Artefacts
Deduction
Epistemology
Experimental control
Validity
Falsifiability
Hypothetical construct
Hypothetico-deductive method
Induction
New paradigm research
Ontology
Operationism
Research ethics

Further reading

Banyard, P. and Grayson, A. (2000) *Introducing Psychological Research.*
  Basingstoke: Palgrave.

Bell, A. (2002) *Debates in Psychology.* Hove: Routledge.

Gross, R. (2003) *Themes, Issues and Debates in Psychology* (2nd edn). London:
  Hodder Arnold.

Richards, G. (2002) *Putting Psychology in its Place.* Hove: Psychology Press.

Rosnow, R. and Rosenthal, R. (1997) *People Studying People: Artefacts and
  Ethics in Behavioural Research.* New York: WH Freeman.

4

Bias in psychology

Route map of the chapter

In this chapter, we look at the problem of bias in psychology. While psychology claims to be an objective, value-free science, we'll see that at various points it has produced theories that support inequality. We consider four main areas of bias; these include ethnocentrism (culture bias), androcentrism (pro-male bias) and racism, and also biases arising from methodology. These are particularly visible examples of bias, but the list isn't exhaustive. We could also have covered homophobia (anti-homosexuality bias) and ageism, for example, but unfortunately space doesn't allow full coverage. Having looked at these areas of bias, we then look at the implications of bias for psychology's claims to objectivity. We conclude by considering some ways in which the problem of bias can be tackled.

Introduction

In Chapter 3 we looked at psychology as a science. A key element of science is that observations are conducted objectively, and theories are developed objectively. However, can psychology, as the study of humans, be objective? There's a growing recognition of the potential for bias in psychology. Such bias threatens psychology's claims to objectivity, and hence to being a science. It also threatens the validity of psychological theories, and can have unfortunate consequences for the victims of bias.

In this chapter we look at the problem of bias in psychology. We start by looking at a number of ways in which bias may be manifested, before identifying some general points about bias. We then consider the implications of these for whether psychology can be

objective, and think about how we can tackle the problem of bias.

Ethnocentrism

Ethnocentrism occurs when we see things from our own cultural viewpoint as the norm, and see things from other cultures in comparison to this norm. In psychology, this means that psychologists have tended to adopt western (American and European) values, and these have shaped the theories and studies developed by psychologists. Ethnocentrism is exhibited in a number of ways, as outlined below.

- Most research studies in psychology are conducted in the USA, and most research described in psychology textbooks is American – over 90 per cent in American textbooks, and over 60 per cent in European textbooks (Smith and Bond, 1998). In addition, non-western research is rarely reported.
- This American research concentrates on studying American participants. This is the group of most interest to the researchers and those who fund research, and American participants are more readily available to study.
- Most studies involve undergraduate students, who themselves aren't representative of the American population (see Chapter 3).
- It is assumed that the results of these studies can be generalised to all humans in all cultures. This isn't a safe assumption – different cultures may show very different results (Smith and Bond, 1998).
- Western psychologists have tended to assume the superiority and desirability of western values. For example, theories of development such as

Maslow's (see Chapter 2) emphasise the need to achieve independence, but independence is less desired in collectivist societies that value self-sacrifice.

The search for universals

As a result of these features, psychology is to a large extent the science of young white Americans. Psychology says little about other groups specifically, and when it does it tends to do so in negative terms, as we shall see. This comes about partly because psychologists are trying to find universal aspects of human behaviour. If we're finding universals, then it doesn't matter what participants we use. However, the problem with this is apparent when we consider the concept of 'self'. The idea of self is fundamental to western views of human nature – though this is relatively recent (see Richards, 2002) – and has led to an emphasis in psychology on individuality and individual differences (Jones and Elcock, 2001). However, other societies place a greater emphasis on the survival of the group. In these societies, psychology would be more likely to emphasise group membership and similarity (Banyard, 1999).

Ethnocentrism arises because we identify with people like ourselves (our *in-group*), and tend to over-value the outputs of our in-group. Against this, we tend to undervalue the outputs of people unlike ourselves (the *out-group*), and show hostility towards out-group members (Banyard, 1999). Because of this, ethnocentrism is, to an extent, inevitable; however,

awareness of it can help us to avoid enshrining it in psychological theories.

Androcentrism

Androcentrism means a 'male-centred' approach. Traditionally, psychology has been dominated by male researchers studying male participants. It has been assumed that results from studies of male participants will simply generalise to females, and little research has been conducted into women's experiences. A considerable amount of work has been done on gender differences (Etaugh and Bridges, 2004), but this has usually taken the androcentric view that women are inferior to men (see Focus Point 4.1).

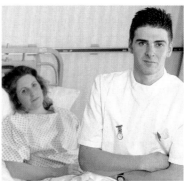

Are gender roles the result of fixed biological differences, or are they determined by society?

FOCUS POINT 4.1

Kohlberg's theory of moral development

Kohlberg (1968) investigated the development of moral reasoning using responses to a set of problems. For example, he described a man, 'Heinz', who couldn't afford to pay for drugs to save his wife's life, and so stole them. Kohlberg asked boys of different ages what they'd do, and identified three stages of moral development:

1 pre-conventional morality – the child responds to other people's definitions of good and bad

2 conventional morality – the child internalises the rules of society
3 post-conventional morality – the child develops his own well thought out ethical principles.

There are two biases in Kohlberg's theory. First, male values are given higher status than female values. Kohlberg assumed that men had better moral reasoning than women, and that women couldn't reach the highest stage. However,

FOCUS POINT 4.1 (CONT.)

Kohlberg didn't actually study women so had no evidence on which to base such claims.

The second bias is a cultural one. Kohlberg conducted a number of cross-cultural studies of moral reasoning and found, not surprisingly, that American boys were more morally advanced than boys from other cultures. This probably reflects the culture-specific nature of Kohlberg's tests more than any real moral superiority of American children.

The search for differences

Difference research investigating gender is an example of a common approach to psychology, which emphasises the search for differences. Psychological similarities between men and women outweigh psychological differences (Barker, 2003), but few psychologists investigate similarities. In part, this reflects the fact that research finding differences is more likely to be published than research that finds similarities. However, there is also a long history of psychology belittling women. Representations of women within psychology include Erikson's view that women's self-concept is defined by their attractiveness and the search for a mate, while Freud accused women of being 'the problem' (Banyard, 1999). In general, psychological theories have tended to characterise women as a problem, or as wives and mothers.

Problems of difference research

A common failing in sex difference research is that any differences that are found between men and women are ascribed to the biological basis of their sex. No account is taken of socialisation, and of the different experiences of men and women. The implication of this is that if gender differences are caused by biological sex, then such differences are unchangeable. On the other hand, accounting for any differences found between genders in terms of socialisation may suggest changes to society to address inequality. This is the project of feminist psychology (discussed under the heading 'Tackling bias in psychology', below). The key point here is that any research on sex differences is quasi-experimental, and as such does not allow us to ascribe causality (see Chapter 3). Whether we ascribe gender differences to biological sex or to socialisation depends on our own preferred form of explanation.

A common aspect of sex difference research is that it often starts from the assumption that males are the norm. Many of the classic studies in social psychology were carried out on male participants, including Kohlberg's theory of moral development and Erikson's model of identity (Kitzinger, 1998). These studies established what was considered normal, and when women differed from this they were considered to be deficient. However, when differences do exist there's no reason, except for one's own personal values, to choose one as 'normal' and another as 'deficient'. This point is highlighted in Tavris's (1991) reformulation of some classic claims from sex difference research (see Focus Point 4.2).

Androcentrism in psychology raises concerns about the validity of theories about 'universal' human nature, when the theories are based on a male perspective. In addition, however, psychology's failure to investigate women also led to a failure to understand the particular experiences of men. Gender-biased research is clearly damaging to women, but also to men – for example, when research suggests that only women should care for children (Barker, 2003).

Racism

The issue of racism should not, sadly, need a definition. It is clear that in the past psychology has produced racist theories. One example is Yerkes's mental testing of army recruits (see Focus Point 4.3). More generally, racism in psychology is illustrated by the project of *scientific racism*, defined by Banyard (1999: 86) as 'the attempt to justify racial policy

FOCUS POINT 4.2

Talking about gender

Tavris (1991) identified a number of conclusions that have been drawn from research on sex differences:

- women have lower self-esteem than men
- women value their efforts less than men
- women are more likely to say they're hurt than admit they're angry
- women have more difficulty in developing a sense of self.

Tavris noted that the way these conclusions are phrased presents women as deficient compared to a male norm. She highlighted this by rephrasing the conclusions as follows:

- men are more conceited than women
- men overvalue the work they do
- men are more likely to attack others when they are unhappy rather than describing their hurt and seeking support
- men have more difficulty than women in forming attachments.

Phrasing the conclusions in this way gives a very different impression of the research results. The difference isn't that one way is right and one is wrong. The difference between the two sets of phrases shows the importance of perspective in interpreting the results of psychology research.

---

through the use of bogus scientific arguments'. Scientific racism claims to find biologically founded differences between races on psychological variables. The approach has a history stretching back to the nineteenth century, and is based on a number of assumptions:

- different races exist, and have been engaged in an evolutionary contest

Are psychologists right when they claim to have found differences between races, or is there more to it than they suggest?

- the contest is over, races can't develop any further, and whites have 'won'
- compared to whites, other races are in a state of arrested development.

Scientific racism believes that there's nothing policy-makers can do about these biological 'facts'. In this view, 'lower races' may be better on 'primitive' characteristics, such as reaction times, but are behind 'higher races' on 'civilised' characteristics, such as intelligence, and always will be.

The assumptions of scientific racism, and their basis in scientific fact, have been widely disputed (see, for example, Richards, 1997). Despite this, scientific racism seems to have an enduring appeal.

The durability of scientific racism

Scientific racism was common from the late nineteenth century to the 1930s, when the excesses of the Nazi regime in Germany made it taboo to advocate scientific racist policies (Jones and Elcock, 2001). In part, they reflected the social context of the time: many people implicitly believed in racial differences. If scientific racism could be dismissed as a historical anomaly, then it would be less of a

FOCUS POINT 4.3

The Army Alpha and Beta tests

When the USA joined the First World War in 1917, American psychologists applied themselves to helping the war effort. One contribution came from Robert Yerkes, who developed group tests of intelligence that were intended to categorise new army recruits into career roles. These tests were known as the Army Alpha and Beta tests. The Alpha test was a written test for literate recruits, while the Beta was a pictorial test. The tests were administered to a total of 1.7 million new army recruits, and were seen as a great success, despite not actually having much of an effect on the military (Jones and Elcock, 2001). However, Gould (1982) describes a range of problems with the tests themselves, and with the interpretation of the test findings.

Gould found that the tests were mis-administered. For example, illiterate recruits were often required to take the Alpha test. Even on the pictorial form of the test, illiterate and immigrant recruits were required to use a pencil and do sums, which were usually unfamiliar skills. The tests themselves were heavily culture biased, asking more about knowledge of American culture than they called for intellectual reasoning. One written question asked 'Crisco is a: patent medicine; disinfectant; toothpaste; food product?' One pictorial item asked respondents to draw in the missing item on a picture of a tennis court with no net. These items clearly required knowledge of toothpaste and tennis, which recent immigrants, for example, may well not have had.

Unsurprisingly, the results of the test showed strong correlations between IQ scores and length of schooling, and between IQ scores and length of residence in the USA. Both of these findings clearly point to an environmental effect on scores. However, the tests were interpreted as providing evidence for racial differences in intelligence. For example, blacks were shown as scoring lowest. This result can be explained readily given that in the USA at the time education was segregated and blacks had considerably less schooling than whites. However, Yerkes and his colleagues preferred to claim evidence for innate racial differences in intelligence.

concern. However, what would you make of an article that claimed to find differences between three races, as shown in Table 4.1? You might think that this must be quite an old example. However, this research was published in *The Psychologist* in 1990 (Rushton, 1990).

Problems with scientific racism

The defence of scientific racism is based on the claim that the research scientific racism is based on is objective, and the data must speak for themselves. Scientists, it is suggested, should not have to suppress scientific fact to satisfy societal concerns.

However, a number of problems have been identified with scientific racist research (Banyard, 1999).

- There are problems in defining race. The concept of race has no biological reality, it is a socially defined construct (see below).
- There is much more variation within each racial group than there is between racial groups.
- It has been impossible to get comparable samples of people from different races to compare, which would allow us to discount other factors (see Chapter 3).

TABLE 4.1

SELECTED RESULTS FROM RUSHTON (1990)

Characteristic	Mongoloids	Caucasoids	Negroids
'Excess neurons'	8.90m	8.65m	8.55m
Age of walking	Slow	Medium	Fast
Age of first intercourse	Slow	Medium	Fast
Age of first pregnancy	Slow	Medium	Fast
Life span	Long	Medium	Short
Aggressiveness	Low	Medium	High
Sociability	Low	Medium	High
Law abidance	Low	Medium	High
Mental health	High	Medium	Low

Source: Banyard, 1999

What these criticisms amount to is that while we might find differences between socially defined groups, these differences could be caused by a number of social factors. We have no real justification for claiming differences are caused by biology. We can observe that the distribution of genes that determine skin colour has no particular correspondence with the distributions of genes for other physiological characteristics (Richards, 1997). As a society, we decided at some distant point in the past to use skin colour to categorise people into groups we call 'races' (hence race as a socially defined construct), but we could equally have used eye colour or hair colour. The implication of this is that it's difficult to claim that there might be a biological correspondence between skin colour and, say, intelligence. Despite this, scientific racist claims continue to be made in psychology.

ACTIVITY BOX 4.1

Evaluating scientific racism

Table 4.1 shows some selected results from Rushton's (1990) article in *The Psychologist*. Rushton's purpose was, first, to argue a case for *neoteny* (see below) and, second, to argue that races differ in how advanced they are.

Neoteny is the idea that evolution has extended the period of childhood in humans compared to our ancestors. Most animals are born with fully formed brains, but primates continue some brain development after birth. Chimpanzees continue to show brain development for nine months after birth. On the other hand, human brains continue to develop into the late teens. This extended period of brain development gives us great adaptability, because the brain is able to shape itself to the environment (which has implications for the nature–nurture debate discussed in Chapter 5).

The idea of neoteny is not widely disputed. What is controversial is the claim, advanced by Rushton in his article, that different races differ in the degree of neoteny they display. Those with more neoteny – that is, a longer childhood – are seen as more evolutionarily advanced than those with a shorter childhood. Rushton's purpose, then, is to show that races differ in the length of their childhood, and hence in how advanced they are.

Rushton's article has been criticised as being 'academically shallow but openly racist' (Banyard, 1999: 85). Certainly, it's worth thinking critically about the basis of Rushton's research. Think about the following questions.

- Rushton divides the world's people into three races. Do you think this classification is appropriate? How else might we classify race? Why might Rushton have chosen only three races?
- Rushton has chosen an eclectic set of variables to consider. Why do you think he's chosen the variables shown in Table 4.1?
- The article claims that differences in the variables listed are the result of biological differences. Can you think of any alternative reasons for Rushton's results? For example, what environmental reasons might account for the low average life span of 'negroids'?

Methodological bias

The examples of bias discussed previously in this chapter arise from the views of psychologists. These views may directly affect what psychologists say, but may also influence the way they go about doing research. In addition, the research methods used by psychologists introduce a source of bias themselves.

Observation and theory

The hypothetico-deductive method (see Chapter 3) suggests that researchers should observe phenomena, and induce theories on the basis of these observations. The theories developed can be used deductively to develop hypotheses, which are tested by conducting research to produce certain data. The idea is that this is conducted in an objective way. However, it is impossible to interpret our observations of phenomena in an 'objective' way, to see things as they really are, even in terms of basic perception.

As a simple example, look at Figure 4.1. What do you see? It's likely that you can't help but see a triangle, even though no triangle is there. How we interpret our observations depends on our existing knowledge, experience and expectations. These expectations include a number of things. In the case of observing psychological phenomena, our expectations include any pre-existing theories we hold, and also pre-existing beliefs. This also affects how we interpret the results of our studies. When we test our predictions, we need to decide what our results mean. This will be affected by what we expect and want the results to mean.

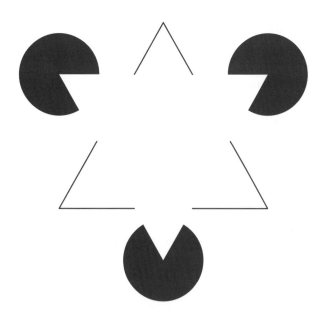

Figure 4.1 *Kanizsa's triangle: most people will see a triangle even though there isn't one, showing how perception is influenced by experience and expectations*

The constraints of methods

The kinds of methods used by psychologists introduce a source of bias because they constrain the kinds of things psychologists can find out about. If we're committed to basing our thoughts on evidence, then we can only think about what we've got evidence for. Different research methods give us different kinds of information, but the 'gold standard' for research in psychology is the experiment. Experiments involve looking for differences between groups. Therefore, psychology becomes a *study of differences*. As Richards (2002: 259) puts it, 'when the only tool you have is a hammer everything begins to look like a nail'.

This preference for difference studies is illustrated by the number of studies looking at differences between genders, and the absence of studies looking at similarities. It's also illustrated by the tendency for journals to publish articles that show a statistically significant difference, but to not publish articles that fail to show such a difference. The reason for this preference is probably that science is seen as a search for cause-and-effect relationships. Using controlled experiments is the only way of showing such relationships with confidence. However, concentrating on showing differences means that there are things that psychology doesn't investigate. The temptation is to assume that such things aren't of interest to psychology, just as behaviourism did with mental processes.

Psychology and objectivity

The problems of ethnocentrism, androcentrism and racism show that psychology sometimes represents the interests of one group over those of others. Richards (1997) suggests that psychology is made up of a number of *constituencies*. This means that different kinds of people are included in the discipline – for example, white middle-class men or lesbian women. These people often represent the interests of their constituency.

At the start of psychology's history, psychologists were overwhelmingly white middle-class heterosexual men, and their theories reflected the concerns and interests of white middle-class heterosexual men. An example of this comes from early studies of intelligence, which investigated gender and racial differences in intelligence. White male psychologists found, unsurprisingly, that white men were more intelligent than other groups (Gould, 1997). In general, the group of white middle-class heterosexual men was seen as the norm, and their privileged position in society was seen as the natural state of affairs.

Theories from this time often tried to show why this state of affairs was natural. Over time, the constituencies represented by psychology have widened, as women and members of minority groups have entered the discipline. This change is reflected in growing awareness of the problem of bias, and changes in the kinds of theory psychology produces. However, there are still structural problems in the discipline that suggest the problem of bias needs to be taken seriously.

Problems in the conduct of psychology

The areas of bias we've covered so far in the chapter show specific examples of bias in action. By examining this biased research, we can draw out a number of features of psychology research that may introduce or reinforce bias. These include the following.

Using hypothetical averages

Studies find the average performance of a group of people, and base findings on this hypothetical average. However, this average performance may not correspond to any particular individual.

Generalising from samples

Psychology research involves taking a group of participants and generalising from them to the population as a whole. This is only reasonable to the extent that the sample is representative.

Emphasising between group differences

Experiments involve looking for differences between the average performances of groups. However, the results usually say little about the variation in performance within groups. Women may score between 85 and 145 on a (invented) measure of 'binkiness' (Banyard, 1999), with an average of 105. Men may score between 84 and 144, with an average of 104. There's a difference between the groups, but this is much smaller than the differences in performance *within* each group (see Figure 4.2).

Ignoring minority groups

When studies rely on a hypothetical average of a group, that average will reflect the majority members of the group more accurately than it will minority members of the group. If, for example, we're looking at differences in intelligence between men and women, our group of men might include 50 young men with an average IQ score of 105, and 10 older men with an average IQ score of 110. The average IQ score for men as a group will be 106, but this isn't really a fair reflection of the performance of the older men. In general, when particular groups (based on race, class, handedness or whatever) represent a minority within a larger group, then that minority is likely to be under-represented by the results of the group as a whole.

Adopting a group as a norm

Difference studies may implicitly or explicitly identify one group as a norm, and see differences between groups as a failing of the other group. As we have already seen, this is common in studies of gender differences, where the male performance is seen as normal and the female performance, if it differs, is seen as deficient.

Believing in fixed differences

Where differences are found, these are often interpreted as being fixed. Alternative interpretations that allow the possibility of change may be ignored.

Ascribing causality

The logic of the experiment says that if we control all factors other than the factor we manipulate, then we can ascribe causality. However, in quasi-experimental studies we cannot ascribe causality if we find a difference. We can only say there is a difference and use reasoning to explain the difference. This reasoning will be affected by our pre-existing theories and beliefs.

Tackling bias in psychology

ACTIVITY BOX 4.2	

Thinking about heterosexism

This chapter describes biases arising from ethnocentrism, androcentrism and racism. Another form of bias is *heterosexism*. This is when heterosexuality is treated as a norm and homosexuality is seen as deviant. Heterosexism in psychology is illustrated by the fact that until 1973 the American Psychological Association's manual for the classification of mental illness, the *DSM*, included homosexuality as a sexual deviation. Similarly, it took nine years and four attempts to establish a Lesbian and Gay Psychology section of the British Psychological Society (Kitzinger and Coyle, 2002).

This heterosexism is apparent in a number of classic theories within psychology. For example, Erikson's theory of life span development includes seeking 'relationships with a partner of the opposite sex'.

Review the description of Freud's psychoanalytic theory in Chapter 2. How does Freud's theory reflect heterosexism in psychology? Can you think of other examples of heterosexism in psychology?

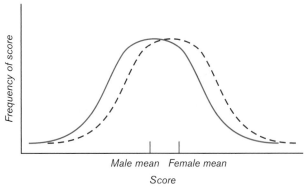

Figure 4.2 Distributions of scores for the invented measure of 'binkiness': the distributions show a small difference between males and females, but a considerable difference within each group
Source: Banyard, 1999

From what we've covered so far in the chapter it's easy to see how bias can be introduced into psychology studies. This is most worrying when psychology influences social policy – for example, when theories of intelligence influence schooling policy. Psychologists may claim that in conducting objective science, they aren't responsible for any policy effects of their theories. They might claim that they are only involved in finding facts, and it's up to politicians, who make policy, to decide what should be done with those facts. However, given concerns about the extent to which psychologists can be objective, and the extent to which they make interpretations of ambiguous evidence rather than finding guaranteed facts, it is important that we try to eliminate bias as much as possible. There are a number of ways of doing this. One is to do scientific psychology better, to prevent bias creeping in. Another is to tackle psychology in different ways.

Improving scientific methodology

There are a number of ways in which we can do scientific psychology better, and these are related to the problems discussed in the sections on methodological bias and psychology and objectivity, above. These include:

- not over-interpreting the results of quasi-experimental studies – a quasi-experiment may find a difference between groups, but this does not prove a causal relationship
- ensuring that samples are representative – in some cases undergraduate students may be representative of the population, but in many cases they will not be
- not over-stating the population – given a particular sample, we should limit claims to the population that is represented by that sample; if we've only tested males, then our results only apply to males
- looking for similarities as well as differences – psychologists prefer to look for differences because of the desire to ascribe causality; however, this means not investigating a range of phenomena in psychology
- considering effect sizes – reports of difference tests usually concentrate on whether a result is

significant or not; however, this says nothing about how big a difference there is between groups, and the difference may be very small; reporting effect sizes, which indicate the size of the difference, allows us to make a judgement about how meaningful a result is (Thompson, 1999).
- recognising the effect of values on interpretation – because of the desire to be objective, scientists usually say nothing about their own value systems when reporting on research; arguably, this makes more sense for the physicist, who probably doesn't care what the accelerative force of gravity is, than it does for the psychologist; being open about our own values makes it easier for others to interpret our claims (Thompson, 1999).

Adopting an alternative approach

There is currently a growing recognition of the need to improve research practice in psychology, as described in the previous section. However, some psychologists reject the use of the scientific method entirely and adopt alternative approaches. One such approach is that of *cross-cultural psychology*. Cross-cultural psychology assumes that culture is a key independent variable. It seeks to investigate differences and similarities between cultures, to identify which behaviours are culture bound and which are universal (Gross, 2001).

Another alternative approach, which adopts a social constructionist perspective, is *feminist psychology*. Kitzinger (1998) states that this is based on two assumptions:

1 women are worthwhile human beings, worthy of study in their own right
2 social change is necessary to improve the situation of women.

The view that psychology can be an agent of social change runs entirely counter to the idea of psychology as an objective, detached science. For feminist psychologists, psychology should be active and engaged in social issues.

The idea that psychology should be engaged in social issues is supported by Howitt and Owusu-

Section 1
Conceptual and historical issues

Bempah (1994). They assert that bias must be rooted out at individual, institutional and cultural levels. For example, individuals should strive to become sensitive to their own and others' biases, should empathise with the victims of bias, and should decide actively to resist bias rather than ignore it. The need to tackle bias is seen as a moral obligation.

Learning outcomes
When you have completed this chapter you should be able to:

- describe the issue of bias, and the threat it poses to objectivity in psychology
- assess how ethnocentrism affects the validity of theories in psychology
- evaluate the impact of androcentrism and racism on psychology's treatment of diverse groups in society
- discuss how bias can be introduced into scientific methodology in psychology
- describe ways in which we can tackle the problem of bias in psychology.

> **Key Terms**
> *Androcentrism*
> *Cross-cultural psychology*
> *Difference research*
> *Ethnocentrism*
> *Feminist psychology*
> *Heterosexism*
> *Scientific racism*

Further reading

Banyard, P. (1999) *Controversies in Psychology*. London: Routledge.

Etaugh, C. A. and Bridges, J. S. (2004) *The Psychology of Women: A Lifespan Perspective* (2nd edn). Boston, MA: Allyn & Bacon.

Gross, R. (2003) *Themes, Issues and Debates in Psychology* (2nd edn). London: Hodder Arnold.

Jones, D. and Elcock, J. (2001) *History and Theories of Psychology: A Critical Perspective*. London: Arnold.

Richards, G. (1997) *Race, Racism and Psychology: Towards a Reflexive History*. London: Routledge.

Smith, P. B. and Bond, M. H. (1998) *Social Psychology Across Cultures* (2nd edn). Hemel Hempstead: Prentice Hall Europe.

Issues and debates in psychology

Route map of the chapter

This chapter introduces three key debates in psychology that shape the kinds of approaches psychologists use to understand human nature. The chapter is divided into four main sections. It begins with an overview of how issues arise in psychology and the ways in which psychologists choose a position in debates. It then goes on to look at reductionism and its value, free will and determinism, and the nature–nurture debate. These topics have been chosen because they affect the fundamental purposes and methods of psychology, and psychologists' views of human nature. Understanding the nature of these debates, and where different psychologists stand in regard to them, is critical for evaluating the theories in psychology that we'll see later in the book. In addition, understanding the debates will help us to evaluate the claims about psychology that are made in everyday life.

Introduction

We saw in Chapter 2 that there are a number of different theoretical approaches in psychology, and each provides a different kind of explanation of the same psychological phenomena. Why are there so many different approaches? You might think that psychology would have developed a standard approach to investigating phenomena. There are a number of reasons why it hasn't. One is that different psychologists are trying to achieve different things. For example, some may be trying to develop therapeutic techniques, while others are striving to explain the structure of memory. Related to this,

different psychologists try to explain things at different levels, as we saw in Chapter 2. Another reason why there are a number of different approaches to psychology is that there are some key philosophical issues that psychologists disagree on. These issues influence our views of human nature, and also affect how research is conducted. In this chapter, then, we'll look at some of the major debates in psychology.

Overview of issues and debates

A number of key philosophical issues divide psychologists. These include:

- reductionism and its appropriateness
- free will and determinism
- heredity and environment.

An individual's viewpoint on these issues affects their conception of human nature, their view of how to explain behaviour, and their choice of methods and interpretation of evidence. In order to understand the complexity of psychology, and particularly in order to appreciate why there may be several competing theoretical explanations of a given phenomenon, it is necessary to understand these issues.

The difficulty psychology as a discipline faces is that these issues lack objective criteria for resolution. How, then, do psychologists choose a position on a particular issue? This is a question that is often overlooked. It is taken for granted that disagreements occur. However, by looking at the factors influencing psychologists' choice of position on these issues we can get a better understanding of the nature of psychology. This is one reason why it can be useful to study the history of psychology, since studying developments in its past can help us to understand these factors (Richards, 2002). Understanding the basis of a particular position, and its effect on the theories that are developed, can also help us to assess the validity of theories in psychology. The kind of approach psychologists take, and the kind of theories they develop, depend in part on their view on these issues.

A full discussion of these factors is beyond the scope of this book, but they will be considered briefly, as relevant, when considering particular issues and particular theories. The suggestions for further reading at the end of the chapter give more thorough coverage. In general, though, we can say that a range of factors outside the discipline of psychology itself will affect a psychologist's views on these issues. Such factors include the socio-cultural context, political beliefs, the background of the theorist, sources of funding and practicality (Jones and Elcock, 2001).

Reductionism

Reductionism is a general term referring to a view that complex phenomena can best be understood by reducing them to separate, simpler parts. In psychology, reductionists may claim that only a single level of explanation is necessary to explain human behaviour.

Types of reductionism

The term reductionism can be used in a number of ways. Malim and Birch (1998) identify four types of reductionism, which will be discussed briefly here.

Physiological reductionism

Physiological reductionism is the general view that psychological explanations can be replaced by physiological explanations. The particular aspect of physiology varies, but most commonly is either that of brain functioning or of genetics. Recently there has been some merging of these two levels, such that Steven Rose (1998) talks of *neurogenetic determinism*, the idea that behaviour is determined by a

combination of brain operation and genetic inheritance. This form of reductionism is particularly amenable to scientific explanation, and it provides (relatively) simple explanations of psychological phenomena. Since we are biological organisms, we assume that there is a neurophysiological basis for behaviour, and hence potentially we can explain all behaviour in neurophysiological terms.

Physiological reductionism has had considerable success, as we saw in Chapter 2 when we considered the physiological approach to psychology. For example, schizophrenia is thought to be due to a malfunction of brain chemistry (particularly a surfeit of dopamine). This explanation has led to successful treatment. However, there are some problems with this explanation. In particular, it doesn't explain what led to the high levels of dopamine (there could be an underlying biological or environmental cause of this). Relatedly, it cannot explain why in Britain black males are ten times more likely to develop schizophrenia than white males, and why the pattern may be different in other cultures. (See Chapter 33 for a fuller discussion of these issues.)

Biological reductionism

Biological reductionism attempts to explain human behaviour in terms of less complex animals. This approach has been an important one throughout the history of psychology, including late nineteenth-century comparative psychology, behaviourism and *ethology*. Modern biological reductionism comes in the form of *sociobiology* (Wilson, 2000), which searches for evolutionary origins of behaviour and studies less complex animals to identify which behaviours may be genetically determined. Biological reductionism in its various forms has contributed greatly to the development of psychology and our understanding of human nature. However, a potential difficulty of the approach is that it assumes a continuity of behaviour between humans and lower animals, such that humans share a behavioural repertoire with less complex animals. Not everyone accepts this, claiming that just as humans are *physiologically* different from other species (for example, we stand on two legs), so humans are also different *behaviourally* (Malim and Birch, 1998).

Experimental reductionism

This is more an issue of methodology than philosophy, and hence a different kind of issue. *Experimental reductionism* attempts to isolate particular factors influencing behaviour, and study the effect of those factors in isolation. This reflects the issue of experimental control discussed in Chapter 3. The view is that the particular behaviour can be explained solely in terms of those factors. As an example, a psychologist might study the effect of noise on memory for word lists, and ask one group to remember a word list in a quiet environment, and another group to remember the list in a noisy environment. As we saw in Chapter 3, applying experimental control can lead to a loss of external validity for the sake of internal validity. However, strong internal validity is necessary if psychology is to produce precise and rigorous scientific theories (Malim and Birch, 1998).

Machine reductionism

Machine reductionism is the use of computer models to explain psychological phenomena, particularly in the area of cognitive psychology. Many theories in cognitive psychology are based on the *mind as computer* metaphor. The application of computer modelling has produced a number of impressive simulations, particularly in the area of problem solving (Malim and Birch, 1998). However, there are some important differences between humans and computers that need to be borne in mind. For example, humans are conscious and forgetful, while computers are neither.

Reductionism and levels of explanation

There is an alternative way of conceiving of reductionism, which is in terms of *levels of explanation*. Rose (1998) suggests a hierarchy of sciences, corresponding to different levels of explanation (see Table 5.1). Sciences lower down the hierarchy are seen as more scientific than those higher up. Reductionism can be seen as an attempt to explain phenomena at a given level in terms of levels below. For example, physiological

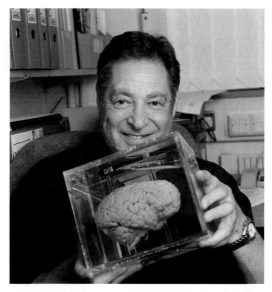

Steven Rose is a leading British critic of reductionism in psychology.

reductionism attempts to explain psychological phenomena (such as extroversion) in terms of physiology (brain operation) or biochemistry (genetics). One attraction of reductionism is that it suggests that we can provide more scientific explanations of behaviour by explaining things at a lower level of the hierarchy. In line with this, the physicist James Watson once remarked 'there is only one science, physics: the rest is just social work'.

Any given phenomenon in psychology can be explained using any level of the hierarchy. As an example, consider the explanation of a handshake. This can be explained in many ways, including the social role fulfilled by a handshake, the thought processes underlying the physical act, the physiological processes necessary to make the hand move, the chemical state of the brain and body tissue at the time, and so on. The question is, what is the most suitable level of explanation? Although it is possible to explain a handshake in terms of physiology, in psychology it might be more important to concentrate on *why* people shake hands.

Psychology asks two kinds of questions about behaviour. These are *how* behaviour was performed

Section 1
Conceptual and historical issues

TABLE 5.1

A HIERARCHY OF SCIENCES

Rose (1998) identifies a hierarchy of sciences. Those at lower levels investigate simpler units than those above.

Science	Units of explanation
Sociology	Society
Social psychology	Groups
Cognitive psychology	Mental processes
Physiology of systems	Brain physiology
Physiology of units	Genes
Anatomy/biochemistry	Chemicals in the brain
Chemistry	Chemicals in isolation
Physics	Subatomic particles within chemicals

ACTIVITY BOX 5.1

Reductionism

In this chapter, we use the example of explaining a handshake to show that we can explain a given thing at different levels of explanation. We saw that a handshake can be explained in terms of sociology, of social psychology, of cognitive psychology, and so on.

Try doing this yourself. Draw up a table showing the levels of the hierarchy, like the one below, leaving a blank column to enter your explanations. Now work down the hierarchy trying to explain telling a joke at each level.

Level	Explanation
Sociology	
Social psychology	
Cognitive psychology	
Physiology of systems	
Physiology of units	

Level	Explanation
Anatomy/biochemistry	
Chemistry	
Physics	

You'll probably find that the kinds of explanations you come up with change as you go down the table, from explanations of *why* people tell jokes to explanations of *how* people tell jokes.

Look back at what you've written, and mark whether each explanation is an explanation of 'why' or an explanation of 'how'. Now try giving the other kind of explanation for each level. For example, at the social psychology level you might have explained that people tell jokes to build up friendships or to break the ice in an awkward situation. These are 'why' explanations. Alternatively, you might give a 'how' explanation in terms of the way people take turns to tell jokes, the way in which jokes rely on shared knowledge of how the world works, and so on.

and *why* behaviour was performed. For each of these questions a different level of explanation may be appropriate.

The 'Why shake hands?' question could be answered at a social level (social psychological in most cases, but sociological in the case of, for example, Gerry Adams and David Trimble), or it could also be answered in evolutionary terms.

The 'How shake hands?' question can't be answered at a social level, and a lower level of explanation is necessary. This may be the cognitive psychological level, which would try to explain the mental processes guiding the motor movements that control the hand. Alternatively, it may be at a physiological level, which explains how nerve fibres carry signals to muscles, how the muscles contract, and so on.

There are advantages to reductionism conceived in this way. It fits in with attempts to be scientific, it provides nice concise explanations, and in some cases (as with dopamine and schizophrenia) it suggests successful interventions. For some questions, we must look for answers at a lower level. However, there are also a number of disadvantages – in particular, the fact that reductionism tends to lose many of the important features of the phenomenon of interest – the

idiom 'can't see the wood for the trees' applies here, since reductionism is really about looking for the trees.

As an example of the difficulties inherent in some reductionist approaches, consider the search for neurogenetic explanations of violence. It has been suggested that there is a 'gene for violence', or that violent people have an excess of testosterone. These seem to be easily understood explanations of violence, but they overlook the fact that violence tends to happen in particular social and cultural contexts. The notion of 'violence' itself is constructed by social agreement. A terrorist who bombs a building would be seen as 'violent', and as requiring explanation. However, a pilot who bombs an enemy building would be seen as serving his/her country, and not needing explanation.

The difference here is one of social interpretation, and biological processes won't necessarily correspond with social categorisations. Fortunately in much of psychology the phenomena being investigated are more clearly defined, and direct correlates between psychological and physiological phenomena can be found. For example, we can usefully identify how memories are physically stored in the brain and we can identify the genes that give people a predisposition for certain illnesses.

One concern about reductionism is that in some cases reductionist explanations have been sought for particular reasons or purposes. Reductionist arguments have been used, for example, to claim that there are racial differences between groups and to argue for the inevitability of inequality in society. This isn't a problem of reductionism in itself, but rather an example of bias in psychology. These concerns are addressed in Chapter 4.

Free will and determinism

Discussing reductionism in the context of neurogenetic explanations brings us to the next issue that concerns psychologists. This is the question of whether we have *free will*, or whether we should accept *determinism* – the view that all behaviour is determined. Neurogenetic explanations are deterministic, in that they assume that behaviour is caused (or determined) by particular brain structures, or particular chemical balances, or a particular genetic make-up. Thus if you have a gene to be violent, you will be violent. Your behaviour is determined by the gene. Reductionism in Rose's (1998) sense is deterministic, since it suggests that a given phenomenon can be explained by (because it is determined by) processes at a lower level.

The debate over whether we have free will or whether behaviour is determined is an ancient one in philosophy, and given psychology's antecedents has inevitably become a debate within psychology too. However, unlike the reductionism issue, the debate over determinism is often obscured, because many psychologists implicitly adhere to the view that behaviour is determined. This is an inevitable consequence of psychology's determination to be scientific (Valentine, 1992). Scientific psychology involves looking for cause-and-effect relationships (see Chapter 3), which of course means that behaviour must be caused. Any scientific approach to psychology is therefore a deterministic approach at heart.

There would seem not to be much of a debate over determinism. Unfortunately, this deterministic view conflicts with our subjective experience of having free will. If asked, most people would say that their behaviour is often the result of conscious choices or

is in some other way undetermined. Much of the time, therefore, psychology keeps quiet on the issue. The main exceptions are in the areas of neurogenetic determinism, where the determinism is made explicit, and humanistic psychology, where free will is championed.

In terms of 'mainstream' psychology, the most prominent exponents of determinism were the behaviourists, who believed that behaviour was determined by learnt responses, and the psychodynamicists, who believed that behaviour was determined by a combination of biology and early experience. The important point is that most researchers in psychology continue to use a behaviourist methodology, and so continue to work on the implicit assumption that behaviour is determined.

To consider the debate between free will and determinism in more depth, let's look at some definitions of the concepts.

Free will

One of the problems psychologists face is what precisely is meant by free will. Valentine (1992) suggests a number of possible interpretations of what we mean when we say that we have free will.

Choice

In everyday terms, people would say they have free will if they have a genuine choice in a particular situation. However we can't test this assertion because we can't guarantee that there isn't some underlying cause that we aren't able to identify, perhaps because of a lack of knowledge or a lack of necessary technology.

Behaviour that is uncaused

This doesn't really mean behaviour that is random, which is what a literal interpretation would suggest. Experience suggests that behaviour is predictable in some way. This interpretation is better phrased as meaning behaviour that is unconstrained (Gross, 2003). This interpretation is adopted by soft determinism, which we shall consider later.

Voluntary behaviour

Voluntary behaviour is behaviour over which we have control, as opposed to involuntary behaviour, which is behaviour that is an uncontrolled reflex. If we have control, then this suggests that we have free will. We can give a more technical definition of 'choice' if we say that choice means exerting control over our behaviour.

None of these explanations is particularly problematic, and all of them seem to express our subjective experience of feeling free. None of them denies that behaviour is predictable, and in some versions of determinism they all fit in with a deterministic view. The advantage of adopting these interpretations is that they fit in with subjective experience. However, they may not fit in with a scientific model. Accepting free will also has the advantage that we can continue to accept our everyday ideas of moral responsibility. Rejecting the idea that people are responsible for their actions, as extreme determinism would suggest, would make responsible social behaviour difficult. The main disadvantage of accepting a strong free will position is that you're then left with the rather difficult task of finding an alternative explanation of how behaviour comes about.

Determinism

Determinism comes in a number of forms, depending on what forces are claimed to determine behaviour. The two extremes are behaviourism, which says that all behaviour is determined by experience, and neurogenetic determinism, which says that all behaviour is explained by evolution and genetics. The contrast between these two positions is at the heart of the heredity/environment debate that is covered in the next section. When we consider that debate, we'll see that the debate is about *what* determines behaviour, not *whether* behaviour is determined.

The common argument in the different flavours of determinism is that all behaviour has a cause. Taken to an extreme, determinism suggests that all future behaviour is predictable, given sufficient information. This has the advantage of fitting scientific explanation, and can allow a degree of

control. However, if all behaviour is determined, then how can we ascribe praise or blame to actions? Other disadvantages of determinism are that modern physics suggests that physical events are not entirely determined, so how can we say that behaviour is, and that it is unfalsifiable (Valentine, 1992).

An intermediate position is that of *soft determinism*, which holds that behaviour is determined to a certain extent, but that in the absence of compulsion people have an element of choice over courses of action. In soft determinism, the focus is on coercion rather than causation. It assumes that there is ultimately a causal explanation, but that the explanation is difficult or impossible to access. The ultimate cause is therefore irrelevant to explaining everyday behaviour.

This view seems to fit subjective experience. The question then changes. Soft determinism is basically saying that many things are determined, but that there is some degree of free will. So the question becomes one of how much is determined, and what is free will. Most debate in psychology, and most differences between theories, is in terms of this. For example, neurogenetic determinism argues for a large degree of determinism, whereas much modern social psychology argues for a large degree of free will. As a rule of thumb, reductionist theories tend to be deterministic, whereas non-reductionist theories tend to allow more free will.

In considering the debate between free will and determinism, it's important to recognise that there may not be a single answer to the debate for all of psychology. Psychologists study many different phenomena, and it's possible that phenomena differ in the extent to which they are determined. One contribution to the development of cognitive psychology came from Chomsky (1957) who argued forcefully that language production is a spontaneous and creative process. We choose what we're going to say, even though there will be a number of factors affecting what it is that we say.

On the other hand, it's clear that some phenomena are strongly determined. For example, many human behaviours are instinctive responses that we have limited control over (try not blinking when someone throws something at your eyes), and there are clearly identified genes for a range of conditions, including *Down's syndrome* and *phenylketunoria (PKU)*. It's also important to recognise that determinism seems to work for psychology, and for the sciences in general (Valentine, 1992).

We will see throughout the book examples of well-founded and well-supported theories that identify determining causes for behaviour. It seems rather unreasonable to adopt a strong free will position given the volume of psychological knowledge which suggests that most behaviours are, to some extent, determined.

Heredity and environment

The question of the relative influences of *heredity* and *environment* on behaviour is one of the most visible and long-running debates in psychology. Many of psychology's most controversial claims rely on the view that heredity is a strong determinant of human nature. This debate is where the influence of psychologists' beliefs on their theorising is most apparent, demonstrated in many discussions of the issue (e.g. Rose, Lewontin *et al.*, 1990; Gould, 1997).

Are a child's character and capabilities determined from birth?

The issue is sometimes known as the *nature–nurture debate*, and concerns whether genetic inheritance (the heredity or nature side) or the environment (the nurture side) determines behaviour. Today, the debate is couched in terms of genetics, but it actually predates the discovery of genes (Gould, 1997). In psychology, the debate is mainly concentrated on the explanation of personality and intelligence.

The opposing views

The environmental outlook suggests that a newborn child is a blank slate, whose nature will be shaped by experience. This allows the possibility of change – if you change the environment then you change the person. Environmental explanations provide a basis for attempts (such as those of the behaviourists) to control and modify behaviour.

Hereditarian explanations provided the basis for the *eugenics* movement, and are also the basis of some of the theories discussed in Chapter 4. The hereditarian position claims that newborn children carry a blueprint that dictates aspects of their character. Behaviours develop over time, where maturation leads to genetically determined behaviours becoming part of a person's repertoire.

Questions of heredity and environment

Early discussions of the heredity–environment debate asked which factor determined behaviour. However, it became clear that both heredity and environment have an effect on the individual (see Focus Point 5.1). The question then changed to how much each factor determined behaviour. This was based on the assumption that heredity and environment had separate effects, which could be added together to explain the totality of behaviour.

For many psychological phenomena, it seems entirely reasonable to suggest that there's both a genetic and an environmental component. However, as the example of height shows, there's an interaction between the two. Two identical twins raised in different environments will differ. Despite the occasional story about twins separated at birth who meet up 50 years later and find they both have purple as their favourite colour, most identical twins are different from one another, reflecting differences in their environment.

The opposite side of the coin is that the same environment acting on two genetically different individuals will have a different effect, depending on the make-up of the individual. The reason for this is that genes are expressed through an environment.

The question then becomes 'In what way do genes interact?' This is likely to differ for different phenomena, and there is considerable debate over how the interaction happens in particular aspects of human psychology.

FOCUS POINT 5.1

The relationship between genes and environment

The hereditarian view is usually taken as denying the possibility of change. If behaviour is innate, then it is fixed. However, even in physical make-up, where there is clearly a strong genetic element, we can see a clear environmental effect. Take height, for example. Tall parents will generally have tall children, and short parents short children. That is in the nature of genes. There are three observations here, however (Lewontin, 2001):

1 the actual height of the child is impossible to predict, because the operation of genes is shaped by chance factors

2 environmental effects can disturb the trend; for example, poor nutrition will inhibit growth
3 the average height of people has increased over time, as a result of improved environmental factors, particularly nutrition.

Even in an area as clearly genetically determined as height, there is a strong environmental effect. A complete explanation of the role of heredity and environment therefore has to account for both.

Interaction between heredity and environment

In trying to explain the nature of the interaction between heredity and the environment, we're trying to explain how individuals get from an initial 'blueprint' encoded in the genes to their adult form. The blueprint, which is a set of genes encoded in the body's chromosomes, is called the *genotype*. The individual's structure and characteristics are known as the *phenotype*. The question we're asking then is what happens to get from the genotype to the phenotype.

The genotype actually contains more genes than we need. Some will only activate under certain conditions, and some are recessive, which means that they are suppressed in the presence of a dominant gene for the same characteristic. Less than 50 per cent of the genotype contributes to the phenotype, although all remain in the chromosomes to be passed on to offspring (Stratton and Hayes, 1999). This apparent wastefulness actually introduces a lot of flexibility into development, but it does mean that the final phenotype cannot easily be predicted from the genotype.

The environment

The environment exerts a significant influence on how a genotype is realised as a phenotype. The term 'environment' covers a broad range of factors. It includes conditions within the womb, and both the physical and social environments throughout life. Environmental factors may be organic or stimulative, and in each case a factor may have a broad or narrow effect.

Organic factors

Organic factors are those that lead to physiological changes. For example, disease and substance abuse will have a negative effect on development, while good nutrition will have a positive effect. Broad organic factors are those that leave permanent changes, such as brain damage, while narrow organic factors are those with a short duration, such as measles.

Stimulative factors

Stimulative factors make up the social context in which the individual develops, ranging from the narrow effects of the kind of school attended to the broad effects of social class and life opportunities.

The genotype

Characteristics represented in the genotype vary along a continuum of how direct an effect they have on the phenotype. Some characteristics are very direct and are resistant to change (for example, Down's syndrome). Others may lead to a susceptibility that will be realised under certain environmental conditions, as may be the case with schizophrenia. Still others may be very indirect, and social stereotypes will exert a greater effect, which may explain gender differences in technical skills. Where genotype characteristics have a very indirect effect, the environment plays a larger role in influencing the development of the phenotype.

It has been estimated that there are over 70 trillion possible human genotypes (Malim and Birch, 1998). The number of possible environments is potentially infinite. Clearly, then, there are many potential phenotypes, which accounts for the human diversity we see all around us. Figure 5.1 illustrates how genotype directness, organic environmental effects and stimulative environmental effects interact.

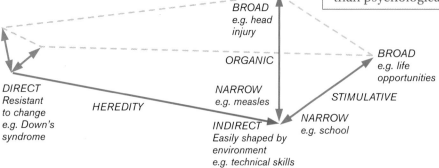

Figure 5.1 Heredity–environment interaction (the more indirect the effect of heredity on a characteristic, the greater the effect of organic and stimulative environmental factors)

Genotypes and psychology

The interaction between heredity and environment described above is certainly true for the physical characteristics of individuals. However, the picture is a little more complicated for psychological characteristics. This is partly because psychological characteristics have no tangible reality. We saw in Chapter 3 that it is difficult to be certain that the psychological characteristics we identify really exist. When we are sure they do exist, it can be difficult to correlate characteristics with our genetic make-up. The reason for this is that there is an intermediate step between the genotype and the phenotype for psychological characteristics. This intermediate step is the brain (Lewontin, 2001).

It is safe to assume that psychological characteristics result from the operation of the brain. If there is a genetic basis for psychological characteristics, it must be because genes specify a certain brain organisation that underlies the characteristic. However, unlike other parts of the body the brain has the properties of self-organisation and plasticity. Over the course of development, the brain develops new connections between the nerve cells that make it up, in response to experience and learning. In addition, the brain prunes itself by allowing to die those cells that are deemed unnecessary. This process starts in the womb, and continues throughout childhood. The result is that the adult brain has half the number of brain cells of the newborn child's brain (Kolb and Whishaw, 2003).

If the genotype sets a blueprint for the brain, then the adult phenotype will necessarily be different from the original blueprint in some ways. The degree of difference will vary for different parts of the brain. Thus the brain stem will differ considerably less than the association cortex in the cerebellum. We can expect also, then, that the degree of difference will vary for different psychological characteristics. However, we need to know more about how different characteristics are represented in brain structures, and how these brain structures develop, before we can come to firm conclusions about the genetic basis of psychological characteristics.

Learning outcomes

When you have completed this chapter you should be able to:

* describe and evaluate different forms of reductionism
* assess how reductionism relates to the explanation of phenomena at different levels of explanation
* compare and contrast free will and determinism, and evaluate the importance of determinism for the scientific method
* evaluate the hereditarian and environmentalist sides of the nature/nurture debate
* explain how heredity and environment interact in shaping human behaviour.

Key Terms

Biological reductionism
Determinism
Environment
Experimental reductionism
Free will
Heredity
Levels of explanation
Machine reductionism
Neurogenetic determinism
Physiological reductionism
Reductionism
Soft determinism

Section 1
Conceptual and historical issues

Further reading

Barker, M. (2003) *Introductory Psychology: History, Themes and Perspectives.*
Exeter: Crucial.

Bell, A. (2002) *Debates in Psychology.* Hove: Routledge.

Gross, R. (2003) *Themes, Issues and Debates in Psychology* (2nd edn). London:
Hodder Arnold.

Gross, R. and McIlveen, R. (1999) *Perspectives in Psychology.* London: Hodder &
Stoughton.

Valentine, E. (1992) *Conceptual Issues in Psychology.* London: Routledge.

Sectiontwo

Chris Chandler

Psychobiology

6	Introduction to psychobiology	66
7	Basic foundations of psychobiology	86
8	Animal learning and cognition	120
9	Motivation, brain reward mechanisms and behaviour	138
10	Emotion and sleep	150
11	Perceptual systems and motor control	161

6

Introduction to psychobiology

Route map of the chapter

This chapter consists of three broad sections. The first is an introduction to the psychobiological perspective and its diversity. The second examines the scientific nature of animal experiments and the use of animals in research within the UK. The third section focuses on evolution and genetics. The process of evolution suggested by Darwin explained how the process of natural selection influences subsequent generations; Mendelian genetics helped clarify how this process occurs, and modern molecular biology has narrowed the focus to individual genes on chromosomes.

Introduction

Psychobiology is a subdiscipline of psychology that seeks to explain behaviour in terms of biological mechanisms. Psychobiology is also known as biopsychology, biological psychology and behavioural neuroscience. Many general textbooks have a section on (or even called) the 'biological bases of behaviour'. This title is somewhat misleading. It implies that the biological influences on behaviour are a one-way street: that biology affects behaviour. In fact, an organism's behaviour and its environment can in turn influence its biology. The use of the term 'environment' here refers to everything outside the organism. As we will see, the process of evolution demonstrates an environmental influence over a long period of time. In this section on psychobiology we will examine how both biology and the environment interact to produce and influence behaviour.

Reductionism

All psychobiological accounts of behaviour use *reductionism*. Reductionism permits us to explain behaviour at the biological level. Within biology there are also different levels of investigation (see Figure 6.1). Investigation can start with large regions of the brain (e.g. the temporal lobes and memory (Milner, 1970)) and then move to smaller identifiable groups of nerves (e.g. the hippocampus and memory (Zola-Morgan and Squire, 1986)). Reductionism also helps answer important questions. For example, 'What does the brain do?' Perhaps one response is that the brain does everything, but this is not a satisfactory answer. By reducing the big questions to smaller elements we can ask more specific questions, such as 'What does the hippocampus do?' This is a much more manageable question, which means that we can give a more precise answer.

In the past 50 years there has been a rapid increase in our understanding of behaviour at the genetic level. Psychologists have embraced genetic research methods and techniques as crucial tools to aiding our understanding of behaviour (Plomin *et al.*, 1997; Plomin, 2002). Behavioural analysis can now take place at the molecular level: the question now is 'What genes are responsible for our behaviour?'

Psychobiology: a multidisciplinary account of behaviour

Psychobiologists use a wide range of information from other subjects to explain behaviour. As the quote in Focus Point 6.1 suggests, psychobiology is truly multidisciplinary. Some of the key areas that contribute to it are indicated in Figure 6.2. In this

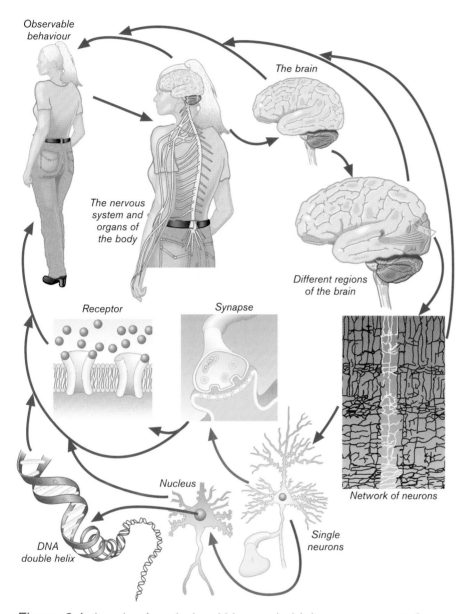

Observable behaviour

The brain

The nervous system and organs of the body

Different regions of the brain

Receptor

Synapse

Network of neurons

Nucleus

Single neurons

DNA double helix

Figure 6.1 Levels of analysis within psychobiology: we can study behaviour at different levels – from large parts of the brain down to the effects of genetics

figure, the disciplines that contribute to psychobiology can be seen as cells that communicate information to psychobiology. The subdisciplines are the cells that make up the region of psychobiology. The nucleus can be seen as the theoretical position that determines the function and activity of the cell (the methods). Psychobiology, then, is the meeting place of many different schools of thought and diverse scientific research, all of which are used to provide an account of behaviour.

Section 2
Psychobiology

Sahgal on psychobiology

Sahgal (1993) said that 'Behavioural neuroscience (psychobiology) is the study of the neural basis of behaviour, but this colourless definition does not do justice to the wealth of scientific expertise that it incorporates.'

It is important to be aware of the dynamic, ever changing nature of psychobiology. There is an almost daily increase in knowledge from all the contributory disciplines. With new information we have to be prepared to adapt and change any previously accepted ideas regarding the biological mechanisms underlying behaviour. We have to be able to account for behaviour within new theoretical contexts and test these theories rigorously via experimentation.

Technological advances, in particular, have permitted a substantial amount of new research to take place within psychobiology. An example of this is the use of functional magnetic resonance imaging (fMRI) and positron emission tomography (PET), a sophisticated X-ray technique that examines the processes of the brain in action (see Research Methods Box 6.1).

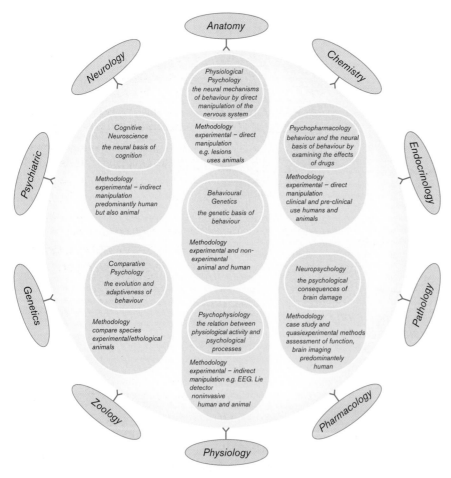

Figure 6.2 Psychobiology in the context of other disciplines and its subdisciplines

RESEARCH METHODS BOX 6.1

Inside-the-headoscope

Vic Reeves in his *Big Night Out* TV programme once tried to see what was going on inside the brain of his assistant Les. He used what he referred to as an inside-the-headoscope. Whilst the show used this idea to good effect, scientists also seek to investigate the brain.

There are a number of methods that allow this, but two are prominent: functional magnetic resonance imaging (fMRI) and positron emission tomography (PET).

PET uses compounds that can be tagged with radioactivity. The PET scanner can detect this radioactivity. Depending on what you tag with radioactivity you can see which parts of the brain are being used during certain tasks or where certain receptors are in the brain.

Functional MRI measures the changes in oxygen flow in the blood. Depending on which part of the brain is being used, oxygen levels will be increased in busy areas.

Similarly, other areas of psychology also benefit from psychobiological investigation. Developmental psychology is able to chart changes in cognitive ability from birth to old age (see Chapter 18). Underlying these changes are biological substrates that change over the life span of the individual. The growth and death of cells are keenly investigated.

If understanding behaviour is like fitting together a jigsaw, then the many disciplines related to psychobiology represent the different pieces. Together they can start to complete the picture, but there are still some elusive pieces yet to find.

Subdivisions of psychobiology

Figure 6.2 illustrates the broad subdisciplines that make up psychobiology and the different methods they use to address questions. In Applications Box 6.1 you can see how one subdivision, psychophysiology, is applied. These areas are strongly represented in the British Psychological

Society's view of important areas within psychobiology.

Figure 6.2 also shows that psychologists do not rely entirely on evidence from humans. Psychology (like the other contributory disciplines) owes a great debt to the study of animals. Studies of animals and their behaviour have been instrumental in shaping theories and advancing our understanding of the biological mechanisms that underlie human behaviour.

APPLICATIONS BOX 6.1

Psychophysiology

It is easy to see that psychobiology has direct and relevant applications to medicine. However, there is one branch of psychobiology that is used to detect lies. Psychophysiology has the key to assessing the truth.

The polygraph, or lie detector, measures the body's response to stress. It does this by monitoring such things as heart rate, blood pressure level and sweat production. Think about what happens when you are under stress: your heart rate and blood pressure may increase and you may start to sweat more. When you are telling lies you are under stress. These are also the telltale signs that you are not telling the truth. Many films have shown polygraphs in use and many daytime television programmes use psychophysiology in the quest to find out, say, if one partner in a relationship is cheating on the other.

Animal and human research

Research is vital to increasing our understanding of behaviour. Only by experimental investigation can we begin to unlock the mysteries of the brain. It is clear that if you wish to understand human behaviour then you need to investigate humans. Indeed, many experiments are conducted each year that use humans to investigate the relationship between biology and behaviour. These experiments are published only if they fulfil all the requirements of an ethically acceptable procedure. A full account of the ethical guidelines is provided by the British Psychological Society (BPS) for experimental conduct (see Chapter 37 for a summary). However, the BPS's jurisdiction only extends to its members and there may be different standards outside the UK.

Research using human participants can answer only some questions. Other questions remain because of the ethical and moral restrictions placed on human research. This is when animal studies are useful in trying to resolve questions that could not otherwise be answered.

Today we are very aware of moral and ethical issues due to the advancement of genetic engineering, its potential use and misuse and the high-profile media debate surrounding it. The concept of a utopian human race and cloned humans remains ethically unacceptable to most people, but we should not become complacent in our position of superiority. There are numerous instances of inhumanity in the name of science. For example, just over half a century ago in Nazi Germany evolutionary theory was used as the justification for eugenics (Brune, 2001) and to further scientific knowledge (Shevell and Peiffer, 2001).

Ultimately we, as humans, are animals. We are highly sophisticated and socialised animals, but we are still animals. Humans as a species have evolved but still share many similarities with other species. This shared heritage is the area in which evolutionary and comparative psychologists work. The society we live in permits a large number of scientific procedures to be conducted on animals that would be regarded as unethical in humans. Scientists can lesion (destroy) part of a rat's brain but cannot do the same to a human for the advancement of knowledge. The rat is the most researched animal on the planet. However, rats are not the only animals used by scientists. Many species have been used, ranging from snails to mice and pigeons to chimpanzees. Which animal is used depends on the question asked, and whether the animal is in a position to provide an answer.

Animal research is an area charged with moral, ethical and emotional debate, and we will not go too far into it here. If you wish to investigate the arguments surrounding vivisection, then the British Union for the Abolition of Vivisection (BUAV) and Research Defence Society (RDS) provide coherent contrasting accounts.

The antivivisection movement (of which some scientists are members) has two main objections to experiments with animals. First, it considers it unethical to experiment with animals. The basis of this view is that such procedures are cruel to the animal, inducing unnecessary suffering to an animal that has no choice. Second, the scientific validity of experimentation is called into question: how can an animal provide us with insights into human behaviour? Those that support the use of animals have challenged this view with statements of the advantages, to animal and man, of experimentation with animals. All groups would agree that unnecessary suffering should never occur. Perhaps the biggest point of contention is the definition of what *is* necessary. However, legislators past and present consider animal experimentation necessary to answer some questions.

This section will explore how animals can best be used to explain the biology of behaviour, and the extrapolation of animal research to humans. However, we must start by placing animal experimentation within the context of the United Kingdom.

In the United Kingdom, the government (via the Home Office) is responsible for ensuring that animal welfare is maintained during experiments. The Home Office also decides if the experiments are really necessary. Its aim is to refine, reduce and replace animal experimentation (the '3 Rs'). This is a goal that remains to be achieved. Under the Scientific Procedures Act 1986 scientists are only allowed to perform certain experiments if they are suitably trained. They also have to provide a good reason for doing the experiments, explaining why they are needed, and can only carry them out in particular laboratories.

Thus three licences are needed from the Home Office.

1 One licence is required for the establishment where the experiment is conducted, ensuring a

high quality of care and a suitable environment for the animal.

2 A second licence is required for the project (or set of experiments). This permits only certain procedures to be carried out on the animal. A scientist cannot just do anything he or she wants.

3 The third licence is a personal licence for a particular individual to conduct the experiment. This is granted only if the applicant has received appropriate training and demonstrated sufficient competence in animal welfare.

The Home Office sends out inspectors and veterinarians, without prior notice, to visit establishments to check that the rules are being maintained. Heavy fines and a custodial sentence may result from successful prosecution of those failing to adhere to the rules governing animal experiments.

The validity of animal models of behaviour

The Home Office deals with the welfare and legal aspects of animal research. However, the scientist has to do more than simply comply with legislation. He or she needs to be clear that the questions asked of an animal in an experiment can actually be answered. Animals are used in many ways within psychobiology and cognate disciplines, but these fall into three key domains (Willner, 1984; 1986; Willner and Mitchell, 2002).

1 The first is the screening test, to find out if a procedure or drug is going to be useful. These are favoured early on in drug development by drug companies.

2 The second is *behavioural bioassay*, which aims to mimic or model a physiological mechanism in the whole animal. Willner (1991) points out that there are good reasons for looking at the behavioural consequences of a physiological event. Behaviour is the result of the integration of many brain mechanisms. Unlike pure physiology we can see how the whole system works to influence behaviour.

3 The third domain, and the one most important to the psychobiologist, is the animal model or simulation of behaviour. More often than not, these are simulations of abnormal behaviour. As we can see in Focus Point 6.2, Willner claims there is a necessity to use animals wisely. To put this another way, are we getting suitable answers to the questions we ask?

FOCUS POINT 6.2

Willner's view

Willner (1991) stated that 'models are tools. As such, they have no intrinsic value; the value of a tool derives entirely from the work one can do with it. Conclusions arising from the use of a simulation of abnormal behaviour are essentially hypotheses that must eventually be tested against the clinical state. An assessment of the validity of a simulation gives no more than an indication of the degree of confidence that we can place in the hypothesis arising from its use.'

Using the concepts behind the development of psychometric testing and questionnaire design (see Chapter 31), Willner (1984) proposed that animal models should be validated. He developed the appraisal of an animal model for psychopharmacology, but it can be extended to other aspects of psychobiology. Three sets of validity are differentiated: *predictive validity, face validity* and *construct validity*. When assessing the utilisation of animals these criteria provide a useful structure.

Predictive validity

This is similar to a screening test, but goes beyond it. If you wish to have an animal model of schizophrenia then the many types of antipsychotic medication should also work in the model (see Chapter 7). Furthermore, you should be able to exacerbate the symptoms in the animal in the same way you can in the human. Experiments in which patients with schizophrenia have been given amphetamine have shown some deterioration in their symptoms (van Kammen *et al.*, 1982). Similarly, if you give a rat amphetamine its behaviour becomes disorganised (e.g. Ellinwood and Escalante, 1977).

Face validity

This is the degree to which there is a similarity between the model and the behaviour to be modelled. Are the symptoms of schizophrenia modelled in the animal? Are the symptoms that are modelled in the animal significant in schizophrenia and schizophrenia alone? If the answer is no, then you may have problems with the animal model because you cannot be sure it is modelling schizophrenia. Additionally, you will have to account for new research findings in the model. Thus a model of behaviour may have face validity one day, but not the next, after new knowledge is assimilated.

Construct validity

A limitation with face validity is that the different species of animals have different overt behaviour. Willner (1991) uses the example of maternal behaviour to demonstrate this point. Maternal behaviour is evident across all species. However, it is expressed differently. The rat keeps her litter close and retrieves strays with her mouth. The rat mother does not change nappies, warm milk or go to rat playgroups, while the human mother, in general, performs some if not all of these behaviours.

The observable behaviours are different. However, they are regarded as homologous – arising from the same physiological substrate. This is the theoretical rationale behind the behaviour. If experimentation supports the theory then the model has a degree of construct validity. It has been argued that some models of schizophrenia score more highly than others for construct validity (Ellenbroek and Cools, 1990). Construct validity is harder to achieve for the animal models of addiction because the theories behind drug misuse do not have a single theoretical rationale: some scientists argue that drug addiction is due to the pleasant actions of a drug, while others claim it is

motivated by the urge to avoid unpleasant withdrawal symptoms (see Goudie, 1991; see also Chapter 9).

Psychobiological accounts of behaviour

To use a legal metaphor, human and animal data contribute circumstantial evidence for a biological case of behaviour. One account alone does not provide conclusive evidence: it is the sum collection of the presented evidence that is required for a conviction (acceptance of a hypothesis). It is for the (scientific) jury to decide if the evidence is sufficient to support the charge (hypothesis). If the hypothesis cannot be supported then we have to accept the null hypothesis. If this is the case then we either have to provide stronger evidence or look for another suspect.

Behavioural genetics

It cannot escape anyone's notice that genetics is an important and rapidly advancing branch of science. We only have to read the more lurid newspaper stories of man's inhumanity to his fellow man to see that genetics is foremost in forensic science (with, for example, the use of DNA testing). Fortunately, genetic science is also used in less negative circumstances, and can offer insight and hope. Recent advances in genetics, such as the Human Genome Project and Dolly the cloned sheep (Campbell *et al.*, 1996), have focused on DNA, but the study of genetics has a much longer and more detailed history than this, and has shaped the formation of our present-day views.

Evolution

The idea that species change and evolve over time is now a well-established fact. While Charles Darwin was not the first to take an evolutionary perspective, he was certainly the most influential. Darwin published *The Origin of Species* (1859) at a time when Christianity stated that God had created all species *de novo* (from scratch). Darwin's account of evolution was revolutionary at the time, and brought about a change in viewpoint very quickly. His account was convincing to biologists because he used evidence to support his theory. Without this supporting evidence his theory would have attracted less attention.

Darwin's evolutionary theory

Darwin proposed that all organisms are related and share a common ancestor. His theory of descent with modification encapsulated how modern organisms are (successful) adaptations of previous generations. How did these modifications occur? The answer, he said, lies in the process of natural selection. Certain characteristics are more beneficial to the organism in a particular environment. Therefore those organisms that possess such beneficial characteristics are more likely to survive and reproduce. Via reproduction, these characteristics are passed to the next generation. Organisms that are not ideally equipped to interact with their environment stand a reduced chance of being able to survive and reproduce. The phrase often used for this is the 'survival of the fittest'; this means that those organisms that '*fit* into' their environment are more successful at survival (note that the word 'fittest' as it is used here does not necessarily have anything to do with physical fitness).

In Activity Box 6.1 you are asked to discuss how and why certain traits are more desirable than others. Natural selection is distinct from selective breeding programmes. With natural selection there is no specific plan, the environment is the influence. However, the breeding of animals is a specific, and intended, act that produces offspring with particular characteristics (as in the case of the thoroughbred racehorse).

ACTIVITY BOX 6.1

Rules of attraction

What do you find attractive in another person? I imagine you would provide a list of physical and personality traits. The male of our species, for instance, is likely to prefer females with larger hips.

There has been a lot of talk in the media regarding booty – that is, the female bottom. Why would having a large bottom be so desirable? Jennifer Lopez is rarely out of the newspapers and photographs of her nearly always focus on her rear.

Ask yourself the following questions.

- Why has the body evolved this way?
- Does the opposite sex like it?
- Why does the opposite sex like this shape?
- How would you assess the desirability of someone's booty?
- Is the desirability of booty a fixed trait?

Fortunately, Singh (1993) has provided a more scientific analysis of the desirability of body shape related to the hips. A waist-to-hip ratio (WHR) that resembles an hourglass shape is seen as desirable and conferring many positive attributes.

Similarly, males are rated more favourably if they have fuller beards (see Barber, 1995). Like the WHR, a beard is linked to dimensions that are seen as positive. I particularly look forward to reading the research that indicates a positive appraisal of male pattern baldness and a beer gut!

Section 2
Psychobiology

Evidence in support of evolution

As with all good science, evidence has to be amassed to support (or refute) a theory. Darwin (and others since) has presented a great deal of evidence in support of evolution via natural selection. The evidence for the case of evolution derives from the following.

* Biogeography: why are some organisms indigenous to particular environments and not others? These organisms are the best fit for their unique environment.
* Fossil records: looking at different geological layers reveals changing fossils. These changes permit the palaeontologist to chart the evolution of species. For example, the change in the size and shape of the skull is important in tracing our ancestors. As

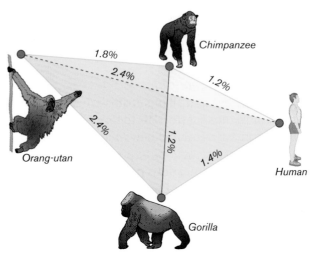

Figure 6.4 The close relationship of species: the human race is not created as new but has evolved from previous species; the human is a close relation of other species
Source: adapted from Lewin, 1984

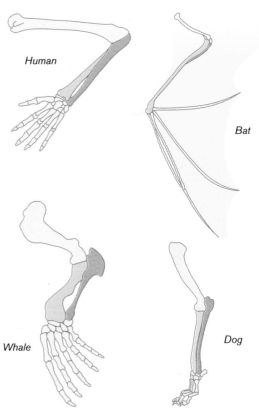

Figure 6.3 The bone structure in the limbs of various animals; in accordance with evolutionary theory these structures share a common ancestor

new fossils are found, established views are challenged and our understanding of evolution advanced.

* Structural similarity: across species there are comparative similarities. Arms, paws, flippers and wings have similar skeletal structures but different functions (see Figure 6.3). In evolutionary terms, these have developed from a common ancestor.
* Embryology: comparing the development of embryos reveals that there are similar stages across species. Campbell *et al.* (1999) point out that both human and fish embryos go through a phase of possessing gills. As the embryo develops, these similarities are reduced and the embryos take on the unique characteristics of their species. (However, please note that we do not start out as fish!)
* Molecular biology: Darwin did not have the benefit of modern science and our knowledge of DNA (more of which later). However, molecular biology supports Darwin's account of evolution and the fossil evidence. Ultimately, we share common strands of DNA with other organisms, and some are closer than others (see Figure 6.4).

The organism and the environment

The Darwinian account is a very good example of how the environment changes biology and behaviour, albeit over an extended period of time. Johnston and Edwards (2002), who provide an integrative model of the development of behaviour, have acknowledged the importance of the environment. Here the development of behaviour is a product of interactions between genetics, the environment and perception. Essentially behaviour will be determined not purely by genetic make-up, but also by experiences, interpretations and perceptions of the environment.

Mendelian genetics

A monk called Gregor Mendel (1822–84) was working on inheritance at the same time as Darwin was explaining evolution. Mendel was able to account for differences in *conspecifics* (members of the same species). Mendel's work (see Campbell *et al.*, 1999) accounted for the inheritance of behavioural as well as physiological and anatomical characteristics. His evidence was derived from his experiments with pea plants. Fortunately, we can extrapolate his work with peas to human inheritance.

Mendel studied seven different observable characteristics of peas, such as seed colour and flower colour. Regardless of the characteristic he looked at, the principles remained the same.

He examined *dichotomous traits*; that is, the characteristics that are in one form or another. One dichotomous trait he observed in the pea was whether the seed was yellow or green. This variant in colour is called a *trait*. If a yellow-seeded plant (Y1) is inbred with another yellow-seeded plant (Y2) then the resultant offspring is also a yellow-seeded plant (Y1:Y2). The same goes for the green-seeded plants (g1:g2). These plants are true breeding lines and produce the same trait in subsequent generations (yellow seeds or green seeds).

But what happens if a true breeding yellow-seeded plant is crossed with a true breeding green-seeded plant? As shown in Figure 6.5, the result is a first generation of yellow-seeded plants. No green seeds can be observed. Mendel then took the first-generation plants and crossed them with one

---

ACTIVITY BOX 6.2

My wife, the love rat, with sex-mad monk

Dear Emma,

I have been married to my wife for seven years. We have two children, aged two and five years old. The problem is I think I might not be the father of one of the children. My wife and I both have dark brown eyes. So does our five-year-old. However, the two-year-old has blue eyes. I do not understand how this can happen.

Well, I confronted my wife about this and accused her of having an affair. She was shocked at my accusation, but said it was down to some monk called Mendel and his peas. Of course, this shocked me even more. I had no idea she was religious or interested in gardening. I have tried to contact this so-called Mendel the monk, but I have not had any success.

When I tell my wife that I am going to track him down and give him a good talking to, she laughs at me. She says that I am the father and it is all in our genes. But how can he have blue eyes when we both have brown eyes?

Yours,
Cheated from Brighton

Dear Cheated from Brighton,

You have not been cheated upon. Your two-year-old is just obeying Mendelian genetics. This is nothing to do with what is in Mendel's jeans. Any first-year psychology student will be able to tell you about the principles of Mendelian genetics.

How would you explain this to Cheated from Brighton? Use the example of pea seeds to explain the difference in eye colour.

Section 2
Psychobiology

another. This produced a second generation of pea plants. In the second-generation pea plants, 75 per cent had yellow seeds and 25 per cent had green seeds.

Only one trait appeared in the first-generation cross – this is the *dominant trait* (yellow seeds). The *recessive trait* (green seed) was not expressed because it was overridden by the yellow seed trait. In the second generation, green-seeded pea plants were produced. Despite not being observed in the first-generation plants, the recessive trait was passed on to the second generation. The first-generation plants were carriers of the recessive trait, but because it was combined with a dominant trait it was not observably expressed. Thus there is a difference between observed traits and genetic traits. What is observed is called the *phenotype* and what is transmitted genetically is called the *genotype*. What you see (the phenotype) and what you get (the genotype) can be different (see Activity Box 6.2).

The observations made by Mendel can be translated into the language of modern genetics. The fact that there are dichotomous traits for pea characteristics means that there is a gene for yellow and a gene for green seeds. Each successive generation inherits two of these genes, one from mother and one from father, or in the case of the peas one from a yellow-seeded plant and one from a green-seeded plant. If the two genes are controlling the same trait (e.g. seed colour) they are referred to as *alleles*. The random inheritance of alleles permits a number of combinations, as can be seen in Figure 6.5.

Huntington's disease: dominant allele in action

The principles of Mendelian genetics can be applied to *Huntington's disease* (HD). This is a case of a dominant allele in action (like Mendel's yellow seeds). HD is a progressive disorder that is characterised by motor disturbances and a subsequent cognitive decline. The manifestation of symptoms occurs between the ages of 30 and 45. The significance of this late onset is that reproduction may have occurred and therefore HD is passed on to

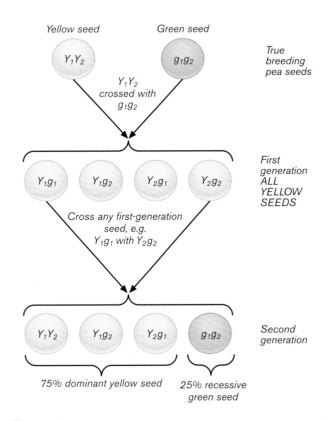

Figure 6.5 Mendelian genetics: the inheritance of dominant and recessive alleles in the pea plant have shown how traits such as pea seed colour (or eye colour) are passed on to subsequent generations

offspring. An early onset would minimise the opportunity to reproduce.

The reason someone contracts HD is because of a dominant allele for HD (H). When this dominant allele is combined with a recessive allele (*h*) the person will develop HD. A parent who has an H*h* genotype will pass on either the H or the *h* allele to the offspring. In Figure 6.6 it can be seen that each parent has two alleles. These are divided during reproduction into the egg or sperm. For example, if the father has a genotype of H*h* then the sperms produced will either be H or *h* carriers. When this is combined with an *hh* mother (the eggs contain the recessive allele *h*), there is a 50 per cent chance of the dominant H allele being expressed in the offspring.

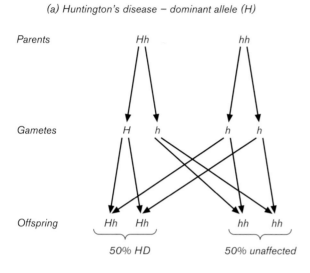

(a) Huntington's disease – dominant allele (H)

Parents   Hh   hh

Gametes   H   h   h   h

Offspring   Hh Hh   hh hh

        50% HD   50% unaffected

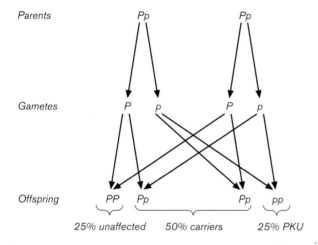

(b) PKU recessive allele (p)

Parents   Pp   Pp

Gametes   P   p   P   p

Offspring   PP Pp   Pp pp

25% unaffected   50% carriers   25% PKU

*Figure 6.6 Mendelian genetics applied to (a)
Huntington's disease (HD), and (b)
Phenylketonuria (PKU): a dominant
allele is responsible for HD and a
recessive allele is responsible for
PKU
Source: adapted from Plomin et al.,
1997*

PKU: recessive allele in action
Phenylketonuria (PKU) is a form of mental
retardation and is due to a recessive allele. If a
recessive allele is to be expressed there have to be
two copies of it. Remember that the green seeds in

Mendel's second-generation pea plants were
expressed only when the genotype was g1:g2. Here
there was no yellow seed to dominate. Similarly, with
PKU, the disorder is only expressed when there is no
dominant allele (P) to override the recessive trait (*p*).
Therefore only 25 per cent of offspring will have the
disorder and 50 per cent will be carriers of PKU but
will not contract the disorder (see Figure 6.6). Here
again is an example of the genotype being very
different from the phenotype. A person can be a
carrier of PKU but not express PKU.

Chromosomes and inheritance

The process of inheritance described by Mendel has
a biological basis. The examples of HD and PKU
demonstrate that the genes (alleles) that each parent
has are not expressed in every gamete (sperm or
egg). The genes are divided. Genes are located on
chromosomes that are contained in the nucleus of a
cell. Chromosomes come in matched pairs; humans
have 23 pairs. The alleles for a particular trait (e.g.
HD or PKU) are found in the same location on each
chromosome.

The exception to this rule is the sex chromosomes.
These are called X and Y. Females have two X
chromosomes (XX), and males have an X and a Y

I HAVE FOUND THE GENE
FOR SLIM, NEUROTIC AMERICAN
LAWYERS... ALLELE McBEAL!

chromosome (XY). All chromosomes apart from sex chromosomes are called *autosomes*.

The pairs of chromosome are divided between gametes by cellular division called *meiosis* (see Figure 6.7). A different path of meiotic cell division occurs in sperm and eggs. Each gamete has half the full complement of chromosomes. Thus meiosis reduces the chromosomes from the diploid number (46) to the haploid number (23) of unpaired single chromosomes. With a sperm and an egg each having 23 unpaired chromosomes, fertilisation allows them to pair up and form a zygote.

Once created, a zygote grows through cellular division. This cellular division is called *mitosis*. During mitosis the cell doubles its chromosomes before division (see Figure 6.8). This doubling permits the new cells to have a full complement of chromosomes. Mitotic division occurs until the organism is complete.

Genes that are located closely on the same chromosome are more likely to be inherited. This is referred to as linkage. However, linkage does not obey Mendelian rules. To account for partial linkage from chance (50 per cent) to full linkage (100 per cent)) Morgan (see Campbell *et al.*, 1999) suggested crossing over. The chromosomes in meiosis duplicate and cross over each other at a random point. At the point of the cross-over they break and reattach with the other chromosome (see Figure 6.9). With the occurrence of crossing over it is unlikely that intact chromosomes will be passed on to the next generation. This process ensures the genetic diversity of a species.

DNA

You will be familiar with the term *DNA (Deoxyribonucleic Acid)* and its label as the 'building block of life'. But what is it and what does it do?

DNA has two functions. First, it replicates itself to make new cells and, second, it eventually makes proteins and determines the function of the cell.

Figure 6.7 Meiosis: pairs of chromosomes are divided between gametes; a different path of meiotic cell division occurs in sperm and eggs

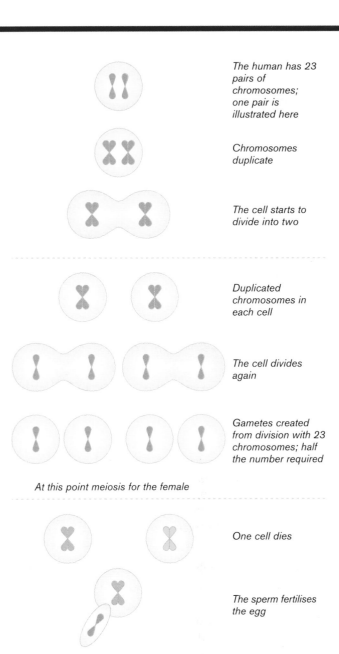

The human has 23 pairs of chromosomes; one pair is illustrated here

Chromosomes duplicate

The cell starts to divide into two

Duplicated chromosomes in each cell

The cell divides again

Gametes created from division with 23 chromosomes; half the number required

At this point meiosis for the female

One cell dies

The sperm fertilises the egg

The cell divides

The cell without the sperm dies

The two gametes combine to create a cell with 23 pairs of chromosomes

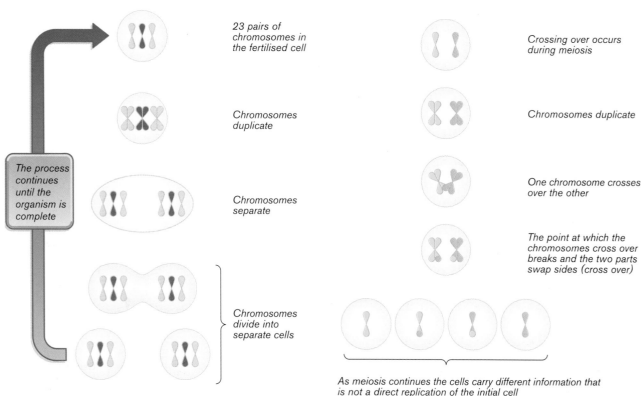

Figure 6.8 Mitosis: during mitosis the cell
doubles its chromosomes before
division, which provides new
cells with a full complement of
chromosomes

Figure 6.9 Crossover: not all genes are faithfully
copied during cellular division;
crossing over accounts for differences

Proteins are extremely important and constitute 50 per cent of the dry weight of a cell (see Campbell *et al.*, 1999). There are many thousands of proteins that are used in a variety of ways. It is beyond the scope of this chapter to provide an exhaustive account of proteins, but it is worth highlighting one example. In Chapter 7 we shall see how cells communicate with each other in the nervous system. This is achieved by a transmitter molecule (a sequence of amino acids that make up polypeptides and proteins) interacting with a receptor protein.

What is DNA?

Each chromosome is made up of two strands of DNA. The strands of DNA are made up of chemicals called nucleotide bases that are attached to a sugar phosphate support, or backbone (Figure 6.10). The

two strands of DNA are held together by a mutual attraction of the *nucleotides*. This double-stranded structure is the famous double helix (Crick and Watson, 1953). The attraction of nucleotides can be seen in Figure 6.11. This pattern of bonding means that each strand of DNA is the complement of the other.

What is the function of DNA?

There are two functions of DNA: replication and protein synthesis.

Replication

Looking more closely at mitotic cell division, here DNA replicates itself before another cell can be created. During DNA replication the two strands of nucleotide bases unravel. The exposure of the

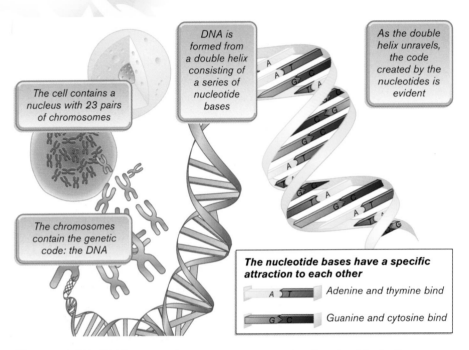

The cell contains a nucleus with 23 pairs of chromosomes

DNA is formed from a double helix consisting of a series of nucleotide bases

As the double helix unravels, the code created by the nucleotides is evident

The chromosomes contain the genetic code: the DNA

The nucleotide bases have a specific attraction to each other

A T Adenine and thymine bind

G C Guanine and cytosine bind

Figure 6.10 DNA: as a chromosome unravels, the double helix can be seen; the double helix is formed of nucleotide bases on a phosphate backbone

unravelled nucleotide bases attracts their complement from unattached bases in the nucleus. The unravelled strand now has a full complement of attached nucleotide bases and is therefore identical to the original.

This process sounds simple but errors in the replication can occur. Such errors are called mutations. Most mutations disappear though evolution and survival of the fittest. Some mutations remain, such as those responsible for HD and PKU. Mutations result in the different alleles that are responsible for HD being expressed. These mutant alleles are called polymorphisms. Mutations are rarely beneficial but, if they are, they are passed on to successive generations.

Protein synthesis

The nucleotide bases are a code. It is this code that permits the construction of amino acids. A series of amino acids can then make up enzymes, proteins and polypeptides (small proteins).

The code for an amino acid is based on a sequence of three nucleotides (see Figure 6.11). The code from

DNA has to be transported outside the nucleus before the amino acid sequence can be formed. The process of reading the DNA code is called transcription (see Figure 6.12). During transcription, a strand of DNA acts as a template for the creation of *messenger Ribonucleic Acid (mRNA)*. Messenger RNA carries the code from the nucleus to the cytoplasm of the cell. Unlike the replication of DNA during mitotic cell division, mRNA is not an exact copy. In the case of mRNA, uracil substitutes for thyamine. The three-nucleotide bases on the strand of mRNA are called *codons*. Each codon specifies an amino acid (Figure 6.13).

The next step in protein synthesis is to read the message contained in the strand of mRNA (Figure 6.12). *Ribosomes* are the translators of the sequence of nucleotide bases contained in mRNA. Ribosomes read the sequence and add amino acids as the codons instruct. The amino acids are taken to the ribosome by *transfer Ribonucleic Acid (tRNA)*. As the ribosome reads the codons, each specific tRNA molecule adds amino acid after amino acid. Eventually the ribosome reaches a codon that

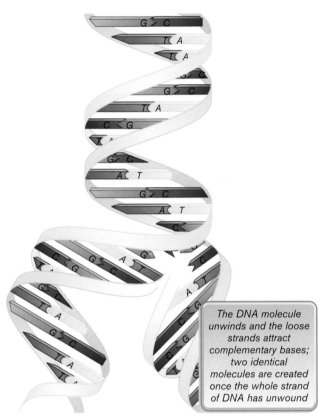

The DNA molecule unwinds and the loose strands attract complementary bases; two identical molecules are created once the whole strand of DNA has unwound

Figure 6.11 The bonding of the double helix: the nucleotide bases have one partner to which they are attracted

indicates that the protein is complete. This codon is like the full stop at the end of a sentence. Thus the sequence on the DNA strand is translated into a sequence of amino acids that go on to make proteins.

Why should psychologists look at genes?

Genetics is clearly a biological science. The examples used to illustrate genetic principals are medical conditions. Other more subtle behaviours may also have a genetic underpinning. In fact, there is a great deal of overlap between the biological sciences and the behavioural sciences.

The understanding that there is a genetic contribution to behaviour has been central to psychological discourse and in particular the nature–nurture debate (see Chapter 5). This has been a long-established argument about the relative contribution of our biology (nature) and the environment (nurture) to behaviour. Often the dialogue between students of psychology regarding nature and nurture adopts polarised points of view – it is either one or the other. Are we intelligent because we have inherited genes for intelligence or have we learned to be intelligent? A more accurate explanation is that the two interact.

One way in which psychologists have sought to understand the genetic and environmental input to behaviour is to look at twins. There are numerous twin studies that have investigated various behaviours. (A more elaborate account of twin studies and intelligence can be found in Chapter 30.)

The rationale behind such studies is to do with the degree of genetic similarity in twins. There are two types of twins: monozygotics (from one zygote) and dizygotic (from two zygotes). Monozygotic twins are genetically identical, whereas dizygotic twins are as genetically similar as any two siblings in a family. Of course, this alone does not help disentangle the nature–nurture issues. Twins are most likely to share the same environment, which could have a great impact on their behaviour. To minimise environmental factors, and focus on the genetics, twins that have been reared apart have been studied. These twins do not share the same environment. The question asked of these groups is to what extent are they similar or different.

DNA and psychology

The growth of biotechnology has permitted a more detailed analysis of genetics. The twin studies have looked at the phenotype with some speculation about the genotype. Now it is possible to look at the actual individual genes themselves. Increasingly, the modern techniques of molecular biology are telling us about the specific genetic basis of disorders such as Alzheimer's disease (Larner and du Plessis, 2003), schizophrenia (McDonald and Murphy, 2003) and drug addiction (Li *et al.*, 1997). While understanding the underlying genetics of disorders is clearly important, behavioural geneticists have also looked at personality traits, e.g. aggression in children (Schmidt *et al.*, 2002)). The search for an understanding of the genetics of personality is an

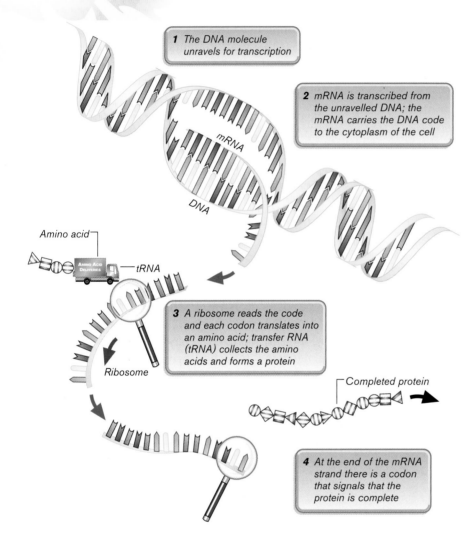

1 The DNA molecule unravels for transcription

2 mRNA is transcribed from the unravelled DNA; the mRNA carries the DNA code to the cytoplasm of the cell

mRNA

DNA

Amino acid

AMINO ACID DELIVERIES

tRNA

3 A ribosome reads the code and each codon translates into an amino acid; transfer RNA (tRNA) collects the amino acids and forms a protein

Ribosome

Completed protein

4 At the end of the mRNA strand there is a codon that signals that the protein is complete

Figure 6.12   Transcription: the genetic code is read in a process called transcription, which makes the protein

ongoing quest, but some headway has been made. One personality trait that has received a lot of attention is sensation-seeking. The possibility that there is a gene for sensation-seeking, and the methodological limitations of some studies are addressed in Research Methods Box 6.2 (p. 84).

Molecular Biotechnology and Psychology

In order to investigate and experiment with DNA, numerous copies have to be made (you need enough DNA to work with). This is known as gene cloning. Once the DNA has been isolated, a number of studies can be conducted (see Stephens *et al.*, 2002). Below is a list of techniques that you may encounter and what they do or can tell us.

- The polymerase chain reaction (PCR): this is one way used to amplify (clone) a specific strand of DNA; during a PCR the DNA is replicated many times by an enzyme.
- *Transgenic mice* (see Carter and Murphy, 1999).
- Knock in: the harvested DNA from the PCR can be incorporated into a mouse zygote; the mouse then codes for this new gene.

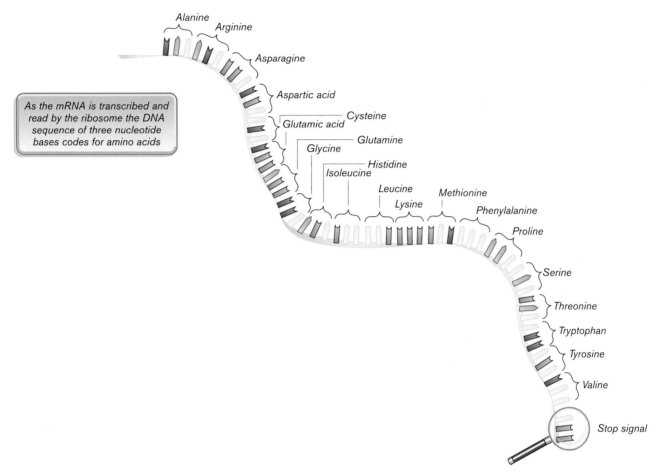

Figure 6.13 The genetic code: the nucleotide bases code for amino acids, which make proteins. Some examples are illustrated above

- Knockouts: here a particular gene is deleted, or knocked out.
- Southern blots: a process looking for a particular sequence of DNA, thus genes can be identified; this is important for evolutionary psychologists as we can see the degree of relatedness between species.
- Northern blots: a process that confirms which cells are using a specific gene.

The Human Genome Project and beyond
This is a collaborative project that has set out to determine the sequence of each human gene. Two of the primary purposes of the project are to identify all the genes in human DNA, and to determine the sequences of the chemical base pairs that make up human DNA.

Frequent reports in the media identifying the location of a gene responsible for some disorder or disease are inescapable. Genetics is being incorporated in forensic science, diagnosis, gene therapy and pharmaceutical design. Since the nineteenth century, when Darwin and Mendel presented their theories of evolution and inheritance, our understanding of genetics has increased enormously, but even in the twenty-first century it is still in an early period of development.

Learning outcomes
When you have completed this chapter you should be able to:

- compare and contrast the different approaches in psychobiology, and the different

methodologies they use
- demonstrate an understanding of the use of animals in UK research
- describe the basic infrastructure required to assess animal models of behaviour
- provide an account of evolution and inheritance
- summarise the role and action of DNA and its use by psychologists.

RESEARCH METHODS BOX 6.2

A gene for bungee jumping?

The idea that there is a gene for sensation-seeking (SS), or novelty-seeking (NS), has been investigated (Ebstein *et al.*, 1996). The early focus for a gene for SS has focused on the DRD4 gene. This is a gene that makes a receptor for dopamine. Dopamine is a neurotransmitter that underlies SS. Since the initial findings that there is a gene for SS a number of other studies have been conducted.

With the scientific rigour of molecular biology one would assume a consistent methodology across laboratories. A review by Lusher *et al.* (2001) points out, however, that there are many methodological inconsistencies.

- Ethnic differences: different ethnic groups have been used; there are genetic variants across ethnic groups, therefore an SS gene may be different in one group from that in another.
- Age: studies that have not found an association between the DRD4 gene and NS in some cases have used older participants; NS declines with age.
- Measures of personality: there are a number of scales to assess NS; the reports used different scales.
- Sex: some studies used only males while others used only females.

The overall position at present is that the DRD4 gene is not associated with NS (Burt *et al.*, 2002; Strobel *et al.*, 2003). The search continues for a gene for NS and to find out what the DRD4 gene

does. The DRD4 gene has been linked with severity of addiction (Lusher *et al.*, 2000), fear (Falzone *et al.*, 2002), nicotine craving (Hutchison *et al.*, 2002), attention deficit hyperactivity disorder (Grady *et al.*, 2003), gambling (Comings *et al.*, 2001) and many more behaviours. The task now is to understand how these genes work to influence behaviour (Plomin, 2002).

Key Terms

Alleles
Autosomes
Behavioural bioassay
Chromosomes
Codons
Conspecifics
Construct validity
Dichotomous traits
DNA (Deoxyribonucleic Acid)
Dominant trait
Face validity
Genotype
Huntington's disease
Meiosis
Messenger Ribonucleic Acid (mRNA)
Mitosis
Nucleotides
Phenotype
Phenylketonuria
Predictive validity
Recessive trait
Reductionism
Ribosomes
Trait
Transfer Ribonucleic Acid (tRNA)
Transgenic mice

Further reading

Barrett, L., Dunbar, R. and Lycett, J. (2002) *Human Evolutionary Psychology*.
   Basingstoke: Palgrave.

Campbell, N. A., Reece, J. B. and Mitchell, L. G. (1999) *Biology* (5th edn).
   Harlow: Addison Wesley.

Dawkins, R. (1989) *The Selfish Gene* (2nd edn). Oxford: Oxford University Press.

Plomin, R., DeFries, J. C., McClean, G. E. and Rutter, M. (1997) *Behavioral
   Genetics* (3rd edn). New York: WH Freeman & Co.

Rosenzweig, M. R., Breedlove, S. M. and Leiman, A. L. (2002) *Biological
   Psychology* (3rd edn). Sunderland, MA: Sinauer Associates, Inc.

Sudbery, P. (1998) *Human Molecular Genetics*. Harlow: Longman.

Web links

Research Defence Society: http://www.rds-online.org.uk

British Union for the Abolition of Vivisection: http://www.buav.org/

Home Office: http://www.homeoffice.gov.uk/comrace/animals/

Human Genome Project:
   http://www.ornl.gov/sci/techresources/Human_Genome/home.shtml

Mendelian genetics:
   http://www.ndsu.nodak.edu/instruct/mcclean/plsc431/mendel/

The Darwin centre: http://www.nhm.ac.uk/darwincentre/

DNA from the Beginning: http://www.dnaftb.org/dnaftb/

The original *Nature* paper on DNA:
   http://www.nature.com/genomics/human/watson-crick/

7

Basic foundations of psychobiology

Route map of the chapter
In this chapter you will be introduced to the nervous system and its numerous divisions. The focus will then move to the brain, looking first at large structures and then at small units of activity. In the second part of the chapter you will be introduced to neural communication and how the action of drugs can influence this process. Finally we look at the action of hormones as communicators within the body.

afferent and efferent nerves. However, the ANS has efferent nerves that can be further subdivided into the sympathetic nervous system and the parasympathetic nervous system. The difference between these two systems is based on location. The sympathetic nerves project from the CNS in the lumbar and thoracic regions, while the parasympathetic nerves project from the brain and the sacral region (Figure 7.3).

In general when the sympathetic nervous system is activated the person/animal is aroused. Energy resources are mobilised ready for flight or fight – in a threat situation your heart rate increases, and your muscles receive more energy either to run away or stay and fight. (The psychobiology of fear and

Introduction
Psychobiology is concerned with how brain functions shape behaviour (see Focus Point 7.1). The brain as part of the nervous system can be investigated at a number of levels. The basic processes of brain activity and functions are addressed within this chapter. However, remember that neuroscience is a dynamic and rapidly changing discipline, and changes in theories will occur.

The nervous system
The nervous system has many subdivisions (see Figure 7.1). In the first instance the nervous system can be split into two branches: the *central nervous system (CNS)* and the *peripheral nervous system (PNS)*. The CNS is contained within the skull and spine, whereas the PNS is on the outside of these structures (see Figure 7.2). The CNS comprises the brain and the spinal cord. The brain has evolved as an outgrowth from the spinal cord.

The PNS is further subdivided into the *somatic nervous system (SNS)* and the *autonomic nervous system (ANS)*. The SNS interacts with the external environment. It receives sensory information along *afferent nerves* (e.g. signals from eyes, skin, muscles etc.) and relays the information to the CNS. The CNS acts on this incoming information and sends motor signals via *efferent nerves* to the skeletal muscles (e.g. your hand grips a pen). Therefore afferent nerves carry sensory information and efferent nerves send out motor commands.

The ANS interacts with the internal environment (internal organs). Like the SNS, the ANS comprises

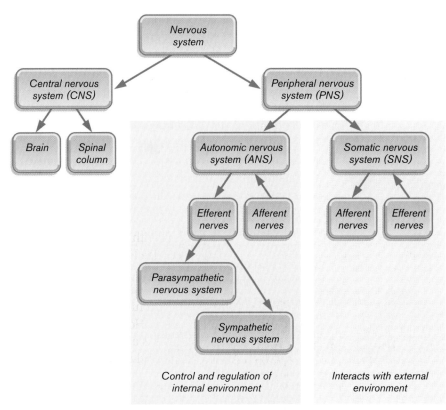

Figure 7.1 Subdivisions of the nervous system

emotion will be covered in greater depth in Chapter 10.) The amount of stimulation an internal organ receives depends on the input of *sympathetic* and *parasympathetic* nerves. Parasympathetic neurons act in the opposite direction to sympathetic neurons and induce relaxation.

The majority of neurons in the PNS come from the spine. However, there are 12 nerves, called the cranial nerves, which come directly from the brain. These are either sensory neurons or both sensory and motor neurons. The cranial nerves and their function are illustrated in Figure 7.4.

The central nervous system (CNS)

The brain and spinal cord are incredibly well protected. However, damage to the brain can have serious consequences, as you will know from your viewing of any hospital drama. The skull is a hard shell, a bit like a hard hat. Under the skull are three protective membranes called the *meninges*

(see Figure 7.5). In between two of the meninges (the arachnoid membrane and pia mater) is the *subarachnoid space*. The subarachnoid space contains blood vessels and *cerebrospinal fluid (CSF)*. The CSF fills the spinal canal (which runs down the spine) and the cerebral ventricles. The cerebral ventricles are chambers within the brain. If you look at the brains of boxers the lateral ventricles are connected due to deterioration of brain tissue (Unterharnscheidt, 1995). Enlarged ventricles are one of the many pathological changes seen in Alzheimer's disease (Soininen *et al.*, 1993).

The brain is also protected by tightly packed blood vessels called the *blood–brain barrier (BBB)*. This barrier only allows certain molecules to pass through it. Drugs that exert their effects in the brain cross the BBB.

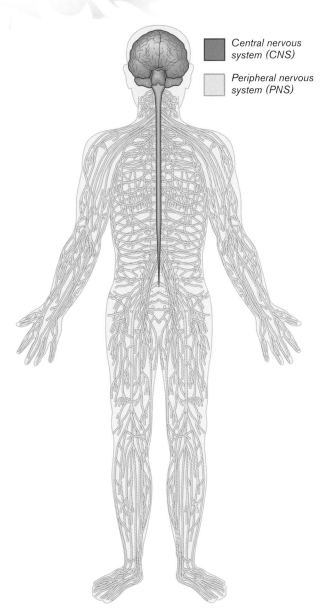

Central nervous system (CNS)

Peripheral nervous system (PNS)

Figure 7.2 The central nervous system (CNS) and the peripheral nervous system (PNS); the PNS connects to the brain and spinal column

Cells of the nervous system

The nervous system uses two types of cells: neurons and support cells. The main area of interest for psychobiologists is the neuron.

Neurons

Neurons are cells that communicate to each other using electrochemical signals. Neurons come in different shapes and sizes, but all share a similar anatomy (Figure 7.6). Around the cell is the cell membrane. The cell membrane is made up of two layers of lipids (fat molecules). These lipid layers have protein channels in them that allow certain molecules to pass from inside the cell (intracellular) to outside the cell (extracellular), or vice versa. There are also receptor proteins that receive information. The importance of both types of proteins will become clear later.

Neurons are the simplest unit of the nervous system and are made up of three components: the *soma*, the *axon* and the *dendrites*. The neuron is wrapped in a cell membrane. The soma contains the *nucleus* and *mitochondria*. The dendrites are the main recipients of information from other neurons. Incoming information is integrated at the *axon hillock* and an electrical message is passed down the axon to the terminal buttons. The axon is like a wire that carries electricity. It is sometimes covered in a *myelin* sheath. Myelin is like the insulation around an electric wire. However, unlike the insulation on a wire, there are gaps in the myelin sheath. These gaps are called *nodes of ranvier*. When a message is received at the terminal button a chemical called a neurotransmitter is released. This neurotransmitter is needed to cross the small gap between different neurons. This gap is the synapse. While most neurons share common features, there are some minor differences (Figure 7.7).

Groups of neuronal cell bodies are called nuclei or a nucleus. This nucleus is not to be confused with the other nucleus that contains the genetic code.

Support for neurons

The neurons are the main actors in the nervous systems, but they require support. *Satellite cells* in the PNS and *glial cells* in the CNS provide this. As steel girders provide support and structure in a building, support cells provide the infrastructure to hold together neural circuits.

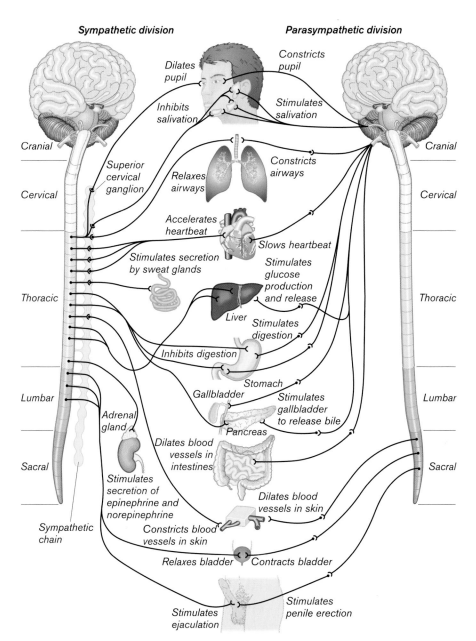

Figure 7.3 The sympathetic nerves of the autonomic nervous system (ANS) connect from the internal organs to the spine; the parasympathetic nerves enter at the base and the top of the spine; both systems work together, but sometimes in opposition, to control physiological processes
Source: adapted from Rosenzweig et al. (2002)

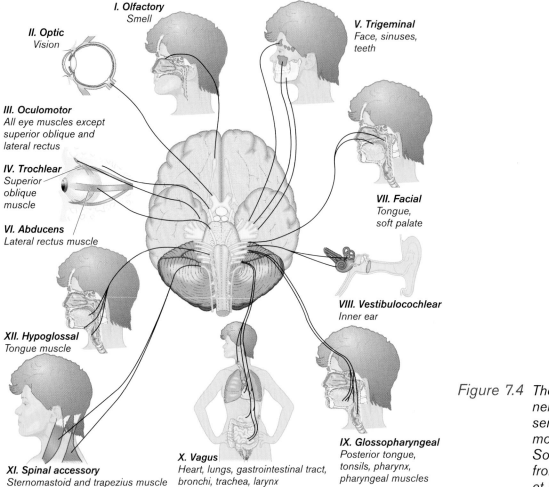

Figure 7.4 *The 12 cranial nerves carry sensory and motor messages Source: adapted from Rosenzweig et al. (2002)*

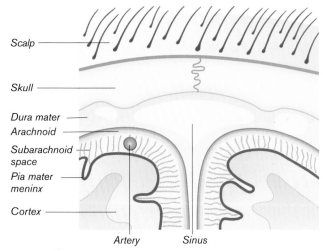

Figure 7.5 *The brain is protected from external forces by the skull and the meninges*

Developmental changes in the brain

The brain undergoes many changes during its life, from conception to death (see Figure 7.8). After conception the cells multiply (this is called mitosis; see Chapter 6). As cellular proliferation continues, the groups of cells fold in on each other to form a *neural tube*. The neural tube eventually becomes the ventricles and the central canal of the spinal column.

The genetic code provides each cell with its location. The cells move to their destination aided by glial cells (Rakic, 1985). Once the cell is in its location, cellular differentiation occurs. Differentiation is the process by which cells take on their unique characteristics and functions. It is this principle that stem cell research is based upon. Stem

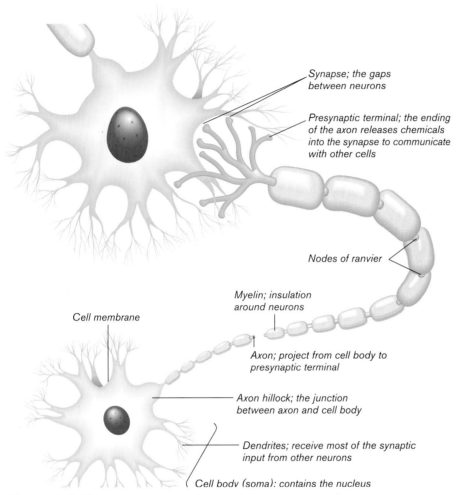

Synapse; the gaps between neurons

Presynaptic terminal; the ending of the axon releases chemicals into the synapse to communicate with other cells

Nodes of ranvier

Myelin; insulation around neurons

Cell membrane

Axon; project from cell body to presynaptic terminal

Axon hillock; the junction between axon and cell body

Dendrites; receive most of the synaptic input from other neurons

Cell body (soma): contains the nucleus

Figure 7.6 The components of an average neuron

cells are undifferentiated cells that can be grown *in vitro* (i.e. in a test-tube or other laboratory environment). When transplanted to a recipient they take on the same function as their neighbouring cells.

The axon and dendrites of the cell grow in a process called *synaptogenesis*. Synaptogenesis spans from embryonic and foetal development throughout life. Synaptogenesis is assisted by *Nerve Growth Factor* (NGF), which is a protein that promotes the survival of only certain neurons (Levi-Montalcini, 1982). Not all the axons are myelinated at birth, and

myelination continues postnatally (Paus *et al.*, 1999). Not all of the cells survive. During a process called apoptosis, unwanted neurons are programmed to die. After cell death, synapses are rearranged.

The brain is not an organ that, once formed, remains stable until death. Throughout the brain's life it undergoes many changes which affect behaviour. The behavioural effects of brain development and the brain's exposure to experiences are clearly visible in the young child. Developmental psychology is often concerned with the child but,

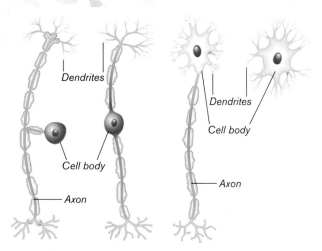

Figure 7.7 Different types of neurons (many types of neurons exist but they are all variations on the theme depicted in Figure 7.6)

with an increasingly elderly population, old age has become a growth industry. A great deal of research is being conducted to determine the effects of time on the brain. Diseases such as Alzheimer's have received considerable attention, with many changes in the brain being evident (Wenk, 2003).

Neuroanatomy
During early brain development the cells become differentiated. Cellular differentiation permits the architecture of the brain to be seen. Some features can be seen clearly, others require scientific techniques to visualise them.

Location within the brain
The brain exists in three dimensions. Therefore the brain can be looked at from three orientations. There is a convention to describe where a particular orientation is or where sets of nuclei are situated (see Figure 7.9). These terms prefix an area and provide a reference point to its location (e.g. the lateral hypothalamus is in an area towards the outer edge of the hypothalamus).

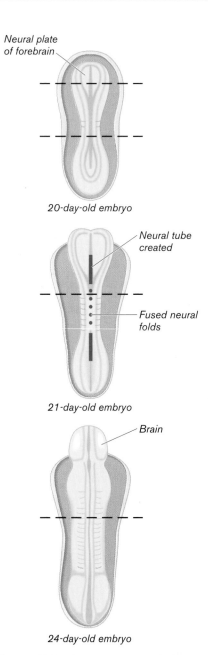

Figure 7.8 The brain develops as cells proliferate; as the number of cells increases they fold over to form a neural tube

RESEARCH METHODS BOX 7.1

Left brain/right brain
The two cerebral hemispheres have been associated with different functions (see Springer

and Deutsch, 1998). Neurological examination indicates that there is a degree of asymmetry between the two sides (see Kolb and Wishaw, 2003). The formation of cerebral lateralisation has taken advantage of both clinical and normal populations.

The notion of functional cerebral asymmetry began when Broca's area was reported. This is an area in the left hemisphere that, when lesioned, produces aphasia. Aphasia is a dysfunction of language comprehension and production. Voluntary motor control was also associated with the left brain, as patients with lesions were apraxic. Apraxia is the inability to perform conscious motor movements. The location of a function in one hemisphere is referred to as lateralisation. The left hemisphere is called the dominant hemisphere.

The dominance of the left hemisphere does not relegate the right hemisphere to a superfluous supporting role. The right hemisphere has been associated with spatial tasks and emotions.

Ascribing a function to a particular hemisphere does not provide it with a precise location. Broca's area is associated with speech production. Another area, Wernike's area, is associated with language comprehension. Both areas produce their own type of aphasia. Geshwind (1970) placed Broca's and Wernike's areas in neural context in the left hemisphere. Basically, incoming language is received by the auditory cortex and sent to Wernike's area for comprehension. If a response is needed a message is sent to Broca's area, which then sends messages to the primary motor cortex. The motor cortex organises the muscles etc. to articulate the response. Visual words are sent to the angular gyrus, which codes the visual information for comprehension in Wernike's area.

This concept of language production and comprehension has been extremely influential, but is rather simplistic. Experimental evidence does not support all the assumptions of Geshwind's model. While the aphasias are evident, the lesions are often widespread, and localisation of function differs across individuals. There are no specifically identified cells for Broca's and Wernike's areas.

An area of hot debate is the difference in cognitive abilities between the sexes (see Weiss *et al.*, 2003). Males are regarded as more right brain oriented and more lateralised. Females are thought to be more left brain oriented and to have less lateralisation. The stereotype goes that women are better communicators and males are better at spatial tasks. A car insurance report points to this stereotype. Females are more likely to claim for accidents in car parks while manoeuvring. Males on the other hand have far more serious (and costly) accidents involving high speeds. Thus the myth about women drivers is perpetuated.

Why should there be a difference in lateralisation between the sexes?

Numerous evolutionary theories have been presented. The case for spatial abilities has emphasised the male as hunter-gatherer. Therefore spatial abilities have been selected via natural selection (see Jones *et al.*, 2003).

Is functional lateralisation fixed?

The functional asymmetry of the brain has been investigated during different phases of the menstrual cycle. Sanders and Wenmoth (1998) used a verbal and musical dichotic listening task to reveal the effects of the menstrual cycle on cerebral asymmetries. The verbal task is a task for the left hemisphere, whereas the music task is a task for the right hemisphere.

A brief explanation of the dichotic listening task is required. In the standard dichotic listening task different sequences of digits are simultaneously presented via headphones to each ear. Thus each ear receives a different input. Kimura (1961; 1967) revealed that people recalled more digits from the right ear (left hemisphere) than the left ear.

In the experiment by Sanders and Wenmoth, one dichotic listening task was to identify either consonants or vowels. The other task was to identify which of four musical chords had been presented. The dichotic listening tasks were conducted at different times during the menstrual cycle. The results of this study demonstrated that the women's ability at these tasks differed as a function of menstrual status. During menses, when oestrogen is low, there was a left-ear advantage for the music task (right hemisphere). During the midluteal phase, when oestrogen is high, there was a right-ear advantage for the verbal task (left hemisphere). The functional cerebral asymmetry was greatest for the music task during menses, and for the verbal task during the midluteal phase.

Brain regions

When we see a building we see it as a whole, like the brain as a whole organ. However, the building can be divided into rooms and then into what they are made of (e.g. bricks and mortar). The levels at which we look at the brain can also be reduced from large structures to smaller components (right down to the nuts and bolts, or neurons). The functions of the different regions of the brain have been associated with different behaviours. Regional function is an area of extensive research and theorising. However, ascribing a particular function to one region is not simple as all the areas communicate with each other.

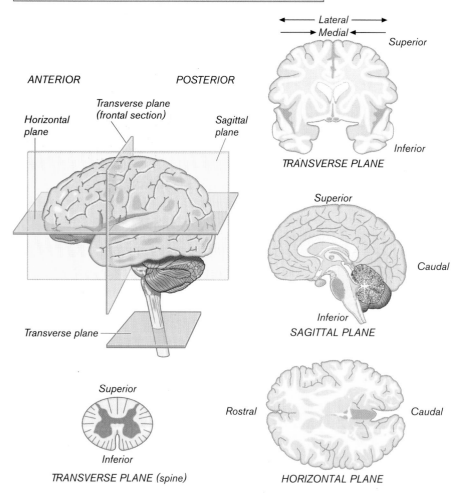

Figure 7.9 The brain can be looked at from different orientations

ACTIVITY BOX 7.1

The frontal lobes

The frontal lobes are perhaps the area of the brain that makes us uniquely human. Early studies of frontal lobe function come from research on patients with lesions to this area. The most famous of these was Phineas Gage. He had an accident in which a large area of the frontal lobe was lesioned. Surprisingly he survived. However, there were notable changes in his behaviour.

Similar problems still occur. As I write, the newspapers are covering the story of an American who fell while drilling a hole. The drill went through his skull and brain and out the other side. Lesions of the frontal lobe miss vital areas of the brain involved in life support. Thus people with such lesions survive.

Many researchers have studied the frontal lobe and provided a theoretical framework to understand its function. Luria (1973) pointed out that an individual creates intentions, plans and programmes of his actions. This individual inspects the plans' performance and regulates his behaviour so that it conforms to these plans, and uses feedback to correct mistakes. Norman and Shallice (1980) presented a cognitive science theory to account for the experimental data derived from experimental evidence. They claim the frontal lobes are important in:

- planning and decision-making
- error correction and troubleshooting
- novel situations
- dangerous situations
- overcoming habitual responses and temptation.

The types of problems a patient with frontal lobe damage may have are:
- a failure to see problems as a whole, instead dealing only with fragments of information
- a failure to use error to correct mistakes
- a failure to plan a solution to a problem
- perseveration where new rules are not learned

- poor performance of the Stroop task (see Chapter 13)
- easily distracted
- a failure to inhibit responses.

Now that you have this information, think what is required in an examination. How are the frontal lobes implicated? What might you expect to see if the frontal lobes are damaged?

The examination and the questions make up a novel situation, which requires the candidate:

- to follow instructions – a failure to read them may lead to insufficient questions being answered or too many being answered; this may be seen as a failure to inhibit responses
- to read the question and see how the words relate to each other – if the frontal lobes are damaged they may just pick key words in the question and write about them; the question will require them to apply their knowledge and not just write everything they know about a given subject
- to plan the answer – a failure in planning may result in a disjointed answer that does not focus on the question
- to evaluate the plan – the plan will need to be checked as the answer progresses; in an examination situation it is easy to drift off-task
- not to perseverate – many students use last year's exam as a revision aid; this is good practice; however, do not become dependent on that one question – a new question will appear in the year that you sit your examination; do not perseverate with last year's solution
- to sustain attention and not be distracted – without the role of the frontal lobe the person crunching mints next to you may result in a sorry end to the paper.

Of course, you need more than just the frontal lobes for an exam – the temporal lobe and hippocampus are also useful. You also need to remember the material and how to navigate your way to the exam hall!

Forebrain: telencephalon and diencephalon

The *diencephalon* is made up of the *thalamus* and *hypothalamus*. The thalamus is a relay station that receives sensory information and sends it to appropriate areas of the brain. The role of the lateral geniculate nuclei of the thalamus is illustrated in Chapter 12.

The hypothalamus is below the thalamus (hence the 'hypo' prefix). The hypothalamus is in close communication with the pituitary gland, and has been a key site of investigation for motivational behaviours such as eating (see Chapter 10).

The *telencephalon* is made up of the two cerebral hemispheres containing the cortex, the basal ganglia and the limbic system.

The cortex

The convoluted area of the brain is called the *cortex*. The cortex is made up of peaks and troughs. The large troughs in the convolutions are called *fissures*. The small troughs are called *sulci*. In between the fissures and sulci are the *gyri* (the peaks). The brain is a bilateral organ with two cerebral hemispheres clearly visible. The bilateral nature of the brain is not a complete mirror image, but it is close. A fissure separates the two hemispheres. This has given rise to the concept of a right and a left brain, with cerebral asymmetries and specialised functions (see Research Methods Box 7.1). Between the hemispheres are small connections called cerebral *commisures*; the *corpus callosum* is the most obvious to the naked eye.

The lateral and central fissures divide the brain into four lobes: the *frontal, occipital, temporal* and *parietal lobes* (see Figure 7.10). These areas have been ascribed various functions: the occipital lobe is the area of visual perception; the temporal lobe is the focus of many theories of memory; and the parietal lobe is associated with visuomotor guidance (see Kolb and Whishaw, 2003).

The frontal lobes are considered to form the area that makes us unique as humans. For an account of the frontal lobes see Activity Box 7.1. In evolutionary terms the cortex is the most recent addition to the brain and is called the neocortex.

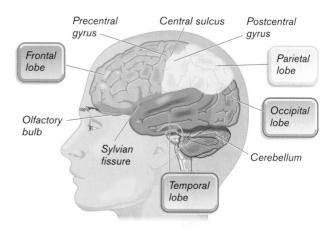

Figure 7.10 The frontal lobes

The limbic system (and hippocampus)

The *limbic system* is a network of nuclei that are thought to be involved in emotions and learning. The limbic system comprises the *hippocampus, amygdala, cingulate cortex, fornix, septum* and *mamillary bodies* (see Figure 7.11).

The hippocampus and the amygdala have been studied extensively. The hippocampus is associated with spatial memory (see Research Methods Box 7.2), and the amygdala with fear and emotion (LeDoux, 2000).

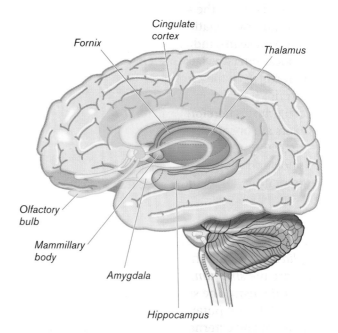

Figure 7.11 The limbic system

RESEARCH METHODS BOX 7.2

The hippocampus and taxi drivers

London taxi drivers have to pass 'the knowledge' before they are licensed. The knowledge consists of knowing many routes around London (e.g. from Buckingham Palace to Harrods).

Maguire *et al.* (1997) tested taxi drivers' knowledge while undergoing positron emission tomography (PET). A PET scan measures radioactivity. If you make oxygen radioactive you can find out which parts of the brain are using the most.

The taxi drivers were given three tasks:

1 to provide the route between two locations (spatial task)
2 to describe landmarks which weren't in London and which they had not visited (non-spatial task)
3 to recall the plot of a film (control task).

A number of brain regions were activated during these tasks, but the one that differentiated was the hippocampus. The hippocampus was activated only in the spatial task.

Further investigation by Maguire *et al.* (2000), using MRI scans, indicated that the posterior hippocampus was larger in taxi drivers. Interestingly, the increase in the size of the posterior hippocampus was a function of years as a taxi driver. Therefore, it is unlikely that taxi drivers are born with an increased posterior hippocampus. The increase in the posterior hippocampus occurs through learning and experience.

'We asked him how to get from north London to south London and there was no hippocampal activity'

The basal ganglia

In some neuroanatomical classifications the *basal ganglia* also contain the amygdala. The basal ganglia comprise the *striatum*, the *globus pallidus* and the *substantia nigra*. The striatum is further subdivided into caudate and putamen. The globus pallidus has an internal and external part. The substantia nigra divides into two areas called the pars compacta and pars reticulata. The basal ganglia are extremely important in motor control and it is this area that contains the underlying fault in Parkinson's disease and Huntington's disease.

Midbrain: mesencephalon

The *mesencephalon* is divided into two: the *tectum* and *tegmentum*. Again, this division is on the basis of location; the tectum is dorsal and tegmentum is ventral. The tectum comprises the *inferior* and

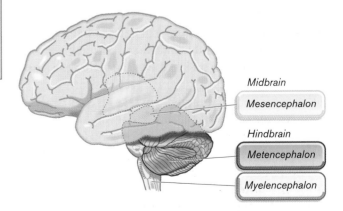

Midbrain
Mesencephalon

Hindbrain
Metencephalon

Myelencephalon

Figure 7.12 The midbrain and hindbrain

superior colliculi. These relate to auditory and visual functions respectively. The tegmentum comprises the substantia nigra (also part of the basal ganglia) and another motor area called the *red nucleus*. The mesencephalon also contains the periaqueductal gray, which is tissue around the cerebral aqueduct that connects the third and fourth ventricle. This site is the target of many analgesics. It also contains the *reticular formation*, which has been implicated in sleep (see Chapter 11).

Hindbrain: metencephalon and myelencephalon

The *metencephalon* comprises the *pons* and the *cerebellum* (see Figure 7.12). The pons contains a part of the reticular formation, and descending and ascending neural fibres. The cerebellum is the cauliflower-like structure you can see in MRI images and is involved in motor control.

The *myelencephalon* (also called the medulla) contains the reticular formation.

Communication in the brain

Neurons do not sit in isolation. They communicate with each other. A neuron receives a message from another at the dendrites and passes it down the axon to the terminal region. The communication of information within a neuron is electrical. The communication between neurons is chemically mediated.

Electrical communication

The basis of electrical communication is the difference in ionic concentrations on either side of the neuron's cell membrane. There are different ions in the intracellular and extracellular fluid. Ions are molecules that have different electrical charges. They can be either positively charged (cations) or negatively charged (anions). There is an electrical force between ions: like charges repel and opposite charges attract. Across the membrane this force, or *electrostatic pressure* as it is known, is in action.

Another force that acts on ions is their movement down the concentration gradient. This is when ions move from where there is a high concentration to where concentration is low, until there is an even distribution. This is somewhat similar to the action of sugar in tea. If you place a spoon of sugar in a cup of tea, there is an initial high concentration of sugar at the bottom. Give the tea a stir and the sugar dissolves and distributes itself evenly throughout the tea.

The resting potential

If we place one electrode inside the neuron and another outside we can measure the difference in electrical charge between the two sides. The *resting potential* is a comparison of charges from the extracellular fluid to the intracellular fluid. The difference is called a membrane potential; the membrane produces resistance. When there are no influences impinging on the neuron it is said to be at rest, thus the 'resting potential'. The resting potential in neurons is about -70m V.

There are four main ions that contribute to the resting potential: sodium (Na^+), potassium (K^+), chloride (Cl^-) and some negatively charged proteins.

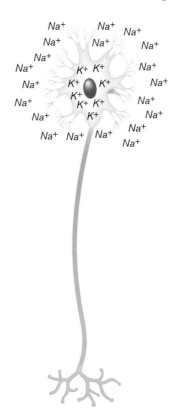

Figure 7.13 The ions across the cell membrane are distributed unevenly

Calcium (Ca^{++}) is also involved, but more so at the synapse. These ions are not equally distributed across the cell membrane (see Figure 7.13). There are two reasons for this uneven distribution. The first is that the membrane is semi-permeable and permits certain molecules to pass through it. The site at which an ion can gain passage to either side is called the *ion channel*. The ion channels are proteins that are configured to allow only certain ions through. The second mechanism responsible for this distribution is the *sodium-potassium pump*. The sodium-potassium pump is an energy-consuming mechanism, which pumps Na^+ out, and K^+ in. It does this in a three-for-two manner: three Na^+ ions for two K^+ ions. The sodium-potassium pump is there to counteract the seepage of Na^+ into the cell via the semi-permeable membrane. Na^+ attempts to gain entry because of the concentration gradient and electrostatic pressure.

Due to the differences at rest, the neuron is *polarised* – that is, the two sides of the neuronal membrane are differentially charged.

The action potential

When a neuron is activated (or fires) it produces an *action potential*. Action potentials are the neural impulses that are involved in communication. An action potential is a rapid reversal of the membrane potential. The change in membrane potential permits an exchange of ions. During the resting potential the neuron is polarised; an action potential reduces the polarity and is *depolarising*. An action potential is a depolarisation of the neuron. Conversely, *hyperpolarisation* is when the neuron becomes even more polarised than when it is at rest.

Postsynaptic potentials

Incoming signals from other neurons are received by receptors on the dendrites and soma. If the message that is received depolarises the receptor it produces an *excitatory postsynaptic potential (EPSP)*. An inhibitory input produces a hyperpolarisation called an *inhibitory postsynaptic potential (IPSP)*. Both types of input vary according to the intensity of the signal received. An EPSP increases the probability that an action potential will occur and an IPSP decreases that probability.

EPSPs and IPSPs are integrated at the axon hillock. The axon hillock acts like a funnel, collecting all the information before passing it down the axon. Depending on the balance of incoming information (EPSPs and IPSPs) a depolarisation of the axon may occur.

The integration of information at the axon hillock accounts for the location and timing of inputs. In *spatial summation* there is integration of information coming in from different sites. With *temporal summation* if the incoming information is close together in time there is an increased change of response in a particular direction. In the case of a barrage EPSP an axon potential will be initiated.

The sequence of events during an action potential

In the case of an action potential there is a depolarisation caused by an EPSP. An action potential can be induced artificially with electrodes. If an electrical stimulus is of sufficient strength it reaches the threshold of excitation. The threshold of excitation is the point at which an action potential can occur. The action potential is an all-or-nothing event. Action potentials either happen or they don't. A big stimulus does not produce a bigger action potential. The action potential is always the same size.

The process of an action potential starts with the opening of Na^+ channels. When the channels open, Na^+ enters the cell causing a change in membrane potential. In response, K^+ channels open and K^+ exits the cell. Na^+ channels close, but K^+ ions are still exiting, producing a repolarisation of the cell. K^+ channels close slowly and an overshoot occurs, which results in a hyperpolarisation. Once all channels are closed the membrane returns to the resting potential (see Figure 7.14). All this happens in the space of 3–4 ms.

After the start of an action potential there is a period of time in which another one cannot occur. There are two preventative periods of an action potential. There is the *absolute refractory period*, which is followed by the *relative refractory period*. The latter requires greater stimulation to obtain an action potential. Thus if a stimulus is of sufficient

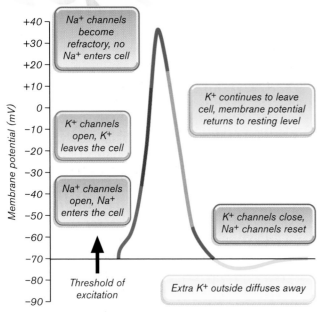

Figure 7.14 *The action potential: the exchange of ions across the cell membrane can be placed on the recording of an action potential*

Labels in figure:
- +40 to -90 (Membrane potential (mV))
- Na+ channels become refractory, no Na+ enters cell
- K+ channels open, K+ leaves the cell
- Na+ channels open, Na+ enters the cell
- K+ continues to leave cell, membrane potential returns to resting level
- K+ channels close, Na+ channels reset
- Threshold of excitation
- Extra K+ outside diffuses away

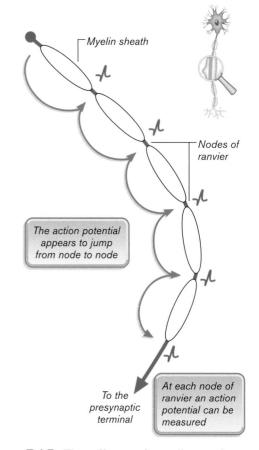

Figure 7.15 *The effects of myelin on the action potential*

Labels in figure:
- Myelin sheath
- Nodes of ranvier
- The action potential appears to jump from node to node
- To the presynaptic terminal
- At each node of ranvier an action potential can be measured

intensity it will produce an action potential during the relative refractory period.

Propagation of the action potential

From the axon hillock the action potential moves down the axon. The exchange of ions at one point influences the neighbouring section of the axon. To clarify this concept think of the axon as a set of dominoes laid out ready to topple over. If you are the electrical stimulus and knock over one domino, the next one falls over too. Eventually, all the dominoes fall without you having to touch each one. Each domino falling represents the sequence of events during action potential: one point on the axon influences the other.

The speed of propagation depends on the size of axon; large axons are faster than smaller ones. The speed is increased in myelinated neurons. Myelin acts as insulation (or a sheath) and prevents the ionic exchange characteristic of an action potential. The signal produced by the action potential passes along the sheathed area passively. The impulse along the myelinated axon is diminished. However, in the

myelin sheath there are gaps, as we have seen, called nodes of ranvier.

The diminished signal is sufficient for an action potential to occur at these gaps. Thus the action potential appears to jump from node to node in a process called *salutatory conduction* (see Figure 7.15). Myleinated neurons send information at great speed. The importance of myelin can be seen in patients with multiple sclerosis (MS). In MS the neurons are there but an immune response attacks and destroys the myelin (see Steinman *et al.*, 2002). This has profound effects on sufferers, who experience motor and sensory difficulties.

Synaptic transmission

Neurons communicate with other neurons – they send messages to one another. Neurons are not physically connected, though. Between neurons there is a small gap. This gap is called the *synapse*. For a neuron to communicate with another neuron the synapse has to be traversed. The presynaptic neuron (the neuron sending the message) releases a chemical called a neurotransmitter, which crosses the synapse. Neurotransmitters interact with receptors on another neuron (the postsynaptic neuron). The neuron that receives the message transforms the message into an action potential. The action potential travels down to the axon and releases a neurotransmitter into another synapse.

Consider this like a telephone conversation with someone. The axon is the wire between the two telephones. To be able to talk to someone we have to speak into the handset. The person speaking has to bridge the gap between mouth and microphone (the synapse). The microphone converts the words into electrical signals. The electrical signals pass down the wire (the axon) to another telephone. The telephone then converts the electrical information (the action

potential) into words via the speaker. The speaker sends information across the space that lies between it and the recipient's ear (another synapse). Of course, in this example we are only speaking in one language. We will come back to the example of conversations when we look at chemical communication between neurons in more detail.

Neurotransmitters

There are many neurotransmitters within the nervous system, and with advances in biochemistry the list of chemicals that act as neurotransmitters is sure to grow.

The neurotransmitters already identified have received extensive investigation. Research has provided detailed accounts of neurotransmission in general and the application of this knowledge to various disorders. Many neurotransmitters are classified into groups or families (see Figure 7.16). Which group a neurotransmitter belongs in depends on its chemical structure.

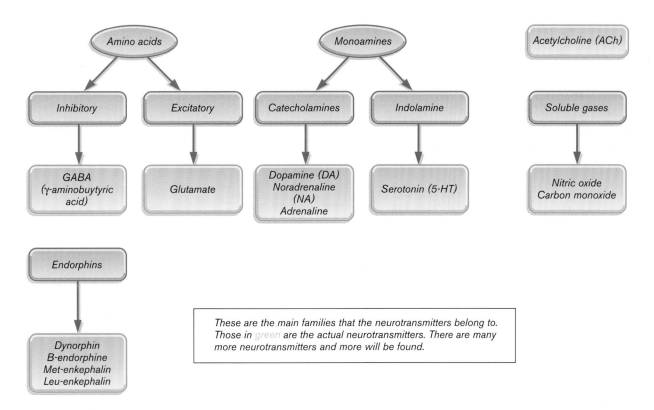

Figure 7.16 Neurotransmitters can be categorised into various groups

Section 2
Psychobiology

Dopamine, noradrenaline and adrenaline synthesis and metabolism

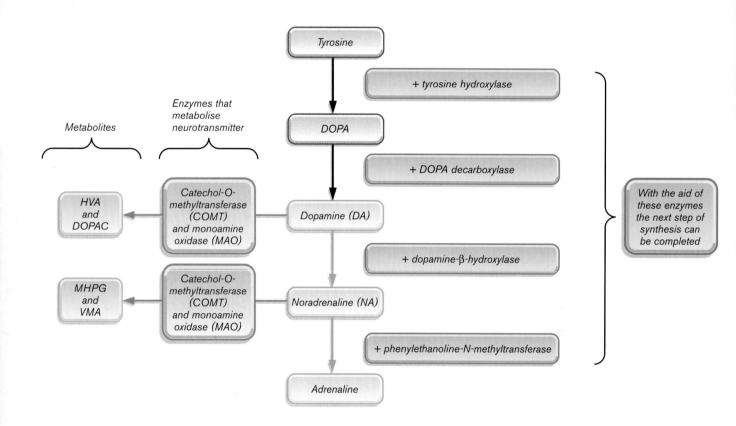

Serotonin synthesis and metabolism

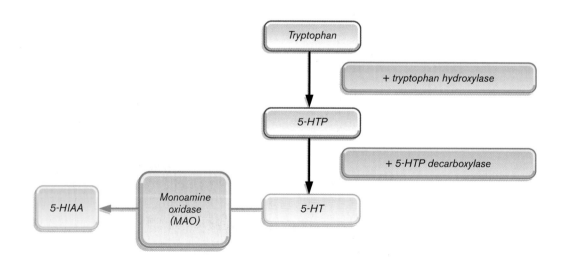

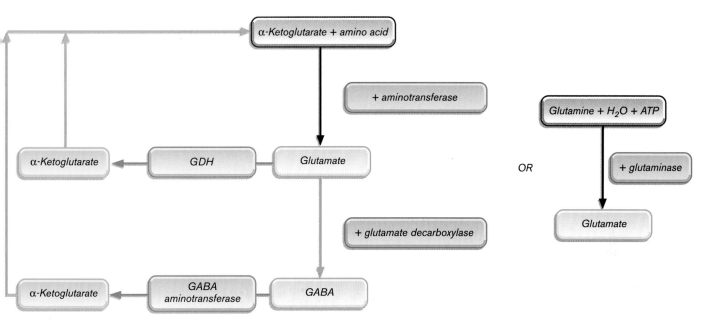

Glutamate and GABA synthesis and metabolism

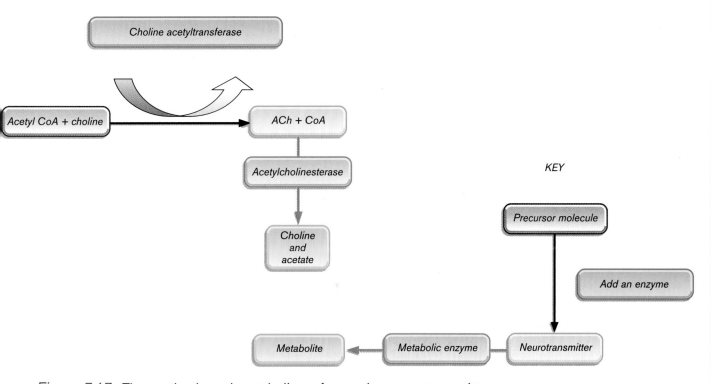

Acetylcholine synthesis and metabolism

Figure 7.17 *The synthesis and metabolism of some key neurotransmitters*

TABLE 7.1	
NEUROTRANSMITTERS AND RECEPTORS	
Dopamine	D1, D2, D3, D4, D5
Noradrenaline	α and β adrenoceptors
Serotonin	$5\text{-}HT_1$, $5\text{-}HT_2$, $5\text{-}HT_3$
GABA	GABA A and GABA B
Endorphins	μ, κ, δ
Acetylcholine	Nicotine and muscarinic
Glutamate	NMDA and AMPA

It is worth noting that for adrenaline and noradrenaline there are differences across the literature. In the USA adrenaline is referred to as epinephrine, and noradrenaline as norepinephrine. Noradrenaline and norepinephrine are one and the same – they are not different (adrenaline and epinephrine are also the same). Also, the chemical name for serotonin is 5-hydroxytryptophan. Serotonin is clearly easier to say, but when reading the literature the abbreviation '5-HT' is used.

Neurotransmitters are made – they do not just appear, they have to be synthesised (see Figure 7.17). Synthesis of a neurotransmitter is like a recipe; all the ingredients must be added before the meal is ready. The synthesis of a neurotransmitter takes place in the soma. The newly made neurotransmitter is put into packages called *vesicles*. The vesicles are transported down *microtubules* to the presynaptic terminal. They stay there until they are released into the synapse.

Synaptic transmission: the events

The vesicles that contain neurotransmitter substances are poised ready for communication. It is the action potential at the presynaptic terminal that causes the neurotransmitter to be released. When the action potential reaches the presynaptic terminal the membrane is depolarised. Depolarisation of the membrane allows calcium (Ca^{++}) ion channels to open and Ca^{++} to enter the presynaptic terminal. The entry of Ca^{++} in the presynaptic terminal makes the vesicles fuse with the presynaptic membrane.

Once fused, the contents of the vesicle are released into the synapse (see Figure 7.18).

Particular neurons release particular neurotransmitters. A neuron that releases dopamine (DA) is referred to as a dopaminergic neuron. Neurons that release glutamate are glutamatergic neurons. This convention can be applied to many neurotransmitters. To use the example of a telephone conversation again, each neurotransmitter can be considered a particular language. A dopaminergic neuron speaks the language of DA, etc. Thus the different neurotransmitters of the nervous system can be considered as the different languages of our world. An example of excitatory and inhibitory messages is given in Activity Box 7.2.

Now that the neurotransmitter is in the synapse, its job is to communicate with the postsynaptic neuron (the neuron at the other side of the gap). The postsynaptic neuron requires a means of receiving the message.

In order to receive the message the postsynaptic membrane of the neuron has specialised *receptors*. These are proteins that are configured so that only certain neurotransmitters can talk to certain receptors e.g. 5-HT with 5-HT receptors (see Table 7.1).

Similarly, if we are to understand a message on the telephone we have to be able to interpret the language being spoken. Our ears are like the receptors for neurotransmitters. We need our ears to hear the other person on the telephone. However, if that person speaks a language we do not understand, the message cannot be conveyed to us. People who

ACTIVITY BOX 7.2

Inhibitory and excitatory pathways in Parkinson's disease

Parkinson's disease is a severe motor disorder caused by a reduction of DA in basal ganglia (Ehringer and Hornykiewicz, 1960). Specifically there is an 80–90 per cent reduction of DA in the substantia nigra and striatum (Bernheimer *et al.*, 1973), which form the nigrostriatal pathway.

That all seems very simple for a severe neurological disorder. However, a loss of DA in the nigrostriatal pathway has knock-on effects in other areas of the brain. These knock-on effects are mediated by two amino acid neurotransmitters. GABA is an inhibitory transmitter and glutamate is excitatory. Think of them as instructions. GABA is saying 'be quiet', whereas glutamate wants to make some noise.

Figure 7.19a (p. 106) shows the communication in the non-Parkinsonian brain, while Figure 7.19b shows what happens in the brain of someone with Parkinson's disease. Looking at the first flow diagram (Figure 7.19a) the basal ganglia is in harmony because there is no loss of nigrostriatal DA. In the second flow diagram (Figure 7.19b) the loss of nigrostriatal DA has profound effects and produces the symptoms of Parkinson's disease.

The DA deficiency fails to inhibit the subthalamic nucleus (STN) because not enough GABA is received from the globus pallidus external section. This is called disinhibition. A lack of STN inhibition means that it sends excitatory glutamate messages to the globus pallidus internal (GPi) section. The GPi is then overactive and sends its inhibitory GABAergic message to the thalamus. That thalamus is in effect told to be quiet by the GABA and therefore does not 'talk to' the cortex.

From this example it can be seen how both excitatory and inhibitory neurotransmitters affect groups of cells. Due to one deficiency the effects are seen throughout the motor system.

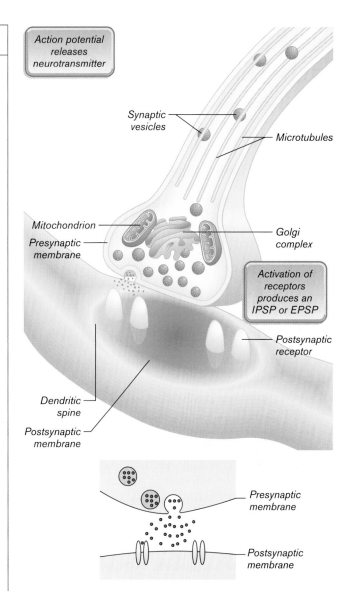

Figure 7.18 *The synapse and exocytosis: neurotransmitter release*

understand only English can act only on a message in English. They cannot interpret a message, for example, in German. However, neurons can be multilingual and can understand other languages (e.g. some DA neurons can understand a message sent by acetylcholine (ACh)).

Receptors

When a neurotransmitter attaches itself to a receptor this is called *binding*. It is not just neurotransmitters

Section 2
Psychobiology

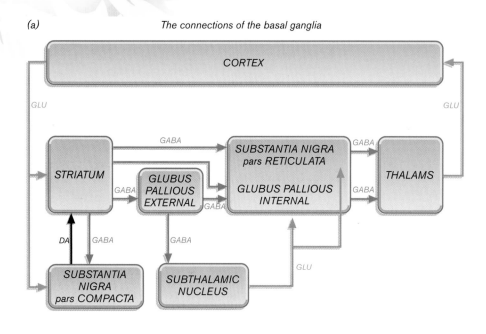

(a)

The connections of the basal ganglia

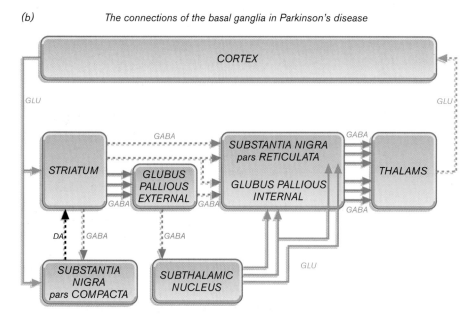

(b)

The connections of the basal ganglia in Parkinson's disease

Figure 7.19 Communication in (a) the non-Parkinsonian brain and (b) in the brain of someone with Parkinson's disease

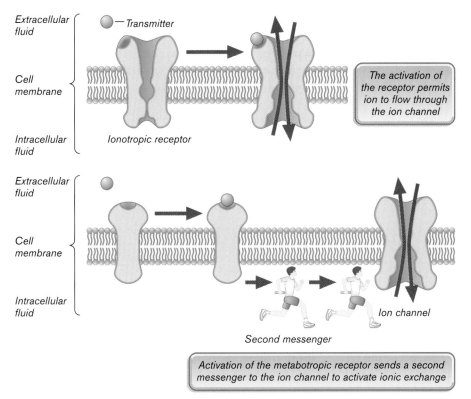

Figure 7.20 *Ionotropic and metabotropic receptors*
Source: adapted from Nicholls et al. (2001)

that bind to receptors – chemicals bind to receptors too. Chemicals that bind to receptors are called *ligands.*

There are two types of receptors: *ionotropic* and *metabotropic receptors* (see Figure 7.20). These two types of receptors respond to messages in different ways. The ionotropic receptor responds quickly to a neurotransmitter. When a neurotransmitter acts as an ionotropic receptor, ion channels are activated. Ions enter the postsynaptic cell. This induces either an EPSP or IPSP, depending on the ion that enters.

Metabotropic receptors respond to ligands with an intermediate step. The metabotropic receptor activates G-proteins. More often than not, the G-proteins activate another chemical called a second messenger. The second messenger takes the signal to an enzyme that alters ion channel activity. If an ionotropic receptor is a straight race, the metabotropic receptor is a relay race.

Synaptic regulation

The released neurotransmitter is monitored by the presynaptic neuron. It does this by using receptors for the neurotransmitter that are located on the presynaptic membrane. These receptors are called *autoreceptors* (see Figure 7.21). They act a bit like a thermostat on a central heating system. If you set the thermostat to 18°C and the temperature in the room rises over 18°C, the heating cuts out. Conversely, if it falls below the temperature, the heating comes on.

We can apply this principle to DA. For example, if there is too much DA in the synapse, the autoreceptor relays the message to the neuron and it shuts down the production and release of DA. If there is too little DA, the neuron increases production and release. The neuron therefore uses feedback derived from the autoreceptor to regulate release of the neurotransmitter.

Heteroreceptors are another type of presynaptic receptor, which modulate synaptic transmission.

Section 2
Psychobiology

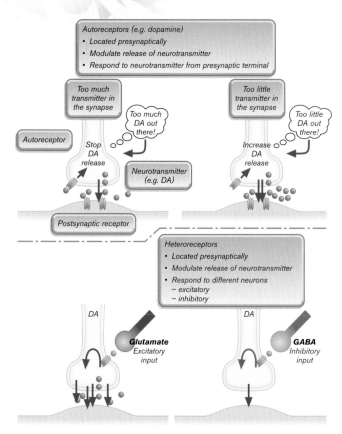

Figure 7.21 Presynaptic modulation by autoreceptors and heteroreceptors

However, they are different from autoreceptors as they receive messages from other neurons. Heteroreceptors on a neuron are responsive to different neurotransmitters. Received signals are either excitatory or inhibitory, and can increase or decrease the likelihood of neurotransmitter release (see Figure 7.21). The neuron can understand other neurotransmitters' messages.

Once a neurotransmitter has been released, its life is very short and is brought to an end by either *enzymatic metabolism* or reuptake. The process of enzymatic degradation involves the conversion of neurotransmitters into other chemicals called *metabolites* (see Figure 7.17). These metabolites are inactive and can be measured in CSF, urine and blood.

Reuptake also stops the action of a neurotransmitter by reclaiming it from the synapse. The presynaptic neuron can have another set of receptors called transporters. A transporter reclaims the neurotransmitter from the synapse and repackages it for further use.

Psychopharmacology

Drugs can influence neurotransmission at many points throughout the entire process of neural communication. We tend to think of drugs as clinical agents; however, we can use drugs as tools to probe the functions of the brain. Drugs can be used to influence

---

APPLICATIONS BOX 7.1

The DA hypothesis of schizophrenia: evidence from psychopharmacology

One of the most remarkably resilient hypotheses about the neurochemistry of schizophrenia focuses on DA. It is thought that there is an increase in DA in the schizophrenic brain.

Some of the evidence used to support this hypothesis comes from the actions of drugs. All anti-psychotics block the actions of DA, and DA agonists can increase or induce schizophrenia-like symptoms.

Amphetamine facilitates the release of DA. People who have abused amphetamine can have a form of psychosis that resembles paranoid schizophrenia (Connell, 1958). Amphetamine has been shown to intensify psychotic symptomatology in patients diagnosed with schizophrenia (Van Kammen *et al.*, 1982), but 29 per cent showed an improvement.

Why is amphetamine therapeutic? This is best explained in terms of positive and negative symptoms (Crow, 1980; Sanfilipo *et al.*, 1996). Hallucinations and delusions are examples of positive symptoms. Apathy and an inability to engage in the world and be active typify negative symptoms. Not surprisingly, patients with these symptoms became more animated after a dose of amphetamine. Their baseline activity was so low that there was only room for improvement.

Further evidence of a DAergic involvement in schizophrenia comes from the treatment of schizophrenia. Chlorpromazine was the first drug used to treat schizophrenia. It was also able to block amphetamine-induced behaviours. Chlorpromazine blocked the DA second messenger system, pointing towards the involvement of DA (Miller *et al.*, 1974). Other anti-schizophrenic drugs also increase DA metabolites (an index of DA turnover) due to a compensatory reaction to DA blockade (Carlsson and Lindqvist, 1963).

However, there is a discrepancy between the clinical effects of the pharmacology (Snyder *et al.*, 1975). Haloperidol, another type of anti-schizophrenic drug, did not have a pronounced effect on the DA second messenger system. Kebabian and Calne (1979) proposed two types of DA receptors to account for this difference: the D1 and D2 receptors. The D1 is linked to the second messenger and the D2 is not.

Anti-schizophrenic drugs are regarded as acting at the D2 receptor, where they exert their therapeutic effect. Other drugs act at the D2 receptor and also at the D1 receptor, which blocks the second messenger.

As drug development has continued, new drugs have started to illuminate the neurochemistry of schizophrenia. New types of anti-schizophrenic drugs, called atypical drugs, point to regions in the brain where the therapeutic action takes place. This is a DA-rich area called the mesolimbic system; atypical drugs act there.

The psychopharmacology of schizophrenia is an ongoing concern. As already stated, the involvement of DA was just a hypothesis and remains such. As the decades have passed, the hypothesis has evolved to include other neurotransmitters (e.g. Grace, 1991). Psychopharmacological research has not provided a definitive account of schizophrenia. There are many questions that remain to be answered as to the biological bases of schizophrenia.

physiology and behaviour. Psychopharmacology has helped develop many theories of abnormal behaviour (for example, the DA hypothesis of schizophrenia; see Applications Box 7.1)) and has helped inform legislation such as the level of alcohol permitted in drivers. Drug research is not conclusive, however, and can at times raise more questions than it answers.

Drug classification

Drugs come from different chemical classes and have different pharmacological actions. The best way to categorise drugs is by what they do (e.g. anti-depressants treat depression and anxiolytics relieve anxiety). The doctor's prescribing guide, the British National Formulary, is laid out by drug effect. For example, anti-depressants come from different chemical classes and have different modes of action, yet are still effective in treating depression (see also Chapter 34, pages 596–597).

Drug action

The fate of a drug is determined by two chief characteristics: *pharmacokinetics* and *pharmacodynamics*. Pharmacokinetics is about the factors that influence a drug as it travels through the body. Route of administration, rate of absorption and termination of the drug action are important pharmacokinetic factors. Pharmacodynamics is concerned with the drug effect – what happens when it reaches its destination.

Types of drug action

Drugs can be divided into four groups: agonists, antagonists, partial agonists and inverse agonists. *Agonists* facilitate the action at the synapse. *Antagonists* (or blockers) inhibit synaptic activity. *Partial agonists* operate somewhere between a full agonist and a full antagonist. *Inverse agonists* produce a response that is in the opposite direction to that of an agonist (see Activity Box 7.3). Inverse agonists should not be confused with antagonists. Antagonists *inhibit* a response, they do not *produce* a response. The main two that we will be concerned with here are the agonist and antagonist.

Drugs can also be seen as either *competitive* or *non-competitive* (see Figure 7.22). Competitive drugs

Section 2
Psychobiology

ACTIVITY BOX 7.3

Anxiety and the inverse agonists: an adaptation of evolution

Why is it useful to have anxiety?

We all get feelings of anxiety and fear. No doubt you will experience anxiety when you have deadlines to meet or examinations looming. This type of anxiety is normal because of the circumstances.

However, when the anxiety response is maladaptive it may be considered a psychiatric problem.

Drugs such as diazepam (Valium) are used to treat anxiety disorders. Diazepam is a benzodiazepine (BZ) and acts at the BZ receptor. Diazepam is an agonist that boosts the actions of inhibitory GABA at the GABA A receptor. Drugs such as diazepam are called anxiolytics because they reduce feelings of anxiety.

What is the evolutionary significance of anxiety?

Is there a case for an endogenous BZ?

De Blas *et al.* (1987) found endogenous compounds that bind to BZ receptors that had a similar structure to benzodiazepines. In the search for endogenous BZs, beta-carbolines were discovered. They were found to displace benzodiazepines and to have a wide spectrum of pharmacological activity. Some were found to be inverse agonists.

If the BZs are agonists, then what do inverse agonists do?

Inverse agonists act at the BZ site to reduce the action of the GABA A receptor. Inverse agonists are anxiogenic, pro-convulsant, activating and promnestic (the opposite to amnesic). It is the inverse agonists that may well be the endogenous ligand. Clearly a substance that promoted flight or fight responses would be of evolutionary significance

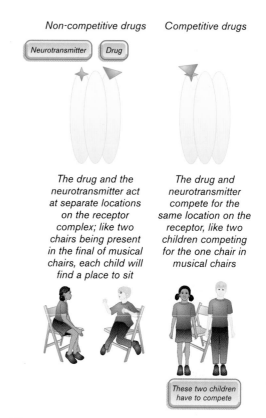

Non-competitive drugs   *Competitive drugs*

The drug and the neurotransmitter act at separate locations on the receptor complex; like two chairs being present in the final of musical chairs, each child will find a place to sit

The drug and neurotransmitter compete for the same location on the receptor, like two children competing for the one chair in musical chairs

Figure 7.22 Competitive and non-competitive drug action

fight for the same place as the neurotransmitter. This can be seen as rather like the last two children competing in a game of musical chairs. Non-competitive drugs act at a different site on the receptor to the neurotransmitter. In this case there is a chair for each child in the final of musical chairs.

Modulation of neurotransmission by drugs

Drugs can influence neurotransmission at a number of different points that can influence behaviour (see Figure 7.23).

Precursor drugs

These drugs enhance the synthesis and increase the turnover of a neurotransmitter by acting as a precursor in the neurotransmitter's synthesis (e.g. L-DOPA therapy in Parkinson's disease provides the precursor for DA where DA is deficient).

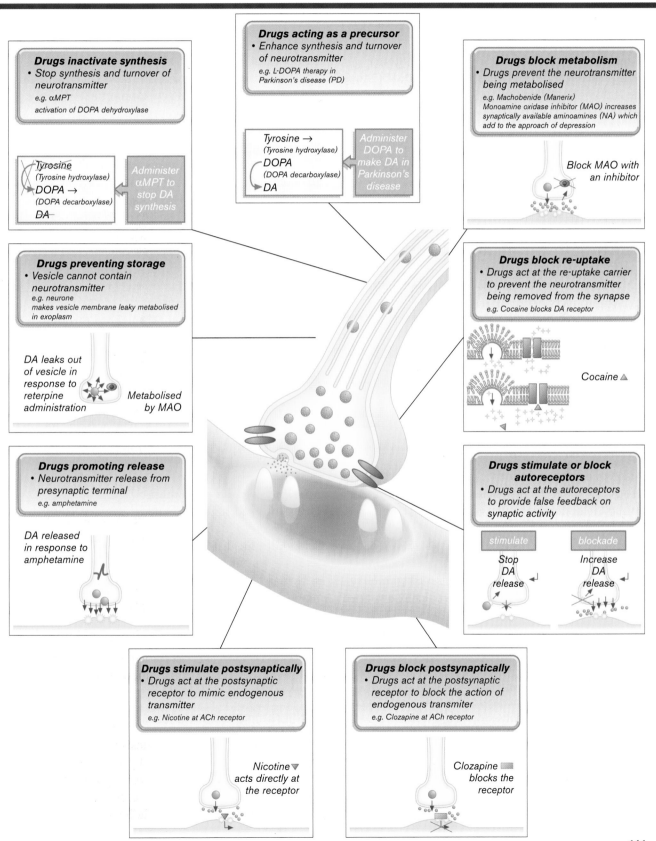

Figure 7.23 Drugs can influence neurotransmission in a number of ways

Synthesis inhibition

Drugs can interrupt synthesis, thus preventing a neurotransmitter from being made (e.g. αMPT stops the action of tyrosine hydoxylase and therefore DA (and NA) cannot be made).

Storage prevention

Drugs can prevent the neurotransmitter from being stored in the vesicle (e.g. reserpine makes monoamine vesicles 'leaky'). Just as a tea bag allows the flavour to flood out into the water, monoamines flood out into the cytoplasm of the cell. Once in the cytoplasm, the monoamines are metabolised. Reserpine was once used as a treatment for schizophrenia, but it has also been used to induce the symptoms of depression in animals.

Enhance neurotransmitter release

Drugs can promote neurotransmitter release from presynaptic terminals (e.g. amphetamine forces the release of DA (and NA) without an action potential). Amphetamine has been reported to induce symptoms similar to paranoid schizophrenia (see Applications Box 7.1).

Postsynaptic stimulation

Drugs can act at the postsynaptic receptor and mimic the endogenous neurotransmitters e.g. nicotine acts at a receptor for ACh and is called a nicotinic receptor. This receptor was discovered using nicotine as a tool to locate its site of action. However, nicotine is not an endogenous ligand like ACh; we do not have a receptor specifically designed for smoking.

Postsynaptic antagonism

A drug can act at the postsynaptic receptor to block the action of endogenous neurotransmitters (an antagonist) (e.g. the antipsychotic haloperidol blocks DA D2 receptors and thus stops DA interacting with these receptors).

Autoreceptor stimulation and antagonism

Drugs can act at the autoreceptor to provide false feedback on synaptic activity (e.g. apomorphine at low doses stimulates the DA autoreceptor to reduce the release of DA). Conversely the DA antagonist haloperidol increases DA. This would appear counterintuitive, as its task is to stop DA activity and reduce the symptoms of schizophrenia (see above for haloperidol's therapeutic target).

Drugs that block reuptake

Drugs can act at the reuptake transporter to prevent the neurotransmitter being removed from the synapse (e.g. cocaine blocks the DA transporter and thus increases DA in the synapse because it cannot escape and be deactivated). This is also how Prozac works, but specifically at 5-HT transporters, hence it is referred to as a selective serotonin reuptake inhibitor (SSRI).

Inhibition of metabolism

Drugs can prevent the neurotransmitter from being metabolised (e.g. the anti-depressant moclobemide is a monoamine oxidase inhibitor (MAOI)). MAOIs increase monoamines in the synapse by inhibiting the enzymes that degrade them. The only drugs available for the treatment of Alzheimer's disease (e.g. donepezil) act in a similar way to block the metabolism of ACh. These anti-dementia drugs are called anticholinesterase inhibitors.

Multiple sites of drug action

Drugs often act at more than just one site. This can lead to increased therapeutic efficacy, e.g. the anti-schizophrenic drug clozapine acts on DA, 5-HT and glutamate systems to be clinically effective. Multiple sites may be required for the pharmacotherapy of Alzheimer's disease; because so much goes wrong in the brains of these patients one target is not sufficient.

Multiple sites of action can also contribute to neurotoxicity and adverse effects (e.g. MDMA (see Applications Box 7.2). The action of drugs, other than the desired target, can lead to side-effects.

Endocrinology: hormones and their action

Hormones are chemicals that are secreted by *endocrine glands* (see Figure 7.24). Hormones enter the bloodstream and travel to their destination. The distance a hormone travels can vary from millimetres to metres. Thus hormones, like neurotransmitters, are chemicals that transmit messages.

APPLICATIONS BOX 7.2

The agony of ecstasy: long-term effects of MDMA

There is controversy surrounding the effects of MDMA (ecstasy) on the brain. MDMA releases DA and 5-HT. The initial release of 5-HT is followed by depletion. The acute behavioural affects of MDMA are well known (e.g. a positive mood) (Downing, 1986). MDMA is self-administered (Lamb and Griffith, 1987), induces a conditioned place preference (Marona-Lewicka *et al.*, 1996), acts as a discriminative stimulus (Baker *et al.*, 1995) and induces locomotor sensitisation (Cheeta and Chandler, 1998).

All of these measures indicate that MDMA is a drug of abuse. However, it is the long-term neurotoxicity of MDMA that gives cause for concern. Ricaurte *et al.* (1988) demonstrated that MDMA administration results in neurodegeneration of 5-HT terminals. McCann *et al.* (1998), using PET scans in humans, found a decreased global and regional reduction in 5-HT transporters in the brain.

Reports on the behavioural consequences of MDMA neurotoxicity are starting to appear. Serotonin is implicated in sexual activity, sleep, pain, circadian and seasonal rhythms, affective behaviours, motor activity and body temperature. Studies have demonstrated that MDMA users had lower scores on measures of impulsivity and indirect hostility (McCann *et al.*, 1994), delayed and immediate recall (Parrott *et al.*, 1998) and verbal recall (Thomasius *et al.*, 2003). They also had low mood problems after drug use (Curran and Travill, 1997), which could last up to a year (Taurah and Chandler, 2003). However, changes in depression were not correlated with changes in 5-HT neurons (van den Brink *et al.*, 2003).

There are methodological problems associated with studying the consequences of MDMA use. Most users do not take just MDMA. They are poly-drug users and may take other drugs too, such as ketamine or cannabis. MDMA is illegal, therefore the recruitment of participants is difficult. Those that volunteer may be different in some way from those that do not. The illegal nature of MDMA means that one cannot determine accurate details of drug-taking. People do not know how much of the drug they are taking and what other drugs it may be combined with (e.g. amphetamine). Ethical considerations mean that controlled studies are not permitted in the human population. Of course, this is not unique to MDMA. Research into the effects of other illegal drugs is also limited by such variables.

A conclusive answer accounting for the long-term effects of MDMA is yet to be found. As time passes and MDMA users grow older, its effects may start to become increasingly apparent. These reports allude to a future danger. The high derived from ecstasy now may well give way to depression in later years.

There are some more similarities between hormones and neurotransmitters:

- both neurons and endocrine glands store their chemicals for release
- both neurons and endocrine glands require stimulation to release their chemicals
- there are many types of hormones; some neurotransmitters also act as hormones
- there are receptors for hormones and these are linked to second messengers.

There are also some differences between hormones and neurotransmitters:

- neurons communicate with adjacent cells; hormones travel throughout the body before they reach their target (Figure 7.24)
- hormones are slow; neural communication is fast
- the action potential is all-or-nothing in neurons, whereas hormone levels alter the intensity of the message.

Section 2
Psychobiology

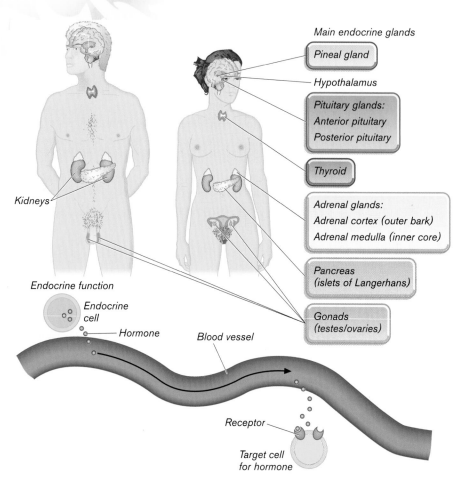

Main endocrine glands
- Pineal gland
- Hypothalamus
- Pituitary glands:
  Anterior pituitary
  Posterior pituitary
- Thyroid
- Adrenal glands:
  Adrenal cortex (outer bark)
  Adrenal medulla (inner core)
- Pancreas (islets of Langerhans)
- Gonads (testes/ovaries)

Kidneys

Endocrine function
Endocrine cell
Hormone
Blood vessel
Receptor
Target cell for hormone

Figure 7.24 Hormones travel to distant targets; the endocrine glands release hormones that travel to their target destination via the bloodstream

Types of hormones

There are three categories of hormones, distinguished by their chemical structure: *protein*, *amine* and *steroid hormones*. Protein hormones and most amine hormones act at receptors on the cell membrane. The receptors initiate second messengers similar to a metabotropic receptor (see Figure 7.20). The protein hormones influence previously made proteins (see Chapter 6). Steroid hormones gain entry to the inside of a cell and, once inside, the steroid acts as a receptor and binds to the DNA. The steroid hormone influences transcription and the creation of new proteins (see Figure 7.25).

The pituitary and hypothalamus

The *pituitary gland* and the *hypothalamus* are considered to be in control of the endocrine system.

The pituitary gland releases tropic hormones that send signals to release other hormones. There are two parts to the pituitary gland: anterior and posterior. The two areas differ in the hormones they release (see Figure 7.26). The pituitary is under the influence of the hypothalamus.

The hypothalamus communicates with the anterior and posterior pituitary using different mechanisms. The paraventricular and supraoptic nuclei of the hypothalamus have neurons that project down the pituitary stalk to the posterior pituitary. The

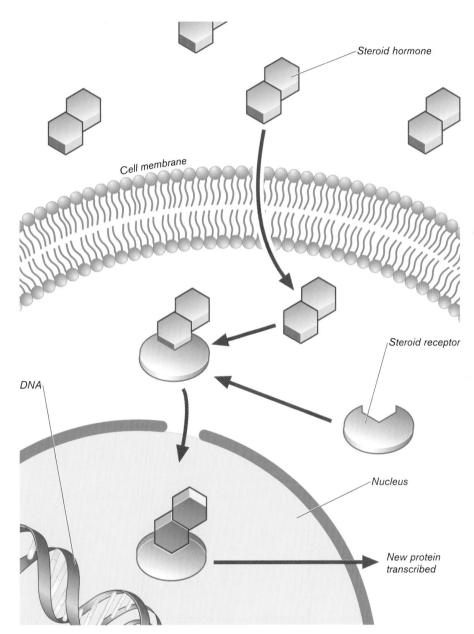

Figure 7.25 Steroid hormones enter the cell to alter the DNA and facilitate the production of new proteins

hormones of the posterior pituitary are transported from the hypothalamus down these neurons. Such neurons are called *neurosecretory cells*.

The hypothalamus influences the anterior pituitary via networks of capillaries called the *hypothalamic-pituitary portal system*. The hypothalamus sends out either releasing or inhibiting hormones to the anterior pituitary.

Endocrine feedback

Hormones exert many effects on the body and ultimately on behaviour. Hormones are not released in a constant stream, but rather in pulses. There is a considerable amount of feedback from the environment, which can affect hormone levels and subsequent behaviour.

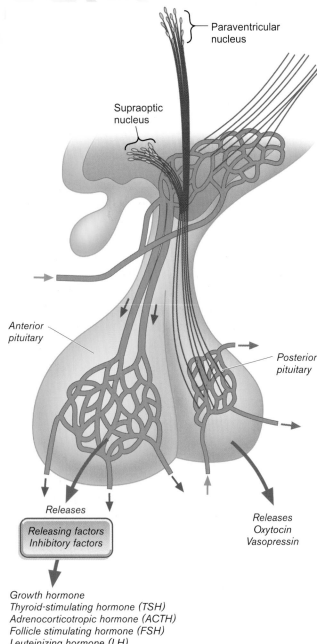

Figure 7.26 The anterior and posterior pituitary glands release different hormones

Labels in figure:
- Paraventricular nucleus
- Supraoptic nucleus
- Anterior pituitary
- Posterior pituitary
- Releases
- Releasing factors
- Inhibitory factors
- Releases Oxytocin Vasopressin
- Growth hormone
- Thyroid-stimulating hormone (TSH)
- Adrenocorticotropic hormone (ACTH)
- Follicle stimulating hormone (FSH)
- Leuteinizing hormone (LH)
- Prolactin

Sex and hormones

Males and females differ in their hormones, in particular the sex hormones. Hormonal changes in females have been studied extensively. There is a whole area of medicine specifically devoted to the female (gynaecology). The menstrual cycle consists of systematic fluctuations in the hormone levels of females, and these naturally occurring changes allow psychologists to identify the effects of hormones on behaviour. For example, Sanders and Wenmoth (1998) were able to identify changes in functional cerebral asymmetry across the menstrual cycle (see Research Methods Box 7.1). Males do not demonstrate such a cycle.

Activational and organisational effects of hormones

There are two processes by which hormones exert an influence: *activational* and *organisational* effects. Organisational processes are those that differentiate the body and brain. Activational processes are when changes in hormone levels influence behaviour.

Sexual differentiation

For the first few weeks after conception the foetus is undifferentiated; it is neither male nor female. The chromosomes for males are XY and the chromosomes for females are XX, as we have seen. The presence of the Y chromosome codes for the release of H-Y antigen. The presence of H-Y antigen allows the testes to grow. Absence of H-Y antigen allows the ovaries to develop.

After six weeks of gestation, the foetus has reproductive ducts. In the male the reproductive ducts are called the Wolffian system. In the female they are known as the Mullerian system. These systems are the start of the seminal vesicles and vas deferens in the male, and the uterus and fallopian tubes in females.

Once formed, the testes of the male foetus release testosterone and Mullerian-inhibiting factor. Mullerian-inhibiting factor suppresses the development of the female system and allows testosterone to develop the Wolffian system. In the female foetus the Mullerian system is allowed to develop. Again it is the absence of hormonal influences that allows the female system to develop.

Meanwhile the external features of sexual differentiation are becoming evident. At about two months there is no external difference. The reproductive organs of males and females emanate from four principal components (see Figure 7.27). The development of the male external genitalia is controlled by the presence of testosterone, whereas it is the absence of testosterone that allows the female genitals to develop.

Sexual differentiation of the brain

The organisational effects of hormones are not restricted to the reproductive systems of the different sexes. Hormones also affect the brain.

The most obvious line of thought is that the presence of androgens, such as testosterone, alters the male brain. The male brain produces male behaviours; an absence of androgens results in a female brain, and subsequently female behaviours. This is not the case. The *aromatisation* hypothesis is at first counterintuitive. The aromatisation hypothesis states that estradiol (a female hormone) is responsible for the masculine brain. Due to the chemical similarities, testosterone can be converted into estradiol (an oestrogen). The female brain is protected from aromatisation by α-fetoprotein. α-fetoprotein binds with estradiol and stops it gaining access to the brain. Testosterone, on the other hand, gets into the brain before it is converted into estradiol.

There are areas of the brain that are structurally different in males and females. The preoptic area of the hypothalamus is larger in males than females (Raisman and Field, 1971; Gorski *et al.*, 1978). This nucleus is referred to as the sexually dimorphic nucleus – that is, it differs between the sexes. Similarly, other areas of the hypothalamus are also larger in males (e.g. Swabb and Fliers, 1985). Lesions on the preoptic nucleus in the rat stop male copulatory behaviour (Hull *et al.*, 1999), whereas stimulation elicits it (Rodriguez-Manzo *et al.*, 2000). The role of the hypothalamus is still subject to further investigation. However, the fact that structural differences exist has prompted researchers to look at the brains of people with different sexual orientations (see Rahman and Wilson, 2003). Some studies have indicated that there are differences in the sexually dimorphic nuclei in homosexual and heterosexual men (e.g. LeVay, 1991). This type of research has many social, ethical and moral implications.

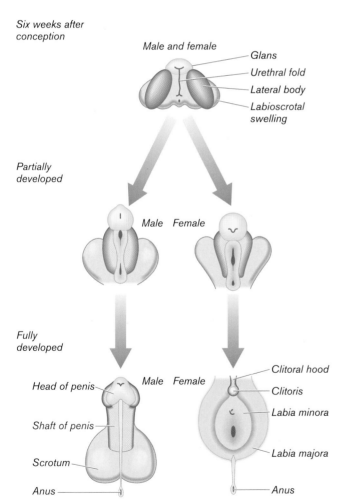

Six weeks after conception

Male and female
— Glans
— Urethral fold
— Lateral body
— Labioscrotal swelling

Partially developed

Male   Female

Fully developed

— Clitoral hood
Male   Female
— Clitoris
Head of penis —
— Labia minora
Shaft of penis —
Scrotum —
— Labia majora
Anus —
— Anus

Figure 7.27 The genitals are undifferentiated after conception and then, during gestation, develop into male and female

Learning outcomes

When you have completed this chapter you should be able to:

- describe the divisions of the nervous system
- describe the different regions of the brain
- provide an account of neural communication
- describe how drugs influence neural communication
- provide an account of endocrine communication.

Section 2
Psychobiology

Key Terms

Absolute refractory period
Action potential
Activational effects
Afferent nerves
Agonists
Amine hormones
Amygdala
Antagonists
Aromatisation
Autonomic nervous system (ANS)
Autoreceptors
Axon
Axon hillock
Basal ganglia
Binding
Blood–brain barrier (BBB)
Central nervous system (CNS)
Cerebellum
Cerebrospinal fluid (CSF)
Cingulate cortex
Commisures
Competitive drugs
Corpus callosum
Cortex
Dendrites
Depolarising
Diencephalon
Efferent nerves
Electrostatic pressure
Endocrine glands
Enzymatic metabolism
Excitatory postsynaptic potential (EPSP)
Fissures
Fornix
Frontal lobes
Glial cells
Globus pallidus

Gyri
Hetereoceptors
Hippocampus
Hormones
Hyperpolarisation
Hypothalamic-pituitary portal system
Hypothalamus
Inferior colliculi
Inhibitory postsynaptic potential (IPSP)
Inverse agonists
Ion channel
Ionotropic receptors
Ligands
Limbic system
Mamillary bodies
Meninges
Mesencephalon
Metabolites
Metabotropic receptors
Metencephalon
Microtubules
Mitochondria
Myelencephalon
Myelin
Nerve growth factor (NGF)
Neural tube
Neurons
Neurosecretory cells
Nodes of ranvier
Non-competitive drugs
Nucleus
Occipital lobes
Organisational effects
Parasympathetic
Parietal lobes
Partial agonists
Peripheral nervous system (PNS)
Pharmacodynamics

Pharmacokinetics
Pituitary gland
Polarised
Pons
Protein hormones
Receptors
Red nucleus
Relative refractory period
Resting potential
Reticular formation
Salutatory conduction
Satellite cells
Septum
Sodium-potassium pump
Soma
Somatic nervous system (SNS)
Spatial summation

Steroid hormones
Striatum
Subarachnoid space
Substantia nigra
Sulci
Superior colliculi
Sympathetic
Synapse
Synaptogenesis
Tectum
Tegmentum
Telencephalon
Temporal lobes
Temporal summation
Thalamus
Vesicles

Further reading

Andrewes, D. (2001) *Neuropsychology from Theory to Practice.* Hove: Psychology Press.

Feldman, R. S., Meyer, J. S. and Quenzer, L. F. (1997) *Principles of Neuropsychopharmacology.* Massachusetts: Sinauer Associates, Inc.

Gazzaniga, M. S., Richard, R. B. and Magun, G. R. (1998) *Cognitive Neuroscience: The Biology of the Mind.* New York: Norton.

Julien, R. M. (2001) *A Primer of Drug Action: A Nontechnical Guide to the Uses and Side Effects of Psychoactive Drugs* (9th edn). New York: WH Freeman.

Nicholls, J. G., Martin, A. R., Wallace, B. G. and Fuchs, P. A. (2001) *From Neuron to Brain* (4th edn). Massachusetts: Sinauer Associates, Inc.

Web links

Society for Neuroscience: http://web.sfn.org/

British Neuroscience Association: http://www.bna.org.uk/

British Association for Psychopharmacology: http://www.bap.org.uk/

The American College of Neuropsychopharmacology (ACNP): http://www.acnp.org/g4/4thgen.php

Synapse Web: http://synapses.mcg.edu/

8

Animal learning and cognition

Route map of the chapter

In the first two sections of this chapter we will address the two dominant theories of learning: classical conditioning and operant conditioning. The application of associative learning theories illustrates how experience can influence biological responses. In the third section of this chapter we will look at cognitive learning. In the final section, the possible underlying neural mechanisms of learning are addressed.

Introduction

It would be easy to assume that biology determines behaviour. In part it does – we are born with the necessary equipment to learn and adapt. This is called preparedness (see Chapter 33, page 560). An organism is not born with a complete set of programmes to deal with every situation it could ever encounter – it has to adapt its behaviour for survival.

An example of this is imprinting (Lorenz, 1937). Imprinting is when a newly born animal attaches itself to a moving object. In the case of Lorenz's ducks, they followed him rather than their mother. These adaptations and experiences shape future behaviour and also physiology. The organism learns from experience.

From an evolutionary perspective, behaviour that favours survival will be selected. Those behaviours that are not useful will not be selected. There are many similarities between the learning theories and evolutionary theories (e.g. adaptation to the environment). The main difference between the two is timescale. Learning is within an organism's lifetime, whereas evolution transcends the life of an individual.

Two notable theorists have dominated the field of animal learning: Pavlov and Skinner. Their initial learning theories have been adapted, refined and supported by empirical study in both animals and humans. The two main theories – classical conditioning and operant conditioning – are referred to as 'associative learning'; this is because associations are made between stimuli and their responses.

Habituation

Habituation is the simplest and most ubiquitous form of learning. It is when you learn to ignore a stimulus that does not convey any meaning.

Habituation can be measured in the rat. A loud noise, say, can induce a startle response in a rat. The rat jumps because it has been startled. If the rat is repeatedly exposed to the noise, and that noise has no consequence, the magnitude of the startle response diminishes.

From an evolutionary perspective, habitation is an adaptation that aids survival. It makes good sense for the animal to respond to a stimulus that it has never experienced before. A novel stimulus may, or may not, pose a threat. However, if the stimulus is repeated with no consequences the animal habituates to it. This enables the animal to get on with the important business of survival. Thus the only stimuli that are attended to are those that may pose a threat to survival. A rat, then, should habituate to traffic noise but not to a cat. The cat is a predator. Habituation is important to the researcher and can influence the conclusion arrived at in an experiment (see Research Methods Box 8.1).

RESEARCH METHODS BOX 8.1

Habituation in psychopharmacology

In Chapter 7 we saw how a drug can increase the action of a neurotransmitter – an agonist. A dopamine agonist, such as amphetamine, makes rats run about (see Clarke and White, 1987). However, different conclusions can be arrived at on the basis of the rat's previous experience.

When an animal is put into a test arena for the first time it explores the environment. This is seen as increased motor activity. Within a one-hour session short-term habituation occurs and the motor activity diminishes. If the rat is exposed to the test environment several times, long-term habituation occurs; the rat does not engage in much exploratory behaviour at all and thus there is a decline in motor activity.

In a study by Chandler *et al.* (1990) two groups of mice were given a DA agonist. The first group had never experienced the test environment before (they were non-habituated). The second group had been exposed to the test environment many times (the habituated group).

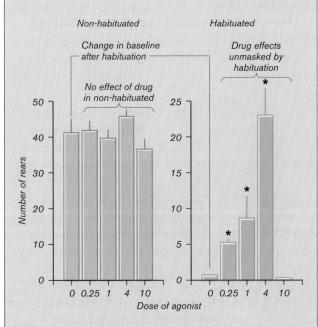

Figure 8.1 Habituation to the test environment

The DA agonist produced very different results in the two groups of mice. Two measures were taken: motor activity and rearing. Rearing is illustrated in Figure 8.1. You can see clearly that the drug appeared to have no effect in the non-habituated mice. Note that the amount of rearing was consistently high (around 40 counts). However, in the habituated mice the baseline of control mice was reduced (about two counts). They had habituated, but after the DA agonist there was a dose-dependent increase in rearing.

This study indicates that the behavioural history of the animal is an important factor in determining the effects of a drug. The response to the drug was dependent on pre-exposure to the test environment. Conclusions from the non-habituated mice would lead to the notion of the drug being devoid of behavioural activity. In the habituated mice the conclusion is different. The DA agonist in these animals produced behavioural activation.

Humans can also habituate (see Applications Box 8.1). If we hear a loud noise behind us we respond by trying to locate its source. This is called the orienting response. If we observe that the source of the loud noise is non-threatening (e.g. a builder hammering) and the noise continues, we habituate to the noise. If the sound is indicative of a threat, like gunfire, we locate it and preferably avoid it.

Reflexes

The response of the organism during habituation is a reflex. A *reflex* is an automatic response to an external stimulus. Leg jerking in response to a tap on the knee area with a tendon hammer is a reflex.

A reflex involves closely related events. For a reflex to occur, an input stimulus is necessary. The input triggers the cellular events of neurotransmission. Stimulus input is via afferent neurons to the spinal column. The afferent neuron communicates with an interneuron. An *interneuron* is a neuron that is neither sensory nor motor but connects the two. The interneuron communicates with an efferent neuron.

Section 2
Psychobiology

The Kiss

An example of habituation to auditory warnings was recently evident in the Sussex town of Lewes. An extremely valuable statue by Rodin – *The Kiss* – was placed on display in a public building. Normally such valuable items come with highly sophisticated security systems. *The Kiss* had a security guard with a whistle.

Why the low-key approach? Because people have learned to ignore (they are habituated to) electronic alarms and buzzers, such as car alarms. People would, however, respond to someone blowing a whistle.

In the city we hear false alarms sounding all the time; they no longer signal an intruder, say. The novelty of the whistle, and the fact that it has to be blown deliberately, means that anyone hearing it will orient to the source of the sound. Thus someone touching *The Kiss* will stop in their tracks on hearing the whistle.

The efferent neuron activates muscles to execute the reflex.

If you touch something hot you automatically retract your hand from the source of the heat (the stimulus). You do not think 'That's hot! I must remove my hand before I suffer tissue damage' (or words to that effect). The thermal information is sent along afferent neurons that connect to efferent neurons (via the interneuron) and the reflex of hand removal is executed (see Figure 8.2). Thus you avoid getting a serious burn to your hand.

Classical conditioning

While they are automatic responses, reflexes can be subject to learning. The reflex is central to Pavlov's theory of *classical conditioning*. Classical conditioning is when a neutral stimulus becomes associated with a stimulus that is able to produce a reflex. The neutral stimulus, which previously had no effect, becomes able to produce the reflex.

Pavlov was investigating digestion in the dog. Incidental to this, Pavlov and his students noticed that dogs would salivate to stimuli that were predictive of feeding time. Like all good scientists they systematically investigated this phenomenon with experiments.

Pavlov put the dogs in a special apparatus that allowed saliva to be collected. When food was put into a dog's mouth, saliva was produced. Saliva

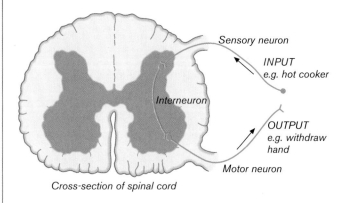

Figure 8.2 A reflex comprises the activation of an afferent nerve connected to an interneuron, which is in turn connected to an efferent neuron

contains enzymes that are used in the digestion of food. The saliva-producing response is a reflex to the orosensory stimulus of food in the mouth. In Pavlovian terms, the food is an *unconditioned stimulus (UCS)* and the production of saliva is an *unconditioned response (UCR)*. A reflex can be described as an unconditioned response to an unconditioned stimulus.

So far nothing had been learned by the dog in the experiment. During the next stage of the experiment a tone was introduced (a bell), which accompanied the presentation of food. Initially the tone was a neutral stimulus and did not produce a response. However, after a number of tone/food presentations the tone was presented alone, and on its own produced salivation in the dog. This tone is referred to as the *conditioned stimulus (CS)*. The response to the tone, in this case salivation, is called the *conditioned response (CR)*. The dog is said to have acquired an association between the tone and the production of food (see Figure 8.3).

Measuring the CR

Measuring a CR is not an all-or-nothing observation. Such a measure would put us in danger of missing the subtleties of the conditioning process. There are three main ways of assessing the strength of a CR.

1 Response amplitude: how large is the CR? In Pavlov's experiments, how much saliva does the dog produce? The more saliva, the stronger the conditioning.
2 Response probability: how many times does a CR occur in response to a CS? A probability of 0.5 (50 per cent) would indicate responding at the level of chance. A CR probability of 0.9 (or 90 per cent) would indicate that there is a strong association between the CS and UCS. How many times does the dog salivate to the CS?
3 Response latency: how long is it after the CS that the CR appears? The closer in time they occur, the stronger the conditioning. How long does it take for the dog to salivate after hearing the CS?

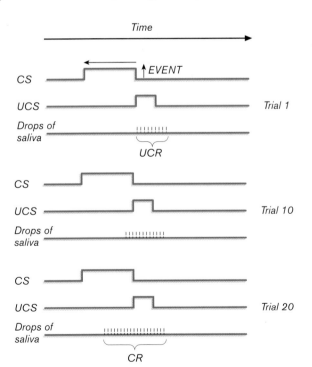

Figure 8.3 The development of classical conditioning: at Trial 1 only the UCS produces salivation; at Trial 20 the CS produces the CR of salivation

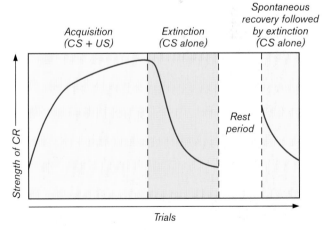

Figure 8.4 The acquisition, extinction and subsequent spontaneous recovery of the CS: acquisition is gradual and when the CS is presented alone extinction occurs in which the animal no longer produces a strong CR; after a period of time the animal is presented with the CS again and a CR is emitted

Pavlov's laboratory provided the basic premise of classical conditioning. Using this framework a large number of behaviours can be described. A human example of classical conditioning in action is a phobia (see Chapter 33).

Acquisition

Over successive pairings the CS gradually becomes associated with the UCS, producing a CR. The more pairings (or trials), the stronger the conditioning (see Figure 8.4). However, numerous CS–UCS pairings do not result in a continual increase in learning – they reach what is called asymptote (a sort of impasse).

Extinction

Once asymptote has been reached, presentation of the CS without the UCS would decrease the CR. Stop giving a dog food after it hears the tone and it will eventually stop salivating to the tone. This is called *extinction*. The CR is extinguished gradually as the animal experiences the CS without the UCS (see Figure 8.4). Although there are many similarities, extinction is different from habituation (no associations have been made in habituation).

Spontaneous recovery

After the extinction of the CR, and a period of rest without experimentation, the CR can appear again in response to the CS. This phenomenon is known as *spontaneous recovery* (see Figure 8.4). The CR is not as strong as it was during earlier training. If training is restarted, learning the CS–UCS pairing will be quicker than it was in the initial learning period. Spontaneous recovery can occur after a substantial rest period, indicating the permanence of learning. Bouton (1994) asserts that extinction is not forgetting, but is similar to proactive interference in which new learning supersedes old.

Stimulus generalisation and stimulus discrimination

Pavlov's experiments used a tone of a particular frequency as the CS. What would happen if another similar, but not identical, tone was used? If the new tone was similar to the CS then the CR would be strong. If the new tone was dissimilar to the CS then

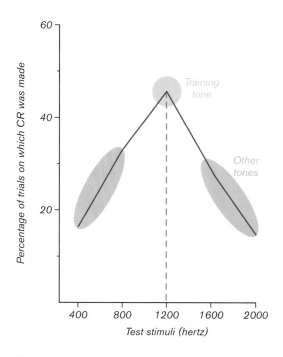

Figure 8.5 *The CS can both generalise to like stimuli or be discriminated from other stimuli*

the CR would be weak. Similarly an organism is able to differentiate between stimuli that are similar but not identical to the CS (see Figure 8.5).

Conditioned emotional response

The *conditioned emotional response (CER)* is the basis for a classically conditioned phobia (see Chapter 33). In experiments to obtain a CER, rats are trained in an operant chamber (see below). In the chamber, the rats press a lever to receive food. Rats are good at this task. Sometimes a tone will sound for 30 seconds. Following the tone an electric shock is given. As training continues, the rat stops pressing the bar for food when the tone is presented. This is called conditioned suppression or the conditioned emotional response (CER).

Is the CR identical to the UCR?

So far in Pavlov's experiments the CR and UCR are both salivation. However, with a more detailed analysis of the saliva, differences in CR and UCR are evident. Saliva contains enzymes that are used for

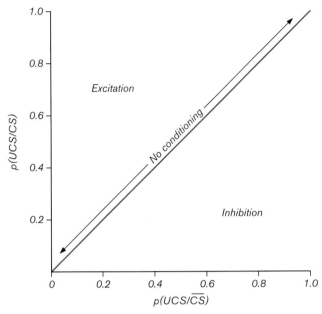

Figure 8.6 *The temporal relationship between the CS and UCS: along the diagonal line there is no conditioning because a CS does not convey any information about the UCS; above the line the UCS has a higher probability of occurring if there has been a CS; below the line the probability of a UCS is higher in the absence of a CS*

digestion. In the CR there are fewer of these enzymes than there are in the UCR.

In the CER experiment in which a rat receives an electric shock, the CR and UCR are different. In response to the UCS (shock) the rat's heart rate increases and it jumps about the chamber. The response to the CS (tone) is different from the UCS.

APPLICATIONS BOX 8.2

Drug tolerance and overdose

The body likes to maintain homeostasis. This means that it does not like external agents upsetting its balance. Opponent processes compensate for changes in the body to achieve homeostasis. If you take morphine for pain relief the body compensates for the drug by producing a reaction in the opposite direction: more pain. After

the drug has been given a number of times its effect is weakened. This is called tolerance. Tolerance could be seen as a pure biological activity in response to a drug. However, classical conditioning is very important in drug tolerance and can account for the overdose effect to a regular dose.

Using the example of heroin, the drug is a UCS that produces a UCR (euphoria and analgesia). However, drugs are not taken in an environmental vacuum and plenty of stimuli are associated with heroin intake (e.g. syringes, tin foil etc.). These stimuli act as a CS. The CS then produces a CR. The CR is the compensatory response from the body in the opposite direction. The CR produces dysphoria and hyperalgesia. Thus the compensatory CR negates the effect of the drug. The effect on the person is one of tolerance and the need for greater quantities of the drug in order to experience an effect.

Classical conditioning can also account for the overdose effect to a regular dose. Most people take their drug in a particular environment. The very nature of heroin use means it has to be taken in a clandestine manner. All the cues in the environment provide the users with a CR. What happens if you take the drug user out of their environment, put them somewhere new, and give them their regular dose? They may well die from their regular dose in what looks like an overdose. In the new environment the cues are no longer there to provide the user with a CR. The absence of the compensatory CR means that the intake of their normal dose of heroin has a greater effect because it does not have to account for the CR.

This is an effect that has been studied systematically in the rat under controlled conditions (Siegel *et al.*, 1982). In this experiment one group of rats was exposed to heroin in the test environment and another in a different environment. A third group received neither (the control group). The group that received the heroin in a different environment showed the overdose effect, whereas the rats that received the same dose in the test environment did not.

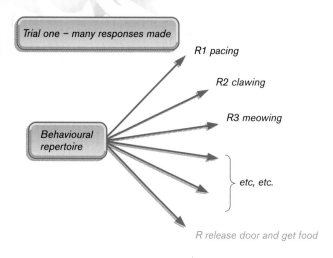

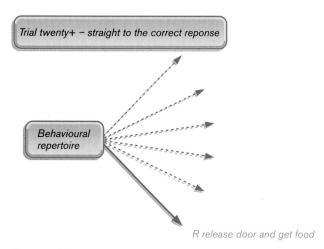

Figure 8.7 The law of effect: after a number of trials the cat emits the correct response

In this case the rat's heart rate decreases and it remains still. The importance of the CR being different from the UCR is exemplified in drug tolerance (see Applications Box 8.2).

The relationship between the CS and the UCS

It should have become clear that the CS becomes associated with the UCS. That is, when there is a CS the chance of a UCS is high. The association between CS and UCS varies in strength depending on the temporal characteristics (see Figure 8.6).

The temporal relationship between the CS and the UCS is important. *Contiguity* is when the CS and UCS are presented close together in time. Rescorla (1968) suggested that contiguity was necessary but not sufficient for conditioning. Differential contingency was also required. Differential *contingency* refers to the likelihood (probability) of a UCS following a CS. If the probability of a UCS following a CS was 0.5, then there would be no learning. If the probability was 0.8, then the CS would be associated with the production of a UCS. If the probability was low (e.g. 0.2), then the absence of a CS indicates a higher likelihood of a UCS.

Applications

Classical conditioning has been used to explain behaviour such as phobias. Classical conditioning can also be used to explain sexual fetishes (see Activity Box 8.1). It is also influential in understanding the phenomenon of drug tolerance and overdose (see Applications Box 8.2). Aversive conditioning, as popularised in the book and film *A Clockwork Orange*, is also used in the psychopharmacological treatment of alcoholism (see Applications Box 8.3).

ACTIVITY BOX 8.1

Fetishes

Fetishes are unusual sexual attachments. You only have to glance at late-night television to see that certain objects are linked with sexual arousal. The boot or high-heel fetish that many men would appear to have can be induced by classical conditioning. Rachman and Hodgson (1968) conducted such an experiment. They exposed people to pornographic images (UCS) along with neutral stimuli (CS). The pornographic images produced sexual arousal (UCR). After a number of UCS–CS exposures the CS was presented and produced sexual arousal in its own right (CR).

Using this framework let your imagination run wild and apply scenarios to whatever fetish springs to your mind. It may be the case that some males like pierced belly buttons because this is associated with their early sexual experiences in which women had staples across their midriffs (e.g. as magazine centrefolds)!

APPLICATIONS BOX 8.3

Preventing alcohol consumption

The saying goes – one's too many and a hundred isn't enough. This is true for alcoholics. They can never have just one drink. Once they start, they just keep on going.

One way of preventing drinking is to stop the first drink. Easier said than done! Alcohol is highly addictive and people may have a genetic predisposition to it.

One method is to make the effects of alcohol unpleasant. This is called counterconditioning (an aversion therapy; see also Chapter 34), in which the pleasant effects of alcohol are replaced with unpleasant effects (see Schwartz, 1984).

To achieve counterconditioning the pleasant effects of the drug are replaced by nausea and vomiting. This can be induced by another drug called an emetic. Thus the unpleasant effects of the drug become associated with the taste of alcohol. Hopefully this should be sufficient for the alcoholic to avoid future drinking.

Another drug called disulfiram (Antabuse) is also used to produce unpleasant effects if alcohol is consumed. If it is consumed there is a rise in toxic metabolites. This toxicity produces facial flushing, nausea, vomiting, dizziness and confusion, shortness of breath and changes in heart rate (see Feldman *et al.*, 1997). Altogether this is an unpleasant effect.

Disulfiram can also be placed within a classical conditioning framework. The benefit of disulfiram is that its pharmacological action lasts a number of days. Therefore the process of conditioning can take place outside a clinic.

Operant conditioning

Operant conditioning (or instrumental conditioning) is about the organism operating in the environment to produce an outcome. If we do something and the outcome is good, then there is a greater chance we will do it again.

The law of effect

Thorndike (1898) put a cat in a cage with a latch on the door. Outside he placed cat food. The cat wanted the food, moved around and scratched at the cage. Eventually, by accident the cat knocked the latch on the door. The door opened; the cat got the food. Successive trials of this nature led the cat to gain access to the food quickly. The behaviour exhibited by the cat was strengthened by its relationship with reward. Thorndike referred to this as the law of effect. In essence, the cat learns which of its many behaviours leads to freedom and food. It is a gradual process (see Figure 8.7), which leads to the strengthening of a stimulus–response (S–R) relationship.

Behaviourism

Skinner was instrumental in shaping behaviourism (see Chapter 2) and put forward the view that behaviour followed laws (see Focus Point 8.1). Skinner experimented with pigeons in a box, which became known as the Skinner box (or operant chamber; see the accompanying photo). Skinner boxes are used with many animals, especially the rat. The basic premise is the same as that of the law of effect: S–R associations.

FOCUS POINT 8.1

Skinner's view

According to Skinner (1971), 'As a science of behaviour adopts the strategy of physics and biology, the autonomous agent to which behaviour has traditionally been attributed is replaced by the environment – the environment in which the species evolved and in which the behaviour of the individual is shaped and maintained.'

The Skinner box (or operant chamber).

Reinforcement

Fundamental to operant conditioning is *reinforcement*. Reinforcement is when the consequences of a response increase the probability that the response will reoccur. If a rat presses a lever and gets food, it will be more likely to press the lever again. If you work hard at an essay and get a good mark, you are more likely to work hard at your next essay. The first example uses a primary reinforcer (e.g. food and water). The latter is an example of a secondary reinforcer. A secondary reinforcer is something that does not satisfy a physical need (e.g. money, praise or attention).

Positive and negative reinforcement

Using reinforcement, behaviours can be selected and strengthened. There are two types of reinforcement: positive and negative. *Positive reinforcement* is when a reinforcer is presented after a response and increases the likelihood of that response recurring.

In the animal experiments, food is a positive reinforcer. For humans, money and praise (particularly in children) are positive reinforcers. Basically you get something you want after you have done something (e.g. wages for working). Recently an experiment with monkeys demonstrated that they would reject unequal pay. In this experiment they would not participate in the experiment if they saw another monkey get a better reward for less work (Brosnan and de Waal, 2003). Clearly there is

something more complex occurring in these monkeys than just associative learning.

Negative reinforcement also increases the probability of a particular response. However, in this case, it is the removal of an unpleasant event or circumstance that strengthens a response. For example, a rat will press a bar or lever to escape an electric shock. When a stimulus is indicative of electric shock, the rat will press a lever and thus avoid the shock. Similarly, humans respond to negative reinforcement. The roles of positive and negative reinforcement have been used to account for drug addiction (see Chapter 9).

Punishment

The first point to note about *punishment* is that it is *not* negative reinforcement (see Figure 8.8). The difference between punishment and negative reinforcement focuses on what it does to a particular behaviour. Negative reinforcement *increases* the likelihood of a particular behaviour, whereas punishment *decreases* the likelihood of a particular behaviour. Thus, punishment is used to stop a behaviour whereas reinforcement is used to promote a behaviour.

Punishment can be subdivided into positive and negative punishment. Positive punishment is when behaviour leads to an undesired consequence. In the rat this could be an electric shock. In the human it could be a fine for illegal parking. Negative punishment is when behaviour results in the removal of or failure to obtain a desired reinforcer. In the rat this could be restricted access to food (e.g. Chandler and Stolerman, 1997). In the child it could be the removal of television time.

In order for punishment to be as effective as possible it should contain three features. First, the punishment has to come straight after the behaviour; there has to be contiguity between the response and the punishment. Second, the behaviour has to be consistently punished; failure to be consistent means that an association between the behaviour and the punishment is not established. Third, the punishment needs to be sufficiently aversive, but not too aversive. If the punishment is not sufficient then the behaviour may continue. A slap on the wrist for

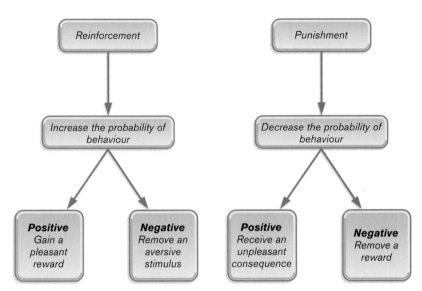

Figure 8.8 *Reinforcement increases the likelihood of a behaviour while punishment decreases the likelihood of a behaviour*

armed robbery is insufficient to stop the criminal reoffending. If the punishment is too aversive then other problems may occur, like high levels of fear and anxiety.

There are also a number of problems with punishment. The first is that the recipient of punishment may, via classical conditioning, come to fear the person giving the punishment rather than the punishment itself. In such a scenario there is a failure to modify the undesired behaviour. Additionally, there is a new problem created – fear – which can be very difficult to eliminate (LeDoux, 2000). For example, a dog requires training. During training the trainer may punish the dog. Consequently the dog may cower at the sight of its trainer (a CER) and not make the association between behaviour and punishment.

Due to the unpleasant consequences of punishment, a person may seek to escape it. To escape punishment, they may cheat and lie. If escape is not possible, the person may consider aggression and attack. Think of a bank robber – the consequence of punishment is sufficient to make the robber challenge police with violence. If eventually caught, the robber may lie about the crime. The robber will still engage in the activity, but become more devious in order to avoid detection.

Punishment may suppress many behaviours rather than eliminate one. The person may just give up and become apathetic. Finally, the punished may start to imitate the punisher. A child will imitate and learn from its parents. If parents use physical punishment, this is likely to be seen in their children.

Schedules of reinforcement

When a particular behaviour is reinforced every time, it is said to be on a continuous reinforcement (CRF) schedule. Behaviourists consider all our actions under the control of operant conditioning. Clearly we are not on a CRF schedule for all our behaviours, so how is behaviour maintained in the absence of a CRF schedule?

The answer can be found when we consider partial reinforcement. With partial reinforcement the organism is not reinforced every time it responds. There are four schedules of reinforcement. The nature of the schedule can influence the response output of the organism (or, as in the examples below, the rat). After reading this section on schedules of reinforcement, try the exercise in Activity Box 8.2.

ACTIVITY BOX 8.2

Schedules of reinforcement

According to behaviourists we are controlled by schedules of reinforcement.

As you go about your daily business you may not be aware that you are being influenced by these schedules. Take a close look at your environment and try to determine what the schedules are.

To help you on your way, simple activities like using a pelican crossing place you on a schedule. You have to press a button to activate the lights. This may happen immediately or you may have to wait a short while.

What are the schedules? (Note that there may be more than one schedule in operation at any time.)

Fixed ratio (FR) schedules

With a *fixed ratio (FR) schedule* the rat is reinforced after a number of bar presses. If the schedule is said to be FR10, this means that the rat is reinforced after the 10th response has been made. Similarly on an FR30 schedule the 30th response is reinforced. People on piecework are on FR schedules (i.e. they get paid for, say, every 100 boxes packed).

A rat on an FR schedule will respond (work) rapidly until the reinforcer is delivered. After reinforcement there is a pause, which is followed by another period of rapid responding (see Figure 8.9).

Variable ratio (VR) schedules

A *variable ratio (VR) schedule* is similar to the FR schedule, except that reinforcement occurs after a variable amount of responses. If the rat is on a VR10 schedule then it is reinforced *on average* after 10 responses. However, this varies around an average of 10. Sometimes the rat receives reinforcement after 5 responses and other times after 15. On a VR schedule the rat does not know exactly when the reinforcement is going to occur. A VR schedule produces a high rate of rapid and constant responding (see Figure 8.9).

The VR schedule is resistant to extinction. This is demonstrated clearly in gamblers. Slot machines are on VR schedules: sometimes you win but many times you do not. A machine is programmed to pay out on a VR schedule. You will get reinforced every so often

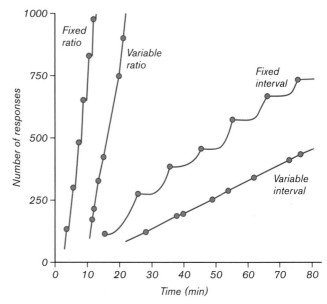

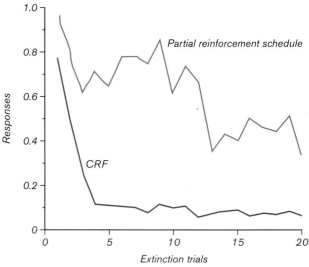

Figure 8.9 (a) Cumulative chart of the different schedules of reinforcement: the chart depicts the responses made; each response is added to the previous one
(b) Extinction of a partial reinforcement schedule

but you cannot predict the payout. This schedule means you keep putting money in the machine.

Fixed interval (FI) schedules

A *fixed interval (FI) schedule* is when, after a specified period of time the rat receives reinforcement only if it has pressed the bar during that time. A rat on an FI30 schedule receives reinforcement every 30 seconds if it has pressed the bar. The rat may press the bar once or many times in the intervening period between reinforcements. A clear scallop is produced in the cumulative response record (see Figure 8.9). This happens because the rat learns not to respond at the beginning of the interval and only starts responding towards the end of the interval.

Variable interval (VI) schedules

A rat on a *variable interval (VI) schedule* receives reinforcement after an average period of time only if it has responded correctly. On a VI30 schedule the rat receives reinforcement on average after 30 seconds, but sometimes after 20 seconds and sometimes after 40. This schedule produces slow but consistent responding (see Figure 8.9). Home Office inspectors (see Chapter 6) visit animal laboratories on a VI schedule to spot-check that the law is being adhered to and animal welfare maintained. If they arrived on an FI schedule then the laboratories could predict an inspection and could put on a 'good show' just for the inspectors.

Acquisition

Animals, like people, do not learn immediately. A number of learning trials have to be completed before a rat can respond to a stimulus reliably. Many of the experiments you will read about have involved long, and sometimes complex, training regimes. The more complex the task, the longer the training. In the example of rats as drug connoisseurs, Garcha and Stolerman (1989) required up to 90 sessions of 15 minutes' duration for the rat to be a reliable detector of nicotine.

Shaping and conditioning by successive approximations

A complex piece of behaviour cannot be learned overnight. In order to train an animal one must start

---

RESEARCH METHODS BOX 8.2

The water maze

A water maze consists of a pool of water (with a circumference of about two metres) from which a rat cannot escape (see fig. 8.10). The water is coloured to obscure a platform just below the surface. The rat is placed in the pool and to get out has to find the platform. Initially the rat just swims about until, by accident, it finds the platform. After a number of trials the rat is able to find the platform relatively easily. The rat uses spatial cues in the environment to locate the platform.

There are a number of measures that can be used to determine spatial learning in the water maze:

- latency
- path length
- average speed
- side wall proximity
- directionality
- quadrant times
- quadrant distances.

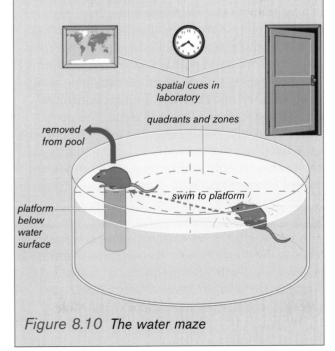

Figure 8.10 The water maze

with simple behaviours, which contribute to the overall goal behaviour. Once acquired, new behaviours can be worked on and refined. This process is called *shaping*. The shaping of the smaller subsets of behaviours is called 'shaping of successive approximations' – that is, one reinforces behaviours that are getting closer to the desired behaviour. Such procedures are used regularly in training animals (dogs in particular).

Extinction

On a CRF the animal stops responding soon after reinforcement stops. Initially the rat presses the lever rapidly, but eventually this diminishes until it stops responding altogether. Partial reinforcement schedules make extinction of a response more difficult (see Figure 8.9).

Spontaneous recovery

As is the case with classical conditioning, spontaneous recovery can occur. After a period of absence from training, the rat, on reacquaintance with the apparatus, will start responding again.

Discrimination and generalisation

The animal is able to discriminate between stimuli that bring about reinforcement and stimuli that do not. These stimuli are called *discriminative stimuli (SD)*. A pigeon will peck an illuminated key for food reinforcement. It will peck any key at first. However, if reinforcement is made contingent upon pressing a green key (and not a red key) the pigeon learns to discriminate between the two stimuli. The green switch is called S$^+$ (a stimulus that is contingent with reinforcement). The red key is S$^-$ (a stimulus that is *not* contingent with reinforcement). The colour of the key is a clear SD. Other discriminative stimuli can be subtler. A pigeon may go on to discriminate between shades of green, for instance.

Unlike discriminative learning, generalisation refers to the phenomenon where an animal responds to different stimuli. The pigeon that is trained to discriminate between coloured switches initially generalises to all coloured switches.

Interoceptive and exteroceptive stimuli

Up to this point the animal has produced a response to an SD (a light or a tone). This is an *exteroceptive stimulus* (sometimes called a stimulus cue). The rat detects the SD, presses a lever and gets a reward.

A rat can also respond to its internal physiological state (an *interoceptive stimulus* or cue). A procedure called drug discrimination is used to understand the stimulus properties of drugs. The rat uses the feelings derived from a drug to determine which bar in the operant chamber leads to reinforcement (see Research Methods Box 8.3).

RESEARCH METHODS BOX 8.3

Drug discrimination: rats as drug connoisseurs

People take drugs for a number of reasons. One is that they like the effects of a drug (e.g. euphoria, alertness). These properties make up the feeling of a drug and thus its stimulus properties. People who smoke are aware of the different amounts of nicotine delivered from various cigarettes. Other drugs of abuse are also readily discriminated in both man and animal (e.g. heroin).

The capacity to detect a drug effect is also mirrored in the animals. After training, drugs can act as discriminative stimuli. By behaving appropriately the animal can indicate its ability to detect the presence of the drug in the body.

Why use animals?

Stolerman (1993) said, 'Data from animals are often more precise, detailed and extensive than that from humans because animals may be trained and tested over longer periods of time and because they have more rigorously controlled behavioural and pharmacological histories.'

How do they do this? They can't talk!

Of course, the use of animals does not permit the verbal measure of drug effects. In order to determine the stimulus properties of a drug the animal has to perform an operant task, such as pressing a bar for food reinforcement.

There are two bars, or levers, in the Skinner box. One is associated with the drug effect and results in reward. The other is associated with the vehicle (an inert injection of saline). This permits the data to be analysed in terms of overall responding (e.g. no specific drug effects) and drug–bar responding (specific discrimination of the bars).

The process of training a rat to discriminate a drug from saline is long. First, the rat has to be acclimatised to the environment and placed on restricted diet to motivate it to bar-press. The rat is introduced to the food delivery system in the operant chamber. Then one bar is put in the chamber and made contingent for reinforcement (FR1). This is reversed the next day so the other bar is associated with reinforcement. Progressively the FR is increased to FR10. When the rat gets good at this the injections of a drug start. Only one bar is contingent for reinforcement. When given a drug only the drug bar yields food; with saline only, the saline bar yields food. The process continues with saline and drug pairings in a random order. Both bars are present in the chamber.

Stolerman then introduces punishment to the process: when the rat makes an incorrect response the FR schedule is reset. If the animal makes nine correct responses and then makes one wrong one, it has to start again at the beginning. Additionally a VI component is introduced and is increased to 60 seconds. The rat is then on a tandem schedule (VI60–FR10). The VI schedule stops the animal from receiving too many reinforcers in a session and also stops it being able to predict reward. Thus the rat works hard for little pay.

This process takes many months. Once the rats can reliably discriminate the drug from saline, tests can be carried out to see if the stimulus properties are dose dependent; they can then generalise to other drugs.

Alternatively, they can be blocked by antagonists of the training drug. A drug that is like the training drug will generalise to the discriminative cue; drugs that are not like the training drug appear to be more like saline.

The stimulus may be important to explain why people smoke. Perkins *et al.* (1994) showed that people can discriminate between different doses of nicotine delivered in a nasal spray. Pratt *et al.* (1983) used the procedure described above and showed that rats could discriminate nicotine from saline reliably without a reduction in the overall response rate. The effects of nicotine are mediated by a receptor for ACh in the brain. They are sensitive to antagonism from nicotine receptor antagonists.

Drug discrimination experiments can tell us a lot about the nature of a drug's effect and the mechanisms underlying that effect.

Cognition in animals

Strict behaviourists reject all forms of cognitive explanation that are in opposition to behavioural explanations. However, recent theories of animal learning do argue that cognition and cognitive processes underlie learning in animals. Cognition here refers to mental processes that are not subject to direct behavioural observation. In fact, according to Lieberman (2000), the behaviourist view and cognitive view of animal learning have become increasingly similar.

Tolman (1948), who championed the cognitive view, presented the idea of cognitive maps and latent learning. Rats learnt to navigate a maze quickly despite an absence of reward. When given reward these rats were quick to learn the whereabouts of the reinforcer. Tolman claimed that the rats had a cognitive map of the maze. After receiving reward the behaviour of the rat became observable, whereas previously learning was not observable. Behaviourists will account for observable behaviour. Clearly from Tolman's studies learning had occurred that was not directly observable. This is referred to as *latent learning*.

Tolman (1932; 1959) argued that behaviour is goal directed and that animals (and humans) act as if they expect certain behaviours to lead to a desired goal. Dickinson (1989) has further accounted for expectancy in both classical and operant conditioning. His concepts of expectancy involve two types of information.

First, the contiguity between events gives rise to a representation of the associative link between those events. In Pavlov's experiments the dog developed a representation of the CS and UCS, which would elicit the CR in response to the CS. That is, the dog develops associative expectations that the bell precedes food and produces salivation in response to the expectation of food.

Second, expectancy involves the belief that a particular behaviour will have a specific effect. In the operant conditioning experiment, the rat presses a bar to get food. That is, there is a *belief* that the behavioural response results in reward. Dickinson (1989) claims that, with increased training, stimulus–response habits emerge that do not involve the expectation that a particular behaviour will lead to reinforcement. Thus, the cognitive phenomenon of expectancy can eventually change into an automatic habit.

The area of animal cognition focuses on how the animal uses experience to form the basis for future behaviour. Of course, how the past affects our behaviour is to do with memory. Cognitive psychologists have demonstrated that there are numerous types of memory (see Chapter 14). One type of memory that has been extensively investigated in the animal is spatial learning, and this has a neurophysiological substrate in the hippocampus.

In the experiments by Tolman a maze was used. These experiments required the animal to retain information about the spatial features of the apparatus. There are numerous other methods of assessing memory in the animal (see Sarter *et al.*, 1992a; 1992b). One method of assessing spatial memory is the water maze, which has been used to study potential treatments for Alzheimer's disease (see Research Methods Box 8.2).

The phenomenon of learned helplessness (Seligman, 1975) also points to cognitive learning.

The animal has to compute the probabilities of affecting the environment and receiving reward. In learned helplessness a chance level of affecting the environment leads to there being no predictive information about reward contingencies. Underlying the computation of probability are neural mechanisms. Recently, DA neurons of the midbrain have been shown to be differentially active on presentation of different probabilities of reward (Fiorillo *et al.*, 2003). Matsumoto *et al.* (2003) identified the lateral and medial prefrontal cortex (mPFC) as a site that is active when there is anticipation of reward. The mPFC was also identified as the place where responses are selected.

It may not be possible, and it may also be unnecessary, to provide a definitive answer to the cognitive versus associative learning debate. Lieberman (2000) states that the two forms of learning can coexist. Cognitive learning involves attention, and concepts of abstraction and expectation. Associative learning may represent automatic processes that are well learnt and do not require conscious attention. This view is rather similar to the cognitive approach to the function of the frontal lobes proposed by Norman and Shallice (1980).

The neural bases of learning: long-term potentiation (LTP)

The above studies provide neural correlates of behaviour. The temporal lobes and the hippocampus are involved in learning and memory. Understanding the neuroanatomy is important but it does not tell us about the processes of learning and memory. Changes in hippocampal activity during associative learning have been identified (e.g. Wirth *et al.*, 2003).

What happens at the neural level?

Hebb's (1949) initial theory of changes in synaptic transmission has since been supported and refined by experimental evidence (Bliss and Lomo, 1973). With the induction of *long-term potentiation* (LTP) there is a facilitation of synaptic transmission. After there has been a period of high-frequency electrical stimulation of the presynaptic neuron by an electrode, the response to low-frequency stimulation is potentiated.

LTP setup

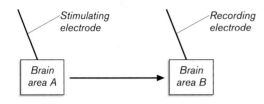

LTP procedure

Step 1: Give single test stimulus to area A and record neural response in area B

Step 2: Give trains of high frequency stimulation to area A

Step 3: Give single test stimulus to area A and record neural response in area B

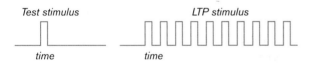

Neural responses

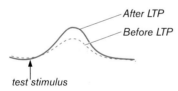

Figure 8.11 *The method to induce LTP in the hippocampus: a stimulating electrode in brain area (a) influences brain area (b); after high-frequency stimulation the response of brain area (b) is increased or potentiated Source: adapted from LeDoux (1998)*

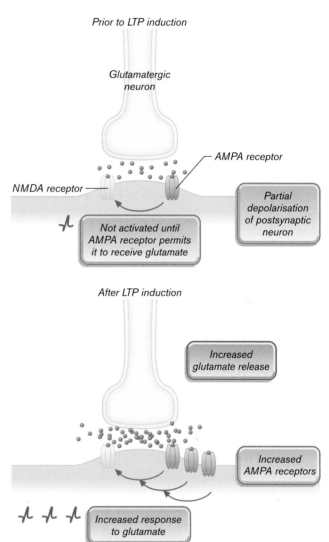

Figure 8.12 *The role of glutamate receptors in LTP: repeated activation of the AMPA receptor leads to long-term potentiation in the synaptic response to glutamate*

LTP can last for a long time and requires the activation of both pre- and postsynaptic neurons (Bliss and Gardner-Medwin, 1973; Sastry *et al.*, 1986). Interestingly, in the context of this chapter on learning, Iriki *et al.* (1989) have found changes in the rat hippocampus after conditioning that are similar to LTP (see Figure 8.11).

The search for the neural mechanisms underlying LTP has focused primarily on the NMDA and AMPA receptors. The NMDA and AMPA receptors are configured to receive messages from glutamate (an excitatory amino acid). The NMDA receptor and LTP share some similarities. Instead of high-frequency stimulation, the NMDA receptor can produce LTP from converging inputs (temporal and spatial summation).

If the NMDA receptor is to respond fully it requires: (i) glutamate to bind to the NMDA and AMPA receptors, and (ii) partial depolarisation of the postsynaptic neuron. In the second requirement, partial depolarisations are produced by inputs to the AMPA receptor or other receptors nearby (see Figure 8.12). Thus, naturally occurring LTP requires the convergence of two inputs.

The postsynaptic neuron responds to stimulation by producing a series of biochemical events. Without going into fine detail, these events increase both glutamate release and the number of AMPA receptors. Therefore the initial stimulation results in synaptic changes that can be enduring. Supporting evidence for the involvement of the NMDA receptor comes from 'knockout mice', which do not express the receptor (Tsien *et al.*, 1996), and psychopharmacological studies that use drugs to block the NMDA receptor (Morris *et al.*, 1986).

While LTP offers great insight into putative neural mechanisms of memory there is still a link to be made with the psychology of learning and memory. The work of the cognitive neuroscientist is never done!

Learning outcomes

When you have completed this chapter you should be able to:

* describe the two main theories of associative learning
* apply the principles of associative learning to real-world situations
* describe the limitations of associative learning
* describe the possible neural mechanisms underlying learning.

Key Terms

Classical conditioning
Conditioned emotional response (CER)
Conditioned response (CR)
Conditioned stimulus (CS)
Contiguity
Contingency
Discriminative stimuli (SD)
Exteroceptive stimuli
Extinction
Fixed interval (FI) schedule
Fixed ratio (FR) schedule
Habituation
Interneuron
Interoceptive stimuli
Latent learning
Long-term potentiation (LTP)
Negative reinforcement
Positive reinforcement
Punishment
Reflex
Reinforcement
Shaping
Spontaneous recovery
Unconditioned response (UCR)
Unconditioned stimulus (UCS)
Variable interval (VI) schedule
Variable ratio (VR) schedule

Further reading

Chance, P. (2003) *Learning and Behaviour* (5th edn). CA: Wadsworth.

Dudai, Y. (1989) *The Neurobiology of Memory: Concepts, Findings, Trends.* Oxford: Oxford University Press.

Lieberman, D. A. (2000) *Learning: Behaviour and Cognition* (3rd edn). UK: Wadsworth.

Pearce, J. M. (1997) *Animal Learning and Cognition: An Introduction* (2nd edn). Hove: Psychology Press.

Skinner, B. K. (1971) *Beyond Freedom and Dignity.* Harmondsworth: Penguin.

Web links

Animal Learning: go.owu.edu/~deswartz/introduction.html

Drug Discrimination: http://www.dd-database.org/

9

Motivation, brain reward mechanisms and behaviour

Route map of the chapter

Why do we eat, drink and sometimes be merry? This chapter addresses the biological basis of three highly motivated behaviours. The first section addresses the possible neural mechanisms underlying addiction. The actions of two illegal drugs, cocaine and amphetamine, and the legal drug nicotine are explored. The actions of these, and other drugs, are placed within the context of the general theories of addiction.

Eating is a behaviour that has generated a great deal of interest, especially because of the increasing prevalence of eating disorders. The brain mechanisms involved in eating are investigated, with particular emphasis on the hypothalamus.

Drinking is an essential behaviour and its neural substrates are described. The motivation to drink is important for our survival and, again, the brain is central to this behaviour.

Introduction

We are highly motivated to engage in some behaviours (see Chapter 27 for the theories about this). This chapter addresses a biological basis of motivation. It is clear that there is a physiological necessity for eating and drinking: without food and water the organism will stop functioning. However, people eat for pleasure and are highly motivated to take certain drugs, which do not appear to have a physiological benefit (see Activity Box 9.1).

ACTIVITY BOX 9.1

Drug-taking motivations

Why do people take drugs?

This sounds like a simple question. Try to answer it.

You should have come up with a number of reasons, such as peer pressure, relief from boredom and escapism. All are valid.

Why do people continue to take drugs?

This is a more difficult question. What is your answer?

I would imagine you would say because they are addicted. This gives rise to the next question.

What is addiction?

There is no simple answer to this. This chapter will focus on the biological mechanisms that are thought to underlie addiction.

Substance misuse

Drug misuse is an increasingly growing concern. Many people are using drugs for recreational purposes. Along with misuse there may be a number of other problems: criminality, poverty, poor health and psychological problems.

The question of why people take drugs defies one definitive answer. There are a number of circumstances that could induce drug-taking behaviour, ranging from peer pressure to stress relief. To understand the factors involved is a multidisciplinary task. However, psychobiology has made advances in the understanding of the neural mechanisms involved once the drug has been consumed. These mechanisms are thought to be responsible for addiction.

To illustrate the themes of substance misuse we will look at the examples of cocaine and amphetamine, two illegal drugs, and nicotine, a legal drug available at a price. The basic premise of these drugs can be applied to numerous other substances.

What is addiction?

The word addiction is often used interchangeably with dependence and abuse. Altman *et al.* (1996) provided a description of these terms (see Focus Point 9.1). The net effect of substance misuse is to impact on daily life . . . and not just the life of the misuser. Once started, the drug user may have severe difficulty giving up (see Activity Box 9.2).

FOCUS POINT 9.1

Altman *et al.* (1996) on addiction, dependence and abuse

Addiction is the extreme or psychopathological state where control over drug use is lost.

Dependence is the state of needing a drug to operate within normal limits.

Abuse is the use of drugs, which leads to problems for the individual.

ACTIVITY BOX 9.2

Giving up is hard to do

It is not a simple task to give up taking drugs.

- In what ways do people try to give up drugs?
- What are the psychobiological roots of these?

It would be convenient if a drug user could take another drug to stop the addiction. Unfortunately, addiction is very difficult to treat; there is no panacea.

There is a range of options for the drug user, from counselling to detoxification using replacement strategies and withdrawal. However, relapse is likely and many do not benefit from intervention.

New ways are being investigated to achieve a greater success rate. Biotechnology companies are attempting to stop the passage of various drugs to the brain, using immunology to fight the drug (see O'Brien, 1997). Such immunological treatments mean the drug cannot gain access to the brain, and its reinforcing properties are negated. This is an area that offers some hope and is still in development.

A reward pathway

A number of methods are used to determine the reward pathways in the brain and the site of action of drugs in animals (see Stolerman, 1992):

- *intracranial self-stimulation* (ICSS)
- *drug self-administration*
- *conditioned place preference* (CPP).

Using the criteria for animal models (see Chapter 6), you may wish to assess how valid these methods are in their effort to model addiction.

Olds and Milner (1954) first used the technique of ICSS, in which they placed electrodes into the rat brain and found that the rat would press a lever to self-administer electrical stimulation to certain areas of the brain. The areas of the brain that mediated electrical stimulation also contained high levels of DA (Corbett and Wise, 1980), in particular the *nucleus accumbens (NAcc)* (Phillips *et al.*, 1975), the striatum (Phillips *et al.*, 1976) and the prefrontal cortex (Mora *et al.*, 1976).

The area that has received most attention as the neural substrate of addiction is referred to as the *mesolimbic pathway* (see Figure 9.1). The mesolimbic pathway runs from the *ventral tegmental area* (VTA) to the NAcc. Destroying the mesolimbic pathway

Section 2
Psychobiology

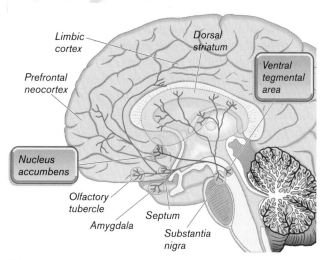

Figure 9.1 *The mesolimbic pathway: activation of dopamine in this pathway, projecting from the ventral tegmental area to the nucleus accumbens, is thought to be the reason for addiction*

with a neurotoxin disrupted ICSS, especially when the electrodes were placed in the NAcc on the same side of the lesion (Phillips and Fibiger, 1978; Fibiger *et al.*, 1987).

Of course, addicts do not self-administer electricity, they take drugs. As you can see in Research Methods Box 9.1, drug self-administration is an operant task in which an animal receives an infusion of a drug after pressing a lever.

Conditioned place preference (CPP) is a non-invasive method for assessing the reinforcing properties of a drug. CPP involves looking at drug-seeking behaviour. It does this by using secondary conditioning: a drug becomes associated with a particular environment (see Figure 9.2 and also Chapter 8). Previously neutral stimuli become associated with the drug. The drug is the UCS that produces pleasurable effects (the UCR), and the environment in which it receives the drug becomes associated with the drug (CS). When tested drug-free, the rat seeks out the drug-associated environment if it is reinforcing (CR).

Amphetamine and cocaine

Amphetamine and cocaine are psychostimulants that act on the dopaminergic system. Both enhance dopamine (DA) transmission. However, they do this in different ways (see Chapter 7). Generally speaking, amphetamine releases DA from the vesicles without the need for an action potential, whereas cocaine blocks reuptake and does require an action potential (Carboni *et al.*, 1989).

A number of studies have been conducted to determine the effects of cocaine and amphetamine on ICSS. Using a rate free method, in which the rat presses a lever to obtain different frequencies of electrical stimulation, cocaine decreased the frequency administered by the rat (Maldonado-Irizarry et al., 1994). This is indicative of cocaine being a substitute for the rewarding properties of ICSS (i.e. the rat does not require as much electrical stimulation after cocaine).

Many experiments have verified that animals will self-administer cocaine and amphetamine (see Katz, 1989). Once established, a more detailed account of amphetamine and cocaine self-administration can be explored.

Roberts and Ranaldi (1995) pointed out that DA antagonists increase responding for cocaine and amphetamine. This is a compensatory mechanism; the animal lever-presses even more to overcome the interruption of the drug effects. This is like the extinction burst in operant experiments.

Looking specifically at cocaine, we can see that its actions are mediated via postsynaptic DA receptors. There are two families of DA receptor: D1 and D2 (Kebabian and Calne, 1979). There are other receptors for DA and these can be classed according to the original categorisation.

One way of probing the receptor mechanisms of cocaine and amphetamine self-administration is to substitute them with more specifically targeted drugs. Woolverton et al. (1984) found that the D2 agonists maintained responding for cocaine or amphetamine in rhesus monkeys. In contrast, D1 agonists failed to maintain responding. The increased responding seen with D2 antagonists was not evident with D1 antagonists. Thus DA is important, but more specifically DA acting at the D2 receptor is important for drug self-administration.

If the NAcc and VTA are destroyed, cocaine and amphetamine responding stops in the rat (Roberts et al., 1977; Roberts and Koob, 1982). Furthermore, Koob et al. (1987), using a PR schedule, demonstrated that lesions of NAcc decreased the number of drug infusions and an unwillingness to work for cocaine in rats. However, lesions of the NAcc are not a realistic treatment for addiction – after all, blockade of this area is achieved by a number of drugs that have not shown any therapeutic efficacy.

Both cocaine and amphetamine produce robust CPPs (e.g. Carr et al., 1989). The amphetamine-induced CPP can be blocked by DA antagonists (Mithani et al., 1986; Leone and Di Chiara, 1987). Lesions of the NAcc also produce a reduction in amphetamine induced CPP (Spyraki et al., 1982).

Cocaine and amphetamine are both DA agonists and increase DA in the synapse. Their powerful addictive properties appear to be mediated by DA in the mesolimbic pathway.

Nicotine

Nicotine is derived from tobacco, which is smoked, and there has been a great debate about its addictive properties (Stolerman and Jarvis, 1995). Nicotine is an agonist at nicotinic acetylcholine (ACh) receptors.

In the previous section we made a case for cocaine and amphetamine mediating their addictive properties via mesolimbic DA. This is not too difficult to comprehend, as both drugs enhance DA directly. Nicotine acts at an ACh receptor, so how is it addictive if it does not act at DA directly?

Nicotine receptors can be found in the VTA and NAcc. A number of studies (e.g. Mirza et al., 1996) have shown that nicotine can also increase the levels of DA in the NAcc. These studies have used a technique called in vivo microdialysis, a method of obtaining sample fluid from the synapse in the functioning animal. The content of the fluid can then

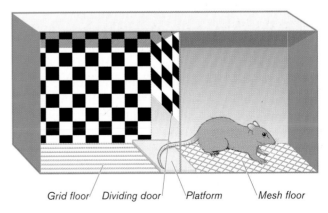

Grid floor　Dividing door　Platform　Mesh floor

Figure 9.2 Typical conditioned place preference (CPP) apparatus as used in the experiments on nicotine

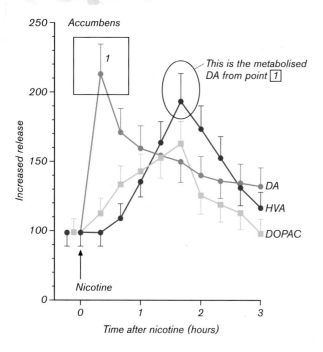

Figure 9.3 Nicotine increases DA and DA metabolites in the nucleus accumbens

be analysed. Imperato *et al.* (1986) found that nicotine increased DA in the NAcc by 100 per cent and also increased the levels of the DA metabolites DOPAC and HVA (an effect that was blocked by nicotine antagonists (Mifsud *et al.*, 1989)).

Looking at Figure 9.3, you can see that nicotine increases the levels of DA very quickly, but these then diminish. As the levels of DA diminish, the metabolites of DA increase. This is indicative of DA being used and eliminated by metabolic enzymes (e.g. MAO). Thus the DA neurons in the NAcc have been very busy after nicotine administration. Nicotine's ability to increase DA from the NAcc is something it shares with many other addictive drugs (e.g. the opiates, such as heroin (Pontieri *et al.*, 1996)).

Nicotine has been shown to affect ICSS (Clarke and Kumar, 1984). Like amphetamine and cocaine, nicotine lowered the frequency of ICSS, indicating its rewarding properties (Huston-Lyons and Kornetsky, 1992). However, some of the main reasons surrounding the scientific debate regarding nicotine's

addictive qualities revolved around the experiments using nicotine self-administration.

Nicotine self-administration has been seen in primates (Goldberg *et al.*, 1981) and, obviously, humans (Henningfield *et al.*, 1983). Surprisingly, rats did not engage in nicotine self-administration. This was because the studies used a continuous reinforcement schedule, which produced low rates of responding. Thus the rat literature was not indicative of nicotine being a reinforcer.

Corrigal and Coen (1989) put rats on an FR5 schedule and found dose-dependent responding for nicotine. The schedule was critical to achieving nicotine self-administration. On a CRF and an FR2 schedule, responding was low (Donny *et al.*, 1995; 2003); the rats needed to work harder for their reward so that a behaviour could be seen. Once obtained, nicotine antagonists blocked nicotine self-administration (Corrigal and Coen, 1989). As with cocaine and amphetamine, lesions of the NAcc also stopped nicotine self-administration (Corrigal *et al.*, 1992). Thus, nicotine also appears to mediate its reinforcing and motivating properties via mesolimbic DA.

The addictive properties of nicotine have not been entirely supported by studies using CPP. Some studies have found a CPP with nicotine (e.g. Fudala *et al.*, 1985), others have not (e.g. Chandler *et al.*, 1995). The reason for this is unclear, but for the majority of cases it is a methodological issue. However, when a CPP was found with nicotine it could be blocked with both nicotine and DA antagonists (Carboni *et al.*, 1989; Iwamoto, 1990).

Nicotine acts at receptors for ACh, and increases DA in the mesolimbic pathway. Detailed studies have shown that its addictive properties are mediated in a similar pattern to that of cocaine and amphetamine. This action of nicotine is not unique; a number of other drugs that are addictive also increase mesolimbic DA, and this pathway is regarded as the common denominator of drug addiction (see Wise and Bozarth, 1987)

Giving up
Therapies for treating addiction are somewhat lacking in their effectiveness. However, a profitable industry surrounds giving up smoking, with

strategies ranging from self-help and acupuncture to pharmacological assistance. Most forms of pharmacological help for smoking involve nicotine replacement. This comes in a number of forms: gum, patches and inhalators. They all involve replacing the cigarette and reducing the dose of nicotine over a period of time. Unfortunately there is no quick fix or antidote to smoking.

Interestingly, there is a drug that bears no relation to nicotine that has been used to help treat smoking addiction. Zyban (bupropion), an anti-depressant, is an agonist for noradrenaline. How does it work for nicotine addiction? It may work in three ways (Cryan *et al.*, 2003):

1 by increasing brain reward mechanisms
2 by blocking nicotine's reinforcing properties
3 by reducing withdrawal.

LSD – the exception to the rule

It has been claimed that the common denominator of addictive drugs is the mesolimbic DA pathway (see Koob, 1992). However, there is a group of drugs that are not addictive, but misused. The psychedelics are typified by D-lysergic acid diethylamide (LSD), an extremely potent hallucinogen. LSD and other hallucinogens are not self-administered by animals. In fact rhesus monkeys will press a lever to turn off a stimulus associated with LSD infusion (Hoffmeister and Wuttke, 1975). The reason for this is that LSD acts on serotonin and does not act in the mesolimbic pathway as do cocaine, amphetamine and nicotine. However, MDMA (ecstasy), a mixed DA and 5-HT drug, is self-administered (Fantegrossi *et al.*, 2002; Schenk *et al.*, 2003) and produces a CPP (Meyer *et al.*, 2002), thus pointing to the role of DA in mediating these behaviours rather than serotonin.

In contrast CPP experiments, LSD produces a conditioned place preference in the rat (Parker, 1996; Meehan and Schechter, 1998). Thus a CPP may be acquired without exclusive activation of the mesolimbic DA pathway.

Theories of addiction

Having established that there is a physiological basis for addiction – mesolimbic DA – these physiological accounts can be placed within a theoretical framework. The main theoretical positions are based on associative learning (see Chapter 8). However, there is increasing evidence to suggest a genetic predisposition (Uhl *et al.*, 2002).

Positive reinforcement

We have seen in Chapter 8 that a rat will press a lever to obtain a reinforcer. In drug self-administration experiments the drug is the reinforcer (see Katz, 1989). If there is a good outcome from the behaviour we are likely to engage in it again.

Physical dependence theories and negative reinforcement

Drugs clearly produce physiological effects. With positive reinforcement this may be getting high. However, drugs often have side-effects – that is, the absence of the drug produces physical reactions in the body, known as withdrawal symptoms. Given the extremely unpleasant nature of withdrawal symptoms the addict is compelled to alleviate them by continuing to take the drug. Therefore drug-taking behaviour is maintained by negative reinforcement: a response (drug-taking) stops a negative consequence (withdrawal symptoms). However, a person can become addicted without exhibiting physical dependence and therefore the theory is inadequate to explain all cases of addiction.

Sensitisation of incentive salience

With continuing exposure to a drug there is a heightened responsiveness to subsequent drug administrations – basically there is a bigger effect (this is called sensitisation). This is an effect that mesolimbic DA may mediate (e.g. Kalivas and Weber, 1988; Kolta *et al.*, 1989).

Wise and Bozarth (1987) presented a view that the common denominator of reinforcing drugs is their psychomotor stimulant properties, which are mediated via mesolimbic DA.

Robinson and Berridge's theory (1993; see also Berridge and Robinson, 2003) has integrated learning and the physiological action of drugs: the incentive–sensitisation theory of addiction. In this theory there are three major features of addiction (see Figure 9.4):

1 there is craving for the drug
2 the drug craving is persistent and can reappear after abstinence
3 as the craving for the drug increases (the wanting of the drug), the pleasure obtained from it decreases (the liking).

The process of drug-taking leads to sensitisation of physiological and behavioural measures. The neural system that is sensitised is hypothesised to mediate a psychological function involved in incentive motivation. In the addict the drug becomes a highly motivating reinforcer and is given incentive salience – the wanting of the drug. Sensitisation, then, enhances incentive salience. Incentive salience is a motivational state, which turns stimuli into desired must-have objects (or drugs).

The theory continues to state that, via conditioning, drug and associated stimuli become more salient. Thus stimuli that are associated with the drug (e.g. drug paraphernalia, such as the syringe with intravenous heroin use) become able to control behaviour – that is, induce the wanting of the drug. This increase in wanting the drug is due to the neural substrate, and the associative learning to it, becoming more sensitised. The bad news is that repeated exposure only sensitises the wanting, not the liking. The pleasure derived from the drug is mediated by another system, perhaps an opiate system (see the interview with Berridge in Phillips, 2003), and is subject to tolerance.

Sensitisation remains for a long period of time, even after the drug-taking has stopped; it may even be permanent. It is this that can lead to the reinstatement of drug-taking (somewhat like spontaneous recovery). Because of the conditioning of drug-related stimuli to the drug, the drug-related stimuli can precipitate relapse. Anecdotal accounts from detoxified drug users have indicated that returning to the drug-taking environment can lead to relapse.

While the theory has generated a great deal of interest and debate, it does not hold out the prospect of an optimistic future for the drug addict. But of all the therapies available, cognitive-behavioural therapy is necessary to reduce the problem (Robinson and Berridge, 2000).

Brain mechanisms for eating

The brain is in control of feeding behaviour, not just the mouth and stomach. The brain's role in feeding

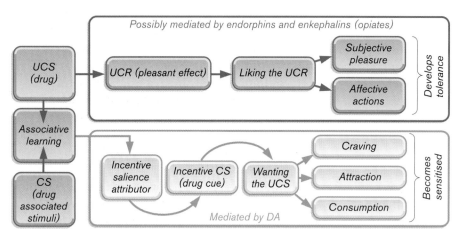

Figure 9.4 Sensitisation of incentive salience: the wanting of a drug becomes sensitised and, through conditioning stimuli that are associated with the drug, promotes craving; the liking of the drug does not sensitise and develops tolerance
Source: adapted from Robinson and Berridge (1993)

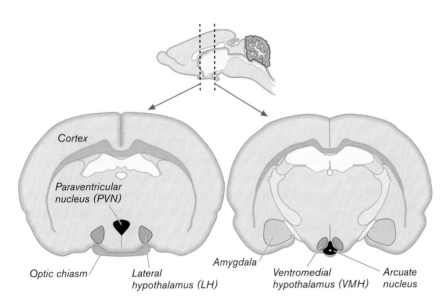

Figure 9.5 The hypothalamic nuclei involved in eating

has been through a number of adaptations that demonstrate the benefits of hindsight and the advantages of modern technology.

The hypothalamus

The hypothalamus has been the main focus of attention regarding feeding behaviour, in particular the *lateral hypothalamus (LH)* and the *ventromedial hypothalamus (VMH)* (see Figure 9.5). The LH is regarded as the hunger centre and the VMH the satiety centre. Satiety is the motivational state that terminates feeding. When the LH is stimulated, the state of hunger is induced and eating commences. The LH is under the inhibitory control of the VMH. There are receptors for glucose, called *glucoreceptors*, in the VMH, and when glucose is low the LH is released from inhibition by the VMH. Conversely, when glucose concentrations are high the VMH inhibits the LH. Glucose is a simple type of sugar and provides energy for cells.

This hypothesis was derived from rat studies. Lesions of the LH produced *aphagia* in rats: they stopped eating (Anand and Brobeck, 1951). The aphagia was accompanied by *adipsia* (they stopped drinking); the animal could recover from both conditions with intensive care (Teitalbaum and Stellar, 1954).

Lesions of the VMH led to *hyperphagia* (overeating) (Hetherington and Ranson, 1940). There were two phases of hyperphagia: the dynamic phase and the static phase. The dynamic phase, during which the rats gained the most weight, was immediately after surgery. During the following static phase they ate enough to maintain obesity.

A reappraisal of the literature calls into question the role of the hypothalamus. Unfortunately, but not surprisingly, the hypothalamus as the control centre of feeding is an oversimplification. Lesions of both the LH and VMH have behavioural consequences other than altering the regulation of feeding per se.

Lesions of the LH produce non-specific deficits, most notably deterioration of motor behaviour. The hypothalamus is a region with both intrinsic nuclei and neurons that pass through without synaptic contact. The nigrostriatal pathway is also lesioned during LH destruction.

Lesions of the nigrostriatal pathway can lead to extreme motor problems; after all, Parkinson's disease is a result of degeneration of this pathway. Selective lesions of the nigrostriatal pathway also induce aphagia (Marshall *et al.*, 1974).

Does this mean the LH has no role in feeding behaviour? More recent studies also point to a role for the LH. In the monkey, neurons of the LH fire in response to the sight of food (Burton *et al.*, 1976). Lesions with ibotenic acid selectively destroy the LH, while leaving the nigrostriatal pathway intact, and produce aphasia (e.g. Dunnett *et al.*, 1985). Ibotenic acid is a neurotoxic agent that acts on glutamatergic neurons. Glutamate in the LH produces eating (Stanley *et al.*, 1993b), whereas antagonists decrease eating (Stanley *et al.*, 1996). Thus, the hypothalamus remains an area of key interest, but the attention is now diverted to the role of various chemicals in LH.

There are two neuropeptides that are released by the LH (and glutamate in the LH) that affect feeding: *melanin-concentrating hormone (MCH)* and *orexin*. Both of these induce eating, and when the animal is deprived of food there is an increase in mRNA levels to make MCH and orexin (Qu *et al.* 1996; Sakurai *et al.* 1998; Dube *et al.* 1999).

Neuropeptide Y (NPY) is a potent stimulator of food intake (Clark *et al.*, 1984), and activates MCH and orexin (Broberger *et al.*, 1998; Elias *et al.*, 1998). When leptin (a hormone released by fat tissue) is released, it inhibits NPY, reducing feeding (Wang *et al.*, 1997). Injection of NPY into the LH makes rats eat under aversive conditions (Flood and Morley, 1991; Jewett *et al.* ,1992). NPY in the *paraventricular nucleus (PVN)* of the hypothalamus increases insulin levels (Stanley *et al.*, 1993a), and inhibition of NPY synthesis suppresses feeding and insulin (Akabayashi *et al.*, 1994). Food deprivation increases NPY and eating (Sahu *et al.*, 1988), an effect that can be blocked by NPY antagonism (Myers *et al.*, 1995). Deprivation of glucose leads to activation of NPY in the *arcuate nucleus* that projects to PVN (Minami *et al.*, 1995) and therefore increases insulin. Insulin is a pancreatic hormone that: (i) aids the entry of glucose into the cell, (ii) aids the conversions of glucose into glycogen (stored glucose) and fat, and amino acids into proteins (all of which can be stored), and (iii) promotes storage of the converted nutrients. NPY thus promotes hunger and preserves energy stores.

The actions of NPY on feeding make it clear that the hypothalamus is still an important structure.

Lesions of the VMH result in more than a loss of inhibitory control of eating. Rats will not eat food that is made bitter – they become fussy eaters (Ferguson and Keesey, 1975). VMH lesions cause an increase in the parasympathetic activity of the vagus nerve, which stimulates insulin secretion and inhibits glucogon (Weingarten *et al.*, 1985). *Glucogon* is a pancreatic hormone that converts stored *glycogen* back into glucose. VMH lesions increase insulin levels, promoting storage and therefore body fat production. VMH lesions also decrease the breakdown of fat for utilisation. Therefore, most of the energy is derived from the absorption of nutrients and not from the release of stored nutrients. If the vagus nerve is cut, thereby blocking communication between brain and pancreas, the effects of the VMH lesion are negated.

There are also anatomical consequences of VMH lesions. In VMH lesions, axons are destroyed that connect the PVN (and its functions) to other brain stem structures, e.g. the ventral noradrenergic bundle (Gold *et al.*, 1977).

Serotonin (5-HT) in the VMH and PVN leads to an inhibition of eating (Leibowitz *et al.*, 1990). Food intake is increased by 5-HT destruction (Saller and Stricker, 1976), inhibition of 5-HT synthesis (Breisch *et al.*, 1976) or 5-HT receptor blockade (Stallone and Nicolaïdis, 1989). Serotonergic antagonism increases NPY secretion, which in turn leads to increased food intake (Dryden *et al.*, 1995). Drugs that increase 5-HT can be used for obesity.

Eating disorders

There are three main eating disorders: obesity, anorexia nervosa and bulimia nervosa. (For a more detailed account of the physiological factors involved in eating disorders, see Chapter 33.)

Obesity

The media love to print stories about an increasingly obese nation, and the diet industry is extremely profitable. Even with our current understanding of feeding, the pharmaceutical industry has yet to deliver a drug alternative to the diet. Part of the problem in treating obesity is a lack of understanding surrounding the aetiology and pathogenesis of this behaviour. There are many reasons why someone may be obese, ranging from hormonal through to genetic and behavioural (see Activity Box 9.3). Some drugs have been used (such as fenfluramine, which is a 5-HT agonist), but side-effects tend to make this limited (Blundell and Halford, 1998).

Anorexia nervosa
A person with anorexia nervosa restricts their food intake, which leads to a dramatic decline in weight. Anorexia nervosa, like obesity, has had several theories associated with it. Again, there is little pharmacological help at hand for the patient with anorexia nervosa (see Chapter 33, pages 586–590).

Bulimia nervosa
Patients with bulimia nervosa binge-eat and then vomit or use laxatives to control their weight.

ACTIVITY BOX 9.3

Why do we overeat?

It cannot have escaped your notice that regular reports in the media claim we are becoming an overweight nation. In nutritional terms we are eating more than we require.

Why are we eating more? Try to think of all the explanations that could account for this increase in food intake.

I would imagine at the top of your list is the type of food we consume. People are eating more fatty foods, etc. Then there is taste. People eat more because they like the taste. A quick look around any supermarket will show you the rich variety of tastes present from around the world.

However, there are other features that can increase food intake, for example:

- smell – the smell of freshly baked bread is often enough to make people feel hungry
- visual appeal – we often 'eat with our eyes'; presentation of food can make people eat more
- variety – the increased variety of foods available can make people eat more; something as simple as the variety of colours in Smarties can make you rate the pleasantness of the sweet higher than if there were just one colour (Rolls *et al.*, 1982).

Fluoxetine (Proxac) is a 5-HT agonist that has been used to treat bulimia nervosa (Kaye *et al.*, 2001). This is contradictory to the actions of serotonergic drugs in the PVN. However, those who suffer with bulimia nervosa also suffer depression. Fluoxetine is an anti-depressant and it may be that once the depression is treated the eating disorder improves.

This highlights an important point in all disorders, not just eating disorders. The symptoms of eating disorders are focused on food intake. Food intake may be a secondary symptom of a psychiatric/psychological disorder (depression), rather than a primary symptom of an eating disorder in its own right (see Chapter 33, pages 589–590).

Drinking and thirst

The entertainer David Blaine was willing to go without food for 44 days but not water during September/October 2003. The consequences of not eating for this period of time are unpleasant but not necessarily life-threatening. To go without water is far more serious.

We have two fluid-filled compartments in the body: there is *intracellular fluid* (in the cytoplasm) and *extracellular fluid*, which includes *intravascular fluid* (blood plasma), *interstitial fluid* (between the cells) and cerebrospinal fluid (CSF). The body needs to regulate these fluid compartments (see Rosenzweig *et al.*, 2002). There is movement between the fluid compartments that allow cells to survive. The extracellular fluid acts in a supporting role to the cells and is controlled by brain mechanisms that monitor its levels.

The brain does this by promoting thirst as the motivator for drinking. There are two types of thirst: *osmotic thirst* and *hypovolemic thirst*. Osmotic thirst occurs when the solute concentration of extracellular fluid increases (it becomes more salty) and takes water from the intracellular fluid (which may place the cells in danger of damage). Basically, salty food changes the constituents of the fluid. Such food increases thirst, and that's why some pubs and bars serve free salted peanuts as these enhance the fluid intake of their customers. *Osmoreceptors*, perhaps located in the anterior hypothalamus and other areas, detect changes in the concentration of the interstitial fluid.

Hypovolemic thirst occurs when the intravascular fluid decreases. A loss of blood volume is detected by *baroreceptors*, which detect blood pressure, and also by receptors in the kidneys. The kidneys secrete *renin* at times of low blood flow.

Renin aids the production of *angiotensin*, a hormone that increases drinking (Epstein *et al.*, 1970). Angiotensin activates two other hormones: *aldosterone* and *vasopressin*. Aldosterone retains salt and water, plus it constricts the blood vessels. Vasopressin (or antidiuretic hormone) reduces the amount of fluid going to the bladder. Vasopressin conserves water, whereas aldosterone conserves salt until more is consumed.

Brain mechanisms in thirst

Signals from the baroreceptors located in the heart are sent to the *nucleus of the solitary tract* (in the medulla). Angiotensisin levels are detected by neurons projecting to the *subfornical organ*. The subfornical organ communicates with the *median preoptic nucleus (MPN)*. According to Thrasher *et al.* (1989) the MPN integrates hypovolemic and osmotic signals. The MPN is therefore instrumental in initiating drinking behaviour.

Learning outcomes

When you have completed this chapter you should be able to:

- describe the main theories of addiction
- describe the physiological bases of drug addiction
- evaluate the hypothalamus as a site of feeding
- describe the mechanisms underlying drinking.

Key Terms

Adipsia
Aldosterone
Angiotensin
Aphagia
Arcuate nucleus
Baroreceptors
Conditioned place preference (CPP)
Drug self-administration
Extracellular fluid
Glucogon
Glucoreceptors
Glycogen
Hyperphagia
Hypovolemic thirst
Interstitial fluid
Intracranial self-stimulation (ICSS)
Intracellular fluid
Intravascular fluid
Lateral hypothalamus (LH)
Median preoptic nucleus (MPN)
Melanin-concentrating hormone (MCH)
Mesolimbic pathway
Neuropeptide Y (NPY)
Nicotine
Nucleus accumbens (NAcc)
Nucleus of the solitary tract
Orexin
Osmoreceptors
Osmotic thirst
Paraventricular nucleus (PVN)
Renin
Subfornical organ
Vasopressin
Ventral tegmental area (VTA)
Ventromedial hypothalamus (VMH)

Further reading

Altman, J., Everitt, B. J., Glautier, S., Markou, A., Nutt, D., Oretti, R., Phillips, G. D. and Robbins, T. W. (1996) The biological, social and clinical bases of drug addiction: commentary and debate. *Psychopharmacology* 125, 285–345.

Berridge, K. C. and Robinson, T. E. (2003) Parsing reward. *Trends in Neuroscience* 26, 507–14.

Koob, G. F. (1992) Drugs of abuse: anatomy, pharmacology and function of reward pathways. *Trends in Pharmacological Sciences* 13, 177–84.

Rosenzweig, M. R., Breedlove, S. M. and Leiman, A. L. (2002) *Biological Psychology* (3rd edn). Massachusetts: Sinaur Associates, Inc.

Wonnacott, S., Russel, M. A. H. and Stolerman, I. P. (1990) *Nicotine Psychopharmacology: Molecular, Cellular and Behavioural Aspects.* Oxford: Oxford University Press.

Web links

Feeding: http://www.psy.plym.ac.uk/year3/psy337EatingNeuralFactors/PSY337EatingNeuralFactors.htm

Eating Disorder Unit at the Institute of Psychiatry:
http://web1.iop.kcl.ac.uk/iop/Departments/PsychMed/EDU/index.shtml

National Institute on Drug Abuse: http://www.nida.nih.gov/

National Addiction Centre:
http://web1.iop.kcl.ac.uk/IoP/Departments/PsychMed/NAC/new.shtml

10

Emotion and sleep

Route map of the chapter

Our emotions make life a colourful experience. This chapter investigates the neural mechanisms that underlie our emotions – for example, the amygdala and fear. It also investigates the neural mechanisms of sleep.

Introduction

If emotion is a heightened state of consciousness, sleep is a lowered state of consciousness. We spend a large proportion of our life asleep. The brain is also responsible for sleep. Changes in sleep can have serious ramifications for other behaviours, and sleep disorders can be debilitating.

Emotion

What is emotion? We all have an idea of what love, anger, fear etc. are (see Activity Box 10.1). Emotions are complex experiences that involve cognition, affect and physiology. What happens when we are confronted by a fierce bear, for example? The cognitive part of the emotion identifies the stimulus as fierce bear. The affective component of the emotion produces the feeling of fear and the physiological response is the activation of the sympathetic nervous system. This gets us ready for fight or flight.

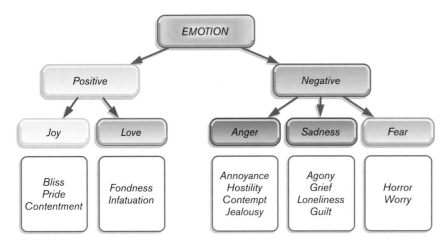

Figure 10.1 Emotions can be placed into different categories

ACTIVITY BOX 10.1

How many emotions can you name?

Much of the research into the biological basis of emotion has focused on fear. Clearly we experience more than fear.

How many emotions can you name?

Figure 10.1 shows a list compiled by Fischer *et al.* (1990) in a hierarchy.

How do you know that someone is experiencing one of these emotions?

Apart from verbal communication we are able to tell the emotional state of an individual by their facial expression. The facial expression is a relatively cross-cultural display of emotion (Russel, 1994).

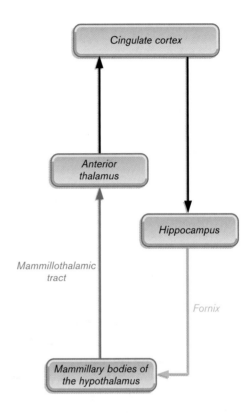

Figure 10.2 The Papez circuit

There have been a number of theories proposed to account for emotions. A full discussion of these can be found in Chapter 26, but all of these theories have involved a physiological component.

Given that emotion is a cross-cultural phenomenon and that the expression of emotions via the somatic nervous system is also universal, this chapter will focus on the neural mechanisms that underlie emotion.

The emotional brain

The theories of emotion have included physiological responses, but they have not provided a detailed account of the neural circuitry involved in emotion. Papez (1937) considered the limbic system to be involved in the emotional experience, and the neural mechanism of emotion has since come to be known as the *Papez circuit*.

Papez circuit

The initial proposal by Papez was a neural circuit for the expression of emotion. This involved the connection of the *cingulate cortex* and the *hypothalamus*. The hypothalamus is connected via the *mammillary bodies* of the hypothalamus to the *anterior nucleus* of the *thalamus*, which then projects to the cingulate cortex. Information from the cingulate cortex projects to the hippocampus and back to the hypothalamus via the *fornix* (see Figure 10.2).

After lesions of the medial temporal lobe, monkeys demonstrated a set of behaviours that became known as *Klüver–Bucy syndrome* (Klüver and Bucy, 1938). There are many behavioural consequences of such a lesion, but in the context of emotion, these monkeys did not demonstrate fear or hostility to humans. They were placid or tamed. The changes in the monkeys' emotional output were considered to be a result of disruption to the Papez circuit.

With subsequent neuroanatomical investigation, other areas of the brain have been implicated, in particular the amygdala. The reduced fear response in Klüver–Bucy syndrome can be accounted for by lesions, specifically to the amygdala.

Section 2
Psychobiology

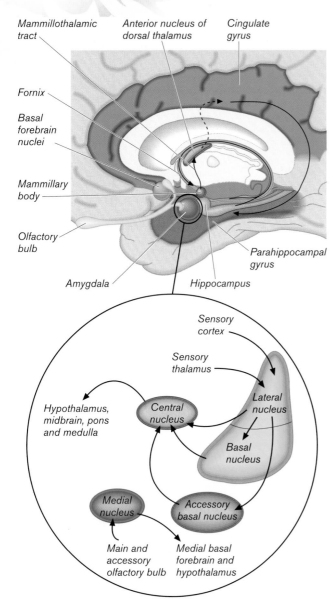

Figure 10.3 The nuclei of the amygdala

The amygdala

The *amygdala* is not one set of nuclei, but rather a complex of different regions (see Figure 10.3), and these different regions have different neuroanatomical connections. The medial nucleus receives input from the olfactory cortex and olfactory bulb. The basolateral nuclei receive input from the cortex, thalamus and hippocampus. The central nucleus receives input from the basolateral nuclei.

The amygdala is the convergence point for the integration of cortical and subcortical information.

The amygdala and fear

The central nucleus projects to a diverse set of brain regions (see Figure 10.4). Unilateral removal of the amygdala in split-brain monkeys revealed the importance of this region (Downer, 1961). By cutting the communication of the hemispheres, stimuli presented to one eye could not be passed to the other hemisphere. Stimuli that would normally provoke an emotional reaction did not if they were presented to the side with the lesion of the amygdala. If the stimuli were presented to the intact side then an emotional response was seen.

One emotion that is very well studied is fear. Fear can be produced under controlled experimental conditions in animals, and therefore experiments can be performed that could otherwise not be undertaken in humans (LeDoux, 1998). Fear responses can be learned by animals (see the section in Chapter 8 on the conditioned emotional response (CER)). Using conditioning procedures to induce fear to an auditory stimulus, LeDoux's laboratory has been able to study the role of the amygdala. By systematically lesioning pathways within the brain that process auditory signals, the pathway that mediates the fear response can be traced. Lesions of the central amygdala prevent a CER developing, whereas lesions connecting cortical processing have no effect (LeDoux *et al.*, 1998). Conversely, when the amygdala is stimulated, animals show signs of fear and agitation (see Davis, 1992).

The lack of CER after damage to the amygdala can also be seen in humans (LeBar *et al.*, 1995). Blood flow to the amygdala is increased when a cue that is associated with an aversive stimulus is presented (LeBar *et al.*, 1988). Studies using fMRI have shown that the amygdala is activated in response to fearful faces (Phillips *et al.*, 1998) and during fear conditioning (Cheng *et al.*, 2003). Lesions of the amygdala prevent negative facial expressions being rated as less favourable than positive facial expressions (Adolphs *et al.*, 1998). Patients with lesions of the amygdala are impaired at recognising the emotional content of complex social scenes only when there is facial expression; they are not affected when the faces are erased (Adolphs and Tranel, 2003).

PET scans have revealed activation of the amygdala when participants have to recall the content of emotionally loaded films compared to neutral films (Cahill *et al.*, 1996) or are shown threatening words (Isenberg *et al.*, 1999). The experimental evidence supports a central role of the amygdala in emotion.

The hippocampus and fear

Many people feel fear when entering a hospital. If you have to attend a hospital for negative reasons, the hospital may become associated with fear. LeDoux (1998) has included the *hippocampus* as an area that is responsible for the conditioning of contextual fear. Lesions of the hippocampus prevent contextual fear conditioning. If the lesions are performed after conditioning, it is only the fear response to the context that is blocked. The hippocampus provides the memory for previous events and experiences (see LeDoux, 1998) (see Figure 10.5).

Beyond fear

The relative ease with which fear can be produced in humans and non-humans has meant that this emotion has been the main focus of attention for researchers, and other emotions have not been as well studied.

Bartels and Zeki (2000) investigated the brain activation of people who claimed to be in love. When looking at pictures of their loved ones, there was an increase of activity in the anterior cingulate cortex and the striatum. This was accompanied by a reduction of activity in the amygdala.

Damasio *et al.* (2000) investigated the recall of happiness, sadness, anger and fear, and the number of brain regions that were activated during emotional experience differed from emotion to emotion. So emotion is much more than the amygdala activation seen with fear conditioning.

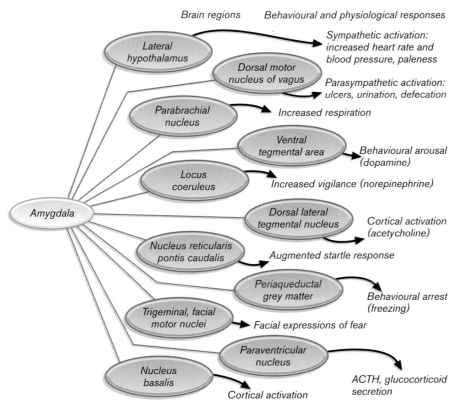

Figure 10.4 The connections of the amygdala

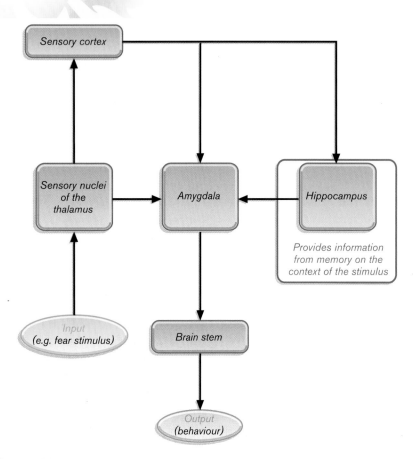

Figure 10.5 A neural circuit of fear, including the involvement of the hippocampus

Aggression

Aggressive behaviour is a subject of great concern for many branches of our society, and the male of the species has been studied at great length to understand aggression and violence.

Neural mechanisms and aggression

In animal studies, the amygdala and hypothalamus have been shown to influence defence behaviours and attack behaviours (see Siegal *et al.*, 1999). The amygdala was activated in the brains of convicted murderers whose crime was impulsive and not premeditated, whereas those who were guilty of premeditated murder exhibited greater prefrontal activity (Raine *et al.*, 1997; 1998).

Research suggests that the job of the prefrontal cortex is inhibiting the amygdala's response (see Carlson, 2004). As the executive controlling mechanism of the brain, the frontal areas are involved in initiating, planning and the execution of behaviours. The frontal lobes would have access to an account of the implications of our actions and thus suppress them if necessary (see Shallice, 1988).

Hormones and aggression

It is predominantly males who display aggression, and this has given rise to evolutionary and hormonal explanations for this behaviour.

The male hormones (in particular, the androgens such as testosterone) have been held responsible for male aggression and, consistent with this belief, castration in rats reduces aggression, while testosterone treatment reinstates it (Beeman, 1947).

Early exposure to androgens during the organisational period of the brain's development results in less androgen being required to produce an aggressive response later in life (vom Saal, 1983).

Research into human aggression has not been entirely conclusive. Methodological limitations, such as the fact that you cannot castrate males, means that many experimental manipulations are not permitted. This leaves us with correlation studies. These have looked at the circulating levels of androgens and attempted to map them with behaviour. The overall view is that there is a possibility that androgens are involved in human male aggression (Albert *et al.*, 1993).

Stress

How many times have you heard someone say that they are 'stressed out'? Do you feel stressed when confronted with exams? There are many events that can lead to stress (see Chapter 35). Stress is big business: whether it is litigation after the event or prevention of its occurrence.

From a psychobiological point of view, stress is the reaction to the perception of an aversive stimulus and automatic responses initiated by the amygdala. The amygdala releases *corticotrophin-releasing hormone (CRH)*, which activates the autonomic and endocrine systems. The activation of these systems mobilises energy for a fight or flight response. Activation of the SNS produces a release of adrenaline, noradrenaline (NA) and stress hormones.

Adrenaline interferes with glucose, allowing more energy to be released, and adrenaline and NA increase blood flow and heart rate.

The stress hormone, a glucocorticoid called *cortisol*, is released by the adrenal gland, and then *glucocorticoids* convert proteins into glucose and increase blood flow. CRH stimulates the release of *adrenocorticotrophic hormone (ACTH)* from the anterior pituitary, and ACTH prompts the adrenal gland to secrete the glucocorticoids.

If the stress continues, the locus coeruleus releases more NA and communicates with the amygdala, causing more CRH to be released, and a vicious circle begins (see Sapolsky, 2003). The behavioural

response to administration of CRH is consistent with the brain's reaction to aversive stimuli, where CRH enhances conditioned emotional response (Cole and Koob, 1988) and decreases the amount of time spent in the centre of an open field – a sign of anxiety and stress (Britton *et al.*, 1982). Blockade of CRH prevented stress in rats (Heinrichs *et al.*, 1992).

The consequences of our bodies' physiological reactions to stressors can give rise to many health problems. If there is a long-term stress reaction, these responses are harmful. The area of health psychology has focused on stress and its effects on, for example, heart disease and immunology (see Chapter 35, pages 626–631).

Sleep

Many of us are preoccupied with our emotions during our waking moments, and sometimes these emotions interfere with the respite of sleep. We spend a great deal of time asleep, and sleep takes us into a different state of consciousness.

The stages of sleep

The brain's activity can be measured by placing electrodes on the scalp; this psychophysiological measure is called an *electroencephalogram (EEG)*. Despite appearances to the contrary, the EEG reveals that the brain goes through a number of different stages of sleep.

The brainwaves present during the various stages of sleep can be seen in Figure 10.6. When we are awake there are two types of brain activity: *alpha activity* and *beta activity* (or waves). Alpha activity predominates during rest and inactivity, whereas beta activity is associated with being alert. The brain's activity changes through the four stages of sleep.

Stage 1 sleep is the initial entry into the sleep state and represents a transitional state. The EEG indicates that the brain activity has changed, producing a theta wave. After a short period the person enters Stage 2 sleep. The EEG recording during Stage 2 is irregular: there is theta activity, with a burst of activity called *sleep spindles*. Stage 3 sleep is characterised by *delta waves*, and during Stage 3 sleep the number of spindles diminishes. The

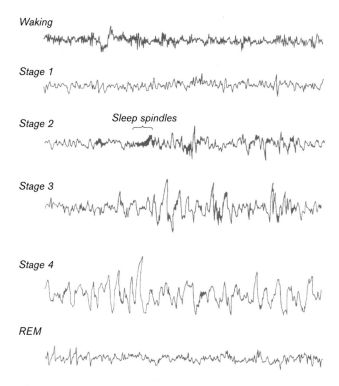

Figure 10.6 *The EEG recording of the different stages of sleep*
Source: adapted from Horne, 1988

difference between Stage 3 and Stage 4 is not clear-cut, but appears to be related to the number of delta waves. In Stage 3 there are less than 50 per cent delta waves, whereas in Stage 4 there are more than 50 per cent. These stages are called slow-wave sleep.

It takes about an hour to go through Stages 1 to 4, and these stages are referred to as non-rapid eye movement (non-REM) sleep. After about 45 minutes of Stage 4 sleep there is a change in the EEG recording. The brain activity is desynchronised, with some theta and beta activity. Electrodes attached to the muscles of the eye to detect movement (an electrooculogram (EOG)) indicate that the eyes are active. This is called *REM sleep*, and during this sleep phase the rest of the body is paralysed.

During a night's sleep there is a cycle of non-REM and REM sleep. Each cycle lasts about 90 minutes, a third of which may be REM sleep (see Figure 10.7).

Dreams

We are in a different state of consciousness when we are asleep, but we are not unconscious. The fact that we dream indicates that the brain is active during sleep, and the visual cortex in particular is active during sleep (Madsen *et al.*, 1991). This may account for REM sleep; indeed the brain activity during REM sleep is similar to that of a person scanning a visual scene (Miyauchi *et al.*, 1990).

The function of dreams and REM sleep is still to be determined. However, many theories have been put forward to account for dreams. For example, Freud attempted to account for dreams as revelations from the unconscious, and claimed that an interpretation of a dream such as posting a letter had a sexual content. Most postal workers may disagree with this, particularly early in the morning, but one has to remember that Freud also worked with cocaine!

The neural mechanisms of sleep

There are many changes in brain activity during sleep (see Maquet, 1999). Three neural systems are thought to produce sleep, and these communicate with each other.

The forebrain

The forebrain can be isolated from the rest of the brain by surgery and is called the *cerveau isole*. The isolated forebrain can generate slow-wave sleep, while lesions of the basal forebrain prevent slow-wave sleep (Clemente and Sterman, 1963). Neurons during sleep became active, resulting in widespread inhibition of other brain regions (Gallopin *et al.*, 2000).

The reticular formation

Stimulation of the *reticular formation* will wake a sleeping animal (Moruzzi and Magoun, 1949), and so the reticular formation appears to function as a wake-up call to the basal ganglia, thalamus and forebrain.

The pons

The *pons* is the focus of REM sleep, and if various cuts are made to transect the brain stem, the action of the pons's ability to trigger REM sleep can be seen.

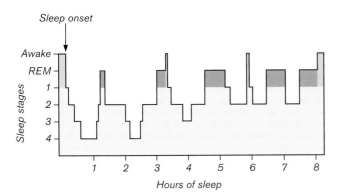

Figure 10.7 *The pattern of REM activity over a night's sleep*
Source: adapted from Kales and Kales, 1970

If the transection is below the pons, the brain shows alternation between slow-wave sleep and REM sleep. A particular waveform is indicative of REM sleep: *PGO waves* (pons, geniculate and occipital cortex) arise from the pons and go to the cortex. If the transection is made higher, leaving the pons in contact with the medulla and spinal cord, then the body shows REM sleep.

Neurotransmitters and sleep

Serotonin and noradrenaline have both been implicated in the control of sleep. Serotonin is found in the raphe nucleus of the reticular formation, where activation of the raphe nucleus produces arousal, and inhibition of 5-HT synthesis reduces it (Peck and Vanderwolf, 1991). Sleep is disrupted in rats with lesions of the raphe nucleus (Jouvet, 1999). When aroused the raphe nucleus is active, when in REM sleep it is silent (Trulson and Jacobs, 1979).

The noradrenergic neurones of the locus coeruleus show increased firing during waking hours and decreased firing during sleep (Aston-Jones and Bloom, 1981). Noradrenaline release is associated with the change from sleep to wakefulness (Mendelson, 2001).

Acetylcholine in the pons produces the activation of eye activity during REM sleep and PGO waves (Baghdoyan *et al.*, 1984; Kodama and Honda, 1996).

The different actions of neurotransmitters promote either sleep or waking. The fact that neurotransmission is altered during sleeping and waking states permits the modification of sleep. However, drugs that are used to induce sleep act elsewhere.

Sleeping pills

Drugs can be used to aid sleep; these are called hypnotics. Barbiturates were once used to induce sleep, and they act at the GABA A receptor and influence such areas of the brain as the reticular formation. However, barbiturates are dangerous drugs with abuse liability. Another group of drugs, the benzodiazepines (such as diazepam (Valium)), are also effective hypnotics. The benzodiazepines act at a receptor complex on GABA neurons; they are anxiolytic and somewhat safer to use than barbiturates. However, benzodiazepines are also used to treat anxiety disorders and there is a high risk of dependence developing.

Why do we need to sleep?

This may seem like a simple question with a straightforward answer: because we are tired! However, although there are several theories about the function of sleep, a definitive answer is elusive.

An evolutionary account of sleep involves animals conserving energy and avoiding danger (Meddis, 1975). Perhaps this is why we sleep best at night. Our visual system is not tuned for night vision and therefore we are vulnerable during the hours of darkness. The opposite is the case for nocturnal animals that function best at night.

When we are awake we are busy. This requires energy and there is wear and tear on the body, so sleep has been considered to be a period in which restoration of the body can take place (Moruzzi, 1972). After a difficult day you may feel like you could sleep for a long period of time. However, a strenuous day does not lead to an increase in sleep. Sleep patterns can change over the life span. Why do babies sleep so much? Perhaps the answer lies in the fact that growth hormone is released when they are asleep.

Another view is that sleep is cognitively beneficial. Sleep aids the retention and consolidation of material learned during the day. REM sleep increases after learning, and brain activity during REM sleep has been shown to be similar to that when performing a task (Maquet *et al.*, 2000). However, other studies have failed to show a specific effect with REM sleep, but have concluded that the density of sleep spindles in Stage 2 sleep is correlated with recall performance on a learned task (Gais *et al.*, 2002).

Sleep disorders

Disorders of sleep – whether it is too much or too little – can have a profound effect on behaviour. Simply not getting enough sleep can produce a number of problems (see Activity Box 10.2).

ACTIVITY BOX 10.2

What are the effects of sleep deprivation?

If you have very young children or very noisy neighbours you will be familiar with the effects of sleep deprivation.

Using your previous experience think about how sleep can affect your behaviour.

Now that you are studying psychology, when and why might you consider a good night's sleep essential?

Many students prior to an examination have difficulty sleeping or engage in last-minute revision. We have already seen how important the frontal lobes are in answering exam questions. Experimental studies have shown the consequences of sleep deprivation to the frontal lobes (see Jones and Harrison, 2001, for a review).

Sleep deprivation has been shown to impair working memory (Smith *et al.*, 2002), creative thinking and attention (Wimmer *et al.*, 1992).

The importance of a good night's sleep for children was highlighted by Randazzo *et al.* (1998). In this study children aged between 10 and 14 had their sleep restricted. These children performed poorly on complex cognitive tasks, whereas simpler tasks remained the same as for non-sleep-deprived children. So when your parents said you needed a good night's sleep on school days they were right!

Insomnia

Insomnia is difficulty in falling asleep or staying asleep. However, there are large individual differences in the amount of sleep a person needs. Margaret Thatcher, for example, reputedly needed very little sleep when she was prime minister. Thus insomnia is relative to an individual's needs. Some people may seek a medical solution to insomnia (see below). However, this can have rebound effects when drug treatment is discontinued.

Narcolepsy

People who cannot resist falling asleep at inappropriate times during the day have a condition called *narcolepsy*. If you were to fall asleep during a tedious lecture, however, this would be quite normal and not a symptom of narcolepsy!

There are specific symptoms of narcolepsy: cataplexy, sleep paralysis and hypnogogic hallucinations. Cataplexy happens when the person is awake, and during cataplexy there is a complete paralysis of the body – the person simply can't move. One view of cataplexy is that the muscle paralysis in REM sleep occurs out of context. Sleep paralysis is similar to cataplexy, but happens either just before or just after sleep. Hypnogogic hallucinations are dreamlike states that happen prior to falling asleep, but while still awake. They occur during sleep paralysis and are not that form of daydreaming you may also experience during a tedious lecture.

Narcolepsy is primarily a genetic disorder (Lin *et al.*, 1999), and the gene that is dysfunctional in narcolepsy codes for the peptide orexin (Kilduff and Peyron, 2000). Orexin has been shown to be reduced in people with narcolepsy (Peyron *et al.*, 2000) and general sleepiness (Martinez-Rodriguez *et al.*, 2003).

A number of pharmacological treatments are available for narcolepsy, but none of these drugs directly influences orexin levels. They are stimulants that act on dopaminergic, serotonergic and noradrenergic systems.

Sleep deprivation

Sleep deprivation can have serious consequences. For example, sleep-deprived rats have reduced immunity, which can be fatal (Everson, 1993); this supports a restorative theory of sleep. In extreme cases most humans with fatal familial insomnia die within two years of the insomnia starting (Manetto *et al.*, 1992).

Obviously death is a dramatic consequence of sleep deprivation, but there are more subtle effects of a lack of sleep (see Applications Box 10.1).

APPLICATIONS BOX 10.1

Doctors work long hours with little sleep: reason enough to activate our amygdala

Performance on many tasks can be impaired by sleep deprivation. There are a number of occupations in which sleep deprivation can have dramatic effects. A lack of sleep on the part of the driver whose car derailed a train in Selby Yorkshire in 2001 was cited as an influence in the accident. Experimental evidence also suggests that partial sleep deprivation can alter driving (De Valck *et al.*, 2003).

The recent wars in Afghanistan and Iraq have required military personnel to be without sleep during stressful situations, and this could have a dramatic effect on combat performance. Indeed, marksmanship has been shown to deteriorate in elite soldiers after nearly 73 hours of partial sleep deprivation (Tharion *et al.*, 2003), as did cognitive performance (Lieberman *et al.*, 2002).

The one profession we hear the most about in relation to sleep deprivation is medicine. Hospital doctors have to work long hours with very little sleep. This is said to affect their judgement, which is sometimes critical to the wellbeing of their patients (see Buysse *et al.*,

2003). For example, a doctor needs to be attentive in giving the correct dose of a drug to a patient, or vigilant in the diagnosis of symptoms.

Recent research looking at sleep deprivation and fatigue in surgeons indicated an increase in errors when they were sleep-deprived (Eastridge *et al.*, 2003).

It would be reasonable to assume that when confronted with a tired doctor our amygdala should be active, and fear expressed!

Learning outcomes

When you have completed this chapter you should be able to:

- describe the role of the amygdala and the hippocampus in fear
- describe the stress response
- explain why we need sleep
- describe the stages of sleep.

Key Terms

Adrenocorticotrophic hormone (ACTH)
Alpha activity
Amygdala
Anterior nucleus
Beta activity
Cerveau isole
Cingulate cortex
Corticotrophin-releasing hormone (CRH)
Cortisol
Delta waves
Electroencephalogram (EEG)
Fornix
Glucocorticoids
Hippocampus
Hypothalamus
Insomnia
Klüver–Bucy syndrome

Section 2
Psychobiology

Mammillary bodies
Narcolepsy
Papez circuit
PGO waves
Pons
REM sleep
Reticular formation
Sleep spindles
Thalamus

Further reading

Gottesmann, C. (1999) Neurophysiological support of consciousness during waking and sleeping. *Progress in Neurobiology* 59, 469–508.

LeDoux, J. (1998) *The Emotional Brain*. London: Phoenix.

Rolls, E. T. (1999) *The Brain and Emotion*. Oxford: Oxford University Press.

Strerade, M. (1992) Basic mechanisms of sleep generation. *Neurology* 42, 9–18.

Taheri, S., Zeitzer, J. M. and Mignot, E. (2002) The role of hypocretins (orexins) in sleep regulation and narcolepsy. *Annual Review of Neuroscience* 25, 283–313.

Web links

Brain and Emotion Research: http://www.news.wisc.edu/packages/emotion/

Brain Basics: Understanding Sleep:
http://www.ninds.nih.gov/health_and_medical/pubs/understanding_sleep_brain_basic_.htm

Perceptual systems and motor control

Route map of the chapter

In this chapter you will be introduced to the mechanics of the sensory systems, such as the eye, the ear and the nose. The route a perceptual signal takes once it has been detected by the senses is further described, with all culminating in the cortex. In the second part of the chapter we will look at motor control and response output.

Introduction

We receive large amounts of information about our environment via our senses and this information is converted into neural impulses that are sent to the brain via afferent neurons. Incoming information from all the senses is integrated in the brain. We are not simply passive recipients of sensory input – we respond to incoming information. For example, we orient to a loud noise (see Chapter 8). Some of the responses are automatic, while some require consideration and selection.

The sensory modalities (see below) are the channels that receive information, but then it is the brain that interprets the signals. It is the brain that perceives and it is the brain that sees, hears, tastes, smells, and feels pleasure and pain.

Sensory modalities

As mentioned above, the sensory modalities are those that receive information and send signals about the environment to the brain.

Vision

More emphasis is given to visual perception than any other sensory modality. The eye, and the brain's interpretation of signals from the eye, have been studied extensively, and this chapter will look at the mechanics of the visual system.

The retina

The eye is made up of a number of structures (see Figure 11.1). Light enters the eye and lands on the retina. Thus an image of the environment is projected directly on to the retina. The *retina* is part of the CNS, and comprises several cellular layers that communicate with each other using neurotransmitters. Most importantly, the retina contains cells receptive to light (*photoreceptors*). There are two types of photoreceptor, which have an uneven distribution over the retina: rods and cones.

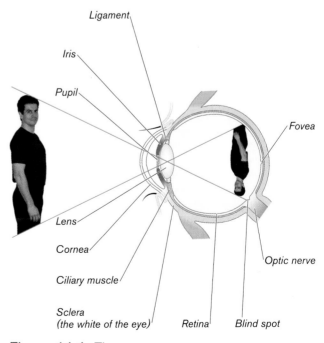

Figure 11.1 The eye

Rods are very sensitive but do not provide high acuity (fine detail) or colour. They are found in greater numbers on the edges of the retina. Cones, on the other hand, provide high acuity and respond to colour. There is a high density of cones in a central area of the retina called the fovea.

Photoreceptors are connected to interneurons and ganglion cells that form the optic nerve (see Figure 11.2). After looking at Figure 11.2 you will probably conclude that the retinal cells appear to be inside-out. You are right; this is an artefact of embryological development, and the retina is equipped to deal with it. The point at which information funnels out of the retina on its way to the brain (via the optic nerve) is called the *blind spot* (see Activity Box 11.1).

ACTIVITY BOX 11.1

The blind spot

The point at which the retinal cells exit the eye is called the optic disk. This produces an area where images cannot be seen.

Close your left eye. Focus on the ✳ below. Maintain your focus and move the book backwards and forwards. There is a point at which the black circle is not visible. Congratulations! You have found your blind spot.

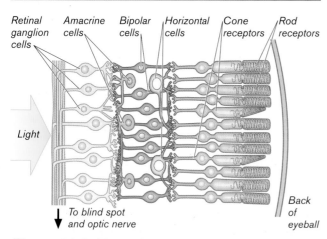

Figure 11.2 The retina
Source: adapted from Pinel (2003)

When light falls on the rods and cones, they convert the image into a neural impulse. The rods and cones contain visual pigments that are photosensitive, and there are different visual pigments that are made from *opsins* and retinal (Wald, 1964). *Rhodopsin*, usually referred to as the chemical for rods, is now also used to refer to the visual pigments for cones.

In the dark, rods are relatively depolarised – about -35 mV (see Bowmaker, 2002). This is achieved because rhodopsin is not activated. Rhodopsin is G-protein linked. A second messenger (cyclic GMP) keeps Na^+ channels open and Na^+ can flow into the rod. To counteract this, K^+ flows out. The rod in the dark state releases glutamate. However, light produces a reaction with rhodopsin – it disrupts the second messenger and Na^+ is no longer permitted to enter the cell. The rod then becomes hyperpolarised and glutamate release stops. In continuous light the rod will recalibrate itself to the ambient light (see Bowmaker, 2002).

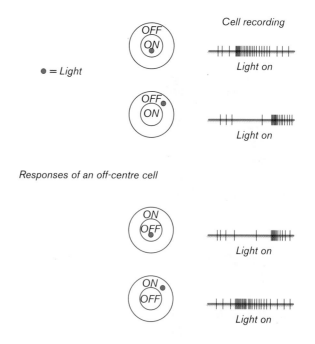

Figure 11.3 Receptive fields can be divided into areas that are 'on' or 'off'; the cell fires more when light is projected onto the on-area

The released glutamate from the photoreceptors differentially reacts with the next cellular layer, the *bipolar cells*. These cells are divided into two receptive fields: off-centre cells and on-centre cells. The cells of the visual system have receptive fields that are sensitive to light (see Figure 11.3). When light is shone in the on-area the cell fires. If a light is shone in the off-area it does not fire. Other cells have off-centres and on-surrounds.

The effect of having two receptive fields is that the cell responds best when there is contrast. If both receptive fields of the cell have light on them the cell does not fire – one field cancels out the other. The consequence of having receptive fields is illustrated in Activity Box 11.2.

ACTIVITY BOX 11.2

Receptive fields

Look at the grid below. You may have to adjust the distance from your eyes to get the full impact. What can you see? Hopefully at the junction of each white line you can see white. However, around the junction you are focusing on there are grey dots. Try to focus on a grey dot, though. You can't!

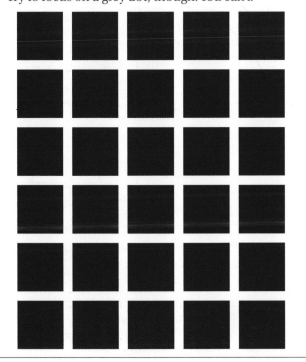

The reason for this effect is due to receptive fields. At the junction there are four inhibitory inputs compared to one excitatory input. Along the white line there are only two inhibitory inputs compared to one excitatory input. The firing of the cell will be influenced by the ratio of input across the receptive field. The information coded by the cell is then passed on to the next set of neurons in the visual pathway.

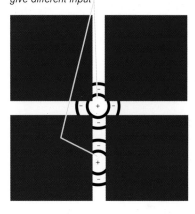

Receptive fields at different points give different input

When the light is off, glutamate is released, which depolarises off-centre bipolar cells. Conversely, in on-centre bipolar cells, the reduction of glutamate in response to the light on photoreceptors results in a depolarisation. Thus glutamate can influence cells in two different ways, depending on the type of receptive field it has.

When activated, bipolar cells release glutamate, which stimulates the *retinal ganglion cells*. Again, there are two types of ganglion cell: on-centre and off-centre (Kuffler, 1953). The retinal ganglion cells respond to incoming information, and relay the coded messages about light and dark to the brain. The retinal ganglion cells form the optic nerve.

Convergence

Cones feed into the bipolar cells with a degree of low *convergence* – that is, each cone speaks to a small number of bipolar cells (both on- and off-centre bipolar cells; see Figure 11.4). The different response

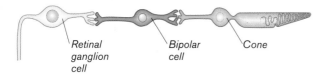

Low convergence in cone-fed circuits

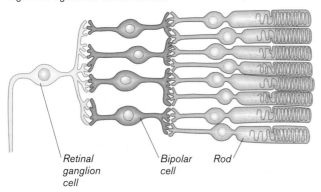

High convergence in rod-fed circuits

Figure 11.4 Rods and cones differ in their degree of convergence onto bipolar cells; many rods feed into one retinal ganglion cell (high convergence), whereas cones have low convergence with fewer cones feeding into the retinal ganglion cell Source: adapted from Pinel (2003)

to incoming information from cones is determined by glutamate receptors. On-centres have metabotropic receptors; off-centres have ionotropic receptors. A decrease in glutamate at the metabotropic receptor produces depolarisation and at the ionotropic receptor, hyperpolarisation.

Rods, in contrast, have high convergence. Large numbers of rods synapse on to a single bipolar cell (see Figure 11.4). This makes the system very sensitive, but it has low acuity (i.e. it detects changes in light relatively easily but is not very good at transmitting fine detail in the visual field).

Lateral inhibition

While it is clear that visual information is transmitted from the eye to the brain, there is also communication between the cells of the retina (horizontal communication). Look at Figure 11.2

again and you will see a set of cells that communicate across the retinal cells: the *amacrine cells* and *horizontal cells*. Horizontal cells synapse

---

ACTIVITY BOX 11.3

Lateral inhibition

Look at the Mach bands below. What do you see? Within each band there appears to be a gradient of tone. Now take two pieces of paper and cover all but one of the Mach bands. Now what do you see?

Hopefully you can see that there is no tonal gradient within a band. What is there and what you see are two different things. How can we account for this effect?

The answer lies in lateral inhibition and what is happening at the edge of each band.

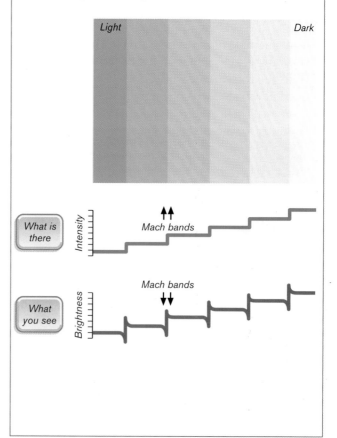

with the photoreceptors and provide feedback that is in opposition to the photoreceptor. If a rod stimulates a horizontal cell it sends a message back saying 'stop it'. Note that horizontal cells synapse with more than one photoreceptor, and horizontal cells are involved in a process called *lateral inhibition*.

Studies on the horseshoe crab have cast light on the mechanisms of lateral inhibition (Hartline *et al.*, 1956). Lateral inhibition is when one neuron inhibits its neighbouring neurons. Light activates a photoreceptor and glutamate release stops. The horizontal cell sends inhibitory messages (using GABA) to all the photoreceptors it is connected to.

Look at Activity Box 11.3 to see the effects of lateral inhibition. The effect is achieved because the edges of the different contrasting bands are being differentially inhibited (see Figure 11.5). The receptor at the edge of the more intense light fires more than the other receptors receiving the same light input. On the darker side, the receptor at the edge fires less compared to the others in the middle of the band. The middle receptors fire at the same rate because they receive the same amount of stimulation and the same amount of inhibition from the horizontal cell. The receptors at the edge of the light receive the same amount of light input, but receive different levels of inhibition. The bright receptor inhibits the darker receptor. Meanwhile the darker receptor has less inhibitory power on the adjacent bright-sided receptor.

A similar process is achieved by the amacrine cells, which communicate with the bipolar and retinal ganglion cells. Depending on the type of incoming information from the bipolar cells, the amacrine cells can inhibit retinal-ganglion cells.

The optic nerve

The *optic nerve* is the collated axons of the retinal ganglion cells. Because we have two eyes we have two optic nerves. Two eyes mean we have slightly different images of the same stimuli; this is called *binocular vision*. Look at an object and close one eye. Close the other eye and open the first eye. You will see that the image of the object is slightly different and it appears to move. The information that is

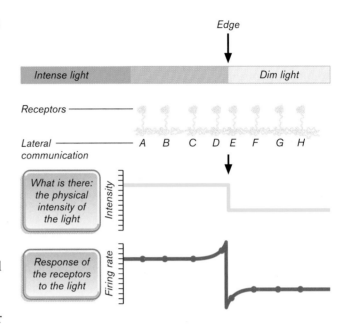

Figure 11.5 *The cells of the retina communicate with each other in a process called lateral inhibition, which is responsible for the contrast enhancement seen in Activity Box 11.2*

transmitted to the brain is sorted according to the visual field.

In Figure 11.6 you can see that the nasal hemiretina projects to the opposite side of the brain (contralateral) and the temporal hemiretina projects to the same side of the brain (ipsilateral). Information from both eyes is integrated.

The point at which the visual fields cross is called the *optic chiasm*. There are no connections in the optic chiasm; the axons of the optic nerve synapse at the *lateral geniculate nucleus (LGN)* of the thalamus.

The LGN

The LGN is a multi-layered structure. Each layer contains a map of the visual field. There are six layers that can be differentiated into two types, depending on the size of the cell: the *magnocellular layer* and the *parvocellular layer* (see Figure 11.7). Signals from cones tend to innervate the parvocellular layer, and signals from the rods innervate the magnocellular layer.

The information from the retina does not appear to be reorganised by the LGN (Derrington, 2002). The information at this point may be integrated with other signals before they are passed to the cortex. The magnocellular and parvocellular layers project to the occipital cortex (visual cortex).

The visual cortex

The visual cortex interprets the signals that are received from the retina via the LGN. Within the visual cortex there are two types of cell that respond to visual input: simple cells and complex cells. Our understanding of these comes mainly from the early experiments of Hubel and Wiesel. Their experiments used animals that had electrodes placed in regions of the visual cortex to record activity. Light was shone on the retina and changes in the firing rate of the cells could be measured.

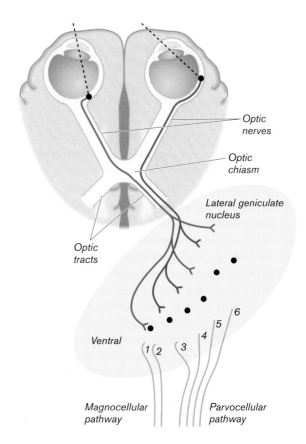

Figure 11.7 *The parvocellular and magnocellular layers of the LGN*

Hubel and Wiesel (1959; 1962; 1968) discovered that receptive fields were round. They also comprised two receptive fields. This was the case for all the cells in the visual pathway.

Simple cells

The *simple cells* of the visual cortex differ from the cells of the rest of the visual pathway inasmuch as they have visual fields that are divided by straight lines (see Figure 11.8). They respond best when the light falls in a particular orientation. The hypothesised manner by which the LGN projects this information to the simple cells is depicted in Figure 11.8.

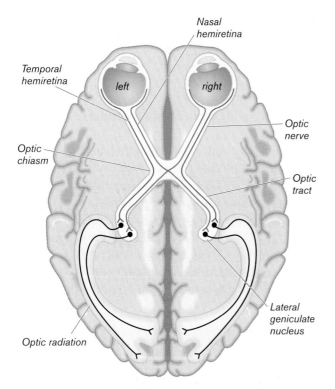

Figure 11.6 *The passage of information from the visual fields of the retina to the LGN and cortex*

information from simple cells to complex cells is depicted in Figure 11.9.

Spatial frequency

The receptive fields of simple and complex cells led to the notion of edge and bar detectors. This somewhat oversimplified account gave way to the *spatial frequency theory*, which states that cells work on the number of light/dark cycles in a receptive field. If you look at the grids in Figure 11.10 you can see high- and low-frequency grids, and how retinal ganglion cells can interpret them. These grids can be described by a sine wave. These sine waves can differ from each other in frequency (width of light/dark cycles), amplitude (the difference between the light and dark parts of the grid) and angle. The complexity of a visual stimulus can be broken down into constituent sine waves by a mathematical process called Fourier analysis.

Presentation of sine-wave grids, in the same way that Hubel and Wiesel presented light, demonstrates that cortical cells are more responsive to this type of stimulus (De Valois *et al.*, 1979). The cells of the visual cortex are thought to perform a biological version of Fourier analysis on the incoming information. This analysis turns the complex spatial

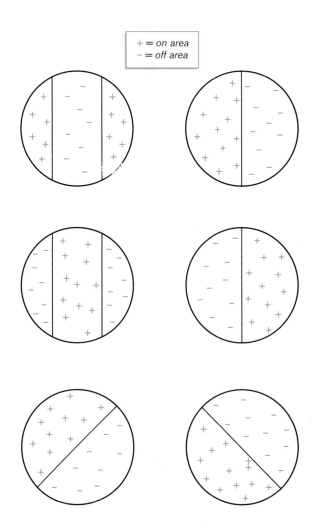

Figure 11.8 *Simple cells have zones that can be mapped into on- or off-areas*

Complex cells

Complex cells are more numerous than simple cells and respond to straight lines of a particular orientation. Complex cells differ from simple cells in three ways:

1 they are large
2 the receptive field cannot divide into on- and off-areas
3 they are binocular, whereas simple cells are monocular (one eye).

Complex cells respond to stimuli in their entire receptive field (see Figure 11.9). The incoming

> Note the receptive field does not have a division between on and off areas

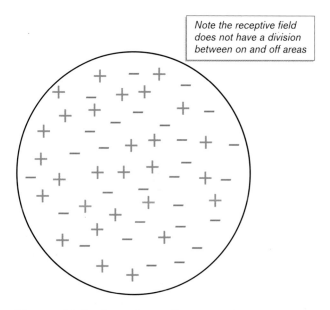

Figure 11.9 *Complex cells do not have distinct zones that are either on or off*

information into its component sine waves. Cortical cells are individually tuned for a particular orientation and frequency. Therefore different groups of cells will be active depending on the spatial frequency of the visual stimuli. The initial work by Hubel and Wiesel can be accounted for in these terms, as they presented stimuli that could be described by spatial-frequency analysis.

Hypercolumns

Cortical cells are organised in columns. Proceeding down a column, all the cells have receptive fields in the same visual field. They also respond to stimuli of the same orientation (Hubel *et al.*, 1978). Cutting across the columns, the next in line has a slightly different input from a different location of the visual field, and responds to stimuli of a slightly different orientation. Each column has a dominant input from either the left or right eye.

A summary of visual perception

The eye receives the complexities of our visual world and converts the information into neural messages for the brain to interpret. The cells of the brain work on the visual input to allow the person to have some understanding of the visual world. However, the brain does not automatically interpret the signals from the eyes. The brain has to learn to see, and without experience has difficulty interpreting the visual world (see Focus Point 11.1).

Sine waves

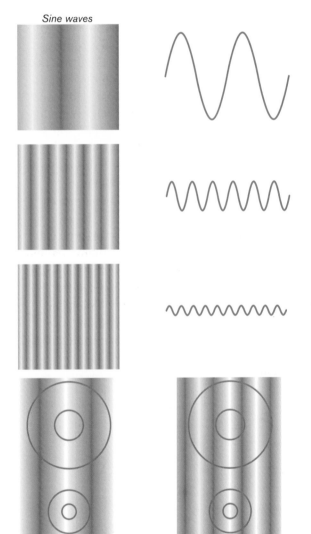

Three vertical sine-wave gratings whose spatial frequency increases from left to right. Superimposed on each are the receptive fields of three ON-centre retinal ganglion cells.

Figure 11.10 Spatial frequency: (a) the sine-wave grids can be described in terms of their spatial frequency; (b) retinal ganglion cells respond to these grids depending on the amount of light falling in an on- or off-area

FOCUS POINT 11.1

The brain requires experience to see

A recent report (Fine *et al.*, 2003) indicated how the brain requires experience to make sense of the world. At the age of three MM lost his sight; 40 years later he received a corneal and stem-cell transplant to the right eye.

After the surgery, MM was tested to see what the impact of the surgery was. He experienced difficulty in interpreting three-dimensional images, and with object and face recognition. With regard to facial recognition, he had difficulty in determining gender and facial expression, and often resorted to individual features like hair length. Functional MRI scans indicated that during such recognition tasks his lingual and fusiform gyri – areas of object and face recognition – were not as active as those of control participants. His occipital lobe (visual cortex) was activated, thus he could see but he could not interpret the image.

His motion perception was good. When he was blind he was an accomplished skier. After surgery he would close his eye because he was frightened of a collision. Two years after surgery he was able to ski with sight, but he had to use the shading patterns of the snow to determine the slope. On difficult ski runs, however, he still chose to 'go blind'.

Audition

We hear many sounds that influence our behaviour and colour our emotions – for example, 'dinner music' can increase food intake in patients with dementia (Ragneskog *et al.*, 1996). As with visual perception, auditory stimuli are converted into signals that are sent to the brain.

The ear

We also have two ears, and having two ears helps us to locate sounds in space. Just as our different eyes have slightly different images, so our ears receive sounds milliseconds apart, and this difference provides information about the location of the sound.

The part of the ear we can see is only the tip of the iceberg. The ear comprises the outer ear, the middle ear and the inner ear (see Figure 11.11). The outer ear is a funnel that collects sound waves and sends them to the middle ear. It consists of the pinna and the auditory canal.

Sound waves vibrate the structures of the middle ear. The first structure to vibrate is the eardrum (tympanic membrane). The vibrations affect a set of three bones behind the eardrum called *ossicles*. These ossicles are called the hammer (malleus), anvil (incus) and stirrup (stapes), and vibration affects each one in turn.

The stirrup communicates with the inner ear by vibrating the oval window; the oval window is a thin membrane that covers the inner ear. The vibrations are conducted to the *cochlea*, a fluid-filled tube with a membrane that is receptive to auditory information. This membrane is called the organ of corti and is made up of three subcomponents: hair cells and the tectoral and basilar membranes.

Movement of the fluid in the cochlea is transmitted to movement of the basilar membrane and the hair cells that are attached to it. The hair cells are mechanoreceptors and they turn movement into action potential.

The auditory nerve and cortex

The auditory nerve synapses with the hair cells and relays auditory signals to the brain, then enters the brain stem and divides in two. The split input projects to dorsal and lateral cochlear nuclei. The projections of the cochlear nuclei go to the *superior olivary nuclei*. This area receives and integrates signals from both ears and is used in auditory location. Other projections from the cochlear nuclei go to the *inferior colliculus* (see Figure 11.11). The superior olivary nuclei also send messages about location to the inferior colliculus.

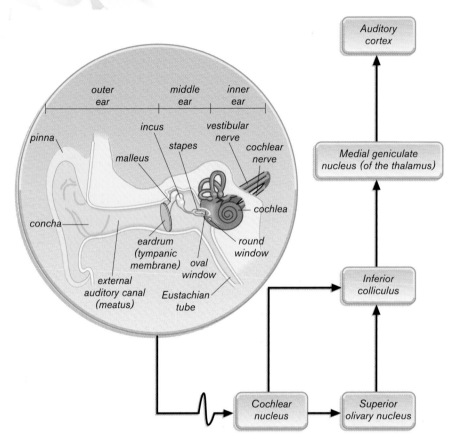

Figure 11.11 The components of the ear and the route to the auditory cortex

The inferior colliculus connects to the *medial geniculate nucleus (MGN)* of the thalamus, and the MGN then projects to the auditory cortex. The cells of the auditory cortex are in columns that respond to similar frequencies.

Olfaction
The perfume and deodorant industries are highly profitable. The increase in sales of aromatherapy products as an alternative medicine highlights the potential of olfactory mechanisms. However, scientific evidence for the effectiveness of aromatherapy is speculative (Martin, 1996). Smells are some of our most emotive stimuli, and – as many of you will know – can retrieve vivid memories (LeDoux, 1998). The smell of a hospital is often a potent cue to aid memory of previous visits.

Odours can also affect cognitive processing – for example bergamot reduces visual vigilance (Gould and Martin, 2001). The sense of smell is called olfaction.

The nasal membrane
The nose has receptors in the *olfactory epithelium,* which is located at the top of the nasal passage. An odour molecule interacts with the olfactory receptor and produces a depolarisation of the cell membrane. There are numerous receptors for different types of odours. (On a hot tube train at rush hour evolution does not appear to have done us any favours!) The action potential from the depolarisation is carried along the olfactory nerve, which then connects to the olfactory bulb, which in turn transmits impulses to the primary olfactory cortex (see Figure 11.12).

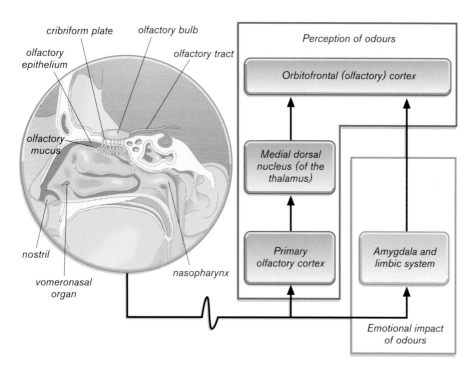

Figure 11.12 The components of the nose and the route to the olfactory cortex

Olfaction does not have to pass via the thalamus on its way to the cortex. After leaving the primary olfactory cortex there are two branches the signals can take. The first is via the amygdala, which may give rise to the emotional response to odours. The second branch is to the medial dorsal nuclei of the thalamus, and the signals from the amygdala and thalamus converge on the olfactory (orbitofrontal) cortex.

Somatosensation
Somatosensation is the process of communicating information from regions of the body, and messages are sent from the skin, muscles and joints etc. to areas of the brain.

The somatosensory system can be divided to account for external stimuli, internal influences (interoception) and where the body is positioned (proprioception).

Clearly the somatosensory system has to integrate a great deal of information, and the remainder of this section will focus solely on the sensation of touch. Touch is a useful mechanism to look at because of its involvement in pain (see also Chapter 35, pages 631–632).

The skin
Touch is mediated through mechanoreceptors responsive to physical changes in the skin. Activation of these mechanoreceptors produces a depolarisation and thus an action potential is transmitted.

The transmission of tactile stimuli to the brain
The action potentials initiated by the mechanoreceptors are sent along the axons of afferent nerves, and enter the dorsal column of the spinal cord. The part of the skin that projects to the dorsal column is segregated and called a dermatome. There are two pathways that carry different information to the brain: the anterior lateral system

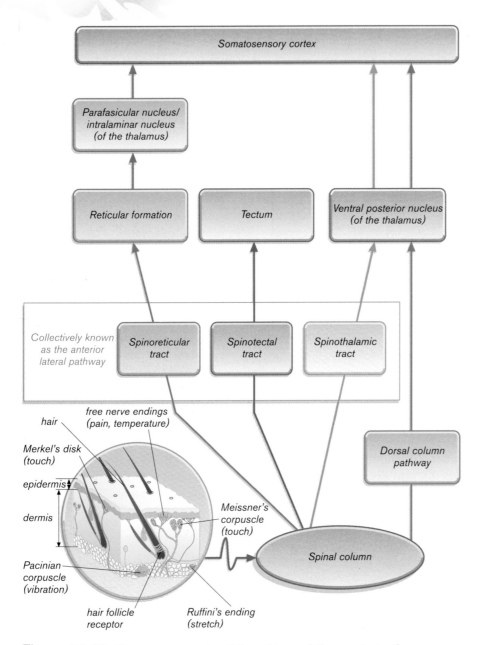

Figure 11.13 The components of the skin and the route to the somatosensory cortex

and the dorsal column system. The anterior lateral system carries thermal and *nociceptive* (pain) messages; the dorsal column system sends touch information.

The dorsal column passes to the dorsal column nuclei where the axons cross over to project to the other side of the brain. The neurons pass through the medial lemniscus where they synapse at the ventral posterior nucleus of the thalamus. From the thalamus, electrical signals are projected to the somatosensory cortex (see Figure 11.13).

Nociception: the perception of pain

The anterior lateral system is divided into three pathways: the spinothalamic pathway, the spinoreticular pathway and the spinotectal pathway. All these pathways begin at the spine and end up at different locations: the thalamus, the reticular system and the tectum respectively. The spinothalamic pathway and the spinoreticular pathway both project to the thalamus and then to the cortex.

This system sends pain information via two afferent nerves: *C-fibres and Aδ–fibres.* Aδ-fibres send fast pain messages, whereas C-fibres send slow pain messages ('ouch!' and 'ache' respectively).

The pain fibres have a diffuse set of projections that can account for perception and reflex actions, and response to pain is mediated via efferent neurons that produce a motor response.

Pain control

Nobody likes pain (except perhaps for masochists), so why should we experience it? Clearly an evolutionary explanation can account for its necessity. Think of what would happen to you if you could not experience pain – it could seriously compromise your chance of survival.

Melzack and Wall (1965) proposed the influential gate control theory of pain. They claimed that cognitive and emotional factors could, via descending brain circuits, mediate the blockade of incoming pain signals (see Chapter 35 for a more detailed account). Such descending circuits have been identified, most notably including the *periaqueductal gray (PAG)* where stimulation is analgesic. The PAG also contains receptors that modulate pain, called endorphin receptors, and that respond to endorphins – our natural painkillers. It is within this system that opiate analgesics are effective. The PAG projects to the raphe nuclei, which then project down the spinal column where the pain signal is blocked (Basbaum and Fields, 1978).

The neural circuitry of pain is complex and challenging to the neuroscientist. There are many features of pain that still require understanding.

Gustatory system

One only has to watch the plethora of celebrity cookery programmes on TV to hear about something 'tickling the taste buds'. It is the gustatory system that mediates the culinary experience.

The tongue and mouth

Taste buds are a collection of receptors configured for particular molecules. The receptors are located on papillae on the tongue, and these papillae are the taste buds.

There are four basic tastes that these receptors mediate: salty, sour, sweet and bitter.

- Salt (or sodium Na^+) passes readily through Na^+ channels and depolarises the cell – thus salt directly activates an action potential.
- Sour tastes are produced by acidic substances. Acidic substances release a hydrogen ion that blocks K^+ channels. Blockade of K^+ channels stops the release of K^+, and the ionic imbalance that is created leads to depolarisation of the cell and an action potential.
- Bitter and sweet tastes are mediated by G-protein linked receptors. On stimulation by a sweet or bitter taste, a second messenger is released before depolarisation.

Taste buds have a short existence and are constantly being replaced.

The brain

Three cranial nerves carry the signal from the taste buds. The facial nerve carries information from the anterior of the tongue, the glossopharyngeal nerve carries messages from the posterior portion of the tongue and throat, and the vagus nerve carries information from the lower part of the throat.

All three cranial nerves project to the nucleus of the solitary tract, which passes the information to the ventral posterior medial nucleus of the thalamus. The thalamic nuclei pass the signal on to the primary taste cortex in the frontal lobe.

The red hot chili pepper

Of course, taste is not the only delight for which the mouth is responsible. Capsicum (better known as the chili pepper) can produce pain. The mouth contains receptors that respond to painful stimuli and temperature. Caterina *et al.* (1997) identified the capsaicin receptor, which is heat activated. For those that like chili one of the interesting findings from this study was that the habanero pepper is the most potent. The message from these heat-sensitive receptors is transmitted via the trigeminal nerve to the brain and the pain pathways.

The vestibular system

The vestibular system detects changes in the position of the head and changes in gravity. It is located next to the cochlea in the inner ear, and comprises the utricle, the saccule and three *semicircular canals* (see Figure 11.14).

The utricle and saccule respond to static positions of the head, while the semicircular canals – which are at 90° to each other – detect motion. The receptors in the vestibular system, as in the ear, are hairs; movement of fluid acts upon these hairs and produces action potentials.

The vestibular system relays information down part of the auditory nerve and synapses at the vestibular nucleus. Projections from the vestibular nucleus are diffuse and connect with many areas of the brain (e.g. the thalamus, the cortex and other motor areas like those that innervate the eye muscles).

Motor control

The brain and the sensory modalities are not just passive recipients of incoming signals – the signals that are received are acted upon. They may be acted upon as reflexes or as motor programmes, and a large area of the brain is concerned with motor control.

Regions of the brain

There are two regions of the brain that control two motor pathways. There is a great deal of communication between the two. The *pyramidal motor system* starts at the primary motor cortex,

which is responsible for fine motor programmes. The *extrapyramidal system* projects from a number of brain regions: the cortex, cerebellum, basal ganglia, reticular formation and the thalamus.

The pyramidal system

The primary motor cortex is located in the frontal lobes. It communicates information to the secondary motor cortex. The secondary motor cortex comprises the premotor area and the *supplementary motor area (SMA)*, and the secondary motor cortex receives information from the association cortex – the latter of which receives sensory inputs.

The primary motor cortex sends messages to the muscles via efferent fibres. The muscles respond, permitting fine motor movement like writing.

The extrapyramidal system

The extrapyramidal system receives input from the primary motor cortex and the SMA, and communicates with a diverse set of structures to

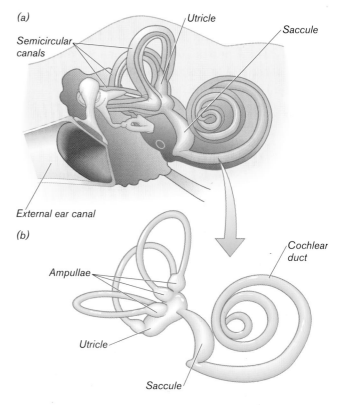

Figure 11.14 The vestibular system

control gross motor movements. There are two key areas in the extrapyramidal system: the basal ganglia and the cerebellum.

The basal ganglia

The *basal ganglia* are a group of subcortical structures that receive information from the cortex. There are a number of routes through the basal ganglia, but essentially they all start at the SMA and go back to the cortex via the thalamus. The role of the basal ganglia is to modulate the motor programmes of the pyramidal system.

APPLICATIONS BOX 11.1

Further destruction of the brain can be beneficial to patients with Parkinson's disease

We saw in Activity Box 7.2 how the architecture of the basal ganglia operates when there is a loss of DA in the substantia nigra. Most therapies for Parkinson's disease have sought to replace the deficit.

Would you consider destroying another part of the brain as a treatment?

Your answer is probably no. It is counterintuitive to treat neurodegeneration with further destruction. However, this is exactly what happens when a patient receives a pallidotomy. A pallidotomy is the destruction of the globus pallidus.

Why should this work?

Gerfen (1995) states that there is an increase in activity in the striatopallidal system (the striatum to the globus pallidus) in relation to the striatonigral system (striatum to substantia nigra) in Parkinson's disease.

If the globus pallidus is overactive in Parkinson's disease, then damping down its effect may be clinically effective. A lesion of the globus pallidus is a dramatic way of achieving silence from the globus pallidus. After pallidotomy, 81 per cent had relief from tremor and improvement

of gait (Laitinen *et al.*, 1992). Ten years after surgery there was still a marked improvement (Hariz and Bergenheim, 2001).

The improvements seen after pallidotomy may arise as a result of the patients being able to tolerate higher doses of therapeutic drugs due to a reduction of side-effects (Dogali *et al.*, 1995). Even with this consideration, namely that the pallidotomy is not a cure, the benefits remain for at least a year (Baron *et al.*, 1996).

PET measures of regional cerebral blood flow before and 17 weeks after pallidotomy show increased activity in the supplementary motor area and the premotor cortex (Grafton *et al.*, 1995). This indicates that the motor circuits of the basal ganglia are being reactivated to some extent because they are seen to be busy once again.

The implications of a dysfunction of the basal ganglia are clearly evident in Parkinson's and Huntington's disease. An increase in our understanding of the architecture of the basal ganglia has given rise to surgical treatment for Parkinson's disease (see Applications Box 11.1). Huntington's disease is a result of degeneration of the striatum (Calabresi *et al.*, 2000) and produces abnormal involuntary movements.

The cerebellum

The *cerebellum* receives sensory input and information from the pyramidal and extrapyramidal systems to coordinate responses, and is important in modifying fine motor movement, posture and the learning of new motor sequences. Damage to the cerebellum can have numerous effects on motor behaviour (such as ataxia, which is the inability to walk in a coordinated manner).

Passage of information to muscles

The aim of the descending motor pathways is to control movement, by influencing muscles. Neural messages are communicated at the *neuromuscular junction (NMJ)*, and at the NMJ the action potential releases acetylcholine (ACh). The muscles react to ACh via nicotinic and muscarinic receptors, producing further action potentials.

Returning information

The whole process of receiving sensory input and acting upon it is a sensorimotor loop. The muscles, whether of the arm or the eye, send back information that helps guide motor programmes. The information is integrated with other sensory modalities. How we interact with our environment is down to afferent and efferent control.

Summary

As an organism, we receive a wealth of information from our environment via our sensory modalities. The senses are the tools for receiving information; it is the brain that interprets the input.

However, we do not merely receive information, we also act on it. The motor system allows us to be far more than passive recipients of sensory input – it enables us to interact with the environment. Between the perceptual systems and the motor systems there is a great deal of cross-communication.

Learning outcomes

When you have completed this chapter you should be able to:

- describe the visual system in detail
- describe the auditory, somatosensory, gustatory and olfactory systems
- provide an account of pain
- describe the neural mechanisms underlying motor response.

Key Terms

Aδ-fibres
Amacrine cells
Basal ganglia
Binocular vision
Bipolar cells
Blind spot
Cerebellum
C-fibres
Cochlea
Complex cells
Convergence
Extrapyramidal system
Horizontal cells
Inferior colliculus
Lateral geniculate nucleus (LGN)
Lateral inhibition
Magnocellular layer
Medial geniculate nucleus (MGN)
Neuromuscular junction (NMJ)
Nociceptive
Olfactory epithelium
Opsins
Optic chiasm
Optic nerve
Ossicles
Parvocellular layer
Periaqueductal gray (PAG)
Photoreceptors
Pyramidal motor system
Retina
Retinal ganglion cells
Rhodopsin
Semicircular canals
Simple cells
Spatial frequency theory
Superior olivary nuclei
Supplementary motor area (SMA)

Further reading

Bruce, V., Green, P. R. and Georgeson, M. A. (1996) *Visual Perception: Physiology, Psychology, and Ecology.* Hove: Psychology Press.

Farah, M. J. (2000) *The Cognitive Neuroscience of Vision.* Oxford: Blackwell.

Jeannerod, M. (1997) *The Cognitive Neuroscience of Action.* Oxford: Blackwell.

Pickles, J. R. (1988) *Introduction to the Physiology of Hearing* (2nd edn). New York: Academic Press.

Roberts, D. (2002) *Signals and Perception: The Fundamentals of Human Sensation.* Palgrave Macmillan.

Web links

Centre for the Neural Basis of Hearing: http://www.mrc-cbu.cam.ac.uk/cnbh/

Thalamus and perception at Washington University at St Louis: http://thalamus.wustl.edu

Pain at University of Pennsylvania: www.uphs.upenn.edu/tbilab/rehab/

Pain Pathways: www2.utmb.edu/acelab/Directory/Pain/PainCourse/PainPathways.htm

Bay Area Pain Medical Associates: http://www.bayareapainmedical.com/

Sectionthree

Christopher Sterling

Cognitive Psychology

12	Perception	180
13	Attention	204
14	Memory	220
15	Language	246
16	Thinking and reasoning	263

12

Perception

Route map of the chapter

The aim of this chapter is to introduce students to some of the important issues in the psychology of perception. It begins with a discussion of the major issues to do with the perception of form. These are referred to as the figure–ground problem, the perceptual constancies and visual illusions. Next we look at how we perceive depth, and the three sections after that deal with the perception and recognition of patterns and objects. These are followed by a discussion of bottom-up and top-down processes in perception. The chapter concludes with a description of some of the processes involved in speech perception.

Introduction

Imagine you are looking out from a high building and that a large part of a town is spread out in front of you. The buildings are crowded together but you have no problem separating them from each other. You know which are close by and which are far away. People are walking on the pavement below, and you know that they are people even though they are as small as ants. Streams of cars and buses drive by and even from your position you have no trouble distinguishing between them – in fact, you can easily recognise different makes of car. A person walking by looks familiar. You recognise their walk and build. They look up and you confirm that it is a colleague.

How does your brain work all this out from such a crowded scene? This chapter begins to explore some of the processes that comprise our perception and recognition of the world.

We have five senses: sight, sound, touch, smell and taste. In this chapter we are concerned mainly with visual perception and the role it plays in cognition. We shall deal briefly with the perception of speech, which is an intriguing aspect of auditory perception. The other sensory modalities are covered in Section 2 of this book, on psychobiology, partly because most of the research in these modalities is on sensation and partly because it is only in the realms of vision and speech perception that the complexities of perception have been investigated extensively.

Researchers distinguish between the *distal stimulus* and the *proximal stimulus*. The distal stimulus is what is out there in the world – the object you are looking at. The proximal stimulus is the pattern of stimulation that hits the retina. While the distal stimulus is invariant, or constant, the proximal stimulus varies, often quite considerably. The book you're looking at remains constant and unchanging regardless of when you look at it, but the image it casts on your retina will change with angle of view, with distance from it, and with changes in light intensity and colour. A major issue for perception is how your perception remains constant when the proximal stimulation is so variable.

Researchers also distinguish between *sensation* and *perception*. Generally, sensation is concerned with the quality of stimulation. How bright is a light? What colour is an object? Is this weight heavier than that weight? Can you see the gap between those two lines or do they appear as one line? Early researchers were very concerned with these kinds of questions and developed a discipline called *psychophysics*.

The goal of psychophysics is to measure the psychological effects of the physical stimulus. One aspect of this is concerned with determining *sensory thresholds*. How bright does a light have to be before it's detected? How loud does a sound have to be before it's heard? Psychophysics is also concerned with how we respond to change in sensory stimulation. If the intensity of a light (measured in physical units) is doubled, will you see it as being twice as bright? What is the smallest change in volume of a sound that you can detect? Investigations of all these questions have to do with the relationship between the physical stimulation and the psychological sensation (see Chapter 11).

Perception is concerned with more complex questions. How do we separate one object from another when they're close together or overlapping? How do we see the shape of an object? How do we perceive the three-dimensional nature of the world when the image falling on the retina is two-dimensional? Does our past experience affect how we see the world? These questions will be addressed in the course of this chapter.

Figure 12.1 *The perception of figure and ground: a crowded scene is viewed as a collection of objects, separated from each other and from the background*
Source: Winston, 1970

The perception of form

Figure–ground separation

No matter how crowded a scene, we always seem able to separate the objects in it from each other and from the background. This is called *figure–ground separation*. We take our ability to do this for granted but a little reflection reveals that it is not a trivial matter. The Gestalt psychologists Koffka (1886–1941), Kohler (1887–1968) and Wertheimer (1880–1943) made up a group of German practitioners who emigrated to the USA before the Second World War. They identified several principles, or *laws of pragnanz*, that contribute to our understanding of how this is done. These psychological principles identify cues that help the brain to put the pieces of a visual scene together in an appropriate way. If you look at Figure 12.1 you can see separate forms, not just a random collection of lines.

One of these principles is the *proximity principle*.

This holds that surfaces or edges that are close together are more likely to belong to the same object than those that are far apart. This can be seen in both Figure 12.1 and 12.2b.

Another is the *closure principle*. This refers to the fact that we tend to complete incomplete forms and generally 'fill in the gaps'. In Figure 12.2a you can see complete figures rather than incomplete ones.

A third principle is the *similarity principle*. This is where similar parts of a form are more likely to be perceived as belonging together than parts that are dissimilar. In Figure 12.2c you can see vertical bars, not horizontal ones.

The final principle is the *continuity principle*. We tend to group stimuli into forms that follow continuous lines or patterns. So we tend to see Figure 12.2d as being composed of two intersecting lines rather than as two angular patterns.

181

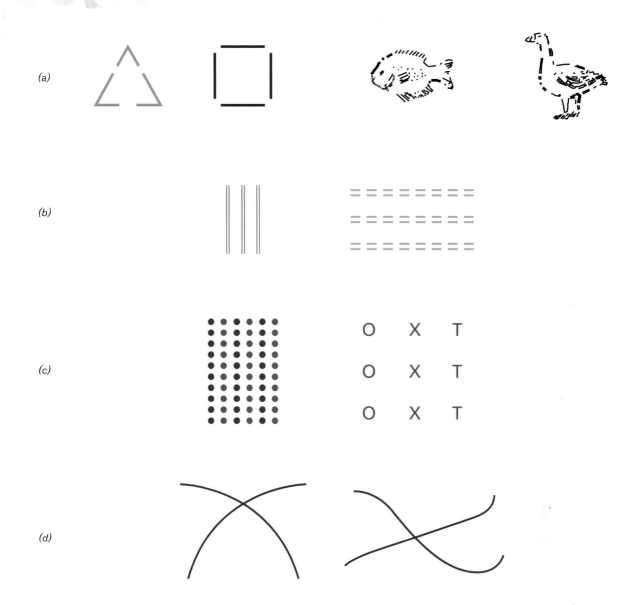

Figure 12.2 Illustrations of the laws of pragnanz: (a) closure; (b) proximity; (c) similarity; (d) continuity
Source: Anderson, 1995b: 46

The constancies

An important characteristic of perception is the tendency to see shape and size, as well as brightness and colour, as being constant across changes in the proximal stimulus. This psychological invariance across physical changes is referred to as 'the constancies'. *Shape constancy* refers to the phenomenon of the shape of an object remaining constant, even though the outline it throws on to the retina depends on the angle from which it is seen.

ACTIVITY BOX 12.1

Shape constancy

Pick up a book. Hold it with the cover upright and facing you. You will agree that it is a rectangular shape with two long sides (of the same length) and two shorter sides (of the same length). The angles between the sides are right angles.

Now start turning and twisting the book through different angles and keep looking at the cover. You will see that opposite sides are no longer the same length and that the angles between sides are not right angles. The shape cast on your retina is no longer rectangular. However, at no time do you consider the shape of the book as having changed, regardless of the shape being cast on the retina. This is shape constancy.

The size of the shape on the retina depends on the size of the object. The bigger the object the bigger the retinal size.

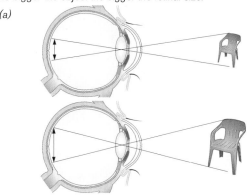

(a)

The size of the shape on the retina also depends on distance from the eye. A close object has a bigger retinal size than a distant object.

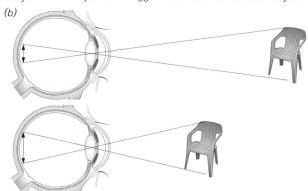

(b)

Figure 12.3 Retinal size as a function of (a) object size and (b) distance

Another constancy is *size constancy*. This is the phenomenon that an object is perceived to be a constant size, regardless of how close or far away it is. This should not happen because a cue to the size of an object is the size of the shape it casts on the retina. A small *retinal size* indicates a small object, and a large retinal size a large object. Figure 12.3a illustrates this.

However, retinal size also depends on distance. A chair ten metres away casts a much smaller shape on the retina than the same chair five metres away. Figure 12.3b illustrates this. So distance also affects retinal size. If retinal size was the only cue, we would perceive the chairs as being of different sizes. But we don't. We perceive them as being the same size. This is size constancy.

Size constancy has been explained by the *size–distance invariance hypothesis* (Kilpatrick and Ittleson, 1953). This says that for a given retinal size (i.e. proximal stimulus) the perceived size is proportional to the perceived distance. In perceiving size we take account of both the retinal size of the object and the perceived distance of the object. So if we perceive it to be far away we then compensate for the fact that the retinal size is small and perceive it as

being of a normal size. If we perceive it as being close then we again compensate for retinal size, but in the opposite direction.

The Ames room (see Figure 12.4) provides a startling demonstration of how perception can be manipulated and size constancy destroyed. The Ames room is built so that it gives the impression of being a perfectly ordinary rectangular room to someone looking in from the outside. In fact, though, it is built so that the two distant corners, which seem equally far away, are not. One is much closer than the other. This distortion is disguised by other distortions such as a sloping floor. The end result of these distortions is that the room seems perfectly normal but is not. In particular the two distant corners seem equally far away but are not.

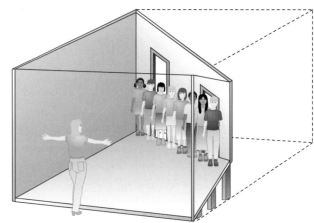

Figure 12.4   The Ames room: deliberate distortions in construction produce an illusion of size differences
Source: Sdorow and Rickabaugh, 2002: 153

The experimenter then introduces people of equal size into the room, one in each of the distant corners. The person in the closer corner seems much bigger than the person in the farther corner because he or she casts a much bigger retinal image. If the room wasn't distorted, the fact that he or she is closer would be taken into account and size constancy would hold. However, the room has been distorted to make the viewer think that the two people are equally far away. As a result, size constancy breaks down and the two people are seen as being of different sizes.

Other constancies are *brightness constancy* and *colour constancy*. A white surface, such as a white shirt, is seen as white, regardless of whether it is looked at in the sunlight or a darkened shop. This is brightness constancy. The fact that it does vary in brightness with the intensity of light can be seen by looking at it through a tube. Under these conditions it goes from a bright white to a dull grey, depending on the lighting conditions. This suggests that brightness constancy is dependent on the context of the stimulus. When there are other objects for comparison brightness constancy holds, but when the basis for comparison is removed the constancy breaks down.

Colour constancy is very similar. A red object, such as a dress, continues to be perceived as red even

though the brightness and/or colour of the ambient light may vary. The effect of context can again be seen by looking at the surface through a tube. Constancy breaks down.

The constancies provide evidence that our perception of the world is not dependent only on the relevant aspect of the stimulus. It depends on other aspects of the stimulus such as its perceived distance, its context and our knowledge of the world. We know a face doesn't change size and we know that a book doesn't change shape. This knowledge mediates the information from our senses, which is telling the brain that the size and shape of an object are changing. Consequently, the percept (the product of perception) remains relatively constant.

Visual illusions

Visual illusions offer powerful examples of how perception can be wrong. Even knowing about an illusion and trying to counter it offers no protection. In this section we have selected two for closer examination: the Ponzo illusion and the Muller–Lyer illusion.

In the *Ponzo illusion* (see Figure 12.5a) the two horizontal lines are exactly the same length (measure them with a ruler) even though the lower line appears to be much shorter than the higher one. In

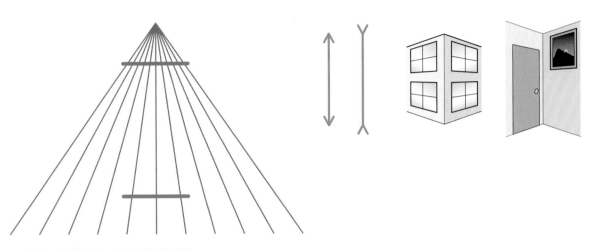

Figure 12.5 *(a) The Ponzo illusion – the two horizontal bars are seen as being of different lengths when they are the same length; (b) the Muller–Lyer Illusion – the two vertical lines are seen as being of different lengths when they are actually the same.*
Source: (a) Sdorow and Rickabaugh, 2002: 154;
(b) Sdorow and Rickabaugh, 2002: 153

the Muller–Lyer illusion (Figure 12.5b) the two vertical lines are again exactly the same length but one line (with the diverging lines at each end) appears longer than the other (with the converging lines at each end). Gregory (1972; 1980) has argued that these illusions can be explained by assuming that previous knowledge of three-dimensional objects is misapplied to these two-dimensional patterns.

In the Ponzo illusion linear perspective is misapplied to the display. The two lines have the same retinal size so they should be the same size. However, the linear perspective created by the converging lines suggests that the top line is further away. If it has the same retinal size but is further away it must be bigger – that is, the illusion occurs because the perceptual system is mistakenly taking apparent distance in account.

In the *Muller–Lyer illusion* Gregory uses the same kind of argument. The left line looks like the outside corners of a building while the right line looks like

the 'inside' corners. The inside corners are, in a sense, further away than the outside corners. So the right line is perceived to be further away than the left line. The two lines have the same retinal size but one is perceived (mistakenly) as further away than the other. Thus the line perceived as being further away must be bigger. Illusions have been used by researchers such as Gregory to argue that perception is influenced by factors other than the stimulus – in these cases, by perceived distance and previous experience.

Depth perception

Depth perception is concerned with how we perceive the three-dimensional nature of the world. Objects are three-dimensional. They have depth. They are also located at different distances from us. The problem lies in the fact that the image the world throws on our retina is two dimensional, flat, but we perceive the world in three dimensions. How do we do this?

Section 3
Cognitive Psychology

Retinal disparity

Focus on a finger close to your face. Shut one eye and look at it with only your open eye.
Remember the view you're getting of your finger. Now look at the finger with only your other eye. Note that this view of your finger is very different from the previous view. This difference is retinal disparity.

Now move the finger away from you and repeat these actions. As the distance increases the retinal disparity decreases.

Knowledge of the cues we use to perceive depth has accumulated over thousands of years. This accumulation is evident in the work of artists from Ancient Egypt to the present day. Psychologists are relative newcomers to this area of perception. In general, perception of depth depends on two types of cue: *binocular cues*, which depend on information from two eyes, and *monocular cues*, which depend on information from one eye. It also comes from the motion of the observer.

Binocular cues

One type of binocular cue is *retinal disparity*. We have two eyes, spaced apart by a few inches. Because

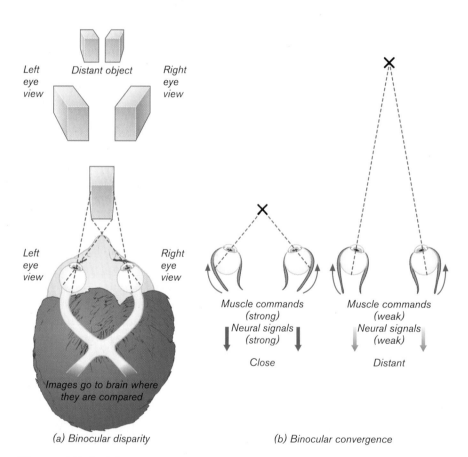

Left eye view   Distant object   Right eye view

Left eye view   Right eye view

Images go to brain where they are compared

(a) Binocular disparity

Muscle commands (strong)
Neural signals (strong)
Close

Muscle commands (weak)
Neural signals (weak)
Distant

(b) Binocular convergence

Figure 12.6 (a) Retinal disparity: the difference between what each eye sees is a cue to distance.
(b) Binocular convergence: a close object elicits stronger neural signals than a distant object.
Source: Sternberg, 1999: 122

of this separation each eye gets a slightly different view of the world. There is a disparity, or difference, between the two retinal images. The crucial fact is that when an object is far away the disparity is small but when the object is close it is large (see Figure 12.6(a)). So the degree of disparity between the two eyes is a cue to how far away the object is.

A second binocular cue is *binocular convergence*. When the two eyes are focused on a distant object the eye muscles are less stressed than when they're focused on a near object. The difference in muscle tension is a cue as to the distance of the object. Distant objects cause less tension than near objects, see Fig. 12.6(b) (see Activity Box 12.3).

Monocular cues

Some cues to depth depend on only one eye for their effectiveness. Several cues have been identified. One is *interposition*. The relative distance of two objects is indicated by the fact that one object obscures the view of the second object because it is interposed between you, the viewer, and the second object. The obscured object is further away. This is illustrated in the photograph opposite. All the mountains are far away but you know that some are closer than others because the closer ones partly obscure the more distant ones.

A second cue to distance is *texture gradient*. The term refers to the fact that the texture or graininess of a scene depends on distance. The texture of the foreground is very grainy, with large grains that are quite far apart. As you recede from the foreground the texture becomes less grainy, with smaller grains that are closer together. Thus the graininess, or texture, is a cue to distance from the viewer. In the photo on the next page, you can see that the graininess resulting from people's heads in the foreground is coarser than that resulting from heads in the distance. Texture changes with distance from the viewer.

A third cue is *linear perspective*. This is a reference to the way that parallel lines converge as they recede into the distance. It is very evident in railway lines receding into the distance. Less obviously, it's also present if you look at a rectangular box with the long sides pointing away from you.

ACTIVITY BOX 12.3

Binocular convergence

Focus on a distant object. The muscles responsible for swivelling the eyes in their sockets are relaxed and there's no feeling of strain. Now focus on a very near object (a finger inches from your eyes). Hold the focus for as long as you can. It becomes evident quite soon that the eye muscles are being stressed.

Although this activity exaggerates the difference, it does convey the idea that the degree to which the eye muscles are stressed is a cue to the distance of the object.

The retinal size of an object is also a cue to distance. We discussed it earlier when talking about size constancy. An object that is close by throws a larger image on the retina than an object that is far away. The relative retinal size is therefore a cue to the distance of the object.

Motion cues

Another set of cues to depth comes from the motion of the viewer. The first of these is *motion parallax*, which is only of use when you, the viewer, are

Interposition: the relative distance of the mountains in this scene is gauged by interposition; closer mountains partly obscure more distant ones.

Texture gradient: relative distance from the viewer can be gauged by texture gradient; the 'grain' caused by people's heads becomes finer with distance from the viewer.

moving. When you look out of a moving train you see that some objects are moving across your line of vision much faster than others. The 'faster' objects (e.g. the fencing and telegraph poles by the railway line) are those that are close by. The 'slower' objects (e.g. cows in a field, farm buildings) are those that are far away. This disparity in their relative movement is

a cue that one is further away from you than the other. The faster one is nearer than the slower one.

Another motion cue to depth comes from the *optical flow pattern* (Gibson, 1950). James J. Gibson was an American psychologist who was an officer in the Army Air Corps during the Second World War. He developed his ideas while making training films for pilots (Reed and Jones, 1982). The following example, taken from Gibson (1950), reflects his background.

Look at Figure 12.7 and imagine yourself in a plane making a pass over the runway, heading towards a focal point on the distant horizon. As you speed towards this point the visual field ahead expands outwards from the focal point on the horizon. The environment is 'flowing' past you and the speed at which it flows depends on the distance from the focal point. This is shown by the length of the arrows. The parts of the ground and sky closest to you are moving the fastest, while the parts near the focal point (and furthest away) are moving the slowest. There is actually no motion at the focal point itself. So the optical flow of different parts of the environment as you move forward are cues to depth and distance.

Linear perspective: the parallel lines of the railway (a) and the sides of the boxes (b) appear to converge with distance from the viewer.

Pattern recognition

The laws of pragnanz tell us how we segregate objects. The constancies tell us that our perceptions are relatively invariant, but illusions remind us that our perceptions can be mistaken. How do we recognise a particular form for what it is (the letter A, a book, a picture of a tree)? In this section we consider several theories of *pattern recognition* Implicit in these theories is that pattern recognition is a two-part process. First, there are perceptual processes that analyse the input and produce a percept. Second, there are recognition processes that identify the percept by looking for a match in memory. Evidence for this distinction comes from visual object agnosia (see Focus Point 12.1).

Template matching

An intuitively appealing explanation of how we recognise patterns is offered by *template matching theory* (Selfridge and Neisser, 1960). This argues that we store templates of the various patterns we come across. So, for example, we have templates for each letter of the alphabet and each number (0–9). Whenever we come across a letter or number, the percept is compared with the store of templates, and recognition occurs when a match is found. Figure 12.8a illustrates how an input 'A' would match a template 'A' in memory. However, Figures 12.8b, 12.8c and 12.8d show how a match could fail because of a change in position (b), of size (c) or of orientation (d).

Although appealing, this theory runs into a number of problems. First, it implies a huge number of templates: one for each and every pattern we come across. This suggests a huge load on memory. However, we know that memory does have an enormous capacity and so this may not be a problem. Second, it implies a very time-consuming process in which each input is compared with thousands, even millions, of templates until a match is found. This is inconsistent with recognition being virtually instantaneous. However, Neisser, Novick and Lazar (1963) showed that participants could search for up to ten target letters in an array of letters as quickly as they could search for one letter. This suggests that comparisons between the letters in the

Figure 12.7 *The optical flow pattern of a pilot flying towards the horizon: cues to depth and distance come from the relative speed at which different parts of the environment flow towards and past the flyer; distant points flow more slowly than nearer points*
Source: Gibson, 1950: 125

array and the templates can be done in parallel (with several comparisons made simultaneously) rather than in serial (one comparison at a time) so this may not be a problem.

However, a serious problem is that stimuli like the letter A can be written in different fonts, handwriting styles, sizes and orientations (see Figure 12.9). We can't possibly have a template for each variant. The problem can be partly overcome by a 'clean-up' of the stimulus in pre-recognition processing. This would standardise the stimulus in terms of the font, the size, the orientation and the general appearance of the stimulus. This prepared stimulus would then be ready for template matching. However, there is a problem with this clean-up proposal (see Activity Box 12.4, p.194).

The logical problem posed by pre-recognition clean-up can be reduced by context in some, but not all, circumstances. You can see from Figure 12.12 (p. 194) that the letter between C and T could be an H or an A. The context resolves the ambiguity.

Visual object agnosia

Agnosia means not knowing. Object agnosia means not knowing objects. *Visual object agnosia* means not knowing objects presented visually. Some people with brain damage suffer from visual object agnosia. The precise nature of the problem varies from patient to patient (people don't have head injuries to suit the convenience of neuropsychologists!), but a useful distinction has been made between *apperceptive agnosia* and *associative agnosia* (Lissauer, 1890–1988). This distinction reflects a distinction in normal object recognition between perceptual processes and memory processes. The end result of perceptual processes is the percept: a representation of the object but no knowledge of what it is. For recognition to occur, this percept has to be used in a memory search to find an appropriate match.

In apperceptive agnosia the person cannot recognise familiar objects (tables, chairs, books etc.) because of a perceptual impairment. This is reflected in the person's difficulty or inability in copying a simple line drawing. She or he can, however, draw the object from memory. In some cases she or he can't point out a shape in a busy picture or recognise an object from an unusual angle (a bus seen from above) or in poor lighting conditions (heavy shadows). Processes that act together to produce a percept have broken down.

However, the person can recognise these same objects when presented through the other sensory modalities (i.e. recognising a dog from its bark, or a book from its touch).

H.J., a patient reported by Humphreys (1999), couldn't recognise his wife when she was standing in front of him but could recognise her when she moved or when she spoke. This indicates that fundamental information about the object is present in memory but is not accessible through vision because visual perception is impaired. For an interesting and readable account of H.J., see Humphreys (1999).

In associative agnosia the failure to recognise common objects occurs because of a memory problem. The perceptual processes that produce the percept are intact. An ideal characterisation would be like someone with normal perception looking at an object they had never seen before. The person is able to copy simple line drawings and can match copies of the same picture but they can't draw the object from memory. In some cases the person is able to recognise the object through other modalities because the damage is to a connection between perception and memory. In other cases the damage is more widespread and the information is lost to all modalities. For a readable account of an associative agnosic called Dennis, see Riddoch and Humphreys (1992).

Feature theory

An attractive replacement for template theory is *feature detection theory* (Neisser, 1967). According to this theory, each pattern can be specified in terms of a list of distinctive features which together make up the pattern. There is a detector for every feature.

You can see from Table 12.1 that patterns, letters in this case, can be specified in terms of a list of features. This list can then be compared with feature lists stored in memory (one for each pattern), and when the input list matches a memory list the pattern is recognised. There is very good biological evidence for the existence of *feature detectors* in the visual system. Hubel and Wiesel (1963) and other researchers have identified single cells that respond selectively to stimulation from edges, bars and corners that are in particular orientations and in particular parts of the visual field (see Research Methods Box 12.1, p. 195).

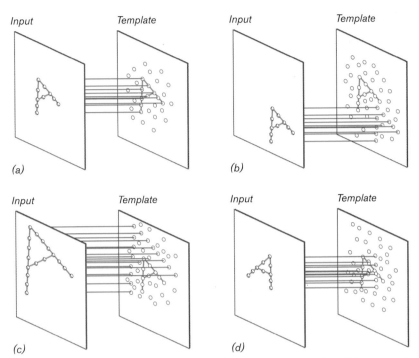

Problems of template-matching. (a) shows an input that matches the template; (b) a mismatch due to change of position; (c) a change of size; (d) of orientation

Figure 12.8 Template matching: the pattern, a letter A, matches (a) or fails to match a stored representation of A depending on the (b) position, (c) size and (d) orientation of the pattern
Source: Neisser, 1964: 51

TABLE 12.1

DISTINCTIVE FEATURES FOR SOME LETTERS OF THE ALPHABET

Letter	Possible features
A	— / \ ∧
K	I ⟍ ⊬⊩
Z	⁻ / ⁊ L

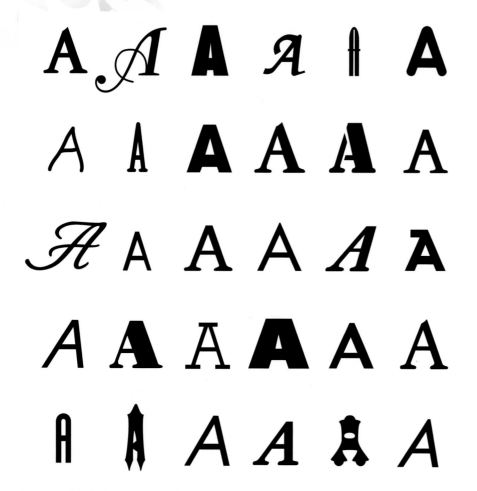

Figure 12.9 Variations of the letter A: these examples of the letter A are very different from each other but all recognisable as As; they illustrate a problem faced by template-matching models of pattern recognition
Source: Solso, 1998: 108

Another source of evidence for the existence of features comes from *visual search* experiments. Neisser (1964) showed that looking for a target letter that consists of straight lines and sharp angles (e.g. Z) in an array of similar letters (e.g. A, H, N, L, T) is harder than looking for it in an array of letters with more curved features (e.g. C, Q, G, O, S). You can confirm this for yourself by doing the exercise in Activity Box 12.5 (p. 197). In the first case the features of the target and background are less similar than in the second case.

While the idea of feature detectors is both plausible and supported, it is not clear how the features are put together. A feature list consists only of the features present. It does not contain information about the spatial relationship between the features. The same feature list can be put together in several ways (see Figure 12.15). A structural description of the percept is necessary to specify how the features are to be combined.

Face recognition

A special case of pattern recognition is face recognition. How do we recognise familiar faces? Are familiar and unfamiliar faces processed differently? These and other questions have received (at least) partial answers from an influential model by Bruce and Young (1986). A particularly interesting aspect of the model is that it has been developed largely on the basis of neuropsychological research and the use of 'double dissociation' methodology (see Chapter 14).

How do we recognise a familiar face? According to the model there is an initial stage of perceptual processing that produces a percept that is expression-independent (i.e. the expression on the face doesn't influence recognition). This percept goes through to a 'face recognition unit'. There is a unit for every face you know. If processing stopped at this point you would be left with a feeling of familiarity but nothing else – you wouldn't know anything about the person. The information from here then feeds through to a 'person identity unit', which does have information about who the person is (i.e. a lecturer from college). Again, if processing stopped here this is all you would know – you wouldn't know his/her name. Finally, this information feeds through to the 'name unit', where the person's name is available.

Harder evidence for the model comes from studies of head-injured patients with prosopagnosia (an inability to recognise familiar faces). First, there is evidence that some prosopagnosia is due to a perceptual deficit (in the perceptual processing unit) rather than to a memory deficit (in the face recognition, person identity or name units).

One patient, called Unteroffizier S. and who was prosopagnosic after being wounded in the head during the Second World War, said that the faces of people he looked at all looked the same and like flat white oval plates with emphatically dark eyes (Bodamer, 1947, cited in Ellis and

Young, 1995). He didn't recognise his mother in a chance meeting, or his own face when he and several others were looking in a mirror! On the other hand, a patient called Mr W. had no significant perceptual impairment. He could copy faces, identify gender and age, and classify expressions correctly. Nevertheless, when their hairstyles were covered up, he couldn't identify the faces of famous people, or himself, his doctor or a patient he was friendly with (Bruyer, LaTerre, Seron, *et al.*, 1983, cited in Ellis and Young, 1995). His problem lay in the face recognition units and stages following.

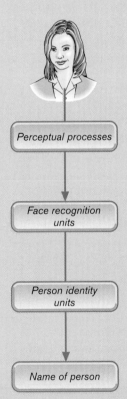

Perceptual processes

Face recognition units

Person identity units

Name of person

Figure 12.10 Part of Bruce and Young's (1986) model of face recognition: after a perceptual analysis, face recognition, person identity and name units are activated by the input, resulting in full recognition

Evidence that naming a person is a separate ability comes from a patient, G.L., who when given 20 photographs of familiar people could describe who they were (e.g. politician) but couldn't name them.

Finally there is some evidence that the ability to recognise faces is distinct from the ability to recognise other objects. De Renzi (1986) reports a patient who had severe prosopagnosia but could recognise other things, such as his belongings, his handwriting, his own car in the car park and Italian coins from other coins.

Object recognition

Patterns are two-dimensional. Objects are three-dimensional. While the basic idea of a feature carries over very well to object recognition, the theory needs modification to cope with the three-dimensional world. Marr (1982) proposed a theory that was specified in sufficient detail to be simulated by a computer. According to Marr the brain computes depth in three stages. First, a 2-D 'primal sketch' based on basic sensory information which is two-dimensional in nature and has information about lines, corners and regions of similarity (similar areas that, therefore, probably belong to the same object). It then creates a 2.5-D representation, which has some depth information such as texture gradients and binocular cues as well as the orientation of the object. The final stage is a 3-D model, which represents the three-dimensional nature of the object and the spatial relationships between the objects in the scene.

This theory influenced Biederman's (1987) *recognition-by-components theory*. The basis of this theory is the idea that objects consist of combinations of *geons*. Geons are three-dimensional building blocks, 'such as bricks, cylinders, wedges, cones and their curved axis counterparts' (Biederman, 1987: 314). There are a total of 36.

In the same sense that letters of the alphabet combine to make words, or features combine to make letters, so geons combine to form objects (see Figure 12.16). Thus object recognition consists of (i) segmenting the object into its component geons, (ii) identifying these geons and (iii) specifying the relationship between them for the given object. This structural description is matched to the contents of memory (also consisting of the same kind of information) and when a match is found the object is recognised.

You can see that the theory is very similar to feature theory, but translated to three dimensions. The relationship between features and geons is also plausible. Geons are themselves composed of

---

ACTIVITY BOX 12.4

The problem with the clean-up proposal

Question: What is wrong with the proposal that poor As can be cleaned up to produce a standard A, which can then be compared with templates until a match is found?

Answer: The problem is a logical one. How can pre-recognition processing prepare an A properly for matching until it knows that it's an A?! A badly written 4 could be mistakenly cleaned up and presented as an A. Mistaken identification is not a rare phenomenon. Indeed people often depend on the similarity between a 4 and an A to personalise their car number plates (see Figure 12.11).

Figure 12.11 A personalised number plate

THE C⊣T

Figure 12.12 Letter identification and context

RESEARCH METHODS BOX 12.1

Biological evidence for feature detectors

Technological advances in the 1950s and 1960s allowed scientists to measure the firings of single cells in the brain. David Hubel and Torsten Wiesel were awarded the Nobel Prize for their work on this in 1981. (See Chapter 11 of this book for further details of the biological aspects of their work.)

Hubel and Wiesel's research (1963; 1968; 1979) measured single cell responses in the visual cortex. They found several types of cell. First, there were *simple cells*. Each simple cell responded to line segments (i) in a particular orientation in (ii) a particular area of the retina (i.e. the cell's receptive field). Each simple cell is therefore a detector for a very specific stimulus in a very specific location (see Fig. 12.13).

Further research revealed that several simple cells fed into a complex cell. Each *complex cell* responded to line segments in (i) a particular orientation (ii) located anywhere in the *receptive fields* of the inputting simple cells. Later research (e.g. De Valois and De Valois, 1980) identified *hypercomplex cells*, which responded to specific stimuli such as corners and angles. This neurophysiological research provides strong support for the notion of feature detectors.

the parts of a face – the nose, ears, eyes etc. – was clearly superior when these were presented as parts of a face than when presented in isolation. More detail was needed when they were presented out of context (see Figure 12.17).

The strongest, clearest evidence for context effects on perception comes from studies of word recognition. These have shown that identifying a letter (e.g. k) is easier when it is presented as part of a word (e.g. work) than either in isolation (i.e. ___k) or as one of a string of random letters (e.g. rwok). This is called the *word superiority effect* and it shows that recognition of the letter is being affected by knowledge of the word in which it appears (see Research Methods Box 12.2, p.197).

Bottom-up and top-down processes

An important debate about the nature of perception began in the middle of the last century. On one side were those such as J.J. Gibson, who argued that perception was *direct*. On the other side were equally eminent psychologists such as Bruner (1957), Gregory (1966) and Rock (1983), who argued that it was *constructive*. More current terms are *bottom-up processing* (*direct perception*) and *top-down processing* (*constructive perception*).

David Hubel and Torsten Wiesel, Nobel Laureates (1981) for their discoveries concerning information processing in the visual system.

features such as edges, corners, curves, and so on. The major problem with recognition-by-components theory is that there are many objects in the natural world that are not easily specified in terms of geons. A bush, the sea and a beach are three examples. Neither does it address the question of how we recognise specific examples of an object (the chair in my living room) or a face (my friend John). It does, however, go some considerable way to explaining how we perceive the three-dimensional world.

Context

The context in which an object is seen can affect its perception. Palmer (1975) showed that recognition of

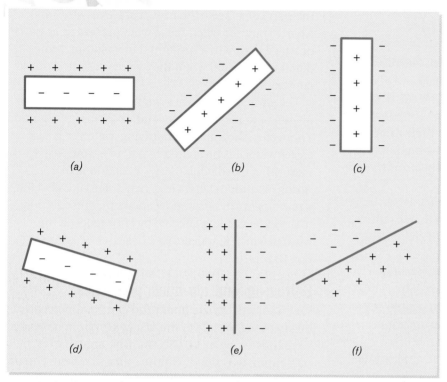

*Figure 12.13 Receptive field of single cells in the cortex: areas marked + are excited by stimulation; areas marked − are inhibited by stimulation; in combination they respond to lines and bars falling on the retina
Source: Kalat, 2001: 170*

The bottom-up view argues that perceptual processes are driven entirely by the stimulus or input. There is enough information in the stimulus for us to perceive the complexities of the world without having to involve higher cognitive processes such as inference and knowledge of the world. The top-down view, in contrast, argues that the stimulus provides the basic working material, but that perceptual processes are heavily influenced by these higher cognitive processes. According to this view, perception involves forming hypotheses about the percept using the sensory data as well as knowledge and inference. Hence the term constructive. Another way of conceptualising the two views is to say that the percept is stimulus driven or is conceptually driven. Reviewing the chapter we find evidence for both points of view.

Gibson's work on depth perception (1950; 1966) is a good example of his theory of direct perception. He argued that all the information we need to perceive depth is present in the stimulus. Linear perspective and texture gradient are properties of depth in the same way that colour is a property of objects. They are invariants of a stimulus involving depth. Similarly, the pattern of optical flow remains the same whenever an observer is moving towards a point. It is an invariant of perception. The existence of invariants is, for Gibson, clear evidence that perception is direct.

The bottom-up approach is also implicit in some of the other theories we have reviewed. In template matching the stimulus is matched to templates in memory and whether a match is obtained depends on the stimulus. Feature theory certainly focuses on

ACTIVITY BOX 12.5

Visual search

Look at Figure 12.14 and, using a watch with a second hand, time how long it takes you to find the letter Z in column 1. Note down the time.

(a)	(b)
ODUGQR	IVMXEW
QCDUGO	EWVMIX
CQOGRD	EXWMVI
QUGCDR	IXEMWV
URDGQO	VXWEMI
GRUQDO	MXVEWI
DUQGRO	XVWMEI
UCGROD	MWXVIE
DQRCGU	VIMEXW
QDOCGU	EXVWIM
CGUROQ	VWMIEX
OCDURQ	VMWIEX
UOCGQD	XVWMEI
RGQCOU	WXVEMI
GRUDQO	XMEWIV
GODUCQ	MXIVEW
QCURDO	VEWMIX
DUCOQG	EMVXWI
CGRDQU	IVWMEX
UDRCOQ	IEVMWX
GQCORU	WVZMXE
GOZUCD	XEMIWV
GDQUOC	WXIMEV
URDCGO	EMWIVX
GODRQC	IVEMXW

Figure 12.14 Searching for Z in two arrays of letters
Source: Neisser, 1967: 70

Now see how long it takes you to find Z in column 2. Again, make a note of the time it takes you.

What do you notice?

The features for A are plausibly

But these can be put together to produce

Figure 12.15 Combining features in different ways

RESEARCH METHODS BOX 12.2

The word superiority effect

Experiments on word recognition using the technique outlined in Table 12.2 (p. 199) were first carried out by Reicher (1969) and Wheeler (1970).

Reicher (1969) found that performance in condition 1 was better than in conditions 2 and 3, which were the same. So letters in words are recognised better than letters in random letter strings (or on their own). This is the word superiority effect.

Subsequent experiments showed that letters in pronounceable strings (e.g. rowk) were also recognised better than on their own or in unpronounceable strings (Baron and Thurstone, 1973). This was called the pseudo-word superiority effect, and is further evidence of context effects. This time the benefit comes from the participant's implicit knowledge of the letter sequences permissible in English. These results suggest that (i) knowledge of the word and (ii) knowledge of the structure of English words influence the recognition of individual letters.

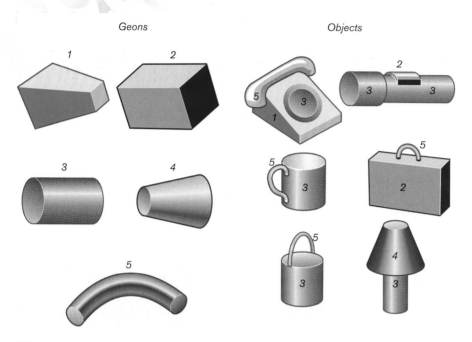

Figure 12.16 Geons and objects: Biederman argued that objects can be thought of as being composed of basic building blocks called geons
Source: Biederman, 1987

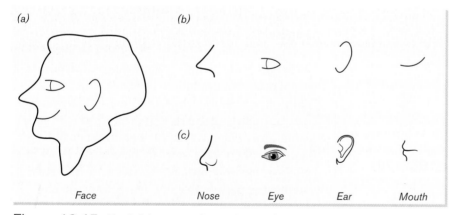

Figure 12.17 Facial features in and out of context: facial features are more recognisable in context (a) than out of context (b), unless they are very detailed (c)
Source: Palmer, 1975

bottom-up processes. Feature detectors are dependent on whether or not the given feature is present in the stimulus.

Finally, if we adopt the findings of Gestalt psychology, then the processes segregating objects from each other and from the background are bottom-up. The cues of similarity, proximity and continuity are all present in the stimulus and are simply waiting to be decoded.

The evidence for top-down processes is equally

TABLE 12.2		
WORD RECOGNITION TECHNIQUES		
Condition 1	**Condition 2**	**Condition 3**
Present stimulus	Present stimulus	Present stimulus
work	___k	rwok
Present test display of alternatives	Present test display of alternatives	Present test display of alternatives
___k ___d	___k ___d	___k ___d
Question: Which letter was in the original word?	Question: Which letter was in the original word?	Question: Which letter was in the original word?

compelling. It could be argued that linear perspective and texture gradient are cues to perception of depth inasmuch as the brain uses them to *infer* the depth and distance of objects. While template theory is consistent with a bottom-up view, recall that for template matching to work with everyday, 'dirty' stimuli, information about context would have to be used to render the input unambiguous.

Context effects are consistent with top-down processing. The experiments on word recognition provided the strongest evidence for how context, knowledge of words and the rules of English word structure affect the perception of single letters. Finally, the constancies and the existence of illusions are consistent with the idea that perception is based on more than only the properties of the stimulus, and that factors such as inference, experience and knowledge of the world play an important part.

Fortunately, a synthesis of the two views is both possible and convincing. Bottom-up processes are dominant early in processing when, for example, feature detectors are doing their work, while top-down processes operate higher up the system when identification and recognition (of often ambiguous stimuli) are at issue.

Speech perception

Speech perception is a particularly complex topic requiring specialist knowledge and a specialist vocabulary. Most of it is beyond the scope of an introductory text like this. However, it is possible to identify some of the issues, especially as some of them are shared with visual perception.

The invariance of speech perception

Our perception of speech remains remarkably consistent across a very large range of physical properties of the speech signal. We understand what someone says regardless of the pitch of their voice. A child's high-pitched voice and the deep bass of a barrel-chested male are equally comprehensible. We understand a range of accents. English speakers as well as speakers of other languages can usually be understood fairly easily. We understand someone speaking either in a whisper or shouting across a busy street. Nor does speed seem to make much difference[i] to comprehensibility. The rapid speech of a sports commentator is perfectly comprehensible, although cattle auctioneers may cause some problems. The invariance of speech perception suggests that it is not the absolute values of the input that matter but

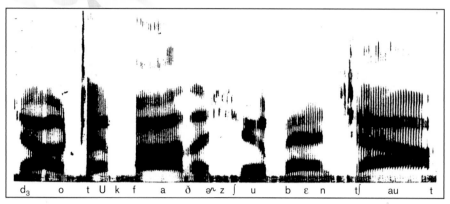

Figure 12.18 A speech spectrogram of the phrase 'Joe took father's shoe bench out': the sounds are represented by the intensity (blackness of pattern) of frequencies (X axis) over time (Y axis); the phonemes being produced are also presented along the Y axis
Source: Tartter, 1986

the relationship between the speech sounds of a particular speaker.

The segmentation problem in speech perception

A major problem in speech perception is known as the *segmentation problem*. To any native speaker of a language, speech is clearly segmented. We 'hear' a string of discrete words separated by very brief periods of silence. This perception is actually an illusion. We can easily confirm this by listening to a language we don't know. This seems to be a continuous stream of sound rather than a string of discrete words.

This is confirmed by looking at the speech spectrogram of an utterance. A speech spectrogram is a visual representation of the speech signal. It shows the frequencies present in a particular speech sound and the amplitude of those frequencies. Both of these are presented over the time course of the sound being made (see Figure 12.18).

The breaks in spectrograms do not correspond in any systematic way to the gaps between words. A similar problem occurs within a word. We perceive a word like 'father's' to consist of the component sounds /f/, /a/, /th/, /e/, /z/, called phonemes, blended together, but this is not evident in the spectrogram (see Figure 12.18). This lack of

correspondence between the acoustic signal and our perception of the component sounds of a word is called the *lack of invariance problem*. This is that there is no invariant (constant) aspect of the acoustic input that allows the extraction of these segments.

This brief summary indicates that there is no direct link between the acoustic signal and the perception of phonemes. There does, however, appear to be a link between the acoustic signal and *distinctive features*, and between distinctive features and *phonemes*.

Consider the sounds /p/ and /b/ (as in pat and bat respectively). Acoustically they differ only in a distinctive feature called *voicing*. In /b/ there is an explosion of air as the two lips open and air comes rushing out. At about the same time the vocal cords begin vibrating and we perceive a resonance. This is called voicing. With /p/ there is the same explosion of air but this time there is a delay of about 60-thousandths of a second (60 msecs) before the vocal cords begin vibrating. There is a delay before voicing. Because of this delay, we hear /b/ and /p/ as being different sounds: /b/ is a voiced phoneme; /p/ is an unvoiced phoneme.

Voicing is a distinctive feature that distinguishes other sounds (e.g. /d/ and /t/, /g/ and /k/). The point to notice is that voicing can be specified in terms of the acoustic signal (the onset of resonance)

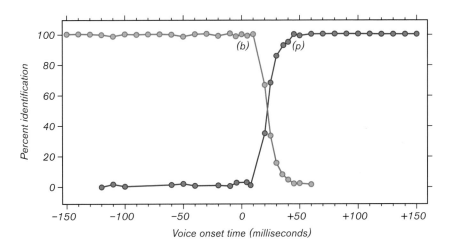

Figure 12.19 Categorical perception: the percentage of times the sound was identified as /b/ or /p/ changes dramatically at a certain point (when voicing begins at about 25 msecs after the bilabial explosion); this indicates that perception is of two categories, /b/ or /p/, not a continuum
Source: Lisker and Abramson, 1970

and in terms of the perception of phonemes (/b/ or /p/).

Categorical perception

The relationship between the acoustic signal and phonemic perception has been tested in experiments on *categorical perception*. Lisker and Abramson (1970) did experiments with computer-generated speech, which allowed them to manipulate the voicing onset time (the delay before the vocal cords begin vibrating). Voicing onset was manipulated from 150 msecs before the explosion to 150 msecs after the explosion. The results are presented in Figure 12.19.

We see in Figure 12.19 that as long as voicing begins before the explosion (at 0 seconds) then /b/ is perceived. When voicing begins after the explosion (25 msecs after, to be precise) then /p/ is perceived. The important point is that there isn't a slow transition from perception of /b/ to perception of /p/. The change is sudden, from one category (/b/) to another (/p/).

Top-down processing

A dramatic demonstration of top-down processing in speech perception comes from the *phoneme*

restoration effect. Warren and Warren (1970) presented the following four sentences to listeners.

1 It was found that the *eel was on the axle.
2 It was found that the *eel was on the shoe.
3 It was found that the *eel was on the orange.
4 It was found that the *eel was on the table.

The * signifies a missing sound.

They found that the participants heard the *eel as wheel, heel, peel or meal, depending on the sentence they heard. They were 'restoring' the missing phoneme but were doing so with a phoneme that was appropriate to the sentence, indicating that context was influencing perception.

Summary

In this chapter we have been concerned with perception. We began by looking at the perception of form or whole figures, and examined the figure–ground problem, the constancies and visual illusions. We then looked at depth perception before moving on to pattern recognition. Here we looked at template and feature theories. The effects of context were seen in the next section, before we moved on to

Section 3
Cognitive Psychology

a brief consideration of the contrasting arguments of the bottom-up and top-down approaches. Finally, we looked at speech perception where we drew some similarities between visual and speech perception.

Learning outcomes

When you have completed this chapter you should be able to:

- outline major characteristics of the perception of form
- describe how figures are separated from each other and from their background
- describe the constancies and their origins
- provide a tentative explanation of selected visual illusions
- describe the different kinds of cues to depth perception
- describe and compare major theories of pattern recognition
- outline two theories of object recognition
- describe the effects of context on perception
- contrast bottom-up and top-down theories of perception
- identify some of the major characteristics of speech perception.

Key Terms

Apperceptive agnosia
Associative agnosia
Binocular convergence
Binocular cues
Bottom-up processing
Brightness constancy
Categorical perception
Closure principle
Colour constancy
Complex cells
Constructive perception
Continuity principle
Depth perception
Direct perception
Distal stimulus
Distinctive feature

Feature detection theory
Feature detectors
Figure–ground separation
Geons
Hypercomplex cells
Interposition
Lack of invariance problem
Laws of pragnanz
Linear perspective
Monocular cues
Motion parallax
Muller-Lyer illusion
Optical flow pattern
Pattern recognition
Perception
Phoneme
Phoneme restoration effect
Ponzo illusion
Proximal stimulus
Proximity principle
Psychophysics
Receptive field
Recognition by components theory
Retinal disparity
Retinal size
Sensation
Sensory threshold
Shape constancy
Similarity principle
Simple cells
Size constancy
Size–distance invariance hypothesis
Speech perception
Template matching theory
Texture gradient
Top-down processing
Visual illusions
Visual object agnosia
Visual search
Voicing
Word superiority effect

Further reading

Bruce, V., Green, P. R. and Georgeson, M. A. (2003) *Visual Perception: Physiology, Psychology and Ecology* (4th edn). Hove: Psychology Press. (Specialist high level text for those with a special interest.)

Eysenck, M. W. and Keene, M. T. (2000) *Cognitive Psychology. A Student's Handbook* (4th edn). Hove: Psychology Press. (Densely packed information with evaluations of research.)

Parkin, A. J. (1996) *Explorations in Cognitive Neuropsychology*. Cambridge, MA: Blackwell. (Very readable coverage of major neuropsychological disorders.)

Sternberg, R. J. (1999) *Cognitive Psychology* (2nd edn). Orlando: Harcourt Brace College Publishers. (Good, general, reader-friendly text.)

13

Attention

Route map of the chapter

The aim of this chapter is to introduce the reader to important aspects of attention. We will begin by looking at vigilance, which is the ability to sustain attention over a period of time. Next we'll examine characteristics and models of *focused auditory* and *focused visual attention*. The final section explores our ability to divide our attention between two tasks requiring simultaneous attention.

Introduction

We are constantly bombarded by stimulation. Even a simple scene presents our senses with a host of shapes, colours and sizes of objects and people. Consider a lecturer working in her office. She hears the roar of traffic outside, people talking in the corridor, doors slamming and the constant hum of a computer. She might be feeling thirsty and a little hungry. Memories – some personal, some work-related – probably fill her mind. A number of problems probably need speedy solutions. Some may be obvious, others not. Students are lining up outside the door, colleagues are telephoning, and e-mails are queued up for response. How is it she doesn't get overwhelmed by these sights, sounds, memories and thoughts?

The answer is *attention*. According to Sternberg (1999: 69), 'Attention acts as a means of focusing limited mental resources on the information and cognitive processes that are most salient at a given moment.' Attention is usually, but not always, a conscious process. When our lecturer is looking at her computer screen, or listening to a colleague, she is consciously directing her attention to the task in

hand. She is focusing her attention and is aware of doing so. It is an intentional act. Similarly, when she divides her attention between taking a telephone call and replying to an e-mail at the same time there is a conscious effort to divide her attention between the two tasks. Finally, towards the end of the day it probably takes conscious effort to keep focused on a particular task when the prospect of a drink with colleagues beckons.

On the other hand, much of attention is not conscious in the sense that she may be aware of what she's doing but what she's doing is not under conscious control. She focuses consciously on the book she's reading, but the cognitive processes of reading are not conscious. They were once, when she was learning to read and rather painfully had to convert the letters to sounds and then blend the sounds. But no longer. She's listening to her colleague tell her about an incident in his lecture and this is conscious, but whatever is involved in listening to his voice and filtering out all the other sounds is not. When she drives her car home the sequence of actions to change gear is not something she thinks about now that she's a skilled driver. She's aware of needing to change gear but everything thereafter is barely in her awareness.

Psychologists have distinguished between *controlled processes* and *automatic processes*. As the examples above indicate, controlled processes require conscious control. They require intentional effort, full conscious awareness and attention. They operate quite slowly and usually do things serially, one at a time. In contrast, automatic processes do not require conscious control. They require little or no intention or effort, and are usually outside conscious awareness. They need very little attention and can be performed rapidly and in parallel with other actions. This distinction between controlled and automatic processes, approximately congruent with the distinction between conscious and non-conscious and between needing and not needing attention, provides a context for the issues to be discussed in this chapter.

Vigilance

'*Vigilance* refers to a person's ability to attend to a field of stimulation over a prolonged period of time, in which the person seeks to detect the appearance of a particular target stimulus of interest' (Sternberg, 1999: 83). A vigilance task usually involves waiting for something unpredictable to happen. The classic example is of radar operators in war time looking at their radar screens for missiles launched by the enemy. It might never happen, but the fact that it might means that they have to be on alert constantly.

Jobs involving vigilance have become increasingly rare with the advance of technology. Whereas industry once employed people to sit on production lines looking for faulty goods they now have robots to do the same job, usually more efficiently. Nevertheless, when vigilance is required it is usually of crucial importance, as in the case of air traffic controllers. Let's hope that the character in the cartoon on this page doesn't exist!

Studies of vigilance have revealed that the ability to detect an event is dependent on various factors, such as training (Fisk and Schneider, 1981) and expectations (Posner, Snyder and Davidson, 1980). An important consideration when researching vigilance is to identify why vigilance fluctuates. The psychological tool used to investigate this is called *signal detection theory* (SDT). This measures two components of a person's ability to detect signals:

1   their perceptual *sensitivity (referred to by d')*
2   the *decision criterion (referred to by ß)* they use.

Consider the following situation. You are a radar operator looking for evidence of a missile attack by a foreign power. You are in a darkened room with a

"Yippee! Join the dots!"

screen in front of you. The screen is alive with signals caused by commercial aircraft, flocks of birds and other aerial events. You are looking for a particular type of signal, which will probably never come. You have been trained to discriminate this signal from all others but the difference is not that great and a mistake is easily made. If you see the signal for a missile attack you have to press a red button. This will automatically alert the local airbase and scramble attack aircraft, closely followed by the firing of retaliatory missiles. Your decision to press the red button will clearly be determined by your perceptual sensitivity to the difference between missiles and a flock of birds (d'). However, it will also be determined by your decision criterion.

If you press the button and you're wrong (it is a flock of birds) then you may start the Third World War. This is called a false alarm. To avoid this, you need to adopt a conservative criterion and only press the button when absolutely certain. On the other hand, if you don't press the button when missiles are coming then your failure to respond could lead to the annihilation of your country. This is called a miss. To avoid this you need to adopt an aggressive criterion and press the button at the first sign of enemy action.

The point is that the response to the same signal and with the same perceptual sensitivity depends on a decision criterion (ß), which can vary from conservative to aggressive. Investigations of vigilance need to take these two factors into account.

Wickens (2002) found that training observers, showing them samples of what they were looking for and varying the event rate, all improved perceptual sensitivity (d'). Providing good instructions, which told the observer of the consequences of different actions, giving feedback on performance and giving false signals, all shifted the observer's criterion.

If you want more information about SDT and to do an online experiment, go to: http://epsych.msstate.edu/deliberate/index.html.

Focused/selective attention

Focused auditory attention

The central question in investigations of *focused auditory attention* is the degree to which we can focus on an attended message while excluding other, undesired messages. To what extent can we select what we attend to? This section reviews several models of focused auditory attention in an attempt to answer this question.

Cherry (1953) first identified the 'cocktail party phenomenon', a reference to the ability to listen selectively to one conversation during a party while ignoring the noise going on around you. Cherry used a *dichotic listening task* to investigate this (see Research Methods Box 13.1). In this sort of experiment different messages are presented to each of a participant's ears and he or she is asked to shadow or repeat one of the messages. This ensures that he or she is attending to the shadowed message.

With a little practice subjects are able to do this quite efficiently. Researchers have asked what happens to the unattended message? Cherry (1953) found that participants could report only the physical characteristics of the message, such as whether it was a man's or woman's voice. They were not able to say whether the message was in English or a foreign language, indicating that non-physical characteristics such as the language (or meaning) had not been processed.

Broadbent's filter model of selective attention

Broadbent (1958) proposed a *filter model* to explain Cherry's findings. He argued that, to prevent us from becoming overwhelmed by sensory input, there is an *attentional filter* that prevents all but the desired, selected message from getting through to perceptual processing. This filter, he argued, is located right after the incoming information is registered at the sensory level. Crucially, it operates on the basis of physical characteristics of the message. So in a crowded room it lets through the voice of the person you're speaking to but everything else is heard only as noises and voices (see Figure 13.2).

It soon became clear that the model was wrong. Moray (1959) found that subjects could recognise their own names in the unattended ear, a common phenomenon in a noisy room. This indicated that the unattended message was being processed for meaning. It wasn't being shut out immediately after sensory analysis. Treisman (1964a) found that subjects noticed if the unattended message was the same as the shadowed message when they were presented with a lag between them. This happened regardless of whether the shadowed message led or lagged behind the unattended message. She also found that bilingual participants were able to recognise the identity of the two messages when the message was the same in the person's two languages. These findings also indicated that the unattended message must be undergoing processing for meaning. This was not consistent with *Broadbent's filter model*.

Treisman's attenuator model of selective attention

Treisman (1964b) proposed her own attenuation model (*Treisman's attenuation model*) of selective attention. She argued that all messages were processed beyond the sensory stage but that the unattended messages were subject to *attenuation*. Broadbent's filter is replaced by an attenuator that 'softens' the unattended message. This is necessary because the system has limited capacity and can handle only a limited amount of information. This limited capacity takes the form of a bottleneck after the attenuator. Stimuli such as one's own name have

---

RESEARCH METHODS BOX 13.1

Dichotic listening task (Cherry, 1953)

The purpose of the dichotic listening task is measure the participant's ability to attend to two simultaneous messages while ensuring that she or he is attending to one. The participant is fitted with a set of headphones. These are set up so that one message can be delivered to one ear and another message to the other. The situation is designed to simulate hearing two messages coming from different locations in space.

The participant has to repeat one of the messages as it is delivered. This is called *shadowing* and the message being shadowed is called the attended message. The other message is the unattended message. The participant is told that whatever else she or he is asked to do they must make shadowing a priority. This ensures that the attended message is being given full attention. The experimenter can then look at what is happening to the message in the unattended ear.

...and then John turned rapidly towards...

–ran–house–ox–cat

and, um, John turned...

Figure 13.1   The dichotic listening task: the participant receives different messages in each ear and has to repeat, or shadow, one of them while ignoring the other
Source: Anderson, 1995: 76

---

low thresholds for activating meaning because of their importance, and so have an impact even in attenuated form (Treisman, 1964b).

Deutsch and Deutsch response selection model

The common feature of these two theories is that they propose a bottleneck that limits what gets through to perceptual processes. Both bottlenecks occur early and so both are known as *early selection models*. They differ in how they function: filter (shut out) versus attenuator (soften). In contrast, *late selection models*, proposed by Deutsch and Deutsch (1963) and Norman (1968), argued that all inputs were processed perceptually and for meaning but with no attenuation. This is why participants recognised their own names and the identity of the two messages. They also argue for a bottleneck because of limited capacity but the bottleneck comes at the response stage, when only one of the messages can be responded to.

A number of experiments tried to distinguish between the Treisman (1964) and the Deutsch and Deutsch (1963) models by asking participants to

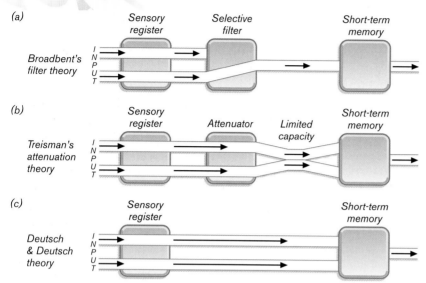

Figure 13.2 *(a) Broadbent's filter model of selective attention: incoming information is filtered very soon after entering the perceptual system. Only one input is allowed through for further processing after this 'bottleneck'. The others are shut out; (b) Treisman's attenuator model of selective attention: incoming information is attenuated very soon after entering the perceptual system. All inputs but one are attenuated (or 'softened') so that they can all pass through the (limited capacity) 'bottleneck'; (c) Deutsch and Deutsch's late selection model of attention: all incoming information is fully processed. There is no early 'bottleneck'. One input is given precedence nearer the time when a response has to be made.*
Source: Eysenck and Keane, 2000: 123

shadow one ear and to signal every time they heard a target word. The target word could occur in either ear. Target detection was never as good in the unattended ear as in the shadowed ear, supporting Treisman's notion of attenuation (Treisman and Geffen, 1967; Glucksberg and Cowan, 1970).

Johnston and Wilson (1980), however, showed that the fate of the unattended message depended on the task. When the listener focused on one ear and expected targets only in that ear then the unattended message was largely ignored. However, if they were told that targets could occur in either ear then the unattended target did have an effect. This notion of

attention being under strategic control is a theme that is repeated during this chapter.

Kahneman's capacity model of attention

Kahneman's (1973) model got away from the notion of bottlenecks, of whatever form. He argued that the limitation on the messages that could be processed occurred because attention is a resource that is in limited supply. His is a *capacity model of attention*. There is a certain 'amount' of attention available at any given time and this is allocated to different messages that need attention. The degree to which more than one message will be processed depends on how demanding each of the messages is, and their relative importance. One important demanding message may require all the attention available, leaving little or nothing for other messages. Several 'easy' messages may all be fully processed.

Focused visual attention

Covert attention and sensory memory

We are all familiar with focusing our attention by swivelling our eyes and fixing on a target, but research shows that we select and focus attention internally – in conditions where there isn't time for eye movements. Posner (1980) calls this *covert attention* to distinguish it from the *overt attention* associated with eye and head movements.

The phenomenon of *visual sensory memory*, also called *iconic memory*, is relevant to this chapter because it provides evidence that selection of specific targets for focused attention occurs early in the perceptual process, before stimuli have been analysed for meaning. See Chapter 14, which deals with memory, for details of iconic memory.

Recall that in Sperling's (1960) experiment participants were able to direct their attention to required parts of the array: to the top, the middle and the bottom, depending on the tone being used. Remember also that this was in conditions where eye movements were not possible because the arrays appeared for only a very short time. This means that participants were able to direct covert attention to different locations in the array *internally*. Later experiments showed that they were actually able to direct their attention to specific locations in the array, indicated by a bar, and report the letter in this location (Averbach *et al.*, 1961). These results indicate that covert visual attention can be directed to specific locations very early in perceptual processing.

Shifting covert attention – the spotlight analogy

An experiment by Posner, Nissen and Ogden (1978) showed more explicitly that we can shift the focus of covert attention. A useful analogy to aid understanding of this is the *spotlight analogy* – that of attention being like an internal spotlight that can be turned on to the target stimulus: anything in the spotlight is given full attention; anything outside the spotlight is given less or no attention (see figure 13.3).

Posner *et al.* (1978) had participants respond to a stimulus that could occur to the left or right of a fixation point. On the majority of trials (condition 1) they were correctly cued as to which side the stimulus would appear. On some trials (condition 2) they were misled as to where the stimulus would appear. In a third, control, condition there was no cueing as to where the stimulus would appear (see figure 13.4 overleaf).

The results were clear (see figure 13.5). Responses were quickest in condition 1, suggesting that participants made use of the cue to shift attention to where they expected the stimulus to come. The cue identified where the stimulus was to come so there was no need to shift attention. Condition 2 was the slowest, suggesting that they shifted attention to where they expected the stimulus, but it came the other side. This required a shift in attention from the wrong to the right location. The control results were midway. This experiment showed the ability to shift attention internally as circumstances demand.

Covert attention and the zoom lens analogy

What happens to a visual stimulus not in the spotlight? Is it completely shut out, as in Broadbent's auditory model? Is it attenuated, as in Treisman's auditory model? Or is it fully processed, as in Deutsch and Deutsch's auditory model? The evidence suggests that whatever happens is under strategic control, as in Kahneman's general model. LaBerge (1983) found that if attention was focused on the central letter of a five-letter word, then much less attention was paid to the letters on the left and right of the central letter than to the central letter (see Figure 13.8).

However, if participants were instructed to attend to the whole word, then as much attention was paid to the peripheral letters as to the central one. This experiment suggests that the way attention is spread over the visual field is under strategic control. The degree to which it can be focused can be varied

Figure 13.3 The spotlight analogy of visual attention: covert or internal attention has been compared to a spotlight, with one part of the stimulus being 'illuminated'

depending on instructions and the demands of the situation. Perhaps the spotlight model should be rebranded as the *zoom lens model*. If the 'lens' is on telephoto then a restricted part is in close focus. If the 'lens' is on wide angle, taking in a larger area, then there is less attention to go round and the overall clarity suffers.

Attention and assembling a percept

Treisman's *feature integration model* (Treisman and Gelade, 1980; Treisman, 1988; Treisman, 1993) is a theory of attention and perceptual processing. She argues that there are two kinds of processing of the visual input. One requires attention, the other does not. She distinguishes between different kinds of features of a stimulus: colour, size, shape, orientation. The particular set of features present will depend, of course, on the characteristics of the

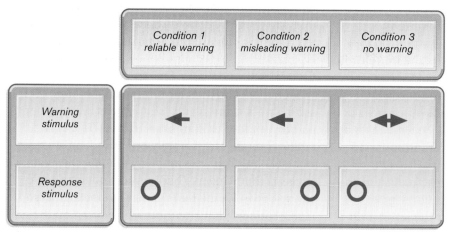

Figure 13.4 Schematic representation of Posner, Nissen and Ogden's (1978) experiment on shifting visual attention. In condition 1 the participant is warned that the stimulus will appear on the left of the fixation point. The participant shifts attention to the appropriate location and this is where the stimulus appears. In condition 2 the participant is given the same warning but the stimulus actually appears on the other side. The participant has to shift attention from the wrong location to the right one. In condition 3 the warning is neither a help nor a hindrance

To summarise, feature detection is done in parallel, is automatic and pre-attentional, but combining features to form the object percept requires attention.

Treisman and Gelade (1980) showed this in an experiment involving visual search. The participants had to look for a specified target in a large array of other stimuli. The size of this array was varied. They argued that if the size of the array *didn't* affect search time then the search processes must be operating in parallel. That is, all items in the array were being examined simultaneously. On the other hand, if array size did make a difference, then search must be serial. Items in the array were being examined one after the other.

They used two types of target in an array consisting of letters of different colours: first, a feature target, which consisted of, for example, an 's' or the colour blue (one of the letters was blue); second, a conjoined target, which consisted of a particular letter in a particular colour e.g. a green 't'. They found that detecting a feature target (e.g. spotting any blue letter) did not depend on array size. However, detecting a conjoined target (e.g. spotting a green 't') did depend on array size. As the array size increased, finding a green 't' took longer. They concluded that features were analysed in parallel but that objects (combinations of features) needed attention to 'glue' the features together.

Divided attention

This section deals with *divided attention*, which is in many ways the opposite of focused attention. Where research into focused attention asks about the extent to which we can focus on one task and ignore others, divided attention asks about the extent to which we can do more than one task at the same time. This research is best understood in the context of theories of limited attentional capacity.

A theory such as Kahneman's (1973) argues that there is:

- a central bank of resources that is available for all tasks requiring mental effort, and
- that the capacity of this bank is limited.

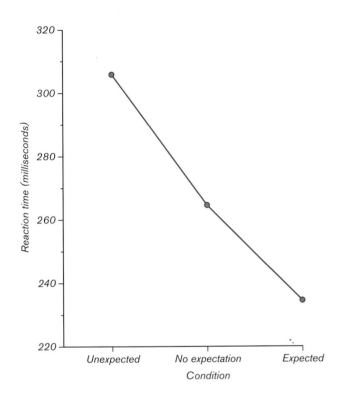

Figure 13.5 Time taken to focus attention on a target: the time taken to respond to the stimulus depends on the extent to which attention has to be shifted Source: Posner, Nissen and Ogden, 1978

scene. She argues that, in the initial stage of processing, these features are processed in parallel and require no attention. The system can 'look' for all the possible colours in the scene simultaneously. Similarly, it can look for all the different shape features (line segments, corners etc.) simultaneously. This simultaneous processing is called *parallel processing* and it needs very little or no attention. It is completely automatic.

In contrast, for an object to be perceived as a whole, its different features (shape, colour etc.) need to be integrated. The different types of feature (i.e. colour, size etc.) that specify the object have to be conjoined so that the final product is an accurate percept. This 'combining' of features is done by *serial processing* (one after the other) and takes attention.

APPLICATIONS BOX 13.1

Unilateral visual neglect

Unilateral visual neglect is a condition that arises out of extensive damage to one of the hemispheres of the brain in the parietal lobe region. Patients with neglect ignore one half of visual space, on the opposite (contralateral) side to the damaged hemisphere. Unilateral left neglect, due to damage of the right hemisphere, is the more common.

This neglect may take several forms. For example, the patient may eat food only from the right side of a plate. The left half of the body will not be dressed and the left half of the face not shaved. In unilateral left visual neglect the person behaves as if they have no visual input from the left half of space. This is reflected in their drawing

Figure 13.6 Patients with unilateral left visual neglect. Notice that details in the left half of the drawings have been omitted or neglected.

and in simple tests like line cancellation when, if asked to cancel through a display of lines, they will omit only the lines on one half of the page (see Figure 13.6).

The condition is not due to a perceptual deficit. There is nothing wrong with vision. This can be shown by the fact that the degree of neglect varies with the importance of the stimulus in the neglected field. For example, Marshall and Halligan (1988) showed left neglect patients pictures of two houses. They were identical except that in one house flames and smoke were pouring out of a left-hand window. The patients reported no difference between the two pictures, presumably because the left half of each house was being ignored. However, when they were asked which house they would like to live in they picked the one without the smoke!

Neglect is also found when these patients are asked to draw something from memory. Bisiach and Luzzatti (1978) asked two patients with left neglect to describe the Piazza del Duomo in Milan from memory and from two perspectives: one looking towards the cathedral and the other away from it. In both cases the patients only described landmarks that were on the right!

Posner, Walker, Friederich and Rafal (1984) have argued that neglect is an impairment of covert attention. They distinguished three aspects of shifts of covert attention: disengagement of attention from its current focus, moving attention to the new focus and engagement of the new focus. In left visual neglect, the patient finds it difficult to disengage his/her attention from the 'good side' (from objects on the right-hand side of space) and move it to the 'damaged side' (to the left-hand side of space). This is why the 'damaged side' is neglected. Posner, Cohen and Rafal (1982) showed this using the cueing experiment reported earlier.

We can see from Figure 13.7 that when the person is cued to expect something in the neglected field it doesn't matter too much whether the stimulus comes there or not (the damaged side is not engaging the stimulus). However, when the person is cued to expect something in the normal field but the stimulus appears in the neglected field it makes a massive difference. This is because the 'good side' has captured the stimulus and won't let go.

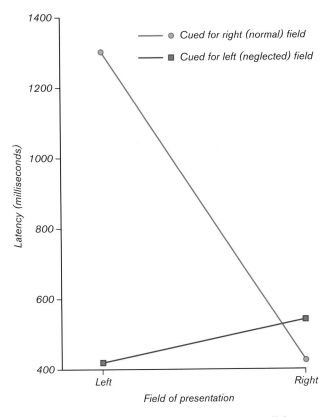

Figure 13.7 *Responses to valid and invalid cues by a patient with right hemisphere damage*
Source: Posner, Cohen and Rafal, 1982

The ability to perform two tasks simultaneously therefore depends on the demands the two tasks make on this central bank. If both tasks can be carried out without exceeding the capacity then they will be performed together as well as they will be performed separately. If the demands of the task exceed capacity then one or both tasks will suffer.

Allocating attention to competing tasks

A pertinent question is whether we have strategic control over how these resources are allocated.

Kahneman (1973) argued that we do. An experiment by Wickens and Gopher (1977) supported this view. Participants were given two tasks. One was a tracking task, which involved keeping a pointer on a moving reference point (called a pursuit rotor – sometimes seen at fair grounds). The second was a task requiring the participant to respond as quickly as possible every time a number came up on a screen.

The participants had to do both tasks at the same time. However, they were given different instructions in different conditions as to the priority each task was to be given. In one condition, 100 per cent priority was to be given to the tracking task and 0 per cent priority to the digit monitoring task. In another condition, the split was 70 per cent priority to the tracking and 30 per cent to the monitoring. In a third condition, the split was 30 per cent and 70 per cent. In the final condition, the split was 0 per cent and 100 per cent. Thus they prioritised according to instruction. The results were clear. As the priorities shifted from one task to the other the relative performance changed (see Figure 13.9).

Practice and automaticity

We all know that 'practice makes perfect'. An interesting question concerns the degree to which practising doing two tasks simultaneously will produce better performance. It seems likely. This was shown in an experiment by Spelke, Hirst and Neisser (1976), which shows, if nothing else, incredible perseverance on the part of the two participants, Dianne and John.

These two (paid) volunteers were required to do two tasks simultaneously: read for comprehension and write to dictation. They received five hours' training a week for the duration of the experiment, which took many weeks. After six weeks of practice they were able to read while writing as well as they could read on its own. There were mistakes but in

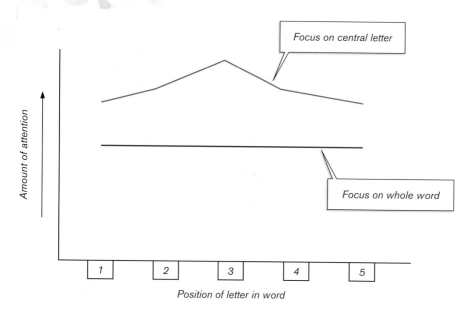

Figure 13.8 Idealised representation of the amount of attention paid to peripheral letters as a function of the degree of focus
Source: based on Laberge, 1983

general the performance was impressive. This suggested that practice had brought the writing task to the point where it needed little or no attention.

However, an analysis of the results also showed that these two people weren't processing the dictated words to any depth because, for example, they weren't aware that some of the words in sequence formed a sentence. With yet more practice they were able to categorise each dictated word (e.g. table – furniture), showing that processing of these words could now be done to a semantic level. This experiment provides impressive evidence of the effects of practice on divided attention.

Other evidence of the fact that highly practised tasks can demand little or no attention comes from Allport *et al.* (1972), who showed that expert pianists (who practise their skill many hours a day) could play from seen music, without detriment, while shadowing.

The theoretical question raised by practice is whether one or both tasks are done by automatic

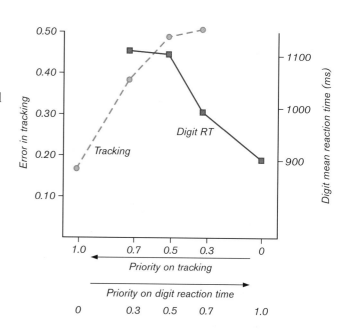

Figure 13.9 Changing priorities in dual task performance
Source: Wickens and Gopher, 1977

processes. (We cover this issue in Chapter 16, on thinking and reasoning.) Recall Anderson's theory, which identified the three stages of skill acquisition:

1 a *cognitive stage*, in which knowledge was declarative and hence in conscious awareness
2 a *procedural stage*, in which this knowledge was implemented as a set of production rules
3 an *automatic stage*, in which the task no longer requires attention, does not require conscious awareness and is difficult to interrupt.

The participants in these two studies seem to be well on their way to this final stage. The practised task seems to need very little attention but it is not clear whether it needs conscious awareness or whether, once started, it would be difficult to interrupt. In Chapter 16, we discuss the Stroop effect, which shows that single word reading is a completely automatic process. When participants were asked to name the ink colour of a word, however, this was much harder when the word was a colour name than when it was a neutral word (e.g. blue vs clue). This was because the brain's processing of the meaning of the word is completely automatic and not under conscious control. The meaning of the word disrupted naming the ink. It's doubtful whether reading continuous text for meaning could ever reach this state of automaticity.

Similarity of competing tasks

The ability to do two things at the same time is also dependent on the similarity of the two tasks involved. We'll see that the evidence supporting this forces us to reconsider the idea that there is a *central* bank of resources that are allocated to tasks as priorities demand. The effect of similarity can be seen clearly in an experiment by Segal and Fusella (1970). They had participants do different combinations of two tasks simultaneously (see Table 13.1).

Participants in condition A (constructing an auditory image and detecting an auditory stimulus) are doing two similar tasks in the sense that they both involve audition. Participants in condition B are doing two less similar tasks in that one involves

audition and the other vision. If similarity of task is important, then condition A should produce worse performance than condition B. By the same logic, condition D should be harder than condition C. So the two similar conditions (A and D) should be harder than the two different conditions (B and C). What they found is illustrated in Figure 13.10.

The ability to detect an auditory or visual stimulus while forming auditory or visual images depended on the combination of tasks. As predicted, two different tasks produced better detection than doing two similar tasks.

Central vs multiple resources

Experiments such as these have great theoretical importance. The fact that performance depends so crucially on the similarity of the tasks casts doubt on *central resource theory*, which says that there is one central 'bank' of resources that are allocated to the two tasks. If this were true, then performance shouldn't be affected by particular combinations of conditions (see Figure 13.11(a)).

Notice that the results can't be ascribed to task difficulty. Suppose constructing an auditory image was a very difficult task and it was this that produced

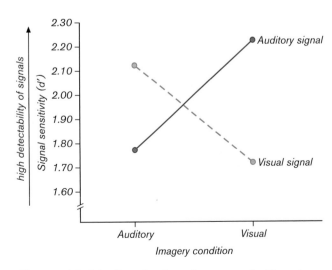

Figure 13.10 *Graph of performance in Segal and Fusella (1970)*
Source: Eysenck and Keane, 2000: 140

APPLICATIONS BOX 13.2

Human error

We all make errors. Fortunately most of our errors do not have serious consequences, although they may cause us considerable embarrassment. In some professions, however, the consequences of error can be very serious. Reports of surgeons removing the wrong leg, soldiers firing on their comrades and nuclear reactors melting down are relatively infrequent but still very disturbing examples of human error.

It's important to understand why errors occur because then we might be able to do something about them. Reason (1990) argues that we can adopt two approaches. The *person approach* places great emphasis on personal responsibility and generally ascribes errors to forgetfulness, inattention, poor motivation and negligence. Generally it has little to say about how errors can be reduced, except by appealing to people's vigilance and sense of responsibility.

The *systems approach* takes the view that we all make mistakes but that these errors often have their origins in faulty systems or practices. Thus, Reason refers to the errors we make as *active failures* and to the circumstances that breed them as *latent conditions*. The systems approach argues that errors can be reduced by actively looking for accident-inducing conditions. For example, if a factory has a high accident rate then we should look at the safety procedures, the shift patterns, training regimes, and so on, for evidence that aspects of the system are inducing accidents.

The systems approach does not mean that we ignore the personal variable. Psychologically, we are looking for the factors (independent variables) that induce human error (dependent variable). We can then try to eliminate the effects of these factors.

Reason (1990) has identified three kinds of cognitive process that underlie errors. First, there are skilled processes. These are automatic in nature and are carried out without much conscious awareness. They are highly practised routines. Everyday examples are brushing your teeth and making a cup of tea. Errors, called slips, occur when you fail to disengage one of these routines. Making a cup of tea when you actually wanted a cup of coffee, or a doctor telling someone in the early stages of meningitis to lie down and take a paracetamol for their headache are examples of an automatised routine being wrongly engaged.

Second, there are *rule-based processes*. These involve following a set of procedures (for example, what you do when the fire alarm rings). Errors occur when these procedures are violated. At the Chernobyl nuclear reactor in the Soviet Union in 1986 the operators broke the rules and switched off successive safety systems in their hunt for the original problem, leading to an explosion in the core.

Finally, there are *knowledge-based processes*. These involve thinking through a problem and arriving at a solution. Errors may occur when a new product is being designed. Examples are the relatively frequent recall of domestic products, especially cars, because they have a design fault that makes them dangerous to use.

Reason argues for adopting a systems approach. Although blaming individuals is emotionally more satisfying than targeting institutions, much the best results in accident reduction are obtained by institutions such as the military and air traffic controllers that actively look for the errors that could occur and then actively look for ways to reduce their likelihood.

poor performance in condition A. This would mean that performance in condition C should also be very poor. But condition C produces relatively good performance. The same argument can be used against the suggestion that any one of the four tasks is particularly difficult.

In contrast, the results can be explained if we abandon the idea of a single all-purpose *central* 'bank' and consider that there might be *separate* 'banks', one for visual processing and one for auditory processing, each with its own attentional resources. This is *multiple resource theory* (Navon and Gopher, 1979; Wickens, 1992) and it says that the degree to which two tasks interfere with each other depends on whether or not they use the same processes (e.g. visual or auditory) (see Figure 13.11(b)).

Central resource theory argues that simultaneous tasks are handled by a central bank of resources. It doesn't matter whether these tasks are similar or different. Think of an open-plan office with a central pool of workers who are qualified to handle any type of task.

Multiple resource theory argues that simultaneous tasks are handled by separate banks of resources. It does matter whether the tasks are similar or different. Think of a divided office where the workers in each part are qualified to handle only 'their' type of task.

Some models, such as Baddeley and Hitch's (1974) working memory model (see Chapter 14), have compromised between one central all-purpose bank of resources, and multiple-resource, modality-specific banks of resources. In their model there is a 'central executive', which is a central all-purpose resource, and two modality-specific resources called the phonological loop and the visual-spatial scratchpad.

Summary

In this chapter we have looked at various aspects of attention. We began with vigilance, the aspect of attention that deals with detecting events. Then we looked at focused auditory attention, and compared several models of how we select one message and (relatively) ignore others. In our coverage of focused visual attention we looked at the idea of a spotlight

(a) Central resources theory

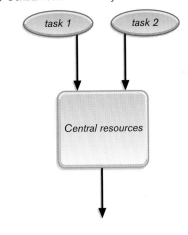

(b) Multiple resources theory

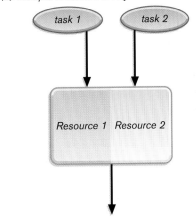

Figure 13.11 *A schematic representation of (a) central and (b) multiple resource theories*

model and then at how constructing a percept in the spotlight takes attention. In the final section we looked at the ability to divide attention between two tasks simultaneously, and examined different models of how this is done.

Section 3
Cognitive Psychology

TABLE 13.1		
THE COMBINATION OF TASKS IN SEGAL AND FUSELLA (1970)		
	Construct an auditory image	Construct a visual image
Detect an auditory stimulus	Condition A	Condition B
Detect a visual stimulus	Condition C	Condition D

Learning outcomes

When you have completed this chapter you should be able to:

- describe the basic concepts in signal detection theory
- compare three models of focused auditory attention
- outline the characteristics of focused visual attention, contrasting the spotlight and zoom lens analogies
- identify and discuss the factors that determine the degree to which we can do two tasks at the same time
- distinguish between controlled and automatic processes
- outline the differences between central and multiple resource models of attention.

Key Terms

Active failures
Attention
Attentional filter
Attenuation
Automatic processes
Automatic stage of skills acquisition
Broadbent's filter model
Capacity model of attention
Central resource theory
Cognitive stage of skills acquisition
Controlled processes
Covert attention
Decision criterion (ß)
Dichotic listening task
Divided attention
Early selection models
Feature integration model
Focused auditory attention
Focused visual attention
Iconic memory
Knowledge-based processes in human error
Late selection models
Latent conditions
Multiple resource theory
Overt attention
Parallel processing
Person approach to human error
Procedural stage of skills acquisition

Rule-based processes in human error
Sensitivity (d')
Serial processing
Shadowing
Signal detection theory
Skilled processes in human error
Spotlight analogy of visual attention
Systems approach to human error
Treisman's attenuation model
Unilateral visual neglect
Vigilance
Visual sensory memory
Zoom lens model

Further reading

Eysenck, M. W. and Keane, M. T. (2000) *Cognitive Psychology. A Student's Handbook* (4th edn). Hove: Psychology Press. (Densely packed information with evaluations of research.)

French, C. C. and Colman, A. M. (1994) *Cognitive Psychology.* London: Longman. (Chapters written by eminent specialists in their field. Clearly written. Attention chapter by Eysenck.)

Parkin, A. J. (1996) *Explorations in Cognitive Neuropsychology.* Cambridge, MA: Blackwell. (Very readable coverage of neglect and other neuropsychological disorders.)

Sternberg, R. J. (1999) *Cognitive Psychology* (2nd edn). Orlando: Harcourt Brace College Publishers. (Good, general, reader-friendly text.)

14

Memory

Route map of the chapter

The aim of this chapter is to introduce some of the key aspects of memory. It begins with an overview of the different memory systems. It then describes three types of memory: visual sensory memory, short-term memory and long-term memory. We then move on to discuss three memory models that seek to explain some of these results, and the next section describes the major memory processes of encoding, retrieval and forgetting. The final two sections describe autobiographical and semantic memory.

Introduction

What is memory? What role does it play in our lives? How important is it? One way to answer these questions is by imagining what it would be like if you lost your memory completely. You wouldn't be able to recognise anything you'd ever seen, heard, tasted, smelt or touched. Suppose you also lost the ability to form new memories of any kind so that everything you experienced or learnt simply 'passed through you'. Nothing would be retained for more than a matter of seconds. You wouldn't even be able to start restoring some of what you'd lost. The world in which you now lived would be completely alien, with no hope of ever becoming familiar.

The importance of memory is best appreciated by looking at people who have lost theirs through brain damage – a condition called *amnesia*. A good example of an amnesic is Clive Wearing, who is the subject of many journal articles, including one by his wife Deborah (Wilson and Wearing, 1995). Clive was a very talented musician who was struck down at the peak of his career with a disease called herpes simplex encephalitis, a virus that attacked his brain and left him with devastating memory loss. He has *anterograde amnesia*, which means he is completely unable to acquire new memories. Anything that happens is lost within minutes. If his wife leaves the room and returns a few minutes later he greets her as if he hasn't seen her for months. He keeps a diary in which he writes 'have just woken up for the first time' every time he looks at it so there can be numerous such entries for the same day. It is as if he is living in a time capsule that extends back only a few minutes.

His memory for his past life is also devastated, a condition called *retrograde amnesia*. He has 'islands' of memory from life before his illness but in general cannot remember much from his childhood, from his university years or from his highly successful career. The only thing Clive has not lost is his musical skill. He can still play the piano and conduct his old choir with deftness and sensitivity.

Memory systems: an overview

Baddeley (1995) suggests we think of memory as an alliance of systems. Rather than there being a single entity that deals with all memories there are a number of related and connected systems, each of which deals with different kinds of memories. Memory has sometimes been likened to a library. Memories are categorised and stored according to type. The filing system ensures that most of the time they can be speedily recalled, but sometimes they cannot be retrieved. They are forgotten.

Memory systems for the senses

We can identify one cluster of memory systems that serve our different senses. There is a memory system for the visual modality which stores information about colours, shapes, objects, faces, works of abstract art etc. There is also an auditory memory system for stimuli such as tones, melodies and voices. Similarly, there are systems for odours, tastes and textures. The majority of our experiences in everyday life are multisensory and have multiple representations. Thus we remember someone not just by their face but also by the sound of their voice, the perfume they wear and even the 'feel' of their handshake.

Memory systems based on duration of memories

One classification of memory systems is based on the length of time for which information is held. *Sensory memories* hold large amounts of 'raw' sensory information for a very short time, less than a second. Researchers have identified a visual sensory memory, called *iconic memory*, and an auditory sensory memory, called *echoic memory*. Second, there are *short-term memory* systems that hold small amounts of information, such as a telephone number, for short periods of time. Finally, there are *long-term memory* systems, which hold very large amounts of information for indefinite periods of time.

Verbal memory systems

Humans, uniquely, have language, and *verbal memory* is concerned with spoken material, such as conversations, and written material, such as text. It is also concerned with other language-based knowledge such as the meaning of words and the kind of facts we need to know for a general knowledge quiz. Research into various aspects of verbal memory has made a major contribution to the development of theory and practice, which also applies to other memory domains such as visual and autobiographical memory.

Long-term memory systems

Episodic, semantic and procedural memory

Long-term memory actually refers to a number of different memory systems. Endel Tulving (1985) has been the architect of a theory that identifies these different types of memory. First, we have memories about episodes in our lives: going to the cinema last night, sitting a psychology exam last term, making a new friend last week, and so on. Tulving calls this kind of memory *episodic memory*. The memories here are time-tagged multidimensional memories about people, objects, places and actions woven together. They are also accompanied by a clear awareness of remembering.

Second, and in contrast, we also have memories of a factual kind. This is evident from listening to any quiz show on television where the contestants can often recall a staggering number of obscure facts – or from your own knowledge of taking exams. In addition we also have a huge store of conceptual knowledge such as what is meant by furniture, animal and truth. These memories are not time-tagged and are stored, according to Tulving, in *semantic memory*, a different system to episodic memory.

Finally, Tulving argues that there is a third kind of memory, called *procedural memory*, which is knowledge of how to do things. It is a system for knowledge of different kind of skills such as riding a bike, playing the piano, doing jigsaw puzzles and solving puzzles such as the Tower of Hanoi (also known as the Tower of London). An important characteristic of procedural memory is that it is not time-tagged and is implicit in the sense that we have no feeling of remembering or even knowing that we are calling upon memory. You know how to ride a bike, but you can't necessarily explain how you do it.

Explicit and implicit memory processes

One of the distinctions between these systems lies in whether the memory processes are *explicit* or *implicit*. Explicit processes are accompanied by conscious activity such as searching. If asked what we did last night we consciously search for the answer. Thus episodic memory is generally characterised by explicit processes. Implicit processes are not accompanied by awareness or conscious processes. The memory is reflected in the behaviour. So when you drive your car you're not consciously remembering what you have to do – your knowledge is implicit and reflected in the fact that you're doing the job reasonably well. Thus procedural memory is characterised by implicit processes. The processes in semantic memory, however, are not so clear. If asked for a fact ('What is the capital of Australia?') or a definition ('What's a ball?') you do have to search consciously, but when you use the term ball in conversation you do so implicitly.

Neuropsychological evidence

One source of evidence for the distinction between these memory systems comes from neuropsychology. Thus amnesics such as Clive Wearing and H.M. have devastated episodic memories, with very little recall of their past lives. Conversely, they seem to have relatively unimpaired semantic memories in that they retain large vocabularies and conceptual knowledge about the world (e.g. Baddeley and Wilson, 1988). Most strikingly, all amnesics retain their procedural knowledge. Recall that Clive Wearing retained his many sophisticated musical skills.

Sensory memory, short-term memory (STM) and long-term memory (LTM)

Visual sensory memory (iconic memory)

Iconic memory was discovered by George Sperling as a PhD student at Harvard in the late 1950s. Sperling (1960) presented participants with an array containing 12 letters, as shown below.

W	J	D	L
R	V	G	M
N	Q	F	S

This array was presented for a very short time (50 msecs). This is such a short time that there is no time for eye movements or checking on what has appeared. When participants were asked to report what they had seen they were typically able to remember about four letters. This was the whole report condition. Sperling was convinced that all the letters were available but that most of them had faded by the time three or four had been reported. To show that all the letters were available for a brief time in sensory memory he devised the partial report condition.

In the partial report condition the visual array was followed by one of three tones. Participants were told to report the top line if they heard a high tone; the middle line if they heard a middle tone and the bottom line if they heard a low tone. Because the tone occurred after the visual display had gone from the screen any letters they reported must have come from their memory of the display. Sperling called this memory store *iconic memory*. Participants were very successful at reporting letters from any of the three lines. This indicated that information about all the lines was present in iconic memory. Perfect performance would have been 12 letters. They actually reported about nine. Sperling then increased the interval between the presentation of the array and the onset of the tone. As this interval increased the number of letters reported fell off. At an interval of approximately one second about four letters were being reported. This is the same as in the whole report condition. Sperling concluded that the duration of sensory memory was actually about one-third of a second (see Figure 14.1).

An intriguing question concerned whether iconic memory occurred before or after the letters had been identified. An experiment by von Wright (1968) presented mixed arrays of letters and numbers, and asked participants to report either the letters or the numbers. If iconic memory is operating after letters and numbers have been identified then the results should have been the same as when the instructions to report were based on location (tones or bars). They were not, indicating that iconic memory holds information at an early stage of processing, before they have been identified.

What is the purpose of iconic memory? Coltheart (1983) argues that it ensures that information is held in raw form for a minimum amount of time, allowing the processes of perception and attention to operate. (This issue is covered in Chapter 13.)

Distinguishing short- and long-term memory

The distinction between short- and long-term memory was first made by William James (1890). He argued that primary memory (STM) holds whatever is in our consciousness, while secondary memory (LTM) contains the sum of our past experiences. In this section we report the evidence for the existence of separate systems for short- and long-term memory.

Capacity

The first major difference between short-term memory (STM) and long-term memory (LTM) is their respective capacities. The capacity of long-term memory is huge. Consider, for example, all the factual information you've acquired, and can remember, over many years of education. In contrast, the capacity of STM is very limited. George Miller (1956) showed that we could hold about seven items in short-term memory, plus or minus two (i.e. between five and nine). This can be demonstrated in a simple experiment on immediate memory span (see Research Methods Box 14.1).

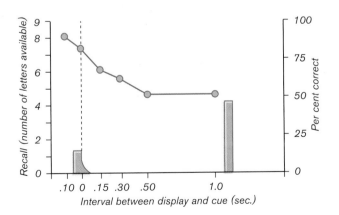

Figure 14.1 *The decay of sensory memory: the number of letters reported decreases with time*
Source: Solso, 1998: 87

RESEARCH METHODS BOX 14.1

Measuring the capacity of short-term memory

A common way of measuring the capacity of short-term memory is to measure a person's *digit span*. Digit span is one of the subtests of the Wechsler adult intelligence scale. The question is: how many digits can the person repeat back, without error and in the right order? Recalling the right digits immediately after presentation in the right order is known as immediate *serial recall*. Recalling the right digits in any order is known as *free recall*.

The steps are as follows.

1 Assemble the test materials, consisting of several rows of digits of increasing length (see below).
2 The experimenter reads out a row of digits at the rate of about one per second.
3 After the last digit, the participant repeats the numbers back, in the correct order.
4 Continue with the following rows until there is an error.
5 The person's digit span is the number of digits in the last errorless row.

```
8 4 7 5
1 9 6 4 3
3 6 1 4 5 3
8 2 7 5 9 4 6
2 5 1 4 9 2 3 9
9 4 6 3 6 1 3 2 5
8 5 1 9 4 6 8 2 4 2
4 3 7 2 5 4 3 9 5 4 7
```

Duration

A second difference between STM and LTM is the length of time for which material is held. Information can be held in LTM for a very long time and in many cases a lifetime. The term *permastore* has been used to refer to the durability of long-term memory (it is analogous to the term permafrost, which describes

223

ACTIVITY BOX 14.1

What is your letter span?

To get an approximate answer to this question, test your memory for each of the rows of letters below. For each row, read the letters out loud, about one per second. After the last letter, cover the line and write the letters down in the correct order. Continue with the remaining rows until you make a mistake. Your letter span is the number of letters in the last error-free row.

d t b j
r k c s t
l n r v z l
m p l x g v t
r t s d h k l b
m b c l j d s r f
k s r t n p v l s b
m r b k n d f z j p t

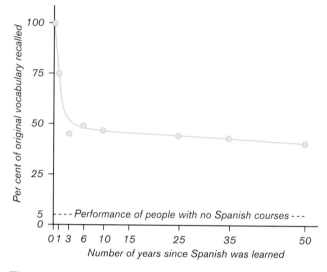

Figure 14.2 *Memory for Spanish vocabulary learnt up to 50 years previously*
Source: graph adapted by Rubin, 1995, from Bahrick, 1984

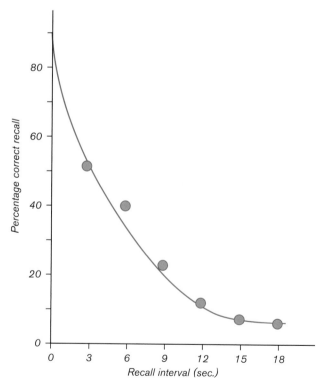

Figure 14.3 *Short-term forgetting: the graph shows loss of information from STM over a period of time*
Source: Peterson and Peterson, 1959

the permanently frozen ground of Arctic regions). This isn't the case for all memories, but certainly for enough of them to be significant. Experimentally, the durability of long-term verbal memory was shown by Bahrick (1984), who found that people who had learnt Spanish some 50 years earlier remembered almost half the vocabulary they had acquired (see Figure 14.2).

In contrast, the durability of material in short-term memory is severely limited. This was shown by classic experiments in the 1950s and 1960s (Peterson and Peterson, 1959) using the Brown–Peterson technique. On each trial of the Brown–Peterson experiment the participant is given a single trigram (a three-letter syllable such as lef or kib), which has to be remembered for a length of time that varies from trial to trial. At the end of the specified time, the participant has to report the trigram. If rehearsal is allowed then performance is always around 100 per cent. However, if rehearsal is prevented by, say, asking the subject to count backwards in threes (100, 97, 94, etc.) then the trigram is forgotten after about 15 seconds (see Figure 14.3).

Notice that the graphs in Figures 14.2 and 14.3 have a similar form. The loss of information is initially rapid, followed by a decrease in the rate until the curve flattens out, indicating that very little is lost from then on. This is the classic 'forgetting curve'. However, it doesn't always indicate the same underlying processes. Forgetting from long-term memory is generally taken to be through *interference*, with new and old memories becoming confused and eventually irretrievable, while forgetting in short-term memory is generally taken to be through *trace decay*, with the neural substrate of the memory fading over time or *displacement*, with early material being pushed out by recent material.

Encoding

A third potential difference between STM and LTM lies in *encoding*, or the form in which incoming information is held. The two main forms are phonological and semantic encoding. A spoken sentence could be encoded in terms of the speech sounds of the words or in terms of the meaning of the words. The former is referred to as *phonological encoding*, the latter as *semantic encoding*.

Generally, encoding is phonological in short-term memory and semantic in long-term memory. This is consistent with our own experiences. If someone gives me their telephone number I rehearse it verbally until I can write it down. But if I want to remember a fact for the longer term then I remember it in terms of the meaning. Interestingly, trying to remember jokes seems to need both memory for the general content of the joke and for the precise wording. A misremembered punchline guarantees puzzled looks and a stony silence.

Evidence for phonological encoding in STM comes from an experiment by Baddeley (1966a), who presented participants with a list of five words (well within the capacity of STM) for immediate serial recall. He found that words that were phonologically similar (man, mad, cap, can, map) were not remembered as well as words that were semantically similar (big, huge, broad, long, tall) or unrelated (pen, rig, day, bar, sup). The similarity of the sounds was disrupting their phonological encoding.

In a second experiment he increased the number of words to ten and inserted an interval between presentation and recall in which rehearsal was prevented. The task now required LTM, first because ten words exceeds the capacity of STM and, second, because of the interval. The semantically similar list produced the worst performance, indicating the use of semantic encoding in LTM (Baddeley, 1966b).

ACTIVITY BOX 14.2

The effect of phonological confusability (Conrad and Hull, 1964)

Read the following letter string once, one letter at a time at the rate of about one letter per second. Then cover the line and write down as many letters as you can, preserving the letter order.

PVBCEDG

How many did you get in the right order?
Now repeat the procedure for this next letter string:

RZAFHNL

How many did you get this time? Most people get fewer letters when they rhyme because of the phonological confusability of the first set.

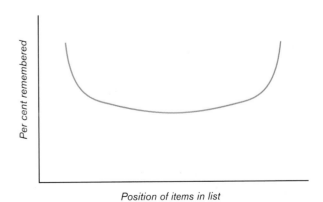

Figure 14.4 Graph of idealised serial position effect

Rugby fans tend to remember the last few games best − a recency effect in long-term memory (Baddeley and Hitch, 1977)

Serial position effect

A phenomenon that seems to distinguish between STM and LTM is the *serial position effect*. If participants are presented with a list of 20 words and then asked to recall them in any order (free recall), we find that the first few items and the last few items in the list tend to be remembered better than the middle items – that is, memory depends on the serial position in the list (Glanzer and Cunitz, 1966) (see Figure 14.4).

The enhanced memory for the first few items in the list is called the *primacy effect*. The enhanced memory for the last few items is called the *recency effect*. How does this relate to the short-term/long-term memory difference? Basically, the first few items are remembered well because they are transferred to long-term memory as soon as they enter the system. The last few items are remembered well because they are still in short-term memory when the list is being recalled. The middle items suffer because the system becomes overwhelmed trying, simultaneously, to encode, to rehearse and to transfer items to long-term memory. However, this interpretation of the serial position curve needs to be treated with caution because we find recency effects in long-term memory. For example, rugby fans tend to remember the last few games of the season better than those in the middle (Baddeley and Hitch, 1977).

Neuropsychology

Perhaps the strongest evidence for separate short- and long-term memory systems comes from neuropsychology. The separation is well illustrated in the case of H.M., an amnesic very similar to Clive Wearing. H.M. has been studied for nearly 50 years and has become a celebrity in his own right. Corkin (Postle and Corkin, 1998) has reviewed H.M.'s case since the onset of his amnesia in the 1950s, and has found that he did not know where he lived, who cared for him, or the date or year. He didn't recognise a picture of himself taken a few years earlier. He didn't remember what he'd seen recently on television and had little awareness of current affairs (e.g. who is the current prime minister). Clearly his long-term memory is severely impaired.

On the other hand, he performed normally on tests of short-term memory such as digit span. Thus H.M. presents a picture of an intact short-term memory but virtually non-existent long-term memory.

The opposite condition was found in the patient K.F. (Shallice and Warrington, 1970), who had a normal long-term memory but a severely impaired short-term memory, with a memory span of only one item. The fact that these two people have complementary impairments of short- and long-term memory provides powerful evidence for separate systems (see Research Methods Box 14.2).

In this section we have looked at representative evidence for distinguishing short- and long-term memory on the basis of their capacity, the duration of memories and the coding system. We also reported ambiguous evidence from the serial position effect and powerful evidence from neuropsychology.

Three models of short-term memory

The modal model of memory

An early model of short- and long-term memory was that of Atkinson and Shiffrin (1968), which was developed specifically to account for the results just

RESEARCH METHODS BOX 14.2

Dissociation and double dissociations of function

This is an investigative tool used extensively in the neuropsychology of cognitive function to make inferences about how the mind is organised. Its purpose is to discover whether two sets of structures or processes are independent of each other.

Suppose we are looking for evidence that short-term memory and long-term memory are the products of different sets of cognitive processes – let's call them STM processes and LTM processes. One source of such evidence would be people who, through disease or injury, have suffered brain damage and are cognitively impaired. In particular we would be on the lookout for a person or persons who have a memory problem (and as few other impairments as possible, to keep matters simple). We would be looking specifically for a person with a long-term memory loss. On finding such a person we would give them an extensive battery of tests to measure precisely their pattern of memory impairments. The question would be 'Which aspects of memory have been lost and which aspects preserved?' The pattern we would be looking for is one in which all measures of long-term memory (acquiring new information, remembering recent events etc.) produce poor scores, suggesting an impairment, but one in which measures of short-term memory (e.g. memory span) produce high scores.

The inference to be drawn would be that the two sets of functions are dissociated, or separated, from each other. The existence of this case would be evidence for a dissociation of the functions of short-term and long-term memory.

It could, however, be argued that the result could be due to something other than different sets of processes that were differentially impaired. The most obvious one is that perhaps the tests of long-term memory were harder than those of short-term memory. The person concerned was therefore able to do the latter but not the former.

The objection would effectively be refuted if we then found another patient with the reverse pattern of impairment. That is, someone who failed all the tests of short-term memory, indicating an impairment, but who passed all the tests of long-term memory. The task difficulty explanation falls down because this patient has passed the hard tests and failed the easy ones. The separate processes explanation survives.

Either one of these patients on his/her own constitutes a *dissociation of function*. Together they constitute a *double dissociation of function*. The principle underlying dissociation of function applies to any area of cognitive psychology, not just memory. It is a much used methodological investigative tool in cognitive neuropsychology. Notice the similarity between dissociation of function and the *dual-task paradigm* (see Chapter 13). They both provide evidence that two sets of processes are independent of each other, one by making inferences from a pattern of impairment and the other from the pattern of response to doing two tasks at the same time.

reported (see Figure 14.5). The sensory store of the model was described briefly above.

In the *modal model of memory*, STM and LTM are presented as connected memory stores, the characteristics of which have been outlined above. In addition, the short-term store has a number of control processes such as rehearsal, coding and retrieval. *Rehearsal* is the means by which information is moved into the long-term store, while *retrieval* is the process by which required information is fetched from its home in the long-term store. Information is lost from STM by trace decay and from LTM by interference.

There were several problems with this model. The claim that information had to pass through STM to reach LTM was wrong. The patient K.F. (see above), who had a badly impaired STM, was still able to acquire and retain new information in LTM. According to the modal model, which says that information has to pass through STM to reach LTM, this should not have happened.

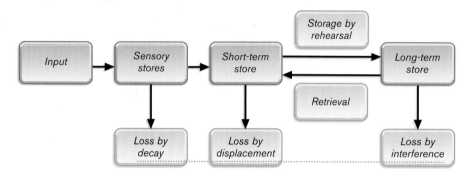

Figure 14.5 *Atkinson and Shiffrin's (1968) modal model of memory: this was developed to account for all the research at the time; it consisted of three memory stores with information that wasn't lost en route passing sequentially through the three stores*

ACTIVITY BOX 14.3

Doing two tasks simultaneously.

The purpose of this activity is for you to get a feel for the role of short-term memory in spelling. You'll need a friend to help.

1 Condition 1: spell one of the words listed below.
2 Condition 2: ask your friend to read out a set of the random digits below. Your task is to hold them in your short-term memory using rehearsal. Once you've begun rehearsing the digits, he or she should then say a (different) word to be spelt.
3 Condition 3: ask your friend to read out a set of random letters. Again, when you're rehearsing he or she reads out another word to be spelt.

Now rank these three tasks in order of difficulty. Which was the easiest? Why?

Words to be spelt: contribution, retribution, attribution
Random digit string: 824963
Random letter string: rfknvj

Answer: the spelling task by itself should be the easiest. Next comes the spelling with the digit load, because even though you were doing two tasks at the same time, the degree of interference between digits and letters is minimal. The letters and spelling should be the hardest because there is both a memory load and maximum interference between tasks.

In addition, rehearsal does not play such an important role in LTM as the model suggested. Most of what we remember is encoded automatically; we don't go around making a point of trying to remember the events in our lives by rehearsing them. Note that these criticisms are not discounting the existence of short- and long-term stores, merely this model of them.

Another major problem with the modal model was that although it identified 'control processes' such as decision-making, the short-term store didn't really seem to have a purpose, other than to remember telephone numbers! In contrast, an alternative model proposed by Baddeley and Hitch (1974) specifically asked what short-term memory is for. They explored the role of STM in everyday cognitive tasks such as understanding spoken sentences and verbal reasoning. They approached the general problem by asking participants to carry out cognitive tasks such as prose comprehension and simple reasoning, while simultaneously remembering a set of digits. What they found was that while performance on the cognitive task was impaired by the simultaneous digit load, the impairment was much less than expected from the Atkinson and Shiffrin model. Atkinson and Shiffrin would predict that the digits would fill the short-term store, leaving no space for the requirements of the cognitive task. This, in turn should lead to badly impaired performance on the cognitive task. This did not happen, suggesting that the structure of memory envisioned by Atkinson and Shiffrin (1968) was wrong. These experiments were the beginning of the *working memory model* (Baddeley and Hitch, 1974; Baddeley, 1986; 1998).

Working memory

In the working memory model the notion of a single, passive holding store (STM) is replaced by a multicomponent system with interacting storage and processing components. It is an active system, geared towards carrying out cognitive processing. We can see that this concept is closer to William James's idea that primary memory is related to consciousness.

Working memory (WM) has three components (see Figure 14.6). First there is the *central executive*, which, as its name implies, oversees the processing of information. It focuses attention and allocates resources to the task in hand. It is an online supervisor of cognitive function.

The central executive is served by two slave systems. One of these is the *phonological loop*. This is a speech-based short-term store with a limited capacity, limited duration (assuming rehearsal is prevented) and phonological encoding. It is similar to the kind of short-term store we've been discussing and therefore accounts for the experimental findings described earlier. The other slave system is the *visuospatial scratchpad*. This is a short-term store for visual information. It expands the horizons of the model beyond verbal memory. It is the locus of visual imagery and plays an important role in the processing of visual information. To get an idea of the kind of task it might be used for, ask yourself this question: 'How many windows are there in my house?' How did you answer it? You almost certainly visualised each room in your house in turn, counting the windows as you went, thus using the visuospatial scratchpad.

Further details of working memory can be found in Baddeley (1997). An evaluation can be found in Eysenck and Keene (2000). A major criticism of WM is that the phonological loop and the visuospatial scratchpad do not seem to play as significant a role in cognitive processing as was expected and that cognitive processing is too often hypothesised to

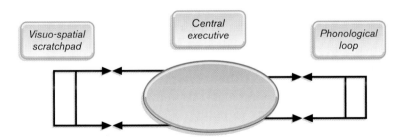

*Figure 14.6 Working memory model: this consists of a central processor or executive served by two slave systems – a phonological loop and a visuospatial scratchpad
Source: Baddeley, 1997: 52*

occur in the central executive, about which very little is known (Donald, 1991). However, Applications Box 14.1 gives a brief description of how the model has been useful.

Levels of processing

An alternative to the two-memory view is the idea that memory consists of one system and that differences between short- and long-term memory can be explained in terms of *levels of processing* (Craik and Lockhart, 1972). This idea holds that shallow processing – processing of superficial perceptual aspects of the to-be-remembered stimulus (e.g. the appearance or sound of words) – would lead to short-term retention, and that deep processing – processing of the meaning – would lead to long-term retention.

The problem with the levels of processing idea is that there is no independent way of distinguishing between deep and shallow processes. Consequently the predictions made are circular: shallow processing leads to poorer memory than deep processing, but the way that shallow and deep processes are distinguished is by the fact that they lead to differences in memory!

APPLICATIONS BOX 14.1

Working memory and learning vocabulary

Gathercole and Baddeley (1989) were investigating a cohort of language-disordered children who had normal non-verbal intelligence but delayed language. They were about two years behind on reading, vocabulary and spelling, and about four years behind on non-word repetition. Non-word repetition is a simple task in which the child is asked to repeat back to the experimenter a set of non-words such as ledmond and bavsimp. Non-word repetition is hypothesised to require efficient operation of the phonological loop.

The co-occurrence of poor non-word repetition and poor performance on language tasks alerted Gathercole and Baddeley to the possibility that there might be a causal relationship – that is, impaired non-word repetition, and hence an impaired phonological loop, might be the reason why these children's vocabulary development was delayed.

Using this information, they tested a group of 100 normal four- to five-year-old children and found a significant correlation between non-word repetition and vocabulary size, both at the start of the study and at subsequent follow-ups. Thus it seems that the phonological loop may be involved in the acquisition of a vocabulary.

Long-term memory: encoding, retrieval and forgetting

Long-term memory is a system with a large – perhaps infinite – capacity. It uses semantic encoding of information and has a duration that can be a lifetime. This section examines the processes of encoding (or learning), of remembering and of forgetting. Again, the research is overwhelmingly verbal in nature but the assumption is that the principles generalise to non-verbal memory systems.

Encoding

Organisation

There is considerable evidence that the key to remembering complex information is to organise it. Many students arrive at this conclusion on their own, covering their walls in the pre-examination period with diagrams, boxes and arrows to denote the key topics and the relationship between them. In the laboratory, Bousfield (1953) showed that memory for 60 categorised words (names of animals, vegetables, professions and boys) presented randomly was better than for 60 random words. Also, the words were remembered in semantically related clusters (e.g. some animal names together, and so on). Bower, Clark, Lesgold and Winzenz (1969) showed that words presented in a hierarchical organisation were remembered better than the same words presented randomly (see Figure 14.7).

Perhaps most impressively, Mandler (1967) showed that instructions to organise were as effective as instructions to learn. One group of participants was given a pack of cards, with a word on each, and asked to sort (organise) the pack in a meaningful way (e.g. groups of related words together). Nothing was said about subsequent recall. A second group was instructed to learn the words for subsequent recall. A third group was told both to organise and learn. There was no difference in the amount recalled between groups.

This study is a strong illustration of the power of organisation and of *incidental learning*, in which we acquire memories without having any intention to do so. We all know that we don't go around constantly making decisions about whether or not we want to remember a particular event. These incidental memories are the product of what Hasher and Zacks (1984) have called *automatic processing*, to be distinguished from the conscious *effortful processing* that we engage in when, say, learning for an exam. (See Chapter 13 for more on the distinction between automatic and effortful or controlled processing.)

An important determinant of organisation is the presence of a *schema*, or mental framework, to guide it. A schema is an organised pattern of thought about some aspect of the world, such as class of people, events, situations or objects (Bartlett, 1932). For example, proficient chess players acquire a chess schema, composed of strategies, situations and past experiences, which they have acquired over the years and which they use to guide their play. Chase and Simon (1973) gave an expert, an intermediate and a novice chess player a few seconds to look at a chess board with about 25 pieces and then reproduce the positions. When the positions were meaningful (as in a game) the expert remembered them best and the novice worst. When the pieces were randomly arranged, however, all three players remembered them equally badly (about three pieces). In the first situation the expert's schema was usable and helped him encode the positions, but in the second case it wasn't.

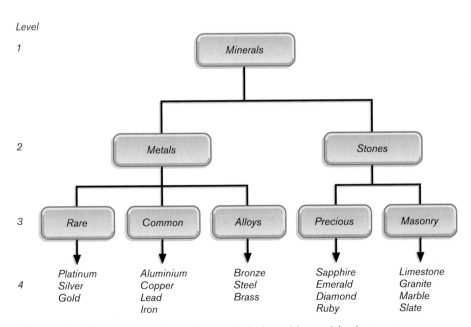

Figure 14.7 Presentation of materials in a hierarchical structure
Source: Bower et al., 1969

APPLICATIONS BOX 14.2

Improving memory for medical instructions

How well do you remember instructions given to you by your doctor? According to a review by Ley (1988), not very well. In a survey of studies looking at this it emerged that you are likely to remember about half of what you're told. Clearly, the information you get from your doctor is important and could be critical.

Ley, a clinical psychologist, looked at different ways in which patients' memory for information and instructions could be improved. In one study, making use of what we know about the primacy effect, he presented the important information at the beginning. There was a significant improvement in memory (Ley, 1972). In another study he found that advice was remembered best if it was explicit rather than general: 'You must weigh yourself every Saturday and lose eight pounds by 30 June', rather than 'You must weight yourself regularly and lose some weight' (Bradshaw, Ley, Kincey and Bradshaw, 1975).

In another study he used the evidence that categorising information enhanced memory. So the instructions went like this: 'I am going to tell you what is wrong, then what tests you need to have, then what the treatment will be. First, what is wrong with you: I think you have bronchitis. Second, what tests you need: some X-rays and a blood test. Third, the treatment I'm going to give you: an antibiotic, which I want you to take three times a day after having eaten something.' Again, memory for this information was improved significantly (after Baddeley, 1997).

Mnemonics

The use of *mnemonics* to remember information was of particular help when the majority of people were illiterate and writing tools were cumbersome. Nowadays, we have so many recording devices that the use of mnemonics is more like a party trick. Some, however, can still be useful.

One of the best-known mnemonic systems is the method of loci, used by Roman orators to remember the key points of their speeches. The technique involves visualising a walk through the rooms in a 'memory theatre', leaving one of the key topics at each location. So, if the speech was to argue against a war that Caesar was about to wage, the orator might visualise leaving a sack of money in the first room to represent the costs of the war, a woman crying over her dead son in the next room to represent the possible consequences, and so on.

Another strategy used by many students (Soler and Ruiz, 1996) consists of reducing what is to be remembered to a few key points and then encoding these with an acronym (e.g. the colours of the rainbow as ROYGBIV). It is an example of a *reduction mnemonic*.

A third technique uses an *elaboration mnemonic*. You've probably come across the rhyme:

One is a bun
Two is a shoe
Three is a tree
Four is a door
Five is a hive
Six is sticks
Seven is heaven
Eight is a gate
Nine is wine
Ten is a hen

The idea, if you're trying to remember something like a short shopping list, is to associate each item on the list with each line of the rhyme, using bizarre images. Thus for toothpaste you might imagine eating a bun spread with toothpaste; for a bottle of milk you might imagine stuffing it into your shoes, and so on (see Figure 14.8). When the time to remember comes, you recite the poem and up pop the items you want.

Notice that mnemonic devices work because they function as retrieval cues that enable you to access the information you want. They don't affect the amount of information that is learnt.

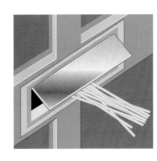

Figure 14.8 An example of an imaging technique that might be used in an elaboration mnemonic

---

ACTIVITY BOX 14.4

Using mnemonics to learn the STM/LTM distinction

We have outlined three mnemonic strategies to remember information that can be put into a list: the method of loci, reduction coding, which produces an acronym, and elaboration coding involving a rhyme.

Now look back at the section that reviewed the evidence for distinguishing short-term and long-term memory. This consists of a series of discrete points that form a list. You should be able to apply each of the aforementioned mnemonic strategies to this list. Apply each strategy in turn and decide which you think would be the easiest to use, and which would be the most effective if you were working for an exam and anticipated a question on the STM/LTM distinction.

Retrieval

Retrieval cues

How do we remember? One of the most important determinants of retrieving information from long-term memory is the presence of a *retrieval cue*. This is simply a piece of information, related to the memory in some way, that enables the memory to be found and retrieved. So if I wanted you to tell me about a film you'd seen last month I would have to

identify it in some way. The title is obviously one retrieval cue but if I didn't know it, then I might say, 'Tell me about the film you saw last Thursday with Rebecca and John'. Of course, if you'd been to a film festival then I would need to be even more specific.

Endel Tulving has shown in a series of experiments over many years that appropriate retrieval cues are essential for the retrieval of memories (Tulving and Osler, 1968; Tulving and Psotka, 1971; Tulving and Thompson, 1973).

Tulving distinguished between the *availability of memories* (they are 'in there somewhere') and the *accessibility of memories* (whether they can or can't

Endel Tulving

be accessed on a particular occasion). Retrieval cues make available memories accessible. In one experiment (Tulving and Pearlstone, 1966), participants were asked to remember a list of words that could be (but weren't) categorised (e.g. names of animals, names of metals). After learning the list, the subjects recalled as much as they could. They were then given the category names (animals, metals, transport) as retrieval cues and this enabled them to remember items they hadn't remembered previously.

A particularly interesting retrieval cue is context: where and when an event occurred. We all know that memory of an experience is improved by information about when it occurred, where it occurred, who we were with at the time, and so on. One of the most spectacular experiments on context was carried out by Godden and Baddeley (1975). They found that divers who were asked to learn a word list on land remembered it better on land than underwater, while a list learned underwater was remembered better underwater than on land. This is a classic example of *context-dependent memory*. This is when something experienced in a particular context is best remembered in that same context.

Another kind of context is one's internal state. Goodwin, Powell, Bremer, Hoine and Stern (1969) found that what their subjects learned while drunk they remembered better when drunk than when sober. Conversely, what they learned sober was better remembered when sober than when drunk. This is an example of *state-dependent memory*. Experiments involving a variety of other drugs, including caffeine, have found the same effect of internal state (e.g. Carter and Cassidy, 1998).

Similar findings exist for *mood-dependent memory* (e.g. happiness and sadness). These ideas were formalised by Tulving (Tulving and Osler, 1968; Tulving, 1983) into his *encoding specificity principle*, which states that a retrieval cue is successful only if it is present at the time of encoding. In other words, the more the conditions at retrieval resemble those at encoding, the more likely is a successful retrieval.

Constructive memory

An important characteristic of memory and remembering is that it is a *constructive process*. We

This still from the film City Lights illustrates state-dependent memory. A drunken millionaire spends the evening drinking with Charlie Chaplin's character after Chaplin saves his life. The next day the millionaire is sober, doesn't recognise Chaplin and kicks him out. On getting drunk, he remembers Chaplain again.
Source: Passer and Smith, 2001: 292

don't just faithfully report the contents of a memory trace, which is probably sketchy and incomplete – we construct the memory from what is stored and from relevant schemata we may have, adding or changing details to produce a plausible outcome. We add in our own details and interpretations so that things make sense (Bartlett, 1932; Neisser, 1984; Schacter, Norman and Koutstaal, 1998).

For example, we have schemata for different kinds of robberies (bank robberies, muggings and so on), which consist of stereotypic characters performing stereotypic actions in a predictable sequence. When a robbery deviates from this we tend to distort what we recall to fit the schema of the robbery rather than what we actually witnessed (Holst and Bezdek, 1992).

Forgetting

How do we forget? Perhaps the best-known theory of *motivated forgetting* is Freud's theory of repression. This states that forgetting occurs because memories are emotionally painful, the remnants of a trauma or unpleasant event. In an effort to cope with the emotional pain, the mind represses the memory. The main problem with this theory is that it doesn't explain the vast amount of forgetting of mundane events that occurs daily.

An early alternative to repression is trace decay (Ebbinghaus, 1885; Broadbent, 1958). The idea here is that a memory is laid down in the brain as a memory trace, a physiological or chemical change, which is subject to 'decay' (i.e. a reversal of the change, over time). However, this theory leaves a lot of unanswered questions, such as why some memories should decay while others are retained for years. Neither does it allow for the fact that forgetting may occur because of the intervention of other events.

Interference theory argues that memories are subject to interference from other memories and that we forget because they become entangled with both earlier and later memories. Early researchers identified two types of interference: *proactive interference* and *retroactive interference* (McGeogh and McDonald, 1931; Underwood, 1957) (see Figure 14.9).

Suppose a participant sees two science fiction films. Proactive interference (Figure 14.9a) occurs when s/he is tested on his/her memory for the second film, and the first film acts 'forward' in time to interfere with his/her memory of it. Retroactive interference (Figure 14.9b) occurs in the same scenario when the participant is tested on his/her memory of the first film, which has been interfered with by the second film.

Consider the following example. Suppose you saw a science fiction film a month ago and another one a week ago, and suppose that on different occasions you are asked to describe both films. If, when describing the first film, you left out bits because your memory system had them coded as coming from the second film, or if you brought bits of the second film into your description of the first film, then you would be experiencing retroactive interference. Memories of the second film would be working retroactively (backwards) to interfere with memories of the first film. Similarly, if your description of the second film was being affected by memories of the first film, you would be experiencing proactive interference.

An important determinant of interference is the similarity of the memories. You are far more likely to experience interference between two science fiction films than between a science fiction film and a musical. Interference theory provides a very powerful account of forgetting and explains the common experience of confusing memories.

Forgetting can be thought of simply as a failure to remember. As we saw in the section on remembering, this often occurs in the absence of the appropriate retrieval cue. A forgotten memory is one that is available but not (currently) accessible. A major problem with this theory is that it is impossible to prove wrong. You could spend years trying to remember a particular piece of information, trying every possible retrieval cue, but your claim that you had forgotten the information (i.e. it was gone for ever) would be met with the argument that you simply hadn't found the right retrieval cue and should keep trying!

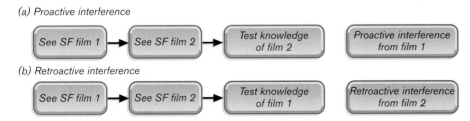

(a) Proactive interference

See SF film 1 → See SF film 2 → Test knowledge of film 2   Proactive interference from film 1

(b) Retroactive interference

See SF film 1 → See SF film 2 → Test knowledge of film 1   Retroactive interference from film 2

Figure 14.9 Diagrammatic representation of the difference between proactive and retroactive interference

Section 3
Cognitive Psychology

Autobiographical memory (AM)

The nature of AM

Autobiographical memory is memory for biographical information and for life experiences. It's your personal memory system, containing information about you and your experiences. At first glance it seems obviously related to Tulving's notion of episodic memory, and many researchers, including Nelson (1989), have thought of it in this way. However, Robinson (1992) points out that we need to distinguish between our *autobiographical knowledge* and memories for *autobiographical episodes*.

APPLICATIONS BOX 14.3

Eyewitness testimony

The importance of knowing how accurate memory is when testifying in a court of law is illustrated by a case described by Loftus (1979).

An assistant manager of a small-town store in the USA was kidnapped by two men. They drove him to his place of work and demanded he open the safe. He managed to get a glimpse of them before they pulled on their masks. Fortunately he managed to convince them that he didn't know the combination to the safe and they let him go. He was able to give a description of one of the men and said that he looked like someone who had recently applied for a job at the store. Three days later the police stopped and arrested Sandie and Lonnie Sawyer, who were driving a similar car but neither of whom looked anything like the photofit that had been constructed. At the trial, the store manager identified the couple as the men who had abducted him and in spite of eight witnesses who testified that they had been elsewhere, they were convicted. The story ends happily because a year later the abductors were tracked down by a private investigator and the Sawyers subsequently released.

The question that immediately arises is: how did the victim make such a catastrophic mistake of identification? Was it because he had been intimidated by the police, who wanted a quick result? Or was it a genuine case of misidentification? (If the latter, what kind of memory factors were responsible?) Perhaps it was a combination of these explanations. The fact that eyewitness testimony can be so unreliable, for a host of reasons, makes it a prime case for psychological investigation.

The American psychologist Elizabeth Loftus is perhaps the most renowned expert witness in psychology, and has been called upon in numerous court cases to inform judges and juries about what needs to be taken into consideration when deciding on the reliability of an eyewitness's testimony.

The work for which she is best known looked at the degree to which misleading questions about an event can affect a witness's memory for that event. Briefly, she (Loftus and Palmer, 1974) showed undergraduate students film of two car accidents, after which they were asked questions about what they had seen. Some participants were asked, 'About how fast were the cars going when they smashed into each other?' Other participants were asked the same question, but the words 'smashed into' were replaced with 'contacted' or 'hit' or 'bumped' or 'collided with'. Participants were then asked to estimate the speed at which the cars were travelling. This varied from 32 mph for 'contacted' to 41 mph for 'smashed into'.

In a later, similar experiment, participants were more likely to report seeing broken glass after the collision if the question had used the words 'smashed into' than if it had used the word 'hit'.

The important conclusion to draw from this is that when we report the contents of our memories we are not simply reporting what is in the memory trace of that event. Instead, memory is more an act of reconstruction, which is susceptible to inaccuracy, distortion and confusion with subsequent events.

Much work has been done since these original experiments. Ridley and Clifford (2002), for example, have been looking at the effects of anxiety on susceptibility to misleading questions and have found that higher levels of anxiety decrease susceptibility.

Cars after a collision.

Elizabeth Loftus

Autobiographical knowledge is information about where and when you were born, your educational history, places you've lived, your work history, your marriage and children. Your memory for autobiographic episodes is, in contrast, less systematic and more idiosyncratic, involving descriptions about specific episodes in your life that you remember particularly well.

Tulving, Schacter, McLachlan and Moscovitch (1988) describe a head-injured patient who knows his life history but cannot remember any specific episodes from it. This suggests that even though episodes overlap, biographical information has its roots in semantic memory while autobiographical episodes are rooted in episodic memory. Another

piece of evidence that autobiographical memory is a system in its own right comes from De Renzi, Liotti and Michelli (1987), who report a patient who had lost much of episodic and semantic memory but whose autobiographical memory was preserved.

Distribution of AM memories over the life span
How much of the past do we remember? Rubins, Wetzler and Nebes (1986) collected the results from several studies that presented participants with cue words such as 'friend', 'home' and 'work', and asked them to respond with memories evoked by these cue words. In response to the cue 'friend', for instance, you might recall a school friend you haven't seen for some years. Their participants were 50 and 70 years

old. When combined, the results of these studies showed that memories were not distributed evenly over the life span (see Figure 14.10).

Rubins *et al.* identified three components. First, there was a *retention function* for the most recent memories. Recent memories were remembered best, dropping off to when the person was about 40–50 years old. Second, there was a rise in memories from the teens and early twenties; they called this a *reminiscence bump*, reflecting a person's tendency to reminisce about events during their youth. Third, there was amnesia for the early years of childhood, with few memories from the preschool years.

Several researchers have speculated about the causes of *childhood amnesia*. There is the Freudian explanation that childhood is full of guilty memories about the anal and genital stages, and that these have been repressed. A more plausible explanation is by Schactel (1947), who argued that memories are coded in different ways before and after children acquire language. Young children's experiences are perceptual before language acquisition, and

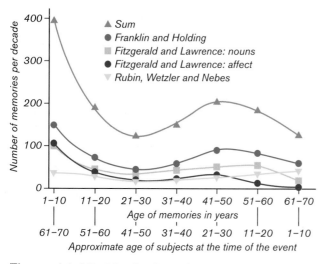

Figure 14.10 Distribution of autobiographical memories over the life span: the graph plots the number of memories remembered from different times in a person's life (lower scale); see text for comments
Source: Rubins et al., 1986

cognitive and linguistic after acquisition. They lose their ability to retrieve these early memories after the change.

Flashbulb memories

Do we remember emotionally charged events particularly well? *Flashbulb memories* are memories for dramatic, surprising, important and emotionally arousing events. Brown and Kulik (1977) reported participants' memories for the assassination of President Kennedy in November 1963. They were able to remember where they were, what they were doing, who told them, what they felt and what happened next. Brown and Kulik (1977) argued that the event was so spectacular that it was caused to be printed on the brain (hence the term flashbulb memory). More recent events like this are Margaret Thatcher's resignation and the death of Princess Diana.

Neisser (1982) disputed the 'flashbulb' interpretation, however. His research found that such memories were not as accurate as they were claimed to be, and that they were remembered vividly because they were the kind of event that would be discussed for many years after. Rubin and Kozin (1984) asked their participants about personally significant flashbulb events (accidents, injuries, and encounters with sexual connotations predominated). The vividness of the memories was related to surprise, emotionality and personal importance.

Forgetting in AM

What about forgetting? Linton (1975) and Wagenarr (1986) both kept diaries about daily events over a period of six years. They thus overcame the verification problem of studying autobiographical memory. How do you know if your memory is correct or not?

Linton (1975) found that repetitive events such as attending meetings quickly merged and she was unable to remember specific examples of these so-called *repisodes*. Trivial events were completely forgotten, with no recollection of them at all. Surprisingly, events she rated as being important and emotional when they occurred were not remembered particularly well either.

Remembering Diana

Think back to when you heard about Princess Diana's death in 1997 and then answer the following questions.

1 Where were you?
2 What were you doing?
3 Who told you?
4 What did you feel?
5 What did you do next?

Try to verify the accuracy of your answers by checking with other people.

Princess Diana's funeral

Wagenaar's (1986) diary recorded the what, when, where and who of an event. Subsequently he used these cues to try to recall an event. He found the 'what' cue best for prompting recall, followed by the 'where' and 'who'. The 'when' cue was almost useless, suggesting that autobiographical memories are not organised by time. He also found that the more recall cues he gave himself, the more likely he was to remember an event. Most interestingly, there were some events of which he had no recollection at all but by accident someone provided him with a cue that enabled him to remember them. Perhaps forgetting is only a matter of not having the right retrieval cue.

Semantic memory – representing knowledge

Concepts

How are concepts represented in memory? How is the knowledge that a canary is a bird, small and yellow with feathers, two legs and a beak represented in our minds? In this section we consider major theories that address this question.

An associative network model

Collins and Loftus (1975) produced the *spreading activation model*, a very influential version of an *associative network model*. In an associative network theory, concepts are represented by the nodes of a network and the relationship between concepts by the links between the nodes (see Figure 14.11). These links are associative in nature. For example, fire engine is associated with the concepts 'red' and 'fire'; it is also similar to other vehicles such as an ambulance and a truck. These associations are represented by direct links between the node for fire engine and nodes for these other concepts.

In the spreading activation model the strength of the association is represented by the length of the link. Short links are strong associations and long links weak ones. In addition, concepts can be linked through 'mediating' concepts. Whether two nodes are linked, whether they're linked directly or indirectly, and the length of the links is determined by asking a sample of people to write down all the characteristics of a fire engine they can think of and then use the frequency with which characteristics are mentioned to construct a network containing, say, fire engine (as in our example above).

The spreading activation model was developed to explain the *typicality effect*, one of the most robust findings in psychology.

It's likely that your list of birds included robin but not penguin, sparrow but not ostrich. Robins and sparrows are typical birds but penguins and ostriches are not. If you were constructing your own associative network of birds then this would be reflected in the relative lengths of the links between bird and robin (short) and bird and ostrich (long). Similarly, dog and cat are typical mammals, while whale and bat are not.

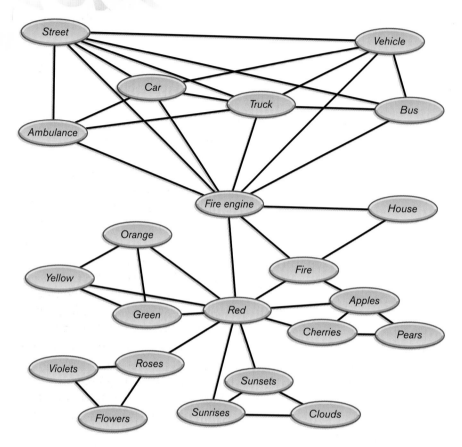

*Figure 14.11 Spreading activation model: concepts are represented
by nodes, and associations between concepts by links
between nodes
Source: Collins and Loftus, 1975*

ACTIVITY BOX 14.6

The typicality effect

1 Write down the first five birds that come to mind.
2 Write down the first five mammals that come to mind.

Now look back at your lists, and ask yourself how many of the birds and mammals you've listed are untypical examples. For example, have you listed an emu as a bird or a bat as a mammal? Probably not.

How does the associative network model work? How can it answer a question like 'Is a dog a mammal?' Collins and Loftus argue that it does so through spreading activation. The dog node is activated by the question and this activation spreads out from the dog node through the network to other connected nodes. As it spreads, the activation becomes weaker with distance from the node until it has dissipated and can spread no further. Because dog and mammal are closely associated (short link) the mammal node will become activated strongly, enabling a quick, accurate response to the question. In contrast, if the question is 'Is a bat a mammal?', then it will take longer to answer because the association between bat and mammal is weaker.

Consequently, the link is longer so the activation has a long way to go and will only activate it weakly. It may even produce the wrong answer because some people don't know that bats are mammals.

An important point about an associative network is that it is individual-specific. It depends on the particular associations a person makes about how concepts are connected. Having said this, associative networks for common concepts are likely to be similar for most people.

The strongest evidence for the spreading activation model comes from experiments involving *semantic priming*. In a classic experiment, Meyer and Schvaneveldt (1971) found that participants' responses when presented with the word 'nurse' were quicker if the word 'nurse' had been preceded by the word 'doctor' than if it had been preceded by 'bus' or 'plumber'. Seeing the word 'doctor' activates the doctor node, from which activation spreads to the nurse node because they are strongly associated. The nurse node is thus primed, or partly activated, so that when the word 'nurse' comes along, the node is already 'prepared'. This would not happen if 'nurse' was preceded by 'plumber' because 'plumber' and 'nurse' are not associated.

Although a much used theory in the psychology of memory, the notion of an associative network has been criticised because it does not explain how the concepts are linked to their referents (what they refer to) in the real world.

The attribute model of semantic memory

The *attribute model of semantic memory* is a different model of knowledge representation (Smith, Shoben and Rips, 1974). Concepts such as 'dog' are represented by lists of attributes such as 'has four legs', 'has fur', 'has a pointy face', 'barks' and so on. The attributes are divided into defining attributes (four legs) and characteristic attributes (has a pointy face). So if we are asked whether a labrador is a dog, we would simply compare the list of attributes for labrador with the list for dog and make a decision on overlap between the two lists. The typicality effect is accounted for because the list for pekinese would not overlap to the same extent (e.g. has a flat face, yaps rather than barks).

The major problem with such a feature list theory is that it's not clear what the defining features of a

concept are. So a dog may not have a bark because of a genetic abnormality, but it's still a dog. It may have had one of its legs amputated, but it's still a dog. There seems to be no one feature that is critical for dogness.

Prototype theory

A third type of knowledge representation theory is the *prototype model of semantic memory*. This follows on directly from the typicality effect because a concept is represented as an abstraction of characteristic features (Posner and Keele, 1970). The concept dog, then, is represented as a prototypical dog, which is quite large, has four legs, has a pointy face and is a pet. Labradors and alsatians would fit the prototype well, but pekinese and chihuahuas wouldn't. The speed and accuracy with which a new instance would be classified as a dog would depend on how closely it fitted the prototype. Notice the potential for error. Wolves fit the prototype very well and it's only particular knowledge that blocks the classification of a wolf as a dog. Dogs are domestic, wolves are wild. This example highlights another feature of natural concepts, which is that they are 'fuzzy'.

The notion of prototypes and typicality also allies to other types of concept, such as the perceptual category of colour and the semantic category of furniture. Much of this work was done by Eleanor Rosch in the 1970s, working across cultures. She argued that not all reds, for example, are equal – some reds are more representative of redness than others.

She worked with the Dani, a tribe who had colour vocabulary that only distinguished between light and dark. They had no words for colours such as red, blue, and so on. Dani participants learnt the associations between names and colours better for prototypical reds than for other reds, suggesting that they too thought some reds better than others, and that the distinction between the different types of red is based on perceptual rather than language differences. Rosch (1975a) also found typicality effect for semantic categories such as furniture. Chair and table were consistently rated as being more representative of furniture than bed or bookshelves (see Table 14.1).

TABLE 14.1

TABLE OF REPRESENTATIVENESS OF FURNITURE (ROSCH 1975b): SOME ITEMS OF FURNITURE ARE RATED AS BEING MORE REPRESENTATIVE OF FURNITURE THAN OTHERS

Furniture category member	Goodness-of-example rank	Vehicle category member	Goodness-of-example rank
Chair	1.5	Automobile	1
Sofa	1.5	Station wagon	2
Couch	3.5	Truck	3
Table	3.5	Car	4
Easy chair	5	Bus	5.5
Dresser	6.5	Taxi	5.5
Rocking chair	6.5	Jeep	7
Coffee table	8	Ambulance	8
Rocker	9	Motorcycle	9
Love seat	10	Streetcar	10
Chest of drawers	11	Van	11
Desk	12	Honda	12
Bed	13	Cable car	13

Source: Rosch, 1975b

Some researchers (e.g. Brooks, 1978) have taken the notion of a prototype to an extreme and argued that all knowledge is episodic, not abstract. Concepts are represented as specific instances so that someone's concept of dog may be represented by, for example, their neighbour's black labrador (see Brooks, Norman and Allen, 1991). This is known as the exemplar theory of concepts.

Schemata

Types of schema

While concepts are quite specific in what they refer to, schemata represent broader categories of knowledge. Bartlett (1932) introduced the notion of schema in the context of cultural knowledge. He gave English students at Cambridge (you might like to reflect on what their cultural background is likely to have been in 1932!) a story about Native Americans and supernatural events. When asked to recall the story, the participants consistently changed and distorted the story to make it consistent with English culture.

Another type of schema is called a *script* (Schank and Abelson, 1977; Schank, 1982; 1986). As the name suggests, this is a schema that consists of a timetable of key events in common situations, such as going to restaurants, travelling to work and sitting an exam. Bower, Black and Turner (1979) asked participants to list what was involved in going to a restaurant and found that certain key events were listed by most of them: entering, giving the reservation name, ordering drinks, discussing the menu, talking, ordering dessert, paying and leaving a tip.

Notice that schemata such as scripts can also be discussed in terms of prototypes. The restaurant script produced by participants is actually a prototype for going to a restaurant. Some visits (e.g. to a French restaurant) will fit the prototype better than others (e.g. to a Japanese restaurant).

A third kind of schema is called a *scene*. Scene schemata are about the contents and layout of different places. Thus there are scenes for kitchens, chemistry labs, public houses, and so on. Friedman (1979) presented participants with line drawings of different scenes (kitchen, office, farm, nursery) containing expected and unexpected objects. Participants spent up to twice as long looking at unexpected objects in a scene (e.g. a garden rake in the kitchen) than at expected objects (e.g. a saucepan in the kitchen). On a subsequent recognition test, changes to the unexpected objects (e.g. the rake replaced by a broom) were spotted quicker than changes to the expected objects. This finding has been replicated many times (Henderson, 1992).

Uses and abuses of schemata

Earlier, we looked at an experiment that showed how schemata helped expert chess players remember meaningful chess positions. An experiment by Anderson and Pichert (1978) showed how schemata also affect retrieval. Participants were asked to read a description of a house from either a home buyer's or a burglar's point of view. They then recalled as much of the house as they could from the perspective they had adopted. Following this, they changed perspective (the burglar became a householder and vice versa). The participants in each group now produced information from their new perspective that they hadn't produced in their original recall. Adopting a new schema had helped them remember information more pertinent to that perspective.

Although schemata are clearly useful psychological constructs, they are open to the criticism that they are too imprecise to be of scientific value. For example, one type of schema is called a story grammar. Each type of story is alleged to have a clearly identifiable structure that most examples of that type follow (e.g. whodunnits, Mills & Boon romances). However, Harley (2001) has argued that on closer inspection there are as many story grammars as there are stories, and a consensus on any particular grammar is hard to find. Eysenck (2000) argued that schemata are good at explaining results after they have been obtained but much less helpful at predicting them.

Summary

This chapter has provided an overview of memory. We have discussed, at various levels of detail, the major memory systems. We have tended to focus on short- and long-term verbal memory, partly because this reflects the literature and partly because our knowledge of this usually generalises to other systems. In the next chapter we will concentrate on the representational aspect of memory – that is, how our knowledge of the world, found in semantic memory, is represented and organised.

ACTIVITY BOX 14.7	

Writing scripts

Write down all the things you usually do for these activities:

1 going to college for a lecture
2 going clubbing
3 writing an essay.

Even though there may be some variation from occasion to occasion, the kinds of things you do and the order in which you do them is likely to be fairly fixed for each of these activities. If this is the case then you have just written scripts for them.

Section 3
Cognitive Psychology

Learning outcomes

When you have completed this chapter you should be able to:

- provide an overview of the different memory systems
- assemble the evidence that distinguishes short-term from long-term memory
- outline Atkinson and Shiffrin's (1968) modal model of memory and its major deficiencies.
- outline Baddeley and Hitch's (1974) working memory model
- describe the major factors in encoding or learning information
- describe the role of retrieval cues in remembering
- describe the major theories of forgetting
- distinguish between episodic, semantic and procedural memory
- describe some features of autobiographical memory
- distinguish between models of semantic memory
- describe several types of schema.

Key Terms

Amnesia
Accessibility of memories
Anterograde amnesia
Associative network model of semantic memory
Attribute model of semantic memory
Autobiographical episodes
Autobiographical knowledge
Autobiographical memory
Automatic processing
Availability of memories
Central executive
Childhood amnesia
Constructive process
Context-dependent memory
Digit span
Dissociation of function

Double dissociation of function
Dual-task paradigm
Echoic memory
Effortful processing
Elaboration mnemonics
Encoding
Encoding specificity principle
Episodic memory
Explicit processes
Flashbulb memories
Free recall
Iconic memory
Implicit processes
Incidental learning
Interference
Levels of processing
Long-term memory
Method of loci
Mnemonics
Modal model of memory
Mood-dependent memory
Motivated forgetting
Organisation and memory
Permastore
Phonological encoding
Phonological loop
Primacy effect
Proactive interference
Procedural memory
Prototype model of semantic memory
Recency effect
Reduction mnemonics
Rehearsal
Reminiscence bump
Repisodes
Retention function
Retrieval
Retrieval cue

Retroactive interference
Retrograde amnesia
Scene
Schema
Script
Semantic encoding
Semantic memory
Semantic priming
Sensory memory
Serial position effect

Serial recall
Short-term memory
Spreading activation model of semantic memory
State-dependent memory
Trace decay
Typicality effect
Verbal memory
Visuospatial scratchpad
Working memory model

Further reading

Baddeley, A. D. (1997) *Human Memory: Theory and Practice* (revised edn). Hove: Psychology Press. This is effectively the 'handbook of memory' for students of British psychology. It provides comprehensive coverage of the important topics in memory from a British perspective.

Eysenck, M. W. and Keene, M. T. (2000) *Cognitive Psychology. A Student's Handbook* (4th edn). Hove: Psychology Press. Densely packed information with evaluations of research.

Hunt, R. R. and Ellis, H. C. (1999) *Fundamentals of Cognitive Psychology* (6th edn). New York: McGraw Hill College. Well-explained, clear coverage of the main ideas in memory and cognition. Uncluttered.

Parkin, A. J. (1996) *Explorations in Cognitive Neuropsychology*. Cambridge, MA: Blackwell. Very readable coverage of amnesia and other major neuropsychological disorders.

Sternberg, R. J. (1999) *Cognitive Psychology* (2nd edn). Orlando: Harcourt Brace College Publishers. Good, general, reader-friendly text at a relatively advanced level.

15

Language

Route map of the chapter

The purpose of this chapter is to introduce you to selected key topics in psychology. It begins with a discussion of the design characteristics of language, which are then used to ask whether animals, particularly primates, can learn human language. The two sections after that deal with key ideas in sentence comprehension and sentence production. The chapter then moves on to a discussion of spoken word recognition before concluding with an examination of the processes involved in reading, the dual route model and written word recognition.

Introduction

While the other cognitive abilities we have discussed in this section (memory, attention, perception and thinking) are general abilities that can be found in other animals, there is a powerful argument that language is a uniquely human ability. It is of enormous importance to our functioning and the advances humans have made. It is the basis of our knowledge and the transmission of this knowledge. It is the basis of our communication, and its sophistication surpasses by some distance the communication systems possessed by other species. It is also the basis of much of our leisure, in the form of books, films and other media. It could be argued that it is one of the defining characteristics of being human.

One of the main proponents of this view has been the linguist Noam Chomsky (1957; 1965), who has argued that humans are innately endowed with language. We are born with a blueprint for language and the process of learning language consists of developing this blueprint into a grammar. The speed with which children learn language, without being taught it in any explicit way, is, Chomsky argues, strong evidence that it is innate. All a child needs is exposure to his/her particular language so that the grammar and vocabulary for that language can be developed (see the section in Chapter 19 on language development).

A crucial test of the hypothesis that language is innate and specific to humans is whether other animals have language. If they do use something comparable to human language to communicate, then we cannot claim it to be uniquely human. This would weaken the 'language is innate' hypothesis. If, on the other hand, they have sophisticated communication systems but these are qualitatively different to human language, then the innate hypothesis remains plausible. In the first section of this chapter we cover this issue in some detail.

Language and animal communication

The design features of language

All animals communicate, but do any of them have language? First, we must answer another question: 'What is language?' Rather than try to answer this with a disputable definition, psychologists and linguists have tried to identify the characteristics of human language.

The linguist Charles Hockett (1960) drew up a list of the design features of language. Many of these have been disputed but most researchers have been able to agree on a subset of between five and ten. The full list is presented in Table 15.1. Have a look at this table, then we'll discuss a subset that is particularly important to answering our question.

The first design feature of human language is *semanticity*. The words we use mean something. They stand for objects and actions in the world. Over time, they acquire associations with other objects and actions as well as emotional connotations. All of these are part of what we mean by the word 'language'.

A related feature is *arbitrariness*. Although words mean something, in themselves they are arbitrary symbols. Except for a few onomatopoeic words such as cuckoo and bang, which sound like the things they refer to, there is no connection between the symbol and its referent. For example, there is no reason why we call a dog a dog. Indeed the French call it *un chien*. Other languages have different names. All have been chosen arbitrarily but they all have the same referent (the thing they refer to).

A third feature of human language is that of *duality of patterning*. This refers to the fact that combinations of arbitrary sounds are combined to form units (words) that mean something. Thus there is a duality to the structure of words – the sound level and the word level. Lest you think this is a relatively trivial characteristic, consider the fact that a mere handful of sounds, such as /p/ and /b/ (between 20 and 30), can be combined to make hundreds of thousands of words. This is a characteristic that contributes to the creative power of language.

A fourth feature is *structure dependence*. This refers to the fact that language combines words in rule-governed ways to convey information. The same word order can mean different things (Jack chased Jill vs Jill chased Jack). Different word orders can mean the same thing (Jill chased Jack vs Jack was chased by Jill) The rules of combination vary from language to language.

A fifth feature is *creativity*. Although the sentences in a language have to conform to rules of structure, the number of combinations is infinite. There is no restriction on what we can say and still be understood. Whatever the message, we can find a combination of words to communicate it. You have probably never heard the sentence 'Aardvarks read Shakespeare regularly' but you still understand it, even if it is nonsense.

The above features have to do with the nature of language. There are other design features that have to do with the ways language is used. One of these is *displacement*, which is the use of language to refer to events in a different place at a different time. A history lecture is a good example of a communication with a displaced content.

Another feature is that of *spontaneous usage*. Language is not used only to respond to another communication or action. It is used freely to express thought and feelings that come from within the individual.

Finally in this particular list there is *cultural transmission*. This refers to the fact that language is passed between individuals, and particularly between parents and offspring.

Do animals have language?

Jean Aitchison (1989), in her eminently readable book *The Articulate Mammal*, tackles the question of whether animals have language by taking each of these features in turn and asking whether it is found in the communications of animals. Her logic is that if we take a given feature, such as cultural transmission, and find it in a species' communication, then it can't be a defining feature of human language. Using this strategy, she arrives at the conclusion that we can always find at least one species that has a particular design feature, and some that have more than one. However, it is doubtful whether any species demonstrates displacement, duality, semanticity, structure dependence or creativity.

Can primates learn language?

Primates may be a different matter, however. There is over 40 years' worth of research on teaching human language to chimps and other primates. It quickly became obvious that it was pointless to try and teach them to speak because they don't have the vocal apparatus. Accordingly the various attempts to teach these animals language have used symbol systems such as deaf sign language and plastic tokens (called lexigrams) instead of spoken language.

The first attempt to teach language to a primate involved the chimp Washoe (Gardner and Gardner,

TABLE 15.1
HOCKETT'S DESIGN FEATURES OF HUMAN LANGUAGE (RATHER THAN TRY TO DEFINE LANGUAGE, HOCKETT IDENTIFIED SEVERAL FEATURES HE CONSIDERED TO BE CHARACTERISTIC OF HUMAN LANGUAGE)
1 Vocal–auditory channel (communication occurs by the producer speaking and the receiver hearing)
2 Broadcast transmission and directional reception (a signal travels out in all directions from the speaker but can be localised in space by the hearer)
3 Rapid fading (once spoken, the signal disappears rapidly and is no longer available for inspection)
4 Interchangeability (adults can access everything about their productions)
5 Complete feedback (speakers can access everything about their productions)
6 Specialisation (the amount of energy in the signal is unimportant; a word means the same whether it is whispered or shouted)
7 Semanticity (signals mean something: they relate to the features of the world)
8 Arbitrariness (these symbols are abstract; except with a few onomatopoeic exceptions, they do not resemble what they stand for)
9 Discreteness (the vocabulary is made of discrete units)
10 Displacement (the communication system can be used to refer to things remote in time and space)
11 Openness (the ability to invent new messages)
12 Tradition (the language can be taught and learned)
13 Duality of patterning (only combinations of otherwise meaningless units are meaningful – this can be seen as applying both at the level of sounds and words, and words and sentences)
14 Prevarication (language provides us with the ability to lie and deceive)
15 Reflectiveness we can communicate about the communication system itself, just as this book is doing)
16 Learnability (the speaker of one language can learn another)
Source: Harley, 2001: 49

Washoe the chimp could use approximately 150 signs

by HAGEN

Sometimes, I think that men imagine us smarter than we really are... What on earth does that mean?...

How smart are animals?

1969; 1975), who was brought up as a child in the Gardners' house (this included toilet training!). She was taught American sign language (ASL). By the age of four Washoe could use about 85 signs and this grew to over 150 within the next few years. She showed some sensitivity to word order (structure dependence). For example, she distinguished between 'you tickle me' and 'I tickle you'. There was some evidence of creativity in that she signed 'water bird', a unique combination, to refer to a duck.

Another chimp, Nim Chimpsky (Terrace, Pettito, Sanders and Bever, 1979), named, loosely, after the linguist Noam Chomsky, was able to combine two symbols quite regularly but longer combinations tended to be either repetitious or meaningless. Nim rarely signed spontaneously: over 90 per cent of his signs were replies and 40 per cent repetitions. Comparisons of chimps' language with that of an average two-year-old child come out in the child's favour. Seidenberg and Pettito (1987) compared the performance of the more intelligent pygmy chimp Kanzi with that of a three-year-old child and, again, found the chimp's performance inferior (see Table 15.2).

It's likely that even these achievements are exaggerated, because there are methodological problems with many of these studies. For example, there is plenty of scope for researcher bias (the tendency of researchers to interpret ambiguous data – unintentionally – in their favour). Pinker (1994) found that independent deaf human signers didn't understand many of the things Washoe signed. There's also the potential problem of selective reporting. Washoe's use of the creative combination 'water bird' seems, at first sight, to be good evidence of grammatical structure and creativity, but, as Harley (2001) points out, if this actually occurred in a stream of other signs such as 'water shoe', 'water food' etc., then its occurrence is far less impressive.

Most commentators on the status of chimp language conclude that the evidence for semanticity, as well as for structured and creative utterances, is flimsy and that, at best, the case for chimps having language is not proven.

Section 3
Cognitive Psychology

Language (sentence) comprehension

Word order and constituents of sentences
The psychology of how we understand sentences and discourse is beyond the scope of an introductory text like this one. However, in this section we have selected some basic and quite robust findings that will give you a flavour of this fascinating but difficult topic.

The meaning of a sentence comes not just from the meaning of its individual words but also from the order in which those words appear. Thus 'Jack kissed Jill' does not mean the same as 'Jill kissed Jack' but does mean the same as 'Jill was kissed by Jack'.

Linguists such as Chomsky have provided strong arguments and robust evidence that the word order of English sentences is rule governed. Each speaker of a language has an internalised *grammar* or set of rules that enables the meaning of a sentence to be extracted from its word order. One of the principal aims of psycholinguistics is to identify the nature of these rules and how they generate the millions of sentences that are used every day, and all the millions that they could generate. The term given to the rules of word order is *syntax*.

The importance of word order is that it tells the listener how the word meanings of a sentence are combined. So if you know, as you do, implicitly, the rules of English word order or syntax, then you know how to extract the meaning of a sentence from the meanings of the individual words. Consider the words in the sentence 'The herd of elephants trampled the trees in the forest.'

The words cluster together into *constituents* in a fairly obvious way and the cluster is related to the meaning. So a first step in deconstructing the sentence might be:

The herd of elephants   trampled the trees in the forest.
This could be further broken down into:
The herd of elephants   trampled   the trees in the forest.
And this into:
The herd of elephants   trampled   the trees   in the forest.

The particular way in which a sentence breaks down to show how the words cluster together is called the *phrase structure* of the sentence. The process by which speakers of English derive the phrase structure of a sentence is called *parsing*. The question of how listeners parse a sentence is a major research topic in the psychology of language. One of the problems faced by a psychological parsing mechanism is that many sentences are ambiguous and can be parsed in different ways. So, for example,

TABLE 15.2	
A COMPARISON OF APES' AND CHILDREN'S LANGUAGE	
Apes	**Children**
• Mainly references to the here and now	• Utterances can refer to other times
• Lack of syntactic structure (rules of word order)	• Clear syntactic structure and consistency
• Need explicit training	• Do not need explicit training
• Rarely ask questions	• Frequently ask questions
• Little spontaneous use of symbols	• Spontaneous use of symbols
Source: adapted from Harley, 2001: 56	

the sentence 'Flying planes can be dangerous' has two possible interpretations and therefore two possible parsings, as follows.

1 The act of flying planes can be dangerous.
2 Planes which fly can be dangerous.

Which is the correct interpretation can't be known without knowing the context in which it was spoken (e.g. by a test pilot or by someone who lives near a military training area). As we'll see shortly, however, ambiguous sentences also provide a window on how sentences are parsed.

The psychological reality of constituents

A question of concern to psychologists (as opposed to linguists) is whether there is experimental evidence to show that listeners (and readers) actually break up sentences into constituents. The evidence is that they do. Jarvella (1971) read sentences to participants, and these were interrupted at various points. When the interruption came, the participants had to write down as much of the sentence as they could remember verbatim (word for word). An example is: 'Having failed to disprove the charges Taylor was later fired by the president.'

Before moving on, break this sentence up into two parts at what you consider to be an appropriate boundary (i.e. the constituent boundary).

Now if this sentence was being processed as a stream of words without any constituent structure we might expect the classic primacy-recency effect (see Chapter 14, on Memory) with the first few words (having, failed, to) and the last few words (by, the, president) being remembered particularly well and the ones in the middle being remembered less well. What Jarvella (1971) actually found was that the whole of the second part of the sentence, 'Taylor was later fired by the president', was remembered very well. All the words were equally well remembered. The first part, 'Having failed to disprove the charges', was remembered much less well. In other words, the sentence had been broken down into two parts and this was reflected by the participants' memory. Did your division of the sentence coincide with the participants' division?

Other evidence of constituent structure comes from an experiment by Aaronson and Scarborough (1977) using reading. (It is assumed that the processes involved in parsing spoken and written language are generally the same. Converging results support this.) Participants sat in front of a screen on which the words of a sentence appeared one at a time. Participants controlled the appearance of each word by pressing a bar. This allowed the experimenters to measure how long a participant spent looking at each word and the length of the intervals between words. So if the reader paused, this would show up as a lengthy gap between looking at two consecutive words. Look at Activity Box 15.1 before you read on.

ACTIVITY BOX 15.1

Testing constituent structure

Here is one of the sentences that was used in Aaronson and Scarborough's (1977) experiment. Break it up into three parts.

Because of its lasting construction as well as its motor's power the boat was of high quality.

Now return to the text.

The results of the experiment for the sentence in Activity Box 15.1 are shown in Figure 15.1, which plots the length of the intervals between words.

Notice first that the graph in Figure 15.1 is not a flat horizontal line, which would have resulted if the reader had been reading at a regular pace, as if to the beats of a metronome. Instead, the line is scalloped, with peaks and troughs. The peaks in the graph indicate where the reader paused. We can see from this that he or she paused between constituents. Do these constituent boundaries agree with the boundaries you identified in the sentence? They should be much the same.

Wrap-up

Both of the experiments discussed above show that sentence comprehension involves breaking the

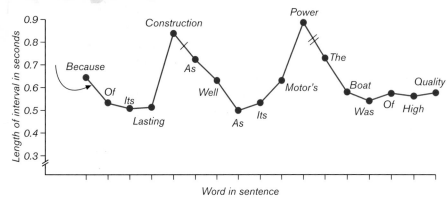

Figure 15.1 Pause time as a function of the position of a word in a
sentence: pauses do not occur evenly across the
sentence; the reader pauses at particular points
Source: Anderson, 1995b: 381

sentence down into constituents. They also suggest
something else. The comprehension processes seem
to 'wrap up' whatever they're doing at the constituent
boundaries, hence the pauses. They seem to 'pack
away' the results of a constituent before moving on
to the next one. *Wrap-up* is also shown in another
early experiment by Sachs (1967). She had subjects
listen to text and then tested their memory for
particular sentences in the text.

Test sentence
. . . He sent a letter about it to Galileo, the great
Italian scientist . . .

Sachs tested this by presenting subjects with a
multiple-choice test of what they'd heard. In addition
to the exact form of the sentence, they were also
presented with one alternative in which the word
order had been changed but the meaning was the
same, and another in which the meaning was
different.

Multiple-choice alternatives to test sentences
He sent a letter about it to Galileo, the great Italian
scientist (identical)
He sent Galileo the great Italian scientist a letter
about it (word order changed)
Galileo the great Italian scientist sent him a letter
about it (meaning changed)

The results showed that participants didn't pick up
on word order changes, suggesting that their
memory for the exact words and word order didn't
last very long. On the other hand, they were quick to
reject alternatives in which the meaning was
different. The conclusion is that listeners extract the
meaning and pack it away, but discard the exact
words and their order very quickly.

These experiments about the psychological reality
of constituent structure seem to imply that the
listener is waiting until she or he has heard all the
words in a constituent before beginning work on the
sentence. This is not the case. Further evidence
suggests they begin working on the relationship
between words (parsing) immediately – from the first
word. This is called the *immediacy principle* (Just
and Carpenter, 1980). You can test the psychological
reality of the immediacy principle for yourself by
reading the following sentence: 'The fireman told the
man that he had risked his life for to install a fire
detector.'

This is an example of a *garden path sentence*, so
called because it leads the listener/reader up the
garden path of interpretation. When you reach 'for' in
the sentence there is a sudden realisation that you
are on the wrong track and that you have to put
together the first part of the sentence in a different
way. Why does the sentence processor begin parsing
immediately rather than adopting a wait-and-see

policy? It would seem much more sensible to wait for a good chunk of speech before starting to put things together. If this were done, the garden path phenomenon would not exist.

The reason for this (according to Just and Carpenter, 1980) is that a wait-and-see policy would put a constant and burdensome strain on working memory. It's much more economical in cognitive terms to begin processing at once. Even though garden path sentences may cause a problem, in broad cognitive terms they are an inconvenience worth suffering.

Language production

A major problem with investigating language production is the difficulty of devising appropriate experiments. With language perception we can manipulate variables such as the type of sentence and then look at the effects of this on comprehension. With production we can't stimulate the speaker into using different kinds of processes. Consequently, language production relies more on naturalistic data such as speech errors, speech problems, and hesitations and pauses.

Levelt (1989) has identified three broad types of process involved in speech production: conceptualisation, formulation and articulation.

Conceptualisation processes operate at the thought level. It's not very clear exactly what's involved but we can identify some aspects. Generally, the speaker has to work out what, in broad terms, she or he wants to say. The form of the message will be affected by its purpose, such as whether it's a question, a command or an assertion (Grice, 1975), and by the conversational context in which it is being delivered. Is it meant to persuade or merely inform? If it has factual content, then the level of detail and the order in which the information is presented need to be decided. Perhaps it includes some personal information. Generally, the message has to be linearised in that it has to be converted into a sequence of sentences. The defining feature of this initial level is that the product of the conceptualisation process is a pre-verbal message (Levelt, 1989).

The second main stage is that of *formulation*. The conceptual message has to be translated into a linguistic form ready to be spoken. This involves

three main processes: appropriate words have to be selected; the appropriate word order has to be worked out; the component sounds of the words have to be specified. This can be thought of as a blueprint for the sounds.

The third stage is that of *articulation*. This takes the blueprint for the sounds and, through the use of the motor (muscular) processes involved, produces the correct sounds in the correct order.

We will deal with formulation in some detail.

Formulation
This section describes some of the processes involved in:

1 selecting the appropriate words
2 putting the words into the appropriate order
3 specifying the sounds of the word.

We'll deal with each of these in turn.

Lexicalisation
Lexicalisation is the process by which a word meaning (animal, four legs, barks, man's best friend) is turned into a blueprint for the sound /dog/. Lexicalisation occurs in two stages. First there is a process of *lexical selection*. The word that fits the desired meaning is selected from the mental lexicon (dictionary). At this point the word is in an abstract form and is called a *lemma*. The errors that occur at this stage are semantic errors (meaning-based). The word that is wrongly selected is related in meaning to the target word. It could be a synonym (same meaning) or an antonym (opposite meaning), or simply an associated word (see Table 15.3).

The second stage of lexicalisation deals with finding the correct *phonological (sound) form* of the lemma. This is a specification of the sound of the word in terms of its component sounds. Evidence for the existence of this stage comes, again, from speech errors. These occur because the wrong word is selected. The result is a *malapropism*. Malapropisms are speech errors named after a character called Mrs Malaprop in Sheridan's play *The Rivals*, who frequently used the wrong word. The distinguishing feature of a malapropism is that it sounds like the target word, particularly at the beginning. Some examples are given in Table 15.4.

Other evidence for the two-stage process of lexicalisation comes from the *tip of the tongue phenomenon* (Brown and McNeill, 1966). When someone is in the tip of the tongue state, he or she is unable to find the word they want. It's on the tip of their tongue. They have a very strong feeling of knowing what the word is, but can't quite find the spoken form. In lexicalisation terms, they have the correct lemma but can't find the phonological form. They are often able to say how many syllables it has and identify the sound it begins with. It's a transient experience, though, and the word usually pops into their head at some point soon afterwards.

TABLE 15.3
TARGET WORDS AND ERROR WORDS IN LEXICALISATION

Target (the word the speaker wants to use)	Error (the word the speaker actually uses)
Barely	Nearly
Today	Yesterday
Spade	Lawn mower

TABLE 15.4
EXAMPLES OF MALAPROPISMS

Target	Error
Incubator	Incinerator
Antelope	Antidote
Equivalent	Equivocal

ACTIVITY BOX 15.2

The tip of the tongue (ToT) phenomenon

Brown and McNeill (1966) induced ToT experiences by presenting participants with definitions of infrequent words and asking them to produce the words. Here are two examples. See if you experience the ToT phenomenon.

1 What do we call a navigational instrument used in measuring angular distances, especially the altitude of the sun, moon and stars at sea?

2 What word means formally to renounce the throne?

The answers are: (1) sextant; (2) abdicate.

Syntactic planning

The second major process in formulation is that of *syntactic planning*. Garrett (1975) distinguishes between two stages of syntactic planning: a functional stage and a positional stage. The functional stage is one at which the main functional components of the utterance are identified and assigned syntactic roles. In less technical terms, different parts of an utterance have specific roles, so in a simple sentence like 'Jack kissed Jill' there is a doer (the subject: Jack), an action (the verb: kissed) and the done-to (the object: Jill).

More complex sentences have other functional components such as describers (adjectives: big, blue etc.), determiners (a, the) and locational terms (prepositions: in, there, out). At the *functional level* the relationship between these parts is specified in general terms but exact word order has not been determined.

Errors that occur at this level of planning are word exchanges. A very robust observation of speech errors is that 'like exchanges with like' so nouns exchange with nouns, verbs with verbs and so on. In particular, *content words* (names of things, names of actions) do not exchange with *function words* (the, in, from), they only exchange with other content words and vice versa. Here are some examples of *exchange errors* from this stage of planning.

The Grand Canyon went to my sister

The red colour was attracted by the hummingbird of the feeder

Don't buy a car with its tail in the engine

In the next stage, the *positional level*, word order is specified more precisely. At this stage, it seems that a sentence 'frame' is constructed. This frame is made up of the function words and word endings such as (-s and -ed). Content words are slotted into this frame. Errors occur when content words are put into the wrong positions.

Consider this sentence. What should have happened is this:

slant   write
She _____s her _____ing (She slants her writing)

When this sentence was involved in a speech error what happened was this:

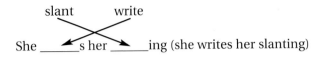

slant   write
She _____s her _____ing (she writes her slanting)

These errors are called morphemic *stranding errors*, because the morphemes (the -s and the -ing) are stranded while their roots, the content words, exchange.

Here are some more examples of stranding errors.

That's why they sell cheaps drink (That's why they sell drinks cheap)

We have a lot of churches in our minister (We have a lot of ministers in our church)

Phonological specification

The third process in formulation is that of producing the phonological blueprint for the sounds of the sentence. Just like sentences are made up of component words, so words are made up of component phonemes. Within the formulation stage is a level at which the sounds of the words are constructed from component phonemes. Evidence from this stage of speech production comes from speech errors called *spoonerisms*. These are named after the Reverend Spooner (1844–1930), an Oxford don, who supposedly made large numbers of these errors. The characteristic of these errors is the exchange of speech sounds. Here are some examples:

You have hissed all my mystery lectures (you have missed all my history lectures)

You have tasted a whole worm (You have wasted a whole term)

lawfully joined (lawfully joined)

Spoken word recognition

Speech perception (see Chapter 12, on Perception) is about how we perceive speech sounds and produce a percept. Speech recognition, on the other hand, is

The Reverend Spooner

RESEARCH METHODS BOX 15.1

Shadowing and speech perception

The purpose of the shadowing task in this context is to examine online processes in speech production.

In contrast to the dichotic listening shadowing task, the participant hears only one message. She or he has to shadow this as closely as possible. The message contains errors of different kinds (omitted sounds, wrong sounds, incorrect grammar, and so on).

The variables of interest are:

1 whether the participant corrects errors
2 which errors they correct
3 the time frame in which they correct them.

The online correction of these errors tells the researcher about processes in speech perception (see the text for an example from Marslen-Wilson, 1975).

about how we recognise a sound as being a word. As in written word recognition, this involves accessing the *mental lexicon*, the memory store that holds words and their meanings.

One critical difference between the written and spoken word is that the whole written word is available at the same time, whereas the spoken word 'arrives' over a period of time. Thus when we hear the spoken word 'trap' we hear the /t/ first, then the /r/, then the /ae/ and then the /p/. This serial entry immediately raises the question of whether the speech recognition system waits for the whole word before beginning lexical search or whether it begins immediately on receipt of the first phoneme.

Marslen-Wilson (1975) had participants listen to spoken passages and repeat what they were hearing as it was being heard. This is called shadowing. Some participants were particularly skilled at this. The message being heard contained errors such as omitted sounds, wrong sounds, grammatical errors and so on. Marslen-Wilson found that the shadowers were often correcting the errors spontaneously (they repeated the correct version of the word, not what they heard) and that this was being done before they'd even heard the whole word. The correction could only be made if they knew what the word was, so this means that they were recognising the word

before they'd heard it all. He estimated from the lag time that they were recognising the word, on average, on the basis of the first 200 msecs (about the first syllable). This was confirmed using a technique called gating.

Grosjean (1980) presented a spoken word in segments: first the /t/, then /tr/ then /trae/ and then /traep/ The subjects tried to identify the word as early in this process as possible. He found that recognition was occurring after about 175/200 msecs, confirming Marslen-Wilson's estimate.

These results lead to the development of the *cohort model* (Marslen-Wilson, 1984; 1989). When the first phoneme enters the speech recognition system all possible words beginning with that phoneme are lined up as possible candidates. These candidates are known as the cohort. When the second phoneme comes, the number in the cohort is automatically reduced (there are fewer words beginning /tr/ than beginning /t/). There is further reduction when the third phoneme comes in. This continues until there is only one candidate left. This is the recognised word.

It seems a little difficult to believe that the number of candidates drops quickly enough to be useful but Wayland, Wingfield and Goodglass (1989) calculated that, on average, the number of candidates for concrete nouns drops to five after the first 300 milliseconds of the word. Marslen-Wilson (1989) has had to modify the model since 1984 but the essentials remain the same. Lexical access begins immediately.

Written language

Reading words

Reading is an acquired skill. It is a relatively recent development in our cultural history, and there are millions of people in the world who cannot read or write. This indicates that, unlike spoken language, reading and writing are not a hardwired product of evolution but are acquired through education.

English is an alphabetic language. The writing system (*orthography*) is built on a relationship between the component sounds of spoken words (phonemes) and the letters of the alphabet. Although English is notorious for its irregular spelling, in general the relationship between the phonemes (/p/, /ae/, /t/) and letters ([p], [a], [t]) is regular and predictable. The enormous advantage of an alphabetic writing system is that once the relationship is learned the user can read or spell any word, even those they haven't seen before. You should, for example, be able to read the following non-words: gand, spruck, lomted and voretin. The only constraint is that the sequence of sounds is permissible according to the rules of English word structure. You won't be able to read dnga, kprucs, tmoedl and tverio.

The dual-route model of reading aloud

The alphabetic basis of English orthography and the fact that there are many irregular words suggests that there are two ways in which we can read. The first is to make use of the regularity of English and read by converting spelling to sound. We call this the *phonological* (or *indirect*) *route to reading*. The

second way is to use the visual characteristics of the word to look it up in the mental dictionary, which will also store its pronunciation. The word can then be read out loud. This is the *visual* (or *direct*) *route to reading*. Between them, the two routes can account for the reading of all English words. The *dual-route model* has been developed over the years but this fundamental aspect of it remains (see Figure 15.2).

APPLICATIONS BOX 15.1

The acquired dyslexias

Acquired dyslexia refers to the general condition of someone who once knew how to read but who has lost this ability because of head injury. It's very important to distinguish acquired dyslexia from developmental dyslexia, which refers to people who have had difficulty learning to read in the first place. There are two kinds of acquired dyslexia relevant to this discussion.

Acquired surface dyslexia (Marshall and Newcombe, 1973) is characterised by severe impairment in the ability to read irregular words (yacht, colonel). Attempts at reading these words result in regularisation errors. That is, they are pronounced the way they are spelt, so 'yacht' would be pronounced 'yacked' and 'colonel' would be pronounced 'col-on-ell'. This is consistent with the loss of the direct or visual route to reading. The acquired surface dyslexic has damaged his or her indirect route. They can read any word (and non-word) that is spelt regularly. This is consistent with the preservation of the indirect route and the ability to convert print to sound.

Acquired phonological dyslexia (Shallice and Warrington, 1975) is characterised by the loss of the ability to read regular non-words. If these dyslexics do not know the word they cannot read it, even if it is regular and potentially readable by conversion. This is consistent with loss of the indirect route. They can read any word they know, regardless of whether it's regular or irregular. This is consistent with the preservation of the direct route.

TABLE 15.5

EXAMPLES OF FOUR TYPES OF WORDS WHOSE READING HAS TO BE EXPLAINED BY THE DUAL-ROUTE MODEL

	Regular words	Irregular words
Frequent words	and, milk	said, people
Infrequent 'words'	crift, gond	myrrh, pyorrhoea

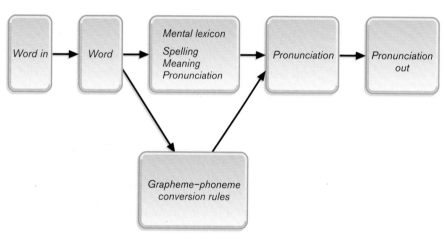

Figure 15.2 *The dual-route model of reading: this argues that there are two routes to reading a word out loud (a direct route and an indirect route)*

To appreciate how the model accounts for reading all English words, consider Table 15.5. Words can vary along two dimensions: how well known they are, measured by how frequently they occur; and how regular they are. At one extreme on the frequency dimension we have words like 'the' and 'and'. At the other end we have non-words, letter strings that could be words but aren't. Examples are 'gond' and 'crift'. At one extreme of the regularity dimension we have words like 'and' and 'milk', whose pronunciations are predictable from their spellings. At the other end we have words like 'yacht' and 'colonel', whose pronunciations you have to be told.

The phonological route can only read words that conform to the rules of English spelling. So it will work for regular frequent and regular infrequent 'words' (and, milk, crift, gond). The direct route will only work for known words. They have to have been seen before and the pronunciation given. So it will work for frequent words (and, milk, said, people). Irregular infrequent words can't be read without previous instruction (myrrh, pyorrhoea).

The most powerful evidence for the dual-route model comes from neuropsychology and the *acquired dyslexias* (see Applications Box 15.1).

Word recognition

This section is concerned with how we recognise words visually and access their meaning. It focuses on the direct route in the dual-route model.

The effects of word frequency and context

Two tasks have been crucial to investigations of word recognition. The *lexical decision task* and the *priming task* (see Research Methods Box 15.2).

RESEARCH METHODS BOX 15.2

Lexical decision task

The purpose of the lexical decision task is to make the participant process a word (usually presented visually) to the point where its meaning may be accessed.

Participants are presented with real words (e.g. band) and plausible (pronounceable) non-words (e.g. gand), and asked to respond 'yes' to words and 'no' to non-words. Because the non-words conform to the rules of English spelling the only way this can be accomplished is by looking up the stimulus word in the mental dictionary, or lexicon. If it is in the mental lexicon it is a word. If not, then it is not a word.

The dependent variable is:

1 the time taken to respond
2 the number of errors made.

The effect of different variables, such as word frequency on processing a word, can thus be determined.

RESEARCH METHODS BOX 15.3

Semantic priming

The purpose of semantic priming is to discover the relationship between words (e.g. associative, categorical).

In a control condition, lexical decision times to a set of target words (e.g. doctor) presented on their own are determined. In the experimental condition the presentation of the target word is preceded by a priming word. This word is usually either related (e.g. nurse) or unrelated (e.g. purse) to the target. The most reliable effects occur if the participant is required to make a lexical decision on both the prime word and the target word.

The comparison of interest is the response time in the experimental condition relative to the response time in the control condition. If, relative to no prime, the prime speeds up the response to the target word, then it is said to be having a facilitating effect and the words are assumed to be positively related. If there is no difference between the prime and no-prime conditions, then the prime and target are thought to be unrelated. If the prime slows down the response then it is said to be having an inhibitory effect, and the target and prime are thought to be negatively related.

The lexical decision task presents the reader with a single word and asks him or her to decide, as quickly as possible, whether the word is an English word or a non-word. The response time to different kinds of words under different conditions generates hypotheses about the nature of word recognition. The priming task primes recognition of the target word by presenting another word or sentence, or picture, before the target. So 'doctor' may be preceded by 'nurse' or by 'purse'. The response time to 'doctor' under these different conditions is the variable of interest.

Many factors affect word recognition but principal among these is *word frequency*. The more frequent or common a word is, the quicker and more accurate the response (Whaley, 1978). Word frequencies are obtained from frequency norms such as that of Kucera and Francis (1967), which counts the number

of times a word appears in a large sample of written texts. 'The' is the most frequent word in English. Response time in a lexical decision task is also affected by the nature of the non-words. It takes longer to reject 'gand' as a word than 'gnda': 'gand' conforms to the rules of English word structure and needs to be checked out, whereas 'gnda' violates the these rules and can be rejected without further checking.

Word recognition is also affected by priming. Meyer and Schvaneveldt (1971) showed that preceding a target word (doctor) with 'nurse' produced faster response times to doctor than when it was preceded by, say, 'purse'. Facilitation can also be obtained by preceding the target word with a sentence context if the word is a highly probable continuation of the sentence (Fischler and Bloom, 1979). For example:

For lunch he had roast beef and Yorkshire _____

Sentence context is particularly facilitatory if the word is difficult to read because of poor light, smudging etc. (Stanovich and West, 1981).

The logogen model

The *logogen model* (Morton, 1969; 1979) has been a very influential model of word *recognition* (as opposed to word *perception*). Every word is represented in a mental lexicon, or dictionary, by a logogen. This is a device that collects evidence that the word is present in the input. This evidence increases the *activation* of the logogen and, if it is strong enough, the activation rises above the *logogen threshold* and it fires. The word is recognised (see Figure 15.3).

For example, if 'book' is presented, then the logogens for 'boot', 'look', 'book', 'foot', 'boon' etc. will all accumulate some evidence because of the shared letters. However, the most evidence is collected by the 'book' logogen and so it, rather than any of the others, will fire.

The threshold of a logogen is determined by the word's frequency. A high-frequency word will have a low threshold and so will be recognised more quickly than a low-frequency word with a high threshold. The level of activation is affected by the evidence collected from the input but also by the context. So

the context 'For lunch he had roast beef and Yorkshire ...' raises the activation of the 'pudding' logogen, making it quicker to recognise when it comes (see Figure 15.3).

Although the logogen model was later modified, the essentials of the model are seen most clearly in the older model. The logogen for a given word collects evidence from (i) the input and (ii) the context until there is sufficient to trigger firing (recognition).

The early version of the model (Morton, 1969) had one logogen per word. It could be fired by either a visual (written) or auditory (spoken) input. However, Winnick and Daniels (1970) showed that priming the written 'book' by itself was more helpful than priming it with the spoken word 'book'. This should not happen if there is one logogen for both modalities. This and other evidence persuaded Morton to modify the model (Morton, 1979). In the new system, there are separate logogens for written and spoken versions of a word.

Summary

This chapter has dealt with the psychology of language. It began with a consideration of whether animals have language and, in so doing, addressed the question of the nature of language. It then went on to describe major processes in the comprehension and production of language. The psychology of spoken word recognition was then discussed, before the chapter ended with a discussion of the psychology of reading and word recognition.

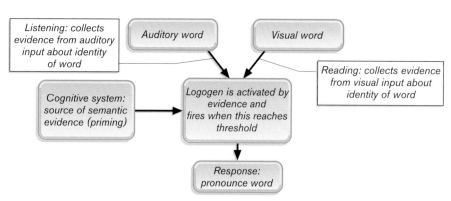

Figure 15.3 The logogen model (1969 version)

Learning outcomes

When you have completed this chapter you should be able to:

- explain Hockett's design features of language
- evaluate whether animals have language and whether primates can learn language
- describe key aspects of how we understand sentences
- describe some of the important aspects of sentence production, citing speech errors as evidence
- describe the cohort model of spoken word recognition and supporting evidence
- outline the dual-route model of reading and show how it explains acquired reading disorders
- describe how the logogen model works.

Key Terms

Acquired dyslexia
Acquired phonological dyslexia
Acquired surface dyslexia
Activation
Arbitrariness
Articulation
Cohort model
Conceptualisation
Constituents
Content words
Creativity
Cultural transmission
Displacement
Dual-route model
Duality of patterning
Exchange errors
Formulation
Function words
Functional level
Garden path sentence
Grammar
Immediacy principle

Lemma
Lexical decision task
Lexical selection
Lexicalisation
Logogen model
Logogen threshold
Malapropism
Mental lexicon
Orthography
Parsing
Phonological (sound) form
Phonological (or indirect) route to reading
Phrase structure
Positional level
Priming task
Semanticity
Spontaneous usage
Spoonerisms
Stranding errors
Structure dependence
Syntactic planning
Syntax
Tip of the tongue phenomenon
Visual (or direct) route to reading
Word frequency
Wrap-up

Section 3
Cognitive Psychology

Further reading

Aitchison, J. (1989) *The Articulate Mammal. An Introduction to Psycholinguistics* (2nd edn). London: Hutchinson University Press. Very readable text on language, but doesn't cover reading or speech recognition.

Eysenck, M. W. and Keene, M. T. (2000) *Cognitive Psychology. A Student's Handbook* (4th edn). Hove: Psychology Press. Densely packed information with evaluations of research.

French, C. C. and Colman, A. M. (1994) *Cognitive Psychology*. London: Longman. Chapters written by eminent specialists in their field. Clearly written. Language chapter by Willem Levelt.

Harley, T. (2001) *The Psychology of Language. From Data to Theory* (2nd edn). Hove: Psychology Press. Very comprehensive, densely packed text with everything you need to know about language.

Parkin, A. J. (1996) *Explorations in Cognitive Neuropsychology*. Cambridge, MA: Blackwell. Very readable coverage of major neuropsychological disorders, including spoken and written language.

Thinking and reasoning

Route map of the chapter

The aim of this chapter is to introduce the reader to important aspects of thinking and reasoning. It begins with a description of theories of problem-solving and of the barriers to solving problems. It then deals with how we learn concepts, and make judgements and decisions, all of which are rooted in inductive reasoning. The elements of deductive reasoning are identified before moving on to a discussion of how skills and expertise develop.

Introduction

According to Solso (1998: 420), 'Thinking is the Crown Jewel of Cognition. It is spectacularly brilliant in some people; . . . sublime amongst average folks; and the fact that it happens at all one of the great wonders of our species'.

Thinking, together with language, is what distinguishes us so clearly from other species. Look around you now and you'll see the product of human thought: the written language you rely on for communication; the transport you use to get to and from college; the pharmaceutical and medical expertise you depend on when you're ill. Although other animals can think, often in quite a sophisticated way, none of them comes close to the human capability.

Thinking is a broad term for many different activities, such as problem-solving, decision-making and reasoning, as we shall see in this chapter. The essence of thinking is the idea that it changes your view of some aspect of the world. You may start with the question 'Which university should I go to?' At this point your mental state is one of uncertainty. After

thinking about it and making a decision your mental state is one of (greater) certainty. Your worldview has changed in one respect. When asked to write an essay your initial mental state is one of ignorance, but after doing the reading and thinking about it your mental state is one of organised knowledge. Again, your worldview has changed.

Here are three general characteristics of thinking. First, thinking is a collection of essentially private mental processes. We are aware that we are thinking and conscious of the products of thought but cannot describe, with any accuracy, the precise sequence of thoughts. Second, thinking involves knowledge. Often this is 'only' general knowledge about the world and how we think the world works, but sometimes it involves very specialised knowledge. For example, the thinking that goes on during a chess game involves specialist knowledge about the rules of chess.

Finally, thinking is usually directed towards some goal or end (but see Wetherick and Gilhooly, 1995, for work on undirected thinking). So thinking about how to get to work when the buses are on strike or trying to understand this chapter in preparation for an exam is thinking directed towards a specific goal.

Problem-solving

According to Evans (1995: 61), 'Problem-solving consists of finding a method of getting from where you are to where you want to be'. We could add that this excludes circumstances in which the solution is given to you through instruction or education, and when it is not readily available through past experience. The sort of *problem-solving* we do regularly includes anagrams and crosswords, trying

Section 3
Cognitive Psychology

to win at backgammon or chess, finding our way round a new area, making friends and trying to plan our careers.

An important distinction is that between *well-defined problems* and *ill-defined problems*. Anagrams and crosswords are examples of well-defined problems: you (i) have all the information you need and (ii) know exactly what has to be done (doing it is the problem!). An ill-defined problem is one in which some aspect of the problem is not well defined. Most real-life problems are ill defined. You may not have the appropriate information ('What do I have to do to become a clinical psychologist?'); you may not know which is the best strategy ('Should I get practical experience before or after doing a degree?'); you may not even know what the goal is ('Do I really want to be a clinical psychologist or do I want to be a counsellor?').

Early theories of problem-solving

The behaviourists (e.g. Hull, 1920) argued that problems are solved either by reproducing previously successful strategies and solutions or by trial and error. If your car won't start on a cold morning you begin by working through all the past causes of this failure: damp wiring, battery low, old spark plugs etc. This is known as a *reproductive strategy* because it reproduces past solutions. If, however, none of these works you might resort to a *trial and error strategy*: poking and prodding, fiddling and fumbling, connecting and disconnecting, and other random actions. After many trials and numerous errors you might stumble across the solution, which would then join your repertoire of reproductive strategies for starting the car.

Trial and error explains some kinds of problem-solving, as is illustrated in an early experiment by Thorndike (1911). He put hungry cats into cages that could only be opened if they hit a bar inside the cage. Food was put within sight outside the cage. After thrashing about frantically for some time the cats usually hit the bar accidentally and released themselves. On subsequent trials the time taken to hit the bar decreased dramatically until a point when the cats hit the bar immediately they were confined. It takes time for the correct association between pressing the bar and escaping to build up. Much

animal learning is like this (see Chapter 8 on animal learning and cognition).

Gestalt theorists (such as Koffka, Kohler and Wertheimer) argued that problem-solving was more of a *productive strategy* than trial and error suggested. New solutions were produced through *insight*, which is based on a reconfiguring, or *restructuring*, of the problem – seeing the problem in a different way.

Insight was demonstrated in a series of famous experiments by Wolfgang Kohler (1927) with apes, including one called Sultan. In one such experiment Sultan could only reach a banana outside his cage by joining together two sticks inside the cage. In another experiment he could only reach food suspended from the ceiling by piling boxes on top of each other and then climbing on them to reach the banana. Although both problems could be solved by trial and error, Kohler observed periods of reflection by Sultan followed by an apparently insightful solution – the 'Aha!' moment when the solution suddenly came to mind.

A problem with the Gestalt concepts of insight and restructuring is that they don't really explain what's

Sultan solving the problem of the suspended banana

going on in the ape's head when the problem is solved. Why does restructuring occur? What mental processes does it involve? Without answering these questions, insight and restructuring are little more than labels for particular aspects of the ape's behaviour.

Another problem is that Epstein (1984) subsequently showed that pigeons could solve the problem in the same way if they'd previously been trained to (i) move a box to the correct location and (ii) climb on the box. This suggests that the ape's 'insight' could be attributed to previous relevant experiences and the building up of a chain of associations rather than a sudden restructuring of the problem.

Barriers to success

The Gestaltists also identified barriers to successful problem-solving. One of these is *functional fixedness*. This is the tendency to focus on the main function of an object and so not see that it could be used in other ways to help solve a problem. Duncker (1926; 1945) gave participants a candle, a box of nails, some matches and several other objects on a table. The task was to attach the candle to the wall beside the table so that when lit it didn't drip wax on the table. Duncker found that participants tried many things, including trying to nail the candle to the wall. Only a few thought of emptying the box of nails and tacking the box to the wall with the nails. It thus became a tray for the candle. Duncker argued that participants were so fixated on the box as a container of nails that they didn't see its potential use as a candle holder.

Another barrier to problem-solving is *mental set*. People learn particular ways of doing things and continue to apply them even when they are clearly inappropriate. This is shown in another series of classic experiments involving water jugs (Luchins, 1942; Luchins and Luchins, 1959). The essence of these experiments is to get participants to learn the strategy for solving a set of problems and then show that they continue using the strategy even when it is clearly inappropriate for a new set of problems (see Table 16.1).

In each of the problems in Table 16.1 the aim is to transfer water from one place to another using three

---

ACTIVITY BOX 16.1

The pendulum problem

In the pendulum problem (see Figure 16.1), two pieces of string are suspended from the ceiling. The problem is to tie them together. However, the strings are not sufficiently long to allow you to grasp one and walk over to the other: if you're holding one piece of string you can't reach the other. On a table in the room are several objects: a glass of water, poles, a book and a pair of pliers. How can you tie the two pieces of string together?

Solution: to solve the problem you need to change your perception of the pliers' normal function; you need to overcome your functional fixedness and see the pliers as a weight that can be tied to one of the pieces of string to make a pendulum; it then becomes possible to catch the swinging pendulum while holding the other piece of string.

Figure 16.1   The pendulum problem
Source: Sternberg, 1996: 350

---

jugs. The amount to be transferred is given in column 5 of the table. The amount of water that the jugs can hold varies across problems (columns 2, 3 and 4 in the table). After solving a few of the problems the participants hit upon the solution, which is the same in each case:

1   fill pitcher B
2   fill pitcher A from pitcher B
3   fill pitcher C twice from pitcher B.

This leaves the required amount of water in pitcher B. The formula is pitcher B – pitcher A – twice pitcher C. This algorithm, or formula, applies to problems 1–6, but is wrong for 9 and is not the simplest solution to 7, 8, 10, 11. Nevertheless, participants persist in applying it because they have acquired a mental set that is difficult to abandon.

Functional fixedness and mental set are both examples of mental inflexibility. Past experience helps develop strategies that are enormously useful in solving the problems we usually come across, but can become a liability when a change in strategy is needed. It is difficult to break free of this. In sports such as football and tennis, for example, players develop tactics and strategies that work against most opponents. In football there is the long-ball game; in tennis the serve-and-volley game. However, against an opponent whose style demands a change in tactics (a new solution), players often find themselves unable to change (e.g. play a passing game or set up baseline rallies).

TABLE 16.1

WATER JUG PROBLEMS USED BY LUCHINS (1942) TO DEMONSTRATE MENTAL SET; THE SAME ALGORITHM (B – A – 2C) APPLIES TO ALL PROBLEMS EXCEPT 9

| Problem | Containers given (capacity in quarts) | | | To get |
	A	B	C	
1	29	63	7	20 quarts
2	21	127	3	100 quarts
3	14	163	25	99 quarts
4	18	43	10	5 quarts
5	9	42	6	21 quarts
6	20	59	4	31 quarts
7	23	49	3	20 quarts
8	15	39	3	18 quarts
9	28	76	3	25 quarts
10	18	48	4	22 quarts
11	14	36	8	6 quarts

Source: Luchins and Luchins, 1950, in Medin and Ross, 1996: 493

Using analogies

Another strategy for solving problems is *analogy*. Experience plays a key part in analogical problem-solving because the problem solver is trying to find a solution on the basis of the problem's similarity to another problem that he or she knows how to solve. However, this doesn't come as easily as one might suppose, as a study by Gick and Holyoak (1980; 1983) showed.

In this experiment the main problem to be solved is the radiation problem. Prior to this some participants are given a similar problem – the fortress problem – which they all solve. The question is whether solving the fortress problem helps them solve the radiation problem.

Here is the radiation problem. A person has a malignant tumour in the middle of his body (e.g. in the liver). The tumour can be removed by radiation therapy but the problem is that the radiation has to pass through healthy tissue to reach the tumour. A dose strong enough to kill the tumour will also kill healthy tissue. How can we destroy the tumour without also destroying healthy tissue? Only about 10 per cent of Gick and Holyoak's participants solved the problem.

Now the fortress problem. A good king wants to attack a tyrant who is in his fortress. The good king has enough troops to ensure success but the problem is that the tyrant has laid mines along all the roads leading to his fortress. However, while the mines will be triggered by large numbers of troops, small numbers can pass over them safely. Accordingly, the good king divides his troops into small groups and each group approaches the castle along a different road. They don't detonate the mines and when they arrive at the fortress together there are enough of them to storm and destroy it (see Figure 16.2).

If you weren't able to solve the radiation problem before can you solve it now? The solution is to rotate the source of radiation through a full circle with the tumour at the focus. Thus while the tumour receives a massive dose of continuous radiation no piece of surrounding healthy tissue receives more than a (safe) fraction of what is delivered (see Figure 16.3).

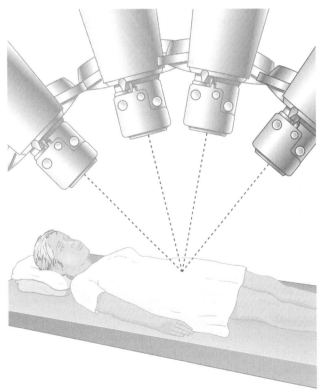

Figure 16.3 The radiation problem
Source: after Sternberg, 1996: 372

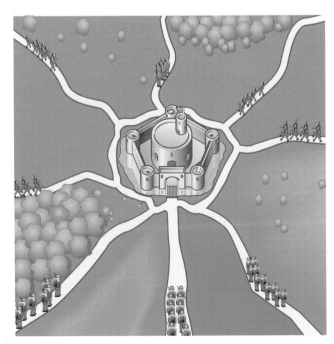

Figure 16.2 The fortress problem

Gick and Holyoak (1983) found that 30 per cent of participants who were given the fortress problem and its solution under the pretext of it being an experiment in memory (the 'no hint' group) subsequently solved the radiation problem. This is only 20 per cent more than the group who had had no exposure to the fortress problem at all. So analogies are not spotted as spontaneously as one might expect. In contrast, 75 per cent of a group whose members were exposed to the fortress problem and who were told it would be helpful in solving the radiation problem (the 'hint' group) were successful. So giving hints about using analogy helps, but even with the hint the remaining 25 per cent didn't get the solution. Again, it seems that analogies are not an obvious problem-solving strategy.

The general problem solver

The most influential and complete model of problem-solving was devised by Newell and Simon (1961). Their 'general problem solver' was developed to provide the basis for computer as well as human problem-solving. They conceptualised solving a problem in terms of a number of states. The first of these is the *initial state*, which is a statement of the unsolved problem. This is followed by a number of *intermediate states*, each being a step on the path to the solution. Finally, there is the *end state*, which is when the problem is solved. The problem solver moves from state to state using an appropriate action (physical or mental) or operation. Appropriate *operations* lead to mental states that lead to the solution, while inappropriate operations lead to a cul-de-sac, which then has to be reversed. The solution depends on the problem solver finding a correct sequence of states (there may be more than one).

This description can be applied to a huge range of problems, such as finding the way through a maze, proving a theorem, solving an anagram, winning a game of chess, doing an experiment, finding the partner of your dreams or becoming prime minister! As it stands, however, it doesn't indicate how the problem is solved. How do we acquire the appropriate operations? How do we know which operations are appropriate? How do we know when

to apply them? Generally, how does the problem solver move from the initial to the end state?

Previous experience and formal instruction play a role. In chess, for example, the moves (operations) that each piece can make are learnt, along with the rules of the game. Selection of the appropriate operations at any stage is governed by several considerations. One is to think through the alternatives to each move and their consequences. In chess, thinking two or three moves ahead for about two or three choices is the most that novices can manage. Newell and Simon (1961) argued that progress is governed by the use of *heuristics*. These are rules of thumb that guide a sequence of operations. They are imprecise and offer no guarantee of success. They stand in contrast to *algorithms*, which are sequences of precise rules that, if followed, will necessarily lead to a solution (see Activity Box 16.2).

ACTIVITY BOX 16.2

Algorithms and heuristics

An algorithm is a problem-solving strategy consisting of a set of rules that, if followed precisely, leads to the correct solution. Think of examples of algorithms. Here are some to start:

- doing the Luchins (1942) water jug problems
- finding the area of a parallelogram
- finding a place from a set of precise directions.

A heuristic is a general principle that guides problem-solving. Think of examples of heuristics. Here are some to begin with:

- doing a jigsaw by putting together all the pieces with the same pattern (blue for the sky)
- trying to win a chess game by controlling the centre of the board
- finding a place by heading in its general direction.

A well-known heuristic is *means–end analysis*, in which the problem solver breaks the problem down into a series of *subgoals*. Subgoals represent milestones on the road to the solution and each becomes an end in itself. In chess, for example, an appropriate subgoal might be to protect the king and this might be achieved by 'castling' at the earliest possible moment. Other subgoals might be to control the main diagonals or to capture the opposition's queen. Subgoals break down the road to solution into more manageable chunks.

Inductive reasoning

According to Anderson (1995b: 323), '*Inductive reasoning* is the term used to describe the processes by which one comes to conclusions that are probable rather than certain'. In this section we cover several topics that deal with people's ability to draw conclusions from information that may not be complete or where several sources of information compete for attention. The conclusion is not something that follows inevitably from what we know. Inductive reasoning underpins the following sections on concept learning, judgement and decision-making.

Concept learning

Concepts are mental representations of classes of object. Our concept of 'table' consists of all those things we consider to be tables. Our concept of 'animal' consists of all those things we consider to be animals, and so on. Research into *concept learning* throws light on the inferential processes that underlie the acquisition of concepts. Sometimes these processes are explicit – the person is actively and consciously trying to learn the concept. At other times these processes are implicit – the person learns the concept without being able to say what it is!

An important distinction is between *logical concepts* and *natural concepts*. Logical concepts are identified by clear and unambiguous rules. For example, a square is a figure with four sides of equal length and where all the angles are 90 degrees. Anything that fits these specifications is a square. Anything that doesn't is not. In contrast, natural concepts, like 'dog', have fuzzy boundaries and can't

be identified on the basis of clear unambiguous rules. What are the 'rules' that distinguish a dog from a wolf (leaving aside specialised biological knowledge)? The different nature of logical and natural concepts may well influence how they are acquired.

While many concepts, such as those you've acquired through reading this book, are acquired through a process of education, most everyday concepts are not acquired through formal instruction. Children acquire a huge number of concepts, such as dog, chair, food, drink, car and clothes, in a very short time and largely on their own. How are concepts acquired?

Associative learning

The associationists (e.g. Hull, 1920) argued that concepts are acquired through a process of *associative learning*. The characteristics of chairs become associated with each other and with the name 'chair'. To show this, Hull presented participants with Chinese characters such as those in Figure 16.4. In the first column of each row is a radical or specific character. This radical is present in the remaining characters in the row and defines the concept for that row. So in row 1 the radical in the first column is found in the characters presented in columns 2–7. These characters are therefore positive examples of the concept or category.

Each row of characters was mixed in with other Chinese characters that were not category members (they didn't contain the radical) and participants were asked to classify each character in the mixed set as being a member of the category or not. Hull simply told them whether they were right or wrong. They learnt to categorise correctly, indicating that they had learnt the concept, but the process was gradual and took many trials. Even when successful, participants couldn't state explicitly why a character belonged in one category rather than another. This pattern of responding is consistent with the building up of associations over a period of time.

Hypothesis testing

This account of concept acquisition was challenged by Bruner, Goodnow and Austin (1956). They gave

Section 3
Cognitive Psychology

Figure 16.4 Chinese characters used in Hull's concept learning experiment: the character in the first column is found in all the remaining columns for that row – it defines the concept
Source: Anderson, 1995b: 352

participants a similar task using complex stimuli such as those presented in Figure 16.5. The task for the participants was to determine the basis on which cards would be classified as being positive or negative instances. In column 1 any card with 'two crosses' is a positive instance; all others are negative instances. In column 2 any card with either 'two circles or two borders' is a positive instance and all others are negative. In column 3 any card with 'equal number of borders and objects' is positive and all others negative.

Note that in these cases a logical concept, or rule, for categorisation is involved. There is a clear classification rule. Bruner *et al*. (1956) found that participants were *forming hypotheses* about the nature of the concept. After a few patterns they would speculate about the rule for classification and classify subsequent patterns on the basis of this rule. However, if the rule was wrong and they made an error, they would abandon the rule and speculate on a new one. This would continue until they got the rule (see Research Methods Box 16.1).

Bower and Trabasso (1963) followed up on this and looked at each participant's performance. They found that until the participant got the correct rule she or he was performing at chance level. Immediately they got the rule, however, they jumped to 100 per cent correct. This sudden change in correctness is difficult to explain as a gradual build-up of associations.

Confirmation bias

A very strong factor in *hypothesis formation* is the phenomenon of *confirmation bias*. This is the tendency to look only for evidence that confirms the hypothesis and to neglect evidence that the hypothesis is wrong. The problem with doing this is that no matter how much confirming evidence we find we can never be certain that the hypothesis is correct. There is always the possibility that a counterexample exists. Finding countless birds that fly supports the hypothesis that 'all birds fly' but it doesn't prove it, because there is always the possibility of coming across birds that don't fly. Instead we should look for evidence that disconfirms, or refutes, the hypothesis. We should be looking for birds that don't fly.

If the hypothesis survives this test, then the probability that we have the right hypothesis is increased significantly. If it doesn't, then we must change the hypothesis. Immediately we came across penguins or kiwis we would have to amend the hypothesis to 'most birds fly'.

Confirmation bias was well illustrated in an experiment by Wason (1960). He provided participants with a set of three numbers: 2, 4, 6. Their task was to find the rule that had generated these numbers. The participants did this by generating new triples of numbers and the experimenter telling them whether each triple conformed to the rule or not. When the participant felt confident that he or she had found the rule they had to report it, and were told whether or not they were right.

Participants tended to generate numbers that increase in twos (1, 3, 5; 33, 35, 37; 102, 104, 106) and were then surprised to find that the rule is not 'numbers that increase in twos'. They continued to

Concept acquisition

Concept 1   Concept 2   Concept 3

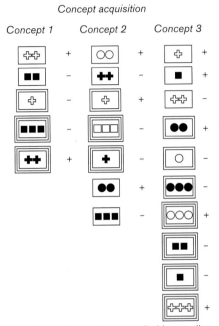

Concept formation has been studied in paradigms
in which subjects see instances identified as
members or non-members of a concept they are
supposed to identify

*Figure 16.5   Some stimuli used in Bruner,
Goodnow and Austin's (1956)
concept learning experiment. Each
column has both positive (+) and
negative (−) instances of a concept
Source: Found in Anderson, p355*

RESEARCH METHODS BOX 16.1

The reception and selection paradigms for testing concept acquisition

This Research Methods Box looks at Bruner, Goodnow and Austin's (1956) *reception paradigm of concept learning* and *selection paradigm of concept learning.*

AIM: the aim of the experiment is to learn how participants acquire concepts.

Reception paradigm

METHOD: the participant is presented with a series of cards, one at a time; some cards contain positive examples of the concept, the remainder do not; the participant is asked to respond 'Yes' (card is an example of the concept) or 'No' (card is not an example of the concept) to each card presented.

DEPENDENT VARIABLE: the experimenters are interested in the sequence of responses; this tells them about the kinds of strategies the participant is using and the hypotheses the participant is testing.

EXAMPLES OF RESULTS: Bruner *et al.* (1956) identified a *wholist strategy*, used by most participants, in which participants tried to recall the characteristics of all the positive instances they could remember and formulate an appropriate hypothesis; this clearly imposes a big memory load but can produce a quick result.

Selection paradigm

METHOD: the participant is presented with *all* the cards; his/her task is to select a card, one at a time, which she or he thinks is an example of the concept; he or she continues to select cards until he or she has acquired the concept.

DEPENDENT VARIABLE: the experimenters are interested in the sequence of responses; this tells them about the kinds of strategies the participant is using and the hypotheses the participant is testing.

EXAMPLES OF RESULTS: with a *conservative focusing strategy* the participant picked one positive card and then systematically changed one attribute at a time to find out which were relevant; with a *focus gambling strategy* the participant picked one positive card and then changed several attributes at a time in the hope they would strike lucky.

generate triples that increase in twos. The rule, decided by the experimenter, was actually 'three increasing numbers' and the best way to get to this is to generate sequences that refute the 'increases by twos' rule (i.e. they should produce a sequence like 2, 4, 5). They would then have to come up with another hypothesis. This is the most efficient strategy in the long run.

Resolution

Anderson (1995a) argues that trying to find a single theory for how concepts are learned may not be very sensible. The type of learning that occurs may be a function of the kind of concept that has to be learned. The Bruner *et al.* (1956) patterns are rule-governed and so are conducive to a hypothesis-formation strategy that people will, very sensibly, adopt.

On the other hand, natural concepts are fuzzy. Some examples of the concept are more typical than others and they don't have defining features. The concept 'dog', as we have seen elsewhere, depends on possessing a cluster of features (four legs, barks, man's best friend etc.) and there is no unambiguous rule that distinguishes dogs from wolves, jackals, hyenas and the like. Anderson argues that association learning may well be how natural concepts such as 'dog' are acquired.

Judgement

Judgements involve drawing a conclusion from a combination of knowledge and observation. We make judgements all the time:

Q1: Is this person I've met someone I can trust to look after my bag?
A1: Yes, I think so. He's got an honest face and plays cricket.
Q2: Am I likely to get mugged if I visit my friend in central London?
A2: Almost certainly. Someone got mugged there last week.
Q3: Are Londoners more intelligent than other people?
A3: Probably. People from other places are always asking for directions. Besides, I'm from London.

In each case we make a judgement about the answer and in each case the answer takes the form of a subjective probability. These examples show that subjective judgements are often based on partial or incorrect information, flawed reasoning and prejudices.

Base rate information

In some cases when we are called upon to make probabilistic judgements, objective data are available to us. We know, or are told, how likely some events are, and our judgements should be based on this objective information. An interesting question asked by researchers has been, 'Do people use this *base rate information* when making judgements?' A number of experiments have examined this question (e.g. Casscells, Schoenberger and Graboys, 1978; Cosmides and Tooby, 1996). See Activity Box 16.3 for a much-cited example from the pioneers in this field.

ACTIVITY BOX 16.3	

Judgement and base rate information 1

Problem 1

Of a sample of 100 people, 30 are engineers and 70 are lawyers. I select, completely at random, one person from the sample. What are the chances that he is an engineer?

Kahneman and Tversky (1973) gave the problem in Activity Box 16.3 to two groups of participants. Members of group A were told that of the sample of 100 people, 30 were engineers and 70 were lawyers; those in group B were told that 70 were engineers and 30 were lawyers. Both groups gave the correct answer. Group A said 30 per cent and group B said 70 per cent. They were both perfectly capable of understanding and using objective base rate information about the relative incidence of engineers and lawyers in the sample. The two groups were then given the problem shown in Activity Box 16.4.

ACTIVITY BOX 16.4

Judgement and base rate information 2

Problem 2

As before, of a sample of 100 people 30 are engineers and 70 are lawyers. One person is selected from the sample. This time we have a bit more information about him:

Jack is a 45-year-old man. He is married and has four children. He is generally conservative, careful and ambitious. He shows no interest in political and social issues and spends most of his free time on his many hobbies, which include home carpentry, sailing and mathematical puzzles.

What are the chances that Jack is an engineer?

Daniel Kahneman, Nobel Laureate 2002 for having integrated insights from psychological research into economic science, especially concerning human judgement and decision-making under uncertainty.

This time, both groups said that Jack was almost certainly an engineer (90 per cent certain). Both groups were ignoring base rate information. The effect was particularly marked in group B. Members of this group knew that only 1 in 3 men in the sample were engineers but were still prepared to say that Jack, chosen randomly, was almost certainly an engineer. This and other experiments show that we are not very good at using base rate information.

Heuristics

Why did these participants become distracted from the base rate information? Kahneman and Tversky (1973) argued that participants use heuristics (rules of thumb) rather than logical thinking or an objective calculation of probabilities because this is less difficult and demanding. In this particular example they used the *representativeness heuristic*. In making their judgement they concluded that the description of Jack was more representative of an engineer than a lawyer. It fitted their stereotype of an engineer. The representativeness heuristic says that we base our judgement more on our subjective impression of

how representative an instance is of a particular category than on objective information.

Tversky and Kahneman (1974) also found that people make likelihood judgements using the *availability heuristic*. In this case the estimate is made on the basis of relevant memories. To illustrate, if people have just seen a television series about street crime they are more likely to feel vulnerable than if they haven't seen the series because examples of street crime are fresher in their memories.

The availability heuristic is about making judgements based on the relative availability of relevant memories. The effects of the availability heuristic have been demonstrated in medical decision-making. Doctors, like everyone else, seem to be very influenced by recent events. They are more likely to make a diagnosis of, say, heart disease if they have recently seen and diagnosed several cases of heart disease (Weber, Boeckenholt, Hilton and Wallace, 1993). The base rate information about the likelihood of heart disease would tend to be swamped by these experiences and so have much less influence on his/her judgement.

Finally, an interesting source of miscalculation in arriving at probabilistic judgements is *gambler's fallacy*, also known as 'the law of averages'. This is the belief that if an event (red coming up on a roulette wheel) has not happened for a while then it must come up soon 'because of the law of averages'. In fact, each spin of the roulette wheel is independent and whether red or black comes up is completely unrelated to what has happened previously. Casinos love gamblers who believe this because they bet on 'runs'. Gambler's fallacy is another example of how baseline information (e.g. the objective probability of red or black coming up on a turn of the roulette wheel) is distorted in the implicit calculation of the subjective probability.

Decision-making

How do people make decisions? What affects the choices we make? Are our decisions logical? The starting point for research on *decision-making* is the assumption that people calculate the *expected utility* of each of the alternatives and then pick the best one (von Neumann and Morgenstern, 1947). Expected utility is calculated by multiplying the value of an alternative ('How much money will this bring me?', 'How happy will it make me?') by the probability or likelihood of it happening (very unlikely, quite likely, and so on) (see Activity Box 16.5).

In both examples in Activity Box 16.5, expected utility theory says that in both cases you make your decision by multiplying the value of each alternative (the money, the attractiveness of the person) by the probability of attaining it (more or less likely).

Biases in decision-making

A factor that affects the decisions we make is called *loss aversion*. A choice that entails a loss counts more than it should according to loss aversion. Kahneman and Tversky (1984) gave participants the chance to toss a coin and win $10 if it came up heads or lose $10 if it came up tails. Most people declined the invitation even though the chances of winning and losing are equal. They were averse to losing. The aversion to losing continued even when they were promised $20 if it came up heads because of the fear of losing $10 if it came up tails! Loss aversion is part

---

ACTIVITY BOX 16.5

Calculating expected utilities

Situation 1

You have a pound to spend on the lottery. You have two choices. You can spend it on a lottery that has one prize of £10 million or on another that offers 100 prizes of £100,000 (i.e. the same total money). Which do you go for? How have you made your decision?

Situation 2

You are at a party. You see two people you find attractive. One is mildly attractive and has been sending you signals that they find you attractive. The second is stunningly attractive and gave you a brief smile when you first came into the room. Whom should you approach with the intention of getting a date?

Making a difficult decision

of our everyday lives. Have you ever decided to stay with the partner you currently have, even though she or he is a bit dull and even though you may have been able to find someone more lively. If so, perhaps it's because you were averse to a certain loss in the hope of a possible gain.

A factor related to loss aversion is the *sunk cost effect* (e.g. Dawes, 1988). This is also known as 'throwing good money after bad'. Suppose you have just bought a car that turns out to be a dud. The repair bills keep coming in and all the indications are that this will continue. Should you keep the car or get rid of it? One factor that affects your decision is the amount you've already spent. If you got rid of the car you would be throwing this away. This is a sunk cost, and it makes you reluctant to get rid of the car in spite of the prospect of more bills.

Another example is deciding how long to wait on the phone when you have been put on hold. The longer you wait the more difficult it becomes to hang up because of the time and money you've already sunk into waiting.

Deductive reasoning

Deductive reasoning is concerned with the ways in which we deduce the conclusion(s) that follow from premises (bits of information we are given initially). In theory this should be a simple matter of following the rules of logic. In practice human beings deviate quite considerably from the rules of logic. Research into deductive reasoning takes the form of presenting participants with premises and then asking them for the conclusion. Their errors and deviations from logic inform us about how they are reasoning. For example, suppose you are told the following.

1   If Jim understands this section of this chapter he will get a good exam mark.
2   Jim understands this section of the chapter.

According to the rules of logic the *valid conclusion must* be that:

3   Jim will get a good exam mark.

As Anderson (1995b) points out, this example illustrates the problems of applying logic to the real world and using it as an idealised model of thought. Psychologically, we all know that many other things will also determine the kind of mark Jim gets, but logically we must conclude that he will get a good mark.

Skill and expertise

Skill

As we have seen, thinking involves solving some sort of problem. The discussion so far has dealt largely with what happens when we encounter a problem for the first time. However, it's clear that we all become skilled at solving the everyday problems we encounter. We learn to read, get on with people, look after ourselves, play games, write essays and pass exams, do a variety of jobs and so on. Each of these was a problem at one time. How does initially effortful, error-prone problem-solving turn into the acquisition of *skills* that facilitate competent or even expert performance?

Anderson's theory of skill acquisition

According to John Anderson (e.g. 1995a) skills are acquired in three stages: a cognitive stage, an associative stage and an autonomous stage. The concept 'skill' applies to: speaking one's native language, reading, maths, interacting with other people, driving a car. We have specific terms for people with skills in particular domains: physicists, doctors, carpenters, counsellors, computer programmers, pianists and lifestyle gurus.

In the initial *cognitive stage of skill acquisition* the task is one of problem-solving. It is the state in which we (i) identify the nature of the problem, (ii) learn or are taught the operations or actions needed to solve the problem, (iii) apply the appropriate heuristics or algorithms, and (iv) solve the problem. All this is conscious and reflective. It is usually hard work and often frustrating. Anderson says that the knowledge involved at this stage is *declarative knowledge*. We can describe what we know and what we are trying to do with this knowledge.

Consider two seemingly different examples. First, driving a car for the first few lessons. We can describe:

- how to start it
- how to make it move forwards
- how to steer it and
- how to stop it.

Our description will involve terms such as clutch, steering wheel, accelerator, brakes and so on. We can also perform all the necessary actions, even though our performance may be somewhat clumsy and error prone. We have to remind ourselves of the sequence or ask our instructor, and we're more or less oblivious to other road users, the route we're taking and the Highway Code.

Consider another example: learning to read. The early stages involve learning the letters of the alphabet, learning the relationship between sounds and letters, and learning to translate the letters in a word into a sequence of sounds. Again, this is declarative knowledge that can be articulated by the novice reader.

Next there is the *associative stage of skill acquisition*, in which this declarative knowledge becomes procedural knowledge (in the *procedural stage of skill acquisition*). What we know becomes a set of procedures. Procedural knowledge consists of 'production rules', which have an 'If . . . then . . .' form. The 'If' specifies when the rule is to be applied and the 'then' specifies what has to be done. Here are some simple production rules for changing gear in a car:

- *If* I want to change gear *then* I need to lift my foot off the accelerator
- *If* I want to change gear *then* I need to depress the clutch
- *If* I want to change gear *then* I need to move the gearstick
- *If* I want to change gear *then* I need to release the clutch
- *If* I want to change gear *then* I need to press the accelerator

Here are some production rules for reading:

- *If* I want to read this word *then* I must break it up into its component letters
- *If* I want to read this word *then* I must find the correct sound for each letter
- *If* I want to read this word *then* I must pronounce each letter
- *If* I want to read this word *then* I must blend the sounds together

In both cases, experience and practice make the associations between the 'If' part (the situation) and the 'then' part (the action) stronger. It's also evident from these examples that the set of production rules that make up a complex action need to become coordinated. Sequence and timing are crucial. We are all familiar with trying to move the gearstick before depressing the clutch (resulting in a harsh grating sound) or letting the clutch out and failing to press the accelerator (the car stalls). The end result of this associative stage is a reasonable ability to perform the sequence of actions, but it stills takes concentration and mental effort.

Finally there is the *autonomous stage of skill acquisition*. In this stage the skill develops to the point where it doesn't need thought or even attention. The sequence of production rules is triggered and implemented rapidly in a smooth sequence. The sequence of actions becomes automatic (these are known as *automatic actions in skill acquisition*). The different components become 'welded' together, a consequence of which is that it becomes difficult to interrupt the sequence (see Figure 16.6). It also becomes possible to do something else at the same time without any obvious detriment to performance. Consider the fact that skilled drivers can hold conversations at the same time as driving. This is not true of the prudent novice.

The Stroop effect

A striking example of the automaticity of skilled performance comes from reading and the Stroop effect. Do the activity in Activity Box 16.6 before reading on.

You should have found naming the ink colours of words in column 1 much more difficult than naming those in column 2. This is because you can't avoid reading the words, and the fact that they are colour names interferes with naming the ink colour (i.e. reading is automatic). (If you want to do an online

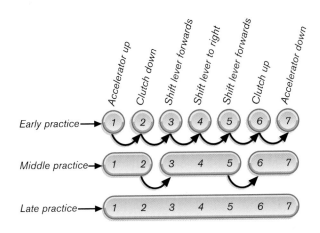

Early practice →
Middle practice →
Late practice →

Accelerator up · *Clutch down* · *Shift lever forwards* · *Shift lever to right* · *Shift lever forwards* · *Clutch up* · *Accelerator down*

Figure 16.6 How the components of a complicated sequence like changing gear become one smooth action sequence
Source: Schmidt, 1992

ACTIVITY BOX 16.6

Automaticity and reading

In column 1 below are several words written in different colours. Your task is to name the colour in which the word is written. Do this as quickly as you can without making errors.

Repeat this for the words in column 2.

Column 1	Column 2
RED	BED
BLACK	SLACK
BLUE	CLUE
YELLOW	FELLOW
GREEN	DREAM
BLACK	SLACK
YELLOW	FELLOW
GREEN	DREAM
BLUE	CLUE
RED	BED

Stroop experiment go to http://epsych.msstate.edu/deliberate/index.html.)

Expertise

While almost everyone acquires a range of everyday skills, and some people some quite unusual ones, only a few people become experts in their chosen field. A little reflection will reveal that *expertise* is a 'fuzzy' concept. At what point does a good chess player, a good carpenter or a good doctor become an expert? Experts seem to have two major characteristics. First, they have a huge fund of declarative knowledge about their field of expertise; chess masters can recall in detail scores of games played by themselves and others. Second, experts can also solve problems that those with less skill can't solve.

A major difference between experts and novices lies in the way they represent a problem. Experts spend more time initially making sure they understand the nature of the problem and what exactly is required. So, in physics, experts will represent problems in terms of their underlying principle, such as Newton's laws of motion, rather than in terms of their superficial characteristics, such as the fact that they involve particular mechanical devices with incline planes, wheeled carts and pulleys (Chi *et al.*, 1989). This time is well spent because it makes it less likely that when they come to solve the problem they will make errors or waste time on false solutions.

Another major characteristic of expertise is the way this vast store of knowledge is structured and organised. Experts' knowledge seems to be stored as *schemata* (De Groot and Gobet, 1996) that, in chess, encode set pieces, different types of board position, different strategies, different end-games, and so on. As we saw in the chapter on memory (Chapter 14), chess masters' ability to reproduce board positions from memory was significantly better than that of less expert players, but only when the board positions were meaningful. They weren't any better when the pieces were placed randomly (Simon and Chase, 1973). Schemata were making the encoding and recall of board positions easier.

These researchers went on to look at the pattern of recall. All players were doing their recalling in chunks: putting a few pieces into place, pausing, then a few more, pausing again and so on. The difference between experts and the lesser players was the size of these chunks. The experts' chunks were bigger.

Differences in knowledge and the organisation of this knowledge are reflected in the way experts go about solving a problem. Experts work forwards (Sternberg, 1999): they start at the beginning and work through to the end of a problem. Novices tend to work back from the intended solution, and change the approach to the problem more frequently. Because of their huge knowledge base, experts have less need of heuristics. They are likely to have come across similar problems before and their approach is more likely to be algorithmic.

However, even experts can make mistakes. Recall the recent problem with the Millennium Bridge across the River Thames, which famously 'wobbled' when the first pedestrians walked across it. The architects and engineers building it were clearly very experienced and expert in their field but nevertheless made a mistake that turned out to be hugely embarrassing, time-consuming and expensive.

Summary

This chapter has been concerned with various aspects of thinking. We began by looking at how people solve problems and some of the barriers to problem-solving. After that we looked at various aspects of inductive reasoning as found in concept learning, judgements and decision-making. We touched briefly on deductive reasoning before discussing the factors involved in skill and expertise.

Learning outcomes

When you have completed this chapter you should be able to:

- describe some of the ways we solve problems and some of the barriers to problem-solving
- compare contrasting theories of problem-solving
- describe how we acquire concepts of different kinds and compare opposing theories
- describe how we make judgements about probabilistic events and the biases that influence these judgements
- describe how we make decisions and also the biases that affect this process
- outline the basic characteristics of deductive reasoning
- describe the main stages of skill acquisition
- describe the main characteristics of expertise.

Key Terms

Algorithms

Analogy

Associative learning

Associative stage of skill acquisition

Automatic actions in skill acquisition

Autonomous stage of skill acquisition

Availability heuristic

Base rate information

Cognitive stage of skill acquisition

Concept learning

Confirmation bias (in hypothesis testing)

Conservative focusing strategy (in concept learning)

Decision-making

Declarative knowledge (in skill acquisition)

Deductive reasoning

End state (of problem-solving)

Expected utility

Expertise
Focus gambling strategy (of concept learning)
Functional fixedness
Gambler's fallacy
Heuristics
Hypothesis formation
Ill-defined problems
Inductive reasoning
Initial state (of problem-solving)
Insight
Intermediate states (of problem-solving)
Judgement
Logical concepts
Loss aversion
Means–end analysis
Mental set
Natural concepts

Operations (in problem-solving)
Problem-solving
Procedural stage of skill acquisition
Productive strategy
Reception paradigm of concept learning
Representativeness heuristic
Reproductive strategy
Restructuring
Schemata
Selection paradigm of concept learning
Skill
Subgoals
Sunk cost effect
Thinking
Trial and error strategy
Valid conclusion
Well-defined problems
Wholist strategy (of concept learning)

Further reading

Anderson, J. R. (1995) *Learning and Memory: An Integrated Approach.* Chichester: John Wiley & Sons. Good coverage of skill acquisition.

Eysenck, M. W. and Keene, M. T. (2000) *Cognitive Psychology. A Student's Handbook* (4th edn). Hove: Psychology Press. Densely packed information with evaluations of research.

French, C. C. and Colman, A. M. (1994) *Cognitive Psychology.* London: Longman. Chapters written by eminent specialists in their field. Clearly written. Chapter on thinking by St B. T. Evans.

Sternberg, R. J. (1999) *Cognitive Psychology* (2nd edn). Orlando: Harcourt Brace College Publishers. Good, general, reader-friendly text.

Sternberg, R. J. and Ben-Zeev, T. (2001) *Complex Cognition. The Psychology of Human Thought.* Oxford: Oxford University Press. This covers advanced material on all aspects of thinking and reasoning.

Developmental psychology

17	An introduction to developmental psychology	282
18	Cognitive development: thinking, information and representations	299
19	Communication, language and literacy	321
20	The self, others and social relationships	340

17

An introduction to developmental psychology

Route map of the chapter

This chapter starts by considering what is meant by the term 'development'. This is followed by a brief review of the way that development is influenced by genetics and experiences. This leads on to a consideration of extreme effects of the environment on development. This in turn is followed by a consideration of the way genetics influences development. The chapter ends with a discussion of the research designs and methodologies used by developmental psychologists.

Introduction

Consider the following.

- A newborn sticking her tongue out in imitation of what her father has just done.
- A nine-month-old crying in distress when his mother leaves him.
- A 20-month-old starting to put words together to communicate with her older brother.
- A child with autism who is having difficulty interacting with people.
- An eight-year-old who is reading quickly and efficiently.
- An adolescent who is arguing with her parents.

Research findings by psychologists have contributed to our understanding of all these behaviours. This area of research is described using various terms; each gives a slightly different emphasis to the type of investigation being conducted (see Activity Box 17.1).

ACTIVITY BOX 17.1

Terminology about change and development

- Child development: the study of changes during childhood (i.e. up to and sometimes including adolescence).
- Child psychology: the study of psychological processes during childhood.
- Developmental psychology: the study of the way psychological processes develop in childhood and sometimes in adulthood.
- Life-span development: the study of development across the life span, with as much attention paid to adulthood as childhood.
- Developmental science: the use of models of cognitive processes to study development.

Particular areas of investigation are often identified by the use of terms like cognitive development or social development.

- *Infants*: children below about 24 months of age.
- *Peers*: children of the same age.
- *Siblings*: brothers and/or sisters.

In developmental psychology there tends to be an assumption that whatever is being studied will be different at different ages. As you can see, a common thread running through the areas of study listed here is a focus on *change* and *development*. Write down what you think is meant by these two terms.

Change and development

It has been suggested that change, unlike development, can involve a decline in the abilities of a person, such as that occurring in very old age. Furthermore, simply getting bigger does not necessarily involve development. For example, corals grow by adding single cells to give the large exotic structures we see in films of underwater life. However, these cells are not specialised or different from any other cell. As the coral grows there is no change in the organisation or structure of the coral. In contrast, when a child develops there is increasing specialisation (e.g. the development of speech from a range of communication) and increasing integration (e.g. the way language becomes incorporated into many cognitive processes).

The idea of development also involves the contradictory ideas of *continuity* and *discontinuity*. If there was no change across different ages then there would be a high degree of continuity, but we would not consider development to have taken place.

The changes shown in Figure 17.1 are dramatic and involve discontinuity in abilities and characteristics, but most of us are happy to accept this as development, because we know that the same individual continues to go through all these changes, and perhaps because we know that there are complex biological processes that enable these changes to take place. Continuity in certain characteristics can also be seen within each part of the butterfly's life cycle – for example, the way the newly hatched caterpillar grows into its mature form.

Development also involves related issues about prediction and individual differences. These are questions about whether the characteristics or the experiences at one point are related to later development. To return to the example in Figure 17.1, this could be a question about whether we can predict that larger caterpillars will become larger butterflies.

A further example may help to clarify these points. If there is some form of continuity then we should be able to predict later characteristics from earlier characteristics, such as scores on an IQ test. Interestingly, it is rare for psychological

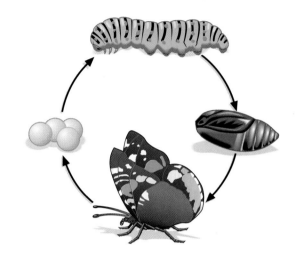

Figure 17.1 Development from egg to butterfly

characteristics to be highly predictable from one age to another. In this sense, discontinuity and unpredictability are features of development. This may be a cause for scientific disappointment, but it is also reassuring that there is flexibility in our life path.

What causes development? A continuing concern

Many of us know about the broad features of human development. Most of us also have ideas about what factors influence development and some type of 'theory' about the mechanisms of these processes. However, such theories are usually based on unsystematic observations. Developmental psychologists seek to remedy this situation by providing information about the growth of a whole range of abilities. In addition, they also seek an understanding of the way that this growth takes place. Thus, developmental psychology can be characterised by asking the following two basic questions.

- Does ability change with age?
- How do these changes come about?

Many of the debates about the mechanisms of development have been concerned, in one form or another, about whether development is the result of experience or the result of our inherited abilities. This is often known as the nature–nurture debate, or sometimes the debate between *empiricists* and *nativists* (see Chapter 5). Given the common-sense notion that we are the result of both *genetics* and experience it may seem surprising that there continue to be arguments about these processes. Part of the reason seems to be that the debate concerns the fundamental mechanisms that underlie development.

The philosophical discussions of nature and nurture during this 'age of enlightenment' provide examples of this debate. John Locke (1632–1704) believed that children's minds were a *tabula rasa* (Latin for 'blank slate') on which experience would write. Another significant figure was Roussou (1712–78), who believed in the essential goodness of children, a capacity that could be influenced by experience, and as such his ideas were a move away from the extreme positions of empiricists and nativists. These discussions were primarily of a theoretical nature, and did not involve empirical studies.

In contrast, work in the nineteenth century provides examples of observations that were linked to theory. Charles Darwin's careful observations in animals and humans provided a basis for his discussion of the development of emotions. The ideas of Freud also had a basis in data collection, but involved case notes about the recollections of clinical patients without the use of data collected from children. Freud's work drew attention to the importance of childhood in the formation of adult characteristics.

Binet (1857–1911) was concerned with the systematic collection of data to enable the construction of the first intelligence test for children (Binet and Simon, 1905). The test originated from concerns about identifying children who were not making good progress in French schools so that alternative provision could be made for them.

At about the same time, G. Stanley Hall (1844–1924) was influential in drawing attention to the need for research into child development and, as

a result, he is often seen as the founding father of modern developmental psychology. His contribution was to emphasise the scientific approach to data collection.

Another important figure in the development of tests is Arnold Gesell (1856–1961), who wanted to chart the milestones of early childhood as a way of documenting the maturation of innate characteristics.

Between the 1930s and 1950s, because of the prominence of behaviourist views (see Chapter 2) much of the theorising in Britain and the United States was limited to observations of behaviour, and explanations of development involved *learning* theory. For example, John B. Watson (1878–1958) concentrated on the way that reward and punishment influenced the developmental process. The same approach could be seen in the work of B.F. Skinner (1904–90), a leading exponent of learning theory. In both cases, the role of *nurture* (or, more precisely, experience) was emphasised and the role of *nature* was largely ignored. However, although learning theory can explain many of our activities, it does not provide a satisfactory explanation of many other developmental processes. This became apparent when Skinner (1957) tried to use the theoretical principles of learning theory to explain language acquisition.

Chomsky's (1959) dismissal of Skinner's account of the acquisition of language was a significant criticism that was part of a general reaction against learning theory at the time. Accompanying this was a reassessment of the role of innate predispositions and an interest in children's thinking.

Other significant findings that fuelled the reaction against learning theory involved the work of Harlow (1958) and of Schaffer and Emerson (1964), who showed that attachment to parents was not based on the availability of the basic reinforcements such as food. From a different perspective, Bandura's (1977; 1986) findings about the effectiveness of observational learning also provided a further attack on the idea that human behaviour is solely the result of direct reinforcement. His work is famous for showing that children who see an adult performing aggressive acts directed towards a large 'bobo' doll

Children with bobo dolls.

will carry out similar aggressive actions when left alone with the doll.

During the 1960s, researchers in Britain and the United States were also becoming better informed about the work of Jean Piaget (1897–1980) and Lev Vygotsky (1896–1934). Both theoreticians had already rejected learning theory, and their ideas found a receptive audience.

The focus of Piaget was on cognitive development, which he showed could be central to psychological research. Part of the appeal of his approach was his suggestion that children actively constructed their knowledge of the world; this was in contrast to learning theory, which seemed to suggest that children were passive recipients of information.

Vygotsky's ideas have appealed to those who believe that social interaction and culture provide the basis for human learning and development. From this perspective, psychological development is not an individual struggle with facts and concepts. Instead, development is facilitated by adults or peers who help children 'nurture' new understandings.

There has also been a growing realisation that children affect the environment around them, and are not necessarily passive recipients of the experiences provided by carers (Bell, 1968). For example, babies who cry more and are more difficult than others to soothe are likely to have a different effect on their parents than babies who do not cry very much and are easy to soothe.

ACTIVITY BOX 17.2

The usual suspects

These are people who have made a significant contribution to our ideas about development (top to bottom: Skinner, Piaget and Chomsky).

Which of these theoreticians do you think would agree with each of the following statements?

1. Human abilities are mostly the result of rewarding appropriate behaviour.
2. Both inherited abilities and the environment play a part in the development of children.

285

The last 20 to 30 years have seen a considerable expansion of research in developmental psychology. Major conferences attract several thousand delegates, who present and listen to research findings. Today there are no widely accepted general theories that dominate developmental research. Instead, each area uses theories and investigative procedures to suit the topic under investigation. After all, there are many different levels of explanation of developmental phenomena – ranging from genetic and neurophysiological to those that focus on cognitive or social processes, and others that are concerned with the wider impact of society as a whole.

The growth in research into child development has also raised questions about whether the whole of adult life should be seen from a developmental perspective. An influential figure who brought this issue to prominence was Erikson (1902–94), who proposed that there are eight stages of psychosocial development across the life span. Another important figure has been Baltes, who has emphasised the need for a 'life span' developmental perspective.

We now turn to an examination of a number of ways in which nurture and nature can be seen to influence development.

Effects of the environment

Extreme effects of the environment: deprivation and recovery

Unfortunately the role of 'nurture' can be seen in cases where there has been a severe lack of care (*deprivation*). In the 1940s and 1950s some institutions for children provided minimal levels of psychological support, play objects were largely absent and care was usually given in an interpersonal and authoritarian manner. This reflected the lack of appreciation of the importance of such experiences on the part of the people in these organisations.

Dennis (1973) documented the dramatic beneficial effects of transferring infants from a Lebanese orphanage to more favourable circumstances. In the orphanage the children were given adequate physical care but minimal social contact. White sheets were even tied round their cots to isolate the infants, and if the babies cried they were unlikely to get a response. These children showed severe delays. Children who were adopted by the age of two, despite having very low IQ scores at this time, achieved normal IQ (intelligence quotient – see Chapter 30) scores when they were older. Girls who stayed in the orphanage and then went on to a school that provided only a very poor level of education had at 16 years an IQ of 50. Boys who went on to a more stimulating school fared better, and their average IQ score was 80.

More recently, similar outcomes have been observed with children who have been adopted into the UK from orphanages in Romania, where care levels were extremely low both in terms of physical and psychological resources (Rutter *et al.*, 1998; O'Connor *et al.*, 2000). Children adopted before the age of six months when tested at later ages functioned at a very similar level to a group of children born in the UK who also were adopted when they were six months old. Children who were adopted from Romania after six months of age showed increasing effects of this delay in adoption. Those adopted when aged between six and 24 months had scores about 15 IQ points below the control group, and those adopted between 24 and 42 months had scores about 25 IQ points below those of the control group (this would be considered to involve learning disabilities).

Extreme institutional conditions.

Disadvantage, resilience, intervention and development

The previous section provided examples of the effects

APPLICATIONS BOX 17.1

Birth difficulties: biology and environment

Can the environment compensate for initial biological vulnerability? One much quoted study that answers this question was conducted by Werner and Smith (1982) on an island that is part of Hawaii. They carried out a study that followed up all the infants born on the island. Their findings indicated that for infants who came from poor economic backgrounds, difficulties at birth such as lack of oxygen (anoxia) were associated with lower scores on IQ tests, but for infants from middle to high economic backgrounds there was no detectable effect of having had adverse birth experiences. Thus, outcome appeared to be an interaction of biological factors and environment. Psychosocial factors associated with higher incomes such as more resources and better-educated parents apparently could compensate for biological vulnerability.

Infants born before 38 weeks after conception are considered to be pre-term and babies born before 32 weeks are considered to be very pre-term. Until recently, the latter group had a very poor chance of survival, but medical advances have changed this. As well as babies who are pre-term being at increased developmental risk, babies who are below their expected weight are also at increased risk. Infants below 2500 gm (5.5 lbs) at birth are considered to be of low birth weight, and those below 1500 gm are considered to be of very low birth weight, while those below 1000 gm are classified as of extremely low birth weight.

Wolke (1998) has argued, on the basis of more recent data, that pre-term infants above 1500 gm only have a slightly increased risk of developmental difficulties, and for these infants the family psychosocial environment can compensate for their early experience. However, he suggests that lower-weight premature infants are more vulnerable, and even the use of intervention programmes has not markedly improved their outcomes.

This is not to say that all high-risk infants will have developmental difficulties, rather that a high proportion will experience these difficulties. A comparison study of 264 very pre-term infants with a sample of full-term infants who had similar family backgrounds (mother's age, family economic status, marital status) was conducted by Wolke and Meyer (1999). At six years, the very pre-term infant group had lower scores than the control sample on information processing, grammatical understanding and production, as well as the naming of letters and numbers. In addition, the average scores of the very pre-term infants were significantly below those expected of typical children.

of extreme deprivation and the way that early rehabilitation can reverse such effects. In relation to this, it should be remembered that even in less extreme environments it is well established that family circumstance (such as income, social class and education) predict children's development, educational attainment and employment (McGurk and Soriano, 1998). Webster-Stratton (1999) identified four factors that put children at risk of later problems:

1. low family income, economic crises in the family
2. family problems such as violence, abuse and family arguments
3. rejection by parents or peers
4. being a member of a deviant peer group.

It was estimated that the presence of two or more of these factors meant that an individual was four times more likely to develop mental health problems, and those who experience four risk factors are ten times more likely to have such problems.

However, it is also the case that many individuals overcome disadvantage and are resilient in the face of adversity (Garmezy, 1983; Masten, Best and

Section 4
Developmental psychology

Garmezy, 1990). In broad terms, *resilience* appears to be promoted by two factors: the presence of an adult who provides responsive care towards the child and the child having personal characteristics such as intelligence, a sense of their own worth and ability, and responsiveness to others. Compensatory intervention programmes have been developed by governments in an effort to counter the effects of disadvantage (see Applications Box 17.2).

Chemicals, biology and early development
Discussions of nurture have tended to place

APPLICATIONS BOX 17.2

Head start
One of the biggest intervention programmes was 'Head Start', which was launched in the USA in 1965. This preschool programme, involving several million children, was designed to assist cognitive and linguistic development, and to prepare children for school. The early evaluation of the programme suggested there were few gains and those that did occur were temporary. However, later evaluations provided a more positive picture. Weikert *et al.* (1970) compared children who were involved in a 12-hour, weekly preschool programme that stressed communication and active learning, with a control group whose members were not enrolled in the programme.

The intervention group showed higher IQ scores than the control group in the first two or three years following the programme. However, this difference decreased as the children became older, and by 14 years the IQ scores of both groups were nearly identical. Nevertheless, more general benefits of the programme were identified. At 15 years of age the intervention group had higher scores on reading, arithmetic and language. In addition, only 19 per cent of the intervention group were placed in remedial school programmes compared to 39 per cent of the control group.

A follow-up of the sample when they were 27 years old revealed that those in the intervention group were much less likely to have been arrested (7 per cent versus 35 per cent), were four times as likely to have higher earnings and three times as likely to own their own homes (Weikert, 1996).

Weikert argued that these positive outcomes were due to the programme empowering:

- children to be active learners and decision-makers
- parents to support their children and work with teachers
- teachers, by providing additional training and support.

More recent discussions of intervention programmes have drawn attention to the benefits of the whole family supporting learning, and making wider changes to the resources available.

emphasis on the role of experience in affecting psychological development. However, the environment can affect the biology of an individual and in this way affect psychological development. Some of the best examples of this process can be seen in what are termed *teratogens*. These consist of a range of agents such as radiation, pollution, alcohol, illegal drugs and prescribed medicines. They can affect the development of the unborn child and can cause anything from mild problems to death (see Applications Box 17.3).

In very general terms, the effects of teratogens are greatest during embryonic development (three to eight weeks after conception); this can be a time when the mother does not realise she is pregnant. However, different teratogens have different effects at different ages. For example, the drug thalidomide was given to pregnant women as a sedative during the 1960s. The most serious effects occurred when the drug was taken between the fourth and sixth week after conception. At this age the limbs are

APPLICATIONS BOX 17.3

Effects of selected teratogens

- Cigarettes: reduce oxygen available to foetus, reduce foetal movement, transmission of cancer-causing agents to foetus, reduced birth weight.
- Alcohol: passes into blood stream of foetus and may cause death of brain cells; excessive drinking can result in foetal alcohol syndrome (FAS), which involves facial deformities, learning disabilities, attention problems and hyperactivity; binge drinking is believed to be particularly problematic.
- Cocaine: associated with premature birth and small head size; there is poor attention in some children and over-arousal in others.

developing, and the drug interfered with their development. Taking the drug at other times had no major effects.

Other teratogens have effects on different systems at other sensitive periods (the ages at which an effect is greatest). The effect of a teratogen will also depend on the amount of the substance and the length of exposure. In addition, there can be cumulative effects of several teratogens (e.g. smoking and alcohol). It also seems to be the case that some mothers and their children are more affected by teratogens than others.

The foetus is not just affected by external chemicals or diseases. Huttunen and Niskanen (1978) investigated the hormones associated with maternal stress to see whether they have an effect on later development. To do this they followed up children born in Europe during the Second World War. They compared individuals whose fathers had died shortly before they were born with children whose fathers had died shortly after they were born. In both cases, the mothers were likely to experience stress, but the hormones could only have been transmitted to the unborn children in the first of these two groups. The investigators were careful to obtain the participant sample from regions where alcohol and cigarettes were unobtainable, to eliminate the common association between stress and these drugs. Those in the sample whose father had died when their mother was pregnant were, in comparison to the other sample, at greater risk in adulthood of developing emotional problems and behavioural disorders.

Genetic effects on development

Genetics and the beginning of life

We will now turn to a consideration of 'nature' accounts of development. We will start by outlining the process of pre-natal development. This is a dramatic period involving remarkable changes that occur in the short space of time before birth. During eight months a single cell develops into the complex organism that is the newborn baby. The start of life can be considered to occur when the male sperm and female egg are united to form a zygote. Each sperm contains a random selection of half the *chromosomes* of the father, and each egg holds a random selection of half the chromosomes of the

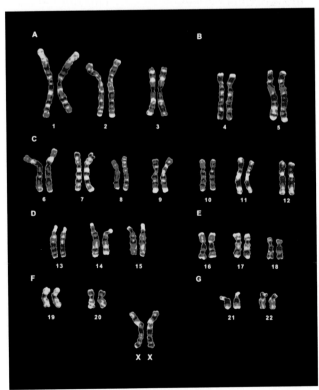

The 23 pairs of human chromosomes.

mother. Chromosomes are structures in cells that contain genetic material (see the accompanying photo). After conception, the human zygote usually contains 23 pairs of chromosomes. The chromosome is made up of *genes*. These are regions of the chromosome that influence the development of a particular characteristic.

Cell division increases the size of the zygote and at about the third week after conception these cells become implanted on the uterine wall. This marks the beginning of the embryonic stage, and from the ninth week until birth the term 'foetus' is used when referring to an unborn child.

The process of cell division and specialisation that occurs before birth is a fascinating one. Every time cell division occurs, the two new cells have the same genetic material as the original. As a result, every cell in our body contains the same chromosomes, and these are unique to each of us. This is why 'genetic fingerprinting' enables scientists to decide whether a piece of hair comes from a particular individual.

As cell division increases, the cells become more specialised and have different functions from those in the original zygote. The genetic material and the environment of the cell influence what type of cell it will become (neuron, muscle cell and so on). A complex process of cell migration (movement), and cell differentiation (the change in the character of cells) enables the formation of different parts of the body, and forms the basis of the development of different regions of the body.

It is often assumed that a newborn infant is a 'pure' example of genetic characteristics that have been isolated from environmental influences. However, this is far from being the case, and even before birth both genetics and environment can affect development. For one thing, a foetus is not a passive creature – he or she can move (from seven weeks), hear sounds (from 24 weeks), and can taste liquids. The foetus also demonstrates a process of learning called habituation (see Research Methods Box 17.1).

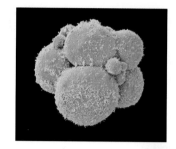

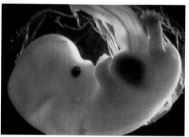

From zygote to newborn.

How do genes affect development?

The term genotype is used to refer to the genetic characteristics of an individual. However, genes usually interact with the environment. The result of these interactions between genes and environment is known as a phenotype. It is important to realise that the genotype is not the maximum potential of an individual; rather, the genotype can give rise to a range of characteristics. For example, a person's height is something that is highly determined by genetics (see below), but someone who is malnourished will be very much smaller than someone growing up in more favourable conditions.

RESEARCH METHODS BOX 17.1

Habituation

Lecanuet *et al.* (1995) repeatedly played the sound 'babi' to nine-month-old foetuses. At first there was a brief but noticeable slowing of the heartbeat, but with repeated playing of 'babi' this response progressively decreased in size. This decrease is called habituation, and involves an initial reaction to a stimulus that becomes smaller with repeated presentations.

The opposite process is dishabituation. This involves the recovery of the response when a different stimulus is presented. In this experiment, after habituation had occurred, the sound 'biba' was played and the heartbeat showed a noticeable slowing to the new sound.

These findings show that learning can take place even before birth. As we will see, habituation is an important research tool in the study of infants.

There are two major ways in which genes can affect development, through:

1. mutations and genetic abnormalities, or
2. the process of inheritance.

Mutations are the result of a configuration of genetic material that would not usually be expected from the genetic characteristics of the parents. Not all mutations have a known cause. However, some do: for example, radiation from the atomic bombs in Japan caused mutations such as deformed limbs because the radiation affected the chemical composition of chromosomes. Although many mutations adversely affect development, some may be positive and could result in evolutionary advances.

There are also a number of mutations that involve the same chromosomes and result in genetic syndromes. These usually involve the removal or duplication of genetic material, and often there is no obvious cause for the change in genetic characteristics. The most common genetic disorder is Down's syndrome, which usually involves an extra twenty-first chromosome. Down's children often have learning disabilities and a range of health problems. In the case of Down's syndrome, increasing maternal age is associated with increased incidence of a child having the syndrome, and there may also be a genetic component that increases the probability of some people having a child with the syndrome.

The genes a person inherits can also have a major impact on development. As already mentioned, two pairs of genes are present for each characteristic. A dominant gene influences the development of characteristics associated with it, and will override the influence of any recessive gene (a well-known example of this is the gene for brown eyes being dominant over the gene for blue eyes).

It is relatively rare for dominant genes to have an extremely adverse impact on development. This is because, in our evolutionary history, individuals with these characteristics were much less likely to be able to reproduce. An example of the adverse effects of a dominant gene is Huntington's disease, where there is neural degeneration in later life. As a result, individuals with this genetic disease are able to have children, and the effects of the disease usually become apparent when these children reach late adulthood.

There are several recessive genes that can adversely affect development. A recessive gene will not adversely affect development if its influence is overridden by that of a dominant gene. However, if a person inherits two of these recessive genes, then development can be adversely affected. An example of this condition is phenylketonuria (PKU), which if untreated can result in learning disabilities. The condition has a one in four chance of occurring when both parents have a recessive gene for this condition (see Figure 17.2).

In many hospitals, a small blood sample is taken from the foot of newborn infants to test for PKU. In this syndrome, learning disabilities are caused by a build-up of PKU that is not removed by the normal chemical processes of the body. However, by adopting a special diet it is possible to minimise the effects of PKU.

Thus, we have a complicated developmental

pattern with PKU where adverse effects on development can be caused by an inherited characteristic. However, these adverse effects can be minimised by modifications to a person's environment.

Genetics, environment and intelligence

Although most psychologists acknowledge that most characteristics of people are the result of both genetics and environment, this topic continues to generate discussion and debate. One area where this debate is particularly fierce is with regard to intelligence. Tackling the exercise in Activity Box 17.3 will help you to understand this topic.

Data similar to those in Table 17.1 are used by behavioural geneticists to try to understand the relative influence of genetics and environment on particular characteristics. Analyses tend to show that about 50 per cent of the variation in intelligence is due to hereditability (Plomin, 1990). What do you think this means?

Think of your class of psychology students and imagine that they have been given an intelligence test. If we say that 0 per cent of the variation in the scores on this test is due to hereditability this would mean that the genetic characteristics had no influence on the scores. On the other hand, if we say that 100 per cent of the variation was due to hereditability, this would mean that differences in the genetics were totally responsible for the high and low scores we see. Thus, if

Father

*Dominant non-PKU gene
+ recessive PKU gene
(parent does not have PKU)*

Mother

*Dominant non-PKU gene
+ recessive PKU gene
(parent does not have PKU)*

If we simply calculate the different combinations of these two genes then we obtain the following.

Dominant non-PKU gene (from father) + dominant non-PKU gene (from mother): this child does not have PKU and does not carry the gene for the condition.

Dominant non-PKU gene (from father) + recessive PKU gene (from mother): this child does not have PKU, but does carry a recessive gene for the condition.

Recessive PKU gene (from father) + dominant non-PKU gene (from mother): this child does not have PKU but does carry a recessive gene for the condition.

Recessive PKU gene (from father) + recessive PKU gene (from mother): this child has PKU.

Figure 17.2 The inheritance of PKU

ACTIVITY BOX 17.3

Nature, nurture and intelligence

The genetic similarity between two individuals can range from:

- 100 per cent similarity, as in the case of identical twins who have exactly the same genetic make-up; these are often termed monozygotic (MZ) twins because they are the result of a single zygote (i.e. fertilised egg) that has divided to make two individuals immediately *after* conception
- an *average* of 50 per cent similarity as in the case of non-identical twins (dizygotic (DZ) twins are the result of two different eggs being fertilised); and children who have the same parents.

The word 'average' is used above because, sometimes, two individuals in the same family will by chance have very similar genes, and sometimes by chance two individuals will have very different genes. Remember that the genes in a baby are a random selection from the *two* sets of the genes from each parent. As a result, in theory, a girl could inherit from her mother exactly the same genes as her sister, or she could inherit exactly the opposite set of genes – these events are, however, highly unlikely to occur. On average, children will have a selection of 50 per cent of the genes of their parents.

When evaluating the influence of genetics on development, it is important to try to make comparisons that take into account the influence of different environmental experiences. For example, identical or non-identical twins who are reared together will have more similar experiences than children who are of a different age in the same family.

The process of adoption also provides a way of looking at the influences of environment. Children who are reared in different families are likely to have different experiences than those reared in the same family. It should be noted, however, that adoption panels often try to place children with families that are similar to their biological parents, thereby limiting the degree of difference between families even in a particular culture.

Having read the above information, look at Table 17.1 and try to answer the following question.

1 What does Table 17.1 tell us about the influence of genetic factors on intelligence?

Try to answer this question before reading further. A correlation of .86 means that if one monozygotic twin has a high score on an intelligence test then the other twin is highly likely to have a high score. A correlation of .24 means that if one sibling has a high score on an intelligence test then it is quite difficult to predict whether the other twin will have a high or low score. (For more details about correlations see Chapter 39.)

Identical twins.

Section 4
Developmental psychology

Non-identical twins.

Children who have the same parents.

TABLE 17.1 THE INFLUENCE OF GENETIC FACTORS ON INTELLIGENCE

GENETIC RELATIONSHIP	CORRELATIONS	GENETICS THE SAME?	ENVIRONMENT THE SAME?
MZ twins reared together	.86		
MZ twins reared apart	.72		
DZ twins reared together	.60		
Siblings reared together	.47		
Siblings reared apart	.24		

50 per cent of variation is due to hereditability, we can assume that about half of the range in intelligence scores we see in this class can be explained by inherited characteristics (see Chapter 30 for a fuller discussion of intelligence and the nature–nurture issue).

Behavioural genetics studies are usually based on the assumption that there are three types of contribution to development: hereditability (variation explained by genetic differences), shared environment (variation explained by individuals sharing the same environment, such as being in the same family), and non-shared environment (variation explained by individual experiences, such as birth order, or the way individual children are treated differently by their parents).

Behavioural genetics is a controversial area of research. For one thing, it is easy to get carried away with figures from behavioural genetics studies and regard the percentages that are supplied as providing some absolute assessment of the effect of genetics and the environment on development. However, it is important to recognise that the figures concerning hereditability are only relevant to a particular sample in a particular environment. For example, if everyone in a sample has the same environment when they develop, then the effect of genetic differences would be very large. In contrast, if people in a sample experienced very different environments, then the effects of genetics would be very much smaller.

Research methods in developmental psychology

Design and development

Many of the same research techniques that are used in psychological investigations of adults are also used with children. However, the design of these studies usually differs from those used with adults. Suppose you wanted to find out whether intelligence increased as people become older or whether as you get older, intelligence declines after a certain age. How would you do this? For the answer, see Research Methods Box 17.2.

In relation to these issues it should be remembered that not all investigators of development involve groups of children. There have been a number of important longitudinal case studies, often conducted by one of the parents of a child. These have been valuable in giving a detailed description of changes and of raising questions about the process of development. However, such studies need to be interpreted with caution as there is uncertainty about the generality of the findings.

Experimental and non-experimental designs

Investigations of development also differ according to whether an experimental or non-experimental design is employed. In experiments there is one group that has an experience, and another group that does not. Children are randomly allocated to these two groups so that any differences can be attributed to the differences in experimental conditions. Such studies may take a few minutes to conduct, or they can take several years.

However, it is often the case that for ethical reasons it is not possible to assign children randomly to conditions. For example, it would be unacceptable to investigate the effect of breastfeeding on sleeping by asking one group of mothers to breastfeed their infants and the other group to bottlefeed their infants. Consequently, many investigations adopt what are termed natural experiments, quasi-experimental or correlational designs.

In these studies, comparisons are made between children who do and do not receive an experience of some sort (e.g. breastfeeding). However, because the children are not randomly assigned to conditions it is always possible that any difference between the groups is the result of some other association in the child's environment. For example, in the case of breastfeeding, mothers who do this tend to be middle class and better educated. So any effect of breastfeeding on sleeping could be the result of the mother's social class or education rather than the effect of breastfeeding.

Thus, to examine the effect of breastfeeding on sleeping it is important to try to rule out confounding variables that could bias the results. This can be achieved by the careful matching of the two groups so that they are as similar as possible in terms of any characteristic that could bias the results.

Methods of collecting data

Studies also vary according to the place where they are conducted. Some studies are conducted in a child's home (such as observational studies of infant attachment to adults (Ainsworth, 1967)), street or school (e.g. studies of cognitive development (Pine and Messer, 2000); see page 316). Other studies are conducted in laboratories that at first will be unfamiliar to the participants (e.g. studies of attachment in the 'strange situation' (Ainsworth and Wittig, 1969; see page 346). The advantage of more naturalistic settings is that children are likely to feel more secure and relaxed in them. The disadvantage is that there will be differences across children in their homes, schools and streets, and this could in some circumstances affect the findings of an investigation.

The opposite set of criticisms can be directed at laboratory settings. Children may behave in their normal manner in the atypical surroundings of a laboratory, but at least the context can be standardised. One should not, however, imagine that the issue is as clear-cut as this. A child might feel 'at home' in a laboratory where she has been carefully

RESEARCH METHODS BOX 17.2

Cross-sectional and longitudinal designs

Two principal designs are used to collect data about development: cross-sectional and longitudinal. If we were conducting a *cross-sectional* study to find out the age at which babies produce the sound 'psy', we would collect data from babies of different ages (see below for an example).

- The names of some of the babies who were observed when they were four months old: Jean Piaget, Margaret Mead, Arnold Gesell . . .
- The names of some of the babies who were observed when they were 8 months old: Mary Ainsworth, Noam Chomsky, John Watson . . .
- The names of some of the babies who were seen when they were 12 months old: William James, John Bowlby, Anna Freud . . .

Thus, different children are seen at each age. The advantage of this type of study is that it is quicker, and therefore less expensive, to collect the data. A drawback is that because each age group contains different children, the statistics that can be used to assess differences are less powerful (see Chapter 39).

If we were to conduct a longitudinal study, then the same children would be seen at each age.

- The names of some of the babies who were seen when they were four months old: Jean Piaget, Margaret Mead, Arnold Gesell . . .

The same babies would be seen when they were eight and twelve months old.

Interestingly, cross-sectional and longitudinal studies can produce different findings. Cross-sectional studies tend to show a decline in raw scores on intelligence tests from age 20 years onwards (Weschsler, 1939). In contrast, longitudinal studies tend to show an increase in scores until age 50 and then a plateau (Schaie and Willis, 1986). Why should this be? (If you wish, write down at least one explanation for each of these two profiles of development.)

There seem to be two major reasons for these different findings. Cross-sectional studies that compare people in their twenties, thirties, forties and fifties encompass groups of people who have experienced different educational systems, different lifestyles, different types of nutrition and are more or less familiar with taking tests. These people belong to different *cohorts*, and this helps to explain why younger people, who have usually experienced higher standards of resources, perform better than older people on intelligence tests.

In the case of *longitudinal* studies, there are always some people who move house and do not keep in contact with the research team, or who simply become bored with taking difficult tests. When comparisons are made between the participants who remain and the participants who drop out of a longitudinal study it is often found that those people who do less well in the tests tend to drop out. As a result, there can be an increase in the average score of the group.

Schaie (1989) overcame some of these methodological problems by conducting what are termed sequential research design studies. These began with a cross-sectional study (i.e. testing people at a range of ages), but also tested these same individuals seven years later and made adjustments for drop-outs. These studies indicated that decline in IQ performance is not noticeable until about 60 years of age, and then for some but not all individuals.

introduced to the people and settings, whereas in her own home she might feel uncomfortable when an intrusive and insensitive investigator is present. Furthermore, infants are likely to respond to a laboratory much as they would to any unfamiliar location.

The actual process of data collection from children also involves a whole range of techniques. Direct observations of their behaviour can be made, or their behaviour can be video recorded and subsequently coded. Observational studies are often time-consuming and it is important to make sure that good inter-observer reliability can be obtained.

Observational studies are not limited to 'natural' situations such as the child's home, but can also take place in laboratories. The ethological approach to investigating animal and human behaviour emphasises the benefits of detailed observations in naturally occurring situations. An extension to this method of data collection, which is based on very different principles is ethnographic observations. Here the observer attempts to become part of the group that is being observed, and evidence about the processes in which the observer is interested is derived from samples of conversation, observations of events, and so on.

Parents can be enlisted to help provide descriptions of behaviours as diverse as language and sleeping. These data can be useful as parents will know more about their children's behaviour than investigators and can provide more extensive records. However, there can be problems with parental responses being influenced by social desirability or by a lack of objective evaluation.

Data can also be collected by interviews and questionnaires directed at children, with the obvious limitations being the communicaton abilities of the children. In addition, psychologists have found to their cost that children do not always provide answers that reflect what they think. Young children, partly because of their reliance on non-verbal cues when interpreting speech, often pay more attention to the context than to the content of the speech they hear. In addition, because of the power relation that makes it more likely that adults are 'right', young children often give the answers they think the adult wants to hear and may use non-verbal cues to help them guess what is the 'correct' answer.

RESEARCH METHODS BOX 17.3

Observations in a laboratory

An example of an observational study conducted in a laboratory involves a study of infant pointing. Murphy and Messer (1977) asked mothers to draw their infant's attention to toys that were positioned on the walls of the laboratory. The sessions were recorded by video cameras positioned behind a one-way mirror. From this semi-structured situation details of the time when mothers pointed at the toys and the direction of the infants' gaze were recorded in tenths of a second by painstakingly analysing the video recordings.

From this it was possible to show that nine-month-olds could follow points to objects directly in front of them, probably by transferring their gaze from the pointing hand to the target object. However, these infants had difficulty when mothers pointed at objects where there was a large gap between the mother's pointing hand and the target object – for example, when the point was across the infant's body to an object in a corner. Fourteen-month-olds, though, were successful at both types of point.

Given the number of these dimensions it should be apparent that there are many different techniques for investigating child development. All research methods have advantages and disadvantages, and as a result the choice of a particular technique will usually be a matter of compromise. However, the important principle linking different techniques is that investigators' work should be able to be replicated and, if necessary, used to challenge the work of other researchers.

Section 4
Developmental psychology

Learning outcomes
When you have completed this chapter you should be able to:
- understand that development can involve change, continuity, discontinuity and predictability
- discuss different views about the mechanisms of development; in particular, be able to distinguish between nature and nurture
- describe the effects of deprivation and disadvantage
- discuss the way that genetic processes influence development
- explain the way that behavioural geneticists estimate hereditability
- describe longitudinal and cross-sectional designs
- explain the difficulties with non-experimental designs
- describe the methods of data collection used by developmental psychologists.

Key Terms
Chromosomes
Cohort
Continuity
Cross-sectional
Deprivation
Discontinuity
Empiricist
Genes
Genetics
Infants
Learning
Longitudinal
Nativist
Nature
Nurture
Peers
Resilience
Siblings
Teratogens

Further reading

Harris, M. and Butterworth, G. (2002) *Developmental Psychology*. Hove: Psychology Press.

Messer, D. J. and Millar, S. (1999) *Exploring Developmental Psychology*. London: Arnold.

Slater, A. and Bremner, G. (2003) *An Introduction to Developmental Psychology*. Oxford: Blackwell.

Smith, P. K., Cowie, H. and Blades, M. (2003) *Understanding Children's Development*. Oxford: Blackwell.

Cognitive development: thinking, information and representations

Route map of the chapter

Cognitive development involves the study of the way children's thinking develops. The topic can be extended to cover almost any aspect of children's activities. This chapter focuses on children's thinking about their physical world, and their ability to solve problems. (Thinking about social aspects of their world is considered in Chapter 20.) Piaget's theory of cognitive development in infancy is the first topic considered here. This is followed by a consideration of his ideas about cognitive development in childhood. Piaget's work has influenced the study of moral judgement, and this is discussed next. The final section outlines more recent views about cognitive development, those involving the information processing approach, children's representations and a social perspective.

Introduction

Look at Activity Box 18.1 and think about the changes that occur in the first two years of life.

ACTIVITY BOX 18.1

The growth of cognitive abilities

Take a look at these photos before answering the questions that follow for each one.

1. Does this infant know where to search if an objected is covered up?
2. Can this infant work out how to get an object behind a screen?
3. Can this infant use words to refer to an absent object?

Infants at the ages of about 4 months, 8 months, 12 months, 18 months and 24 months.

Section 4
Developmental psychology

The growth of cognitive abilities

Piaget's theory of cognitive development

How do we account for the changes described in Activity Box 18.1? Jean Piaget has had a particularly powerful influence on the study and understanding of infancy because he identified a number of puzzling behaviours and developed challenging explanations for them. He argued that infant thinking is different from that of adults because it involves sensations and motor movements and, unlike that of adults, is not based on language. Piaget put forward a general theory of cognitive development involving powerful processes that could be applied to any stage of development.

Piaget and his ideas about development

Piaget (1897–1980) was fascinated with the issue of

ACTIVITY BOX 18.2

Terms used by Piaget to explain development

Piaget believed that advances in thinking occur through the processes of *assimilation* and *accommodation*. Assimilation consists of responding to stimuli using existing ways of thinking. Accommodation consists of altering existing ways of thinking/actions to adapt to new stimuli.

1. What process happens when a young child who knows the word 'duck' sees a swan and then calls this a 'duck' – is it assimilation or accommodation?
2. What happens when this child learns the word 'swan' – is it mostly a process of assimilation or accommodation?

A good way to remember this distinction is that a sofa can accommodate several people, but assimilation and movement is needed for them to be seated comfortably. Although it is easier for us to think of accommodation and assimilation as occurring one after the other, Piaget believed

---

that most of the time assimilation and accommodation occur together, but that there could be different ratios of the two processes. These ideas provided an important alternative to behaviourism and learning theory, which largely ignored cognitive processes.

Piaget used a number of other terms when explaining his theory. For example, the word *schema* was used to refer to the cognitive structures that provide the basis for actions and thinking (e.g. sucking or grasping schema, or in older children a schema about the mother). Schema can be thought of as providing the units of thinking.

Other important terms are *adaptation* and *equilibration*. Adaptation involves a change in thinking to a more effective way of responding to the world. Equilibrium occurs when the cognitive system has been adapted to new information or stimuli so that for the moment there is no need for further accommodation. However, in childhood this stability is usually only temporary as it can be further disturbed by new experiences. Piaget thought that all these processes were involved not only in learning specific information, but also in changing from one developmental stage to another.

Piaget accepted that there is a 'specific heredity', such as the innate reflexes that infants have at birth, our sensory abilities and the processes of accommodation and assimilation. He also argued, however, that our experiences bring about the construction of ever more complex schemata that allow us to go beyond these limitations, so that as human beings we can develop ways to think, understand and detect things that we cannot sense (e.g. ultra-violet light, gravity).

Activity: when infants modify their sucking responses to take account of the different shape of objects, this can be described as a process of (i)_____ and this results in (ii) _____ of the sucking schema (fill in the gaps using words from the following list: accommodation, adaptation, assimilation; you will find the answer below).

Answer: (i) accommodation (ii) adaptation.

the way that children acquire knowledge about their world. He originally trained as a biologist and, after working with Binet on the development of intelligence tests, devoted his life to the study of children. He produced over 200 articles and more than 30 books. A summary of his ideas about development is given in Activity Box 18.2.

Piaget developed what is termed a *stage theory* (for the substages in infancy, see Focus Point 18.1; we will discuss the other stages later in the chapter), through which children progress in a fixed order. Each stage is characterised by a certain cognitive process that influences thinking and reasoning (see Figure 18.1).

A stage theory of development assumes that cognitive advances will occur in a step-like manner, but many studies have found that development is in fact a more gradual process, especially when there are only small gaps between age points.

More recently there have been suggestions that the level of children's thinking differs according to the topic (for example, they master language much earlier than mathematics).

Details of Piaget's *sensorimotor* stage are presented in Focus Point 18.1.

Issues about object permanence

Object permanence involves the capacity to understand that objects continue to exist even if they are no longer visible. Piaget observed that infants below the age of eight months who are shown an interesting object, which is then covered, do not try

---

FOCUS POINT 18.1

Piaget's sensorimotor stage

Substage 1: reflex activity, 0–1 months

Infants refine their innate responses (e.g. the sucking schema is modified to accommodate different-shaped nipples).

Substage 2: primary circular reactions, 1–4 months

Actions which by chance result in satisfying outcomes are repeated (e.g. moving a thumb to the mouth to suck it). There is no awareness of object permanence: if infants cannot see an object then they have no awareness of its existence ('out of sight is out of mind').

Substage 3: secondary circular reactions, 4–9 months

Infants use established schemata to explore new objects (e.g. suck and/or shake new objects). They begin, intentionally, to change their environment by repeating actions that cause interesting events. They have little awareness of object permanence.

Substage 4: coordination of secondary schemata, 9–12 months

Infants use established actions for new effects (e.g. they knock down a barrier to obtain a toy) or they use different schemata on the same object. They can imitate others. They are aware of object permanence, but make 'A not B errors' (see page 302).

Substage 5: tertiary circular reactions, 12–18 months

Trial-and-error strategies are used to obtain goals, and infants experiment with objects by varying their behaviour (e.g. dropping objects on the floor). Object permanence occurs in many, but not all, circumstances.

Substage 6: new means through mental combinations, 18–24 months

Symbolic activity starts to occur, so a sound or action can signify an absent object. There is imitation in absence of the original model. Infants can solve problems without manipulation and testing, showing that they can think about the best way to solve a problem.

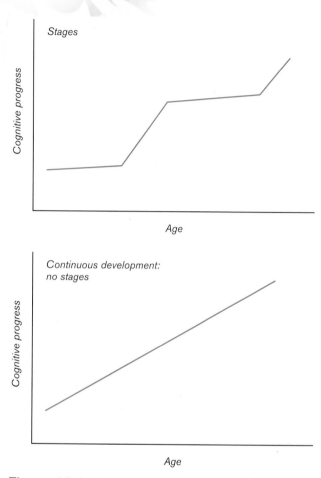

Figure 18.1 *Stages or continuous development?*

to uncover it. These and other observations led Piaget to claim that, initially, infants do not understand that objects continue to exist when they can no longer see them.

Support for this idea came from a study by Bower and Wishart (1972). They found that six-month-old children could retrieve an object from under a transparent cup but not an opaque cup, indicating they had the hand coordination, but not the cognitive understanding, to carry out the task.

However, other findings have challenged Piaget's claims. Bower and Wishart (1972; see also Hood and Williats, 1986) found that five-month-old children would reach for objects in the dark when the light was turned off at the start of their search, contradicting Piaget's claims that an object ceases to exist for infants when they can no longer see it.

A related topic concerns what has been termed the 'A not B error'. Piaget (1954) observed that one of his children could find a ball that had rolled to the same place under a sofa on a number of occasions (location A), but when the ball was rolled to a different place (location B) the search was made at the original location (A). Piaget interpreted this as an incomplete understanding of object permanence, the response seeming to be based on learning that certain actions are successful. Older children, of about 12 months, are successful at this task, but they still do not have the same awareness as adults. This can be seen when an object is placed under a cover, but the cover and object are moved by the experimenter so the object can secretly be dropped into a box. The cover is then returned to its original position. Infants will look only under the cover and do not search the box. At about 18 months, however, they will also look in the box.

Other explanations have been put forward about the A not B error. One is that infants simply have a poor memory. Support for this explanation was obtained by Harris (1973), who found that errors were reduced if infants were allowed to search immediately on the B trials. In addition, Gratch *et al.* (1974) found fewer errors at B if the delay was less than one second. They suggested that the direction of a search is based on postural orientation, and supposed that this information is lost when a delay occurs. However, the memory explanation has been undermined by Butterworth's (1974) findings that B errors occur even when the object is visible. A further difficulty for all these accounts is that infants will exhibit the error even if someone else retrieves the object at A (Landers, 1971; Butterworth, 1974).

All the previous research involved infants making motor responses to discover where an object is located. A different approach was used by Wilcox *et al.* (1996) who showed ten-week-old to six-month-old infants an object that disappeared at one location. The object then reappeared in the same location (regarded as a possible event) or at another nearby location (regarded as an impossible event). The infants looked longer at the impossible event, which suggests in these circumstances that they were not susceptible to the A not B error. The effect still occurred after 15 seconds' delay between disappearance and reappearance.

Diamond (1988) has suggested that the development of the frontal cortex is implicated in the A not B error. The frontal cortex is involved in the inhibition of typical or learned responses – a process known as *executive functioning* (see also page 354). Bell and Fox (1992) provide evidence consistent with this claim. They found that infants who were successful on tasks involved in sensorimotor substage 4 had more developed EEG patterns in the frontal cortex. However, this account has difficulty in explaining why the effect occurs when infants observe someone retrieving the object at A.

Thus, after 50 years of research there is still no totally satisfactory explanation of Piaget's observations about the A not B error!

Challenges to Piaget's theory about sensorimotor development

Gibson (1966) is sometimes seen as providing an alternative view to that of Piaget because of his suggestion that there is a rich array of perceptual information about the world and that infants have a capacity to make use of this information. Part of this process is *direct perception*, which involves immediate and automatic perceptual understanding (such as instantly knowing how far away an object is). In discussing these issues, Gibson emphasised innate perceptual abilities, but accepted that there will be some perceptual learning.

If infants directly perceive perceptual characteristics then one would expect them to show evidence of *cross-modal integration*. Cross-modal integration involves understanding the relationship between different senses – for example, knowing that there is a relation between a sound and the location of that sound. Several studies investigated whether newborn infants would turn in the direction of a sound, but these studies produced inconclusive findings. In a comprehensive study, Crassini and Broerse (1980) found that appropriate movements occurred, but there were often failures to make responses due to the unpredictability of infant behaviour.

Another type of inter-modal perception involves touch and vision. Meltzoff and Borton (1979) allowed four-week-old infants to suck for 90 seconds on dummies (pacifiers) that had either a plain or stippled surface. Then the infants were shown two objects. They looked longer at the object they had just sucked. Thus, both studies suggest that cross-modal integration is present in young infants.

A study by Slater *et al.* (1990) indicates that newborns also exhibit the principles of size constancy. As things (e.g. a person on a bicycle) move away from us, their size on the retina in our eye decreases. However, we do not perceive the objects becoming smaller. Instead, we perceive them as remaining the same size.

Newborns were shown a cube six times, and each time it was positioned at a different distance from the infant. The infant was then shown this cube and another one. The two cubes were positioned so that they both produced the same-sized image on the infant's retina, and to do this they were at different distances from the infant. Despite the fact that the retinal size of the two cubes was the same, the infants preferred to look at the new cube. This suggests that even newborns possess size constancy, and their perceptual systems do not have to learn to take account of the relation between retinal size and distance.

Another group of important investigations has concerned infants' visual attention and whether they look longer at events that violate physical laws. One of the first of these studies was conducted by Baillargeon *et al.* (1985). Five-month-old infants sat in front of a screen that was attached by a hinge to a table, rather like a drawbridge that could move through 180 degrees. This arrangement allowed the screen to lie flat in front of the infant, be raised to vertical and drop down to lie flat, 180 degrees from its starting position (see Fig. 18.2). The infants were allowed to habituate to the screen moving back and forth in this way. Then a cube was introduced into the sequence and infants saw one of two sets of events. They either saw the flap of the screen come to rest on a cube, or saw the flap falling to the ground and by implication flattening the cube.

If infants have little or no understanding of the physical properties of objects one might expect them to pay more attention to the flap resting on the cube, because this is a different event from the *habituation* sequence. In fact, infants looked longer at the flap falling to the ground and appearing to squash the cube. This suggests that infants have an appreciation of the properties of objects and that objects should continue to exist and not simply disappear in these circumstances.

Later, Baillargeon (1987b) demonstrated the same effect with 14-week-old infants, and showed that

seven-month-old infants appeared to expect the screen to stop sooner if the cube was larger or closer to the flap.

In another study, Spelke *et al.* (1992) familiarised two-and-a-half-month-old infants with the following sequence: a ball rolled down a slope, it went behind a screen and then the screen was lifted to show the ball against an end wall (see Figure 18.3). In the test trials the infants saw a box placed in the path of the ball and then a screen was placed in position so they could see only the top of the box visible behind the screen. The screen was then lifted. Some infants saw the ball resting against a box, others saw the ball resting against the end wall. Infants looked longer at the ball against the end wall. Again, this study suggests that the infants could distinguish between possible and

The infants at first see a rectangular screen that moves back and forth from a position lying flat in front of them, through a vertical position, to a position where the screen is lying flat away from them.

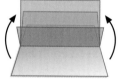

All the infants then see a box placed in the path of the screen.

Next, some infants see the box flattened by the screen.

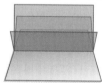

Other infants see the screen coming to rest on the box.

Which group of infants look longer at these two events?

Figure 18.2 Stimuli used by Baillargeon et al. (1985)

Infants see the following sequence a number of times. A ball rolls down a slope and behind a screen.

The screen is lifted to show the ball resting against a wall.

For all infants, a box is placed in the path of a ball and the screen is then lowered, and the ball rolls down the slope.

The infants then see one of two test events – either the ball resting against the box (possible)

or resting against the wall (impossible).

The looking time of the infants is recorded.

Figure 18.3 Stimuli used in the study by Spelke et al. (1992)

impossible physical events, and paid more attention to the impossible events.

All these studies suggest that infants have expectations about some of the important physical characteristics of their environment. Furthermore, it seems unlikely that infants as young as this could have discovered these properties by acting on the environment using the cognitive processes suggested by Piaget. However, more recently, the disparity between the findings about infant abilities in studies of attention and in studies of actions has been commented upon. The studies of attention appear to show that infants have abilities that are not present in their actions until a number of months later (see Bremner, 1999; Hood, 2003). For example, the studies of visual attention suggest that before the age of six months infants have an awareness of object permanence. However, studies of infants' actions when they uncover an object that is hidden indicate that success only occurs a number of months later. Thus different methods give us different findings about infant capabilities. One explanation for this difference is that actions increase the cognitive demands placed on infants, with the result that they are much more likely to be unsuccessful in these tasks (e.g. planning, retaining information in short-term memory).

Cognitive development: preschool to adolescence

Piaget's theory of cognitive development has also had a profound effect on the study of children in the preschool and the school-age years (see Focus Point 18.2).

Evaluation of Piaget's ideas

One criticism of Piaget's work was his general lack of appreciation of the way that social processes could affect development. However, it is inaccurate to say that he did not consider social processes. A number of his studies into children of school age were concerned with the way that discussions involving peer interaction could be more beneficial than discussions with adults. He supposed that children would accept the accuracy of adult viewpoints without any accommodation of their schemata.

However, research by Margaret Donaldson and her colleagues has shown that Piaget did not fully appreciate that many of the abstract tasks he gave children could make it more difficult for them to work out the correct answer, and the way that children were asked questions could undermine their confidence in their own answers (see Research Methods Box 18.1).

Despite these criticisms, and despite the fact that much of developmental psychology has moved beyond the issues Piaget identified, he still remains the most important figure in developmental psychology. This is partly because of the breadth of his writings across a range of ages. Another factor that contributed to his impact was the way he identified differences between children's and adults' thinking, and was able to demonstrate these differences by obtaining simple but dramatic findings. Piaget's work has had a profound influence on early education and has resulted in emphasis being given to so-called discovery play, where children find out about the properties of objects through their own exploration and efforts (see the accompanying photograph).

Discovery play in young children.

The stages of development identified in Piaget's theory

Pre-operational stage: two to six years

The beginning of this stage is marked by the use of symbolic representations. These allow children to use one thing to stand for another, such as words for objects or a banana to be treated as a telephone. This capacity makes humans very different from other species.

Piaget also identified two limitations of children's thinking during this stage, *egocentrism* and *centration*. The egocentrism that Piaget described was not deliberate selfishness, rather it involved the tendency to see the world from one's own point of view. A well-known study that describes this is Piaget's 'three mountains task'. As you can see from Figure 18.4, a child is seated in front of a table that has three model mountains placed on it. Piaget asked the children sitting at the table to choose a picture that showed what a doll, seated in a different position, could see. Children below six years usually chose the picture showing what they could see, not what could be seen from the position of the doll.

Centration refers to children focusing on one aspect of a task and ignoring others. For example, when children are asked which side of a balance scale (such as that shown in Figure 18.5) will go down, they tend to respond according to the number of weights on each side and ignore the effects of distance (Piaget and Inhelder, 1956).

Another task that Piaget used to show children's lack of *conservation* abilities involved setting out two rows of beads, each with the same number of beads, and the beads in each row matching the position of the beads in the other row. The experimenter would make sure that the children understood there was the same number of beads in each row. Then one of the rows of beads was extended to make it longer than the other row. Children were asked whether there were more beads in one row than in the other.

Usually children younger than six would reply that there were more beads in the longer row. This was taken to show that the children were not able to conserve the number of items. The children appear to make a mistake due to centration, concentrating on only one aspect of the problem.

Concrete operations: seven to twelve years

At this stage children are less likely to be affected by egocentrism or centration. As a result they can understand reversibility (e.g. that volume and weight remain the same despite being changed in shape). This enables children to be successful at conservation tasks; Figure 18.6 gives one of the best-known examples of this. However, children at this stage tend to be better at 'concrete' tasks that are tied to objects or events around them, rather than abstract tasks. An example of a concrete task is: if James is bigger than Adam, and Adam is bigger than John, is James bigger than John? An example of an abstract task is: if A is greater than B, and B greater than C, is A greater or less than C?

Formal operations: twelve years and over

This stage involves the ability to think abstractly, hypothetically and systematically, but it is a stage that is not necessarily reached by everyone. An example of this form of thinking occurs in the task of identifying the variables that influence the length of swing of a pendulum. Children tend to evaluate in an unsystematic manner variables like weight of pendulum, length of string and the force used to push the pendulum. In other words, they fail to study the effect of changing one of the variables while holding the others constant.

In contrast, systematic strategies are adopted by individuals at the formal operations stage. Thus, formal operations involve the principles of scientific thinking, especially the development and systematic testing of hypotheses.

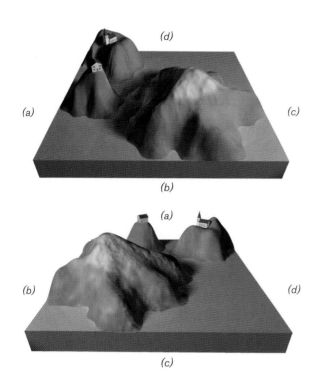

Figure 18.4 *The three mountains problem: children can see one view of the mountains and have to decide what someone else (a doll in one test) can see from a different viewpoint*

Figure 18.5 *A balance scale*

Present beakers A and B. Check that child agrees there is the same amount of water in each. Then pour water from B into C, and ask child whether there is the same amount of water in A and C.

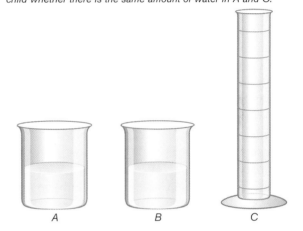

Figure 18.6 *The conservation of liquid*

Moral judgements: thinking about social situations

Piaget's findings about children's rules and judgements provided an important starting point for the study of moral judgements. This topic concerns the way that children develop the ability to decide about the appropriateness of their own actions and those of others, and this is usually distinguished from the study of moral behaviour, which concerns the actual actions that children and adults carry out.

As one would expect, there is usually a reasonably close relationship between moral judgements and moral behaviour, but it is not a perfect one. Thus, the study of moral judgement concerns children's thinking about social situations, and as we will see, this thinking can be influenced by the wider cultural context.

Piaget's (1932) investigations of children's rules provided a starting point for the study of moral judgement. His studies concerned boys playing marbles and girls playing hide-and-seek. The conclusions he drew were based on watching children play the games, playing the games with them and pretending to be ignorant of the rules, asking children about rules, and asking children where the rules came from.

Piaget claimed that in the first stage, below about four years, children do not understand rules. At the second stage, between four and ten years, children believe that rules come from a higher authority, such as God, the government or adults. In the third stage, children realise that rules can be negotiated between people, and that rules can be changed by agreement. This distinction between stages 2 and 3 is sometimes referred to as a distinction between *heteronomous* and *autonomous* morality. The former involves obeying authority, the latter involves individual decisions. These findings were broadly confirmed by Linaza (1984) in a study of English and Spanish children.

RESEARCH METHODS BOX 18.1

Getting the best from children

A group of investigators working in Edinburgh devised a series of clever studies which showed, when given the appropriate circumstances, that children could perform better than Piaget had predicted. One of these is a version of the three mountains task. It involved a model brick wall built in the shape of a cross, a model robber and two policemen. The children were asked to place the robber so that he could not be seen by the two policemen (See Figure 18.7).

Children as young as 45 months could successfully accomplish this task; to be able to do this involves the ability to understand what the policemen could see. Hughes and Donaldson (1979) argued that these young children could accomplish this task because it was like a hide-and-seek game and so was a familiar problem to them.

The usual design of conservation experiments is that the experimenter asks a question (e.g. 'Are there the same number of beads in both rows?'), something is done to the materials and then the experimenter asks the question again. McGarrigle and Donaldson (1974) pointed out that the repetition of questions to children often occurs when the first answer is incorrect, and the implication is that the child should give a different answer (see Rose and Blank, 1974).

For these reasons McGarrigle and Donaldson had a character called 'naughty teddy' who muddled up the test material. As a result, in the conservation of number task, naughty teddy would make one row of beads longer than the other. In these circumstances, about 80 per cent of children aged between four and six years gave the correct answer to the conservation problem. McGarrigle and Donaldson argued that the actions of naughty teddy provide a much more reasonable case to ask the same question again and, as a result, children may not feel they had to change their answers.

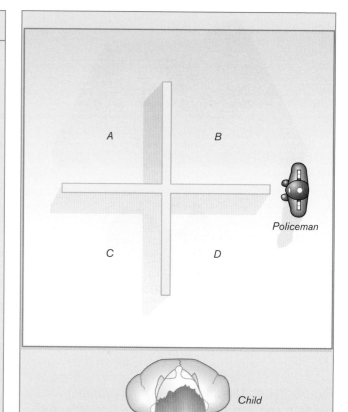

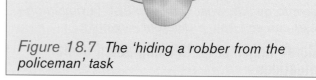

Figure 18.7 The 'hiding a robber from the policeman' task

Another important study of Piaget's (1932) involved telling children two related imaginary stories that involved a moral dilemma. The pairs of stories were made to differ so that the children could express their views about these differences. For example, one pair of stories concerned a boy who accidentally broke 15 cups, and another who broke one cup when trying to get some jam while his mother was out. Children were asked to say which child was the naughtiest. Up to nine or ten years, children often made judgements about the amount of damage, a stage Piaget referred to as *moral realism*. However, above this age children's judgements started to be made about the motivation or intention of the children, a stage referred to as *moral subjectivism*.

These studies were conducted at an early stage in Piaget's career when psychological methodology was not well established. Have you spotted the problems with these studies? One criticism (see Turiel, 1998) is that they do not systematically investigate one variable at a time (the story above involves different intentions and different amount of damage) and the situations used in the two stories were different. Thus it would have been better if Piaget had counterbalanced the content of the stories, so that one story had accidental damage to 15 cups on half the occasions, and accidental damage to one cup on half the occasions.

Moral dilemma stories were also used by Kohlberg in his extensive research on this subject (see Research Methods Box 18.2)

In the 1950s Kohlberg started a longitudinal study of 50 males who were seen every three years to give a sample of people whose age spanned between 10 and 36 years. Kohlberg identified three stages of *moral reasoning*, each of which was subdivided into two further stages. The stages are given in the table in Activity Box 18.3.

Kohlberg's proposals have had a substantial impact on the study of moral reasoning. Even so, a number of criticisms have been levelled at his methodology and conclusions. For example, Kurtines and Greif (1974) argued that the different stories had been selected on an intuitive basis and that the answers across different stories were not always consistent. Damon (1977) raised the issue of the stories having different meanings to different-aged individuals: think about the way the story in Research Methods Box 18.2 might affect a six-year-old and a fifteen-year-old. Damon devised alternative proposals that assessed the idea of positive justice, involving principles such as sharing, fairness and distributive justice.

Another type of criticism was made by Gilligan (1982). She argued that because Kohlberg's initial sample was all male, his stages reflected a male bias, particularly at the higher end of the scale. She suggested that female morality was based more on issues of responsibility to others than on justice. This was supported by findings from females who were attending an abortion and pregnancy counselling service.

Kohlberg and Colby revised the assessment procedures to take account of some of these criticisms (Colby and Kohlberg, 1987). The new

RESEARCH METHODS BOX 18.2

The hypothetical dilemma, 'Joe and his father'

Read through the following hypothetical dilemma that Colby and Kohlberg (1987: 3) set their participants. There are some questions that go with it and you will be asked to answer these yourself in Activity Box 18.3.

Joe is a 14-year-old boy who wants to go to camp very much. His father promises him he can go if he saves up the money for it himself. So Joe works hard at his paper route and saves up the $100 it costs to go to camp and a little more besides. But just before camp is going to start, his father changes his mind. Some of his friends have decided to go on a special fishing trip, and Joe's father is short of the money it will cost. So he tells Joe to give him the money he has saved from the paper route. Joe doesn't want to give up going to camp, so he thinks of refusing to give his father the money.

1. Should Joe refuse to give his father the money? Why? Why not?
2. Does Joe's father have the right to tell Joe to give him the money? Why? Why not?
3. In general, why should a promise be kept?
4. In general, what should be the authority of a father over his son?
5. What do you think is the most important thing a son should be concerned about in his relationship with his father?

system was applied to the original data: it reduced the number of individuals who were at stage 5 and no one was identified at stage 6 (Colby *et al.*, 1983).

Despite the research of Kohlberg being based on a North American sample, the sequence of stages has for the most part been found to exist in other societies. In a review of 27 cross-cultural studies, Snarey (1985) concluded that most found evidence of stages 1–4, but stage 5 was rare, suggesting that higher levels of moral reasoning may be related to cultural values.

Section 4
Developmental psychology

ACTIVITY BOX 18.3

Kohlberg's stages of development of moral judgement

Note down your answers to the questions in Research Methods Box 18.2 and then try to see where you fit in the stages below.

LEVEL AND STAGE	WHAT IS RIGHT?
LEVEL I PRECONVENTIONAL	
Stage 1 Heteronomous morality	• Adherence to rules backed by punishment; obedience for its own sake
Stage 2 Individualism, instrumental purpose and exchange	• Acting to meet one's own interests and needs, and letting others do the same
LEVEL II CONVENTIONAL	
Stage 3 Mutual interpersonal expectations, relationships and interpersonal conformity	• Living up to what others expect
Stage 4 Social system and conscience	• Fulfilling the actual duties to which one has agreed • Upholding laws except in extreme cases when they conflict with other fixed social duties • Contributing to a society, group or institution

LEVEL AND STAGE	WHAT IS RIGHT?
LEVEL III POSTCONVENTIONAL OR PRINCIPLED	
Stage 5 A social-contract orientation, generally with legalistic and utilitarian overtones	• Being aware that people hold a variety of values and opinions; these are often relative to the group that holds them • Upholding rules in the interests of impartiality and because they are the social contract • Non-relative values and rights, such as *life* and *liberty*, must be upheld in any society, regardless of majority opinion
Stage 6 Universal ethical principles	• Following self-chosen universal principles of justice: the equality of human rights and respect for dignity • Judging laws in relation to these principles • When laws violate principles, acting in accordance with the principle

Information and representations

Kohlberg's study of moral judgement adopted a developmental model similar to that used by Piaget. Other approaches to cognitive development provide a greater contrast and we now turn to these. Piaget saw cognitive development as involving the assimilation of stimuli and the accommodation of schema. These are general mechanisms and, as a result, it is difficult to break cognitive development into identifiable components. This is made even more difficult because accommodation and assimilation are supposed to occur at the same time. Work carried out subsequently to that of Piaget has been concerned with the changes in the way that information is coded and processed. The following two sections concern information processing theories about representations.

Information processing theories
According to this approach, cognitive development

FOCUS POINT 18.3

Children's memory
Several aspects of children's memory have been studied. Memory span is assessed by giving random sets of items (usually letters or digits) to children and seeing how many are recalled. Four- and five-year-olds can usually recall four digits; most nine- and ten-year-olds can remember six (Siegler, 1996).

Case (1995) has suggested that this change might be due to older children being able to process information more quickly and, as a result, they can encode, store and retrieve more items. In particular, older children can say words faster than younger children, and this may help them by allowing more items to be rehearsed in short-term memory (Case et al., 1982).

It also seems that increasing knowledge about a topic enables children to process and remember information more successfully. A study by Chi (1978) compared the ability of college students and children to memorise the arrangement of pieces on a chessboard. The children were better at the task than the students. The children were chess experts and the students were chess amateurs. However, the students were better than the children at recalling a random set of numbers.

Research has also been conducted into children's accuracy as eyewitnesses. Varendonck (1911), in the first study of this topic, concluded that children were too suggestible to be witnesses. More recent research on eyewitness experiences has revealed that children produce only a limited amount of information in free-recall settings and the amount increases with age (Martin et al., 1979). Furthermore, when given objective questions (i.e. ones that did not suggest a particular answer) six-year-olds were as accurate as older children and adults. However, when children are given leading questions ('He had blonde hair, didn't he?') they are more likely than adults to give the answer implied by the question (Goodman and Reed, 1986).

In addition, Leichtman and Ceci (1995) have shown that if three- and six-year-olds are repeatedly given misleading information when questioned, they eventually seem to incorporate this information into their memories. Thus they are accurate at the immediate recall of information, but after being given misleading questions on a number of occasions they report the misleading information as fact.

Research into memory has also concerned *metamemory*. This involves knowledge about memory itself. Flavell et al. (1970) report that eight-year-olds are much better than five-year-olds at judging whether they would be able to remember a set of ten pictures. In addition, the five-year-olds said they were ready to be tested before they had taken sufficient time to study the pictures.

occurs because information is processed in more effective ways over the course of development, new aspects of a problem are noticed, new strategies are developed and/or greater *information processing* capacity brought to bear on a task. The suggestions made by Brainerd (1983) illustrate the way that information processing involves much more specific aspects of cognition than Piaget's more general ideas about development.

Brainerd supposed that 'encoding limitations' could result in children failing to notice and process information. For example, in the balance scale shown in Figure 18.5 (page 307), some children notice the number of weights on each side but cannot remember the position of the weights.

Interestingly, this is similar to Piaget's ideas of centration, where children attend only to certain aspects of a problem. Brainerd also suggested that computational limitations occur when there is an absence of appropriate strategies. When predicting whether the scale will balance, this might incorrectly involve simply adding up the weights on each side and predicting that the side with most weights will go down. Retrieval limitations were believed to occur when children have the appropriate strategy (among others) in long-term memory, but retrieve the incorrect one – for example, dividing when the appropriate strategy would be multiplying.

Another difficulty could arise because of storage and cognitive workspace limitations. These occur when children forget information or fail to use information because they are dealing with too many factors for their information processing capacity to cope with (see Focus Point 18.3).

A good example of the information processing approach is Siegler's work on the balance scale (see Figure 18.5). Children were given different arrangements of weights on the rods, and were asked whether the beam would stay level or would go down to the right or to the left. What do you think would happen to the scale shown in the figure?

Siegler varied the arrangements of weights to help him understand the principles behind children's answers. This involved task analysis to identify the variables that govern the balancing of the scale; in this case weight, distance and the multiplication of these two variables can be used to make predictions. From the children's answers he identified four 'rules' that they follow when giving their answer. These rules give an idea of children's understanding of the problem (see Figure 18.9).

Siegler also conducted a series of studies to identify what brought about the change in the rules. He found that the youngest children who were adopting rule 1 did not encode (i.e. pay attention and process) information about distance. Siegler briefly showed children a balance scale with an arrangement of weights on it. He then took the scale away and asked the children to reproduce what they had seen on another balance scale using another collection of weights.

Five-year-olds tended to remember the correct number of weights, but they often positioned them on the wrong rod, while eight-year-olds were more accurate in remembering the number of weights and their position. However, the performance of young children was improved by asking them to count the number of weights on each rod. This also resulted in almost all of the younger children, when later given the prediction task, using a rule that was more advanced than rule 1.

An issue facing information processing theories concerns what developments allow children to become better at information processing. One possibility is that there is a general increase in capacity – for example, more items can be stored in memory (Kail, 1990). Another possibility is that children become more efficient at coding information so that they can deal with more information at any one time (Case, 1985).

One aspect of this is the speed of processing information. Case described a set of stages based on children's information processing abilities. This has been described as a 'neo-Piagetian' approach because it uses new ideas to describe development in terms of stages.

More recent work by Siegler and his colleagues has developed what he has termed the *overlapping waves* theory (Siegler, 1996). This supposes that children when attempting to solve a problem use a variety of strategies, and that eventually the most successful strategy will 'win' and become the predominant one.

This can be seen in a study of addition conducted by Siegler and Jenkins (1989). They focused on what has been termed the *min strategy*. For a problem like adding up 2 and 5, the min strategy involves identifying the larger number and simply counting up from that to give the answer (e.g. 5 + 1 = 6; 6 + 1 = 7).

The investigators studied eight children aged between four and five, who did not yet use this strategy. The children were given these problems three times a week for eight weeks. This is termed a *microgenetic study* because there was an intense period of data collection over a comparatively short space of time. From video records and interviews it was apparent that the children used several strategies. It had been assumed that children would count up from either number they were given and then start to realise that it is more efficient to count up from the larger of the two numbers. However, this does not seem to have been the case. What was discovered was that, when adding 2 and 5, children would use a strategy of simply counting from 1 up to 7 to obtain the correct answer. When they had used this strategy only a few times they then started to use the min strategy. Interestingly, the min strategy was adopted more quickly when the children were given problems like 20 + 2, where the min strategy is especially effective.

The information processing approach has provided important insights into the development of children's thinking. By focusing on the way children overcome their limitations in the way they process information, we have gained a better understanding of the changes in their reasoning and the best ways to assist their development. However, it has been difficult to go beyond the descriptions of the information processing in specific tasks so that one can predict what will need to change for children's performance to improve.

The nature of representations

Information processing theories tend to assume that all stimuli are processed in similar ways. However, a feature of human thinking is that we have different types of representations. Bruner's (1966) ideas about representations provide a good example of this. He described three modes of representing the world. Enactive representations involve actions and experiences (similar to Piaget's sensorimotor stage). These representations can occur at later ages and involve automatic patterns of motor activity such as typing and riding a bicycle. Iconic representations are coded as images; these occur during the last six months of sensorimotor development and throughout most of the pre-operational stage. At around six to seven years, Bruner suggested, there is a change to the symbolic mode. This enables children to deal with logical relations and reversability.

More recently, increasing interest has been shown by psychologists in thinking that involves non-consciousness processes. Studies of adults have often drawn a distinction between implicit and explicit knowledge. An example of implicit knowledge is children's use of language: children usually follow the rules of grammar, but if you ask them how they do this or why a particular sentence is correct then they (and many adults) cannot give an explanation.

In addition, there are examples of learning taking place without conscious awareness. Reber (1967) gave adults long sequences of letters, which unknown to them involved certain sequences being more likely than others (e.g. J usually follows X). When they were asked to predict which letter occurs next there was evidence of implicit knowledge. The adults often gave the correct answer, but were not aware that they had learnt something about the sequence of letters – they thought they were just 'guessing'.

In contrast, other forms of knowledge are explicit: a person can explain the rules of chess or how to reach a place they know. In these cases, the knowledge about the answer is accessible and can be put into a verbal form.

There is also work on children's speech and gestures, which suggests that children have different representations underlying these two forms of communication. McNeill (1992) described the way that gestures are often iconic – this means that one can understand their meaning from the form of the action. For example, children will use appropriate sideways movements of their hands when talking about width, and vertical movements to indicate height in conservation tasks (Church and Goldin-Meadow, 1986).

However, on occasions there is discrepancy between speech and gesture (Alibali and Goldin-Meadow, 1993). These children seem to be in a state of readiness to learn and this may be because their non-verbal representations are more advanced than their performance or verbal reports. Research findings show that children who exhibit this discrepancy are more likely to benefit from instruction in conservation tasks, mathematics and balancing tasks (Pine, Lufkin and Messer, under review).

Karmiloff-Smith (1992) in her *representational redescription* (RR) model suggests that one form of cognitive development involves a progression from implicit to explicit representations. Thus, her concern is about the way that thinking becomes more sophisticated in terms of higher levels of awareness about our own thought processes. The term representational redescription captures the idea that cognitive development involves simple implicit forms of representation being changed into more sophisticated forms of representation that are easier to access and that, eventually, can be expressed through language.

One of the tasks she used to study cognitive development involved the balance beam (see Fig 18.8), where a wooden rod-like beam is balanced on a fulcrum. Some beams are symmetrical and have the same number of small blocks of wood stuck to both ends of the beam. As a result, the beams balance in their geometric centre. Other beams are asymmetrical, and have a different number of small blocks of wood at each end of the beam. As a result these beams do not balance in the geometric centre.

Karmiloff-Smith suggested that children start with an *implicit* level of representation. On the balance beam task, these children can balance both symmetrical and asymmetrical beams. However, if the experimenter asks them how they achieve this, they will say they 'don't know', they might try to show by gestures how they balanced a beam or they might give a spurious explanation such as 'I balanced it where that bit of paint is' (Pine and

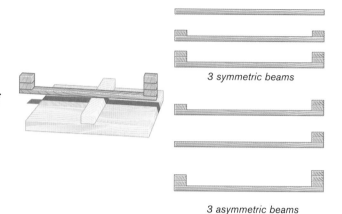

Figure 18.8 Balance beam

Messer, 2003). Karmiloff-Smith believes that, at this level, children do not have any unified strategy or theory about balancing, but solve each problem by trial and error.

At the next level children start to use a general strategy to solve problems, but still cannot explain their own behaviour. In the case of the balance beam they try to balance all the beams at their geometric centre. This is successful with symmetrical beams, but results in failure with asymmetrical beams. Consequently, although children are making cognitive progress, because they have adopted a general strategy, their performance actually declines. This dip in success rates is often termed a u-shaped curve. Pine and Messer (2000) have termed this the abstraction level because children seem to have 'abstracted' a strategy that often, but not always, results in success.

Karmiloff-Smith believes children at this level do not yet have conscious access to their representations. As a result they are not aware of their strategy or able to explain it. However, their strategy has a powerful effect on their behaviour. Children at this level will deny that an asymmetrical beam can be balanced, and they have more difficulty than children at other levels in learning from observations about someone balancing an asymmetrical beam (Messer and Pine, 2000).

Karmiloff-Smith also argues that there might be a further level where children *do* have conscious access to their representations, but are not able to

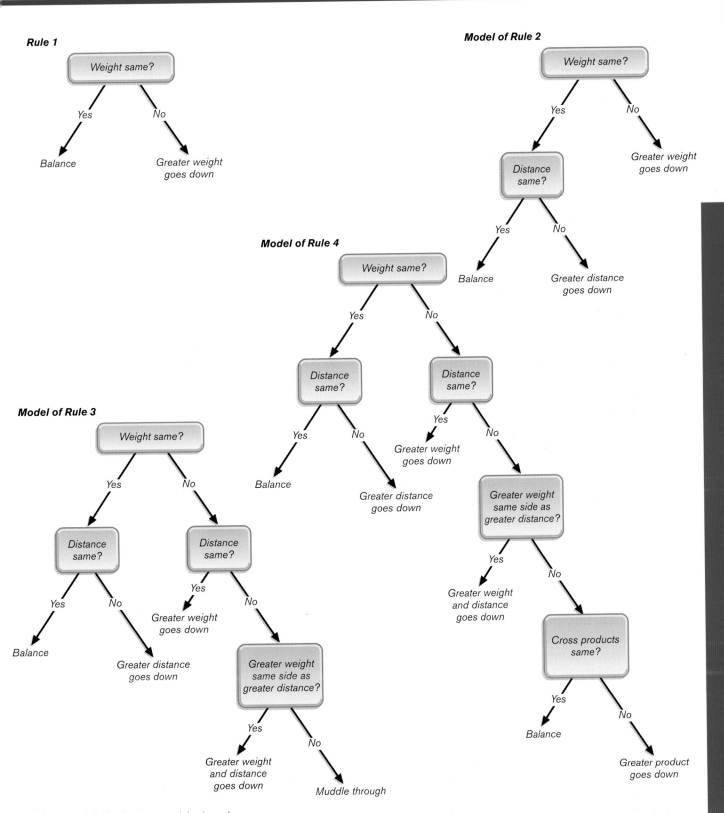

Figure 18.9 Rules and balancing

explain what they know. She terms this level E2. This seems to corresponds to being able to make predictions about whether a beam will balance, but not being able to explain the prediction (see Pine and Messer, 2000). The final level identified is the *explicit* level. At this level children are able to explain their success in terms of weight and distance, and are also able, once again, to balance both symmetrical and asymmetrical beams.

Karmiloff-Smith rejects the idea that development involves a series of stages as claimed by Piaget. Instead she proposes that different levels of development occur within particular domains, so that children can be at one level for, say, spelling and at another for balancing. This is why she uses the term level rather than stage. She also rejects the idea that at birth there are modular systems separate from other cognitive processes (e.g. that language is a separate modular system). Instead she believes that modules are the result of development resulting in specialised cognitive processing. Thus a language module could develop as a result of the time spent in listening and talking, as well as the importance of this cognitive operation to children.

Investigations conducted by Pine and Messer using balance beam tasks have provided support for the general features of the representational redescription theory. A microgenetic study (which involves detailed observations over a short period) that collected data from children on five successive days revealed that in almost all cases they showed progress to higher levels of representation. In addition, there were very few regressions to lower levels. Furthermore, the children showed a gradual progress through the levels. They did not jump from implicit to explicit levels as might be expected if all that was necessary for cognitive development was to work out how to explain something verbally (Pine and Messer, 2003).

Another important finding was that the level of representation in the balance beam task was not related to children's vocabulary size, so that the levels did not seem to be simply the result of better language abilities (Messer and Pine, 2000). Furthermore, they found that children who were at the abstraction level had the most difficulty in making progress. It seemed as if having a strategy that is difficult to put into words makes further progress more difficult.

The study of implicit and explicit representations shows that cognitive development can involve a progression from implicit levels where success occurs but children are unable to explain this success, to abstraction levels where there is an inappropriate strategy and the success rate is lower, and then to the explicit level where there is success and the ability to explain why the success has been achieved. Thus limitations in children's cognitive operations occur because the underlying representations are difficult to integrate or access.

In contrast, Piaget saw limitations of children's cognitive operations as occurring because of inappropriate assumptions (e.g. object permanence) or failure to process all the information that was available (e.g. centration), while information processing theories tended to treat all cognitive operations as involving the same type of cognitive representations. Thus the study of children's representations provides an additional perspective about the cognitive development of children by alerting us to the way that not all representations have the same status.

FOCUS POINT 18.4

Vygotsky

Vygotsky (1896–1934) grew up in Tsarist Russia and his research work was carried out under the repressive communist regime of Stalin, in a context where there was considerable personal danger associated with having independent and challenging views. The predominant view during the 1930s and 1940s in both communist Russia and the West was to put consciousness and the complexities of social processes beyond the remit of psychological investigations. Vygotsky's work only became widely known in the West through translations made available in the 1960s and 1970s.

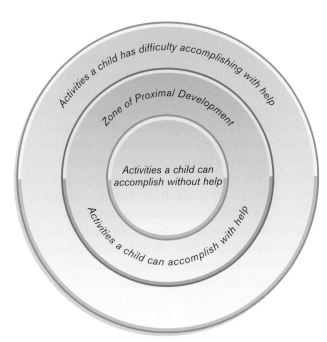

Figure 18.10 The zone of proximal development (ZPD)

Social process and cognitive development

Vygotsky: bringing cultural, social and cognitive processes together

A general criticism of many cognitive theories of development is that social processes are largely ignored, and for humans it is possible to argue that learning in social settings rather than individual voyages of discovery are responsible for many of the abilities we have. Lev Vygotsky is seen by many as being the first psychologist to discuss and theorise extensively about the role of speech, social settings and culture (see Focus Point 18.4) in relation to cognitive development.

In many ways, Vygotsky's contribution to developmental psychology is difficult to pin down. Unlike Piaget he did not produce a detailed model of development through the life span. Despite this, it is possible to argue that his views have a more direct relevance to contemporary research than those of Piaget. Part of the reason for this is Vygotsky's preoccupation with children's participation in social and culturally based activities as the primary means of extending their capabilities. For example, the way

children think about the world around them and the issue of causation can be influenced by the religious and scientific beliefs of a culture (e.g. believing that the world is flat). This is different from the way that Piaget portrayed the independent scientific thinking of the formal operations stage, where the highest level of thought involves a scientific approach.

Vygotsky was concerned with the relationship between thought, language and consciousness. Part of this concern involved an interest in private speech; this occurs when young children talk to themselves in an apparent effort to help themselves think and reason. Children's use of private speech provided a basis for suggesting that language enables thought and language to be integrated in the reasoning process. Vygostky also made the point that language allows reflection and restructuring of one's own thought processes.

Another important aspect of Vygotsky's work was his belief that an important feature of cognitive development is the way children learn from others who are more knowledgeable than themselves. This idea has been taken up with the use of the term *zone of proximal development (ZPD)*. The activities a child can accomplish alone form the first 'zone'. Beyond this is the ZPD; in this zone children can accomplish things with partial help from others (e.g. a one-month-old appearing to engage in taking turns in a 'conversation' because the adult carefully inserts their speech between infant vocalisations). Beyond the ZPD are activities that a child will find difficult to accomplish even with assistance (e.g. trying to teach a one-month-old to talk). The importance of the ZPD is that, through social interaction, individuals with more advanced abilities can help children make cognitive developments by supporting their learning processes.

These ideas have had an impact on the way teachers try to extend pupils' own ideas and abilities, and has emphasised the way that this can be achieved in social settings.

A good example of this is the idea of *scaffolding* proposed by Wood, Bruner and Ross (1976). They observed mothers and children jointly attempting to solve the problem of building a pyramid made from blocks. The most effective mothers were those who anticipated the difficulties of their child. Wood *et al.* describe a number of processes that contribute to effective scaffolding. It might help to imagine these in relation to helping a young child solve a jigsaw puzzle. The strategies include the recruitment and maintenance of a child's interest and motivation in a task by, for example, pointing out where to look and by offering encouragement.

Another strategy is modelling to show a child what to do – for example, putting some jigsaw pieces together and then undoing them again. Adults can simplify the task by reducing the number of possibilities: an adult might give one jigsaw piece to a child that will fit in part of the already constructed jigsaw. During scaffolding, adults also highlight critical features of the task when an incorrect attempt is made or when an insightful action is accomplished. What is seen as important in effective scaffolding is matching the level of assistance to the children's capabilities, so the help puts children in a position to accomplish something they would be unable to do by themselves.

A related idea is that of *guided participation*, where adults model, guide and regulate the activities of children (Rogoff, 1990). The difference between this and scaffolding involves the emphasis given to the acquisition of particular activities of a culture. Rogoff *et al.* (1995) identified three levels of analysis. These involved the community plane (people interacting in culturally organised activities such as education); the interpersonal plane (the actual interaction between

Peer interaction: children discussing a problem

people), and the personal plane (the way children change through their engagement in the activity).

There is also a body of research about the beneficial effects of group collaboration on children's learning (e.g. Doise and Mugny, 1984). On the whole, children have been shown to learn more if they work together with a group of peers than if they solve problems individually (see Joiner *et al.*, 2000).

However, simply putting children together is no guarantee of improvement, and several factors have been identified that mediate the facilitative effects. These include the relative competence of the children, the presence or absence of feedback, task design (Howe *et al.*, 1995), the role of modelling, friendship patterns, and the degree of active participation (see Messer and Pine, 2000).

Cultural psychology as applied to child development has drawn on many of these ideas. Crook (1999) has identified three concerns of cultural psychology within a developmental context. The first is the way that individual human activities and development are mediated by objects or organisations that have been created as part of human culture (i.e. cultural tools). These can be simple objects, such as a spoon, or complex organisations like the Internet. These cultural tools make humans and human development different from most animals who act directly on their environment; instead human actions take place in a cultural environment that has been created by humans. Adults assist children in using cultural tools, and by using the cultural tools, children change their own skills and thinking.

The second concern is about the importance of interpersonal experience to human development. Interpersonal experiences allow personal meanings and views to be negotiated and changed during the process of interaction. Such experiences can involve the development of a whole range of ideas. These might include the views a person has of him/herself. The third concern is about the importance of ecological settings: the precise way that social and physical settings influence the development of children.

Thus, the socio-cultural perspective emphasises the way that children are influenced by and influence their cultural settings – for example, the widespread use of computer games can be seen as the result of a complex set of influences that involve technical innovation, children's interests and changes in family structure, as well as the wider values and organisation of the culture.

Learning outcomes

When you have completed this chapter you should be able to:

- describe and discuss Piaget's ideas about cognitive development in infancy
- describe and discuss Piaget's ideas about pre-operational and concrete operational thinking
- evaluate the information processing explanation of cognitive development
- describe the differences between the information processing and representational accounts of children's development
- discuss the contribution of social and cultural processes to cognitive development.

Key Terms

Accommodation
Adaptation
Assimilation
Autonomous
Centration
Conservation
Cross-model integration
Direct perception
Egocentrism
Equilibration
Executive functioning
Explicit
Guided participation
Habituation
Heteronomous
Implicit
Information processing
Metamemory
Microgenetic study
Min strategy
Moral realism
Moral reasoning
Moral subjectivism
Overlapping waves
Representational redescription
Reversibility
Scaffolding
Schema
Sensorimotor
Stage theory
Zone of proximal development (ZPD)

Section 4
Developmental psychology

Further reading

Bremner, G. (1999) Knowledge of the physical world in infancy. In D. Messer and S. Millar (eds) *Exploring Developmental Psychology*. London: Arnold.

Pine, K. (1999) Theories of cognitive psychology. In D. Messer and S. Millar (eds) *Exploring Developmental Psychology*. London: Arnold.

Siegler, R. S., DeLaoache, J. S. and Eisenberg, N. (2003) *How Children Develop*. Basingstoke: Palgrave Macmillan.

Wood, D. (1998) *How Children Think and Learn*. Oxford: Blackwell.

Communication, language and literacy

Route map of the chapter

This chapter is divided into four sections. The first begins with a discussion of the development in the first year of the ability to process speech and produce vocalisations. This is followed by discussion of the role of social interaction in language acquisition, and the differences between communication and language. The second section considers explanations of language acquisition that emphasise the role of innate abilities, while the third considers the opposite perspective, which emphasises the role of experience. Evidence for and against these perspectives is evaluated and discussed. The final section considers the development of literacy; reading is a way of acquiring information that involves language, and the development of literacy appears to be associated with a number of linguistic abilities.

Introduction

Children's acquisition of language is a remarkable achievement. At birth infants can give only rudimentary signals of pleasure and discomfort, while by 30 months they have a reasonable command of their mother tongue. This is achieved despite initial cognitive immaturity, it is achieved without explicit teaching and it is achieved despite the fact that human language is remarkably complex.

In terms of wider issues of development, language is a medium through which children are educated about their world. It is associated with the transmission of culture, and it is a characteristic without which many human achievements would be that much more difficult, if not impossible. Furthermore, language is a human characteristic that makes us different from most, if not all, other species. Given this importance it is not surprising that language acquisition has been a focus of research interest and debate, a debate that focuses on the nature–nurture argument.

Hearing, vocalising and speaking

Hearing and vocalising

To process speech we need to be able to identify phonemes. These are the smallest units of sound that can be identified in speech, such as the 'ba' of 'bath' or the 'pa' of 'path'.

Adults' perception of phonemes is categorical: we hear sounds as either 'ba' or 'pa' and do not perceive there to be intermediate sounds. This has the advantage that we hear a 'pa' sound even when it is spoken by different people and in different circumstances. Do infants process sounds in this way?

In the case of adults we can ask them whether they hear a sound as 'pa' or 'ba', although obviously this will not work with a baby. However, as we have already seen in the previous chapter, the principle of habituation can be used to find out whether infants perceive one stimulus as similar to or different from another. Eimas *et al.* (1971) did just this, by measuring sucking on a dummy (pacifier) so that a high rate of sucking produced a phoneme such as 'ba'. Infants learnt to do this, but after a while habituation occurred and the rate of sucking decreased (see Figure 19.1).

This study involves presenting the sound 'ba' to infants. They habituate to the sound 'ba' (i.e. they become familiar with it) and as a result their rate of

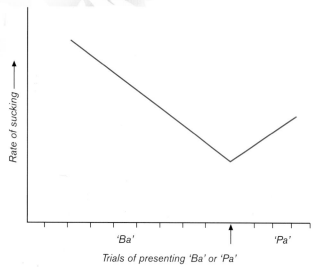

Figure 19.1 Habituation to 'ba'

sucking decreases. When 'pa' is presented, the infants' rate of sucking increases in response to hearing a new sound. The fact that sucking increased shows that the infants could distinguish between the two phonemes (dishabituation). If the sucking did not increase, then this would indicate that the

---

ACTIVITY BOX 19.1

Nature, nurture and language acquisition

Decide which of the views in Figure 19.2 are compatible with 'nature' or 'nurture' viewpoints. What would a compromise position between nature and nurture involve? Which viewpoint do you think is most likely to be correct?

Figure 19.2 Nature, nurture and language acquisition

Answer: all viewpoints except that involving an innate capacity involve nurture.

infants could not tell the difference between the two phonemes.

It was found that one- and four-month-old infants showed dishabituation when a new sound crossed the boundary of a phoneme, but not when the sounds differed by the same extent and were within a phoneme boundary. This indicates that infants identify phonemes in a very similar way to adults.

Further research, however, has revealed that monkeys, chinchillas and even quails also process sounds in a similar way (Kuhl and Padden, 1983; Kluender *et al.*, 1987). Thus the categorical perception of phonemes occurs in a range of biological species, and so human speech may be structured in a way that reflects our perceptual abilities rather than human infants being specifically adapted to human speech. Whatever the reasons, the ability of infants to distinguish between phonemes means that their hearing is already tuned in to the important distinctions present in the speech of adults.

Different human languages make use of different sets of phonemes. For example, Japanese people often find it difficult to identify the difference between 'l' and 'r', because their language treats them as being similar. How do infants perform on these tasks?

A process known as 'conditioned head turning' was used to investigate this ability. The infants learnt that if they heard a change in a series of sounds and then turned their head to a display, they would see interesting objects light up. In this way the researchers were able to discover whether infants could detect a difference between certain sounds. Findings indicate that, initially, Japanese infants are better than their parents at this task, but by 12 months they perform in a similar way to adults (Werker, 1989). In other words, they lose their early ability to distinguish between sounds that are not important in the language they hear.

There is a similar pattern of development in the production of sounds. Initially, infants produce long vowel-like sounds at around seven weeks ('oooh', 'aaa'), which are often referred to as 'cooing'. These sounds are adapted to social circumstances, so that higher-pitched sounds occur when interacting with their mothers than with their fathers (Boysson-Bardies, 1999).

Babbling starts at around seven months, and consists of a sequence of alternating vowels (e.g. 'a', 'e') and consonants (e.g. 'p', 'd') to produce vocalisations such as 'bodadada'. At first, babbling includes phonemes that are not used in the language heard by a child, but these gradually drop out of the child's repertoire (Boysson-Bardies, 1999).

As infants become older, babbling takes on the characteristics of adult speech, and adults can identify whether or not an eight-month-old infant is learning a language, such as French or Arabic (Boysson-Bardies, Sagart and Durant, 1984). Interestingly, there are also suggestions that children learning sign languages will use a manual form of babbling, employing hand gestures (Petitto and Marentette, 1991).

These findings show that infants are equipped to deal with the range of human languages. However, it also seems to be the case that the speech heard by infants results in adaptation to the characteristics of this speech. Thus, by the end of the first year, infants have made considerable progress in their *phonological awareness*. These achievements put infants in a position to identify and produce words – an important step along the route to acquiring language.

Social interaction, words and attention

Social interaction in the first five or six months of life often revolves around body games and activities or the reactions of the infant and adult. In many ways this can be seen as a period when caregivers and infants get to know one another. In western societies, the character of social interaction starts to change at around five to six months, with more attention and speech being paid to objects and events (Sylvester-Bradly and Trevarthen, 1978).

At the same time, infants become able to follow the gaze of adults to objects located in a room (Scaife and Bruner, 1975), although it is unclear how often this happens in naturalistic circumstances. In addition, at around nine months (as we saw in an earlier chapter), infants start to be able to follow the pointing of adults to easy targets such as objects in front of the pair, and by 14 months are able to use geometric principles to follow points at more difficult locations (Murphy and Messer, 1977).

Adults often play what has been termed 'the

original word game' with young children, by asking 'Where's the X?' In addition, much of the time adults match their speech so that it is about things that infants are looking at (Collis, 1977). Not only is adult speech matched to the infant's interest, but at about eight to nine months infants begin to be able to point at objects themselves (see Messer, 2003). Thus, adult speech is structured around infant interests, with both adults and infants being able to draw the interest of their partner to objects and events.

All these activities involve *joint attention* and there has been growing appreciation of the importance of this activity for the development of vocabulary. Tomasello and Farrar (1986) were able to show that mothers who named objects more often when 15-month-old infants were looking at them, had 18-month-old infants with larger vocabularies. However, this correlation does not establish causation, so that it is of interest that Tomasello and Farrar also used an experimental situation to show that infants learnt the words they heard when looking at an object.

Joint attention.

The importance of joint attention: language development in twins

Studies in the 1930s (Davis, 1937) revealed that the speech of twins was often delayed in comparison to that of 'singletons' (children who are not twins) in terms of when speech starts, a reduced vocabulary and more simple sentences. Davis also observed that these deficiencies decreased during the preschool years. These findings have been broadly confirmed by more recent studies, with catch-up occurring by the school years (Mogford, 1988).

What are the explanations of this early delay in language? One is that the delay might be due to the greater sharing of biological resources during pregnancy or to complications during delivery. Lytton (1980) failed to find strong relations between perinatal complications and language in a group of two- to three-year-old boy twins. Could sharing a rearing environment cause an early delay in language? Two explanations have been put forward. One is that the close

relationship between the twins reduces the need for verbal communication. 'Secret' languages have been observed between twins (in the sense that these are unintelligible to others) (Thorpe *et al.*, 2001), and Zazzo (1978) suggests that these secret languages impede the acquisition of the mother tongue.

There is even stronger evidence for the delays being caused by division of resources. Tomasello *et al.* (1986) examined the speech of twins and singletons between the ages of 15 and 21 months. The singletons were matched to the language level of the twins. The study showed that the mothers talked as much with the twins as with the singletons, but that each child received less speech matched to the focus of their attention, and fewer maternal responses that extended the number of turns in conversation. These characteristics were found to be associated with poorer language development. Thus the difficulties that carers face in dividing resources between twins may lead to the delay in early speech.

Further research by Tomasello and his colleagues has shown that children around this age are very sophisticated in being able to work out the relation between a word and its referent. For example, an experimenter told 18 month olds that she was looking for a 'gazzer', picked up one object with disappointment and was pleased when they picked up another object. The children deduced from this that the second object was labelled a 'gazzer' (Tomasello *et al.*, 1996). Focus Point 19.1 outlines the way that fewer opportunities for joint attention in twins may slow down the initial acquisition of language.

In general, children make progress in the comprehension (i.e. understanding) of speech before the same achievements in production (i.e. saying a word). Six-month-olds will often look towards their mother or father when they hear the appropriate word, such as 'mama' or 'dada' (Tincoff and Jusczyk, 1999). Ten-month-olds can respond appropriately to between 10 and 150 words (Fenson *et al.*, 1994). Somewhat later, between 8 and 12 months, infants start to produce sounds that appear to be recognisable words, although it is surprisingly difficult to be sure when infants use words in a similar way to adults.

The ability to produce words seems to be the result of several processes. Joint attention plays an important part, and so does the infant's ability to start to control the complex muscle movements involved in producing sounds. Interestingly, the words employed with young children (such as 'dada', 'papa' and 'mama') match the type of sounds infants find easy to produce. There are also suggestions that early words are tied to particular contexts and objects, so that an infant says 'duck' only about a toy that is used in the bath (Barrett, 1996) and not in connection with other ducks or birds.

What is surprising is that children produce only one word at a time until about 18 months. During this period the use of words undergoes a considerable change, from the uncertainties about the use and meaning of the first words, to what can be quite assertive communication at 18 months. Indeed, there have been suggestions that the first words can have a variety of communicative functions and, because a single word often seems to stand for a whole phrase, these utterances are sometimes termed *holophrases*.

From words to language

At about 18 months children go through a vocabulary spurt when the number of words they produce can increase by several hundred in a few weeks. At around the same age children start to produce two-word utterances such as 'want milk'. Interestingly, the order of words in these utterances does not appear to be random: children do not often say 'milk want'. Some believe this is because children are starting to use linguistic rules, while others think this simply reflects the organisation of the speech that children hear (Radford, 1995; Tomasello, 2000).

There are also uncertainties about the cognitive changes that enable this achievement. At around the same age children start to engage in symbolic play (see Chapter 18). Piaget has argued that this general capacity enables children to treat words as symbols, so words can 'stand for' something else.

The next advance is the production of telegraphic speech, with utterances like 'I want milk'. These utterances are much closer to adult language, but elements such as past tense (-ed), plurals (-s), many pronouns (he, she, it) are still absent. Between 24 months to about 30 months many of these linguistic elements become incorporated into children's speech.

The progression that has just been described raises the question of when children start to use language. In everyday speech we often use the terms communication and language interchangeably. *Communication* is usually defined as the transmission of information. It is certainly the case that other species can communicate: there are the warning cries of animals when they detect danger, and most of us have experience of pets who seem to know what certain signals mean (such as fetching a dog lead or saying 'walkies').

However, most psycholinguists regard *language* as a special form of communication. Two features are considered to make it different from other forms of communication. The first is that meaning depends on the arrangement of the elements ('John loves Jane' vs 'Jane loves John'). The second is the presence of structural dependency. This involves different

---

Terms used in the discussion of language

- The arrangement of words in a sentence involves syntactic rules (i.e. 'John loves Jane' is acceptable, but 'John Jane loves' is not).
- The smallest linguistic unit of meaning is a morpheme (so the word 'birds' contains two morphemes 'bird' and '-s'). The arrangement of these elements involves morphological rules.

- What people often think of as grammar is sometimes described as *morphosyntax*.

Note that psycholinguists are interested in the rules people actually use, rather than laying down rules that should be used. Therefore, British dialects are considered as acceptable as 'BBC English'.

---

elements of an utterance influencing one another. Whether we say 'love' or 'loves' depends on the subject of a sentence (e.g. 'John loves Jane' vs 'They love Jane'). Most forms of animal communication do not have these characteristics. Some of the technical terms used to discuss language are given in Focus Point 19.2.

Innate characteristics and language acquisition

Although reinforcement (see also Chapter 8) can account for many aspects of learning, Skinner's attempt to explain language acquisition in this way failed to find acceptance. Skinner suggested that children initially produce sounds at random and that the reinforcement of appropriate sounds results in the production of recognisable words. Following this, the reinforcement of certain arrangements of words provided the basis for language development.

A review by Noam Chomsky (1959) of Skinner's (1958) book *Verbal Behavior* made a number of very important criticisms. One was that a finite number of words can be combined using linguistic rules to generate an infinite number of different utterances. As a result, language cannot be learnt by specific associations – instead, children need to acquire general linguistic rules in order to generate the infinite number of utterances that are possible. Chomsky's review was a starting point for a renewed interest in the possibility that language acquisition is the result of innate predispositions.

The language acquisition device (LAD)

In the 1960s Chomsky and his associates proposed that children have an innate language acquisition device (LAD). The LAD enables children to abstract linguistic rules from the speech they hear. Not much detail was provided about this process, except it was supposed that children have access to what is termed universal grammar (this is the rules that lie behind different human languages). As a result, they can simply match the language they hear to one of these sets of rules.

According to this model children hear speech and match what they hear with one of the human languages present in universal grammar. This enables them to produce language without having to learn its grammar.

Several forms of evidence supported the idea of an LAD. One was that children make overgeneralisation errors (e.g. 'goed', 'wented') that cannot be learnt by imitation as adults do not say such words, and so the words appear to be the result of the inappropriate use of a linguistic rule. Young children also have the ability to generalise linguistic rules to new words. Berko (1958) presented four-year-olds with a picture of an imaginary animal and called it a 'wug'. When she presented two of these animals and asked what they were, the children replied 'wugs'. This demonstrated the ability to create new linguistic forms without modelling or reinforcement.

Principles and parameters theory (PPT)

The LAD explained language acquisition but did not provide much in the way of detail about the process. For these and other reasons a new model of language acquisition was developed by Chomsky and his colleagues. The new model has been termed

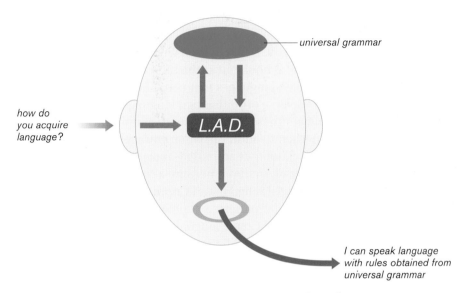

Figure 19.3 The language acquisition device (LAD)

principles and parameters theory (PPT) or sometimes government and binding theory (GB theory) (Chomsky, 1986). The 'principles' referred to in the name of the theory are the elements that are present in all human languages. The parameters refer to characteristics that are different across different languages. For example, it is believed that all languages contain nouns – a principle. But English and Japanese have different subject–verb order – a parameter.

PPT supposes that children identify parameters from the speech they hear. At first this was seen as similar to setting a switch to one of several positions, much as you might switch a light on or off. Thus children acquiring English would have a parameter set for one type of subject–verb order, whereas children acquiring Japanese would have a different parameter set. In this respect, PPT shares similarities with the LAD – children are assumed to have innate access to the basic rules governing all human languages. As there are many linguistic rules in a language it is supposed that parameter setting can simultaneously involve a number of these rules.

Related to these ideas is the assumption made by some researchers that human cognition involves a number of modules. A module consists of a set of operations that are largely independent of other cognitive processes and are considered to be fast,

automatic and usually without conscious awareness about how decisions are made (Fodor, 1983). Language is a prime candidate for modular operations. Furthermore, the idea of a language module is compatible with the system being inherited rather than learnt.

Willam's syndrome is a rare condition that appears to be caused by the deletion of genetic material. It involves cardiovascular problems, what has sometimes been termed an 'elfin' facial appearance and an uneven profile of abilities. Children suffering from this condition have been described as having advanced language capacities relative to other areas of functioning and this has been interpreted as providing support for the modular view of language (Pinker, 1994).

However, more recent research has questioned this interpretation by the use of careful investigation of a range of abilities possessed by these children (Karmiloff-Smith, *et al.*, 1997; Karmiloff-Smith and Thomas, in press; but see also Clahsen and Almazan, 1998). In particular, individuals with William's syndrome have low scores on assessments involving the comprehension of grammar, and French children with William's syndrome have difficulties with the gender of their language (e.g. being able to use masculine and feminine nouns appropriately).

Research into PPT has usually involved finding out the age at which children are able to produce particular grammatical forms and then assuming that this involves parameter setting. It is important to recognise that such findings do not actually test PPT, rather evidence is produced that is consistent with it.

Findings that suggest young infants are searching for patterns in the speech they hear provides support for PPT. Aslin *et al.* (1998) played four nonsense 'words' (i.e. utpiro, golabu, bidaku, padoti) to eight-month-old infants. The 'words' were presented in a random order, with no pauses between them, for two minutes. Then infants either heard the same nonsense words or they heard the words combined in different ways. It was found that the infants listened longer to the new combinations, showing that they had learnt the way these words had been combined and were interested in the new combinations.

Other evidence supports the claim that humans have innate linguistic abilities. A study by Goldin-Meadow and Mylander (1990) investigated whether sign language would develop spontaneously. The sample consisted of ten deaf children of hearing parents who were in oral programmes that discouraged the teaching of sign language. The gestures of these children appeared to involve a primitive form of grammar that involved their ordering and the positioning of gestures (the position of the hands is an important component in many sign languages).

There are also findings about the creation of a sign language that accompanied a change in schooling in Nicaragua. Deaf children were brought together in a special school, but at the time adults did not know any sign languages that could be taught to them. However, a primitive sign language emerged out of the gestures children used to communicate with one another. In addition, when younger children joined the school they started to make this system more elaborate so that it became a fully developed sign language (Senghas and Coppola, 2001).

A similar pattern is claimed to occur in the use of pidgin and Creole languages. Pidgin languages develop when different language groups meet and a common set of words starts to be used that borrows from these different languages. However, pidgin language lacks many features of a full language, such as the use of grammatical endings to words. The development of a pidgin into a Creole language occurred when people with several different language groups came to Hawaii to work on sugar plantations. Bickerton (1990) claims that children introduced more sophisticated linguistic elements into the pidgin language to create a Creole language (see Focus Point 19.3).

Examples of sign and Creole languages support the idea that language is an inherited human characteristic. However, the findings are not totally consistent with the idea of PPT, because languages seem to develop spontaneously without any clear model for the parameter-setting process. It is

---

FOCUS POINT 19.3

Creole language

The Creole language Tok Pisin has become a national language in Papua New Guinea. The following lines are taken from a famous comic strip published there.

- 'Sapos yu kaikai planti pinat, bai yu kamap strong olsem fantom.'
- 'Fantom, yu pren tru bilong mi. Inap yu ken helpim mi nau?'

The translation of these is as follows.

- 'If you eat plenty of peanuts, you will come up strong like the phantom.'
- 'Phantom, you are a true friend of mine. Are you able to help me now?'

possible, however, to argue that a 'default' parameter is used in the absence of any input.

A debate about the innate basis of language between Chomsky and Piaget (Piattelli-Palmarini, 1980) resulted in the former predicting that blind children would acquire language with little difficulty because all that is necessary for this process is exposure to language. Children who are blind (and have no other disabilities) acquire language at about the same rate as sighted children. This supports Chomsky's prediction.

However, it can be argued in the case of children who are blind that language acquisition does not occur by exposure to a disembodied stream of speech, but by caregivers matching their speech to what a child shows an interest in touching. This view is supported by findings that appear to show that merely hearing speech is insufficient for language acquisition. Children whose main source of speech input is from television, either because their parents are deaf or because they watch cartoons that are in a different language, make little or no progress with the language they hear (Sachs and Johnson, 1976; Snow, 1977). And as we have seen, there are delays in the language of twins, which can be attributed to only half the speech they hear being linked to their own activities and interests.

Other issues concern the nature of the parameters that are set when sign languages are acquired and how the same parameter can be set in different positions when bilingual children acquire two or more languages. In addition, concerns have been expressed about the neurophysiological plausibility of PPT. Many complex biological systems are not 'hardwired' in the way that PPT suggests, and this has the advantage of allowing adaptability to environmental variation.

The dual-route model

In English we add '-s' to nouns to make them plural (e.g. egg → eggs), or '-ed' to create the past tense of verbs (e.g. walk → walked). These are words that follow the regular rules of English. However, there are also irregular items that do not follow these rules (e.g. the singular and plural of sheep are 'sheep', and 'went' is the past tense of 'go').

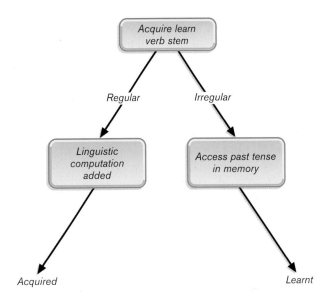

Figure 19.4 *The dual-route model*

The *dual-route model* has been used to explain the acquisition of regular and irregular words within the PPT tradition. This theory supposes that regular words are produced by a computational process, such as adding '-ed' to make the past tense of verbs. Obviously this route will produce errors like 'goed' if it is applied to irregular words.

According to this model, children produce speech in different ways according to whether the word is regular or irregular. For a regular word like 'acquire' children form the past tense simply by adding '-ed' to give 'acquired'. For irregular verbs like 'learn' the children have to locate the past tense in memory, i.e. 'learnt'.

In the dual-route model the irregular words are learnt individually, and when they are learnt they block the regular computational process from occurring. The predictions of the model have been tested by giving people the present tense of a verb and measuring how quickly they produce the past tense. The speed of producing the past tense of regular verbs does not depend on how common the verb is in a language, suggesting that the same computational process occurs for rare and common regular verbs. However, the speed of producing irregular verbs depends on how common they are:

rare irregulars are produced more slowly than common irregulars, suggesting that familiarity with these verbs influences how quickly they are retrieved.

Section summary

PPT has been very influential. Supporters of the theory believe that it provides a framework for understanding language acquisition and argue that it offers a coherent theory about the acquisition of grammatical rules that is lacking in other approaches. Furthermore, it makes sense that humans have biological and cognitive predispositions that enable them to acquire language so easily. What is still debated is the extent to which the environment plays a role in the acquisition process.

The role of the environment

Imitation and simplification

Imitation of adult speech seems an obvious way in which children could acquire language – after all, French children acquire French and Japanese children acquire Japanese. However, examples like the one in Focus Point 19.4 show that providing model utterances does not always help children. This strengthens the case for an innate LAD.

Investigators in the early 1970s also realised that speech to children is not the same as to adults. The investigators recorded mothers talking to their children and to another adult. It is worth pointing

---

ACTIVITY BOX 19.2

How do you speak to children?

In the late 1960s some people were so taken with the idea that powerful innate processes made language acquisition possible that statements like the following were made.

> ... the language learning environment of the child does not differ in any useful way from that of an adult ... it must contain a very substantial number of false starts, slips, grammatical mistakes and so forth.
>
> (Fodor, 1966: 109)

This claim strengthened the argument that something like an innate LAD is present in humans. However, try to rehearse in your mind how you would speak to a young baby or child, and spend a few seconds writing down the differences between your talk to a young child and an adult. What did you find?

---

out that writing down (transcribing) speech is a laborious process: it can take an hour to transcribe five minutes of conversation. As many of you will no doubt realise, speech to children was found to be different from speech to adults. This sort of speech

---

FOCUS POINT 19.4

The failure of modelling and imitation

The following is a widely quoted example of a conversation between a child and his mother that appears to show the difficulty of teaching children by getting them to imitate correct utterances.

> *Child:* Nobody don't like me.
> *Mother:* No, say 'Nobody likes me'.

This sequence is repeated eight times.

> *Mother:* Now listen carefully, say 'NOBODY LIKES ME'.
> *Child:* Oh! Nobody don't like*S* me.

has been called *motherese, baby talk* and, more recently, *child directed speech (CDS)*. Some of the differences that have been found are shown in Figure 19.5.

CDS is found in many language groups, ranging from Apache to Arabic (Ferguson, 1964), and even four-year-olds use simplified CDS with infants (Shatz and Gelman, 1973). Furthermore, infants prefer to listen to CDS than to other speech (Cooper and Aslin, 1990).

It also appears that adults modify sign language in ways that could aid acquisition. For example, adults tend to sign near to relevant objects rather than in the usual position for certain gestures (e.g. near their face or upper body). Signing in the usual position would make it difficult for children simultaneously to see both the appropriate gesture and the relevant object (Harris *et al.*, 1989).

An important question is whether these simplifications assist language development, and there is still no consensus about the answer to this question. Part of the reason is that, for ethical reasons, correlational rather than experimental studies have to be conducted (see Research Methods Box 19.1). In addition, many of these studies have failed to find relations between the extent of speech simplification at one age and children's language development at a later age (Furrow and Nelson, 1986; Scarborough and Wyckoff, 1986). Thus, the evidence that CDS helps language acquisition is not particularly convincing.

There have also been claims that in some cultures children do not receive CDS in the simplified form that is common in the middle-class families of the West. As those children develop language, then CDS cannot be considered necessary for language acquisition (Heath, 1983; Ochs and Schieffelin, 1984). However, Snow (1995) has pointed out that while some features of CDS are absent in some cultures, it remains to be established whether there are cultures that totally fail to modify speech in ways that could assist language acquisition.

Feedback and contrast

Another topic about which there has been controversy concerns whether children are provided with feedback about grammatical errors. This issue is important because if children do not receive feedback then it is difficult to explain how they 'learn' language, and so claims about innate processes are strengthened. A classic study by Brown and Hanlon (1970) examined adults' reactions to children's ungrammatical speech. They found overt correction of errors was extremely rare: if a child said 'he goed', adults were likely to accept this and not reply 'that's incorrect, you should say he went'.

Additional studies in the 1980s confirmed Brown and Hanlon's findings, but also revealed that when children make a grammatical mistake adults are likely to produce an expansion that usually involves the adult supplying a grammatically correct version of the child's utterance, or they ask a follow-up question (as shown in Focus Point 19.5) (Hirsh-Pasek *et al.*, 1984; Demetras *et al.*, 1986; Penner, 1987; Bohannon and Stanowiccz, 1988; Bohannon *et al.*, 1990). When a child's utterance is grammatically

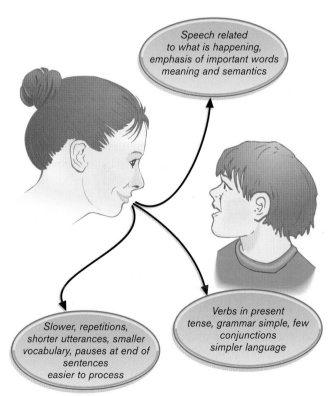

Figure 19.5 *The characteristics of child directed speech (CDS)*

RESEARCH METHODS BOX 19.1

Correlations and causation

Investigations into the effects of CDS have usually involved seeing whether the mother's simplified speech at time 1 is correlated with children's language at time 2 (see Figure 19.6). This would mean that mothers who simplify their speech more at time 1 have children who have more advanced language at time 2. Even if a significant correlation is found, why does this fail to establish that mothers who simplify their speech are responsible for (i.e. cause) the growth in the language of their children? If you are not sure about this, look at Fig. 19.6.

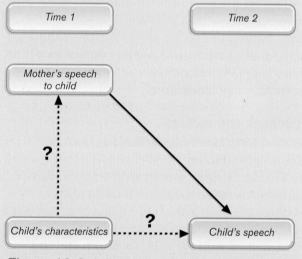

Figure 19.6 Influences that are possible on mother's speech at time 1 and children's language at time 2

correct, adults tend to continue the topic of conversation.

Constructivist views

Tomasello and his colleagues have rejected many aspects of PPT and emphasised the role of speech to children. Tomasello (2000) starts with the assumption that children and adults need to be both conventional in the sense of using language in a

similar way to other people, and creative in the sense of being able to use language in new ways to create new meanings. (A similar point to that made by Chomsky!)

However, Tomasello has argued against children having access to a universal grammar. He believes that if children have a universal grammar, they should be able to take a new word and start to use it in the same way as other nouns or verbs (or any appropriate linguistic class) that they have in their vocabulary. Instead he suggests that children construct their grammar *gradually*, first by producing utterances similar to those they have heard, and then by noticing that groups of words are used in similar ways (e.g. that nouns are used in certain utterances and verbs in others).

Various pieces of evidence have been produced to support this claim. For example, a study by Tomasello *et al.* (1997) investigated children's ability to treat a new word as a verb or noun. These were 'nonce' (i.e. made up) words, such as 'tam' and 'gop', to ensure the children had not heard them before.

Children aged between 18 and 23 months heard two novel words used as verbs (e.g. 'it's tamming'), and two novel words used as nouns (e.g. 'that's a gop') over many sessions. It was found that the children could use the new nouns in a similar way to the other nouns they had in their vocabulary (e.g. they said 'some gops'). But new verbs were used only in utterances similar to the ones in which they had heard the new verb; they did not use the new verbs in a similar way to the other verbs in their vocabulary (e.g. saying 'it tammed' to produce the past tense of a verb).

Additional evidence comes from observations by Tomasello (1992) of his own daughter. He found that each verb tended to be used in an individual way, so that his daughter was not operating with a general set of linguistic rules to create utterances with verbs; rather, she was using each verb in a restricted manner. This he termed the *verb-island hypothesis*.

In addition, work by Lieven, Pine and their colleagues has revealed that many of children's first utterances are extremely similar to the speech they have already heard (Pine and Lieven, 1997; Theakston *et al.*, 2001). These findings and claims

FOCUS POINT 19.5

Contrast between child and adult speech: example of an adult providing a correct grammatical structure

> *Child:* That policeman FALLED all the way down to the tiger.
> *Adult:* He FELL down.

An interesting perspective about these reactions has been provided by Saxton (1997). He argues that expansions supply a useful *contrast* between the child's incorrect speech and the 'correct' adult utterance. This provides a mini-learning session for the child. Supporting evidence comes from observations that children are more likely to repeat an adult expansion than other adult utterances (indicating that they are processing the information in expansions (Farrar, 1992)) and from experimental investigations of the effect of providing expansions (Saxton, 1997).

These suggestions are extremely interesting but there are still uncertainties about their significance for the general process of language acquisition.

provide a direct challenge to the idea that children have access to innate specifications about linguistic rules and classes.

Connectionist networks

PPT suggests that there are specific cognitive systems devoted to language acquisition. A contrasting perspective involves connectionist networks, neural networks and parallel distributed processes (these terms are often used interchangeably), and involves the idea that language acquisition is just one of many aspects of cognition that involve general learning processes (Plunkett *et al.*, 1997). This approach uses computer programs that are designed to imitate the changes that occur during development.

To study language acquisition, computers are usually given speech relevant to a specific aspect of grammar (e.g. they might be given verbs in the present tense such as 'like' and have to learn to produce the past tense such as 'liked'). Usually the computers are given this speech after it has been converted by some means into numeric form. At first the computer makes random connections between the 'input' (e.g. the present tense of a verb) and a range of outputs (e.g. various possible past-tense forms). After this 'guess', the computer is usually given information about whether or not its response is correct. If the response is correct the tendency to produce the connection in future is strengthened by adjustments being made to the hidden layer. If the response is incorrect the tendency is weakened (these adjustments are known as *backpropogation*).

Using these techniques, computers can learn aspects of language such as the past tense of verbs (see Research Methods Box 19.2). It should be noted that few people claim that connectionist systems imitate exactly the process of language acquisition or are the same as the network of neural connections in the brain.

The research described in Research Methods Box 19.2, along with other research, has challenged PPT in several ways (see Plunkett, 1995). First, the learning mechanisms are not specialised for language – they are general learning processes that can be used to model a range of cognitive developments. Second, the computer does not contain any linguistic rules (all the learning is in terms of mathematical adjustments that govern the choice of output), yet the computer behaves as if it was governed by rules. Third, there is no specific innate knowledge of the rules of grammar supplied to the computer. Thus, it would seem that

RESEARCH METHODS BOX 19.2

Modelling the past tense

The difficulty of learning the regular and irregular past tense of verbs presents a considerable challenge to connectionist systems. However, these systems can be successful, and when they make errors these tend to be similar to the errors made by children. The first attempt to do this was made by Rumelhart and McClelland (1986); however, their model was criticised for using speech input that would help produce the findings the experimenters wanted.

Later connectionist systems took account of the criticisms and were still able to show learning of both regular and irregular words (Plunkett and Marchman, 1993). Part of the reason for this success seems to be that although irregular verbs do not follow general rules and would be expected to be more difficult to learn, they are much more common in CDS (think how often we say 'went' rather than 'started'). As a result, connectionist networks (and possibly children) are able to learn irregular verbs because they are so common in CDS, and this learning occurs while the computer also abstracts a general principle of adding '-ed' to regular verbs (see Smith *et al.*, 2003).

non-specialised but sophisticated learning systems can acquire rules in a very different way to PPT.

However, there are two important limitations of connectionist systems. The first is that most systems are given feedback about the correctness of every response they make, and this does not occur with children. The other issue is that most connectionist

APPLICATIONS BOX 19.1

Children with language difficulties

In recent years there has been a considerable amount of research into children who have specific language impairment (SLI). These children have difficulties with language that would not be expected on the basis of their other abilities (e.g. non-verbal reasoning). It has been estimated that somewhere between 5 and 10 per cent of children have SLI.

The causes of SLI are still not very well understood. There is a range of profiles and there is a strong possibility that the condition might be caused by different factors (Conti-Ramsden *et al.*, 1997). Research using twin studies has revealed that SLI is highly inherited, but this in itself does not tell us what cognitive difficulties give rise to the condition (Bishop, North and Donlan, 1995).

One explanation of SLI uses ideas derived from PPT and findings from a family who had language difficulties over three generations. These individuals had problems producing regular endings to words (e.g. walk + ed).

An explanation put forward by Gopnik and Crago (1991) was that these individuals were not able to follow the computational route of the dual-route model (see page 329). As a result, any language learning would be on a word-by-word basis rather than using a rule to generate the past tense or some other aspect of language. This explanation has been extended to children with SLI.

The explanation has difficulties in accounting for some forms of language disability such as those to do with word-finding difficulties that involve problems in retrieving words that the child knows (Dockrell *et al.*, 1998; 2002).

A different explanation for SLI has been put forward by Leonard (1998). He suggested that children with SLI have difficulties with those grammatical features of languages that are difficult to hear and identify (e.g. the '-ed' of the past tense is said without emphasis). Thus one would expect that children with SLI would have different types of difficulties with different languages. Comparisons between English and Italian children with SLI tend to support this hypothesis (Leonard *et al.*, 1998).

modelling involves only one aspect of language (e.g. the past tense) and the speech given to the computer is usually selected by the researcher to contain only these forms. Children, on the other hand, seem to learn a number of linguistic forms at the same time (e.g. tense, plurals, word order and so on). It remains to be established whether connectionist systems can be devised to deal with a much higher level of complexity in the input and output.

Section summary
Several aspects of children's environment could help language acquisition but there is an absence of compelling evidence that this help is effective. However, the detailed research in the *constructivist* tradition and in connectionist modelling provides indications that though language may be innate it is not necessarily acquired through a process of parameter setting. Look back at Activity Box 19.1. How would you answer these questions now?

Literacy
Unlike with language, most children have to be taught to read, write and spell. Furthermore, until comparatively recently, few people possessed these abilities. The precise origins of writing are uncertain, but a number of cultures developed symbolic systems they could use to make records of agricultural produce, taxes and events. Because of the importance of literacy to individuals and to society it has been the topic of extensive research.

Models of reading: the dual-route model
When we read, we usually convert the letters we see into a word that we have in our *lexicon*. Traditionally,

the lexicon is thought to contain details about the phonological characteristics, meaning and linguistic properties of each word. This is one of the routes proposed by Coltheart in his dual-route model (see Figure 19.4). However, we can also read the following: 'One day the mib fell in the feg', which contains words that are not in our lexicon. Observations such as this provided a basis for a second route that involves grapheme–phoneme (letters to sounds) conversion, but does not involve the lexicon.

More recently, it has been found that some patients with brain damage are not able to say what words mean but can read them, and this has provided the basis for the description of a third route. Although the dual-route model provides a good overview of the process of reading, it is descriptive rather than quantitative and does not address the issue of learning to read. In addition, it has been found that the lexical and non-lexical routes are not totally independent (Kay and Marcel, 1981).

Several models of reading development have been proposed. One of these was put forward by Frith (1985) (see Focus Point 19.6).

Frith's stage theory and others like it have provided a very useful description of children's strategies when reading. However, the order of the stages does not appear to be universal and can depend on the type of teaching and the nature of the language being read. In addition, Ehri (1992) has suggested that skilled readers will start to recognise words as a whole and this might be thought of as a further developmental stage, which in some respects is like the original logographic stage but involving a much greater vocabulary of written words.

Another problem with the stage theories is that they do not capture the way that reading involves building on and developing phonological skills. As adults, it is easy to forget that reading involves not only identifying letters but also being able to identify the sounds of our language so that we can relate printed letters to these sounds (i.e. phonemes).

In addition, most of us do not remember that before we began to read we had only a very limited ability to process phonemes. Preschool children can tell the difference between the words 'bat' and 'mat'

ACTIVITY BOX 19.3

Differences between language and literacy
Literacy involves reading, spelling and writing. Language and literacy differ in a number of important ways.

Write down some of the ways in which you think they differ.

Frith's stages of reading development

At the *logographic* stage children learn to read a few words on the basis of visual recognition – for example, their own name.

The *alphabetic* stage involves *decoding* words into single letters and converting these into sounds (phonemes).

At the *orthographic* stage words are broken down into smaller (orthographic) groups of letters. Goswami and Bryant (1990) suggest that children break written words into 'onset' and 'rime' (i.e. the rhyming part of a word). For example, the beginning sound 'c' of 'cat' is the onset, while the rime is the sound of the rest of word, the 'at' of 'cat'.

but they have great difficulty splitting words up into separate phonemes (Liberman *et al.*, 1974). They also have difficulty in saying which words begin with the same sound (alliteration) or end with the same sound (rhyme). Both of these tasks are often used to assess phonological awareness.

An important landmark in studying reading was the findings of Bradley and Bryant (1983). They reported that preschool children who were better at phonological awareness tasks involving rhyme and alliteration were, three years later, better at reading. Furthermore, the children who were better at phonological awareness in preschool were no better than other children at mathematical tasks.

Bradley and Bryant's work also showed that young children who were given help to develop phonological skills tended, when they were older, to be better readers than children who were not given this training. Thus both correlational evidence and evidence from interventions suggest that phonological awareness plays an important part in helping children learn to read. These studies established the importance of prereading phonological skills and the findings have been replicated by a number of investigators and in different languages.

Languages differ according to how close a correspondence there is between letters and sounds. Languages such as English are often termed *opaque languages* as it is often difficult to work out the sound of a word from the way it is spelt (think about the different ways of saying 'c' in 'cat' and 'chat'). In contrast, other languages, such as Turkish and German, are termed *transparent languages* because the spelling of words closely corresponds to their sound.

Although it is difficult to make comparisons between languages that are not confounded by other variables (such as the way reading is taught), a number of findings indicate that it is easier to learn to read in transparent systems. For example, Wimmer and Goswami (1994) compared English and German children. There were similarities in the speed and accuracy of reading numerals (1, 2, 3 etc.), and number words (one, two, three etc.) but English children were slower and more inaccurate in reading non-words.

Up to now our discussion has focused on the influences of various cognitive processes on literacy. However, there is also evidence that the development of reading has its own effect on a range of cognitive skills – in particular, being able to read seems to assist the development of vocabulary and phonological skills. Evidence to support this claim comes from a study by Morais, Alegria and Content (1987), which compared Portuguese people who had been taught to read in adulthood with a group who were still illiterate. The adults who could read were much better at phonological awareness tasks.

Another interesting example comes from studies of Chinese children. Chinese writing involves the use of what are termed 'pictograms'. These symbols correspond to elements of meaning rather than sounds. This makes the acquisition of reading a difficult process. As a result, when reading is being taught, Roman letters (i.e. the letters we use in writing) are sometimes given to accompany pictograms. The use of Roman letters is phased out over time. Read *et al.* (1986) found that Chinese adults who had been exposed to Roman letters were able to add or delete phonemes from words and then were able to say the resulting sound (i.e. in English the task would be to remove the first sound of the word 'cat' and say what the remainder of the word sounds like: 'at'). However, individuals who had not been taught with the help of Roman letters had great difficulty with this task. This suggests that learning about the relation between letters and sounds helps children to break down words into phonemes.

Another area of research has revealed connections between memory, vocabulary and reading. Short-term memory (STM), as assessed by auditory digit span (repeating a series of digits) and non-word repetition (repeating nonsense words), and vocabulary size are reasonably closely related in young children. This means that a child who has a large STM tends also to have a large vocabulary (e.g. Michas and Henry, 1994).

Baddeley, Gathercole and Papagno (1998) have argued that this relation occurs because phonological short-term memory helps children to remember words and this supports language development (although they also acknowledge that larger vocabulary sizes might help with the memorisation of words). In addition, Baddeley *et al.* suggest that children with higher phonological STM capacities and larger vocabularies develop literacy abilities faster than other children.

Connectionist modelling provides yet another perspective on reading. A print-to-speech connectionist system was designed by Seidenberg and McClelland (1989) to learn the relation between letters and sounds (see page 336). The connectionist system was reasonably successful, and the types of errors were similar to those found in children. More recently, Plaut *et al.* (1996) have developed a model that more closely corresponds to what is known about the development of reading. In this model graphemes and phonemes were available to the connectionist system. As would be expected, this improved the system's performance. The use of connectionist modelling has been useful in drawing attention to the learning processes underlying reading. However, as with many connectionist models of development, the learning environment is assumed to contain consistent feedback about the production of correct and incorrect phonemes – something that children rarely receive.

Dyslexia and literacy difficulties

It has been known for over a century that there are children who appear to have a special difficulty with literacy that would not be expected on the basis of their other abilities (such as non-verbal reasoning). This is usually considered to involve developmental dyslexia, which is distinct from acquired dyslexia. The former is present from the early stages of reading; the latter is not present in childhood but is usually the result of a brain injury in later life. In this chapter, the term *dyslexia* will be used to refer to developmental dyslexia.

As we have seen, phonological abilities appear to play an important part in the development of literacy abilities. Stanovich's (1986; Stanovich and Siegel, 1994) 'phonological core hypothesis' supposes that difficulties with phonological processes are the main cause of dyslexia. One way of explaining this link is the suggestion that children with dyslexia have imprecise or, as they are sometimes termed, 'fuzzy' representations of phonemes. As a result, when they are learning to read it is more difficult for them to detect consistent patterns between the letters and sounds (Swan and Goswami, 1997).

There are many studies that have findings consistent with the phonological core hypothesis. Bradley and Bryant (1978) found that children with dyslexia were worse at phonological awareness tasks than children with a similar reading age, but who were much younger.

Other evidence comes from a study conducted by Scarborough (1990), who followed up 32 children from two to seven years who had at least one parent with dyslexia. 65 per cent of the children were later identified as having dyslexia; these children were found to have at two-and-a-half years the same vocabulary size, but more speech mispronunciations and simpler sentences, than other children in the sample. At five years they performed less well on assessments of phonological awareness.

However, there are also findings which suggest that the nature of literacy difficulties may differ from language to language. German children have a comparatively easy task in learning to relate letters to sounds because this relation is very consistent in German (unlike English). Wimmer *et al.* (1998) found that German children with literacy difficulties tended to be slower at reading than their peers but they did not have appreciable difficulties in decoding (i.e. converting letters into sounds). Thus it may be that phonological skills are not as important in languages where there are regularities between letters and sounds.

In addition, there have been suggestions that dyslexia could be the result of two types of problem, one involving phonological awareness and the other involving speed of processing. This is an idea put forward by Wolf and Bowers (1999) in their double deficit model of dyslexia. More recently, there have been findings to suggest that both phonological abilities and speed of reaction time are independently related to reading abilities (Catts *et al.*, 2002).

Explanations of dyslexia have also concerned the visual system. Many clinical reports exist of children with reading difficulties who have problems with: letters moving on a page; letters changing place in words; or letters like 'c' and 'l' being fused and read as 'd'.

Miles (1983) argued that dyslexia involves a range of difficulties, including: unstable vision when reading print, difficulties with the sequencing of sounds, attentional difficulties and poor motor coordination. Recently, Talcott *et al.* (2000) have shown that the visual abilities of children with dyslexia are different from those of other children. Children with dyslexia had higher thresholds for perceiving coherent motion across a large display of random dots (kinematograms). In addition, correlations were found between performance on these tasks and literacy skills. These findings suggest that dyslexia may involve other difficulties beyond phonology, at least in some groups of children.

Learning outcomes

When you have completed this chapter you should be able to:

- discuss the way that early speech perception and vocal development are the result of both inherited and acquired dispositions
- describe the way that social interaction helps children acquire their vocabulary
- distinguish between communication and language
- discuss the role of universal grammar in relation to PPT
- describe the evidence for and against PPT
- explain why correlational studies do not establish causation
- describe the reason why constructivists do not think children have access to universal grammar
- explain how a connectionist system arrives at the past tense of verbs
- describe the phonological hypothesis about reading
- discuss the causes of dyslexia.

Key terms.

Backpropogation
Child directed speech (CDS)
Communication
Constructivist
Contrast
Dual-route model
Dyslexia
Holophrases
Joint attention
Language
Language acquisition device (LAD)
Lexicon
Morphosyntax
Opaque languages
Phonemes
Phonological awareness
Principles and parameters theory (PPT)
Specific language impairment (SLI)
Transparent languages
Universal grammar
Verb-island hypothesis

Further reading

Barrett, M. (ed.) (1999) *The Development of Language.* Hove: Psychology Press.

Bishop, D. (1997) *Uncommon Understanding.* Hove: Psychology Press.

Dockrell, J. and Messer, D. J. (1999) *Language Disabilities in Children.* London: Cassell.

Messer, D. (1999) The development of communication and language. In Messer, D. and Millar, S. (eds) *Exploring Developmental Psychology.* London: Arnold.

Nicolson, R. (1999) Reading skill and dyslexia. In Messer, D. and Millar, S. (eds) *Exploring Developmental Psychology.* London: Arnold.

Snowling, M. (2000) *Dyslexia.* Oxford: Blackwell.

20

The self, others and social relationships

Route map of the chapter

The way that children think about themselves and the relationships they have with others are important and inter-connected aspects of development. The beginning of this chapter describes some of the possible representations infants have of their self, and the further development of this concept is then discussed. This is followed by a consideration of attachment, the history of this research, the way attachment develops and the consequences of separation. Attachment forms a bridge between the self and others; another bridge involves children being able to understand what goes on in the minds of others. This is the topic of the third section. The final section considers another aspect of the self and others – the way that relationships with parents and peers change in adolescence and the factors that may be responsible for this.

Introduction

A newborn baby comes into a world that can be categorised in lots of different ways and with many different possibilities to capture their attention. There are all sorts of objects that differ in terms of colour, shape and size. There are all kinds of things that differ both in their physical characteristics and in the way they move; some movements are relatively regular, like those of a tree waving in the wind, others are more irregular, such as the movements of people. How do infants place themselves in relation to all these things that are around them? When do they recognise that they can cause events to happen? When do they become aware of their own characteristics and identity?

These questions are related to a number of different topics about the development of the self and the development of identity. A distinction is often made between 'the I' and 'the me' (James, 1890; Lewis and Brooks-Gunn, 1979).

The 'I' refers to the recognition of the self as an agent, an awareness that one can cause events to occur (this is sometimes termed the existential self or *executive self*).

The 'me' involves an understanding that we as individuals are known and evaluated by others (e.g. a naughty/good boy). This is also termed the *categorical self*.

The development of an understanding of self is a continuous process. As children's cognitive abilities develop, this permits a greater awareness of their own characteristics. In addition, for both children and adults, the self is continually changing along a large number of dimensions such as status, abilities and family relationships. As a result this awareness needs to be updated with the developmental changes that occur. Furthermore, the view of the self can feed into and motivate children's actions, which results in further change and development.

The self and identity

Indications of self and identity

Studies indicate that almost from birth infants have a preference for people, or to be more precise the stimuli generated by people. Newborns show a marked interest in human faces or face-like stimuli (Kleiner and Banks, 1987). Although it is unclear whether this is a result of a general preference for stimuli that have similar properties to those of the human face (being symmetrical, containing eye-like stimuli and moderate degrees of contour) or whether this reflects an innate preference for the human face (Johnson and Morton, 1991). It would also seem that newborn infants will look for longer at faces that adults rate as being attractive than those rated as unattractive (Slater *et al.*, 1998; 2000).

One way of explaining this preference for faces is that infants have some awareness that they are similar to people. In a fascinating study, Meltzoff and Moore (1977) showed that newborn babies could imitate adult models. The adult model either repeatedly stuck their tongue out, opened their mouth or pouted. Infants were significantly more likely to show similar facial movements to those they had just seen than the other types of movement.

To be able to do this, infants need to match the movements of someone else to the movements of their own body that they cannot even see. In a discussion of these and other findings, Meltzoff and Gopnik (1993) suggested that newborns recognise at some level that adults are 'like me'. Consequently, they can relate the movements they see to themselves. This is an interesting, if controversial, claim because it suggests that from the very beginning of life children have the ability to recognise that they share characteristics with other people, and this could be considered a primitive form of the categorical self.

Trevarthen (1977) has also emphasised the communicative capacity of young infants and their recognition of the communicative abilities of other people. He believes that young infants act in a purposeful manner and appreciate some of the intentions of others – they have *intersubjectivity*. Trevarthen has described the way that two-month-old infants will move their limbs when interacting with their mother in ways that suggest a communicative desire. They will also move their lips and tongue in what he has called 'prespeech mouth movements'.

Thus some argue that, almost from birth, infants have an understanding that they share characteristics with other living things, particularly people. However, an alternative view is the 'hard-nosed' interpretation which maintains that infants' reactions are part of inbuilt automatic responses in

the case of imitation, or reflect levels of excitement in the case of prespeech movement. It is surprisingly difficult to devise ways to test these different interpretations.

Is there evidence for the early presence of the existential or executive self? Watson and Ramey (1972) found that not only could two-month-old infants learn to turn their heads to one side to make a mobile move above their cot, but they also showed enjoyment at being able to do this. Infants in control conditions where head-turning had no effect on the mobile did not show such pleasure. Furthermore, during an extinction phase when their actions no longer controlled the mobile, infants showed what appeared to be distress and frustration. We cannot be sure what is going on in these infants' minds, so again it is possible to adopt a more hard-nosed interpretation which says that these are simply automatic responses.

There seems to be a change in infants' executive abilities at around eight to ten months, when they begin to solve problems in new ways, not simply by repeating past successes. This is something Piaget described as involving new means to obtain an objective. Significantly, at this age infants appear to recognise that they can achieve their objectives through communicating with people (Bates *et al.*, 1975).

For example, Bates *et al.* describe the way a young infant tried to tug a toy out of the hands of an adult without communicating with them, but when the child was slightly older (around eight to nine months), she made pleading noises and looked at the adult.

Infants at this age also appear to have a better idea of the distinction between themselves and others. They start to check adult interest or reactions. Such behaviour implies an awareness of the agency and importance of others. Examples of these behaviours are: social referencing (checking to see the reactions of others to an event), following the points and gazes of other people, showing objects to people and producing points to indicate their own interest (see Messer, 2003).

The ages of emergence of a number of these behaviours are significantly correlated, suggesting that they are part of the same cognitive system (Carpenter *et al.*, 1998). Furthermore, as we will see in the next section, at between eight and ten months, attachment and separation become a significant feature of the infant's world. The beginning of an appreciation of the security provided by another or distress at her departure are likely to be associated with a new level of understanding of the infant's own agency in relation to other people (see Baldwin and Moses, 1996). There is also more direct evidence that there are changes in the categorical self at about this age. Lewis and Brooks-Gunn found that between nine and twelve months infants look longer at pictures of themselves than at those of other infants (Lewis and Brooks-Gunn, 1979).

In older, two-year-old, children the majority (63 per cent) are able to pick out photographs of themselves (Bullock and Lutkenhaus, 1990), and this figure rises to 97 per cent by about 30 months. Lewis and Brooks-Gunn (1979) also conducted a classic study that indicated another important change in the categorical self at around 20 months. Infants initially saw themselves in a large mirror for 90 seconds and very few touched their nose or face. Then the infants had their noses wiped, and some red make-up was put on their noses. The infants were again put in a position to see themselves in the mirror: 12-month-old infants did not touch their faces despite their red noses; only a few 15- and 18-month-old infants touched their faces; however, the majority of 21- and 24-month-old infants touched their faces.

These findings indicate that the ability to recognise violations of one's own appearance occurs towards the end of the second year. More recent work by Povinelli *et al.* (1996) used stickers rather than make-up. Instead of the mirror, the children saw pictures or video clips that had been taken a few minutes earlier and stickers replaced the red make-up. Children who were under three and a half years did not try to remove the stickers, but children above this age did. Povinelli *et al.* argued that this is because the younger children had difficulty understanding that the pictures had relevance to their current appearance.

With older children it is possible to ask them to describe themselves. Harter (1999) has concluded on

the basis of an extensive body of data that three- to four-year-olds typically talk about themselves in terms of concrete, observable characteristics ('I have brown hair'). They also tend to be optimistic about themselves and the future. Children in the early school years tend to engage in social comparisons with other children of a similar age (Frey and Ruble, 1985). However, children between eight and eleven years have a more integrated view of themselves, which accepts both strengths and weaknesses, and shows awareness of links between behaviour and social relationships (Harter, 1999).

The multicultural nature of modern western societies and the presence of disadvantaged minority groups have focused attention on the development of ethnic identity. The techniques used to study this are often similar to those used to study self-identity (toys, model dolls and photographs). Children above four years of age appear to be able to identify photographs of someone from their own ethnic group (e.g. Aboud, 1988).

Furthermore, between the ages of four and seven years, black and other minority-group children have been found to give a preference for white identities over their own. This has occurred when they are asked which group they would like to be similar to, or with which group they would like to play. After the age of seven children show a preference for their own ethnic group (Davey, 1983).

As one might expect, family and cultural influences can affect the nature of these responses. African-American parents who emphasised civil rights issues were found to have children who developed more positive attitudes to their own ethnic group (Davey, 1983; Milner, 1983).

Identity and gender differences
Another aspect of self-identity concerns gender. Usually the term 'sex differences' is used to refer to exclusively biological differences, such as the presence of a beard. 'Gender differences' is used to refer to differences that can be the product of biological and cultural experiences, such as boys being more aggressive than girls.

Stereotypical behaviours of boys and girls.

At around two years, about three-quarters of children identify pictures of boys or girls that match their own sex; by three years 90 per cent of children identify the appropriate picture (Thompson, 1975). The ability of children to match a picture to their own sex indicates that they have an awareness of their *gender identity*. This is followed at about four years by an awareness of gender stability, where there is recognition that one remains the same gender across the life span. Following this is the achievement of gender constancy, with the recognition that gender remains the same although appearances may change, such as when a girl wears trousers or a boy grows long hair.

Many reports suggest that constancy is achieved at about seven years, although it may be achieved earlier by those children who are educated about the nature of genital differences between children (Bem, 1989).

Considerable interest has been shown in the question of whether the differences that we see between males and females are the result of environmental or biological influences. The answer to this question has important implications for the way that we see ourselves and for the way that we might want children to be educated. It is clear that there are physical differences between the two sexes and that the sexes experience different levels of sex hormones such as testosterone and oestrogen. In terms of biological explanations, it is supposed that these hormones form the basis of differences between males and females. After reviewing the evidence, Collaer and Hines (1995) suggest that the effect of male sex hormones is most apparent in activities like play, where the presence of male sex hormones is associated with more physical play and aggression.

Another explanation of gender differences involves social learning and social reinforcement. According to this account, girls receive reinforcement for stereotypically female activities, and boys for stereotypically male activities. However, observation learning could also play a part (Bandura, 1969). Research findings indicate that adults appear to reinforce different behaviours with boys and girls. For example, observations of two-year-olds in their homes revealed that boys were encouraged to play with toy vehicles, discouraged from asking for help or playing with dolls. In contrast, girls were encouraged to play with dolls, dance and dress up, but were discouraged from jumping and climbing (Fagot, 1978).

Similar patterns are seen in older preschool children (Langlois and Downs, 1980). However, we should not assume that just because reinforcement occurs it is effective. Fagot (1985) also found that nursery school teachers rewarded quiet activities and discouraged physical activities equally in boys and girls. Despite this reinforcement of stereotypical female patterns, boys engaged in more physical play activities.

Some of the more recent work on issues connected with gender has tried to bring these different ideas together and has stressed that there are multiple influences at work. A good example of this is the work of Maccoby (1998; 2000), who has focused on the strong tendency of children to play with same-sex individuals. She discussed a range of influences from innate biological tendencies to the way social identity can limit interaction with the opposite sex.

Self and others: attachment and relationships

Attachment

The previous section discussed the development of children's ideas about the self and others. This section discusses the attachment relation between children and others who are special to them. As we will see, attachment between children and their parents is a significant feature of children's lives. It is a topic that has been studied extensively by developmental psychologists.

Freud drew attention to the importance of first relationships to later development and believed that babies become attached to the people who feed them because of the associated relief from hunger. From a very different perspective, learning theory also explained attachment as being the result of the person who feeds infants becoming a secondary reinforcer through their association with the primary reinforcement of food.

During the 1950s and 1960s these assumptions were challenged by a number of research findings. An important landmark was an experiment by Harlow in which he provided two wire mesh cylinders for isolated infant monkeys. One cylinder contained a nipple so that the monkeys could obtain milk, the other was covered with towelling material (terry cloth). The views of Freud and learning theorists predicted that infant monkeys should show attachment to the wire cylinder because of the reinforcing properties of the milk. The opposite occurred. The monkeys spent more time on the towelling cylinder and, when scared, would jump back on this cylinder.

Another significant study was conducted by Schaffer and Emerson (1964). They also showed the inadequacies of reinforcement explanations. They followed up a group of Glaswegian infants and found that attachments were not always formed with people who provided care. Instead children formed attachments to people who communicated and played games with them, even if these people were not associated with the process of feeding.

FOCUS POINT 20.1

Imprinting

The work of Lorenz and others on imprinting had an influential effect on thinking about attachment. An example of imprinting is newly hatched ducks following the first moving thing they see, and seeking security from this object when threatened. The first object a duckling sees is likely to be its mother, but in experimental situations imprinting can occur with bizarre objects such as watering cans. In the wild, imprinting increases the chances of survival as the ducklings can be defended by their mother and will stay close to her.

There is often a critical period for imprinting, a time after hatching during which certain experiences have to occur for there to be an effect on development. However, more recent research has suggested that there is greater flexibility over the time-frame than was previously thought and so the term 'sensitive period' has been used.

These findings indicate the importance of evolution in shaping attachment behaviour. They also show that developmental changes can occur relatively quickly if an organism is primed to learn something, and that primary reinforcement need not be involved in the process.

At this time Bowlby was formulating an alternative to learning theory. His ideas drew on findings from *ethology*, which is the study of behaviour from an evolutionary perspective (see Focus Point 20.1).

Bowlby identified four phases in the development of attachment behaviours, although some of his descriptions have been superseded by more recent findings. For example, he identifies a first phase in which infants do not discriminate between different people. However, there is evidence that a very young infant will look longer at his or her mother's face (Bushnell *et al.*, 1989), prefer to hear her voice (De Casper and Spence, 1986), and prefer her odour (Cernoch and Porter, 1985). These early preferences may be the result of familiarity – for example, a newborn's preference for his or her mother's voice appears to be the result of hearing her voice while in the womb. In addition, a newborn prefers to hear her or his mother's voice when it has been transformed so that it sounds as it did when the infant was in the womb, rather than an undistorted recording of her voice (Fifer and Moon, 1989). These initial preferences are not, however, the same as attachment, and young infants do not appear to be upset by *separation*. Indeed, research findings suggest that before four months of age, there is minimal behavioural disturbance by adoption (Yarrow, 1964).

The second phase that was identified by Bowlby (six weeks to six to eight months) involves preferences being shown for particular adults, such as the mother in terms of smiling, vocalising and being soothed. Clear-cut attachment was seen as developing in the next phase (seven to eighteen months) when protest occurs at separation from particular people, and infants show wariness of strangers. Bowlby believed that reciprocal relationships begin between 18 and 24 months, when toddlers start to understand their caregivers' motives better and organise their own behaviour to mesh with that of the caregiver.

Although the development of attachment had been reasonably well described, there was at one point a difficulty in assessing attachment relationships. A breakthrough came with Ainsworth and Bell's (1969) use of the *strange situation* (see Research Methods Box 20.1).

Doubts have been expressed about the validity of the strange situation (i.e. whether it provides an accurate assessment of attachment). For example, Kagan (1984) argued that it could be an assessment of temperament, avoidant infants being difficult to stress, while ambivalent infants were easy to stress. However, van IJzendoorn and De Wolff (1997) conducted a systematic review of published findings (a meta-analysis). They concluded that infants often have a different type of attachment to their mother from that to their father (i.e. an infant might have a secure attachment to the mother and an insecure attachment to the father). This suggests that attachment is more a feature of the relationship than a feature of infant temperament. If it were a feature of infant temperament the children should have the same attachment to both parents.

There have also been worries that the strange situation is not valid in different cultures. Grossman *et al.* (1981) reported that 40–50 per cent of German infants were avoidant, and supposed this might be because of the value placed on independence in that country, although it should be noted that other studies have found percentages more similar to those reported in the United States and Britain. In Japan, Miyake *et al.* (1985) reported that 35 per cent of infants were ambivalent, and Takahashi (1990) drew attention to the possibility that 12-month-old Japanese infants might be extremely distressed in the strange situation because they were seldom left alone by their mothers. Rothbaum *et al.* (2000) argued that such differences in attachment patterns between North American and Japanese samples indicate that the strange situation is not valid cross-culturally.

The origins of attachment type
What causes different patterns of attachment? On the basis of Bowlby's views, Ainsworth *et al.* (1978) supposed that caregivers who were responsive to infant distress and demands would have secure infants, inconsistent responsiveness would result in ambivalent infants, and a low level of response would result in avoidant infants. However, a meta-analysis by De Wolff and van IJzendoorn (1997) indicated that there is only a moderate relation between maternal behaviour and infants' later

attachment type. It could be that the measures did not assess maternal responsiveness accurately or it could be that other variables are more important.

There are indications that maternal belief systems as assessed by the *adult attachment interview (AAI)* (Main *et al.*, 1985) are related to infant attachment. The AAI involves a semi-structured, one-hour interview, which is then transcribed and coded. The concern is not with the accuracy of the reports but with the coherence and attitudes expressed during the interview. The four main attachment types from the AAI are given in Research Methods Box 20.2.

RESEARCH METHODS BOX 20.1

The strange situation
The eight episodes that make up the strange situation are as follows.

- Episode 1: experimenter takes caregiver and infant into unfamiliar room and caregiver brings the infant to a pile of toys.
- Episode 2: child and caregiver left alone in room.
- Episode 3: an unfamiliar adult enters the room, sits and reads, then starts to play with the infant.
- Episode 4: caregiver departs, leaving infant with unfamiliar adult.
- Episode 5: caregiver returns, unfamiliar adult departs.
- Episode 6: caregiver leaves again and infant is alone in the room.
- Episode 7: the unfamiliar adult returns.
- Episode 8: caregiver returns in the 'reunion episode'.
- Most episodes take three minutes.
- A complex coding scheme is used to code behaviour so that infants can be classified in terms of the type of attachment that they show.
- Type A – Avoidant Infants: during separation from the caregiver there is little sign of distress;

the infant does not interact or come close to caregiver at reunion.
- Type B – Secure Infants: infants sometimes show distress at separation; infants actively seek interaction and proximity with caregiver especially at reunion.
- Type C – Ambivalent Infants: at reunion, show both contact-seeking and resisting behaviours.
- Type D – Disorganised (introduced by Main *et al.*, 1985): no clear pattern shown across the episodes, and bizarre responses to separation and reunion may be shown.

North American studies often report the following: 21 per cent of infants are avoidant, 67 per cent are secure and 12 per cent ambivalent. For statistical analyses, avoidant and ambivalent groups are often combined and termed insecure.

Episodes in the strange situation.

RESEARCH METHODS BOX 20.2

The adult attachment interview: classification of adult answers into four types of attachment

The four types of attachment are autonomous, dismissive, enmeshed and unresolved.

Autonomous

These adults can recall particular events in childhood and have a willingness to see the positive and negative features of experiences with their own parents. Adults who have this attachment type often have children of their own who are classified in the strange situation as securely attached.

Dismissive

These individuals regard the attachment processes between an adult and his/her parents as being of little relevance or importance. Individuals who have this adult attachment type often have children of their own who are avoidant.

Enmeshed

These people have difficulty distancing themselves from their parents. Adults who have this attachment type often have children who are ambivalent.

Unresolved

This is often the result of a trauma around the loss of a parent, in which the issues are still unresolved. Adults who have this attachment type often have children who are classified as having disorganised attachments.

A meta-analysis by van IJzendoorn (1995) revealed a strong relation between the way mothers were classified on the AAI and the way their infants were classified in the strange situation. The relation was even found between maternal AAI before the birth of her baby and later attachment type (Fonagy *et al.*, 1991). This is an important finding because it largely eliminates the possibility that birth experiences or characteristics of the infant could have influenced the mother's responses in the AAI. It is also relevant that behavioural genetic studies indicate that attachment type is not a highly heritable condition (14 per cent genetic, as estimated by O'Connor and Croft, 2001) and so the relationship between AAI classification and infant security is not a result of powerful genetic processes.

ACTIVITY BOX 20.1

Longitudinal studies of attachment

Bowlby's theory supposed that attachment security would become part of children's internal working model of their world. Thus, a secure infant would have a more confident approach to new situations than an insecure child. A number of studies have indicated that children's attachment classification is predictive of later characteristics.

Securely attached infants tend to be more cooperative with their mother during problem-solving tasks at 24 months (Matas *et al.*, 1978), they are seen as social leaders by preschool teachers (Sroufe, 1983), are more positive at reunion with parents at six years of age (Main and Cassidy, 1988) and have a more positive self-concept at eleven years (Elicker *et al.*, 1992). There are also indications that disorganised attachment predicts later aggressive behaviour and child psychopathology (van Farrar *et al.*, 1999). However, it has also been found that attachment type changes even in the second year, with this often being related to changes in family circumstances (Vaughn *et al.*, 1979).

Do these connections establish causation? What other explanations are there (think about the stability of parental characteristics)?

From the previous findings it would appear that there could be a tendency for cross-generational continuity. Maternal classification on the AAI is related to infant *security of attachment*. However, this does not always occur. A study of survivors of the Holocaust illustrates the way that attachment

APPLICATIONS BOX 20.1

Attachment and separation

The short-term effects on young children of separation from parents, usually the mother, have been reasonably well documented. Many of these studies were conducted in the 1950s and 1960s when there was a lack of appreciation of the effects of separation. Bowlby observed that the short-term response of young children involved protest (crying and anger), despair (absence of play) and detachment (recovery of interest but detachment from parents/caregivers).

Films made by the Robertsons showed these short-term reactions in a boy who was separated when his mother went into hospital (Robertson and Robertson, 1967–73). In contrast, another child was prepared for the separation. She visited the Robertsons before the separation, took photographs of her mother with her and the Robertsons talked to her about her mother during the separation. The effects of separation on this child appeared to be minimal. Observations such as this have changed our awareness of the issues of separation, and hospital practice is now designed to ensure that young children do not have to be separated from their carers.

The separation of children from their parents during the Second World War raised concerns about the long-term effects of separation. Concern was increased by Bowlby's findings about a group of delinquent boys in London. Earlier in their lives these boys had often been separated from their mothers. Bowlby concluded that separation from the mother was largely responsible for their delinquency. However, later work by other investigators, and by Bowlby himself, involving careful comparisons between children who had experienced separations and other children, revealed that separations were not associated with later developmental problems. Instead it seemed more likely that the stress and chaotic lifestyles of some families were associated with the negative outcomes (Rutter, 1987).

One common cause of separation is parental divorce. Children's reactions to divorce appear to be related to their age when the separation occurs (Heatherington and Stanley-Hagan, 1999). Not unexpectedly, with increasing age children better understand the divorce process. Children in middle childhood often have recurring wishes that their parents will reunite, while adolescents often show more anger and shame, and are more likely to take sides with one parent.

Heatherington *et al.* (1982), in one of the first studies of this topic, compared young children with an average age of four years from divorced and non-divorced families. One year after their parents' divorce, children were more likely to exhibit emotional distress and behavioural problems than the comparison group. After two years, these differences had diminished, although some boys whose fathers had left continued to have poor relationships with their mothers and exhibited more anti-social behaviour.

Six years later, comparisons revealed that children whose parents had divorced had more independence and had a greater role in decision-making, although mother–son relationships continued to be problematic.

When interpreting these findings it is important to bear in mind that the extent and type of conflict between parents prior to a divorce may influence children's adjustment. Using the UK National Child Development Study and the US National Survey of Children, Cherlin *et al.* (1991) came to this conclusion after investigating the relationship between divorce, school achievement and behavioural problems. Furthermore, the impact of divorce is likely to vary from cohort to cohort as attitudes, incidence and support change from generation to generation.

patterns can change across generations. Individuals who had experienced the terrible suffering of the Holocaust, usually with their family having been killed, were not surprisingly classified as 'unresolved' on the AAI. One would expect this pattern to continue into the next generation, but there was only a slightly higher percentage of unresolved individuals than would be expected, and the next generation showed no difference in attachment patterns to those found in the general population. Thus the devastating psychological effects of the Holocaust did not appear to cause a downward cycle of psychological problems in subsequent generations.

Relating to others: helping and harming

Attachment is central to young children's relationship with a limited number of adults. However, children show both positive and negative behaviours with a wide range of people. Two examples of this are pro-social behaviour and bullying.

Pro-social behaviour

Pro-social behaviour involves helping, comforting and sharing. Empathy and sympathy are often seen as providing the basis for pro-social behaviour. Hay, Nash and Pedersen (1981) report that six-month-old infants show interest and attempts at intervention when a peer is distressed. Radke-Yarrow and Zahn-

Pro-social behaviour

Waxler (1984) found that 10- to 14-month-old infants were disturbed by the distress of others. However, it is difficult to know whether these are examples of genuine empathy or more simple responses such as social contagion or imitation.

Responses are clearer around two years, when children are more likely to respond by comforting others than by becoming distressed themselves (Zahn-Waxler and Robinson, 1995). Between two and three years the frequency and range of pro-social behaviours increase to include sharing and providing assistance. However, it should be noted that pro-social behaviours are still relatively infrequent. Longitudinal studies indicate that there is continuity in the expression of pro-social behaviours between childhood and adolescence (Eisenberg *et al.*, 2002).

Bullying

Bullying can be considered to be almost the opposite of pro-social behaviour. Olweus (1991) defined bullying as negative actions to others that occur repeatedly over time. Bullying can range from severe physical attacks to verbal name-calling, teasing and taunting. Research has indicated that physical bullying is more common in boys, and that relational aggression (spreading of rumours, name-calling, influencing friends) is more common in girls (Crick and Grotpeter, 1995).

Wolke and Stanford (1999) suggest that about one in five pupils are bullied, with the incidence of the activity decreasing between eight and fifteen years. They also summarise the methods used in research on this topic, together with their advantages and disadvantages (see Research Methods Box 20.3).

Sutton and Smith (in press) have identified a number of different roles in the bullying process. These involve the bully plus an assistant and a reinforcer who yell and laugh. Children who bully or who are assistants are rarely victims but children who mainly adopt the reinforcer role are often both bullies and victims. Somewhat surprisingly, it appears that bullies are better at mind-reading and similar tasks than other children (Sutton *et al.*, in press), whereas victims show the poorest performance in these types of task. Thus, the bullies appear to understand the thinking of others but

---

RESEARCH METHODS BOX 20.3

Methods of researching bullying in schools

Table 20.1 highlights some of the different methods available for researching bullying in schools.

TABLE 20.1 METHODS RESEARCHING BULLYING IN SCHOOLS

	ADVANTAGES	DISADVANTAGES
SELF-REPORT QUESTIONNAIRE	• *Whole-class administration (quick and economical)* • Ideal for quantitative surveys • Anonymous (honest information) • Reliable	• *Differences in measures lead to varying frequencies* • Reliance on reading and comprehension skills (not suitable for young children) • Self-perception bias
ONE-TO-ONE INTERVIEW	• *Can be used with young children* • In-depth enquiry, e.g. reasons for bullying and attributions • Probing if inconsistent information is given	• *More expensive* • Time-consuming • Cannot be anonymous (older children may not own up to being bullies/victims)
PEER-NOMINATION TECHNIQUE (children reporting on their peers)	• *Whole-class administered in older children (quick and economical)* • Anonymous (honest information) • High re-test reliability	• *Time-consuming with young children (interview)* • Liable to 'reputation effect' • Children talking about their nominations between each other
OBSERVATION TECHNIQUE	• *Offers qualitative detail that survey studies may miss* • Captures bullying in social context	• *Expensive* • Time-consuming • Observer effect/bias • Not useful for prevalence investigations (e.g. hidden bullying)

Source: Messer and Millar, 1999

---

ignore or distort the effects of their actions on other children.

Olweus (1992; 1993) has advocated a whole-school approach to reducing bullying, where all children are given guidelines about unacceptable behaviour and intervention occurs with whole classes as well as individual children. Olweus (1993) reports a 50 per cent reduction in bullying for schools adopting the programme. Other studies, however, have not reported such dramatic improvements (Roland, 1993, in Norway; Sharp and Smith, 1995, in the UK), and report that any effects appear to diminish over time (Eslea and Smith, 1998).

RESEARCH METHODS BOX 20.4

Theory of mind tasks

Wimmer and Perner (1983) devised a 'false belief task' to address this question. They used some toys to act out the following story.

Maxi left some chocolate in a blue cupboard before he went out. When he was away his mother moved the chocolate to a green cupboard. Children were asked to predict where Maxi will look for his chocolate when he returns.

Most children under four years gave the incorrect answer, that Maxi will look in the green cupboard. Those over four years tended to give the correct answer, that Maxi will look in the blue cupboard. The incorrect answers indicated that the younger children did not understand that Maxi's beliefs and representations no longer matched the actual state of the world, and they failed to appreciate that Maxi will act on the basis of his beliefs rather than the way that the world is actually organised.

A simpler version of the Maxi task was devised by Baron-Cohen *et al.* (1985) to take account of criticisms that younger children may have been affected by the complexity and length of the story in the task described above. The new task was the same in structure and involved two characters, Sally and Anne, and the location of a marble (see Figure 20.1). Again younger children gave the incorrect answer and older children gave the correct answer (although children were able to pass the Sally/Anne task at a slightly earlier age than the Maxi task). Further simplification of these tasks can result in even greater success in even younger children (Lewis and Osbourne, 1990; Mitchell, 1996).

Understanding others' minds: a cognitive approach

Interactions between people are very complex processes. Part of the complexity is that most of us are continually evaluating what another person is saying in terms of their beliefs, feelings and desires. Quite often these beliefs, feelings and desires are different from our own, and many of us find it an interesting challenge to try to understand what other people think and feel.

A considerable amount of research since the mid-1980s has been concerned with what has been termed children's *theory of mind* (see below). This involves children's ability to understand that people can have different beliefs and representations of the world – a capacity that is shown by four years of age. Furthermore, this ability appears to be absent in children with autism.

Theory of mind (TOM)

How can we tell whether young children have a theory of mind (see Research Methods Box 20.4)?

The origins of theory of mind

The ability to work out what another person is thinking is clearly an important aspect of both cognitive and social development. Furthermore, one important explanation for *autism* is that children suffering from this condition do not have a theory of mind (TOM). Consequently, the development of children's TOM has attracted considerable attention.

One set of explanations traces the development of TOM back to infancy. At around nine months joint attention is a noticeable feature of interaction. This involves infants and adults attending to the same object or event. Hobson (1993) has argued that these triadic relations put infants in a position to notice that other people can have different emotional reactions to the world (the mother may find something funny that the child finds frightening). From these triadic relationships infants begin to understand that they can construct more than one representation of an entity.

A more cognitive explanation of this process has been proposed by Baron-Cohen (1993). He suggested that infants are born with a module that processes information about the direction of other people's eye gaze: eye direction detector (EDD). At around six to

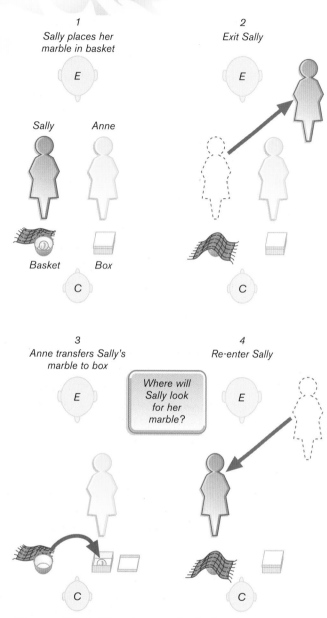

1
*Sally places her
marble in basket*

E

Sally   Anne

Basket   Box

C

2
Exit Sally

E

C

3
*Anne transfers Sally's
marble to box*

E

Where will
Sally look
for her
marble?

C

4
Re-enter Sally

E

C

Figure 20.1 The theory of mind task

nine months EDD is able to note triadic relationships. This forms a basis not just for monitoring gaze, but also allows infants to start to process information about mental states like interest, attention, and so on. In this way children develop the ability to form two different representations (their own and those of the other person) about an object or event.

In both explanations it is supposed that having two different representations of the same thing provides the basis for the later development of pretend play. Pretend play involves object substitution (e.g. a banana is used as a pretend telephone), giving false properties to objects and things (e.g. 'teddy is tired') and pretending that an object is present (e.g. pretending to eat).

Leslie (1987) argues that, before 18 months, children treat the world in a literal way and rarely demonstrate pretence. He also argues that it is necessary for the cognitive system to distinguish between what is pretend and what is real. If children were not able to do this, they would not be able to distinguish between imagination and reality. Leslie suggested that this pretend play becomes possible because of the presence of a *decoupler* that copies primary representations to secondary representations. For example, children, when pretending a banana is a telephone, would make a secondary representation of a banana. They would manipulate this representation and they would use their stored knowledge of 'telephone' to build on this pretence.

Being able to play pretend games might not at first seem to have much relevance to understanding the mind of others. However, both processes involve *metarepresentations*, which means being able to create thoughts (i.e. representations) about things that are different from what is happening in the world.

There is also evidence that social processes play a part in the development of TOM. Meins and her colleagues have found that what they term *mindmindedness* in maternal speech to six-month-old infants is related to both security of attachment and to TOM abilities (Meins *et al.*, 1998; Meins *et al.*, 2002). Mindmindedness involves speech that discusses infants' feelings and explains their behaviour in terms of mental states (e.g. 'you're feeling hungry').

Lewis *et al.* (1996) investigated older children living in extended families in Crete and Cyprus. They found that children who socially interact with more adults, who have more friends, and who have more older siblings tend to pass TOM tasks at a slightly earlier age than other children. Furthermore, because young children are more likely to talk about their thoughts and feelings with peers than with their mothers, peer interaction may provide a special impetus to the development of a TOM (Brown *et al.*, 1996).

A similar point has been made by Dunn (1999), who argues that peer interaction is more likely to contain pretend play and that it is likely to be more challenging because other children, unlike adults, do not make large adaptations to the communicative needs of other children.

In addition, there has been concern that some aspects of the TOM approach underestimate children's understanding of other people. After all, infants will point to objects apparently in an effort to change a person's direction of gaze and interest; they can interact quite effectively with other people; they will express their ideas in opposition to the wishes of others; and they will show empathy for the feelings of others. All this suggests that they have some level of understanding that their own thoughts are different to those in another person's mind.

Evidence to support this position comes from a variety of sources. When a card with a different picture on each side is shown to a child and an adult sitting opposite her, then three year olds understand that they see a different picture to that seen by the adult (Masangkay *et al.*, 1974).

Schatz *et al.* (1983) studied the spontaneous speech of three-year-olds and found that these children used mental terms, and used them in circumstances where there was a contrast between, for example, not being sure where an object was located and finding it, or between pretending and reality. Thus the social abilities of children indicate that they are aware of the difference between mental states and external reality at ages younger than four.

What changes to enable children to pass TOM tasks? Wellman (1990; Wellman and Gelman, 1998) claims the change involves children's theory about other people. He suggests that two-year-olds have 'desire' theory about people, because they assume that desires will influence behaviour. For example, children of this age were told a story about Sam, who was looking for his rabbit so he could take it to

school. Some children were told that he found his rabbit, some were told he found a dog. All the children were asked whether Sam would go on searching or whether he would go to school. Both groups gave the appropriate answer. This indicates that even young children who do not pass TOM tasks appreciate that others can have different desires depending on the circumstance.

However, children of this age give incorrect answers to the following story. They were told that Sam thinks a puppy is under a porch, but that the puppy is actually in the garage. When asked where they think Sam will look, they said in the garage, and so did not appear to take account of Sam's belief. Wellman suggests that three-year-olds progress to a 'belief–desire' theory about people. They can understand people's belief if it corresponds to the state of the world but still have difficulties with TOM tasks.

A different explanation has been put forward by Harris (1989). He proposed that children use 'simulation'. This involves putting yourself in the other person's position, and then trying to predict what the other person would do. Thus success on false belief tasks can be explained by children trying to imagine what they would do if they were a character in the stories, rather than children being able to appreciate the beliefs of other people. Such thinking about situations that do not exist involves what is termed *counterfactual reasoning* (Harris, 2000).

The theory of mind explanation of autism

We have just seen that there are various explanations for the development of TOM. In addition, over the last 20 years a considerable research effort has been devoted to increasing our understanding of autism. One explanation that has been central to this work is that children with autism fail to develop a TOM. Before we discuss this, however, the characteristics of children with autism will be outlined. Autism was first described in the 1940s by Kanner (1943), who was working in Chicago, and by Asperger (1944) working in Austria. Wing (1988) has proposed that autism involves a triad of impairments (see Focus Point 20.2).

The triad of impairments in autism

1. Impaired non-verbal and verbal communication
- Delayed or absent speech
- Inability to initiate and sustain conversations
- Stereotyped and repetitive speech

2. Impaired social relations
- Failure to develop peer relations
- Lack of spontaneous sharing of enjoyment
- Lack of social and emotional reciprocity

3. Restricted, repetitive and stereotyped behaviours
- Unusually intense interests in restricted topics
- Adherence to rituals
- Stereotypes and repetitive motor movements
- Persistent preoccupation with parts of objects

Many, but not all, children with autism also have low scores on intelligence tests. Some have areas (islets) of ability such as drawing, music or the ability to perform calculations. Often, symbolic and pretend play is absent or restricted (Libby *et al.*, 1989). Over half of children with autism do not acquire language (Bailey *et al.*, 1996). In addition, many children who can speak will echo back speech they have heard (echolalia) and will also reverse personal pronouns, using 'you' when they mean 'I ' or 'me'. However, it is important to emphasise that autism involves a range of abilities and characteristics.

In 1985 Baron-Cohen and his colleagues gave the Sally/Anne task (see Research Methods Box 20.4) to a group of children with autism and a group of children with Down's syndrome. Both groups were similar in terms of their general abilities and both had higher abilities than a typical four- to five-year-old. So these children would be expected to pass the task. About 80 per cent of the children with autism failed the task but most of the children with Down's syndrome passed.

A subsequent study by Leslie and Frith (1988) confirmed these findings with a real-life task. One experimenter put a coin under a cup, then another experimenter who had been present left the room and the coin was moved under another cup. Children with autism gave incorrect answers to the question 'Where will Uta [the second experimenter] look?' They thought she would look where the coin was now positioned.

Baron-Cohen (1993) has suggested that these

Executive functioning, central coherence and autism

Adults who have had damage to the frontal lobes of their brains have been described as having difficulties with *executive functioning*. This involves inflexibility in action plans. For example, on the Wisconsin card sorting task, which involves picking out cards with particular characteristics, patients with frontal brain damage have difficulty changing their strategy when asked to pick out cards with a different set of characteristics. In addition, these patients are often socially unresponsive or insensitive to social cues.

Ozonoff *et al.* (1991) drew attention to the similarities between high functioning individuals with autism and patients with executive functioning deficits. A dramatic illustration of these difficulties has been shown in a 'windows task' used by Russell *et al.* (1991). The main part of this task involves two boxes, one of which contains a sweet. If children point to the empty box they can have the sweet. Children with autism have considerable difficulty inhibiting their response.

Another explanation of autism is that the children have a difficulty with *central coherence*. This view has been put forward by Frith and

Happe (1994). Central coherence refers to the ability to identify the relationship between separate items of information, and Frith and Happe believe it involves a style of thinking rather than a primary deficit. A number of studies show that children with autism have superior performance to typical children on tasks where there is an advantage in not being able to 'see things as a whole'.

In the embedded figures test (see Figure 20.2), children have to pick out a shape that is hidden in a picture. Children with autism are better at this task than children of a similar cognitive ability (Shah and Frith, 1983).

Happe (1994) also found that children with autism, who could read and had passed TOM tasks, had difficulty using contextual information. Some words have the same spelling but are pronounced in different ways (e.g. a tear in a cloth and a tear in an eye). Children with autism, unlike typical children, had difficulty using information provided in the rest of a sentence to pronounce these words correctly.

Another finding related to central coherence is that when children with autism draw something they start with detail and then build up a complete picture. In contrast, typical children start with the overall shape of what they are drawing and then fill in the details. Thus there is a range of findings that support the idea that children with autism have 'weak' central coherence.

How well do you think TOM, executive functioning and central coherence explain the following characteristics of children with autism?

1. Lack of pretend play
2. Inability to lie
3. Lack of communication
4. Repetitive and stereotyped behaviours
5. Failure on TOM tasks

Don't read the following two paragraphs unless you want help in answering these questions.

The executive functioning explanation is consistent with a range of characteristics of children with autism (e.g. not inhibiting incorrect answers in TOM tasks, not inhibiting inappropriate social behaviours). However, there are also problems with the theory. Surprisingly, patients with frontal lobe damage do not have impaired TOM.

Another problem is the finding that children with PKU have impaired executive functioning but not an impaired TOM (Welsh et al., 1990). Thus it would seem that impaired executive functioning does not always result in an impaired TOM.

The false photograph test also creates problems for this theory. In this task the children are shown a camera, which is used to take a photograph of a scene. The scene is changed and the child is asked about what the photograph in the camera will show. Children with autism can respond correctly, and therefore seem able to inhibit a response in these circumstances. However, they cannot answer correctly in TOM tasks when asked about what is in a person's mind (Leekham and Perner, 1991; Leslie and Thaiss, 1992).

Central coherence theory can be used to explain a lack of TOM, as children with autism fail to see the wider implications of situations in assessments such as the Sally/Anne task. In a similar way, central coherence theory can be used to account for the difficulties of children with autism in dealing with social situations and pragmatics. It can even account for the obsession that some children with autism have for order (e.g. arranging toys in a line) and for detailed knowledge about some aspect of the environment (e.g. makes of car), because they fail to take a more general perspective.

There are criticisms of this theory, however, for example, Jarrold and Russell (1997) reported no difference in the analytic skills of children with autism and children with learning disabilities. Another criticism is that the predictions of central coherence theory are not particularly clear when it comes to deciding the type of task children with autism will find difficult, so that explanations tend to be *post hoc*.

Section 4
Developmental psychology

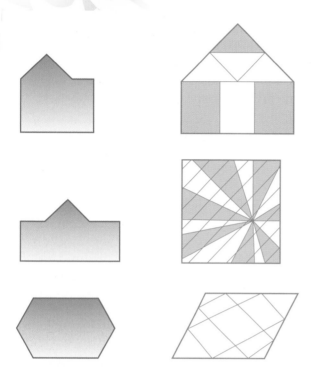

Figure 20.2 The embedded figures test

findings indicate that children with autism have *mindblindness* due to the failure to develop a theory of mind module (TOMM), and this can be traced back to a failure of shared attention mechanisms (see page 351). More recently, Baron-Cohen has taken this argument further by suggesting that autism is a form of extreme male thinking associated with the amygdala region of the brain. This involves an obsessive interest in some topics and a lack of appreciation of social processes.

The presence of mindblindness helps to explain a number of characteristics of autism but there are some difficulties with this explanation. For one thing, only about 80 per cent of children with autism fail TOM tasks, and an absence of TOM fails to account for the repetitive and stereotyped behaviours of these children. Other competing explanations have been put forward (see Activity Box 20.2).

Section summary
In this section we have seen the way that research into children's theory of mind has:

- produced new methodologies
- generated discussion about the way this ability develops
- provided an explanation for the characteristics of children with autism.

Think about each of these points and the conclusions you have come to about this work.

Adolescence: new relationships

Biology, culture, storm and stress
Adolescence is a period of changing views about the self, changing relationships, and a greater sensitivity to the views of peers. While there is no generally agreed definition of adolescence, most definitions include some aspect of biological maturation, an increasing adoption of adult roles and a transition from childhood to adulthood. Deciding when adolescence ends is especially problematic in western cultures as there has been an increase in the age at which conventional adult roles are adopted (such as the age at which people start to have a regular income from employment).

The biological changes of adolescence enable individuals to engage in functional sexual relationships. These biological changes are well known and involve the development of the sexual organs, the beginning of menstruation or the capacity for the ejaculation of sperm, the development of secondary sexual characteristics (pubic hair, breasts and deeper voices), and then a growth spurt that often signals the ending of increases in height.

Lack of appropriate nutrition is associated with delays in the age at which these biological changes take place. Furthermore, in countries where there are large disparities in wealth, those in higher social classes are likely to reach puberty at younger ages (Katchdourian, 1977). Puberty also appears to have occurred at progressively younger ages over the last century. Records from Finland and Norway indicate that the age of menarche (the first menstruation) declined from about 16 years in the 1860s to about 13 years in the 1960s (Tanner, 1973; but see Bullogh, 1981). These effects are usually regarded as being caused by better nutrition and healthcare, and possibly by smaller family sizes.

There is evidence that an earlier onset of puberty relative to other individuals has consequences for psychological development. A study by Magnusson *et al.* (1985) in Sweden found that girls who mature earlier, in comparison to those who are late maturing, tended at 14 years to be more involved in drinking alcohol, taking illegal drugs and missing school. Part of the reason for this seems to be that the early-maturing girls mixed with older adolescents who were more likely to engage in these activities.

A follow-up of these individuals at 25 years revealed that those who matured early were more likely to have married and to have had children, and less likely to have continued with their education. The general pattern of these findings has been supported by other studies in various countries (Silbereisen and Kracke, 1997). In the case of boys it would appear that those who mature early tend to feel more positive about themselves, be popular and do well at school (Silbereisen and Kracke, 1997). This is probably because of their strength, size and sporting abilities, features that tend to be valued by peers.

Is adolescence a period of storm and stress?

Freud's theory of development suggested that adolescence is an especially difficult time because of the emergence of biologically based sexual motivations. He believed that these disrupt the equilibrium achieved during childhood.

A different explanation has been that the transition between childhood and adulthood cultural roles is responsible for the difficulties of this age group (e.g. making decisions about new relationships, careers and responsibilities). It has also been suggested that these difficulties are particularly common in western societies because of the ambiguous status of adolescents (i.e. countries often specify different ages at which sexual intercourse, drinking alcohol, driving, entering the army and voting are legal), and that this increases uncertainties about roles and responsibilities. This can be contrasted with other cultures where ceremonies mark the transition from childhood to adulthood, and after the ceremony has taken place the person is treated as a member of the adult community. It is also worth pointing out that the view that adolescence is a period of *storm and stress* coincided with the period of adolescent rebellion in the 1960s and 1970s.

It has been suggested that part of the reason for any storm and stress is the *generation gap* between adolescents and adults, particularly parents. Many studies suggest that adolescence involves a change in the orientation, from the family to the peer group.

However, studies also indicate that for many young people this transition is not necessarily a difficult one. For example, in one of the first studies of this topic, Rutter *et al.* (1976) used questionnaires and interviews to collect information from parents and adolescents on the Isle of Wight. Most parents (five-sixths of them) reported that they did not have arguments about matters such as their children going out or their activities, although one-third said that there was conflict over clothing or hairstyle (remember this study was conducted when there was a marked change in youth culture and appearance). Similarly only about one-third of the adolescents made criticisms of their parents during the interviews.

Another significant study was conducted by Coleman (1974), who asked adolescents to complete a sentence such as 'My friends are ...'. This technique is likely to obtain responses that reflect current concerns and attitudes. The analysis of the answers revealed that, in general, anxiety and fear of rejection by friends increased from 11 to 15 years, but declined around 17 years. Similarly, a longitudinal study conducted by Galambos and Almeida (1992) revealed that conflict with parents about chores, appearance, politeness, finance and substance abuse declined with the increasing age of the adolescents.

Research into the more general issue of storm and stress has not usually shown adolescence as a period of widespread difficulty for all individuals at all ages. Instead, Coleman (1980), in his *focal theory*, suggested that difficulties occurred for some individuals at some times. Evidence to support his view came from questionnaires and interviews with adolescents (see Coleman and Hendry, 1999).

Section 4
Developmental psychology

Adolescent appearance and identity. What are these adolescents communicating about their identity?

Issues of identity

As we saw earlier in this chapter (pages 340–344), identity increases in complexity with age. Harter (1999) has shown that in adolescents this process continues. Adolescents, in comparison to younger children, use more abstract terms when describing themselves. They also recognise that they act differently in different circumstances and with different groups of people. In addition, Harter describes the way that during adolescence there is an increasing integration of these different perspectives, and that there is less dependence on the views of others.

Adolescence is also different in that it is a period when individuals are able to make choices about a coherent identity, but when there can also be difficulties in achieving this. Erikson, who worked within a psychoanalytic framework, proposed that this is a major issue facing adolescents (Erikson, 1959; 1968). He described a number of different states that occur during the identity formation process. One involves adolescents trying out different types of identity involving such things as politics, religion, choice of career, appearance and so on; and to some extent adults were tolerant and expected changes of this nature. Erikson termed this a 'psychosocial moratorium'.

Other states concern identity diffusion, where individuals have not yet experienced a crisis; identity foreclosure, where there has not been a crisis and the identity promoted by others is accepted; and identity achievement, where the crisis is resolved. Erikson pointed out that adolescents sometimes choose a negative identity, which is the opposite to that of a parent or another member of their family. In such cases the adolescent will dress, act and have attitudes that are the opposite to this person.

Marcia (1966) investigated these ideas by carrying out interviews about attitudes to politics, religion, careers and sexual behaviour. He found that the responses corresponded to Erikson's description of the different states of adolescent identity. More quantitative research has documented the way that the percentage of individuals who achieve a coherent self-identity increases across the adolescent age range (Meilman, 1979). Other research has revealed that the failure to achieve a coherent identity is associated with a lack of intimate relationships, being apathetic and being more likely to engage in drug abuse (e.g. Grotevant, 1998). In contrast, those who are experimenting with identity (moratorium stage) tend to have high self-esteem and anxiety, but are also likely to have experimented with drugs (e.g. Jones, 1992).

Learning outcomes

When you have completed this chapter you should be able to:
- define self-identity and describe its development
- discuss the influences on the formation of attachment
- define theory of mind and discuss its development
- compare theories about the causes of autism
- evaluate whether adolescence is a time of storm and stress.

Key terms

Adult attachment interview (AAI)
Attachment
Autism
Categorical self
Central coherence
Counterfactual reasoning
Decoupler
Ethology
Executive functioning
Executive self
Focal theory
Gender identity
Generation gap
Imprinting
Intersubjectivity
Metarepresentations
Mindblindness
Mindmindedness
Security of attachment
Separation
Storm and stress
Strange situation
Theory of mind (TOM)
Triadic relations

Section 4
Developmental psychology

Further reading

Coleman, J. C. and Hendry, L. B. (1999) *The Nature of Adolescence*. London: Routledge.

Eckensberger, L. (1999) Socio-moral development. In Messer, D. and Millar, S. (eds) *Exploring Developmental Psychology*. London: Arnold.

Mitchell, P. (1997) *Introduction to Theory of Mind*. London: Arnold.

Powell, S. (1999) Autism. In Messer, D. and Millar, S. (eds) *Exploring Developmental Psychology*. London: Arnold.

Van IJzendoorn, M. H. and Schuengel, C. (1999) The development of attachment relationships in infancy and beyond. In Messer, D. and Millar, S. (eds) *Exploring Developmental Psychology*. London: Arnold.

Ian P. Albery

Social Psychology

21	Issues and themes in social psychology	362
22	Attitudes, persuasion and attitude change	376
23	Attribution	395
24	Impression formation and social interaction	409
25	Social influence and group processes	429

21

Issues and themes in social psychology

Route map of the chapter

The aim of this chapter is to provide you with a basic introduction to the various themes and issues that are important for the study of social psychological processes. Our starting point will be to look at how social psychology has been defined and the historical basis to these definitions. The next part of the chapter focuses on two approaches that social psychologists take in their studies. The first is the experimental approach. We shall see that the main proponents of this approach are those who come from a social cognition perspective. The second approach is called critical social psychology; we will focus on one perspective – social constructionism – from this school. We then move on to study the types of experimental and non-experimental research methods and strategies that social psychologists use, and the ethical considerations that this work involves.

Introduction

Social psychology is the field of psychology that is to do with how we think about other people, and how we interact with other people or interact in groups. It is a subdiscipline of general psychology. Over the years a number of definitions of social psychology have been offered (see Focus Point 21.1).

FOCUS POINT 21.1

Defining social psychology

'. . . the scientific field that seeks to understand the nature and causes of individual behaviour and thought in social situations' (Baron and Byrne, 2003: 5).

'Social psychology is all about the give-and-take of influence – on behaviour, beliefs, and feelings – between individuals, between groups, and between an individual and a group' (Carr, 2003: 3).

'. . . the scientific investigation of how the thoughts, feelings and behaviour of individuals are influenced by the actual, imagined or implied presence of others' (Hogg and Vaughan, 2002: 2).

Social psychology

You will see throughout this section that the sorts of questions social psychologists have been interested in answering are designed to understand how people or groups of people interact, and the results of those interactions. Social psychologists are concerned with the social world in which people and groups coexist.

They are also interested in how people think about and behave in their social worlds.

Social psychology is concerned with people's thoughts, feelings, intentions, goals, beliefs and attitudes, as well as their behaviour. For instance, in Chapter 22 we will come across the idea of attitudes as a concept for understanding how we and others behave towards each other. In Chapter 23 we will look at how people explain their own behaviours and those of others. Chapter 24 is concerned with how we form impressions of others and interact with others, while Chapter 25 looks at how groups of other people affect our own thoughts and feelings. These areas are all key aspects of understanding our social world and together form the bulk of what social psychology is about.

As social psychologists we study behaviour because behaviour can be 'seen', but we also study beliefs, intentions, feelings, attitudes and so on, which can't directly be 'seen'. We can infer these from people's behaviour and they may be important for predicting how a person will behave in social situations. These are the psychological dimensions of social behaviour. As we shall see in this chapter and in the chapters that follow, some social psychologists try to relate these dimensions to more fundamental cognitive or thinking processes. In other words, they are interested in those processes that occur within the human mind.

A brief history of social psychology

Where does social psychology as a discipline come from? The earliest influence came from the German

folk psychologists, or *Völkerpsychologie*, in the 1860s. These people were interested in what they called 'group mind', or 'the collective mind', that basically described the ways in which societal thinking is reflected in the individual. This approach was the main way in which people understood social behaviour in the late nineteenth and early twentieth centuries. For instance, LeBon (1908) used this approach to try and understand why people behave differently in crowds.

Experimental work in social psychology, and the adoption of empirical methods derived from behaviourist principles, really began in 1898 with Norman Triplett's work on competition and *social facilitation* (see Chapter 25) in which cyclists were shown to ride faster when competing with others. For many, however, the 'father' of experimental social psychology is Kurt Lewin, who founded a research centre at the University of Michigan, USA, in 1945 to study group processes. Some of his work looked at the role of leadership in group behaviour.

Many influential experimental studies were carried out in the first part of the twentieth century. These include the work of Leon Festinger, Soloman Asch, Muzafer Sherif and Carl Hovland, to name but a few, and focused on areas like impression formation, attitude change, attribution and group processes.

It seems, therefore, that although the foundation of social psychology can be attributed to the European scholars, the Americans soon took over leadership in the discipline. However, the latter part of the twentieth century has seen a rapid rise in influence on the part of European social psychologists, particularly in the area of group processes and social influence. These particularly influential psychologists include Henri Tajfel and Serge Moskovici.

While all this work has been dominated by experimental approaches, more recently some Europeans have adopted a more critical approach to social psychology by questioning the empirical assumptions of the experiment (e.g. Potter and Wetherell, 1987; Gough and McFadden, 2001; Stainton Rogers, 2003).

Kurt Lewin: the 'father' of experimental social psychology

Section 5
Social Psychology

Key paradigms in social psychology

We now turn to the key paradigms that are of contemporary importance in social psychology. Specifically, we are going to look at experimental social psychology (and social cognition as the main paradigm associated with it) and social constructionism.

Social cognition

Social cognition developed from theories and ideas from general cognitive psychology (see Chapters 12 to 16), except that the emphasis was specifically on our experience of the social world. In a landmark publication, Susan Fiske and Shelley Taylor (1991) outlined the main assumptions behind the social cognition approach (see also Fiedler and Bless, 2001). They argued that people should be seen as active thinkers who use complex cognitive strategies to bring meaning to their experience in the social world.

Social cognition is that part of social psychology that looks at how people perceive their social worlds. It is concerned with how we attend to, store, remember and also use information received about other people and ourselves. Social cognition researchers are interested in understanding the types of systematic cognitive strategies that people use in this process. We will come across examples of work that adopt the social cognitive approach in this chapter and those that follow. We will also see that much work that predated Fiske and Taylor's proclamation is really social cognitive accounts. These include attitude work (Chapter 22), attribution work (Chapter 23), impression formation work (Chapter 24), and also work on group processes and social influence (Chapter 25). For now, though, let's look at some of the key assumptions of social cognition.

People as cognitive misers

This idea basically argues that people are exposed the whole time to a barrage of information that needs processing. To do this we would probably need heads the size of small planets to give us the necessary processing space. Nisbett and Ross (1980) introduced the term *cognitive miser* to describe the

idea that people have limited cognitive resources available to them and therefore use all sorts of short-cuts to cope with incoming information (see also Taylor, 1991).

One example here is the use of stereotypes in forming impressions of others (see later in this chapter), and other forms of heuristic processing or using general 'rules of thumb' in decision-making (see Chapter 16).

People as motivated tacticians

In their social cognition account, Fiske and Taylor (1991) see people not so much as cognitive misers but more as *motivated tacticians*. They see cognition as more strategic than limited. So, for instance, a person can actively select from a number of available strategies based on the needs, goals and motives of the thinkers at that time. I think you will see that this idea of the person as a motivated tactician is the other side of the coin to being a cognitive miser.

People as naïve scientists

The idea of the *naïve scientist* is derived from Heider's (1958) 'common-sense psychology' and is discussed in Chapter 23 on attribution. The basic idea here is that we use various strategies to understand why we and others behave in particular ways in certain social situations. In effect, we work out causes for particular events or make attributions in predictable ways.

Given that these main assumptions propose that various processes are important for understanding the thinking social being, let's now look at a few examples of these processes. We are going to restrict ourselves to categorisation, schema and an example of these processes in action: stereotyping.

Categorisation and schema

Cognitive social psychologists argue that the way in which meaning is given to information being received is through categorisation. Categorisation itself describes the idea that we classify similar things together and treat them as a discrete category. These categories are stored in our long-term memory. For instance, the category 'footballers' includes people like David Beckham, George Best and the like, but it will also include people specific to the individual perceiver, like those people who play five-a-side with you, and so on. Figure 21.1 gives an example of how football as a category can be organised hierarchically.

In addition, these categories can also have other attributes associated with them. For instance, when we think about footballers we may well associate them with being 'stupid', 'spoilt' or even 'attractive'. However, these types of traits can also be appropriate to other categories and may also form a category in their own right.

For instance, you may well be asked to recall anything that is associated with the concept of being 'spoilt' and recall footballers as well as other people. This shows that we do not necessarily represent categories as being completely independent of one another.

There are also connections between different social categories. This is called an *associative network* (Fiedler and Bless, 2001). These associative networks describe how categories are related semantically and give meaning to our social world. For instance, categories that share many features, and have quite similar meanings are closer and more strongly connected than more dissimilar ones. For example, when we think about the category 'footballer', related categories like 'rich people', 'stupidity', 'being male', 'aggression', 'unintelligent' and so on are also all closely connected (unless you are a footballer!). Fiedler and Bless (2001) give a nice example of an associative network involving categories related to being a feminist (see Figure 21.2).

In associative networks the links between the categories are organised in a semantic way. For example, if you were to think of the category 'feminist', other related categories would also be thought of (or activated), on which we may base attributions for events or behaviours, or the impressions we form of others.

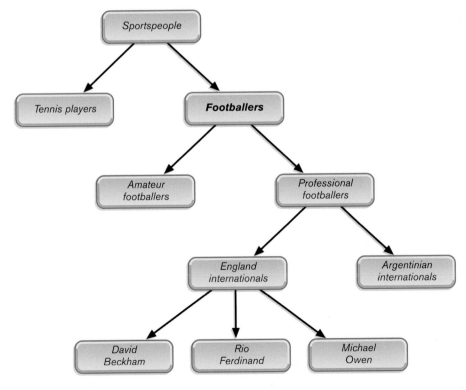

Figure 21.1 Hierarchical representation of how the category 'footballers' is organised

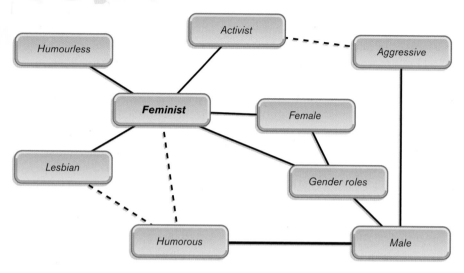

Figure 21.2 Associative network of categories related to being a feminist

---

FOCUS POINT 21.2

Types of social schema

Person schemata

These are expectations about other people based on past experience with them and knowledge about them. For example, it is likely that we have all built up over time a detailed person schema for a close friend. Among other things, this is based on the behaviours we expect of that person, their beliefs and attitudes, and possibly their personality type. The types of schema we have might also govern how we behave towards that person or towards other people in the presence of that person. We can also have schemata that characterise our ideal person. These are called prototypes. These contain the ideals, beliefs, behaviours etc. we expect of that person.

Role schemata

These schemata represent knowledge we have of the roles we play in different situations. For example, we all have an idea of the roles we have in lectures, in an interview, in a restaurant or even at a football match. They are expectations of how we should behave that come into play when we are in a particular context. In other words, they are the roles we play in different contexts. For example, you as readers of this book are likely to have a student role schema that acts to predict the way you behave when you are at college or university.

Self-schemata

These guide how we process information related to ourselves. Certain characteristics are defining for each human being and these help to define the self. For instance, you might hold particular beliefs or opinions that help define the self; these are called 'schematic'. We also know of other possible characteristics that are not useful for defining the self; these are called 'aschematic'.

Event schemata

This refers specifically to representations we have of what we normally expect in a whole host of situations. For example, we would have an event schema for going to the pub or for being in a lecture and so on. They are also called scripts.

Fiske and Taylor (1991) adopted the concept of schema from cognitive psychology (see Chapter 14) to describe how social knowledge is represented in our heads. A social *schema* is a cognitive structure that represents our knowledge about something in our social world. This representation includes the attributes of the stimulus and also the relationship between these attributes. Schemata are based in memory and are dependent upon past experience with the stimulus. They may also form the basis for making judgements about social objects.

In essence, these schemata are 'shorthand summaries of our social world' (Pennington, 2000: 69). A number of social schemata have been identified over the years, including person schemata, self-schemata, role schemata and event schemata (see Focus Point 21.2)

ACTIVITY BOX 21.1

The stereotypical librarian

For the next minute write down as many words as you can that describe a librarian. Do this before reading the following paragraphs.

I hope you didn't find this very taxing. What sorts of characteristics did you identify as relevant to being a librarian? Did you include personality-based traits like shyness, introversion or being boring? What about more external characteristics like the way they dress? For example, did you write down the word 'glasses'? I bet if you compared your list of words with those of a friend there would be quite significant overlap in how you both characterised a librarian.

Getting you to write down this word list was designed to show you that we all have characteristic, or stereotypical, beliefs about others. The fact that different people report the same or similar characteristics shows how generalised these beliefs are. Also, getting you to write down the words as quickly as possible and within a small timeframe hopefully got you to write down the first things that came to mind – in other words, the traits most easily retrievable or accessible from memory about what a librarian is like.

Stereotyping

Before you read this section have a look at Activity Box 21.1.

What sorts of words did you write down to describe a librarian? These words to some extent will form the basis of a stereotypical image you have of a librarian. The trouble is that it is highly unlikely that every librarian will be exactly the same. People are different from one another. Not all librarians are boring and shy! (See the photo on p. 368.) So the *stereotypes* we have of certain people or groups of people might not be accurate.

Our social schemata, of which the stereotyping process is an example, lead to errors and bias in inferences. They might even guide the way we behave towards people. An extreme example here is prejudice and discrimination (see Chapter 25). In general, stereotypes are generalisations that a large number of people have about particular social groups (Macrae *et al.*, 1994; Brown, 2000a).

Evidence suggests that stereotypes act in an automatic manner (see Biernat and Billings, 2003). For instance, on encountering a librarian you are likely to infer that they are 'boring' and 'shy' because your librarian stereotype or schema has been activated without you having control over it.

Some studies have shown that you may well behave in accordance with the stereotype that has been activated. For instance, Bargh *et al.* (1996) got participants to form sentences from a series of scrambled words. One group was asked to form sentences that included a word related to being elderly (e.g. shoes give replace *old* the) and another group was asked to form sentences that did not include an old-age-related concept (control group). Participants in the first group were subsequently shown to walk more slowly than those in the control group. When debriefed, the participants were not aware that they had been primed with the scrambled sentences. The idea was that being presented with the words had activated, or cognitively primed, the old-age stereotype and resulted in a behaviour change. Other work has demonstrated automatic racial stereotyping at work (e.g. Lepore and Brown, 2002).

In general, most of the work that has applied a social cognitive account of how people understand

Section 5
Social Psychology

Does this match your stereotype of a librarian?

and interpret their social worlds has attempted to establish general causal laws for behaviour through controlled experiments. Social cognitivists argue that there is a predictable and objective reality in the world that is observable through experimentation (Fiske and Taylor, 1991; Augoustinos and Walker, 1995). What if these types of assumptions are not thought of as being totally valid? Some social psychologists are now questioning these types of assumptions. One of these is a critical social psychological approach called social constructionism.

Social constructionism

As an approach, *social constructionism* has its roots in work undertaken by Gergen (1973) and Berger and Luckmann (1967). The basic idea is that because social life is ever-changing all we can try and do is to ask how the world looks at the point of time at which we are looking at it. For social constructionists, any knowledge we have of the social world is created (or constructed) by language, culture and history (McGhee, 2001).

The way in which we understand the world does not show how the world really is. That is to say,

experiments do not reflect objective reality. Reality is argued to be constructed by people in their everyday interactions. For social constructionists, experiments do not allow for context to play a role. To understand human behaviour and existence you need to study what people say, in what contexts, and take into account the person's own personal history as well as your own (Gough and McFadden, 2001). An example of this is discourse analysis, which is described later in this chapter.

Social constructionists have criticised 'scientific' or experimental social psychology as being too positivistic. *Positivism* is the non-critical acceptance that science is the best and only way to arrive at a true understanding of what is going on in the social world. It is argued that because, ultimately, social psychologists are actually studying themselves, because they are interested in human behaviour and experience, they cannot be totally objective in their interpretations of behaviour. Because psychologists cannot be objective, then the scientific methods that have been used in experimental social psychology can be questioned.

Some would argue that social psychology can at best only pretend to be an objective science. It can never be a true science in the sense that chemistry, physics and biology are (see Stainton Rogers, 2003; see also Chapter 5 of this book).

We have already seen in our look at social cognition – and will also see throughout all the chapters in this section on social psychology – that experimental social psychology is based on a number of core processes. These are virtually laws and give reasons why we behave in predictable ways. These processes describe how our perception of the social world around us uses cognition, or thinking, to guide the behaviours we produce. These processes include causal attribution, categorisation (how people organise and think about information perceived from the social world) and attention (how people may selectively seek out certain information to guide behaviour and interpretation).

Social constructionists, and other critical social psychologists, argue that these fundamental processes are only estimations or approximations to explain observations that are biased by our own lack of objectivity. Also, they argue that the scientific approach acts to dehumanise people by considering them as objects that are manipulated in the experimental setting.

So social constructionism seeks to understand people as whole human beings that are constructed by the historical and cultural context within which they exist. Experimental methods and quantitative data analysis are not useful in understanding the 'real' constructed person because they are too objective. Social constructionists therefore rely on more qualitative approaches (see the section on discourse analysis, below) that allow more in-depth and subjective accounts of how people think, feel and behave.

They believe that language is central to understanding the constructions people hold about their social worlds. For them, language is not just seen as a communication tool for conveying our feelings and thoughts, it is an action that performs the role of helping with the construction of the social world.

Research methods in social psychology

In this section we will take a brief look at the numerous methods that are used in social psychological studies. As you will have seen in Chapter 3, psychologists have traditionally adopted the scientific method. You will also have seen that this scientific method involves us stating precise predictions, or hypotheses, about how one variable affects another.

Social psychology is no exception to this rule. If we see social psychology as a science then there are broadly three types of research method that are employed (see Manstead and Semin, 2001). These are descriptive research, correlational research and experimental research.

Descriptive research

This approach is concerned with getting an accurate description of behaviour. The question we ask is 'Does behaviour X happen?' For instance, in Chapter 25 you will come across Stanley Milgram's work on obedience to authority (e.g. Milgram, 1974). The question he initially asked was 'How many people would obey orders from an authority figure?' To get

an answer to this he observed people in a situation in which they were asked to deliver electric shocks to other people. Milgram's answer was that about 65 per cent of his participants were completely obedient to an authority figure's request. But why? To go some way to answering this 'Why?' question, social psychologists use either correlational methods or experimental methods (see also Chapter 39).

Correlational research

The question we ask here is 'Is variable X related to variable Y?' If we use the Milgram example again here, the question could be 'Do those people who obey orders from authority figures tend to be particular types of individuals?' For instance, we may be interested in finding out whether introverts are more likely to obey than extroverts. So the question we are asking is 'Is there an association or relationship between personality type and obedience to authority?'

While finding relationships between variables is a useful step in helping psychologists to understand why two variables may correlate, such work is limited because it does not allow us to see whether one variable caused another. For this we must turn to experimental work.

Experimental research

This type of research is designed to get to the cause of observed phenomena. Using experiments, social psychologists see what happens to one measured variable when they deliberately manipulate other factors in the environment. The question we ask is 'By changing variable X (the independent variable) will there be a change in variable Y (the dependent variable)?' For example, you may be interested in finding out whether people on average make more risky decisions when they are in a group of people than when they are alone (see Chapter 25). You might, on the other hand, be interested in seeing whether 'scaring' smokers with information about the risks of continuing smoking – like telling them that their chances of dying from lung cancer are significantly increased – changes their beliefs about smoking and the likelihood that they will give up (take a look at the attitude change and persuasion sections in Chapter 22). In this second example we're asking the question 'Are smoking-related beliefs and actual smoking cessation changed when a smoker is given information about the health risks of continuing smoking?'

Throughout this section on social psychology you will come across many examples of the experimental approach in operation. For instance, you will see work from Asch (1956) in Chapter 24 that looked at whether first impressions count in impression formation.

Having looked briefly at the types of research approaches that social psychologists use, let's take a look at some of the important research strategies that are used in these approaches.

Research strategies in social psychology

The types of research strategies used by social psychologists can broadly be divided into two types: experimental and non-experimental methods.

Experimental methods

Social psychologists use laboratory-based experiments and field experiments. Laboratory-based studies enable the researcher to control many potentially confounding variables when looking at the effects of manipulating one variable (the independent variable) on another variable (the dependent variable).

For instance, we may want to look at the effects of an audience on how a person performs on a task. To do this we would get a person to do the task under conditions where they were being watched by others or were alone (see Chapter 25). Task performance is the dependent variable, and the presence or absence of an audience the independent variable. If all other confounding variables are controlled for in the laboratory, by comparing performance levels between the audience and no audience conditions we can see whether or not a difference in performance is dependent upon being watched. Laboratory experiments are useful because they let us claim that one variable *caused* an effect in another.

Field experiments are those that are undertaken outside the laboratory in the 'field', or the real world. In these circumstances not as many confounding variables can be controlled for and the exact

relationship between variables is more difficult to claim. We could do the audience experiment in the field. We could go to a gym and observe how people behave under conditions of being alone on a treadmill as compared with being watched by the experimenter or any number of other people.

Non-experimental methods

In some instances either it is not possible or it is inappropriate to use an experiment to test a particular idea or hypothesis. For example, some variables cannot be manipulated so that we can see their effects on other variables. We cannot change a person's gender, for example, if we are interested in looking at the effects of gender on exposure to media violence.

In the same vein, at times we cannot manipulate particular variables for ethical reasons (see the section on this later in the chapter). For instance, it would not be ethically correct to expose people to a violent attack from somebody else because we wanted to look at what effect this would have on levels of self-esteem, depression or anxiety.

It is for this reason that social psychologists also use non-experimental methods in their research. These include survey research, archival studies and field studies. On the whole these approaches do not allow us to claim that one variable caused an effect in another. This is because non-experimental methods do not involve the manipulation of one variable and testing its effect on another variable. The best we can usually do is claim that there is a relationship between the variables being studied (i.e. a correlation).

Survey research

Survey research is a widely used tool for acquiring data. Just think of the number of times you have been approached on the street and asked if you would mind spending a few minutes answering questions about this, that or the other. Think too about the numbers of occasions you have seen this or that public opinion poll in the media, showing so many people are in favour of whatever.

These are examples of survey research. To get the data, researchers either ask people directly about their opinions and note down the answers that are given, or else the respondents are asked to fill in a questionnaire containing a number of items relevant to the topic area. The questions people are asked are not just plucked out of thin air – the survey instrument has usually been through an intensive pilot phase so that the researchers can be fairly sure that the questions they are asking are relevant to the issue they are studying. People's responses might even be tape-recorded so that the researcher does not have to note everything down.

The important point about survey research is that the people asked to answer the questions (known as the sample) are representative of the population from which they are drawn. For example, it would not be representative if the only people asked about whom they were going to vote for in the next election were young when we know that they make up only a small proportion of the population as a whole. The researchers would not be able to claim that the sample opinions were representative of the true population picture.

Archival research

This involves researchers using data and information gathered by others in the past to study the question they are interested in. This sort of data can involve diaries and media accounts (from the television, radio, the newspapers and so on), as well as biographies about events or even autobiographies of people involved in events.

In Chapter 25 you'll come across an example of this approach in action. We'll look at how Janis (1982) used other people's reports, and also media reports of events surrounding various situations in which groups had made disastrous decisions, in developing his theory of groupthink. As you will see when you read Chapter 25, groupthink describes which factors are important for describing the circumstances important for group decision-making in stressful situations.

Field studies

Field studies involve the observation and recording of naturally occurring events and behaviour. For instance, we might want to look at how people behave while drinking alcohol. So we go to a pub to observe and record how people are behaving. Compare this to the field experiment in which we manipulate one variable and see its effects on another. In the field study there is no manipulation of variables.

As we have seen, some people question the idea that social psychology is a science and as such is accountable to the laws of science through experimentation. If we seek to understand the 'true' nature of human behaviour by trying to understand people as whole human beings, and not as the by-products of experimental manipulations, we need to adopt a more in-depth qualitative approach for research. Qualitative methods allow researchers to focus more on the qualities or characteristics of a person's behaviour.

With the continuing interest in social constructionism as another approach to understanding social psychology, researchers have been using other techniques in designing and analysing their studies. These include grounded theory, conversation analysis and the Q method (see Stainton Rogers, 2003), although the most widely used is discourse analysis.

Discourse analysis

This approach was developed by Jonathan Potter and Margaret Wetherell (1987). It involves the detailed analysis of language that is provided from a number of sources. These include the texts of interview transcripts, newspaper and other media articles, and even the transcripts of people in conversation.

Discourse analysis does not try to test causal predictions or hypotheses. The idea is that the person using discourse analysis provides a 'reading' or 'interpretative account' of the text or conversation. Of course, the researcher's account itself then becomes a source of text for the next discourse analyst! Discourse analysis allows the researcher to study how talk is used to manage interactions between people.

Discourse analysis has a number of aims, as described below.

Isolating the interpretative repertoires of discourse
Interpretative repertoires are the types of metaphors and images we use in everyday talk to

construct an object. According to Wetherell, these *interpretative repertoires* are 'sets of recurrent and coherently related stylistic, grammatical and lexical features . . . including metaphors . . . and figures of speech' (1997: 162). For any object in our social world there will be range of these repertoires that we can and do use. In addition, the same person can use these repertoires in contradictory ways depending upon the context of the interpersonal situation, including the goals that people bring to their interactions.

An example of the types of repertoire that people may use about a particular issue is given by McGhee (2001). He identifies two repertoires that may be used when discussing 'students in higher education'. One interpretative repertoire is that students are lazy, always drunk, drug-crazed, left-wing, irresponsible and enjoying three years of loan-funded clubbing. Another is that students are poor, brainy bookworms who struggle day in and day out to make ends meet, while keeping up with university assessments and assignments. These repertoires may be used by the same person discussing the category 'students' and, as you can see, can be contradictory.

Looking at how rhetorical actions are achieved in talk

When discourse analysts talk about rhetorical actions they mean those that are used for communicating and persuading when interacting with another. So, for example, the use of blaming, justification and presenting information as fact are all examples of rhetorical actions.

The most common use of discourse analysis is with interview transcripts between a researcher and a participant or group. For example, Reavey and Gough (2000) were interested in the subject of childhood sexual abuse. They interviewed ten counsellors, therapists and psychiatrists, and studied how their discourses reflected how female abuse survivors were seen (see Applications Box 21.1).

Whatever the approach we take in designing and running studies that involve trying to understand how people think, feel and behave, we need to be aware of a number of ethical issues. It is to this area that we will turn now.

APPLICATIONS BOX 21.1

Therapists' constructions of women survivors of childhood sexual abuse

The extract below is taken from interview transcripts reported by Reavey and Gough (2000). In this study they interviewed ten professional therapists, such as psychiatrists, counsellors and clinical psychologists, on the area of childhood sexual abuse. The study aimed to explore how female abuse survivors were positioned in professionals' discourses in terms of sexuality and also femininity.

Take a look at the transcript example below. Remember that the researcher and the participant are discussing the female abuse survivors.

The following is an extract of part of the interview between the researcher and a clinical psychologist called Oliver.

Oliver: I think always, think the choice of partners often fascinating.
Researcher: Right, why?
Oliver: So often they choose a partner who will in turn abuse them in some form.
Researcher: Right.
Oliver: Cos it's like, it's almost like kids build up some kind of internal working model of um the environment still being abusive in some way, and I think in some unwitting way also [women] seek that out, it's like that's what you know . . .

In this extract women survivors of childhood sexual abuse are constructed by Oliver as making illogical or irrational choices of partner. In fact he constructs these women as recreating the abusive scenario in their choice of partner.

Ethics in social psychology

When doing social psychological studies we have to take account of a number of ethical issues. For example, is it right or ethical to put people into a situation in which they may feel uncomfortable or that might lead to longer-term suffering? Is it ethically sound deliberately to deceive a study participant?

FOCUS POINT 21.3

Zimbardo and colleagues' prison study

Participants were recruited for the study through newspaper advertisements. They were told that they were needed for a study of prison life and that the study would last for two weeks. In total, 24 males were accepted on to the study. They were all emotionally and physically healthy. They did not have any criminal convictions and had not been in trouble with the police. In other words, they did not differ very much in their personal characteristics.

In the summer of 1971 the basement of Stanford University's psychology department was converted into a mock prison. The idea was to recreate the prison environment as closely as possible so as to look at the impact of prison life on people who live or work in prison.

The participants were randomly assigned to be either a prisoner or guard in the simulation. The experiment began with the arrest by local police of those who would be portraying prisoners. The participants were not expecting to be arrested like this. Think, though, whether this part of the experiment is ethically sound. Should people be subjected to something they are not expecting in this way?

Having been arrested the participants were charged, searched, handcuffed and taken to the police station. From the police station they were then taken, still handcuffed and now also blindfolded, to the mock prison.

On arrival at the prison they were stripped naked, searched again, deloused and issued with standard prison clothes. They also had a chain placed around one of their ankles. The prisoners were only referred to by their prison numbers, which were on the front and back of their uniforms. The guards wore standard uniforms and carried clubs, whistles, handcuffs and keys.

The prison was guarded all day, every day by the guards, who worked eight-hour shifts. The guards had complete control over the prisoners. One point to remember is that none of the participants had been told or instructed how to behave – they were just given the role of either prisoner or guard.

It wasn't long until the guards became quite abusive and aggressive towards the prisoners, who themselves became very passive. After 36 hours one prisoner had to be released because he was showing signs of being very affected by the experience. He cried uncontrollably and seemed to be depressed. Another three of the prisoners were also released over the next few days for similar reasons. The prisoners were completely demoralised. It was no surprise that after six days the experiment was halted.

The important point about this study is that it showed the effect of a situation on how a person behaves and how roles can easily be adopted. Do you think you would have behaved as the guards did? If not, why not?

An often cited example here is Milgram's work on obedience to authority, which is dealt with in some detail in Chapter 25. Another example is the infamous prison study (the 'Stanford prison experiment') undertaken by Philip Zimbardo and his colleagues on social roles and power in social situations (Haney, Banks and Zimbardo, 1973) (see Focus Point 21.3).

The results obtained from Milgram's work and also from that of Zimbardo are important because they spawned a great deal of interest in obedience, conformity and power relations. (You may recall that Zimbardo's study was replicated in a television show on British television in 2002 (see Reicher and Haslam, 2002).)

When undertaking social psychological studies we are guided by a number of ethical principles, as described below. (For a broader view of ethical issues in psychology generally, see Chapter 36.)

Protection of participants from harm

This includes both physical and mental harm. We should design our studies so that people participating in them are not subjected to any form of physical or mental harm. At times this is very difficult to achieve. For example, getting a person who has been involved in a serious road accident and then asking them about the accident could lead that person to feel anxious or a bit 'down'. The act of recalling the accident itself could be in some way harmful. One way to help reduce this effect is to debrief the participant fully (see below).

Right to privacy

Many social psychological studies involve situations in which a person's privacy is to some extent invaded. Examples here include studies that observe people without their knowledge, or that ask very intimate questions. The question we need to ask ourselves is whether the research aims justify this invasion of privacy. For example, asking people about committing an illegal act, like drink-driving (Albery and Guppy, 1995), is fundamental if we are to understand what motivates these people to behave in the ways they do. To get around the problem of privacy we ensure that any information we get from participants is completely confidential. No one knows who said what, who ticked which box on a questionnaire or who responded in a particular way to a computer-generated task.

Deception

To avoid bias in responding, people taking part in experimental research are usually not told what the hypotheses of the study are. Experimenters sometimes do not say what the true nature of an experiment is. People are deceived. With the odd exception (such as Milgram's obedience work) most social psychological studies involve trivial deception. For example, social influence studies might be advertised as being studies to do with group decision-making.

Informed consent

Before the study people should be asked to consent freely to taking part in it. This means that they are provided with full information about the study so that they are in a position to make their consent in an informed way. Also participants are assured that

Two images from Zimbardo's prison experiment

they can withdraw at any point from the study. Theoretically, this is all fine. However, in practice it is not always that clear what 'full information' means. For example, some studies might require that the person is not told about the precise study aims or is deceived in some way.

Debriefing

This is a very important ethical principle. After finishing the experiment people should be told about the experiment, what was expected and what the significance of the work they have just taken part in is. This full debriefing can be quite time-consuming but is fundamental, especially in those studies that have involved any sort of deception.

Learning outcomes

When you have completed this chapter you should be able to:

- describe how social psychology has been defined
- describe and evaluate the historical background to the study of social psychology

- critically assess a number of paradigms that have been developed in the general area of social psychology
- describe how social cognition as a scientific account is consistent with or differs from social constructionism as a critical account

- describe key experimental and non-experimental methods used in social psychology
- evaluate the role of ethical considerations in the area of social psychology.

Key Terms

Associative network
Cognitive miser
Discourse analysis
Interpretative repertoires
Motivated tactician
Naïve scientist
Positivism
Schema
Social cognition
Social constructionism
Social facilitation
Social psychology
Stereotype
Völkerpsychologie

Further reading

Fiedler, K. and Bless, H. (2001) Social cognition. In Hewstone, M. and Stroebe, W. (eds) *Introduction to Social Psychology* (3rd edn). Oxford: Blackwell, 115–50.

Fiske, S. E. and Taylor, S. T. (1991) *Social Cognition* (2nd edn). New York: McGraw-Hill.

Gough, B. and McFadden, M. (2001) *Critical Social Psychology: An Introduction.* Basingstoke: Palgrave,

Manstead, A. S. R. and Semin, G. R. (2001) Methodology in social psychology: tools to test theories. In Hewstone, M. and Stroebe, W. (eds) *Introduction to Social Psychology* (3rd edn). Oxford: Blackwell, 73–110.

McGhee, P. (2001) *Thinking Psychologically.* Basingstoke: Palgrave.

Stainton Rogers, W. (2003) *Social Psychology: Experimental and Critical Approaches.* Buckingham: Open University Press.

22

Attitudes, persuasion and attitude change

Route map of the chapter

The aim of this chapter is to present you with an overview of attitudes, persuasion processes and attitude change. Initially, we will explore how the term 'attitude' has been defined, what functions attitudes serve, how attitudes are structured, how they develop and how we measure them. We then move on to look at the relationship between attitudes and behaviour, and at what psychologists know about how attitudes change. Finally, we look at how people may be persuaded to change their attitudes and, theoretically, their behaviour.

Introduction

Unlike some psychological terms, attitude is part of our everyday, or common-sense, language. We try to explain our own and other people's behaviour

Ask these people and they'd report negative attitudes towards the 2003 war in Iraq!

towards another person or issue in terms of our own or others' attitudes towards that person or issue.

For instance, ask yourself why so many people demonstrated against the war in Iraq in spring 2003. What could account for the fact that millions of people took to the streets in London, Paris and across the world? Your answer is likely to focus on the types of attitudes these people had towards the war in Iraq or conflict in general. You might explain the demonstrators' behaviour by saying that 'the marchers had a negative attitude towards the war, they were anti-war and pro-peace'. It is this sort of language we use when talking about our own and other people's attitudes.

Attitudes have been of interest to social psychologists for many years. Some have argued that social psychology as a discipline is really the scientific study of attitudes (Watson, 1930). The prominence of attitudes as a theme was highlighted as early as 1935 when Gordon Allport commented on the importance of attitude work (see Focus Point 22.1).

In this chapter we look at a number of key questions about attitudes (see the list below), and the theories and evidence behind these questions.

1 How do we define attitudes? How are attitudes structured? Are attitudes made up of distinct and predictable psychological components?
2 How do we develop the attitudes we hold about particular issues, events or people?
3 How do we measure attitudes?
4 How do attitudes relate to behaviour? Is how people behave towards an 'attitude object'

dependent on their thoughts and feelings towards that object?

5 Are an individual's attitudes stable over time or do they change? Which factors are important in describing how and why attitudes may alter?

6 How can we persuade people to change their attitudes?

These questions have been of enduring interest to social psychologists over the past 80 years (Stainton Rogers, Stenner, Gleeson and Stainton Rogers, 1995; Eagly and Chaiken, 1998). However, the first thing we need to do is to define what we mean by 'attitude'.

Defining attitude

An *attitude* is a hypothetical construct. As a hypothetical construct an attitude cannot be directly observed, it can only be inferred from other responses that *can* be observed (such as what a person says about what they think and how they feel towards an attitude object). Attitude objects (those things we have attitudes about) may be concrete (e.g. Brussels sprouts), abstract (e.g. Marxism), people

---

ACTIVITY BOX 22.1

The war in Iraq

You will probably remember that in 2003 the UK, the USA and some other countries went to war with Iraq. Were you pro- or anti-war? Write down as many attitudes of yours that you can towards the war in Iraq, then think about the following questions.

1 What do you think caused you to hold the attitudes you have towards the war?

2 Do you think you would hold different attitudes if the coalition had had the backing of the United Nations?

3 Have your attitudes changed in the aftermath of the war?

4 What role did the media play in your attitudes towards the war?

5 Did you ever find yourself doubting your attitudes after discussing the war with other people? If so, why do you think this was?

FOCUS POINT 22.1

The importance of attitudes

According to Allport (1935: 798), 'The concept of attitudes is probably the most distinctive and indispensable concept in contemporary American social psychology. No other term appears more frequently in the experimental and theoretical literature.'

(e.g. President George W. Bush), groups of people (e.g. immigrants) and even inanimate objects (e.g. telephones). Our behaviour towards another person is assumed to be the result of the attitude we hold about that object. These general comments show that numerous definitions have been offered for the term 'attitude' (see also Focus Point 22.2).

When we think about a social object or some other social stimulus we evaluate it by asking ourselves how positive or negative it is. Do we like or dislike the object? For some psychologists this liking or disliking, or the feelings we have about an object, forms the basis of what attitudes are about (Petty and Cacioppo, 1996).

Functions of attitudes

Why have attitudes? What purpose do they serve for us? Shavitt (1989) proposes four different functions for attitudes:

1 maintenance of self-esteem

2 a utilitarian function

3 a knowledge function

4 a social identity function.

We will now look at each of these in turn.

Section 5
Social Psychology

Some definitions of attitude

'... a psychological tendency that is expressed by evaluating a particular entity with some degree of favour or disfavour. ... Evaluating refers to all classes of responding, whether overt or covert, cognitive, affective or behavioural' (Eagly and Chaiken, 1993: 1).

'... a summary evaluation of an object of thought. An attitude object can be anything a person discriminates or holds in mind. Attitude objects may be concrete (e.g. pizza) or abstract (e.g. freedom of speech), may be inanimate things (e.g. sports cars), persons (e.g. Slobodan Milosevic, oneself) or groups (e.g. conservative politicians, foreigners' (Bohner and Wänke, 2002: 5).

'... a mental and neural state of readiness, organised through experience, exerting a distinctive or dynamic influence upon the individual's response to all objects and situations with which it is related' (Allport, 1935: 810).

'... an evaluative disposition toward some object. It's an evaluation of something or someone along a continuum of like-to-dislike or favourable-to-disfavourable' (Zimbardo and Lieppe, 1991).

Maintaining self-esteem

This assumes that negative attitudes operate to distance us from others or groups of others that may pose a threat, like minorities or out-groups (see Chapter 25). For example, being a member of the far-right political wing will not be beneficial for your own self-esteem if you define yourself as the typical student who traditionally holds opposing political views. As such you'll likely have a negative attitude towards these groups.

At the same time, positive attitudes serve the function of aligning us with favoured groups. For example, back in 1930s Germany you would probably have had a more favourable attitude towards the far right and Nazism in particular. In psychoanalytic terms these factors can be seen as acting in an ego-defensive way (Katz, 1960).

Utilitarian function

This approach is based on operant learning processes (see Chapter 8). It means that attitudes are used to gain positive outcomes and at the same time avoid negative outcomes. In essence, we favour or disfavour attitude objects because they become associated with punishments and rewards and we learn to adapt our behaviour to maximise reward and minimise punishment. We might, for instance, come to learn that aligning ourselves with the views of a 'popular' group (e.g. the 'in-crowd') will result in us getting social approval from other group members. Also behaving in ways consistent with those views and in ways consistent with other members of the group will again result in positive reinforcement.

Knowledge function

All attitudes serve a knowledge function inasmuch as they help us to organise our social worlds. They provide a means of interacting with and making sense of events in our environment (Smith *et al.*, 1956). Social cognitive accounts see attitudes as types of schema that guide the information processing of socially relevant experiences (Fiske and Taylor, 1991; Eagly and Chaiken, 1993). This 'guiding' role makes it easier for us to respond to objects in consistent ways. Attitudes allow us to think about how to respond to objects in our environment without too much effort.

Social identity function

Basically, attitudes enable us to express our individual core values. Katz (1960) called this the value-expressive function. Expressing our attitudes also allows us to establish an identification with other groups (Smith *et al.*, 1956). For instance, wearing a replica Chelsea football shirt acts as a marker of identification with other Chelsea fans.

Having looked at what functions attitudes serve for us in our social world we now turn to the issue of how attitudes are structured in our minds.

The structure of attitudes

Over the years psychologists have argued about the structure of attitudes. As we have seen, some believed that an attitude equals a general evaluation of an object (Edwards, 1957; Petty and Cacioppo, 1981). This evaluation represents an emotional judgement – how an individual feels towards an object – and has been called the *unidimensional approach* (Thurston, 1930; Petty and Cacioppo, 1981). But is that all there is to an attitude as an evaluative tool? Are attitude objects only evaluated on the basis of how they make us feel? Proponents of the *multidimensional approach* think not (Rosenberg and Hovland, 1960; Eagly and Chaiken, 1993).

As shown in Figure 22.1, psychologists have argued that there are three types of responses that are used when we evaluate another person's behaviour or other attitude object. These evaluation types can be summarised by the acronym ABC: affective, behavioural and cognitive components. The cognitive component refers to the thoughts people have about the attitude object. The affective component (or emotional component) refers to the

feelings or emotions that we have about the attitude object. Finally, there's the behavioural, or conative, component.

This last component has consistently been confused as meaning that instead of predicting actual behaviour, behaviour itself is part of the attitude. This is not the case. The behavioural component does not refer to actual behaviour but *intentions* to behave. In other words, our attitudes are made up of our thoughts, feelings and behavioural intentions towards the attitude object.

The important point about the multidimensional approach is that there is no inconsistency between the cognitive, affective and behavioural responses to an attitude object. In other words, the way we feel about an object is usually consistent with our beliefs about that object. The three components of this model are thought of as being of equal importance for the definition and expression of an attitude. An individual expresses an attitude when he or she has thought about the object, interpreted how they feel about it and understood the different ways of responding to it.

As an example, take a positive attitude towards New Labour. According to the multidimensional approach this positive attitude will comprise thoughts and expectations that, for example,

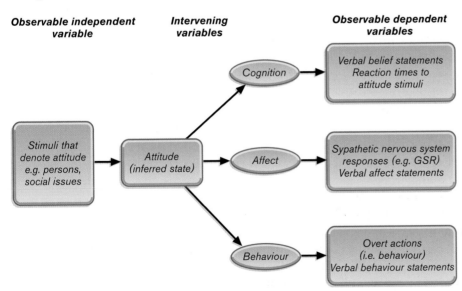

Figure 22.1 The three-component view of attitude structure
Source: developed from Eagly and Chaiken, 1993: 10

university students will not have to pay for their education (a positive belief or cognition), a liking or respect for New Labour representatives (a positive feeling or affect) and the intention to join the Labour Party (positive behavioural intention).

Since attitudes are the process through which we evaluate social objects, it seems reasonable that attitudes need to be represented in a person's memory. So when an attitude object is encountered, the memory for the response to that attitude has to be retrieved. This retrieval can either be deliberate and controlled or spontaneous and uncontrolled (i.e. automatic).

For instance, when asked to make a judgement about an attitude object (in other words consciously deliberate) a person will construct their response from what they have stored in memory about that object (Schwartz and Bonner, 2003). Alternatively, the mere presence of the attitude object itself without any conscious awareness of the judgement process is enough to elicit an evaluative response from memory. These have been called *implicit attitudes* (Greenwald and Banaji, 1995).

Attitude development

Up to this point we have seen how attitudes have been defined by psychologists, what functions attitudes serve for us, and how attitudes are structured and organised in our minds. We now turn to how attitudes develop.

Although some have argued that attitudes are derived from a genetic or biological basis (see Waller, Kojetin, Bouchard, Lykken and Tellegen, 1990), most social psychologists think, or believe, that attitudes develop as a result of experience – they are learnt in some way.

Allport (1935) believed that attitudes are learnt by the same principles as other learnt responses. The result of this learning experience is that a new or redefined attitude is stored in memory for future use when the same attitude object is encountered (Eagly and Chaiken, 1993). *Operant conditioning* and *classical conditioning* have been massively influential in the study of learning processes in general, and the formation of attitudes is no exception. (Turn to Chapter 8 for a description of the principles involved in operant and classical conditioning.)

One early but influential study using operant conditioning principles was conducted by Hildum and Brown (1956). In this study participants were asked questions about their university education policies. Some participants were reinforced when their answers were favourable about the policies, and others were reinforced when their answers were unfavourable. Also for half the participants the verbal reinforcement was the word 'good' and for the other half it was 'mm-hmmm'. The study showed that 'good' was more successful in getting the required conditioning response from the individual (i.e. either favourable or unfavourable attitudes).

Insko (1965) replicated these results but found, in addition, that participants who were conditioned to express positive attitudes also showed greater favourability a week later. The same was true for those conditioned to show more negative opinions.

Other psychologists have described how classical conditioning operates in the development of attitudes. The most influential of these is Arthur Staats (see Staats, 1983, for an overview of his ideas). He argued that people learn attitudes in much the same way as Pavlov's dogs learned to salivate on the presentation of a light or sound.

He showed that with the experience of emotional responses (feelings of uneasiness or pleasure) a person learns the evaluative message of words like 'good' and 'bad' because these words (the conditioned stimuli) are paired with unconditioned stimuli, such as physical punishment or the desire to be respected by others. These established attitudes are then available as unconditioned stimuli and, when paired with other conditioned stimuli, will produce a new conditioned response.

These ideas can be used to understand how people come to hold prejudiced attitudes towards minority groups. For instance, imagine that, while growing up, a child repeatedly hears words like 'bad', 'stupid', 'untrustworthy', paired with the name of minority groups (e.g. illegal immigrants, Jews). Over time it is likely that this repeated pairing will result in a conditioned response – in this case a negative attitude towards minority groups. If attitudes guide behaviour, it may be that some people will then act on their learning experience. (See Chapter 25 for a discussion of prejudice.)

Measuring attitudes

Attitudes cannot be observed directly. Because of this, psychologists have had to find ways of measuring them, either directly or indirectly. Direct measures usually involve asking a person about their attitudes and beliefs towards another social object or issue, whereas indirect measures use other cues to *infer* the attitude the person holds. Some indirect measures have been designed to measure the attitudes that people are even unaware that they hold – these are called implicit attitudes.

Direct measurement

The most common form of direct measurement is to question a person about their attitudes towards an object and ask them to mark their response on a numeric response scale. The most frequently used of these are the *Likert scale* (Likert, 1932) and the *semantic differential scale* (Osgood *et al.*, 1957). These will be the focus of this section (other less frequently used techniques are the Thurstone scale and the Guttman scale).

The scales are all known as multi-item scales because they use more than one statement to tap the overall attitude towards an object (see Oppenheim, 1992, and Bohner and Wänke, 2002, for reviews of these scales). Research Methods Box 22.1 gives examples of semantic differential and Likert-type scales.

RESEARCH METHODS BOX 22.1

Examples of semantic differential and Likert scales

Likert scale

Items assessing primary healthcare workers' attitudes towards working with drug users (from Albery, Heuston, Ward, Groves, Durand, Gossop and Strang, 2003). Each statement is presented with a scale ranging from 1 to 7: 1 represents total disagreement and 7 total agreement. Higher scores indicate a more favourable attitude towards working with drug users. Because of this the item marked with an asterisk (*) is reverse-scored before analysis.

- I often feel uncomfortable when working with problem drug users.*
- One can get satisfaction from working with problem drug users.
- It is rewarding to work with problem drug users.
- I feel I can understand problem drug users.
- I like problem drug users.

Semantic differential

Applied to attitudes towards using cannabis in the next three months (from Conner and McMillan, 1999).

Using cannabis in the next three months would be …
Bad   −3 −2 −1 0 +1 +2 +3 Good
Pleasant +3 +2 +1 0 −1 −2 −3 Unpleasant

Higher scores indicate a more positive attitude towards using cannabis in the next three months.

In the Likert method people rate how far they agree or disagree with a number of statements. These statements are designed to measure aspects of the overall attitude towards an object or issue. The statements are usually derived from extensive pilot work that includes many more statements than those actually used. The statements selected are those for which agreement unambiguously corresponds to either a positive or negative attitude. The ratings are on five- or seven-point scales, and are summed to get the overall attitude score.

Semantic differential scales are made up of what are known as bipolar adjective scales. They are bipolar in the sense that one end of the scale is marked with one adjective, such as 'Good', while the other end is marked with the opposite of 'Good' (i.e. 'Bad'). These scales are usually divided into seven response categories and are scored -3 to +3, with positive numbers for the positive adjective (e.g. 'good') and negative numbers for the negative adjective (e.g. 'bad'). The ratings are summed across all differentials to arrive at the overall attitude score for each person.

The main criticism levelled at direct measure techniques is that because people know that their attitudes are being measured they may respond in ways that are not consistent with their 'real' attitudes (a validity issue). This is known as 'impression management'.

The 'bogus pipeline technique' (Jones and Sigall, 1971) was designed to counteract this. Basically, a participant is rigged to what they are told is a psychophysiological indicator of a person's true attitudes. A few practice trials are then given. In these the participant knowingly gives some false answers to questions that the experimenter knows are actually correct. This demonstrates how powerful the bogus pipeline apparatus is – it has the effect of removing the participant's motivation to distort responses.

Another way to minimise the risk of impression management is by using indirect measures of attitudes.

Indirect measurement

Numerous methods have been introduced to measure attitudes indirectly, including projective techniques and physiological measures, such as galvanic skin response (GSR). The chances of getting 'real' attitudes is thought to be increased if the participant is not aware that their attitudes are being studied. (Note that, with physiological measures, although a person may know their attitudes are being measured they do not have control over their physiological responses.)

One interesting example of an indirect measure is the lost-letter technique (Milgram *et al.*, 1965). This involved leaving addressed letters in public places as if they had been lost and then recording how many were returned or posted on, and also the condition of the letter. The attitude object was given by the address printed on the letter. Examples from Milgram's studies included the Friends of the Nazi Party, the Friends of the Communist Party and Medical Research Associates. The assumption was that people with positive attitudes towards the object would post the letter back unopened. (A more up-to-date version of this procedure is the lost e-mail technique (Stern and Faber, 1997).)

Other indirect measures developed out of the need to produce techniques that could measure unconscious cognitive processes – those thoughts that are automatic or spontaneous (Bargh, 1997). The possibility of implicit attitudes, or evaluations, which are out of our conscious control, has led to the development of priming techniques (Greenwald and Banaji, 1995; Fazio *et al.*, 1996). In a *priming paradigm* an uncontroversial target word (e.g. 'untrustworthy') is presented immediately after the participant has been exposed to the attitude object (e.g. 'estate agents'). By pressing response keys, participants are asked to respond as quickly as they can to the target word in terms of how 'good' or 'bad' it is. If evaluations of the prime and the target word are the same (e.g. for those people who have a negative attitude towards estate agents) responses to the target should be quicker than if evaluations are incongruent. The idea is that the prime serves to activate the evaluative response in memory and make it more accessible when other consistent stimuli are encountered.

Another indirect measure is the *implicit association test* (Greenwald, McGhee and Schwartz, 1998). This measures people's implicit attitudes – or those attitudes that are not available to conscious reflection – by measuring the strength of association between a category, concept or person (like Tony Blair) and an evaluation (like 'good' or 'bad') (see Bohner and Wänke, 2002: 41–5, for a detailed description of the test).

The attitude–behaviour relationship

We've already seen that the attitude a person holds about an object is supposed to predict how they behave towards it. Is this true? Some psychologists have reported low attitude–behaviour correspondence or correlation (e.g. Wicker, 1969; Sutton, 1998). Wicker (1969), for instance, reported correlations that ranged between .00 and .30.

LaPiere's (1934) study was one of the first to question attitude–behaviour consistency. In the company of two Chinese people, LaPiere travelled around the USA staying in various hotels and motels. Their expectation was that they would encounter attitudes of an anti-Chinese nature and that they would not find it easy to get accommodation. This was not the case and very few hotel managers refused them accommodation. However, when these same hotels were sent a letter asking whether they would accept Chinese guests, over 90 per cent replied 'No'. There is a clear inconsistency here between attitudes and actual behaviour.

Although this seems to confirm the adage that 'the only completely consistent persons are dead' (Aldous Huxley, novelist, 1894–1963), some psychologists have argued that evidence such as LaPiere's does not give a true reflection of the attitude–behaviour relationship. Fishbein and Ajzen (1975) and Ajzen (1988) in their *correspondence hypothesis* (also *principles of compatibility)* proposed that attitudes *do* predict behaviour – provided that specific behaviours are predicted from specific attitudes. In addition, because all behaviour is made up of specific actions, specific context, specific time and in response to a specific target, attitudinal measures have to reflect this specificity.

A study by Davidson and Jaccard (1979) highlights the importance of correspondence or compatibility. They looked at correlations between married women's attitudes towards birth control and the use of oral contraceptives over a two-year period. When 'attitude towards birth control' was used as the attitude measure, a low correlation was shown (r = .08). When 'attitude towards oral contraceptives' (r = .32), 'attitude towards using oral contraceptives' (r = .53) and 'attitude towards using oral contraceptives during the next two years' (r = .57) were used as attitude measures, the correlation increased steadily.

In this case it is clear that when action, object and time correspond, the attitude–behaviour relationship is more consistent. Context was not included in this study although, hypothetically, the inclusion of context would increase still further the relationship.

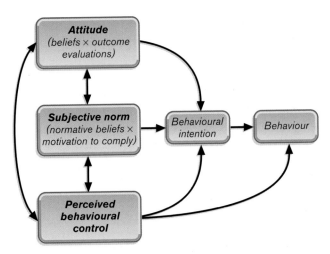

Figure 22.2 Ajzen's theory of planned behaviour

The theory of planned behaviour

Many studies have looked at the so-called attitude–behaviour relationship. One approach was Ajzen's (1991) *theory of planned behaviour* (*TPB*). He was interested in studying how the beliefs held by an individual are important for understanding how they decide to behave towards an attitude object and also how their beliefs predict how they subsequently behave. Ajzen's TPB model was derived from the earlier *theory of reasoned action* (*TRA*) (Fishbein and Ajzen, 1975) and differs only in that the TPB was aimed at understanding types of behaviour that are not necessarily under a person's volitional control.

Figure 22.2 shows the structure of the TPB. Basically, Ajzen proposed that beliefs are structured according to an *expectancy–value framework*. In other words, people hold expectancies about what *outcomes* they should get if they behave in a particular way. At the same time, they hold beliefs about the *value* of that outcome for themselves. So consider, for example, submitting your first essay on time; you may think that submitting your essay on time will result in the outcome of getting feedback before you sit your exam (outcome expectancy) and that getting feedback before your exam is a good thing (value association).

So if we look at Figure 22.2 we see that the immediate antecedent of actual behaviour is behavioural intention. If we intend to submit our first essay on time it is likely that we will. This intention to behave is determined by three belief-based factors: attitude, subjective norm and perceived behavioural control. Attitude is made up of core beliefs about the outcomes of a behaviour and the value we hold about these outcomes (we saw an example of this earlier). Subjective norms are those beliefs we have about how other important people want us to behave (normative beliefs) and the value we hold about behaving that way in line with others' wishes (motivation to comply).

Think back to the example of submitting your first essay on time. It may be that one of the people you believe wants you to submit your essay on time is your lecturer – and of course you'd be right! This is a normative belief. Of course, you like to do what your lecturer wants you to do; this then is motivation to comply. In this instance it is likely that you will form the intention to submit the essay on time.

Perceived behavioural control comprises those beliefs that relate to how much control a person thinks they have over a certain behaviour. For instance, you are likely to form an intention to submit your essay on time if you believe that it is under your own control. Ajzen argues that we hold many different types of association about single behaviours. It is the sum of these expectancy–value relations that predicts a person's intention to behave in that way, which subsequently predicts their actual behaviour.

Evidence suggests that the TRA and the TPB accurately predict between 40 and 50 per cent of variance in behavioural intention and between 19 and 38 per cent in actual behaviour (Sutton, 1998). Because of this there has been some speculation as to which other factors may be important as extensions to the TPB for predicting behavioural intention and actual behaviour. These include more affective factors, moral norms and self-identity (see Conner and Armitage, 1998; Sheeran, 2002).

One factor that has been the subject of considerable attention in recent years is habit or past behaviour. It is thought that the effect of past behaviour predicts behaviour directly, and that this relationship is not necessarily dependent upon subjective norms, attitude or perceived behavioural control (Bentler and Speckart, 1979; Triandis, 1980; Sutton, 1994; 1998).

Ouellette and Wood (1998) argue that past behaviours affect future behaviour in two ways. The first is that well-learned behaviours may occur repeatedly in the same context (e.g. wearing a seat-belt). For this reason, cognitive control over this behaviour eventually becomes automatic. Behaviours that are not so well learned, or those that occur in more unstable contexts, remain under conscious control.

The TPB is used extensively in health psychology to predict health-related behaviours (such as practising safe sex) and this use of the model is discussed in Chapter 35.

The dual-process model of attitude–behaviour relations

Fazio's (1990) *MODE model* (MODE stands for 'Motivation and Opportunities as DEterminants') studied the conditions under which attitudes towards an object predict behaviour automatically. Fazio proposes that when motivation and the opportunity to think consciously about a potential behaviour are low, attitudes towards the target will activate behaviour immediately and automatically – as long as these attitudes are accessible and easily retrievable from memory. When people can consciously deliberate about a behaviour and motivation is high, the automatic attitude–behaviour relationship will be overridden. In other words, the more we think about it, the more our behaviour will be characterised by *deliberative processing*. This is very similar to the dual-process model of persuasion presented later in this chapter.

Attitude change

We now turn to how and why attitudes change. Why do you think it is important for a person to change their attitudes? If we assume that attitudes are a predictor of behaviour, then there are ramifications for understanding behavioural change from altering attitudes. This is especially important nowadays in an applied context. For instance, because of the focus on understanding behaviours that are thought of as unhealthy, applied psychologists have undertaken to change behaviour by changing a person's attitude and beliefs towards that behaviour. Some examples of this are driving dangerously (e.g. Parker, Stradling and Manstead, 1996) or cyclists *not* wearing a cycle helmet when riding (Quine, Rutter and Arnold, 2002).

We are bombarded with education campaigns that try to alter our beliefs and convince us to drive less dangerously, to 'kill our speed, not a child', or to stop smoking. If we can identify which beliefs are important in an individual's decision to drive in a dangerous way, and actually change those beliefs, we should be able to change their behaviour. We will see a specific example of this when we look at persuasion models.

Our starting point for understanding attitude change is to examine those approaches that take as their starting point the idea that humans are motivated to maintain consistency between their different beliefs and attitudes, and also consistency between these beliefs and their behaviour. Unsurprisingly, these approaches are labelled *consistency theories* and have been the subject of much research during the lifetime of contemporary social psychology. A number of consistency approaches have been proposed, including Heider's

balance theory (Heider, 1958) and *Festinger's theory of cognitive dissonance* (Festinger, 1957).

Heider's balance theory

Fritz Heider's *balance theory* was especially interested in how attitudes and beliefs about issues, and also attitudes and beliefs about people, are related in a perceiver's mind. He argued that these relationships are best described as existing in a series of cognitive triads, some of which can be thought of as comprising a consistency pattern and others an inconsistency pattern. If there is inconsistency among these various beliefs then people will try to restore equilibrium by changing one or more of the belief states.

Think about the following example. Imagine that P is you, O is a friend of yours called Tony and X is New Labour. You really like New Labour and, of course, you also like Tony (given that he is your friend). However, in deciding whether these two beliefs are stable you also have to consider whether you perceive Tony to be pro- or anti-New Labour. So we now have a series of triads comprising you (the perceiver, or P), another person (Tony, or O) and finally a non-person attitude object (New Labour, or X). Heider argued that these elements are linked through positive and negative evaluations or feelings.

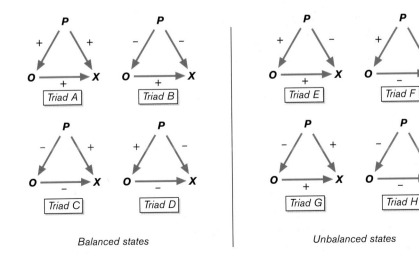

Balanced states   Unbalanced states

Figure 22.3 Heider's balance theory

Figure 22.3 presents all the possible balanced and unbalanced states. Balanced states are those triads that yield a positive figure after multiplying the signs between the elements in the triad (e.g. triads A to D). If the result of this multiplication is negative, an unbalanced cognitive state is said to exist. So, for instance, if you perceive that Tony dislikes New Labour (a negative O–X relation), while remembering that you like Tony (positive P–O relation) and New Labour (positive P–X), an overall negative triad will result (i.e. negative x positive x positive) (Triad F in Figure 22.3).

Heider argued that this state of imbalance results in psychological discomfort, and therefore you will be motivated to restore a state of *equilibrium* to your cognitions. How do you do this? Well, you could change your attitude towards New Labour and adopt a more negative one. You could change your attitude towards Tony and believe he cannot be such a nice person if he feels negatively about New Labour. Or you could attempt to change Tony's negative beliefs about New Labour such that you perceive him to actually have a positive belief about it too. These would make your liking for New Labour and your liking for Tony consistent.

Balance theory, therefore, describes what happens when the internal cognitions we have about our relationship with other attitude objects are consistent or inconsistent. What happens, though, when the inconsistency lies in a mismatch between our attitudes and our actual behaviour towards that object? We now turn to the theory of cognitive dissonance.

Festinger's theory of cognitive dissonance

Like Heider's approach, the *cognitive dissonance theory* assumes that people want to avoid feelings of discomfort by maintaining consistency among their cognitions. Leon Festinger (1957) argued that a person's attitudes or beliefs could be consonant (in line with one another), dissonant (at odds with each other) or unrelated to each other. If a person has a set of dissonant beliefs, the result is an unpleasant state of arousal. Because of this unpleasant feeling, the person is motivated to change all or some of their beliefs so that they become consistent again and the unpleasant state is alleviated.

Festinger and Carlsmith (1959) demonstrated this effect in their famous *induced compliance experiment*. In this experiment participants first had to perform a series of very lengthy, extremely tedious tasks (like turning pegs in peg holes). Afterwards they were asked to tell the next participant (who was in fact a confederate) that the tasks they would do were actually really interesting! In effect the participants were asked to lie. The idea was to create in each participant the dissonant cognitions that, on the one hand, they had disliked the experiment but, on the other hand, they had told another person that they enjoyed it.

In addition, half of the participants were given $20 for compliance with the 'lying' request and the other half a meagre $1. The idea here was that those in the $1 group would experience a higher level of cognitive dissonance than those in the $20 group because they had insufficient justification for the inconsistency between their attitudes (i.e. 'that really was a boring task') and their actual behaviour (i.e. lying about the behaviour to another person). The $20 group had the justification of a decent money payout and would thus experience less dissonance. It was predicted that the $1 participants, being highly cognitively dissonant, would change their attitude towards enjoying or liking the tasks so as to re-establish consonance; those in the $20 condition would not. This was exactly what happened when attitudes towards the task were measured after the experiment.

Further studies over the years have added to the original work by showing other conditions under which attitude change may result. These include the need for the person to feel some physiological arousal as a result of dissonant beliefs (Zanna and Cooper, 1974) and the need for the person to feel personal responsibility for the behaviour (Linder, Cooper and Jones, 1967).

Bem's self-perception theory

Although well over a thousand studies have been published on cognitive dissonance, the theory is not without its critics. The main opposition is Bem's (1965; 1972) *self-perception theory*. Daryl Bem took a more attributional approach. His starting point was not a rejection of the findings of dissonance experiments but to disagree with the interpretation offered for these findings. He claimed that people infer their attitudes by attributing events in the same way as an outside observer would. In other words, people act as observers of their own behaviours and only infer their attitudes from this observation.

In essence, behaviour can have internal (dispositional) and external (situational) causes. According to Kelley (1972), internal causes (like attitudes) are inferred when external attributions cannot be made (see Chapter 23). So when people are forced to act in a way that is counter to their true attitudes (like lying about how interesting a study is), and do not get sufficient justification for doing so (such as being paid) they are more likely to make an internal inference or attribution, such as 'the tasks in the experiment really were interesting'. If sufficient reward is given (like the $20 condition in Festinger and Carlsmith's study), then they are able to make the default external attribution and no internal appraisal is necessary.

Based on this reasoning, Bem argued that the effects seen in induced compliance experiments with reward – like writing a counterattitudinal essay and being paid for it or the forced compliance paradigm adopted in Festinger and Carlsmith's work – are best explained in terms other than a feeling of psychological discomfort or negative physiological arousal (the main tenet of dissonance theory). He showed that identical inferences to those people doing an induced compliance technique were found for individuals who had only been told about the technique. For Bem, therefore, attitude change occurs when a person has information about the behaviour and the conditions under which it happened, not because of arousal states.

How inconsistent are dissonance theory and self-perception theory? At first you may think they are very different. Some authors have argued that it is very difficult to distinguish conceptually between the two approaches and that both may be relevant under different circumstances or in different contexts (e.g. Eagly and Chaiken, 1993; Eiser and van der Pligt, 1988). Indeed Fazio, Zanna and Cooper (1977) provided a synthesis of the two

approaches. They argue that dissonance is a better explanation when a person makes an argument that is very distant from their original attitudes (attitude-discrepant), whereas self-perception processes are more appropriate when an individual makes arguments proximal, or close, to their initial attitudes (attitude-congruent).

Another approach for induced compliance effects comes from *impression management* theorists (e.g. Tedeschi, 1981). Impression management refers to the processes people use to present a desirable image of themselves to others when in a social interaction. Impression management assumes that people are motivated to appear to be consistent, in order to avoid feelings of social embarrassment such as anxiety. This motivational assumption is similar to that underpinning dissonance theory.

Where the approaches differ, however, is at the level at which this motive acts. The impression formation approach argues that it operates at a public level in social interaction, whereas dissonance theory assumes a more private level in the cognitions of individuals. In other words, participants are thought of as deceiving the other person in the interaction by faking an attitude that is in line with a discrepant behaviour, even though they have not really changed their attitudes. If attitudes do change, as in Festinger and Carlsmith's $1 group, the motivational basis for the change happens at a more social level than a strictly cognitive level.

Persuasion processes

Having looked at those processes that are important in describing how attitudes change we now turn to models and theories that have been developed to examine the persuasion process. For psychologists, *persuasion* refers to how attitudes change as a result of exposure to messages and information about the attitude object.

We are exposed daily to persuasive messages that are designed to alter our attitudes towards an object or behaviour (from favour to disfavour or vice versa) with the assumption that changing the attitude in the desired direction will result in a behavioural change in line with the new attitude. We are bombarded with these from the television screen, the

We are constantly subjected to persuasion processes

radio, billboards, newspapers, magazines and from other people around us; they also come in the form of advertising campaigns and health-promotion literature. It seems that we are constantly subjected to persuasion processes during our everyday lives (Petty and Cacioppo, 1996).

So what are these persuasion processes? The primary questions psychologists interested in persuasion ask are 'Which cognitive processes are important for describing how attitudes change after exposure to a persuasive communication?' and 'Based on this knowledge, can we design persuasive communications that are likely to evoke long-lasting attitude change?'

Early work on persuasion processes at Yale University identified a number of factors that are important for describing the conditions necessary for a persuasive communication to be effective (Hovland and Janis, 1959) (see Figure 22.4). These factors are the message *source* (Who is doing the persuading?), aspects of the *message* itself (e.g. Does scaring people persuade them to change?), the message *recipient* (Who is being persuaded?), and the *context* of the persuasion attempt (Under what conditions is the person being persuaded?).

What this work did not show is which specific cognitive processes are important for manipulating attitudes, and then behaviour, through persuasive communication. For this let's look at models that propose two modes of cognitive processing that differ in the extent to which a person uses more effortful thinking about the information and arguments included in any persuasive message. Two of these models are the *elaboration likelihood model* (*ELM*) (e.g. Petty and Cacioppo, 1996) and the *heuristic systematic model* (*HSM*) (Bohner, Moskowitz and Chaiken, 1995; Chen and Chaiken, 1999). These approaches have been the focus of much persuasion work since the late 1970s and were based on earlier work from the so-called cognitive response approach to persuasion (see Greenwald, 1968).

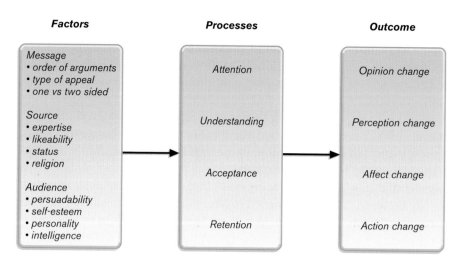

Figure 22.4 *The Yale model of persuasive communication*
Source: adapted from Fishbein and Ajzen, 1975

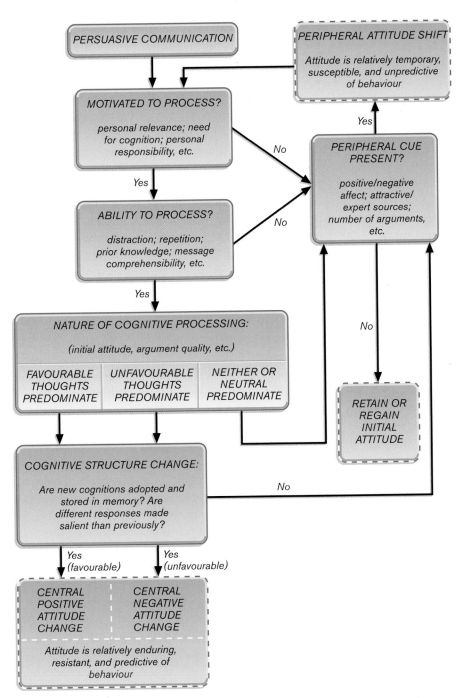

Figure 22.5 Petty and Caccippo's (1986) elaboration likelihood model of persuasion
Source: Eagly and Chaiken, 1993

Elaboration likelihood model of persuasion

In the ELM (Petty and Cacioppo, 1986) the modes of thinking that lead to changes in attitudes and behaviour following exposure to a persuasive communication are (i) the central processing route and (ii) the peripheral processing route (see Figure 22.5). These types of processing form the extreme ends of what can be thought of as an 'effort-based cognitive processing continuum'.

At one end of the continuum is the pure *central processing route* or mode, which is characterised by the message recipient being fully engaged with the content of the message and the information it contains. This means that the perceiver is engaged in effortful cognitive processing. At the other end of the continuum is the *peripheral processing route* or mode, which is dependent on resources that require very little cognitive effort, such as *heuristics*. These are general rules of thumb used in decision-making. An example of a heuristic in the context of persuasion could be 'what experts say is always correct'.

The idea behind the ELM is that to achieve central route processing people need to elaborate on the details of the message, which means that they engage in an *effortful* way. One way of doing this is using the thought-listing technique (Cacioppo, Harkins and Petty, 1981). During and after being exposed to a persuasive message, participants are asked to report any thoughts that come to mind. Because people have only limited cognitive processing capacity (see Fiske and Taylor, 1991, on the assumptions of social cognition; see also Chapter 21), people cannot elaborate every persuasive message they come across. As such, peripheral processing is thought of as the default mechanism in the ELM.

What determines whether a person elaborates? The ELM assumes that (i) motivation to process the information (e.g. personal involvement with the message and accountability for a behavioural decision (Petty and Wegener, 1998)) and (ii) the actual ability to process the information (e.g. the presentation of strong versus weak arguments (Petty, Cacioppo and Goldman, 1981)) are crucial. If a person is motivated and able to engage with a message, the likelihood is that they will elaborate the message and engage in central processing. Decreased motivation and ability are associated with less cognitive effort and more peripheral processing.

Attitudes formed via the central route are more persistent, harder to change and good predictors of behaviour. Those formed via the peripheral route are more transient in nature and less likely to lead to long-term behaviour change. More recently, the ELM has been used in trying to change attitudes and behaviour in applied contexts, including health-related (e.g. Jones, Sinclair and Courneya, 2003) and advertising-related contexts (e.g. Lammers, 2000). Applications Box 22.1 gives an example of how the ELM has been used in persuading school children to use cycle helmets when bike-riding (Quine, Rutter and Arnold, 2002).

Heuristic-systematic model (HSM) of persuasion

Like the ELM, the HSM of persuasion is characterised by two modes of processing (Chen and Chaiken, 1999). One of these is an effortless heuristic mode, the other a more demanding systematic mode. Also like the ELM, the HSM assumes a 'processing continuum', and that this processing effort is dependent upon a person's motivation and ability to process the persuasive message.

When a person is engaged in systematic processing he or she undertakes comprehensive and analytical appraisal of the message when forming a judgement. This is similar to how the central processing of the ELM works. The heuristic processing mode uses general rules of thumb – like 'if an expert thinks that, it must be right' – which are stored in long-term memory for decision-making. Little cognitive effort is required to use this latter processing mode.

The activation in memory and use of this mode depend on the presence of a heuristic cue in the message. An example of a heuristic cue could be mere delivery of the message by what is perceived to be an expert source. You can see that heuristic processing is more precise than the peripheral route of the ELM inasmuch as it focuses specifically on heuristics. Like the peripheral route of the ELM, heuristic processing is the default process when presented with persuasive messages. We are not 'set up' to be motivated to process all information intensively, which is required for systematic processing in the HSM.

However, unlike the ELM, the HSM makes different predictions of what happens with fluctuations in motivation and cognitive activity. It is argued that, even at higher levels of motivation and activity, although systematic processing is strong, people may still be using heuristic processes. This interaction between processing types has been labelled the *co-occurrence hypothesis* (Bohner *et al.*, 1995). For instance, if a message contains both strong and weak points (i.e. it is ambiguous), the initial heuristic processing of the information will bias subsequent systematic processing. Attitudes will therefore follow that are to some extent consistent with the original heuristic applied (Chaiken and Maheswaran, 1994). This highlights how intrinsically related both processing modes are in the HSM.

The HSM also proposes which factors are important for levels of motivation to use either processing type. One important factor is called the *sufficiency principle*. This is the assumption that people want to have confidence in their attitudes, but whether or not this confidence is sufficient is dependent upon the sufficiency threshold (or desired confidence) and actual confidence. When actual confidence is lower than desired confidence a person will be more motivated to process information at the systematic level. The bigger the difference between these types of confidence the greater will be the processing needed to reduce the gap.

Other factors – such as accountability and how relevant the message is to the individual – have also been found to be important for desired confidence or sufficiency threshold levels. To illustrate if an issue raised in the persuasive communication is highly personal for you – for example, that you will leave your children fatherless or motherless if you continue to smoke – the likelihood is that you will strive for greater certainty in the judgement you make than when the information is not personally relevant (see Eagly and Chaiken, 1993: 326–46).

Fear appeals

Another approach to persuasion and attitude change, which has been the focus of considerable work over the past 50 or so years, is that based on what are called *fear appeals.* Fear appeals have been used over the years to try to stop people from performing behaviours, like smoking, that will have negative effects on their health.

The assumption here is that the fear aroused in a person will motivate them to change their attitudes and behaviour. Evaluations of fear appeals suggest, however, that they are not always successful (Witte, 1992) and some have questioned the effectiveness of evoking fear when attempting to persuade individuals to change (Ruiter, Abraham and Kok, 2001).

Nevertheless, McGuire (1969) conducted many studies in which he altered the levels of fear evoked by different messages. He found that the relationship between the amount of fear aroused and the degree of attitude change was best represented by an inverted U-shaped curve (see Figure 22.7). This means that when too little or too much fear is evoked there is weak attitude or behaviour change, but that moderate doses of fear bring optimal levels of change.

Why is this the case? Well, when only a little fear is aroused, the message fails to grab the attention of

Would you be put off?

APPLICATIONS BOX 22.1

An example of attitude change using the ELM: the case of encouraging cycle helmet wearing among school children (Quine, Rutter and Arnold, 2002)

This study aimed to use the ELM to change the attitudes of school-age children towards wearing cycle helmets when riding their bicycles.

Background

Pedal cycle accidents are one of the leading causes of death and injury among school-aged children. The UK Department for the

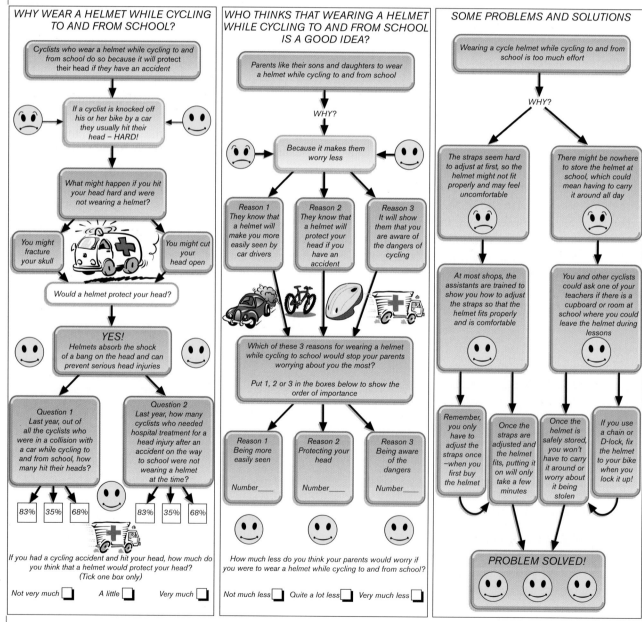

Figure 22.6 **The persuasive communication used in the Quine et al. (2002) study**

Environment, Transport and the Regions reported that in 1999 nearly 4000 people aged 8 to 19 were killed or injured as cyclists. This accounted for 37 per cent of all injuries to cyclists (DETR, 2000).

Quine *et al.* used elements of the ELM to change certain beliefs drawn from the theory of planned behaviour that previous work had shown to be important in determining that a child would not wear his or her helmet.

Method

A total of 97 adolescents aged between 11 and 15 years who reported not using cycle helmets were randomly assigned to receive an intervention booklet or a control booklet. The intervention booklet contained persuasive messages in the form of flow charts based on behavioural beliefs ('protecting one's head'), normative beliefs ('the expectations of parents for wearing a cycle helmet') and control beliefs ('overcoming the barriers to helmet use'). Participants were asked to respond to and elaborate on the information contained in the message and also to list the thoughts that came to mind while reading the persuasive information.

The control group was given a booklet that was concerned with attending a cycling proficiency course. The independent variable in this study was intervention vs control group, and the dependent variables were cycle helmet wearing behaviour five months after the intervention, and attitudes immediately after the intervention and five months later.

Results

After five months, 25 per cent of the intervention group wore a helmet when riding. None of the control group did so. Results also showed changes in behavioural, normative and control beliefs for the intervention group and not in the control group. Intervention participants showed more positive beliefs about wearing cycle helmets when riding.

Conclusion

School-aged children can be persuaded to change their attitudes and subsequent behaviour in regard to wearing helmets. The TPB and methods within the ELM are useful tools for designing effective interventions.

---

the perceiver, and when fear is extreme, attention to the message will be adversely affected. This is because the individual is diverting cognitive resources to dealing with the negative arousal (e.g. anxiety) produced by being frightened. The challenge is to produce messages that involve neither too much nor too little fear, so that a person attends to the message and does not have to divert resources away from the message to deal with the fear.

Fear appeals have been present in many models developed to understand decision-making processes about health behaviours. Examples here include the health belief model and protection motivation theory (see Conner and Norman, 1996, Rutter and Quine, 2002).

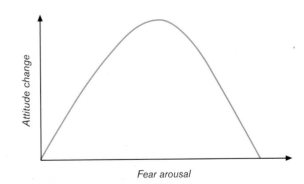

Figure 22.7 McGuire's inverted U-shaped curve hypothesis for describing the relationship between levels of fear and attitude change

Section 5
Social Psychology

Learning outcomes
When you have completed this chapter you should be able to:

- describe how the concept of attitude has been defined
- describe why we have attitudes and what functions they serve
- describe how attitudes are structured
- describe how attitudes develop according to principles based on learning theory
- describe various direct and indirect measurement techniques that are used to study attitudes
- critically assess theories and models that have been used to understand the belief–behaviour relationship, such as the theory of planned behaviour
- discuss 'consistency' approaches that attempt to explain how attitudes change, like balance theory and cognitive dissonance
- evaluate models that have been proposed for explaining how people are persuaded to change their attitudes, like the elaboration likelihood model
- evaluate how applied psychologists have adopted attitude change theory for understanding and changing health behaviour.

Key Terms
Attitude
Balance theory
Central processing route
Classical conditioning
Co-occurrence hypothesis
Cognitive dissonance theory
Consistency theories
Correspondence hypothesis (also principles of compatibility)
Deliberative processing
Elaboration likelihood model
Expectancy–value approach
Fear appeals
Festinger's theory of cognitive dissonance
Heuristic systematic model
Implicit association test

Implicit attitudes
Impression management
Induced compliance experiment
Likert scale
MODE model
Multidimensional approach
Operant conditioning
Peripheral processing route
Persuasion
Priming paradigm
Self-perception theory
Semantic differential scale
Sufficiency principle
Theory of planned behaviour
Theory of reasoned action
Unidimensional approach

Further reading

Ajzen I. (1988) *Attitudes, Personality and Behavior.* Chicago: Dorsey.

Bohner, G. (2001) Attitudes. In Hewstone, M. and Stroebe, W. (eds) *Introduction to Social Psychology.* Oxford: Blackwell, 239–84.

Bohner, G. and Schwartz, N. (2003) Attitudes, persuasion and change. In Tesser, A. and Schwartz, N. (eds) *Blackwell Handbook of Social Psychology: Intraindividual Processes.* Oxford: Blackwell, 413–35.

Bohner, G. and Wänke, M. (2002) *Attitudes and Attitude Change.* Hove: Psychology Press.

Eagly, A. H. and Chaiken, S. (1993) *The Psychology of Attitudes.* New York: Harcourt Brace.

Attribution

Route map of the chapter

The aim of this chapter is to present you with an introduction to many of the theories and models psychologists have developed to explain how people attribute behavioural outcomes to different types of causes. We will explore the nature of the attribution process by looking at a number of different models. We will focus on what attributions 'look like' and the circumstances that lead to different kinds of attributions. The second part of the chapter will focus on various errors and biases that result from the attribution process.

Introduction

Imagine that you are walking along the street one night after a good time at the local pub. The street is fairly empty and it is getting late. Walking towards you are two people who are talking with each other. Just as they pass you, both begin to laugh but continue staggering down the road.

In this instance you would probably be thinking to yourself '*Why* did they laugh? What possible reasons could there be for these people to behave in the way they did? Did they laugh because of the way I look? Did they laugh because one had just told the other an amusing story and it was just coincidence that they passed me at that time? Did they laugh because they had been drinking too much and that's what drunk people do? Did they laugh because they are rude people who try to embarrass perfect strangers?'

This example shows that we search for answers to these 'Why?' types of question and invariably arrive at a conclusion for understanding what could have possibly caused another person's behaviour. We don't just register the events we experience; we try to explain them as well. We search for explanations of events in our social world. Every day we are exposed to situations or information that require us to try and understand causes for events. In this sense forming attributions, or going through the psychological processes that allow us to offer explanations for events, is a common-sense activity (see Heider, 1958). We have a desire, or are motivated, to understand cause-and-effect relationships in our social world in order to derive meaning about events (van Overwalle, 1998).

We can all easily give examples of when we have made attributions and, if we think about it (see Activity Box 23.1), whether the attributions we make are consistent or can be grouped into different types. Psychologists over the years have been concerned with uncovering those factors that are important for individuals arriving at explanations for observed events. The kinds of questions they have been concerned with include the following.

- What types of information do people use in explaining events?
- How do we process this information?

This *causal attribution* process is inferential. We infer effects (e.g. how a person behaves, what they say, how we feel) by attributing them to causes. In the example at the beginning of this chapter, you might conclude that the people are laughing for external reasons, such as the effects of alcohol, or for more internal reasons like they are just 'rude' and 'nasty' people.

Section 5
Social Psychology

Understanding the reasons for people answering the 'Why?' questions is the cornerstone of *attribution theory* (Försterling, 2001). Attribution theory is concerned not only with how we explain other people's behaviour but also how we explain our own. Strictly speaking, it is a collection of mini-theories that together go some way to explaining how we ourselves account for events (Gilbert, 1998). Attribution theory is not concerned with *actual* causes for our own or another's behaviour but focuses specifically on *perceived* causes.

As we shall see, research and theorising on attribution has a long history, in excess of 50 years. *Attribution* has played a major role in the development of social psychology, and its principles have been employed in many applied psychology disciplines including clinical, organisational, occupational, forensic and educational psychology.

In this chapter we will take a look at various theories and approaches that have been proposed so that we can build a picture of how people attribute causes to events. As you will see, some of these theories focus on very distinctive aspects of the attribution process. What they have in common is that they use a mainly cognitive approach for understanding causal attribution. These approaches focus on how people select, store, recall and evaluate relevant information (in other words, how they process such information) and how they utilise this information in making causal decisions.

Recently, however, discursive psychologists have introduced other approaches to understanding causal attribution (for more information, see Gough and McFadden, 2001; Stainton-Rogers, 2003). In general, however, social psychologists have attempted to provide answers to a number of broad questions concerning the attribution process (see

Fincham and Hewstone, 2001; Försterling, 2001). These are as follows.

- What are the main characteristics of the attributions we make?
- Under what circumstances do we make attributions?
- How do we make attributions for our own and other people's behaviour?
- Are there any biases in the attributions people make and are these biases systematic? Are these biases universal across people?

This chapter will present you with theories, models and evidence that have been developed to address these issues. Our starting point is a look at the various theories that have been proposed to explain the causal attribution process. We begin with Fritz Heider's work, which is generally perceived to be the foundation of attribution theory.

Heider's 'common-sense' approach

In his book *The Psychology of Interpersonal Relations*, Heider (1958) proposed an approach that took as its starting point the idea that 'everyday' humans are *naïve scientists* (see Chapter 21). He meant by this that people link observable behaviours to unobservable causes. These causes are perceived, and it is these perceived causes that give meaning to what people (and themselves) do, not the actual behaviour itself. Heider argued that it is therefore fundamental to 'know' what others believe because, by knowing these beliefs, we can understand their behaviour and also predict their future intentions and behaviour.

Two fundamental propositions were derived from Heider's common-sense approach. The first concerns the idea that, when making causal attributions, people frame their responses either in terms of reasons internal or external to the observed person. Heider was the first to make the explicit distinction between internal and external causes. Some authors use the term *dispositional causes* to refer to internal causes and *situational causes* to refer to external causes.

Heider believed that when making an attribution the person is actively trying to work out whether the behaviour they have seen is something to do with the observed person themselves – like effort, ability or mood – or about things external to the person – like how complex a task is or what the weather was like. Internal causes lie within the individual while external causes lie in the environment around the individual. People use these types of attribution to make their world more predictable or controllable.

Heider's second main idea was that, when making an attribution, people tend to favour using internal or dispositional attributions for explaining another's behaviour. They seem to ignore – or at least downgrade – the role of situational or external causes. He noted that explaining another's behaviour in terms of their personal motives or intentions (internal causes) are seen as 'final causes', in that we are usually satisfied with an explanation grounded in a person's motives. We are less inclined to ask any more questions.

Figure 23.1 shows Heider and Simmel's (1944) classic geometrical figure experiment, which demonstrates the general tendency to make attributions to personal motives and intentions.

As we shall see in the following sections, Heider's ideas have been the focus of much experimental work by social psychologists and the basis of other theories of attribution. One such theory is Jones and Davis's (1965) *correspondence inference theory*.

Jones and Davis's correspondence inference theory

This theory focuses on how people make judgements about the dispositions of other people. It is specific to understanding how we use the observation of another person's behaviour (i.e. the actor) to infer dispositional attributions of that person.

According to Jones and Davis, the behaviour of the actor is not the only source of information we use in making the judgement – we also observe the effects the behaviour has. In addition, the theory assumes that the actor has knowledge about the effects of their action or behaviour. Also, this approach assumes that the actor has the ability to produce the action with the desired effect. One problem with the theory is that is does not specify how we understand that an actor has knowledge of the effects of an action and also the ability to produce the desired effects.

FOCUS POINT 23.2

Do inanimate objects have motives and intentions?

Heider and Simmel's (1944) participants watched a series of short films that involved a number of geometrical shapes. For instance, one of these films showed a large triangle (T), a small triangle (t), a circle (c) and a rectangle (R) (see Figure 23.1). The rectangle had one section that opened and closed like a door or gate. The film showed the triangles and circle moving about in different directions and at different speeds. The rectangle was stationary. After watching the film participants were asked to report 'what they saw'.

The striking result of this experiment is that virtually all the participants reported seeing intentions and motives in the behaviour of the shapes, and also that these intentions and motives were seen as being the property of either humans or animals. In addition, people attributed personal traits to these characters. For instance, one participant reported that:

Triangle number one shuts his door (or should we say line), and the two innocent young things walk in. Lovers in a two-dimensional world. No doubt, little triangle two and sweet circle. Triangle one ... spies the young love. Ah! He opens his door, walks out to see our hero and his sweet. But our hero does not like the interruption ... he attacks triangle one rather vigorously.

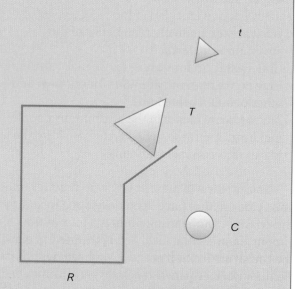

Figure 23.1 Geometrical figures used in the Heider and Simmel (1944) study
Source: Försterling, 2001: 28

(Originally reported in Heider and Simmel, 1944: 247; reprinted in Försterling, 2001:29)

This shows how people seem to structure a number of unconnected events involving objectively inanimate objects into a meaningful sequence of events involving people or animate objects with intentions and motives.

As you have no doubt guessed, central to the theory is the idea of correspondence. Jones and Davis believe that the ultimate goal in attribution is to make correspondent inferences. What does this mean? Basically the assumption is that people need to be able to infer that the behaviour, and also the intention that led to the behaviour, *correspond* to some underlying dispositional characteristic(s) within the individual. These dispositional characteristics are a stable feature of the person.

Correspondence is high when we think, or believe, that the behaviour (with its effects) reflects completely the underlying disposition. For example, on seeing a person help a mother and baby in a pushchair up some steps, we are likely to infer that this person is 'caring, unselfish and kind' – the behaviour and the disposition correspond with one another. Similarly, correspondence is high if we see a person walking past and ignoring a mother trying desperately to get her baby and pushchair up some steps. We would be likely to infer that this person is 'uncaring, selfish and unkind'. On the other hand, if we are not certain or other information is available that casts doubt on the reasons for the behaviour of the actor, correspondence is low. For instance, it could be that the only reason the actor helped the person carry the pushchair up some steps is because they were forced to by another person.

What predicts whether correspondence is high or low? One factor is called the analysis of *non-common effects*. The idea here is that the observer believes that in a given situation the actor has alternative actions available to the one seen. People are assumed to compare the different possible actions in terms of the effects each would have. A common effect is one that would be reached irrespective of the action alternatives, whereas non-common effects are specific to the behaviour observed.

Pennington (2000) provides us with a nice example of the operation of these effects. He offers a scenario in which there are two cinemas that are equidistant from your home. These cinemas are both showing the same film that you want to see. One cinema sells the brand of ice cream you really like, the other does not. You of course choose to go to the cinema that sells your favourite brand of ice cream. The non-common effect in this example is that you get to eat your favourite ice cream while watching the film. It is these non-common effects, and how desirable they are, that are used to make inferences about intentions and dispositions. When non-common effects are high, correspondence is low, and vice versa.

This analysis of non-common effects can lead to ambiguous interpretations. For this reason, it is argued that we use other factors in arriving at a dispositional attribution. We are likely to make a dispositional attribution when the behaviour is *not* socially desirable. This relates to the norms in behaviour associated with different situations. When someone behaves in a manner that does not reflect the preconceived norms of the situation, we are likely to infer that things internal to them (a

dispositional explanation) have caused the behaviour.

We also make dispositional attributions when we observe a person behaving in a way that is at odds with the role we perceive of them, like seeing a member of the clergy dancing all night at a rave. Our past experience with a particular individual's behaviour in particular situations is also important. The question we ask in this case is 'Is their behaviour typical of 'them'?' An example here could be bumping into your mother or father at a nightclub one evening, even though 'parents never go out'. If the behaviour is atypical we usually explain their behaviour in terms other than dispositions – such as situational factors.

We will now turn to approaches that consider the preconditions for making internal (dispositional) or external (situational) attributions.

Kelley's covariation and configuration models.

What information is required to make a causal attribution? To answer this question, Kelley (1967; 1973) developed two accounts of the attribution process. These accounts differ in the amount of

What can explain this person's behaviour?

information needed to make a causal attribution. The first comprises instances where we base our attributions on multiple observations, made at different times and in different settings. This is called the *covariation model*. The second comprises instances where we can only base our attributions on a single observation, and is called the *configuration approach*.

The covariation account

Kelley proposed that to arrive at a causal attribution for another's behaviour, people try to work out which effects can be attributed to which of a number of factors. To do this he suggested that we use the *covariation principle*. This states that, given time and motivation, a person can make attributions on the basis of perceiving the covariation of an effect and its hypothetical causes. The effect is attributed to the factor that is present when the effect is present, and absent when the effect is absent.

This model is also called the *ANOVA approach* (i.e. analysis of variance approach), which is a statistical test that looks for changes in a dependent variable

(the effect) by varying independent variables (the factors). Kelley classified the potential causes of events as being located within the person (internal), the entity (external) and the circumstance (external). He also suggested that we use three kinds of causal information to arrive at the cause being accounted for by the person, the entity or the circumstances in which the behaviour took place. These are *distinctiveness*, *consistency* and *consensus* information.

Let's demonstrate these types of information by using an example reported by McArthur (1972). He describes a situation in which a student called Neil falls asleep in Professor Brown's lecture. If we observe this behaviour the question we ask is 'What could explain this behaviour?'

Distinctiveness

How distinctive is Neil's behaviour? Does Neil fall asleep in other lectures? In other words, we are asking ourselves the question 'Does Neil behave in a similar way when confronted with other similar entities?' If the answer to this question is 'Yes', then the behaviour is said to be low in distinctiveness –

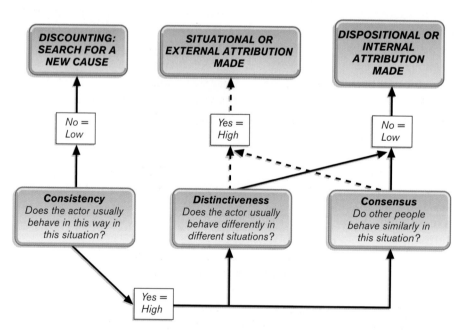

Figure 23.2 Kelley's covariation, or ANOVA, model of causal attributions

there is nothing special about Professor Brown's lecture. If the answer is 'No', then Neil's behaviour is said to be high in distinctiveness.

Consistency

How consistent is Neil's behaviour? Is he forever falling asleep in Professor Brown's lectures? A 'No' answer will imply low consistency, and a 'Yes' answer high consistency.

Consensus

Do other people behave in the same way as Neil? Did other people also fall asleep during Professor Brown's lecture? If other people fell asleep, consensus is said to be high but if only Neil fell asleep, consensus is low.

Kelley argued that high and low distinctiveness, high and low consistency and high and low consensus information vary with each other in specific ways that lead to either a person attribution (internal), entity attribution (external) or circumstance attribution (external).

Figure 23.2 gives the relationship between levels of the three factors and the attribution that will be made. For example, when Neil's behaviour is perceived as low in consensus (only he fell asleep) and low in distinctiveness (he falls asleep in other lectures in other subject areas) but high in consistency (he is always falling asleep in Professor Brown's lectures), then the cause of Neil's behaviour is located within him (i.e. 'Neil'). An internal attribution, like 'Neil can't help but stay out too late at night', has been made. Any other combination of the factors will result in an external attribution about the entity (e.g. Professor Brown being a boring lecturer) or the circumstances (e.g. it being particularly hot in the lecture theatre) being made. When consistency is low, people will discount one potential cause and look for another potential cause of the behaviour.

Evaluation of Kelley's covariation model

While empirical evidence has been offered in support of the general principles of the ANOVA model (e.g. McArthur, 1972), it is not without its critics (e.g. Cheng, 1997). One criticism suggests that not all types of causal information are used all of the

time in arriving at causal decisions. For instance, Nisbett and Borgida (1975) found very weak effects for consensus information. They argued that people are less likely to use information based on base rates (which have to form the basis of consensus-related information) and are more likely to use information based on the observed person at that time.

Hilton and Slugoski (1986), in their *abnormal conditions focus (ACF) model*, proposed that people make causal attributions from consistency, distinctiveness and consensus information by selecting as a cause the condition that is 'abnormal' when compared to the background of the behaviour. In other words, people use the three sources of information as contrast cues. So high distinctiveness information ('the target person does not act in this way to other similar entities') is used as a cue for the entity as being 'abnormal', low consensus information ('not many other people do it') for the target person as being 'abnormal', and low consistency ('the event has hardly ever happened in the past') as the circumstances being 'abnormal'.

Another problem with the covariation model is that it requires multiple observations to draw together consistency, distinctiveness and consensus information, whereas in the 'real world' this may not always be the case. This questions the covariation model in terms of its rather idealistic approach. Kelley (1972) recognised this and so produced another model that was designed to understand causal attribution based on a single observation – the configuration model.

The configuration account

In cases where there is incomplete data on which to base consensus, distinctiveness and consistency information, Kelley proposes that we use *causal schemata*. These are incumbent beliefs and preconceptions about how causes interact to produce particular effects, and are derived through experience. One such schema is known as the *multiple sufficient causal schema*, which suggests that any of a number of potential causes acting by themselves can produce the same effect.

For instance, what caused the England football captain David Beckham to transfer to Real Madrid in the summer of 2003 can be explained by a number of potential causes (better money, playing with the best footballers in the world, pressure from his partner to move to a sunnier climate etc.) all of which are sufficient causes in their own right.

There are also attribution principles attached to these schemata. The one attached to the multiple sufficient cause schema is known as the *discounting principle*. This suggests that because distinct causes can create the same effect, the role of one of the causes is discounted if possible alternative causes are present. For example, we are likely to discount the idea that a friend of yours failed to turn up at the pub to celebrate your birthday because they are selfish and inconsiderate if we also learn that they had been taken seriously ill that day.

Another principle is called the *augmentation principle*. This suggests that the role of a cause is augmented, or increased, if the effect occurs at the same time as an inhibitory cause. For instance, a friend who turns up at the pub to celebrate your birthday even if they are ill that day may be thought of subsequently as more considerate and selfless (an internal attribution) than one who also turns up but who is not ill. This principle applies to the multiple cause schema and also another schema called the *multiple necessary cause schema*. This proposes that causes operate together to produce the effect, and is especially important when events are unusual or extreme (Cunningham and Kelley, 1975).

Weiner's attribution model of motivation

Weiner (1986; 1995) focused specifically on attributions of success and failure as means of examining human motivation and its relationship to emotion. He suggested that the attributions we make result in identifiable emotional responses (Weiner, 1985b). His approach is important because it takes the traditional internal/external perceived causes idea of Heider and Kelley, and adds two other dimensions that interact with it and with each other to provide an understanding of the structure of perceived causality.

Weiner, then, suggests that three causal dimensions are used to predict the types of attribution made. *Locus* concerns whether the cause is perceived as being internal or external to the actor; *stability* refers to whether the causes are temporary or permanent in nature; and *controllability* concerns whether the cause is perceived as being controllable or uncontrollable. It is the covarying nature of these factors that will predict the attribution for success or failure, and how one will feel as a result.

Let's take an example here. Imagine you have just been given a very poor mark for a recent assignment. You could attribute the mark to the fact that you found the assignment very taxing and particularly difficult. If this is the case you are likely to have made an external, unstable and uncontrollable attribution that will leave you feeling rather frustrated and angry. Another option is that you may attribute your poor performance to a general lack of ability. This is an example of an internal, stable and uncontrollable attribution that will make you feel rather gloomy or ashamed.

Weiner's basic premises can be summarised by the flow diagram in Figure 23.3. You will see that the diagram identifies what are called outcome-dependent affects. These are the primitive emotions that may be elicited without thought as a result of success or failure at a task. For instance, irrespective of the attribution process, people will feel sad or frustrated after failing but happy and content after being successful. They are outcome-dependent because they depend on the attainment, or failure to attain, a desired goal (they like to succeed in getting a good mark for an assignment), and not the causal attributions themselves. As we saw in the above example, the causal attribution process has psychological consequences including emotional

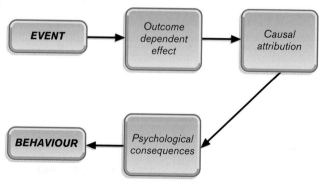

Figure 23.3 A summary of Weiner's model

APPLICATIONS BOX 23.1

Attributing blame and responsibility

Ever been involved in a road accident, however minor? If you have, you will know that insurance companies are always interested in who is to blame for an accident. Sometimes the police too are interested in trying to work out who is to blame. If you are to blame, your insurance premium goes up and driving becomes that bit more expensive. In general, internal attributions result in a person being held responsible for an outcome. External attributions result in blame being ascribed elsewhere, like the poor state of the road causing a puncture.

One approach to understanding attribution of responsibility comes from Shaver (1985), who identifies a number of factors that govern whether or not an internal attribution is made. These are:

- whether the behaviour can be deemed as originating from a specific person
- if there is no justification for why the behaviour was adopted in the first place
- a belief that the actor could have predicted the consequences of their behaviour
- that the actor had free choice in behaving in the manner they did.

Take the example of a driver who is involved in an accident when he is over the drink-driving limit; assume that the other driver was sober. In this instance, we are likely to attribute blame to the drink-driver and think of that person as being 'dangerous', 'untrustworthy' and a 'menace to other road users'. Why? Because we can identify a specific person involved in the accident who is over the limit, we do not know why the person chose to drive after drinking in the first place, we think that this driver is well aware that alcohol impairs driving performance and they could have chosen not to drink that day.

It has also been shown that severe outcomes lead to more responsibility being placed on the actor. A number of studies focusing on driving behaviour have found that attributions of blame and responsibility increased as severity of the outcome of the road accident depicted increased (e.g. Dejoy and Klippel, 1984; Kelley and Campbell, 1997).

Other psychologists have shown that responsibility attributions decrease if you believe yourself to be similar to the actor (Burger, 1981). Wilson and Jonah (1988) showed that drink-driving offenders reported decreased attributions of blame to hypothetical drink-drivers when compared to the attributions made by non-drinking drivers. This is an example of a defensive attributional bias.

ones and the expectancies we might have for our own achievement in the future.

More recently, Weiner (1995) has taken his approach and applied it successfully to attributions of responsibility and blame. For example, if we judge the cause of the behaviour leading to a road accident

To what will this person attribute her success or failure?

as internal, controllable and either stable or unstable, we will make the driver of the vehicle responsible or to blame.

Applications Box 23.1 provides a brief overview of other work that has used attribution principles in understanding blame and responsibility.

Although a significant amount of supportive evidence has been reported for this theory (see Weiner, 1995) it has been criticised by others. Some have provided evidence that people do not necessarily classify ability, effort, luck and task difficulty in terms of stability, controllability and internal/external properties. For instance, Krantz and Rude (1984) found that many people classified ability as unstable.

Section summary

The attribution theories we have looked at in this chapter can be seen as presenting different approaches to the study of attribution and all have distinct foci. Correspondence inference theory is concerned with explaining dispositional attributions, while the covariation model addresses instances in which people have been presented with detailed information about a person's behaviour and the behaviour of others over time. Both these approaches are likely to require deliberative (effortful) thinking (see below). In comparison, the configuration model is based on causal schemata, and may be more prone to spontaneous (non-effortful) thinking.

We have now covered the most influential theories of attribution. One issue that does arise from the theories seems to be the inherent assumption that the attribution process is a deliberative one, requiring significant cognitive effort. Is this the case or does the nature of the attributional process go beyond effortful, conscious deliberative thought and into the realms of spontaneous attributions?

Spontaneous and deliberative attributions

The conditions that give rise to either spontaneous or deliberative attributions have been the subject of more recent work. Spontaneous attributions are those that are made without the person consciously thinking about alternative causes. Stereotypes (see Chapter 21), for instance, might lead a person to make a spontaneous attribution. Some people hold the stereotype that young drivers are irresponsible drivers. This may lead a person spontaneously to attribute the cause of a road accident to a young person's dangerous driving without thinking about any contextual information, such as the fact that a tyre on their car might have blown and caused the accident, and so on.

These types of attributions require little cognitive effort. Contrast this with deliberative attributions, which require us to expend significant cognitive effort in analysing and observing behaviour and the context within which it occurs. Langer (1978) was the first to claim that people were not at all times actively seeking causes, that a lot of attribution work was 'mindless', and that the process may in fact be fast-acting and require only limited information processing (see Fincham and Hewstone, 2001).

Gilbert et al.'s three-stage model for attribution

In this model Gilbert, Pelham and Krull (1988) and Gilbert (1998) propose the attribution process to be a sequence of events involving (i) an initial identification phase, followed by (ii) an automatic (spontaneous) attribution phase, which in turn is followed by (iii) an effortful (deliberative) attribution phase (see Figure 23.4).

A series of experiments showed that after identifying or perceiving a behaviour or event a person will then enter an attribution process characterised by a spontaneous operation requiring limited cognition (Gilbert et al., 1988). The likelihood is that this automatic phase will result in a dispositional attribution. Indeed, studies have shown that trait inferences are made very quickly (Smith and Miller, 1983).

The second stage in the attribution process is characterised by being more cognitively taxing and deliberative. According to Gilbert and colleagues, this stage results in what they call situational correction. In other words, the person realigns their attribution on becoming aware of other relevant information about the situation within which the behaviour occurs.

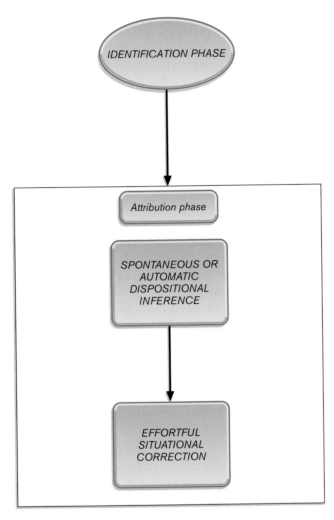

Figure 23.4 *Gilbert's three-stage model of attribution (1995)*

For instance, you may have originally thought that a road accident involving a young person driving fast was due to the irresponsible and dangerous way in which all young people drive – a dispositional attribution based on the stereotypical young driver. However, if you learn that the passenger in the car was the driver's pregnant partner who was in labour at the time, more deliberative processing will occur and you will realign your attribution to make a more situational attribution: the person was driving too fast because he needed to get his partner to hospital as quickly as possible.

Attributional bias and errors

In this section we are going to pose the question of whether there are systematic biases or errors in people's judgements of causes. What factors are important for understanding any such errors as systematic? Kelley's covariation model sees people as logical perceivers of causal information, who use standard ways of making inferences. However, it does appear that there are attributional biases that operate in predictable ways. In this section we will look briefly at the *fundamental attribution error, correspondence bias,* the *actor–observer difference, self-serving bias* and the *false consensus effect.*

Correspondence bias

Imagine that you are out at dinner with some people whom you do not know very well. One of your companions arrives 30 minutes late for the meal. On entering the restaurant they trip and fall over. After getting to their feet they come over to the table and, while sitting down, knock over a glass of wine. Later on during the meal the person spills their cup of coffee over their clean white shirt.

How would you explain these events? In all likelihood you would come to the conclusion that this person is rather 'clumsy', and that his or her clumsiness led to them falling over, knocking over the wine glass and spilling the coffee.

Is this an accurate attribution to make? Not necessarily, because there could be other possible explanations for the events. Perhaps the floor of the restaurant was wet, causing the person to slip over when entering. Maybe he or she spilt their coffee because the cup was far too hot to hold. You could probably think of many possible reasons for these events.

The fact that you are not likely to consider these possible external causes has been labelled the *correspondence bias* (Jones, 1979). This is the tendency for people to explain others' behaviour as the result of (or corresponding to) dispositions even when information about possible situational causes is apparent or even more likely (see Gilbert, 1995). This bias is so general in scope that some psychologists call it the *fundamental attribution error (FAE)*. This states that people tend to underestimate the role of situational (external) factors and to overestimate the role of dispositional (internal) factors in causing behaviour (Ross, Amabile and Steinmetz, 1977; Ross and Nisbett, 1991).

What factors are important in the operation of the correspondence bias? One motivational explanation argues that dispositional attributions give the perceiver *control* (Miller, Norman and Wright, 1978). An example here is the *just world hypothesis* (Langer, 1978; Lerner and Miller, 1978; Lerner, 1980). As a means of protecting their self-esteem, people have been shown to attribute negative outcomes to the victims themselves. When bad things happen to other people it is because they are bad people and deserve the outcome. We blame the victim. Why?

One cognitive explanation rests on the idea that a person's behaviour is more distinctive than the situational context in which the behaviour takes place (Rhodes and Pryor, 1982). In this sense, the person's behaviour is more *salient* in the mind of the perceiver, rather than the context in which the behaviour takes place. These explanations seem to assume that situational and dispositional attributions are totally distinctive. Others have provided accounts that see these attributions in a more sequential manner (see Gilbert's three-stage model, discussed previously).

Although the evidence seems to be quite consistent with the FAE or correspondence bias, there are occasions on which people are more likely to attribute causes to situational rather than dispositional factors. These include when attention is focused on situational information, when the observers are in a negative mood, highly motivated or when behaviour is inconsistent with the perceiver's expectations (see Gilbert, 1998).

Actor–observer differences

This is when people assume that their own behaviour is caused by situational factors, and other people's identical behaviour is determined by dispositional factors (Jones and Nisbett, 1972). For instance, if you see another person trip over, you are likely to attribute this to them being clumsy or inattentive (internal or dispositional). If you yourself trip and fall over you are more likely to attribute this to an uneven or slippery pavement (external or situational).

There is an obvious difference in the type of attributions we make about ourselves as the actor (situational) and those we make about others as actors (dispositional). Why are there these actor–observer differences? One account argues that there is greater information available to self-raters. We know more about our own behaviour than about the behaviour of others.

Another account proposes that the effect is due to greater attention being focused on situational factors when judging causes of our own behaviour, and attention being more behaviour-orientated when we attribute cause to others' behaviours (Storms, 1973). Storms (1973) showed this by making situational factors more salient and attention-grabbing for the observer, and dispositional factors more salient for the actor, which resulted in a reversal of the effect.

Self-serving biases

These biases refer to the tendency for people to take credit for any successes they have by making a dispositional attribution (e.g. to do with ability), and in the case of failure deny any responsibility and make a situational attribution (Fiske and Taylor, 1991). Taking credit for a success is an example of the *self-enhancing bias*, and denying responsibility for failure an example of *self-protective bias*. These biases have been explained in motivational terms as the need to maintain self-esteem and protect one's ego (Zuckerman, 1979; Taylor and Brown, 1988).

An interesting extension to these biases is the idea of self-handicapping (Jones, 1990). In order to make the link between their performance and evaluation more unambiguous, people will often manipulate the causes of an event before it has occurred. For example, if we expect to fail an exam, we might therefore stay out very late at a nightclub the night before we are due to take it. This provides a self-serving explanation for the predicted failure.

These biases all operate at the individual level. Hewstone (1989) has also identified such biases as existing in groups of people. In-groups (those you identify with) favour dispositional attributions for success, whereas out-groups tend to have situational causes attached to their behaviour. This group-level bias has been called ethnocentric bias or group-serving attributional bias.

The false consensus effect (FCE)

Ross, Greene and House (1977) demonstrated that people tend to overestimate how many of their own behaviours, attitudes and beliefs are shared by other people (*false consensus effect (FCE)*). In their study, students were initially asked if they would walk around the university wearing an advertisement stating 'Eat at Joe's'. Of course some refused and some agreed. Those who refused stated that the majority of other students would also refuse. Those who agreed estimated that the majority of other students would also agree.

These findings have been confirmed in many other areas, including attitudes related to body shape in women (Muller, Williamson and Martin, 2002) and perceived prevalence of drug use (Wolfson, 2000; see Applications Box 23.2).

APPLICATIONS BOX 23.2

False consensus effect (FCE) in drug use

Drug and alcohol use among young people is not uncommon. Some studies have found that children as young as 13 have taken illicit drugs (e.g. Miller and Plant, 1996). Wolfson (2000) studied the FCE in 350 university students who were classified as being either drug users or non-drug users. Participants estimated the prevalence of drug use among other students.

In line with the FCE, drug users gave higher estimates of drug use than non-drug users, who in turn increased their estimates of non-drug users compared to drug users. It seems that students are motivated to exaggerate relatively the behaviour of others to favour their own personal behaviour.

One explanation for the FCE argues that our own beliefs, attitudes and so on are at the forefront of our own minds. We know them and experience them,

and as such they are salient. Encountering others who hold similar views acts to reinforce this saliency, which has the effect of creating the impression that more people than are objectively realistic hold the same opinions. A motivational account focuses on the idea that one good way to manage, maintain and enhance our own self-esteem is to believe that other people hold similar views to ours (see Fiske and Taylor, 1991).

Learning outcomes

When you have completed this chapter you should be able to:

- describe what is meant by the term 'attribution'
- describe different types of attributions people make and give examples of these types of attributions
- critically assess a number of attributional models, and identify various similarities and differences between them
- describe and evaluate the differences between deliberative and spontaneous attributions
- describe a number of errors and biases in the attributional process that have been of interest to social psychologists.

Section 5
Social Psychology

<table>
<tr>
<td>

Key Terms

Abnormal conditions focus (ACF) model
Actor–observer differences
ANOVA approach
Attribution
Attribution theory
Augmentation principle
Causal attribution
Causal schemata
Configuration approach
Consensus
Consistency
Correspondence bias
Correspondence inference theory
Covariation model

</td>
<td>

Covariation principle
Discounting principle
Dispositional cause
Distinctiveness
False consensus effect (FCE)
Fundamental attribution error (FAE)
Just world hypothesis
Multiple necessary cause schemata
Multiple sufficient causal schema
Naïve scientists
Non-common effects
Self-enhancing bias
Self-protective bias
Situational causes

</td>
</tr>
</table>

Further reading

Augoustinos, M. and Walker, I. (1995) *Social Cognition: An Integrated Introduction.* London: Sage.

Försterling, F. (2001) *Attribution: An Introduction to Theories, Research and Applications.* Hove: Psychology Press.

Fincham, F. and Hewstone, M. (2001) Attribution theory and research: from basic to applied. In Hewstone, M. and Stroebe, W. (eds) *Introduction to Social Psychology* (3rd edn). Oxford: Blackwell.

Gilbert, D. T. (1998) Ordinary personology. In Gilbert, D. T., Fiske, S. T. and Lindzey, G. (eds) *Handbook of Social Psychology* (4th edn). New York: McGraw-Hill, 89–150.

Hewstone, M. (1989) *Causal Attribution: From Cognitive Processes to Collective Beliefs.* Oxford: Blackwell.

24

Impression formation and social interaction

Route map of the chapter

The aim of this chapter is to provide you with an overview of some of the theories and evidence that social psychologists have used to study impression formation and social interaction. The chapter will begin with a section on how we form impressions of others and also why we attempt to manage the impressions others form of us. The second part of the chapter will look at non-verbal communication in social interaction. Finally, we will move on to look at a few examples of social behaviour including attraction, aggression and helping.

Introduction

People spend an awful lot of time thinking about other people. We spend a large proportion of our waking life forming impressions of new people we have met or just heard about, or rejigging our opinions of people already known to us. One way we do this is thorough social interaction. We meet people all the time, we talk to them and we 'behave' with them. Aside from language, we also use non-verbal skills to tell people what we think and feel, and also interpret what others think and feel from what they do.

Of course, forming impressions and interacting with other people go hand in hand. On one side of the coin, the way we think about people can be influenced by the impression we have formed of them. On the other side, interpersonal interaction with people can also provide us with information that allows us to adapt our impression of them, the impression we subsequently have of other people who are similar to them, and also the way we behave towards them.

In extreme circumstances, the impressions we have formed of people and the result of interpersonal interaction with them can result in either aggressive or loving thoughts and behaviours. In other instances, the impressions we have of people can also result in whether we would help that person in the future.

Why do we form impressions and take part in social interaction? We do so in order to understand and predict other people's behaviour. For some this is important because it gives the social world 'meaning' for us (Fiske and Taylor, 1991). (The social cognition section in Chapter 21 outlines these ideas.) How do we form impressions of others? What governs our social interactions with others? What effects are there on our behaviour as a result of these processes? Well, that is what the rest of this chapter is concerned with. We will be studying some classic and contemporary evidence that has been used to answer the following questions.

- How do we form impressions of others in our social world? Do first impressions count?
- What factors are important for understanding how we form these impressions?
- How does non-verbal communication influence interpersonal perception and behaviour?
- Why are we attracted to some people but behave aggressively to others?
- Why do we decide to help people?

These types of questions have been asked by social psychologists over the past 50 or so years.

Take a look too at the social cognition section (Chapter 21), the attitude section (see Chapter 22),

ACTIVITY BOX 24.1

First impressions

You have probably all heard the adage 'never judge a book by its cover'. What does this mean? Think about a person you formed an impression of before meeting them and then changed your opinion about after having met them. Write down some words that describe what you originally thought of that person. Now write down what your overall initial impression of that person was.

Did you find yourself basing your impression on certain key things like what the person was doing at the time, their appearance or what you had heard about them from other people? Maybe your impression was based on the fact that the person was in some way different from or similar to you? Maybe they held different political views to you, supported a different football team, or even wore the 'right' clothes? Whatever the reasons, you created an impression of that person and probably behaved in line with the impression you formed.

Now think about what happened when you actually met the person. Think about the occasion when you interacted with the person. Where were you and what were you doing? What went through your head? Think about how you behaved. Again write down some words that describe what you thought of the person and how the new overall impression was based on these descriptions.

Compare your new impression with the initial one. How different are the two sets of words used to describe the first and second impressions? What do you think made you change your mind? Was it something the person did, something they said or is it something you can't put your finger on?

We form impressions because they help us to understand why other people are behaving in the ways they are and also to predict how they will behave in the future. Solomon Asch showed that first impressions are important and seem to be based on us focusing on certain key traits in

people (see the section headed 'First impressions', below).

Take another look at the key characteristics you listed for this activity and work out how consistent or inconsistent some factors were in your first and second impressions of the person.

Figure 24.1(a) *What are your impressions of this person?*

Figure 24.1(b) *Now what are they?*

the section on attribution processes (see Chapter 23), as well as those on social influence and group processes (see Chapter 25) for other processes that are important in understanding both the impression formation process and social interaction.

Impression formation

Social psychologists have been studying *impression formation* since the 1940s. They have primarily been interested in how we form initial impressions of other people, whether these impressions are permanent or stable, and also how we try to manage the impressions others have of us (this latter process is called *impression management*).

First impressions

Soloman Asch is the godfather of impression formation research. He argued that when forming an impression we use all available perceived information about a person in a dynamic way. This may include what they say, how they behave, how they are dressed, and other non-verbal cues. Asch took an information processing approach in his work. In his configural model he suggested that we attend to specific pieces of information about a person when we are forming an impression. In particular, we attend to what are called *central traits*. This attentional or selection bias guides the impression formed and is fundamental to the content of it. Central traits affect the meanings of other identified traits and are also important for allowing us to perceive relationships between traits.

Asch also identified other more *peripheral traits* that people use but that are of far less importance for the impression developed. Although these are of less significance they too give meaning to other traits, but not as much as central ones. Together, central and peripheral traits guide the configuration of the impression formed.

Asch (1946) showed this effect in an experiment in which participants were presented with one of two lists of words (see Table 24.1), which described an imaginary person. From the table you can see that the only difference between List A and List B is one word, *warm* (List A) and *cold* (List B). After reading one or other of these lists, participants were then asked to rate the person, using a series of semantic differential scales (see Chapter 22 for a description of these types of scale), on dimensions like generous or ungenerous, reliable or unreliable and happy or sad.

Those people presented with the *warm* list formed a very positive impression of the person, those in the *cold* condition a much more negative impression (see Figure 24.2). This finding has also been used to demonstrate the *halo effect*. If the information we get about a person is positive we form a positive impression (a positive halo), while negative information brings with it a poor impression (a negative halo). In addition, when the words *warm* and *cold* were replaced with *polite* (List C) and *blunt* (List D) there was no difference in the favourability of the impression formed between the word list groups.

Asch interpreted these findings as supporting his view that the traits *warm* and *cold* act as central traits because they had such a major effect on the impression formed of the imaginary person. In comparison he concluded that words like *polite* and *blunt* were more peripheral. They had much less impact on the impression formed or the attribution of traits to the imaginary person.

Although Asch's work is important, do the same processes occur in a more naturalistic setting? Is

(a) Central traits

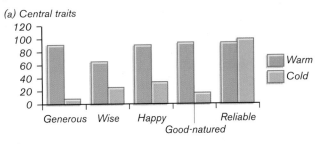

(b) Peripheral traits

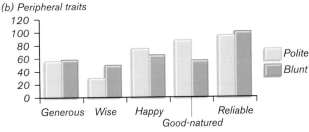

Figure 24.2 Percentage of participants' agreement with other traits based on central and peripheral traits
Source: Asch (1946)

Section 5
Social Psychology

there support for the central–peripheral trait distinction when the person is not imaginary but real? The answer here seems to be 'Yes'. Kelley (1950) demonstrated this by introducing students to a guest lecturer as being 'a rather warm (or cold) person, industrious, critical, practical and determined'. Half the participants were given the *warm* introduction, the other half the *cold* introduction. They were then actually lectured to by the person and afterwards asked to form an impression of him based on a number of evaluative dimensions.

Kelley's findings replicated those of Asch. Those in the cold condition rated the lecturer with more unfavourable traits, like unpopular, formal and unsociable, than those in the warm condition. Interestingly, the students' behaviour also differed between conditions. Those in the warm group asked more questions and interacted more with the lecturer than those in the cold group. Impressions seem to influence how we behave.

The conclusion we can draw from Asch's and Kelley's work is that impressions seem to be generated by the integration of wholes based on specific and central cues. When at least two traits are thought of as belonging to a person, the traits no longer exist in isolation from each other but combine to form the whole impression (Asch, 1946). This idea has been encompassed into *implicit personality theory* (Bruner and Tagiuri, 1954), which argues that people have preconceptions of what a person is broadly like based on knowledge about central traits.

Other work has criticised Asch's approach as being far too simplistic, and has stated that the centrality of any trait is dependent upon the context in which the impression is being formed (Rosenberg *et al.*, 1968). The idea is that Asch's results can be explained because the central traits (e.g. warm, cold) contrasted with other cues, and were also linked semantically with evaluative dimensions (we can see this from Table 24.1).

Rosenberg and colleagues proposed that in different contexts we use two evaluative dimensions, good/bad in intellectual terms and good/bad in social terms. Applying this to Asch's stimuli, warm/cold is good/bad in social terms as are the traits used by the participants to evaluate the

TABLE 24.1

ASCH'S LISTS OF WORDS FOR SHOWING THE INFLUENCE OF CENTRAL AND PERIPHERAL TRAITS

Central trait lists		Peripheral trait lists	
List A	**List B**	**List C**	**List D**
INTELLIGENT	INTELLIGENT	INTELLIGENT	INTELLIGENT
SKILFUL	SKILFUL	SKILFUL	SKILFUL
INDUSTRIOUS	INDUSTRIOUS	INDUSTRIOUS	INDUSTRIOUS
WARM	*COLD*	*POLITE*	*BLUNT*
DETERMINED	DETERMINED	DETERMINED	DETERMINED
PRACTICAL	PRACTICAL	PRACTICAL	PRACTICAL
CAUTIOUS	CAUTIOUS	CAUTIOUS	CAUTIOUS

imaginary person. The other traits (e.g. intelligent, skilful) are good/bad in intellectual terms. It is not surprising, therefore, that the warm/cold conditions showed an effect and the polite/blunt ones did not.

Primacy and recency effects

We have all heard the adage 'first impressions count'. Is this the case, though? Is there a bias towards the first things we hear, read or observe in another person (*primacy effect*) or a bias towards the latest information we get (*recency effect*)?

By presenting two lists of words that were identical except that one list was the reversal of the other (see Table 24.2), Asch (1946) demonstrated a primacy effect. He showed that earlier traits had the greatest influence on the impression formed. So, being presented with List A produced a more favourable impression and List B a more unfavourable impression. Asch argued that first information affects the meaning of later information.

It is not uncommon to change the meaning of information received later in light of what you were told first about a person. This suggests that early information may act in much the same way as central cues. People naturally seem to pay more attention to facts presented first (primacy) and pay less attention to later information. This shift in

attention is most apparent when we are presented first with negative facts about a person (Fiske, 1980), and we will form an impression based on that.

Why should this be? Well, the *person-positivity bias* argues that we seem to assume that people are good (Sears, 1983), so if negative information is seen or heard it tends to grab our attention (Skowronski and Carlston, 1989; Peeters and Czapinski, 1990).

This primacy effect was replicated by Luchins (1957), who also provided evidence of conditions under which a recency effect may be evident. He presented participants with a description of a man called Jim. One of these gave the description of Jim's behaviour as being extroverted, the other as being introverted. Participants were randomly assigned to four different groups based on the order in which they received introversion and extroversion information. Research Methods Box 24.1 shows the four groups.

Impression ratings of Jim's introversion and extroversion showed the predicted difference between groups 3 and 4. Those who got the extroversion information before the introversion account (group 3) viewed Jim as more extroverted than those who received the reverse order (group 4);

TABLE 24.2

WORD LISTS IN ASCH'S TRAIT REVERSAL EXPERIMENT TO ASSESS PRIMACY AND RECENCY EFFECTS

List A	List B
INTELLIGENT	ENVIOUS
INDUSTRIOUS	STUBBORN
IMPULSIVE	CRITICAL
CRITICAL	IMPULSIVE
STUBBORN	INDUSTRIOUS
ENVIOUS	INTELLIGENT

RESEARCH METHODS BOX 24.1

Luchin's four experimental groups for impression formation of a character called Jim

Story	Description
Group 1	Read Jim the extrovert description
Group 2	Read Jim the introvert description
Group 3	Read Jim the extrovert description first and then Jim the introvert description
Group 4	Read Jim the introvert description first and then Jim the extrovert description

Note: groups 1 and 2 are control groups. People were assigned to these conditions to rule out the idea that any effects are due to people being able or unable to identify introvert and extrovert traits. Obviously people in group 1 rated Jim as the most extroverted and those in group 2 rated him as the most introverted.

this is known as the primacy effect. Luchin explained the effect by suggesting that when people are given information that contrasts with what they already have about a person, they treat the information they received first as indicative of what that person is 'really like'.

Luchin also showed that after a delay between getting information about a person and actually being asked to form the impression, people were more likely to make recency judgements. Also, if motivated to attend to later information (like asking the person not to make any immediate impression) they would base their impressions on the most recent information. He also showed that the recency effect is used more when we are forming impressions of people we know. When we learn something about someone after having already formed an impression (recency effect), we sometimes adjust the impression we have of that person (have another look at Figure 24.1!). Although it seems that the primacy effect is more common than the recency effect, and that first impressions do count, it also looks like there may be limits to the primacy effect (Jones, Goethals, Kennington and Severance, 1972).

Other factors have also been shown to be important in impression formation. Two examples here are stereotypes and physical appearance. *Stereotypes* are widely held assumptions about the attributes, attitudes, behaviours and personalities of other people, based on group membership (see Chapter 21 for more information on this).

When we come across a person for the first time we usually categorise them by how they look and behave, and form an initial judgement or impression of them based on these stereotypes. We also seem to form impressions based on physical appearance. Ever remember complaining to your mother or father about having to wear your 'best clothes' when visiting relatives, and asking them why you have to dress up like that? The response was probably the same for many of us: 'Because you want to make a good impression.'

Evidence shows that because the physical appearance of a person is usually the first thing that we encounter it may have a dramatic effect on the impression we form (see the section on attraction later in this chapter). For instance, attractive male professionals were rated as more able than unattractive ones (Heilman and Stopeck, 1985). Attractiveness is also related to the impression of being a 'good' person (Dion, Berscheid and Walster, 1972).

The assumption we made at the beginning of this chapter is that we all form impressions when presented with information about people from our environment (Hastie and Park, 1986). The work we have looked at so far basically shows that when people are asked to form impressions they do so in quite predictable ways. This may well be correct but what this work does not tell us is at what cognitive level these impression formation goals operate.

Level of processing in impression formation

Do we have to be aware that we are making an impression for us actually to do so? Does having an impression formation goal predict actually forming the impression? When we see a person behaving in a way that is clearly linked to a trait stored in our memory (e.g. a person punching somebody else is indicative of them being 'angry', 'frustrated') it activates the trait concept regardless of whether you want to form an impression or not (see Bargh and Pietromonaco, 1982; Bargh, 1997).

It is argued that traits like honesty, aggressiveness, intelligence and so on, when repeatedly paired with behaviour that we see as fitting them, can eventually become activated automatically by the mere presence of the behaviour. So, for example, over time we have learnt that seeing a person being violent will automatically evoke a view that they are the angry type or the frustrated type.

One study showed that by getting people to form sentences from a set of scrambled (jumbled-up) words (e.g. 'he fell her kicked'), people were likely to form an impression of another person that was in line with a hostility trait (Srull and Wyer, 1979). The idea is that the hostility trait has become accessible in a person's memory because unscrambling the sentences has triggered the stored representation of the trait, and also its association with the behaviour in a person's mind. This was the case even though participants had not been instructed or told that they would be forming an impression until after the so-called 'language test'.

Similarly, John Bargh and others have also shown that impression formation goals – motivating an individual to form an impression of another person – can also be kicked into action implicitly, when a person is not consciously aware that they are forming an impression. Chartrand and Bargh (1996) used scrambled sentences and also what is called subliminal priming to activate the impression formation goal (see Research Methods Box 24.2 for a description of scrambled sentence and subliminal priming techniques). They found that people who were primed with impression formation goal words were more likely to go on to form impressions of other target individuals.

So, we've now got some idea of how we form impressions of other people, and of course we also know that other people form impressions and then change or update them about us. Because we all want to be in control of how other people see us and think about us, we are also in the game of trying to *manage* the impressions these people have of us. How do we do this?

RESEARCH METHODS BOX 24.2

Scrambled sentence and subliminal priming techniques used in social psychology

These techniques allow the researcher to look at how a concept or representation of an environmental event we have in our memory leads to the types of impression we form, the types of attitude we display, and the types of behaviour we emit. The idea is that priming activates the representation we have of an event automatically, or without our conscious control. We are not aware that we are necessarily thinking in the ways we do.

Let's take an example here to make things a little easier. What about driving a car? Initially when you are learning to drive you 'think' the whole time about the environmental events going on around you. You also have to think about when to change gear, when to put your foot on the accelerator, the brake and the clutch, and so on and so forth. Over time, however, these behaviours all become habitual. In other words, you no longer consciously 'think' about how to drive – it just happens. This is an example of a behaviour becoming automatic in the presence of environmental events – in this case events encountered while driving.

Scrambled sentence priming and subliminal priming techniques are particularly useful because they are designed to study how events are interpreted and acted upon in this non-conscious way (see Bargh and Chartrand, 2000, for a description of these techniques, with examples).

Scrambled sentence priming

For this technique participants are initially told that the task is about language ability. They are instructed to make sentences from a number of strings of words. In an experiment looking at the effects of priming the old age stereotype on subsequent behaviour, Bargh, Chen and Burrows (1996) used 30 scrambled sentences to activate the old age stereotype, including:

1 should now withdraw *forgetful* we
2 sunlight makes temperature *wrinkle* raisins
3 shoes give replace *old* the
4 the push wash frequently clothes
5 they obedient him often meet

In the course of doing this task the participant is exposed to some concepts the experimenter wishes to prime, sentences 1, 2 and 3 above (the concepts are not italicised in the actual priming task but are italicised here for easy identification), and to other concepts that are not related to the concept, sentences 3 and 4. Sentences are usually randomly presented.

The participant is then required to do some other task. For example, in the example above, participants for whom an elderly stereotype was primed walked more slowly down the hallway when leaving the experiment than did control participants, consistent with the content of that stereotype.

To make sure that the people are not aware that there is a link between the scrambled sentence priming and measured task (e.g. how quickly someone walks) participants are asked a number of questions, including 'Did you think that any of the tasks you did were related in any way?' and 'When you were completing the scrambled test, did you notice anything unusual about the words?' This is called the funnelled debriefing procedure. Any participant who gives replies which indicate that they are aware of the purposes of the experiment or have made a link between the scrambled sentences and the test phase are not used in any subsequent analysis.

Subliminal priming

Ever been the subject of a subliminal message? You wouldn't know if you had! This type of priming gets over the need to question participants about whether they make the link between the priming phase and test phase of an experiment. How? Well, the most basic form of subliminal priming presents words related to the concept to be primed (e.g. 'old' and 'wrinkled' for the old age stereotype) very rapidly on a computer screen. The presentation is so rapid that the person sees only a flash at best; they cannot see the word itself. (Images are sometimes used with this technique too.)

In other words, the prime is presented below the visual recognition threshold. In this case the participant is primed without their being consciously aware that this is happening because the prime does not register at all in conscious thought (see Chartrand and Bargh, 1996).

Impression management

People behave differently in public from how they do in private (Leary, 1995). They seem to take on different roles when their audience changes, just as actors do in the theatre. What types of motive are there to explain this? Snyder (1974) demonstrated that people who self-monitor, or those who are careful about how they present themselves, adopt strategic self-presentation tactics, while low self-monitors apply expressive self-presentation strategies. The adoption of these strategies may have the effect of guiding the impressions others make of us as a result of social interaction.

Strategic self-presentation is about changing or managing others' perceptions of you. The motives we have for self-presentation are (Jones and Pittman, 1982; Leary, 1995):

- ingratiation (trying to get others to like you)
- self-promotion (trying to persuade others that you are a competent person)
- intimidation (trying to get others to think you are dangerous)
- supplication (trying to get others to think of you as helpless and take pity on you)
- exemplification (trying to get others to think of you as morally respected and someone to be trusted).

If you think about it, you should be able to recall occasions when you have used one or all of these strategies.

Expressive self-presentation is about people trying to get some validation of their self-concept through their behaviours. For instance, we might try to reinforce the idea we have of ourselves that we are selfless by always agreeing to help other people. However, the *self-concept* we have is irrelevant, and does nothing for our *self-esteem* if others do not reinforce or even recognise it (Swann *et al.*, 1992). What is the point of having the idea that you are selfless if everyone thinks you are selfish?

This idea that we use self-presentation to define our self-concept has been shown in work on delinquency. For instance, Emler and Reicher (1995) argue that delinquency is always performed publicly so that others can validate it and recognise it as part of a person's make-up, thus reinforcing the delinquent self-concept. Other work has shown that when asked about which behaviours are important to their self-concept, people invariably report publicly performed ones (Tice, 1992).

Social interaction, non-verbal communication and behaviour

Having looked at how impressions are formed and the motives behind how we manage these impressions, we now turn to social interaction. The way we interact with people is of course central to how we communicate our thoughts, feelings, motives, goals, intentions, beliefs, desires and so on to others. Interaction is the main vehicle for expressing ourselves to others and also allows us to understand and make sense of the beliefs and behaviours of others in our environment. Social interaction is basically a form of communication, and for human beings communication can be verbal or non-verbal. As such, communication depends on a common understanding of what words, sounds, and gestures mean.

The cognition underlying language and how language develops have already been covered in Chapters 15 and 19 respectively. Here we will concentrate on *non-verbal communication* and behaviour, and also cover attraction, aggression and pro-social (e.g. helping) behaviour. All of these are examples of behaviours that reflect social interaction and interpersonal relationships.

Non-verbal communication
Speech allows us to convey things to people in our immediate social environment and provides meaning for interactions. Searle (1979) has identified five types of meaning that people use language to communicate. These are:

1 to describe how something is
2 to express feelings and attitudes
3 to get someone to do something

What is this person trying to 'say'?

Would you employ this person?

4   to make a commitment
5   to accomplish something directly.

For some psychologists language or discourse tells us a lot about how people operate in their social worlds (Potter and Wetherell, 1987; Potter, 1996).

However, speech rarely happens in isolation from other non-verbal signs. Gestures, facial expressions, postures and even the distance we put between another person and ourselves are all examples of non-verbal cues (Argyle, 1988; DePaulo and Friedman, 1998). For example, people who are telling a lie tend to put their hands to their faces or fiddle with their fingers (DePaulo, 1994).

People acquire the use of non-verbal cues very early in life. Most of the time we don't know we are using them, they just happen automatically, like smiling to convey being happy or grimacing to show disapproval (Erickson and Schulkin, 2003). On other occasions these cues are used deliberately, just as the person in the photo on page 417 is doing.

Patterson (1983) points to five reasons why we use non-verbal communication in our social interaction:

1   to give out information about how we are feeling and what our intentions are – we use cues to show other people whether we like them or not, and also interpret others' non-verbal cues to decipher whether or not they like us
2   to direct the social interaction – for instance, non-verbal cues are used as signals in turn-taking (showing a person that it is their turn to speak)
3   to express intimacy with another through touching or forms of eye contact
4   to help attain a goal, like pointing at something you desire
5   to give out information about your desire to be the dominant one in a social interaction by the use of non-verbal threats.

One form of non-verbal communication that does not involve explicit parts of the body – like the hands, the face or the eyes – to convey information is interpersonal distance (also called proxemics). You have probably all heard the phrase 'don't invade my personal space'. This expression is really saying that a person is getting too close and that you feel threatened by them in some way; this is because interpersonal distance is used to convey intimacy, liking or privacy (Hayduk, 1983). The further away you are the easier it is to disguise the non-verbal cues you are giving off, and the other person in the interaction will be less able to use your non-verbal cues to understand your intentions. The opposite, of course, is the case the closer you are (Kahn and McGaughey, 1977).

One classic study showed that when asked to convey either friendliness or unfriendliness to another, those participants who were asked to show unfriendliness placed their chair significantly further away from the other person (Rosenfeld, 1965). From thousands of observations, Hall (1966) identified four *interpersonal distance zones* that describe the function of non-verbal communication in social interaction. These are shown in Focus Point 24.1.

Attraction, liking and loving

We have just noted that more positive impressions are formed of physically attractive people. In terms of faces, some have argued that we are attracted to 'averageness' (see Bruce and Young, 1998). Other work has shown that we experience *attraction* to others who are similar to ourselves. For instance, people seek out and associate themselves with those who hold similar attitudes to them (Tesser, 1993) (see Chapter 22). Accordingly, opposites do not attract. So why is it that we choose certain people to have a *liking* or *loving* relationship with?

Various theories have been developed to answer these questions. The *reinforcement-affect model* says that people learn to associate particular feelings (liking, loving, hating etc.) with particular people. They come to do this because of the pairing of the presence of a person with either environmental rewards or punishments that come in the form of emotions (Byrne and Glore, 1970).

Social exchange theory proposes that people like or dislike others in terms of the rewards they exchange between each other (Berg and McQuinn, 1986; Sprecher, 1998). Their liking or disliking is dependent on what is called the *cost–reward ratio*. This suggests that we all undergo an appraisal of what it will cost to

FOCUS POINT 24.1

Hall's (1966) interpersonal distance zones: 'How close is close enough?'

Intimate distance

Your proximity to the other person is anywhere up to about 0.5 metres away. A lot is exposed about a person in this zone. The cues you get about another person in this zone include smell, how heavily they are breathing, body temperature and other visual cues. In this zone there may well be some touching.

Personal distance

This ranges between 0.5 and 1.25 metres and is thought of as the transitional region between intimate contact and more formal contact. It is characteristic of our interactions with friends and other close acquaintances. At this distance many cues are still available, including touching, although other more intimate cues are not as strong.

Social distance

This ranges from 1.25 to 4 metres. It is the distance we usually put between ourselves and other people we are having a casual interaction with. It is also characteristic of the normal business meeting arrangement. Furniture is set up so that the distance between you and the other person is across a table. Many cues are available, and of course speech is still there too.

Public distance

This is characteristic of very formal communication occasions like speeches and lectures. The distance ranges from about 4 to about 8 metres. In these types of situation communication is usually unwanted and the distance between perceiver and communicator conveys this.

---

seek reward from another. If the costs outweigh the rewards then the relationship will not work.

Surely, though, the rewards we seek and the costs we try to avoid have to differ across individuals? Yes, they do. Everyone entering a relationship brings with them different expectations about what they should receive from the other person. This is called the comparison level. For instance, if you have just come out of an abusive relationship you may think that a relationship without abuse is highly profitable.

Factors shown to be important for influencing levels of reward, and hence attractiveness or liking of another, include familiarity, exposure and proximity. Familiarity suggests that the more we are exposed to another person the more we like them, even strangers (Moreland and Zajonc, 1982). This is called the *mere exposure effect* (see Focus Point 24.2). For example, Moreland and Beach (1992) showed that students rated as most likeable those lecturers they had contact with most often.

Proximity has also been shown to be important for relationship development (Kahn and McGaughey, 1977). Living close to another person increases the chances that you are more likely to enter a relationship with them than if you live further apart. A classic study showed the effect of proximity on entering friendships (Festinger, 1950) (see Figure 24.4). Proximity may be important because the nearer you are to a person, the greater the likelihood of exposure, repeated exposure and of course familiarity.

Look at Figure 24.4. Compared to other residents on the ground floor, people who lived in flats 1 and 5 interacted most with residents who lived on the upper floor. Why? Because flats 1 and 5 are near communal staircases, which the other residents have to use to go in and out of their homes. The probability of encountering the first-floor residents is greater, then, for those who live next to a shared space. Also, Festinger found that more friendships

FOCUS POINT 24.2

The mere exposure effect

Familiarity does not breed contempt! Many studies over the years have shown that the more you are exposed to all kinds of things the more you like them or rate them more favourably. The graph in Figure 24.3 illustrates this idea. This effect has been shown for our liking of nonsense words (i.e. those that mean nothing), music, faces and so on. We also seem to prefer letters that appear in our own names or that occur frequently in our own languages (Kitayama and Karasawa, 1997).

Furthermore, Zajonc's work has demonstrated that exposure leads to liking even when you do not know that you have been exposed (e.g. Kunst-Wilson and Zajonc, 1980). Can you think of ever immediately liking or disliking something or someone without knowing why? This shows that exposure can have its effects at an unconscious level (Zajonc, 1998).

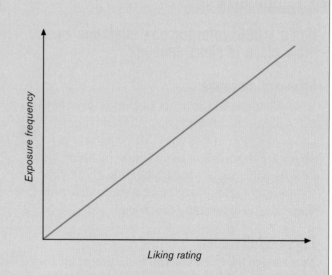

Figure 24.3 *The mere exposure effect*

were seen between flats 1 and 6 than between 2 and 7. The same was the case for flats 5 and 10 than between flats 4 and 9.

Based on the core assumptions of social exchange theory, *equity theory* suggests that, along with a cost–reward analysis, liking is dependent on how fair people think the exchange is (Adams, 1965). For example, have you ever been in the situation where you think that you put an awful lot into a relationship but receive very little in return? This is an example of inequity.

Consider the relationship between two people, Henry and Beth. Equity exists between these people when the ratio between the outcomes of a relationship and the inputs into the relationship for both Henry and Beth are equal. If inequity occurs then one or other of the individuals will alter their perceived inputs to, or outcomes from, the

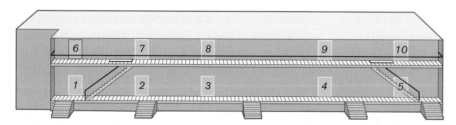

Figure 24.4 *Festinger's housing complex study*
Source: *Festinger et al., 1950*

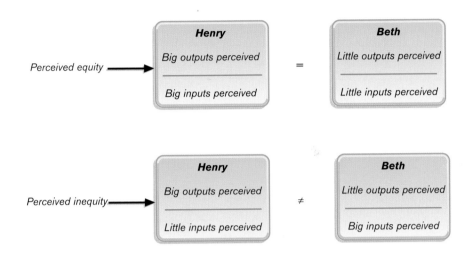

Figure 24.5 Perceived equity and inequity in a personal relationship
Source: adapted from Hogg and Vaughan, 2002

relationship so as to maintain a balance (See Figure 24.5).

Thus far we have really just looked at some of the evidence that shows why people become attractive and why we like some people and not others. Other psychologists have been addressing the question of whether loving someone is different from liking someone (Dion and Dion, 1996). The lay perception is that it is.

Rubin (1973) believed that liking is completely distinct from loving and suggested that loving comprises attachment, caring and intimacy. Also, Lamm and Weismann (1997) have suggested that 'liking' is about wanting to interact with a person, 'loving' about trusting a person and 'being in love' about being aroused by another person.

In his *triangular model of love*, Sternberg (1988a) proposed three aspects of love: intimacy (e.g. feelings of closeness), commitment (e.g. the decision to be fully in the relationship) and passion (e.g. sexual desire). Look at Figure 24.6. The three components of love form the three points on the triangle. If a relationship has only the passion component the relationship is described in terms of infatuation (the external points on the diagram). If there are two dimensions, like passion and intimacy, the type of relationship is seen by reading the appropriate diagonal that links the dimensions, in this case romantic love. Having intimacy, passion and commitment is called consummate love (the circle in the middle of the triangle).

Pro-social behaviour

Pro-social behaviour refers to acts that are evaluated positively by your society, those that contribute to the psychological and physical well-being of others (see Eisenberg *et al.*, 1996; Dovidio and Penner, 2003). Fire-fighters and paramedics indulge in pro-social behaviour. These behaviours include *helping*, altruism, cooperating, comforting and bystander intervention (Batson, 1998). Simple examples here are helping an old person across the road or diving into a swimming pool to assist a person who is obviously drowning.

We have already seen, in Chapter 23 (on attribution), that the *just world hypothesis* predicts that we have a tendency to believe that people get what they deserve (Lerner and Miller, 1978). If people deserve bad things to happen to them, why help them? In this section we are going to focus on altruism and bystander intervention as examples of pro-social behaviour, and ask the question 'Why do people decide to help?'

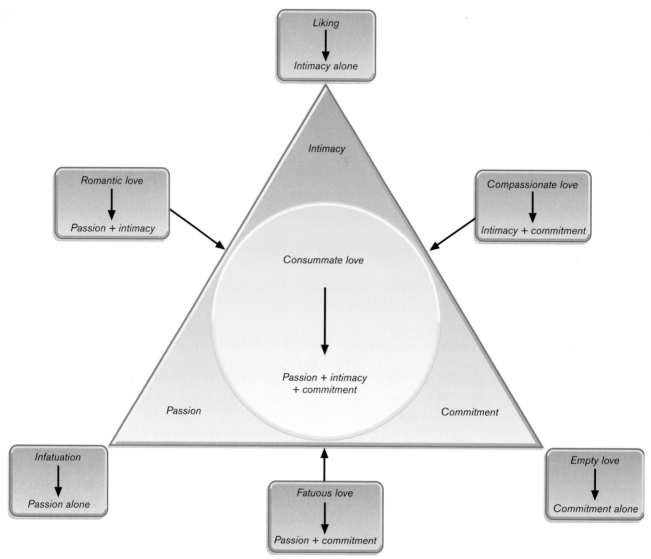

Figure 24.6 The triangular model of love (Sternberg, 1988)
Source: based on Kosslyn and Rosenberg, 2004: 697

Altruism

Altruism is a special form of helping behaviour. It describes those behaviours that are acted out without any expectation that you will be rewarded for them. Do we ever perform behaviours that will not result in some form of reward (or punishment)? We may not get immediate external feedback, but surely we know that helping will make us feel good and bolster our own self-worth.

This debate was taken up by social psychologists studying empathy. *Empathy* is the ability to

experience the emotions that somebody else is experiencing. Some have argued that only behaviour associated with empathy feelings is truly altruistic – this is Batson's *empathy–altruism hypothesis* (Batson *et al.*, 1981; Batson *et al.*, 1999). In contrast, Robert Cialdini's (Schaller and Cialdini, 1988; Cialdini *et al.*, 1997; Maner *et al.*, 2002) *negative state relief theory* argues that we act pro-socially to relieve our own state of distress about another's misfortune. He and his colleagues have shown that willingness to help was predicted not by people's empathy scores for a hypothetical person in need, but by how sad that person's predicament made them feel (Cialdini *et al.*, 1987).

In an ingenious extension to this work, some of the participants were given a so-called 'mood-fixing placebo'. They were told that this pill would make it impossible for them to alter their moods. As a placebo, of course, this was not the case. The results showed that after taking this pill fewer people were willing to help, and this included those who scored highly on empathy for the hypothetical person. So it is still not clear whether empathy or relief of distress accounts for altruistic behaviour.

Bystander intervention

The infamous case of the murder of Kitty Genovese in 1964 sparked interest in trying to understand factors that are important for helping (or not helping) someone who is in immediate need. Read about the case in Focus Point 24.3 and then think about what you might have done in similar circumstances? Would you have helped if nobody else did?

At no point during the attack did the 38 people who witnessed the murder described in Focus Point 24.3 try to help. This has become known as the *bystander effect*. This spurred John Darley and Bob Latané to undertake a programme of work designed to understand why people do not help or act in the presence of others (Latané and Darley, 1968; 1970). Their cognitive model of bystander intervention identified five steps in the decision to help, or not help, when others are present (see Focus Point 24.4).

In one of their experiments Latané and Darley (1970) had students attend an interview to discuss life at their university. While they were filling in a preliminary questionnaire smoke was pumped into the room. Participants were either by themselves, with two research confederates who completely ignored the smoke, or with two other people (non-confederates) but who were strangers to them. About 75 per cent of the people who were alone reported the smoke, and only about 38 per cent of those in the other two groups did. Why?

Latané and Darley introduced the idea of *diffusion of responsibility* as an explanation of the bystander effect (Latané, 1981). This is when a person assumes

that other people will take responsibility for dealing with an emergency, with the result that nobody does. The same pattern emerged when people were exposed to a situation in which a person was having an epileptic fit. By themselves people helped, but helping behaviour decreased as the number of bystanders increased.

Another explanation is known as *pluralistic ignorance*. This view argues that individually each person believes that their personal perceptions and feelings are different from other people's, while at the same time their behaviour is the same as everyone else's (i.e. not helping). Because of this co-occurrence, people come to think that other people in the emergency situation believe the event to be harmless and that, therefore, they do not need to do anything about it.

An alternative proposed by Piliavin *et al.* (1981) is called the *bystander-calculus model*. It proposes a central role for both cognitive determinants and arousal in the bystander effect. It proposes three steps that people proceed through when faced with an emergency involving another person.

1 Physiological arousal: this is the first response and may include things like faster heartbeat and breathing.
2 Arousal labelling: in this stage the person feels personal distress (anxiety and tension) and comes to label their physiological responses as reflecting this.
3 Evaluation of consequences: this suggests that, before acting, people weigh up the costs of acting and the costs of not acting. For instance, if the costs of helping are high (e.g. being attacked by the person mugging somebody else) and the costs of not helping are low (e.g. not feeling that people will blame you for not helping) a person is not likely to help. If, however, the costs of helping are low and the costs of not helping are high, a person is likely to offer direct assistance.

See Chapter 25 for a discussion of other theories and approaches that might be useful in understanding how people behave in the presence of others.

The murder of Kitty Genovese (adapted from the New York Times, 27 March 1964)

The article below was originally reported in the *New York Times* two weeks after the murder of Kitty Genovese. The case spawned a significant amount of research into reasons why people may or may not help others in need.

Thirty-eight who saw murder didn't call the police

by Martin Gansberg

For more than half an hour 38 respectable, law abiding citizens . . . watched a killer stalk and stab a woman in three separate attacks. . . . Twice their chatter and the sudden glow of their bedroom lights interrupted him and frightened him off. Each time he returned, sought her out, and stabbed her again. Not one person telephoned the police during the assault; one witness called after the woman was dead.

Kitty . . . was returning home from her job as a manager in a bar. . . . [S]he parked her red Fiat in a lot . . . turned off the lights, . . . locked the door and started to walk the 100 feet to the entrance of her apartment. . . . Miss Genovese noticed a man at the far end of the lot. . . . She got as far as a street light in front of a bookstore before the man grabbed her. She screamed. Lights went on in the 10-story apartment house. . . . Windows slid open and voices punctuated the early morning stillness.

Miss Genovese screamed: 'Oh, my God, he stabbed me! Please help me! Please help me!' From one of the upper windows in the apartment house, a man called down: 'Let that girl alone!' The assailant looked up at him, shrugged, and walked . . . away. Miss Genovese struggled to her feet.

Lights went out. The killer returned to Miss Genovese. . . . The assailant stabbed her again. 'I'm dying!' she shrieked. 'I'm dying!' Windows were opened again, and the lights went on in many apartments. . . . It was 3:35 a.m. . . . The assailant got in his car and drove away. . . . The assailant returned. . . . He stabbed her a third time – fatally.

It was 3:50 by the time the police received their first call from . . . a neighbour. . . . In two minutes they were at the scene. The neighbour . . . and another woman were the only persons in the street. Nobody else came forward. The man explained that he had called the police after much deliberation. . . . 'I didn't want to get involved,' he sheepishly told police.

[W]itnesses from the neighbourhood . . . find it difficult to explain why they didn't call the police. . . . A man peeked out of a slight opening in the doorway to his apartment and rattled off an account of the killer's second attack. Why hadn't he called the police at the time? 'I was tired,' he said without emotion. 'I went back to bed.'

It was 4:25 a.m. when the ambulance arrived to take the body of Miss Genovese. It drove off. 'Then', a solemn police detective said, 'the people came out.'

Aggression

We have seen why people are attracted to others and why they like them or love them. At times, however, people are aggressive to others. *Aggression* refers to behaviour that is intended to harm another person who does not wish to be harmed.

Every day, through the media, we are bombarded with images and reports of people acting aggressively. Think about 'road rage'. Have you ever been the victim of road rage, or even the perpetrator of road rage? It is highly likely that if you drive a car you have. What could explain why people become

FOCUS POINT 24.4

Latané and Darley's cognitive stage model of decision-making in emergency situations (based on Latané and Darley, 1970)

Stage 1
Does the bystander notice the event or notice that something is wrong, like an emergency?

Stage 2
Does the bystander interpret the event as one that may require help to be given? Verbal distress cues like screaming are effective in increasing the likelihood of helping.

Stage 3
Does the bystander accept personal responsibility for helping? This decision is influenced by whether there are other onlookers and how competent the bystander feels in a particular situation.

Stage 4
Does the bystander decide what to do in the situation?

Stage 5
Does the bystander decide how to implement what they have decided to do?

If the answers to all of the above questions are 'Yes', then help will be given. If, however, at any stage during the decision-making processes the answer to the question is 'No', help will not be given. So, for example, if we do not think that the event is really an emergency, or we do not really know what to do, it is likely that the behaviour of other people around us will influence our actions (or inaction).

---

aggressive – and at times violent – as a result of getting stuck in heavy traffic? (See Applications Box 24.1 and the accompanying photo)

What have social psychologists offered to explain aggressive behaviour? In general they have attempted to understand aggression in terms of learning processes and factors related to the social context of the behaviour – although biosocial approaches have also been proposed. These approaches incorporate the view that social context triggers a basic drive or instinct to be aggressive.

The biosocial approach
One such model is the *excitation-transfer approach* (Zillmann, 1988). This proposes that aggression is the product of learned behaviour, arousal (or excitation) from another stimulus, and the person's interpretation of this aroused state (i.e. aggression is appropriate). The model seems therefore to combine biological, learning-based and cognitive factors for the understanding of aggressive behaviour.

The main premise of the model is that arousal in one context transfers to another. When a second stimulus (or context) is encountered, the already aroused person might interpret it in a way that, for

Ouch, that really hurt!

Section 5
Social Psychology

Road rage in three European countries

Reports in the media seem to suggest that road rage is on the increase. We regularly come across reports about how aggressive people appear to become in reaction to how other people drive. While this behaviour usually involves verbal aggression, at times people have become physically violent towards other drivers and road users.

This sort of behaviour is not restricted to drivers. Some reports have been made about 'office rage', and even 'trolley rage', where people act aggressively when pushing supermarket trolleys. It's virtually laughable, isn't it? Yet it has stirred some recent work.

For instance, Diane Parker and colleagues looked at how angry and aggressive a number of different driving situations make drivers feel. They studied this in three countries: the Netherlands, the UK and Finland (Parker, Lajunen and Summala, 2002). They developed the Driver Anger Questionnaire. Drivers were asked to rate how angry each of 22 driving situations would make them feel. Those situations that made drivers most angry were: when someone cuts in and takes the parking spot you have been waiting for; when at night someone is driving behind you with bright lights on; someone is driving very close to your rear bumper; when someone speeds up when you try to pass them. I can hear your blood boiling now!

For each of these situations, drivers were also asked how they would react. They were given a number of options, including 'no reaction', 'beep the horn or flash the lights', 'swear at or verbally abuse the other driver' and 'get out of the car, prepared to engage physically with the other road user'. While reports of fighting with the other driver were not common, those situations that produced the greatest amount of anger in the drivers also provoked the more extreme reactions. For instance, it is probably worth remembering that nicking somebody else's

parking space could lead to you being on the end of the other driver's unfriendly hand gestures and horn-blowing. You have been warned!

And, surprise surprise, the study also found that males are more likely to be angrier and react more than females. Got the stereotypical angry driver yet?

them, requires an aggressive act. One example here could be the verbal and physical violence we see among football fans after a game. Kerr (1994) has noted that after-match violence between fans could be caused by the heightened states of arousal generated while watching the game.

The learning approach

The major proponent of this approach is Albert Bandura, who applied his *social learning theory* (1977b) to understand aggression. By adopting the principles of reward and punishment from operant conditioning (see Chapter 8), he proposed (Bandura, 1977a; 1973; Skoler, Bandura and Ross, 1994) that a person's aggressive behaviour in a given context is predicted by:

- their previous experience with their own and others' aggressive behaviours
- how successful this aggressive behaviour has been previously
- how likely they think it is that aggressive behaviour

in the current context will be rewarded or punished
- the effects of environmental factors within the current context.

Bandura also proposed that *modelling* is the key vehicle through which learning occurs. Modelling is a form of observational learning in which people reproduce the attitudes, beliefs and behaviours displayed by another person. It was demonstrated in the classic bobo doll experiment (Bandura *et al.*, 1963) (See Chapter 17 and photo p. 285).

In this study four- and five-year-old children were randomly assigned to one of four aggressive behaviour conditions, as follows.

1. The live condition: an adult came into the room, played for a bit with the child and then started to behave aggressively towards the bobo doll.
2. The video condition: this was exactly the same as the first condition except that the child watched the adult's behaviour on video.
3. The cartoon condition: the bobo doll itself acted in the same way as in the first two conditions except that it was dressed in a catsuit.
4. A control condition: the child was just allowed to play with the doll.

The dependent measure was the number of aggressive acts the child made towards the bobo doll when left alone to play with it. Children exposed to any aggressive acts by adults towards the bobo doll also behaved aggressively towards the poor thing when left alone to play with it.

Importantly, this study showed modelling of behaviour when the child was exposed to a real person and also when the child watched television images.

Bandura's experiment fostered much research into the role of learning in aggressive behaviour. For example, it has been applied to the possible role of the media (e.g. violent TV programmes) in promoting future aggressive behaviour (see Freedman, 2003), and to investigating whether smacking a child leads to increased aggressive behaviour in the child (Strauss *et al.*, 1997).

In this chapter you have been presented with some of the theories and evidence that social psychologists have used to study impression formation and social perception. Specifically, we looked at how we form impressions of others (and manage these impressions), non-verbal communication strategies in interpersonal or social perception, and what we can say about why people like and love others, why they are aggressive to others and why they may help others in particular situations.

Learning outcomes

When you have completed this chapter you should be able to:

- describe the key factors involved in forming impressions of others
- evaluate theories and evidence that have been used to understand impression formation processes
- describe strategies people use in managing the impressions of others
- describe the role of language in social interaction and communication
- describe the role of non-verbal cues in social interaction and communication
- discuss theories and evidence that ask the question 'Why are we attracted to some people and not others?'
- discuss ideas that have been proposed to explain aggressive behaviour
- critically assess evidence and theory that have looked at why people help others in need.

Section 5
Social Psychology

Key Terms

Aggression
Altruism
Attraction
Bystander effect
Bystander-calculus model
Central traits
Cost–reward ratio
Diffusion of responsibility
Empathy
Empathy–altruism hypothesis
Equity theory
Excitation-transfer approach
Halo effect
Helping
Implicit personality theory
Impression formation
Impression management
Interpersonal distance zones
Just world hypothesis

Liking
Loving
Mere exposure effect
Modelling
Negative state relief theory
Non-verbal communication
Peripheral traits
Person-positivity bias
Pluralistic ignorance
Primacy effect
Pro-social behaviour
Recency effect
Reinforcement-affect model
Self-concept
Self-esteem
Social exchange theory
Social learning theory
Stereotypes
Triangular model of love

Further reading

Argyle, M. (1988) *Bodily Communication* (2nd edn). London: Methuen.

DePaulo, B. M. and Friedman, H. S. (1998) Nonverbal communication. In Gilbert, D. T., Fiske, S. T. and Lindzey, G. (eds) *The Handbook of Social Psychology* (Vol. 2). New York: McGraw-Hill, 3–40.

Duck, S. (1998) *Human Relations* (3rd edn). New York: John Wiley.

Hogg, M. A. and Vaughan, G. M. (2002) *Social Psychology* (3rd edn). London: Prentice Hall.

Schroeder, D. A., Penner, L. A., Dovidio, J. F. and Piliavin, J. A. (1995) *The Psychology of Helping and Altruism: Problems and Puzzles*. New York: McGraw Hill.

Social influence and group processes

Route map of the chapter

This chapter provides an introduction to some of the theories and evidence that social psychologists have used to study social influence and other group processes. We begin by identifying different types of groups and then move on to research that has been used to understand how groups can influence people to change their attitudes, beliefs and behaviours. The second part of the chapter looks at work on how a person's performance can be influenced by other people watching them. The third part looks at group decision-making, group performance and what happens when poor decisions are made. We then turn to conditions when people behave in ways they normally would not. For instance, we will look at the conditions under which people obey authority. The role of leaders will also be discussed in terms of group performance. Finally, we study how groups behave towards one another, with special reference to conflict and discriminatory behaviour.

Introduction

Groups are made up of two or more people. According to Rupert Brown, 'a group exists when two or more people define themselves as members of it and when its existence is recognised by at least one other' (2000b: 3). So you may be a member of a group of people who like watching soap operas on television. Within that, you may be a member of a group of people who particularly like *EastEnders* over the other soaps. You are also likely to be a member of a group of people who are studying, or are interested in, psychology. Try to think of the groups you are a member of. The list could go on for ever.

It should be clear by now that we are all members of groups. One important characteristic of the term group that is drawn out in Brown's definition above is that the group should be known to others. These 'others' are people who do not define themselves as members of the group. For instance, the *EastEnders* group is a group because people who do not like watching soaps or who prefer *Coronation Street* recognise that there are people out there who do like *EastEnders*.

Groups are important because, as we shall see, membership can define who we as individuals think we are. Groups are also important because group membership (even artificially produced groups of strangers) can lead to changes in our own beliefs, attitudes and behaviours. This means that groups are important vehicles for how social influence works.

Other factors may also be important in guiding how we behave around others. These include obedience and the role of the group leader. In addition, because a lot of decision-making occurs in groups, it is important to understand how and why these decisions differ from those we would make as individuals. Take, for example, the case of juries in criminal trials. Could it be that the decision the jury makes differs from the decisions each jury member would make if left to their own devices?

Understanding group processes is also important because there are occasions when different groups do not get on. In other words, there is intergroup conflict. In our newspapers, on television and on radio we see examples of this all the time. Examples include conflict between union members and employers, violence between football supporters,

Section 5
Social Psychology

racial tensions and so on. The sad thing about this is that we have all at one point or another been a member of a group that has been in conflict with another group, however trivial the issue over which the conflict erupted. This chapter will look at all these issues and focus on the following questions.

1   What types of groups are there?
2   How are people's beliefs, attitudes and behaviours influenced by others?
3   How do people behave when in the presence of others? Does performance get better or worse?
4   Do group decisions differ from the decisions we would make as individuals? Are two heads better than one?
5   Why are these decisions different?
6   Why do we obey authority figures?
7   What is the role of the leader in groups? Is group behaviour dependent on the type of leader the group has?
8   What gives rise to intergroup conflict and how can we reduce it?

Types of group

Kelley (1952) proposed two types of group. One he called *reference groups*, the other *membership groups*. Reference groups are those that are significant for our own personal beliefs, attitudes and behaviour. A person may try to behave in line with the norms of the group or against the norms. In other words, reference groups can be significant for us in either a positive or negative way. Membership groups are those that we are a member of for some objective reason (e.g. because you are the prime minister). Your reference groups can also be your membership groups. For instance, for Tony Blair the Labour Party, or even the cabinet, are both reference and membership groups.

Stainton Rogers (2003) proposes three types of group: incidental groups, membership groups and identity-reference groups. The latter two are really the same as Kelley's. Incidental groups are transient in nature. People in these groups have minimal commitment and involvement with each other (e.g. perhaps you have been randomly assigned to a small group by a lecturer to do one particular exercise).

Membership groups are those defined by being a member. People are committed to the group's norms and values (e.g. membership of committees, clubs etc.). *Identity-reference groups* are those where belonging to the group has an effect on one's own social identity. This means that these groups act as a reference frame for a person knowing and understanding who they are. These groups involve identification with the opinions, goal and motives of the group.

The best way to think about the differences between these groups is in terms of commitment and cohesiveness. As we move from incidental via membership to identity-reference your commitment to the group will increase. Also, identity-reference groups will tend to be more cohesive (i.e. people act as a group) than, say, incidental groups, where people will act in a more individualistic way. Again for many people these distinctions are not always clear-cut.

Social influence

Social influence refers to ways in which a person's thoughts, their feelings and the ways in which they behave are influenced by other people or groups (Lord, Brown and Harvey, 2003). You've probably at some time or another been in a situation where you have agreed with other people's opinions and have complied with their requests publicly but have not changed your 'real' internal opinions, which may be different. This is called *compliance*. On other occasions, you've probably changed these innermost thoughts and feelings as a result of less direct pressure from other individuals or groups. This is called *conformity*.

Power and influence

For compliance to operate, a person needs to think of the source of influence as being powerful. According to Hogg and Vaughan (2002), power is the ability to exert influence over another person and not be influenced themselves. Raven (1965) identified six sources of power perceived by the person doing the influencing or the person being influenced. These are reward power, coercive power, informational power, expert power, legitimate power and referent power (see Table 25.1). For example, *obedience* can best be thought of as being to some extent dependent on legitimate power, and conformity on referent power. Sources of power may all be operating together in the social influence process.

TABLE 25.1	
RAVEN'S SOURCES OF POWER	
Reward power	The ability to promise rewards for being compliant
Coercive power	The ability to give or to threaten punishment for not being compliant
Informational power	The belief of the person being influenced that the person doing the influencing has more information than themselves
Expert power	The belief of the person being influenced that the person doing the influencing has greater expertise and knowledge than themselves
Legitimate power	The belief of the person being influenced that the person doing the influencing is authorised by a recognised power to command and make decisions
Referent power	The person being influenced identifies with, is attracted to or has respect for the person doing the influencing

Source: based on Hogg and Vaughan, 2002

Conformity or majority influence

Majority influence is when social influence occurs after a person has been exposed to the opinions, beliefs or behaviours of the majority of people in a group of which they are a member (see Martin and Hewstone, 2003). Work in this area has investigated whether people change their opinions after learning what the majority thinks. Is this change only there when they give overt responses – out loud in front of others – but not when they respond in private – so that nobody else knows their answers? Under what conditions do people resist conformity pressure?

Sherif's autokinetic effect experiment

When in a totally darkened environment people often perceive a small stationary bright light as moving. This is an example of the autokinetic effect. Sherif (1935) used this effect to explore majority group influence. He asked participants to give an estimate of how much the light moved when viewed by themselves and then in groups of two or three. He found that when participants were by themselves, they gave estimates that revolved around their own established reference (personal norm).

When participants were brought together into groups of people with varying personal norms, their judgements appeared to converge towards a common position or group norm. So, for an unstructured and ambiguous stimulus these people appeared to disregard their own reference points in favour of that of the group. Sherif also showed that when people were asked to judge the movement of the light first in groups and then by themselves (the reverse of the first condition), there was no difference between the alone and groups conditions.

In other words, the *group norm* had already been established and carried over for their responses when by themselves. The effect occurs at the group level and social influence seems to carry on even after the source of influence has been removed. Sherif showed how powerful group norms are in social influence.

Strictly speaking, Sherif's experiment is not a majority group influence experiment because he had people form groups who all held different beliefs. To demonstrate majority influence we need evidence that a person will change their opinions when in the presence of a *majority* of others who unanimously agree on a response. Soloman Asch did just this – but he was also interested to see whether majority pressure occurs for an unambiguous task when there is a right answer to the task.

Asch's lines experiments

During the 1950s Asch conducted a series of studies looking at majority group influence (Asch, 1951; 1952; 1956). In one study he asked participants to make judgements between the length of a standard line and the length of three comparison lines. In each of 18 trials one of the comparison lines was equal in length to the standard line, and the other two either longer or shorter.

Figure 25.1 gives an example of the stimuli used. After seeing the lines, participants were asked to say which of the comparison lines was the same length as the standard line. Of a control group of 37 people, 35 judged the correct line, showing how unambiguous the task was.

In the experimental condition participants were asked to give their judgements out loud. They were seated in a semi-circle in groups of seven people: six research confederates and themselves. The confederates always gave the same predetermined answer as each other. Sometimes this was a correct answer but on 12 trials they gave an obviously incorrect answer. To make sure the participants were subjected to influence they were also seated in position six out of the seven. This meant that they would hear the responses of five confederates (seated in positions one to five) before having to give their own answer.

The results were astounding. Compared to the control group, where less than 1 per cent of errors were made, the experimental participants made on average 37 per cent incorrect responses. The amount of influence differed across participants: 25 per cent gave no incorrect responses, which means that 75 per cent made at least one error; 5 per cent conformed to the group opinion every time! When asked about their feelings after the experiment, those who had conformed said they felt uncomfortable, anxious, sad and lonely. They said that they knew they were seeing different things from the rest of the group but felt more and more uncertain about their own private judgements. Others remarked that they knew they were correct but did not want to stand out from the rest of the group and so went along with them.

On the basis of this work, Asch thought that the fear of social disapproval was a central component in majority influence. He tested this by replicating the lines experiment but this time participants either made the judgements out loud (publicly) or privately. Although the error rate dropped to 12.5 per cent, some people continued to conform. The thing that seems to reduce the likelihood of conformity most is when a participant has a supporter in the group and is not the only dissenter.

Informational and normative social influence

Two important explanations for conformity have focused on the role of *informational* and *normative social influence* (Deutsch and Gerard, 1955; Cooper, Kelly and Weaver, 2003). When asked to make a judgement in the presence of other people, we want

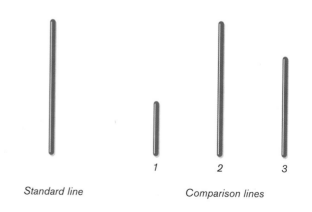

Figure 25.1 Asch's line-judgement task to study conformity

to be 'right' and also want to make a good impression on other people. To try to be 'right', people can use their own ideas or their perceptions or what other people say.

The conformity experiments we have looked at put the person in the position of choosing between these information sources. Informational influence is the notion that we seem to go with information derived from others, rather than from ourselves, because it removes ambiguity in the situation. Support for this idea has come from numerous studies (e.g. Allen and Levine, 1971; Baron, Vandello and Brunsman, 1996).

Recall Sherif's autokinetic experiment, which comprised a truly ambiguous task. The effect he found is consistent with informational influence because participants could not rely only on their own judgement, they needed help from others. The less you can rely on your own perception of the world, the more likely you are to be influenced by others. This is called the social reality hypothesis (Sherif, 1936).

Normative influence says that conformity is caused by the desire to be liked and accepted, and also the desire to avoid being disliked and not accepted by others. If we agree with the majority, this should maximise the chances of our being liked, whereas non-conformity may lead to negative evaluations about us by others in the group. For instance, by making group members dependent on each other it has been shown that conformity rates increase (Deutsch and Gerard, 1955). Cross-cultural work has shown more conformity in cultures that place a high value on collectivism versus those that have more of an individualistic society (see Bond and Smith, 1996).

The degree of informational and normative influence varies across situations but in some instances they both play a role. For example, people may conform and change their judgements *publicly* to be in line with the majority because they want to be liked by others. In this case the likelihood is that they will not change their *inner beliefs*. However, if they also respect and use information provided by others they may also change their private thoughts and beliefs. These findings have led to a distinction between compliance (or public conformity) and conversion (or private conformity). The distinction between normative and informational social influence is an example of a *dual process dependency model* (Abrams and Hogg, 1990; Turner, 1991).

Social identity and social influence

The dual process view has been criticised as a complete appraisal of conformity processes because it underestimates the role of *social identity* as an influence factor. Social identity is basically a person's sense of who they are, derived from being a member of a particular group (Tajfel, 1982; Brown, 2000b).

Social identity theorists propose that another type of influence, called *referent informational influence*, is important in conformity. This argues that we conform because we are group members and *not* to avoid social disapproval. We conform not to other people but to group norms (Hogg and Turner, 1987). We do this through a *self-categorisation process*, which suggests that members of a group seek out the group norm to minimise differences between members of the group (the in-group) and maximise differences with other groups (the out-group). This process leads us to behave in ways consistent with our group's norm and it is this that produces social identity (see Turner, 1985; Brown, 2000b).

This approach has also been influential in studying group and intergroup behaviour (see later in this chapter). Having found that people seem to be influenced by a majority position, we now turn our attention to situations in which a minority can also influence individual decisions.

Conversion or minority group influence

History tells us that minorities can exert significant powers of social influence. For example, the suffragette movement of the 1920s gradually changed opinions to a degree that allowed women eventually to gain the vote. Try to think of other examples where minorities have, over time, changed the majority viewpoint.

Serge Moskovici was the first social psychologist to look at how minorities can influence other group members, in his *genetic model* of *minority influence* (see Moskovici, 1976; Wood *et al.*, 1994). He argued that because minorities do not have access to normative influence (they are, of course, fewer in

Minority influence in action: the suffragette movement of the 1920s

number than the majority), and are often thought of by the majority as a 'bit strange' for holding their dissenting views, they have to rely on behavioural style. For instance, minorities have to be consistent in their arguments over time and with other members of the minority (i.e. show consensus).

Moskovici, Lage and Naffrechoux (1969) demonstrated the role of consistency by getting participants to rate the colours of different slides in groups of six. They were presented with a total of 36 slides, all obviously blue but differing in intensity, and asked to judge aloud the colour of each slide. Of the six group members two were confederates who in one condition answered 'green' on all the trials (consistent condition) and in another condition answered 'green' on 24 trials and 'blue' to 12 slides (inconsistent condition). There was also a control group that did not contain any confederates.

Figure 25.2 shows that members of the majority in the consistent minority condition gave the obvious incorrect response of 'green' significantly more often than either the control or inconsistent minority conditions, and that the inconsistent minority condition was not very different from the control condition. It seems that a consistent minority has an impact on the public judgements of a majority.

Another study, by Moskovici and Lage (1976), compared inconsistent and consistent minorities and inconsistent and consistent majorities using a similar paradigm as before but also including the private responses of people after the influence. As expected, those participants exposed to a consistent majority conformed 40 per cent of the time. Those exposed to a consistent minority conformed 10 per cent of the time, replicating the earlier work, and those to an inconsistent majority 12 per cent of the time.

This shows that consistent minority influence is just as effective as inconsistent majority influence. But the main finding of the study was that the only people who actually changed their private views were those in the consistent minority condition. This raises the question 'Do minorities and majorities show influence because of different processes?' Moskovici's answer was 'Yes!'

Moskovici's dual process model

This model extended Moskovici's genetic model and argued that majorities bring about direct public compliance because of normative and informational influence, without much 'thinking' going on. Minorities, on the other hand, bring about indirect and private change because majorities actively think about the minority view, which leads to cognitive conflict and more cognitive resources applied to the judgement (Moskovici, 1980). Moskovici calls this the *conversion effect*. So the rule of thumb seems to be that majority influence equals compliance, minority influence equals conversion. This position has been supported by a number a studies (e.g. Moskovici and Personnaz, 1986; Nemeth, 1986).

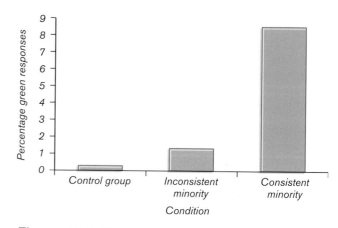

Figure 25.2 Percentage green responses given by majority participants in the Moskovici, Lage and Naffrechoux (1969) study

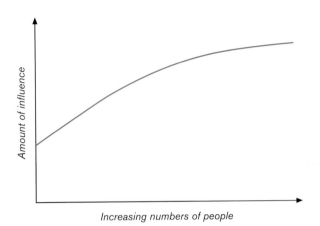

Figure 25.3 Degree of social influence by numbers of people: the relationship is in a negatively increasing fashion

Single process account

Latané and Wolf (1981) argue that social influence is a single process. There is a quantitative difference between majority and minority influence, not a qualitative one. They differ only in the strength of their influence effects. Drawing on *social impact theory*, Latané and Wolf propose that there are more sources of influence evident in majority conditions. This is important because influence seems to increase with an increase in the number of *sources* of influence. The main sources of influence in conformity experiments are the numbers of people. This influence is in a negatively increasing fashion so that the first source has the biggest effect, the second also shows an effect but not as big as the first, and so on (see Figure 25.3).

Because majorities contain more people they should have a greater effect, and as we have seen they seem to. Wolf (1985) showed that in mock jury situations, when participants were asked to make their response privately, minorities and majorities showed influence but the latter produced greater influence – a difference in size, not kind (see Brown, 2000b, for a review of this issue).

So far we have looked at how groups of people can influence the thoughts, feelings and behaviour of others. With this in mind let's turn now to look at how groups make decisions. The first thing to do is to see how the performance of individuals is affected by

the presence of others in our social environment. The questions we are asking are 'Does a person's behaviour change in the presence of others?', 'Does an audience or being a member of a group affect their performance?' and 'Why is this?'

Social facilitation and social inhibition

Social facilitation and social inhibition refer, respectively, to the findings that people appear to get better at well-learned tasks and worse at difficult tasks when in the presence of others (Kerr and Park, 2003). Zajonc (1965) produced a model to explain these processes, which he called *drive theory* (see Figure 25.4). He argued that the presence of others when performing a task causes us to be in a state of arousal: we are alert and ready. This arousal acts on a person's most likely responses. So, for instance, a good runner will perform better when being watched

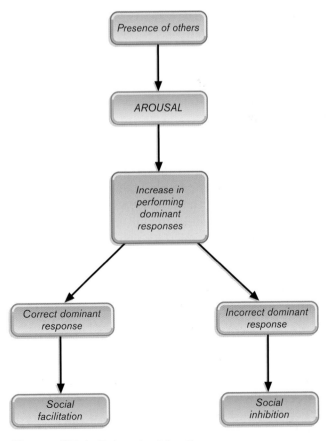

Figure 25.4 Zajonc's drive theory

because his or her most likely response is running fast (i.e. social facilitation). In contrast, a poor runner's likely response is not running fast. In this case the arousal will lead to decreased performance, or social inhibition.

Cottrell's (1972) *evaluation apprehension model* extends Zajonc's work by stating that people are aroused in the presence of others because people learn that social approval and disapproval (or perceived rewards and punishments) are dependent on how we are evaluated by others. Support for this position comes from studies that have shown no facilitation when the audience is not attentive to the participant's behaviour, but facilitation when they do attend (Cottrell *et al.*, 1968). Other psychologists have argued that facilitation occurs only when people are unable to monitor the audience because they do not receive any cues about how the watchers are evaluating their performance (Guerin, 1989).

More recent work has focused more on how attention processes (see Chapter 13) alter when in the presence of others (e.g. Manstead and Semin, 1980). The general argument is that attentional capacity is overloaded when people perform a task in the presence of others. Do they attend to the task, the audience or what? Overload leads the person to focus on only a few central cues.

For instance, in one study people were shown actually to increase their performance on difficult attentional tasks (such as the Stroop colour-naming task) when in the presence of others (Monteil and Huguet, 1999). This showed that people were better at reporting the colour of the ink in which a colour word is written (e.g. 'green' written in red) when others were present. Attention has been focused on the colour of the ink, which is what participants were instructed to do. (Go to Chapter 16 for a discussion of the Stroop effect.)

So we see that other people can affect our performance on tasks – they can change the way we behave. This focuses on an individual's behaviour, so the question we now ask is 'What is different about the performance of people in a group scenario compared to individual performance?'

Group size and performance

Increasing group size leads to a decrease in individual effort and performance. In 1931 Ringelmann showed that as group size increases, the amount of effort each individual person puts in decreases. For instance, people in groups of eight, nine or ten will put less effort into a task compared to individuals in groups of two, three or four (See Focus Point 25.1).

This is called *Ringelmann effect*. One explanation for this effect is *social loafing* (Latané *et al.*, 1979). This says that people work less hard on tasks when they think that others are also working on the task. In effect, they can 'loaf' about. People are less motivated to try at the task.

Another explanation is referred to as *free-riding* (Kerr, 1983). This is the idea that group members sometimes come to believe that their own efforts are not that important to the group because of the efforts of other group members. They effectively leave the decision to other group members while reaping any rewards that result.

This all sounds rather depressing. When in a group we are motivated to leave things to other people. All is not lost, however, because at times we *socially compensate* for other group members. This is the tendency for some group members to work harder on tasks when they perceive other members cannot do the tasks or are not prepared to put in the effort (Guzzo and Dickson, 1996). Can you think of occasions when you have socially compensated another person in a group situation, or when you have been compensated for yourself?

Group decision-making

Groups are responsible for many decisions we make and how we behave every day. This includes rather innocuous decisions like which pub to go to while on a pub crawl with a bunch of friends (hic!), to more important ones such as those that juries make in criminal trials. You have probably heard the adage that 'two heads are better than one' in making decisions. Is this true? What sorts of decisions do groups make? Are they the same or different from those that individuals make? What sort of psychological processes are important in group decision-making?

FOCUS POINT 25.1

The Ringelmann effect

Max Ringelmann was an agricultural engineer who was interested in the efficiency of various types of pulling techniques used in farming. During the later part of nineteenth century he did a number of experiments. In one of these he got students to pull on a horizontal pole that was connected to a machine that measured the force exerted. The students either pulled by themselves or in groups of different sizes.

As you'd expect, Ringelmann found that the force exerted increased as the group size also increased. No great surprise there. However, he also observed that the force exerted did not increase in proportion to the numbers of people pulling. For example, if by themselves people on average pull about 85 kg you would expect that in a group of five the amount pulled would be five times the original. This was not the case and, in fact, the force exerted per person decreased as group size increased. It seemed that the bigger the group the less hard individual people pulled.

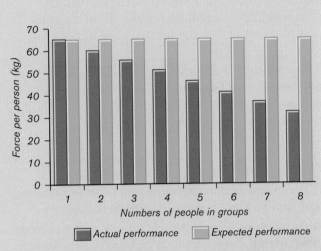

Figure 25.5 *An example of the Ringelmann effect*

Figure 25.5 shows how much force was exerted per person for different group sizes. It's clear that the bigger the group the less force is exerted by each individual.

Group polarisation

Early work showed that the decisions made by groups tended to be more risky than those made by individuals (Wallach *et al.*, 1962). This is called the risky-shift phenomenon (Stoner, 1968). However, later work showed that group decisions can also be more conservative than individual decisions. This led to the idea of *group polarisation* (Wetherell, 1987; see also Myers and Lamm, 1976).

Formally this suggests that group decisions become more polarised than individual ones (Cooper *et al.*, 2003). For example, getting individuals who already favoured the war in Iraq in 2003 into a group discussion with other like-minded people would result in a consensual group decision that favoured the war *even more*. Myers and Kaplan (1976) showed that mock juries become more extreme in their decisions of guilt or innocent if they are shown to favour guilt or innocence before the group discussion.

Look at Figure 25.6. Group polarisation in decision-making groups is the tendency to shift their opinions towards more extreme views. For example, if groups begin with a position that is slightly in favour of a particular view they will end up holding a view more strongly in favour of the position. Exactly

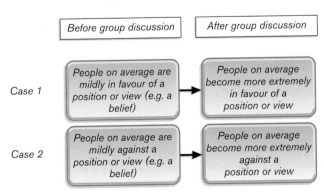

Figure 25.6 *Group polarisation*
Source: based on Baron and Byrne, 2003: 508

the same will happen when the initial position is slightly against a particular view. In other words, groups shift their opinions towards more extreme points of view, but in the same general direction as the original opinion.

According to Hogg and Vaughan (2002), group polarisation can be explained from three perspectives: a persuasive arguments perspective, a social comparison perspective and a self-categorisation perspective.

Polarisation through persuasive arguments

The idea here is that in groups people are persuaded by new information that supports their original thinking on an issue. People in groups of like-minded individuals will not only hear arguments that they have heard before but also new ones that support their beliefs (Larson *et al.*, 1994). Because of this, the views of each member of the group will become more ingrained, with the result that the view of the group as a whole becomes more polarised. Repeated expressions of one's own and other's arguments or beliefs to supportive group members have also been shown to lead to polarised group opinions (Brauer, Judd and Gliner, 1995).

Polarisation through social comparison

This approach is based on two assumptions. First, people need to evaluate their own opinions and behaviours by comparing themselves with other group members. Second, people seek a positive image of themselves, and need to get approval and avoid social disapproval. Because of this, in group discussions like-minded people will move their position to one that reflects the socially desirable opinion. This will maximise rewards.

Codol (1975) has suggested that during the process of learning which beliefs are the most socially desirable, a person will compete with other group members to appear as the person most strongly in support of the position. This is called the *primus inter pares* effect, or first among equals effect.

Polarisation through self-categorisation

We have already met self-categorisation when we talked earlier on about conformity. Recall that as group members we create an impression of what the group norm is for our group (the in-group) compared to the perceived norm for other groups (the out-groups). We effectively set up a *prototype* that describes best what the group has in common and what makes it different from an out-group (Turner *et al.*, 1987).

The person who is the least different from other *in-group* members but the most different from *out-group* members is the prototype. This prototype person is the norm for the in-group and his or her arguments are the most persuasive. The movement of group members' opinions towards the prototype leads to polarisation.

Groupthink

Probably the most famous example of a group's decision becoming polarised is *groupthink* (Janis, 1972; 1982; Janis and Mann, 1977). Groupthink is a type of thinking among very cohesive groups that is based on members wanting to reach a unanimous decision irrespective of a motivation to use logical and reasoned decision-making processes. Based on actual accounts of poor group decision-making (such as the Bay of Pigs fiasco in 1961 when President Kennedy and a team of advisers sent some Cuban exiles on a disastrous invasion of Cuba), Janis and Mann were able to describe the antecedents, symptoms and consequences of such faulty decision-making (or groupthink); these are shown in Figure 25.7.

Groupthink occurs when a number of conditions are present. These are:

- when the group is cohesive
- when the group is isolated from external sources of information
- when the group leader clearly favours a certain outcome judgement
- when the decision is made in stressful or demanding circumstances
- when members of the group are ideologically consistent with each other.

These conditions give rise to various outcomes, which together combine to give rise to poor

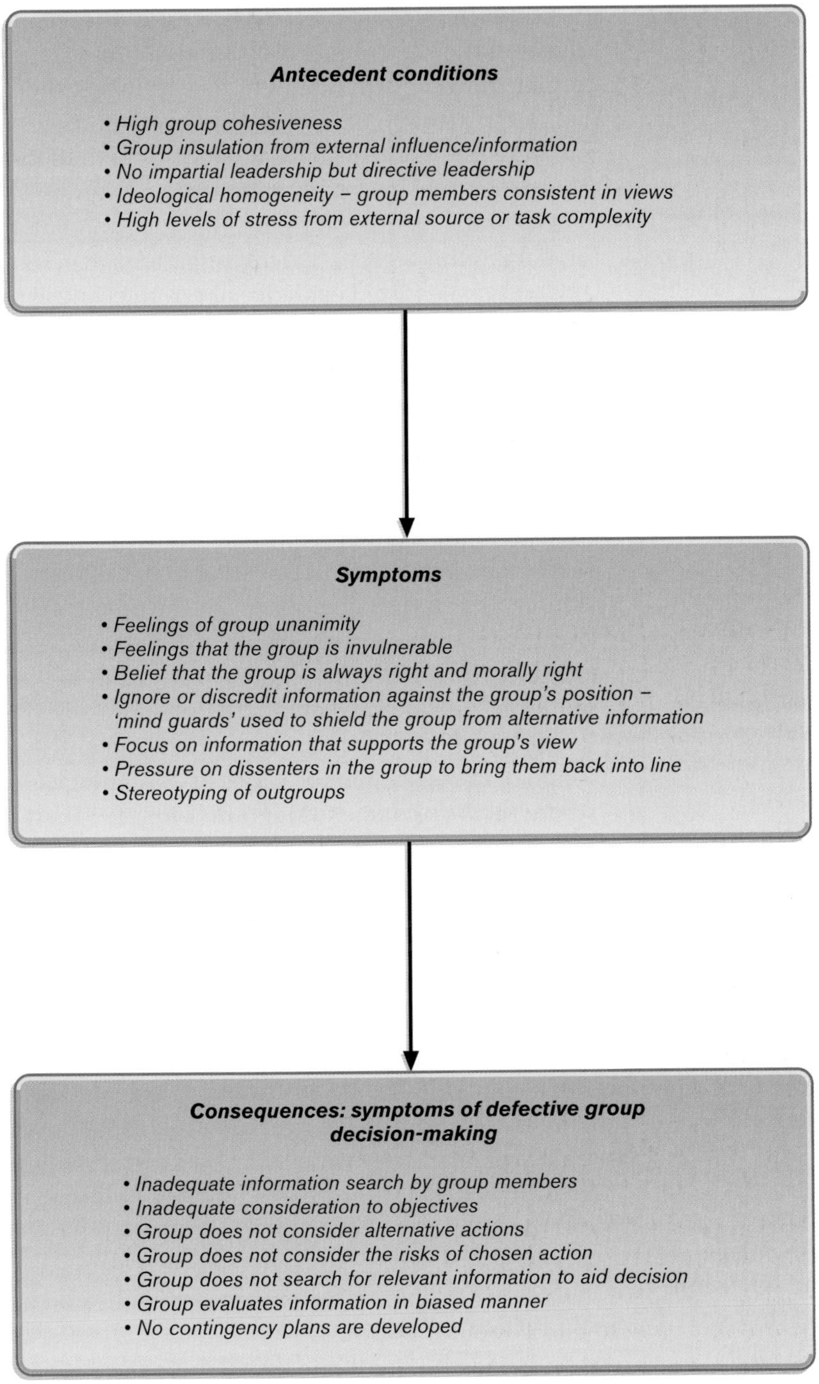

Antecedent conditions

• *High group cohesiveness*
• *Group insulation from external influence/information*
• *No impartial leadership but directive leadership*
• *Ideological homogeneity – group members consistent in views*
• *High levels of stress from external source or task complexity*

Symptoms

• *Feelings of group unanimity*
• *Feelings that the group is invulnerable*
• *Belief that the group is always right and morally right*
• *Ignore or discredit information against the group's position –*
  'mind guards' used to shield the group from alternative information
• *Focus on information that supports the group's view*
• *Pressure on dissenters in the group to bring them back into line*
• *Stereotyping of outgroups*

**Consequences: symptoms of defective group
decision-making**

• *Inadequate information search by group members*
• *Inadequate consideration to objectives*
• *Group does not consider alternative actions*
• *Group does not consider the risks of chosen action*
• *Group does not search for relevant information to aid decision*
• *Group evaluates information in biased manner*
• *No contingency plans are developed*

*Figure 25.7 Antecedents, symptoms and consequences of groupthink
Source: adapted from Janis and Mann, 1977*

Section 5
Social Psychology

Overcoming groupthink
Imagine yourself in the following situation.

You are a Chartered Occupational Psychologist and have been employed to advise the UK government cabinet on what makes for a good group decision. The prime minister, who leads the cabinet, is a strong-minded and autocratic type. She doesn't really listen to everyone's opinions when making policy decisions. However, the cabinet members agree on most things, including their underlying political principles. One day another country invades and captures an island that, as far as the cabinet is concerned, belongs to the UK. The trouble is, it has been only a few years since this same cabinet has sent troops there, which was not very popular at the time among the voters. However, as far as the cabinet was concerned this was justified on humanitarian grounds. The invading country is led by someone whom no one in the ruling political party seems to like very much, although members of other political parties – and a lot of the British people – seem to think the invading leader is OK. The cabinet seems to think that members of other political parties do not know what they are talking about. You have heard it remarked that 'It is just the typical reaction you'd expect from them' and that 'Anything they say is not worth listening to.'

Now take a look at the antecedents and symptoms of groupthink in Figure 25.7. What advice would you give the cabinet and the prime minister to avoid making a totally disastrous decision in these circumstances? What kinds of things do you think can be done to try and ward off the likelihood of this group suffering groupthink?

decisions being made. For instance, groups will not question their belief that they are right, they ignore or play down information that may question their belief, they feel invulnerable, they exert extreme pressure on people who disagree with them in the group and they invariably stereotype out-groups.

While some studies have been able to validate the model in other descriptive investigations (e.g. Hart, 1990), there is mixed evidence about the central role of cohesiveness based on experimental studies. Cohesiveness has been shown to increase, decrease or neither with faulty decision-making (e.g. Leana, 1985; Turner *et al.*, 1992).

Obedience to authority
In most of the examples of social influence we have seen so far, the source of the influence is indirect. Conformity studies do not answer the questions 'What happens when people are explicitly pressurised by authority figures to conform to requests?', 'Will people obey at all costs?'

Stanley Milgram's work on obedience to authority is one of the most famous series of psychological studies ever conducted (Milgram, 1963; 1974). In one of his studies participants were told that they were going to do a study on the effects of punishment on learning and that they would be either a 'teacher' or 'learner' in the study. In reality the participants were always assigned the 'teacher' role while the 'learner' was a confederate.

The participants saw the learner being strapped into a chair and having electrodes attached to them. They also overheard the experimenter explaining to the learner that they were using paste to attach the electrodes to try and stop any burning or blistering, and that although the shocks might be painful there should be no lasting damage. They also overheard the learner telling the experimenter that he had a heart condition.

Participants were then taken to an adjacent room and told that they were to give an electric shock to the learner every time the learner made a mistake on a paired associates learning task. They were sat in front of a shock generator (see Figure 25.8) and told that the voltage in the shock would increase with every mistake made: 15 volts for the first, 30 for the

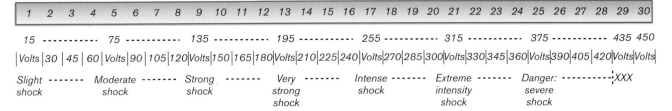

Figure 25.8 Milgram's shock generator

second and so on. They were told to administer these progressive shocks by pressing the appropriate buttons, each marked with a voltage ranging in intensity from 15 to 450 volts. In addition, certain shock levels were labelled with, for instance, 15 volts labelled 'slight shock', 375 volts 'danger: severe shock' and 450 volts 'XXX'. Finally, participants were given a 45-volt shock themselves to give the impression that the shock generator was real.

As well as giving correct answers, the learner also made errors for which the teacher was to administer progressively greater shocks. At different shock levels the teacher heard the learner say various standard things. For instance, at 120 volts they heard the learner say that the shocks were getting uncomfortable; at 150 volts the learner demanded to be allowed to leave the study and at 250 volts the teacher heard the learner scream in agony. At 300 volts and above, the learner stopped responding completely to the task and the participant was told to treat these responses as errors and administer the next shock level. The first time a participant (the

FOCUS POINT 25.2

Key factors in obedience

Milgram conducted a total of 18 experiments in which he changed different aspects of the experiment to look at which factors are important in obeying authority. These factors are listed below.

Persuasion

The experiments start with participants having to administer rather harmless shocks. The participants have thus committed themselves to this course of action, which subsequently makes it difficult for them to change their minds.

Immediacy of the victim

This refers to the social proximity of the participant to the victim. Higher obedience scores are found when the victim is 'anonymous' ('out of sight out of mind'). In one study Milgram actually got the participants to hold the victim's hand on to the electrode to receive the shock. It seems that empathy with the victim plays a role here.

Immediacy of the authority figure

This refers to the social proximity of the participant to the authority figure. Obedience decreased when the authority figure was not in the same room as the participant and relayed instructions by telephone. It decreased even further when no instructions were given at all and the participant was allowed to choose their actions freely.

Group pressure

Participants were shown to increase their obedience when in the presence of other obedient peers and decrease obedience when disobedient peers were present. The presence of others behaving in either a similar or dissimilar way gives the behaviour legitimacy or illegitimacy.

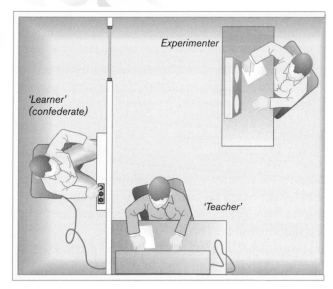

Figure 25.9 Layout of one of Milgram's obedience-to-authority experiments

teacher) questioned giving more shocks they were told to 'continue'; the second time, that 'the experiment requires you to continue'; the third time, that 'it is absolutely essential that you continue'; and the fourth time, that 'you have no other choice, you must go on'. So the teacher was exposed to social influence from both the learner and the experimenter. The study finished when the participant refused totally to administer any more shocks or when they had administered three of the maximum voltage.

A leader in full flow!

A quite astounding result showed that 62.5 per cent of people gave the highest-intensity shock, the average being about 360 volts (marked 'danger: severe shock'). These obedience effects have been replicated in many countries (Smith and Bond, 1998). Milgram subsequently went on to do a total of 18 studies looking at the factors that were important in obedience. These factors are described in Focus Point 25.2.

Leadership and group processes

In many of the groups of which we are members, we come across leaders. *Leadership* is basically a role designated in a group for encouraging other members to realise the group's goals (Chemers, 2003). It's another form of social influence in this sense. The role is given to one person by other group members. Much research has been carried out on how leaders lead, who becomes a leader and the role of leaders in group decision-making. For instance, we have already seen the importance of leadership style in groupthink. More recently, applied psychologists have been studying the role of leadership in the workplace (see VanYperen and van de Vliert, 2001).

The trait approach

Early views held that leadership qualities were inherited and this gave rise to the idea that some people are 'born leaders'. Later work has focused on whether there are particular personality characteristics or traits that leaders have and that non-leaders do not have (House, 1977). Most studies have produced only rather weak associations between certain characteristics and effective leadership (Yukl, 1998). For instance, leaders are more physically attractive, self-confident and sociable. Believe it or not, they are on average taller than non-leaders! Of all the factors that have been investigated, intelligence and talkativeness have been shown to be associated best with leadership. On the whole, the evidence that leaders have particular personality traits is equivocal.

Leaders' behaviours

A clearer picture of leadership comes when we look at the behaviours leaders use in their groups. In a

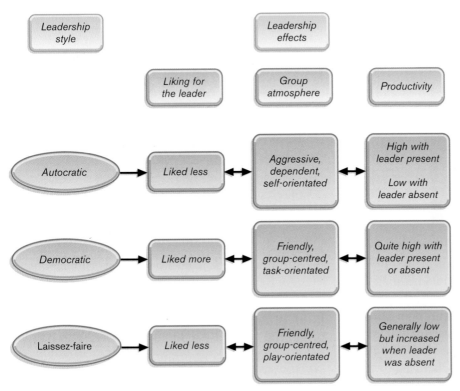

Figure 25.10 *Lippitt and White's leadership styles and their effect on group behaviour and group productivity*
Source: Hogg and Vaughan, 2002: 313

classic study, Lippitt and White (1943) investigated the effect of different leadership styles on group atmosphere, liking for the leader and group productivity. School children were assigned to one of three leadership style groups (with the leader in each group being a confederate), as follows.

1 An autocratic leader group: leaders were remote, focused only on the task, were very organisational in approach and dished out orders to group members.
2 A democratic leader group: leaders were always prepared to consider others' opinions, and called for discussion and suggestion.
3 A laissez-faire leader group: leaders hardly intervened at all in this group. In effect, they left the group to do whatever it wanted.

From Figure 25.10 it is clear that group members disliked the *laissez-faire* and *autocratic leaders* and liked the *democratic leaders*. Group productivity also differed between the styles. It was low in the laissez-faire condition, but high in the democratic one. Interestingly, Lippitt and White measured

Discrimination on the basis of which football team is supported

Robert Mugabe, Prime Minister of Zimbabwe

Mikhail Saakashvili, who took 95% of votes in Georgia's 2003 presidential elections

Which of these is an autocratic leader and which a democratic leader?

productivity when the leader was present or absent from the group. They showed that when autocratic leaders were present productivity was high but their being absent lead to decreased productivity. Productivity in the democratic group was always high whether the leader was present or absent. Based on these results, it was proposed that the most effective form of leadership is a democratic one.

Situational perspective

This argues that effective leadership depends on the situation, or context, of the group. For instance in his contingency approach, Fiedler (1965) argued that group performance is produced by the interaction between leadership style and three situational characteristics. These are:

1 the relationship between leaders and members (leader–members relations)
2 how well the group's task is structured (task structure)
3 how much legitimate power the leader has.

Sound leader–member relations, a well-structured task and high legitimate power will lead to high situational control, thus making it easy for the leader to manage.

Inter-group behaviour, discrimination and prejudice

Having looked at conformity group processes and obedience we will now consider how groups get along, or do not get along, with each other (see Brown and Gaertner, 2003). *Intergroup behaviour* can be thought of as the actions of one group's members towards members of another group (Brown, 2001). Sometimes these actions are about conflict. Every day we are bombarded with media images of groups of people being in conflict with other groups. Just think of football violence and abuse when groups of opposing fans chant at each other, and even become physically violent. What have psychologists to say about how groups behave and interact with one another? What explains intergroup conflict and *prejudice*? Why do groups *discriminate* against other groups?

Broadly speaking, we can think of prejudice and discrimination as being caused by three general factors (see Brown, 2000a):

1 personality type
2 environmental factors
3 group membership.

Personality and prejudice

The argument here is that certain aspects of an individual's personality predispose them to act in a discriminatory way to people or other groups they perceive as being different to them. Adorno *et al.* (1950) identified the authoritarian personality as being particularly important here. People with this type of personality are thought to be uneasy and hostile with people they think to be inferior, and overly subservient to people they believe to be superior to them. Adorno developed the F-scale (potential to fascism scale) to measure this personality type.

Although generating a lot of research, the personality approach has been severely criticised (see Brown, 2001). First, the approach ignores the effect of social context on the development of attitudes. People are attracted to a group because they see that group as holding norms they feel happy with. At the same time, group membership will affect how our beliefs change over time. Second, how does a person-centred approach that emphasises differences between people explain the observation that prejudice types are widespread in society? Third, the approach cannot account for changes in prejudice over time. Many examples of prejudice develop rapidly (e.g. the recent rise in anti-asylum-seeker attitudes in the UK) and this does not allow sufficient time for parents to change the ways in which they rear their children to take account of this new belief system. Finally, this personality approach takes an individualistic approach: that the behaviour of people when by themselves is essentially the same as when they are in groups. The fact that this is *not* the case has led to the study of environmentally based factors.

Environmental factors

This is also referred to as the conflict approach and sees intergroup conflict as a 'normal' response by everyday people in situations involving intergroup contact. The basis for the approach is group goals. In a given situation, if one group's goals are incompatible with another group's goals, conflict is more likely. The reverse is the case when goals are compatible (or concordant). In effect, in the first instance, groups are working against each other because they have different goals while in the second instance groups may be working together to achieve

the same goals. The best-known supporter of these ideas is Mustafa Sherif (see below).

Sherif's realistic conflict theory

Sherif (1966) argued that intergroup conflict is the outcome of a conflict of interests between an in-group and an out-group. When these groups both desire the same goal, but cannot both attain it, then conflict arises. There is hostility between the groups reflected in negative attitudes towards the other group, competitiveness and discriminatory behaviour.

This approach (the *realistic conflict theory*) is seen in a series of three classic studies by Sherif and colleagues at the Robber's Cave State Park summer camp for boys in the USA (see Sherif, 1966). Before coming to camp the 12-year-old boys did not know each other. The studies involved three phases

1 forming the groups
2 creating intergroup competition
3 reducing conflict.

Groups were formed by first assigning boys to one of two experimental groups. In two of the studies the groups were arranged so that any 'new friends' were assigned to different groups. In the other study the boys never actually met prior to being assigned their group; they could not have made friends at all. Even before conflict had been introduced into the experiments Sherif observed that in-group favouritism had started.

To get the groups to compete, contests such as a tug-of-war were arranged. The boys were told that the winners would receive a prize and the losers would receive nothing. In other words, when one group won, the other lost. There was a conflict of interest between the groups. This is called negative interdependence and created hostile behaviour between the groups. For instance, the groups actually fought each other, and destroyed and stole each other's property. In one study each group was given a flag but prior to the competition one group set fire to the other's flag.

In addition, the groups exhibited in-group favouritism. They held negative attitudes towards members of the other group (e.g. they were 'sneaky') and positive attitudes towards members of their own group (e.g. they were 'friendly').

With the conflict generated, Sherif *et al.* wanted to see if they could reduce it. One way they tried was to create goals that no one group could attain by themselves. These types of goals are called *superordinate goals*. The boys in one group would have to work with those in the other group and they were therefore dependent upon each other for achieving the goal.

One situation involved a truck in which the boys were travelling breaking down, and the only way to get it started again was for both groups to work together and pull the truck. This was just before lunchtime so the superordinate goal was getting back to camp in time for lunch. Having to work together for the common goal generated a decrease in aggression towards the other group and a decrease in in-group favouritism.

Sherif's work is important because it highlights the role of competition in intergroup conflict. Other work has shown, however, that discrimination or prejudice can happen when interests do not conflict.

Group membership

Henri Tajfel and colleagues (1971) argued that the perception of others as belonging to other groups is enough to create discrimination. They demonstrated this using the *minimal group paradigm* in which people were first assigned to one of two groups depending on their preference for one of two artists:

Vassilij Kandinsky and Paul Klee. This is important because liking for an artist is a very arbitrary distinction. Also, participants only knew which group they had been allocated to – they did not know to which group other people had been assigned. Then each person worked on their own on a task in which they were asked to allocate points to in-group members (i.e. people with a preference for the artist they preferred) and out-group members based on matrices like the one shown in Figure 25.11. They were told that these points would be converted into money. They did not allocate money to themselves.

Look at Figure 25.11. This is just one of the matrices presented to participants. They were asked to allocate points to members of their own group based on their liking for either Klee or Kandinsky (the in-group) and also for out-group members – people who preferred the other artist. For example, I personally prefer Klee. When given the matrix above I may choose that member 74 of my in-group (other Klee lovers) gets 25 points and member 44 of the out-group (the Kandinsky lovers) gets 19 points. Each matrix was presented at least twice so that the allocations could be reversed for recipients.

The results showed that people had a tendency to allocate greater rewards to members of their own group (the in-group) compared to the out-group. People will show favouritism to the in-group under circumstances when group allocation is arbitrary and when they have not met other members of either the in-group or the out-group. This is a very powerful effect and has been replicated in many studies over

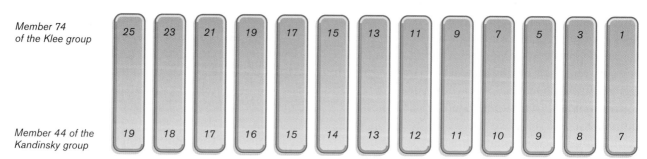

Numbers are rewards for:

| Member 74 of the Klee group | 25 | 23 | 21 | 19 | 17 | 15 | 13 | 11 | 9 | 7 | 5 | 3 | 1 |
| Member 44 of the Kandinsky group | 19 | 18 | 17 | 16 | 15 | 14 | 13 | 12 | 11 | 10 | 9 | 8 | 7 |

Figure 25.11   One of Tajfel et al.'s matrices used in the minimal group paradigm
Source: Brown, 2001: 494

the years (see Brown, 2000a). However, there are conditions under which the paradigm does not show the discriminatory effect. For instance, when a person's responses result in negative outcomes for their own group members, no favouritism is shown (Mummendey and Otten, 1998; see Bourhis and Gagnon, 2003).

Tajfel explained the minimal group effect in terms of social identity theory (Tajfel and Turner, 1986a). This says that people are motivated to maintain a positive self-image. They do this through personal identity and social identity. Personal identity is those characteristics that make a person unique. Social identity is a person's sense of who they think they are, which is based upon their group membership.

In general terms, the more positive the image people have of a group, the more positive the social identity and the greater the self-esteem of the group member. So in terms of the minimal group effect the only way a person can distinguish the two groups is in terms of a label (i.e. Klee preference vs Kandinsky preference) and the fact that they are in one of the groups. They are even anonymous to other members of the group. Because of this the only source of identity can be the in-group. Given that the in-group is so ill-defined, the person initially does not derive much positive self-esteem. To change this they have to make their own group distinctive from the out-group, which leads to in-group favouritism (e.g. the allocation of greater rewards to the in-group members).

Reducing intergroup conflict

We have seen how easy it is artificially to induce intergroup conflict and, just from media reports, it seems that we are surrounded by instances of group conflict. What have psychologists told us that we can do about this? We have already seen from Sherif's work that creating conditions where groups are working towards superordinate goals may be effective. Another approach revolves around the *contact hypothesis* (Allport, 1954; Pettigrew, 1998). This view suggests that contact between members of different groups lessens intergroup hostility.

On the whole, the contact hypothesis has been shown to be valid for reducing intergroup conflict and discrimination (Brewer and Gaertner, 2003). But

how does contact work? Pettigrew (1998) argues for four main processes through which contact has a positive effect on reducing intergroup hostility:

1 learning about the out-group in terms of understanding their behaviours and the beliefs they hold
2 changing beliefs and attitudes through behaviour; some argue that contact works as long as the groups are working towards common goals (Hewstone and Brown, 1986); it has also been shown that the best form of contact between groups is through representatives who are seen as 'typical' members of the groups
3 getting members of the in-group to reappraise their own position, views or attitudes, which have led to intergroup conflict
4 trying to establish ties based on emotional processes; for example, one study showed that contact can reduce anxiety between Hindus and Muslims in Bangladesh (Islam and Hewstone, 1993), and between Catholics and Protestants in Northern Ireland (Paolini *et al.*, in press).

In this chapter you have been presented with some of the theories and evidence that have been proposed to study social influence and group processes. We looked at the types of groups people are members of, how groups can influence the beliefs and behaviours of others, why people obey an authority figure's instructions, how groups make decisions, and the causes and consequences of intergroup conflict.

Section 5
Social Psychology

Learning outcomes

When you have completed this chapter you should be able to:

- describe those factors that are important in social influence from either a majority or minority group
- evaluate theories and evidence that have been used to study conformity and conversion
- describe factors that have been used to understand group decision-making
- assess evidence that group performance may be affected by leadership style
- evaluate evidence and theory which show that people obey authority figures
- describe theories that have aided the understanding of intergroup behaviour in relation to conflict and prejudice.

Key Terms

Autocratic leaders
Compliance
Conformity
Contact hypothesis
Conversion effect
Democratic leaders
Discrimination
Drive theory
Dual process dependency model
Evaluation apprehension model
Free-riding
Genetic model
Group
Group norm
Group polarisation
Groupthink
Identity-reference group
Informational social influence
In-group
Intergroup behaviour
Laissez-faire leaders
Leadership

Majority influence
Membership group
Minimal group paradigm
Minority influence
Normative social influence
Obedience
Out-group
Prejudice
Prototype
Realistic conflict theory
Reference group
Referent informational influence
Ringelmann effect
Self-categorisation process
Social comparison
Social compensation
Social facilitation
Social identity
Social impact theory
Social influence
Social loafing
Superordinate goals

Further reading

Brown, R. (2000a) *Prejudice: Its Social Psychology* (2nd edn). Oxford: Blackwell.

Brown, R. (2000b) *Group Processes* (2nd edn). Oxford: Blackwell.

Brown, R. (2001) Intergroup relations. In Hewstone, M. and Stroebe, W. (eds) *Introduction to Social Psychology* (3rd edn). Oxford: Blackwell, 479–518.

Brown, R. and Gaertner, S. (2003) (eds) *Blackwell Handbook of Social Psychology: Intergroup Processes.* Oxford: Blackwell.

Forgas, J. P. and Williams, K. D. (2001) *Social Influence: Direct and Indirect Processes.* Hove: Psychology Press.

Gass, R. H. and Serter, J. S. (1999) *Persuasion, Social Influence and Compliance Gaining.* New York: Allyn & Bacon.

Hogg, M. A. and Tindale, S. (2003) (eds) *Blackwell Handbook of Social Psychology: Group Processes.* Oxford: Blackwell.

Section six

Simon Moore

Personality and Intelligence

26	The psychology of emotion	452
27	Motivation	464
28	The self and social identity	477
29	Personality	487
30	Intelligence	514
31	Psychometric testing	530

26

The psychology of emotion

Route map of the chapter

The main function of this chapter is to describe what emotions are, what their function is and how they are researched. This chapter will outline the contribution of both physiology and cognition to emotional experience and describe the debate that discusses the importance of these two factors. The chapter also describes how emotions are measured and uses examples such as lie detection, ADHD in children, and temperature and violence, to demonstrate the applied nature of emotional research.

Introduction

We experience many emotions in a single day. If, like me, for instance, you have a PC, you can run the whole gamut of emotions in five minutes if you experience problems with it. Just how many different types of emotions are there? Robert Plutchik (1980), an American psychologist, proposed that there is a basic set of emotions that all people experience. These are fear, anger, joy, disgust, acceptance, sadness, surprise and anticipation. These eight emotions are also universally recognised by people from different locations and cultures worldwide. In fact, different cultures seem to express and recognise these emotions in almost identical situations (Hejmadi *et al.*, 2000). They are innate and directly related to adaptive behaviour that is designed to enhance our survival in just the same way as the fight or flight response is designed to help us survive.

ACTIVITY BOX 26.1

What emotions do you encounter in a typical day?

Spare a few moments to think about a typical day for you. Think of all the people and situations you encounter. What types of feelings do you experience in a typical day? Make a mental list of these.

How many did you list? Psychologists have identified eight basic emotions that seem to be experienced universally (across gender, age and cultural groups). Can you name them?

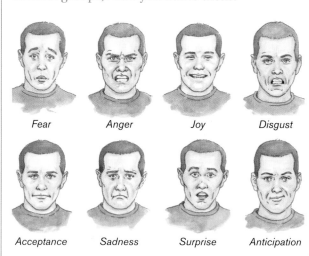

| Fear | Anger | Joy | Disgust |
| Acceptance | Sadness | Surprise | Anticipation |

The eight basic human emotions (fear, anger, joy, disgust, acceptance, sadness, surprise and anticipation are generally recognised in all cultures around the world.

TABLE 26.1   PLUTCHIK'S EIGHT EMOTIONS AND THEIR ACCOMPANYING CHARACTERISTICS

EMOTION	TRIGGERED BY	BEHAVIOURAL RESPONSE
Anger	Being prevented from doing something you want	Destroy the thing in your way
Fear	Any threat or danger	Protection often through 'freezing' so you are not noticed
Sadness	Loss of something important	Search for help and comfort
Disgust	Something gruesome, awful	Reject or push away the thing that is revolting
Surprise	A sudden unexpected event	Focus on the new thing, wide eyes take in as much as possible

The basic emotions

Table 26.1 shows some of the basic eight types of emotions, what triggers them and how we usually respond when experiencing them.

Plutchik suggests that emotions are made up of four pairs of opposites: joy and sadness, acceptance and disgust, fear and anger, and surprise and anticipation. According to Plutchik we cannot experience opposite emotions at the same time. They are also either positive (joy, acceptance, anticipation and surprise) or negative (anger, fear, disgust and sadness). Positive emotions are seen to have a positive impact on our health, while negative emotions can make us ill (Verrier and Mittelman, 1996).

Plutchik also suggests that we can experience blends of emotions. So, for example, joy and acceptance produce the complex emotion of love.

What exactly are emotions?

Now we have a clearer picture of what the main emotions are, the next question we need to ask is 'What exactly is an emotion?' In answer to this question, emotions are feelings that accompany thinking. An emotion involves physiological arousal, expressive behaviour and conscious experience. So when we are scared, our heart beats faster, our eyes become wide, and we consciously judge that the situation is dangerous and we should be scared.

What psychologists agree on is that emotions contain both a cognitive and physiological element.

TABLE 26.2   THE BASIC CHARACTERISTICS OF EMOTIONS

- Pure emotions do not last long and have a short duration. Mood, on the other hand, tends to last longer.
- Emotional experience can act as a motivation for action: the disgusted diner, for example, sending his uncooked steak back to the chef and putting his coat on to leave the restaurant. Where motivations are internal stimuli, emotions are reactions (responses).
- Emotional experience is elicited in part by conscious mental assessments. Such perceptual assessment can lead to very different emotional expressions. So getting an annual bonus might bring joy, which might turn to anger when you learn your co-workers all got bigger bonuses than you. Therefore cognitive appraisal is central to emotional experience.
- Emotional experience is either positive or negative, pleasant or unpleasant to us.

What they do not agree on is which comes first. When we encounter a situation that scares us, do we become aroused and from this state of arousal deduce that we are scared? Or do we decide mentally that the situation is scary, which then causes our physiology to react? Such questions sum up the key differences between the main theories of emotion.

For more on the basic characteristics of emotions, see Table 26.2.

What are the functions of emotions?
We all feel and express emotions, but what are they for? What is their purpose? There are possibly five main functions of emotional behaviour.

1. They are a source of information (they tell us if we have transgressed social and moral standards, or tell us that something important is happening in our environment).
2. They prepare us for action (arousal caused by emotional experiences makes us ready for action).
3. They help us communicate with others (they let others know our feelings, and let us know others' intentions). Ekman (1999) maintains that this is the primary function of emotion: to mobilise the individual to deal quickly with important interpersonal encounters. For example, *facial expressions* are involved in the formation of attachments between mother and baby prior to language acquisition.
4. They regulate social behaviour (through *reinforcement* we learn to avoid situations and people that bring about fear, shame and guilt, and seek out those stimuli that promote joy and happiness).
5. They can create cognitive bias and maintain *self-esteem* (it has been shown that people who are in a good mood are not only more confident and optimistic about their own abilities, they are also more likely to rate others as being more honest, creative and helpful. The downside is that the reverse can be true for people in a negative mood (Forgas, 1995).

What is the basis of emotional experience: physiology or cognition?
One of the main debates as far as emotions are concerned is whether emotions result from biological arousal to a stimulus or from *cognitive appraisal* of a stimulus. At one extreme, emotions can be seen as biological responses to situations over which we have little control. At the other extreme, there are psychologists who define emotions more by the conscious experience than the biological response (Lazarus, 1991).

This issue has been at the forefront of research into *emotional experience* for over a century now. It has yielded a number of significant theories. Each attempts to provide a universally accepted definition of the psychological basis of emotional experience.

Proponents of the biological explanation of emotion
Theorists, such as William James and Carl Lange, suggest that emotional experience is a direct result of *physiological arousal*. They differ, though, in terms of where physiological arousal fits into the time frame of emotional experience. For some, physiological arousal is seen to cause the emotion, for others such arousal is a signal system for the brain to act and produce emotions. Indeed, when reading about characters in literature who are attracted to someone, we are often told that their heart rate quickens. When we are disappointed we expect a sinking feeling in our stomachs, or 'butterflies' when

RESEARCH METHODS BOX 26.1

Ax's emotion experiment

Ax (1953) designed an ingenious study, if somewhat ethically questionable by today's standards. He undertook an experiment to investigate the potential physiological correlates of emotion as suggested by the James–Lange theory. Recruited participants were told that they would be involved in an experiment to observe the physiological correlates of people with and without hypertension. This was a deception and used as a cover story to distract participants from the real nature of the study.

When the participants turned up for the study they were instructed to lie on a bench for one hour and listen to personally selected music. While doing this, their breathing rates, heart rates and *electro-dermal activity* (measured by monitoring changes in perspiration rate on the skin) was under constant measurement via electrodes attached to them, which led to recording machines in an adjacent room. Ax wanted to see if participants' physiological arousal differed between induced states of anger and fear.

Ax stage-managed the inducement of anger by having a technician enter the room to check the electrode attachments. The technician was instructed to be rough with the participants, and to make critical and sarcastic remarks about them out loud. Fear was induced rather alarmingly by administering electric shocks to one of their fingers, after which the technician would shout loudly about faulty wiring. This would be followed by a loud bang and lots of smoke from the adjacent room. Provided that his poor participants survived (!), Ax debriefed them as to the true nature of the experiment. His findings were interesting.

Under the anger condition, it was seen that blood pressure rose significantly more than under the fear condition, while heart rate decreased and muscle tension was seen to be greater. In the fear condition, electro-dermal activity was greater, as was the rate of respiration, than under the anger condition.

Ax concluded that different physiological reactions seem to accompany different emotions. We should be cautious, however, about how we interpret these results. For one thing, we cannot be sure that the physiological changes under the fear condition were not instead due to the threat of receiving an electric shock rather than a reaction to the shock itself. In the anger condition, some people may have been more irritated or shocked than angered by the comments and actions of the stooge technician.

Finally, Ax's experiment did little to untangle whether physiological arousal serves to produce emotions or merely accompanies them. Needless to say in today's world of research, from an ethical point of view, Ax would at the very least face a lawsuit – he might even be throttled on the spot!

... AND SO CAN YOU DESCRIBE WHAT EMOTION YOU ARE FEELING NOW?

we are nervous. When angry, we talk of our blood boiling or being hot under the collar. When we are scared we feel our blood turn to ice, it feels as if someone is running a cold finger down our backs and the hair on our necks stands on end.

Is there any basis for these expressions? Does physiological arousal really decide which emotion we shall feel next?

James–Lange somatic theory of emotions

Psychologists William James and Carl Lange both reached a similar conclusion in the last decade of the 1800s. This was that the body informs the mind. For example, we know we are sad because we cry.

This became known as the James–Lange *somatic theory of emotions*. This theory suggested that distinctive body changes/symptoms accompanied different emotions and that the perception of these changes/symptoms determined the experience of emotion.

Differences between emotions are a direct result of the different patterns of physiological response associated with them. Thus seeing something frightening instinctively triggers an integrated set of physiological reactions in our bodies. These specific patterns are perceived by individuals consciously and are subsequently experienced as the particular emotion of fear. At the core of this theory is the supposition that our brains are able to distinguish between different forms of physiological arousal. Thus feedback to the brain from such things as muscle tension, blood pressure, breathing rate and so on, signals what type of emotion we are experiencing, which the brain then labels accordingly.

Sometimes events get on top of us.

More recent evidence for the physiological basis of emotion

The view that distinct physiological arousal accompanies different emotions has also received more recent research support. Levenson, Ekman and Friesen (1990) reported distinctive patterns of *autonomic nervous system (ANS)* activity for anger, fear and disgust, and there is also some evidence of a distinctive pattern for sadness (Levenson *et al.*, 1991).

Rimm-Kaufman and Kagan (1996) have reported that hand and face temperatures were different in a sample of females viewing different film clips and being asked a series of questions. Those film clips rated as being positive resulted in an increased skin

Figure 26.2 Order of events according to the James–Lange theory

ACTIVITY BOX 26.2

Does distinct physiological arousal give rise to distinct emotions?

It is not just things such as blood pressure, heart rate and breathing that the somatic theory considers important in providing the basis of emotional experience. Muscle movement and brain temperature have also been suggested as physiological feedback mechanisms influential in emotional experience.

The facial feedback hypothesis suggests that the facial muscles involved in emotional displays feed sufficient information to the brain for it to realise emotional experience. So this theory suggests that feeling yourself smile would make you happy. Smile now. Do you feel happier or just plain silly? This might sound too good to be true – if we simply make the appropriate facial expressions that go with emotions we should experience them. In all probability the major pharmaceutical companies would not like to hear this. Their production of anti-depressants would take a massive market dive overnight!

Is there any research evidence that this works? Well, there is, and it is called the *facial feedback hypothesis of emotion*. Davis and Palladino (2000) report a study where participants were either prevented from smiling or encouraged to smile by being instructed how to hold a pencil in their mouths. Holding a pencil in your teeth uses the same muscles that are used when you smile. Try it. Holding the pencil in your teeth does not prevent you from using your smile muscles, but holding it in your lips does.

Participants were then given cartoons to watch. Those who held a pencil in their teeth and thus were able to smile rated cartoons as funnier than did those who held the pencil in their lips and thus could not smile.

A second study that sounds equally bizarre had participants pronouncing different sounds such as 'eee' and 'ooh'. According to the researchers, making the 'eee' sound activates those muscles used in smiling, making the 'ooh' sound does not.

It also results in more air being inhaled through the nostrils compared to when making the 'ooh' sound.

Go on, try making the sounds, and breathe through your nose. If you didn't feel a fool with the pencil trick you certainly will now! Because more air is being inhaled, this acts to cool the forehead, which obviously houses the frontal lobes (the area of the brain associated with emotions). Results from this study indicated that the 'eee' speakers were more positive and happier than the 'ooh' speakers (Zajonc *et al.*, 1989). The effect of tensing facial muscles altering blood temperature through breathing has been called the *vascular theory of emotional feedback* (McIntosh *et al.*, 1997).

temperature, while skin temperature was cooler when the participants were asked a set of threatening personal questions.

While it would seem that physiological arousal is intertwined with emotional experience, the question still remains: 'Are these physiological differences actual causes of emotional expression or merely consequences of it?'

Progression of the James–Lange theory

Physiologist Walter Cannon put forward the first formal challenge to the James–Lange theory. For Cannon (1927/1987) emotional encounters were emergency situations that directly triggered a central brain process in the thalamus. Such brain stimulation had two simultaneous but independent outputs.

1. One output led to the arousal system, which prepared the body to cope with the emergency (flight or fight response).
2. A second led to the cortex, where the conscious experience of the emotion was registered (am I feeling happy or sad based on past experience?).

Thus the symptoms of increased heart rate and quicker breathing were side-effects of general arousal, the body engaging in energy mobilisation. This physiological arousal, according to Cannon, was irrelevant to the subjective awareness of emotion. In other words, bodily changes were consequences rather than causes of emotion; emotional experience, then, began in the brain.

So according to the James–Lange theory we might see a large snake moving towards us, wait to see what our physiology does and then react accordingly. Cannon argued that this would be too slow. The snake would have bitten us and be trying to swallow us (depending on what sort of snake it was, of course) before we even knew we were scared.

Cannon maintained that emotional experience is instantaneous with stimulation. In other words, we would see the snake, our body would become aroused anyway due to the new stimulus (sight of snake), and the brain would then automatically give meaning and purpose to this energy (avoid snake).

Despite Cannon's point about the slowness of recognising how we are feeling if we follow the James–Lange theory, his own theory also contains a flaw. If the brain decides upon emotional experience based upon physiological arousal, then individuals who receive no physiological arousal signals should not experience emotion (as the brain has no information to act upon). This is not true, of course. Have you ever been in a situation when you did not know whether to laugh or cry, or been excited but nervous? How would the brain decide from your physiological arousal which emotion to choose?

Other contradictory evidence comes from work with physically injured individuals. Chwalisz *et al.* (1988) reported that people who had sustained spinal injuries, in which their spinal cords has been severed, still experienced the whole range of emotions as clearly as those people with fully intact spinal cords.

Are we any good at judging our arousal levels?

Two other theories of emotion point to how inaccurate our levels of physiological arousal are. These are known as *false autonomic feedback* (Valins, 1966) and *excitation transfer theory* (Zillman, 1978). Both theories suggest that there has to be more to emotional experience than mere physiological arousal.

Valins argued that the role of arousal in emotion was not as a direct energiser of emotional reactions but as a source of information to be used in a self-attributional process: in other words, not the feelings of physiological arousal but our interpretations of

why we are aroused. It is therefore not the arousal itself that is important but the cognitions about the arousal that define arousal.

To test this theory, Valins gave male students false heart rate feedback when they viewed pictures of naked women. Some participants were given false fast heart rate signals and others were given false slow heart rate signals. Participants, when given a choice, chose to keep the pictures of the women they had seen when they heard the highest heart rate signals. Valins suggested that this was because participants had wrongly attributed their arousal (heart rate) as an indicator of attraction. This is known as the Valins effect.

The knock-on effect of arousal and emotional experience

Zillman (1978) argued that arousal is usually attributed to a single cause, even when it is usually derived from a number of factors. He suggested that arousal that resulted from a primary emotional cause may be carried over to a secondary source. He had people either exercise or rest prior to viewing an erotic film. Those participants who had exercised prior to the film reported the greatest levels of sexual arousal to it. Zillman argued that they had misattributed the arousal caused as a result of the exercising as a product of the second stimulus, the film. This process might explain why we sometimes bite people's heads off for the slightest inconvenience, when normally we would not bat an eyelid.

Imagine having an argument with your partner just prior to going shopping. You drive to the shops (still physiologically aroused by the disagreement), you search for a parking space, eventually finding one only to be beaten to it at the last moment by another driver. Already aroused by the earlier argument, it does not take much for you to perceive your arousal levels shooting up again in response to the selfishness of that other driver. You wrongly assume your current feelings are produced solely by this new situation. If you had not had the argument prior to going shopping, however, it is likely that you would simply have shrugged off the parking space incident. Now, though, you sit in your

Situations like these can create very emotional episodes, especially on a hot summer's day

car planning the total destruction of the other driver's car while they are blissfully unaware in a shop.

This principle might explain the rise of violent crime in hot weather. Anderson *et al.* (2000) report evidence from a variety of sources, centuries and continents that aggressive acts and violence increase during periods of hot weather. It could be that the irritation caused by the heat is transferred to secondary events so that we lose our patience more quickly and are less tolerant than usual of other people's behaviour.

Evaluation of the biological basis of emotion

Is it possible for us to detect the differential changes in our body between fear and, say, attraction? If you could anaesthetise your thought processes, would you be able to judge if you were scared, excited or angry simply by how your breathing, blood pressure and heart rate responded?

This is questionable and is the major line of attack of the opponents of a purely biological explanation of emotion. For example, nervousness often feels similar to excitement. You may feel no real difference between waiting to go on a big rollercoaster and waiting to give a presentation in front of a group of people (despite a probable preference for one over the other).

A major criticism levelled at the biological approach to emotion is that we are not very good at detecting our levels of physiological arousal. If we cannot detect changes in our physiology accurately, how then do we decide which emotion we should be experiencing? If we *are* to be able to judge which emotion we should be experiencing in a given situation, surely we must also take into consideration the nature of the stimulus and any past experience we have of it? If these two things are important, then cognition should play a major role in emotions.

We cognitively appraise situations we find ourselves in and compare them with past experience to try to produce the appropriate behavioural response. Thus, if you have been chased by a lion in the past, it is doubtful that you will hang around checking your own pulse and monitoring your breathing the next time you encounter one! You'll probably feel scared straight away: your memory will quickly remind you what happened last time you encountered a lion. So it will be your thoughts that will probably produce the feeling of fear before you have time to take stock of your physiological reaction. Presumably, your cognition will also question how on earth you came to be in this situation in the first place.

Cognitive explanations of emotional experience

Emotions must have some biological underpinnings. For example, some studies have shown that up to 60 per cent of children with *ADHD* have increased behavioural problems (e.g. increases in aggression and violence) after consuming synthetic colourings such as tartrazine (E102), flavourings, preservatives, dairy foods and chemicals such as detergents and perfumes (Ward, 1997).

As another example, viewers of fearful faces show more distinct *amygdala* brain activity than when they watch pictures of angry faces (Whalen *et al.*, 2001), and the complexity of the relationship between the brain and emotions is seen with Parkinson's patients, who seem to show deficits in recognising fear and disgust in facial expressions compared to non-sufferers (Kan *et al.*, 2002).

Biological factors alone do not, however, account for emotional experience. What is evident is that

---

APPLICATIONS BOX 26.1

Lie detection

Think about some of the crime dramas you may have seen on TV. Someone accused of a crime is undergoing stringent questioning while hooked up to a so-called 'lie detector' machine. Do you think there is such a thing?

The machine associated with *lie detection* is called a *polygraph*; it measures the physiological arousal of the body (in terms of such things as breathing and heart rate). The individual is asked a series of questions while his or her physiological arousal is monitored via the output on the polygraph. It should be remembered, though, that polygraphs are designed to detect emotional arousal and not, specifically, lies. Some questions are going to lead to a reaction regardless of whether the person being interrogated is guilty or innocent.

Suppose you were stopped in the street and asked if you would do a routine lie-detection test about a murder that had taken place near where you live. 'No problem,' you might think. You are hooked up to the machine and the interrogator asks questions like 'Do you like watching violent films?' With such questions it's hard to interpret what the questioner is trying to get at, so you might think he's trying to suggest you like watching violence because you are a violent person. You start to worry that you might give the wrong answer. Your physiology becomes aroused at your 'cognitive' anxiety, the arousal indicates stress on your part and, before you know it, you have been arrested for murder! Of course, it's unlikely it would end in this way, but you get the point.

Leonard Saxe (1994) has been a major critic of the lie-detector test. He suggests, unlike James, that our arousal is much the same from one emotion to another and so the polygraph will not be able to distinguish between irritation, anxiety, guilt and annoyance. He notes that around one-third of all lie-detection tests reach inaccurate conclusions.

emotions involve physiological responses that are regulated by the brain and mental activity.

The proponents of the cognitive explanation of emotional experience suggest that we recognise different emotions because of our mental evaluations of our current situation. Erickson and Schulkin (2003) suggest that no specific emotion centre exists over and above cognitive systems in the brain, and that emotion cannot be divorced from cognition.

The relevance of situation in emotional experience

Schachter and Singer (1962; 1964) put forward a theory that emphasised the importance of both physiological and situational factors in determining emotion. They called this the *two-factor theory of emotion*. This theory revised James's view that emotions are dependent upon feedback from bodily changes, and incorporated Cannon's point that emotions share the same bodily response of a generalised state of arousal.

The basis of the theory suggested that autonomic arousal provided the energy and intensity of an emotion. In other words, physiological arousal by itself could determine the *quantity* but not the *quality* of arousal. Physiological arousal acted as a 'volume control' to emotional experience. As the same state of arousal seemed to accompany a wide diversity of emotions, Schachter argued that there had to be some other variable that gave each emotional state its distinctive feeling (quality).

This factor was the situation in which the arousal was experienced. For example, feeling aroused after eight shots of strong coffee will lead to less intense emotional arousal than realising the coffee shop is closed and being unable to get your morning caffeine rush. You would be aroused in both situations but you can cognitively attribute the cause of your arousal (to either the caffeine or lack of it).

Therefore the kind of emotion felt depends on how the situation is interpreted and explained by the person experiencing it. So Schachter and Singer proposed an element of *cognitive attribution* as the critical factor in emotional experience. If a state of arousal is caused by a wild dog chasing you, this should be attributed to fear (wild animals can be dangerous), but if the dog chasing you was your pet, then the attribution would not be one of risk but one of play and enjoyment.

Schachter and Singer tested their theory by injecting participants with epinephrine (a drug that produces high states of arousal). The participants were then placed in one of two conditions: either with another person who acted happily or with another person who acted angrily. It was found that those participants who had had the injections reported themselves to mirror the emotions of the people they were placed with. When participants were told about the effects of the drug the same effects were not seen, and participants attributed their feelings to the drug and not to the presence/mood of the other person.

The two-factor theory signalled a crucial rethink of emotional phenomena. Prior to this theory, social

TABLE 26.3 COMPARISON OF THE JAMES–LANGE, CANNON–BARD AND SCHACHTER–SINGER THEORIES OF EMOTION

THEORY	INITIAL REACTION	SECONDARY REACTION
James–Lange	Physical reaction	Emotion occurs
Cannon–Bard	Emotion occurs at the same time as the physical response	
Schachter–Singer	Physical and emotional reactions occur at the same time	Situation–search environment

factors were seen only to modify the expression of biological arousal. Following this theory, there was recognition that cognitive interpretations could shape emotional experience.

The role of cognitive appraisal

The suggestion that cognitive attributions are crucial in engaging in appropriate emotional responses was also proposed by Lazarus (1991). Cognitive appraisal of a situation determines the level of physiological arousal and the specific type of emotion to be experienced. In other words, in most emotional episodes interpretation and appraisal of the situation provide an immediate template for emotional experience.

Learning principles are important here. If we have learnt that snakes have been dangerous in the past, then the next time we see a snake we will be wary and exhibit the appropriate emotion of fear. Cognitive appraisal also explains why we can be disappointed by the actions of others through expectation. For example:

> Every time I come around for a visit I bring you flowers – flowers make you happy. So you associate my visits with flowers, which make you happy. So via learning you expect to get flowers and expect to feel happy. When I turn up without flowers you will be more disappointed with me than if I had never brought you flowers in the first place!

Lazarus suggested that cognitive appraisals include such things as values, goals, beliefs and expectations. Zajonc (1984) maintains that cognitive appraisal theories might explain long-term emotional behaviour (such as depression and jealousy of others) but not instantaneous reactions like shouting out loud when you see a mouse.

Summary

An emotion is a temporary experience, generated by a mental assessment of a situation, and is accompanied by both learned and innate physical responses. These emotions motivate a person's thoughts and actions, and provide a way for

---

RESEARCH METHODS BOX 26.2

Measurement of emotions

How do we go about measuring emotions? From a psychological research methods perspective, there are two ways we can try to achieve this. We can try to measure physiological arousal and assume it is a viable correlate of emotional experience. Physiological events such as heart rate, breathing, electro-dermal activity and muscle tension have all been used as physiological indicators of emotional arousal. Many of these are measured by a polygraph, as we saw earlier in this chapter. The problem here is that we cannot easily separate what the emotion being experienced is from the physiological arousal input. All we can do is look at the levels of general arousal.

If we want to be more specific about the nature of the emotional experience, we can also ask people how they feel by employing *self-report questionnaires*. So we can ask them if they feel sad, how much do they feel sad and how long they have felt sad.

Examples of questionnaires presently being employed to measure people's emotions are the Positive and Negative Affect Schedule (PANAS; for more details on this see Watson *et al.*, 1988: 1063–70) and the Mood Adjective Checklist (MACL). Both ask individuals to rate themselves on different types of emotional scale.

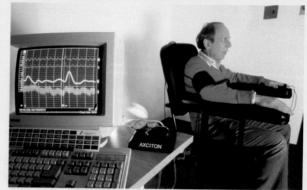

Polygraphs are often used to measure our underlying physiological behaviour in relation to emotional experiences.

individuals to communicate their internal states and intentions to others. While cognitive processes produce emotional responses, physiological arousal provides the intensity of emotional feeling.

Learning outcomes

When you have completed this chapter you should be able to:

- describe the main theories of emotion and evaluate their contribution to our understanding of it
- consider the extent to which physiological arousal plays a role in emotional experience
- consider how our cognition influences our emotional experience
- appreciate that emotions can be influential in changing behaviour
- appreciate how research on emotions has been used to inform other areas of psychology.

Key terms

ADHD
Amygdala
Autonomic nervous system (ANS)
Cognitive appraisal
Electro-dermal activity
Emotional experience
Excitation transfer theory
Facial expressions
Facial feedback hypothesis of emotion
False autonomic feedback
Lie detection
Physiological arousal
Polygraph
Reinforcement
Self-esteem
Self-report questionnaires
Somatic theory of emotion
Two-factor theory of emotion
Vascular theory of emotional feedback

Further reading

Davidson, R. J. (2003) Seven sins in the study of emotion: correctives from affective neuroscience. *Brain and Cognition* 52(1): 129–32. This brief commentary highlights 'seven sins' in the study of emotion that are explicitly treated in contemporary affective neuroscience.

27

Motivation

Route map of the chapter

This chapter will deal with motivation and the 'whys' of behaviour. We will consider the major theories of motivation in attempting to evaluate what motivates us. The chapter is divided into three sections. The first considers biology as a motivational force. The second evaluates the role of our cognitive and mental processes in deciding what does and what does not motivate us. Lastly, we consider other motivational forces such as sexual motivation, sensation-seeking and the need for achievement. We will also look at hunger and thirst as forms of motivation. The chapter will also differentiate between intrinsic and extrinsic motivational factors.

Introduction

Ever wonder why some people seem to be very successful, highly motivated individuals? Where does that energy, drive or direction come from?

Motivational research has been applied to many areas of psychological investigation, such as health and work behaviour. For example, it has been established for many years that in healthcare, rehabilitation professionals commonly believe that the motivation of patients has an important role to play in determining their health outcome (Ibbotson, 1978).

Korabik (1994) has suggested that lack of confidence in their own abilities has resulted in a lack of motivation for business women in China and Hong Kong, and may be a factor in explaining why they have failed to reach managerial levels comparable to those of their male colleagues.

Motivation is an area of psychology that has been paid a great deal of attention, especially in recent years. This is because we all want to be successful, we all want direction and drive, and we all want to be seen as motivated.

FOCUS POINT 27.1

A definition of motivation

Motivation is that which gives the impetus to behaviour by arousing, sustaining and directing it towards the successful attainment of goals.

So motivation energises people to act and moves them from a resting state to an active state. Motivation directs behaviour – it organises behaviour towards a particular goal state. It maintains behaviour until that goal is achieved.

Some individuals seem highly motivated to achieve their goals in life.

Money, the motivator

Take a little time to consider what would motivate you to work harder. If your boss paid you more money, would that make you work harder? Would you enjoy your job more? While your answer to these two questions may well be 'Yes', such experiences would probably be short-lived.

In general, money is a good motivator for those who need or value it enough. Generally speaking, the more you need money the stronger it is as a motivational force. Pay rises motivate us when they lead to noticeable effects – so large lump sums would make us feel better off and would probably motivate us, at least temporarily. However, due to adaptation, we soon get used to the new standard of living brought to us by a pay rise and so the motivational effect offered by pay rises does not last long (Furnham, 1997).

For money to be a successful motivator, a clear relationship needs to be seen by the worker between his/her input (work) and subsequent output (money).

Biological explanations of motivation

Most motivation theorists assume that motivation is involved in the performance of all learned responses – that is, a learned behaviour will not occur unless it is energised.

Where does the energy to engage in behaviour come from? Some theorists propose that our biological systems produce the *drives* for the attainment of goals.

Instincts and motivation

Among the first of the theories about this was the instinct theory of motivation.

Instinct-based theories suggested that people are motivated to act in certain ways by their *instincts*. William McDougall (1908) suggested that humans have thousands of instincts (for example, reproduction, competition, work), which provide the motivation for our behaviour. However, it has been

Instincts

Instincts are automatic, involuntary and unlearned patterns of behaviour triggered by the presence of particular stimuli.

recognised more recently that humans have fewer instinctive behaviours and so interest in instinct theory has waned.

For example, babies are born with a unique ability that allows them to survive – they are born with the instinct to cry. Without this, how would others know when to feed the baby, when he needed changing, or when she wanted attention and affection? Crying allows a human infant to survive.

Another instinct that has been studied recently is the desire to pass on our genes to the next generation. Buss (1999) has suggested that this desire may provide the motivational forces for such things as love, romantic relationships, attraction and marriage.

Drives and motivation

Drive theory also emphasises the biological factors behind human motivation and is based on the concept of our body's *homeostasis* (see Focus Point 27.3).

QUICKSAND

FOCUS POINT 27.3

Homeostasis

Homeostasis is where an organism attempts to keep its physiological systems at a constant steady level. This works very much like a heating thermostat in your home – adjusting to rises and falls in temperature and responding accordingly. Homeostasis is therefore the natural tendency to keep the body in a state of equilibrium.

Clark Hull (1943) suggested that physiological disruptions to homeostasis produce drives (states of internal tension that motivate an organism to engage in behaviour that reduces this tension). So, for example, if we get too hot we take measures to try to cool ourselves down: wearing fewer clothes, keeping physical movement to a minimum, sipping cold drinks etc. Hull maintained that reducing these tension drives is the ultimate goal of motivation.

Hull also proposed the existence of secondary drives. So, for example, people learn that money can be used to satisfy the basic drives of food, drink and shelter – so earning money becomes a secondary drive. Drive theory is less influential now than it has been, probably because it is recognised that people do not always act in ways to reduce these so-called drives. Dieting, for example, flies in the face of the drive to eat, while taking a trip on a rollercoaster runs contrary to the drive for safety. Freud also proposed that psychic drives, urges of the id (as described in Chapter 34), serve to drive our behaviour and so act as motivational forces.

FOCUS POINT 27.4

Thirst

Thirst is the psychological experience of the need for water. Satisfying our thirst is an important homeostatic process. There are two kinds of thirst: *extracellular thirst* and *intracellular thirst.*

Losing water due to exercise or lack of drinking results in extracellular thirst. Water lost in urine and sweat is extracted from the body by the kidneys, and mostly comes from the water in the blood supply. Reduction of the water levels in the blood results in the loss of blood volume, which in turn signals reduced blood pressure. Under such conditions the brain sends a neural signal to the kidneys that makes them release the hormone renin. Renin reacts with another substance in the blood to produce another hormone called angiotensin. *Angiotensin* triggers neurones in the brain that produce the desire to drink. So in effect the response of our biological system motivates the desire to drink in order to maintain homeostasis.

Osmosis (the tendency of water to migrate from areas where it is abundant to areas where it is scarce) causes intracellular thirst. As we lose water the concentration of salt levels in the blood rises. This rise in salt concentration of the blood causes water from areas where it is more abundant to move into the blood system. The effect here is the same as when a sponge is placed in a part-filled bowl of water. Neurones in the hypothalamus activate when water is pulled away from them. Such activation results in the experience of thirst. So intracellular thirst does not necessarily have to result from water loss – indeed, eating lots of salty food can have the same effect by raising salt concentration relative to the amount of water in our blood. We need to drink more water to lower that concentration level. Again such a reaction is based on the principles of homeostasis.

Thirst is a basic motivational force.

Maintaining arousal as a basis of motivation

A third biologically based theory of motivation, *arousal theory*, maintains that people are motivated to act in ways that keep them at their optimum levels of arousal (Hebb, 1955).

This optimum level is obviously different for different people. So, for example, some people seek greater arousal by parachute jumping while others shudder at the prospect of jumping out of a plane and hurtling towards the earth. Motivation to behave, then, is induced by sets of positive and negative reinforcers in terms of maintaining this optimum level of arousal. We learn what keeps our own arousal levels at the optimum level.

However, these theories of motivation fail to account for all the reasons why we engage in behaviour. Biological theories fail to take into account cognitive influences on what motivates us. Why is it that, for some, money can motivate while for others it is not important? For example, why do some people work as volunteers for no wages and other people seek highly paid jobs? There must, then, be something else other than pure biological energy that motivates different people for different reasons.

The influence of cognition on motivation

How can we explain why some things motivate only some people and why these do not always motivate the same person twice? The contemporary view of motivation emphasises the importance of cognitive processes. How important something is to you and how confident you are in your ability to succeed are cognitive factors that will influence motivation. So if passing your driving test is essential in gaining that ideal job you might become too stressed and not perform as well.

Incentive, expectancy and cognitive theories of motivation

The role of incentives

Incentive theory maintains that external stimuli motivate behaviour. Accordingly, individuals are attracted to behaviours that offer positive *incentives*, and discouraged from those behaviours they associate with negative outcomes. So getting a top grade in an exam might act as an incentive for that student to work hard to maintain this level.

The value of an incentive is influenced by cognitive and biological factors. So drug-taking behaviour might be motivated both by biological addiction (craving) and cognitive evaluations (taking the drug in the past has made the person feel relaxed and happy). Incentives might also explain some sports motivation. Improving on personal bests for athletes, or triumphing against a rival team for footballers, are powerful incentives to perform well.

Achieving success over a rival can be a strong motivational force for performance.

How do our expectations influence our motivations?

Expectancy theory, developed by Edward Tolman in the 1930s, is based on cognitive processes, and motivation here is provided by people's thoughts about engaging in behaviour. Expectancies refer to beliefs about how you will do if you engage in a certain behaviour. So if we expect to do well then we will be more likely to engage in the behaviour. If we feel that the chance of succeeding is poor we will be less likely to become involved.

The *cognitive x value theory* states that goal-directed behaviour is motivated by two cognitive judgements: first, the strength of an individual's expectation that engagement in a particular behaviour will lead to goal obtainment (expectation value); second, the value the individual places on the goal (incentive value).

Let us consider an example concerning successful job promotion. Paul studies hard for his upcoming promotion interview, as he believes that this will increase the probability that he will be promoted

APPLICATIONS BOX 27.1

Hunger

There are a number of social and biological mechanisms underlying hunger (the state of wanting to eat) and satiety (the state of no longer wanting food). From a biological perspective (as noted in Chapter 9), there are two sets of signals that are associated with hunger. Empty stomachs might increase appetite and produce hunger 'pangs' and a full stomach usually results in a decrease in appetite through bloating. Yet it has been found that people who have had their stomachs removed still get hungry and eat normal levels of food. If the stomach does not seem to signal food satiation, what does?

More precise signals probably come from the brain and its monitoring of blood-borne nutrients such as glucose (sugar used by body cells), amino acids and fatty acids. When glucose levels drop, eating increases. Even animals that have been deprived of food for long periods will not eat

again if injected with large doses of glucose.

Hormones also play a role in satiety. High levels of *leptin*, a hormone produced by fat cells, send signals directly to the hypothalamus to indicate satiety. It has been seen that animals that do not produce leptin (due to natural abnormalities) are often obese.

There are also non-biological signals for eating. Appetite is the motivation to seek pleasure from food. Take chocolate craving as an example. It has been shown that if people who crave chocolate are given substances that taste like chocolate but do not have the same chemical composition as real chocolate, their craving is satiated. However, if people who crave chocolate are given substances that have the same chemical composition as chocolate (but do not taste like it), they go on craving chocolate (Michener and Rozin, 1994). This suggests that flavour also acts as a motivational force in some kinds of eating.

It has also been shown that our social environment can influence our eating. People tend to eat more when they are with others. However, individuals who are concerned with how they look to others consume more food when eating on their own than when eating with others. This suggests that social cues can also act to influence our eating habits.

(high expectation value), and he really wants to develop his career with this company (high incentive value). Paul is therefore highly motivated to study for his interview.

Rachel believes that studying hard for the promotion interview will lead to greater interview performance (high expectation value) but is not completely sure if she wants a long-term job with this company (low incentive value). Rachel is therefore moderately motivated to study for her interview.

Sam thinks performance in an interview is down to luck and places little value on studying for it (low expectation value). In addition, he is not that bothered about staying with this company (low incentive value). Sam is therefore not particularly motivated to study for his interview.

Heckhausen's expectancy-value model (1991)

Heckhausen (1991) attempted to integrate a number of different approaches to motivation. The resulting model distinguished between four different types of expectancy: situation–outcome (subjective probability of attaining an outcome in a specific situation without acting), action–outcome (subjective probability of attaining an outcome by one's actions), action-by-situation–outcome (subjective probability that situational factors facilitate or impede one's action–outcome expectancy), and outcome–consequence (subjective probability of an outcome to be associated with a specific consequence).

It is important to note that in Heckhausen's model outcomes are the immediate results of one's actions. These immediate results are or are not followed by various consequences (e.g. self-evaluation, external evaluation). They do not have any incentive value on their own. Incentive value is only attributed to the consequences of one's actions. Therefore the motivation to act depends mainly on the value attached to the consequences of one's behaviour.

The role of self-efficacy

Another model of the cognitive basis of motivation has been suggested by Bandura (1997). He proposed a social cognitive model of motivation focused on the role of perceptions of efficacy and human agency. Bandura defined *self-efficacy* as an individual's confidence in their ability to organise and execute a given course of action to solve a problem or accomplish a task.

He distinguishes between two kinds of expectancy belief. First, outcome expectations, which are beliefs that certain behaviours will lead to certain outcomes (e.g. the belief that practising will improve one's performance). Second, efficacy expectations, which are beliefs about whether one can effectively perform the behaviours necessary to produce the outcome (e.g. 'I can practise sufficiently hard to pass my driving test').

These two kinds of expectancy belief are different because individuals can believe that a certain behaviour will produce a certain outcome (outcome expectation), but may not believe they can perform that behaviour (efficacy expectation). So, for example, an individual might believe that a good presentation will impress their boss (outcome expectation), but judge that they get very anxious about public speaking and so probably cannot give a good presentation (efficacy expectation).

The self-efficacy construct has been applied to behaviour in many domains, including school (how well children think they will do in exams), healthcare (patients' ratings of their chances of recovery), sports (athletes' expectations of winning a race), therapy (individuals' judgements on self-improvement) and even snake phobia (a phobic's attitude towards success in beating the phobia).

For example, St Charles (2002) reported a significant correlation between self-reported self-efficacy scores of lecturers and their subsequent teaching performance. Those academics that reported high self-efficacy in being able to teach were those rated as the best teachers. This study therefore strongly suggested that motivation to teach was influenced by self-efficacy.

D'Amico and Cardaci (2003) investigated self-efficacy and scholastic achievement as measured in 151 schoolchildren (mean age 13.4 years). They reported that all self-efficacy scores were significantly correlated with scholastic achievement. Therefore studies such as these seem to suggest that

TABLE 27.1   THE FOUR ATTRIBUTIONS THAT RESULT FROM A COMBINATION OF INTERNAL OR EXTERNAL LOCUS OF CONTROL

	INTERNAL LOCUS OF CONTROL	EXTERNAL LOCUS OF CONTROL
No control	Own natural ability with maths	Pure luck (how I am feeling on the day; if I get a lucky break with the right questions)
Control	The amount of effort I put into studying maths	Task difficulty (how hard the questions are going to be)

judgements of self-efficacy do have an impact on motivation levels.

How we try to explain the world and motivation

Attribution models include beliefs about ability and expectancies for success, along with incentives for engaging in different activities, including valuing of achievement. *Attribution theory* proposes that every individual tries to explain success or failure of self and others by offering certain 'attributions'. So when running for the bus to work in the morning and missing it, we could make a number of attributions regarding our failure to catch it. We might attribute our failure to the fact that we got up late or we might judge that the driver was being unreasonable and did not wait for us.

Different attributions lead to different outcomes in terms of our attitude towards an event. So attributing getting up too late will lead to us being cross with ourselves, while attributing our failure to the bus driver's impatience will make us cross with him/her.

Weiner's attribution theory has been a major theory of motivation for the past 20 years (Weiner, 1985a). Weiner (1992) identified ability, effort, task difficulty and luck as the most important achievement attributions that serve to motivate action. These attributions were classified into three factors: locus of control, stability and controllability. The locus of control dimension has two poles: *internal* versus *external locus of control*. The stability dimension refers to whether or not causes change over time.

Controllability contrasts causes one can control (such as skill/efficacy) with causes one cannot control (e.g. mood, climate, others' actions and luck).

Table 27.1 shows the four attributions that result from a combination of internal or external locus of control and whether or not control is possible when faced with a maths exam.

Weiner (1985a; 1992) demonstrated that each of these causal dimensions has unique influences on various aspects of achievement behaviour. Stability influences individuals' expectancies for success: attributing an outcome to a stable cause such as ability or skill has a stronger influence on expectancies for future success (producing greater motivation to engage in action) than attributing an outcome to an unstable cause such as effort. So, for example, we try some things but often give up quickly on them as we soon realise that – while we might be able to expend effort – we do not possess the skill (playing a musical instrument, for example).

The locus of control factor is linked most strongly to affective reactions. For instance, attributing success to an internal cause enhances one's pride or self-esteem, but attributing that success to an external cause enhances one's gratitude. So we might want to do well in an exam. We could cheat and pass, but we would attribute that pass to dishonesty rather than our own ability. If we studied hard and passed, then we would feel proud of ourselves for achieving that goal.

As another example, attributional processes have also been shown to play an important motivating role in the rehabilitation of criminals with drug habits. In accordance with the model, motivation has been found to affect engagement in treatment, a variable that includes attendance, cooperation and dependability (Hiller, Knight and Simpson, 1999)

Cognitive strategies designed to improve motivation have been shown to lead to increased engagement in treatment, including commitment to treatment and the strength of the therapeutic relationship between client and counsellor (Simpson, Joe and Rowan-Szal, 1997).

The role of goals as a motivating force

Goal theories assume that all actions are given meaning, direction and purpose by the goals that individuals seek out, and that the quality and intensity of behaviour will change as these goals change.

The work on goal theory (Ames, 1992; Urdan and Maehr, 1995) has differentiated three separate types of goals:

1. *mastery goals* (also called learning goals), which focus on gaining competence or mastering a new set of knowledge or skills
2. *performance goals* (also called ego-involvement goals), which focus on achieving normative-based standards, doing better than others or doing well without a lot of effort
3. *social goals*, which focus on relationships among people.

Further research has suggested the existence of other goals. For example, Nicholls *et al.* (1990) defined two major kinds of motivationally relevant goal patterns or orientations: *ego-involved* goals and *task-involved* goals. Individuals with ego-involved goals seek to maximise favourable evaluations of their competence and to minimise negative evaluations of competence. Questions like 'Will I look intelligent?' and 'Can I outperform others?' reflect ego-involved goals. Motivation here is provided by the perception that engagement in the behaviour will enhance one's ego.

In contrast, with task-involved goals, individuals focus on mastering tasks and increasing their competence. Questions such as 'How can I do this task?' and 'What will I learn?' reflect task-involved goals. Here individuals perceive that engaging in the behaviour will aid learning and skill competence.

Much of the development of *goal-setting theory* has been carried out in connection with motivation in sports, business, education and health. For example, Locke and Latham (1985) reported that goals affected sports performance by affecting effort, persistence and attention, and by motivating strategy development.

Fisher and Hardie (2002) examined the value of goal attainment scaling (GAS) as a therapeutic tool and an outcome measure in a rehabilitation programme for the management of chronic pain. The GAS measures individuals' likelihood of attaining a specific goal. A total of 149 patients (mean age 42.5 years) with chronic pain completed a 15-day pain management programme (daycare or residential) in an NHS regional rehabilitation centre. Goal theory correlated significantly with walking improvement and pain experience.

Dowson and McInerney (2001) found a positive relationship between students' social goals and effective engagement in learning. Students' concerns about fitting in with others, social affiliations and social responsibilities were the most salient academic motivators and directly influenced students' academic achievements.

The need for self-development

Some psychologists believe that our desire to better ourselves and improve our skills and situation in the world are the strongest factors that motivate our behaviour.

Humanistic theory provides one of the best-known accounts of motivation. According to this view, humans are driven to achieve their maximum potential and will always do so unless obstacles are placed in their way. These obstacles include hunger, thirst, financial problems, safety issues or anything else that takes our focus away from maximum psychological growth. According to Maslow's (1970) hierarchy of needs we are motivated to seek basic needs such as food and shelter and then move up to higher psychological needs.

Maslow's work has led to additional attempts to develop a grand overarching theory of motivation. For example, Leonard, Beauvais and Scholl (1995) proposed five factors as the sources of motivation:

1. instrumental motivation (rewards and punishers)
2. intrinsic process motivation (enjoyment, fun)
3. goal internalisation (self-determined values and goals)
4. internal self-concept-based motivation (matching behaviour with internally developed ideal self)
5. external self-concept-based motivation (matching behaviour with externally developed ideal self).

APPLICATIONS BOX 27.2

Theories in focus

There is an impressive body of research showing the relationship of expectancy, attributions and values to different kinds of performance, and it supports the continuing viability of these models. However, expectancy theory, attribution theory, goal theory and self-efficacy theory can all be criticised for emphasising the rational cognitive processes leading to motivation and behaviour.

Fischoff *et al.* (1982), for example, argued that individuals do not realistically engage in the logical, rational decision-making processes of determining expectancies and values. They found that people prefer more fallible and optimistic decision-making strategies in terms of motivating them to act.

Goal theory has also been criticised in one area, namely that it leaves largely unaddressed the question of why individuals choose one goal over another. The humanistic approaches to motivation, while interesting, are somewhat rigid. Maslow's contention that we must first satisfy basic needs prior to attending to higher needs is not reflected in daily life. For example, someone who is dieting may be hungry but is more motivated by how the diet will make them look than by satisfying their hunger.

So their model has two sources of motivation: internally driven and externally driven. Factors one and five in the list above are both externally oriented. The main difference is that individuals who are instrumentally motivated are influenced more by immediate actions in the environment (e.g. operant conditioning), whereas individuals who are self-concept motivated are influenced more by their constructions of external demands and ideals (e.g. social cognition).

Factors two, three and four are more internally oriented. In the case of intrinsic processes, the specific task is interesting and provides immediate internal reinforcement (e.g. cognitive or humanistic theory). The individual with a goal-internalisation orientation is more task-oriented (e.g. humanistic or social cognition theory), whereas the person with an internal self-concept orientation is more influenced by individual constructions of the ideal self (humanistic or psychoanalytic theory).

What is the difference between intrinsic and extrinsic motivation?

From a review of motivational theories it can be seen that there are, generally speaking, two different kinds of motivational factor: those that are internally generated and those that are externally generated. These are called, respectively, *intrinsic motivation* and *extrinsic motivation*. Examples of intrinsic motivation are feeling good about doing something (ego boosts) and gaining knowledge or competence as a result of engaging in a behaviour.

In contrast, examples of extrinsic motivation include money, materialistic gains (new car, bigger office, more friends) and basically engaging in a task merely to obtain rewards or avoid punishments from sources outside oneself.

When people pursue activities for their intrinsic interest, they are especially likely to become and remain fascinated and absorbed by them and feel happy. Conversely, when people concentrate on the external rewards of particular tasks, they experience decreased emotional involvement and more negative feelings. Hence, intrinsic motivational factors seem to motivate us for longer periods of time. Previous findings have shown that students who are intrinsically motivated persist longer, conquer challenges and demonstrate accomplishment in their academic endeavours more than those who are extrinsically motivated (Ames, 1992).

Twemlow *et al.* (1996) researched why people (170 martial arts students, ranging from the ages of 5 to 63) studied martial arts. Responses supported the view that both intrinsic and extrinsic factors motivate people:

- physical and recreational (extrinsic motivation) needs, such as self-defence, the need for physical exercise or the experience of competing
- intellectual and emotional (intrinsic motivation) needs, such as self-discipline and self-confidence.

One also has to distinguish between immediate reasons (e.g. enjoyment) and ultimate reasons for behaviour (e.g. survival). Intrinsically motivated behaviour can be conducive to ultimate goals even though the individual is motivated only by immediate incentives. A typical case is exploratory or play behaviour. Play helps to increase an individual's competence but it is also performed because play is exciting, pleasurable or enjoyable.

APPLICATIONS BOX 27.3

Increasing motivation in the classroom using intrinsic and extrinsic factors

There is a variety of specific actions that teachers can take to increase *motivation* in classroom tasks. In general, these fall into the two categories: intrinsic motivation and extrinsic motivation, as shown in Table 27.2.

Other motivational forces

Sexual motivation

There is a difference between *sexual motivation* and the hunger and thirst motivation drives. When a hungry or thirsty animal ingests a sufficient quantity of food or water, this restoration of energy or fluid returns the organism to a state of homeostatic balance. Sexual activity, however, depletes the organism's energy stores and the sex drive is satiated only when fatigue and exhaustion override it. Additional important differences arise because sexual motivation is largely elicited by environmental cues, whereas hunger and thirst reflect internal changes.

As noted in the section of this book on psychobiology, sex hormones released by the brain play an activating role in sexual behaviour. While both males and females have both types of sex

TABLE 27.2 TWO CATEGORIES OF MOTIVATION: INTRINSIC AND EXTRINSIC

INTRINSIC	EXTRINSIC
- Explain or show why learning a particular content or skill is important - Create and/or maintain curiosity and interest - Provide a variety of activities and sensory stimulations: reading, stories, video - Provide games and simulations - Set clear goals for learning - Relate learning to student needs and examples from their daily lives - Help student develop plan of action	- Provide clear expectations - Give corrective feedback - Provide valuable rewards - Make rewards available

hormones, oestrogens and progestogens are the female sex hormones and androgens are the male sex hormone. Females obviously have greater amounts of oestrogens and progestogens, and males greater levels of androgens.

Despite the fact that sexual behaviour in humans is controlled and driven by our brains, at the same time it is strongly influenced by learned experience from interaction with our environment. This being the case, social, ethnic and cultural experience also regulates our sexual preference and habits.

Learning must be an important factor in sexual motivation because what is considered 'normal' and 'abnormal' in human sexual behaviour is highly variable across cultures and times. Sexual motivation is therefore a unique blend of physiological and psychological stimulation.

Sensation-seeking

Many individuals seek out stimulation, which as we have said runs contrary to the drive-reduction goal theories.

Sensation-seekers seem less reactive to stimulation and therefore require stronger levels of it than low sensation-seekers (Zuckerman, 1994). So people who have high *sensation-seeking* tend to be motivated to engage in more risky behaviour, more high-risk jobs (fire-fighters, pilots) and more extreme sports (Jack and Ronan, 1998). Slanger and Rudestam (1997) investigated the role of sensation-seeking as a source of motivating people to partake

Sensation-seekers seem less reactive to stimulation and therefore require stronger levels of it in order to experience its effects.

in extreme sports, using Zuckerman's sensation-seeking scale (1974).

Results indicated that the extreme sports participants were in fact seeking the highest levels of sensation and self-efficacy. Researchers discovered that in terms of intrinsic motivation, the participants' desire for mastery of their sports allowed them to overcome the fear of imminent injury or even death. Those who scored as low risk takers were more interested in the safer, aesthetic aspects of their sport.

High sensation-seekers are also more likely to engage in illegal activities (Slobodian and Browne, 2001) and in a wider range of sexual activities with a greater number of partners (McCoul and Haslam,

---

FOCUS POINT 27.5

Cross-dressing and transvestism

Let's look at the motivational factors responsible for transvestism, or cross-dressing. For every 100 male cross-dressers there will be probably be only one female cross-dresser. The major difference between male and female transvestites is the underlying motivation for cross-dressing. Whereas male cross-dressing is generally associated with fetishism (sexual arousal elicited by an inanimate object such as lingerie or shoes), this is not the case for female cross-dressers. For female transvestites there tends to be little or no erotic component to cross-dressing. Instead, their cross-dressing seems to emanate from a desire to embrace and experience male power and status, and what is perceived to be male privilege.

Thus these two sets of cross-dressers have acquired such behaviour through different associated learning patterns, which result in differing motivations.

Sensation-seeking
Sensation-seeking is the motivation to seek out stimulation and novelty.

2001). They also express a greater liking for 'unpleasant' paintings and photographs than do low sensation-seekers (Rawlings, 2003). It has also been shown that high sensation-seekers within security forces are those most likely to engage in bomb disposal work (Glicksohn and Bozna, 2000).

Achievement motivation
The need for achievement (*achievement motivation*) is the desire to accomplish tasks, achieve goals and excel. David McClelland *et al.* (1953) and John Atkinson (1981) have contributed greatly to this area of study. There may be two reasons people strive to succeed: motivation for success and fear of failure.

The motive of success reflects intrinsic motivational forces, the desire to master skills or goals. Success motivation develops when parents reward success and achievement but do not punish failure (Koestner and McClelland, 1990). Fear of failure produces motivation that drives us to outperform peers. Such motivation is not always conducive to better performance. Indeed it has been shown that individuals who have high fear-of-failure attitudes are also very anxious. Such anxiety produces stress, and stress as we have seen elsewhere in this book interferes with effective cognitive functioning (such as concentration, attention and memory). It has been shown that fear of failure seems to develop in children whose parents take success for granted but punish failure (Weiner, 1992).

There are four characteristics of those with strong need for achievement motives:

1. preoccupation with own performance
2. tendency to struggle with tasks rather than seek help
3. plan more
4. prefer honest no-nonsense feedback from competent critics.

Borucki (1985) studied the role of the need for professional achievement in perceived organisational stress in 107 male junior managers in Gdansk, Poland. The need for achievement was examined in its effect on stress levels for perceived role conflict, role overload and role ambiguity (a job that is poorly defined in terms of what it entails).

High need for achievement diminished experience of negative emotions and perceived stress within role-conflict and role-overload situations. Borucki (1985) reported that the need for professional achievement appears to be a significant determinant of resistance to organisational stress in relation to job roles.

Summary
Motivation is an internal state experienced by individuals. Motivation is engaged in by choice or intention. Some theorists see motivation as a psychological force by which we achieve goals, others see it as a tool to fulfil our needs. There are two different motivational forces: intrinsic motivational factors and extrinsic motivational factors. Motivational research has been applied in such settings as health behaviour, criminal activity and work performance.

Learning outcomes
When you have completed this chapter you should be able to:

- describe the major theories of motivation
- distinguish between intrinsic and extrinsic motivation
- describe motivational forces such as sexual motivation, sensation-seeking and need for achievement
- use examples of where motivational research has been applied in other areas of psychology.

Section 6
Personality and Intelligence

Key terms

Achievement motivation
Angiotensin
Arousal theory
Attribution theory
Cognitive x value theory
Drives
Expectancy
External locus of control
Extracellular thirst
Extrinsic motivation
Goal-setting theory
Homeostasis
Incentives

Instincts
Internal locus of control
Intracellular thirst
Intrinsic motivation
Leptin
Mastery goals
Motivation
Osmosis
Performance goals
Self-efficacy
Sensation-seeking
Sexual motivation
Social goals

Further reading

Barker, K. L., McInerney, D. M. and Dowson, M. (2002) Performance approach, performance avoidance and depth of information processing: a fresh look at relations between students' academic motivation and cognition. *Educational Psychology* 22(5), 571–89.

Laming, D. (2004) *Understanding Human Motivation: What Makes People Tick?* Malden, MA: Blackwell.

Piët, S. (1987) What motivates stunt men? *Motivation and Emotion* 11, 195-213.

Sanna, L. J., Meier, S. and Wegner, E. A. (2001) Counterfactuals and motivation: mood as input to affective enjoyment and preparation. *British Journal of Social Psychology* 40(2), 235–56.

28

The self and social identity

Route map of the chapter

This chapter is divided into several sections. The first begins with a discussion of what we understand by the concept of self, its function and how it develops. We will then focus on how we gather and organise information about ourselves from both our own behaviour and how we are treated by others around us. We will also describe some of the strategies we deploy as defence mechanisms when the concept of our identity comes under threat. We will then consider how culture and the social groups to which we belong also play vital roles in the understanding of who we are. Lastly, we will discuss what happens when we lose our way and become confused about who we are and what we represent.

Introduction

It doesn't take long for someone to form an impression of us when we meet for the first time (probably around 60 seconds). These 60 seconds will form the basis of what that other person sees as our 'self' and will influence their future behaviour towards us. So think very carefully about what you say and how you say it! Even how we present ourselves can provide useful information to others about who they think we are. In reality, most of the people we encounter, meet and bump into get less than a minute to form an impression of us. Something worth thinking about!

ACTIVITY BOX 28.1

Spontaneous self-concept

Take a clean sheet of paper and give yourself five minutes to write down and describe who you are.

Finished? So how did you describe yourself? Out of all the things you are and you think you represent what did you give priority to in your self?

The information you chose to write down in this activity is called your spontaneous self-concept. For some people, five minutes will be too little time to do descriptive justice to who they think they are, while for others spending five minutes describing themselves is a daunting challenge.

What is the self?

The self encompasses such things as our conscious thoughts of our uniqueness from others, and of course our similarities to them. Higgins (1999) suggests that the self is divided into two parts: the ideal self (what individuals would like to be) and the ought self (an understanding of what others want us to be).

Stainton Rogers (2003) suggests that we have three selfs: a *personal self* (the me that is conscious of my own thoughts and feelings), a *social self* (the me defined by whichever social context I am in) and a *relational self* (the me that comes from interconnected relationships with others around me).

SOCIAL ID : FANCY DRESS SHOP

People generally strive to have traits that will support these interpersonal relationships. We are particularly concerned with how other people will perceive ourselves. The self organises this feedback from others and also buffers us against negative feedback.

The self allows us to make choices. It typically comes to have a collection of values, preferences and priorities that can be evoked whenever we need to make a decision.

The self organises our thoughts, feelings and actions, and is the primary centre of our personalities. It reflects our hopes, dreams and plans. Lewis (2003) argues that the self also acts as our moraliser. Thus we are able to reflect on the past, consider the future, develop ideas about ourselves, consider what others think about us and decide how we would like to be seen by other people.

Only a few, closely related, species (chimpanzees and orang-utans) have our developed capacity for

Functions of selfhood

The self is an interpersonal tool. Having some form of identity is a prerequisite for social life and human interaction. To hold a conversation requires understandings of 'you' and 'I'. To maintain a long-term relationship requires the identities of the two people involved to remain stable over time.

FOCUS POINT 28.1

The self defined

Sedikides (1992: 273) defines the self as follows: 'a person's self is the person's mental representation of information pertaining to him or her'.

TABLE 28.1 DEVELOPMENT OF THE SELF

AGE	HOW THE SELF IS MANIFESTED
3–4 years	Children describe themselves in terms of their favourite activity or the behaviours they often engage in; so 'I watch TV', 'I do painting' are examples of how children here might describe themselves
8–9 years	Children at this age tend to describe who they are in terms of their age, name, and what they like and dislike; they still describe things that they do but now also start to describe how good they are at them compared with other children they know
11 years	Children describe themselves in terms of their relationships with others; so they might say they are 'sporty' or 'smart'
Adolescence	Descriptions of ethnic and national identity seem to be the final stage in the development of the self

self-recognition, although this is not as sophisticated as ours. This ability is called *self-concept*. Self-concept reflects our sense of our own identity and our individual worth. The concept of self has been used by psychologists and philosophers as a way of describing the core of our personalities, our central motivations in life and our higher cognitive functioning.

Self-concept has also been shown to be influential in guiding behaviour. For example, Corte (2003) showed that an impoverished self-concept contributes to negative affect and can lead to high levels of alcohol use, and that this might be one factor in explaining alcohol addiction. Similarly, Mizell and Andre (2003) proposed that a child's self-concept mediates the effects of inter-parental discord on subsequent bullying behaviour.

Development of the self
We start to develop a sense of who we are from an early age (see Table 28.1). Infants as young as 15 months appear to recognise themselves in a mirror – studies have shown that they become startled when a red line has been placed on their noses and they look back into the mirror (Butterworth, 1992). At about 18 months we gain the knowledge that we exist as individuals separate from anyone else. The self develops largely through 'social identity'. For every individual, our social identity is crucial in defining who we are, what we do and how we evaluate ourselves.

An individual's social identity stems from our personality, our self-concept and the roles we undertake. We acquire each of these three elements of social identity through social interactions of the various groupings of people with whom we identify (groups such as race, religion, sex type, political affiliation, age and occupation).

As we go through life we each acquire information about ourselves from how others react to us, and this information develops our appraisal of our 'self'. This can be from *direct social comparison* with others (students do this with coursework when the results come out, each wanting to know how they have done in comparison with other students' marks).

It can also be from observing our own behaviour, which is called *self-perception*. There are times when

we become self-conscious and scrutinise our own behaviour. A good example of this is going on a first date. We start to ask ourselves questions by self-observing our behaviour. For example, should I have worn that jumper Granny knitted me? Do I sound interesting, yet cool and sexy at the same time? Will my date like me compared with other dates they have been on?

Hirsch, Clark, Mathews and Williams (2003) reported that when social-phobic participants held a negative self-image in their minds they experienced greater anxiety, rated their anxiety symptoms as being more visible and rated their performance as poorer than did those people who were not told to imagine a negative self-image. The researchers suggested that holding negative self-concept images has a causal role in maintaining social phobia.

The importance of self-presentation
The way we present ourselves is important to maintaining both our own awareness of who we are

> **ACTIVITY BOX 28.2**
>
> ### What are you wearing?
> Let's have a look at what you are wearing. Some of you reading this will be embarrassed about what you are wearing and, quite frankly, some of you who are not should be! If you had known we would be scrutinising what you are wearing you'd have tried harder. Some of you would have tried harder but it would have made no difference.
>
> The point here is that even our clothes are props in the presentation to the world of who we are. We would probably dress differently for a job interview than we would going out to the pictures with friends. We are the same person inside, so why change our clothes? What difference does it make? Well it must make some difference or else fashion would be redundant and you would have no need for a clothes collection.
>
> We make different statements about who we are with different people and in different circumstances.

and that of the people we are with. The good news is that we are all assigned our own PR agent in life, who is free; the bad news for many of us is that it is ourselves! *Self-presentation* is the conscious effort to control the impression we make to others in an effort to maintain our self-identity.

Erving Goffman (1959) suggested that self-presentation is important in maintaining self-image to others. It is a tool that we use to maintain ego and self-esteem. He likened the engagement of self-presentation to that of preparing to act in a play.

- We pay special attention to our *appearance*. (Many of you probably do not make such an effort with how you look if you know you are not going to venture out, and some of you spend more time getting ready than you do actually being out!)
- We use *props* to further our self-presentation image. (We might wear glasses when at home with the family or contact lenses when out with friends.)
- We often set the *stage*. (We might take a date to a specific club or restaurant to create an impression.)
- We often *rehearse*. (Just before making a phone call many people rehearse what they are going to say; some individuals prepare mock interviews with friends prior to the real thing.)
- Much of the preparation for our performances takes place *backstage*. (We might slave away over a meal the entire day, laying waste to our best saucepan set and persuading the fire brigade it wasn't a full-scale kitchen fire, only a bit of smoke.)
- The backstage preparation leads to our *frontstage* performance. (When your dinner guests turn up and exclaim their delight at your culinary skills you simply reply 'Oh, it's just a little something I threw together'.)

But none of these would be meaningful if we didn't have an audience to play to. So paradoxically the development of the self through the process of social identity is reliant upon experience with others. Without the presence of others with whom we might compare ourselves and learn from, we would be impeded perhaps in the development of a sense of

who and what we are. The funny thing is that we seem to be more worried about what people think about us than they are. Gilovich, Kruger and Medvec (2002) have suggested that people around us are more *unaware* of the variability of our appearance and behaviour that we actually give them credit for.

How is the information we hold about ourselves organised?

An individual's *self-schema* organises memories about the self and also controls the processing of self-relevant information. Consider again how you described yourself in Activity Box 28.1. Those traits that you listed are the traits that are probably central to your own self-schema. These are the core elements of how you view yourself.

Generally people tend to see themselves as having rich, well-developed and adaptable personalities, and judge that they are less predictable than other people. Traits that are considered central to one's own self-schema are valued more highly than other characteristics.

For example, students who do well in a subject would probably rate that subject as a more important part of their personality than would those students who got poorer grades at it. So if you said you are honest, you would probably be very sensitive to other people's honesty. Your self-schema would view that characteristic as being important to you.

Our information, judgements and feelings about ourselves are influenced by many factors. We will now consider how we come to form an impression of our 'self' and who and what we represent.

Factors contributing to knowledge of our 'self'

There are a number of important factors that shape the information we hold about our 'self'. You will probably recognise some of these as you are likely to engage in them on a daily basis.

Socialisation and group membership

Our treatment by our parents, relatives, teachers, peers and friends can be influential in how we come to view ourselves. Our self-schema organises this feedback and looks for consistencies in how we are treated by people and in certain situations. The more that different people treat us the same in more different situations, the greater the importance our self-schema attaches to this information. So if lots of people laugh at us wherever we go, our self-schema might formulate that being funny was a core part of who we are (either that or we should upgrade our fashion sense, and fast!).

This process of information gathering by our self-schema is called *reflected appraisal*. We appraise the feedback and treatment we get from others around us. Cooley (1902) called this tendency for self-appraisal our 'looking glass self'. In other words, everyone around us is a mirror by which we get to see how our own behaviour is received and judged. Meade (1934) described this process as our 'reflexive self': a self that is able to observe, respond to and plan our own behaviour.

How we are socialised and how we interact with others gives us our sense of social identity. So in many cases the sense of our own identity is linked closely with our various group memberships. Participation in recreational, religious, ethnic, occupational and cultural activities provides us with who we are and where we fit into our society.

Since part of our self-identity is derived from group membership and since we strive to keep a positive self-concept of ourselves, we also have a tendency to view the groups we belong to more positively than those groups we do not. This is called *social identity theory* (Tajfel and Turner, 1986b). In essence, people come to identify with social groups and then tend to define themselves as having the characteristics of those groups to which they belong. So being a smoker or having a disability are examples of groups by which we are judged by the stereotype of that group of people. Such perceptions, obviously, can lead to misjudgements, heralding stereotypes and prejudice.

Reflected appraisal and explicit feedback

Not only do we appraise how others treat us and respond to our actions, we also reflect on our own behaviour. Bem (1972), through his theory of self-perception, suggested that we know who we are by observing our own behaviour. So in an emergency, if you observe yourself acting calmly, you may come to think that you are a calm person in a crisis. If you attend church regularly of your own free will, then you would conclude you are religious. So just as someone who observes us would infer a reason for our current behaviour, we try to do the same with our own behaviour.

We also tend to have an ego defence system that operates in this judgement of our own behaviour, which is called *egocentricity*. In judging our own behaviour we tend to rate our contributions as being more important than anyone else's. People who have been asked to rate their own and their work colleagues' relative contributions in solving a task while working in pairs give very different assessments according to when you ask them. When asked immediately after working in the pair, individuals judge the other person to have contributed more than themselves. However, after a three-day break, judgements are reversed and they now judge themselves to have been the one in the pair who contributed most.

Direct and explicit feedback by others also informs the development of our self-perception, and explicit feedback starts at an early age. Proud parents delight at their children's first steps and words, and show disappointment when they do something wrong.

The feedback directed at us from our teachers also shapes the perception of our 'self'. For example, take

---

ACTIVITY BOX 28.3

Make a new friend

Let's see how good your social skills are. When you get the opportunity, ask someone you do not know very well to describe themselves to you. Make a note (mental or otherwise) of how they describe themselves to you.

What you will notice, quite paradoxically, is that while you asked them to describe themselves they will usually describe to you how they fit in relation to others around them. For example, 'I am a mother', 'I work as a nurse', 'I come from London'. It is very hard to define ourselves without reference to at least one group membership.

a person's skills at chemistry: for many people (like me), if chemistry gets any more complex than understanding that coffee gets weaker the more milk you add to it, they are left way behind. This is probably because such individuals were not confident at chemistry when they were at school, and received feedback from both their teachers and classmates confirming their lack of ability.

Our peers also provide targeted feedback. Being picked last for team games in the break at school and constantly being asked by colleagues at work for advice are examples of direct feedback.

Bias in self-perception

Biases in our self-perception also influence the information we hold about ourselves. These biases help maintain positive self-esteem in the face of disappointment and failure, and there are several mechanisms we engage in to protect our self-image. One is *positivity bias*, resulting in a systematic, positive distortion of memories.

Let's say someone is given an intelligence test and then the false impression that their score represented that of a highly intelligent person. They are then asked to remember how high their grades were at school on average. The chances are that they would falsely remember that they got higher grades than they actually achieved. This is because the recency effect of being informed that they are highly intelligent creates a positive distortion of the memories of their past intellectual ability.

There is also the tendency for people to accept very general or vague characterisations of themselves and take them to be accurate. A good example of this can be seen when people believe what is said about them in psychometric tests, personality profiles and astrological predictions. This is known as the *Barnum effect*, named after the famous showman P.T. Barnum, who believed that a good circus had 'a little something for everybody'.

More recently this has been termed the *subjective validation effect*. Even though the descriptions we read or that are given to us could apply equally well to other people, some individuals are gullible enough to believe they are unique to them. This is exactly what happens with horoscopes and palm reading.

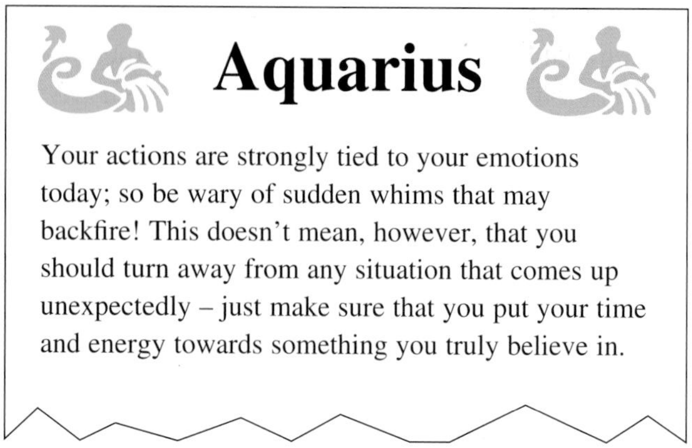

 Aquarius

Your actions are strongly tied to your emotions today; so be wary of sudden whims that may backfire! This doesn't mean, however, that you should turn away from any situation that comes up unexpectedly – just make sure that you put your time and energy towards something you truly believe in.

Figure 28.1 Even though the descriptions we read are sometimes generalised to a group of people some individuals believe they are unique to them.

Psychologist B.R. Forer (1949) found that people tend to accept vague and general personality descriptions as uniquely applicable to themselves without realising that the same description could be applied to just about anyone. Forer gave a personality test to his students, ignored their answers and gave each student the identical generally positive descriptive evaluation. He asked them to rate the evaluation from 0 to 5, with 5 meaning the recipient felt the evaluation was an 'excellent' assessment and 4 meaning the assessment was 'good'. The class average evaluation was 4.26. That was in 1948. The test has been repeated many times since and the average is still around 4.2.

Interpretation of self-relevant information

We are constantly monitoring ourselves and reflecting on the information we receive about ourselves. This information is also used to shape and update our self-schema. This evaluative process of evaluating 'me' is called *self-esteem*, and it is therefore our evaluation of our self-concept (Brown and Marshall, 2001). The greater the discrepancy between the actual self, the ideal self and the ought self, the lower our self-esteem will be. Also, the more important these attributes are to us, the greater the negative effect on our self-esteem (Boldero and Francis, 2000).

This probably sounds alarming to many of you who are reading this, because you may well have the opinion that there is a gap between your actual self and your ideal self. However, we have a couple of tricks up our sleeve to try and limit the effects of despair and disappointment brought on by thoughts of inadequacy and failure.

We actively try to maintain positive self-image. In an attempt to maintain our acceptable self to ourselves we often enhance our self-esteem by interpreting self-relevant information in a biased self-serving manner. The aim of this is to make ourselves feel good by minimising the difference between our actual self and our ideal/ought self (Dunning and Hayes, 1996).

A second defence mechanism involves *self-handicapping hurdles* (Tice and Baumeister, 1990). These protect positive self-esteem and also help to maintain positive self-image. We have all engaged in this kind of behaviour before. How many of you have used the following excuses:

* blamed the dog for eating homework
* blamed the room temperature for poor exam performance
* blamed public transport for being late?

Self-handicapping hurdles de-emphasise our own failings and excuse them in terms of unexpected or uncontrollable events. They buffer our positive self-image by pretending that we have the ability to succeed although some other 'X' factor not under our control spoiled our chances. We see football managers excusing their teams because they were wearing the wrong colour shirts, public transport officials blaming train delays on leaves on the line and politicians blaming just about everything save themselves.

Students engage in this process when results are published after their examinations. Success in an exam is often put down to intelligence and ability, whereas failure is interpreted as bad luck, poor questions or the bad mood of the examiner when marking the scripts. This is called self-serving bias. It is the tendency to take personal credit for success but to blame failure on external causes. In general, it

IF ONLY I'D BROUGHT MY LUCKY RABBIT'S FOOT!

seems that men use more alcohol/drug/external excuses while women tend to use more stress or physical illness-related excuses.

We also know that culture can influence self-esteem. Tashakkori (1993) has reported that for white students, physical appearance was closely related to self-esteem, for African-Caribbean boys it was power, and for African-Caribbean girls it was popularity. So the basis for self-esteem can be different for different groups and cultures of people, just as it can from one individual to the next.

Social comparisons

How do you know how intelligent you are? How funny you can be? How patient you are? Another source of information that shapes the development of our 'self' is that of comparing ourselves with others around us. Social comparison is when we evaluate our own accomplishments by comparing them with those of others. Our self-esteem suffers if others are judged to outperform us (Kulik and Gump, 1997).

If you lived alone on a desert island and engaged in activities such as coconut shaving and grass skirt weaving, how would you know how good you were at these skills? You might be able to shave a coconut but is there someone else in the world who can do it faster? You need other individuals so that you can compare how you stand in relation to them. Better? Worse? The same?

We also tend to look to others most when we find ourselves in a novel situation. We look around us to see if someone near us has the answers or skills needed in this new situation. Say you find yourself in the middle of the dance floor on a Friday night in the wee small hours, strutting your stuff and generally getting on down. Suddenly, without warning, the DJ slaps on a new tune. It's one you haven't had a chance to practise in your room. Your legs freeze and your arms suddenly fall by your side, losing all animation. Panic! What do you do? Walk away defeated, to the accompaniment of the sneers and jeers of all the other disco divas, or lock on to someone who is in the middle of their finely choreographed dance number and copy them?

This is a perfect example of using others around you to learn when faced by novelty. Another good example of this is crossing a busy road with which you are unfamiliar. Faced with this task, many people refer to other people around them in deciding when or where to cross the road.

Maintaining positive self-image with others

We also have a number of ways in which we can preserve our self-esteem when comparing ourselves with others. These techniques are known as *self-enhancement strategies*, and are aimed at seeking positive information about ourselves or interpreting ambiguous information in the most favourable light to maintain our self-esteem (Sedikides, 1993). These strategies enable us to maintain a positive impression of ourselves through reference to others around us.

An example of this is when you compare yourself with those who are less capable than you. This has been termed *downward comparison* (Lockwood, 2002). However, only people with low self-esteem will benefit from downward comparison. So the next time your friend beats you at tennis, give your 101-year-old granny a call and book a court.

Another way to try and recover lost self-esteem through social comparison is to exaggerate the ability of those who outperform you. By making out that the person who beat you is in actual fact superman/woman you can still perceive yourself as being at least good or above average.

A third strategy that works is to change your belief in the task at hand so that it is no longer important to your self-concept (Pilkington and Smith, 2000). So that degree in figure skating you failed recently, despite breaking every bone in your body twice and taking eight years to complete it, wasn't really that important to you – it was just a hobby!

The role of culture

What role does culture play in the development of who we understand ourselves to be? Our culture provides another form of social comparison. Cousins (1989) employed a questionnaire (called the Twenty Statements Test) to investigate how the concept of 'self' is viewed across different cultures. He tested students in America and Japan. He found that American students tend to have a more individualistic sense of self, while Japanese students, in contrast, have more of a sense of a relational self. This would therefore seem to suggest that not only do individuals have different concepts of 'self' but that cultures are also influential in developing our self-concepts.

One major difference in world culture is that of the *collectivist identity* versus the *individualist identity*. Individualist cultures tend to promote the drive for personal control, independence and individual achievement, and individualistic values tend to be associated with the western world. People from individualistic cultures who move countries show more concern for establishing a career and gaining achievement than they do for establishing relationships and maintaining family ties (Boneva and Frieze, 2001).

In contrast, the collectivist identity gives priority to the aims of the group (family, clan or company). These group principles bring a sense of belonging, a set of understood and shared values and a secure environment. Collectivist societies are associated more with oriental cultures. For example, it has been shown that in Korea that people place more emphasis on cultural tradition and shared practices, and give less value to promoting a unique self-concept (Choi and Choi, 2002).

There is also evidence to illustrate the powerful impact of collectivist cultural identities on an individual's self-concept. Examples of collectivist culture and self-sacrifice are activists (such as animal and environmental rights activists) and in extreme cases suicide bombers (Drury and Reicher, 2000). In each case the individual sacrifices their personal self for the good of the collective self.

The role of social norms

Our societies and cultures also help shape our self-concept with the production of *social norms*.

Each cultural group will evolve its own norms for behaviour among its group members. So the British norm of queuing in an orderly fashion for a bus runs in stark contrast to the chaotic free-for-all in some other countries. Knowing what cutlery to use in which order at a wedding reception or giving your seat up to an elderly person are both examples of social norms. Shaking someone's hand or kissing them in greeting will be decided by the norm of the group you belong to. These unwritten rules are absorbed by our self-concept and become part of our 'self'.

Identity crises: challenges to identity

We have considered the factors that contribute to who you and others think you are, but what happens when your identity is challenged? People change jobs, sometimes quite dramatically (from banker to teacher), go from being single to married and vice versa, and face the challenge of new identities – parent, aunt, uncle or grandparent. Baumeister (1997) has suggested two distinct forms of personality crises: *identity conflict* and *identity deficit*.

Cultural identity also serves as an important informer of who we are and what we represent.

Identity conflict arises when we are faced with aspects of our identity that are incompatible. Strong examples of identity conflict are seen in some women who want a family but also want a career. Refugees who seek new lives in new countries away from persecution also face a crisis as they face the challenge of assuming a new cultural identity while trying to preserve some of their former cultural identity. Such conflicts often result in anxiety, stress and feelings of guilt, and can have a significant impact on welfare and mental health.

Identity crises, on the other hand, arise when an individual does not have an adequately formed or stable identity. This unstable identity is threatened further by facing major decisions. Many people can make an important decision straight away as they know their own values and are aware of their own preferences. For other people, their insecure sense of who they are, and of their skills and abilities, makes the decision harder.

Take the example of attending university. Faced with this decision some individuals will question their intellectual capacity to complete a degree successfully; others might question whether further study is right for them; yet others might wonder which course might suit them. Individuals who do not have established or clear personal identities can also be more vulnerable to propaganda and persuasion by others. They are curious about others who seem to 'know who they are', and impressed by those who seem to know what they are doing. People with identity deficits are probably more susceptible to the recruitment strategies of cults and other extreme groups (Singer and Lalich, 1995).

Summary

The self is a cognitive representation of who we are. It informs us where we stand in relation to others and acts as a tool for directing our interpersonal relationships. It allows us to make choices in our behaviour. Our self develops through interaction with others and is influenced by how others treat us. We constantly self-evaluate and this process forms the basis of self-esteem.

Learning outcomes

When you have completed this chapter you should be able to:

- describe what is meant by 'self' and what its functions are
- describe how the perception of self develops
- appreciate how our self-concept is influenced and shaped by social factors (such as society and culture)
- describe the mechanisms that we employ to maintain a positive self-image
- describe what is meant by identity crises and how these might arise.

Key terms

Barnum effect
Collectivist identity
Direct social comparison
Downward comparison
Egocentricity
Identity conflict
Identity deficit
Individualist identity
Personal self
Positivity bias
Reflected appraisal
Relational self
Self-concept
Self-enhancement strategies
Self-esteem
Self-handicapping hurdles
Self-perception
Self-presentation
Self-schema
Social identity theory
Social norms
Social self
Subjective validation effect

Personality

Route map of the chapter

This chapter discusses the psychological factors that contribute to our personalities. We will consider several important questions about the nature and development of our personality characteristics in relation to the main theoretical paradigms in this field. Consideration will be given to the environmental, cognitive and biological factors that contribute to the shaping of our personalities. We will also investigate personality in terms of gender difference, stability over the life span and the influence of motivational forces.

Introduction

Scientists have only explored the notion of personality systematically since the 1930s. This represents a relatively short period of time in terms of scientific study. As such, psychologists are still finding their way in this area. So to some extent we are still struggling to identify the questions and issues that need to be addressed if we are to understand fully what personality is. We have, however, made some inroads in our understanding.

Personality similarity can bring us together with friends and also set us apart from them too.

ACTIVITY BOX 29.1

How aggressive are you?

Consider how aggressive you are, and then think about the following questions.

1. How often do you get aggressive?
2. Do you tend to find yourself getting angry in lots of different situations or is your anger aroused by more specific stimuli?
3. Do the same people make you angry?
4. Have you felt more or less angry at different stages in your life?

The answers you give to these questions reveal much about you, in terms of whether your behaviour is motivated by your personality or people/events around you. They also reveal how stable your personality is in terms of consistency (for example, angry in most situations with lots of different types of people) and over time (for example, feeling less angry as you get older).

In this section we will explore such questions in relation to personality as a whole. Psychologists have been looking for answers to them for some time, to help them understand what personality is.

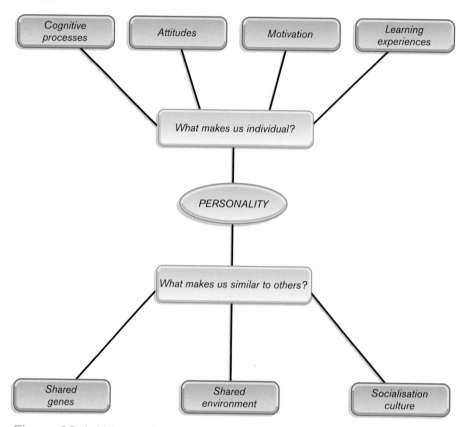

Figure 29.1 *What makes us similar to/different from others?*

Psychologists, generally speaking, view personality as the unique combination of psychological and behavioural characteristics by which each individual can be compared and contrasted with everyone else. This is neatly summarised by Mischel when he defines personality as 'the distinctive patterns of behaviour (including thoughts and emotions) that characterise each individual's adaptation to the situations of his or her life' (1986: 4).

Defining personality

Attributes of personality

Personality as a construct, therefore, has a number of attributes (Peterson, 1992). In essence these are as follows.

- Personality is an integrated part of an individual – it is something a person is, does or has. People bring their personalities to situations and take them away with them when they leave.

- Personality is psychological – it refers to the individual (actions, thoughts, feelings) and not to material things such as possessions or status.
- Personality is made up of smaller units called characteristics (the combination of these individual characteristics creates a unique psychological signature).
- Personality can be functional or dysfunctional – that is, our characteristics can help us succeed and prosper in some situations, but they can also disadvantage us or make us vulnerable in others.

Broadly speaking, much of the work by therapists and academics within the field of personality seeks to understand what factors make us consistent in ourselves but at the same time different to, or individual from, other people.

Defining personality

Child (1968: 83) described personality as the 'more or less stable, internal factors that make one person's behaviour consistent from one time to another, and different from the behaviour other people would manifest in similar situations'.

To appreciate what makes us individual we also need, therefore, to consider what factors make us similar to, or the same as, others.

What makes us similar to/different from others?

As Kluckhorn and Murray (1953) stated, 'every person is in certain respects like all other people, like some other people and like no other person'. Some of these factors are illustrated in Figure 29.1.

Armed with these considerations, modern personality research offers valid and useful insights into human psychology. It is concerned with such questions as the role played by personality in physical health and sickness, job success, attraction and criminal behaviour. Are certain individuals more prone to stress? Are specific personalities more likely to succeed in specific occupations? Are certain personalities more attractive than others? Is there such a thing as a criminal personality? We will consider some of this applied research throughout this section.

Perspectives of personality research

There are many theories of personality and these can be neatly categorised into subgroups using two concepts. These two concepts are 'perspectives' and 'paradigms'.

A perspective is an approach or outlook, and it should be recognised that there are two perspectives

Personality and observation

Consider the following famous people: Tony Blair, Madonna and Hugh Grant. Write down one word that you think best describes each of them. Ask someone else who is at hand to do the same.

Compare your descriptions. Why do you think you have the same or different words to describe them? Do you really think these words best describe their personalities or are you merely describing what you know of them?

This is one problem with personality research – simply relying on observation of people does not allow us to gain a full three-dimensional picture of that person. For example, we generally see famous people in one setting – in the media – but would they be different in other settings? How would these individuals describe themselves?

Thus, to understand the nature of personality we need to employ multiple methods of investigation, namely observation and self-report.

that guide work relating to personality research. These are clinical psychology and academic psychology. Both have made significant contributions to our understanding of the nature of personality and both perspectives have well-known psychologists allied to them. While these two different perspectives seek greater understanding of the formation, regulation and influence of personality, they differ in a number of significant ways.

Clinical psychology

Clinical psychologists working within personality research tend to focus on how people generally adapt to everyday life, and how the individual copes with the stresses and challenges of daily life. Clinicians are primarily concerned with those individuals who fail to adapt. Clinical psychologists, therefore, often seek to intervene by studying each person in depth in order to improve the lives of these individuals through therapy.

The study of one individual without comparing them to any other is called the *idiographic* approach to studying personality. Gordon Allport, a well-known personality theorist, argued that personality should be studied idiographically, otherwise unique aspects of individuals could be overlooked.

Many well-known personality theories have evolved out of clinical practice and the idiographic approach. Indeed, many of the best-known personality theorists were clinicians: Freud, Jung and Rogers, for example.

The advantages of this approach are as follows.

- It recognises that everyone has a unique combination of personality characteristics and as such each person should be studied in their own right.
- Any attempts to improve people's lives must be based on individual study and intervention. To suggest an intervention based on group prediction might be inaccurate.
- The study of individuals allows us to investigate unconscious processes more accurately.
- By studying an individual we can see how they progress over time (if intervention works).

This approach is not without its suggested drawbacks, however.

PEOPLE THINK I HAVE BIG EARS, BIG EYES, AND BIG TEETH!

- The clinical method poses methodological problems. It has been criticised for being too subjective. There is over-reliance on the clinician's observational abilities and record-keeping skills.
- Gaining insight from clinical populations only reveals information about clinically diagnosed individuals. It would be wrong to generalise any observed findings to non-clinical populations.

Academic psychology

In contrast to the clinical perspective in studying personality, academic personality researchers study groups of people. They examine selected aspects of personality rather than attempting to deal with the whole person. So, for example, they might see how shyness manifests itself across a variety of people (gender, age, culture, occupation) in a variety of situations. This approach to studying personality is often called the *nomothetic* approach.

Researchers from this perspective try to describe personality in terms of sets of dimensions (personality traits) that can be applied to describe any person. They thus tend to express their observations in quantitative terms such as statistical means and other statistical concepts.

By assigning quantitative scores to each individual, researchers can then see how people compare with one another. For example, imagine you have just completed a questionnaire to find out how aggressive you are. The researchers give you a final score. This score is practically meaningless to you unless you can compare it with other people's scores to see where you fit in relation to them (e.g. less aggressive, as aggressive, more aggressive).

Well-known academic personality theorists are Eysenck, Cattell and Allport.

The main advantages of the academic approach are as follows.

- It seeks to obtain precise, valid and reliable measures of personality in an attempt to establish what is common or usual across people.
- Personality dimensions can be used to describe all people. Thus neuroticism is assumed to be a personality dimension upon which all people can

be located (some people are highly neurotic, most people are average and some are hardly neurotic).

It does, like the clinical perspective, also have some suggested weaknesses.

- Its focus on groups of people rather than individuals tends to disadvantage itself in terms of being able to identify deep-rooted unconscious processes.
- Describing people's personalities in terms of numbers rather than the richer and more in-depth method of words brings accusations of shallowness and reductionism.

Paradigms guiding personality theories

We are now aware of the perspectives that guide research into this area of psychology. However, before we can start to evaluate the contributions of the various theories concerning personality we need to place them within the broad context of the differing paradigms they are influenced by. In other words, while there are many individual personality theories, many of them are related by the strategies or methods they employ, and so can be placed into subgroups called *paradigms* or domains.

As you will remember from earlier chapters, a paradigm is 'the language, theories, methods and limits of the science. It determines which aspects of the world the scientist studies and the kinds of explanations he considers' (McCain and Segal, 1973: 81). Domains are a 'speciality area of science and scholarship, in which psychologists have focused on learning about some specific and limited aspects of human nature' (Larsen and Buss, 2002: 15).

There are five main paradigms/domains guiding research into personality psychology and these are outlined in Table 29.1.

Each of the five paradigms described in the table focuses on a different aspect of personality. If we are to have a better understanding of the whole concept of personality we should see these domains as pieces of a jigsaw puzzle that, together, create a complete picture. We can evaluate each dimension's contribution to our understanding of personality within the context of a specific question about the nature of personality.

Personality: a conscious or unconscious process?

Are you always aware of why you have done something or what you will do or say next? There are times when even we are surprised by what we do and what we say.

One of the questions that is of interest to psychologists is whether personality is a conscious process (we have to think actively about being who we are) or whether the manifestation of our personality is unconscious (rather like autopilot on a plane).

The interpersonal (*psychodynamic*) approach contends that some elements of personality manifestation (particularly problem behaviour) reside in the person's unconscious (the part of the mind outside the individual's immediate awareness). Focusing on the unconscious will give us a better understanding of how personality is manifested individually (Ellenberger, 1970). So past traumatic events can be forgotten yet still cause psychological problems and influence our personality (Bass and Davis, 1988). Interpersonal theories of personality have developed mainly out of clinical practice.

What evidence is there to suggest that unconscious mental processes are responsible for how our personalities develop?

Freud and psychoanalysis

Sigmund Freud (1856–1939) is known as the father of psychoanalysis. He suggested that unconscious mental processes and experiences can shape the development and manifestation of personality. Such processes, he maintained, start in infancy (with what he termed primary processes, characterised by impulses) and develop into adulthood (secondary processes, the realisation that our impulses have to fit in with the demands of the world around us).

For Freud, the unconscious part of human thinking was one of the fundamental driving forces of personality. He conceptualised the mind as being like an iceberg (see Figure 29.2). The smallest part of

TABLE 29.1 THE MAIN PARADIGMS GUIDING THEORIES INVESTIGATING PERSONALITY PSYCHOLOGY AND THEIR BASIC DEFINING PRINCIPLES

PARADIGM	MAIN THEORIES	CHARACTERISTICS
Psychodynamic	Sigmund Freud Carl Jung Alfred Adler Anna Freud Erik Erikson	Assumes individual's personalities are motivated by unconscious emotional conflicts (mainly originating in childhood) Seeks understanding via case studies (in terms of dreams, free association and creativeness) Aims to change individuals by freeing the energy devoted to neurotic symptoms and therefore allowing the development of a more positive personality **Example:** a childhood experience that may be buried in the unconscious and that affects negatively how an individual might relate to others
Humanistic	Abraham Maslow Carl Rogers George Kelly	Interested in personality in terms of how people's conscious experiences and drives help or hinder their ability to reach their full potential Criticises scientific psychological methods in trying to measure personality in that such an approach is too mechanical and misses the essence of individuals; case studies have been used by some humanistic personality theorists as the favoured method of study However, it remains mostly empirically unsubstantiated and is criticised for this reason **Example:** success in family life may give an individual happiness, contentment, reward and satisfaction, which they may take to other parts of their life (such as work), or vice versa
Trait	Gordon Allport Raymond Cattell Hans Eysenck Costa and McCrae	Assumes that individuals have stable personality characteristics evident in behaviour across a multitude of situations Tries to describe and predict how individuals might behave based on their personality traits Measures personality via questionnaires **Example:** using Eysenck's Personality Inventory (EPI), which measures introversion–extroversion to predict music-listening choices

TABLE 29.1 CONTINUED

PARADIGM	MAIN THEORIES	CHARACTERISTICS
Cognitive-behavioural	Albert Bandura Julian Rotter George Kelly Walter Mischel	Assumes people's thoughts and beliefs are central to personality Seeks to measure these thoughts/beliefs and to see how they lead to behaviour in specific situations (personality), and how the expression of personality through behaviour shapes future cognitive processes Seeks to measure and understand personality using self-report measures (questionnaires or interviews) and in some cases via observation Aims to facilitate harmony between individuals and the world around them (by changing either the individual or the environment) **Example:** if a child learns that tantrums achieve a desired result then the rewards for such behaviour condition and establish a set of behaviours that will probably be used in later life
Biological	William Sheldon Robert Plomin Hans Eysenck C. Robert Cloniger	Assumes people's personality characteristics are either inherited and/or are biologically influenced by hormones Seeks to understand personality via work with twins and through neurological research Aims to improve personality through medication or gene manipulation/selection **Example:** finding a relationship between the existence of a specific gene and a personality trait, such as anxiety
Behavioural	Burrhus Skinner John Dollard and Neal Millar	Forces of conditioning and reinforcement have shaped personality Seeks to understand personality via observation Emphasises the role of learning in the development of personality and aims to enhance positive personality characteristics through reward and punishment **Example:** If a child learns that aggression in the playground will bring immediate gratification of a need or goal then it is likely that aggression will be reinforced and used more often; if such aggression is punished, however, its use as a strategy should diminish

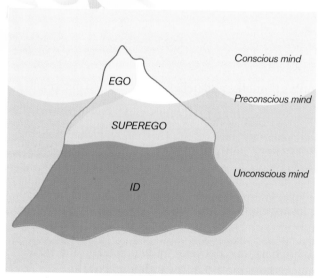

Figure 29.2 *Freud's view of the mind as an iceberg*

the mind, the tip of the iceberg, is composed of conscious thought processes – those mental abilities that we are fully aware of.

Freud referred to preconscious mental processes as those thoughts or memories that we may not be consciously thinking of but that we can easily and readily bring into our conscious awareness. So while you are not currently thinking of your telephone number, if I asked you what it is you should be able to bring it into conscious thought.

According to Freud, however, by far the largest part of the mind comprises unconscious processes. For Freud, evidence of the unconscious was provided by 'slips of the tongue' and through the interpretation of dreams. The unconscious, he believed, contains instincts and drives, childhood memories and memories of traumatic events which may deliberately be forgotten (cast out of conscious awareness) or even repressed.

Stages of personality development
Freud proposed that personality developed in early childhood through a series of what he called 'psychosexual stages' (see Table 29.2). A fixation at one stage or another has implications at an unconscious level in adult life.

Development of Freud's work
Freud's suggestion that unconscious mental processes are influential in how our personalities develop and are manifested gave rise to an immediate debate. Many criticised his work (as we shall see later) and many of his initial followers disagreed with elements of his theories. Psychodynamic theory then splintered into two groupings: the neo-Freudians and the ego-psychologists.

The neo-Freudians maintained many of Freud's initial ideas but many went on to develop their own approaches to the study of personality and expanded them in new directions. Carl Jung (1875–1961), via his theory of 'analytic psychology', agreed with Freud's proposal that the unconscious played a significant part in personality, but disagreed with his theory in its entirety. Jung (1964) argued that complexes reside in our unconscious. These complexes can be either positive (perfection) or negative (power).

Alfred Adler (1870–1937), on the other hand, in his individual psychology theory, emphasised the importance of social factors rather than sexual urges in the development of personality. He did not agree with Freud about the extent to which unconscious processes were influential in personality. Unlike Freud, Adler saw conscious processes as the major contributing factor to personality; however, he did recognise that one unconscious process might play a part (Adler, 1930).

Ego-psychologists such as Anna Freud (1895–1982), who was Sigmund Freud's daughter, and Erik Erikson (1902–94) emphasised the role of *ego* development in personality. Anna Freud (1936) identified three sources that the ego responds defensively to: displeasure, danger in the outside world and unconscious impulses from the *id*. One of the ways in which her work differed from that of her father was that, rather than trying to derive childhood experiences from adult patients, Anna worked directly with child patients. One of her main contributions was that she helped adapt psychoanalytic techniques for use with children.

Other theorists developed Sigmund Freud's work. Erikson's life span theory moved psychoanalytic thought out of childhood. He maintained that

TABLE 29.2 FREUD'S PSYCHOSEXUAL STAGES AND IMPLICATIONS OF STAGE FIXATION FOR BEHAVIOUR IN ADULT LIFE

PSYCHOSEXUAL STAGE	DEFINING FEATURES	ADULT SIGNS OF FIXATION
Oral	*First year after birth.* The mouth is the centre of pleasure at this stage. Babies use their mouths to eat and explore everything around them.	Problems arise when oral needs are either under- or over-stimulated. So early or late weaning may lead to adult behaviours such as overeating, smoking and drinking to excess. Over-dependence on others is also, according to Freud, a by-product of fixation at this stage.
Anal	*During the child's second year.* Here according to Freud there is a clash between free bowel movements at will and parental demands for appropriate toilet training. Thus it is at this stage that the ego starts to develop.	Fixation at this stage can occur when toilet training is too harsh or starts too early or too late. Associated adult behaviours might be excessively concerned with control and cleanliness, or they might be reckless or impulsive.
Phallic	*Between the ages of three and six.* Focus of attention diverts to the genital area. Here, according to Freud, boys develop sexual feelings for their mothers and form a desire to eliminate the competing affections of the father (known as the Oedipus complex). Girls, on the other hand, develop penis envy and try to compensate for their lack of a penis by identifying with the father (the Electra complex). Here the superego starts to develop.	Freud believed that fixation at this stage could lead to problems later in life via unresolved conflicts with one's same-sex parent. These could be manifested by aggression, difficulty with authority, inability to hold down a stable relationship and, in extreme cases, socially disapproved-of sexual behaviour.
Latency period	*Following on from phallic stage through to the onset of puberty.* Here the ego represses sexual instinct internally, and this is reinforced externally by parents' and teachers' suppression of sexual matters. Child learns values of family and culture.	
Genital	*At puberty and during adolescence and spanning the rest of the individual's life.* Via hormonal changes, sexual impulses reappear. The genitals again become the focus of pleasure.	Individuals reach the genital stage only when they have successfully resolved the conflicts at the prior stages.

adulthood was a continuing process of development that was influenced by past experience. Like Freud, he did propose a number of stages in terms of personality development (Erikson, 1978), but he rejected Freud's notion that identity was fixed in childhood. He argued that the formation of identity was in fact a lifelong process. He did not agree that unconscious processes accounted entirely for personality manifestation. He also recognised the importance of the societies we live in and their effect on our thoughts, beliefs and behaviour.

Freud's work still gives rise to strong opinions. Some personality theorists argue that his work (or a major part of it) is still very relevant (Weston, 1998), while others argue that psychoanalysis should be abandoned (Eysenck, 1985).

What are the positives and negatives that can be taken from Freud's work?

Evaluation of Freud's theory

There is no question that Freud was influential in the development of psychology and research into personality. His theory of the stages of personality provided the springboard for the field of developmental psychology. His work also provided the first comprehensive personality theory and stimulated the development of personality assessment techniques. In addition, he drew attention to the possible influence of unconscious mental processes on the development and manifestation of personality.

Does research support Freud's ideas? There has been some empirical support for facets of his work, and recent research by Myers (2000) has provided support for concepts such as a repressive coping style.

Major critics of Freud's theory maintain that his work is out of date and would not apply to the very different society we live in today. They think that he over-emphasised the importance of unconscious principles in respect of personality. However, it should be remembered that Freud lived in the Victorian era with its very conservative attitudes towards sex and women. His work is based on a small, select group of paying clients (mainly wealthy and educated women) and his observations were restricted to therapy sessions only.

His work on the stages of personality development has been criticised by many psychologists who do not agree that personality stops developing at around five or six years of age. They believe that personality can dramatically change throughout the life span. One of the most potent criticisms is that Freud's work and that of psychodynamic theory in general are not open to scientific investigation. It is hard to refute Freud's theories, which deal with theoretical concepts that are difficult to measure and test scientifically (Holzman, 1994).

Object relations theory: rethinking unconscious influence

Freud's emphasis on sexuality and unconscious processes has now been rethought. Contemporary psychodynamic theories instead focus on social relationships and their origin within childhood development. Object relations theory is one example; it deals with how individuals internally conceptualise (in terms of feelings and attitude) the people and objects around them.

While there are several versions of this approach, which emphasise different aspects, all object relations theories share some common assumptions. One is that the child's developing relationship with others around them (external forces) are more important than internal urges and desires (internal forces).

Children create their own unconscious mental representation of others around them. So important others (e.g. the mother) become internalised by the child. Each child has an internal representation of their mother to whom they can relate. Thus children can have a relationship with this internalised object (mother) even when she is not present (so children can still imagine what their mothers might say if they do something they are not supposed to, even when the mother is not physically present).

In essence, then, object relations theorists attempt to understand personality in terms of how children develop relationships with others around them based on how they mentally represent this relationship. So if children have formed the impression that they do not like someone, this will influence how they behave with that person in the future.

Melanie Klein (1964), John Bowlby (1988) and Heinz Kohut (1977) developed their accounts of personality based on the principles of object relations theory. This has been applied to investigating why children of divorced parents might themselves have difficulty with relationships. Judith Wallerstein *et al.* (2000) suggest that the ghost image of the parents' failed marriage and the strong emotions of their own fear of subsequent relationship failure produce ambivalent internal images of relationships in general.

Evaluation of the role of unconscious processes in personality formation

One way of verifying whether unconscious processes account for the way our personality develops is to evaluate psychotherapy as a therapy technique. For example, psychoanalysis focuses on unconscious processes. If this method of psychotherapy is seen to be effective, then we might conclude that personality is largely influenced by unconscious processes.

What is the evidence for this? It would seem that psychotherapy is neither more nor less effective than other forms of therapy that do not aim to uncover unconscious mental processes. Some research has supported the influence of unconscious processes. Fiona Gardner (1991), for example, has used object relations theory in her attempts to explore factors linked to self-harming behaviour in young women. Jodeyr (2003) has employed psychoanalysis in her research into the emotional and personality development of second-generation refugees, and by working on these unconscious thoughts and attitudes has witnessed positive improvements in these groups.

Other research has contradicted the work of psychotherapy. For example, Pennington (2003: 50) states, 'how can you have an unconscious if you are not aware of it?' Wallerstein (1989) reported a 30-year longitudinal study that compared psychoanalysis with alternative forms of therapy that did not focus on the unconscious. No significant differences were found between these.

Daly and Wilson (1990), using incidents of family murders, found that the Oedipal hypothesis (sons envying their fathers as they want to have the sole attention of their mothers, and daughters envying their mothers in terms of attention from their fathers) is not supported. Rather than finding greater same-sex (son/father, daughter/mother) murder links, it was found that males were the more frequent murderers of fellow family members and they were also the more frequent victims. Such findings suggest that simply concentrating on unconscious behaviour will not account sufficiently for personality development.

What is the function of personality?

This question allows us to explore two other paradigms of personality research: the *humanistic* approach and the *cognitive-behavioural* approach. The humanistic, or phenomenological, theorists see personality as a tool for personal growth and development, and suggest that our characteristics can serve us in terms of seeking improvements in our quality of life (by, for example, gaining success, friends and satisfaction). The cognitive-behavioural paradigm sees personality as an interface between what we would like and what the world will allow. In other words, personality allows us to interact with the world, form social relationships, learn what is right, what is wrong, and what is good and what is bad for us.

The humanistic or phenomenological paradigm

Humanistic psychologists emphasise personality in terms of growth potential and, like the psychodynamic psychologists, delve into self-understanding. However, this attitude differs sharply from the negativity of the psychodynamic movement. It instead attempts to focus on the positive aspects of human personality. Humanistic theorists look at the way 'healthy' people strive for their own positive development through their personalities.

MacDonald and Freidman (2002) provide an overview of the research findings exploring the relation of humanistic/transpersonal phenomena/concepts to human functioning. Some examples of the humanistic paradigm are described below.

Abraham Maslow (1908–70): hierarchy of needs

Maslow conceptualised individuals as being driven by needs, and believed that all needs were organised hierarchically. He divided human needs into five levels, with the most pressing needs at the base of the hierarchy (see Figure 29.3). Maslow proposed that we must satisfy the lower needs before we can progress and concentrate on obtaining those higher up in the hierarchy. So finding food and water, in Maslow's theory, takes precedence over, for example, obtaining respect from our peers or fitting in with them.

He also suggested that the levels develop with age – so that the first levels occur in childhood (such as need for food, need for safety) and the others develop throughout the life span. Maslow (1968) recognised that the higher-level needs are not necessary for survival, and so motivation to achieve these is weaker than for the more basic needs such as water. The final need stage is that of *self-actualisation*, where an individual seems to know who they are and has little confusion regarding the route their life should take. Our personality is a tool that we use to gain these needs and to attempt to achieve this self-actualisation.

Research evidence and humanistic approaches to personality

Hagerty (1999) has provided some evidence from a cross-cultural perspective that people from different countries do try to achieve needs within the sequence Maslow suggested. Baumeister and Leary (1995) have demonstrated that we do possess a need to belong to social groups (such as clubs, gyms and teams, for example). Betz (1984) offers mixed support for Maslow's theory. She found that there was a positive relationship between need fulfilment and satisfaction with one's life. She also reported, however, that there was no relationship between need importance and need deficiency.

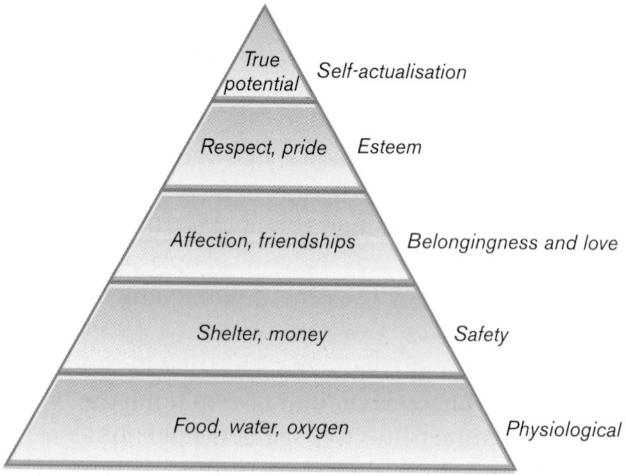

Applications of humanistic theory

Sonnekus (1998) has tried to develop a system, using self-actualisation principles, to aid first-year students in their academic environment. Pennebaker (1990) has suggested that the need to belong is an important concept in people facing life-threatening illness. Such support groups include those for people suffering from all types of serious illness. Indeed Pennebaker suggests that membership of these groups may even be life-prolonging. Thus humanistic principles have been used successfully in areas such as health psychology.

Maslow's need theory has also been applied to employment. So, for example, if pay and security needs are fulfilled, workers might then concentrate on improving their relationships with their co-workers and then finally on developing their own skills, thus moving up Maslow's need hierarchy (Muchinsky, 1997).

The cognitive-behavioural paradigm

Cognitive-behavioural theorists see personality as a package of behaviours that people have acquired through learning and interaction with their environment, and which they employ to help them navigate through their environment. While recognising that behaviour is learned through classical and operant conditioning (see Chapter 8), the cognitive-behavioural approach expands this by assuming that much of personality is learned through social interaction. So we gain both our behaviour and cognitive processes via experience in our social worlds. We then use this experience to survive within our environments.

Figure 29.3 **Maslow's hierarchy of needs**

- True potential — *Self-actualisation*
- Respect, pride — *Esteem*
- Affection, friendships — *Belongingness and love*
- Shelter, money — *Safety*
- Food, water, oxygen — *Physiological*

The function of personality is, then, to test our theories of the world around us in order that we might learn how to survive and behave. The cognitive-behavioural approach to personality seeks to understand (i) how learned cognitive thought patterns influence behaviour, and (ii) how the consequences of a behaviour inform cognition for future actions.

Do cognitive representations of the world influence our personalities?

Kelly (1905–67) maintained that to understand personality we need to consider how people conceptualise the world around them and how this is represented cognitively in their minds. He viewed people as 'informal scientists', always generating and testing hypotheses about the world around them. He believed that people are motivated to understand the world around them and predict what might happen. Kelly (1955) termed this process personal construct theory. In order for us to interpret and predict, we develop cognitive structures, which he termed personal constructs.

Through experience and learning in the world, everybody develops his or her own unique set of constructs (cognitive representations of people, events, environments). Kelly suggested that these personal constructs were represented via a bipolar scale (either/or representation). For example, personal constructs you might apply to your boss could be: helpful/unhelpful; intelligent/unintelligent; effective/ineffective.

Kelly argued that we engage in a process of template-matching with these constructs. So if your boss engages in ways consistent with your construct, then it is retained. If the behaviour is not consistent, then it is modified. We learn which descriptions to apply to which people and, based on these descriptions, we react to them accordingly. So, for example, different people might use different personal constructs to describe the same person. Some might describe Tony Blair as a decent, hard-working, honest man, while others might say he is arrogant, dishonest and power-mad.

The way we test these constructs is through our personalities and engagement with our

Figure 29.4 *What's your view of Tony Blair?*

environments. So if you are hard-working and you hit a problem at work with which your boss refuses to help, then you will form the construct that your boss is unhelpful. Future behaviour will either reinforce or weaken this construct.

Kelly proposed that some personal constructs are more important than others for predicting and interpreting our world. He called these superordinate constructs. The less important ones he called subordinate constructs. Subordinate personal constructs for one person might be superordinate for another person. So Jane might be conscientious in everything she does and Karen can be conscientious in some of the things she does.

Kelly also recognised that everyone has a different perception of world reality, and that this would influence the behaviour that people engage in. He called this constructive alternativism.

Personality: a tool of social environmental interpretation?

Bandura envisaged personality from a social-cognitive perspective. He proposed two theories which suggested that personality affects how we react to environmental stimuli. These were cognitive *social learning theory* (1977b) and reciprocal determinism (1986). He viewed behaviour, internal personal factors and the influences of the environment as inseparable parts of each other. So people's eating habits (past behaviour) influence their eating preferences (personal factor), which in turn influence how different foods (environment) affect their behaviour.

Bandura recognised that different people choose different environments (some people like to go to a large cinema complex to watch a film, others prefer a smaller local cinema and other people would prefer to watch it in the comfort of their own home). He proposed that personality influences how we interpret and react to events/stimuli (so a snake is a cute pet to some people and a loathsome reptile to others).

Bandura also argued that our personalities often contribute to situations that we react to (so if we expect someone to be rude to us, we may be offhand to them in the first place, which then causes the behaviour we had expected).

In essence, then, personality is the sum of our internal personal factors, our cognitions and the behaviours we use to deal with our environments.

One important concept that Bandura suggested was self-efficacy. This is a person's self-rated judgement of success for any behaviour they may engage in. For example, before we try and lift anything heavy we ask ourselves what are our chances of succeeding. If we feel they are good we will try, but if we judge the odds of lifting to be low, we probably will not try and will seek help instead. Self-efficacy is therefore learned.

Other psychologists have emphasised that personality enables us to learn about the success or failure of our actions, and the consequences of behaving in certain ways in certain environments. Mischel (1984) believed that learned expectations are different for each individual and therefore make that individual unique. These expectation dimensions Mischel labelled 'person variables'. In Mischel's view, the most important person variables were: expectations (what the individual expects to happen after a behaviour and what he/she thinks they are

capable of doing – self efficacy); perceptions (how the environment is perceived by each individual); competencies (what thoughts and actions the person can perform); values (the individual's subjective world ideals) and plans (a person's plan for reaching their goals).

Mischel argued that it is not enough to measure someone's traits to predict how they might act; we also need to take into account the situation in which the action occurs. So a helpful person might help someone who trips over in the street but might not help someone who gets mugged at knifepoint. The perception of the situation (in this example risk of injury for offering help) Mischel argues can override a trait.

Evaluation of the social learning approach to personality

The greatest strength of these cognitive and behavioural theories is the generation of empirical research based on objective observations to test their assumptions. This approach to understanding personality has also yielded a number of effective therapeutic approaches to the treatment of a variety of psychological disorders, such as depression (Furlong and Oei, 2002) and obsessive compulsive disorders (Salkovskis, 1999). So it would seem that personality does act to some extent as an interface between our cognitive representation of the world and how we should behave in that world in order to succeed and survive.

Personality is a tool by which we learn the trial and error of our behaviour in relation to our environment. A child who throws tantrums to get what he wants (aggression as a tool of personality) might develop two different personalities depending on how the environment treats such outbursts. If the child is scolded every time he throws a tantrum, then this personality aspect should diminish. If the child is rewarded with what he wants to stop the tantrum, then such reinforcement will develop these tantrums as a useful personality tool.

FOCUS POINT 29.3

Personality and the environment

Personality is also subject to environmental pressures. So while personality is usually expressed at an individual level, the social relationships we have will also guide and influence our behaviour. There are examples to show that our personalities can be influenced by the social groups we belong to (for example, culture). The expression of our personalities via behaviour can also be altered by these groups.

Culture

Personality psychologists believe that exploring personality expression across cultures is important (Church, 2000). This allows us to investigate whether certain personality concepts are prevalent in certain cultures. So, for example, western society is based on individualistic principles – that is to say independence and uniqueness are held as positive characteristics. (Most western films, for example, depict lone heroes overcoming evil groups. Eastern society, however, reflects a more collectivist ideology, where each individual is a contributing member to a successful group).

Do these differing cultural perspectives have an impact on how our personality develops? It seems so. Kitayama *et al.* (1997) reported that Japanese students had a greater sense of positive feeling if they felt they had contributed to establishing interpersonal relationships with others. In contrast, American students associated feelings of positivity with their own individual personal accomplishments. It is not just between different countries that overarching personality

differences have been reported. Nisbett (1993) reported that people from the northern United States were less likely to engage in violence (physical) to avenge a personal slur than were those from the southern United States. Homicide rates for crimes related to defending one's own reputation were far higher in the southern United States than in the northern part of the country.

Conformity and obedience

There are times when it would be foolish or dangerous to follow our own personality. We might risk sanction or punishment from society for doing so (for example, breaking the formal laws in our society), or hostility and ostracism from the smaller groups we belong to (parents, friends). So despite being an individual there are times when we abide by the rules and regulations provided to us, so that we resemble everyone else around us.

Our environment can, therefore, be quite potent in reining in our personalities. However, our personality characteristics can regulate our obedience to rules. It has been seen that people who score highly on authoritarianism tend to conform more often, as do people who score highly on external locus of control (Blass, 1991). In addition, Forbes (2001) investigated, among other factors, personality differences in individuals with and without tattoos or body piercings. Results showed that tattoos and piercings in college students are associated with significantly more risk-taking behaviour, greater use of alcohol and marijuana, and less social conformity.

What is personality?

Just what does personality consist of? This is another important question in the field of personality research: what constitutes personality? We have

descriptive terms for personality, such as 'dispositions' or 'characteristics'. The most widely accepted term in personality is *trait*.

Section 6
Personality and Intelligence

FOCUS POINT 29.4

Traits defined
Personality traits are the tendencies we use to describe how someone thinks and behaves most of the time.

Exactly how many or how few traits make up your personality? Do we all have the same traits at the basis of our personalities or do we have different combinations of traits? Such questions have given rise to a fourth paradigm of personality research: the trait approach to understanding personality.

However, people do not always behave in accordance with traits they possess. For example, if Matthew has a leadership trait, this does not mean that he will take charge in all social situations. In some situations, leaders might already have been chosen and so Matthew will override his leadership trait's need for expression.

While there are many trait theorists, they all share three common assumptions and are guided by three fundamental questions.

The three assumptions are as follows.

1. Individuals each possess particular personality traits to either a greater or less extent. Perhaps the best analogy here is to think of individual traits as having a volume control. In some people the volumes on certain traits are high, in others they are medium and in others they are low. So while we all possess the same personality traits, different combinations of sound volume across these traits create unique personalities.
2. Traits remain relatively stable across time, so a sociable person will probably remain generally sociable throughout his or her lifetime.
3. Traits remain stable across a wide diversity of environmental and social situations. Someone who is competitive, then, will probably be competitive at work as well as on the tennis court.

Trait theories are also concerned with the following three questions.

1. How should traits be conceptualised? In other words, how are traits defined?
2. How can those traits that are most important to personality be identified among the huge numbers of ways people differ?
3. How can all personality traits be identified?

Just how many traits are important in personality?

Three traits?

Jung, though a psychoanalyst, launched the work that influences the trait movement. He proposed that individuals develop and vary along three important dimensions (traits): introversion–extroversion, thinking–feeling and sensation–intuition. He believed that people can differ in their levels of sociability, indicated by having different levels of introversion (a tendency to reflect within oneself – characterised by shyness, submission and quietness) and extroversion (a tendency to focus on the world around us – characterised by enthusiasm, sociability, dominance over others).

For Jung, extroversion is a focus on things, people and events outside oneself, and introversion relates to looking inside oneself and concentrating on our feelings and thoughts. Jung maintained that an individual could have tendencies towards both introversion and extroversion, but that one of these would be dominant.

Like Jung, Eysenck (1991) proposed a model of personality based on three broad traits that he believed were inherited and had psychophysiological foundation. These are extroversion, psychoticism and neuroticism.

Extroverts have a high energy level, are sociable, and like activity and people around them. Introverts, on the other hand, like to spend more time alone, prefer routine and are more evenly paced. A person scoring highly on the neuroticism dimension is anxious and can often be depressed as a result. Low scores reflect people who are emotionally stable, cope better with stressful events and can return to normality faster than a neurotic person.

People scoring high on psychoticism lack empathy and have little sympathy for the suffering of others,

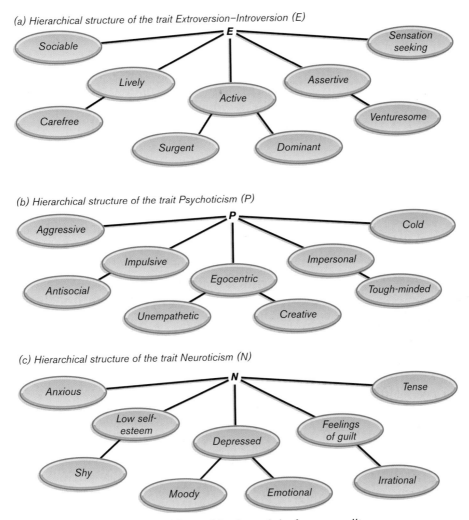

(a) Hierarchical structure of the trait Extroversion–Introversion (E)

Sociable · E · Sensation seeking · Lively · Assertive · Active · Carefree · Venturesome · Surgent · Dominant

(b) Hierarchical structure of the trait Psychoticism (P)

Aggressive · P · Cold · Impulsive · Impersonal · Antisocial · Egocentric · Tough-minded · Unempathetic · Creative

(c) Hierarchical structure of the trait Neuroticism (N)

Anxious · N · Tense · Low self-esteem · Feelings of guilt · Depressed · Shy · Moody · Emotional · Irrational

Figure 29.5 *Eysenck's hierarchical model of personality*

can be aggressive and are often described as anti-social loners. Each of these has a number of underlying associated subtraits (see Figure 29.5).

For Eysenck, the basic personality traits should have high *heritability*. He also linked his proposed traits to the working of the central nervous system. So, for example, introverts would be more easily aroused and show greater physiological arousal reactions.

Eysenck's work has been criticised, however, on a number of grounds and in particular in terms of the terminology employed in the theory. For example, the term 'psychoticism' is outdated and negative, and

might better be superseded with a more acceptable label such as 'anti-social personality'.

Sixteen traits?

Cattell (1946) employed factor analysis to identify and describe the underlying structure of personality. He used a 'psychometric' approach (a way of studying both personality and intelligence in terms of underlying structures) in his bid to describe the structure of personality. We will consider the psychometric method in more detail in Chapter 30.

Cattell sees personality as a cocktail of characteristics that can be used to predict behaviour.

RESEARCH METHODS BOX 29.1

Factor analysis

Factor analysis is a statistical procedure for analysing a complex phenomenon with the aim of simplifying it into more basic and more manageable patterns of description. For example, take a sample of earth from your back garden. What is it made of? Well, if we separated it all out into its basic elements we would probably find soil, maybe traces of clay, peat, flint, granite, pebbles, leaves, roots, twigs and so on. This is a very long-winded way of describing what earth is made up of.

Why not instead make life simple by saying earth is made up of stones/rock, soil components and decaying vegetation? What we have done here is to form subgroups of related items. This idea can be applied to psychology too.

What if we wanted to describe personality? There are hundreds of potential personality traits but we could make life simpler by seeing if certain traits are related to one another. For instance, nervousness, anxiety and worrying are probably all related, so if you score highly on one of these you are likely to score highly on the others. We might call these three concepts 'neuroticism': we have taken three separate descriptions and placed them into a category where we can now employ one description.

This approach can be useful for describing personality because, rather than describing each person in terms of all their traits (which would take a very long time), we can instead simplify things by describing their dominant traits.

traits would be humble versus assertive or emotional versus stable.

If there are 16 of these, and people can either be high, medium or low on each of these source traits, how many combinations would there be? Around 43 million to be precise – that is 43 million different types of people! Cattell (1984) developed the Sixteen Personality Factor (16PF) test based on these source trait groupings. He has applied this test to investigation of structure of the 'abnormal personality'.

One major criticism has been that many researchers have failed to replicate the existence of 16 main personality traits, and others have suggested that a smaller number of factors is sufficient in encompassing how the majority of people differ. There has also been criticism that the 16PF test is not applicable to all cultures – for example, black mother-tongue speakers in South Africa (Abrahams, 2002).

Five traits?

It has been seen over the past 50 years that certain traits seem central to many personality theories and so there are those psychologists who suggest that the core of personality is determined by five central traits, known as the 'Big Five' (Costa and McCrae 1982). The five that have been most commonly suggested are 'extroversion', 'neuroticism', 'agreeableness' (cooperation, trusting and helpful at one end of the trait, and critical, irritable and suspicious at the other), 'conscientiousness' (self-reliant, careful and knowledgeable at one end and careless and ignorant at the other) and 'openness' (creative, daring and independent at one end with conforming, conventional and unadventurous at the other).

While there has been considerable support for the existence of four out of the five factors (McCrae and John, 1992) there has also been some disagreement over the fifth, which Costa and McCrae labelled as 'openness'. This could be due to the fact that different cultures may attach different meanings to the word openness and it is therefore difficult to pin down a definitive label that semantically reflects such a term cross-culturally.

He also makes a distinction between what he calls surface traits and source traits. Surface traits represent the near infinite differences that can be observed between people. He suggested that there are 171 surface traits, such as conscientiousness, competitiveness and flexibility. These surface traits can be grouped together into related groups of traits, which he called source traits. Examples of source

Are some traits more important than others?
Allport (1897–1967) suggested that each person has unique key qualities. He proposed the existence of so-called 'common traits' and 'personal dispositions'. For Allport, common traits are those characteristics shared by a population (because of a biological similarity or common cultural heritage). He viewed personality characteristics in terms of an individual's goals or motives, which are governed by personality dispositions (a trait peculiar to each individual). Those traits that have the greatest influence on our behaviour Allport labelled cardinal traits. Not everyone has these, but they are characterised as being the main driving passion in an individual's life (so, for example, Mother Teresa's desire to help the suffering of others governed her life).

A second set of traits, called central traits, form the main basis of personality; and these are qualities that we all possess and that guide our behaviour. So if you were asked to note down five words to describe yourself these would be your central traits.

Lastly, Allport suggested that we possess secondary dispositions that do not appear in many situations or that influence a variety of behaviours. For example, you may be able to paint walls and ceilings and lay some tiles, but that may just about sum up your relationship with DIY. Allport differed from the views of other theorists such as Cattell by arguing that factor analysis (a statistical representation) could not do justice to the richness of an individual's personality (Allport, 1961).

Allport differs from most other trait theorists in suggesting that we have cardinal traits that are unique to individuals. Most trait theorists, as we will see, propose that people differ in their personalities due to different combinations of traits. They argue that we all possess the same traits in essence, but the difference we see is that for some people the influence of a trait is high, while for others it is medium and, for others still, low. They do not, like Allport, agree that some traits exist in some people and not in others.

Allport's work on cardinal traits is also problematic in terms of research evidence. Deciding on any one individual's cardinal trait is a matter of subjective opinion. For example, one friend might describe my key trait as the 'the desire to have fun', while another might label it 'recklessness'. Who is right?

Evaluation of the trait paradigm
There is evidence that traits provide stability in personality in similar types of situations (Izard *et al.*, 1993). People who are confident meeting new people in a bar will generally be fairly confident in that type of environment. However, are traits stable across a diversity of situations?

One of the leading criticisms of the trait perspective is that personality traits may not be stable and enduring. In other words, the assumption of the trait theorists that personality characteristics influence an individual's behaviour always in the same way, regardless of the situation they are in, might be optimistic. Such an approach takes no account of the power of the environment to change how behaviour manifests itself.

While, on the whole, you may say you are fairly outgoing and socially confident, you might get a little nervous before you give a public presentation. Trait theorists would argue that your social confidence trait would be stable and so given all situations where you might give a speech in public you should feel and perform in the same way. Yet when you gave the leading speech at your best friend's birthday party you were the most nervous you had ever been speaking in public. The fact that you were speaking in front of friends and relatives who knew you quite well made the whole situation much more nerve-racking than when you made a speech in front of strangers. So your perception that the environment was different caused a change in your behaviour, which according to trait theories should have been stable. Mischel (1984), a critic of the trait paradigm, argues that people do not act with predictable consistency.

Biological factors and personality
One of the most significant questions guiding personality research is the extent to which our personalities are influenced by biological factors such as heredity and hormones. Such a question has been tackled by the last paradigm we will discuss, that of biological explanations of personality.

TABLE 29.3   GALEN'S BODILY FLUID THEORY

PERSONALITY LABEL	ASSOCIATED BODILY FLUID	DESCRIPTION
Phlegmatic	Phlegm	Abundance of phlegm made a person calm, thoughtful and passive
Sanguine	Blood	Abundance of blood made a person happy, lively and sociable
Choleric	Yellow bile	Abundance of yellow bile made a person unstable, aggressive and excitable
Melancholic	Black bile	Abundance of black bile made a person pessimistic and unhappy

ACTIVITY BOX 29.3

Ageing and personality: is personality stable over time?

How stable are personality traits across the life span? If there were evidence that traits are fairly consistent across an individual's life, then this would support the trait theorists' proposals. How might we go about researching this fact? There are two approaches we might take.

First, we might ask someone to judge how similar their present personality is to their personality in their past. This approach is called a 'retrospective study', so called because it asks people to remember their past behaviour. However, an individual's memory might not be very reliable and so the accuracy of their accounts might be questionable.

Second, some people may not want to view their personality as inconsistent. They might simply assume, then, that their present personality is very much like their personality was when they were younger because they feel more comfortable with that image of stability.

A more reliable method of assessing the stability of personality traits would be to assess someone's personality now and then assess it again after a period of years has passed. This method of research is called a longitudinal study and is a popular method with personality theorists interested in assessing whether personality is indeed stable over a lifetime.

So the burning question, then, is 'Is it?' Recent research evidence seems to suggest that traits are not completely fixed and can be changed over time by events in a person's life.

Ardelt (2000) reviewed the findings from 206 sets of results investigating the stability of Costa and McCrae's Big Five personality traits over time. He found that personality tends to be less stable if (i) the time between the tests is large, (ii) if age at first measurement is low or over 50, and (iii) if a change in individual aspects of personality, rather than overall personality, is measured.

Srivastava et al. (2003) reported that in a large sample of adults aged 21 to 60 (129,515 people) who completed a Big Five personality questionnaire over several time points, conscientiousness and agreeableness increased throughout early and middle adulthood at varying rates. Neuroticism declined among women but did not change among men. They concluded that the variety in patterns of change suggests that the Big Five traits are complex phenomena subject to a variety of developmental influences and therefore not completely independent of the influence of life-changing events.

Maiden et al. (2003) conducted a longitudinal study of 74 elderly women with a mean age of 80. They were assessed on the personality traits of neuroticism, extroversion and openness, and were seen to be moderately stable on all three traits over time. The authors also found that stability was influenced by negative changes in life circumstances. For example, decreased social support and increased unmet needs were subsequently associated with more neuroticism.

The notion that facets of personality are the products of bodily, or biological, processes is not a modern concept. In the second century AD, Galen, a Roman physician, proposed that it was the presence or absence of four bodily fluids that determined personality (see Table 29.3). While this view remained in favour for many centuries, today it seems rather antiquated. It was one of the first recorded physiological approaches to personality.

Biological approaches are founded on the premise that psychological characteristics (such as aggression and shyness) are based on an underlying physiological system. For example, a biologically oriented personality psychologist might argue that a person is introverted because they have an overly sensitive nervous system (a physiological characteristic) and thus try to avoid stimuli that might lead to over-stimulation.

The role of arousal and personality

Arousability theory

Eysenck first proposed the view that people can be described as being either introverted or extroverted. From a biological perspective, introversion and extroversion have been described in terms of arousal levels. That is, an extrovert will seek more stimulation than an introvert because their arousal system requires more stimulation to become aroused. If this is true then we should see that extroverts' arousal levels respond less quickly to arousal than introverts' arousal levels. Studies by Bullock and Gilliland (1993) and Brocke, Tasche and Beaducel (1997) have all supported this observation. It does seem to take extroverts more stimulation over a longer period to reach the same arousal levels as introverts.

Jeffrey Gray's (1985) reinforcement sensitivity theory

Gray has proposed a model of personality that is based on two hypothesised biological systems within the brain. The first of these is what he calls the behavioural activation system (BAS). This responds to incentives and is responsible for behaviour engagement. Thus when the BAS recognises a stimulus that offers a potential reward, it encourages approach behaviour. The other system Gray postulates is the behavioural inhibition system (BIS). This is responsive to punishment cues.

So you might be hungry after a night on the town and see a kebab shop, and this activates your BAS to encourage you to enter the shop to buy some food. However, you were violently ill the last time you mixed alcohol with a late-night kebab, so on nearing the shop the smell of the food activates your BIS (memories of being ill), which terminates your approach towards the shop. Instead you decide to go home and settle for a cup of tea and a biscuit. So personality is determined to some extent by the balance between your BAS and BIS.

Hebb and Zuckerman's work on sensation-seeking

Hebb (1955) initially suggested that people are motivated to seek out an optimal level of arousal with which they are personally comfortable. So if they are under-aroused relative to this level, further arousal will be considered rewarding, and if they are over-aroused, a decrease in arousal will be rewarding. Adopting sensory deprivation research techniques, Zuckerman (1978) observed that some people were not as distressed as others by depriving the senses of stimulation. Zuckerman proposed the term 'high need for *sensation-seeking*' and applied this to those individuals who actively seek out stimulation.

Some people seek out stimulation while others are happy to avoid it.

Zuckerman developed the Sensation Seeking Scale, which measures the degree to which people seek out stimulation. His theory suggested that high sensation-seekers seek stimulation while low sensation-seekers tend to avoid it more often. He reports various findings to support this – for instance, that those police officers volunteering for riot duty have higher sensation-seeking scores than those officers who do not volunteer for such duties (Zuckerman, 1991).

Zuckerman proposes a physiological basis for sensation-seeking behaviour focusing on the role of neurotransmitters (see Section 2 of this book). Just to remind you, neurotransmitters are chemicals in the nerve cells that are responsible for communication between cells using nerve impulses. Monoamine oxidase (MAO) is an enzyme related to maintaining proper levels of neurotransmitters – too much MAO, and nerve transmission will be reduced. In other words, MAO acts like the brakes of the nervous system. Zuckerman (1991) has reported that people who score highly on sensation-seeking seem to have lower MAO levels, so they have less inhibition in their nervous system.

Hormones and personality
Theorists working with hormones argue that sex differences between genders occur because each gender has different levels of underlying hormones. Men, for example, have on average 100 times the amount of testosterone in their blood as females (Hoyenga and Hoyenga, 1993). Higher testosterone levels have been linked to aggressive behaviour, and Dabbs and Hargrove (1997) reported that female prisoners with high levels of this hormone received more disciplinary punishments from the prison authorities than those female inmates with lower testosterone levels.

Cashdan (2003) investigated hormone levels and self-reported expressions of competitive feelings in a sample of women. Results indicated that women with low levels of androstenedione and testosterone were less likely to express their competitive feelings overtly, while women with high levels of androstenedione were more likely than other women to express their competitive feelings through verbal aggression.

We need to be cautious when interpreting such research, however. Most studies of this nature are correlational (see Chapter 36) and so we cannot be sure if the testosterone has caused the behaviour or if the behaviour has caused the increase in the hormone.

Evolutionary perspectives on personality
Evolutionary psychology maintains that there will be differences in behaviour between men and women in behaviour domains where they have faced different sorts of adaptive pressures (Buss, 1994). So, for example, men and women face differing information-processing information in reproductive behaviour. For men there is the question of assured

---

FOCUS POINT 29.5

Sex differences in personality
Are women from Venus and men from Mars? Not exactly. We often hear that men and women are different and think differently. This may be the case at times. Men are seen to be more individualistic in their relationship with their environments, whereas in general women tend to be more collective and to foster more social networks (Triandis et al., 1990).

What we are not reminded of as often, however, is that on closer examination there is greater within-sex difference in personality than there is between the sexes (Griffen, 1991). For example, Harris and Schwab (1990) report that individuals with high levels of masculinity (regardless of whether they are male or female) seem to experience lower levels of depression than those who score more highly on femininity.

So rather than two potential planets, we may have a whole number of planets reflecting the different personalities that are evident both across the sexes and within them.

paternity as fertilisation occurs internally within the female. Men who fail to solve this problem of whether they are the biological father risk investing resources in offspring that are not theirs. For women, the problem is securing reliable sources that will support them and their child through pregnancy and the period immediately after.

Evolutionary psychologists argue that it is these differing needs across the genders that motivate different types of personality development. So biological differences might account for why people have different personalities.

Such biological differences can also shape within-sex differences in personality too. A muscular man, for example, might be more confident using confrontational or aggressive behaviour to achieve his goals than a skinny one (as he has more muscles and is physically stronger and more intimidating). The skinny one might have too much to lose to employ such a confrontational approach to life – after all, he has not got the physical muscle to support or defend himself. Instead, the skinny man may opt for a more cooperative approach that does not have to rely on physical presence or fitness.

So through the processes of reinforcement and punishment we learn what we can and cannot do, based on our biological make-up. Tall people, for instance, have a greater chance of being more successful at playing basketball; or a short person might be loud as they feel they need to be heard if they cannot be seen.

Behavioural genetics

What is the role of genetics in influencing personality? The human genome was first drafted in June 2000 and refers to the complete set of genes that humans possess (between 30,000 and 50,000 genes). Most of these genes are shared commonly between all humans, and this is why we physically resemble one another in our main features.

However, a small number of genes are different for different people (hair colour, for instance). So while we have the sequence for our DNA we do not as yet fully understand the role these genes play in such things as behaviour, cognitive ability and personality.

Work in the area of *behavioural genetics* is

Researchers seek to understand the similarity in personality between family members.

attempting to discover the extent to which individual differences in personality are determined by environmental or genetic factors. This is arguably one of the most controversial areas of psychology for a number of reasons. If scientists can identify set genes that are related to personality, then these findings might be used for political purposes. For example, if we found that addiction was related to a specific gene it *could* be argued that rehabilitation of drug and alcohol addicts may represent a thankless task because such programmes cannot override a genetic basis for this behaviour.

There is also concern that if scientists identify certain behaviours with the presence of certain genes, this will lead to misuse. For example, if criminal behaviour is related to the presence or absence of a specific gene, this may raise concerns that such information could lead to genetic screening at birth. This is known as eugenics and espouses the view that we can design the future of the human race by encouraging people to reproduce in a way that promotes so-called 'desired' traits and discourages reproduction of 'undesired' traits. The Nazi philosophy during the Second World War, for example, reflected this extreme view.

However, just because a personality trait is

RESEARCH METHODS BOX 29.2

How do geneticists research genetic influences on personality?

Behavioural geneticists employ the notion of heritability. Heritability refers to the extent to which genetic inheritance is responsible for the variability (the degree to which we differ) of a trait in a population of people. So how much of the variability in scores on an aggression test given to people might be accounted for by their inherited differences in aggression from their parents?

There are two general methods that have commonly been employed by behavioural geneticists investigating the genetic basis of personality. These are called twin studies and adoption studies.

Twin studies investigate the similarity of identical (monozygotic, or MZ) twins – who share 100 per cent of their genetic material – and fraternal (dizygotic, or DZ) twins – those who develop from two separate eggs and are no more related than normal brothers and sisters (i.e. they share only 50 per cent of their genetic material) – in terms of how similar or dissimilar their personalities are.

Stein *et al.* (2002) examined the heritability of negative evaluation fears by using a twin sample (437 twin pairs aged between 18 and 86 years). Genetic correlations between twin scores on submissiveness, anxiousness and social avoidance facets of a personality test were high. A study in Germany by Borkenau, Riemann, Angleitner and Spinath (2002), testing 525 identical twins and 268 fraternal twins, reported that identical twins were more alike in their personalities than fraternal twins.

Adoption studies attempt to see if identical twins who have been adopted by different families differ in their personalities. (Obviously researchers cannot make this happen – it would be rather unethical to storm into someone's house, take a set of twins, purposely separate them and give them to two different families to see how their personalities develop. Instead they have to wait for natural separations of twins from their natural parents for whatever tragic reason.)

If researchers observe that the separated adopted twins are still similar in their behaviour as they grow up, this would suggest a strong biological underpinning to personality manifestation (as they share the same biology but have different environments). If, on the other hand, they grow up to have different personalities, this would suggest, instead, that the environment is more influential in shaping personality.

Bouchard *et al.* (2003), in a study called the Minnesota Study of Twins Reared Apart, found that there was still evidence of strong similarities in personality between identical twins who had been reared apart. Bouchard also found that separated fraternal twins do not exhibit similarities to the same extent as separated identical twins.

Similarly, Pederson *et al.* (1988) reported that of 99 separated identical twins and 200 fraternal twins, compared with equivalent numbers of non-separated identical and fraternal twins, separated twins had more dissimilar personalities. Thus identical twins reared apart appear to have more similar personalities than fraternal twins reared apart.

The similarity between parents and children might also reveal something of the genetic bases of personality. It has been interesting to note that the behaviour of adoptive children in general resembles more their biological parents' behaviour than that of their adopted parents (Rowe, 1990; Pederson, 1993).

Adoption studies have a number of recognised methodological weaknesses, however. It is assumed that the adoptive children, their adoptive parents and their circumstances are representative of the general population. But how can we be sure that people who adopt children are similar to those people who do not seek to adopt?

A second problem is the placement of the children themselves into an adoptive environment. Children who are placed with adoptive parents that are matched closely to their biological parents (as often happens) confuse matters further. Are the children behaving as they do because of their genes (sharing similar genetic make-up with their biological parents) or because of environmental influences, as their adoptive parents are so similar to their biological parents. It would become difficult to unravel this question.

To what extent do our genes influence our personalities?

identified with a certain gene it does not mean the environment cannot also play a role in how this behaviour is shaped.

Molecular genetics

Most recently, biological research into personality has moved away from the issue of whether genes influence personality and towards a much more focused set of questions such as 'how much' they influence personality and 'which precise genes' influence which behaviour (*molecular genetics*).

One of the main areas in which this approach is currently being applied is in the search for genes that are associated with genetically influenced disorders. So families with a history of these disorders are studied, blood or saliva is taken from those members of the family that have the disorder and those who do not, so that a DNA comparison can be made.

Other biological indicators of personality

Research into hormones and brain hemisphere use has also been used to investigate influences on personality. For example, Compton *et al.* (2003) investigated hemisphere involvement in emotions in 170 people. Results indicated that brooding and dwelling on the negative may be associated with decreased left hemisphere involvement, whereas openness to emotion may be associated with increased right hemisphere involvement.

Other areas of investigation involving biological indicators of personality differences concern blood sugar levels. Svanborg (2000) investigated blood glucose levels and personality. Results indicated that in males, low blood glucose is associated with extroverted and impulsive, acting-out behaviour, which includes breaking societal norms. Such studies highlight the different kinds of research exploring the biological link to personality.

Evaluation of the biological approach to personality

Theoretical concepts do not have a physical existence and so are difficult to prove or disprove. One main advantage in the biological approach is that physiological characteristics can be measured reliably (the brain, genes and blood are all physical entities). Brain activity and differences can be monitored via PET scans (positron emission tomography, a powerful brain-imaging technique). For example, Johnson *et al.* (1999) have shown that extroverts might seek more arousal because their

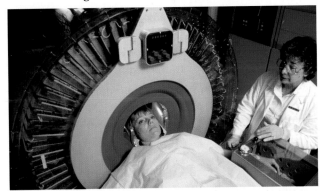

Brain activity and differences can be monitored using PET scans in an effort to explain differences in personality.

511

normal brain arousal (as measured via a PET scan) is relatively low in the frontal lobe area compared to introverts, whose normal arousal level is higher. Introversion, on the other hand, is associated with increased blood flow in the frontal lobes and in the anterior thalamus. In this case a direct physiological indicator has demonstrated a difference in an aspect of personality.

The biological approach, in terms of hormone and brain activity, offers interesting insights into how biology is linked to the expression of personality, but there is a danger here that the complexity of human nature is forgotten in such a specifically focused area.

Bunge (1990), among others, would argue that reduction to biological processes cannot fully explain personality. Behaviour is rooted in a rich cocktail of

---

APPLICATIONS BOX 29.1

Applications of personality research

Personality research has been applied to many areas of human behaviour. Presented below are research findings snapshots from just three areas of application.

Personality and health

Patients who demonstrate 'fighting spirit' in response to cancer diagnosis seem to fare better than those who do not. Indeed, cancer patients who gave higher ratings of helplessness and negative beliefs about their future had poorer outcomes (Goodkin *et al.*, 1986).

Personality seems to play an influential role in the post-treatment stage too. Allison, Guichard and Gilian (2000) investigated the role of dispositional optimism (DO) as a predictor of health-related quality of life (HRQL) in a sample of stomach cancer patients. Following treatment, optimists reported better role and cognitive functioning, and less pain.

Personality and criminal behaviour

Mak, Heaven and Rummery (2003) investigated the impact of personality factors on self-reported delinquency among 224 male and 196 female

---

Australian high-school students. Results indicated that the strongest predictor of delinquency among both males and females was Eysenck's psychoticism factor, and that extroversion scores predicted delinquency – but only for males.

Nussbaum *et al.* (2002) reported personality differences in violent, non-violent and sexual offenders incarcerated at a medium-security federal penitentiary in America. Violent offenders were found to be more impulsive and less empathic than non-violent offenders. Sexual offenders were found to be less impulsive, more empathic and more attached than non-sexual offenders.

Personality and television violence

Haridakis (2002) examined whether several viewer personality characteristics (disinhibition and locus of control) mitigated how people view and respond to watching television violence. Results supported the notion that individual characteristics and expectations influence the effects of exposure to televised violence.

Kiewitz and Weaver (2001) explored the short-term impact of exposure to violent mass media content while accounting for personality (i.e. trait-aggression). Following exposure to either a violent or non-violent film, 268 participants reported their perceptions of violent interpersonal incidents described in four written

There is research evidence which suggests that personality can influence engagement in or avoidance of criminal behaviour.

scenarios. High-scoring trait-aggressive individuals generally displayed more callous and hostile tendencies in their perceptions of interpersonal conflicts than low-scoring trait-aggressive individuals. Moreover, high-scoring trait-aggressive males were found to be most extreme in reporting aggressive thoughts and actions. These studies suggest that personality can be influential in how we interpret and respond to social stimuli.

influential factors, with biological indicators being just one, along with others that can be equally powerful – such as cognitive processes or environmental pressures.

The main problem with the biological approach to understanding personality is that a number of misconceptions have become attached to this view. First, that heredity means permanence. This is not the case. People can change over their lives due to environmental factors (such as changing jobs, becoming a parent). There is then the misconception that everyone inheriting a trait will act in the same way. Again this is untrue. Only twins inherit all the same genes – the majority of us inherit different combinations of traits. So two individuals might inherit a particular trait but they will also inherit other different traits too. In this way genes can be seen as a kind of chemistry set – mix the same substance with lots of different substances and you'll get different results each time.

Summary

We have seen how research within this field has been directed by a number of significant questions regarding the nature of personality. The term 'personality' refers to the unique sets of psychological and behavioural characteristics/dispositions by which individuals can be compared and contrasted.

There are five main approaches to personality research: psychodynamic, humanistic, trait, cognitive-behavioural and biological. Contrasting factors across gender and culture tend to exert some influence on the development of personality. Biological factors also offer some insight into how personality develops.

Applications of personality research are making positive contributions to our understanding of many applied areas of psychology (such as health, criminal behaviour and social issues).

Learning outcomes

When you have completed this chapter you should be able to:

- describe the main personality theories and evaluate their contribution to our understanding of personality
- understand the role that biology might play in influencing personality
- describe how social influences might impact on personality
- describe some of the ways personality research has been applied to contemporary social issues.

Key terms

Adoption studies
Behavioural genetics
Cognitive-behavioural
Ego
Extroversion
Heritability
Humanistic
Id
Idiographic
Introversion
Molecular genetics
Nomothetic
Paradigm
Psychodynamic
Self-actualisation
Sensation-seeking
Social learning theory
Trait
Twin studies

Further reading
Cooper, C. (2002) Individual Differences. London: Arnold.

30

Intelligence

Route map of the chapter

This chapter is divided into three parts. The first deals with the history of intelligence research and the issue of defining it as a psychological concept. The second part considers whether intelligence is a single ability or made up of smaller, more specific intellectual skills. Lastly, we will discuss the influence of heredity and biological factors on intelligence. Throughout this chapter we will aim to evaluate the main theories of intelligence and their contribution to our understanding of human intellect. We will consider how social influences might impact on intellectual development and review the research on racial and gender aspects of intelligence.

Introduction

Intelligence is a fundamental concept in our time. The term has become a convenient evaluative expression covering a wide variety of domains (for example, singers are described as having intelligent voices, footballers as having intelligent feet, horses as running intelligent races). However, while many people use the term in their daily language in a way that suggests there is agreement about what intelligence is, the truth of the matter is that psychologists cannot agree at all!

The *Oxford English Dictionary* defines intelligence as 'quickness of understanding', while the *Cambridge Advanced Learners Dictionary* defines it as 'the ability to learn, understand and make judgements or have opinions that are based on reason'.

Psychologists, as mentioned above, do not yet agree on a universally acceptable definition. While they may agree that intelligence is not a physical

---

ACTIVITY BOX 30.1

Are you as intelligent as you think?

Take a few moments to judge how intelligent you consider yourself to be. You probably made judgements about your intellect, maybe on the basis of your education or your general knowledge skills. Now also ask yourself the following questions.

1. Can you change the engine on a car?
2. Could you use the stars to navigate your way home if you got lost?
3. Do you know how many square feet of tiles you would need to cover your bathroom?
3. Can you walk a tightrope?

If you cannot do any of these things, then would you be considered unintelligent?

---

entity but rather a concept (idea or notion), they disagree on what that concept it. For example, as we shall see later in this chapter, some psychologists see intelligence as being a single aptitude, while others see it as representing a cluster of aptitudes or mental skills. Other psychologists look to definitions of intellectual inheritance, contrasting with those who view intellect as a learned behaviour.

Definitions of intelligence over the last century can be seen in Table 30.1.

The problems with defining intelligence are in part due to how we define intellectual behaviour as part of everyday life. In other words, the term intelligence is *socially constructed* – that is, different cultures and

TABLE 30.1   HISTORICAL DEFINITIONS OF INTELLIGENCE

1916	Binet and Terman: motivation and adaptation to the environment
1923	Spearman: understanding relationships between objects and understanding correlations
1943	Stoddard: taking on difficult tasks and carrying them out despite resistance
1955	Freeman: adaptation to the environment, the ability to learn, the ability to think abstractly using symbols
1958	Wechsler: to act rationally and purposefully, and interact with the environment
1973	Das: planned behaviour based on desired goal
1979	Humphrys: acquiring new information, retrieving it when necessary and applying it to new situations
1983	Gardner: problem-solving and acquiring new knowledge
1986	Sternberg: adaptation to and selection of environments relevant to one's life

groups of people see intelligence as being whatever attribute leads to success within that group (Sternberg and Kaufman, 1998).

In the western world we take for granted that our definition of intelligence – which revolves around high academic attainment – applies the world over. As we shall see later in this section, however, this is not the case. For example, within the Sahara regions of North Africa, intelligence might be considered in the context of being able to find water. In the jungles of Brazil the identification of edible plants is viewed as a sign of intellect.

Another distinction that is evident is the difference between academic and non-academic definitions of intelligence. Sternberg and Detterman (1986) asked experts working in the field of intelligence for their views on what intelligence was. Learning and adaptive abilities were considered important, as was the ability to understand and control oneself. This contrasted with the non-expert definitions, which emphasised practical problem-solving, verbal ability and social competence as indicators of intelligence (Sternberg *et al.*, 1981).

This distinction raises the issue of how we go about defining intelligence. Do we define it as higher intellectual functioning or do we define it in terms of successful day-to-day survival?

In terms of academic investigations of intelligence, there have been three main types of definition. These can be seen in Table 30.2.

FOCUS POINT 30.1

Intelligence defined

A working definition that would encompass both academic and non-academic definitions of intelligence, and apply to people worldwide and from all geographical contexts, might be that intelligence is the ability to learn from experience, apply knowledge to solve problems, and to adapt and survive in different environments (social and geographical).

In more simple terms, then, intelligence equals survival. If we exhibit intelligence, then we will survive and prosper within the social and geographical contexts we encounter. This does not mean just finding food and shelter, but building successful social relationships with those individuals that share our community.

TABLE 30.2   THE THREE TYPES OF INTELLIGENCE DEFINITIONS

INTUITIVE DEFINITIONS

These maintain that intelligence relies upon experience and judgement. Such definitions can be further subdivided into:
* those concentrating on adaptation to the environment
* those emphasising the capacity for learning
* those stressing the capacity for abstract thinking.

LOGICAL DEFINITIONS

These focus on what the actual word 'intelligence' implies to people. Such an approach recognises that different groups of people will use different words and abilities to describe intelligence.

EMPIRICAL DEFINITIONS

These start from facts that have been scientifically established (for example, the observation that many academics lack practical intelligence) and try to derive further hypotheses from these facts by seeking evidence to test out these hypotheses via research and observation.

History and origins of the scientific study of intelligence

A history of the debate about human intelligence can be traced back over the past 25 centuries. Table 30.3 summarises those who have been influential in discussing the nature of intelligence over this period.

Intelligence: a general ability or a number of defined abilities?

Modern theories of intelligence consider the question of whether intelligence is a single mental ability (you are either intelligent or not) or whether a number of specific abilities make up overall intellectual ability. If intelligence comprises a number of abilities, there is also the question of what these specific abilities might be. The distinction is a vital one. If we are to view intelligence as a single trait, then someone who performs badly on a test measuring that trait could be labelled as unintelligent. However, if intelligence is made up of sub-abilities, then a poor score does not necessarily mean that person is unintelligent in everything they attempt to do.

In addressing these issues, contemporary research on intelligence originates from two main perspectives: the psychometric perspective and the cognitive and contextual perspective.

FOCUS POINT 30.2

Sample tasks from Binet and Simon's mental tests

Binet and Simon's tasks (see Table 30.3) were organised depending on the age category of the child, as outlined below.

Four years of age
* Name objects (key, knife, penny)
* Repeat three figures
* Compare the lengths of two lines

Eight years of age
* Compare two objects from memory
* Count down from twenty to zero
* Repeat five numbers

Twelve years of age
* Produce more than 60 words in three minutes
* Define three abstract words
* Comprehend a jumbled-up sentence

TABLE 30.3   THE LEADING INDIVIDUALS ASSOCIATED WITH THE ADVANCEMENT OF A SCIENTIFIC FOCUS ON INTELLIGENCE

Socrates (fourth century BC)
Greek philosopher. He hypothesised that individuals have inborn, or innate, knowledge systems that are inherited. He viewed intelligence not as a single construct but as a sum of several different capacities.

René Descartes (seventeenth century)
French philosopher and mathematician. Intelligence was mostly God-given; knowledge was thus innate and resided in the mind, so was without physical attributes, and was separate and distinct from the body. The argument that the mind and body are separate entities is called 'dualism'.

John Locke (seventeenth century)
British philosopher. Disagreed with Descartes about intelligence being innate. Saw the mind as a blank piece of paper that was to be filled through experience and interaction with one's environment. He is credited with founding the British empiricists, who argue that experience is the basis of all knowledge.

Immanuel Kant (eighteenth century)
German philosopher. Attempted to bring together the two opposing stances taken by Descartes and Locke. Kant argued that the human mind comes ready-furnished with the ability to make 'categories' (such as relation, time and space, and quantity). The human mind perceives the world in ways that are determined by its innate categories. Thus we all see the world in terms of time, space, quantity and quality. Kant also suggested that we make mental representations of our world through 'schema'.

TABLE 30.3 CONTINUED

Wilhelm Wundt (nineteenth century)

German academic professor. Credited with establishing the first experimental psychological laboratory. From work in his laboratory, Wundt concluded that a number of basic mental processes were required to solve problems. Some of these he named as perception, cognition, judgement and reflex.

Francis Galton (nineteenth century)

Half-cousin to Charles Darwin. Proposed that intellect was inherited. He studied the children of notable and eminent men in Victorian society, and observed that such men bred intelligent offspring. He focused on sensory indications of intelligence, such as pitch detection, and colour and weight differentiation, but was criticised for not taking into account that such eminent families at that time could provide educational stimulation to their children when the majority of the population could not afford to. Galton is credited with coining the word 'eugenics' (enhancing humans' mental abilities by improved selective breeding).

Alfred Binet (twentieth century)

French psychologist. Opposed to the sole use of the sensory skills approach pursued by Galton. He also focused on what he called higher-order skills, such as reasoning, invention and comprehension. In 1904 the French Ministry of Public Instruction commissioned Binet to devise a test to identify children who were not learning in ordinary schools but who might benefit from remedial education. Binet and Theodore Simon published their first tests of children's mental ability in 1905 (Binet and Simon, 1916; 1973). (See Focus Point 30.2 for examples taken from this test.)

Edward Thorndike (1900–1940s)

American educational psychologist. Reported via his work with animal behaviour that repetition increases the rate of problem-solving ability. Saw the mind as a blank sheet of paper which, via learning and exposure to environmental interaction, could acquire intellectual skills and competences.

We will explore these perspectives and their respective theories in relation to the question of whether intelligence is a single ability or a reflection of a finite number of specific abilities.

Psychometric perspective

Most standard IQ and intelligence tests have been forged out of psychometric approaches to understanding the structure of intelligence. While we will consider the psychometric method in more detail in a separate section, we will describe the main psychometric theories of intelligence here. The psychometric approach to intelligence is among the oldest of approaches, and dates back to Galton's (1883) psychophysical account of intelligence.

Let us now consider some of the contributions of psychometric theories in understanding the structure of intelligence.

FOCUS POINT 30.3

Intelligence quotient defined

Intelligent quotient (*IQ*) was defined originally as the ratio of mental age (ma) to chronological age (ca) multiplied by 100 (IQ = ma/ca x 100).

FOCUS POINT 30.4

Do you have more than one intelligence?

Think about the skills you have. Are you good with numbers or do you need a calculator? Are you good at languages or do you have difficulty mastering just one? Are you musically minded or do your efforts to hum in the shower sound more like those of a drowning ostrich? Are you good with mechanical things or if you took your car apart and put it back together would you end up with two smaller cars, neither of which worked?

Chances are there are few of you reading this who are good at all the things I have just mentioned. If you are one of them I guess you are feeling fairly proud of yourself right now! But are the skills I have just mentioned indicators of separate forms of intelligence or are they all part of a general intellectual ability? Do we have a single intelligence or *multiple intelligences*?

Charles Spearman (1863–1945): two-factor theory

Spearman was a statistician at the turn of the last century. He observed that individuals who tended to do well on one test of intellectual ability tended also to do well on other tests related to intelligence. He also helped develop factor analysis in his work. So he suggested that different abilities seemed correlated with one another and therefore under the direction of the same system. Spearman called this general overarching system general intelligence (g).

FOCUS POINT 30.5

A definition of general intelligence (g)

General intelligence is believed to underlie specific mental abilities. Spearman saw this as a neurologically based power that drives the ability to engage in and complete intellectual activity.

While Spearman believed that our intellectual ability is represented by 'g' he also suggested we have a number of specialised skills or abilities, which he labelled *specialised intelligence (s)*. These were the specific skills and knowledge needed for particular mental tasks. He believed 'g' could be used to improve our abilities in these other areas. So someone who had a high 'g' but an average ability in maths, could divert some of their 'g' intellect to help them improve their maths standing. Thus 'g' was the crucial component of whether someone was intelligent or not; 'g' represented a single intelligence.

L. L. Thurstone (1887–1955): factor analytic theory

Thurstone opposed Spearman's assertion that there was a single underlying 'force' guiding intellectual ability. Thurstone employed factor analysis to analyse correlations among 56 intelligence tests to see if there was any related underlying factor. His work did not reveal a single dominating 'g' factor. While he did not deny 'g' existed, he did not believe it was as important as Spearman suggested.

He did, however, report finding around seven groupings or clusters of what he called primary mental abilities (numerical ability, verbal fluency,

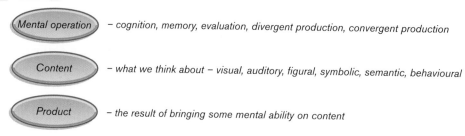

Figure 30.1 **Guilford's structure of intellect model (1967)**

spatial visualisation, reasoning, perceptual ability, verbal comprehension and memory). As a result, Thurstone believed that intelligence was not a united single entity but a linked system of mental abilities.

J.P. Guilford (1967): structure of intellect model

Guilford's model (see Figure 30.1) did not hold with the importance of 'g', nor did it propose a single concept for intelligence. Guilford's structure of intellect model contained 120 factors in three dimensions – often represented as a 4 x 5 x 6 cuboid.

Guilford visualised intelligence as having a number of subcomponents, all of which contributed to an individual's intellectual ability. So intelligence comprised a single concept subdivided into different aptitudes.

Philip Vernon (1950): hierarchical model of intelligence

The British psychologist Philip Vernon suggested that 'g' intelligence was made up of two groupings of abilities. Higher-order abilities, called v:ed, which generally reflected educational type abilities (language, numbers etc.), and k:m, abilities associated with spatial ability and mechanical understanding.

John Horn and Raymond Cattell (1966): fluid and crystallised intelligence

Horn and Cattell agreed with Spearman. They proposed two components to intelligence, but rather than 'g' and 's', they labelled them 'fluid' and 'crystallised'. Fluid intelligence ('gf') was the ability to think logically and to relate concepts through reasoning. Crystallised intelligence ('gc') refers to specific (or set) knowledge as a result of the

application of fluid intelligence to a task. So an ability to engage in multiplication is a form of crystallised intelligence in the western world.

Horn (1989) added to the earlier work on this model and suggested a hierarchical basis for the two 'gf' and 'gc' systems of intelligence in his gf–gc theory of intelligence.

Horn also recognised that the expressions of these abilities 'are outcroppings of distinct influences operating through development, brain function, genetic determination, and the adjustments, adaptations, and achievements of school and work' (Horn, 1989: 76).

Carroll (1993): hierarchical model of intelligence

Carroll analysed more than 460 intelligence data sets obtained between 1927 and 1987, involving more than 130,000 people from varying countries. Carroll's model of intelligence is a hierarchy comprising three levels, which he called strata. The first stratum includes many specific abilities (e.g. spelling); the second stratum includes various group-factor abilities (e.g. flexible thinking) and an accumulated knowledge base; the third stratum is a single general intelligence, much like Spearman's 'g' factor.

Evaluation of the psychometric approach

At least some psychometric theories agree with each other in conceptualising intelligence as a single construct, while others suggest that intelligence comprises different subfactors. It would seem to some extent that theory is often influenced by the type of research statistical tool employed:

> Given the same set of data, it is possible, using one set of factor analytic procedures, to come

RESEARCH METHODS BOX 30.1

Researching intelligence

There are several research methodologies that can be employed to investigate the issues (such as the composition of intellect) and questions (such as 'To what extent is intelligence inherited?') discussed in this chapter.

Longitudinal studies

These enable the observation of the development of intelligence over a time period, usually starting in childhood and continuing into adulthood. This method is useful for studying how intellectual ability develops and how life events might impact on intelligence. This type of research can be costly and time consuming.

Cohort studies

These are longitudinal studies involving everyone from a particular group. For example, all babies born in the first week of March 1968 would be a cohort group for a longitudinal study. The weakness with this type of study (as with the longitudinal study design) is that people drop out along the way (they may die or voluntarily remove themselves from the study). The problem here is that the people who drop out could be very different to the people who stay in the study, and this will obviously bias any conclusions we might make at the end of the study.

Cross-cultural studies

These allow researchers to compare intellectual ability across different groups/cultures worldwide. This method is useful in exploring both the development of intelligence within individuals from different groups and also the potential differences in intellectual abilities from a cross-cultural perspective. This method is not without its drawbacks. It is expensive and also requires accuracy in universally translating concepts and questions (for example, asking people to define sexual harassment would be difficult as this means different things to different people from different cultures).

Twin and adoption studies

These are employed to investigate whether aspects of intelligence are genetically inherited. This gives researchers an opportunity to focus on the relative importance of genetic and environmental markers of intellect. One of the drawbacks here is that twins that are adopted are either placed in the same adoptive environments or, if adopted by separate adoptive families, these are often comparable in terms of socio-economic profile. So even though twins may go to different families in different locations, these families (due to the nature of adoptee profiles) are often similar in socio-economic status. The twins, then, are raised in similar environments, which makes it difficult to separate clearly the impact of environment and/or genetics on intellectual development.

up with a picture that supports the idea of a 'g' factor; using another equally valid method of statistical analysis, it is possible to support the notion of a family of relatively discrete mental abilities.

Gardner (1993: 17)

Critics of the statistically based approach to intelligence also suggest that it is limited in its focus, and that it takes no account of context. In other words, the ability to produce intelligent behaviour is a joint product of the knowledge and resources available – within the person, from others or from the environment (Salomon, 1993).

For example, consider learning a new language. People of equal language ability may have learned through a variety of means: some may have learned by going to a place where the new language is spoken, others may have used books and audio-visual education, while others may have used a combination of both.

LEARN ANOTHER LANGUAGE

I WANT TO LEARN ANOTHER LANGUAGE. I WANT TO EXPERIENCE THE WONDERS OF OTHER LANDS AND THE MYSTERY OF OTHER CULTURES. I WANT TO IMMERSE MYSELF IN THE SPIRITUAL ASPECT OF OTHER PEOPLE. I WANT TO BE ABLE TO ORDER STEAK AND CHIPS FOR MY DINNER.

Intelligent behaviour is needed by some to navigate potentially hazardous environments and elements.

Intelligence: a universal concept or culture-specific?

Cognitive, or information processing, approaches to intelligence investigate what mental processes (such as memory, attention and processing speed) contribute to intelligent behaviour. Do differences in these abilities lead to differing intellectual ability?

In essence these cognitive theories attempt to evaluate what cognitive factors might contribute to intellectual functioning. For example, Earl Hunt (1983) reported that individuals with greater attention spans seem to score higher on intelligence tests, whereas Eysenck (1986) suggested that intelligence was error-free cognitive processing. However, it has also been implied that only a quarter of the variation evident in people's performance on intelligence tests is accounted for by differences in cognitive processes (Miller and Vernon, 1992).

Cognitive-contextual theories of intelligence deal with the way that cognitive processes operate in various environmental contexts. As well as considering the nature of intelligence, cognitive-contextual theories try to understand what cognitive abilities in what environments are conducive of intellectual behaviour.

For example, getting a pass mark in maths might be considered a marker of intelligence for students in Britain, whereas using the stars to navigate treacherous reef-strewn seas successfully and safely is considered to be a sign of intelligence for night fishermen in New Guinea.

So if intelligence is a single construct as defined by people like Spearman, then we should find that this definition is applicable to every person all over the world, and therefore would not be measured by individual skills but by the efficiency and effectiveness of the more basic cognitive processes.

Howard Gardner (1983): theory of multiple intelligences

While the psychometric theorists debated how intelligence might comprise multiple abilities, Howard Gardner went beyond this suggestion and proposed that we possess independent intelligences. Rather than arguing that there were multiple abilities, he proposed that there were multiple intelligences that operated independently from one another. He did not recognise the existence of a single intelligence.

Working with brain trauma patients, he observed that individuals who had suffered brain injury may have diminished ability in one area, but not all areas. His evidence also stems from his work with people with *savant syndrome* (individuals who score poorly on intelligence tests in general but who possess exceptional skills in one ability). People (usually

TABLE 30.4 GARDNER'S MULTIPLE INTELLIGENCES

LINGUISTIC
The ability to use and learn languages. Poets exemplify linguistic intelligence, and it is a useful asset for lawyers and journalists.

LOGICAL-MATHEMATICAL
The ability to manipulate numbers and engage in abstract reasoning.

SPATIAL
The ability to perceive visual or spatial information and mentally to manipulate shapes and objects.

MUSICAL
The ability to identify, create and communicate rhythm, pitch, tempo and sounds.

BODILY-KINESTHETIC
The ability to control fine and gross motor actions, eye–hand coordination, athletics, dexterity and dance.

INTERPERSONAL
The ability to recognise correctly and make distinctions between, among other things, feelings, beliefs and intentions.

INTRAPERSONAL INTELLIGENCE
The ability to distinguish and recognise our own feelings, thoughts and actions.

NATURAL INTELLIGENCE
Recently added by Gardner, this is the ability to classify plants and animals in terms of their usefulness and potential danger for survival purposes (e.g. the ability to identify poisonous plants).

males) who suffer from this syndrome often have poor language ability but may have incredible ability in music, art or mathematics. (Dustin Hoffman portrayed the fictional savant Raymond Babbit in the film *Rain Man*.)

Gardner suggests that 'the human mind is better thought of as a series of relatively separate faculties, with only loose and non-predictable relations with one another, than as a single, all purpose machine that performs steadily at a certain horsepower' (Gardner, 1999: 32).

In addition, Gardner thought that the psychometric definitions of intelligence were not flexible enough to represent the different abilities around the world that are considered by different groups to be indicative of intellectual behaviour.

Based on his observations of brain trauma patients and of different ethnic groups' definitions of intelligent behaviour, Gardner offered a new model of intelligence. He proposed the existence of multiple intelligences (see Table 30.4).

Standard intelligence tests measure only the first three of the intelligences (as seen in Table 30.4) proposed by Gardner. Gardner argues that traditional tests are biased towards western definitions of intelligence and do not encompass the diversity of intelligences. He proposed that, whereas most concepts of intelligence had been ethnocentric and culturally biased, his model was universal and based on biological and cross-cultural data, as well as on data derived from the cognitive performances of a wide array of people.

Critics, particularly those that favour the model of a single intelligence, argue that Gardner is confusing intelligences with talents: abilities in music and athletics, for example, are talents rather than forms of intelligence (Scarr, 1989).

Robert Sternberg (1988b): triarchic theory of intelligence

Sternberg agreed with Gardner that conventional notions of intelligence were too narrow. However, unlike Gardner, Sternberg believed that musical and bodily-kinesthetic abilities are talents rather than intelligences. He viewed them as fairly specific and not essential for successful adaptation in most cultures.

For Sternberg, intelligence has three aspects (*triarchic theory*): *analytic intelligence* (academic-based problem-solving with a single right answer, which is assessable through intelligence tests); *creative intelligence* (reacting to and producing novel ideas); *practical intelligence* (required for day-to-day tasks that are often poorly defined or have a number of potential solutions).

Sternberg's theory, like that of Gardner, extends the concept of intelligence beyond traditional academic definitions and reflects the use of intellect in everyday life.

Section summary

Psychometric and cognitive-contextual perspectives therefore seek to understand intelligence in terms of underlying hypothetical constructs, whether these constructs are psychometric factors (e.g. mathematical ability), cognitive processes (e.g. memory retrieval) or constructs defined by environmental context (e.g. survival and adaptation).

These two perspectives also investigate the question of whether intelligence is a single construct or a combination of specific intellectual abilities. Important debate also revolves around the question of whether the definition of intelligence should be

---

FOCUS POINT 30.6

Intelligence and context

Both Sternberg and Gardner, while not in total agreement in their definitions of intelligence, do agree on one thing: they both acknowledge that intellectual behaviour is context-driven to a large extent.

For example, you may achieve a first-class degree in psychology – an excellent academic achievement and measure of intelligence in the western world. On gaining your first-class award you decide to take a well-earned holiday – a trek across the Sahara. You arrive ready for your adventure and meet your guide. Midway into the month-long trek you awake to find that your guide has died in his sleep. You are alone in the middle of all that sand and weeks away from the nearest settlement. 'Aha,' you think, 'I have a first-class degree. I am quite intelligent. I should be able to cope.' But will your first-class degree in psychology indicate where the nearest water will be or what direction you should be heading or how to survive a sandstorm?

Macabre as this example is, it shows that some forms of intelligence are *context-specific*. Skills that are deemed indicative of intelligent-type behaviour in one group or one place are not necessarily useful to indicate intellectual functioning in another group or setting. Answering timed essay questions bears little relationship to being able to find water in a desert.

Indeed, other researchers have recognised that different climates and survival challenges could lead to different sets of aptitudes (Rushton, 1998; Lynn, 2001). So all the exams you sit might only be measuring part of your intellectual capacity. Your ability for practicality or survival is hardly tested, nor is your skill at being a member of a social group.

Should not a definition of intelligence include those areas of intellect that are important to us on a daily basis? After all, we will probably use our practical skills more than our essay-writing skills in life!

Gender and race differences

On tests of general ability, or on summary scores of large test batteries, men and women tend to come out with about the same scores, although there are differences in some specific abilities (Carroll, 1993).

It is widely accepted that females score higher on average than males on tests of verbal abilities (Stumpf, 1995; Halpern, 1996), and that males score higher on average than females on tests of mathematical (Hyde, Fennema, and Lamon, 1990; Halpern, 1996) and spatial abilities (Masters and Sanders, 1993; Hedges and Nowell, 1995; Voyer, Voyer and Bryden, 1995). These differences also vary in size: differences in verbal and mathematical abilities are small; however, differences in spatial abilities and vocational information and aptitudes are moderate to large.

The issue of ethnic differences in intelligence has been an ongoing debate. It is acknowledged that there are observed ethnic differences in IQ, with consistent reports of poorer performance on intelligence tests in certain racial and ethnic groups (Herrnstein and Murray, 1994). However, several important points need to be raised when considering these results.

It has been shown that many students from disadvantaged families have lower confidence in their academic abilities (Steele, 1997). Individuals who are labelled as being less intelligent (by the media, their peers or even academics) could have low confidence in their academic potential and form a negative self-image of their worth. Under the principles of self-efficacy (as defined when we looked at personality in Chapter 29) this could be detrimental to their ability to learn and improve their intellectual standing.

For example, Mayer and Hanges (2003) found that black students reported themselves to be more threatened by completing an intelligence test (due, perhaps, to the pressure of stereotypical attitudes and negative labelling of black people and lower intelligence) than the white participants. Results of the test matched self-reported test anxiety levels, with the less threatened white participants scoring better than the more threatened black participants on the Raven Advanced Progressive Matrices test.

Another potentially important factor might be motivation and its relation to academic achievement. Peer, parental and cultural attitudes towards education could determine children's motivation towards learning. A study by Steinberg, Darling and Fletcher (1995) reported that students' academic performance matched the motivations of their parents towards academic skills. Those children whose parents were highly motivated for their children to do well did so, while those with parents who expressed less motivation for their children's academic levels did not do as well.

Lastly, Zuckerman (1990) is quick to remind us that, just as with gender differences, variation in intelligence is greater *within* ethnic groups than *between* them.

flexible. Different cultures should have different definitions of what is intellectual ability, and intelligence should be determined to some extent by the environment in which it is being used (and for what purpose).

There is one further issue driving psychological research into intelligence. This concerns the extent to which biological factors play a role in intellectual functioning.

What role do biological factors play in the acquisition and operation of intelligence?

The biological perspective seeks to understand two questions. First, the extent to which biology plays a role in the acquisition of intelligence, through inheritance. Second, what parts of the brain are associated with intellectual functioning. Thus biological theorists seek to understand intelligence directly in terms of its biological bases without the use of intervening hypothetical constructs.

Intelligence, brain structure and brain size

Halstead (1951) was perhaps the first to focus on the biological aspects of intelligence, and suggested that there are four biologically based abilities and that all four of these can be traced to the functioning of the frontal lobes in the cortex.

Hebb (1949) distinguished between two basic types of intelligence: intelligence A and intelligence B. Intelligence A is innate potential; intelligence B is the functioning of the brain as a result of the actual development that has occurred. Hebb also suggested that these two intelligences were different from the intelligence as measured by conventional psychometric tests, which he labelled intelligence C. He suggested that learning encourages more and more complex connections among neurons, which form the basis of intellect.

Luria (1980) continued the work on intelligence and brain anatomy by suggesting that the brain comprises three main components in relation to intellectual functioning:

1. arousal in the brain stem and midbrain structures
2. sensory input in the temporal, parietal and occipital lobes
3. organisation and planning in the frontal cortex.

Willerman *et al.* (1991) correlated brain size (controlling for body size) with the Wechsler Adult Intelligence Scale (WAIS-R). They found that IQ was significantly correlated (r = 0.65 in men and 0.35 in women, with a correlation of 0.51 for both sexes combined) with larger brain size. But the question has been raised as to whether brain size causes higher intellect or intellect creates a larger brain size.

Some researchers have also reached the conclusion that intelligence is part of the nervous system. Jensen (1998) suggests that individuals who have higher 'g' scores (general intelligence) have nervous systems that respond more quickly to stimuli, and that these individuals also possess more capacious short-term memory than those people with lower 'g' scores.

Work on brain anatomy and neurology in relation to intelligence is ongoing, and with the advance of new technology in this specialised area it is certain that interesting findings are still to come.

Acquisition of intelligence: behaviour genetics

Recall from Chapter 29, on personality, that behaviour geneticists attempt to determine the extent to which individual differences in personality and intelligence are determined by either environmental or genetic factors. The research literature in relation to intelligence is complex and again – like that for personality – controversial (for the same reasons). The main question is, to what

FOCUS POINT 30.8

Neurological effort and intelligence

Some interesting research has been conducted by Haier and colleagues. Using positron emission tomography (PET) scan analysis, Haier *et al.* (1988) showed that intelligent people solving psychometric intelligence tests had lower cortical glucose metabolic rates than less intelligent people who did not solve as many tasks. This suggests that the more intelligent subjects needed to expend less effort than the less intelligent ones to solve the reasoning problems.

We need to exercise some caution with this interpretation as the causal direction of this research remains unclear. For example, one could as easily argue that the smart people expend less glucose because they are smart (and therefore do not need to think much), rather than that people are smart because they expend less glucose. As you have no doubt seen in other chapters, correlatory studies suffer from this inability to make a causal prediction.

extent do our parents' intellectual abilities reflect our own? What proportion of our intellectual abilities do we inherit from them?

The methods used to investigate these questions are the same as those employed in personality research (e.g. *twin studies* and *adoption studies*). It has been found that identical twins reared apart, in separate homes and with different families, have strikingly similar IQ levels, with correlation of their IQs reported in some cases as high as .72 (Plomin, 1990).

Even with a conservative estimate, advocates of the view that intelligence is inherited claim that about half the total variance in IQ scores is accounted for by genetic factors (Loehlin, 1989; Bouchard, 1997; Plomin, 1997). This is a significant relationship, especially when research also suggests that the IQs of fraternal twins (non-identical) sharing the same household have a correlation coefficient of .60, and the correlation coefficient of the IQs of ordinary siblings (brothers and sisters) raised together is .47.

The highest reported association in IQ scores is reported in identical twins reared together: a correlation coefficient of .86 (Gardner, Kornhaber and Wake, 1996).

Evaluation of behaviour genetic approaches
Critics of the behaviour genetic view argue that the effects of heredity and environment cannot easily or clearly be separated from one another (Bronfenbrenner and Ceci, 1994; Wahlsten and Gottlieb, 1997). The methods of adoption studies have also been the focus of questioning, as many researchers have suggested that identical twins are usually adopted by matched-type families (as was mentioned in Chapter 29), which adds further to the confusion of neatly separating out environmental and genetic influences.

It is recognised that no matter how heritable intelligence is, some aspects of it are still malleable. *Heritability* of a trait is independent from its malleability. Height, for example, is 90 per cent

---

FOCUS POINT 30.9

'Emotional intelligence'
In 1995, Daniel Goleman published a book called *Emotional Intelligence*. It was written for a non-academic audience and argued that mainstream psychology has ignored the ability to recognise one's own and other people's emotions. Goleman calls this *emotional intelligence.*

He argues that being able to regulate our own emotional behaviour (such as aggression, fear and jealousy) and to interact successfully with others on an emotional level is a form of intelligence. He cites the fact that many successful people would not score highly on standard intelligence tests, but instead have succeeded because they have successfully manipulated both their own and other people's behaviour.

Goleman's theory was met with a barrage of interest and criticism in equal measure. Presently, research in this area is directed at answering several fundamental questions.

First, 'Is emotional intelligence different from other factors suggested by previous intelligence theories?' The research literature (Schutte *et al.*, 1998) would seem to suggest that emotional intelligence correlates negatively with *alexithymia* (limited emotionality – lack of empathy etc.).

Second, 'Is there a single emotional intelligence?' Research findings employing factor analysis indicate that emotional intelligence does seem to measure one single dimension (Geher *et al.*, 2001).

Lastly, is emotional intelligence a major facet of intelligence per se? Research to date views emotional intelligence, at best, as a lower-order factor within intelligence and personality as a whole (Petrides and Furnham, 2001) and some would even argue that the concept of emotional intelligence falls into the hinterland of mainland intelligence (Gardner, 1999).

heritable, and the best predictor of height is the height of an individual's parents.

However, as a result of improved nutrition and healthcare, average heights in industrial countries have increased during the twentieth century. This shows that even highly heritable traits can be modified. This principle also holds true for intelligence. As we are presented with more and more opportunities to learn (for example, all the information that can now be found on the World Wide Web) we would expect that the IQ average among the world's population might also increase.

Contemporary issues in intelligence

As well as the debate on the nature and acquisition of intelligence, other issues have recently been driving research in this area of psychology. These include questions concerning the stability of intelligence over time, diet and IQ, and the application of intelligence testing as a useful prediction tool (of future intellectual behaviour).

Intelligence across the life span

Does intellectual functioning change over our life span? If it is seen to change, then this suggests that intelligence is not a stable construct. This could be due either to learning and the influence of our experiences throughout our lives (such as jobs and role changes) or to our changing biological system (reduction in brain efficiency with age, cellular decay and reduced repair capability).

The IQs of a sample of Canadian men between the ages of 25 and 65 were studied over a 40-year span. Findings suggested that the stability coefficient of individual differences in these men over this period for verbal ability was around 0.9, but for non-verbal ability it was around 0.6. This finding implies that different aspects of human intelligence show different degrees of stability across adulthood.

Schwartzman *et al.* (1987) suggested that verbal abilities and knowledge hold up well or increase until old age, though fluid intelligence decreases in most people after young adulthood. Abilities that are concerned with stored information and knowledge (*crystallised intelligence*) are more consistently stable over time than abilities that are concerned with thinking under time pressure with new materials (*fluid intelligence*) (Schaie, 1996). So, for example, older adults have in general less cognitive flexibility, are less likely to consider alternative solutions (Salthouse and Prill, 1987) and have less ability to focus attention than younger adults (Kramer, Larish and Strayer, 1995).

Several factors could be linked to maintaining mental ability level – namely being free of chronic disease, living in an intellectually stimulating environment (which will be defined differently by each individual), living with a partner of high ability, maintaining speed of information processing and being satisfied with life in middle age.

Diet and IQ

McCall (1979) conducted a study on baby diet and later IQ. This prospective, blinded, randomised outcome trial, with follow-up of 98 per cent of survivors still in Britain, found that the diet assigned to a premature baby for an average of just four weeks after birth had a significant effect on IQ – notably verbal IQ in boys – seven and a half to eight years later when IQ scores are highly predictive of subsequent scores.

These findings suggest that suboptimal early nutrition in pre-term infants can have a permanent effect on their cognitive function, emphasising the potential importance of dietary management decisions in this population. In biological terms, these findings offer support to the long debated hypothesis that nutrition during critical or vulnerable periods of brain growth may have lasting consequences for cognition and intellect.

Other researchers (Smart, 1977; Dobbing *et al.*, 1981) have demonstrated no link between childhood diet in infancy and later intelligence. For example, Malloy and Berendes (1998) reported no difference in later IQ levels in those infants either breastfed or not breastfed ten years previously.

Benton and Cook (1991) studied the effect of different dosages of vitamin and mineral allowance on 47 six-year-old children. Another group of children simply received placebo tablets (containing no vitamin or mineral content). The children completed four subscales of the British Ability Scales test and also completed delayed reaction time (RT) tasks, both before and after the diet period. The intelligence scores of the children taking the vitamin tablets increased, while the scores of those taking the placebo declined, primarily on non-verbal rather than verbal measures. When faced with a difficult task, participants who had taken the active supplement were also more likely to concentrate on the task.

Intelligence in the workplace

There are many issues regarding psychometric testing of intelligence in relation to job selection (see Chapter 31, on psychometrics, for more details). One important question that has been asked within occupational psychology is whether intelligent individuals gain higher-status jobs. Research does seem to predict that high scores on intelligence tests correlate fairly well with subsequent occupational status (Cronbach, 1990; Robbins, 1991).

However, there seems to be a less clear relationship between intelligence and how well you will perform in your job, and motivation seems to be a better predictor of high performance (Robbins, 1991). It has been shown that there is little association between intelligence scores and sales performance in salespeople, but more of one for intelligence scores and performance in managers, doctors, academics and lawyers (Jenson, 1980).

More recent research has concentrated on specific abilities in relation to occupational success. For example, Ponomarenko, Aleshin and Zhdan'ko (1996) suggested that three basic factors are distinguished in the structure of intelligence of successful Russian pilots in training. Sternberg (2002) argued that successful leaders require some very specific intellectual abilities (in terms of logico-symbolic, spatial and working memory) such as a vision of where to lead people (creative intelligence) and how to convince them that this is indeed where they need to go (practical intelligence).

Summary

Intelligence refers to the ability to learn from experience, apply knowledge to solve problems and to adapt and survive in different environments (social and geographical). There are three broad approaches to intelligence research: psychometric, cognitive-contextual and biological. The need for intelligence to operate in context-specific situations might explain differences observed in intelligence across gender and culture. It has been shown that both the environment and hereditary factors influence intellectual development. Intelligence tests have been employed in occupational selection and screening. This will be discussed in greater depth in the following chapter.

Learning outcomes

When you have completed this chapter you should be able to:

- describe the main theories of intelligence and evaluate their contribution to our understanding of it
- evaluate the biological influences on intelligence
- describe how environmental and contextual factors might impact on intellectual development
- describe some of the ways intelligence research has been applied to contemporary life.

Key terms

Adoption studies
Alexithymia
Analytic intelligence
Context-specific
Creative intelligence
Crystallised intelligence
Emotional intelligence
Fluid intelligence
General intelligence (g)
Heritability
IQ
Multiple intelligences
Practical intelligence
Savant syndrome
Socially constructed
Specialised intelligence (s)
Triarchic theory
Twin studies

31

Psychometric testing

Route map of the chapter

This chapter is divided into three sections. The first looks at the different types of psychometric tests. Attention will be given to the different types of intelligence and personality tests. The second section covers the main underlying principles of psychometric tests and considers such things as standardisation, reliability and validity. The final section focuses on the limitations and criticisms of the construction and use of psychometric tests. The chapter as a whole aims to describe the main types of psychometric tests and the principles that guide them. It also seeks to show examples of how these tests have been employed within the various disciplines of psychology.

Introduction

Psychometrics deals with the scientific measurement of individual differences (personality and intelligence). It attempts to measure the psychological qualities of individuals and use that knowledge to make predictions about behaviour.

What is psychometrics?

The use of psychometric measurement illustrates a fundamental characteristic of psychological investigation. Psychology employs scientific methods to investigate its claims and psychometrics is one such method of scientific investigation. Indeed, Dawis (1992) suggests that the invention and development of psychometric tests in psychology is comparable in its impact with the invention of the microscope in biology.

ACTIVITY BOX 31.1

Remember all those exams at school?

Take a few moments to consider how intelligent you think you are. How have you come to this impression of your intellectual capacity? Probably the main source of your opinion of your skills and abilities has been through feedback: feedback from peers and family, and feedback from standardised academic tests. Yes, that's right – all those long years spent at school and your academic effort was measured by psychometric principles.

Cast your mind back to Chapter 30, on intelligence. Remember Alfred Binet, who developed a set of tests to measure the intelligence of French children at the turn of the century? His work provides the foundation for nearly all education systems worldwide. All those essays, reports and exams that you slaved over and were awarded marks for provided feedback on your intellectual ability. In other words, you used these school marks to compare yourself realistically with your classmates to see if you were better or worse than them. Probably more memorable were your teachers' and your parents' comments about the marks you did or did not get!

Psychometric tests, then, allow for realistic comparison between people on scores of intellectual ability and personality.

We engage in psychometric measurement at a very early age and the whole of our schooling is based on psychometric principles

We have seen in the previous chapters on intelligence and personality that people differ. Such differences have consequences for all individuals, whether in relation to their education, occupation or interpersonal skills. Being able to predict the best outcome from two or more situations is important. So choosing appropriate subjects to study at school, choosing an appropriate career, and the ability for employers to choose the best applicant for a job or for promotion are important decisions that have far-reaching consequences. Psychometric tests provide standardised techniques we can use to make predictions about our choices.

FOCUS POINT 31.1

Tests defined

A test can be described as an objective, systematic and standardised measure of a sample of behaviour.

What is a test?

'Objectivity' is where every observer of an event would produce an identical account of what took place. 'Systematic' refers to a methodical and consistent approach to understanding an event. 'Standardised' means that observations of an event are made in a prescribed manner. In other words, any differences that are observed can be attributed to differences in test participants and not to variations in the way the observations are made.

For example, if two people are given a painting to assess they will each use their own assessment methods and criteria to judge it. However, if they both receive some form of assessment guidelines, such as a good painting should have at least six different colours, be in watercolour and be a recognisable likeness of someone, something or somewhere, then they would have a more standardised form of assessment to which they could both refer.

A test is also different from an assessment. Assessment refers to the entire process of collating information about individuals and subsequently using it to make predictions. Tests, on the other hand, represent only one source of information within the assessment process. Spelling is one aspect of writing, and so to assess it we would use a spelling test, whereas if we wanted to gauge someone's general writing ability we would have to assess the entire process (spelling, style, grammar, punctuation etc.).

Types of psychometric tests

Two types of psychological tests are used by personnel selection practitioners:

1. tests of cognitive ability
2. tests of personality measures.

Cognitive assessment tests attempt to measure an individual's ability to process information, and include general intelligence (g) and its various subcomponents, such as spatial ability, numerical ability, problem-solving and reasoning ability, and verbal ability.

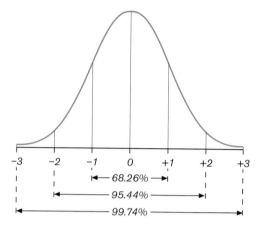

Figure 31.1 *Normal distribution curve representing percentages of the population between standard deviations*

Personality measures are more concerned with people's dispositions to behave in certain ways in certain situations. So tests can measure, for example, characteristics such as aggression, leadership, conformity and extroversion.

Different categories of psychometric tests

There are three categories of psychometric tests in use by psychologists. These are normative, criterion-referenced and idiographic tests.

Normative tests

Most psychometric tests in use today are *normative tests*, or norm referenced tests, which means that data exist that tell us what range of scores is expected from the population under consideration. For example, if someone has a language ability score of 120, this means nothing to us on its own. We need some other vital information by which we can compare the score to a standard.

To make more sense of this score of 120 we would need to know the range (worst possible and best possible score), the mean score (average) and the standard deviation for this test. The mean score (as described in Section 8, on research methods and statistics) is the average score (the total of the items divided by the number of items). The standard deviation is the most important measure of dispersion; it is used to determine how far on average a score is from the mean (see Chapter 38).

So if we know that the mean score for people on a language ability test was 100 we now have something to compare our own score with and we can conclude

that we are better than the average person on verbal ability. If we also had the standard deviation we could also work out more precisely what our score means compared to others by using the normal distribution of scores for this verbal ability test. The *normal distribution curve* for this verbal ability test is presented in Figure 31.1

We can see from the data presented in Figure 31.1 that the mean score for the test is 100 and the standard deviation is 15. A score of 120 is between 1 and 2 standard deviations above the mean. So we could be quite precise in concluding that not only is the score above average, but that 14 per cent of people have a very similar score to this, only about 2 per cent score better than it, while about 84 per cent of people have a score lower than this. This is the advantage of norm-based tests – they allow us to predict quite precisely where people fit in relation to others on psychometric tests. Thus most intelligence tests will be constructed to produce scores with a mean of 100.

Shown in Table 31.1 are the labels and frequency of the Wechsler IQ scores – including the, thankfully, now defunct labels that used to be used to describe people!

Criterion-referenced tests

Criterion-referenced tests are used in the assessment of competencies and are commonly used in

TABLE 31.1 WESCHLER IQ SCORES

IQ	ARCHAIC DESCRIPTION	CURRENT DESCRIPTION	SCORE LOWER/HIGHER THAN:
10	Idiot	Profound mental retardation	Fewer than 1 out of 100,000
25		Severe mental retardation	Fewer than 1 out of 100,000
40	Imbecile	Moderate mental retardation	3 out of 100,000
55	Moron	Mild mental retardation	13 out of 10,000
70		Borderline	2 out of 100
85	Dull normal	Low average	16 out of 100
100		Average	Half
115		High average	84 out of 100
125		Superior	95 out of 100
130	Genius	Very superior/gifted	98.5 out of 100
145			9,913 out of 10,000

education. For example, if a child is presented with a set of reading problems the criterion for entering a particular class might be that the child will correctly solve each problem. If they fail to meet this criterion, then they are assigned to a lower-grade class.

Idiographic tests

Normative psychometric tests rely on the respondent being placed in some position relative to others. Sometimes this is not completely relevant. Suppose you wanted to see how psychoanalytic counselling is helping an individual overcome aggressive tendencies. We want to see if this individual has improved since attending therapy. *Idiographic tests* would be employed in this case to monitor individual progress under treatment. So the respondent is usually given a number of questionnaires over a set time period to investigate his or her progress.

Cognitive testing

Intelligence tests are commonly used in two main areas: occupational psychology for job selection and promotion, and educational psychology for academic and career assessment.

FOCUS POINT 31.3

Employee selection tests

According to Kanfer, Ackerman and Goff (1995), 'tests of intellectual abilities are the single most predictive element in employee selection. Such tests are generally more valid than the use of academic and employment credentials – and certainly more valid than the use of personnel interviews – in predicting training and on-the-job success.'

Cognitive ability tests fall into two categories in terms of administration of the test: individually administered tests, which occur in one-to-one situations and are given by a psychologist trained in test administration; group-administered tests, which are taken by a number of individuals at the same time.

There are also several different types of cognitive tests: speed tests, power tests and knowledge tests. These three types of test are known collectively as maximum performance tests, because the person taking the test is asked to perform to the best of their ability.

Some top quiz shows are based on the psychometric principle of quick answers.

- *Speed tests* are where the person taking the test attempts to answer the questions in a set time period (a timed exam is an example of a speed test).
- *Power tests* are where a person attempts to complete a task in their own time, and the measures of success are (i) whether they succeed or not, and (ii) how long they take. Swimming certificates, for example, ask individuals to swim a set distance.
- *Knowledge tests* are those that get the person taking them to rely on their general and specific knowledge of the world around them (for example, the game of Trivial Pursuit® is based on this type of cognitive test).

Tests can also be combined. So, for example, a short-answer timed examination would be a combination of a speed test and a knowledge test.

Personality testing

Personality tests are concerned with attempting to measure people's characteristics or traits. They are also more standardised and economical (in terms of both time and money) than methods such as interviewing and observation.

There are two forms of personality test employed by psychologists. These are objective tests and projective tests.

APPLICATIONS BOX 31.1

Applications of intelligence tests

Psychological tests are administered in a variety of settings, including schools, colleges and universities, hospitals, outpatient healthcare settings, social agencies, prisons and employment or human resources offices. They come in a variety of formats, including written, verbal and computer administered.

In terms of measuring school achievement, Jenson (1980) reports that the Wechsler verbal IQ score correlates well with achievement in elementary school. Performance on the Weschler tests also has strong correlations with subsequent job status, with individuals scoring highly achieving jobs in science and law, and those who score low tending to have less prestigious occupations (Cronbach, 1990).

IQ tests measuring general intellectual ability (g) have been reported to predict success in job training (Ree and Earles, 1991), and Ackerman and Kanfer (1993) have used the assessment of spatial ability as a selection criterion for air traffic controllers.

Objective personality tests

Objective tests involve questions administered to individuals who are asked to rate their own actions or feelings in set situations. For example, an individual might be given the following statement: 'At a party I am the life and soul', and be asked to choose a further statement that best applies to themselves in this situation. The options might be: (a) This would always apply to me, (b) this sometimes applies to me', (c) This would never apply to me. Such a method is called self-report and self-report personality inventories provide a convenient way of gaining a snapshot of a candidate's disposition at any given moment in time. As discussed in Chapter 29, personality does change over the life span, and so in order to be more accurate a test would need to be administered on several occasions over a longer time period.

Some objective personality tests focus on measuring one personality characteristic, such as extroversion, while others measure a small group of related traits such as empathy and social responsibility.

Projective tests

Projective tests require individuals to formulate an unstructured response to some form of ambiguous stimulus or task. So individuals may be presented with an ambiguous picture and asked to describe what it represents to them. These tests are widely

Figure 31.2 Sample TAT picture

used to attempt to identify personality characteristics related to abnormal psychological functioning. The most commonly used projective instruments (Watkins *et al.*, 1996; Wilson and Reschly, 1996) fall into one of the following three categories: drawings, inkblot techniques and verbal/storytelling techniques. The best known of these is the Rorschach inkblot test (Rorschach, 1921).

The use of the Rorschach test declined in the 1960s and 1970s, and has been overtaken by the thematic apperception test (TAT) (Bellak, 1993), which can be used for adults as well as children down to the age of four years. Also widely used is the children's apperception test (CAT) (Bellak, 1993), which was designed for children aged from three to ten years.

Whereas the TAT consists of sets of black-and-white pictures depicting various scenes, the CAT

APPLICATIONS BOX 31.2

Applications of personality tests

Psychological tests are administered for a variety of purposes in many applied psychological settings. For example, criminal psychologists might employ questionnaires to measure impulsivity and its relationship to crime, or they might use tests to evaluate criminal defendants in order to determine their competence to stand trial, and/or to determine sanity as it relates to criminal responsibility. Health psychologists might measure people's optimism in relation to their response to cancer diagnosis.

Occupational psychologists often employ personality tests to predict job performance and job suitability. For example, Barrick and Mount (1992) concluded that extroversion was a valid predictor of job performance for people with jobs based on social interaction, such as managers and salespeople, and Furnham (1992) has reported that workers who score highly on 'negative affect' (neuroticism, anxiety, irritability) tend to be less productive, have less job satisfaction and are more prone to absenteeism.

depicts cartoon-like pictures of animals in human situations that relate to various developmental themes (e.g. toilet training, feeding, sibling rivalry). The task is for the examinee to tell a story based on the picture. Projective tests are based on the assumption that, in ambiguous situations, a person will impose meaning and structure dictated by his or her own unique personality.

Objective tests are often criticised for lacking complete objectivity. The test scorer's interpretation of open-ended information is often said to be subjective and arbitrary. For example, if two different scorers had to interpret someone's story based on a picture they had just seen would they both draw the same conclusions? If not, how do we know which is right and which is wrong? For this reason, projective tests have been criticised for having lower validity than objective tests.

Principles of psychometric testing

Just because a personality test or intelligence test is written on a piece of paper, this does not guarantee that it is either reliable or valid. Nor does it mean that the test has been standardised. These three concepts – reliability, validity and standardisation – are essential criteria for a good psychometric test.

Test standardisation

Test *standardisation* ensures that the conditions are as similar as possible for all individuals who are given the test. Standardisation also ensures that no matter who gives the test and scores it, the results should be the same.

To enable meaningful comparisons between individuals, test makers have first to give the test to a representative sample of people. So if everyone takes the test under the same conditions and they are all scored in the same way, we can make viable comparisons between them.

Let's say we wanted to investigate a psychology undergraduate class's knowledge of chemistry. We give them all the same chemistry test under the same conditions and we score them in the same way. In order for us to assess their relative chemistry knowledge we should compare their scores with those of other psychology undergraduates as they are

all from the same population (psychology undergraduates). It would be wrong to compare their scores with chemistry undergraduates' scores, as chemistry undergraduates study chemistry and should therefore be better at it! We need to compare like with like to get an accurate estimate of people's test scores.

Both IQ and personality tests often summarise the test taker's performance in terms of scores. Scores allow the calculation of norms, and norms are descriptions of the frequency of particular scores. Many psychometric tests are designed for use with individuals from diverse ethnic, socio-economic and age groups. Norms tell us what percentage of a group of people obtained each possible score on an exam, for example. How many of them scored 5 per cent, 50 per cent or 90 per cent as a basis of their ethnicity, age and socio-economic status? Norms have been useful in education to produce criteria for standards.

Test reliability

As you will have seen elsewhere in this book, *reliability* refers to something that is stable and repeatable. In other words, a test must measure the same thing in the same way every time someone takes it. The greater the reliability of a test the more confident we are that the testee's scores are real and do not reflect such things as luck, being in a good/bad mood, being hungry or being too hot.

There are two types of test reliability, as described below.

Internal consistency reliability

Internal consistency reliability ensures that all the parts of your test questionnaire are reliable. For example, is every question throughout the test a reliable question in terms of what you are trying to measure? One method that can be used to test this is called 'split half reliability'. Split half reliability is a correlational test that compares either the first half of the test with the second half, or all the odd-numbered questions with all the even-numbered questions. If the questionnaire has internal reliability among all its questions then we should get a positive correlation (i.e. the questions are all measuring the same thing).

TABLE 31.2 THE FOUR TYPES OF TEST VALIDITY

1. *Face validity* relates to the appearance of a test. Does an aggression test actually look like it is a test to measure aggression?

2. *Concurrent validity* predicts that if you made up your own test of 'honesty' and correlated scores on it with scores on an existing standardised test of honesty, you should get a high correlate if your test is valid. In other words, standardised psychometric tests serve as benchmarking devices for the construction of new tests.

3. *Predictive validity* suggests that your test should be related to future behaviour. So if someone scores high in social anxiety on your test then we should see that person getting anxious in social situations in their future behaviour. If they do not, then your test is invalid as it does not relate to actual behaviour. Sternberg *et al.* (2001) suggest that tests where the results are carefully interpreted, after extensive training, offer the best predictive validity for future behaviour.

4. *Construct validity* suggests that if all our hypotheses about the test variable (construct) are supported, we have a high degree of construct validity. For example, with an anxiety test we might test the following hypotheses:
   - high scorers would be more likely to be receiving psychiatric/psychological support than low scorers
   - high scorers would be less likely to be in stressful or dangerous occupations
   - the anxiety test will have positive correlations with other anxiety tests
   - the anxiety test will not correlate with personality tests not measuring anxiety
   - the anxiety tests should have zero correlation with tests that measure ability and motivation.

The more of these hypotheses that we find to be true, the greater the construct validity of the test.

Test-retest reliability

Test-retest reliability ensures that your questionnaire remains valid over time. If a test is given on two separate occasions (on different days of the week, say) and different scores are achieved, then one (or both) of the scores must be wrong. A reliable test would measure what it was supposed to measure at *any time* it was administered. Time should not make the test score different.

To measure test-retest reliability the test should be given out on more than one occasion with a time delay. The greater the positive correlation between these two time-separated scores, the more reliability the test has. It must yield consistent results over time.

Test validity

A test might have high reliability but still possess low *validity*. Let's suppose you wanted to find a new person to fill a vacant job position in your firm of lawyers. The test you decided to administer was whether they could touch their nose with their tongue. The fact is that if you you can touch your nose with your tongue you can, and if you can't you can't! So this is a reliable test – the same results would be obtained over a time period with the same challenge.

However, your test lacks any validity. What on earth does being able to touch your nose with your tongue tell you about whether that person will make a good lawyer? Aiken (1997) suggests that the validity of a test reflects the degree to which it measures what it sets out to measure.

There are four types of test validity. These are presented in Table 31.2.

Example intelligence tests

The *Wechsler intelligence scales* are the most popular among intelligence tests (Watkins *et al.*, 1996; Wilson and Reschly, 1996). There are three different Wechsler intelligence tests that are structurally similar but differ with regard to the target age range.

The Wechsler Preschool and Primary Scale of Intelligence-Revised (WPPSI-R) (Wechsler, 1989) is the most recent version of the test normed for ages 3 to 7.3 years; the Wechsler Intelligence Scale for Children-Third Edition (WISC-III) (Wechsler, 1991) is normed for ages 6 to 16 years, 11 months; and the Wechsler Adult Intelligence Scale-Third Edition (WAIS-III) (Wechsler, 1997) is normed for ages 16 to 74 years. All three are well normed with considerable data supporting their reliability and validity.

The fourth edition of the *Stanford–Binet test* (SB-IV) (Thorndike *et al.*, 1986) represents several advances over previous versions of this first of all intelligence tests. Like the Wechsler tests, the SB-IV is an individually administered test that requires extensive training to administer. It is well normed for ages two through to adulthood, thus allowing assessment of younger children than does the WPPSI-R.

The SB-IV is composed of 15 tests divided into four cognitive areas: verbal reasoning, abstract/visual reasoning, quantitative reasoning and short-term memory. Its reliability coefficients are excellent, and validity data indicate high correlations with other intelligence tests, with older versions of the Stanford–Binet test, and with measures of academic achievement (Thorndike *et al.*, 1986; Laurent *et al.*, 1992).

Problems with psychometric tests

There are several potential problems associated with psychometric testing. These are generally divided into two types of problem:

1. those that derive from how the respondent goes about completing the test
2. those that derive from the nature of the test contents themselves.

Acquiescence and social desirability

When faced with a psychometric test, many people feel they are being judged. For example, if a test is measuring hostility, then the person might assume that hostility is a negative behaviour and amend his or her answers accordingly so that they will be seen in a more positive light. This phenomenon is called *acquiescence* or *social desirability*, and is a way of faking responses.

So people try to answer the questions on the test in a way that they feel presents them in a more socially desirable way. This problem tends to be associated more with personality tests than intelligence tests. We would all like to do better on intelligence tests, but if we do not know an answer we can't easily fake greater intelligence. With personality tests, however, we can at least make a judgement regarding what might be a more acceptable way of presenting ourselves.

People might engage in social desirability for two reasons.

1. Self-deception: here individuals are overly optimistic in their perceptions of their own positive personality features and play down their perceived negative aspects; Furnham *et al.* (2002) have shown that both males and females tend to rate their father's IQ scores as higher than their mother's, their brother's scores higher than their sister's and their son's scores higher than their daughter's, regardless of the reality of the relative intelligences.
2. Impression management: individuals trying to appear 'nice' because they fear social disapproval and reprimand for negative behaviour.

Mood and environmental influence

Another set of factors that might influence psychometric performance are those associated with mood and environmental conditions. On personality tests, people in a good mood might answer a questionnaire completely differently from how they would if they were in a bad mood. Features of the environment – such as noise, heat and light – might also have an impact on our mood, as well as on our cognitive abilities. Hancock (1986) has demonstrated that high temperature has a significant negative effect on vigilance, attention, memory and reaction time – all important elements of intelligence-based tests.

Ecological validity

Ecological validity is the extent to which research findings and methods can be generalised to common behaviours and natural settings. Research that lacks ecological validity focuses on what an individual can do in a research environment instead of what they are usually doing in their everyday lives. For example, IQ tests that ask general knowledge questions about areas that are not important to individual's daily lives will lack ecological validity.

It has been shown, for example, that in general many people perform badly when dealing with calculating fractions on IQ tests. This is probably due to the fact that in many people's daily lives being able to calculate fractions has no bearing on their existence. However, people who attend slimming clubs, who have to calculate calorie intake and use fractions on a daily basis, are much better at IQ-based fraction-type questions.

In other words, if a test is not relevant to an individual's lifestyle, they are unlikely to perform well at it. This might be more to do with a lack of motivation or experience with the type of problem set than any deficit in intellectual capability.

Cultural bias

One area of rightful contention in the field of psychometric testing is the possibility of bias in such tests against members of ethnic subgroups of the population.

Standardised tests are widely criticised as culturally inappropriate for many groups, both in content and process. This criticism usually centres on the differing relevance of the content to people from different cultures. For example, newly arrived immigrants can be expected to have greater difficulty

---

ACTIVITY BOX 31.2

Problem-solving around the world

Consider the following. Ivan always eats his breakfast with Boris. Boris is presently eating his breakfast. What is Ivan doing?

Most of us would probably answer that Ivan too was eating his breakfast, as this seems logical from the information we have been given. However, in some cultures such a question would yield a completely different answer. In some cultures the answer would more probably be that they do not know what Ivan was doing as they have never met him and so could not possibly comment on his behaviour!

This might sound strange to those brought up in the west, but it is a totally logical answer. In other words, we should not assume that people around the world use the same problem-solving parameters.

ACTIVITY BOX 31.3

All in the same boat?

Consider the following problem. A farmer wishes to take a fox, a chicken and a bag of grain from one side of a river to the other. He has space in his boat for himself and one more thing. He cannot leave the chicken alone with the grain, otherwise it will eat it, and he cannot leave the fox alone with the chicken as the fox will eat the chicken. Can you work out how many trips he will need to make to get them all safely to the other side of the river?

The solution is below. Did you get it right? If we presented this abstract problem in other parts of the world we might get some of the following responses.

- How does the farmer help me if I help him?
- I don't know the farmer so I won't interfere.
- What on earth is a farmer doing with a fox in the first place?!

None of these responses is unintelligent – they are all based on logic. So it is important to be aware that most standardised psychometric tests are based on western definitions and western cultural practices.

Solution: the farmer would need to make four trips. He first takes the chicken to the far bank. He then comes back for the grain, takes it across to the far bank and then takes the chicken back with him again to where he started. He leaves the chicken at the near bank and collects the fox. He drops the fox off with the grain on the far bank and comes back one final time for the chicken.

with an intelligence test that asks them to name past leaders of the country in which they have recently arrived.

Tests that are based on English discriminate against the language ability of minority groups whose mother tongue is not English. Furthermore, translation into native languages does not always help because many words or phrases may not have direct translations.

Attempts have been made to develop culture-free and culture-fair (culture-neutral) tests of intelligence, but on the whole these have not been successful. Conceptions of intelligence vary widely from culture to culture (in the west speedy answers are linked to intelligent behaviour, whereas in parts of Africa you are considered intelligent if you take your time and give a considered answer), and abstracting the few common elements, or what appear to be the few common elements, cannot be depended on to produce a reliable guide to intelligence. Furthermore, even if the content of a test can be made culture-free or fair to all cultures, culture will still affect the results because of cultural attitudes towards tests, test-taking, competition and so on.

For example, white and Asian Americans achieve higher scores than black Americans on many IQ tests developed in America. However, a test developed by Professor Robert L. Williams to reflect black American lifestyles and cultural values – the Black Intelligence Test of Cultural Homogeneity (BITCH) – gives higher overall scores in general to black Americans than white/Asian Americans. This generally highlights that most tests are not culture-free and that, as a result, bias exists in many tests against certain subgroups of the population.

There is no simple solution to this problem of culture bias. No one has as yet been successful in devising an intelligence test that does not produce discrepancies in scores between subgroups.

Some researchers have tried to address cultural bias. The *Leiter International Performance Scale-Revised* (Roid and Miller, 1997) is an untimed test that is normed for ages two to twenty years, and is administered using essentially no verbal instructions. Each set of items begins with a simple example that is prompted through mime. This revised version covers four domains of functioning: reasoning, visualisation, attention and memory. Unlike its predecessor, the revised Leiter generates standard scores rather than the cruder ratio IQ scores.

Another test that is relatively free of cultural bias is the *Ravens Progressive Matrices* (Court and Ravens, 1995). This test comes in three forms, two of which are appropriate for use with children: the Coloured Progressive Matrices (normed for ages five and a half to eleven and a half years) and the Standard Progressive Matrices (normed for ages six to eighty years). The Ravens Matrices are administered in a multiple-choice format. The test begins with simple visual discrimination and gradually moves to more difficult perceptual analogies and reasoning problems. The Ravens Matrices are untimed and can be administered using virtually no language.

Summary

The term 'psychometrics', then, refers to tests measuring both personality and intellectual functioning. The principles of psychometric testing include standardising and ensuring validity and reliability of the content of tests. Tests have been applied in many areas of psychology, such as health, criminal and occupational psychology. Tests are not yet culture-free, nor are there tests that seem to be applicable to all people in all situations. We need to recognise that many tests are at best only a reflection of a particular academic theory about the nature of personality or intelligence. These theories are still evolving, as are psychometric tests (Jackson, 1996).

Learning outcomes

When you have completed this chapter you should be able to:
- describe the main types of psychometric tests
- understand the difference between intelligence and personality testing
- describe the main principles of psychometric tests
- understand the problems associated with psychometric tests, such as ecological validity and cultural bias
- give examples of how psychometric testing has been used within the field of psychology.

Section 6
Personality and Intelligence

Key terms

Acquiescence
Criterion-referenced test
Ecological validity
Idiographic test
Internal consistency reliability
Knowledge tests
Leiter International Performance Scale-Revised
Normal distribution curve
Normative test
Objective tests
Power tests
Projective tests
Ravens Progressive Matrices
Reliability
Social desirability
Speed tests
Standardisation
Stanford–Binet test
Test-retest reliability
Validity
Wechsler intelligence scales

Further reading

Saville & Holdsworth is a major British developer and publisher of psychometric tests. Its website is at http://www.shldirect.com/.

Graham Davey

Abnormal, Clinical and Health Psychology

32	Basic issues in psychopathology	544
33	Psychological disorders	558
34	Treating psychological disorders	595
35	Health psychology	618

32

Basic issues in psychopathology

Route map of the chapter

This chapter provides a necessary introduction to clinical and abnormal psychology, and is concerned with how we identify, define and classify psychopathology and psychological disorders. The chapter is divided into three main sections covering the concept of madness (i.e. how we try to explain mental illness), definitions of abnormality and the classification of psychological disorders. Finally, the chapter briefly discusses what it means to have good psychological health.

Introduction

How regularly do you use the terms 'madness' and 'insanity'? Probably quite often in relation to your own behaviour (e.g. 'I must have been mad to pay money to watch England play cricket!'), and just as frequently to describe the behaviour of others (e.g. 'Brian McFadden must have been insane to leave Westlife!').

We tend to use terms like madness and insanity in a number of circumstances. For example:

- when someone's behaviour deviates from the expected norm
- when we are not sure of the reasons why someone is doing something
- when a behaviour seems to all intents and purposes to be irrational
- when a behaviour appears to us to be maladaptive or potentially harmful.

This discussion of the terms 'madness' and 'insanity' leads us on to those areas of thinking and behaving that seem to deviate from normal modes of functioning. For psychologists, the study of these deviations from normal functioning is labelled *psychopathology* or *abnormal psychology*; the branch of psychology responsible for understanding and treating psychopathology is known generally as *clinical psychology*.

However, deciding what are proper and appropriate examples of psychopathology is not easy. As we shall see, just because someone's behaviour deviates from accepted norms and patterns does not mean that they are suffering from a mental or psychiatric illness. Nor are we able to define psychopathology simply on the basis that some 'normal' functioning (psychological, neurological or biological) has gone wrong. This is because we are still far from understanding the processes that contribute to many psychological disorders – so we don't yet know whether some disorders *are* caused by the disruption of normal functioning. So before we discuss some of the psychological disorders that we do know something about (Chapter 33), it is important to discuss how we define and classify mental illness.

Models of psychopathology

Throughout history we have always been willing to label some people as 'mad' or 'insane', usually on the basis that their behaviour is unpredictable, irrational or harmful, or simply that it deviates from accepted contemporary social norms. Examples include the Roman Emperor Caligula, King George III, Vincent Van Gogh, King Saul of Israel, Virginia Woolf, to name but a few. However, while we have always been willing to label some individuals as 'mad', we have not always understood what causes them to behave in the way they do, and it is how we attribute the causes of mental illness that can determine how we conceptualise madness.

Demonic possession

When an individual displays signs of mental illness or psychological disorder, the first thing that is usually noticed is a change in their personality. The reserved person may become manic and outgoing, the gregarious person withdrawn and sombre. They may even start behaving in ways that are distinctly out of character, and that may be harmful to themselves and others.

The fact that an individual's personality seems to have changed (and may do so very suddenly) has historically inclined people towards describing those with psychological disorders as being 'possessed' in some way – that is, their personality has been taken over and replaced by the persona of someone, or something, else.

Explanation in terms of 'possession' has taken many forms over the years. It has, sadly, ensured that many who have been suffering debilitating and distressing psychological disorders have been both persecuted and physically abused rather than offered the support and treatment they needed. In Ancient Egyptian, Chinese, Babylonian and Greek civilisations, individuals with psychological disorders were regularly believed to be possessed by bad spirits (this is known as *demonology*), and the only way to exorcise these bad spirits was, at best, with elaborate ritual ceremonies or, more likely, with direct attacks on the victim's body to force the demons out (e.g. through torture, flogging or starvation). Not surprisingly, such actions usually had the effect of driving the sufferer even deeper into their malaise.

Demonology survived as an explanation of psychological disorders right up until a couple of centuries ago, and was prominent in the seventeenth and eighteenth centuries when witchcraft and demonic possession were common explanations for mental illness. This contrasts with the Middle Ages in England, when, in comparison, individuals with mental illnesses were treated in a relatively civilised fashion. From the beginning of the thirteenth century, lunacy trials were held to determine an individual's sanity, and if a person was found to be insane, they were given the protection of the law (Neugebauer, 1979).

Nevertheless, demonic possession is still a common explanation of mental illness in some less developed areas of the world, especially where witchcraft and voodoo remain important features of the local culture (e.g. in Haiti and some areas of western Africa) (Desrosiers and Fleurose, 2002).

The medical or disease model

As we began to understand some of the biological causes of physical diseases, so our conception of 'madness' moved very slowly towards treating it as a disease (hence the term 'mental illness'). The impetus for this came in the nineteenth century, when it became apparent that many forms of behaviour that we would label as 'mad' were the result of physical illnesses, such as strokes or viral infections.

For example, without proper treatment, the late stages of the sexually transmitted disease syphilis are characterised by the inability to coordinate muscle movements, and by paralysis, numbness, gradual blindness and dementia; many of these symptoms cause radical personality changes in the individual, which were once labelled 'madness'. When it was discovered that syphilis had a biological cause, and that it was also one of the main contributors to the mental disorder known as *general paresis*, it became clear that many other examples of mental illness might also have medical or biological explanations. This became known as the *somatogenic hypothesis*, which advocated that the explanation of psychological disorders could be found in physical or biological impairments.

The medical model of mental illness was an important development because it moved psychopathology out of the dark ages when explanation was dominated by superstitious and religious beliefs, and into an era when sufferers could begin to be treated rather than punished for their ailments.

The medical model has given rise to a large body of scientific knowledge based on medicine (known today as *psychiatry*), which attempts to identify the biological causes of psychological disorders, and attempts to treat such disorders with medication or surgery. In Chapter 33, you will notice that many psychological disorders have putative explanations that are biological in nature, and range from explanations in terms of genetic inheritance (e.g. schizophrenia, bipolar disorder), brain dysfunction and brain injury (e.g. OCD), to imbalance in brain and body biochemistry (e.g. ADHD, schizophrenia), and the physical effects of pathological activities (such as the hyperventilation theory of panic disorder).

However, as well as its obvious importance in developing some influential treatments, the medical model of psychological disorder has some important implications for the way we conceive of psychopathology and mental illness.

First, An obvious implication of the model is that it implies that medical or biological causes underlie psychological disorders; while this is true in some cases (e.g. schizophrenia), it is not so obviously true in many others. For example, maladaptive behaviour labelled as disordered can often be the result of perfectly normal and intact psychological processes. Focus Point 32.1 gives an example of how apparently bizarre behaviour in a schizophrenia sufferer can be produced through a normal learning process.

Indeed, both psychodynamic and contemporary cognitive accounts of psychopathology argue that many psychological disorders are the result of normal psychological processes, and it is the *experiences* an individual has that may cause a disorder, not their biology or biochemistry.

Second, the medical model adopts what is basically a reductionist approach (see Chapter 5) by

---

FOCUS POINT 32.1

Can perfectly normal processes cause bizarre behaviour?

A revealing study by Ayllon, Haughton and Hughes (1965) provides insight into some of the processes that might generate the kinds of bizarre and apparently irrational behaviour that make up some forms of psychopathology.

They used operant reinforcement methods (see Chapter 8, page 130) to reward a female patient diagnosed with schizophrenia for carrying a broom. Whenever she was observed holding the broom a nurse would approach her, offer her a cigarette or give her a token that could be exchanged for a cigarette. After a period of this reinforcement, the patient carried the broom around for most of the day, even taking it to bed with her when she slept.

At this point, the researchers called in two psychiatrists (who were unaware of the reinforcement schedule) to give their opinions on the nature of the behaviour. One of them gave the following reply:

Her constant and compulsive pacing, holding a broom in the manner she does, could be seen as a ritualistic procedure, a magical action. . . . Her broom would be then: (1) a child that gives her love and she gives him in return her devotion, (2) a phallic symbol, (3) the scepter of an omnipotent queen . . . this is a magical procedure in which the patient carries out her wishes, expressed in a way that is far beyond our solid, rational and conventional way of thinking and acting.

(Ayllon *et al.*, 1965: 3)

First, this psychodynamic explanation given by one of the psychiatrists is a good example of how easy it is to overspeculate about the causes and meaning of a behaviour when the real causes are unknown.

Second, it shows how behaviour that is viewed as representative of psychopathology can be acquired through a perfectly normal learning mechanism (in this case operant reinforcement).

attempting to reduce the complex psychological and emotional features of psychological disorders to simple biology. It is arguable whether the phenomenology (i.e. the personal experience of mental illness) or the complex cognitive factors involved in many psychological disorders can be reduced to biology. Indeed, when we take a look at the psychological disorders described in Chapter 33, it is hard to believe that many of the dysfunctional beliefs that maintain anxious and depressive disorders, and the personality factors that constitute vulnerability to disorders such as PTSD, GAD and depression, can be reduced to simple biology.

Third, there is an implicit assumption in the medical model that psychopathology is caused by 'things not working properly'. That is, either your biochemistry is imbalanced or, for example, disorders result from deficits in brain or central nervous system functioning. This 'something is broken and needs to be fixed' view of psychopathology is problematic for a couple of reasons.

First, it is becoming clear that not all psychopathology is the result of a deficit or dysfunction in either biological or psychological mechanisms – instead psychopathology may merely represent a more extreme form of normal behaviour (Davey, 2003).

For example, everyone worries, but for some of us it becomes such a prevalent and regular activity that it becomes disabling. When worry becomes chronic in this way, it may well lead to a diagnosis of generalised anxiety disorder (GAD) (see Chapter 33, pages 565–570). However, there is no reason to suppose that the mechanisms that generate the occasional worrying bout in each of us are not the same ones that generate chronic worrying in others.

Second, implying that psychopathology is caused by a normal process that is broken, imperfect or dysfunctional has implications for how we view people suffering from psychological disorders (and how they view themselves). At the very least, it can be stigmatising to be labelled as someone who is biologically or psychologically imperfect, and we often view individuals with psychological disorders as second-class citizens – even when their symptoms

are really only more prominent and persistent versions of the characteristics that we exhibit ourselves (i.e. we all have bouts of anxiety and depression, we all worry, we will all display obsessive or compulsive tendencies, and we will all behave bizarrely enough at one time or another to be called 'mad'!).

Focus Point 32.2 illustrates the differences in people's reactions to someone with a psychological disorder, and how these can often lead to loss of respect and consideration when people perceive that individual as no longer being a properly functioning member of society.

Psychological models

Moving away from the medical illness model of psychopathology, some approaches still see psychological disorders as symptoms produced by an underlying cause (what is known as the *pathology model*), but that the cause is a psychological rather than biological one. These types of approach often view the cause as a perfectly normal and adaptive reaction to difficult or stressful life experiences (e.g. psychoanalysis sees psychopathological symptoms as the consequence of perfectly normal psychodynamic processes that are attempting to deal with conflict).

As such, many of these psychological models view symptoms as normal reactions mediated by intact psychological or cognitive mechanisms, and not as the result of processes that are 'broken' or malfunctioning.

The psychoanalytic model

The *psychoanalytic model* method of understanding psychological disorder originated with Sigmund Freud, and views psychopathology as unconscious conflicts being dealt with by various psychological mechanisms designed to defend against anxiety and depression. It argues that the origins of adult anxiety and depression frequently stem from childhood conflicts.

While psychoanalysis is still practised, it is no longer the therapy of choice for most psychological disorders, nor is it a paradigm in which most current researchers attempt to understand psychopathology.

FOCUS POINT 32.2

A question of dignity (written by Louise about her own experience with depression)

During an episode of depression accompanied by anxiety, I shared my illness with a large number of people. In retrospect, now that the depression is lifting, I realize that this was a grave mistake, at least in light of the way society functions. . . . What has occurred?

When I was deeply depressed, I noticed that some friends departed. I understand now that they could not cope with depression and withdrew. In a few cases the rejection was rude and cruel and those who had seemed to be friends were found not to be so. Other friends stayed and offered their help.

In some cases I became a 'second-class citizen'. I could be treated with a briskness and dismissive air that had never been present before. I could be rudely dismissed and ignored on special occasions. My presence was clearly thought to be potentially threatening. Perhaps I wouldn't be happy enough or introduce inappropriate topics. I had laid bare my weakness and others were not about to forget it. These people, like all human beings, probably thought that they were doing the right thing. They were saving others from my presence. They also probably thought that they were treating me as my merits deserved. I had permanently lost the respect and consideration that I had once received.

It is no wonder that people conceal serious illness, whether cancer, heart disease or mental illness. Once exposed, these illnesses prove to be unforgettable to others. People never walk with the same dignity again. To some this weakness justifies treatment that shows no respect to the person as a human being. Somehow the person is seen to be responsible for the weakness and therefore appropriately blamed. The person has lost the right to be treated with honour. This honour is accorded only to those who are strong, healthy, and successful.

Source: http://www.mentalhealth.com/story/p52-dp11.hmtl

The learning model

The *learning model* method of understanding psychological disorder derives from the behaviourist approach to psychology (see Chapter 2) and argues that many forms of psychopathology are the result of maladaptive learning – that is, individuals have encountered unusual combinations of experiences that have caused them to learn unusual patterns of behaviour. For example, this approach would argue that individuals with specific anxieties (e.g. phobias) have learnt those anxieties because of experiences (usually frightening or traumatic) they have had in their past.

People can also learn maladaptive behaviour patterns through normal learning processes (Focus Point 32.1 provides a striking example of this). The learning model approach is exemplified in contemporary *behaviour analysis*, which applies learning procedures such as classical and operant conditioning to treating symptoms caused by maladaptive learning.

The cognitive model

Perhaps the most widely adopted current psychological model of disorders is the *cognitive model*. Primarily, this approach considers psychopathology to be the result of individuals acquiring irrational beliefs and dysfunctional 'ways of thinking'. It also argues that individuals (especially those with anxious or depressive disorders) may have acquired biases in the way that they process information (e.g. attend to stimuli or retrieve information from memory), and that these biases may cause or maintain the disorder (see page 569) (Williams, Watts, MacLeod and Mathews, 1997).

The popular press can often present mental illness in a way which propagates the stigmas attached to mental illness. In September 2003, the ex-heavyweight champion boxer Frank Bruno was treated for depression at a psychiatric hospital, and the mental health charity Sane (www.sane.org.uk) subsequently criticised unsympathetic coverage of his illness in the media.

The BBC News website reported that an early edition of the Sun newspaper had the front page headline 'Bonkers Bruno Locked Up', which was later changed to 'Sad Bruno in Mental Home'.

Sane chief executive Marjorie Wallace said: 'It is both an insult to Mr Bruno and damaging to many thousands of people who endure mental illness to label him as "bonkers" or "a nutter"'and having to be "put in a mental home".'

This approach has had some success in explaining many anxious and mood-based disorders, and has given rise to an influential set of treatments called cognitive behaviour therapy (CBT) (Wells, 1997). The assumption here is that if psychological disorders are caused by faulty beliefs and faulty ways of thinking, then successful therapies can be constructed by challenging and changing these faulty cognitions.

Definitions of abnormality

The models of psychopathology discussed in the previous sections are different ways of trying to *explain* psychological disorders, but they do not necessarily help us to *define* exactly what kinds of symptoms or behaviours should be considered as examples of psychopathology. For example, are all murderers mentally ill? Are the violent and antisocial tactics adopted by most terrorists indicative of mental illness? Is someone who decides to see if they can walk alone across the Arctic suffering a psychological disorder?

In each of these cases, the behaviours are unusual ones that most people would never contemplate indulging in, but does that make them examples of psychopathology? Below we explore some of the possible definitions of abnormal behaviour that may contribute to us defining psychopathology.

Deviation from the statistical norm

An activity or a psychological attribute might be classified as abnormal if it deviates substantially from the statistical norm (see Chapter 38). In some

Is someone who decides to see if they can walk alone across the Arctic suffering a psychological disorder?

TABLE 32.1	
WHAT'S THE DIFFERENCE BETWEEN A PSYCHOLOGIST AND A PSYCHIATRIST?	
Title	**Description**
CLINICAL PSYCHOLOGIST	Anyone who has been awarded a degree in psychology (most in the UK are accredited by the British Psychological Society) can call him/herself a psychologist. However, there are many different types of psychologist (see Chapter 40), and those that are qualified to offer therapy and undertake clinical assessments have undertaken an extra three years' specialised training.
PSYCHIATRIST	These are medically trained doctors who have undergone the normal medical training, and have then chosen to specialise in mental illness. Their approach to mental illness is primarily medical, but some do offer some forms of psychotherapy. They are the only practitioner group qualified to prescribe medication.
PSYCHOTHERAPIST	Psychotherapy is an umbrella term that covers almost all forms of therapy, but psychotherapists tend to specialise in only one type of therapy (e.g. psychodynamic, humanistic). Psychotherapists do not necessarily have a basic training in psychology.
COUNSELLOR	These are individuals who have been trained specifically in counselling skills, and may be skilled in the use of one or more forms of psychotherapy.
SOCIAL WORKER SPECIALIST	These are fully trained social workers who have received further training that enables them to undertake certain forms of psychotherapy.

areas of clinical psychology this can be used as a defining feature of psychopathology.

For instance, in the area of learning difficulties, if an IQ is significantly below the norm of 100 (usually 70 or less) it is considered indicative of learning difficulties requiring remedial help and attention. However, deviation from the statistical norm itself does not imply psychopathology – no one, for instance, would consider members of Mensa or the fastest sprinters (or those who win the National Lottery jackpot) as abnormal.

Deviation from social norms

On an everyday basis we tend to label a behaviour or activity as indicative of psychological disorder if it is far removed from what we consider to be the social norms for our culture. We assume (perhaps wrongly) that socially normal and acceptable behaviours have evolved to represent adaptive ways of behaving, and that anyone who deviates from these norms is behaving in a maladaptive or disordered way. However, it is very difficult to use deviation from social norms as a way of defining psychopathology, for a number of important reasons.

First, different cultures often differ significantly in what they consider to be socially normal and acceptable. For example, in the Soviet Union during the 1970s and 1980s, political dissidents who were active against the communist regime were regularly diagnosed with schizophrenia and incarcerated in psychiatric hospitals. This does not appear to have been purely a cynical method of political repression, but for many people represented a genuine belief that anti-Soviet activity was a manifestation of mental illness. ('Why,' they claimed, 'would anyone want to demonstrate against the perfect social system?'!)

Soviet psychiatrists even added to the official symptoms of schizophrenia by including '*reformist delusions*: a belief that an improvement in social conditions can be achieved only through the revision of people's attitudes, in accordance with the individual's own ideas for the transformation of reality' and '*litigation mania*: a conviction, which does not have any basis in fact, that the individual's own rights as a human being are being violated and flouted' (Ben Goldacre, *Guardian*, 16 July 2002). Since the collapse of the Soviet system, few would suspect that these kinds of beliefs and activities are representative of mental illness.

Second, it is difficult to use cultural norms to define psychopathology because cultural factors seem to affect known psychological disorders in very complex ways. For example, (i) social and cultural factors will affect the vulnerability of an individual to causal factors (e.g. poor mental health is more prevalent in low income countries) (Desjarlais *et al.*, 1996), (ii) culture can produce 'culture-bound' psychopathological syndromes that appear only in particular cultures, and can also influence how anxiety and depression manifest themselves (Weisz *et al.*, 1997), and (iii) society or culture can influence the course of a disorder (interestingly, schizophrenia in developing countries has a more favourable course than in developed countries) (Weisman, 1997).

Maladaptive behaviour

It is often tempting to define psychopathology in terms of whether it renders the individual incapable of adapting to daily living and, in particular, whether its manifestation is harmful to the individual or to others.

FOCUS POINT 32.3

Ataque de Nervios

Psychopathology can manifest itself in different forms in different cultures, and this can lead to some disorders that are culture-specific (i.e. have a set of symptoms that are found only in that particular culture). One such example is *Ataque de Nervios*, which is an anxiety-based disorder found almost exclusively among Latinos from the Caribbean.

Its literal translation is 'attack of nerves', and symptoms include trembling, attacks of crying, screaming uncontrollably and becoming verbally or physically aggressive. In some cases, these primary symptoms are accompanied by fainting bouts, dissociative experiences and suicide attempts.

Research on *Ataque de Nervios* has begun to show that it is found predominantly in women, those over 45 years of age, and from poor socio-economic backgrounds and disrupted marriages (Guarnaccia *et al.*, 1989). The symptoms appear to resemble many of those found in panic disorder, but with a coexisting affective disorder characterised by emotional lability and anger (Salman *et al.*, 1998).

From this research, it appears that *Ataque de Nervios* may be a form of panic disorder brought on by stressful life events (such as economic or marital difficulties), but whose expression is determined by the social and cultural norms within that cultural group. In particular, Latino cultures place less emphasis on self-control and emotional restraint than other western cultures, and so the distress of panic disorder in Latinos tends to be externalised in the form of screaming, uncontrolled behaviour and aggression. In contrast, in western cultures the distress of panic disorder is usually coped with by adopting avoidance and withdrawal strategies – hence the common diagnosis of panic disorder with agoraphobia.

"I keep having this terrible nightmare, that I'm really a legal secretary from Croydon with a Wagner fixation."

There are some examples of psychopathology that clearly fit this definition – suicide is a good example, and so are many of the symptoms of schizophrenia, where the thought-disordered individual is unable to understand and respond adaptively to the world. It is also true that most psychological disorders for which people seek treatment are characterised by the individual being unable to continue with their normal day-to-day living (Wakefield, 1992).

However, while many forms of psychopathology may fit this definition, there are many other forms of behaviour that we can define as maladaptive, but that we would not want to label as forms of mental illness. The behaviour of most murderers, for example, is certainly harmful to others, but it is only rarely the case that murderers commit their crimes because they are suffering from a mental illness (for an interesting current example of this discussion, see Chapter 33, Activity Box 33.2).

The same could be said for most forms of criminal and anti-social behaviour. In addition, it can be argued that some forms of psychopathology may be *adaptive* rather than maladaptive. For example, a case can be made for suggesting that phobias such as height phobia, water phobia, snake phobia and even spider phobia are adaptive responses that help us to avoid potentially harmful situations (Seligman, 1971).

Distress and impairment
Later in this chapter (under the subheading 'Classifying psychological disorders', below) we will be looking at the ways in which psychologists and psychiatrists have classified psychopathology. In order to be classified as a disorder, one of the main requirements of symptoms is that they must cause 'clinically significant distress or impairment in social, academic, or occupational functioning'.

It is clearly the case that individuals with severe psychological disorders do suffer considerable personal distress, and that this can drastically affect their day-to-day living. Witness the fact that psychological disorders can often be so distressing that they lead the individual to radical actions, such as attempting suicide (see Chapter 33, pages 579–580).

Personal distress and disruption of day-to-day living are now considered to be important defining features of psychological disorders (but see Wakefield, 1992) and are factors that are enshrined in the diagnostic criteria for most disorders. However, to be indicative of psychopathology, distress and disruption must be a relatively *chronic* feature of the problem, and must have a significant psychological or cognitive component.

For example, many medical conditions, such as cancer, can cause significant distress and disruption to daily life, yet we would not want to consider cancer a psychological disorder. Psychological problems may be one of the outcomes of severe medical conditions (such as cancer or AIDS), and the relatively new area of health psychology has been developed in part to help analyse and deal with the psychological consequences of what are primarily medical disorders (see Chapter 35).

Classifying psychological disorders
We have already discussed the different models of psychopathology and the problem of defining it. The next issue is how we classify psychological disorders. Classifying psychological disorders can be problematic because we have to have a diagnostic system that (i) can be independent of the many

theoretical approaches to understanding psychopathology, and (ii) does not allude to the possible causes of the psychopathology (because, as yet, we are still unsure of many of the causes of common psychological disorders).

Instead, like medical practitioners, psychiatrists and clinical psychologists have turned to classifying disorders on the basis of the *symptoms* the sufferer displays. This does at least specify that classification is based on some common, objective criteria that can be used reliably by different practitioners.

Classification can also be important for understanding the causes of disorders and for developing effective therapies. Once we have defined a category we can then effectively study those individuals who fit into it.

The development of classification systems

The very first extensive systems for classifying psychopathology were developed by the World Health Organization (WHO), which added psychological disorders to its *International List of Causes of Death (ICD)* in 1939, and the American Psychological Association (APA), which first published the *Diagnostic and Statistical Manual* (DSM) in 1952. The DSM has now come to be accepted as the most influential diagnostic system in most developed countries, and has been revised several times up to the publication of the most recent

version, *Diagnostic and Statistical Manual IV (DSM-IV)*, in 1994.

DSM-IV

Defining mental disorder

Before attempting to classify psychological disorders it was necessary for the DSM to define what it considered to be a mental disorder. As we have already seen, this is not easy nor is it clear-cut, but the DSM did attempt to rule out behaviours that were purely socially deviant as symptoms of psychopathology (but see Chapter 33, pages 586–588), and put the emphasis on *distress* and *disability* as important defining characteristics.

Focus Point 32.4 shows the relevant section from DSM-IV that attempts to define what should be classified as a mental disorder.

The dimensions of classification

DSM-IV encourages clinicians to rate individuals on five separate dimensions or *axes (I–V)*. These *dimensions of classification* are listed in Table 32.2. Axes I and II cover the classification of abnormal behaviour, with Axis I comprising the majority of common diagnostic categories such as anxiety disorders, depression and schizophrenia. Axis II consists of personality disorders and learning difficulties (mental retardation), and covers

---

FOCUS POINT 32.4

The DSM-IV definition of psychological disorders

In DSM-IV, each of the mental disorders is conceptualized as a clinically significant behavioral or psychological syndrome or pattern that occurs in an individual and that is associated with present distress (e.g. a painful symptom) or disability (i.e., impairment in one or more important areas of functioning) or with a significantly increased risk of suffering death, pain, disability, or an important loss of freedom. In addition, this syndrome or pattern must not be merely an expectable and culturally sanctioned

response to a particular event, for example, the death of a loved one. Whatever its original cause, it must currently be considered a manifestation of a behavioral, psychological, or biological dysfunction in the individual. Neither deviant behavior (e.g. political, religious, or sexual) nor conflicts that are primarily between the individual and society are mental disorders unless the deviance or conflict is a symptom of a dysfunction in the individual

Source: DSM-IV, xxi–xxii

TABLE 32.2	
THE FIVE DIMENSIONS OF CLASSIFICATION IN DSM-IV	
Axis I	Clinical disorders (e.g. anxiety disorders, mood disorders, schizophrenia and other psychotic disorders) Other conditions that may be a focus of clinical attention
Axis II	Personality disorders (e.g. anti-social personality disorder, schizotypical personality disorder) Mental retardation
Axis III	General medical conditions (e.g. infectious and parasitic diseases, diseases of the circulatory system, injury and poisoning)
Axis IV	Psychosocial and environmental problems (e.g. problems with primary support group, educational problems, economic problems)
Axis V	Global assessment of functioning

abnormalities that may be more chronic and long term.

Practitioners are encouraged to explore the possibility that sufferers may have both an Axis I and Axis II disorder, because if they do, then the Axis I disorder may be significantly more difficult to treat.

Axes III, IV and V are not usually required to make a psychopathology diagnosis, but were included so that a fuller appreciation of an individual's life situation could be made. As we will see later, it is just as important to define what we mean by psychological health as it is to define psychological disorder.

Problems with classification

While DSM-IV provides an objective and reliable set of criteria by which psychopathological symptoms can be diagnosed, it is in many senses imperfect. First, it does not define disorders in terms of their causes, and this leaves open the possibility that disorders that may seem the same on the surface (and so may be classified as the same disorder), may have different causes and therefore require different forms of treatment.

For example, the collection of symptoms that would be defined as schizophrenia can be generated in many ways (by severe stress, drug dependence or overdose, personality disorder), and schizotypical diagnoses can be found in a range of Axis I and Axis II disorders.

Second, with successive revisions of the DSM, more and more disorders have been identified and defined (relatively new disorders include eating disorders, post-traumatic stress disorder and schizotypical personality disorder). This may look like good progress in defining and identifying psychological disorders, but it is equally important to note that as we increase the number of diagnostic categories, we find that more and more individuals are being diagnosed with more than one Axis I disorder (e.g. if someone is diagnosed with an eating disorder, it is also quite possible that they will be diagnosed with major depression). This is known as *co-morbidity*, and it is becoming the norm rather than the exception (Kessler *et al.*, 1994).

If many disorders are co-morbid, then this tends to suggest that we haven't yet got classification quite right, and that what we have defined as separate disorders may in many cases be clusters of symptoms that have a single underlying cause.

Third, diagnostic classification (whether by DSM or any other system) tends to define disorders as discrete entities (after being assessed you will either be diagnosed with the disorder or you will not). However, much recent evidence has begun to suggest that psychological disorders may be dimensional rather than discrete (Krueger and Piasecki, 2002). That is, symptoms diagnosed as a disorder may just be more extreme versions of everyday behaviour.

For example, we all worry about our own life problems at times – some of us more than others. In extreme cases, this activity can become so regular and persistent that it will interfere with our daily living and may meet the DSM-IV criteria for diagnosis as a disorder (i.e. generalised anxiety disorder, see pages 565–570). In such circumstances, the cut-off point for defining an activity such as worrying as a disorder becomes relatively arbitrary.

Defining psychological disorders as discrete entities rather than existing on a dimension can also have other negative implications for the sufferer. For example, someone who may just meet the criteria for a disorder is suddenly labelled with that disorder when the individual who might have just failed to meet the criteria is not. This can significantly affect how that individual feels about themselves and how others react to them (see Focus Point 32.2).

Good psychological health

So far in this chapter we have focused on abnormal behaviour, psychopathology, mental illness and psychological disorders, but we must remember that it is often useful to view psychopathology in the light of what we would normally consider to be the criteria for *good psychological health*.

Axis V of DSM-IV attempts to measure the individual's current level of adaptive functioning, and assumes that good psychological health is dependent on adaptive functioning in areas of social relationships, employment and use of leisure time. In most cases, good psychological health can be indicated by the presence of most of the following attributes:

- an efficient perception of reality
- good self-knowledge and awareness of one's own feelings
- the ability to exercise voluntary control over behaviour
- good self-esteem and an appreciation of one's own worth
- an ability to form and maintain affectionate relationships with others
- productivity – a positive and planned approach to life.

TABLE 32.3

THE GLOBAL ASSESSMENT OF FUNCTIONING (GAF) SCALE

Score	Criteria
100–91	Superior functioning in a wide range of activities, life's problems never seem to get out of hand, is sought out by others because of his or her many positive qualities. No symptoms.
90–81	Absent or minimal symptoms (e.g. mild anxiety before an exam), good functioning in all areas, interested and involved in a wide range of activities, socially effective, generally satisfied with life, no more than everyday problems or concerns (e.g. an occasional argument with family members).
71–80	If symptoms are present, they are transient and expectable reactions to psychosocial stressors (e.g. difficulty concentrating after family argument); no more than slight impairment in social, occupational or school functioning (e.g. temporarily falling behind in schoolwork).

TABLE 32.3 CONTINUED

THE GLOBAL ASSESSMENT OF FUNCTIONING (GAF) SCALE

Score	Criteria
61–70	Some mild symptoms (e.g. depressed mood and mild insomnia) or some difficulty in social, occupational or school functioning (e.g. occasional truancy or theft within the household), but generally functioning pretty well, has some meaningful interpersonal relationships.
51–60	Moderate symptoms (e.g. flat affect and circumstantial speech, occasional panic attacks) or moderate difficulty in social, occupational, or school functioning (e.g. no friends, conflicts with peers or co-workers).
41–50	Serious symptoms (e.g. suicidal ideation, severe obsessional rituals, frequent shoplifting) or any serious impairment in social, occupational or school functioning (e.g. no friends, unable to keep a job).
31–40	Some impairment in reality testing or communication (e.g. speech is at times illogical, obscure or irrelevant) or major impairment in several areas such as work or school, family relations, judgement, thinking or mood (e.g. depressed man avoids friends, neglects family and is unable to work; child frequently beats up younger children, is defiant at home and is failing at school).
21–30	Behaviour is considerably influenced by delusions or hallucinations or serious impairments in communication or judgement (e.g. sometimes incoherent, acts grossly inappropriately, suicidal preoccupations) or inability to function in almost all areas (e.g. stays in bed all day, no job, home or friends).
11–20	Some danger of hurting self or others (e.g. suicide attempts without clear expectation of death, frequently violent, manic excitement) or occasionally fails to maintain minimal personal hygiene (e.g. smears faeces) or gross impairment in communication (e.g. largely incoherent or mute).
1–10	Persistent danger of severely hurting self or others (e.g. recurrent violence) or persistent inability to maintain minimal personal hygiene, or serious suicidal acts with clear expectation of death.
0	Inadequate information.

Source: American Psychological Association, 1994: 32

Table 32.3 shows the *global assessment of functioning (GAF)* scale, which is used to assess adaptive functioning. This acts as a measure of psychological health that can be contrasted, when required, with measures of psychological dysfunction and clinical diagnoses.

Learning outcomes

When you have completed this chapter you should be able to:

- discuss from a historical perspective how the concept of madness has developed
- compare and contrast the usefulness of a variety of definitions of abnormality
- describe the basic features of a system for classifying psychological disorders, such as DSM-IV
- compare and contrast a number of different approaches to the explanation of psychopathology.

Key Terms

Abnormal psychology
Axes (I–V)
Behaviour analysis
Clinical psychology
Co-morbidity
Cognitive model
Demonology
Diagnostic and Statistical Manual IV (DSM-IV)
Dimensions of classification
General paresis
Global assessment of functioning scale (GAF)
Good psychological health
International List of Causes of Death (ICD)
Learning model
Pathology model
Psychiatry
Psychoanalytic model
Psychopathology
Somatogenic hypothesis
Symptoms

Further reading

Cave, S. (2002) *Classification and Diagnosis of Psychological Abnormality.* Hove: Psychology Press.

Davison, G. C. and Neale, J. M. (2001) *Abnormal Psychology* (8th edn). New York: Wiley & Sons.

Oltmanns, T. F. and Emery, R. E. (1998) *Abnormal Psychology* (2nd edn). New Jersey: Prentice Hall.

33

Psychological disorders

Route map of the chapter

This chapter describes some of the main psychological disorders, and discusses contemporary accounts of their causes (aetiology). It is divided into six main sections covering anxiety disorders, mood disorders, schizophrenia, personality disorders, eating disorders, and disorders of childhood and adolescence. These topics have been chosen because they represent some of the most prevalent of psychological disorders (e.g. depression, anxiety disorders and schizophrenia), they consist of some of the most thoroughly researched disorders where our understanding of their causes has become relatively well developed (e.g. schizophrenia, anxiety disorders), and they also represent disorders that are of contemporary interest, either because of media interest (e.g. eating disorders) or because they give the reader an insight into broader ethical and political issues related to psychopathology (e.g. PTSD, anti-social personality disorder).

Introduction

In Chapter 32 we discussed many of the important matters that surround how psychological disorders are understood and defined. We now turn our attention to some of the specific issues that face clinical psychologists and psychotherapists when it comes to diagnosing and explaining various specific disorders. As our understanding of psychopathology has increased over the past 30 to 40 years, the number of specific diagnostic categories has expanded enormously. This expansion has largely been based on the fact that we now have a better understanding of the causes, or *aetiology*, of

psychopathology, and clinicians now have a better sense of both the symptoms and the causes of many disorders.

In a textbook of this nature, there is insufficient space to discuss all of the psychological disorders listed in DSM-IV, but this chapter presents a selection of the most common and prevalent disorders. In the case of each of these disorders we will discuss both their symptoms and a selection of the most recent theories that attempt to explain how they are caused and what maintains them.

Anxiety disorders

All of us experience anxiety at some time or other, and we are also aware that the intensity of this sensation can differ depending on the situations in which we experience it. *Anxiety* is a feeling of apprehension or fear, usually resulting from the anticipation of a threatening event or situation. It is often accompanied by various physiological symptoms that may include muscle tension, dry mouth, perspiring, trembling and difficulty swallowing. In its more chronic form, anxiety may also be accompanied by dizziness, chronic fatigue, sleeping difficulties, rapid or irregular heartbeat, diarrhoea or a persistent need to urinate, sexual problems and nightmares.

Most people experience feelings of anxiety quite naturally in many situations, such as just before an important exam, while making a presentation at college or work, during an interview or on a first date. Most anxiety reactions are perfectly natural, and are essential for us to perform effectively in challenging circumstances. However, anxiety can often be so intense or attached to inappropriate events or situations that it becomes maladaptive and problematic for the individual. This is when an anxiety disorder may develop.

An *anxiety disorder* is an excessive or aroused state characterised by feelings of apprehension, uncertainty and fear. The anxiety response (i) may be out of proportion to the threat posed by the situation or event (e.g. in specific phobias), (ii) may not be easily attributable to any specific threat (e.g. in generalised anxiety disorder or some forms of panic disorder), and (iii) may persist chronically and be so disabling that the individual is unable to continue normal day-to-day living.

The following sections discuss the most common forms in which anxiety manifests itself in an anxiety disorder.

Specific phobias

Phobias are normally defined as an 'unreasonable fear of a particular situation or object'; they are extraordinarily common, with surveys suggesting that a clear majority of the general population (60.2 per cent) experience 'unreasonable fears' (Chapman, 1997). Around 15 per cent of people will meet clinical

Most people have a phobia of some kind, but there are some unusual ones – such as a fear or anxiety of cotton wool or of buttons. Both of these odd phobias are more common than you think!

(*DSM-IV*) criteria for a simple phobia within their lifetime, which suggests that severe and disruptive phobic symptoms can be quite common.

Phobics are normally aware that their fear of the phobic situation or event is excessive or unreasonable (in comparison either with the actual threat it represents or with the less fearful responses of other people), but they do acquire a strong set of 'phobic beliefs' that appear to control their fear (Thorpe and Salkovskis, 1995). These beliefs normally contain information about why they think the *specific phobia* is threatening and how to react when they are in the phobic situation (e.g. avoid contact).

The nature of specific phobias

Common phobias tend to focus on a relatively small group of objects and situations, and the main ones are animal phobias (including fear of snakes, spiders, rats, mice, cockroaches and invertebrates such as maggots and slugs), social phobia, dental phobia, water phobia, height phobia, claustrophobia, and a cluster of blood, injury and inoculation fears (known collectively as BII).

Most other types of phobia are less common and can be thought of as quite unusual given the degree of threat they might realistically pose. Such phobias include fear of cotton wool, buttons, chocolate, dolls and vegetables (see McNally, 1997).

Aetiology: how do we acquire phobias?

Classical conditioning and phobias

Attempts to explain phobias in terms of classical conditioning date back to the famous 'Little Albert' study reported by Watson and Rayner in 1920. Albert was an 11-month-old child, and Watson and Rayner attempted to condition in him a fear to his pet white rat. They did this by pairing the rat (the conditioned stimulus, CS) with a loud noise produced by striking an iron bar (the unconditioned stimulus, UCS). After several pairings of the rat with the noise, Albert began to cry whenever the rat was introduced into the room. This type of explanation of phobias has been common over the past 80 years or so, and certainly seems capable of explaining the acquisition

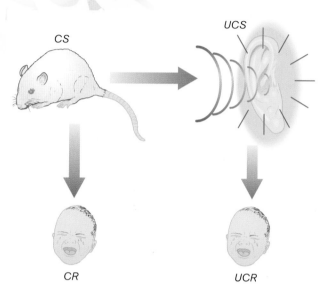

Figure 33.1   The 'Little Albert' classical conditioning study by Watson and Rayner: every time Little Albert was shown his pet white rat (CS), it was associated with a loud noise (UCS); eventually the fear of the noise (UCR) transferred to the white rat (CR)

of some phobias where the phobic event or object has been associated with a traumatic experience (e.g. dental phobia, choking phobia and most dog phobias).

Evolutionary accounts of phobias

The fact that phobias tend to be focused on a limited set of fears that seem to have evolutionary significance has led some researchers to suggest that we may be biologically prepared, or pre-wired, for certain phobias. Two facts are important here:

1 it can be argued that those things that are commonly the focus for phobias are truly dangerous and perhaps life threatening (e.g. heights, water, and venomous animals such as snakes and spiders)
2 they have all been around for many thousands of years; through evolutionary selection processes, those of our ancestors who feared and avoided

these types of objects and events will have survived and passed their fears on through genetic inheritance to their offspring.

The most common of these evolutionary explanations are *biological preparedness* (Seligman, 1971) and *non-associative fear acquisition* (Poulton and Menzies, 2002).

These evolutionary explanations appear to explain (i) why many of these phobias appear to be acquired through a normal developmental process without any apparent pairing with trauma during the lifetime of the individual (e.g. Poulton and Menzies, 2002), (ii) why many phobias appear to have an inherited component, and (iii) why it is more difficult to classically condition fear to something that does not have evolutionary fear significance (e.g. a gun) than to one that does (e.g. a snake) (Hugdahl and Johnsen, 1989).

Multiple pathways to phobias

However, there is no reason why the acquisition of all phobias should be explained by just a single process – and evidence is now accumulating to suggest that different types of phobia are acquired in quite different ways. Some do appear to be acquired through simple classical conditioning processes, where the individual has a traumatic experience paired with the subsequent phobic object or event (e.g. dental phobia, choking phobia, dog phobia, accident phobia).

Recent studies have also shown that children can acquire fear beliefs about objects through the kinds of information they receive about those objects (Field, Argyris and Knowles, 2001). This is likely to be a means by which many children acquire transitory fears during vulnerable developmental years.

Other types of phobias appear to have other origins. Many animal phobias – especially small animal phobias – appear to be related to the disgust emotion rather than fear alone. People who have a highly developed disgust reaction are likely to be more fearful of a whole range of disgust-relevant animals, and these include snakes, spiders, rats, mice, insects and invertebrates (Davey, 1994b).

Disgust is an emotion that has evolved to prevent the spread of disease, and it is hypothesised that we tend to be fearful of these kinds of animals because they have historically been associated with the spread of disease (e.g. rats, cockroaches) or because they possess features that naturally elicit disgust (e.g. they are perceived as slimy in the case of snakes and slugs).

Situational phobias, as the name suggests, are a group of phobias that are focused on specific situations (e.g. height, water and claustrophobia). In most cases, these phobias do not have a history of trauma, but are closely associated with panic and panic attacks (Antony, Brown and Barlow, 1997). There is evidence to suggest that they also share some of the same features as panic disorder (see below), and may develop because the individual has learnt *catastrophically to misinterpret bodily sensations* when in the phobic situation (e.g. when in

Famous Dutch international footballer Denis Bergkamp was well known for his chronic fear of flying. He was often unable to travel to important away matches that required a lengthy aeroplane journey.

an enclosed space or high up) (Davey, Menzies and Gallardo, 1997) (see pages 564–565).

Panic disorder (PD)

The nature of panic disorder

As the name suggests, *panic disorder* is characterised by repeated panic or anxiety attacks. These attacks are associated with a variety of physical symptoms, including heart palpitations, perspiring, dizziness, hyperventilating, nausea and trembling. In addition, the individual may experience real feelings of terror or severe apprehension, as well as depersonalisation (a feeling of not being connected to your own body or in real contact with what is happening around you).

Most people will experience at least one panic attack in their lifetime, but PD is diagnosed when unexpected panic attacks keep occurring (they are recurrent), and are followed by at least one month of persistent concerns about having a further attack. For some individuals, panic attacks are unpredictable, but for others they may become associated (perhaps through classical conditioning, see Chapter 8) with specific situations or events (e.g. riding on public transport).

At least 1.5 per cent of the population will be diagnosed with PD during their lifetime. It is twice as common in women as men. PD is closely related to agoraphobia (a cluster of fears of being in public places and unable to escape to a 'safe' place), and up to half those diagnosed with PD will usually also suffer from agoraphobia.

The aetiology of panic disorder

Interestingly, current theories of PD can conveniently be categorised as either biological or psychological. Because of the intense nature of the physical symptoms of PD, some clinicians believe the causes lie in biological factors (e.g. the physical effects of hyperventilation (Ley, 1987)). However, others have argued that panic disorder is caused primarily by cognitive biases in the way that individuals interpret ambiguous bodily sensations (e.g. Clark, 1986).

FOCUS POINT 33.1

The experience of panic disorder

Here are some different people's descriptions of their experience of panic disorder.

'It started 10 years ago. I was sitting in a seminar in a hotel and this thing came out of the clear blue. I felt like I was dying.'

'For me, a panic attack is almost a violent experience. I feel like I'm going insane. It makes me feel like I'm losing control in a very extreme way. My heart pounds really hard, things seem unreal, and there's this very strong feeling of impending doom.'

'In between attacks there is this dread and anxiety that it's going to happen again. It can be very debilitating, trying to escape those feelings of panic.'

'When a panic attack strikes, most likely your heart pounds and you feel sweaty, weak, faint, or dizzy. Your hands may tingle or feel numb, and you might feel flushed or chilled. You may have chest pain or smothering sensations, a sense of unreality, or fear of impending doom or loss of control. You may genuinely believe you're having a heart attack or stroke, losing your mind, or on the verge of death. Attacks can occur any time, even during nondream sleep. While most attacks average a couple of minutes, occasionally they go on for up to 10 minutes. In rare cases, they may last an hour or more'.

Source: www.algy.com/anxiety/panic.html

Biological theories

Hyperventilation is a common feature of panic attacks, and Ley (1987) has suggested that dysfunctional breathing patterns may trigger a series of autonomic reactions that precipitate a full-blown panic attack. Hyperventilation is defined as a 'minute ventilation that exceeds metabolic demand' and has an end result of raising blood pH level. Oxygen is then delivered less efficiently to body cells, and this can lead to cardiovascular changes that try to compensate for the lack of oxygen in the cells, which in turn produces the symptoms of PD that are recognised as anxiety (Zvolensky and Eifert, 2001).

This type of explanation has been partially supported by evidence from what are called 'hyperventilation and carbon dioxide challenges', where panic attacks have been induced by administering carbon dioxide-enriched air (CO_2) (Ley and Walker, 1973). Similarly, sensitivity to increases in CO_2 have been suggested as a risk factor for PD (Papp, Klein and Gorman, 1993), and have given rise to what are known as 'suffocation alarm theories' of PD, where a combination of increased CO_2 intake in particular situations (e.g. riding on public transport) may signal suffocation and give rise to the intense terror and anxiety experienced during a panic attack (Klein, 1993).

Psychological theories

There are a number of difficulties with those biological accounts of PD that are based on hyperventilation. First, studies that have monitored individuals with PD indicate that hyperventilation occurs in only a small minority of panic attacks, and so could not easily be the cause of the majority of those attacks (Garssen, Buikhuisen and Van Dyck, 1996). Second, the sensations and experiences caused by hyperventilation are not always perceived by everyone as threatening and anxiety-provoking – some individuals actually find the light-headedness and depersonalisation caused by hyperventilation enjoyable and relaxing (Salkovskis and Clark, 1990) – the kind of exhilarating effect that many people experience on, say, a rollercoaster ride.

This led British clinical psychologist David Clark to propose that PD was caused primarily by the way in which the individual interpreted the bodily

The hyperventilation model of panic disorder

The hyperventilation model posited by Ley suggests that panic results from dysfunctional breathing patterns which cause chronic hyperventilation. The theory maintains that stress-induced arousal produces an increase in the volume of air breathed so that respiration exceeds metabolic demands. As a result body tissue suffers excess loss of CO_2, the direct result of which is an increase in blood pH and a decrease in arterial CO_2 tension. The increased blood pH reduces the amount of oxygen that hemoglobin can release to body tissue (hypoxia) while reduced CO_2 in the blood reduces the caliber of the arteries, thus impeding the flow of blood to body tissue (ischaemia). In order to compensate for the decreased CO_2 and increased pH the heart has to beat with greater rapidity and power. Heart palpitations, shortness of breath and breathing difficulties follow, with intensity of symptoms a direct consequence of the degree of hyperventilation.

Source: Edelmann, 1992: 84–5

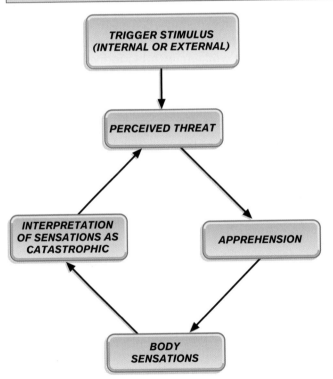

sensations they experienced. In particular, many body sensations are ambiguous, e.g. the heart skipping a beat could mean either an imminent heart attack (negative interpretation) or that

Figure 33.2 Clark's (1986) psychological model of panic disorder: perception of a threat triggers apprehension and then bodily sensations that are interpreted catastrophically (e.g. 'I am going to faint or have a heart attack'); this causes further anxiety which feeds into a vicious cycle that triggers a full-blown panic attack

Professor David Clark of the Institute of Psychiatry, London, first suggested in 1986 that panic disorder may result from psychological rather than biological factors. His groundbreaking article, published in the journal Behaviour Research & Therapy *is one of the most widely cited papers in the areas of clinical psychology and psychiatry*

someone you like has just walked into the room (positive interpretation).

However, individuals who tend to develop PD appear catastrophically to misinterpret bodily sensations – that is, they have a cognitive bias towards accepting the more threatening interpretation of their sensations (Clark, 1986). Clark argues that this leads to a vicious cycle where any apprehension is interpreted threateningly (e.g. 'my heart beating faster means I'm going to have a heart attack'), thus increasing the perceived threat and leading to an escalation of anxiety symptoms, which then precipitate a panic attack.

There is a good deal of evidence to support this psychological account. Individuals with PD have been shown (i) to attend to and discriminate their bodily sensations more closely than individuals without PD (Ehlers, 1993), and (ii) to possess a 'fear of fear' – that is, they find any symptom that may be indicative of fear very threatening and anxiety-provoking (Goldstein and Chambless, 1978).

In addition, individuals with PD will experience a panic attack when they have been told they will receive a CO_2 challenge, but in fact are given only compressed air (Sanderson, Rapee and Barlow, 1989), suggesting that the mere expectancy of an attack is enough to trigger one.

All of these findings suggest there is likely to be a psychological component to the development of PD that involves a bias in how the individual interprets and reacts to their own bodily sensations. Such psychological accounts of PD have already been used successfully to develop cognitive behavioural therapies for the treatment of PD.

Generalised anxiety disorder (GAD)

The nature of GAD

There is unlikely to be a single reader of this textbook who has not worried catastrophically about something at one time or another. Worry is an important activity that is triggered by anxiety. In particular, worry is a central feature of *generalised anxiety disorder (GAD)*; this disorder is characterised by constant worrisome thoughts and tension about a range of aspects of life and daily routine.

The cardinal diagnostic criterion for GAD is excessive or uncontrollable chronic worry that has lasted for at least six months. An individual with GAD usually finds it difficult to control their anxiety and worry, and this may be accompanied by physical symptoms such as fatigue, trembling, muscle tension, headache and nausea. GAD is twice as common in women as in men, and can often be a disorder that lasts from adolescence to old age (Barlow, Blanchard, Vermilyea, Vermilyea and DiNardo, 1986).

Over 5 per cent of the population will be diagnosed with GAD at some point in their lifetime, and over 12 per cent of those who attend anxiety disorder clinics will present with GAD.

The aetiology of GAD

The challenge in explaining GAD is to understand why individuals with GAD worry chronically and pathologically, while many other individuals – often with more stressful lifestyles – worry significantly less. The chronic worrying of those with GAD possesses a number of important features:

- it is always associated with high levels of anxious and depressed mood
- it is perceived by the individual as uncontrollable
- individuals with GAD often catastrophise their worries (i.e. make them significantly worse) when they worry about them.

Any theory of GAD needs to be able to explain these various features of worrying.

Table 33.1 shows the catastrophising sequences generated by a chronic worrier (top) and a non-worrier (bottom). These sequences were generated using the catastrophic interview procedure in which the individual is first asked 'What is your main worry at the moment?' In this case both participants replied, 'Getting good grades in school'. The interviewer then passes this response back to the participant by saying 'What is it that worries you about getting good grades in school?' Each time the participant responds, the interviewer passes that response back by asking what it is about the response that worries them. The interview continues

FOCUS POINT 33.3

The experience of generalised anxiety disorder

The example of Lesley shows how chronic and pathological *worrying* can not only take over all of a person's daytime thoughts, but can also have serious deleterious effects on sleep, health, job performance and relationships.

'Lesley readily admitted that she was a "born worrier". She had seen a school counsellor at the age of 15 when anxious about examinations, but had not previously received psychological treatment when she was referred for help at the age of 28. Her main complaint at assessment concerned severe headaches, with pain behind her eyes. She was worrying about the possibility that the headaches might never go, and that the pain would interfere with her performance at work. She held a temporary, and junior, post in a small publisher, and in her spare time helped to teach on the introductory copy-editing course that she herself had recently completed. In quick succession she spoke about the potential she believed she had and her fear that she would never be able to realise it. Her ability to do the job well was jeopardised by poor concentration, indecisiveness, and tiredness following nights of disturbed sleep. She was frustrated and angry with herself, as well as anxious about how her work was being appraised. She spent many evenings preparing for her teaching commitments, and no longer had time to go to her exercise class or see her friends.

'Lesley's partner Andrew worked for a local estate agent and she relied on him to listen whenever she was bothered about something. She commented that he did not help her in the right way and no longer seemed to take her worries seriously. They enjoyed the same kinds of music, visiting new places and cooking for friends, when they had time to do it – and when Lesley's worries permitted.'

Source: Butler, 1994, in Davey, 1994a: 214

until the participant can no longer think of any reasons.

By looking at the catastrophising sequences in the table, we can deduce a number of things about chronic worriers:

- they produce significantly more catastrophising steps than non-worriers
- they experience increasing emotional distress as catastrophising continues
- the content of their catastrophising steps becomes more and more threatening and catastrophic.

Biological theories

There is some evidence for a genetic component to both anxiety generally and GAD specifically (Noyes, Woodman, Garvey *et al.*, 1992), which suggests that GAD has an inherited component. However, this evidence is somewhat equivocal and does not indicate very clearly what any inherited component might consist of – it certainly does not imply that individuals with GAD are 'born worriers' (Kendler *et al.*, 1992)! In contrast to biological accounts of GAD, most emphasis in research has recently been placed on understanding the cognitive and psychological processes that contribute to excessive and pathological worrying.

TABLE 33.1

CHRONIC WORRIER AND NON-WORRIER TOPICS

Chronic worrier topic: getting good grades in school

Catastrophising step	Discomfort	Likelihood
I won't live up to my expectations.	50	30
I'd be disappointed in myself.	60	100
I'd lose my self-confidence	70	50
My loss of self-confidence would spread to other areas of my life.	70	50
I wouldn't have as much control as I'd like.	75	80
I'd be afraid of facing the unknown.	75	100
I'd become very anxious.	75	100
Anxiety would lead to further loss of self-confidence.	75	80
I wouldn't get my confidence back.	75	50
I'd feel like 1 wouldn't have any control over my life.	75	80
I'd be susceptible to things that normally wouldn't bother me.	75	80
I'd become more and more anxious.	80	80
I'd have no control at all and I'd become mentally ill.	85	30
I'd become dependent on drugs and therapy.	50	30
I'd always remain dependent on drugs.	85	50
They'd deteriorate my body.	85	100
I'd be in pain.	85	100
I'd die.	90	80
I'd end up in hell.	95	80

Non-worrier topic: getting good grades in school

Catastrophising step	Discomfort	Likelihood
I might do poorly on a test.	3	20
I'd get a bad grade in the class.	3	100
That would lower my grade-point average.	2	100
I'd have less of a chance of getting a good job.	2	60
I'd end up in a bad job.	2	80
I'd get a low salary.	2	100
I'd have less money to spend on what I want.	2	100
I'd be unhappy.	2	35
It would be a strain on me.	2	10
I'd worry more.	2	5

Source: after Vasey and Borkovec, 1992

Cognitive factors in pathological worrying

Information processing biases in GAD
A good deal of research has indicated that anxious individuals, and especially those suffering GAD, have a series of information processing biases that appear to maintain their hyper-vigilance for threat, create further sources of worry and maintain their anxiety. For example, individuals with GAD appear to have an information processing bias that causes them to pre-attentively (i.e. rapidly and unconsciously) focus in on any threat-related stimulus, or to selectively attend to threatening stimuli (Mathews and MacLeod, 1994; Mogg and Bradley, 1998), and these characteristics of anxious individuals have been demonstrated using a number of experimental techniques.

It is not yet clear whether these information processing biases are caused by anxiety or whether individuals who go on to develop anxiety disorders, such as GAD, always displayed these biases, which made them vulnerable to acquiring GAD (Williams, Watts, MacLeod and Mathews, 1997). However, if such information processing biases do not represent a vulnerability factor, they are certainly an important factor in the maintenance of anxious psychopathology.

RESEARCH METHODS BOX 33.1

The emotional Stroop procedure
During the 1980s and 1990s, clinical psychology borrowed a number of very useful experimental techniques from cognitive psychology that allowed researchers to investigate some of the important cognitive processes involved in anxiety and depression.

The 'emotional Stroop' is one such example, and this procedure allows the researcher to determine whether individuals with anxiety or depression have a bias towards attending to and processing anxiety-relevant or depression-relevant information (e.g. Mogg, Bradley, Williams and Mathews, 1993) – a factor that may maintain their anxious state.

In this procedure, participants are presented with individual words in coloured ink. Some of these words are anxiety-relevant (or depression-relevant) words, and others are emotionally neutral words. For example:

- DEATH (an anxiety relevant word), or
- CARPET (a neutral word).

The participant has to name the *colour of the ink* as quickly as possible, and their reaction time is recorded.

The implication of this procedure is that if individuals automatically attend to the meaning of threatening words (such as death), then this will delay them processing the colour and responding to it. So, if there is an attentional bias to anxiety-relevant words, then reaction times to name the *colour* of the word will be slower with anxiety-related words than neutral, control words.

Most emotional Stroop studies and their associated procedures do indicate that individuals suffering anxiety have an attentional bias towards anxiety-relevant words and stimuli, including anxiety-relevant faces (Mogg, Millar and Bradley, 2000), and that this attentional bias occurs pre-attentively (i.e. before the individual becomes consciously aware of the meaning of the word).

Beliefs about worrying
The worrying of GAD sufferers appears to be driven by a set of beliefs that worrying is an important and necessary thing to do to avoid 'bad' things happening (Borkovec and Roemer, 1995; Wells, 1995; Davey, Tallis and Capuzzo, 1996). This suggests that for pathological worriers, worrying serves a very specific function, and this gives rise to the rather paradoxical situation where worriers feel the need to worry, yet are aware that such worrying causes them a good deal of emotional discomfort (Davey *et al.*, 1996).

Although it is not yet clear what developmental factors help to fashion these global beliefs about worry, cognitive behavioural therapy techniques are being developed that attempt to change these dysfunctional beliefs about worry into functional ones (see Chapter 34).

FOCUS POINT 33.4

Dysfunctional beliefs in worry

A number of studies have indicated that pathological worriers possess a very strong and stable set of beliefs about worry being an important activity to indulge in – largely because they believe that if they do *not* worry, then bad things will happen to them.

It is far from clear how worriers have developed this set of dysfunctional beliefs, but it is possible that they are maintained through superstitious reinforcement. For example, the majority of things that pathological worriers worry about have very low probabilities of actually happening (e.g. a family member is late home, therefore they must have had a serious car accident). When these events don't happen (i.e. the family member turns up late but quite healthy), this implicitly reinforces their belief that worrying actually prevents bad things happening.

The following are some of the positive beliefs that worriers hold about worry being a necessary thing to do:

- worrying allows me to work through the worst that can happen, so when it doesn't happen things are better
- worrying leads me to explore different possibilities
- worrying is a process that helps me to meet new situations
- worrying makes me reflect on life by asking questions I might not usually ask when happy
- in order to get something done, I have to worry about it.

Source: Davey, Tallis and Capuzzo, 1996

Dispositional characteristics of worriers

While there is still some way to go in understanding the psychological and developmental processes that lead to individuals becoming pathological worriers, there is a good deal of knowledge available about what kinds of psychological features they possess. For example, worriers are intolerant of uncertainty (Ladoucer, Talbot and Dugas, 1997), are high on perfectionism (Pratt, Tallis and Eysenck, 1997) and have feelings of responsibility for negative outcomes (Wells and Papageorgiou, 1998) – all of which suggest that they possess characteristics that will drive them to attempt to think about resolving problematic issues.

However, worriers also have poor problem-solving confidence (Davey, 1994a) and couch their worries in ways that reflect personal inadequacies and insecurities (Davey and Levy, 1998). This contrasting combination of characteristics appears to drive the individual to try and resolve problems, but the process is thwarted by their personal doubt about their own ability to solve them successfully (Davey, 1994a).

Obsessive-compulsive disorder (OCD)

The nature of obsessive-compulsive disorder

We have all on occasions gone back to check whether a door is locked, and we have all experienced a sudden intrusive thought that we find disturbing and out of place (e.g. harming our own child). But for *obsessive-compulsive disorder (OCD)* sufferers such experiences are a distressing way of life.

There are two specific characteristics of OCD. First, OCD is characterised by persistent, intrusive, and usually disturbing, thoughts, images or impulses that are known as obsessions. These obsessions in their turn cause anxiety and emotional discomfort, which give rise to a set of strategies or rituals designed to alleviate this anxiety. These strategies or rituals are known as compulsions.

OCD normally takes one of three prevalent forms:

1   repeated, *unwanted thoughts*, images or compulsions
2   *compulsive washing*, usually to avoid fear of dirt, contamination or illness
3   *compulsive checking*, usually undertaken to ensure that the individual will not be responsible

for any potentially harmful event occurring (if, for example, the gas cooker is left on or the door left unlocked).

OCD can also manifest itself less regularly as compulsive hoarding, superstitious ritualised movements or the systematic arranging of objects. Often, the compulsive rituals developed during OCD can be so demanding that they significantly interfere with the daily life of both the individual and his or her immediate family.

FOCUS POINT 33.5

The case of Howard Hughes

'It would appear that during his declining years Howard Hughes suffered from a severe obsessional disorder, among many other problems. Although the information is scanty and of unknown reliability, it seems extremely probable that he had a strong obsessional fear of contamination. In order to avoid infection, he constructed for himself a sterile, isolated environment in which his contact with potentially contaminated people was kept to a minimum. For the most part he successfully avoided touching any person or object directly – instead, he covered himself with paper tissues and other protective materials. His barber was required to repeatedly sterilise all of his instruments by immersing them in alcohol. There was a complicated ritual for handling objects. Before handing Hughes a spoon, his attendants

had to wrap the handle in tissue paper and seal it with cellophane tape. A second piece of tissue was wrapped around the first protective wrapping to ensure that it would be protected from contamination. On receiving the protected spoon. Hughes would use it only with the handle covered. When he finished with it, the tissue was discarded into a specially provided receptacle. The spoon itself had to be carefully cleaned.

On one occasion he observed that a bottle had been broken on the steps of his range. He wrote out a series of instructions that involved marking out a grid of one-inch squares on each step and then meticulously cleaning one square at a time to ensure that every splinter of glass had been removed.'

Source: Rachman and Hodgson, 1980: 25–6

OCD onset is usually gradual and frequently begins to manifest itself in early adolescence or early adulthood following a stressful event such as pregnancy, childbirth, relationship or work problems (Kringlen, 1970). Recent community surveys have suggested that OCD is more common than was once believed, with around 2.5 per cent of the population being diagnosed with OCD during their lifetime.

The aetiology of obsessive-compulsive disorder

Biological factors

Onset of OCD can be associated with traumatic brain injury or encephalitis (Jenike, 1986), which suggests that there may be a neuropsychological deficit in some forms of OCD. This neuropsychological deficit may give rise to the 'doubting' that things have been done properly, which is a central feature of many forms of OCD.

Areas of the brain that have been identified as important in this respect include the frontal lobes and the basal ganglia, but as yet there is no convincing evidence that deficits in the functioning of specific areas of the brain have a direct causal role in the development of OCD.

Some neuropsychological studies have indicated that OCD sufferers appear to demonstrate a variety of basic information processing and executive functioning deficits. These include deficits in spatial working memory, spatial recognition, visual attention, visual memory and motor response initiation (Greisberg and McKay, 2003). However, while such executive deficits may contribute to 'doubting' that something has been done properly, the evidence is equivocal as to whether these cognitive deficits are linked to any physiological brain dysfunction.

Psychological factors

Memory deficits
'Doubting' is a central feature of OCD, and especially the compulsions associated with the disorder. As a result, it has been suggested that OCD may be characterised by memory deficits that give rise to the doubting that, for example, doors have been locked or hands have been washed properly.

Researchers have suggested that OCD sufferers may have:

- a general memory deficit (Sher, Mann and Frost, 1984)
- less confidence in the validity of their memories (Watts, 1995), or
- a deficit in the ability to distinguish between the memory of real and imagined actions (Brown, Kosslyn, Breiter, Baer and Jenike, 1994).

However, while OCD sufferers do claim to have doubts about their recollection of having either checked or washed properly, recent evidence suggests that lack of confidence in recall may be a consequence of compulsive checking or washing rather than a cause of it (Tolin *et al.*, 2001; van den Hout and Kindt, 2003). In effect, the more we check, the less confident we are about what we have checked.

Inflated responsibility
The most notable of contemporary psychological accounts of OCD are those claiming that inflated responsibility can be a vulnerability factor that generates obsessive and compulsive tendencies (Salkovskis, 1985; Rachman, 1998). Excessive or inflated responsibility is defined as the 'individual's belief in their power to cause harm' (Rheaume, Ladoucer, Freeston and Letarte, 1994), and this inflated responsibility both generates negative affect and motivates the individual to persist with rituals and compulsions until they are fully confident they have avoided negative outcomes (such as avoiding getting contaminated if they are a compulsive washer or avoiding being burgled if they are compulsive checkers).

Inflated responsibility is also hypothesised to play a role in the development of compulsive, unwanted thoughts. For example, most individuals would simply dismiss an intrusive thought about killing their child. However, individuals with inflated responsibility appear to believe that if that thought entered their head, they must be responsible for it. This causes considerable emotional discomfort and leads to attempts to suppress the thought, which then often has the paradoxical effect of projecting it more regularly into the stream of consciousness (Salkovskis, 1985).

RESEARCH METHODS BOX 33.2

Doing research in clinical psychology
Our understanding of psychological disorders is critically dependent on our ability to undertake scientific research into the factors that cause and maintain these disorders. Many different types of research contribute to understanding psychological disorders, and these include the following.

Survey studies

Where epidemiological and demographic factors are investigated (e.g. to see how prevalent a disorder is, or if it affects people from different social backgrounds or from different parts of the country).

Questionnaire studies

Many validated questionnaires have been developed that measure particular aspects of psychological disorders (e.g. these can be used to measure attributes such as levels of trait anxiety or characteristics such as obsessional tendencies). Such studies often provide correlational information about how various characteristics are related – for example, measures of low self-esteem and perfectionism are highly correlated with measures of eating disorder (Hewitt *et al.*, 1995; Fairburn *et al.*, 1997). These types of study, of course, do not imply a causal relationship between these variables, but they do suggest relationships that may be worthy of further research.

Qualitative methods and discourse analysis

One of the important first steps in understanding a particular disorder is understanding its phenomenology – that is, what do individuals with a particular disorder actually experience? Using qualitative methods (such as structured interviews) can help achieve this. Understanding the phenomenology of a disorder is often crucial to determining how you will proceed in trying to discover its causes and the psychological mechanisms that maintain it.

Retrospective questionnaire studies

We may want to ask whether a history of negative life experiences is a factor that might influence whether someone develops depression, an anxiety disorder or an eating disorder. On some occasions, retrospective questionnaire studies have been used to investigate this (e.g. individuals are assessed for current psychological disorders and then asked to recall whether various types of events have happened to them in the past). However, these types of questionnaires are not entirely reliable because (i) people tend to have imperfect memories of past events, and may even have suppressed memories of past negative events, and (ii) we know that current levels of anxiety and depression cause information processing biases (see page 569), which will bias such people to interpreting past events as negative, and more readily to recall negative events than individuals who are not suffering anxiety and depression.

Prospective studies

To overcome some of the disadvantages of retrospective questionnaire studies, researchers can use prospective techniques. These involve taking measures of a variety of characteristics at time one (T1) and then again at time two (T2). (These two time points may be only a few weeks apart or a number of years apart.) This allows objective assessment of characteristics at T1, and these can then be related to whether an individual has developed a psychological problem at T2.

Experimental psychopathology

One of the most effective ways of discovering whether a variable has a causal effect on a psychological disorder is to manipulate experimentally that variable in controlled conditions. For example, Webb and Davey (1993) wanted to see if the disgust emotion was involved in fear of animals. They did this in the laboratory by assessing participants' fears of a range of animals, then manipulating their levels of experienced disgust (by showing videos with disgust-relevant material such as an open-heart operation), and then seeing if this manipulation had changed the participants' fear levels. It did indeed increase fear of certain types of animals, and they concluded that disgust levels play an important causal role in determining fear levels to these animals.

Section 7
Abnormal, Clinical and Health Psychology

Analogue studies

It is often very difficult to carry out research on clinical populations because:

- access to clinical populations is often restricted and difficult to obtain
- there are important ethical issues in doing research with people suffering distressing disorders, especially if the research might make their symptoms worse
- such individuals are often undergoing treatment or therapy, which may make the results of particular studies difficult to interpret.

For reasons such as these, much useful clinical research has been carried out on what are known as 'analogue populations' – that is, people who are not diagnosed with a disorder. The rationale for this is that many psychological disorders (especially those related to anxiety and depression) are dimensional in nature, and the processes that contribute, say, to making anyone feel mildly depressed are the same ones that contribute to major depression. So what we learn about the factors that influence depression or anxiety in non-clinical populations will also be relevant to understanding clinical depression (Davey, 2003).

Post-traumatic stress disorder (PTSD)

The nature of PTSD

Post-traumatic stress disorder (PTSD) is rather unusual among the anxiety disorders because the diagnostic criteria specify exposure to a traumatic stressor as an essential causal factor. In effect, PTSD is a set of persistent symptoms that occur after experiencing or witnessing a traumatic event such as combat during a war, rape or other types of criminal assault, child abuse, car or plane crashes, or natural or human-caused disasters.

The symptoms of PTSD are somewhat different from those experienced in other anxiety disorders, and can be grouped into three main categories:

1 increased arousal – includes an exaggerated startle response, difficulty sleeping, hypervigilance and difficulty concentrating
2 avoidance and numbing of emotions – the individual will attempt to avoid all situations or events that might trigger memories of the traumatic event, and there is a sense of detachment and lack of feelings of positive emotion
3 re-experiencing – the individual regularly recalls very vivid flashbacks of events experienced during the trauma, and these images often occur in recurrent nightmares.

The aetiology of PTSD

PTSD is a complex disorder that has a number of very different symptomatic features. Because of this, explanations of PTSD have been many and varied (Brewin and Holmes, 2003; McNally, 2003) Some theories address specific features of the symptomatology (e.g. the flashbacks), and others address the chronicity of the disorder and its emotional phenomenology.

Vulnerability factors

What is interesting about PTSD is that not everyone who experiences a life-threatening trauma develops PTSD, so there may be factors that make some people more vulnerable than others. In this respect, a number of factors have been identified that characterise those individuals likely to develop PTSD after trauma. These include:

- a tendency to take personal responsibility for the traumatic event and the misfortunes of others involved in the event (Mikhliner and Solomon, 1988)
- developmental factors such as early separation from parents or an unstable family life during early childhood (King *et al.*, 1996)
- a family history of PTSD (Foy *et al.*, 1987)
- existing high levels of anxiety or a pre-existing psychological disorder (Breslau *et al.*, 1997).

Low intelligence is also a vulnerability factor (Vasterling *et al.*, 2002) and high IQ is the best predictor of resistance to the development of PTSD (Silva *et al.*, 2000).

Theory of shattered assumptions

Many people develop schemata of the world that portray it as a benevolent, safe place, and the people who live in it as good, moral and well-meaning. Therefore, when a traumatic event occurs that severely challenges these beliefs (e.g. being assaulted by a stranger or injured in a disaster that was not of their own making), the individual is left in a state of shock and conflict. This challenges the individual's core beliefs and leaves them in a state of 'unreality' (Janoff-Bulman, 1992; Bolton and Hill, 1996).

However, while this may sound like a reasonable explanation of why some individuals exhibit shock and numbing following trauma, the facts do not entirely support this. Paradoxically, it is those who have already experienced the world as an unsafe place (i.e. have experienced previous trauma) who are most likely to develop PTSD, *not* those who have a core belief that the world is safe and benevolent (Resick, 2001).

Emotional processing theory

Foa *et al.* (1989) have suggested that the intense nature of the trauma in PTSD creates a representation of the trauma in memory that becomes strongly associated with other contextual details of the event (e.g. if a person has been assaulted in an alleyway, subsequently walking down any alleyway would selectively activate the fear network in memory). The avoidance of any contexts that might activate this fear network means that there is little opportunity for the PTSD sufferer to weaken these associations between fear and the everyday cues that will activate that fear.

This account of PTSD has been elaborated more recently to take account of the fact that individuals with more rigid pre-traumatic views of the self and the world would be more vulnerable to PTSD (Foa and Riggs, 1993), and the emotional processing theory has been influential in the development and success of prolonged exposure as a therapy for PTSD. Prolonged exposure therapy helps PTSD sufferers to relive their traumatic experiences and, in so doing, weakens the associations between contextual stimuli (e.g. alleyways) and the fear network.

'Mental defeat'

Ehlers and Clark (2000) have suggested that there is a specific psychological factor that is important in making an individual vulnerable to PTSD. This is a specific frame of mind called 'mental defeat', in which the individual sees him/herself as a victim, process all information about the trauma negatively, and view themselves as unable to act effectively. This negative approach to the traumatic event and its consequences simply adds to the distress, influences the way the individual recalls the trauma, and may give rise to maladaptive behavioural and cognitive strategies that maintain the disorder. These maladaptive strategies include thought suppression, avoidance of trauma cues, use of alcohol or medication to control anxiety, and abandonment of normal everyday behaviour patterns.

Mood disorders: depression

Depression is an emotion that everyone will have experienced at some point in their lives. It is usually associated with either some form of loss (e.g. loss of a loved one or loss of a job) or with failure (e.g. failing an important exam). It can be triggered by contextual or external factors, such as inclement, dull weather, or the time of year in the case of *seasonal affective disorder (SAD)*. While acute episodes of depression are quite normal and adaptive in response to certain types of life event, for some individuals depression can become a chronic and disabling problem.

Depression is a *mood disorder* that is characterised by sadness, lethargy, low self-esteem, lack of initiative, and loss of sleep, appetite and sexual desire. It is often associated with a generally pessimistic view of the world. In western cultures, major depression can affect up to 15 per cent of individuals at some point during their lifetime. A bout of major depression can last between three and nine months if untreated, but around 85 per cent of bouts resolve themselves within one year.

ACTIVITY BOX 33.1

Controversies in the study of PTSD

In many ways, post-traumatic stress disorder is a controversial topic. Controversy has arisen because of:

- the way it is diagnosed
- the potential that individuals have to fake the disorder (especially when they are involved in lawsuits to secure financial compensation for involvement in a disaster or accident)
- the issue of whether repressed and then recovered memories of sexual abuse play a role in PTSD.

Harvard psychologist Professor Rich McNally (2003) has reviewed some of these controversial issues in an article in the *Annual Review of Psychology*. They include the following.

'Conceptual bracket creep' in the definition of trauma

Recent changes in the criteria for diagnosis of PTSD mean that PTSD can be diagnosed if 'the person experienced, witnessed, or was confronted with an event or events that involved actual or threatened death or serious injury, or a threat to the integrity of self or others'. McNally points out that PTSD could now be attributed (i) to someone who merely learns about someone else being threatened with harm, or (ii) to a range of non-life-threatening stressors, such as exposure to sexual jokes in the workplace (Avina and O'Donohue, 2002).

Erroneously equating PTSD with merely experiencing stress

After the terrorist attack on the World Trade Center on 11 September 2001, surveys suggested that a majority of Americans were suffering substantial levels of stress as a result of the attack. Technically this would allow almost anyone to claim to have developed PTSD according to the broadened diagnostic criteria, yet it clearly fails to distinguish between normal stress and a psychological disorder.

Faking symptoms of PTSD

It is notoriously easy to fake most of the symptoms of PTSD, and because it is a diagnosis linked to explicit traumatic experiences, there are many cases of individuals faking the disorder in order to obtain financial compensation or damages against those who might have been involved in causing the trauma, or to obtain disability payments (McGrath and Frueh, 2002). Indeed, it is estimated that around 75 per cent of Vietnam War veterans who are currently claiming PTSD compensation are either faking symptoms or never actually saw combat (Burkett and Whitley, 1998).

Recovered memories of trauma

A highly controversial debate has raged for many years now about whether disorders such as PTSD may be caused by traumatic experiences (such as childhood sexual abuse) that are repressed in memory but then subsequently recovered using contentious techniques like hypnosis (Brown *et al.*, 1998). The jury is still out on this issue, but as McNally points out, there is accumulating evidence that those individuals who claim to have recovered memories of previous trauma are prone to exhibit false memory effects (i.e. in laboratory tests of memory, they claim to recall and recognise items that they have not previously been shown). Indeed, Clancey *et al.* (2002) found that individuals who had reported being abducted by space aliens (see Figure 33.3) also exhibited these false memory effects in the laboratory!

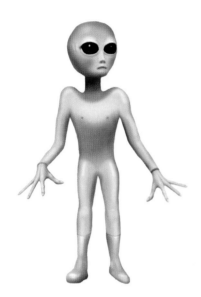

Figure 33.3 Individuals that reported being abducted by space aliens also exhibited false memory effects

In this section we will look at two important types of depression, and at one of the most distressing outcomes of depression: suicide.

Bipolar disorder

The nature of bipolar disorder
Bipolar disorder – previously known as manic depression – is a form of mood disorder that results in unusual shifts in an individual's mood, energy and ability to function. Swings in mood from extreme mania to severe depression may occur in as short a time as a few hours or, more normally, over a period of several months.

The causes of bipolar disorder
Bipolar disorder appears primarily to have some important biological determinants. First, there is clearly an inherited component to the disorder, suggested by the fact that bipolar disorder runs in families, and is also associated with an enzyme

---

FOCUS POINT 33.6

The experience of bipolar disorder
Descriptions offered by people with bipolar disorder (such as those below) give valuable insights into the various mood states associated with the disorder.

Depression
'I doubt completely my ability to do anything well. It seems as though my mind has slowed down and burned out to the point of being virtually useless ... [I am] haunt[ed] ... with the total, the desperate hopelessness of it all. ... Others say, "It's only temporary, it will pass, you can get over it," but of course they haven't any idea of how I feel, although they are certain they do. If I can't feel, move, think or care, then what on earth is the point?'

Hypomania
'At first when I'm high, it's tremendous ... ideas are fast ... like shooting stars you follow until brighter ones appear. ... All shyness disappears, the right words and gestures are suddenly there ... uninteresting people, things become intensely interesting. Sensuality is pervasive, the desire to seduce and be seduced is irresistible. Your marrow is infused with unbelievable feelings of ease, power, well-being, omnipotence, euphoria ... you can do anything ... but, somewhere this changes.'

Mania
'The fast ideas become too fast and there are far too many ... overwhelming confusion replaces clarity ... you stop keeping up with it – memory goes. Infectious humour ceases to amuse. Your friends become frightened ... everything is now against the grain ... you are irritable, angry, frightened, uncontrollable, and trapped.'

deficiency and colour blindness associated with genes on the X-chromosome (Hodgkinson, Mullan and Gurling, 1990; Hyman, 1999).

Second, there are also important changes in certain brain neurotransmitters when the individual is in either a depressed or manic state. During the depressed state, norepinephrine is low, but increases significantly when the individual becomes manic (Schildkraut, Green and Mooney, 1985). The fact that the switch from depression to mania and vice versa is very rapid leads some researchers to believe that the specific problem in bipolar disorder may be related to how the brain controls the levels of different neurotransmitters (Hirschfeld and Goodwin, 1988).

Major depression (unipolar)

The nature of major depression

When experiencing a major depressive episode, the individual often describes themselves as 'depressed, sad, hopeless, discouraged' or 'down in the dumps'. To be diagnosed as *major depression* this feeling must persist for most of the day, nearly every day, for at least two weeks, and be accompanied by 'clinically significant distress or impairment in social, occupational, or other important areas of functioning' (American Psychological Association, 1994: 320).

The causes of major depression

Our understanding of what causes major bouts of depression has progressed significantly over the past 20 years, and a knowledge of the biological factors that can contribute to depression has now been supplemented by a number of psychological theories of why people develop depressed ways of thinking.

Biological causes

There is some evidence for an inherited component to unipolar depression, but this appears to be significantly less important than in bipolar disorder (Kendler *et al.*, 1993), suggesting that psychological factors may play a more central role in the aetiology of major unipolar depression.

In addition, there is some evidence that the neuroendocrine system may also be involved in major depression, and depressed individuals do exhibit high levels of cortisol, which causes enlargement of the adrenal glands. High levels of cortisol in turn may lower the density of serotonin transmitters in the brain (Roy *et al.*, 1987), and low levels of serotonin have been hypothesised to cause depressed mood (McNeal and Cimbolic, 1986). Indeed, the effectiveness of many anti-depressant medications is dependent on them increasing levels of serotonin (and in some cases a related neurotransmitter, norepinephrine).

Psychological and cognitive factors

Beck's cognitive theory

Aaron Beck was probably the most influential of all theorists attempting, in the latter part of the twentieth century, to understand depression. He was arguably the first to suggest that depression was linked to a chronic way of thinking about the world, rather than about either fixation on a stage of psychodynamic development, as Freud had suggested, or simply the result of biological imbalances in the body.

Beck (1967; 1987) suggested that the thinking of depressed individuals was biased towards negative interpretations. In particular, their thinking was negatively biased in three specific areas. They had negative views of *themselves* (e.g. 'I am unattractive'), negative views of their *future* (e.g. 'I will never achieve anything'), and of the *world* (e.g. 'the world is a dangerous and unsupportive place'). These beliefs, known as the *negative triad*, form the basis of a negative cognitive schema through which the depressed individual views the world and interprets everything that happens to them. These negative schemata eventually generate self-fulfilling prophecies: the depressed individual interprets events negatively, fails to take the initiative and then inevitably experiences failure.

According to Beck's theory, depression is caused by a set of core dysfunctional cognitive beliefs about the self and the world, and so successful treatment requires that these beliefs should be changed. This

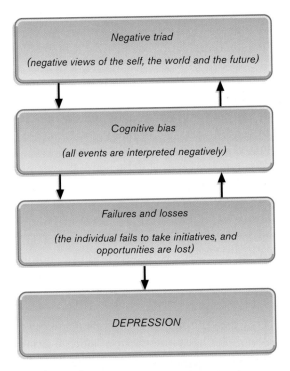

Figure 33.4 *Beck's negative schema: the self-fulfilling prophecy in cognitive models of depression*

has led Beck to develop his highly successful *cognitive therapy for depression*, which involves replacing negative beliefs with more positive ones.

Learned helplessness theory
During a person's lifetime they may experience a number of unavoidable and uncontrollable negative life events. These may include the sudden death of a close friend or relative, or being made redundant from a job. Seligman (1975) proposed that depression could be linked specifically to these kinds of experiences, and that they give rise to a 'cognitive set' that makes the individual learn to become 'helpless', lethargic and depressed. It is the perceived uncontrollability of these negative life events that is important, and leads the individual to the pessimistic belief that negative life events will happen whatever they do.

Seligman (1974) first derived this hypothesis from animal learning experiments in which dogs were first given unavoidable electric shocks and then subsequently taught to learn a simple response that would allow them to avoid the shocks. He found that dogs that were given these unavoidable electric shocks were subsequently unable to learn the avoidance response and simply lay down in the apparatus and 'quietly whined'.

However, while animal experiments on *learned helplessness* do appear to have a formalistic similarity to human depression, there are a number of reasons for believing that it is not a full or comprehensive account of depression. First, some studies with humans have suggested that prior experience with uncontrollable negative events may actually facilitate subsequent performance (Wortman and Brehm, 1975). Second, many depressed individuals see themselves as being responsible for their failures and

	Internal (personal)		External (environmental)	
Degree	stable	unstable	stable	unstable
Global	I lack intelligence	I am exhausted	These tests are unfair	It's an unlucky day
Specific	I lack mathematical ability	I am fed up with maths	The test is unfair	My maths test was numbered 13

Figure 33.5 *Attributional schema of depression: 'Why I failed my GCSE Maths'*

losses, yet someone who perceives themselves as helpless should not blame themselves for these events.

Attributional theories

There is a motivation in all of us to attempt to understand the events that befall us, and this is particularly true when we experience loss or failure. In psychological terms, how an individual attempts to explain his or her behaviour is known as *attribution*, and the way in which we attribute causes to events can have an important influence on our view of both the world and ourselves.

In particular, Abramson, Seligman and Teasdale (1978) suggested that the way in which we attribute causes to our losses and failures could be an important determinant of whether those events will make us depressed. They specified three features of the way we attribute causes to losses and failures. These are whether the reasons are (i) internal (personal) or external (environmentally caused), (ii) stable or unstable (i.e. is the reason likely to be around all the time, or was it just a one-off, freak occurrence?), and (iii) global or specific (i.e. is the reason likely to cause other failures or losses generally, or is it specific to that one failure?).

They argued that individuals are likely to become depressed if they attribute losses and failures to stable and global causes. This is because stable attributions would make the causes of negative life events long term, and the individual might therefore expect more of them. Global attributions, on the other hand, would imply that negative life events should be expected across a whole range of life activities. Finally, attributing losses and failures to internal, personal causes (e.g. 'I failed an exam because I am not very intelligent') also facilitates depression by generating low self-esteem.

Since this theory was formulated, good evidence has accumulated for a relationship between depression and attributional style (e.g. Metalsky, Haberstadt and Abramson, 1987), and attribution theory has provided the basis for more sophisticated models of depression, such as hopelessness theory (Abramson, Metalsky and Alloy, 1989).

Suicide and parasuicide

Suicide and parasuicide are included in this section because suicide attempts or suicidal thoughts form part of the diagnostic criteria for major depression. However, suicide attempts usually occur in the context of psychiatric illness generally (90 per cent of suicide victims have a psychological disorder at the time of death), and suicide is not just something that happens to individuals suffering depression.

Suicide has been found to be related to diagnoses of depression, schizophrenia, borderline personality disorder, panic disorder and alcoholism (e.g. Isometsa *et al.*, 1995). However, it is worth noting that the large majority of individuals with diagnosed psychological disorders do not commit or attempt to commit suicide (e.g. Frances, Fyer and Clarkin, 1986).

Risk factors for suicide

One of the best predictors of future suicide attempts is a history of at least one previous suicide attempt

Michael Hutchence, formerly lead singer of the Australian rock band INXS, committed suicide in his hotel room in November 1997. Such celebrity suicides are usually followed by a brief increase in suicide rates, which suggests that suicide has a sociological aspect to it, as well as a psychological one

TABLE 33.2

CHARACTERISTICS THAT DEFINE SUICIDE ATTEMPTERS AND COMPLETERS

Characteristics	Attempters	Completers
Gender	Mainly female	Mainly male
Age	Mainly young	Increased risk with age
Method	Pills, cutting	More violent (guns, jumping)
Common diagnoses	Mild depression, borderline personality disorder, schizophrenia	Major depression, alcoholism
Dominant affect	Depression with anger	Depression with hopelessness
Motivation	Change in situation, cry for help	Death, self-annihilation
Source: Fremouw *et al.*, 1990		

(Leon *et al.*, 1990). However, since only 20–30 per cent of those who attempt suicide have made a previous attempt, it is important to look at other *risk factors* too.

When risk factors are explored more generally, it is clear that suicide is a complex phenomenon with many potential causes, including social factors, psychiatric factors, psychological factors and familial factors. Recent studies suggest that factors such as subjective depression, hopelessness, suicidal ideation, aggression and impulsivity, a history of physical or sexual abuse, childhood abuse, alcoholism, smoking and drug abuse are all predictors of suicide attempts (Farber, Herbert and Reviere, 1996; Tanskanen *et al.*, 1998; Mann *et al.*, 1999).

Psychological factors in suicide and parasuicide

From a review of the known risk factors, it is clear that suicide and parasuicide have a variety of inter-related causes (Mann *et al.*, 1999). Suicide is seen by many as an attempt at problem-solving under severely stressful circumstances in which the individual experiences a deep sense of 'hopelessness'. The relatively poor social problem-solving skills possessed by individuals in such a state often means that they choose self-annihilation from a very narrow range of alternative solutions (Linehan and Shearin, 1988).

However, suicide is also a sociological as well as a psychological phenomenon, with media reports of suicide often triggering a significant increase in such cases (Bandura, 1986), and suicide rates differing significantly in different societies and cultures (Cutright and Fernquist, 2000).

Schizophrenia

The experience of schizophrenia

One of the most prevalent and severe of all the psychological disorders is schizophrenia. The term comes from the Greek *schizo* (split) and *phrene* (mind). The term *schizophrenia* was first used by the Swiss psychiatrist Eugen Bleuler (1857–1939) to describe the dramatic disturbances in thought and perception that are the main features of this disorder.

Section 7
Abnormal, Clinical and Health Psychology

Individuals suffering schizophrenia often cannot tell the difference between what is real and what is imaginary. They may experience *hallucinations* and *delusions*, and there are disturbances of the most basic functions, which render the individual incapable of feelings of individuality, uniqueness, self-worth and productivity.

The experience of schizophrenia will usually involve many of the following:

- delusions – strange beliefs that have little basis in reality (you may think you have special powers or that others are spying on you)
- hallucinations – hearing, seeing, feeling and smelling things that are not there (you may hear voices talking to you or about you)
- disordered thinking – your thoughts will jump between completely unrelated topics
- inappropriate moods or behaviours – you will do inappropriate things that are entirely out of context (such as taking your clothes off in the supermarket) or express emotions that are inappropriate (such as laughing at a funeral)
- lack of insight into the motives and feelings of others – you will fail to understand why others are doing the things they do
- flat affect – you will often appear withdrawn, fail to express any emotion and present a blank expression
- cognitive deficits – you will have difficulty concentrating, making decisions, planning or remembering things
- negative mood – you will feel chronically depressed and anxious.

Schizophrenia is relatively prevalent, with about half a million sufferers in the UK alone, and with around 1–2 per cent of individuals needing treatment for schizophrenia at some point in their lives. Around 75 per cent of individuals with schizophrenia develop the disorder between 16 and 25 years of age; onset is uncommon after 30 years and very rare after 40 years of age.

Diagnosing schizophrenia
There is no single specific symptom that is required for a diagnosis of schizophrenia but, as a group, people with schizophrenia do display an identifiable set of symptoms. The symptoms that are most commonly associated with the disorder are called *positive symptoms* (such as thought disorder and hallucinations); these characterise its main abnormalities. *Negative symptoms* are arguably less prevalent than positive symptoms, but represent the absence of normal behaviour, and include withdrawal from social contact, flat affect and lack of emotional expression.

DSM-IV describes schizophrenia as 'a disturbance that lasts for at least 6 months and includes at least 1 month of active-phase symptoms (i.e. two [or more] of the following: delusions, hallucinations, disorganized speech, grossly disorganized or catatonic behavior, negative symptoms)' (American Psychological Association, 1994: 273).

Schizophrenia can be divided into a number of different subtypes, depending on the combination and severity of the symptoms. These include

- disorganised schizophrenia
- catatonic schizophrenia
- paranoid schizophrenia
- undifferentiated schizophrenia
- residual schizophrenia.

Full descriptions of these subcategories are given in Table 33.3.

The aetiology of schizophrenia
There has always been some disagreement about whether the basic causes of schizophrenia are biological in nature (e.g. the result of imbalances in brain neurochemistry) or whether they are psychological (e.g. resulting from psychological disturbances caused, for example, by life stressors). However, research over the last 30 to 40 years has indicated that there is almost certainly an inherited component to schizophrenia that is accompanied by abnormalities in brain neurotransmitters, but that psychological factors can affect its severity, its duration and tendency to relapse, and that life stressors generally may play a role in triggering schizophrenia in vulnerable individuals.

TABLE 33.3

CATEGORIES OF SCHIZOPHRENIA IN DSM-IV

Category	Subcategory	Description
Disorganised schizophrenia		Disorganised speech, flat affect and shifts of emotion; behaviour is generally disorganised, neglects appearance and may be incontinent
Catatonic schizophrenia		Alternate between catatonic immobility and excitement; may echo back the speech of others, states of stupor
Paranoid schizophrenia	Grandiose delusions	Exaggerated sense of own importance, power, knowledge
	Delusional jealousy	Delusions of being persecuted or being spied on; belief that partner is being unfaithful
	Paranoia	Delusions of persecution generally
Supplemental types	Undifferentiated schizophrenia	Category reserved for those who meet the criteria for schizophrenia, but not for any of the above three categories
	Residual schizophrenia	Individual shows some signs of the disorder, but no longer meets the full criteria for schizophrenia

This has given rise to a *diathesis-stress model* of schizophrenia, which suggests that individuals have an inherited vulnerability to the disorder, but that it is only triggered when stressful life events are experienced at particular critical ages (e.g. during early adulthood). Given this view, the different theories and explanations outlined below are not necessarily competing ones (i.e. one is not necessarily correct and all the others wrong), but they complement each other by explaining different facets of the disorder at different levels of explanation.

Biological explanations

Schizophrenia as an inherited predisposition

While the majority of individuals diagnosed with schizophrenia do not have schizophrenic parents, there is clear evidence that the disorder does run in families. That schizophrenia has an inherited component has been supported by the results of *concordance studies*. If an individual is diagnosed as schizophrenic, Table 33.4 shows the probability with which a family member or relative will also develop the disorder. This shows that the probability the family member or relative will develop schizophrenia is dependent on how closely they are related – or, more specifically, how much genetic material the two share in common (Gottesman, McGuffin and Farmer, 1987; Cardno *et al.*, 1999).

These types of study are cited as evidence for an inherited component to schizophrenia, but note that the concordance rates for individuals that have an identical genetic make-up (i.e. identical or monozygotic twins) is far from 100 per cent, which it should be if schizophrenia is *entirely* inherited. This implies that factors other than pure genetic inheritance are involved, and suggests that what is inherited in schizophrenia is a vulnerability to the disorder. Other components may determine whether the *vulnerability factors* are translated into full-blown schizophrenia.

Biochemical factors

Cognition and behaviour are very much dependent on the efficient working of brain neurotransmitters, which enable effective communication between brain cells and functionally different parts of the brain itself (see Chapter 7). It is not surprising, therefore, that many researchers have suspected that the thought disorders, hallucinations and behaviour problems characteristic of schizophrenia may be caused by malfunctions in these brain neurotransmitters.

A link between schizophrenia and dysfunctional brain neurotransmitters was indicated by early experiments investigating the effect of amphetamines on both humans and animals. When taken in large enough doses and for lengthy periods, stimulants such as amphetamine produce what is known as amphetamine psychosis, which in humans shows symptoms very similar to paranoid schizophrenia, and in animals as repeatedly stereotyped behaviour patterns, also similar to many form of schizophrenic behaviour (Angrist *et al.*, 1974).

Overdoses of stimulants such as amphetamine have the effect of increasing dopamine activity in the brain, and it is this effect of amphetamines on dopamine levels that is one of the factors that led to the development of the *dopamine hypothesis* of schizophrenia.

The dopamine hypothesis assumes that schizophrenic symptoms result from high levels of dopamine in the brain. This hypothesis can take many forms, including an overabundance of dopamine itself, the increased sensitivity of dopamine receptors, or abnormal interactions between dopamine and other brain neurotransmitters (Van Kammen and Kelley, 1991).

Further support for the dopamine hypothesis comes from the fact that many successful anti-psychotic drugs (i.e. drugs that successfully treat the symptoms of disorders such as schizophrenia) appear to have their effect by reducing brain dopamine levels (e.g. drugs like thorazine, haldol and phenothiazine) (Davis, 1978).

Nevertheless, this is only part of the story and most recent research suggests that schizophrenic symptoms may be caused by complex interaction effects between dopamine and other transmitters such as glutamate (Carlsson *et al.*, 1999) and serotonin (Kapur and Remington, 1996; Megens and Kennis, 1996).

Psychological explanations

Neo-analytic perspectives

In the 1950s and 1960s, many explanations of schizophrenia were related to dysfunctional family dynamics, and championed by such contemporary psychodynamic theorists as Gregory Bateson and R. D. Laing. Prior to this, Fromm-Reichmann (1948) had developed the concept of the 'schizophrenogenic mother' – literally a mother who causes schizophrenia!

According to Fromm-Reichmann, schizophrenogenic mothers were cold, rejecting, distant and dominating. Such mothers demanded dependency and emotional expressions from their children, but simultaneously rejected displays of affection and even criticised the dependency that they implicitly attempted to foster in their children. This account suggests that when subjected to such conflicting messages and demands from a dominant close relative, the child withdraws and begins to lose

TABLE 33.4

CONCORDANCE RATES FOR INDIVIDUALS WITH SCHIZOPHRENIA

Relation to proband	% with schizophrenia
Spouse	1.00
Grandchildren	2.84
Nieces/nephews	2.65
Children	9.35
Siblings	7.30
Dizygotic (fraternal) twins	12.08
Monozygotic (identical) twins	44.30
Source: after Gottesman, McGuffin and Farmer, 1987	

touch with reality – at least in part as a way of avoiding the stresses and conflicts created by the mother.

A very similar neo-analytical account of schizophrenia is Bateson *et al.*'s (1956) *double-bind hypothesis*. This is where the individual is subjected within the family to contradictory messages from loved ones (e.g. a mother may both request displays of affection, such as a hug, and then reject them as being a sign of weakness). This leaves the individual in a no-win situation, in which they may then eventually withdraw from all social interaction.

Today, such neo-analytic accounts are considered as only tangential explanations of schizophrenia, and – while dysfunctional family dynamics may be a cause of the stressors that may trigger schizophrenia in vulnerable individuals – they are not considered to be substantial explanations of the disorder.

Expressed emotion (EE)

While it is not clear what role family dynamics might play in the development of schizophrenia, it is clear that dysfunctional family dynamics can have an important impact on the duration of symptoms and on recovery from the disorder. A study by Brown *et al.* (1966) investigated the family life of schizophrenics in London who had been discharged from hospital to live with their families. They found that three aspects of family interactions were important in determining relapse and whether the individual was readmitted to hospital. These were:

- the number of critical remarks made by family members
- the number of expressions of hostility towards the individual
- the number of comments indicating emotional over-involvement with the individual.

Together, these factors have been labelled as a variable called *expressed emotion (EE)*. High levels of EE have been shown to be related to high levels of relapse and to faster re-hospitalisation (Butzlaff and Hooley, 1998).

Most recent research tends to suggest that EE has these effects on relapse rates though a vicious cycle effect in which expressed emotion elicits higher levels of unusual thoughts in the sufferer, and these increased levels of unusual thoughts elicit increasing levels of expressed emotion in family members (Rosenfarb *et al.*, 1994).

Personality disorders

Classifying personality disorders (PDs)

As we saw in Chapter 29, personality is an elusive concept, and there are many different ways of categorising and measuring an individual's personality characteristics. Personality traits are considered to be relatively enduring features of the individual that determine how they perceive the world, and how they think about the world, themselves and others. Most people can be adaptable in the way they perceive the world and react to it, but it is when personality traits become inflexible, causing distress to the individual and to others, that they begin to constitute a psychological disorder.

Table 33.5 shows the DSM-IV general diagnostic criteria for a PD. The important features of these criteria include:

- behaviour that deviates from that normally expected in a particular culture or society
- inflexible behaviour patterns
- dysfunctional behaviour patterns that are stable and long lasting, and can be traced back at least to adolescence or early adulthood
- behaviour patterns that lead to distress or impairment in a number of important areas of functioning.

Personality disorders are among the most controversial diagnostic categories in clinical psychology, and there is considerable debate about whether functionally different PD categories exist in their own right or whether all PDs represent differences of degree rather than kind (e.g. Haslam, 2003). However, the enthusiasm for diagnosis in psychological and psychiatric practice has led to PDs being categorised for diagnostic purposes into a number of different clusters, depending on their main features.

There is insufficient space here to discuss all of these different PDs, but we will look more closely at one particular category – *anti-social personality disorder* – as a means to understanding how the behaviour and thinking of some individuals diagnosed with PDs can be so radically different from normal standards.

Anti-social personality disorder (ASPD)

Features of ASPD

The example given in Focus Point 33.7 shows how significantly the behaviour of individuals with ASPD can differ from what we consider to be normal standards of social behaviour, morality and remorse. The main features of DSM-IV that categorise ASPD are 'a pervasive disregard for and violation of the rights of others occurring since the age of 18 years', as indicated by at least three of the following:

- failure to conform to social and legal norms
- deceitfulness and impulsivity
- irritability and aggressiveness
- consistent irresponsibility (e.g. repeated failure to honour obligations)
- lack of remorse.

ASPD is also often associated with depressed mood, addiction, and dramatic or erratic anti-social behaviour.

ASPD was previously known as psychopathy (hence, the psychopathic personality), but in 1980 the definition of psychopathy was renamed ASPD and defined by radically different criteria. Prior to 1980, psychopathy was defined primarily by personality traits such as egocentricity, deceit, shallow affect, manipulativeness, selfishness and lack of empathy. Subsequently, however, ASPD has been defined mainly in terms of violations of social norms.

The argument for this shift in diagnostic criteria was that personality traits are difficult to measure, and that it is easier to agree on well-defined behaviours (such as breaking laws or aggressive behaviour) rather than the reasons why they might occur (such as selfishness, lack of empathy) (Widiger and Corbitt, 1995).

This shift in the diagnostic criteria for ASPD has meant that it has become very closely associated with criminal activity rather than being purely a psychological disorder requiring treatment.

TABLE 33.5

THE GENERAL DIAGNOSTIC CRITERIA FOR A PERSONALITY DISORDER

A   An enduring pattern of inner experience and behaviour that deviates markedly from the expectations of the individual's culture. This pattern is manifested in two (or more) of the following areas:

1. cognition (i.e. ways of perceiving and interpreting self, other people and events)
2. affectivity (i.e. the range, intensity, lability and appropriateness of emotional response)
3. interpersonal functioning
4. impulse control.

B.   The enduring pattern is inflexible and pervasive across a broad range of personal and social situations.

C.   The enduring pattern leads to clinically significant distress or impairment in social, occupational or other important areas of functioning.

D.   The pattern is stable and of long duration and its onset can be traced back to adolescence or early adulthood.

E.   The enduring pattern is not better accounted for as a manifestation or consequence of another mental disorder.

F.   The enduring pattern is not due to the direct physiological effects of a substance (e.g. a drug of abuse, a medication) or a general medical condition (e.g. head trauma).

Source: American Psychological Association, 1994: 633

ASPD is very common in criminal populations (Hare, 1996) and in 1999 the UK Home Office and the Department of Health published a white paper that introduced a new term: 'dangerous people with severe personality disorders (DSPD)'. This white paper discussed how individuals with ASPD should be managed.

Because of our profound lack of understanding of the aetiology of PDs generally, and the failure, to date, to find effective and long-term treatments for these disorders, the white paper concluded that individuals diagnosed with ASPD and who carry, in addition, a diagnosis of at least one other type of PD should not be released from prison or hospital if they represent a threat to the public, and may be required to be detained indefinitely.

Personality disorders, morality, criminal activity and politics

The example of DSPD (see Activity Box 33.2) raises a number of issues, including:

- the difficulty of defining and categorising some disorders on the basis of personality traits
- how the relationships between psychological dysfunction and moral and criminal behaviour can become blurred

FOCUS POINT 33.7

Anti-social personality disorder

People with antisocial personality [disorder] (ASPD) show little or no concern for the rights of others. ASPD is seen about three times as often in males as in females, and symptoms of conduct disorder must appear by the time the person is 15 years old if the person is to be diagnosed with ASPD, which cannot be diagnosed before the person is 18.

This diagnosis is sometimes given the names 'psychopathic personality' or 'sociopathic personality' or 'dyssocial personality'. People with the disorder are deceitful and manipulative; they may be charming and accomplished liars, what we think of as the typical 'con man' (or woman). In more extreme cases, they are overt criminals. In either case, they are often arrested, and many people with ASPD are in jail. They are both reckless and irresponsible. They show little ability to plan for or work toward remote goals. They rationalize hurting other people by saying that everyone does it, that the victim deserved it etc. Much of their antisocial behavior is directed toward obtaining the usual goals – money, sex and power. Thus their disorder lies not in their goals but in their means of obtaining them!

If the person with ASPD lives into his or her 40s, her or his aggressive and criminal behaviours are likely to decrease, along with the other symptoms of ASPD. Little is known about whether ASPD can be prevented by giving therapy to high risk children (who show early signs of conduct disorder or attention-deficit/hyperactivity disorder), but there are clear indications that bad parenting increases the probability that conduct disorder will lead to ASPD. It is likely that family and individual therapy for high-risk children would be a good bet for both the individual and society.

Source:
http://healthinmind.com/english/antisocl.htm

- how easy it is for treatment to become entwined with detention and prevention in a political context
- how little as clinical psychologists we know about the aetiology and treatment of DSM-IV categories such as ASPD.

Eating disorders

Eating disorders make up a relatively new category of psychological disorders, and reflect the fact that psychological or emotional problems can manifest themselves as severe disturbances in eating behaviour. The most prevalent of these disorders are *anorexia nervosa (AN)* and *bulimia nervosa (BN)*. These are normally considered as separate disorders, although both are associated with an obsessive fear of gaining weight and the individual's dissatisfaction with their own body shape (as compared, for example, with media-projected ideal images of body shapes). Prior to the 1960s, both AN and BN were relatively rare disorders, but have since become considerably more prevalent in western societies.

Diagnosing eating disorders

AN is characterised by a refusal to maintain a minimally reasonable body weight, and the DSM-IV criteria for the disorder include:

- refusal to maintain body weight at or above 85 per cent of normal weight for age and height
- intense fear of gaining weight or becoming fat
- disturbances in normal perception of one's body shape
- in postmenarcheal females, the absence of at least three consecutive menstrual cycles.

The modal age of onset is between 14 and 18 years, and rarely occurs in females over 40. Among females in late adolescence and early adulthood, around 0.5–1.0 per cent will meet the full criteria for AN.

ACTIVITY BOX 33.2

Can we identify those who will behave violently in the future?

In July 1999, the UK Home Office and the Department of Health published a paper entitled *Managing Dangerous People With Severe Personality Disorder*. This described proposals that the government hoped would be effective in reducing the risk posed by people with dangerous personality disorders.

They coined the term 'dangerous severe personality disorder' (DSPD), but this is not a term that has a medical, psychological or psychiatric definition, and many regard it as a political intervention designed to address public concerns about crime and violence. However, DSPD seems to cover individuals with a diagnosis of anti-social personality disorder (ASPD) who may present a further risk to the public following release from secure hospitals or prison.

The government white paper recommended that individuals with severe personality disorders should not be released from prison or hospital if they are considered a risk to the public, and that powers should be provided for the indefinite detention of people with DSPD. This has led to intense debate about the morality of detaining people purely on the basis of psychological diagnosis, and who have not been convicted of an offence.

It also raises questions about whether it is possible to identify individuals who will commit an offence or behave violently in the future, and whether it is possible successfully to treat people with DSPD. A study by Buchanan and Leese (2001) suggested that DSPD was so loosely defined that six people would have to be detained for a minimum of a year in order to prevent one from acting violently during that year – raising the issues of (i) whether it is moral to detain individuals against their will who will not commit an offence and have not been convicted of an offence in the past, and (ii) whether individuals should be detained purely on the basis of a psychological diagnosis.

You might find it useful to discuss such issues with fellow students in seminars or discussion groups.

In contrast, BN is characterised by recurrent episodes of binge eating (at least two episodes a week for a minimum of three months), inappropriate behaviours adopted to prevent weight gain (e.g. self-induced vomiting, misuse of laxatives, diuretics, excessive exercise etc.), and a tendency to consider body shape and weight as overly important in all areas of self-evaluation (i.e. 'If I am overweight, I am not worth knowing').

BN is found to be more prevalent than AN, with 1–3 per cent of adolescent females meeting DSM-IV criteria for it. Nevertheless, the incidence of both AN and BN has increased significantly over recent years, with a progression from less to more severe disturbances (Shisslak *et al.*, 1995; Wakeling, 1996). Treatments for eating disorders generally are still in their infancy, which means that about one in three sufferers continues to meet the diagnostic criteria for AN or BN for at least five years after initial diagnosis (Fairburn *et al.*, 2000). Sadly, mortality rates (including suicides) in AN and BN are still unacceptably high, ranging from 5–8 per cent (Herzog *et al.*, 2000; Steinhausen *et al.*, 2000).

The aetiology of eating disorders

Biological factors

Because disruptive and avoidant eating practices themselves cause many biological changes in the individual, it is often difficult to determine whether biological factors are the causes or just simply the effects of eating disorders.

However, there may be an inherited component in eating disorders, as evidenced by some family studies. These suggest that eating disorders aggregate in families, and some researchers have suggested that inherited factors may account for between 50 and 83 per cent of variance in such disorders (Spelt

FOCUS POINT 33.8

'Insecurity' (a poem written by an anorexia nervosa sufferer)

Being empty is my only security,
Being empty is my only immunity.
Rejecting food is a desire I cant fight,
Reinforcing hope to which now is far outta sight.

Stabilising my ability to stay in control,
Emptiness comforts me and makes me feel whole.
The coldness perishes my skin,
My blood feels cold against my bones to which I can feel within.

The desire to stay in control is unbearable,
The decisions impossible, confusing me terribly.
My feelings so strong penetrate my thoughts,
Tortured by temptations which I manage to resist, makes my family distraught.

The strength of my soul has disappeared,
Losing my insecurity is truly feared.
Depriving my body is the only thing that keeps me sane,
My head blocks out feelings but my stomach complains.

I ache inside, traumatized, my body feels pain,

For this thing controlling my life I have given a name.
Annie still remains part of my life, part of me,
Something to which I control and is my only security.

No matter how skinny I get I will always want to be thinner,
To me, unless I confront her she'll take over and be a winner.
I feel so alone, like no one understands me,
Please help me get rid of this so called thing (Annie).

My spirit has died, leaving Annie undefeated . . . alive,
Will I ever fight her off?
My body is screaming out for food, for warmth, for hope,
For now I cant cope,
If I don't give in Annie will win allowing her to control me forever.
I just cant bear to eat, so now am I defeated????

Emie

Source: http://www.edauk.com/poetry.htm (copyright)

and Meyer, 1995; Klump *et al.*, 2000). However, Polivy and Herman (2002) point out that such studies also seem to suggest that dysfunctional attitudes associated with eating are also inherited, and it is difficult to understand how genes might influence these attitudes.

At least some attempts to explain eating disorders are in terms of neuroendocrine dysfunction (e.g. hormonal dysfunction or life stressors causing hormonal dysfunction), and these accounts allude to the fact that appetite is very sensitive to changes in hormonal levels. The evidence for such causes is weak.

First, there is no real evidence for disturbances in the hypothalamus – the brain area responsible for influencing appetite – in individuals with eating disorder (Study Group on Anorexia Nervosa, 1995). Second, it has been suggested that AN and BN may be affected by brain serotonin levels. The argument here is that AN and BN sufferers have behavioural and cognitive traits that are very similar to obsessive-compulsive disorder (OCD) (Pryor *et al.*, 1995), and it is known that serotonin levels influence OCD symptoms. However, individuals who have recovered from AN do not show persistent anomalies in serotonin regulation (O'Dwyer *et al.*, 1996), suggesting that fluctuations in serotonin levels in AN may be an effect of the disorder rather than a cause of it.

The biopsychosocial model of eating disorders

It is very clear that a whole range of factors affects whether an individual will develop an eating disorder. These include cultural or socio-cultural factors (e.g. cultural values relating to thinness), family influences (e.g. the attitudes of mothers to eating), individual experiences (e.g. childhood abuse) and individual psychological characteristics (e.g. body dissatisfaction, perfectionism). These various influences suggest that the aetiology of eating disorders is complex and multicausal. The following sections describe just a few of these possible influences.

Media and peer pressure

It will not have escaped your notice that AN and BN are disorders restricted primarily to females (Striegel-Moore, 1997), and a number of researchers have suggested that these eating disorders are influenced by western media representations of idealised, slim physiques. While the media in western cultures are often blamed for broadcasting overly idealised female images, it is clear that most females in these cultures do not develop eating disorders. However, media projection of these ideals may foster feelings of body dissatisfaction that may be an essential precursor to eating disorders (Polivy and Herman, 2002).

As with the media, peer pressure is also seen as a contributor to eating disorders, with adolescent girls often under strong pressure to adopt stylised attitudes towards thinness, body shape and eating habits (Levine *et al.*, 1994; Stice, 1998).

Familial influences

Individuals that develop AN and BN often report living in family environments with some very specific negative characteristics. Such factors include parents who exhibit coercive parental control (Haworth-Hoeppner, 2000) and mothers who are generally critical, especially about their daughters' appearance (Vanfurth *et al.*, 1996; Hill and Franklin, 1998). The families of eating-disordered individuals also tend to be overly concerned with parenting (Shoebridge and Gowers, 2000), and intrusive, hostile and unresponsive to the individual's needs (Minuchin *et al.*, 1978).

Such family factors may well foster problems of identity and/or control that in turn may precipitate eating disorders (Polivy and Herman, 2002). However, as Polivy and Herman point out, most of these family studies are correlational in nature and do not imply causation. In addition, if such factors were found to be causally linked to eating disorders, we still do not know how they specifically trigger eating disorders. For example, why should such factors trigger an eating disorder rather than some other emotional or psychological disorder?

Life experience factors

Individuals with eating disorders report significantly more stressful life events than individuals without eating disorders (Raffi *et al.*, 2000), and individuals who have experienced childhood sexual abuse exhibit an increased tendency to develop BN (Everill and Waller, 1995). However, events such as these may cause eating disorders only indirectly, by influencing susceptibility to depression and anxiety, and other forms of psychopathology (Casper and Lyubomirsky, 1997).

For example, such events may cause severely distressing emotions that affect personal identity and lead to eating disorders (Rorty and Yager, 1996) or eating disorders may simply represent ways of coping with these life traumas (Troop, 1998). In fact, a popular account of eating disorders is that control over one's food intake, weight and body shape offers a form of control in a generally hostile and uncomforting world, and it is certainly the case that the need to *control* eating is a central feature of eating disorders generally (Fairburn *et al.*, 1999).

Psychological factors

Individuals with eating disorders have a number of psychological characteristics in common. They have low self-esteem (Fairburn *et al.*, 1997), high levels of negative affect generally (i.e. anxiety and depression) (Ball and Lee, 2000), high levels of perfectionism

(Garner *et al.*, 1983), and negative feelings about their body and their body shape (*body dissatisfaction (BD)*) (Stice, 2001).

Of all these factors, BD is the most interesting, and is seen as a direct causal factor in many theories of eating disorders (Polivy and Herman, 1987; Stice, 2001). BD is seen as directly causing bingeing in BN and dieting in AN, and most other socio-cultural, familial and experiential factors in eating disorders may have their effect through the way they influence BD.

However, there is still more to understanding eating disorders than this, because not everyone who has dissatisfaction with their body or body shape develops an eating disorder. There are clearly other factors that combine with BD to determine whether AN or BN will develop. These other factors have yet to be clearly identified.

Disorders of childhood and adolescence

The psychological experiences of children are by their very nature not as well developed as those of adults, so although children can suffer many of the psychological disorders we have already described in this chapter (such as phobias), basic emotions like anxiety and depression may manifest themselves in very different ways early in life.

Because children are less able than adults to communicate their psychological problems to us, childhood disorders have tended to be categorised in terms of whether symptoms are externalised or internalised. *Externalising disorders* are those that are manifested as disruptive within the child's external environment, or reflect behaviours that are considered to demonstrate a lack of control as defined by normal standards of conduct.

Externalising disorders include syndromes associated with behaviour problems, such as attention deficit hyperactivity disorder (ADHD), characterised by poor attention span and impulsivity, and *conduct disorders (CD)*, in which the child's behaviour is defiant and violates accepted societal norms.

Externalising disorders are the most commonly diagnosed of childhood psychological disorders. They account for around 50 per cent of problems in

children undergoing psychological treatment (Kazdin, 1995).

Internalising disorders, however, represent the child's experience of emotions such as anxiety and depression, and can reflect the difficulties that a child is having in understanding and expressing their emotions.

During the time they develop physically and psychologically, children are bound to experience events and circumstances that trigger either acute or chronic bouts of anxiety or depression. What is striking about these episodes is that even the best-intentioned of parents often fail to identify bouts of anxiety and depression in their children, and do not have a good insight into the levels of distress their offspring suffer (Kazdin, French and Unis, 1983).

Thankfully, most bouts of anxiety and depression relate to perfectly normal developmental processes and experiences, and these periods of fear, anxiety and depression often disappear as quickly as they developed – especially as the natural development of children leads them to confront and understand their fears (King *et al.*, 1989).

DSM-IV lists a large number of disorders that are usually first diagnosed in childhood, and it is not intended that we should cover them all here. The following sections pick out a couple of examples. The first is an externalising disorder, attention deficit disorder (ADD), and the second example reviews a list of factors that are thought to be important in the development of internalising disorders, such as childhood anxiety.

Attention deficit disorder (ADD)

ADD is primarily a behavioural disorder that is characterised by persistent difficulties with attention span, impulsivity and hyperactivity. A well-known and common subtype of ADD is *attention deficit hyperactivity disorder (ADHD)*. This affects approximately 3–6 per cent of the population, and the ratio of boys to girls with ADD is roughly three to one.

Up to 30 per cent of children with ADHD may have specific learning disabilities that include academic skills such as mathematics, spelling and reading (Casey, Rourke and DelDotto, 1996). Children diagnosed with ADD may not necessarily exhibit both poor attention and impulsivity/hyperactivity, but may manifest only one of these symptoms.

However, at times, all children are usually active, distractible and difficult to control, and care has to be taken to ensure that the ADD label is not misused.

FOCUS POINT 33.9

Attention deficit hyperactivity disorder (ADHD): understanding the problem

Mark, age 14, has more energy than most boys his age. But then, he's always been overly active. Starting at age 3, he was a human tornado, dashing around and disrupting everything in his path. At home, he darted from one activity to the next, leaving a trail of toys behind him. At meals, he upset dishes and chattered non-stop. He was reckless and impulsive, running into the street with oncoming cars, no matter how many times

his mother explained the danger or scolded him. In the playground, he seemed no wilder than the other kids. But his tendency to overreact – like hitting playmates simply for bumping in to him – had already gotten him into trouble several times. His parents didn't know what to do. Mark's doting grandparents reassured them, 'Boys will be boys. Don't worry, he'll grow out of it.' But he didn't.

Source: http://www.nimh.nih.gov/publicat/adhd.cfm#adhd2

The causes of ADD

Biological theories

A number of studies have suggested an inherited component to ADD. ADD does tend to run in families, and around 50 per cent of individuals diagnosed with ADD or ADHD are likely to have an offspring with the disorder (Biederman *et al.*, 1995). Like all other genetic accounts of psychological disorders, however, it is not clear what is inherited in ADD. Some possibilities include abnormalities in brain structure generally (Filipek *et al.*, 1997), specific dysfunction in the frontal lobes that may make the inhibition of behavioural responses more difficult (Barkley, 1997), and a specific genetic disorder (that produces generalised resistance to thyroid hormone) and is specific to ADHD but not other psychological disorders (Hauser *et al.*, 1993).

Some early accounts of ADHD did allude to the possibility that hyperactivity resulted from various biochemical imbalances caused by such factors as food additives (Feingold, 1975), refined sugar cane (Goyette and Conners, 1977), lead poisoning (Thompson *et al.*, 1989), and nicotine (Milberger *et al.*, 1996). While there is little evidence to suggest that food additives generally influence ADHD (Wolraich *et al.*, 1995), there is some support for the

theory that both the levels of lead in the blood and chronic exposure to nicotine increase hyperactivity (e.g. Fung and Lau, 1989).

Psychological theories

Psychological theories of ADD are still in their infancy, and many theories of the disorder tend to focus on how its behavioural component is established or how environmental factors interact with genetically determined characteristics. However, impulsivity has been attributed to the fact that children with ADD have been shown to lack the ability to delay gratification, and choose immediate small rewards over larger longer-term benefits (Mischel, 1983).

In addition, children with ADD may also lack control and show disruptive characteristics either because they fail to understand the motivations and intentions of others (Crick and Dodge, 1994) or their goals during individual activities are personal and sensation-seeking rather than socially appropriate (Melnick and Hinshaw, 1996).

In fact, some theories of the development of ADD are based on the possibility that the child's disruptive and impulsive behaviour may create a vicious cycle with peers and adults. Because the reactions of adults and peers to their disruptive behaviour is

TABLE 33.6

PREVALENCE OF SYMPTOMS IN ADHD AND NORMAL ADOLESCENTS

Symptom	ADHD	Normal
Fidgets	73.2	10.6
Difficulty remaining seated	60.2	3.0
Easily distracted	82.1	15.2
Difficulty waiting turn	48.0	4.5
Blurts out answers	65.0	10.6
Difficulty following instructions	83.7	12.1
Difficulty sustaining attention	79.7	16.7
Shifts from one uncompleted task to another	77.2	16.7
Difficulty playing quietly	39.8	7.6
Talks excessively	43.9	6.1
Interrupts others	65.9	10.6
Doesn't seem to listen	80.5	15.2
Loses things needed for tasks	62.6	12.1
Engages in physically dangerous activities	37.4	3.0
Source: adapted from Barkley *et al.*, 1990		

likely to become increasingly negative (e.g. parents of hyperactive children have more negative interactions with them than do parents of non-hyperactive children), this may incline children with ADD to become increasingly isolated and extreme in their behaviour (Whalen and Henker, 1985), or to develop less of a 'conscience' than would be expected during normal development (Kohlberg, 1985).

Childhood anxiety

The study and diagnosis of childhood psychopathology generally are fraught with difficulties. Children express their worries and emotions differently from adults. They often have poor self-knowledge and undeveloped communication skills that are poorly suited to transmitting their feelings, and their rapid physical and psychological development means that psychopathologies may represent quite normal, and fleeting, stages of development.

Categories of childhood anxiety

Prior to 1994 there was a specific diagnostic category for childhood anxiety, but that has since been removed, and DSM-IV views childhood anxiety disorders as 'downward extensions' of adult anxiety disorders. However, specific to childhood anxiety is *separation anxiety disorder (SAD)*, which is characterised by excessive worry about separation from major caregivers and may often take the form of school refusal.

Prevalence rates of SAD drop from around 4 per cent of prepubescent children to around 2.5 per cent of adolescent children (Benjamin *et al.*, 1990; Verhulst *et al.*, 1997), but this may be because the focus of anxieties and worries changes from childhood to adolescence – for example, while the frequency of separation anxiety decreases compared with childhood, the frequency of social phobia increases (King *et al.*, 1994).

Other specific anxiety disorders that are found in childhood and prepubescent children include specific phobias, GAD and OCD, although there are relatively few reports of panic disorder in children under the age of 11 (Anderson *et al.*, 1987).

Childhood anxiety and depression

As we indicated at the beginning of this section, mood disorders in children are often labelled as internalising disorders generally, and this has led to some difficulty in differentiating childhood anxiety from childhood depression. Indeed, some researchers have suggested that anxiety and depression cannot be differentiated in childhood, but form part of a larger construct of general negative affectivity (i.e. the child simply feels bad about things) (King *et al.*, 1991).

Others have hypothesised that anxiety and depression lie on a developmental continuum, and experiences of anxiety predate experiences of depression. Even so, when measures can differentiate effectively between childhood experiences of anxiety and depression, they are frequently found to co-

occur in a large proportion of children (Brady and Kendall, 1992).

Differentiating childhood anxiety from other disorders

Mood disorders are conceptualised as internalising disorders and behaviour disorders as externalising disorders (see page 592), and anxiety disordered children tend to be 'shy, inhibited, and are likely to demonstrate low risk behaviours, whereas behaviour-disordered children tend to be aggressive, uninhibited, and demonstrate high-risk behaviours' (Schniering *et al.*, 2000: 400).

Werry *et al.* (1987) identified three factors that differentiated anxious children from children with ADD and conduct disorders:

1 children with externalising disorders were more likely to be boys
2 anxious children are likely to have anxious parents
3 anxious children are more likely to show avoidant responses and to interpret ambiguous scenarios as threatening than are children with externalising disorders.

However, there still remain substantial difficulties in assessing and diagnosing childhood anxiety. Research suggests that children below eight to nine years of age are not able to provide accurate reports of their own emotions, and children take some time to develop self-awareness skills that allow them to identify and report their inner states (Stone and Lemanek, 1990).

It should also be remembered that fears and anxieties go through perfectly normal developmental stages in childhood, and so should not be considered as psychopathy. For example, in infancy, typical fears include strangers, loud noises and separation, but by adolescence these have changed into more abstract fears such as fear of evaluation and social situations (Gullone, 1996).

Learning outcomes

When you have completed this chapter you should be able to:

- describe the characteristics and diagnostic criteria of at least three or four important psychological disorders
- describe, compare and contrast at least two contemporary theories of the aetiology of (i) an anxiety disorder, (ii) a depressive disorder, (iii) schizophrenia and (iv) eating disorders
- distinguish between biological and psychological explanations of psychological disorders
- describe the relevance of a variety of research methodologies used in clinical psychology research, particularly questionnaire and experimental methodologies
- describe some of the important phenomenological characteristics of a range of psychological disorders.

Key Terms

Aetiology
Anorexia nervosa (AN)
Anti-social personality disorder
Anxiety
Anxiety disorder
Attention deficit hyperactivity disorder (ADHD)
Attribution
Bipolar disorder
Biological preparedness
Body dissatisfaction (BD)
Bulimia nervosa (BN)
Catastrophic misinterpretation of bodily sensations
Cognitive therapy for depression
Compulsive checking
Compulsive washing
Concordance studies

Conduct disorders (CD)
Delusions
Diathesis-stress models
Dopamine hypothesis (in schizophrenia)
Double-bind hypothesis
DSM-IV
Expressed emotion (EE)
Externalising disorders
Generalised anxiety disorder (GAD)
Hallucinations
Hyperventilation
Internalising disorders
Learned helplessness
Major depression
Mood disorders
Negative symptoms (in schizophrenia)
Negative triad
Non-associative fear acquisition
Obsessive-compulsive disorder (OCD)
Panic disorder
Personality disorders
Positive symptoms (in schizophrenia)
Post-traumatic stress disorder (PTSD)
Risk factors
Schizophrenia
Seasonal affective disorder (SAD)
Separation anxiety disorder (SAD)
Specific phobia
Suicide and parasuicide
Unwanted thoughts
Vulnerability factors
Worrying

Further reading

Davison, G. C. and Neale, J. M. (2001) *Abnormal Psychology* (8th edn). New York: Wiley & Sons.

Oltmanns, T. F. and Emery, R. E. (1998) *Abnormal Psychology* (2nd edn). New Jersey: Prentice Hall.

34

Treating psychological disorders

Route map of the chapter

This chapter describes a broad range of therapies and treatments that have been developed to treat psychological disorders and psychological problems. The treatments discussed cover biological treatments (such as drug-based treatments) and the major psychotherapies that have been developed from a range of different theoretical perspectives (e.g. psychoanalysis, humanistic therapies, behaviour therapies and cognitive therapies). Each section introduces the reader to the main principles on which these therapies are based. Finally, this chapter discusses methods for assessing the effectiveness of therapies.

Introduction

What is very apparent from the previous two chapters is that psychological disorders are both distressing and disruptive for the individual sufferer. Because of this, there is an immediate need to find ways to alleviate these conditions through therapy or treatment.

Those of you that have been through periods of psychological distress – such as an acute period of depression or anxiety – will be aware that many different kinds of things can make you feel better. Just talking to a friend or family member about the condition, trying to distract yourself (e.g. retail therapy!), taking mild forms of medication prescribed by your GP . . . or simply popping bubble wrap. These are all potentially therapeutic in that they may alleviate (temporarily or permanently) the distress caused by the symptoms of the psychopathology.

This need to alleviate the distress and disruption to daily living caused by psychological disorders has led to the development of a very wide range of treatments and therapies. Some have established themselves as treatments of choice for many disorders (e.g. behaviour therapy and cognitive therapy), others are based on attempting to treat physical or medical correlates of the disorder (e.g. ECT, psychosurgery), and others have stood the test of time as well-developed therapeutic paradigms still advocated by many psychotherapists (e.g. psychoanalysis).

This chapter will describe some of the more important and prevalent of the treatment paradigms developed to alleviate psychological disorders and the principles on which they are based, and then finally describe how we go about effectively evaluating the success of various therapies.

Biological treatments

In Chapter 32 we discussed how some of the earliest attempts to explain psychopathology looked for underlying medical causes. For example, in the nineteenth century some forms of mental illness were traced to physical illnesses such as syphilis. Discovering that some causes of mental illness had biological or medical origins quite obviously led to attempts to explain and then treat mental illness by medical means.

However, while there are some psychological disorders that do seem to have biological causes, there are very many others where a physical cause cannot easily be identified, and that appear to be caused by dysfunctional 'ways of thinking' rather than direct biological dysfunction (see Chapter 33). Because of this, biological therapies have developed into a mixed bag of treatments:

- some do appear to deal with the direct causes of the disorder (e.g. pharmacological treatments for schizophrenia)
- some provide relief from the distress and emotional discomfort caused by the disorder (e.g. anti-depressant and anxiolytic drugs that provide relief from depression and anxiety)
- some are used because they appear to have beneficial effects on symptoms even though it is

far from clear why they might have these effects (e.g. electroconvulsive therapy (ECT)).

Pharmacotherapies
One of the most important developments in the treatment of psychological disorders has been the growth in our understanding of the use of drug-based treatments for a variety of important disorders. These include the use of *anti-psychotic drugs* to treat schizophrenic symptoms, and *anti-depressants* and *anxiolytic drugs* to treat mood and anxiety disorders.

TABLE 34.1

SOME REGULARLY USED DRUG MEDICATIONS FOR PSYCHOLOGICAL DISORDERS

Primary therapeutic use	Drug class	Generic or chemical name	Trade name
Anti-depressants	MAO inhibitors	Phenelzine Tranylcypromine	Nardil Parnate
	Tricyclics	Clomipramine Imipramine	Anafranil Tofanil
	Selective serotonin reuptake inhibitors (SSRIs)	Fluoxetine Paroxetine Sertaline	Prozac Paxil Zoloft
Anti-psychotics	Butyrophenones	Haloperidol	Haldol
	Phenothiazines	Chlorpromazine Thioradazine	Thorazine Mellaril
Anxiolytics (anxiety-reducing medications)	Benzodiazepines	Alprazolam Chlordiazepoxide Diazepam Lorazepam	Xanax Librium Valium Activan

Drug treatment of schizophrenia
Drug therapies for schizophrenia have revolutionised the way that schizophrenia sufferers are treated and cared for. The use of effective anti-psychotic drugs became common in the 1960s and 1970s, and this

had the effect of drastically reducing the number of schizophrenic sufferers that need long-term institutionalised care. It has also led to such sufferers reaching a level of normal functioning that permits care to take place in the community. Prior to the

1980s, it was estimated that two out of three schizophrenia sufferers would spend most of their lives in a psychiatric institution; beyond the 1980s the average length of stay is down to as little as two months (Lamb, 1984).

Anti-psychotics (such as chlorpromazine and haloperidol) have their effects by blocking dopamine receptors, and help to reduce the high levels of dopamine in the brains of schizophrenics (see Chapter 33, pages 583–584). This not only reduces the major positive symptoms (such as thought disorder and hallucinations), but can also reduce the major negative symptoms (such as social withdrawal). However, while these drugs have had a remarkable effect on reducing schizophrenic symptoms and, as a consequence, reducing the burden of institutionalised care for schizophrenics, there are some negative factors to consider. For example, most anti-psychotics do have some undesirable side-effects for some people (such as blurred vision, muscle spasms, blood disorders and cardiac problems), and these side-effects can cause relapse or make sufferers unwilling to take their medication on a regular basis (which needs constant monitoring if the individual is being cared for in the community).

The fact that the success of anti-psychotics has led to more sufferers being treated in the community requires that these suffers be properly monitored and supported in that environment, and this increases the importance of the role of the community psychiatric nurse in longer-term treatment and rehabilitation.

Drug treatment of depression

Drug treatments for depression were first successfully developed in the 1960s and the drugs used were called *tricyclic anti-depressants* (because of their chemical structure). These drugs have their effect by increasing the amount of norepinephrine and serotonin available for synaptic transmission.

Other anti-depressants introduced during this period were *monoamine oxidase inhibitors (MAOIs)*, such as phenelzine and tranylcypromine. MAOIs are effective for some people with major depression who do not respond to other anti-depressants. They are

also effective for the treatment of panic disorder and bipolar depression.

Most recently, we have seen the development of the first 'designer drugs' for depression, and these include fluoxetine (Prozac), sertraline (Zoloft), paroxetine (Paxil) and citalopram (Celexa). These newer drugs are collectively known as *selective serotonin reuptake inhibitors (SSRIs)*, because they selectively affect the uptake of only one neurotransmitter – usually serotonin. SSRIs can reduce the symptoms of depression as rapidly as tricyclic anti-depressants, and have far fewer side-effects.

SSRIs – especially *Prozac* – have often been viewed as the miracle drugs for depression. However, they can cause some side-effects, such as a loss of sexual desire in up to 30 per cent of users (Montgomery, 1995), and are perhaps at the point where they are becoming over-prescribed by GPs, who may be failing to look further for more structured psychological treatment for their depressed patients (Olfson and Klerman, 1993).

Drug treatment of anxiety

There are a number of psychological disorders that are characterised by chronic, high levels of anxiety. The more prevalent of these include clinically diagnosable specific phobias, panic disorder, generalised anxiety disorder (GAD), obsessive-compulsive disorder (OCD) and post-traumatic stress disorder (PTSD).

The symptoms of these disorders can usually be treated with anxiolytics (tranquillisers) such as the *benzodiazepines* (which include the well-known tranquilliser Valium). They have their effect by increasing the level of the neurotransmitter GABA at synapses in the brain. Benzodiazepines are usually prescribed for only short periods because they can encourage dependence if taken over a longer period, and can also be abused if available in large doses.

It is important to be aware that anxiolytics will usually offer only symptom relief, and do not address the psychological and cognitive factors that may be maintaining the anxiety. These latter factors can be specific to different anxiety disorders (see Chapter

597

33, pages 561–576) and probably need attention through structured psychotherapy.

Electroconvulsive therapy (ECT)

There are a number of other therapies that can be considered as examples of biological treatments (others include forms of psychosurgery), but one of the most controversial is *electroconvulsive therapy (ECT)*. ECT is where an electric current is passed very briefly (usually for 0.5 secs) between two electrodes attached to the head of the patient. It was dramatically illustrated in the film *One Flew Over the Cuckoo's Nest* starring Jack Nicholson.

ECT induces a convulsive seizure similar to an epileptic fit and is a treatment still regularly practised in psychiatric hospitals throughout the world, although only when most other forms of therapy have failed. Individuals given ECT treatment are usually severely depressed, and may have some residual schizophrenic or manic symptoms. Although its use is still controversial (Johnstone, 2003), there is some evidence that it is successful in alleviating the symptoms of depression for as many as 80 per cent of those patients that have failed to respond to drug treatment alone (Andreasen and Black, 1996). This beneficial effect may, however, be short-lived and limited to as little as four weeks (Breggin, 1997), and the relapse rate is high (Royal College of Psychiatrists, 1995).

It is still very unclear how ECT has the therapeutic effects it does, but it is known to produce widespread effects on brain neurotransmitters generally, and on the secretion of hormones that may influence depressed mood. Other researchers have argued that the short-term beneficial effects of ECT are nothing more than would be expected following *any* trauma to the brain – immediate symptoms of confusion, headache and nausea followed by a period of emotional shallowness, denial and artificial euphoria that may last for a few weeks (Breggin, 1997).

Psychotherapies

Psychotherapy is the general term used for any form of treatment that attempts to address the psychological factors (rather than biological factors) that may be associated with a psychological disorder.

Jack Nicholson was subjected to ECT treatment in the film One Flew Over the Cuckoo's Nest

Many explanations of psychopathology argue that psychological problems are caused by the nature of the life experiences that an individual has, which in turn may have shaped dysfunctional 'ways of thinking' that act to maintain and foster psychological disorders, or developed inappropriate responses through unusual learning experiences.

Psychotherapies usually attempt to address psychopathology by:

- providing the individual with insight into the life experiences that may have given rise to their condition (e.g. psychoanalysis)
- dealing directly with the dysfunctional ways of thinking that are maintaining the disorder (e.g. cognitive behaviour therapy)
- correcting the 'faulty' learning that gave rise to inappropriate responses (e.g. behaviour therapy).

There are very many different forms of psychotherapy, some more accepted than others, and some have been developed to address very specific disorders. Not all psychotherapists have training in psychology, but many have skills in a closely related profession, such as counselling.

Psychoanalysis

Psychoanalysis was developed by Sigmund Freud in the early part of the twentieth century, and was a revolutionary way of understanding emotions and attempting to help people with their psychological problems. Central to psychoanalysis is the assumption that individuals are often unaware of the factors that contribute to their psychological condition, and that such unconscious factors may be the source of psychological conflict. These inner conflicts can then manifest themselves as recognisable psychological symptoms, troubling personality traits, difficulties in relationships, or disturbances in mood and self-esteem.

Psychoanalysis uses a number of techniques to attempt to demonstrate to the individual what these unconscious factors are, what experiences in the individual's past may be responsible for them, and how the individual might deal better with them.

Psychoanalysis and psychopathology

Before discussing the methods that psychoanalysis uses to help alleviate psychological distress, it is useful to understand how psychoanalysts believe that psychological distress is caused. Freud's theories of personality structure and *stages of development* are important here (see also Chapter 2, pages 15–18).

For Freud, there were three main components to an individual's psychological make-up.

1   Freud believed all individuals are born with reflexes and instincts that are called the *libido.* The libido contains an energy force that drives the *id*, and the id is that part of the individual's psyche that unashamedly attempts to satisfy instinctive and biological needs.
2   As the individual child begins to develop and interact with its environment, he or she begins to develop a sense of self that develops into the psychic structure called the *ego*. Inevitably, the functions of the id and ego begin to conflict and the ego will attempt to suppress some of the needs required by the id.
3   Finally, extensive interaction with the world enables the individual to internalise principles related to social norms and values, and this

develops into the third psychic structure, the *superego*. Conflict between the needs of the id and the values inherent in the ego and superego eventually lead to the repression of instincts into the 'unconscious', which leads to the development of guilt and the psychological distress associated with that. Eventually the ego develops *defence mechanisms* whose function is to deal with the conflict by keeping them in the unconscious. Such defence mechanisms include repression, denial and rationalisation.

Freud also believed that, as children, individuals have to negotiate four different stages of development, and each stage centres on a different theme. These stages are the oral stage, the anal stage, the Oedipal or Electra stage, and the latency stage (see Chapter 2, pages 15–18). If the child is able successfully to negotiate these four stages, then a psychologically healthy individual results. However, if conflicts within stages are not properly resolved, then potentially problematic personality traits may develop (e.g. someone who does not properly negotiate the anal stage may develop personality characteristics such as stubbornness or obsessive orderliness).

Techniques of psychoanalysis

The aim of psychoanalysis is to bring any unconscious conflicts into awareness, to help the individual understand the source of these conflicts (perhaps by identifying past experiences or discussing the nature of important relationships), and to help the individual towards a sense of control over behaviour, feelings and attitudes.

There are a number of basic techniques used by psychoanalysts to achieve these goals.

1   *Free association*: here the client is encouraged to verbalise all thoughts, feelings and images that come to mind while the analyst is normally seated behind them. This process functions to bring into awareness any unconscious conflicts or associations between thoughts and feelings.
2   *Transference*: here the analyst is used as a target for emotional responses, and the client behaves

TELL US ABOUT YOUR MOTHER

Serious Freud Squad

or feels towards the analyst as they would have behaved or felt towards an important person in their lives. This allows the client to achieve understanding of their feelings by acting out any feelings or neuroses they have towards that person.

3 *Dream analysis*: Freud believed that unconscious conflicts often revealed themselves in symbolic forms in dreams, and this made the analysis of dream content an important means of accessing unconscious beliefs and conflicts.

4 *Interpretation*: finally, the skilled psychoanalyst has to interpret information from all of the above sources, and help the client to identify important underlying conflicts and to develop ways of dealing with these conflicts.

An appraisal of psychoanalysis

Psychoanalysis represents a quest for self-knowledge, where an individual's problems are viewed in the context of the whole person and, in particular, any conflicts they may have repressed. It can be an effective treatment for many people with moderate to severe anxiety or depression-based problems, especially when other, more conventional, therapies have failed.

However, psychoanalysis does put significant emphasis on sexual drives and the motivations of children in understanding psychopathology – a view that is not necessarily consistent with our current knowledge of many disorders.

Finally, psychoanalysis is a long-term form of therapy, in that the individual is required to attend therapy sessions on a regular basis, often for many years. Therapy is not considered to be complete until all problems and conflicts have been resolved, which makes an objective evaluation of its effectiveness almost impossible to conduct (therapy is only considered to be finished when the client is better!). For this reason, psychoanalysis has come to be considered more as a process of self-understanding than a form of treatment for specific psychological disorders.

Humanistic therapies

Throughout the twentieth century, many psychotherapists felt that psychological therapy was becoming too focused on psychological and behavioural mechanisms, or on psychological structures (such as personality), and was losing sight of both the feelings of the individual and the individual themselves. As a consequence, a number of what are called 'humanistic' therapies developed. The most prominent of these are *client-centred therapy* (Rogers, 1961) and Gestalt therapy (Perls, 1969).

These therapies had a number of factors in common:

- they were *holistic therapies*, in that they emphasised the need to consider the 'whole' person, and not just those 'bits' of the person that manifest psychopathology
- therapy should be seen as a way of enabling the individual to make their own decisions and to solve their own problems rather than imposing structured treatments or ways of thinking on the individual
- humanistic therapies espouse the need for the therapist–client relationship to be a genuine reciprocal and empathetic one, rather than the limited skilled professional–referred client

---

FOCUS POINT 34.1

When to use brief humanistic and existential therapies

Humanistic and existential therapies can be useful at all stages of recovery in creating a foundation of respect for clients and mutual acceptance of the significance of their experiences.

Client-centred therapy, for example, can be used immediately to establish rapport and to clarify issues throughout the session.

Existential therapy can be used most effectively when a client is able to access emotional experiences or when obstacles must be overcome to facilitate a client's entry into or continuation of recovery (e.g. to get someone who insists on remaining helpless to accept responsibility).

Narrative therapy may be used to help the client conceptualise treatment as an opportunity to assume authorship and begin a 'new chapter' in life.

Gestalt approaches can also be used throughout therapy to facilitate a genuine encounter with the therapist and the client's own experience.

Transpersonal therapy can enhance spiritual development by focusing on the intangible aspects of human experience and awareness of unrealised spiritual capacity. These approaches increase self-awareness, which promotes self-esteem and allows for more client responsibility, thus giving the client a sense of control and the opportunity to make choices.

Source: http://www.aa2.org/philosophy/briefxistential.htm

---

relationship that exists in many forms of psychological therapy

• increasing emotional awareness is a critical factor in alleviating psychological distress, and is necessary before the client can begin to resolve their life problems.

There is an ever-growing number of psychotherapies that espouse these basic principles (existential therapies, primal therapy, narrative therapy, transpersonal therapy), but lack of space dictates that we can discuss only one in detail here.

Client-centred therapy

Most humanistic therapies focus on the individual's immediate conscious experience, and client-centred therapy is no exception. Crucial to client-centred therapy is the creation of a therapeutic climate that allows the client to progress from a state of rigid self-perception to one that encourages them to become independent, self-directed and to pursue self-growth.

For Carl Rogers (1902–87), *empathy* ('putting yourself in someone else's shoes') was the central important feature of any therapist–client relationship, and it is this ability that is essential in guiding the client towards resolving their own life problems. Empathy has at least two main components in this context:

1 an ability to understand and experience the client's own feelings and personal meanings
2 a willingness to demonstrate *unconditional positive regard* for the client.

This latter feature involves valuing the client for who they are and refraining from judging them.

Another important feature of client-centred therapy is that it is not directive. The therapist acts primarily as an understanding listener who assists the client by offering advice only when asked. The overriding goal is to develop the client through empathy, congruence and unconditional positive regard to a point where they are successful in experiencing and accepting themselves, and are able to resolve their own conflicts and difficulties.

In much the same way that psychoanalysis has evolved, client-centred therapy has developed not just as a therapy, but also as a process for fostering personal self-growth. Like psychoanalysis, it may not be especially effective with severe psychopathologies – such as schizophrenia and some severe forms of anxiety and depression – and because many of the central concepts are very loosely defined (e.g. empathy, congruence, unconditional positive regard) it is difficult to assess objectively its effectiveness as a therapy.

Behaviour therapies

In the 1940s and 1950s there was a growing dissatisfaction with the medical or disease model of psychopathology, and also with the unscientific approaches to psychopathology being generated by many psychodynamic theories. These dissatisfactions led psychologists to look towards the developing area of experimental psychology for objective knowledge that might be used to inform treatment and therapy.

The body of knowledge that psychologists turned to was that of conditioning (see Chapter 8), and this gave rise to the development of what came to be known as *behaviour therapies*. First, such therapies stressed the need to treat symptoms of psychopathology as bona fide behavioural problems rather than the mere symptoms of some other, hidden underlying cause. Second, at the time, many psychologists believed that numerous psychological disorders were the result of what was called *faulty learning*, and that symptoms were acquired through simple conditioning processes.

For example, it was believed that anxiety symptoms could be acquired through classical conditioning – e.g. a phobia might be acquired through the pairing of the phobic stimulus with a traumatic event (Watson and Rayner, 1920) (see Figure 33.1), and that behavioural problems might be acquired through processes of operant conditioning – for example, bizarre and inappropriate behaviours might be acquired because they have been reinforced or rewarded in the past (see Chapter 32, Focus Point 32.1). The reasoning here was that, if psychological problems were acquired through learning, then we could use conditioning principles to develop therapies that effectively helped the individual to 'unlearn' those problematic associations.

Two distinctive strands of behaviour therapy developed from these assumptions. The first was a set of therapies based on the principles of classical conditioning. The second was based on principles of operant conditioning. While the former group of therapies continues to be known as behaviour therapy, the latter group has also come to be known as *behaviour modification* or *behaviour analysis*.

Therapies based on classical conditioning principles

Behaviour therapy effectively originates from the writings of Wolpe (1958), who argued that many forms of emotional disorder could be treated using the classical conditioning principle of *extinction*. The assumption was that if emotional problems such as anxiety disorders were learned through classical conditioning, they could be 'unlearned' by disrupting the association between the anxiety-provoking cues or situations and the threat or traumatic outcomes they have become associated with (see Chapter 8, page 126, for details of extinction procedures).

In practice, this means ensuring that the anxiety-provoking stimulus, event or situation (the conditioned stimulus, CS) is experienced in the absence of accompanying trauma (the unconditioned stimulus, UCS) so that the former no longer comes to evoke the latter.

The most famous behaviour therapy techniques to apply extinction principles are *flooding, counterconditioning* and *systematic desensitisation*. These have, collectively, come to be known as *exposure therapies*, because they are all based on the need to expose the client to the events and situations that evoke their distress and anxiety – so that they can learn that these are no longer threatening.

Wolpe (1958) also introduced the principle of *reciprocal inhibition*, in which an emotional response is eliminated not just by extinguishing the relationship between the CS and the UCS, but also by attaching a response to the CS that is incompatible with anxiety (e.g. relaxation). It has often been assumed that these techniques can only be applied to the treatment of emotional problems such as anxiety disorders, but they have in fact been applied to a range of disorders including addictive disorders (O'Leary and Wilson, 1975), marital conflict (Jacobson and Weiss, 1978) and sexual dysfunction (Mathews *et al.*, 1976).

Flooding

This is an extinction-based therapy that involves therapist-led prolonged exposure to the emotionally provoking event or situation. Flooding can be conducted *in vivo* (through direct exposure to the anxiety-provoking events or stimuli) or *in vitro* (by asking the individual to imagine extended contact with these events and stimuli).

Exposure to the anxiety-provoking event or situation needs to be prolonged and therapist-led (to avoid excessive distress on first confronting these events and situations) – brief exposures can actually make the anxiety worse! So curing your sibling of spider phobia won't be achieved by the abrupt action of putting a spider in their clothing; exposure needs to be structured and prolonged (usually at least 30 minutes or more per structured exposure session).

Counterconditioning

This is a technique also based on extinction, but where the therapist attempts to attach a response to the anxiety-provoking events and situations that is inconsistent with anxiety. Usually, the counterconditioned response is some form of relaxation – people cannot be both anxious and relaxed at the same time.

Systematic desensitisation

This is arguably the most effective, widely used and successful of the behaviour therapies based on classical conditioning, and it is still used today as a treatment of choice for many anxiety-based problems (especially phobias).

In systematic desensitisation, the therapist helps the client to construct a ranked list of events that cause increasing fear or anxiety (known as the *fear hierarchy*). The client is then trained in the use of relaxation techniques. Therapy proceeds as the

---

ACTIVITY BOX 34.1

Creating a fear hierarchy for one of your own fears or phobias

This activity provides a step-by-step guide to how to create a fear hierarchy. Read through this example – related to fear of flying – and then use these steps to create a fear hierarchy for one of your own fears or phobias.

Overview

The fear hierarchy will contain situations or scenes involving some aspect of making a flight. These situations will most likely be those you have actually experienced, but they can also be situations that you fear experiencing even though they have never actually happened to you. For example, you may want to include the item 'The airplane has to turn around and return to the airport in an emergency' even though this has never actually happened to you. The important point is that items included in an anxiety hierarchy describe situations that produce varying levels of anxiety, some more worrisome than others – this is what hierarchy means, and the details of this will be presented below.

You should describe the items on your anxiety hierarchy in sufficient detail to enable you to imagine each one vividly. It might be sufficient to say 'Standing in line at the ticket counter', but saying, 'Standing in a long line at the crowded ticket counter, with nothing to do but wait to get my luggage checked', might be more graphic. Remember that items are most effective if they can help you experience the event in your imagination, not just describe it.

Creating your anxiety hierarchy

You should attempt to create about 16 or 17 situations at the beginning. Most people tend to discard some items in the sorting process, so you can expect to end up with about 10 to 15 items in your final hierarchy. To aid in sorting the items, write each one on a separate index card.

As was mentioned earlier, the situations or scenes in your hierarchy should represent a fairly well-spaced progression of anxiety. The best way to achieve this goal is first to grade the anxiety of each item by assigning it a number on a scale from 0 to 100, where 100 is the highest level of anxiety imaginable and 0 is no anxiety (complete relaxation). Write this number on the back of the index card for the item being graded. At this point, you need not worry about how well spaced the items are; just give each item the first number grade that 'pops into your head'.

When each item has an anxiety grade, your next step will be to sort the cards into five piles. Each pile will represent a different category of anxiety, as follows:

Pile	Anxiety grade
Low anxiety	1–19
Medium–low anxiety	20–39
Medium anxiety	40–59
Medium–high anxiety	60–79
High anxiety	80–100

The goal here is to end up with at least two items in each pile. If this happens, congratulations. If not, you will have to go back and re-evaluate some items or create some new items. When you have finished, combine all the cards into one pile that is ordered from lowest to highest anxiety. This is your personal fear of flying anxiety hierarchy. Set the cards aside for one day.

It helps to check the accuracy of your ordering by shuffling the cards in the next day or so. Without looking at the grades on the back of the cards, re-order them. Then check the grades to see if your second ordering is the same as the first. If not, make some adjustments. You don't have to waste a lot of time with this; just try to get an order that feels right and that represents a fairly smooth progression from low to high anxiety.

Sample fear of flying anxiety hierarchy

The following is a sample hierarchy to help you develop your own hierarchy. Your items should, of course, be more fully detailed. Also note that any item's relative anxiety level does not necessarily relate to its temporal sequence.

- Packing luggage
- Making reservations
- Driving to the airport
- Realising you have to make a flight
- Checking in
- Boarding the plane
- Waiting for boarding
- Taxiing
- In-flight service
- Moving around the cabin
- Climbing to cruising altitude
- Descending
- Waiting for departure
- Taking off
- Landing
- Turbulence

Source: http://www.guidetopsychology.com/sysden.htm

individual is exposed to the anxiety-provoking situation at the bottom of the hierarchy and learns to relax in that situation. Once the client feels quite relaxed with this, therapy then moves on to relaxation in the presence of the next highest-ranked situation on the fear hierarchy.

Thus the technique involves extinction of anxiety through *graduated exposure* and counterconditioning of a relaxation response that is incompatible with anxiety. The success of systematic desensitisation has been shown to be dependent on the principles of extinction and exposure (Kazdin and Wilcoxon, 1976), and has also been shown to be more effective than both no-treatment conditions and almost every other type of psychotherapy with which it has been compared (Rachman and Wilson, 1980).

Aversion therapy

This is rather different from the therapies discussed above because *aversion therapy* attempts to condition an aversion to a stimulus or event to which the individual is inappropriately attracted. For example, aversion therapy is most widely used in the treatment of addictive behaviours such as alcoholism, and in these procedures the taste of alcohol is paired with aversive outcomes (e.g. sickness-inducing drugs) in order to condition an aversive reaction to alcohol (e.g. Voegtlin and Lemere, 1942; Lemere and Voegtlin, 1950).

Since the 1950s and 1960s, this type of procedure has been used to treat a wide variety of problems, including inappropriate or distressing sexual activities (e.g. Feldman and MacCulloch, 1965), drug and alcohol addiction (McRae, Budney and Brady, 2003), and even obsessions and compulsions associated with anxiety (Lam and Steketee, 2001). Aversion therapy was popularised in the 1971 cult film *A Clockwork Orange*, where the lead character's excessive violence was treated by 'conditioning' him to vomit whenever he saw a violent act.

However, while aversion therapy for some problems (e.g. alcoholism) has been shown to have some therapeutic gains when used in conjunction with broader community support programmes (Azrin, 1976), addictive responses are often very resistant to this form of treatment, and there is little evidence that aversion therapy alone has anything other than short-lived effects (e.g. Wilson, 1978).

Therapies based on operant conditioning principles

The principles of operant conditioning offer some rather different approaches to treatment and therapy than do those of classical conditioning. Operant conditioning is concerned with influencing the frequency of a behaviour by manipulating the consequences of that behaviour. For example, if a behaviour is followed by rewarding or reinforcing consequences, it will *increase* in frequency. If it is followed by punishing or negative consequences, it will *decrease* in frequency (see Chapter 8, pages 130–131).

Operant conditioning principles have mainly been used in therapy in three specific ways:

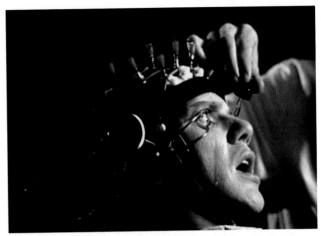

Alex, the leading character in the 1971 film A Clockwork Orange undergoes aversion therapy to cure his violent tendencies

1. to try to understand what rewarding or reinforcing factors might be maintaining an inappropriate or maladaptive behaviour – this is known as *functional analysis* (e.g. trying to understand what factors might be maintaining challenging or aggressive behaviours in individuals with severe learning difficulties)
2. to use reinforcers and rewards to try and establish new or appropriate behaviours (e.g. to establish self-help or social behaviours in individuals who have become withdrawn because of their psychopathology)
3. to use negative or punishing consequences to try and suppress or eliminate problematic behaviours in need of urgent attention (e.g. to eliminate or suppress self-injurious behaviours in individuals with serious learning difficulties).

Functional analysis

This is where the therapist attempts to identify consistencies between problematic behaviours and their consequences – especially to try and discover whether there might be a consistent event or consequence that appears to be maintaining the behaviour by rewarding it. For example, self-injurious or challenging behaviours may be maintained by a range of reinforcing consequences, such as the attention the behaviour may attract or the sensory stimulation it provides. Identifying the nature of the consequence allows the therapist to disrupt the reinforcement contingency and, if necessary, reduce the frequency of that behaviour through extinction (Wacker *et al.*, 1990; Mazaleski *et al.*, 1993).

Functional analysis has been adopted across a range of clinical settings, and has been successfully applied to controlling aggressive/challenging behaviour (O'Reilly, 1995), tantrums (Darby *et al.*, 1992), ADHD (Northrup *et al.*, 1995), depression (Ferster, 1985), anorexia nervosa (Slade, 1982) and self-injurious behaviour (Iwata *et al.*, 1985).

Token economy schemes

One of the enduring advantages of operant reinforcement is that it can be readily and easily adapted to *group therapy* and group management schemes. The first systematic group management procedure in therapeutic use was the *token economy* (Ayllon and Azrin, 1968). In the psychiatric setting, a token economy involves participants receiving tokens (a generalised reinforcer) for engaging in behaviours defined by the programme. At a later time these tokens can be exchanged for a variety of reinforcing or desired items (e.g. access to the hospital grounds or a visit to the cinema).

In psychiatric care, the token economy was first used to foster pro-social or self-help behaviours (e.g. combing hair, bathing, brushing teeth) in previously withdrawn patients. Programmes such as this help to establish behaviours that encourage socialisation in withdrawn individuals, and foster behaviours that are likely to be required in life outside the psychiatric institution. A number of studies have indicated that token economies can have significant therapeutic gains, and patients involved in such schemes earn discharge from the institution sooner than patients not on such a scheme (Hofmeister *et al.*, 1979; Paul and Lentz, 1977).

However, despite their positive effects, the use of token economies in clinical settings is in sharp decline because of a wide variety of factors, which are discussed more fully in Focus Point 34.2.

Response shaping

Behaviours can only be reinforced after they have been performed, so this makes it quite difficult to encourage new behaviours that are not already occurring at a reasonable frequency. This may be a particular problem with withdrawn individuals or individuals with restricted behavioural repertoires (such as those with severe learning difficulties). However, the technique of *response shaping* by successive approximations is a way around this problem.

Here, the therapist will first reinforce a behaviour that does occur quite frequently and is an approximation to the specific target response. Once this general response is established, reinforcement is given only for closer and closer approximations to the target response.

An early study by Isaacs, Thomas and Goldiamond (1960) demonstrates this method. They attempted to reinstate verbal behaviour in a psychiatric in-patient who had been mute for 19 years. In this example the target behaviour was talking, but the researchers might well have waited many years before the patient made any verbal response that could be reinforced. However, they broke down the target behaviour so that it could be achieved by reinforcing a series of approximations to verbal behaviour (using chewing gum as a reward). They started by rewarding the patient for moving his eyes towards the gum, then for moving his mouth and lips. When this was established, they rewarded him only for making audible sounds, and in the next stage the experimenters repeatedly asked him to say 'gum'.

After six weeks of regular sessions, the patient then spontaneously said 'gum please!', and this subsequently led on to the patient verbally responding to questions from the researchers.

Behavioural self-control

The use of operant conditioning principles for behaviour change purposes does not have to be overseen or administered by a therapist. The principles are quite clear and can be used by any individual to control and manage their own behaviour. This personal use of operant conditioning principles has come to be known as *behavioural self-*

FOCUS POINT 34.2

The decline of the token economy

Despite its apparent therapeutic advantages, recent surveys indicate that the use of token economies in clinical settings is in serious decline (Hall and Baker, 1973; Boudewyns, Fry and Nightengale, 1986; Corrigan, 1995). A number of reasons have been put forward for this decline.

- There are legal and ethical issues that need to be considered. This is especially so when decisions have to be made about who will participate in token economies, for how long, and what will be made available as positive reinforcers. Legislation over the past 25 years has sought to protect patients' rights, and treatment staff are severely constrained with regard to the use of more basic items as reinforcers (Glynn, 1990), especially now that patients have a legal right to their own personal property, humane treatment including comfortable bed, chair, bedside table, nutritious meals, cheerful furnishings and so on.
- One of the major challenges for token economies has been maintenance and generalisation of therapeutic effects. To the extent that patients can obtain reinforcers outside the programme and avoid punishment by exiting from it, the therapeutic benefit of token economies becomes less useful (Glynn, 1990). It is true that some studies have shown

that behaviours targeted for improvement in a token economy scheme return to low baseline levels outside the programme (e.g. Ayllon and Azrin, 1968; Walker and Buckley, 1968). However, there are other studies that have shown positive effects of maintenance and generalisation (Banzett, Liberman and Moore, 1984). Nevertheless, it should be pointed out that generalisation is not a passive process, and clinicians must actively build into the programme strategies that transfer positive effects to settings outside the treatment scheme (Stokes and Baer, 1977; Stokes and Osnes, 1988).

- Some other proponents of the token economy have argued that its decline has been the result of unfounded misconceptions about the nature and efficacy of such programmes (e.g. Corrigan, 1995). These include such misconceptions as token economies not being therapeutically effective, their benefits do not generalise, they do not provide individualised treatment, they are abusive and coercive, and they are not practical to implement in the context of present-day attempts to treat patients in the community. Corrigan (1995) argues that these are all unfounded, and that the token economy remains an important and valuable tool for the management of patients and staff in treatment settings.

Source: adapted from Davey, 1998

control (e.g. Thoresen and Mahoney, 1974), and has since been developed into multifaceted behavioural programmes to deal with a variety of personal problems, including addiction, habits, obsessions and other behavioural problems (Stuart and Davis, 1972; Lutzker and Martin, 1981).

A programme developed by Stuart (1967) provides a good example of a multifaceted behavioural self-control scheme designed to

address obesity by controlling behaviours contributing to overeating. The main elements of this programme were:

- recording the time and quantity of food consumption (self-observation)
- weighing in before each meal and before bedtime (helping the individual to discriminate how eating might have contributed to weight gain)

- removal of food from all places in the house except the kitchen (so that only the kitchen comes to act as a cue for eating)
- pairing eating with no other activity that might make eating enjoyable, and so reinforce it (e.g. eating should *not* occur while watching an enjoyable TV programme)
- setting a weight loss goal of one to two pounds per week (setting clearly attainable goals)
- slowing down the pace of eating (defining appropriate responses)
- substituting other activities for between-meal eating (programming acceptable competing responses).

These principles are relatively easy to apply to your own behaviour. Applications Box 34.1 provides some suggestions as to how you might develop your own behavioural self-control programme to promote an activity such as studying.

APPLICATIONS BOX 34.1

Developing your own behavioural self-control programme: promoting studying behaviour

How often do you sit down to write an essay or a lab report or do some reading for a seminar, only for your attention to begin to wander almost immediately? After just a few minutes, you are up making a cup of coffee to distract yourself from the difficulty of concentrating on the task in hand.

Below are some examples of how you might apply behavioural self-control principles to help you concentrate more easily when you are studying. All of these are based on operant or classical conditioning.

When you have read these principles, sit down and write a behavioural self-control programme for your own studying behaviour that takes into account your own learning environment and your personal circumstances.

Reinforcement/punishment

Always try to find some way of rewarding yourself whenever you have achieved a study goal, and make sure that you take this reward immediately on completion of the task. It may be something as simple as a refreshing cup of coffee, a chat with friends, a trip to the cinema or just listening to your favourite music CD.

Response-reinforcer contiguity/contingency

While many people claim to be aware of the principle of operant reinforcement, most rarely apply it consistently. For instance, you may decide to spend two hours in the library writing an essay and then reward yourself for this effort by going off for a coffee and a chat with friends. However, you may find that you are working so well that you continue writing until your concentration and motivation begin to wane – then you go off for coffee.

With all the good intentions in the world, what has happened is that you have inadvertently reinforced behaviours consistent with falling levels of concentration and motivation rather than the two hours' focused work that preceded this. Always ensure that the things you like doing (i.e. rewards) occur *immediately after* the behaviour you want to foster (i.e. concentrating).

Stimulus control (environmental planning)

If you study in an environment that also controls other behaviours, then you will inevitably find it difficult to concentrate solely on studying. For example, if you try and write an essay in your kitchen, that could be very difficult, because a kitchen will also have come to elicit other competing behaviours such as eating, putting on the kettle, and so on. To study effectively, you need to do this in an environment that does not control alternatives to studying (a library is a good example).

Response shaping and the setting of attainable targets

All behavioural programmes set attainment targets of some kind, and it is extremely important that any subgoals in the programme are attainable. For example, if studying you must set yourself a goal that you are certain you can achieve (e.g. reading a textbook for 15 minutes rather than six hours!). It is critical that goals are attainable: if they are not met because they are over-ambitious, then this is tantamount to punishing the effort that was expended in attempting to meet the goal.

Response discrimination/feedback

Can you recall accurately how many hours you have spent studying in the last week? Probably not, and this is because most people have poor recall of the frequency of the behaviours they are trying to develop or reinforce. This being the case, it is perhaps not surprising that you may have difficulty controlling your studying – because you are unable accurately to discriminate it or to remember it.

One way in which this can be overcome is by including in the programme a period of self-observation, where you record or chart information relevant to studying behaviour (e.g. how many hours you studied each day, what you achieved and where you studied). This will give you an idea of the baseline frequency with which you study and will allow you to set some future goals that can increase this baseline level.

Cognitive therapy

Over the latter part of the twentieth century, one of the most impressive developments in our understanding of psychological disorders has been our evolving insight into the cognitive factors that play important roles in causing and maintaining psychopathology.

For example, some psychopathologies are caused by dysfunctional 'ways of thinking', either about the self or the world (e.g. in major depression). In other cases, psychopathologies are characterised by dysfunctional ways of processing and interpreting incoming information. For instance, many anxiety disorders are characterised by a bias towards processing threatening or anxiety-relevant information (e.g. generalised anxiety disorder) or towards interpreting ambiguous information negatively (e.g. panic disorder). In both cases these biases act to develop and maintain anxiety.

If such cognitive factors are maintaining psychopathology, then developing treatments (*cognitive therapy*) that try to address and change these dysfunctional cognitive features is important.

Early examples of cognitive therapy

Ellis's rational-emotive therapy (RET)

How people construe themselves, their life and the world is likely to be a major determinant of their feelings. Albert Ellis developed one of the first cognitive therapies to address these factors. In particular, he believed that people carry around with them a set of implicit assumptions that determines how they judge themselves and others, and that many of these implicit assumptions may be irrational and cause emotional distress. For example, two irrational beliefs are (i) demanding perfection from oneself and from others, and (ii) expecting approval from others for everything one does. Clearly, there will be many occasions when these goals are not met, and this will cause anxiety, depression and emotional discomfort.

Rational-emotive therapy (RET) attempts to challenge these irrational beliefs and to persuade the individual to set more attainable life goals. As such, RET is a good example of a group of therapies that attempt to change a set of core beliefs about the world that may be dysfunctional (i.e. either fallacious or a source of conflict and emotional distress). However, make no mistake about it, changing an individual's core beliefs, which have been developed and refined over a period of many years, is no easy thing.

This is why highly structured cognitive therapies are required for successful treatment, and these therapies will normally go through a process of challenging existing dysfunctional beliefs, replacing these with more rational beliefs, and then getting the individual to test out this new set of beliefs in structured behavioural exercises.

Beck's cognitive therapy

Aaron Beck's cognitive theory of depression (Beck, 1976) is outlined in detail in Chapter 33 (pages 578–579), and from this theory he developed a cognitive therapy for depression. Beck argues that depression results when the individual develops a set of cognitive schemata (or beliefs) that bias the individual towards negative interpretations of the self, the world and the future, and any therapy for depression must therefore address these schemata, deconstruct them and replace them with more rational schemata that do not always lead to negative interpretations.

Beck's cognitive therapy does this by engaging the depressed individual in an objective assessment of their beliefs, and requires them to provide evidence for their biased views of the world. This enables the individual to perceive his or her existing schemata as biased, irrational and overgeneralised.

There is accumulating evidence that Beck's cognitive therapy is effective for a range of disorders, not just depression. These include panic disorder, generalised anxiety disorder, social phobia, chronic pain, irritable bowel syndrome and bulimia nervosa (Chambless *et al.*, 1996). Evidence is also available which suggests that when cognitive therapy is effective, it is so because it changes the individual's cognitions and beliefs (Hollon *et al.*, 1996).

Contemporary cognitive therapies

Chapter 33 reviews a range of theories of the aetiology of psychological disorders, and it is clear from these discussions that we have progressed to identifying a range of cognitive factors that are important in psychopathology. Often, these cognitive factors are specific to individual disorders.

For example, in generalised anxiety disorder, sufferers develop a set of dysfunctional beliefs about worrying being a necessary activity to indulge in (page 570); in panic disorder, individuals have a bias towards catastrophically misinterpreting bodily sensations; in obsessive-compulsive disorder, the individual holds a set of dysfunctional beliefs about being responsible for things that happen and this causes them to become obsessive about some of their activities. Because some cognitive factors are particular to specific disorders, this has meant that we can develop cognitive therapies that are geared towards quite individual disorders and their specific cognitive features.

Focus Point 34.3 gives some examples of how a cognitive therapist would approach the treatment of panic disorder. This example, taken from Adrian Wells's book, *Cognitive Therapy of Anxiety Disorders*, shows how the therapist attempts to challenge the client's catastrophic interpretation of their symptoms and bodily sensations, and then tries to provide counter-evidence about the causes and meaning of bodily sensations.

Group therapies

Therapy can also be undertaken in a group and not just on a one-to-one therapist–client basis. Group therapy can be useful:

* when a group of individuals share similar problems or psychopathologies (e.g. self-help groups), or
* when there is a need to treat an individual in the presence of others who might have a role in influencing the psychopathology (e.g. family therapy).

Group therapies can have a number of advantages, especially when individuals:

* may need to work out their problems in the presence of others (e.g. in the case of emotional problems relating to relationships, feelings of isolation, loneliness and rejection)
* may need comfort and support from others
* may acquire therapeutic benefit from observing and watching others.

There are now many different types of group therapy (Bloch and Crouch, 1987), and these include experiential groups and encounter groups (which

FOCUS POINT 34.3

Cognitive therapy for panic disorder

The following transcript gives an example of how a cognitive therapist (T) would try to challenge the catastrophic beliefs of a panic disorder sufferer (P) who believes that signs of an impending panic attack are signals for an imminent heart attack.

P: When I'm panicking, it's terrible I can feel my heart pounding; it's so bad I think it could burst through my chest.

T: What thoughts go through your mind when your heart is pounding like that?

P: Well I'll tell you what I think; it's so bad that I think I'm going to have a heart attack. It can't be good for your heart beating like that.

T: So you're concerned that anxiety can damage your heart or cause a heart attack.

P: Yes, it must do you some damage. You hear of people dropping down dead from heart attacks caused by stress.

T: Do you think more people have stress in their lives than die of heart attacks?

P: Yes, I suppose so.

T: How can that be if stress causes heart attacks?

P: Well, I suppose it doesn't always cause problems. Maybe it does only in some people.

T: Yes, that's right; stress can cause some problems in some people. It tends to be people who have something wrong with their hearts in the first place. But stress is not necessarily the same as sudden anxiety or panic. When you panic your body releases adrenalin which causes the heart to speed up and your body to work faster. It's a way of preparing you to deal better with danger. If adrenalin damaged the heart or body, how would people have evolved from dangerous primitive times? Wouldn't we all have been wiped out?

P: Yes, I suppose so.

T: So maybe panic itself doesn't cause heart attacks, there has to be something physically wrong for that to happen. When people have had heart attacks they are often given an injection of adrenalin directly into the heart in order to help start it again. Do you think they would do that if it damaged the heart even more?

P: No I'm sure they wouldn't.

T: So, how much do you now believe that anxiety and panic will damage your heart?

Source: Wells, 1997: 123–4

---

encourage therapy and self-growth through disclosure and interaction), and self-help groups (which bring together people who share a common problem, in an attempt to share information and to help and support each other, such as Alcoholics Anonymous).

Family therapy is a specific form of group therapy that is becoming increasingly helpful as a means of dealing with psychopathology that may result from the relationship dynamics within the family (Dallos and Draper, 2002). Family therapy has a number of purposes:

- it helps to improve communications between members of the family – especially where communication between individuals might be the cause of psychopathology in one or more family members
- it can resolve specific conflicts – for example, between adolescents and their parents
- it may apply systems theory (attempting to understand the family as a social system) to treatment by trying to understand the complex relationships and alliances that exist between family members, and then attempting to remould

these relationships into those expected in a well-functioning family (the latter step may usually involve ensuring that the primary relationship in the family – between the two parents – is strong and functional) (Minuchin, 1985).

Focus Point 34.4 gives an example of the kind of case history that family therapy has to deal with.

Assessing the effectiveness of therapies

All of the therapies and treatments we have discussed in the previous sections have at least some degree of intuitive plausibility as treatments for psychological problems. Nevertheless, how do we assess how effective a therapy is?

This is not as simple as it sounds, because we have to decide on what constitutes a therapeutic gain (i.e. on what particular measures are we expecting to see improvement?), we often have to try and compare the efficacy of therapies that have quite different assumptions about what 'successful therapy' is (e.g. cognitive therapies would expect to see some significant improvement after a few months, whereas psychoanalytic and humanistic therapies are seen as life-long processes promoting self-growth).

However, there are some good reasons for wanting to try to assess objectively how successful therapies are:

- psychological disorders are distressing to the individual, and we have an obligation to try to find ways of alleviating this distress rapidly and effectively
- some therapies may have short-term gains, but are significantly less effective over the longer term and may leave the individual open to relapse – we need to be sure that therapies have lasting therapeutic effects
- individuals with psychological problems are a very vulnerable group of people, and we need to ensure that they are not exploited financially and psychologically by what is a growing industry of essentially bogus therapies with shallow – but often beguiling – rationales, and little or no medium-term therapeutic benefit.

What are the criteria for judging a therapy as successful?

On what basis do therapists decide whether their treatments are successful? Focus Point 34.5 provides an interesting example of this that was described by Davey (2002). In effect, it seems that the therapist he describes in this example assumed that her treatment was being effective because no one ever returned to complain about it!

There are many reasons why individuals may not complain, and the client in this example is quite happy to return for more therapy even though her first session was unsuccessful. Such is the enmeshed relationship between some therapists and their clients that they may well satisfy the needs of each other (the client helps the therapist earn a living, and the therapist provides the client with some care and attention) without necessarily achieving any substantial therapeutic gain for the client.

The moral of the story in Focus Point 34.5 is that a client saying they are satisfied with the outcome of the therapy does not mean either that any objective therapeutic gain has been achieved or, if some therapeutic gain was achieved, that it was due explicitly to the type of therapy that was used. It is issues such as these that make assessing the efficacy of therapies difficult. We will discuss some of the factors that can confound these assessments in the next section.

Spontaneous remission

Just because some people get better after therapy does not necessarily mean that the therapy has been effective. The famous British psychologist Hans Eysenck argued that many people who have psychological disorders will simply get better anyway over a period of time, even without therapy (Eysenck, 1961). This is known as *spontaneous remission*, and the current estimate is that around 30 per cent of those diagnosed with anxiety- and depression-based disorders will get better without structured treatment (Jacobson and Christenson, 1996).

So if we are assessing the effectiveness of a therapy, we would expect to see improvement rates *significantly greater* than 30 per cent in order to take into account the fact that many of those undertaking

FOCUS POINT 34.4

A family therapy case history: the Sinclairs

Sandy, aged 17, had been suffering with anorexia for over two years of such severity as to require two brief stays in hospital. She was living with her parents and older brother. Two older brothers had left home.

Though all were invited, only Sandy and her parents attended for family therapy, which took place at intervals of three to four weeks over 18 months. The sessions, with the full permission of all of the family were of one-hour's length with the therapist in the room with them and a team observing from behind a one-way mirror. The team usually joined the family and the therapist after 40–50 minutes and held a reflective discussion with each other in front of the family in which they shared their ideas about the family's problems, ideas, understandings and feelings. The family were then invited to comment and then held a closing discussion with the therapist when the team had left the room. The core idea of family therapy is that problems such as anorexia are not simply, or predominantly, individual but are related to wider stresses and distress the family is experiencing. In addition, it is recognised that the sense of failure and blame associated with conditions such as anorexia can paralyse family members' ability to help each other.

Initially each member of the family was asked to describe what they saw as the main problems, and invited to offer their explanations of the causes of the problem.

This was followed by a focus on two broad areas: (i) the impact of the problems on each of them and their relationships with each other and, in turn, (ii) the influence that they could exert on the nature of the problems. Initially the parents indicated that the distress caused by Sandy's anorexia was the main problem for all of them. However, it quickly emerged that the parents had very different ideas about what caused the

problems and what to do to help. Mr Sinclair had a medical and practical view and Mrs Sinclair a more relational and emotional one. Through the use of a genogram (family tree) it was revealed that both parents had themselves had very negative experiences of being parented that made it hard for them to know how to comfort and help their children. It also transpired that their marriage was in serious difficulty. Sandy commented that her parents' conflicts upset her and she felt caught in the middle in trying to meet the emotional needs of both of her lonely parents. In effect she felt like she was a therapist for her own family. (Interestingly, she has gone on to study psychology at university.)

The therapist and the reflecting team discussed the possible impacts that the parents' own experiences may have made on how they acted towards Sandy. Along with this there were discussions of a variety of related issues, such as the pressure on young women to conform to stereotypes of thinness and starving as an attempt to exert control in one's life. Some marital work was done separately with the parents to look at their childhoods, their marriage, their own needs and how these impacted on Sandy. Mrs Sinclair in particular felt she had failed as a mother but was relieved to hear that the team did not see it in this way. Sandy gained considerable insight into how the family dynamics across the generations had impacted on her and her parents. She became independent enough to go to university but initially struggled, as did her parents to separate. Some struggle with her weight continues but she is confident that she will cope in the long-term.

Source: case history provided by Dr Rudi Dallos, Consultant Clinical Psychologist (Somerset Partnership Trust) and Director of Research, Clinical Psychology Teaching Unit, University of Plymouth

FOCUS POINT 34.5

Stop smoking in one session

As I was passing a local 'holistic' health clinic, I noticed a sign outside which – in large letters – implored 'STOP SMOKING IN ONE SESSION' (which session – surely not the first one?!). Having interests in both clinical and health psychology areas, I was intrigued to find out more. As it turns out, a friend of mine had just recently visited the clinic and had received a single one-hour session of hypnotherapy in an attempt to stop smoking – cost £50. Knowing the literature on psychological treatments for smoking and how difficult it is to achieve abstinence, I decided to find out a little more about these treatment claims. I e-mailed the hypnotherapists who were offering services at the clinic, asking them if stopping smoking in one session of hypnotherapy was achievable, and what their success rates were like. I did get a reply from one of the practitioners, who had worked as a hypnotherapist for seven years. She replied: 'I did not do follow-up calls as I thought this would be intrusive so therefore I did not have stats on my success rates. However, I knew I had a high success rate as people referred others to me and came back to me for help on other issues.' Interestingly, my friend who had attended the clinic was smoking regularly again within three days of the hypnotherapy session, and – despite having long discussions with me about the validity of the treatment and its lack of success – said she was thinking of attending again (this time in relation to other aspects of her life) because the hypnotherapist had been so caring, understanding and interested in her problems!

Source: Davey, 2002: 499

the therapy would have spontaneously got better anyway.

Placebo effects

If an anxiety sufferer is given a sugar pill but is told that it is an anxiolytic medication, they often report significant improvements in their anxiety symptoms. This suggests that individuals will often get better because they *expect* to get better – even though the actual treatment they have been given is effectively useless (Paul, 1966). This is known as the *placebo effect* (Paul, 1966).

Thus, it may be the case that many psychological therapies have beneficial effects because the client *expects* them to work – and not because they are therapies that are effective in tackling the factors maintaining the psychological problems. Unfortunately, the positive gains produced by placebo effects are short-lived, and comparative studies of placebo effects with actual structured psychotherapies strongly suggest that structured psychotherapies lead to greater improvement than placebo control conditions (Andrews and Harvey, 1981; Robinson *et al.*, 1990).

Unstructured attention, understanding and caring

We know too that people with psychological problems also show some improvement in symptoms when they can simply talk abut their problems in an unstructured way with either a professional therapist or a friend or relative (Lambert *et al.*, 1986). This suggests that many forms of social support may have a therapeutic effect in and of themselves (Borkovec and Costello, 1993), and this factor must be taken into account when judging how effective a structured therapy is.

One of the important things that we want to find out about therapies is not just whether they are effective in making people better, but whether they make people better specifically because of the principles they contain. (For example, does psychoanalysis work because of the psychodynamic principles on which that form of therapy is based?)

Determining whether a therapy works because of the principles it contains is known as assessing its *internal validity*.

Methods of assessing the effectiveness of therapies

Randomised controlled trials (RCT)

The current methodology of choice for assessing the effectiveness of therapies is the *randomised controlled trial (RCT)* (Barker *et al.*, 2002: 153–9). This procedure compares the effectiveness of the therapy being assessed (across a range of objective measures) with a variety of control conditions, and with other forms of therapy and treatment (if necessary). Participants in the study are assigned *randomly* to each of these conditions.

Apart from the therapy being assessed, the control conditions used in RCT are those that will control for the kinds of effects described above. These will include:

- a no-treatment or a 'waiting list' control group of participants who will receive no treatment (to control for the effects of spontaneous remission); this condition is often difficult to achieve because of the ethical issues involved in withholding treatment from clinically distressed individuals
- an expectancy and relationship control group, to control for placebo effects and for the beneficial effects of contact with a therapist
- a comparative treatment group, in which the original therapy can be compared with a plausible alternative therapy that is known to have beneficial effects.

For the original therapy to be deemed effective and possess internal validity, participants receiving that therapy must show greater improvement than those in either the no-treatment or the expectancy and relationship control conditions, and at least equivalent improvement to those in the comparative treatment group.

While providing an objective way of assessing the effectiveness of therapies, RCTs do have a number of practical limitations:

ACTIVITY BOX 34.2

Evaluating your new 'fairy tale' therapy for anxiety and insomnia

Imagine that you have just had a great idea: that reading fairy tales every night before you go to bed will relax you and help you sleep better. You are so excited by this idea, and are so sure that it will be successful that you recommend it to all of your friends as a sure way of alleviating anxiety and encouraging restful sleep. You decide to construct an elaborate – but plausible – theory about how your fairy tale therapy works. Your theory argues that 'fairy tale' therapy alleviates anxiety because thinking about imaginary stories helps people to realise that most of their own problems are really quite insubstantial.

After trying it for a couple of weeks, some of your friends tell you that reading fairy tales seems no better than having a mug of cocoa at bedtime. They are not convinced that reading fairy tales makes them less anxious or helps them sleep better.

After reading the section of text headed 'Assessing the effectiveness of therapies', try to construct a study that would enable you to assess objectively whether your fairy tale therapy:

- has any therapeutic benefit at all
- is better than simply having a mug of cocoa.

Finally, if your new therapy does have therapeutic benefits, how would you find out if your theory of *how* it works was correct?

- participants do drop out of these studies, and may do so from some conditions (e.g. the no-treatment conditions) more than from others
- RCTs are costly and time-consuming
- because participants are assigned randomly to conditions, it does not take account of the fact that some participants may prefer some types of therapy to others (Brewin and Bradley, 1989).

What therapies are effective?

So much for attempting to find an empirical and objective way of assessing whether therapies are effective, but what do these studies tell us? Comparative studies tend to suggest that most of the accepted therapies are all more effective than no treatment or expectancy control conditions, but that the therapies themselves do not differ in their relative effectiveness.

For example, in a study of depressed individuals, Gibbons *et al.* (1993) found that cognitive therapy, interpersonal therapy and anti-depressant medication were all as effective as each other, and all more effective than a placebo control condition (after 16 weeks of treatment). Other consumer-based studies have suggested that structured psychotherapy is more effective than no therapy at all, and that those who receive psychotherapy plus medication do not improve any more than those who have received just psychotherapy (Seligman, 1995).

Over the past 10 to 20 years a large number of studies assessing the efficacy of therapies for psychological disorders has been carried out, and there is now good empirical evidence to support the effectiveness and internal validity of many of these therapies. There are too many to mention here, but the interested reader is referred to Chambless and Ollendick (2001) for a review and analysis of many of these studies.

Learning outcomes

When you have completed this chapter you should be able to:

- describe the principles underlying a range of contemporary therapies, including biological therapies and psychotherapies
- describe the techniques involved in a variety of therapies for psychological disorders
- compare and contrast the approaches to therapy implicit in two or more psychotherapies
- understand the main principles necessary for evaluating the effectiveness of a therapy technique.

Key Terms

Anti-depressants
Anti-psychotic drugs
Anxiolytic drugs
Aversion therapy
Beck's cognitive therapy
Behaviour analysis
Behaviour modification
Behaviour therapy
Behavioural self-control
Benzodiazepines
Client-centred therapy
Cognitive therapy
Counterconditioning
Defence mechanisms
Dream analysis
Ego
Electroconvulsive therapy (ECT)
Empathy
Exposure therapy
Extinction
Family therapy
Faulty learning
Fear hierarchy
Flooding
Free association

Functional analysis
Graduated exposure
Group therapy
Holistic therapies
Id
Internal validity
Interpretation
Libido
Monoamine oxidase inhibitors (MAOIs)
Placebo effects
Prozac
Psychoanalysis
Randomised controlled trials (RCTs)
Rational-emotive therapy (RET)
Reciprocal inhibition
Response shaping
Selective serotonin reuptake inhibitors (SSRIs)
Spontaneous remission
Stages of development
Superego
Systematic desensitisation
Token economy
Transference
Tricyclic anti-depressants
Unconditional positive regard

Further reading

Oltmanns, T. F. and Emery, R. E. (1998) *Abnormal Psychology* (2nd edn). New Jersey: Prentice Hall.

Wells, A. (1997) *Cognitive Therapy of Anxiety Disorders: A Practice Manual and Conceptual Guide*. Chichester: Wiley.

35

Health psychology

Route map of the chapter

This chapter introduces the reader to the relatively new area of health psychology. It begins by describing the topics and activities that make up health psychology, and some of the aims that health psychology has set itself in terms of understanding and changing health-related behaviour. The chapter is then divided into three broad areas, and gives the reader a flavour of how psychological factors play an important role in (i) predicting health-related behaviours, (ii) understanding how people interact with healthcare professionals, and comply with their advice, and (iii) understanding physical illness.

Introduction

Who do you think is responsible for your health? Your doctor or GP? Your local health authority? The government? Those who create the environment in which you live and work? Your parents or ancestors, who determined your genetic make-up? Or are you responsible?

The traditional approach to health and illness has been that fostered by the biomedical model of medicine. This model seeks the causes of illness in physical entities such as germs and viruses, and sees the corollaries of illness – such as pain – as being caused by physical factors such as tissue damage. Indeed, even recovery from illness within this model is attributed to external physical factors such as surgery and medication.

This *biomedical model of health* and illness is still one that is held today by many in the prominent health professions – but, interestingly, it is a model that practically excludes the individual from any responsibility for either their illnesses or their good health.

However, what has become clear over the last 30 years or so is that the individual *is* responsible for many aspects of their own health and well-being – and, because of this, psychology has a great deal to offer in terms of understanding and practical advice in matters of health and illness. For instance, many people indulge in activities that are clearly bad for their health (e.g. smoking, excessive drinking and overeating), and fail to indulge in activities that are good for their health (e.g. exercising regularly, eating healthy foods).

Even when they are ill, many people continue to put their recovery at risk by not seeking professional medical help or by not complying with medication regimes prescribed to treat their illnesses. In the late 1970s and early 1980s, these issues gave rise to the area now known as *health psychology* (Matarazzo, 1980).

What is health psychology?

Health psychology is the scientific study of the psychological processes of health, illness and healthcare, and, in particular, its contribution to:

- the promotion and maintenance of health
- the prevention and treatment of illness
- the identification of aetiological and diagnostic correlates of health, illness and related dysfunctions
- the analysis and improvement of the healthcare system and health policy information.

The British Psychological Society set up a division of health psychology in December 1997, and health psychologists now serve a wide variety of functions within healthcare systems (see Appendix 1i).

Our definition of health psychology illustrates how wide and varied this area of psychology must be. It not only encompasses the promotion of a nation's health and health policy, it also examines how individuals communicate with healthcare professionals, and how their own health beliefs might influence both their physical and emotional well-being. It is also concerned with how *stress* in a person's life can influence their physical and psychological health, and how *coping* styles can modulate these effects of stress.

The past 100 years have seen important changes in the patterns of disease, illness and treatments. Many diseases that were once fatal, such as smallpox, diphtheria and polio, are now treatable, and are all but eradicated. However, new threats to health continue to appear, and lifestyle factors rather than bacteria or viruses cause many of these.

These lifestyle factors are known as *behavioural pathogens*, and because they represent ways of living, behaving and thinking, they are often more amenable to psychological interventions than physical or medical interventions. In its 2002 report on promoting healthy life, the World Health Organization (WHO) identified the top ten worldwide risks to health as: underweight; unsafe sex; high blood pressure; tobacco consumption; alcohol consumption; unsafe water, sanitation and hygiene; iron deficiency; indoor smoke from solid fuels; high cholesterol; obesity. Clearly, a majority of these risks are lifestyle ones, which appropriate psychological campaigns and interventions could begin to address.

For example, unsafe sex and tobacco consumption need to be addressed through behavioural interventions designed to educate individuals about the risks associated with these activities, and to find effective ways of changing their behaviours. To this extent, psychologists can play an active role in the prevention and treatment of illness and the promotion of good health.

Both governments and health organisations spend large amounts of money mounting campaigns designed to change the health behaviours of people around the world. These often take the form of high-impact posters – of the kind shown here – but can also be in the form of sophisticated education and intervention programmes managed by organisations like the WHO (www.who.int)

Predicting healthy behaviour

In order to begin effectively to change behaviours that might be detrimental to health, we must first understand why people indulge in them. For example, those individuals who smoke or indulge in unsafe sex are almost certainly aware of the health risks involved in these activities, yet many millions of people continue with them. So what are the psychological factors that determine whether they continue with behaviours that are a risk to health?

Health locus of control

The first factor that is important to whether an individual will take up healthy behaviours relates to the question asked at the very beginning of this chapter: 'Who is responsible for your health?' Research on *locus of control* in social psychology (Rotter, 1966) suggests that people differ as to whether they regard events as controllable by them (an internal locus of control) or whether the events that happen to them are controlled by external factors (an external locus of control). This is a view that can be readily applied to health and illness, and has given rise to the *health locus of control* model (Wallston and Wallston, 1982).

Table 35.1 shows the items in the health locus of control scale, which measures whether you feel in control of your own health (e.g. 'If I take care of myself I can avoid illness') or whether you believe that your health is determined by factors external to you (e.g. 'I can only do what my doctor tells me to do').

There is now an accumulation of evidence suggesting that if you score high on the internal locus of control scale, then you are more likely to adopt healthy behaviours and reject unhealthy ones (e.g. give up smoking) (Wallston and Wallston, 1984; Pitts *et al.*, 1991). Similarly, if you score high on the external locus of control scale, you are less likely to comply with general medical advice given by your doctor or GP (e.g. to change from an unhealthy to a healthy lifestyle), because the individual high on external locus of control does not see themselves as responsible for their health.

TABLE 35.1

THE HEALTH LOCUS OF CONTROL SCALE ITEMS

1. If I take care of myself, I can avoid illness (I)
2. Whenever I get sick it is because of something I've done or not done (I)
3. Good health is largely a matter of good fortune (E)
4. No matter what I do, if I am going to get sick I will get sick (E)
5. Most people do not realise the extent to which their illnesses are controlled by accidental happenings (E)
6. I can only do what my doctor tells me to do (E)
7. There are so many strange diseases around that you can never know how or when you might pick one up (E)
8. When I feel ill, I know it's because I have not been getting the proper exercise or eating right (I)
9. People who never get sick are just plain lucky (E)
10. People's ill-health results from their own carelessness (I)
11. I am directly responsible for my health (I)

Note: I = internally worded, E = externally worded

Source: Wallston *et al.*, 1976

Unrealistic optimism

People are far from objective about assessing the risks they take with their health. Generally, people have an *optimistic bias*. That is, if asked to respond to the statement 'Compared with others my age, my chances of developing cancer are greater than them/same as them/less than them', most people will judge themselves as being less at risk than their contemporaries.

This optimistic bias covers a range of health risks including lung cancer, AIDS, being involved in a traffic accident and heart disease, and the bias is particularly prevalent during adolescence, where it has come to be known as *adolescent invulnerability* (Quadrel *et al.*, 1993).

The optimistic bias will tend to act to prevent individuals from adopting healthy behaviours, and will continue to provide some justification for indulging in unhealthy or risky behaviours. However, the bias may have some psychological benefit, in that research has shown that those who adopt optimistic perspectives on their life are generally more likely to have better physical and psychological health than those who have pessimistic views (Sheier and Carver, 1992).

Nevertheless, Wallston (1994) has argued that there is a distinction between 'cautious' optimists and 'cockeyed' optimists. The former hold optimistic views about their health, but do all they can to ensure that their health is fine. The latter are those who simply 'live in hope' and do little or nothing to influence their health.

Health belief models

The previous section describes just two individual factors that might affect whether or not a person indulges in healthy behaviours (health locus of control and unrealistic optimism). However, there are many more factors than this that will determine whether you act healthily or not, and researchers have attempted to put these together in what have come to be known as *health belief models*.

These tend to describe those factors that predict health behaviours, and try to explain how these predictors influence the set of 'health beliefs' that every individual has. The models derived in this way are usually based on the *biopsychosocial view of health*, which incorporates:

- the biological and genetic factors that are involved in many illnesses
- the psychological factors, such as beliefs, that may inform behaviour change
- sociological and demographic factors, such as age, race, peer or reference group etc.

Also, many of these models attempt to explain how the 'costs' and 'benefits' of health behaviours are weighed up and contribute to health beliefs. For example, if an individual believes that giving up smoking will prevent them from getting lung cancer, then they are more likely to give up smoking. But this has to be weighed up against the 'costs' of giving up, one of which might be the discomfort of nicotine withdrawal.

The health belief model (HBM)

One of the first models of this kind was the original health belief model developed by Rosenstock (1966), which was subsequently modified by Becker and Maiman in 1975 (see Figure 35.1). This model attempts to explain health behaviour in terms of both health beliefs and compliance with treatment, and is a valuable tool for predicting health behaviours before the onset of illness by calculating risk factors and the probability of compliance with treatment after diagnosis.

In particular, the health belief model predicts that an individual is most likely to take preventative health action if:

- they feel susceptible to disease through either genetic or behavioural factors (perceived susceptibility)
- they believe the disease could have potentially serious consequences (perceived severity)
- they think that taking preventative action will be beneficial in preventing the illness (perceived benefits)
- they believe the costs (such as pain) do not outweigh the perceived benefits of the health action

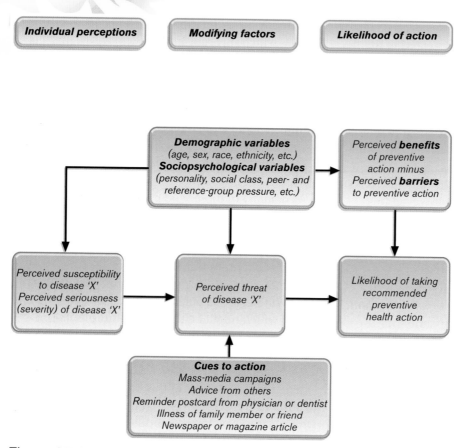

Individual perceptions   Modifying factors   Likelihood of action

Figure 35.1 The health belief model

- they consider that health promotions and motivators (e.g. government health campaigns) prompt some kind of action by the individual (cues to action).

This model has been relatively helpful over the years, and has been successful in predicting compliance with vaccination and screening programmes (Harrison *et al.*, 1992).

The theory of planned behaviour (TPB)

Arguably, the most popular of the current crop of health belief models that have been directly applied to health promotion is the *theory of planned behaviour* (Fishbein and Ajzen, 1975; Ajzen and Madden, 1986). This model was derived from research in social psychology, and in particular from the theory of reasoned action. It is based on the view

that an individual's behaviour is always planned, and that planning is determined by an individual's intentions. This being the case, the model attempts to define those factors that are important in determining intentions. In particular, intentions are a function of three discrete factors:

1 personal attitudes towards a particular behaviour defined by weighing up the pros and cons of that behaviour (e.g. 'I will enjoy giving up smoking because I will save money')
2 the individual's beliefs about what is an acceptable way to behave and what others will think of them (e.g. 'My family will approve if I give up smoking')
3 whether the individual believes he or she can achieve the behavioural goal and have the internal resources and ability to overcome any

obstacles (e.g. 'I think I can give up smoking because I've been able to kick bad habits in the past').

The TPB model has been successful in the past at predicting a number of health-related activities, including testicular self-examination (Brubaker and Wickersham, 1990) and attaining weight loss goals (Schifter and Ajzen, 1985). However, as many people point out, the model has one major drawback: it relies heavily on the assumption that intentions lead to behaviours and, as we all know, that is not necessarily the case!

Communication and compliance

Good health can also be dependent on two other important factors:

1 whether or not we decide to seek professional medical help for our illness symptoms
2 how we communicate our symptoms to these health professionals.

Understanding the psychological processes that contribute to these two factors is therefore of some importance.

'Going to the doctor': seeking professional healthcare advice

On what basis do we decide that we need to visit our GP? Some individuals – such as those often labelled the *worried well* – visit their GPs for a consultation at the slightest opportunity or with the most minor of symptoms. However, others will resist visiting their GP's surgery at all costs – even to the point where an illness requires hospitalisation and urgent attention.

Last (1963) first coined the phrase 'illness iceberg' because the majority of illnesses are never reported to a healthcare professional. From a random sample of individuals who were asked to complete a symptom checklist, Hannay (1980) found that 26 per cent of sufferers who reported one severe symptom did not actually consult a doctor. So what are the factors that make an individual decide to visit a doctor for a consultation?

Pendleton *et al.* (1984) argued that noting a *change* in their health led to an individual making one of three decisions about their condition:

1 a decision for no care (e.g. we may wake up one morning with a headache, and probably decide that it is due to drinking too many beers the night before; we assume this condition will get better before the day is out and that it does not require further help or advice)
2 a decision for self-care (e.g. if we wake one morning with a sore throat and runny nose we may well decide we have a cold, and treat this ourselves by going to the local chemist or pharmacy for some basic medication)
3 a decision for alternative care (e.g. if we wake up one morning and have a violent headache, runny

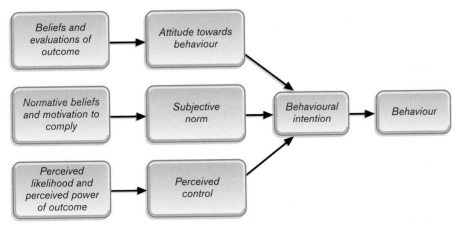

Figure 35.2 The theory of planned behaviour

nose, sore throat and a high temperature, and these symptoms last for some considerable time, we will most likely make a decision to consult a doctor).

There is also a number of demographic factors that are important in determining whether you will consult your doctor. Age is important, with the young and the old most likely to consult a doctor or healthcare consultant (the former because growing up involves childhood diseases and vaccinations, and the latter because old age usually means a frailer body and susceptibility to infection and disease). Gender is also important, with women more likely to consult than their male counterparts. This is not just because women consult more on pregnancy and contraception matters (Verbrugge, 1985), but probably because consultative healthcare for females is more developed in western cultures than it is for men (i.e. there are more 'well woman' clinics than there are 'well man' clinics).

Communication and compliance

Making a decision to visit your doctor or GP for a consultation is the first step in the process towards getting suitable treatment for illness symptoms. The next two stages are equally important. These are (i) how you communicate with the doctor during the consultation, and (ii) how you receive and comply with the advice and treatment given by your doctor.

Doctor–patient communication

According to Pendleton *et al.* (1984), 'the consultation is the central act of medicine and as such deserves to be understood'. A GP will normally see around 6000 patients a year, making a total of around 10,000 GP consultations per day in the UK alone. What is unusual about the doctor–patient consultation is that, unlike many other types of conversation and discussion, the topic of the consultation is very specific (i.e. the patient's immediate symptoms), and both doctor and patient bring to the consultation expectations about the outcome.

The expectations brought to the consultation by both parties can often confuse the diagnostic process. For example, Tate (1994) estimated that doctors usually made an initial diagnosis within 30 seconds of the consultation, and the effects of this tendency towards rapid diagnosis can be far-reaching, especially since it is unlikely that the patient will have divulged their major symptomatology first, but are more likely to build up to their main symptoms. This often leads to doctors systematically distorting the information given later in a consultation to fit the diagnosis that had been made earlier (Wallston, 1978).

On the patient's part, they will often enter a consultation with their own view of what is wrong with them, and they will describe their symptoms to fit their own theory.

Such are the complexities of the doctor–patient consultation that studies have estimated that:

- up to two-thirds of all psychosocial or psychiatric problems are missed during GP consultations (Pendleton *et al.*, 1984)
- over half of patients' actual symptoms fail to be identified during a consultation (Pendleton *et al.*, 1984)
- around 50 per cent of all consultations end in the doctor and patient failing to agree on the main presenting problems (Pendleton *et al.*, 1984).

With such potential for disagreement and misinformation, the doctor–patient consultation needs to be carefully conducted, and guided by a clear set of goals that need to be achieved. Pendleton *et al.* (1984) have outlined a set of guidelines by which the consultation should be conducted.

The doctor should:

1 ensure that the *reason* for the patient's attendance is clearly defined
2 consider problems other than the specific ones mentioned by the patient
3 together with the patient, choose an appropriate action for each problem
4 achieve a shared understanding of the problem with the patient

5 involve the patient in the management of the problem and encourage them to accept appropriate responsibility for this management

6 use time and resources appropriately and effectively

7 establish and maintain a relationship with the patient that will help to achieve future goals.

Compliance

In the context of health psychology, the term 'compliance' can be defined as 'the extent to which the patient's behaviour (in terms of taking medication, following diets or other lifestyle change) coincides with the medical or health advice' (Haynes *et al.*, 1979). This is an important topic for study – not least because the cost of non-compliance, in terms of the patient's health and the economic cost of wasted prescriptions and medications, is enormous.

Some important factors have been identified that appear to influence whether a patient will be compliant or not, and are summarised in Ley's (1989) cognitive model of compliance. First, the degree to which a patient actually *understands* the terminology and the explanations given by the doctor will affect compliance, and many GPs confuse their patients by using technical language and terms that have different medical and lay meanings (e.g. depression, hysteria) (Hadlow and Pitts, 1991).

RESEARCH METHODS BOX 35.1

A closer look at GP consultations on self-diagnosis of ME and CFS

In 1995, Scott, Deary and Pelosi published an intriguing article in the *British Medical Journal* describing the attitudes of GPs to patients who presented for a consultation with a self-diagnosis of ME (myalgic encephalomyelitis) or chronic fatigue syndrome (CFS).

Method

They selected 200 GPs at random and sent them a written case history that described Mrs M, a 28-year-old personnel officer for a computer firm who had a history of good health. The case history described how she attended the surgery complaining of general malaise that had lasted for six months. The malaise had increased in severity and by the time she consulted the doctor she also had intermittent stomach pains, severe tiredness and insomnia. She also reported crying for no apparent reason. Mrs M said she had no financial, marital or social problems. A physical examination that included a full blood count, urea and electrolytes, liver function and thyroid tests produced no abnormalities.

Half of the GPs received the description with Mrs M's occupation changed to that of an office cleaner. The following sentence was also included in 50 per cent of the descriptions: 'Mrs M had read newspaper articles about CFS and believed that this was her problem'. This meant the study was a simple 2 x 2 design in which the researchers varied (i) Mrs M's occupation and (ii) information about whether or not Mrs M had knowledge of CFS.

All GPs were asked how they would manage the hypothetical patient described in the case history, and their attitudes towards her.

Results

The results showed that GPs:

- were more likely to refer Mrs M for counselling if she was described as a personnel officer and not when she was described as an office cleaner
- believed that self-diagnosis would make the patient less likely to comply with treatment and would take up more of their time
- were less inclined to have patients who self-diagnosed on their lists, and were more likely to refer them for a second opinion.

Conclusion

This study shows quite clearly how factors such as social class and self-diagnosis can influence the diagnostic process, and result in GPs adopting negative attitudes towards their patients.

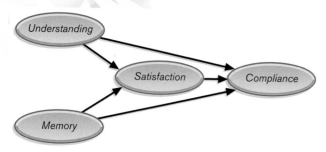

Figure 35.3 Ley's model of compliance

Second, even if patients understand what has been discussed during the consultation, they are likely to *remember* only a small percentage of what they are told; Ley and Spelman (1965; 1967) found that around 40 per cent of what had been said during a consultation was immediately forgotten by the patient. Since there is likely to be a link between understanding and recall of the consultation, then there is also a link between poor recall and compliance.

Third, Korsch *et al.* (1968) found a clear relationship between patients' *satisfaction* with the consultation and subsequent compliance. Patient satisfaction appeared to derive from:

- the doctor being friendly rather than businesslike
- the doctor appearing to understand the patient's concerns
- the patient's expectations about the consultation and treatment being met
- the doctor being perceived as a good communicator
- the doctor providing full and clear information.

However, while the involvement of these factors in compliance may make intuitive sense, Ley's model is largely a correlational one. This means that although there is good evidence for significant relationships between these variables, there is no evidence yet that they exert a *causal* influence on compliance.

The psychology of illness

Psychology plays a central and important role in many forms of physical illness. Have you ever developed a rash or a headache because you were worried about something? Or picked up a cold, tonsillitis or a sore throat while you were taking a series of exams? Psychological factors can influence physical illness in a variety of ways. They can make you more susceptible to picking up infectious illnesses by affecting your immune system (this is known as *psychosomatic illness*).

For example, stress is associated with reduced numbers of lymphocytes, reduced levels of sIgA (a particular form of antibody), reduced NK cell activity (the 'natural killer' lymphocyte), and raised antibody levels to herpes viruses (Herbert and Cohen, 1993). Stressors can also cause changes in behaviour, which may have illness-related consequences. For example, stress has been linked to:

- the onset of smoking in adolescents (Wills, 1985) and to an increase in the desire to smoke (Perkins *et al.*, 1992)
- an increase in the consumption of alcohol (Gupta and Jenkins, 1984)
- an increase in eating – especially in females (Michaud *et al.*, 1990).

All of these behaviours are ones that would be categorised as unhealthy consequences of stress.

Not only do psychological factors have a direct and indirect impact on physical health, they can also influence how we experience some aspects of illness, especially pain. The experience of pain is not simply an inevitable consequence of tissue damage; it is something that is determined in important ways by psychological and cognitive factors.

This section of the chapter will discuss two important elements of psychology and illness. The first is the effects of stress, and the second is the experience of pain.

Stress, stressors and coping

The term 'stress' has traditionally been a difficult one to define, not least because what is stressful for one person often isn't stressful for another. There are three ways in which stress can be defined:

1 as external or environmental forces that create a stressful reaction (e.g. difficulties at work)

2   as something experienced by the individual (e.g. feelings of tension or pressure)

3   as a physiological reaction that affects the autonomic nervous system (ANS), causing changes in arousal, hormone secretion and general physiological alertness.

The role of life events

Stress doesn't normally 'just happen' to people, it is usually triggered by some external or life event, or a series of *life events*, most of which will represent either challenges (e.g. a new job), losses (e.g. death of a close relative) or threats (e.g. the threat of redundancy). Stress-inducing life events can come in a number of forms. Holmes and Rahe (1967) studied the kinds of life events or life changes that preceded periods of illness or stress, and drew up a table of events according to their seriousness or likelihood of inducing stress or illness.

The ranked list of 43 events is shown in Table 35.2. This is Holmes and Rahe's (1967) social readjustment rating scale (SRRS), which ranks life events according to their severity and intensity, and the amount of time required to adjust to them. While this will give you an indication of the kinds of life events that cause stress, remember that this list was compiled over 30 years ago, and some of the items may not now be relevant to contemporary life.

While there is little doubt that most people would consider those life events near the top of the list as possible major stressors, identifying these life events is not alone sufficient to enable us to predict either that an individual will be stressed or the level of stress they will experience. For example, divorce or the death of a close family member are events that may not be so stressful if they are expected or predicted, and being able to predict a stressor gives the individual time to adapt to it (Parkes, 1993). Similarly, life events are usually stressful only if they are perceived to be uncontrollable (Brown, 1986).

The life events described by Holmes and Rahe are relatively discrete events that are experienced over a fixed period of time. However, many stressors may be chronic and ongoing, and result in chronically experienced stress that is more enduring and debilitating than single life events.

Moos and Swindle (1990) identified the most serious of these chronic stressors as:

- physical health stresses and chronic medical conditions
- home and neighbourhood stressors (e.g. safety, cleanliness)
- financial stressors
- work stressors (work pressure, interpersonal problems)
- spouse/partner stressors (e.g. emotional problems with partner)
- child stressors (e.g. childcare)
- extended family stressors (e.g. caring for an elderly or ill relative)
- friend stressors (e.g. maintaining cordial relations with close friends).

Finally, while major life events may act as triggers for stress, it is clear that stress can be caused on a day-to-day basis by a wide variety of minor irritants. These are known as *daily hassles* and are defined as 'the irritating, frustrating, distressing demands that to some degree characterize everyday transactions with the environment' (Kanner *et al.*, 1981: 3).

Stress levels can be predicted more accurately by the frequency of the 'daily hassles' you experience – such as sitting in a traffic jam – than by the frequency of major life events such as divorce or death of a spouse

TABLE 35.2

HOLMES AND RAHE'S (1967) SOCIAL READJUSTMENT RATING SCALE (SRRS)

Rank	Life event	Weighting
1	Death of spouse	100
2	Divorce	73
3	Marital separation	65
4	Jail term	63
5	Death of close family member	63
6	Personal injury or illness	53
7	Marriage	50
8	Fired at work	47
9	Marital reconciliation	45
10	Retirement	45
11	Change in health of family member	44
12	Pregnancy	40
13	Sex difficulties	39
14	Gain of new family member	39
15	Business readjustment	39
16	Change in financial state	38
17	Death of close friend	37
18	Change to different line of work	36
19	Change in number of arguments with spouse	35
20	Mortgage over $10,000	31
21	Foreclosure of mortgage or loan	30
22	Change in responsibilities at work	29
23	Son or daughter leaving home	29

TABLE 35.2 CONTINUED		
HOLMES AND RAHE'S (1967) SOCIAL READJUSTMENT RATING SCALE (SRRS)		
Rank	**Life event**	**Weighting**
24	Trouble with in-laws	29
25	Outstanding personal achievement	28
26	Wife begins or stops work	26
27	Begin or end school	26
28	Change in living conditions	25
29	Revision of personal habits	24
30	Trouble with boss	23
31	Change in work hours or conditions	20
32	Change in residence	20
33	Change in schools	20
34	Change in recreation	19
35	Change in church activities	19
36	Change in social activities	18
37	Mortgage or loan less than $10,000	17
38	Change in sleeping habits	16
39	Change in number of family get-togethers	15
40	Change in eating habits	15
41	Vacation	13
42	Christmas	12
43	Minor violations of the law	11

Daily hassles include losing things, traffic jams, inclement weather, finding the coffee jar is empty, arguments and so on. A number of studies have indicated that the frequency of 'daily hassles' is a better predictor of stress and physical health than major life events (Kanner *et al.*, 1981; Weinberger *et al.*, 1987).

In addition, the severity and frequency of daily

hassles have been shown to mediate the relationship between major life events and psychiatric symptomatology (Johnson and Sherman, 1997), to be associated with diagnoses of chronic fatigue syndrome (CFS) (Van Houdenhove *et al.*, 2002) and to predict eating bouts in women identified as binge eaters (Crowther *et al.*, 2001).

Coping and transactional models of stress
The individual is not just a passive recipient of stressful life events, but indulges in a variety of activities designed to appraise the stressor and to cope with its effects. What these activities are and how they are conducted can have important ameliorative effects on the stressor's impact.

Lazarus and Folkman (1984) argued that stress involves a transaction between the individual and their world, in which their first reaction to a stressor is to appraise it. First, the individual initially appraises the event itself; this is known as *primary appraisal*. During primary appraisal, the individual will appraise the event as (i) irrelevant, (ii) benign and positive or (iii) harmful and negative. If the event is appraised as harmful or negative, the individual then undertakes a *secondary appraisal*, which involves their assessing the various coping resources they have available and deciding on the best way to deal with the stressor (Lazarus and Folkman, 1984).

The primary appraisal process itself is important, and people use a variety of appraisal strategies, many

TABLE 35.3

EXAMPLES OF COGNITIVE STRATEGIES FOR 'DOWNWARDLY' APPRAISING A STRESSOR

Appraisal strategy	Example	Effect
Downward comparison	'This is not as bad as the things that happen to other people – they are much worse off than me'	Reduces the *relative* impact of the stressor
Positive reappraisal	'I will come out of this experience better than I went in'	Redefines the stressor as a challenge from which personal growth is a positive outcome
Cognitive disengagement	'This situation isn't worth getting upset about'	Downgrades the stressor as something that is irrelevant
Optimism	'Everything will work itself out OK in the end'	Reduces the impact of the stressor by focusing on a positive rather than negative outcome
Faith in social support	'I have others who can help me through this'	Focuses on a positive outcome based on existing support and resources
Life perspective	'I can put up with this as long as everything else in my life is OK'	Reduces the relative impact of the stressor by comparing it with positive features of life

Source: Davey and McDonald, 2000

of which function explicitly to reduce the stressful impact of the stressor. Such strategies include those described in Table 35.3, each of which enables the individual cognitively to reduce the negative impact of the stressor (e.g. downward comparison) or to redefine it as an event possessing positive characteristics (e.g. positive reappraisal).

People often use a variety of cognitive strategies for 'downwardly' appraising a stressor, and these function either to reduce the stressful impact of the stressor or to redefine it as an event that possesses positive characteristics. Some examples are given in the table. Studies have shown that the use of these 'neutralising' appraisal strategies reduces experienced stress, increases subjective well-being and facilitates the use of active, task-oriented coping with the stressor (Taylor *et al.*, 1983; Gibbon and Gerrard, 1989; Aspinwall and Taylor, 1990).

Pain

Most early theories of *pain* did not consider psychological factors, and pain was seen as being a simple physiological consequence of tissue damage. However, three factors played an important role in alerting researchers to the role of psychological factors in pain (Ogden, 2000). First, drugs and other medical treatments for pain were found to be effective only for treating acute pain and were relatively ineffective for chronic pain.

Second, a study reported by Beecher (1956) suggested that the perception and experience of pain might depend on factors other than simple tissue damage. He noted the requests of civilians and soldiers for pain relief in a hospital during the Second World War; although the extent of the physical injuries found in both civilians and soldiers was very similar, over 80 per cent of the civilians requested pain relief, while only 25 per cent of the soldiers did. Beech suggested that the *meaning* of the injury for the soldiers was different from that for the civilians: for the soldiers it meant they were alive and were due to go home. Thus it appeared that the meaning attached to an injury could attenuate experienced pain.

Third, it has often been noted that individuals who have had a limb amputated still continue to report experiencing pain in the non-existent limb (the *phantom limb phenomenon*). This can occur even after the wounds caused by amputation have fully healed. Consistent with this is the finding that fewer than 15 per cent of persons with back pain have an identifiable physical problem with their back (Fordyce, 1995). This suggests that experiences of pain can be generated even when there is no evidence of physical injury or tissue damage.

The gate control theory of pain

One of the first theories of pain to include psychological factors was Melzack and Wall's (1965; 1982) *gate control theory of pain*. They argued that a gate exists at the level of the spinal cord that integrates three sources of input:

1 information about the injury received from the site of the injury
2 descending input from the brain, providing information about the individual's behavioural state (e.g. attention towards the pain) and emotional state (e.g. anxiety or fear), and information about previous pain experiences (e.g. 'I know from previous experience that this type of pain doesn't last long')
3 input from the large and small fibres that make up some of the physiological input into pain perception.

The gate integrates the information from these three types of input and then produces an output that determines the perception of pain. The greater the output, the greater the perception of pain. Melzack and Wall argue that the gate's output can be influenced by the physical extent of the injury, or by psychological factors such as anxiety or worry, and focusing on the pain.

While the gate control theory was appealing as the first model to integrate physical and psychological factors into an explanation of pain perception, it has a number of deficiencies. First, there is as yet no evidence that a 'gate' that integrates the three sources of information exists. Second, it is a model that still relies heavily on physical factors as the initiators of pain, and some evidence – such as the

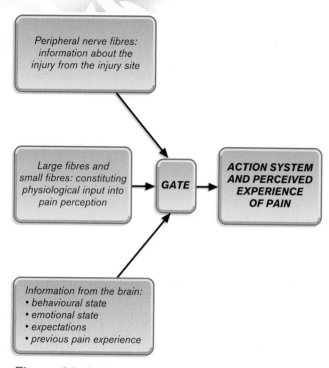

Figure 35.4 The gate control model of pain

phantom limb example – suggests that pain can be experienced without *any* physical input.

Cognitive models of pain

More recent conceptualisations of pain rest heavily on psychological and cognitive factors as critical determinants in the perception of pain. In particular, there appears to be an important link between pain, anxiety and depression, with catastrophic interpretations of pain being associated with higher levels of depression (Rosenteil and Keefe, 1983) and anxiety (Asmundson *et al.*, 1996).

Because of their affliction, it seems intuitively reasonable to suppose that pain sufferers should be more anxious and depressed than others. However, a number of theorists have suggested that it is the high levels of anxiety and depression that *cause* heightened pain perception rather than vice versa (Lethem *et al.*, 1983; Philips, 1987).

This has been related to the concept of *pain anxiety* (McCracken *et al.*, 1992), which suggests that some individuals are fearful of pain, and as such have developed a phobia of pain that makes them

hypervigilant for pain cues and anxious about these cues when they detect them. The subsequent anxiety then leads to the catastrophising of pain symptoms, and heightened experience of pain (Crombez *et al.*, 1998).

Similarly, how the individual interprets the pain experience also has an impact. Those who interpret their pain as being indicative of more tissue damage or illness tend to be more avoidant and more disabled than those who do not have such an interpretative bias (Vlaeyens *et al.*, 1995), and, indeed, fear of pain is a better predictor of disability than either pain severity or physical pathology (Crombez *et al.*, 1998).

While cognitive theories of pain such as these are still in their infancy, they are already capable of generating a range of useful interventions for alleviating and controlling pain in chronic pain sufferers (Turner, 1996; Eccleston *et al.*, 2002; McCracken and Turk, 2002).

Learning outcomes

When you have completed this chapter you should be able to:

- describe the topics that make up health psychology, and describe the aims of health psychology as an academic and applied field of study
- compare and contrast at least two models developed to predict health behaviour
- describe some of the psychological processes that contribute to doctor–patient communication, and the patient's compliance with treatment and health advice
- critically assess how psychology contributes to an understanding of physical illness.

Key Terms

Adolescent invulnerability
Behavioural pathogens
Biomedical model of health
Biopsychosocial view of health
Coping
Daily hassles
Gate control theory of pain
Health belief models
Health locus of control
Health psychology
Life events
Locus of control
Optimistic bias
Pain
Pain anxiety
Phantom limb phenomenon
Primary appraisal
Psychosomatic illness
Secondary appraisal
Stress
Theory of planned behaviour
Worried well

Further reading

Marks, D. F., Murray, M., Evans, B. and Willig, C. (2000) *Health Psychology: Theory, Research and Practice.* Thousand Oaks: Sage.

Ogden, J. (2000) *Health Psychology: A Textbook.* Buckingham: Open University Press.

Pitts, M. and Phillipis, K. (1999) *The Psychology of Health* (2nd edn). London: Routledge.

Taylor, S. E. (2003) *Health Psychology* (5th edn). Boston: McGraw-Hill.

Research methods and statistics

36	Why do we need research methods?	636
37	Collecting data	652
38	Summarising data	671
39	Going beyond your sample	692

36

Why do we need research methods?

Route map of the chapter

The question on most psychology students' lips as they discover that they have to do two years of research methods is 'Why do we need research methods?' On the face of it, it might seem that we just like torturing psychology students by making them learn lots of complicated statistics and such like. Actually, that's not the reason: most of us are nice, really. The reason is that psychology is a scientific discipline that tries to understand human behaviour by using research to test and develop ideas about what drives our thoughts and behaviours. This chapter attempts to describe the research process in general terms, in order to give you some background to why we need research methods, and to discuss the important issues that we need to consider when conducting psychological research. We start by looking at how theories and research are intrinsically linked, before changing our focus to how we can test theories (and why it's important to measure things). We then look at how we can try to identify cause and effect relationships, and how we analyse data.

Introduction

If you ask yourself why you're studying psychology (or reading this book) the answer would probably be something like 'Because I'm interested in why people do the things they do'. You might have a particular interest in why people do everyday things ('Why do we sleep?'), why they do unusual things ('Why does my friend sing "You've lost that loving feeling" by the Righteous Brothers after four pints of Stella?'), or why groups of people do things ('Why does the England football team always seem to play so badly?'). In all

these cases you're interested in answering a question. Scientists are curious people and psychologists are curious *about* people. To answer these questions you need to have two things: data and an explanation of those data.

Linking theories and research

Let's start by looking at an example. It's very curious why people who clearly cannot sing in tune go to the *Pop Idol* TV show auditions. These people are humiliated in front of millions of people and their motivation is a mystery. Having made this casual observation we could collect some data to see if this observation is correct. Let's assume that we managed to collect some data and found that 40 per cent of contestants could sing but the remaining 60 per cent could not. The next logical thing is to try to explain these data.

One explanation is that the people who cannot sing don't know that they sound like a dog howling at the moon. This is a *theory*. Having come up with a theory we can test it. We might go to the contestants who can't sing and simply ask them 'Do you think you're a good singer?' We might find that 80 per cent of them think they are good singers. Is our explanation a good one? Well, it does explain the data: we proposed that the bad singers don't realise they are bad, and for 80 per cent of them this is true. However, it doesn't explain all of the data: there are 20 per cent who are fully aware that their voices sound like fingernails being scratched down a blackboard. It also doesn't explain *why* the 80 per cent don't realise they are bad.

One reason why they might not realise they are bad is because they are tone-deaf. This is another theory, and we can test it by looking at what predictions can be made from the theory. If they *are* tone-deaf, then we would predict that they are unable to distinguish between the sounds of different notes on a keyboard. A prediction from a theory, like this one, is known as a *hypothesis*. We could test this hypothesis by playing them pairs of notes and asking them whether the notes are the same or different.

Imagine we did such a test and found that these people were not tone-deaf. What does this say about our theory? Well, obviously the theory is wrong: the data collected are not consistent with the prediction that arose from the theory.

It's unlikely that we would be the only people interested in why individuals who cannot sing put themselves through the ritual humiliation of a *Pop Idol* audition. There would be other researchers studying *Pop Idol* contestants who cannot sing. Imagine these researchers discovered that:

- those that cannot sing don't notice when they blush or sweat
- those that cannot sing think they are great dancers even when it is clear to others that they cannot dance
- those that cannot sing think they are attractive even when the majority of viewers would think they are not.

This is even worse news for our theory: if they were simply tone-deaf then this shouldn't affect their perception of their dancing or their physical attractiveness. All in all, it's looking pretty bad for our theory: it cannot explain all of the data, predictions from the theory are not supported by subsequent data, and it cannot explain other research findings.

At this point, a rival scientist, Dr Knowitall, comes up with an alternative theory to ours. She suggests that perhaps the contestants who cannot sing have a general attention deficit towards themselves (put another way, their attention is externally focused rather than focused on themselves). One prediction from her model is that if people are confronted by information about themselves and information about other people at the same time, they will be more likely to pay attention to the information about the other person.

To test this, Dr Knowitall showed the contestants that couldn't sing two pictures on a screen (one on the left and one on the right). One of the pictures was always a picture of themselves and the other was always a picture of someone else. She measured which of the two pictures the person's eyes moved towards. She found that the people who couldn't sing did tend to look at the pictures of other people. This supports her theory that these people do not pay attention to themselves.

Dr Knowitall's theory is quite good, then: it explains the initial observations, brings together a range of research findings and also has obvious implications. One implication is that if these people don't pay attention to what they themselves do or say, then they might accidentally leave the house one day without any trousers on, they'd offend their neighbours and probably get arrested. The end result of this whole process is that we should be able to make a general statement about the state of the world. In this case we could state that '*Pop Idol* contestants who cannot sing find it difficult to pay attention to themselves'.

You may not realise it, but in just a few paragraphs we have described the process that underlies all

'Did I put my trousers on this morning …?'

science. We begin with an observation that we want to understand; we generate theories (explanations) of those observations; hypotheses (predictions) are generated from these theories; we test these hypotheses; and the data we collect may support our theory or give us cause to modify it. The processes of data collection (research) and generating theories are intrinsically linked: theories lead to data collection and data collection informs theories!

In describing this process we've also seen that a good theory should:

- explain the existing data
- explain a range of related observations
- allow statements to be made about the state of the world
- allow predictions about the future
- have implications.

In these respects Dr Knowitall's theory is good: it explains the original observation, ties together a range of other related observations, allows predictions about the future, and has implications. Conversely, our theory is of little use: although it explains the original observation, its predictions weren't true, it cannot explain the other related evidence, and it doesn't really have any implications.

Testing theories

When is a hypothesis not a hypothesis?
We've seen what a theory is and we've also seen that theories need to be tested. One important point from the previous section is that a good theory should allow us to make statements about the state of the world. However, there is a distinction between scientific and non-scientific statements. *Scientific statements* are those that can be verified with reference to empirical evidence, whereas *non-scientific statements* are those that cannot be empirically tested. So statements such as 'The new Gareth Gates record is a load of rubbish', 'Chocolate is the best food' and 'This is the best introduction-to-psychology book in the world' are all non-scientific – they cannot be proved or disproved.

On the other hand, scientific statements can be

confirmed or disconfirmed empirically: 'Listening to Gareth Gates makes adolescent women want to marry him', 'Drinking water from the local pond makes you vomit' and 'Prolonged use of amphetamines makes you psychotic' are all things that can be tested empirically (provided you can quantify and measure the variables concerned).

Non-scientific statements can sometimes be altered to become scientific statements, so 'Chocolate is the best food' is non-scientific, but by changing the statement to 'Chocolate is the best food for improving your mood' it becomes testable (we can collect data about the change in mood resulting from different foods and prove or disprove the statement). Karl Popper, the famous philosopher of science, believed that non-scientific statements were nonsense and had no place in science. Good theories should, therefore, produce hypotheses that are scientific statements.

Types of hypothesis
So far we've seen that good theories should allow us to generate scientific statements. These statements should lead to hypotheses, which are testable statements derived from a theory. Any hypothesis has two forms: the *experimental hypothesis* (a.k.a. the *alternative hypothesis*) is denoted by H_1 and is the prediction that comes from your theory. The *null hypothesis*, denoted by H_0, is simply the opposite. Taking our *Pop Idol* example, one hypothesis from our theory was as follows.

- Experimental hypothesis: contestants that cannot sing *don't* realise that they cannot sing.

The null hypothesis is simply the opposite.

- Null hypothesis: contestants that cannot sing *do* realise that they cannot sing.

This is all very well but why do we actually care about the null hypothesis? The reason we care is because we cannot actually prove the experimental hypothesis, but we can disprove the null hypothesis. If our data give us confidence to reject the null hypothesis, then this provides support for our experimental hypothesis. However, be aware that even if we can reject the null hypothesis, this doesn't prove the experimental hypothesis but merely supports it. Just to make life even harder, we cannot ever really say anything definite about either hypothesis. All we can ever do is draw vague conclusions based on collecting data. So rather than talking about accepting or rejecting a hypothesis (which some textbooks tell you to do) we should be talking about 'the chances of obtaining the data we've collected if the null hypothesis is true'.

Using our *Pop Idol* example again, when we collected data from the contestants who couldn't sing, we found that 80 per cent of them thought they were good singers. So when we analyse our data, what we are really asking is 'Assuming that contestants who cannot sing *do* realise that they cannot sing, is it likely that in the group we tested 80 per cent would tell me they think they are good singers?' Intuitively the answer is that the chances of this are very low: if the null hypothesis is true, then most people in the group we tested should realise that they are bad singers and so would not report that they are good singers. Therefore we're very unlikely to have got the data that we did if the null hypothesis were true. What if we had found that only 10 per cent reported that they thought they were good singers? Clearly if the null hypothesis is true, and contestants who cannot sing do realise they are bad singers, then only a small number would be expected to think they are good singers. The chances of getting these data are therefore high.

When we collect data to test theories we have to work in these terms: we cannot talk about the null hypothesis being true or the experimental hypothesis being true – we can only talk in terms of the probability of obtaining a particular set of data if, hypothetically speaking, the null hypothesis were true.

Another distinction we make with hypotheses is whether they are one- or two-tailed. A *one-tailed* hypothesis states that an effect will occur but it also states the direction of the effect. For example, 'A mouse can run up your leg faster than a tarantula' is a one-tailed hypothesis because it states the direction of the effect (the mouse will be

faster than the tarantula). A *two-tailed* hypothesis states that an effect will occur but it doesn't state the direction of the effect. For example, 'Mice and tarantulas differ in the speed with which they can run up your leg' does not tell us whether mice or tarantulas are quicker, just that they differ. This is a two-tailed hypothesis.

Measuring things

Variables

To test hypotheses we need to measure variables. *Variables* are just things that can change (or vary). They might vary between people (e.g. IQ) or vary across time (e.g. mood). Most hypotheses can be expressed in terms of two variables: a proposed cause and a proposed outcome. Let's take one of our previous statements, 'Prolonged use of amphetamines makes you psychotic'. In this case, the proposed cause is 'prolonged amphetamine use' and the proposed effect is becoming psychotic. Both the cause and the outcome are variables: for the cause, people will vary in the amount of amphetamines they have used; and for the outcome, people will also have different levels of psychoticism.

The key to testing such statements is to measure these variables. In psychology particularly we can rarely directly measure variables and instead rely on indirect measures such as self-report, questionnaires and computerised tasks (to name a few).

Why is it so important that we measure things? Well, imagine you were a psychopharmacologist and you wanted to show that amphetamine use does make you psychotic. You force-feed ten people with amphetamines (also known as 'speed') over a six-month period and, lo and behold, after six months they start hallucinating (although see the section on ethics in Chapter 37). These results are then written up and published for others to read. A few years pass and another scientist, Dr L. Dopa, comes along and shows that when he gave people amphetamines over six months they were not psychotic. How could this be? There are two measurement-related issues here:

1. Dr L. Dopa might have fed his participants less amphetamine than you did (and it may be that

psychotic states depend on a certain critical mass of the chemical)

2. Dr L. Dopa might have measured the outcome differently – did you and Dopa assess 'psychotic states' in the same way?

The former point explains why chemists and physicists have devoted many hours to developing standard units of measurement. If you had reported that you'd fed your participants 100 grams of amphetamine per day, then Dr Dopa could have ensured that he had used the same amount – because grams are a standard unit of measurement we would know that you and Dopa used the same amount of the chemical. Direct measurements such as the gram provide an objective standard: an object that weighs 10g, for example, is known to be twice as heavy as an object weighing only 5g.

Levels of measurement

Although scales of *measurement* can be developed for properties that can be directly observed (such as height, mass and volume), we mentioned before that in psychology we usually have to take indirect measures. For example, to measure psychoticism we might use a questionnaire that asks people to report the frequency of various symptoms that we associate with psychotic states (such as delusions, hallucinations, paranoia and so on). This might give us a number from 0 (not psychotic) to 100 (completely psychotic). Could we claim that someone who scores 60 is, in reality, twice as psychotic as someone who scores 30? Probably not. However, we might be able to claim that someone scoring 60 was more psychotic (to whatever degree) than someone scoring 30. This relationship between what is being measured and the numbers obtained on a scale is known as the *level of measurement*.

Thinking back to the reasons why Dr L. Dopa's results differed from yours, the second proposed explanation was that you and Dr Dopa measured the outcome differently. In both cases the observed outcome was 'psychotic states'. What constitutes psychoticism? Do you have to have the odd grandiose idea, or do you constantly have to spend all day thinking that you've just invented the solution to the world's energy problems (or something similarly grand). Perhaps you measured only hallucinations in your experiments, whereas Dr Dopa was more inclusive and required delusions and paranoia as well.

These differences in how you measured your outcome can affect the results you get. An inability to measure directly what we want to measure is a problem psychologists face all the time. When we cannot measure something directly there will always be a discrepancy between the numbers we use to represent the thing we're measuring and the actual value of the thing we're measuring (i.e. the value we would get if we could measure it directly). This discrepancy is known as *measurement error*.

As we have already mentioned, there are different levels at which variables can be measured. *Nominal data* are measured on a scale on which two things that are equivalent in some sense are given the same name (or number). With this scale, there is no relationship between the size of the number and what is being measured; all that you can tell is that two things with the same number are equivalent, whereas two things with different numbers are not equivalent.

One example is the numbers that players in a rugby or football team wear. A rugby player with number 10 (e.g. England's Jonny Wilkinson) on his back is the fly-half, whereas a player with number 1 on his back is the hooker (the nasty-looking player at the front of the scrum). However, a number 10 player is not necessarily better than a number 1 (most managers would not want their fly-half stuck in the front of a scrum). The numbers on the back of shirts could equally well be letters or names (in fact, until recently many rugby clubs denoted team positions with letters on the back of shirts).

It's meaningless to do arithmetic on data from a nominal scale. For example, imagine if the England coach found that Jonny Wilkinson (his number 10) was injured. Would he consider replacing him with his number 4 (Martin Johnson) and 6 (Richard Hill)? The answer is no, not unless he wanted all of his penalty kicks to be missed! The only way that nominal data can be used is to consider frequencies. For example, we could look at how frequently number 10s score tries compared to number 4s.

Would you replace your number 10 with (some weird genetically modified hybrid of) your numbers 4 and 6?

Ordinal data

Ordinal data tell us not only that things have occurred but also the order in which they occurred. However, these data tell us nothing about the differences between values. Imagine you went to a 'ghostly' horse race in which there were three horses: Red Rum, Desert Orchid (who, strictly speaking, isn't actually dead yet, but retired from racing in 1991) and Shergar. The names of horses don't give us any information about where they came in the race, but labelling them according to their performance – first, second and third – does. These categories are *ordered*.

In using ordered categories we now know that the horse that came first was better than the horse that came second. However, we still know nothing about the differences between categories; we don't know how much better the winner was than the horses that came second and third: it might have crossed the line 100 metres in front of the other horses or only one centimetre in front of them. Nominal and ordinal scales don't tell us anything about the differences between points on a scale

A lot of psychological data, especially questionnaire and self-report data, are ordinal. Imagine you were asked to rate on a ten-point scale how bored you are reading this chapter. We might be confident that a reader who gives a rating of 10 was more bored than one who gave a rating of 1, but can

we be certain that the first reader was ten times as bored as the second? What about if both readers gave a rating of 10? Even then, could we be sure they were equally bored? Probably not. Their ratings will depend on their subjective feelings about what constitutes boredom. For these reasons, in any situation in which we ask people to rate something subjective (e.g. their confidence about an answer they have given, how anxious they feel or how popular they are) we should regard these data as ordinal, although many psychologists do not.

Interval data

Interval data are considerably more useful than ordinal data and most of the statistical tests we use in psychology rely on having these data. To say that data are interval, we must be certain that equal intervals on the scale represent equal differences in the property being measured. Imagine that a psychologist took several spider-phobic individuals, asked them to place a tarantula down their trousers and then to rate their anxiety on a ten-point scale. For this scale to be interval, it must be the case that the difference between anxiety ratings of 3 and 4 is the same as the difference between, say, 1 and 2 or 9 and 10. Similarly, the difference in anxiety between ratings of 2 and 5 should be identical to the difference between ratings of 5 and 8. If we had four phobic individuals (their anxiety ratings in brackets)

– Graham (10), Andy (9), Leonora (2) and Benie (3) – an interval scale would mean that the extra anxiety that Benie subjectively experiences compared to Leonora is equal to the extra anxiety that Graham experiences compared to Andy.

Ratio data

Ratio data go a step further than interval data by requiring that in addition to the scale meeting the requirements of interval, the ratios of values along the scale should be meaningful. A good example of a ratio measure that's used in psychology is reaction time (i.e. the time taken to respond to something). When we measure a reaction time, not only is it true that, say, the difference between 300 and 350ms (a difference of 50ms) is the same as the difference between 210 and 260ms or 422 and 472ms, it is also true that distances along the scale are divisible: a reaction time of 200ms is twice as long as a reaction time of 100ms and twice as short as a reaction time of 400ms.

A final property of variables is that they can be discrete or continuous. A *discrete variable* is one for which no underlying continuum exists. In other words, the measure classifies items into non-

---

ACTIVITY BOX 36.1

Hypotheses

Listed below are some popular theories in psychology. For each one, try to generate a hypothesis that might arise from the theory. For each hypothesis, state the null hypothesis and say whether it is a one-tailed or two-tailed hypothesis.

1. Galton suggested that intelligence is hereditary (runs in families).
2. Bandura suggested that people learn their behaviours from watching others (observational learning).
3. Paivio (1969) suggested that things are easier to remember if you visualise them.
4. Piaget suggested that children develop logical thinking skills as they get older.

Some possible answers

1. One hypothesis would be 'People with intelligent parents will be more intelligent than those with stupid parents'. This is a one-tailed hypothesis because we've stated that people with intelligent parents will be more intelligent. The null hypothesis would be that 'People with intelligent parents will not be more intelligent than those with stupid parents'.
2. One hypothesis would be 'The more violent films a person watches, the more aggressively they behave'. This is a one-tailed hypothesis because we've stated that watching violent films increases aggressive behaviour. The null hypothesis would be 'Aggressive behaviour is not influenced by watching violent films'.
3. One hypothesis would be 'There will be a difference between the number of words remembered by people who read a list of words and are asked to visualise each word and people just asked to read the list of words'. This is a two-tailed hypothesis because we've just stated that there will be difference and not what that difference is. The null hypothesis would be 'There will not be a difference between the number of words remembered by people who read a list of words and are asked to visualise each word and people just asked to read the list of words'.
4. One hypothesis would be 'Older children can solve logical problems better than younger children'. This is a one-tailed hypothesis because we've stated that older children will be better at logical tasks than younger ones. The null hypothesis would be 'Older children cannot solve logical problems better than younger children'.

overlapping categories. One example would be being dead: a person can be only dead or alive. A *continuous variable* does have an underlying continuum. For example, intelligence runs along some kind of continuum (from village idiot at one end to Einstein at the other). The distinction between discrete and continuous variables can be very blurred. Gender, for example, seems like a discrete variable (you can be only male or female). However, there are genetic males who feel female and vice versa; there are also chromosomal disorders that can confuse the genetic gender of a person. Continuous variables can be measured in discrete terms. For example, although depression is probably a continuous variable, clinicians tend to make a distinction between clinically depressed people and non-clinically depressed people.

Validity

So far we've seen that it's important to measure things in research and that we should try to measure things as accurately as possible. There are two properties that a measure should have if it is to be accurate: validity and reliability. A good measurement instrument should measure what you designed it to measure and this is called *validity*. So an intelligence questionnaire that actually measures aggressiveness is not valid; however, an intelligence questionnaire that does seem to equate with how clever people are is valid. Things like reaction times and physiological measures are valid in one sense because a reaction time does in fact measure the time taken to react and skin conductance does measure the conductivity of your skin. However, if we're using these things to infer psychological states (for example, using skin conductance to measure anxiety) then they will be valid only if there are no other factors other than the one you are interested in that can influence them. If you choose a self-report measure there are different flavours of validity to consider, as outlined below.

The items in your self-report measure/questionnaire must relate to the construct being measured (*content validity*). Content validity is really the degree to which your items are representative of the construct being measured, so ensure that

questions cover the full range of the construct. *Criterion validity* is whether the questionnaire is measuring what it claims to measure. In an ideal world, you could assess this by relating scores on your measure to real-world observations. For example, if you developed the 'attitudes about our own singing' questionnaire, you could give people the questionnaire and then see whether they can actually sing. This is often impractical and, of course, with attitudes you may not be interested in the reality so much as the person's perception of reality (you might not care whether they can actually sing – you might care only whether they think they can).

Reliability

Validity is a necessary but not sufficient condition of a self-report measure. A second consideration is *reliability*, which is the ability of the measure to produce the same results under the same conditions. To be reliable, the questionnaire must first be valid. The easiest way to assess reliability is to test the same group of people twice: a reliable questionnaire will produce similar scores at both points in time (*test-retest reliability*). In reality, if we did test the same people twice, then they might remember their responses from last time and give the same ones (or different ones if they are trying to mess up your research!) and this will bias your assessment of reliability. Also, imagine you are trying to measure something like depression. Obviously, depression will fluctuate over time, so you'd want your measure to be sensitive to these changes and *not* produce the same scores!

Sometimes people use a statistical technique called *split-half reliability*. You simply split questions on your measure randomly into two groups and then compare participants' scores on the two halves: the scores should be roughly the same. A more sophisticated version of this technique is not just to split the items in half once, but to split the measure into two halves in all possible ways. You can then compare people's scores on the two halves for all of the different splits and compute an average split-half reliability score known as *Cronbach's alpha*. For psychological measures, if Cronbach's alpha is above about 0.7 then you're doing pretty well.

Measurement error

On page 640 we came across the concept of measurement error, which is the difference between the scores on our measurement scale and the level of the construct we're measuring. For example, imagine you know as an absolute truth that you weight 73kg. One day you step on the bathroom scales and they say 75kg. There is a difference of 2kg between your actual weight and the weight given by your measurement tool (the scales): there is a measurement error of 2kg. Although properly calibrated bathroom scales should not produce a measurement error (despite what we might want to believe when they've just told us we're really heavy!), self-report measures like the ones used in many psychology experiments do produce measurement error because they are an indirect way of tapping the construct we're trying to measure.

One reason (of many) for this is that other factors will influence how people respond to our measures. Imagine you were completing a questionnaire about your 'intrusive thoughts' (see Chapter 33, page 568), would you want to admit to thinking about harming someone or drowning puppies or something? Probably not. You'd want to keep your strange ideations to yourself! Also, people's responses can be influenced by what they think the person testing them wants them to do. This is known as a *demand characteristic*.

Causes vs correlations

So far we've learnt that psychologists are interested in answering questions, and that to answer these questions they have to collect data, then generate theories, which in turn generate hypotheses, which then have to be tested. We've also learnt that to test a hypothesis we need to measure variables.

If we simplify things a bit, then there are basically two ways to test a hypothesis: either by observing what naturally happens, or by manipulating some aspect of the environment and observing the effect it has on the variable that interests us. The main distinction between what might be termed *correlational* or *cross-sectional* research (where we observe what naturally goes on in the world without directly interfering with it) and *experimental research*

(where we manipulate one variable to see its effect on another) is that experimentation involves the direct manipulation of variables. In correlational research we do things like observe natural events (e.g. the aggressive behaviour of children in a playground) or we take a snapshot of many variables at a single point in time (e.g. administering several questionnaires about sexual practices).

Correlational research provides a very natural view of the question we're researching because we are not influencing what happens, and the measures of the variables should not be biased by the researcher being there (this is an important aspect of *ecological validity*). Imagine you wanted to answer the question 'What factors affect condom use in teenagers?' We could administer questionnaires about sexual practices (such as condom use, previous condom use, number of sexual partners, perceptions of risk of unsafe sex etc.). By looking at these variables we could see which predict condom use (which has obvious important implications). This is the only real way to answer this question because we cannot really manipulate any of these variables particularly easily: although we might be able to change perceptions of the risks of unsafe sex, ethical considerations would probably prevent us from encouraging people to acquire more sexual partners for the benefit of our research! However, there is a price to pay, which relates to causality.

Cause and effect

Psychologists are interested in answering questions such as 'Does drinking cause memory loss?', 'Is sexual impotence all in the mind?' and maybe 'Does stress trigger depression?' Research questions such as these often imply a causal link between variables. Sometimes this could be in a direct statement such as 'Does drinking cause memory loss?' Sometimes the implication might be subtler, such as 'Is sexual impotence all in the mind?' Here the implication is that a person's mental outlook causes them to be sexually impotent.

Many research questions can be broken down into a proposed cause (in this case mental outlook) and a proposed outcome (poor sexual performance). Both the cause and the outcome are variables: for the cause, some people will worry about their sexual performance, whereas others won't (so it is something that varies); and for the outcome, well, some people will be able to perform sexually and others won't (again, this is something that varies). The key to answering the research question is to uncover how the proposed cause and the proposed outcome relate to each other. Is it the case that the people who worry about their performance are the same people that cannot perform?

Early philosophers, such as David Hume (1748; 1739–40), said that to infer cause and effect:

- cause and effect must occur close together in time (contiguity)
- the cause must occur before the effect does
- the effect should never occur without the presence of the cause.

These conditions imply that causality can be inferred through corroborating evidence: cause is equated to high degrees of correlation between contiguous events.

In our impotence example, to infer that worry caused impotence, it would be sufficient to find that whenever someone worried about their performance they would be impotent, that the worry should precede the impotence, and that the person should never be impotent if they haven't just been worrying about it!

Already we can begin to see one fundamental problem with correlational evidence: the variables are measured *at the same time*. That is, we get no information about the contiguity between different variables. We might find from a questionnaire study that people who worry a lot about impotence do tend to be impotent, but we would know nothing about whether that worry precedes the impotence.

Let's imagine that we also find that sometimes a person worries about their sexual performance but does not become impotent. This doesn't violate any of Hume's rules: he doesn't say anything about the cause happening without the effect. It could be that both worry about sexual performance and impotence are caused by a third variable (for example, the behaviour of their partner, which might quite reasonably mediate how anxious the person feels and whether they rise to the occasion).

This illustrates a second problem with correlational evidence: the *tertium quid* ('a third person or thing of indeterminate character'). Field and Hole (2003) use the example of how you might observe a strong correlation between having dreadlocks and supporting environmental issues. However, it is unlikely that having dreadlocks causes an interest in the environment – presumably, there is an external factor (or factors) that causes both. These extraneous factors are sometimes called *confounding variables*, or confounds for short.

The shortcomings of Hume's criteria led John Stuart Mill to suggest that, to infer cause, not only should cause precede effect, and cause and effect correlate (as Hume had said), but that all other explanations of the cause–effect relationship must be ruled out. Put simply, confounding variables should be ruled out.

To rule out confounding variables, Mill proposed that an effect should be present when the cause is present *and* when the cause is absent the effect should be absent also. Field and Hole (2003) sum up Mill's ideas by saying that the only way to infer causality is through comparison of two controlled situations: one in which the cause is present and one in which the cause is absent. These situations should be identical in all senses except the presence of cause.

We'll come back to these ideas in the next chapter when we look at different methods for collecting data. For now, just bear in mind the conditions necessary to draw conclusions about causes of effects.

Two important variables

We've seen that most research questions can be broken down into cause and effect. We've also seen that it's important to measure things when we do research. It will come as no surprise, then, that to answer research questions we need to measure the proposed cause and the proposed effect. Any variables that we think are a cause are known as *independent variables* (because their value does not depend on any other variables); these are the variables that are manipulated in experiments. Any variable that we think is an effect is known as a *dependent variable* (because the value of this variable depends on the independent variable or cause).

These terms are very closely tied to experimental methods. In cross-sectional research we don't manipulate any variables and we cannot make causal statements about the relationships between variables. So it doesn't make sense to talk of dependent and independent variables because all variables are dependent variables in a sense.

One possibility is to abandon the terms 'dependent' and 'independent variable' and use the terms *predictor* and *outcome*. In experimental work the cause (or independent variable) is a predictor, and the effect (or dependent variable) is simply an outcome. This terminology also suits cross-sectional work where, statistically at least, we can use one or more variables to make predictions about the other(s) without needing to imply causality.

Testing theories with numbers

Once we've come up with a theory and collected some data by measuring some variables, we need some way to assess whether or not the theory is supported. One approach is to use mathematics to help us out with this task (*quantitative research*). In fact, Britain can be very proud of the fact that it produced arguably the two most important figures in modern statistics: Ronald Fisher and Karl Pearson. These two men (both of whom worked at University College London, although not at the same time) are largely responsible for the statistical techniques that psychologists use.

There's also an extremely interesting history between the two men who, on the face of it, hated each other! Pearson was the elder and a famous statistician when Fisher was a young academic. Fisher published a paper that Pearson publicly criticised (based on some misunderstandings of Fisher's work) without informing Fisher. Pearson subsequently ignored Fisher's re-explanation of his work and, to add insult to injury, some of Fisher's papers were withdrawn from the Royal Society (an extremely important forum for this kind of work) because they corrected some errors in Pearson's work and Pearson was revered at the time within this society. The hostility between the men was such that Fisher refused Pearson's offer of a job at University College London, and accepted the post only after Pearson retired. Who said statistics is dull?

The easiest way to illustrate how we use statistics to tell us whether our data support our theories is to use an example that Fisher (1925/1991) describes. Fisher wanted to test a female friend's claim that she

Figure 36.1 Fisher's 'tea test'

could determine, by tasting a cup of tea, whether the milk or the tea was added first to the cup (see Figure 36.1). Fisher reasoned that, if this claim were true, then if he gave the lady some cups of tea, some of which had the milk added first and some of which had the milk added last, she should be able to distinguish the cups correctly. In all cases, all the lady knows is that there is an equal number of cups in which milk was added first or last.

Imagine first that there are only two cups; the lady has a 50 per cent chance of guessing correctly. Would this be sufficient to convince Fisher that she had the talents she claimed to have? Probably not. She could perform well on this task just by guessing. However, if we had four cups (two with milk added first and two with milk added last), then there are six different orders in which these cups can be arranged. If the lady got the order correct, then she could do this by guessing only one in six times. Therefore, our confidence in her talent should increase. If we used six cups, there are twenty orders in which these can be arranged and the lady would only guess the correct order one time in twenty (or 5 per cent of the time). If she got the correct order then we would be very confident that she could genuinely tell the difference.

These principles underlie science: we draw inferences about theories based on confidence about a given set of data. If it's very unlikely that we would get a particular set of data if our hypothesis is untrue, then we become more confident that our hypothesis is true. Fisher actually suggested that an appropriate level of confidence is 0.95 (95 per cent), so that if the probability of our results being due to chance is less than 0.05 (5 per cent or one in twenty – just as in the six-cups example) then we should conclude that a result is genuine.

This example lays the foundations of the statistical ideas presented in subsequent chapters. It is worth remembering, however, that this value is completely arbitrary, even though some psychologists use it as if it has some kind of magical power. The truth is that Fisher could just as easily have decided that 0.1 was a suitable criterion, or 0.01, if he'd woken up in a different mood on that fateful morning!

Figure 36.2 illustrates the idea that you begin with an initial observation or research question that is probably informed by data. You then generate a hypothesis to explain your observation and in doing so identify variables that can be measured. You then collect data to test your theory (and measure the variables you previously identified). Finally, you analyse these data and the results should feed back into your theory by either supporting your ideas or, more often, provoking modification of your original theory. The modified theory is then tested (so you get stuck in this eternal loop of generating and testing theories until the day you die).

One question we haven't yet answered is how we know whether it's likely or unlikely that we would get the data we have if our hypothesis is untrue. Well, put simply, we fit a statistical model to the data and see whether it fits the data well. This is best explained by analogy.

Field (2004) likens statistics to an engineer wishing to build a bridge across a river. An engineer doesn't just go out one morning, with a pile of bricks and steel, and build whatever bridge she happens to feel like, because it would probably fall down. Instead, she looks at bridges in the real world and sees what materials they are made from, what structures they

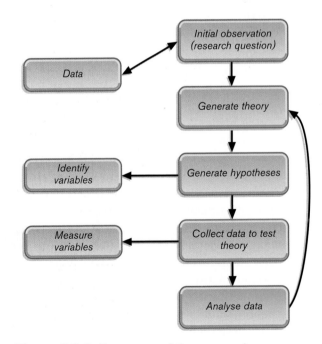

Figure 36.2 Summary of the research process

use and so on. (She might even collect data about whether these bridges are still standing!) This information is used to construct a model. She builds a scaled-down version of the real-world bridge. The engineer will try to build a model that best fits the situation of interest based on the data available. Once the model has been built, it is used to predict things about the real world. For example, its strength might be tested by placing weights along it. Obviously it's vital that the model is an accurate representation of the real world.

Psychologists do much the same thing: we build statistical models of real-world psychological processes based on our theories. We then test these models by collecting data. Unlike engineers, though, we don't have access to the real-world situation and so we can only ever infer things about psychological processes based upon the models we build. For our inferences to be precise, the statistical model we build must accurately represent the data collected (the observed data). The degree to which a statistical model represents the data collected is known as the *fit* of the model. If our statistical model fits our data well, and this model is based on our original theory, then it's likely that the initial theory was correct.

Testing theories without numbers

An alternative to reducing psychological processes to statistical models is to attempt to extrapolate support for a theory from what people say or write (*qualitative research*). Describing qualitative research is not easy: the term has tended to be associated with the researcher being more interested in meanings and contexts rather than the precision and control associated with quantitative research. This has also led to rather unhelpful attributions (in some people) of quantitative research being 'better' because of its association with strict control of variables and causal inference. Of course, the reality is that both methodologies have their strengths and their weaknesses. Hammersley (1992) distinguished qualitative and quantitative research in terms of seven components (as shown in Table 36.1).

Some people would disagree with Hammersley on almost all of these points. For example, quantitative data are not always collected in strictly controlled

laboratory settings; conversely, qualitative data can be collected in a reasonably controlled manner. It is also the case that many psychologists who use qualitative data would object to the implications that they are not interested in human behaviour or trying to uncover scientific laws. The important point is not to get bogged down in these debates but just to see these methodologies as two different approaches to understanding human behaviour.

The wealth of qualitative approaches cannot be summarised adequately here – we can provide only a flavour. One popular method that illustrates qualitative analysis generally is *discourse analysis*. Discourse analysis operates on the basic assumption that by studying what we say (and how we interact) we can gain access to psychological processes. For example, if we say we are 'depressed', our expression of depression is not based just on some internal experience that only we have access to, but rather the label of 'depression' that we have attached to how we feel at that moment is socially constructed – we have used that label because we have observed how others have used the label.

Discourse analysts are interested in what people are doing when they say things and the functions of statements that people make. So our declaring that 'we are depressed' should be taken within the context of our social environment (perhaps we are just trying to elicit sympathy, perhaps we are crying out for help). By studying these interactions we can learn a lot about how the social world is constructed and also about how psychological processes manifest themselves in the real world.

The starting point for a discourse analysis could be an individual interview (which has the advantage of control) or a group discussion (which has the advantage that you can look at natural interactions). These discussions would then be transcribed. The first thing to realise is that not all of the material will be analysed but, instead, topics or themes are identified, often through reading the material and looking for recurring features of conversation or intuition about important parts of the dialogue. You would then begin to index the transcripts according to the themes identified. You should re-read the material to try to find counter-examples of things

TABLE 36.1   HAMMERSLEY'S (1992) DISTINCTION OF QUALITATIVE AND QUANTITATIVE RESEARCH

	QUALITATIVE	QUANTITATIVE
Data	Qualitative	Quantitative
Setting	Natural	Artificial (laboratory)
Focus	Meanings	Behaviour
Model	Holistic	Philosophy of science
Approach	Inductive	Deductive
Aim	Uncover cultural patterns	Uncover scientific laws
Basis	Idealism	Realism

you've identified (this is especially important if you're working on intuitions).

The analysis itself is based on writing an account of the themes you've identified or the intuitions you're following, and extracting data from the transcripts to back up (or contradict) your ideas. The analysis should be iterative: you should reassess your analysis and redraft it as readings of the transcripts throw up new ideas and examples. Billig (1997) gives an excellent real-life example of the process.

There are of course other techniques, and the whole process can be both theory- or data-driven. In theory-driven analysis you analyse discourse or interactions with respect to existing theory. In data-driven analysis you collect data with no particular theory in mind and let the analysis inform the development of a theory (sometimes called *grounded theory*).

Summary

This chapter has shown us how theories and research are intrinsically linked and has tried to give you a flavour of the research process by explaining the various stages of psychological research. You begin with an initial observation or research question that is probably informed by data. You then generate a

hypothesis to explain this observation and, in doing so, identify variables that can be measured. You then collect data to test the theory (and measure the variables you previously identified). Finally, you analyse these data (either by fitting a statistical model if we've collected numeric data, or through an analysis of text, discourse or interactions). The results should feed back into your theory by either supporting your ideas or, more often, provoking modification of your original theory. The modified theory is then tested.

Sir Ronald Aylmer Fisher wondering whether he was right to suggest 0.05!

Section 8
Research methods and statistics

Testing theories

'Little Miss Muffet sat on a tuffet, Eating her curds and whey. There came a big spider, He sat down beside her. And frightened Miss Muffet away!'

Thinking about what you've learnt in this chapter, how would you discover whether the spider really did scare Miss Muffet away? (Think about what your hypotheses would be, use what you know about cause and effect to suggest what you'd need to do to test these hypothesis, what variables would you measure and so on.)

Answer

Your theory is that 'Spiders scare Miss Muffet'. The experimental hypothesis would be 'When Miss Muffet sees a spider, she runs away' and the null hypothesis would be 'When Miss Muffet sees a spider she does not run away'.

Thinking about these in terms of a scientific statement, what are your cause and effect? Well, the cause is spiders and the effect is running away. Therefore these are your two variables: spiders are the independent variable (predictor) and running away (well, anxiety, really) is your dependent variable (outcome).

Thinking about what you know about isolating cause and effect (Hume and Mill), we would need to compare two situations: one in which cause is present and one in which cause is absent.

Therefore we need to have some instances where Miss Muffet sees a spider and some instances where she doesn't. This would be how we manipulate our predictor variable: we would make sure there were some occasions when a spider came and sat beside Miss Muffet and some occasions when it didn't. If the spider causes anxiety, then when the spider is there we would expect anxiety to go up, and when it's not there anxiety should be normal.

How would we measure anxiety? We could just see whether she ran away (yes or no) or perhaps go for something more sophisticated like measuring her heart rate or her skin conductance (how much she's sweating), both of which are indicators of fear.

How would we gain confidence that our theory was correct? If we took many observations, and found that in general when the spider was there Miss Muffet was anxious and when it wasn't there she wasn't anxious, we could be fairly confident that the spider causes anxiety (although we would need to be careful to control the woodland environment to make sure there weren't any other creepy crawlies that appeared when the spider did!).

Knowing that the spider causes anxiety, we can generate new research questions: 'Why does the spider scare her?', 'Is it because it's hairy?', 'Is it because it sat beside her (would it be different if it stood)?', 'Is it because it has eight legs?'

Learning outcomes

When you have completed this chapter you
should be able to:
- describe why research is important in
  psychology
- describe what a theory is and how hypotheses
  are generated
- describe the reasons why we measure things,
  and critically assess the issues involved in
  measuring psychological variables
- discuss the difference between a cause and a
  correlation
- critically assess how data can be analysed with
  either quantitative or qualitative methods.

Key terms

Alternative hypothesis
Confounding variable
Content validity
Continuous variable
Correlational research
Criterion validity
Cronbach's alpha
Cross-sectional research
Demand characteristic
Dependent variable
Discourse analysis
Discrete variable
Ecological validity
Experimental hypothesis
Experimental research

Fit
Grounded theory
Hypothesis
Independent variable
Interval data
Levels of measurement
Measurement
Measurement error
Nominal data
Non-scientific statements
Null hypothesis
One-tailed
Ordinal data
Outcome
Predictor
Qualitative research
Quantitative research
Ratio data
Reliability
Scientific statements
Split-half reliability
Tertium quid
Test-retest reliability
Theory
Two-tailed
Validity
Variable

Further reading

Field, A. P. and Hole, G. (2003) *How to Design and Report Experiments.* London: Sage.

Hayes, N. (1997) (ed.) *Doing Qualitative Analysis in Psychology.* Hove: Psychology Press.

Miles, J. (2001) *Research Methods and Statistics.* Exeter: Crucial.

37

Collecting data

Route map of the chapter

In the last chapter we saw the importance of collecting data to inform theories and to try to explain human behaviour. This chapter looks at how we conduct research. We begin by looking at a very important aspect of research: ethics. We overview some important issues to consider in conducting ethical research, such as informing people about what you're doing, deceiving people, debriefing participants, confidentiality, and the right to withdraw from the experiment. We then turn our attention to experimental designs. We learnt a bit about cause and effect in the previous chapter and we will now build on this to find out why control conditions and randomisation are important in experimental research. We then look at different ways to measure and manipulate variables, and overview some commonly used experimental designs. After that, we turn our attention to non-experimental designs before considering how we actually find people to test.

Introduction

As professionals, it is important that psychologists have a code of conduct that guides their everyday activities (including treatment, research, and interactions with other psychologists, the media, students, patients and members of the public). The purpose of a code of conduct is mainly to protect the people within our care (be they patients, students or participants in our research).

Ethical considerations in research

Ethical guidelines aim to ensure that we treat our colleagues and participants in an appropriate

manner. This section looks specifically at some ethical issues that need to be considered when conducting research.

The British Psychological Society (BPS) has a detailed code of conduct that covers all aspects of a psychologist's activities. In terms of research, the general guiding principle is that the consequences of the research should be considered from the standpoint of all participants; foreseeable threats to their psychological well being, health, values or dignity should be eliminated. In a multi-cultural and multi-ethnic society, and where investigations involve participants of different ages, gender and social background, the researcher may not have sufficient knowledge of the implications of any study – the best judge of whether an investigation will cause offence may be members of the population from which the participants in the study are to be drawn.

Participants should have confidence in the experimenter, and mutual respect and confidence between the experimenter and the participants should be encouraged.

Informed consent

Whenever possible, researchers should inform all participants of the objectives of the study and about all aspects of the research that might be expected to influence willingness to participate. Should the participant enquire about any other aspect of the research, the investigator should normally oblige. A related issue is that of deception (see page 654).

It is important to gain *informed consent* because researchers are often in a position of authority or influence over participants, who may be their students, employees or clients. This relationship can

Figure 37.1 *An example of a consent form*

The form itself contains the following text:

Consent form

Information sheet

Participant code: _____

Age (years): _____

Gender (please tick box): male ☐ female ☐

In this experiment you will be asked to take part in 4 short computer-based tasks. Each task will take around 5 minutes. In all tasks you will be asked to categorise words or pictures as falling into one of two categories. All of the words and pictures are ones that you would normally come across in everyday life. We would also like to weigh you and measure your height before the study begins.

You have been assigned a code so that your name will never be attached to the data collected from you, so the information is completely confidential.

You do not have to take part in this study if you don't want to. If you decide to take part *you may withdraw at any time without having to give a reason.*

Consent form

If you have:

• Read the information above

• Had an opportunity to ask questions

• Got satisfactory answers to your questions

• Understood that you're free to withdraw from the study at any time, without giving a reason

Please sign below to indicate that you agree to take part in the study.

Please sign: _____ Date: _____

Name in block letters: _____

Page 1

---

be allowed to pressurise the participants to take part in, or remain in, an investigation that they find upsetting. Milgram's obedience to authority experiments (see Chapter 25) are a very good example of how people might be encouraged to do things they're uncomfortable with (like giving someone an electric shock) just because an experimenter is telling them to do so. Therefore it's customary to use a consent form in which participants are informed about any aspect of the study that might influence their willingness to participate. They would then sign an agreement saying that they had understood what the study involved, understood that they were entitled to withdraw at any point (see page 655), and had agreed to take part.

Two obvious threats to consent are work with children or with adults who have impairments that may compromise their understanding of the experimental procedures. If research involves any person under 16 years old, consent should be obtained from parents or from those *in loco parentis* (for example, teachers within a school). If the nature of the research precludes consent being obtained from parents or permission being obtained from teachers, the researcher must obtain approval from an ethics committee before commencing the study. Where real consent cannot be obtained from adults with impairments in understanding or communication, wherever possible the investigator should consult a person well placed to appreciate the participant's reaction (e.g. a member of the person's family), and must obtain approval from independent advisers.

A final issue is paying participants for their participation. Payment can induce participants to risk harm beyond that which they would be prepared to risk, without payment, in their normal lifestyle. For example, someone who would not normally take drugs may be induced into taking them in a research context because of the financial rewards. Related to this point is that when research involves potential harm, unusual discomfort or other negative consequences, the researcher must obtain the approval of independent advisers, inform the participants and obtain informed, real consent from each of them.

Figure 37.1 shows an example of a consent form. Note that the information reveals all the important aspects of the research without necessarily giving away its purpose, and without boring the participant with a detailed account of the 'computer task' (because the task is a simple reaction-time task that doesn't have any ethical implications). However, note that specific mention is made that the person will be weighed. It is important to mention this here as it might cause offence. Finally, note that specific mention is made of the fact that the participant can withdraw at any time, and also note that a code is assigned to the participant.

On the actual consent form, the participant signs to agree that they have had the opportunity to ask questions and have got satisfactory answers to any questions they have asked, and that they have understood that they can withdraw at any point. The consent part of the form then needs to be detached so that the name of the participant cannot be connected to the code assigned to them.

Deception

Misleading participants is hugely problematic because it compromises their ability to make an informed choice about whether to participate (and of course it's not nice to lie to people!). The guiding rule in the BPS Code of Conduct is that withholding information or misleading participants is unacceptable unless there is extremely strong scientific or medical justification for this, and is especially reprehensible if the participants are likely to object or show unease once debriefed. If this is the case, the BPS recommends that you consult individuals who share the social and cultural background of the participants in the research (to gauge their objection/unease at the *deception*), although the advice of ethics committees or experienced and uninvolved colleagues may be sufficient.

Nevertheless, the BPS respects the fact that sometimes it's impossible to study psychological processes without withholding information about the true object of the study or deliberately misleading the participants. It therefore suggests that before engaging in such a study the researcher should:

- ensure that alternative procedures avoiding concealment or deception are not available
- ensure that the participants are provided with sufficient information at the earliest stage
- consult appropriately upon the way that the deliberate deception or withholding of information will be received.

Debriefing

If participants are aware that they have taken part in an experiment, it is only fair that the experimenter tell them something about the experiment. The researcher should provide any necessary information to complete the participant's understanding of the nature of the study. In addition, the investigator should discuss the participant's experience of the study to monitor any unforeseen negative effects or misconceptions.

However, this isn't an excuse to be incredibly unethical or to deceive people (under the pretence that they'll find out the truth eventually), because some effects of an experiment cannot be negated by a verbal description following the research. The BPS therefore encourages active intervention before participants leave the research setting.

Freedom to withdraw

You'll remember on our consent form (Figure 37.1) there was a phrase informing the participant that they were free to leave the experiment at any time. It is vital that this principle is upheld, even if money has been offered to participate. In fact, it's good practice still to pay people who withdraw (otherwise you're offering an inducement to stay and complete a task that a participant would otherwise stop doing).

The right to withdraw can be difficult in observational or organisational settings; nevertheless, the investigator must attempt to ensure that participants (including children) know of their right to withdraw. There is an issue of how to tell if a child wants to withdraw. The BPS suggests that if a child tries to avoid the testing situation, then this can be taken as evidence of failure to consent to the procedure. Having done research with children, I'm also encouraged by the fact that some children at least are perfectly happy to tell you that they'd rather be doing something else!

A related issue is that having done an experiment, a participant has the right to withdraw retrospectively (resulting from their experiences or the debriefing). This withdrawal would mean their withdrawing their consent to you using their data (which must then be destroyed).

Confidentiality

Legislation, including the Data Protection Act, means that information obtained about a participant during an experiment is confidential unless otherwise agreed in advance. Participants in psychological research have a right to expect that information they provide will be treated confidentially and, if published, will not be identifiable as connected with them. Note that in the consent form (Figure 37.1) the participant is explicitly told that their data will remain confidential. (You can explicitly say in consent forms that participants' data may be published but that, if it is, their confidentiality will be maintained.) If confidentiality and/or anonymity cannot be guaranteed, the participant must be warned of this in advance of agreeing to participate.

Protection of participants

The primary responsibility of researchers is to protect participants from physical and mental harm during the study. The risk of harm should, ordinarily, be no greater than in everyday life. Where the risk of harm is greater than in ordinary life, independent advice should be sought (see the section on 'Informed consent', above). Participants must be informed about factors in the procedure that might create a risk, such as pre-existing medical conditions, and must be told of any action that will help them avoid risk.

After the experiment, participants have the right to contact the experimenter regarding issues to do with their well being. Procedures for contacting the investigator within a reasonable time period following participation should be made explicit, as should the situations in which contact is appropriate (i.e. if stress, potential harm, or related questions or concern arise despite the precautions taken). Researchers also have an obligation to remove any consequences that might arise from the experiment.

Issues also arise when the research involves collecting personal information. The participant must be protected from stress by all appropriate measures (e.g. assurance that answers to personal questions need not be given). If the experiment involves collecting personal data, there should be no concealment or deception.

Section 8
Research methods and statistics

ACTIVITY BOX 37.1

Ethics

What are the ethical issues in the following study?

Campbell, Sanderson and Laverty (1964) were interested in the effects of traumatic experiences on learning. You should be familiar with the learning account of anxiety, in which anxiety about a stimulus develops as a result of that stimulus being associated with some negative outcome (like 'Little Albert' becoming afraid of his rat because he associated it with Watson and Rayner making a loud noise with an iron bar). Campbell *et al.* wanted to extend these ideas to see whether anxiety would subsequently subside when the stimulus was presented without the associated trauma.

Stimuli

The conditioned stimulus was a tone (which was affectively neutral) and the traumatic outcome was respiratory paralysis induced by Scoline (succinylcholine chloride). This drug has the effect of paralysing the participant without acting as an anaesthetic, so participants are fully conscious except that they can no longer breathe.

Participants

Eleven alcoholic patients volunteered, having been told that the experiment 'was connected with a possible therapy for alcoholism' (1964: 629): five experimental participants and six controls (three of whom only heard the tones and three of whom only received the respiratory paralysis). These six participants were either 'discharged from hospital or ran away' (1964: 629) before the experiment was over.

Method

In essence, participants first habituated to the tone and then the Scoline was administered. As the drug took effect, 'the most noticeable feature of the onset of the paralysis was a fibrillation of the facial muscles followed by closing of the eyes.

The impression which one got ... was that he had been taken by surprise' (1964: 629). Paralysis lasted between 90 and 130 seconds, after which participants 'recovered partial use of their limbs first and made ineffective jerky movements which appeared to be an attempt to remove something which was covering their faces' (1964: 629). At a later date the tone was presented without paralysis to see the time over which the conditioned anxiety response would continue.

How traumatic was the paralysis? Campbell *et al.* report the following.

- 'Once the paralysis had passed off the subject lay very quietly on the table. Several of them asked for a reassurance that they would not be given a second trial' (1964: 631).
- 'After the conditioning each subject was asked to describe what had happened to him and to say what he had felt. The impression which one obtained from listening to these accounts was that, although each subject found it difficult to put his sensations into words, and that many of the feelings arising from the skeletal paralysis were so unfamiliar that they could not be referred to any ordinary conception of bodily function, the suspension of breathing was an experience that was horrific to a degree' (1964: 631).
- 'All the subjects ... said that they thought they were dying. One subject made this comparison: he had been a rear-gunner in a Stirling bomber which had flown, during one operation, straight and level for 5000 yards on a radar beam over Dusseldorf; he rated the Scoline trial as the more traumatic experience of the two' (1964: 631–2).
- 'The subjects described their movements as part of a struggle to get away from the apparatus and to tear off the wires and electrodes. Though in fact their movements were small and poorly controlled the subjects were under the impression that they had been making large movements' (1964: 632).

Results

Participants produced physical reactions associated with anxiety when they heard the tone. Even when the tone was no longer followed by the paralysis, the anxiety did not subside (even a week later and after 100 presentations of the tone alone).

Answers

This experiment is amazing if only because it's hard to believe that people used to get away with doing this kind of thing (for the record, it's an appallingly designed study, but more on that later). It really has got everything: deception, traumatic consequences and no debriefing.

To begin with, the researchers used a vulnerable group (alcoholics) and there is no evidence in the published article that they informed them at all about what would happen to them. They were encouraged into the experiment by being told that the research was connected with a possible therapy for alcoholism. Although this may well have been true, it is taking advantage of the alcoholics' desire to be cured (remember they were all hospitalised).

Participants were not returned to their original state (or debriefed). Neither is there anything in the paper to suggest that any kind of counselling was given to the participants. They also underwent a procedure that compromised their right to withdraw: once the paralysis had set in, there was nothing that could stop it!

Finally, psychologists have a responsibility when disseminating the results of their work to others (including parents and teachers). The main problem here is that evaluative statements may carry unintended weight.

Giving advice

During research, you may (especially if you do clinical work) obtain evidence of psychological or physical problems of which a participant is, apparently, unaware. In such cases, the psychologist should inform the participant if, and only if, they believe that by not doing so the participant's future well being may be endangered. So, for example, if you had reason to believe that your participant was suicidal, it would be a good idea to encourage her or him to seek professional help.

If as a result of your research, or because you detected a problem, a participant solicits advice concerning educational, personality, behavioural or health issues, caution must be exercised. If the issue is serious and you are not qualified to offer assistance, the appropriate source of professional advice should be recommended. Sticking with our suicidal participant, if you're not a qualified clinical psychologist then you shouldn't try to help this person but of course you can take practical steps to assist them in getting the help they need (for example, giving them the phone number of their university counselling service or phoning it on their behalf and with their permission).

Appreciating the limitations of your expertise is one of the key guidelines of the code of conduct that extends beyond research settings. As a psychologist, you should not comment on things about which you are unqualified to give an opinion. So, although an expert on child anxiety could reasonably appear on *Richard and Judy* to discuss anxiety in childhood, the same person should not appear on television offering opinions about the neurological consequences of boxing matches (unless, of course, he also happens to be an expert on this in his spare time!).

Experimental designs

We saw in the previous chapter that experimental designs seek to answer research questions by manipulating one variable to see its effect on another. For example, if we wanted to see whether 'practice makes perfect' in the context of, say, playing the drums, we could manipulate the variable 'practice' by getting different groups of people to practise for different amounts of time each day, then we could see the effect this had on their performance. This section looks at experimental designs – that is, designs where the researcher actively manipulates one or more variable(s) to uncover the effect on other variables.

The function of control groups

It's one thing to manipulate a variable and look at the effect that this manipulation has, but it's another step then to draw inferences about cause and effect. Mill proposed (see page 645) that causal factors could be isolated only by comparing two conditions: one in which supposed cause is present and one in which supposed cause is absent.

In our drumming example, it wouldn't be sufficient just to vary the amount of practice that people had; there would need to be a condition in which the proposed cause (practice) was absent. In other words, we'd have to have some people who didn't practise at all. Mill called this a *control condition*. A control condition is simply a condition that is identical in every respect to your other conditions, except that the proposed cause is not present. A control condition acts as a baseline against which to compare behaviour when a proposed cause is present.

For example, imagine you wanted to test the notion that women become anorexic because the media constantly bombard them with images of skinny, ill-looking waifs. Our proposed cause is the images of skinny, ill-looking waifs, and our effect is dieting or anorexia. To verify that the images are the cause of dieting, we would need to have one condition in which images of skinny waifs are presented to people and one where those images are not presented.

As we've seen before, in experiments we manipulate one variable to observe its effect on another. The variable we typically manipulate is the one we have proposed as a cause and in the simplest situation we manipulate it by changing whether the cause is present or absent. These manipulations are known as *levels* of the variable. The most basic experiment manipulates the causal variable so that it has two levels (supposed cause present vs supposed cause absent). However, we can have more than two levels. For example, we could manipulate not just whether people are exposed to pictures of skeletal celebrities and models but also the *degree* to which they're exposed to these images. We could look at when a person isn't exposed to any images (the control), when they're exposed to 20 images a week, 40 images a week and 100 images a week. The 'images' variable now has four levels (0, 20 per week, 40 per week, 100 per week).

It was mentioned in passing that the control condition needs to be identical to all other conditions *except* that the cause is absent. In fact, all experimental conditions should be identical in every respect except for the manipulation that you've made. Put another way, all random factors should be held constant. To do this, we have to ensure that all aspects of our experimental conditions are the same. You can take this idea to varying degrees of extreme. In the imagery experiment, for example, it might be sensible to make sure that everyone was roughly the same weight to begin with because, presumably, the weight you are has some influence over your desire to diet. In general, you would hope to test everyone in the same room and use identical instructions to ensure that these factors aren't contributing to whatever effects you get.

Random sampling and why it is important

In the previous section, I mentioned that in the imagery experiment we might want to make sure that all participants were roughly the same weight. This comment alluded to an important point about how we allocate participants to experimental conditions. We can rule out many random influences on our experiment simply by *randomising* parts of the study. The first important thing to do is to make sure participants are randomly allocated to your experimental and control groups.

Imagine we went to Weight Watchers© and showed the people there images of waif-like celebrities and then measured the amount of weight they lost over the next few weeks. We then went to a 'fat and proud' group meeting to collect our control data (where no images are shown). We might find that those who were shown images are more likely to lose weight than those not shown images. However, this result is of course because those who were shown images were already at Weight Watchers (therefore wanting to lose weight) whereas those not shown images had a positive attitude towards their bodies and didn't feel the need to diet. The effect of imagery has been confounded with the fact that we used two very different groups of people in which to collect data.

There's nothing inherently wrong with using these two groups of people, but we must randomly (and preferably evenly) allocate them to both groups (that way we know that any people from Weight Watchers are present in both groups and so the effect of Weight Watchers will cancel out). If you think of how complex the average human is (how much humans differ in intelligence, motivation, emotional expression, physical characteristics), you should realise how important it is randomly to allocate people to experimental groups: it ensures a roughly equivalent spread of attributes across all groups.

The same people or different?

Let's take a step back for a minute and think what would happen if we did not introduce an experimental manipulation (i.e. we didn't bother showing anyone any images of skinny women). If there is no experimental manipulation, then we expect the people in the experimental group to behave in roughly the same way as the control group. However, performance won't be identical; there will be small differences in performance created by unknown factors. For example, there will be subtle differences in people's natural desire to diet, they will differ in their upbringing (whether their parents thought it was great to be skinny people), their IQ and all sorts of other variables. These other factors are known as *extraneous variables* and variation in performance created by these variables is known as *unsystematic variation*.

Now imagine we introduce an experimental manipulation (in this case present some of the people with images of skinny women), then we do something different to the participants in condition 1 compared with what we do to those in condition 2. This should have an effect on the performance in the two groups. Differences in performance created by a specific experimental manipulation are known as *systematic variation*.

The key to any research is to work out which variation is caused by the manipulation and which is caused by extraneous variables. So far, I've used the example of when we have different people in our

experimental conditions. This type of design is known as an *independent measures design* (also called a *between-group design*). In these designs there will be lots of extraneous variables at work and that's why it is absolutely vital to allocate different people to different conditions randomly. Randomisation ensures that none of these extraneous variables has too much of an impact on the outcome.

A second alternative is to control some of the obvious extraneous variables. In our imagery study we could weigh everyone, then for each person that we allocate to the experimental group, we find someone of roughly the same weight and allocate them to the control group. You can do this with other variables too, and it's not uncommon to see designs in which the researcher has for every person in one group found someone with the same IQ, gender and age for the control group (IQ, gender and age being the extraneous variables that most psychologists commonly worry about). This is known as a *matched design*.

We can take things even further just by using the same people but at different points in time (testing the same people two or more times). This has the obvious advantage that virtually all individual differences between participants are controlled because they're the same people and so only things like mood and motivation could change over time. This is known as a *repeated measures design* (also called a *within-subjects design*).

In a repeated measures design, differences between experimental conditions can be caused by only two things:

1. the manipulation that was carried out on the participants
2. any other factor that might affect the way in which a person performs from one time to the next.

The latter factor is likely to be fairly minor compared with the influence of the experimental manipulation. In an independent design, differences between the two conditions can also be caused by one of two things:

1. the manipulation that was carried out on the participants
2. differences between the characteristics of the people allocated to each of the groups.

The latter factor in this instance is likely to create considerable random variation both within each condition and between conditions. Therefore the effect of our experimental manipulation is likely to be more apparent in a repeated measures design than in a between-group design.

However, repeated measures designs do have their price. When the same people participate in more than one experimental condition, although they are naïve during the first experimental condition they come to the second experimental condition with prior experience of what is expected of them. At the very least they will be familiar with the task they're performing or what you're measuring. Therefore you will get *practice effects*, where participants perform differently in later conditions simply because of familiarity with the experimental situation.

A second problem is *boredom effects*, where participants perform differently in later conditions because they are tired or bored from having completed the earlier conditions.

Although these effects are impossible to eliminate completely, we can again use randomisation to minimise the effect they have. Imagine we wanted to test the effect of frustration on aggression. We got people to sit in a room and every so often the experimenter would flick their ears. We counted how many times the participant punched the experimenter. Obviously, in the control condition the experimenter doesn't flick the person's ears. If everyone did the experimental condition first, then it's likely that by the time they took part in the

control condition they would already be pretty hacked off (from having their ears flicked for an hour) and so still might be quite aggressive to the experimenter. Therefore we have to make sure that some people do the experimental condition first and the control condition second, whereas others do the control condition first and the experimental condition second. This is known as *counterbalancing*.

Designing the study: some common experimental designs

The exact experimental design that you use will depend on what question you're trying to answer. We can look at a few common designs that may give you some inspiration. The post-test only control group design is the most straightforward type of true experiment you can perform (see Figure 37.2). It has two experimental conditions and uses different people in each. So you randomly divide participants into two groups and do something to one group (the experimental group or treatment group) that you don't do to the other group (the control group or no-treatment group). The performances of the two groups are then measured. If they differ, you can be reasonably confident that the difference is attributable to your experimental manipulation.

There are times when you might have more than one experimental manipulation; in which case you can simply add a third group that engages in a different experimental procedure (see Figure 37.3). In fact, you can add as many different experimental groups as are required.

Although the post-test only design is common in psychology, it has a problem: although participants are randomly assigned to the two conditions to make sure that the groups are equivalent, there is no check

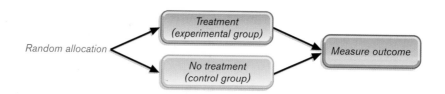

Figure 37.2 The post-test only control group design

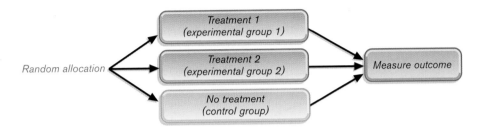

Figure 37.3 The post-test only control design with serveral experimental conditions

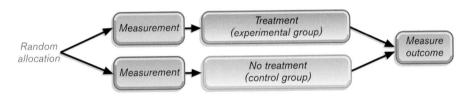

Figure 37.4 The pre-test/post-test control group design

within the design that the groups actually *are* equivalent. One improvement is therefore to measure behaviour before the manipulation in addition to after. If randomisation has been successful, then the groups should behave the same on the measure before the experimental manipulation, but their behaviour will differ *after* the experimental manipulation. (To be specific, behaviour in the experimental group should change because its members have had the experimental manipulation, whereas behaviour in the control condition shouldn't change because that group's members haven't had the experimental manipulation). This design is called a pre-test/post-test control group design (see Figure 37.4).

As with the post-test only design, this design can be extended to include more than one experimental condition. One thing to note is that in the pre-test/post-test design we have one variable that uses different participants (the experimental groups) and one that uses the same participants (measures are taken at two points in time). When there is a mixture of independent measures and repeated measures, the design is called a *mixed design* (or *mixed-plot design*).

One problem with pre-testing participants is that this pre-testing might influence their subsequent behaviour. Therefore if you're feeling really paranoid you can control for this possibility by adding an extra two groups that do not have their behaviour measured before the experiment. This way, not only do we have the advantages of the pre-test/post-test design, we can also check whether the pre-testing has any effect. This is known as the Soloman four-group design (see Figure 37.5). Although this is an extremely rigorous design it is very expensive in terms of time and participants, and so is rarely used.

So far, we've looked at designs that use different groups of participants. There are also some basic designs that use only repeated measures. The post-test only two-condition group for repeated measures uses the same participants. They take part in the experimental condition and then have their behaviour measured, then take part in the control condition and have their behaviour measured again. To control for practice effects, a different group of participants goes through exactly the same process but in the opposite order: they do the control procedure first and then the experimental procedure. Participants must be randomly allocated to these two

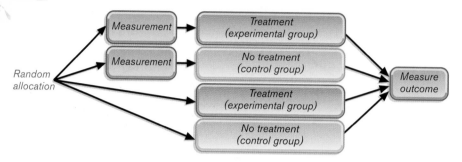

Figure 37.5 The Soloman four-group design

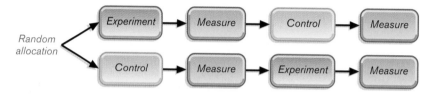

Figure 37.6 The post-test only two-condition repeated measures design

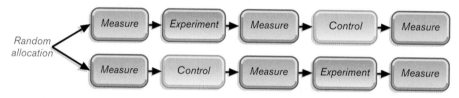

Figure 37.7 The pre-test/post-test two-condition repeated measures design

counterbalancing conditions (see Figure 37.6). A variation on this theme is to measure behaviour in both conditions before participants engage in any of the conditions (see Figure 37.7).

Obviously there are more complex designs than these (see Field and Hole, 2003, for some examples), but these 'simpler' designs should give you a flavour of the types of things that can be done.

APPLICATIONS BOX 37.1

How some standard experimental designs have been used in real research

Below are descriptions of some famous experiments (some of which have been mentioned elsewhere in this book) that use the standard experimental designs described in this chapter.

Festinger and Carlsmith (1959): cognitive dissonance

Festinger (1957) put forward the idea of cognitive dissonance: inconsistencies in our cognitions generate unpleasant feelings (dissonance) and therefore people are motivated to change their cognitions to be consistent with their behaviour. Festinger and Carlsmith (1959) put this theory to the test by getting students to engage in an extremely tedious task (turning pegs in a tray for 30 minutes), and then asking them to tell the next participant that the experiment was really interesting, exciting and fun. Participants were paid either $1 or $20 as an incentive to express these views to the next participant (and a control group did not interact with the next participant). Afterwards a questionnaire was used to measure their attitudes about the research.

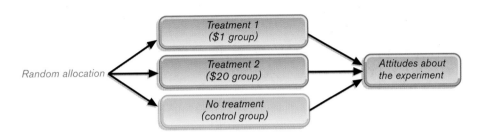

Figure 37.8 Festinger and Carlsmith (1959), an example of a post-test only control group design with several groups

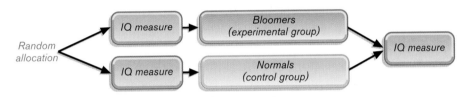

Figure 37.9 Rosenthal and Jacobson (1966), an example of a pre-test/post-test control group design

Given that all participants would have found the experiment boring, the idea was that those paid $20 would express the opinion that it was exciting and fun (and believe it) because they could reason that 'they lied about the experiment being fun because they received a large reward for that lie'. Those paid $1, however, would change their view of the experiment and believe that it really was fun because they had no incentive to lie. The design is a post-test only control group with several groups (Figure 37.8).

Rosenthal and Jacobson (1966): blame the teachers

This study wanted to examine whether teachers' expectations about their students influence how those pupils develop academically. They went into a school and labelled some of the children as 'bloomers' (i.e. children whose intellect, based on their psychological assessment, should develop rapidly). Of course, the children were labelled completely randomly! A total of 20 per cent of pupils were randomly labelled as 'bloomers'

(these were the experimental participants) and the remaining 80 per cent were control participants. IQ was measured at the beginning of the experiment, the 'bloomers' were assigned by the experimenters and then the experimenters returned eight months later to measure IQ again.

The theory was that the change in IQ scores would be bigger in 'bloomers' compared to 'non-bloomers' because teachers *expected* these children to 'bloom' (remember, though, that the bloomers were not really any different to the other children at all). This is an example of the pre-test/post-test control group design (Figure 37.9).

Greenwald *et al.* (1988): implicit attitudes

Greenwald *et al.* created the implicit association task (IAT) to measure implicit attitudes. The IAT is based on the simple idea that it should be easier to map two concepts on to a single response when those concepts are related in memory than when the concepts are unrelated. For example, Greenwald *et al.* (experiment 1)

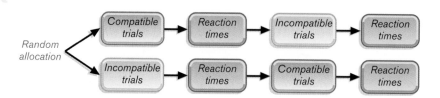

Figure 37.10 Greenwold et al. (1988), an example of a post-test only two-condition repeated measures design

presented names of flowers (e.g. ROSE), insects (e.g. WASP), positive words (e.g. LOVE) and negative words (e.g. ROTTEN) on a computer screen. Participants categorised these words by pressing one of two keys on a computer keyboard and their latency to respond in ms was recorded.

If 'flowers' and 'positive' are associated categories, and 'insects' and 'negative' are associated categories, then when responses to the concept 'flower' are assigned to the same response key as responses to the concept 'positive', and the concepts of 'insects' and 'negative' are both assigned to the other key, response times should be fast. These trials would be *compatible*.

However, when the concepts of 'flowers' and 'negative' are assigned to the same key, and 'insects' and 'positive' are assigned to the other, then response times should be relatively slow because the categories assigned to the same key are *incompatible*.

In a typical IAT, participants do compatible trials (as described above) and incompatible trials at different points in time, and the order in which these two types of trial is done is counterbalanced across two groups. Therefore, we have the post-test only repeated measures design (Figure 37.10).

ACTIVITY BOX 37.2

Experimental design
Think back to the experiment described in Activity Box 37.1. Can you spot the big flaw in the design of this study?

Answer
The problem is that the control participants didn't complete the experiment (they ran away or were discharged from hospital). Therefore for some of the data there was no control group to make the necessary comparisons that would allow us to say something about cause and effect.

Non-experimental designs

Quasi-experimental designs
A *quasi-experimental study* is one in which the experimenter does not have complete control over the manipulation of the predictor variable. The experimenter has control over measuring the outcome but, for whatever reason, cannot randomly allocate participants to experimental conditions. A good example of this is clinical psychological research, where ethical considerations prevent you from manipulating certain variables. For instance, if you wanted to look at the effect of having depression on the way you think, it would be unethical to randomly allocate people to 'depression', in which clinical depression is induced, and 'control' conditions. Instead we wait for people to develop depression naturally and then compare them to those that haven't developed depression. The important

thing is that these groups are not randomly allocated: the depressed people are self-selecting.

There are other predictor variables that simply cannot be manipulated even if ethics permitted it. For example, we're often interested in the effects of things like gender. In this case we again cannot randomly allocate people to conditions of 'male' and 'female', we instead have to use males and females.

The consequence of not randomly allocating people to experimental conditions is that it is not possible to isolate cause and effect as conclusively as with a 'true' experimental design.

Cross-sectional designs
Cross-sectional designs are when many variables are measured simultaneously but none are manipulated. This is sometimes called *correlational* research, because all we can do with this kind of research is to look for relationships between the variables we've measured. We can't look for cause–effect relationships because we haven't manipulated any of the variables, and also because all of the variables have been measured at the same point in time (I mentioned this point on page 645). In psychology, probably the most common cross-sectional research that you'll come across is when someone has administered several questionnaires that measure different aspects of behaviour to see which aspects of behaviour are related.

Observing people
One way to find out about human behaviour is simply to watch it. Many sciences that like to think of themselves as 'hard sciences' rely heavily on observational methods. In fact, possibly the most classic example of how observation can inform scientific theory is the case of a certain Isaac Newton, who observed (well, *experienced* might be a better word than 'observed') an apple falling out of a tree and onto his head. Shortly afterwards we had the theory of gravity, which is still used today. Physicists, chemists, ecologists and the like often observe the behaviour of things (particles, atoms, subatomic particles, birds, worms etc.) before trying to explain their behaviour. Psychology can likewise benefit immensely from observing the behaviour of people.

Psychologists will often video-tape people, or watch them from an unobtrusive location (it has even been known for them to hide up a tree!). They will then attempt to analyse, or 'code', the behaviour they observe. Coding behaviour simply means that you try to find regularities in what people do (so, when watching children in a playground, you might distinguish between an aggressive act and a non-aggressive act). The strength of observational methods is that they enable one to get a good idea of how people normally behave (it has ecological validity). This may be quite different from how they behave in an experiment.

The downside to observational methods is that because of their non-intrusive nature, they don't allow the identification of cause and effect in the same way that a well-designed experiment does. However, systematic observations may often provide hypotheses about cause and effect that can then be tested more directly with experimental methods.

Observational methods also have specific ethical considerations. If you do an observational study you must respect the privacy and psychological well-being of the individuals studied. Unless consent to being observed is first obtained, observational research is acceptable only in situations where those observed would expect to be observed by strangers. Local cultural values need to be considered and you should ensure that you're not intruding upon the privacy of individuals who, even while in a normally public space, may believe they are unobserved.

For more information on observational techniques see Martin and Bateson (1993).

Single-subject designs and case studies
A *case study* is an in-depth analysis of a single person. Often this person will be unusual in some respect (for example, it might be useful to do a detailed study of someone with multiple personality disorder or someone who has brain damage). Case studies can be an extremely good way to generate theories and are based on what's known as the *idiographic* approach to research, which just means developing knowledge on a case-by-case basis. The opposite is the *nomothetic* approach, which is the approach of using experimental methods: knowledge

APPLICATIONS BOX 37.2

How some standard non-experimental designs have been used in real research

Below are descriptions of some famous experiments (some of which, again, have been mentioned elsewhere in this book) that use the non-experimental designs that have been described in this chapter.

Gray *et al.* (2003): psychopaths like violent words

Gray *et al.* used the IAT (described in Applications Box 37.1) to look at whether different groups of people found violent words pleasant or unpleasant. Participants had to classify positive words (e.g. LOVE) and negative words (e.g. ROTTEN), and violent (e.g. KILL) and peaceful words, on a computer screen. They categorised these words by pressing one of two keys on a computer keyboard, and their latency to respond in ms was recorded.

Compatible trials were deemed to be trials in which responses to pleasant and peaceful words were made by pressing the same key, and responses to negative and violent words were made by pressing the same key. Incompatible trials were ones in which responses to pleasant and violent words were made by pressing the same key, and responses to unpleasant and peaceful words were made using the same key. If people found violent words unpleasant then response times should be shorter for compatible trials than incompatible ones.

They tested four self-selecting groups: psychopathic murderers, psychopathic other offenders, non-psychopathic murderers and non-psychopathic other offenders. They found that psychopathic murderers showed a reduced IAT effect – that is, they found violent words more pleasant than did other people!

This design is quasi-experimental because the different groups of people are not randomly sampled (because they belong to specific naturally occurring groups). It would have been unethical to do a true experiment and to try to induce people to become psychopathic murderers (although if we had done this, it turns out that writing book chapters on research methods is a good way to induce this ...!).

Watson and Rayner (1920): Albert the Great

Watson and Rayner's study showing that 'Little Albert' could be taught to fear his pet rat just through experiencing traumatic consequences is one of the most famous psychological examples of a case study (see Chapter 33).

Rosenhan (1973): you don't have to be mad to be treated here, but it helps

Rosenhan (1973) demonstrated elegantly that diagnostic labels change perceptions of the person. Over some time, he got eight 'normal' people to report to twelve psychiatric hospitals with symptoms of hearing voices saying 'empty', 'hollow' and 'thud' (see Field, 2003). All were consequently diagnosed as schizophrenic despite not having the disorder.

Rosenhan reported that subsequent to the diagnosis, the way doctors and staff treated these pseudo-patients was different. For example, staff would ignore the pseudo-patients' attempts at conversation, their normal histories were distorted into tales of ambivalent relationships, and outbursts were attributed to the pathology of the pseudo-patients and not to the behaviour of staff and so on. This showed how 'labels' affect the way in which people are treated.

This was an *observational design* as the pseudo-patients were observed and it was noted how people treated them after their diagnosis.

is developed by studying small numbers of variables in large numbers of people.

The advantage of case studies is that they give us much richer data and allow individual differences between people to shine through. Although it's convenient to think that all schizophrenics experience the same things, in reality they have extremely varied experiences. The downside of case studies is obviously that it isn't possible to generalise the results from them beyond the person you've tested. There are many ways to conduct research on single individuals, and case studies can be experimental. For some information about doing experimental research on single cases see Field and Hole (2003).

The relationship between design and analysis

Having looked at different ways that data can be collected, I want to turn briefly to two really important issues about data analysis.

Design affects analysis and analysis affects design!

Design and data analysis tend to get treated as two different and independent processes. However, they are very much related and although I won't be talking in any depth about data analysis until the next two chapters, I do want to drum it in that you should be thinking about how you will analyse your data when you design your research and not after you've collected the data!

Speaking from experience, there is nothing more frustrating than colleagues presenting you with data they've collected and asking you how to analyse them. Usually the answer is that they can't analyse them (statistics does have some limitations), which means that they've wasted their time, or that they have to engage in highly inappropriate data analysis.

So, having designed your study, ask yourself 'How will I analyse the data?' If, having read the next two chapters, you find an appropriate statistical procedure to analyse the data you are going to collect, then, fine, pat yourself on the back and go and collect the data. If, however, there doesn't seem to be an obvious way to analyse the data you're going to get, then *stop!* Try to find out why you can't find an appropriate statistical procedure and how you can adjust your research design so that the resulting data can be analysed with an existing statistical technique.

Causal inferences

A second point about statistics is that there is sometimes a misconception that certain statistical techniques allow you to make causal inferences. For example, although you won't know what an ANOVA is for another two chapters, some people think that ANOVAs allow causal inferences, whereas correlations do not. This isn't true – it's just that an ANOVA is often used to analyse experiments in which causal variables have been manipulated. However, it's not the ANOVA that allows causal inferences; it is the way the experiment was conducted.

Similarly, multiple regression is a technique for predicting values of one variable from values of other variables (see page 700). Some people think that this is causal (if hours spent writing a book chapter predict the desire to swallow sulphuric acid, then the writing must cause the desire for painful death). However, statistically, there is nothing to say that the desire for a painful death couldn't cause the writing! The point is that statistical procedures do not allow causal inferences: the way you conduct your research does.

How do you find people to test?

Having considered all of the numerous aspects of designing research that we've covered in this chapter, the final stage of the process is to think about how you're actually going to find people to test.

Populations and samples

Psychologists are typically interested in looking for general rules about all people (e.g. 'How do people learn things?'). The best way to find these general rules is obviously to gather data from every single person on the planet. A complete collection of things (be they humans, cats or mice) is known as a *population*. Populations can be very general (e.g. all people), more specific (e.g. all men) or extremely specific (e.g. all men who sing 'You've lost that loving feeling' by the Righteous Brothers when they've had too much Stella® to drink).

If a psychologist wanted to access the entire population, this could mean gathering data from everybody on the planet, which, as you might well imagine, would be impossible. Therefore we collect data from a small subset of the population we're interested in, known as a *sample* from the population. We use this sample to estimate what we would have found had we actually gathered data from the entire population.

Intuitively you might think that larger samples are better than small ones – if your population contains 10 billion people and you collect data from 1 billion, then you should get a more accurate picture of the population than if you collected data from five people. Think of it like this: imagine you're in the pub one night (that serves Stella Artois) and at the end of the evening a bearded man stands up and sings 'You've lost that loving feeling'. Would you be prepared to assume that everyone sings this song when drunk? Probably not. You'd just think there was a drunken weirdo in the pub. What about if you went to ten different pubs and in each one a bearded man sang that song? You might start to think that perhaps there was something going on: Stella Artois does cause bearded men to sing songs by the Righteous Brothers. How about if we go to a very big pub (serving Stella Artois) full of men with facial hair and observe 1000 of them singing 'You've lost that loving feeling'? You'd probably think you were in Belgium, but after that your confidence that Stella genuinely has this strange effect on bearded men should be really high because you've seen the same behaviour in a large number of bearded men.

Jacob Bernoulli termed this the 'law of large numbers' (the fact that large samples are more representative than small ones – not that bearded men sing 'You've lost that loving feeling'!). The behaviours we observe in different samples will differ slightly, but because large samples are more representative of the population than small ones the behaviour observed in different large samples will be relatively similar, whereas the behaviours observed in different small samples is likely to be quite variable. As such, *sampling* is the process of finding people who are representative of the population you want to make inferences about.

Methods of sampling

Random sampling is where every person in the population of interest has an equal chance of being selected to take part in the research. This rarely, if ever, happens. The only way to achieve this is to take the name of every person in the population and stick their name in a hat (or other receptacle), and then pick out names (or do some computerised analogy of this). This is extremely complex, because even if you have some snazzy computer to do it for you, then you could literally spend your life in endless debates with statisticians about how randomly the computer was selecting names!

An easier method is *systematic sampling*, in which you still have your list of names from the entire population but you just pick every nth person from that list (where n is just a convenient number). So, we could test just every 13th person on the list of names.

Another way to try to make the sample as representative as possible is to use *quota sampling*, in which you try to control the characteristics of your sample to match those of the population. So, for example, if it turns out that your population contains 60 per cent women, has an average IQ of 103, average age of 24, and certain cultural or ethnic distribution, then you make sure that your sample also has 60 per cent women, an average IQ of 103, average age of 24, and the same cultural and ethnic characteristics.

In reality psychologists don't always do this: they tend to do research on whoever they can get hold of at the time. One way of doing this is to sample a specific group of people. For example, if your population is sewage workers, then you might test all sewage workers in Brighton (the assumption being that sewage workers in Brighton are not that different from sewage workers in Oxford or anywhere else in the UK). This is called *cluster sampling* because you're using an established group of people who are representative of the population of interest.

You can also use *opportunity sampling*, which is a sample of people willing to take part in your research when asked. So, for example, you go around people within the population of interest, ask them if they'd mind you sticking a huge electrode in their brain, and those that say 'yes' are tested. This is subtly different from *volunteer sampling*, which is when you test people who put themselves forward to take part in research (perhaps in response to an advertisement).

Opportunity and volunteer sampling are fairly similar. However, Miles (2001) points out that it's worth considering that people who volunteer for experiments may be different from people who will take part if asked, but might not volunteer themselves otherwise. In any case, these sampling methods are by far the most common in psychology.

A final method is known as *snowball sampling*, which is when you use participants to obtain other participants. The idea is that you might test someone and then ask 'Do you have any friends who might want to take part?' The obvious downside of this is that you could end up with a very biased sample (at least if you believe that people are friends because they have certain things in common).

In reality, the sampling you use won't fit nicely into these boxes. Whatever your good intentions, after a few months of trying to collect data you'll soon be asking anyone and their dog to take part in your study.

Summary

This chapter has looked at how we conduct research. We began by considering ethics. We saw that it's important to inform people about what you're doing and to get their consent. It's also important not to deceive people and to debrief them properly. We then looked at experimental designs and saw how they allow us to make causal inferences provided we use control conditions and randomisation. We discovered that we can manipulate variables using the same people (repeated measures) or different people (independent measures), before we took an overview of some commonly used experimental designs (and real examples of them). We also saw that non-experimental techniques, such as observation and case studies, can be useful as well. Finally, we looked at lots of different ways to find people to test.

Learning outcomes

When you have completed this chapter you should be able to:

- understand the BPS code of conduct for conducting ethical research
- understand why experiments allow us to make causal inferences
- understand basic experimental research designs
- have a basic understanding of non-experimental methods such as quasi-experimental, cross-sectional, observational and case study methodology
- know the differences between sampling methods.

Section 8
Research methods and statistics

Key terms

Between-group design
Boredom effects
Case study
Cluster sampling
Compatible
Control condition
Correlational
Counterbalancing
Cross-sectional design
Deception
Extraneous variables
Idiographic
Incompatible
Independent measures design
Informed consent
Levels
Matched design
Mixed design

Mixed-plot design
Nomothetic
Observational design
Opportunity sampling
Population
Practice effects
Quasi-experimental design
Quota sampling
Random sampling
Randomising
Repeated measures design
Sample
Sampling
Snowball sampling
Systematic sampling
Systematic variation
Unsystematic variation
Volunteer sampling
Within-subjects design

Further reading

Banyard, P. and Grayson, A. (2000) *Introducing Psychological Research* (2nd edn). Basingstoke: Palgrave. A really great book that describes 70 well-known psychology experiments. For each one, it describes the design results and theory behind it. This is a really interesting way to explore research methods in the real world.

Field, A. P. and Hole, G. (2003) *How to Design and Report Experiments*. London: Sage. Gives a lot more detail on experimental design and data collection.

Martin, P. and Bateson, P. (1993) *Measuring Behaviour: An Introductory Guide* (2nd edn). Cambridge: Cambridge University Press. Essential reading for observational studies.

Miles, J. (2001) *Research Methods and Statistics*. Exeter: Crucial. A very well written overview of all aspects of experimental design and basic statistical analysis.

Web links

British Psychological Society (2000). *Code of Conduct, Ethical Principles and Guidelines,* available online at
http://www.bps.org.uk/documents/Code.pdf. Leicester: BPS.

Summarising data

Route map of the chapter

Imagine you have just collected your first set of data. What on earth are you going to do with them? This chapter explains the basics of summarising and presenting your data. To begin with we look at histograms, which are a way of graphing raw data to see the distribution of scores. We'll discover some of the properties of histograms and find out about a special kind of distribution known as the normal distribution. It's important that, as a scientist, you summarise your data so that others can quickly and easily see what you have discovered. This chapter looks at some of the ways we can summarise data both in terms of what a typical score is (the mean, mode and median) and how diverse your scores are (the range, interquartile range and variance). After that, we look at some common ways of graphing these values, in particular bar charts, line charts, boxplots and scatterplots. Finally, we end with a few comments about how *not* to draw graphs!

Introduction

In Chapters 36 and 37 we discovered why and how psychologists collect data to tell them about how humans behave and the processes that might underlie this behaviour. Having collected data, psychologists often want to show other psychologists what they have found. One obvious way to do this is just to let other psychologists see all the data that you have collected. However, most of us have better things to spend our time doing than trawling through other people's data (although if you are your department's resident statistics 'expert', then other psychologists think you love nothing more than trawling through their data!). Therefore, we need ways to summarise our findings in succinct ways that can be easily understood by everyone. There are two ways to summarise data:

1. we can reduce our data down to a single value (or a few values if the data are complex)
2. we can display our data graphically.

This chapter looks at some of the conventional ways that psychologists summarise and display their data.

Histograms, distributions and their properties

Frequency distributions

Once we have collected data from a sample of participants we need to summarise them so that we (and others) can see the general pattern of the data. One way of doing this is to reduce the data down to a few summary statistics, which is extremely useful in allowing other people to get a quick and easy picture of what's going on.

However, in doing this we lose a lot of information, and so when exploring the data yourself, the best first step is to create some kind of summary that includes all of the data you have collected. One way to do this is to plot a graph of all of the data. The best graph is one that shows how many times each score occurs. This is known as a *frequency distribution*, or *histogram*.

ACTIVITY BOX 38.1

Draw a histogram

Imagine we did a 'Little Albert'-style experiment (see Chapter 33) in which we took 50 children and placed them in a room with a white rat. Every time the rat came near them we played a short blast of a Cradle of Filth CD at loud volume (enough to scare anyone!). After a few hours of this, we measured the length of time for which the children would cry when they saw the rat (without the death metal music).

Time spent crying: 27, 27, 28, 26, 21, 12, 9, 22, 22, 26, 24, 23, 14, 20, 26, 27, 14, 25, 22, 25, 20, 25, 25, 21, 22, 24, 25, 23, 22, 15, 27, 22, 22, 27, 22, 18, 25, 28, 25, 9, 17, 27, 27, 24, 19, 23, 6, 25, 26, 18

The first thing we can do is to arrange these scores into ascending order:

Time spent crying: 6, 9, 9, 12, 14, 14, 15, 17, 18, 18, 19, 20, 20, 21, 21, 22, 22, 22, 22, 22, 22, 22, 22, 23, 23, 23, 24, 24, 24, 25, 25, 25, 25, 25, 25, 25, 25, 26, 26, 26, 26, 27, 27, 27, 27, 27, 27, 27, 28, 28

It's now easy to count how many times each score occurs (this is called the frequency). So, for example, we can easily see that only one child cried for 6 seconds, but eight children cried for 25 seconds. To plot a frequency distribution, we simply count the frequency for each score and then plot a graph with the time spent crying on the horizontal axis (also called the X-axis, or abscissa), and the frequency on the vertical axis (also called the Y-axis, or ordinate). The graph of the data above would look like Figure 38.1.

Even with this relatively small amount of data some things become clear that were not obvious from the unordered raw scores:

1. there were no children who didn't cry at all (in fact, all children cried for at least 6 seconds)
2. the majority of children cried for 22 seconds or more (the bars get higher at this point)
3. the most frequent amounts of time spent crying were 22 and 25 seconds, because these two values have the highest bars.

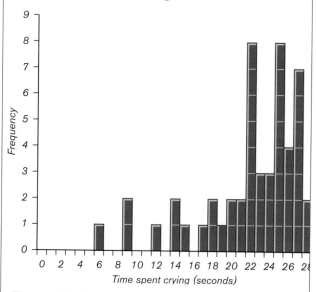

Figure 38.1 The sample data represented graphically

Properties of frequency distributions

Different frequency distributions can look very different (as you might expect!); therefore statisticians have come up with several properties that allow us to describe and compare distributions. These properties can be compared to values that we would find in a 'perfect' distribution. A perfect distribution would be distributed symmetrically around the centre of all scores: if we drew a vertical line through the centre of the distribution it should look the same on both sides. This ideal distribution is known as a *normal distribution* and is characterised by a bell-shaped curve, as in Figure 38.2.

The bell-shape of the normal distribution implies that the majority of scores lie around the centre of the distribution (so the largest bars on the histogram are all around the central value). As we get further away from the centre, the values become less frequent (the bars get smaller).

There are two main properties of distributions: *skew*, which refers to the symmetry of the distribution, and *kurtosis*, which refers to the 'pointiness' of the distribution. In a skewed distribution the most frequent scores (the tall bars on the graph) cluster at one end of the scale. In *positively skewed* distributions, the frequent scores

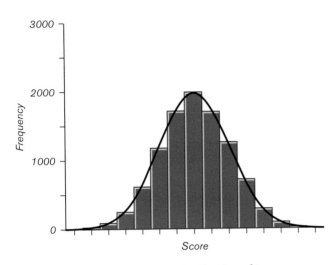

Figure 38.2 The normal distribution (the curve shows the idealised shape of the distribution)

are clustered at the lower end and the tail of the distribution points towards the higher, or more positive, scores. In *negatively skewed* distributions the opposite is true: frequent scores cluster at the higher end and the distribution tails off towards the lower, more negative, scores (see Figure 38.3).

Kurtosis is the degree to which scores cluster in the tails of the distribution: A *platykurtic* distribution has many scores in the tails (often called a heavy-tailed distribution) and so is quite flat, whereas a *leptokurtic* distribution is relatively thin in the tails and so looks quite pointy (again, see Figure 38.3). We can measure skewness and kurtosis and, importantly, these values are 0 in a normal distribution. Therefore if your frequency distribution has positive or negative values of skewness or kurtosis, this tells you

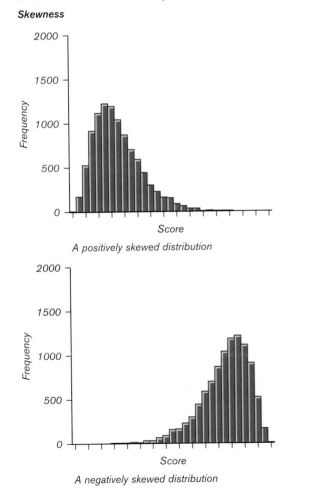

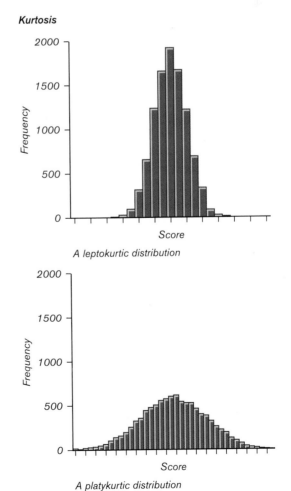

Figure 38.3 Some distributions with different properties

Section 8
Research methods and statistics

that your distribution deviates somewhat from a normal distribution.

Summarising your data with numbers

The mode

We have just seen that we can summarise our sample of data using a graph, but we can also summarise it using numbers. When we looked at these distributions, we saw that, ideally, scores should be clustered around a central point. This being so, the central point should be a value that is consistent with most of the data collected. This is why measures of the centre of the distribution (also called measures of *central tendency*) are often used as a way of summarising a set of scores.

There are several ways to find the centre of a distribution: the simplest is just to look for a score that is typical of the data set – for example, the score most frequently observed. This most common score is called the *mode*, and its value is often self-evident from the frequency distribution (it is the score with the highest bar). However, to calculate the mode, simply place the data in ascending order (to make life easier), count how many times each score occurs, and the score that occurs the most is the mode!

Thinking back to the data in Activity Box 38.1, there are actually two scores that have the highest bars (22 and 25 seconds). Therefore this distribution has two modes and is known as a *bimodal* ('bi' just means 'two') distribution. This illustrates one disadvantage of the mode: there often isn't a single value; in fact, it's possible to have three or more modes (a *multimodal* distribution)!

A second disadvantage is that the mode can be changed dramatically if only a single case of data is added. In Activity Box 38.1, there were two modes, 22 and 25 seconds. Now imagine we collected data from one more child. If this child cried for 22 seconds, then the mode would be 22, but if they cried for 25 seconds, then the mode becomes 25. This one extra child is making a difference to the mode – this makes it an unrepresentative measure.

The median

An alternative way to find a score that represents the data set is to look for the middle score when scores

are ranked in order of magnitude. This is called the *median*. So, for example, imagine a psychologist was interested in how much students hated their statistics lecturers. They pinned a photo of the resident statistics lecturer to a dartboard and then let a sample of 11 students into the room one at a time and counted how many darts they threw at the photo in two minutes.

Number of darts:

20, 35, 100, 15, 22, 27, 18, 11, 21, 23, 22

To calculate the median, first arrange these scores into ascending order:

Number of darts:

11, 15, 18, 20, 21, 22, 22, 23, 27, 35, 100

Next we find the position of the middle score by counting the number of scores we have collected (n), adding 1 to this value, and then dividing by 2. With 11 scores, this gives us $(n + 1)/2 = (11 + 1)/2 = 12/2 = 6$. Then we find the score that is positioned at the location we have just calculated. So, in this example we find the sixth score:

11, 15, 18, 20, 21, ㉒ 22, 23, 27, 35, 100

Median

This works very nicely when we have an odd number of scores (as in this example) but when we have an even number of scores, there won't be a middle value. Imagine the psychologist above replicated her experiment but put the actual statistics lecturer in the room (not a photo). Again, the number of darts thrown at the lecturer was counted, but this time only ten students took part in the study.

Number of darts:

30, 44, 137, 25, 32, 36, 28, 21, 38, 33

Again we arrange these scores in ascending order:

Number of darts:

21, 25, 28, 30, 32, 33, 36, 38, 44, 137

And again we calculate the position of the middle score as before. With ten scores, this gives us $(n + 1)/2 = (10 + 1)/2 = 11/2 = 5.5$. This means that the median is halfway between the fifth and sixth scores. To get around this problem, we add these two scores and divide by two (i.e. we take the average). In this example, the fifth score in the ordered list was 32 and the sixth was 33. We add these together ($32 + 33 = 65$)

and then divide this value by 2 (65/2 = 32.5). The median in this case is 32.5.

The median has several advantages.

- It is relatively unaffected by extreme scores at either end of the scale (known as *outliers*), so if someone behaves really oddly it won't bias this measure too much.
- If the distribution is skewed, then the median is less affected by this than the mean.
- It can be used with ordinal, interval and ratio data (it cannot, however, be used with nominal data as these data have no numerical order).

However, there are two disadvantages.

- Behaviours observed in different samples will fluctuate slightly (remember we said earlier that large samples are more reliable). The median is quite sensitive to these fluctuations. So if you repeated the same experiment on two samples, you'd be likely to see a greater difference between the medians of those samples than the means of those samples.
- The median is not very useful mathematically because it ignores all but one (or two) of the scores in the data set.

The mean

The *mean* is the measure of central tendency that you are most likely to have heard of (although you might know it as the average). The mean is the sum of all scores divided by the number of scores. To calculate the mean we simply add up all of the scores and then divide by the total number of scores we have. We can write this in equation form as:

$$\bar{x} = \frac{\sum_{i=1}^{n} x_i}{n}$$

This may look complicated, but the top half of the equation simply means 'add up all of the scores' (the x_i just means 'the score of a particular person', we could replace the letter i with their name instead), and the bottom bit means divide this total by the number of scores (n).

Let's take the data on the number of darts thrown (by the ten students) for which we calculated the

ACTIVITY BOX 38.2

Calculating medians and means

I've talked in the text about how extreme scores (outliers) can influence the mean more than the median. As a way of practising calculating these statistics, and to illustrate a point, let's try recalculating the data for the example of the number of darts thrown at the stats lecturer. The original data were:

Number of darts: 30, 44, 137, 25, 32, 36, 28, 21, 38, 33

We calculated a median of 32.5 and a mean of 42.4.

Let's now exclude the extreme score of 137, so our data are:

Number of darts: 30, 44, 25, 32, 36, 28, 21, 38, 33

Before you read on, calculate the median and mean of these data (remember there are now nine scores, not ten as before).

Answers

For the median, we reorder the data: 21, 25, 28, 30, 32, 33, 36, 38, 44. Then calculate the position of the median: $(n + 1)/2 = (9 + 1)/2 = 10/2 = 5$. So the median is the fifth number, which for these data is 32. Bear in mind that the median we calculated before (when the outlier was included) was 32.5; the value without this extreme value is very similar.

For the mean we add the scores: $21 + 25 + 28 + 30 + 32 + 33 + 36 + 38 + 44 = 287$. We then divide this by the number of scores (9): $287/9 = 31.89 = 32$. Bear in mind that the mean we calculated when the outlier was included was 42.4; the value without this extreme value has fallen dramatically. This illustrates how the mean is affected by extreme scores. Another way to view this is that when the extreme score is excluded, the median and mean are the same (both are 32), but when one extreme score is added it drags up the mean (to 42.4) but basically doesn't affect the median.

median. To calculate the mean, we first add up all of the scores:

$$\sum_{i-1}^{n} x_i = 30 + 44 + 137 + 25 + 32 + 36 + 28 + 21 + 38 + 33$$

$$= 424$$

We then divide by the number of scores (in this case ten):

$$\bar{x} = \frac{\sum_{i-1}^{n} x_i}{n} = \frac{424}{10} = 42.4$$

The mean is 42.4, which is not a value we observed in our actual data (no one threw 42.4 darts). Interestingly, this value is a lot higher than the median (the median was 32.5). The reason for this is, as was pointed out earlier, the median isn't heavily affected by extreme scores. Well, one disadvantage of the mean is that it can be influenced by extreme scores. In this case there was one person who threw 137 darts, which is a lot more darts than everyone else threw. This has biased the mean (see Activity Box 38.2). The other downsides of the mean are that it is affected by skewed distributions and can be used only with interval or ratio data.

Nevertheless, the mean has important advantages. The mean uses every score (the mode and median ignore most of the scores in a data set) and is the most accurate summary of the data (see Field and Hole, 2003). However, most important is that the mean is resistant to *sampling variation*. Basically, if you took one sample from a population and measured the mean, mode and median, and then took a different sample from the same population and again measured the mean, mode and median, the mean is the most likely of the three measures to be the same in the two samples. This is very important because psychologists usually use samples to tell them about the entire population. Therefore it's unhelpful to use measures that differ from sample to sample because this means that the answers you get depend on the sample you happen to have used!

How good is my measure of central tendency?

The mode, median and mean are simple statistical models – if no other data were available, and we were asked to predict a given person's score, they would be the best guess we could make. It's important with any model that it accurately represents the state of the real world. For example, you wouldn't build a tower block without first constructing many scaled-down models of the building and sticking them in wind tunnels to make sure they don't fall over, would you? If you were building a tower block, it would be essential that the test models behave in the same ways as the real building will, otherwise the tests on the model are inaccurate and pointless.

We can draw a direct parallel with statistics. Imagine the population is the tower block, the sample is a scaled-down version of the population and we use it to build models (like the scaled-down models of the tower block). It's important that these models are accurate, otherwise the inferences we draw about the population (or building) will be inaccurate.

This section really looks at ways we can assess how accurate our summaries of the data are. Put simply, the summaries we have come across all measure the centre of the distribution of scores. As such, if the scores lie close to the centre, then the centre of the distribution will be a good summary of how most people behaved (because most scores are indeed close to that central point). However, if scores are very spread out (some are high above the centre and some are far below it), then the centre of the distribution won't be a good summary of how people behaved because some people produced data points that were very far away from the mean. Therefore to measure how good our summary of the data is, we need to assess how spread-out the data are. This is known as *variability*.

Let's look at an example. Amazon is an Internet company selling CDs, books and just about anything else. For any product, customers can write reviews and rate the product on a scale from 1 (very bad) to 5 (excellent). I looked up the customer ratings for two albums: Britney Spears's *Britney* and Fugazi's *In on the Killtaker* (which, by the way, is one of the greatest albums ever made!).

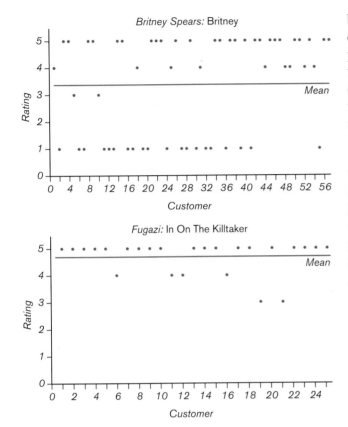

Figure 38.4 The top graph shows the customer ratings from Amazon.co.uk for Britney Spears's album Britney, *whereas the bottom graph is distribution of customer ratings from Amazon.com for Fugazi's masterpiece* In on the Killtaker

Figure 38.4 shows the ratings of each customer along with the mean rating (displayed as a horizontal line). The first thing to notice about these graphs is that for Britney's album customers are divided: they either loved it (and gave it 5) or hated it (and gave it 1); there are very few people between the two extremes! For Fugazi, however, the ratings are universally very high (most are 5s, with only a few 4s and 3s, and no 2s and 1s).

Now let's look at the means. For Fugazi the mean is very close to nearly all of the scores – because the data are not very spread out it is a fairly accurate representation of most people's scores (most of the dots are not too far from the line). Looking at the mean for Britney, this line doesn't really represent anyone much (the dots are all very far from the line)

because the data are very spread out around this central point. So the mean is a lot lower than all the people who loved the album, and a lot higher than those who hated the album! Hopefully, these rather extreme examples illustrate that the variability in data tells us something about whether or not the measure of central tendency (in this case the mean) is accurate.

The range

The easiest way to look at variability is simply to calculate the *range* of scores. To do this, take the highest score that you observed and subtract from it the lowest score. Let's go back to the data about the number of darts thrown at the statistics lecturer. Remember that if we order these scores we get 21, 25, 28, 30, 32, 33, 36, 38, 44, 137. The highest score is 137 and the lowest is 21, therefore, the range is 137 – 21 = 116.

One problem with the range is that because it uses only the highest and lowest score it is affected dramatically by outliers. For example, with these data, the person who threw 137 darts is somewhat unusual (anger management clearly needed!), given that the next highest score was 44. What would the range be if we'd never tested our psychopath dart thrower? The highest score would be 44 and the lowest would still be 21, so the range would be 44 – 21 = 23. This is a dramatic reduction – about a fifth of the size.

One way around this problem is to calculate the range when we exclude values at the extremes of the distribution. One convention is to cut off the top and bottom 25 per cent of scores and calculate the range – known as the *interquartile range*. Let's do this with the dart-throwing data. First we need to calculate what are called quartiles. The calculation of these is similar to how we calculated the median. First arrange the scores into ascending order (if you haven't done so already):

Number of darts: 21, 25, 28, 30, 32, 33, 36, 38, 44, 137

Next we need to split the data into four equal (or roughly equal) groups. The simplest way is to divide the number of scores, *n*, by 4. With ten scores, this gives us $n/2 = 10/4 = 2.5$. The first quartile (known as the *lower quartile*) should therefore contain the first 2.5 scores in your ordered list, the second quartile

Section 8
Research methods and statistics

should contain the next 2.5 scores, the third quartile the next 2.5 scores, and the final quartile (known as the *upper quartile*) the final 2.5 scores. One obvious problem with our data is that you can't have 2.5 scores in each quartile, you can have only 2 scores or 3 scores (we can't cut a score in half and put one half in one quartile and the other half in the next quartile). In these circumstances we'd probably split the data something like this:

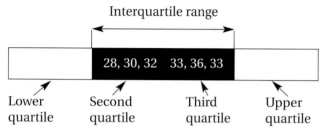

In an ideal world, each quartile should have the same number of scores within it, and often textbooks use examples that conveniently split into four groups; however, I've deliberately used an example that is inconvenient because data often are! Although there are more sophisticated ways of calculating quartiles, this gives you a simple flavour of what they represent. The bottom quartile contains the lowest 25 per cent of scores, the upper quartile contains the top 25 per cent, and the second and third quartiles collectively contain the remaining 50 per cent of the data. The interquartile range is simply the range when you ignore the upper and lower quartile: put another way, it's the highest score of the third quartile minus the lowest score of the second quartile (in this case it

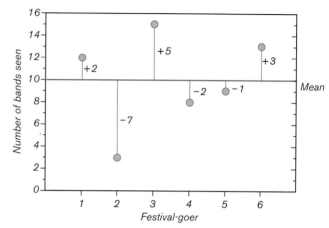

Figure 38.5 Number of bands seen by six people at the Glastonbury Festival

would be 38 – 28 = 10). The advantage of the interquartile range is that it isn't affected by extreme scores at either end of the distribution. However, the problem with it is that you lose a lot of data (half of it, in fact!). Also, cutting off the upper and lower 25 per cent of scores is completely arbitrary (why not the top and bottom 10 per cent or 5 per cent?).

Variance

A more sophisticated way to measure the spread of data is to use all of the scores you have collected and look at how different they are from the centre of the distribution (this is known as the *deviation*). I'm getting a bit tired of the darts example, so let's imagine the organisers of the Glastonbury Festival were interested in how many bands the average

TABLE 38.1   TOTAL DEVIATIONS ADD UP TO ZERO

RAW SCORE x_i	MEAN $\bar{x}$	DEVIATION $(x_i - \bar{x})$
12	10	2
3	10	−7
15	10	5
8	10	−2
9	10	−1
13	10	3
		$\Sigma(x_i - \bar{x}) = 0$

TABLE 38.2 SQUARE EACH OF THE DEVIATIONS

RAW SCORE x_i	MEAN $\bar{x}$	DEVIATION $(x_i - \bar{x})$	SQUARED DEVIATION $(x_i - \bar{x})^2$
12	10	2	4
3	10	−7	49
15	10	5	25
8	10	−2	4
9	10	−1	1
13	10	3	9
		$\Sigma(x_i - \bar{x}) = 0$	$\Sigma(x_i - \bar{x})^2 = 92$

punter sees during their three days there (there are usually over 100 bands playing). (In the unlikely event that you don't know what I'm talking about, Glastonbury Festival is a great three-day music event held near Glastonbury in June most years.)

The data are presented in Figure 38.5, which shows the number of bands that each of six festival-goers saw during the festival, and also the mean number (which, as it turns out, is 10). The diagram has a series of vertical lines that connect each observed value to the mean. If we use the mean as our summary, or modal, of the data, then these lines represent the differences between what our model predicts (the mean) and the data we actually collected; these differences are the deviations. The magnitude of these differences is calculated by subtracting the mean value $\bar{x}$ from each of the observed values (x_i).

For example, the first festival-goer saw 12 bands and so the difference is $x_i - \bar{x} = 12 - 10 = 2$. The fact that the difference is a positive number tells us that our model underestimates the number of bands that this person saw: it predicts that he or she saw 10 bands when he or she actually saw 12. The simplest way to use these deviations to estimate the accuracy of the model would be to add them (this would give us an estimate of the total error). If we were to do this, we would find that the total deviations add up to zero, as in Table 38.1.

The fact that the total of all deviations is zero implies that there is no error within the model or, put another way, the mean is a perfect way to predict how many bands people saw. This clearly isn't true because we know that scores deviate from the mean. The reason why the sum of all deviations equals zero is that the mean measures the centre of the distribution. Therefore about half of the scores are greater than the mean and about half are less. Consequently, about half of the deviations will be positive and about half will be negative and, when we add them up, they cancel each other out. To overcome this problem we square each of the deviations (see Table 38.2) so that they are all positive (the negative ones become positive when squared because you are multiplying two negative numbers).

If we add the squared deviations we get the sum of squared deviations, which is more commonly referred to as the *sum of squared errors* (or *sum of squares* for short). In itself, the sum of squared errors is a good measure of the accuracy of the mean. However, because it is a summed value, it will get bigger if we collect more data. So if we collected data from another six festival-goers, our sum of squares will probably get about twice as large. This makes it difficult to compare across different sets of data. Therefore we need to take account of the number of scores on which the sum of squared deviations is based. The obvious way to do this is just to divide by the number of scores (N) to get the mean squared error. In fact, if we're interested only in the average error for the sample, then this is exactly what we do.

However, we are generally interested in using the error in the sample to estimate the error in the population and so we actually divide the sum of squares by the number of observations minus 1 (if you are interested in why, then read Field and Hole, 2003: Chapter 4). This measure is known as the *variance*:

$$s^2 = \frac{SS}{N-1} = \frac{\sum (x_i - \bar{x})^2}{N-1} = \frac{92}{5} = 18.4$$

The variance tells us on average how much a given data point differs from the mean of all data points. This makes it an incredibly useful measure because we can compare it across samples that contain different numbers of observations. However, by using squared data we change the units of measurement. So for these data we couldn't say that the average deviation was 18.4 bands, we'd have to say it was 18.4 bands squared! It makes very little sense to talk about 'bands squared' (try squaring a band and see how upset they get!). More commonly we'd convert the average error back into the original units of measurement by taking the square root of the

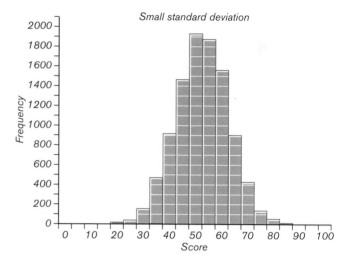

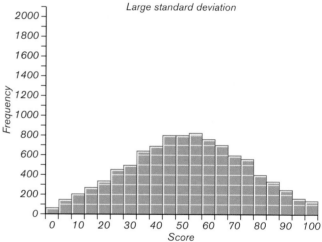

Figure 38.6 *Two distributions that have the same mean but different standard deviations*

variance. This measure is known as the *standard deviation*. In this example the standard deviation is:

$$s = \sqrt{18.4} = 4.29$$

The sums of squares, variance and standard deviation are all measures of the same thing: the variability of the data. Bearing in mind that the mean will be most accurate when the scores are similar, and will be most inaccurate when the scores are very different, this also tells us about the accuracy of the mean as a summary of the data. These measures are all proportionate: if one value is large, then all of the others will be too. Small standard deviations relative to the value of the mean indicate that data points are

---

ACTIVITY BOX 38.3

Calculating standard deviations

Use the Amazon customer ratings for Fugazi's *In on the Killtaker* (see above) and calculate the standard deviation. You can read the ratings from Figure 38.4, but to save your eyesight they are:
  Customer ratings: 5, 5, 5, 5, 5, 4, 5, 5, 5, 5, 4, 4, 5, 5, 5, 4, 5, 5, 3, 5, 3, 5, 5, 5, 5

Answers

First we calculate the deviations and square them, as in Table 38.3 (p. 681).

Once we have added up the squared deviations ($\sum (x_i - \bar{x})^2 = 9.44$), we divide this value by $N - 1$. There are 25 ratings, so we get $9.44/24 = 0.393$. This is the variance. We then take the square root of this to get the standard deviation ($\sqrt{0.393} = 0.627$).

Now have a go with the *Britney* ratings.

TABLE 38.3 CALCULATE THE DEVIATIONS AND SQUARE THEM

RAW SCORE x_i	MEAN $\bar{x}$	DEVIATION $(x_i - \bar{x})$	SQUARED DEVIATION $(x_i - \bar{x})^2$
5	4.68	0.32	0.1024
5	4.68	0.32	0.1024
5	4.68	0.32	0.1024
5	4.68	0.32	0.1024
5	4.68	0.32	0.1024
4	4.68	−0.68	0.4624
5	4.68	0.32	0.1024
5	4.68	0.32	0.1024
5	4.68	0.32	0.1024
5	4.68	0.32	0.1024
4	4.68	−0.68	0.4624
4	4.68	−0.68	0.4624
5	4.68	0.32	0.1024
5	4.68	0.32	0.1024
5	4.68	0.32	0.1024
4	4.68	−0.68	0.4624
5	4.68	0.32	0.1024
5	4.68	0.32	0.1024
3	4.68	−1.68	2.8224
5	4.68	0.32	0.1024
3	4.68	−1.68	2.8224
5	4.68	0.32	0.1024
5	4.68	0.32	0.1024
5	4.68	0.32	0.1024
5	4.68	0.32	0.1024
			$\Sigma(x_i - \bar{x})^2 = 9.44$

close to the mean and large standard deviations (relative to the mean) indicate that the data points are distant from the mean. Now look at Activity Box 38.3.

The standard deviation and the shape of the distribution

As well as telling us about the accuracy of the mean as a model of our data set, the variance and standard deviation also tell us about the shape of the distribution of scores. If the mean represents the data accurately, then most of the scores will cluster close to the mean and the resulting standard deviation is small relative to the mean. When the mean is a less accurate representation of the data, the scores cluster more widely around the mean (see Figure 38.4) and the standard deviation is larger.

Figure 38.6 shows two distributions that have the same mean (50) but different standard deviations. One has a large standard deviation relative to the mean ($SD = 25$) and this results in a flatter distribution that is more spread out. The other has a small standard deviation relative to the mean ($SD = 15$) resulting in a more pointy distribution in which scores close to the mean are very frequent but scores further from the mean become increasingly infrequent. The main message is that as the standard deviation gets larger, the distribution gets fatter.

Z-scores: what are they good for?

Another way to look at frequency distributions is in terms of probability: they give us some idea of how likely a given score is to occur. Think back to the 'Little Albert' example in Activity Box 38.1 and the frequency distribution that we drew. If someone was to ask you 'How likely is it that a child in this experiment cried for less than 10 seconds?', what would your answer be (look at the frequency distribution)?

The chances are you will respond 'Not very likely' because you can see from the graph that only three children out of the 50 that were tested cried for less than 10 seconds. What about if someone asked 'How likely is it that a child in this experiment cried for 25 seconds or more?' Again, by looking at the graph, you might say 'It's actually quite likely' because 21 out of the 50 children cried for that amount of time (that's nearly half of them).

Looking at this a slightly different way we can work out the probability that a particular score will occur. So we could ask, based on our data, 'What's the probability of a child crying for six seconds?' A probability value can range from 0 (there's no chance

whatsoever of the event happening) to 1 (the event will definitely happen). So, for example, the publishers of this book set me a deadline for finishing this chapter and they obviously want to know the probability of me meeting this deadline. When I talk to them I would say the probability is 1: I will definitely have completed the chapter by Friday 1 August 2003. However, when I talk to my girlfriend I might, more realistically, tell her that there's a .25 probability of me finishing the chapter (or, put another way, a 25 per cent chance, or one in four chance that I'll complete it in time). Of course, in reality, the probability of me meeting the deadline is 0 because I never manage to meet publishers' deadlines!

If probabilities don't make sense to you, then just ignore the decimal point and think of them as percentages instead (i.e. .25 probability that something will happen = 25 per cent chance).

So far we have looked in fairly vague terms at how we could use frequency distributions to get a rough idea of how likely a given score is to occur. Most of the time in science it's not good enough to be vague: we need precise estimates. For any distribution of scores we could, in theory, calculate the probability of obtaining a score of a certain size. However, it would be incredibly tedious to have to do this every time we collected some data. Therefore statisticians have identified several common distributions. For these distributions they have worked out tables of

TABLE 38.4 CALCULATE THE CORRESPONDING Z-SCORES

RAW SCORE x_i	MEAN $\bar{x}$	DEVIATION $(x_i - \bar{x})$	STANDARD DEVIATION (s)	$Z = \dfrac{(x_i - \bar{x})}{s}$
12	10	2	4.29	0.466
3	10	−7	4.29	−1.632
15	10	5	4.29	1.166
8	10	−2	4.29	−0.466
9	10	−1	4.29	−0.233
13	10	3	4.29	0.699

the probabilities of getting particular scores based on the frequencies with which a particular score occurs in a distribution of a particular shape.

One of these 'common' distributions is the normal distribution (see Figure 38.2). With this particular distribution, statisticians have calculated the probability of certain scores occurring in a normal distribution with a mean of 0 and a standard deviation of 1. Therefore if we have any data that are shaped like a normal distribution, then if the mean and standard deviation are 0 and 1 respectively, we can use the tables of probabilities for the normal distribution to see how likely it is that a particular score will occur in the data.

The obvious problem is that not all of the data we collect will have a mean of 0 and standard deviation of 1. For example, we might have a data set that has a mean of 75 and a standard deviation of 13.24. Luckily it is easy to convert any data set into a data set that *does* have a mean of 0 and a standard deviation of 1. All we have to do is take each score and subtract from it the mean of all scores (this centres the data set around 0), and then divide the resulting score by the standard deviation (this ensures that resulting data have a standard deviation of 1). The resulting scores are known as *z*-scores and, in equation form, the conversion I've just described looks like this:

$$z = \frac{x_i - \bar{x}}{s}$$

Let's go back to our data about the number of bands that people saw at the Glastonbury Festival. We worked out that these data had a mean of 10 and a standard deviation of 4.29. Let's calculate the corresponding *z*-scores, as in Table 38.4.

Now try calculating the mean and standard deviation of these *z*-scores: you should get a mean of 0 and a standard deviation of 1!

The table of probability values that have been calculated for the normal distribution (with a mean of 0 and standard deviation of 1) is shown in the Appendix of this book. Why is this table important? Well, if we look at our person who saw 15 bands at Glastonbury, we can answer the question 'What's the probability that someone saw 15 or more bands?' by finding the corresponding *z*-score (1.166 or 1.17

when rounded off) in the Appendix and looking at the value in the column labelled 'smaller portion' (i.e. the area above the value 1.166). You should find that the probability is .121 or, put another way, only a 12.1 per cent chance that someone saw 15 or more bands. By looking at the column labelled 'bigger portion' we can also see the probability that someone saw 15 or fewer bands! This probability is .879 or, put another way, there's an 87.9 per cent chance that someone at Glastonbury saw 15 or fewer bands!

Hopefully you can see from these examples that the normal distribution and *z*-scores allow us to go a first step beyond our data, in that from a set of scores we can calculate the probability that a particular score will occur. So we can see whether scores of a certain size are likely or unlikely to occur in a distribution of a particular kind. You'll see just how useful this is in the next chapter.

Reporting data

So far we have seen various ways to summarise data so that we can easily communicate our findings to other psychologists and scientists. This section looks at how to present these summaries. In general terms, we have a choice of reporting these summaries either in words or graphically.

Reporting data in words

When we present the summaries of central tendency (the mean, mode and median), we will usually include information about the accuracy of that statistic. So we might simply report the mean followed by the standard deviation. However, we sometimes report other things such as the standard error and *confidence intervals*, which are described in the next chapter. For the time being, don't worry about what these things are (you'll find out in due course), because at the moment I just want to give you a flavour of how data can be presented.

As a psychologist, if you have collected some data and found a result that is interesting to other psychologists, then you'll typically write up a report to be published in an academic journal. Journals are just like magazines (only usually more boring) and contain articles from scientists. These articles are usually either in the form of an empirical report (where a scientist has tested some theory using the types of techniques we have discussed and written up the results) or a review paper (in which a scientist appraises a body of research that has addressed the same research question). When these articles are submitted to a journal, they are almost always sent to other experts in the field, who assess the work on its quality and importance to the field. For the paper to be accepted by the journal and subsequently published, these experts must have deemed the work to be methodologically rigorous and important.

When submitting manuscripts to journals for consideration, results have to be summarised in a standard way, and many psychology journals have adopted the conventions laid out by the American Psychological Association (APA) in its publications manual, which is now in its fifth edition (American Psychological Association, 2001). Usually we report any numbers to two decimal places and there are various standard abbreviations for statistical values:

- M = mean
- Mdn = median
- SE = standard error
- SD = standard deviation.

Let's take a look at some examples of how to report a mean and the associated standard error in correct APA format. It's most common to parenthesise both the mean and standard error within a sentence that would otherwise make sense even if these parenthesised values were excluded. For example:

- Men (M = 10.94, SE = 4.32) urinated on the toilet seat substantially more than women (M = 2.07, SE = 0.52).
- Peanut consumption increased dramatically after alcohol (M = 500.67, SE = 42.39) compared to before (M = 36.89, SE = 8.29).

There may also be times when you want to report the median, and in these cases you should also report the range of scores or the interquartile range.

- Dogs sniff people's groins (Mdn = 37, $Range$ = 20 – 89) more than cats (Mdn = 3, $Range$ = 0 – 5).

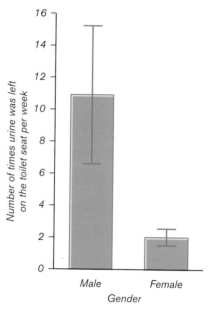

Figure 38.7 Graph of two means (with error bars)

- Cats stick their claws into their owner's groin (Mdn = 62, $Range$ = 40 – 102) more than dogs (Mdn = 40, $Range$ = 18 – 63).

Graphing means

The second approach is to report means and medians by using a graph and then not report the actual values in the text. The choice of using a graph or writing the values in the text largely depends on what you want to report. If you just have one or two means you might decide that a graph is superfluous, but when you have lots of means to report, a graph or a table can be a very useful way to summarise the data. In this section we'll look at how to graph means, before moving on to look at what to do if you want to report the median.

If you do use a graph then you shouldn't really report values in the text as well because the reader should be able to use the graph to get the values for themselves. Means can be displayed either with a *bar chart* or a *line chart*, but in both cases it is very important to include error bars, which are bars that indicate the variability within the data. Figure 38.7 shows an example of a bar chart showing the mean number of times (per week) that men and women urinated on toilet seats; the gender of the person is displayed as different bars and each bar represents

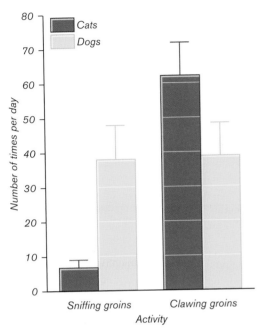

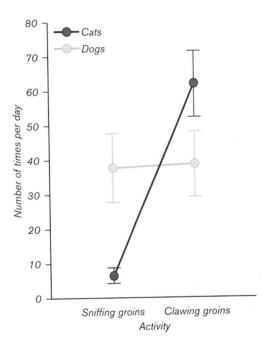

Figure 38.8 A line graph and a bar chart of the same data

the mean, but each mean is also spanned by a funny 'I' shape. This is called an *error bar*.

Error bars can represent the standard deviation of the sample, the standard error estimated from the sample, or a confidence interval for the mean. The error bars in Figure 38.7 display the 95 per cent confidence interval, which we'll come across in the next chapter. All I'll say at this stage is that this tells us something about the range of means we could expect to get across several samples from the same population. Actually, if we were to take 100 samples from a population and calculate the mean of each, then the confidence interval represents the limits within which 95 of those 100 means would fall.

Given that we use samples to estimate what's happening in the population, this statistic is incredibly useful: if the confidence interval is small, then it means that even if we had tested a different sample, the likelihood is that the mean we would have got would be similar to the one we did get. Conversely, a large confidence interval would mean that had we tested a different sample of people we might have got a mean that was very different to the one that we did get. *So remember, small error bars are good, large error bars are bad!*

Figure 38.8 shows how both line charts and bar charts can be used to present the same data. However, use one or the other: *never display the same data with two different charts!* Also, if you do a line chart, don't be tempted to superimpose bars on it, or conversely don't superimpose a line chart over bars: this is completely pointless and just over-complicates the graph!

The charts in Figure 38.8 show the number of times cats and dogs engage in two different activities: sniffing groins, or sticking their claws into them! The task engaged in is shown on the X-axis (the horizontal) but because we have more than one animal (we have cats and dogs) we can represent these activities as different lines, or bars. We have four means in total and each one has an error bar. In the line chart we use the lines to connect means that relate to the same animal, and in the bar chart we use different-coloured bars to represent the different animals.

These charts allow us to examine different patterns in the data for different activities. If we look at groin sniffing first, we can see that dogs engage in rather a lot of it whereas cats do not. This is because dogs are foul animals that love to stick their noses where others wouldn't dare, unlike cats, which have far

685

more sense. If we look at sticking claws into groins then the pattern is reversed: cats love nothing more than to test their owner's love for them by sticking their razor-sharp claws in the most sensitive area of their owner's anatomy (but we still love them, fools that we are), whereas dogs are nice loyal creatures that protect rather than harm their owners (hmm, thinking of trading the cat in, now I think about this …). These graphs should highlight how useful charts can be to show trends in the data.

Graphing medians

Typically if you want to graph the median, then you don't use a bar chart or a line chart (although that's not to say you can't). Instead you use something called a *boxplot*, or *box-whisker diagram* to give it its full name.

Figure 38.9 shows such a graph of the number of grams of peanuts eaten by two groups of students: one group had drunk alcohol, whereas those in the other group were sober. There are several important features of this graph: namely a box and two whiskers! The box shows the interquartile range that I described earlier, so 50 per cent of the scores are bigger than the lowest line of the box but smaller than the top line of the box. You'll also notice another horizontal line within the box. This shows the value of the median. The box also has two whiskers: one

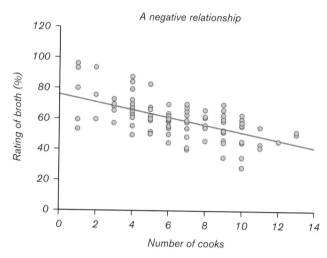

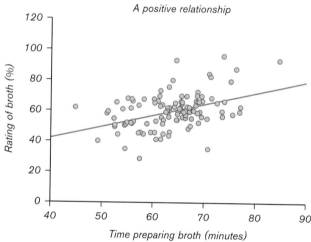

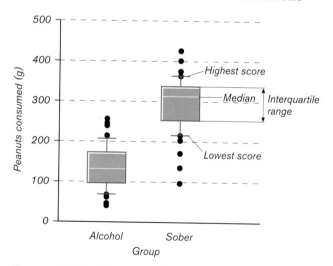

Figure 38.9 A boxplot (or box-whisker diagram) of the quantity of peanuts eaten after alcohol and when sober

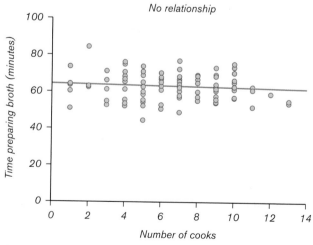

Figure 38.10 Scatterplots showing the relationships between the number of cooks, the preparation time and the quality of broth

sticking out of the top and one sticking out of the bottom. The top line of the whisker that sticks out of the top of the box shows the highest score, therefore the distance between the top edge of the box and the bottom of the lower whisker shows the lower quartile (i.e. the range within which the bottom 25 per cent of scores fall). The final thing worth noting is that the distance between the horizontal line at the bottom of the lower whisker and the horizontal line at the top of the upper whisker represents the range of scores.

'Now,' I hear you ask, 'what are those strange black blobs?' They are outliers or extreme scores. When you plot boxplots with a computer package, they generally identify extreme scores for you and display them as dots above and below the whiskers.

Graphing relationships

Sometimes you won't want to display means or medians of different groups of people, but instead you will want to display relationships between variables. Imagine we wanted to test the proverb 'too many cooks spoil the broth'. We could collect data about the quality of broth (by getting people to rate it on a scale of 1 to 10) and also find out how many cooks were involved in the preparation. Now we're looking for a relationship between the number of cooks and the quality of the broth. If we just calculated the mean rating of broth for each number of cooks (or the mean number of cooks for each rating of broth) then we could end up with a lot of averages. Instead, we can just plot all of the data on a graph. If we plot the number of cooks on the X-axis and the corresponding rating of both on the Y-axis (or vice versa) then we can look at the relationship between these variables very easily. This type of graph is known as a *scatterplot*.

A scatterplot is simply a graph that plots a score on one variable against the corresponding score on another (and a corresponding score on a third variable can also be included on a 3-D scatterplot). A scatterplot tells us many things about the data, such as whether there is a relationship between the variables, what kind of relationship it is and whether any cases look like outliers.

Now imagine we collected data about how long the broth took to prepare. We'd have three variables: the number of cooks, the time spent preparing (in minutes) and the quality of the broth (as a percentage score). Figure 38.10 shows three scatterplots depicting the various relationships between these variables. The top graph shows that as the number of cooks increases, the ratings of the broth decrease. This is known as a negative, or inverse, relationship. That is, as one variable changes in one direction, the other variable changes in the opposite direction (as the number of cooks increases, the quality of the broth decreases, or it would be equally correct to say as the quality of the broth increases, the number of chefs decreases!). So too many cooks do indeed seem to spoil the broth.

The second graph shows the relationship between the time spent preparing the broth and the quality of the broth. This shows that as the time spent preparing the broth increases, the ratings of the broth also increase. This is known as a positive relationship: as one variable changes in one direction, the other variable changes in the same direction (as the time spent preparing the broth increases, the quality of the broth increases, or it would be equally correct to say that, as the quality of the broth increases, the time spent preparing increases, and in fact you could also say that as time spent preparing the broth decreases, the quality of the broth decreases!).

So taking time to prepare the broth appears to be beneficial. The final scatterplot shows the relationship between the number of cooks and the time taken to prepare the broth. This shows no relationship at all: as one variable changes in a particular direction, the other variable stays the

---

ACTIVITY BOX 38.4

Draw some graphs

Use some of the data sets in this chapter to draw each of the following graphs:

- a boxplot
- bar charts
- line charts.

Try to remember Tufte's rules when you draw them!

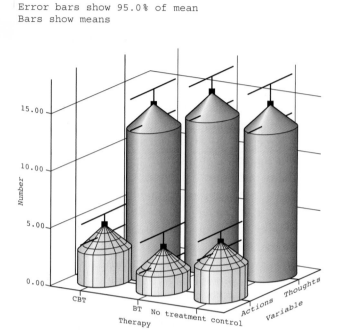

Error bars show 95.0% of mean
Bars show means

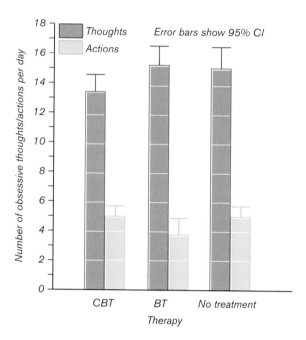

Error bars show 95% CI

Figure 38.11 A cringingly bad example of a graph from Field (2000) (left), and an example of how it should be done (right)

same. So as the number of cooks increases (or decreases) the time taken to prepare the broth doesn't change much at all.

As you can see, there's an awful lot we can tell from a scatterplot and they're extremely useful graphs. You'll notice on all of these graphs that there is a line that summarises the pattern of data (a line that is an approximation of the general trend shown by the dots). This is called the *line of best fit*, or *regression line*, and we'll find out more about it in the next chapter.

How not to graph data

So far I've shown you some of the different graphs that can be used to display data. In this final section I want to highlight some points about good graphing practice. The advent of computers has allowed people to spend vast amounts of time producing very snazzy-looking graphs but I hope to convince you that snazzy is not always best!

Tufte (2001) has written an excellent text about how data should be presented. He points out that graphs should do, among other things, the following:

- show the data
- induce the reader to think about the data being presented (rather than some other aspect of the graph, like how nice the colour scheme is)
- avoid distorting the data
- present many numbers with minimum ink!
- make large data sets coherent
- encourage the reader to compare different pieces of data
- *reveal* data.

However, graphs often don't do these things. Let's look at a few examples of some bad graphs.

Unnecessary whistles and bells

Fortunately, from the point of view of copyright and offending other people, one of the most truly appalling examples of bad graphics was done by some gibbering imbecile called Andy Field in his book *Discovering Statistics...* (2000). It's a graph showing the mean number of obsessive thoughts and behaviours experienced by groups of people suffering from obsessive-compulsive disorder after

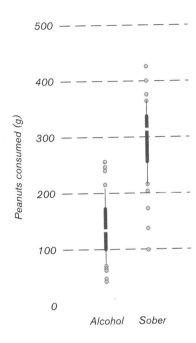

Figure 38.12 A 'minimal' boxplot

three types of therapy: cognitive behaviour therapy (CBT), behaviour therapy (BT) and no treatment. Figure 38.11 reproduces this graph and shows an alternative display of these data. What's wrong with the original?

- The bars have a 3-D effect: never use 3-D on a 2-D graph because all it does is obscure the data; in particular, it makes it hard to see the values of the bars because of the 3-D effect. This graph is a great example because the 3-D effect makes the error bars almost impossible to read.
- Patterns: the bars also have patterns, which although very pretty, merely distract the eye from what matters (namely the data). These are completely unnecessary.
- Cylindrical bars: what's that all about, eh?
- Badly labelled Y-axis: 'number' of what ... delusions? Fish? Cabbage-eating sea lizards from the eighth dimension? Idiots who don't know how to draw graphs?

Now, take a look at the re-done version. What improvements have been made?

- 2-D: the completely unnecessary third dimension is gone, making it much easier to compare the values across therapies and thoughts/behaviours.
- The Y-axis has a more informative label: we now know that it was the number of obsessive thoughts or actions per day that was being measured.
- Distractions: there are fewer distractions like patterns, cylindrical bars and the like.

Tufte (2001) actually goes a step further and recommends trying to minimise the amount of ink used to present data. Now throughout this chapter you'll notice that many of my graphs don't have axis lines and suchlike. I've tried to strike a compromise between Tufte's minimalist approach and conventional graphical displays, because for most readers it could be confusing if I'd just used some of the minimal displays that Tufte recommends. Figure 38.12 shows the kind of thing that Tufte might recommend: it's a redrawn version of the boxplot in Figure 38.9. The median is shown by a white dot, the interquartile range is shown by a

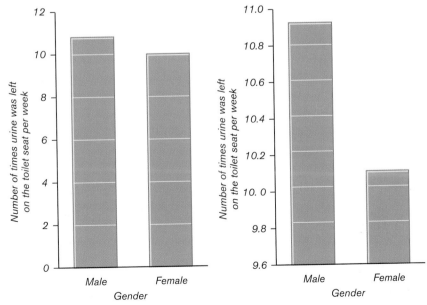

Figure 38.13 Lies, damned lies and statistics!

thickened line rather than a box, and the ends of the whiskers have been deleted. This chart shows exactly the same information as the original boxplot, but with less ink, and fewer distractions.

Distractions such as patterns on bars or excessive 3-D or shading are known as *chartjunk* – that is, stuff that doesn't add anything to the display of data. One innovation of Tufte's that I particularly like is to eliminate grid lines on charts and instead put grid lines only on the bars of the chart (you'll notice I've done this on nearly every chart in this chapter). This really does facilitate a quick interpretation of the data.

Lies, damned lies and statistics

Governments love to lie with statistics, but scientists shouldn't. How you present your data can make a huge difference to the message conveyed to the audience (and politicians know this!). Figure 38.13 shows two graphs that, believe it or not, display exactly the same data. The first panel shows how the graph should probably be scaled. The important thing is that the Y-axis begins at 0, and this creates the correct impression: that there isn't any difference between the amount that men and women urinate on the toilet seat.

However, imagine that you wanted to create the impression that men urinated on the toilet seat more than women (OK, so we know they do, but bear with me), all we have to do is rescale the graph (by *not* starting the Y-axis at zero) and there suddenly seems to be a huge difference. In fact, the difference is numerically very small, but the graph makes it look really big! Tempting as it is, don't do this!

Some final tips

If you want to draw a graph, follow a few of Tufte's recommendations.

- Don't create false impressions of what the data actually show (likewise, don't hide effects!).
- Abolish chartjunk: don't use patterns, 3-D effects, shadows, pictures of hippopotami, photos of your grandma or anything else.
- Avoid excess ink: this is a bit radical, but if you don't need the axis, then get rid of it!

Learning outcomes

When you have completed this chapter you should be able to:

- plot a frequency distribution
- describe what a normal distribution is and what properties it has
- calculate a mode, mean, median, the range, the interquartile range and standard deviation of a data set, and describe what these statistics tell us about the data
- present summaries of your data.

Key terms

Bar chart
Bimodal
Boxplot
Box-whisker diagram
Central tendency
Chartjunk
Confidence interval
Deviation
Error bars
Frequency distribution
Histogram
Interquartile range
Kurtosis
Leptokurtic
Line chart
Line of best fit
Lower quartile
Mean
Median
Mode
Multimodal
Negative skew
Normal distribution
Outliers
Platykurtic
Positive skew
Range

Regression line Sampling variation Scatterplot Skew Standard deviation	Sum of squared errors Sum of squares Upper quartile Variability Variance

Further reading

Field, A. P. and Hole, G. (2003) *How to Design and Report Experiments*. London: Sage.

Rowntree, D. (1981) *Statistics Without Tears: A Primer for Non-Mathematicians*. London: Penguin. Still one of the best introductions to statistical theory (apart from this book, obviously!).

Wright, D. B. (2002) *First Steps in Statistics*. London: Sage. Chapters 1 and 3 are very accessible introductions to descriptive statistics.

If you want to learn about doing statistics using a computer, then the package called SPSS is very useful. The following are recommended.

Field, A. P. (2004) *Discovering Statistics using SPSS for Windows: Advanced Techniques for the Beginner* (2nd edn). London: Sage.

Kinnear, P. R. and Gray, C. D. (2000) *SPSS for Windows Made Simple* (Release 10). Hove: Psychology Press.

For graphing and displaying data I strongly recommend:

Tufte, E. R. (2001) *The Visual Display of Quantitative Information* (2nd edn). Cheshire, Connecticut: Graphics Press.

Web links

A good site for revising basic maths is http://www.easymaths.com.

http://www.math.sfu.ca/~cschwarz/Stat-301/Handouts/node8.html has some good examples of bad graphs!

For more on graphs, see http://www.siggraph.org/publications/newsletter/v33n3/contributions/davis.html.

39

Going beyond your sample

Route map of the chapter

This chapter brings together everything you've learnt so far to try to explain how we use statistics to test hypotheses. The first step is to see whether summaries of our data (for example, the mean) are representative of our population; we can do this using the standard error and confidence intervals. We then look at the rationale behind fitting statistical models to test hypotheses. You will discover that the experimental and null hypotheses can be conceptualised in terms of a statistical model that is fitted to our data. The exact model depends on what data you have and what your hypotheses are but in general terms every model throws out a statistic with known properties. Based on these properties, we can work out whether a value as large as the one we have would be likely if the null hypothesis is true. The final part of the chapter is spent giving you a brief overview of a range of statistical models and giving examples of when they should be used.

Introduction

Over the last two chapters we have discovered that psychologists use samples as a way of trying to understand what goes on in much larger populations. We have also seen that we can summarise these samples using statistical models such as the mean. Finally, we saw that we can use measures such as the standard deviation to tell us whether our model is a good fit of our data. Measures like the standard deviation tell us whether our mean is a good fit of the sample but perhaps a more important question is whether our mean (or whatever model we are fitting to the data) is a good fit of the population.

The standard error

On page 678 we looked at calculating the mean number of bands that a person watched at the Glastonbury Festival. Imagine our population of interest is all the people at the festival (this seems like a reasonable population) and that we actually did ask all of them how many bands they saw. We might find that, on average, people watched 11 bands. This is known as the *effect in the population*. As we have seen, we don't normally have access to this effect, so instead we take samples (see Figure 39.1).

Some samples might be very representative of the population (as you can see in the diagram, some have the same mean as the population), but others will be less representative and will have a mean that is different from the population. This illustrates *sampling variation* – that is, samples will vary because they contain different members of the population. Interestingly, if we were to plot a frequency distribution of the sample means, we would find that we get a nice symmetrical distribution known as a *sampling distribution*.

Just as frequency distributions tell us something about the behaviour of individuals within a sample, a sampling distribution tells us about the behaviour of samples within a population. One important fact is that the sampling distribution will be centred at the same value as the mean of the population (11 in this case). Put another way, if we took the average of all the means of all possible samples from a population, we would get the value of the population mean. Therefore if we could work out the accuracy of this average, then we would know something about how likely it is that a given sample is representative of the population.

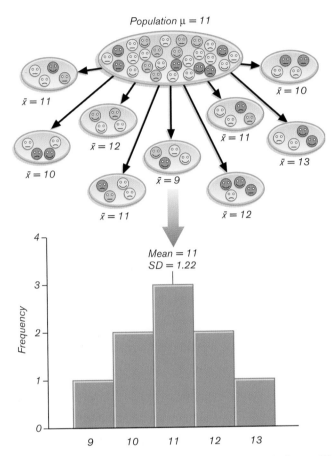

Figure 39.1 Samples taken from a population will have different means

When we wanted to know how well the mean fitted the sample data we used the standard deviation: small standard deviations meant that most data points were close to the mean, while a large standard deviation meant that data points were widely spread from the mean. Therefore if we could calculate the standard deviation between sample means, then this would give us a measure of how much variability there was between different samples from the same population. In fact, we can estimate the standard deviation of sample means (without actually having to collect lots of samples) and it's called the *standard error of the mean* (SE).

We estimate the standard error by dividing the standard deviation in the sample by the square root of the sample size. The resulting value is interpreted in much the same way as the standard deviation: small values tell us that sample means are, in general, quite similar and so the sample mean is representative of the mean in the population, and large values tell us that samples can be very different and so the sample mean might not be representative of the population.

Confidence intervals

A different approach we can use to assess how well a sample statistic represents the population is to calculate boundaries within which most sample means will fall. The best way to think of this is to imagine that, going back to our Glastonbury example, we collected data from 100 samples. Typically we work out the boundaries within which 95 per cent of samples fall. If we calculated the mean for each sample we could draw a frequency distribution and calculate fairly easily the boundaries within which 95 per cent of those sample means lie. This is known as a *confidence interval*.

As I said earlier, psychologists usually deal with 95 per cent confidence intervals (another throwback to Fisher's 5 per cent criterion, which we found out about in Chapter 36), and sometimes 99 per cent confidence intervals. All confidence intervals have a similar interpretation: they are the limits within which a certain percentage (be it 95 per cent, 99 per cent or whatever) of sample statistics will fall. So when you see a 95 per cent confidence interval for a mean think of it like this: if we collected 100 samples, then 95 per cent of these samples would have a mean within the boundaries of the confidence interval.

Probability and hypotheses

In Chapters 36 and 37 we came across the idea that to test theories we had to generate hypotheses from these data and then collect data to see whether the data support our hypothesis. I also mentioned that when we use numbers to test theories we do so by fitting statistical models to our data and then seeing whether or not they fit the data well. These models can be simple, such as saying that the mean in one group will be different from the mean in another group, or complex, such as saying that 20 variables are related to each other.

Test statistics

Regardless of the complexity of the model we use, the underlying principles when we use statistical methods are more or less the same. We saw in Chapter 37 that there are two types of variation: systematic and unsystematic. The systematic variation is due to some genuine effect (be that the effect of an experimenter doing something to all of the participants in one sample but not in other samples, or natural variation between sets of variables). You can think of this as variation that can be explained by the model that we have fitted to the data because we know from where it comes. Unsystematic variation, however, is variation that isn't due to the effect in which we are interested and can come from a variety of unknown sources. Therefore this variation is the error in the model or the variation that the model can't explain.

So we have a hypothesis, we fit some kind of statistical representation of that hypothesis to our data and then test whether that statistical model is a good representation of what's going on. To test whether the model is a good fit we use a *test statistic*. A test statistic is simply a statistic that has known properties; specifically, we know how frequently different values of this statistic occur. By knowing this, we can assess the likelihood of obtaining particular values of that statistic.

Field and Hole (2003) suggest that you think of a test statistic as being a bit like the age at which people die. Past data have told us the distribution of the age of death. For example, we know that, on average, men die at about 75 years old, and that this distribution is top-heavy – that is, most people die above the age of about 50 and it's fairly unusual to die in your teens (you will be relieved to know). So the frequencies of the age of death at older ages are very high but are lower at younger ages. Having a detailed knowledge of the distribution of the age of death, if we met a man of 98, we could calculate the probability of him having lived that long (it would be a small probability because most people die before they reach that age). Test statistics are the same: we know their distributions in detail, so once we have calculated a test statistic, we can discover the probability of having found a value as big as we have.

The computation of these test statistics is way beyond the scope of this chapter (and Field, 2004, covers most of the ones you're likely to come across), but essentially most of them are some function of the systematic variance divided by the unsystematic variance. Put another way, they are all related, in some way, to how much variance the model can explain (and usually a function of how much variation there was in total, or how much variation the model can't explain).

Statistical significance

In Chapter 36 we discovered that there are two types of hypothesis: a null hypothesis and an alternative hypothesis. Theories are tested by generating these hypotheses and then seeing which of the two hypotheses are supported by the data. If we reduced our two types of hypothesis down into very general terms we could express the alternative hypothesis as 'there is an effect' and the null hypothesis as 'there is not an effect'. The statistical model we fit to our data will crudely reflect this. As such, whatever statistical model we apply to our data, our alternative hypothesis is 'there is an effect' (be that effect a difference between two or more groups or a relationship between variables), and the null hypothesis is 'there is no effect' (be that no difference between groups or no relationship between variables).

The test statistic we calculate for a particular model reflects whether the model is a good fit of the data. Given that the model we fit necessarily reflects the alternative hypothesis, this means that the test statistic gives us an idea of whether the alternative hypothesis is true. The better the fit of the model to the data, the bigger the test statistic will be, and the more unlikely it is to occur by chance (like our 98-year-old man). Therefore, for most test statistics, a big value is desirable.

As test statistics get bigger, the probability of them occurring (the *p-value*) becomes smaller. When this *p*-value falls below 0.05 (Fisher's criterion), we accept this as giving us enough confidence to assume that the test statistic is as large as it is because our model is a sufficiently good fit of the data. Put another way, we become confident that our experimental hypothesis is likely to be true. In fact, we can go a bit further than this and infer that the experimental hypothesis is likely to be true not just in our sample but in our population too. We say that our effect is *statistically significant*.

If our test statistic is statistically significant you will often hear people say that it means we can 'reject the null hypothesis' and 'accept the alternative hypothesis'. If the test statistic is small, and not significant, you often hear of people 'accepting the null hypothesis as true'. These are all misconceptions of what the test statistic actually means. It may shock you to discover that the null hypothesis is *never* true: there is always some effect; it's just whether that effect is big enough for us to consider it important (see Cohen, 1990; 1994). For this reason, you should never say that you rejected the null hypothesis. A non-significant test statistic only really means that the effect was very small.

A significant test statistic tells us that *if* the null hypothesis were true, then it is unlikely we would get a test statistic as large as the one we have got. People usually take this as evidence that the alternative hypothesis is true. However, we have just said that the null hypothesis is never true, so the whole reasoning behind this kind of hypothesis testing is fallacious! It's also worth remembering that the criterion of 0.05 is completely arbitrary: it is not magical and it could just as easily have been 0.127, 0.92 or 0.01, depending on Fisher's sanity at the time!

One- and two-tailed tests

We saw in Chapter 36 that hypotheses could be *one-tailed* or *two-tailed*. Given that statistical models reflect our hypothesis, it should not surprise you to find that this distinction applies to our statistical models too: we can test them either one- or two-tailed. Imagine we wanted to discover whether psychopathic murderers eat more or less meat than normal people. We could either do this quasi-experimentally by taking two groups (one of psychopathic murderers and one of normal people) or correlationally (by measuring psychopathic tendencies and meat consumption). If we have no directional hypothesis then there are three possibilities.

1. Psychopaths eat more meat than normals: the mean for psychopath minus the mean for normals is positive or, correlationally speaking, the more psychopathic you are the more meat you eat – a positive relationship.
2. Psychopaths eat less meat than normals: the mean for psychopath minus the mean for normals is negative or, correlationally speaking, the more psychopathic you are the less meat you eat – a negative relationship.
3. There is no difference in meat consumption between psychopaths and normals: the mean for psychopaths minus the mean for normals is exactly zero or, correlationally, there is no relationship between psychopathy and meat consumption. This is the null hypothesis.

The direction of the test statistic (i.e. whether it is positive or negative) will depend on whether the difference, or relationship, is positive or negative. Assuming the test statistic is positive (psychopaths eat more meat), then to assess whether or not this test statistic is likely to have occurred we have to look at the positive end of the distribution (see Figure 39.2).

Therefore if we have predicted incorrectly and actually psychopaths eat less meat, then we would miss this effect (because we would be looking at the wrong end of the distribution). To overcome this, we can hedge our bets and make a two-tailed

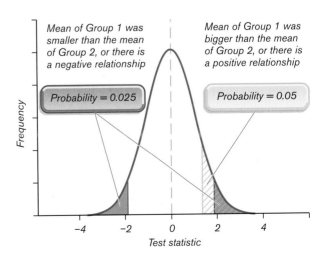

Figure 39.2 One- and two-tailed tests

hypothesis. In doing so we look at both ends (or tails) of the distribution of possible test statistics. Doing this has a price because to keep our criterion probability of 0.05 we have to split this probability across the two tails: so we have 0.025 at the positive end of the distribution and 0.025 at the negative end (see Figure 39.2). In the figure you will note that if we make a specific prediction, then we need a smaller test statistic to find a significant result (because we are looking at only one tail).

Errors

We have seen that we use test statistics to tell us whether there is an effect in our population. If we take a conventional view of hypothesis testing, then there are two possibilities in the real world: there is, in reality, an effect in the population, or there is, in reality, no effect in the population. We use samples to decide which of these possibilities is more likely. However, even though we are fairly conservative about deciding that an effect exists (we have to be 95 per cent confident), there is still a margin for error.

In fact there are two mistakes we can make. A *Type I error* occurs when we infer that there is a genuine effect in our population, when in fact there isn't. If we use Fisher's criterion, then the probability of this error is 0.05 (or 5 per cent) when there is no effect in the population – this value is known as the α-*level*. Assuming there is no effect in our population, if we replicated our data collection 100 times we could expect that on five occasions we would obtain a test statistic large enough to make us think that there is a genuine effect in the population even though there isn't.

The opposite is a *Type II error*, which occurs when we believe that there is no effect in the population when, in reality, there is. In an ideal world, we want the probability of this error to be very small (if there is an effect in the population then it's important that we can detect it). Cohen (1992) suggests that the maximum acceptable probability of a Type II error would be 0.2 (or 20 per cent) – this is called the β-level. That would mean that if we took 100 samples of data from a population in which an effect exists, we would fail to detect that effect in 20 of those samples (so we would miss one in five genuine effects).

There is obviously a trade-off between these two errors: if we lower the probability of accepting an effect as genuine (i.e. make α smaller) then we increase the probability that we'll reject an effect that does genuinely exist (because we have been so strict about the level at which we'll accept that an effect is genuine).

How important is my effect?

Effect sizes

We have just described the traditional way that psychologists conceive of hypothesis testing using test statistics. However, we have already alluded to the fact that the logic behind this approach is flawed. One of the problems that I mentioned was that the null hypothesis is never true: there is always an effect of some description. We have also hinted that the criterion of having a *p*-value less than 0.05 is completely arbitrary. One way to get around these problems is to become less concerned with 'significance' and more concerned with quantifying the size of effect.

When we measure the size of an effect (be that an experimental manipulation or the strength of relationship between variables), this is known as an *effect size*. An effect size is simply an objective and standardised measure of the magnitude of observed effect. The fact that the measure is standardised just means that we can compare effect sizes across different studies that have measured different variables or have used different scales of measurement (so an effect size based on speed in milliseconds could be compared to an effect size based on heart rates).

Many measures of effect size have been proposed, the most common of which are Cohen's *d*, and Pearson's correlation coefficient, *r* (see Field, 2001; 2004). Pearson's correlation coefficient, *r*, may be preferable as an effect size measure because it is constrained to lie between 0 (no effect) and 1 (a perfect effect).

Effect sizes are useful because they provide an objective measure of the importance of an effect. So it doesn't matter what effect you're looking for, what variables have been measured or how those variables have been measured, we know that a correlation coefficient of 0 means there is no effect, and a value of 1 means there is a perfect effect. Cohen (1992; 1988) has also made some widely accepted suggestions about what constitutes a large or small effect:

- $r = 0.10$ (small effect) – in this case the effect explains 1 per cent of the total variance
- $r = 0.30$ (medium effect) – the effect accounts for 9 per cent of the total variance
- $r = 0.50$ (large effect) – the effect accounts for 25 per cent of the variance.

We can use these guidelines to assess the importance of our effects (regardless of the significance of the test statistic). Just as with means, we are actually interested in the size of the effect in the population but because we don't have access to this value we use the effect size in the sample to estimate the likely effect size in the population (Field, 2001)

Statistical power

The effect size in a population is linked to the sample size on which the sample effect size is based, the probability level at which we will accept an effect as being statistically significant and the ability of a test to detect an effect of that size (known as the *statistical power*). As such, once we know three of these four properties (effect size, sample size, significance level and statistical power), then we can always calculate the remaining one. The *power* of a test is the probability that a given test will find an effect, assuming that one exists in the population. Now there are two useful things we can do, knowing that these four variables are related.

1. Calculate the power of a test

Given that we have conducted our experiment and we will already have selected a value of α (it will be 0.05), we can estimate the effect size based on our sample, and we will know how many participants we used. If we did not get a significant result, then this could be because we didn't have enough power to detect it. We can use these values to calculate the

power of our test. If this value turns out to be 0.8 or more we can be confident that the lack of significance was not because we didn't have enough power to detect the effect.

2. Calculate the sample size necessary to achieve a given level of power

We can set the value of α (0.05) and the level of power (0.8), and we can use past research to estimate the size of effect that we would hope to detect in an experiment. Knowing these three things we can calculate how many participants we would need to detect that effect. Deciding how many participants you need is an important aspect of research design and this gives you a good statistical foundation on which to base this decision.

Assumptions of parametric tests

Statistical models usually have *assumptions* of some description. These are conditions under which the procedures are known to be accurate. Many of the tests described in this chapter are parametric tests based on the normal distribution. A parametric test is one that requires data from one of the large catalogues of distributions that statisticians have described, and for data to be parametric, certain assumptions must be true. If you use a parametric test when your data are not parametric, then the results are likely to be inaccurate. The assumptions of parametric tests based on the normal distribution are as follows.

1. *Normally distributed data*: it is assumed that the data are from one or more normally distributed populations.
2. *Homogeneity of variance*: this assumption means that the variances should be the same throughout the data. In designs in which you test several groups of participants, this assumption means that each of these samples comes from populations with the same variance. In correlational designs, this assumption means that the variance of one variable should be stable at all levels of the other variable.
3. *Interval data*: data should be measured at least at the interval level (see page 641).

4. *Independence*: the behaviour of one participant should not influence the behaviour of another. In repeated measures designs, we expect scores in the experimental conditions to be non-independent for a given participant. For example, if we tested a person's memory when sober and after 20 pints of vodka, we'd expect these scores to be related in some way because the person we've tested has a natural ability to remember things that he brings to both experimental tasks. However, behaviour between different participants should still be independent, so if we tested another person's memory when sober and after vodka, her scores should be unrelated to the previous person's – her natural ability to remember things should not have any effect on the other person's ability to remember things.

The assumptions of interval data and independent measurements are, unfortunately, tested only by common sense. The assumption of homogeneity of variance is tested statistically (see Field, 2004) and the assumption of normality can be checked crudely by looking at whether the distribution of scores in the sample is normal (again, see Field, 2004, for more detail).

Statistical models of relationships between variables

The remainder of this chapter looks at different statistical models (tests) and the situations in which they are used.

Correlation

It is often interesting for researchers to know what relationship, if any, exists between two or more variables. A *correlation* is a measure of the linear relationship between variables. For example, I might be interested in whether there is a relationship between how old you are and how much you like the music of Satan-loving Swedish death metallers Dimmu Borgir. These two variables could be related in several ways.

1. They could be positively related, which would

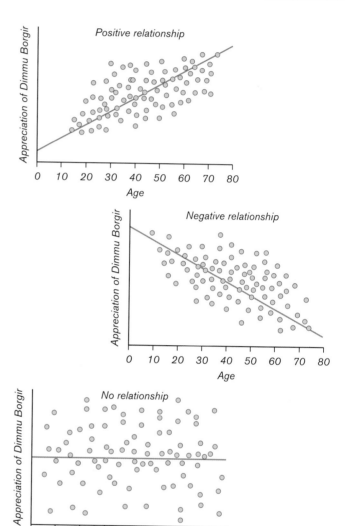

Figure 39.3 An example of a correlation

mean that the older you were the more you enjoy listening to Dimmu Borgir.
2. They could be negatively related, which would mean that the older you get the less you enjoy listening to Dimmu Borgir.
3. They could be not related at all, which would mean that as age changes the enjoyment of Dimmu Borgir stays the same.

An important thing to remember about correlations is that they tell us nothing about causality (this point should have been sufficiently drummed in by now). If we found a negative relationship between age and listening to Dimmu Borgir, even though it might be tempting to interpret this as age causing you to like Dimmu Borgir less, statistically speaking there's no reason why it's not true that listening to Dimmu Borgir makes you young!

Pearson's r

Pearson's correlation coefficient, *r* (*Pearson's r*), is a parametric measure of the relationship between two variables invented by Karl Pearson (remember, Fisher's nemesis – see page 646). It can have a value between -1 and 1, where -1 is a perfect negative relationship (as one variable increases, the other variable decreases by exactly the same amount), and +1 is a perfect positive relationship (as one variable increases, the other variable also increases by exactly the same amount). A value of 0 means that the variables are completely unrelated. As we saw on page 697, values of 0.1 (or -0.1) represent a small effect, values of 0.3 (or -0.3) represent a medium effect size and values of 0.5 (or -0.5) represent a large effect.

The other useful thing about *r* is that if we square it, then the resulting value, the *coefficient of determination*, R^2, tells us the proportion of variance that is shared by the variables. So if *r* is 0.28, then $R^2 = 0.078$. If we multiply this by 100 it tells us this proportion as a percentage. In this case the two variables would share 7.8 of their variance.

However, Pearson's correlation coefficient is dependent on the assumptions of parametric tests. If one of these assumptions is not met, then we have to use an alternative method.

Spearman's ρ

Charles Spearman came up with an alternative method for producing a measure of the relationship between variables, which is not dependent on the assumptions of parametric tests. In short, it is the same as Pearson's correlation except that it is calculated on the ranks of data rather than the data themselves. Ranked data are when you take all of the scores, list them in ascending order and then starting with the lowest score you assign it a rank of 1, then the next highest score a rank of 2, and so on. Like Pearson's correlation, Spearman's test statistic (*Spearman's* ρ) lies between -1 and +1 and can be interpreted in the same way (except we can't square it to find out how much variance the variables share because we analysed the ranks, not the raw data).

Partial and semi-partial correlation

Sometimes when we want to quantify the relationship between two variables, we want to control for the effect of some other variable. We can do this using something called a *partial correlation* or a *semi-partial correlation*. The difference between these two test statistics is quite subtle. Both of these correlations look at the relationship between two variables, controlling for the effect that a third variable has. However, when we do a partial correlation, the effect that the third variable has on *both* variables in the correlation is controlled. In a semi-partial correlation we control for the effect that the third variable has on only one of the variables in the correlation.

For example, we might want to explore the relationship between age and listening to Dimmu Borgir, controlling for whether you worship Satan. Worshipping Satan is likely to relate to listening to Dimmu Borgir (because they themselves are Beelzebub-loving folk). It would also be likely to relate to age if by worshipping Satan he rewarded you with eternal youth.

Figure 39.4 shows the difference between a partial and semi-partial correlation. The partial correlation looks at the relationship between age and listening to

I think I'll invent the correlation coefficient ... that'll annoy Fisher!

Pearson invents the correlation coefficient.

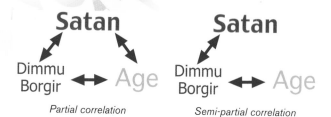

Figure 39.4 Partial and semi-partial correlations

Dimmu Borgir, but controls for the effect that devil worship has on both age and listening to Dimmu Borgir. The semi-partial correlation also looks at the relationship between age and listening to Dimmu Borgir, but controls only for the effect that devil worship has on listening to Dimmu Borgir.

Regression

Regression takes the correlation a step further by fitting a predictive model to the data. In the simple two-variable situations this model is just:

$$\text{Outcome}_i = b_0 + b_1 \text{Predictor}_i + \varepsilon_i$$

The bs in the equation are constants: b_0 is the value of the outcome variable when the predictor is 0, and b_1 tells how important a particular predictor is for predicting the outcome; ε is an error term. Put simply, this model just means that the outcome variable can be predicted from the predictor variable multiplied by its importance in predicting the outcome, plus the value of the outcome when the predictor is 0, plus a bit of error.

One common misconception is that because we are predicting the outcome, this somehow magically tells us that the predictor causes the outcome. It doesn't. Remember, the researcher decides which variable is which in the model. So if we wanted to predict appreciation of Dimmu Borgir from age the model would be:

$$\text{Dimmu Borgir}_i = b_0 + b_1 \text{Age}_i + \varepsilon_i$$

However, we could calculate the model the opposite way around:

$$\text{Age}_i = b_0 + b_1 \text{Dimmu Borgir}_i + \varepsilon_i$$

So as you can see, it's not a causal model, it just tells you how to predict one variable from another.

Interestingly, we can easily extend the regression model to include more than one predictor. If we had a second predictor it simply becomes:

$$\text{Outcome}_i = b_0 + b_1 \text{Predictor 1}_i + b_2 \text{Predictor 2}_i + \varepsilon_i$$

b_0 is the value of the outcome variable when all predictors are 0; b_1 tells us how important the first predictor is for predicting the outcome; b_2 tells us how important the second predictor is for predicting the outcome; ε is again an error term. We can keep extending the model by adding predictors, and each predictor we add will have an associated value that tells us the relative importance of that predictor for predicting the outcome. So in our Dimmu Borgir example, we might add devil worship as a second predictor:

$$\text{Dimmu Borgir}_i = b_0 + b_1 \text{Age}_i + b_2 \text{Devil Worship}_i + \varepsilon_i$$

In regression analysis we first test whether the model is a significant fit of the data (i.e. do the predictors generally do a good job of predicting the outcome?), using a test statistic called F. We then test the predictors individually to see whether they significantly contribute to predicting the outcome. We do this using a t-statistic.

Multiple regression is often used in cross-sectional research: lots of questionnaires are administered at one point in time and then multiple regression is used to look at which variables can be used to predict an outcome. For example, we might predict condom use from age, gender, previous use, social norms and beliefs about condom use (see Sheeran *et al.*, 1999).

Statistical models of differences

We have seen in previous chapters that often researchers use groups of people or different experimental conditions to try to discover causal relationships between variables. Therefore we need statistical models that look at situations where we want to compare different conditions of groups of people. This section looks at these models.

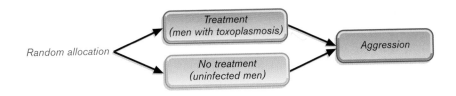

Figure 39.5 Example of a t-test

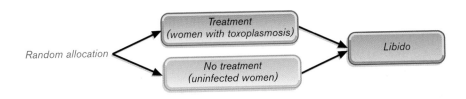

Figure 39.6 Example of a Mann-Whitney test

One predictor with two levels

Independent t-test

The simplest situation is where there is just one predictor (one variable that has been manipulated) and we have manipulated this variable in just two ways (a treatment group and a control). This is the situation represented by the post-test only control group design (Figure 37.2). When we use different people in the two conditions, we have an independent design, and we analyse this situation with an *independent t-test*.

There's been fuss in the news recently about toxoplasmosis, which is a disease caught by humans from cats (pregnant women have to be particularly careful). Although lots of humans are infected with this virus and remain unaware of the fact, recent reports suggest that it increases aggression in males. If we wanted to test this we could get a group of infected males and group of uninfected males and then simply test their aggression by perhaps giving them a very frustrating task and seeing how many times they hit a punch bag. These groups would have to contain different males because you can't be infected and uninfected at the same time!

The *t*-test is a statistic that comes from the *t*-distribution, which is a family of distributions. To know which family a particular *t* comes from we

need to know the *degrees of freedom* (df). This is just the total number of people tested minus 2 (so if we had ten infected men and ten uninfected men, we would have df = 10 + 10 − 2 = 18).

When we know which distribution the statistic comes from we can calculate the probability of that value occurring by chance given the data we have. If this probability is less than 0.05 then we conclude that the test statistic is big because there is a genuine difference between our groups. We can look at the mean of the two groups to tell us the nature of the effect (in this case we would expect the mean aggression to be higher in the infected men than in the uninfected men).

Finally, the *t*-test is parametric and is therefore accurate only when the assumptions of parametric tests have been met.

Mann–Whitney

If the assumptions have not been met, then we have to use a test that does not rely on these assumptions. The *Mann–Whitney test* is used in the same situations as the independent *t*-test but when the assumptions of parametric tests have been broken. Like Spearman's correlation, it gets around the assumptions of parametric tests by analysing the data after they have been ranked (rather than the raw scores).

The fuss about toxoplasmosis also extends to women. Apparently, rather than getting more aggressive, infected females become more amorous: their libido goes up. If we wanted to test this we could get a group of infected females and group of uninfected females and then simply test their libido in some way that we can leave to your imagination. We might find, however, that levels of libido were not normally distributed.

The Mann–Whitney test produces a test statistic, U, which, like the t-test, has known properties, so we can calculate the probability of that value occurring by chance given the data we have. If this probability is less than 0.05, then we conclude that the test statistic is big because there is a genuine difference between our groups. We should look at the median of the two groups to tell us the nature of the effect (in this case we would expect the mean libido to be higher in the infected women than the uninfected ones).

Related t-test

Sometimes we might want to look at differences between two experimental conditions when we have used the same people in each condition (a repeated measures design). This is the situation represented by the post-test only repeated measures control group design (Figure 37.6). When we use the people in the two conditions, we have a repeated measures design, and we analyse this situation with a *related t-test*.

Students often leave things until the last minute. So they'll have an essay deadline that is three months away and yet write the essay in the 12 hours before the deadline. This surely can't be good for their grades, so we could test this with a group of students. For one of their essays we ask them to come in every week over the three-month period to work on their essay at fixed times of the week. For a different essay, we lock them in a room for the 12 hours before the deadline. Obviously it's important to control for the natural ability of the students, so we could use the same students (although we should vary the order in which they complete the tasks, we ignore this in the analysis – we compare all the marks for essays that took 'three months' with all the marks for essays that took '12 hours').

The related t-test, like the independent t-test, comes from a family of t-distributions. To know which family a related t comes from, we again need to know the degrees of freedom (df), but this time it is simply the number of people we have used minus 1 (so, if we had 20 students, df = 20 – 1 = 19).

When we know which t-distribution the statistic comes from, we can calculate the probability of that value occurring by chance given the data we have. If this probability is less than 0.05, then we conclude that the test statistic is big because there is a genuine difference between our groups. We can look at the mean of the two groups to tell us the nature of the effect (in this case, we would expect the mean essay

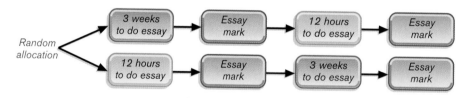

Figure 39.7 Example of a related t-test

Figure 39.8 Example of a Wilcoxon signed-rank test

mark to be higher when the students had spent three months doing them).

Finally, the *t*-test is parametric and so is accurate only when the assumptions of parametric tests have been met.

Wilcoxon signed-rank test

If the assumptions of parametric tests have not been met, then we have to use a test that does not rely on these assumptions. The *Wilcoxon signed-rank test* is used in the same situations as the related *t*-test but when the assumptions of parametric tests have been broken. Like the Mann–Whitney test, it gets around the assumptions of parametric tests by analysing the data after they have been ranked.

Rather than looking at how long the students took to write their essays, we could look at the effect of how many deadlines they have. So for one essay we could set them two other pieces of work due in on the same day (so three deadlines to meet) and for another essay we set them no other deadlines (so they can concentrate on the one essay). We might find that the essay marks were not normally distributed.

The Wilcoxon test produces a test statistic, *T*, for which we can calculate the probability of that value occurring by chance given the data we have. If this probability is less than 0.05, then we conclude that the test statistic is big because there is a genuine difference between our groups. We should look at the median of the two groups to tell us the nature of the effect (in this case we would expect the mean essay mark to be higher when there is only one deadline).

One predictor with several levels

One-way independent ANOVA

The next most complex scenario is when we still have just one predictor (one variable that has been manipulated) but we have manipulated this variable in more than two ways (for example, two treatment groups and a control). This is the situation represented by the post-test only control group design with several experimental conditions (Figure 37.3). When we use different people in all of the conditions, we have an independent design, and we analyse this situation with an *analysis of variance (ANOVA)*. Because there is only one predictor, this is called a one-way ANOVA.

Pets are supposed to be therapeutic: owning a pet extends your life (well, unless they give you toxoplasmosis). A researcher wanted to study whether different pets were more anxiety-reducing. He took three groups of people. One group was given cats to look after, another group was given dogs to look after, and those in a control group were not given a pet. He could then test how relaxed they were after a month.

ANOVA produces a test-statistic, *F*. We can calculate the probability of that value occurring by chance given the data we have. If this probability is less than 0.05, then we conclude that the test statistic is big because there is a genuine difference between our groups. The ANOVA just tells us there is a difference: it doesn't tell us which groups differ from which. If the overall ANOVA is significant we should conduct *post hoc tests*. These are basically lots of *t*-

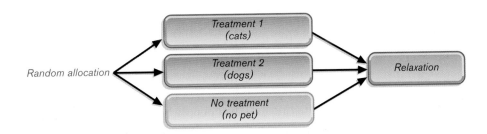

Figure 39.9 Example of a one-way independent ANOVA

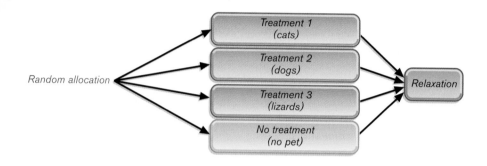

Figure 39.10 Example of a Kruskal–Wallis test

tests that compare all of the different groups (dog vs cat, dog vs control, cat vs control).

ANOVA is parametric and so is accurate only when the assumptions of parametric tests have been met.

Kruskal–Wallis test

The *Kruskal–Wallis test* is used when you have one predictor that has several levels (three or more) and you've used different people in each group but the assumptions of parametric data have been violated. Like the Mann–Whitney and Wilcoxon tests, it analyses the ranked data rather than the raw scores.

Imagine we did our pet study but added a new group of people (bear in mind ANOVA and Kruskal–Wallis can be used with any number of groups). This new group was given lizards as pets. The relaxation scores were not normally distributed, so ANOVA could not be used.

The Kruskal–Wallis test produces a test statistic, *H*, and we can calculate the probability of that value occurring by chance given the data we have. If this probability is less than 0.05, then we conclude that the test statistic is big because there is a genuine difference between our groups. Like ANOVA, it doesn't tell us which groups differ from which. If the overall ANOVA is significant we should conduct post hoc tests. These would be lots of Mann–Whitney tests that compare all of the different groups (dog vs cat, dog vs control, cat vs control, dog vs lizard, cat vs lizard, lizard vs control).

One-way related ANOVA

Sometimes we might want to look at differences between more than two experimental conditions when we have used the same people in each condition (a repeated measures design). When we use the same people in the two conditions, we have a repeated measures design, and we analyse this situation with a *one-way related ANOVA*.

MP3 music files can be encoded at different qualities: 128 kbps (CD quality), 96 kbps (near CD quality), 64 kbps (FM radio quality). The lower the quality, the less room the file takes up on your computer. A company developing MP3 Walkmans was interested in whether people could actually tell the difference between these qualities (because if they can't, then they can encode the files at lower qualities and fit more on their Walkmans). Therefore the company played a group of people a song (not by Dimmu Borgir this time, you'll be pleased to know) at each of the three qualities and then asked the people to rate how good the quality of the recording was. It's important to control for the natural hearing ability of the people, so the same people were used.

Each person hears the three MP3s and rates them, but people hear them in different orders. Figure 39.11 shows a *Latin square counterbalancing* order. The important thing to note is that each experimental condition appears in every location (so each type of MP3 is heard first by some people,

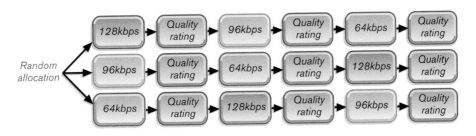

Figure 39.11 *Example of a one-way related ANOVA*

Figure 39.12 *Example of Friedman's ANOVA*

second by others and last by the remainder). Again, for the purpose of analysis we ignore the counterbalancing and just analyse all the quality ratings for the 128 kbps MP3, the 96 kbps MP3 and the 64 kbps MP3.

Like independent ANOVA, related ANOVA produces a test-statistic, *F*. We can calculate the probability of that value occurring by chance given the data we have. If this probability is less than 0.05, then we conclude that the test statistic is big because there is a genuine difference between our groups. The ANOVA just tells us there is a difference: it doesn't tell us which groups differ from which. If the overall ANOVA is significant we should conduct post hoc tests. These are basically lots of *t*-tests that compare all of the different groups.

ANOVA is parametric and so is accurate only when the assumptions of parametric tests have been met.

Friedman's ANOVA
Friedman's ANOVA is used when you have one predictor that has several levels (three or more) and you have used the same people in each condition but the assumptions of parametric data have been violated. Like the Mann–Whitney, Wilcoxon and Kruskal–Wallis tests it analyses the ranked data rather than the raw scores.

Imagine we wanted to look at the effects of sleep deprivation on mood. We could prevent people from

having sleep for 72 hours but measure their irritability after 24 hours and 48 hours. We could also measure their irritability before the study. So we have four experimental conditions: before, after 24 hours, after 48 hours, after 72 hours. Irritability could be measured in terms of how many times they told people to clear off and leave them alone. The irritability scores are not normally distributed so ANOVA cannot be used.

Note that we haven't counterbalanced the orders: we have just measured people at four different points in time. This is known as a *time-series design*.

Friedman's ANOVA produces a test statistic that has a Chi-square distribution χ^2, and we can calculate the probability of that value occurring by chance given the data we have. If this probability is less than 0.05, then we conclude that the test statistic is big because there is a genuine difference between our groups. Like ANOVA, it doesn't tell us which groups differ from which. If the overall ANOVA is significant we should conduct post hoc tests. These would be lots of Wilcoxon tests that compare all of the different groups.

More than one predictor
Sometimes we have more than one predictor when we have used experimental manipulations. In these cases each of the variables could be manipulated using the same people (a repeated measures design),

different people (an independent design) or a mixture (some variables use the same people and some use different people – a mixed design). In all of these cases we can use ANOVA to analyse the data.

Depending on the number of predictor variables (variables we have manipulated), the name changes slightly. For example, a two-way ANOVA has two predictors, a three-way ANOVA has three, and so on. Likewise, we usually insert a word or two to describe whether the predictors were measured using the same or different people. So if we had two variables and we used different people in all experimental conditions, then we would call it a *two-way independent ANOVA*. If, however, we had manipulated two variables and used the same people in all experimental conditions, then we would analyse the data with a *two-way repeated measures ANOVA*. A final scenario is that we manipulate two variables: we manipulate one of them using the same people and the other one using different people. In this case we use a *two-way mixed ANOVA*.

All of these ANOVAs have a lot in common. They will produce *F* statistics for the effect of each of the two variables (the same as if we analysed each variable separately in a one-way ANOVA). We get a test statistic for the interaction between the two. So, that's three test statistics in total!

We'll look at just one of these cases because they are all similar.

Two-way mixed ANOVA

Imagine we wanted to look at whether Lucozade® (a glucose drink in the UK) really does enhance sporting performance. We got some volunteers and we put them on a treadmill and told them to run until they could run no further. We measured the time it took them to give up. Each person did the treadmill task twice: once after drinking nothing and once after drinking Lucozade.

However, so that we could see whether we were just getting a placebo effect (i.e. an effect caused by the fact you *believe* that Lucozade will make you run further and not caused by the fact that Lucozade actually does make you run further), we had a second group of people who did the same task, except they only believed they were drinking Lucozade; in reality they were given something that tasted like Lucozade but had none of its nutritional value.

This is a mixed design: each person is in two conditions (i.e. they experience both 'drink' or 'no drink' conditions) and different people also engage in different conditions (Lucozade or placebo).

The resulting ANOVA will give us an *F*-value for the effect of 'drink'. That is, a difference caused by the fact that in some conditions people had a drink before running whereas on a different occasion they had no drink. If the *F* is sufficiently large, and the probability of this effect occurring by chance is less than 0.05, then we assume that this has happened because there is some difference in the amount of running when people had a drink and when they did not. The expectation would be that people ran for longer when they'd had a drink (regardless of whether that drink was Lucozade or the placebo).

The ANOVA will also give us an *F*-value for the effect of 'group'. That is, a difference caused by the fact that some people drank Lucozade, whereas others drank a placebo. If the *F* is sufficiently large and the probability of this effect occurring by chance is less than 0.05, then we assume that this has happened because there is some difference between the people that had Lucozade and those that had the placebo drink. The expectation would be that people ran for longer when they'd had Lucozade.

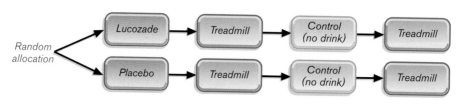

Figure 39.13 Example of a two-way mixed ANOVA

Finally we would get an interaction effect. This would tell us whether the effect of one variable was different at different levels of the other variable. Put simply, we could ask 'Is the difference in how long we run when we have a drink compared to when we don't different when the drink is Lucozade rather than a placebo drink?'

Interpreting interactions

Figure 39.14 shows an interaction graph like the one we might get for our Lucozade example. A significant interaction just tells you that the effect of one of your variables is different at the levels of the other variable. So, with our Lucozade example, if we look first at the condition when nothing was drunk, it doesn't matter whether people were in the Lucozade condition or the placebo condition – they ran for about the same amount of time (the triangle and square are in more or less the same location). So when nothing was drunk, performance was the same.

Now let's look at when a drink was consumed. There's now a huge difference between the Lucozade and placebo group (the square is much higher than the triangle). Therefore, when a drink is consumed performance is different. This is all an interaction is.

Another way to look at this is to examine the slope of the lines. For the placebo group the line is very flat: it doesn't matter if they had a drink or not, they ran for

about the same amount of time. However, for the Lucozade group this isn't true. The line is very sloped because when this group drank Lucozade they ran for a lot longer than when they didn't drink anything. Combine all this and we have shown that Lucozade did affect performance but the placebo did not.

When you have an interaction effect, always draw a graph like this because it helps interpretation. There are a couple of general rules we can extrapolate from this example (see Field, 2004).

1. Significant interactions are shown by non-parallel lines on an interaction graph. However, it's important to remember that this doesn't mean that non-parallel lines automatically indicate that the interaction is significant – whether the interaction is significant will depend on the degree to which the lines are not parallel!

2. If the lines on an interaction graph cross over, then obviously they are not parallel and this can be a dead giveaway that you have a possible significant interaction. However, contrary to what some textbooks might have you believe, it isn't always the case that if the lines of the interaction graph cross, then the interaction is significant.

Categorical data

Chi-square

Sometimes we might have only nominal data – that is, we have collected information about the frequencies with which certain events occur. When we have frequency data we have to use a test called the *Chi-square test* (again devised by Pearson).

Imagine you are interested in the number of people voting for two potential student representatives, Tiddle and Twazzock, and that you have already broken down the voting by whether the voter was male or female. Now each person can be only male or female, and they can vote only for one candidate. Therefore, each number in Table 39.1 represents a quantity of people. For example, six different males voted for Twazzock and 21 different females voted for Tiddle.

The Chi-square test produces a test statistic that has a Chi-square distribution χ^2, and we can

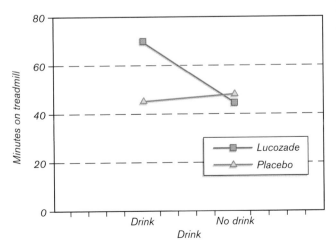

Figure 39.14 An interaction graph

TABLE 39.1 EXAMPLE OF THE CHI-SQUARE TEST

		CANDIDATE		
		TIDDLE	TWAZZOCK	TOTAL
Gender	Males	15	6	21
	Females	21	25	46
	Total	36	31	67

ACTIVITY BOX 39.1

Which test?

For each of the examples in Applications Box 37.1 decide which test would be most appropriate to analyse the data.

Answers
Festinger and Carlsmith: cognitive dissonance

This would be analysed with one-way independent ANOVA because there is one predictor (monetary incentive) with more than two levels (no incentive, $1 and $20). It's an independent ANOVA because different people were used in each of the incentive groups. If the data broke any assumptions, then we could use the Kruskal–Wallis test instead.

Rosenthal and Jacobson (1966): blame the teachers

This would be analysed with two-way mixed ANOVA because there are two predictors (the label attached to the child and the time at which IQ was measured). One is measured using different people (children were labelled either 'bloomers' or not) and the other is a repeated measure (each child's IQ was measured at two points in time).

Greenwald *et al.* (1988): implicit attitudes

This would be analysed with a related *t*-test because there is one predictor (the type of trial) with two levels (compatible trials vs incompatible trials). It's a related *t*-test because the same people see both types of trials. If the data broke any assumptions, then we could use the Wilcoxon signed-rank test instead.

calculate the probability of that value occurring by chance given the data we have. If this probability is less than 0.05, then we conclude that there is a relationship between our variables. So we would say that the distribution of males and females was different for Tiddle and Twazzock.

Summary

You are probably exhausted because this chapter has covered a lot of ground. We started off by looking at how we see whether summaries of our data (for example, the mean) are representative of our population by exploring the standard error and confidence intervals. We then moved on to look at the rationale behind fitting statistical models. We saw that basically we conceptualise our experimental and null hypotheses in terms of a statistical model that we then fit to our data. This model throws out some kind of test statistic, which is simply a statistic with known properties. Because we know the properties of the statistic, we can work out whether a value as large as the one we have is likely to have occurred by chance assuming that the null hypothesis is true. We also saw that we can conceptualise the process in terms of merely establishing how large the effect is. Finally, we looked at a variety of different statistical models that we can apply in a variety of contexts.

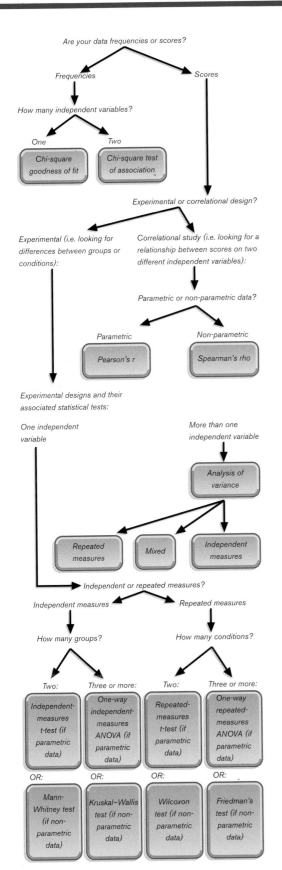

You now know everything you need to know to do some research!

Learning outcomes

When you have completed this chapter you should be able to:

- explain how we use the standard error and confidence intervals
- describe the use of hypothesis testing, and its limitations
- describe different experimental scenarios that would require data analysis using each of the following tests – t-test, Mann–Whitney test, Wilcoxon signed-rank test, one-way ANOVA, two-way ANOVA, Friedman's ANOVA, Kruskal–Wallis test
- explain when correlations and regression should be used to analyse data.

Key terms

α-level
Analysis of variance (ANOVA)
Assumptions
Chi-square test
Coefficient of determination
Confidence interval
Correlation
Degrees of freedom
Effect in the population
Effect size
Friedman's ANOVA
Homogeneity of variance
Independence
Independent t-test
Interval data
Kruskal–Wallis test
Latin square counterbalancing
Mann–Whitney test
Normally distributed data
One-tailed and two-tailed tests
One-way related ANOVA
p-value

Figure 39.15 Which test do I use?

Section 8
Research methods and statistics

Partial correlation
Pearson's r
Post hoc tests
Power
Regression
Related t-test
Sampling distribution
Sampling variation
Semi-partial correlation
Spearman's ρ
Standard error of the mean

Statistical power
Statistically significant
Test statistic
Time-series design
Two-way independent ANOVA
Two-way mixed ANOVA
Two-way repeated measures ANOVA
Type I error
Type II error
Wilcoxon signed-rank test

Further reading

Field, A. P. and Hole, G. (2003) *How to Design and Report Experiments*. London: Sage.

Field, A. P. (2004) *Discovering Statistics using SPSS for Windows: Advanced Techniques for the Beginner* (2nd edn). London: Sage. Covers the theory of all the tests mentioned in this chapter in more detail than Rowntree and Wright, but not as much as Howell!

Howell, D. C. (2002) *Statistical Methods for Psychology* (5th edn). Belmont, CA: Duxbury. Very detailed on theory and quite advanced, but really is one of the best books around.

Rowntree, D. (1981) *Statistics Without Tears: A Primer for Non-Mathematicians*. London: Penguin. Doesn't cover everything in this chapter, but is a nice gentle introduction to the important bits.

Wright, D. B. (2002) *First Steps in Statistics*. London: Sage. Covers most of the tests in this chapter in a bit more detail, but not too much, and very accessible.

Appendixone

Careers and
study skills

i	*Being a psychologist*	*712*
	– Jon Sutton	
ii	*Study skills in psychology*	*723*
	– Nick Hammond and Annie Trappp	

Appendix 1
Careers and study skills

i

Being a psychologist

Route map of the chapter

This chapter will give you a brief introduction to some of the careers open to you as a psychologist. We will focus on areas where there is a recognised training route leading to 'Chartered' status – the seal of approval from the British Psychological Society (BPS), which many employers require. Psychologists in each area will give you a flavour of their lives, and we will conclude with some views on new opportunities and challenges for psychologists of tomorrow, such as you.

Introduction

When you first picked up this weighty tome, perhaps you already felt like a psychologist. Perhaps you were fascinated by what makes people tick – anyone from the brattish brother to the predatory psychopath. Now that you have started your studies and used this book, you have taken the first steps on the path that will take you from being an amateur psychologist to a professional one. How can you turn your new knowledge of psychological theory and research into a career in which you solve practical problems in society and improve people's quality of life?

This chapter can't give you a complete map of how to make it in your chosen career. Psychology is a thriving profession, changing all the time, and a lot of the detail you need is best kept on the website associated with this book: www.completepsychology.co.uk.

What this chapter will try to do is to give you enough of a picture of different areas to help you to decide whether you want to find out more. Along the way we'll meet psychologists working all around us –

in schools, hospitals, prisons and workplaces – to find out how they have put the knowledge in this book to work, and what they love and hate about their jobs.

Where do all the psychologists go?

Psychology graduates are pouring out of universities as the popularity of the subject continues to rise. In 2002, there were over 6500 new graduates. Can there really be jobs for them all?

In fact, only around 15 to 20 per cent of psychology graduates end up working as professional psychologists, after obtaining relevant experience

'A psychology degree will teach some solid science, some tough statistics, some powerful thinking skills and some sensitivity in relating to other humans. That's a sound foundation for many jobs, and also for a rich and full life.'

and postgraduate training in the roles covered in this chapter (see www.prospects.ac.uk for the latest figures). But this doesn't mean that the majority of graduates do not use what they have learnt. On the contrary, many employers recognise and appreciate the skills a psychology graduate has gained.

According to Zander Wedderburn, President of the British Psychological Society 2003–2004, 'a psychology degree will teach some solid science, some tough statistics, some powerful thinking skills and some sensitivity in relating to other humans. That's a sound foundation for many jobs, and also for a rich and full life.'

Of those graduates who go into permanent employment as psychologists, a third enter public services (such as the health service, education, the civil service and the armed forces), and a third go into industry or commerce (market research, personnel management etc.). Of the remainder, about a tenth teach and research in schools, colleges and universities.

This chapter will cover areas in which you can register as a *Chartered Psychologist* with the British Psychological Society, where there is a recognised training route leading to membership of a Division of the Society and eligibility for the Register of Chartered Psychologists. Employers often prefer to appoint a Chartered Psychologist because the title is the public's guarantee that the person is properly trained and qualified, and answerable to an independent professional body. If your degree is recognised by the Society for the 'Graduate Basis for Registration', you could become a Chartered Psychologist in one of the following areas:

- clinical psychologists, working in health and care settings
- counselling psychologists, in private practice and commercial settings
- educational psychologists, in local education authorities, schools and special schools
- forensic psychologists, working in penal establishments, special hospitals and with young offenders
- health psychologists, working in hospitals, health authorities and health research departments

- neuropsychologists, helping people with brain injury
- occupational psychologists, in management, personnel, training, selection and careers services
- teaching and research in institutions of higher education.

ACTIVITY BOX 1

Chartered Psychologists and this book

Although the types of Chartered Psychologist may seem fairly specialist, psychologists working in any of these settings are likely to use knowledge from a range of different areas that you have covered in this book.

Clinical psychologists will draw heavily on their knowledge of psychological disorders and therapies, but they will also be thankful they were listening in lectures on, for example, attention and psychobiology. A forensic psychologist trying to understand a young offender would need to consider a range of factors, potentially applying their knowledge of personality, developmental psychology, and social influence and group processes.

As you read the following accounts from specialist psychologists, take the time to flick back through the book and consider what areas would feed into your practice if you chose to go down each route. Are they the areas of psychology you have enjoyed studying?

Clinical psychology

Psychology is a helping profession, and perhaps nowhere is this more evident than in the field of clinical psychology, which aims to reduce psychological distress and promote psychological well being. It's demanding work. You would deal with a wide range of psychological difficulties and serious mental illnesses, including phobias, depression and schizophrenia.

Clinical psychologists work largely in health and social care settings, including hospitals, health centres, community mental health teams, child and adolescent mental health services, and social

Appendix 1
Careers and study skills

Could you get them to stroke it?

services. They usually work as part of a team with, for example, social workers, medical practitioners and other health professionals. Most clinical psychologists work in the National Health Service, but some work in private practice. Others work as trainers, teachers and researchers in universities, adding to the evidence base of the profession.

The work is often directly with people, assessing their needs and providing therapies based on psychological theories and research. But as Glenda Wallace (Consultant Clinical Psychologist with Bradford Hospitals) explains, these people can be a great resource themselves:

> You are face to face with another human being who can bring you richness, and if you are lucky you can give them something back. This is not dismissing our profession, but acknowledging that people are a wonderful resource even without the wealth of theory under their belt that we are supposed to have.

Places for training are in short supply and a first- or an upper second-class degree is required. A clearing house scheme then operates for applications to all clinical psychology training courses. Candidates make one application to the Clearing House for Postgraduate Courses in Clinical Psychology (see www.leeds.ac.uk/chpccp), which is then distributed to their selected institutions. Application packs and handbooks are available from September to December for courses commencing in September/October of the following year.

Relevant experience is also important: this could involve working as a psychological assistant, research assistant or care nurse/assistant, either before or after graduation. Some graduates get their foot in the NHS door by working as an assistant psychologist on a voluntary basis, or get involved in charities working with mental health client groups.

After this challenging start, job opportunities for qualified clinical psychologists are good. Salaries start at around £17,000 but can rise to over £60,000 for senior experienced psychologists managing departments or large specialist sections.

Counselling psychology

If you love to talk people through their problems – really get to the bottom of them – perhaps you should consider counselling psychology. You would work with others to explore issues underlying a diverse range of human problems. How, for instance, would you go about helping a man who had just lost his wife of 50 years? Perhaps more importantly, how would you help him to help himself?

As human problems are pretty universal, you could end up working virtually anywhere. *Counselling psychologists* work within the NHS, in general and psychiatric hospitals and GP surgeries; in private hospitals and in independent practice; within education in schools, colleges and universities; in industry and in public and private corporate institutions. It's this diversity that keeps Linda Papadopoulos (London Guildhall University) hooked:

> I've done everything from work on acute psychiatric wards and GP surgeries, to giving

lectures to dermatologists and plastic surgeons. I've battled with statistical analysis, travelled all over the world to listen to and talk about research, even sat on Richard and Judy's couch! The fact is my day is never boring. Whether working with patients, doing research or giving a comment to the media, I get to tap into my knowledge of counselling psychology and apply it in so many ways that I always feel challenged and excited about my work.

Postgraduate training is most likely to be self-financed and total costs (including fees) will be approximately £2500 per year. Institutions may be able to provide information on Research Councils and other funding agencies (such as charitable trusts, foundations and companies).

Based on the nationally agreed scales for clinical psychologists, counselling psychologists should expect to receive between £16,000 and £60,000, depending on age, experience and level of responsibility. For counselling psychologists working as lecturers the nationally agreed lecturers' scales apply. The website of the British Psychological Society's Division of Counselling psychology, www.counsellingpsychology.org.uk, has a lot of useful information.

Educational psychology

The small girl sits sullenly in the corner, her education (her future?) slipping away before the teacher's eyes. What's her problem? Can you find it? Can you solve it?

As an *educational psychologist* you would tackle all kinds of problems encountered by young people in education, from learning difficulties to social or emotional problems. Work can be either directly with a child (assessing the problem through observation, interview or test materials, or giving counselling) or indirectly (with parents, teachers and other professionals).

The majority of educational psychologists are employed by local education authorities (LEAs), working in schools, colleges, nurseries and special units. They liaise regularly with other professionals from the departments of education, health and social

services. A growing number work as independent or private consultants.

The path to Chartered Educational Psychologist is under review – see www.bps.org.uk/careers/careers.cfm for the latest. At the moment, however, if you want to become an educational psychologist in England, Wales or Northern Ireland you need to qualify as a teacher first (there are different routes in Scotland). A degree in a National Curriculum subject is normally required to enter a teacher training course, so you may wish to consider a joint/combined honours degree to meet both requirements. You will then usually need two years' teaching experience, followed by an accredited postgraduate course in educational psychology.

Remember, though, that a rewarding job awaits you at the end of this long route to qualification. Kairen Cullen, a senior educational psychologist with CEA@Islington, says:

This is, unarguably, a satisfying and rewarding occupation and will use an individual's academic and personal qualities to the full. Most important of all, in my view, is the possession of a total commitment to one's own learning and ongoing development.

The psychological processes around how individuals, groups and organisations function most effectively – cope with and use difficulties constructively and learn – are complex and fascinating. As an educational psychologist I

use my knowledge of psychological theory, training in hypothesis formulation, and testing and analysis, and create unique solutions for unique problems.

Forensic psychology

Every year when the figures show another rise in the number of applications to study psychology at university, the newspapers call it 'the *Cracker* effect' and chuck in a picture of Robbie Coltrane. There's no doubt that depictions of forensic psychology on TV and in books have encouraged some people into the profession, but is the job all it's cracked up to be?

'The work of a *forensic psychologist* is much more diverse than that depicted by the media,' says Jane Ireland, a Chartered Forensic Psychologist and Reader in Forensic Psychology at the University of Central Lancashire and Ashworth High Secure Hospital.

You may be disappointed if you see yourself as a full-time 'offender profiler', helping the police catch criminals. But if you're interested in working with challenging groups of individuals, in developing and delivering offending-behaviour programmes, conducting in-depth offender assessments to inform on decisions about the risk an offender poses to themselves and the general public, in training staff, conducting applied research and providing a consultancy service, then this may be the profession for you.

As a forensic psychologist you could find yourself drawing on a range of areas in this book, including those on memory (allowing you to assess the reliability of eyewitness testimony), the developmental and social psychology of the self and others (giving you an insight into possible influences on offending across the life span), intelligence and psychometric testing (knowledge you might use to assess prisoners) and psychological disorders (which often accompany offending behaviour). You could put this know-how to use in a variety of legal contexts, from criminal investigation, through courts and mental health tribunals, to understanding and treating criminals (e.g. anger management or social skills training).

There's clearly a lot riding on this type of work and, according to Dr Ireland, a Chartered Forensic Psychologist and Reader in Forensic Psychology at the University of Central Lancashire and Ashworth High Security Hospital,

is not a career that should be taken lightly. We often find ourselves making decisions that impact significantly on others. The compilation of forensic risk assessments, for example, can contribute to the length of time that a prisoner or patient will remain detained. It's also not a career for those seeking a '9 to 5' job or whose primary wish is to make individuals 'better'. Rather, the focus of some psychological intervention with offenders, for example, is on making them 'safer' for their eventual return to the community and in doing so increasing their quality of life. This can be one of the hardest lessons learned by those new to the profession. You either accept the reality of how difficult the work can be or become disillusioned with it and seek a career within another branch of applied psychology.

To become a Chartered Forensic Psychologist, you will need Graduate Basis for Registration followed by either an accredited MSc plus stage 2 of the Society's Diploma in Forensic Psychology, or stages 1 and 2 of the Diploma. HM Prison Service (which includes the Home Office Research and Development Unit as well as prisons) is the largest single employer of forensic psychologists in the UK, and further information on the training, work, pay and recruitment of forensic psychologists in the Prison and Probation Service can be found at www.hmprisonservice.gov.uk. Forensic psychologists can also be employed in the health service (including rehabilitation units and secure hospitals), the social service (including the police service, young offenders units and the probation service), and in university departments or in private consultancy.

Health psychology

'Just say no!', 'If you do drink, don't do drunk', 'Smoking kills', 'Eat five a day' ... We are constantly bombarded with health-related messages, and the relatively new field of health psychology uses theory and research to make sure they work, and to understand *how* they work.

Charles Abraham (University of Sussex) explains how psychological principles are used to promote changes in people's attitudes, behaviour and thinking about health and illness.

> Many professionals aspire to change people's health behaviour. Health psychologists work on understanding *how* behaviour change happens; how the processes that underpin behaviour patterns and behaviour change can effectively be altered. So in the case of preventive health behaviours (such as using condoms) and adherence to medical advice (e.g. taking medication as directed) health psychology research can help professionals offer their patients and clients the right advice in the most effective manner. Recently we have analysed the messages contained in leaflets promoting condom use and moderate alcohol use across a number of European countries. We were able to distinguish between research-based leaflets (which are more likely to be effective) and those containing messages that do not correspond to the psychological antecedents of behaviour change. This work provides guidelines for the production of health texts and helps to establish a foundation for evidence-based health promotion practice.

Usually following a British Psychological Society accredited MSc, *health psychologists* find work in a number of settings, such as hospitals, academic health research units, health authorities and university departments. They may deal with problems identified by healthcare agencies, including NHS Trusts and Health Authorities, health professionals such as GPs, nurses and rehabilitation therapists, and organisations and employers outside the healthcare system.

Posts are not necessarily advertised as being for 'health psychologists'. Employers may request applications from psychologists with the relevant skills to work in the health area, such as clinical or counselling psychologists, or from health professionals in general.

Neuropsychology

Imagine you are in an accident and your brain is injured. If you can't remember your life pre-injury, including giving birth to your son, how do you relate to him now? Or if you can't lay down new memories – you're stuck in the past – what is your emotional life like? If you can only respond with an eye blink, how do you share your thoughts with others?

These are the kinds of questions that fascinate Camilla Herbert, a Consultant Clinical Neuropsychologist with the Brain Injury Rehabilitation Trust and Hurstwood Park Neurological Centre. She says:

> Neurorehabilitation is about people struggling with events and injuries that none of us would choose to endure. The courage and resilience that many people show is inspiring, and compensates for the day-to-day frustrations of slow progress, chaotic lives and missed appointments. What can you expect? The joys of home visits, sitting on vaguely damp sofas

GAME OVER

traffic is the biggest single killer of 12-16 year olds THINK!

Health psychologists find out if and how campaigns like this work

Appendix 1
Careers and study skills

drinking brown liquids out of dirty cups ... laughing with a client as they describe their latest memory failure, whether it was leaving the dog outside the post office or a bucket of dirty water in the boiler cupboard 'to come back for later'.

Professor Barbara Wilson OBE also points to

the intriguing mixture of normality and abnormality that one finds in neuropsychology. Most people with neuropsychological impairments are not psychiatrically disturbed, they do not have developmental learning difficulties, they are people who have sustained an insult to the brain that has resulted in specific problems to be examined, understood and alleviated in some way.

Neuropsychologists most commonly work in the following areas.

- Acute settings: working alongside neurosurgeons and neurologists and the allied disciplines, usually in a regional neurosciences centre. They are concerned with the early effects of trauma, neurosurgery and neurological disease.
- Rehabilitation centres: providing post-acute assessment, training and support for people who have sustained brain injury, or who have other neurological problems. The neuropsychologist will play a central role in the multidisciplinary team preparing the client for return to the community or to a residential placement.
- Community services: performing a similar role as above, but supporting those who have returned to community living.

Research is an important aspect of neuropsychological practice. In fact, Professor Wilson believes that

neuropsychology is a wonderful field if one wants to combine theory and practice. It is a broad discipline encompassing many theoretical models and approaches, and it

welcomes creativity and flair in adopting and adapting theories and models in the quest to improve the lives of patients and their families.

Specialised training in neuropsychology is currently based on prior training in one of the other areas of applied psychology, so graduates interested in entering neuropsychology are advised first to seek a professional qualification in clinical psychology (or educational psychology if they are interested in paediatric neuropsychology).

As Professor Wilson explains:

a generic training in clinical psychology is an important requirement for people specialising in neuropsychology and neuropsychological rehabilitation. Such training provides neuropsychologists with knowledge about mental health issues, gives them expertise in dealing with emotional and psychosocial problems, provides training in working with families, and develops an understanding of the different psychological models that underpin our work.

There is a serious national shortage of neuropsychologists, most acutely in paediatric neuropsychology, and prospects for professional advancement are very good. Pay is on the same scales as for clinical psychologists, but many senior neuropsychologists substantially supplement their income by undertaking private medicolegal consultancy as expert witnesses in personal injury cases.

Occupational psychology

If you want to use your psychological knowledge to change the lives of large numbers of people in one shot, perhaps occupational psychology is for you. The wheels of industry are oiled by happy workers, performing to the best of their ability in a safe and healthy environment. This is where you would come in as an *occupational psychologist*. What psychological knowledge would you use to increase

Could you train a manager to keep his staff motivated and task-focused?

the effectiveness of organisations, and to improve the job satisfaction of the individual?

Occupational psychologists usually work alongside managers, trades union representatives, training officers and specialist staff from the firm or industry concerned. Their work is broad, touching on research from the social psychology, personality and intelligence sections of this book, as well as related disciplines such as ergonomics and personnel management.

Work can be in advisory, teaching and research roles and, to a lesser extent, technical and administrative roles. You could find yourself doing anything from creating a new image for a company, to teaching leadership and conflict resolution, to increasing awareness of ethnic minorities, women and people with special needs.

Frank Bond, a Chartered Occupational Psychologist based at Goldsmiths College, University of London, thinks size matters. He says:

> The best thing about occupational psychology is that I get to have a positive impact on a large number of people. I work with big organisations to find ways of helping them make their workplaces less stressful but, at the same time, more productive. This is very challenging, but so rewarding when you get it right.

Of course, the downside of working with large, sometimes multinational, corporations is that they can seem like a closed shop. You may really have to 'sell' what you have to offer. 'I sometimes feel like a travelling salesperson, selling my wares,' Dr Bond admits. 'Dealing with the inevitable rejection, and thus wasted time, is not the best bit of my job.'

Some would argue that big business is becoming increasingly 'person focused' in the drive for profits, and the services of occupational psychologists are certainly in demand. Rewards can be high: there is perhaps more variation in salary in this area of psychology than in any other. A trainee may earn just £17,000, but a senior psychologist in the private sector can earn well over £100,000, particularly when consultancy work is taken into account.

Teaching and research

David Shewan (Glasgow Caledonian University) isn't your stereotypical bearded, shuffling Prof with tatty tweed jacket adorned with leather elbow patches. He spends a lot of time in the pub. 'Much of my job involves waiting around in Glasgow bars in order to talk to interesting people,' he explains.

> Then I go back to university and tell all (well, mostly all) about this and get paid for it. Sometimes I hang about in jails instead of bars, but the rest remains the same. The people I talk to are drug users, sometimes drug dealers. I summarise and analyse what they tell me, get it published and incorporate it into lectures.

This is a good example of how teaching and research in psychology usually go hand in hand. Some teaching staff will have qualified in one of the applied psychological professions already mentioned. They may return to teaching to develop professional practice and conduct research, or simply to share their knowledge. All university lecturers are expected to help extend their subject by gathering psychological evidence on key research questions, and then disseminating it through journal articles, conference presentations and books. Securing funding for this research is a vital part of the career of a *teacher and researcher of psychology.*

719

Teachers and researchers usually have to be administrators too, although most would rather not be. Admin can take up a great deal of time. It includes student selection, devising new teaching programmes, sitting on committees that allocate resources and coordinating aspects of the life of the department.

Rowan Myron (University of Hull) admits that

admin can be hell – so much paperwork you think you're going to drown – but you do it to support the department as a part of a team. The teaching can be wonderful, it's a great feeling when students really get fired up by the stuff you've introduced them to. But the research is why I do it – the freedom and flexibility to test out those questions you can't wait to answer, and the conferences to exchange ideas . . . it's the best way to earn a living.

If you go down the academic path you will get a taste of this freedom and flexibility while studying for a PhD; most applicants for lecturing posts have one. Essentially an attempt to answer an original research question under the supervision of an established academic, a PhD is a rite of passage that can vary wildly depending on the way you work, the way your supervisor works, even the way your finances work.

If you are not used to ploughing your own furrow and you have a supervisor who favours the hands-off approach, you might find yourself tearing out clumps of hair in front of a computer screen, wrestling with some complicated statistical analysis or struggling to commit your dissertation to paper, one tortuous sentence at a time.

If you have found an area you love, however, a question that genuinely interests you, a productive relationship with your supervisor, and funding or part-time work to take the pressure off your purse strings, then your time as a PhD student can be a delight of independent intellectual endeavour that will give you a flying start in your academic career.

For more information, contact the British Psychological Society and ask for its booklet *So you want to do a PhD?*, and visit its website at www.bps.org.uk/careers/careers.cfm for information on potential supervisors and funding.

Finding funding for a PhD can be particularly important given that a newly qualified lecturer can start on just £20,500; salaries for academics have struggled to keep pace with comparable professions in recent years. The scale for professors starts at around £38,000, and some supplement this with consultancy or expert witness work. In addition, the idea of long holidays may be misleading – many academics find that the long summer 'break' is the only chance they get to crack on with their all-important research.

Many schools and sixth-form colleges of further education now offer psychology as a subject at GCSE and A-level. Teachers work to an exam board syllabus, but there is considerable choice in what to offer and in terms of practical coursework projects. You'll need a PGCE to teach psychology in a state school; formal qualifications in psychology are not always required. In fact, psychology graduates sometimes find it difficult to find places on PGCE courses because psychology is not a National Curriculum subject.

For more information contact the Graduate Teacher Training Registry or the Teacher Training Agency (www.teach.org.uk).

The future

Hopefully, you will now have a healthy stash of psychological knowledge and a good idea of how it is possible to make your living putting it to use. But is the profession in good health? How will opportunities for graduates change in the coming years? I put these questions to the chairs of the two major British Psychological Society Boards, covering research and practice.

ACTIVITY BOX 2

Qualifications and experience

Buy the *Guardian* on a Tuesday and look in the Education supplement. What kinds of qualifications and experience are needed for the psychology lecturer posts?

According to Dominic Abrams, Chair of the BPS Research Board, career prospects for psychologists will continue to expand and improve.

There are good reasons for this. First, the undergraduate entry levels for psychology are high within most universities, so psychology students tend to be academically capable from the start. Second, the BPS requirements for the psychology curriculum ensure that university courses generally provide a mix of training in scientific methods, written communication, use of computer systems and software packages, and last (but not least) statistical skills. Psychology graduates and postgraduates have a tremendous range of skills that employers in many organisations are looking for.

In addition, employers in the public and private sector are also finding that psychological knowledge and expertise is often what they need to deal with behavioural questions, and the financial value of being able to anticipate people's behaviour is central to the marketing strategies of most large commercial and retail organisations. Finally, as the organisation and structure of political and social life become more flexible and less dominated by particular political ideologies, people seem to be increasingly interested in the psychological dimension of one another's decisions, actions and fate.

Ray Miller, Chair of the BPS Professional Practice Board, was similarly optimistic.

If the first 100 years of the BPS have been about establishing psychology as a science, the next 100 will almost certainly be dominated by developments in the applications of psychology. It is becoming widely recognised that the main forces that shape the life we live are psychosocial rather than physics or chemistry. Starting from the predispositions inherited in genetics, through the influence of environmentally mediated learning, to the philosophies that drive our social structures and the behaviours that determine our health and well being, psychology is fast becoming the major means of interpreting and understanding what society has been, is and what it may become.

Like any good tool, it is being put to use. We are seeing applied psychologists taking an increasingly leading role in education, health, social care, justice and the workplace. Not all of it is good psychology. We have seen the term 'psychological' becoming a devalued coinage in everyday use, but at the same time there is a rising tide of professionalism. This has been spearheaded by the standards of the BPS and will be continued by the government's 'Statutory Regulation' of psychology through the Health Professions Council (see www.hpc-uk.org).

We will see more flexible, modular-based training that is not necessarily tied to the divisional descriptors currently in use. Boundaries will be blurred and we may find the current adjectival descriptors falling into disuse as we come to see ourselves first and foremost as 'applied psychologists'.

So, remember all those subheadings you just worked through? Don't get too hung up on them. They are the current recognised training routes, but psychology is expanding into new areas all the time, such as sports psychology. It's an exciting time to be embarking on a career in psychology.

The best way to give yourself the start you need is to talk to people. Talk to other psychologists: find out what they love about their jobs, think about whether you would love that too. In fact, just talk to anyone – perhaps you'll come across a human problem and you will remember an approach or a piece of research from this book and, before you know it, you are a pioneering figure in a completely new area of psychology.

As a science and as a profession, psychology is still relatively young. It's up to you to make an impact and help people in the process.

Appendix 1
Careers and study skills

Learning outcomes

When you have completed this chapter you should be able to:

- list the areas in which you could become a Chartered Psychologist
- comment on how areas with Chartered status relate back to some of the research areas you covered in previous chapters
- visit the relevant websites for further information about the specific training routes in psychology.

Further reading

So you want to be a Psychologist? Leicester: British Psychological Society; also available from http://www.bps.org.uk/careers/careers.cfm.

Handley, J. (2002). *Getting into Psychology* (4th edn). London: Trotman.

Study skills in psychology

Route map of the chapter

This chapter is intended to do two things. It aims to help you with your study during your psychology degree course: for example, how to get the most out of working in groups with others, how to go about structuring an essay and how to approach revision for an exam. It also aims to illustrate how and why psychological knowledge is relevant to studying – so after reading the chapter you may know a little more about psychology as well as a little more about studying. The coverage is necessarily selective because of space limitations. Nevertheless, we hope that the rationale and the examples provided will help you develop more extended study skills. The chapter starts with some preliminary definitions and then introduces five key principles for study. These principles are based in psychology theory and research. The chapter then gives examples of the application of these principles within a number of common study activities, such as attending lectures, writing reports, revision, taking exams and accessing information resources.

Introduction

How you study matters. Suppose you wanted to improve how well you could recognise and remember people's faces. You might feel a reasonable approach would be to learn how to categorise different features of faces (such as different types and sizes of noses, different colours and shapes of eyes, and so on), and then practise using this categorisation scheme to 'code' particular faces you wanted to remember. This is a technique that has long been used for training the police and others to

improve how well an individual can remember faces. However, it turns out that when people are trained according to this method, they can actually become worse at remembering faces than a group of people who have had no training at all (Woodhead, Baddeley and Simmonds, 1979).

This is a rather extreme example of an ineffective study skill, but serves to make a couple of points. The first is that it's not always obvious just what the best way to go about studying a particular skill is. The second is that an understanding of the psychological principles that underlie the particular study skill may help in deciding what techniques might be the most effective. In the case of learning to recognise faces, the training method is based on a misguided principle. Adults are generally highly skilled at perceiving and recognising faces, and this skill is based on the overall pattern of the features. So adopting an approach of focusing on individual features probably disrupts the smooth running of our normal face-recognition skill, and that's why it can degrade performance.

So considering study skills as a psychologist is relevant not only because this may help you study better but also because it provides a practical application of psychology. In turn, an appreciation of *why* particular approaches to study can be effective may help you think about, choose and apply the right study methods for the right circumstance – and as you get more skilled, your study skills will become more refined and automatic.

What are study skills?

There is a good deal of educational jargon around the term 'skill'. You may have come across 'basic skills',

Appendix 1
Careers and study skills

'key skills', 'transferable skills', 'critical thinking skills', 'employability skills', maybe even 'metacognitive skills'. There's a danger that skills of this sort are seen as optional extras, perhaps largely irrelevant to your course and hard to apply in real situations. It would be a mistake to view study skills in this way.

In this chapter we are concerned with study skills which are very much embedded in the learning activities that make up typical psychology degree programmes. That is, skills that, directly or indirectly, result in more effective learning.

In your course you will attend lectures, during which you may well take notes. You will take part in small-group discussions sessions, and perhaps sometimes have to make a presentation to the group. You will be required to write essays and reports, read and summarise research papers, find evidence from a variety of sources, revise for and take exams, and more . . . and make sense of and learn from all these activities. You may already be pretty good at some of them but probably not all of them.

Study skills are concerned with working in a variety of ways so that optimal learning occurs with the least effort; so you need to know about what techniques will help, but also you need to have an overview of what will work when. For example, in the limited time before an exam, what's the best way to revise and what suits your particular learning style?

It's important to distinguish three related classes of skill that are relevant to studying for a psychology degree: prerequisite skills (which you are generally assumed to have when you start your course), graduate skills (which you are expected to acquire during the course) and study skills (which help you

---

FOCUS POINT 1

Three categories of skill relevant to the study of psychology

Prerequisite skills

These are skills that you are generally assumed to have acquired before starting your course. They include relevant literacy, numeracy and IT skills (often termed 'key skills'). You will also be expected to have some basic skills in such areas as critical analysis of materials you read, note-taking, essay writing, and communication and presentation skills. You will be expected to improve these skills during your course.

Graduate skills

These are skills you are expected to learn during your course. They include both general skills, such as teamworking skills or good analytical and communication skills, and more psychology-specific ones, such as psychology research skills or technical ability with statistical analysis. As a graduate you are not only expected to know the facts from your course (the discipline knowledge), but also to be able to demonstrate a set of skills that can be applied and used within the world of work (hence the term 'transferable skills'). Some of the skills psychology graduates are expected to have are listed in a guidance document for all psychology courses in the UK, known as the 'the subject benchmark statement'. You can see this on the web at: www.qaa.ac.uk/crntwork/benchmark/phase2/psychology.pdf.

Study skills

These are the skills that help you deal most effectively with the activities involved in your course. The particular skills involved will naturally depend on what you want to get out of the course and what forms of study are most effective for you. Some will be general purpose, others will be more psychology-specific. For example, tips on how to make the best of lectures or of small-group teaching would probably be much the same were you studying psychology, geography or biology. However, how best to structure a practical report, or how to evaluate psychological evidence, will be more specific to the discipline.

study effectively during the course). It is the last category – how you go about studying – that is the focus of this chapter.

Focus Point 1 provides some further details and examples of these three categories of skill.

In this section we have indicated that study skills can be of benefit on your course in two ways. They can be applied directly to your learning activities (e.g. 'it's a good idea to think of your own concrete examples'), but also they provide a framework for you to reflect about your own study methods in view of your own strengths and weaknesses, goals and preferences (e.g. 'I tend to be better at practical applications than at comparing theories, so I'll look for exam questions that best match my strengths'). In the next section we consider briefly some of the principles underlying study skills that relate directly to effective learning.

Five key principles for study

Learning at university level is becoming more student-centred. For example, you may well find that, compared to studying for A-level psychology, studying psychology at university involves much less discussion with a teacher or tutor. You are expected to take more of a lead in getting on with studying on your own or working with other students.

This change in emphasis is in part a result of the belief that learning to take responsibility for one's own learning is seen as a desirable skill in itself, but it would be disingenuous not to mention other factors too: the changes in the funding of higher education, the increasing availability and accessibility of electronic resources to support self-study, and not least the changes in social and political attitudes towards a more market-driven approach to education. Whatever the reasons, there is an increasing pressure on you, the student, to be an independent learner and take responsibility for your own learning.

Student-centred learning doesn't necessarily mean more time working on your own. Many departments are placing increasing emphasis on collaborative or group-based activities, such as student-led discussion groups, collaborative problem-based learning or enquiry-based learning. The days of

weekly individual or small-group tutorials with members of staff may be gone in many universities, but staff input continues through lectures, larger group sessions, and individual support and advice through occasional electronic or face-to-face contact. Generally speaking, however, departments expect students to be motivated to study their subject and to have, or be able to develop, the skills for working independently and effectively.

In this chapter we separate study skills into two categories, as follows.

1. Skills that are intended to maximise understanding and learning from teaching and study activities typical of most psychology courses: lectures, note-taking, seminars, self-study, taking exams and so on.
2. Skills that help you conceptualise or analyse materials, or help you carry out tasks that are expected of you: writing essays and reports, weighing up evidence, critically reflecting on your work.

In short, the first of these categories is concerned with maximising learning, and the second with moving towards thinking and acting as a psychologist. The next main section of the chapter (under the subheading 'Applying your study skills') focuses on some of these skills in more detail.

In this section we introduce some of the underlying principles that are particularly pertinent to the study skills in the first category: enhancing understanding and learning.

Table 1 lists five principles relevant to skills of understanding and learning, together with a number of recommendations or aspects. Each of the principles is considered in detail below.

Principle 1: stay relevant

It is perhaps a truism to say that learning is likely to be most effective if you stay focused on the materials or skills to be mastered, and that the longer you focus on the task, the more you'll learn. However, it's not always obvious either what is most relevant or how to stay on-task. Is repeating material over and over again effective? Should I have a heroic four-hour

Appendix 1
Careers and study skills

TABLE 1 FIVE KEY PRINCIPLES FOR EFFECTIVE STUDY; LISTED UNDER EACH PRINCIPLE IS A NUMBER OF RECOMMENDATIONS RELEVANT TO THE PRINCIPLE				
PRINCIPLE 1 STAY RELEVANT	**PRINCIPLE 2 MAXIMISE MEANING**	**PRINCIPLE 3 BE ACTIVE**	**PRINCIPLE 4 BE REFLECTIVE**	**PRINCIPLE 5 PLAY TO YOUR STRENGTHS**
The longer the study of factual material, the more is retained	Capitalise on your existing knowledge	Learning-by-doing enriches learning-by-studying	Think critically at all levels – about your goals as well as about the details of your work	Identify your learning preferences and learning styles
Spacing out learning with breaks is more effective than unbroken study	Develop encoding and retrieval schemata to help you memorise	New things are hard: don't panic, get feedback, keep trying	Evaluate your current work and skills against your goals, and plan what to address	Adjust the situation to suit your preferences
Maintain your interest and attention	Think about what you are learning from different perspectives: elaborate and differentiate	Identify the components of a skill or task that require the most practice	Reflect on and share your aspirations and progress with others	Adapt your strategy to suit the learning situation
Understand and stay relevant to your personal goals and perspectives				

revision session without a break or would I be better advised to space things out a bit? Should I focus on a single activity or jump between a number of different activities?

We'll give the practical advice first.

- In general, when studying do whatever is necessary to maintain your interest and attention.
- For simple factual learning, the amount of time spent studying is generally what matters; with more complicated material the focus should be on understanding.

- Have breaks: spacing out your practice really does help, and particularly when you feel your concentration waning.
- Alternate between different activities (such as switching between reading and writing assignments), but make sure you do so in such a way that the two activities don't get confused.
- Vary your study methods. For example, intersperse studying on your own with working collaboratively (discuss your ideas with a colleague, get a friend to test your knowledge).

So what principles underlie this advice? Certainly one of the oldest and most robust findings in memory research is that in learning *simple* material, the best predictor of how much and how well a person learns is simply how long they spend on the task, more or less regardless of how they go about memorising the material. This is known as the *total time hypothesis*, and was first investigated in the 1870s by a German philosopher, Hermann Ebbinghaus. It has been explored extensively since, not only in the lab with meaningless materials, but also in the classroom (e.g. Bloom, 1974). However, the more *complex* the material to be memorised, the more important the nature of *how* you study activities becomes – total time of study is still important, but so too is doing the right sort of study.

How the total study time is distributed is also important for the learning of material: for a given amount of study time, memorisation will generally be more effective if the study periods are spaced out rather than grouped together. Initial observation of this phenomenon is again attributed to Ebbinghaus, and it has been investigated and put to practical use ever since. Not only is immediate memory improved by *distributed practice* (as the technique is known), but so also is longer-term retention (e.g. Baddeley and Longman, 1978). So when learning material, avoid the four-hour slog – it might be better to break your learning into, say, half-hour or 45-minute sessions.

This effect may in part be due to the boredom and sagging attention of long sessions, but also seems to be related to the advantage of encoding materials in a wider variety of situations (a phenomenon known as *encoding variability*; Maki and Hasher, 1975). This idea – that learning under a range of conditions strengthens subsequent recall – is behind the suggestion for alternating activities or varying study methods.

Relevance also depends on your personal goals and perspectives. Surveys exploring the motivations of psychology students (e.g. Newstead and Hoskins, 1999) demonstrate that most tend to be *extrinsically* motivated (that is, motivated by factors external to the focus of study, such as by the need to get a good degree or obtain useful skills to get a job), but some are primarily motivated by *intrinsic* interest in the subject. So think about the following questions.

- What motivates you?
- Are your motivations different for different parts of the course?

If you are primarily concerned to get a good degree and high marks in your assessments it may make sense to focus your study strategically on what you reckon to be most effective to meet this goal. Don't forget, though, that a broad interest early on might pay dividends in assessment later in the course – that topic you ignored in the first year because it seemed a bit boring at the time may be crucial in understanding some more advanced concept in the third-year module.

A related aspect of relevance relates to your personal enthusiasm and interests in the subject. Naturally it makes sense to pursue those topics you find the most compelling and motivating, but of course it is unwise to do so to an extent that damages attaining your overall goals. It is up to you to be strategic in finding the appropriate balance.

A final aspect of relevance relates to your individual *learning styles* and preferences: these are covered in the section below entitled 'Playing to your strengths'.

Principle 2: maximise meaning

Two friends are watching the football results on the television. A little later they go to the pub and get into conversation with the barman about the Premier Division rankings. One of the friends has total recall of the match scores and the goal scorers, the other has virtually no idea of who has played whom, let alone the scorelines. Why should this be? They both heard the same information, and both seem to have equally good memories when it comes to their courses.

This is a common enough situation, and the explanation is equally straightforward in everyday terms: the first is an avid football fan, and already knows a great deal of information about the teams and their current form; the second has no interest in and little knowledge of football. It is an awful lot easier to learn new information when it ties in with a rich set of existing knowledge than when it makes little connection with what we already know. In fact, the term 'learn' seems almost inappropriate for our football enthusiast; the new knowledge about match results and who scored the goals seems to be retained with no effort at all.

This phenomenon is the basis for perhaps the most powerful of the study skill principles: try to make sense of things and find ways of relating them to your existing knowledge. Learning of conceptual material occurs as a by-product of understanding it; learning is not an optional activity that can be switched on or off independently of comprehension. This general principle has a number of implications for study. For example:

- capitalise on what you know already – for example, by linking concepts to personal experiences or concrete examples that make sense to you
- try to form analogies or parallels based on familiar situations, to make concepts seem less abstract
- search actively for links with information you have learnt in other course modules.

A different implication of the importance of linking new knowledge to existing knowledge is that it can be effective to develop 'ways of remembering' that will help you encode new information and retrieve it later, even if this requires some extra effort early on. A simple example is the use of mnemonic tricks: imagining items placed along a familiar route, or linking a list of items to a mnemonic rhyme ('One is a bun, two is a shoe' etc.), or using first letters of words to be remembered to make up a memorable sentence. These are examples of *retrieval schemata* – structures to which you can link new knowledge in a distinctive or meaningful way, which will assist later retrieval.

While such techniques are perhaps most powerful when dealing with relatively simple factual material, they should not be underestimated when remembering 'prompts' for more complex material. For example, suppose in an exam you are faced with the question 'Critically evaluate two theories of selective attention in accounting for relevant

experimental evidence'. If, in your revision, you have encoded the 'headings' for the main strengths and weaknesses of different theories using some mnemonic, you are less likely to forget some crucial point under the stress of exam conditions as you have a systematic way of retrieving the key information.

The power of retrieval schemata is illustrated in a classic study, where one heroic participant increased his digit span (the number of random digits one can correctly repeat back after a single presentation) to over 80 items after many hours of training. This subject based his encoding and retrieval on a structure of times for athletic events (Chase and Ericsson, 1982). In another study, a waiter was able to memorise complete dinner orders from tables of up to eight guests by using a system of first-letter mnemonics (Ericsson and Polson, 1988).

An interesting feature of both studies is that, following a complete session (an hour's testing in the digit span study, an evening shift for the waiter), the participants were able to recall nearly all of the material from the entire session.

A final implication for study is to try to elaborate the *meaning* of the material you are studying.

- Think about the study materials from different perspectives. For example, how they might be applied in different situations.
- Look for comparisons or contrasts that emphasise or bring out particular aspects or highlight differences.
- Try reworking a description or a concept into different words.

These recommendations tie in to a couple of well-established principles from memory research: *depth of processing*, whereby information that is processed more deeply (elaborated) is remembered better, and *encoding specificity*, whereby material that is encoded to be distinctive from other knowledge can more easily be retrieved (provided you are able to use the distinctive cues when you are trying to recall the information). *Elaboration* has been shown to be a much more effective strategy for learning than rote practice, and particularly for longer-term retention. It is especially effective with more complex materials.

Principle 3: be active

Doing things with the material you are learning rather than merely studying it tends to result in better learning (see the following examples).

- Don't just read through the material for an essay-based exam: practise writing answers under exam conditions. Practising writing essay plans will help too.
- Try representing some topic in a different way from how it's presented in the textbook or lecture, perhaps as a diagram (such as a concept map or spider diagram) or as a poster.
- Where practical, try out phenomena or techniques for yourself: see whether visual illusions really work with your non-psychologist friends, or whether the Stroop effect works in French. Be imaginative!

Why does this help? First of all, there are a number of memory effects which suggest that action results in better learning. One is the *enactment effect* (Cohen, 1984) where, for example, if one group is asked to remember the descriptions of simple actions (such as breaking a match) and a second group actually carries out the actions, subsequent recall is higher for the second group.

A related phenomenon is known as the *generation effect* (Gardiner, 1989). This refers to the fact that people tend to be better at remembering material that they have generated for themselves than equivalent material provided by someone else.

A deeper explanation comes from the distinction between *declarative knowledge* and *procedural knowledge*, and how reliance on procedural knowledge tends to increase as a person becomes more expert at a skill. Declarative knowledge concerns facts and concepts, things that can be explicitly expressed or 'declared' – usually in words. Examples include knowing who the prime minister is or how many legs a spider has. Procedural knowledge, on the other hand, is knowledge of actions and how to do things: tying a shoelace, walking, riding a bicycle, playing the piano. Once procedural knowledge is acquired, it is expressed implicitly, through performance or action, and indeed experts may have little awareness of or access to the underlying knowledge that drives performance.

You may feel that not much of the knowledge you learn in a psychology course is procedural in nature; if so, you'd be quite wrong. The knowledge underlying tasks that you practise a lot, such as structuring an essay or a practical report, is likely to become procedural. In addition, as you become more expert about the concepts and ways of thinking within an area, the learning of new materials itself becomes more proceduralised or automatic. As your course proceeds, you will become more familiar with, for example, the technical language, with the way theories are tested, with the way research papers are structured, with how statistical tests are chosen and carried out. The greater this familiarity becomes, the easier it is to make sense of the next specific example.

The downside is that, even if the expert version of a skill is based on procedural knowledge, the learner has to pass through a painful stage of using declarative knowledge in order the learn the new skill, and this may require a good deal of explicit planning and effective use of feedback. (Learning to drive a car is a typical example.) So we have some more recommendations, as follows.

- If a new topic or activity seems really difficult, don't panic! New things are hard. Remember those early days of learning to ride a bike, swim or drive a car? The same can be true for new topics.
- Get feedback on how you are doing. Comments from a critical friend or your tutor may well help.
- Keep looking for meaning, trying different perspectives, elaborating and collaborating, and the topic will start to make more sense.

The idea that many of the activities involved in your course involve calling on a mix of procedural and declarative knowledge brings us back to the recommendations at the start of this section: learn by doing. If writing essays or answering multiple-choice questions involves procedural knowledge (which it does), then you will get better at these tasks by doing them, or components of them, over and over again. After all, you wouldn't get very far learning to ride a bike just by thinking about it.

However it may not be practical, and it will certainly not be enjoyable, to spend your time writing hundreds of essays. Instead, it's helpful and more efficient to identify what the 'task components' are that would benefit most from practice. One of the answers in the study of psychology is likely to be 'critical thinking' skills. For example, when considering an essay or other assignment:

- think actively about, talk about and make notes about topics and ideas in a critical and open-minded way
- evaluate whether the evidence is really as good as it is claimed to be, and what other evidence might support, counter or have implications for the topic in question
- consider alternative explanations or theories, and whether or not 'common-sense' explanations accord with more formal explanations.

Remember that getting into the habit of asking critical questions will in itself become a skill.

Principle 4: be reflective

This principle concerns three related aspects of study: reflecting about what and how you are studying, reflecting about your plans and how you are getting on (for example, your *learning goals*, achievements and progress), and reflecting with others on both of these. In current educational parlance, the term *reflective practice* is often taken to mean only the middle of these – reflecting on personal plans, goals and their achievement – but we will consider a wider view of reflection in order to be more helpful.

Reflection about content is partly a matter of critical thinking, as mentioned above. But it is also important to take a step back and think about issues such as the following.

- How do the different aspects of the module (content, activities) interrelate, and how do different modules relate to each other within the programme as a whole?
- What bits of the module do I understand and what am I confused (or just plain ignorant) about? What do I need to work on and how should I go about it?

- What preparatory work should I do before a teaching session?
- How should I plan my revision in the three days left before the exam?
- What study techniques might it be useful to apply to some part of the course?

You can no doubt add to this list. The point is that a little reflection and planning will help build a feeling of responsibility for your own work, help you use your time effectively, reduce anxiety and worries, and even perhaps avoid an unforeseen catastrophe.

The second form of reflection relates to your personal plans and goals, how they develop and the extent to which you feel you are achieving them. It may well be that your course includes some form of *personal development planning (PDP)*, perhaps directed towards skills for employability, and this may provide a helpful framework for reflection.

You will have plans and goals at different levels, from a long-term view of your degree, future

---

ACTIVITY BOX 1

Reflective checklist for graduate skills

Use Table 2 to reflect on the skills you hope to acquire during your course. You may wish to add to or modify the list. This is a reflective checklist that might be helpful in considering the extent to which you are achieving the graduate skills you hope to gain from your psychology degree programme. Employers will be less interested in the specifics of your knowledge (even if your experimental project has made you a world expert on some interesting wrinkle on the pseudohomophone effect) but rather more interested in what skills you have in being articulate, reflective or analytical, in showing an ability to learn, to negotiate or to work with others.

For each skill listed in the box, note your current skill level, what evidence you could provide to convince a potential employer and what more you might do to enhance or make evident your skill.

TABLE 2   SKILLS I HOPE TO ACQUIRE DURING THE COURSE

SKILL AND SUBSKILLS	MY CURRENT LEVEL 1 = LOW, 4 = HIGH	EVIDENCE FOR MY SKILL LEVEL. WHAT COULD I PUT ON MY CV OR SAY AT A JOB INTERVIEW?	PLANS AND COMMENTS. WHERE DO I WANT TO BE? HOW DO I GET THERE?
Numeracy • Understand and use graphs and tables • Work with descriptive statistics • Carry out and understand a range of statistical analyses			
Writing skills • Use correct grammar and spelling • Be able to put my own ideas into words • Organise ideas coherently • Write a clear and well-organised report • Summarise information from different sources			
Information skills • Use e-mail • Find relevant information (on web or in library) • Evaluate web resources • Word-processing • Spreadsheets and databases • Statistical analysis			
Teamworking • Contributing to a group discussion • Speaking in a group without dominating • Listening carefully to others and being open to ideas • Negotiating and compromising • Putting points across tactfully • Summarising a discussion			

Careers and study skills

TABLE 2 SKILLS I HOPE TO ACQUIRE DURING THE COURSE CONTINUED			
SKILL AND SUBSKILLS	**MY CURRENT LEVEL 1 = LOW, 4 = HIGH**	**EVIDENCE FOR MY SKILL LEVEL. WHAT COULD I PUT ON MY CV OR SAY AT A JOB INTERVIEW?**	**PLANS AND COMMENTS. WHERE DO I WANT TO BE? HOW DO I GET THERE?**
Communication and presentation • Put ideas across succinctly and clearly • Prepare and give a presentation to a group • Know when to use diagrams • Prepare a poster • Answer questions			
Time management and organisation • Able to meet deadlines such as handing in coursework • Plan and allocate my time on a complex task • Prioritise tasks • Juggle competing demands • Organise a busy schedule			
Analysis and problem-solving • Identify the key issues that are a problem • Marshal relevant facts • Clearly outline the available options • Consider alternative solutions in a balanced manner			

education or employment, down to how on earth you can survive the next week. It can be all too easy for the short-term pressures – the looming deadlines and the tendency to procrastinate until the last possible moment – to dominate, and for little explicit thought to be given either to longer-term issues or indeed to reflecting on your current work and skills.

There are many handbooks and guides that provide checklists and forms to aid personal reflection. For example, Collins and Kneale (2001) is written particularly for psychology students.

Is the kind of PDP activity in Activity Box 1 worth the effort? A thorough systematic review of the effects of PDP on learning in higher education (Gough, Kiwan, Sutcliffe, Simpson and Houghton, 2003) concluded that 'the processes and actions that underlie PDP do have a positive impact on student attainment and approaches to learning'. However, the authors add that 'there is also not sufficient evidence to state which balance of the many PDP approaches is more or less effective in impacting on student learning'.

So while you can have some confidence that some sorts of PDP will help you, you would be wise not to adopt these approaches blindly, but rather (as with many other aspects of learning) take responsibility yourself in deciding just what approach to adopt and how best to use it.

The third form of reflection is to share thoughts and feelings with others. Although a good deal of study at university is necessarily an individual activity, much informal working, and some formal sessions, are collaborative. The tradition of students interacting to learn stems from the Ancient Greeks, the so-called *Socratic dialogue* method, with emphasis upon the student working with an expert. This approach, where the guidance of an expert helps the student to move into less familiar territory, forms the basis for the tradition of education and research that has blossomed from the work of Vygotsky (1962).

However, this 'master–apprentice' model is somewhat diluted in university teaching nowadays, with much larger groups and often student-led sessions. All is not lost, though: research does suggest that student-based groups can be effective in terms of motivation and achievement. Such approaches put a greater onus on the student to contribute and collaborate. Issues in group-based teaching and learning are reviewed by Bennett, Howe and Trusswell (2002).

Regarding informal collaboration, students are sometimes unduly concerned that collaboration will be seen as a form of cheating or 'unfair', as assessment focuses on the individual. While much assessed work should of course reflect individual effort and knowledge, many aspects of study can profit from collaborative work or discussion. Some departments encourage collaborative work through group problem-based learning or enquiry-based activities; many allow group final-year projects.

All courses will include collaborative discussion of one form or another. Informal discussion concerning the sorts of issues listed earlier in this section is likely to be helpful. For example, sharing aspirations, worries, achievements and evaluations with others. Not only will friends and colleagues help you formulate and develop plans and ideas, discussion with others acts as a reality check on expectations and progress.

More specific advice on making the best of group learning situations is given in the section entitled 'Working in groups', below.

Principle 5: play to your strengths

People differ. This is as true for approaches to learning as it is for other aspects of life. However, by the time a person has reached higher education, it is likely that he or she will be a fairly flexible learner, able to adapt learning activities to the demands of the situation. This doesn't mean that individual preferences are not important; they are and they can have a major influence on *learning outcomes*. Nevertheless, it is generally more productive to think of different learning styles as a matter of preference and strategic choice rather than as unchanging personal attributes. After all, we have evolved to perceive and learn about complex abstractions from a rich and varied environment. That environment is not going to present itself differently to individuals who prefer a serialist to a holist style of learning, say. We have to adjust our learning style to suit the external conditions.

A study conducted on psychology students makes the point rather well (Newstead and Findlay, 1997, reported in Newstead, 2002). The students were

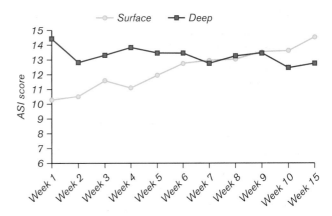

Figure 1 Changes in students' approaches to studying in the lead-up to an examination: scores are measured on the sheet form of the approaches to studying inventory (ASI)
Source: adapted from Newstead, 2002

Appendix 1
Careers and study skills

TABLE 3	CHARACTERISTICS OF HONEY AND MUMFORD'S FOUR TYPES OF LEARNING STYLE			
	LEARNING STYLE			
	ACTIVIST	**REFLECTOR**	**THEORIST**	**PRAGMATIST**
Learn best with:	New experiences and challenges Short 'here and now' tasks Teamwork and problem-solving Excitement and variety High-visibility tasks such as leading discussions	Encouragement to watch, think or ponder on activities Time to think before acting Tasks allowing careful, detailed research Time to review their learning No pressure or tight deadlines	Tasks where what is offered is part of a system, model, concept or theory Exploration of interrelationships between ideas, events and situations Tasks where they are asked to analyse and evaluate, then generalise Tasks where they can question basic assumptions or logic	Tasks with an obvious link between the subject matter and a real-life problem Tasks that involve techniques for doing things with practical advantages Tasks with a model they can emulate, or that allow them to concentrate on practical issues Immediate opportunities to implement what they have learned
Learn poorly when:	Listening to lectures or long explanations Reading, writing or thinking on their own Absorbing and understanding data Following precise instructions to the letter	Acting as leader or role-playing in front of others Doing things with no time to prepare Being thrown in at the deep end Being rushed or worried by deadlines	They have to participate in situations that emphasise emotion and feelings The activity is unstructured or briefing is poor They have to do things without knowing the principles or concepts involved They feel they're out of tune with the other participants, e.g. with people of very different learning styles	There is no obvious or immediate benefit that they can recognise There is no practice or guidelines on how to do it There is no apparent payback to the learning, e.g. shorter meetings The event or learning is 'all theory'

tested to ascertain the extent to which they were adopting a deep or surface approach to their studies on a weekly basis during the lead-up to a formal exam. (A *deep approach to learning* favours an emphasis on understanding and elaboration; a surface approach concentrates on learning the facts in more of a rote fashion.)

Fifteen weeks before the exam a deep approach was favoured, but as the exam got closer the prevalence of a surface approach to study steadily increased. The results are shown in Figure 1. An explanation is probably that students perceived a sensible strategic approach was to 'cram' for this exam as the deadline approached. Of course, the most effective strategy will depend on the sort of exam, and your state of knowledge and understanding beforehand. The point here is that the students were able to change their learning styles in a strategic fashion depending on their perception of the demands of the situation.

This example has probably raised a number of questions for you. What are the important dimensions of individual difference in learning? How can I tell what my preferences are? When should I adopt one style rather than another? These are valid and sensible questions, but are quite hard to answer because there are so many claimed 'learning styles'.

One aspect of individual difference relates to the working environment. People differ in when and under what conditions they work effectively. For example, some people are much more effective working in the morning, some are better late at night. You probably have some feel for this already. If so, adjust your working habits to suit your preferences whenever it is practical to do so. Likewise, some people are much more tolerant of noise or interruption than others – so, again, try to adjust your working environment to suit your preferences.

There are many models of learning style, and even more of cognitive style, which also influence learning. A new UK project (at the time of writing) based in a number of psychology departments is reviewing this confused area and will make available a set of tests for students to assess aspects of their own learning style. It will also provide advice to students on how to adapt their learning style to suit the situation, and how to adapt learning situations to suit their preferred learning style. This is called the Cognitive Learning and Student Strategies Project (CLaSS) and is led from the University of Central Lancashire. If you wish, visit the website at http://www.uclan.ac.uk/facs/science/psychol/fdtl/, where further details are available.

A couple of examples of learning styles will illustrate the flavour of this area. One influential and popular model of learning style has been proposed by Honey and Mumford (1992), who identified four main learning style preferences: activist, reflector, theorist and pragmatist. Table 3 summarises some of the key differences between these four types of learning style.

A second, and rather different, categorisation is provided by Sternberg *et al.* (2000), based on Sternberg's conception of human intelligence, in which individuals vary in their analytical, creative and practical abilities. This distinction is taken up later in this chapter, in the section on 'Assessment'.

We can offer a number of recommendations, as follows.

- Identify aspects of your learning preferences, both in terms of situations (time of day, the sort of environment) and in terms of learning styles.
- Adjust your working habits to suit your learning preferences, and look for ways of playing to your strengths in terms of your learning styles. If, for example, there are choices for some assessed coursework, it may be that one particular question suits your style.
- Bear in mind that you also need to adapt your style to the situation. Be a flexible learner!

Applying your study skills

Being aware of the cognitive processes and different strategies that facilitate learning gives you the ability to consider and monitor your own progress. It enables you to question what you already know, what you need to know, what strategies you should use and what corrective action to take if things are not going well. Psychologists refer to this ability as *metacognition*. In this section, we will focus on how

Appendix 1
Careers and study skills

you can use this 'metaknowledge' to optimise your opportunities for learning in different situations, such as lectures, *small-group work* and assessment.

Lectures and note-taking

How you apply your study skills in different situations is both the responsibility of the course staff and yourself. Staff design the teaching and learning activities that you, the student, will engage in. This still leaves plenty of room for variability between staff performance and student performance! For example, we all know that some *lectures* can be dull. Perhaps you have already experienced being in a large, over-crowded lecture theatre with a lecturer presenting one overhead after another in rapid succession. In contrast, you may have sat spellbound through a lecture in the same overcrowded lecture theatre feeling entertained by a lecturer telling a good story about some aspect of psychology you are interested in.

Use your psychological knowledge to get the most out of both situations. For example, in both cases it would be well to remind yourself that being a passive listener is not the most effective route to learning.

There is some debate among university staff as to whether students should be given handouts of lecture notes prior to lectures. There is a concern that students will not bother to attend the lecture if they already have the notes. However, it is increasingly common for some information to be provided either on the departmental website or handed out prior to the lecture. You can use handouts to highlight areas you do not understand, or to note ideas you have for asking questions, or to jot down a link to something that you have learned previously.

Some students claim that note-taking helps them remember, sustains their attention, provides material for reflection and revision, and identifies areas they are unsure about. There is psychological evidence to support this. Earlier in this chapter it was noted that we retain more knowledge if we have encoded it in a variety of ways (for example, through seeing, hearing, thinking, doing). Having notes provides an additional representation of the knowledge; reorganising notes helps you to structure the knowledge in a way that is meaningful for you; rereading and revising your notes reduces the likelihood of you forgetting. Which technique you use is up to you; the important thing is to find ways of being an *active learner*.

If the topic area is difficult, make sure that you have read something about it before the lecture – you will find the language more familiar and it will be easier to identify what it is you are finding difficult. Sometimes lecturers will pause in order to let students reflect on what has been said, or proffer some questions for you to consider either individually or with others sitting near you. Allowing the audience to predict the answer to a question by voting (as in 'ask the audience' in *Who Wants to be a Millionaire?*) is another technique. These are all methods that lecturers use to help students engage with new material – in other words, to take an *active approach* to their learning.

Lecturers are aware that students may feel shy about asking questions – particularly in front of a large group of their peers. One method that some lecturers use is to ask students to note down things they found unclear, and then to provide a box for queries or comments that students can use as they leave the lecture hall. Reading through these can help the lecturer identify points that were unclear during the lecture and allow them to be revisited, maybe at the beginning of the next lecture or in a subsequent seminar.

If you leave the lecture room worried that you have not understood something, it can be helpful to

Being a passive listener is not the most effective route to learning.

discuss it with other people who were at the lecture, to read around the subject again or to contact the lecturer to seek clarification. It's good to talk! This is another thing we know about learning: trying to articulate our thoughts can be a powerful way of realising what it is that is proving difficult to understand.

Working in groups

During your course there will be opportunities to work with other students in smaller groups, such as in seminars, tutorials and practicals. The psychology of groups is well researched and course staff have some responsibility to apply this knowledge when setting up group work. The size, degree of familiarity, the nature of the tasks, and the way these tasks are assessed affect the performance of the group (McKenna, 2000).

The activities that students are required to engage in during seminars and tutorials will vary according to the intended learning outcomes for the module. They may provide an opportunity for students to explore lecture topics in more detail through discussion, reasoning and problem-solving in order to develop *critical thinking skills*. In this situation, there is a tendency for students to avoid eye contact with the tutor in case they get asked a 'difficult' question. Indeed some tutors find the long silences after a question has been posed as awkward as the

You will have opportunities to work with other students in smaller groups, such as in seminars, tutorials and practicals.

students and will end up answering the question themselves or, worse, avoid asking 'difficult' questions at all.

Remember that we learn by making sense out of nonsense or, more formally, as Piaget described it, through the processes of assimilation and accommodation. Again, it can be difficult to articulate what it is that you do not understand, but the very process of trying will help to clarify the problem.

In other cases, there may be a focus on developing your *oral and communication skills* through student presentations, debates or role-play. Again, this can be an anxious time for students, but try to remember that it is normal to be apprehensive about speaking in public and, more often than not, it becomes less scary with practice. Being well prepared and practising your presentation beforehand (preferably aloud in front of a mirror) are good ways of coping.

Focus Point 2 offers some guidelines to help with the preparation and delivery of oral presentations.

Small-group sessions also provide a valuable opportunity to try out your new-found knowledge on others. Perhaps during the week you have made a tentative link between your own life experience and what you have been studying, or wondered whether there is any connection between the psychological concept under study and something you have observed or learned about elsewhere. By raising these new constructions of your understanding in the group you may be reinforcing your own understanding, and you may receive valuable feedback that will enable you to adjust your understanding and help others to make valuable connections themselves.

Seminars and tutorials are often led by a postgraduate, who will have received guidance from the lecturer on organising the work to be covered. The postgraduate may approach the material from a different perspective or even disagree with the lecturer's viewpoint. This is normal behaviour among academics! It is important to understand that there are few 'right' answers in psychology. Aspects of mental health, for example, can be analysed from a

FOCUS POINT 2

Guidelines for preparing and delivering oral presentations

Preparing your presentation

- A good start helps to calm the nerves, so plan to start with something easy such as a short introduction that gives the title of your presentation and a description of what you are going to talk about.
- As in an essay, try to ensure that your talk has a beginning, a middle and an end, with a logical progression through the points you wish to make. Make sure you use your own words rather than jargon or technical phrases that you do not feel comfortable with or fully understand.
- Practise your talk in a situation as close to the real one as you can. Talking out loud will help you to check the timing and to identify any ideas you find difficult to articulate or that don't flow.
- Visual aids such as overhead or PowerPoint© slides can help you structure the talk and provide extra interest for your audience. These should contain a few bullet points and should be in a large font size (at least 24-point) so they are easy for the audience to read.
- If it helps you to feel more confident, write notes for yourself on cards – one for each of the overheads.

Giving the presentation

- Speak clearly and try not to read directly from notes.
- Try to engage the audience with a smile or eye contact.
- If it is a group presentation, try to hand over to the next speaker in a way that keeps the presentation flowing.
- Try not to mumble, talk in a monotone or talk too fast. Taking a sip from a glass of water can be a useful way to stop, relax and start off again.

medical illness viewpoint or from a societal perspective. Evidence can be provided to support both views. Understanding that there may be *different perspectives* on topics is in itself a valuable skill.

Courses will contain a mixture of individual and group activities. Studies have shown that problem-solving and critical thinking can be improved by working in groups. A National Institute for Science Education study (Springer *et al.*, 1997) showed that students who learned in small groups demonstrated greater achievement, persisted to a greater extent through their courses and expressed more favourable attitudes towards their courses than students who did not work collaboratively or cooperatively.

In practice, students often report problems working on team or group projects. There can be concern that not all members pulled their weight, which may well be true, and fear that as a result their own assessed mark may be affected. In these situations it is important to agree some ground rules early on within your group. Use your *personal skills* to get to know others in the group, find out what their constraints are, which methods of communication will work best for them (for example, face to face or over the Internet) and agree deadlines in advance.

Focus Point 3 provides a checklist of good practice when working in groups. Remember, learning to work with others, reaching compromises, understanding differences, sharing workloads, solving problems – these are the kind of *group skills* that employers are looking for.

Writing essays

Many students feel unsure of what is required of them when they are asked to write an *essay*. In brief, essays are used to assess your depth of knowledge, to provide evidence of critical thinking and to show off your creative ideas.

FOCUS POINT 3

Checklist of good practice for working in groups

1. Make the best use of each person's special skills.
2. Try to work in a collaborative rather than competitive way.
3. Share your ideas with others in the group.
4. Show others respect, even if you disagree with them.
5. Listen to another group member when that person is speaking.
6. Encourage others to speak.
7. Stay on the group's task.
8. Help the group to stay on-task.
9. Do not allow yourself to be distracted.
10. Allow others to present their ideas, even when you think you know the answers.

In this section we offer some practical advice for writing essays.

Plan ahead

A rule of thumb for essays is to spend 50 per cent of your time planning the essay, 40 per cent reading and note-taking, and 10 per cent writing. Once you know when you are required to submit an essay, work out how long you will need to prepare and write the essay, and set aside this time in your work and social calendar.

Gather together as much of the reading material and references as soon as you can. If you leave this until you are ready to start work on your essay you may well find that the resources are not available because they are being used by other students. Photocopying material is one solution, although it can be expensive and sometimes it is hard to know at the outset what will be the most relevant material for your essay.

FOCUS POINT 4

Some hints on understanding essay titles

Discuss 'levels of processing' and 'working memory' theories in relation to memory in humans

This calls for more than a description of each theory. You should provide evidence for and against the theories, give examples of how the theories can be applied to memory tasks and evaluate their importance.

Critically evaluate 'levels of processing' and 'working memory' theories in relation to memory in humans

Note here that the word 'critically' does not necessarily mean a discussion of negative points. A proper critique will put forward positive aspects as well.

Compare and contrast 'levels of processing' and 'working memory' theories as accounts of memory in humans

Avoid structuring your essay in such a way that a discussion of levels of processing is followed by a discussion of working memory with a brief concluding summary. Instead, focus on shared features and discuss these together, followed by features that differentiate them, or try to identify the key concepts that 'levels of processing' and 'working memory' address: for example, the storing and processing of information. Arguments could then be developed around how the different theories account for memory tasks such as mental arithmetic, holding telephone numbers in memory and so on.

Appendix 1
Careers and study skills

Planning an essay

To begin with, it is best to read overview material that sets the essay topic in context and then to consider the essay title more closely. It should be easy enough to identify what the topic of the essay is, but in addition the essay title will tell you what to focus on and the kind of arguments you are expected to put forward.

Some hints on understanding essay titles are given in Focus Point 4.

Deconstructing the essay title after preliminary broad reading will enable you to plan the basic structure of the essay. Remember that an essay is not the place to list all the facts you know about the essay topic. The essay should follow a theme and flow, as if telling a story, with one paragraph leading on to the next.

Your next task is to decide on the specific issues you wish to discuss and to consider how you wish to present these issues in the main body of the essay. This will require more focused reading. Highlighting short sections of reading material *that you own* (to deface books or articles that do not belong to you is unacceptable) can be useful as a reminder of where to find key points. This should not replace the active learning technique of making a brief note in your own words about why the key point is relevant to your essay.

Use spider diagrams and notes to summarise points, and to raise questions that you want to discuss or ideas that you want to develop as you read. Remember to note down the references that you have used as you take notes – this will make the job of referencing much easier.

Writing the essay

The key fact here is that essays have a beginning (the introduction), a middle and an end (the conclusion).

The introduction to the essay is where you set the scene for what comes next. It is the place to give a succinct description of the topic area and why the essay question is worthy of discussion, followed by a guide (or route map) to the arguments you will be presenting in the main body of the essay.

The main body of the essay will be a series of paragraphs centred on concepts or issues. Typically the paragraphs will provide a description of the issue, an example supported by evidence, a statement of why the example is relevant to your essay, followed by any counter-examples or critique that weaken the impact of this point. This provides you with the link to your next point, where you repeat this process, and so you continue until you have discussed all the issues you had put down in your plan.

Finally, use the concluding paragraph to summarise what you have discussed and to return to the theme of the essay by providing your considered response to the essay title.

At the end of the essay you should include a list of all references you have cited in the text ordered alphabetically according to the authors' names. Focus Point 5 shows examples of how to reference a journal article, a book, a chapter from a book and a reference taken from the Internet.

FOCUS POINT 5

Examples of how to format references

A journal article should be listed and formatted like this:

Baddeley, A. D., Thomson, N. and Buchanan, M. (1975) Word length and the structure of short-term memory. *Journal of Verbal Learning and Verbal Behavior* 14, 575–89.

A book should be listed and formatted like this:

Gathercole, S. and Baddeley, A. D. (1993) *Working Memory and Language: Essays in Cognitive Psychology*. Hove: Psychology Press.

A chapter in an edited book should be listed and formatted like this:

Chou, C. and Bentler, P. M. (1995) Estimates and tests in structural equation modeling. In R. H. Hoyle (ed.), *Structural Equation Modeling: Concepts, Issues, and Applications*. Thousand Oaks: Sage, 37–55.

A reference taken from the Internet should be listed and formatted like this:

Muter, P. (2001) The nature of forgetting from short-term memory. Accessed 7 November 2003, at http://cogprints.ecs.soton.ac.uk/archive/00001963/00/cowanmuter.htm.

TABLE 4 EXAMPLE ESSAY ASSESSMENT CRITERIA

CLASS	MARKING GUIDELINES
First	*An excellent answer, well written, logical and critical, showing appreciation of major points and integration with points that go beyond the basic module material. An outstanding essay will also show originality and flair.*
Good 1st	Could be used as a 'model answer' on the module; contains relevant material that would not have been anticipated on the basis of module content.
Solid 1st	A full, organised account; evidence of extra reading.
Low 1st	Well argued and full account, perhaps missing some relevant (but not critical) material. Showing some evidence of originality, whether in content or presentation of argument.
Upper second	*Comprehensive, well-organised and accurate answer. Evidence both of having understood the issues and of being able to think about them effectively.*
Good 2.1	Well-organised and full description of core material, lacking the originality or organisation that would qualify for a first-class mark.
Solid 2.1	As above, perhaps missing some relevant details.
Low 2.1	Relatively full account of core material, missing a relevant study or some part of the core argument, but showing evidence of appreciation of the core material.
Lower second	*An adequate answer that is mostly accurate, but there may be some errors or omissions. Limited organisation and scope with no real development of argument.*
Good 2.2	Good answer, as far as it goes; perhaps introducing irrelevant material or missing a sufficient amount of core argument not to qualify as a comprehensive answer.
Solid 2.2	Pedestrian account of a selection of the core material.
Low 2.2	As above, with some errors or many irrelevancies.
Third	*Incomplete answer, sparse information, substantial errors or omissions, poorly organised. Perhaps relating to a different aspect of the core topic.*
Good 3rd	Incomplete knowledge of module material.
Solid 3rd	Confused knowledge (with errors) of module material.
Low 3rd	Very confused and incomplete knowledge account of relevant material.
Pass	Provides some evidence of (disorganised) knowledge from the module material. Inaccurate with numerous errors and omissions; very poorly organised; irrelevancies; shows little grasp of issues.

Appendix 1
Careers and study skills

CLASS	MARKING GUIDELINES
TABLE 4	**EXAMPLE ESSAY ASSESSMENT CRITERIA CONTINUED**
Fail	*A very deficient to totally inadequate essay. Serious errors or omissions. May include only personal opinion with no evidence of having read anything or attended the module.*
Marginal fail	One or two relevant ideas.
Clear fail	No real idea.
Zero mark	No answer, no psychological content.

When the essay is complete, make sure you use a spellchecker (judiciously – they are not foolproof!) and read the essay through. If you have the time, put it to one side for a couple of days and then reread it. Coming back to the essay will allow you to look at it in a more objective way and to check that the structure seems logical and makes sense to the reader. Finally, make sure you have a copy of your essay before you hand it in.

Many departments will make available the criteria used for determining how an essay is assessed, perhaps including how marks are distributed, and this can help you to structure your essay and decide how to distribute your efforts.

An example (from the University of York) is given in Table 4. It is a useful exercise to review your completed essays against criteria before handing them in, and assessing for yourself how well you think you have met these requirements. If after having received feedback on your marked essay it is not clear what you should have done differently, then it is important to seek advice. Reading an essay that received a higher grade or looking at a model answer that the lecturer has provided can be helpful.

Writing reports

The purpose of a report is to convey specific research-based information concisely and accurately. In psychology, when describing a quantitative study, you are expected to follow a standard structure as outlined below. If the study is a qualitative or an exploratory study it is not appropriate to include a hypothesis or prediction. Instead, there should be

more emphasis on why a particular analytical method was chosen and a detailed analysis section will replace the results section.

This section provides some practical advice to help you organise a report on a quantitative experiment. Reports are a real test of effective communication as they require you to capture why you did the experiment, how you did it, what the results were and what the implications are. This will provide the reader with the rationale for the work and provide full details of an experiment so that it can be replicated. Laboratory reports for writing up experiments take the following format.

Title

The title of the report should be a concise statement of the main topic. In 10 to 15 words you should be able to convey what the experiment is about.

Abstract

The abstract of the report is a brief summary of the content and purpose of the report. It should be short and informative, stating the problem, the method, the results, the findings and the conclusion. It is easiest to write the abstract after you have written the rest of the report.

Introduction

The introduction should give readers a brief overview of the topic that you are studying, followed by a rationale for why you are doing the study. To do this you will need to indicate what other relevant research has been done in this area and how your study will provide added value to understanding the topic under consideration. As in an essay, you should cite previous work – for example, 'Gathercole and Baddeley (2002)', with the full reference given in the references section. Remember to state your hypothesis explicitly and to identify the independent and dependent variables.

Method

This section should be split into different sections to cover the design, participants, apparatus or materials, and procedure. This is where you describe exactly how the study was conducted. It should contain all the details necessary to allow another experimenter to replicate the study and typically falls into the following four sections.

Design

A brief sentence or two here should provide details of the formal design of the experiment. In a quantitative study this will include whether participants performed each condition (repeated measures design) or whether different participants performed separate conditions (independent measures). You should also state what the independent variables (what was manipulated) and dependent variables (what you measured) were.

Participants

This subsection should tell the reader who participated in the study. This should include the number of participants, how were they selected for the experiments, whether they were volunteers or paid and how they were assigned to different conditions. You should also give details of their age, sex and any other factor, such as reading age, that is relevant to the experiment.

Apparatus

In this section you should describe all the apparatus and materials used in the experiment. This might include laboratory equipment, software or questionnaires. Include details of any commercial products, including the name plus version or model number.

Procedure

In this section, describe exactly what happened to the participants. This might include instructions they were given, where they were seated, what training they received, what tests or stimulus materials were administered and what data were collected.

Results

In the first part of the results section, provide summary statistics from the data including the mean and standard deviations for each group. Then you should report the results of the statistical tests you used to ascertain whether there were any differences between the conditions. Use clearly labelled tables and graphs to display the results but make sure that the text can be understood in its own right. You should record all the results, not just those that support your hypothesis.

Discussion

This is the section where you relate the findings of your study to previous work mentioned in your introduction. Start with a brief statement of the main results and whether they support your original hypothesis. You can then move on to discussing the implications of your study for other research. Does your study advance knowledge in the research area? Does it provide different results from other studies? This is also the place to consider ways in which your study could have been improved and to suggest ways in which the work could be taken forward.

References

All publications and commercial products cited in the report should be listed in this section.

Avoiding plagiarism

Plagiarism occurs when you present in your written work someone else's words or work as if they were your own. It does not matter whether you do this deliberately or accidentally – it is still plagiarism. Plagiarism includes:

- exact copying of phrases from another source
- copying of phrases from another source with only minor changes of wording

Appendix 1
Careers and study skills

Illustrative examples of plagiarism

Example A

Let's assume that you, a student, write the following sentences.

> The distinction between left-hemisphere processing and right-hemisphere processing in the brain is complex. Recent research indicates that infants show patterns of hemispheric specialization for musical processing (Balaban, Anderson and Wisniewski, 1998).

- The first sentence is a general statement. Perhaps it is your opinion after you've read a number of sources on the topic. Therefore, it does not need a citation.
- The second sentence refers to evidence from a paper that you've read. The sentence is written in your words, not copied or paraphrased from the authors. Therefore, as long as you cite the source to show where the information came from, you are not plagiarising.

Example B

If an exact quote is necessary to convey an idea, use quotation marks and give the proper citation, like this:

> A recent study of infants' musical abilities found 'hemispheric specialization for different components of auditory perceptual processing' (Balaban, Anderson and Wisniewski, 1998: 45).

Example C (an instance of plagiarism)

Without the quotation marks, the following statements are plagiarised, even though the source is listed.

> A recent study of infants' musical abilities found hemispheric specialization for different components of auditory perceptual processing (Balaban, Anderson and Wisniewski, 1998).
>
> A recent study of infants' musical abilities found hemispheric specialization for different components of auditory perceptual processing (Balaban, Anderson and Wisniewski, 1998: 45).

- This is because, in psychology papers, sources of ideas and information are cited even when the writing is in your own words (see Example A). The statements above would be presumed to be in your own words, but they are not – the phrase 'hemispheric specialization for different components of auditory perceptual processing' is from the original article. Thus, these are examples of plagiarism.
- Note that, because you did not use quotation marks, the statement is considered to be plagiarised even if you listed the page number from the source.

Example D (another instance of plagiarism)

The following statement is considered to be plagiarised because it paraphrases the authors' words too closely.

> A recent study of infants' musical abilities found that the brain's hemispheres were specialised for various parts of perceptual processing in audition (Balaban, Anderson and Wisniewski, 1998).

- You cannot take phrases or sentences from another source and simply move around words or insert synonyms.

Source: adapted from Professor Maire Balaban, http://www2.eou.edu/psych/mb/plagiarism.html Accessed 7 November 2003.

• failing to acknowledge the proper source and not including it in your reference list.

To avoid unintentional plagiarism, it is wise not to write down chunks verbatim out of books or journals. Make notes using your own words and put quotation marks round any extracts or phrases that are not your own, together with the necessary reference information. A useful guided example is shown in Focus Point 6.

Many universities are introducing electronic plagiarism detection systems that can detect whether your written work is similar to other work on the Internet. This includes the detection of subtle alterations to online texts, paragraphs from online essay banks, small chunks of online papers and false citations. You have been warned!

Interestingly, plagiarism has not escaped the interest of cognitive psychologists. Indeed, research has shown that inadvertent plagiarism, or cryptomnesia, is a memory problem that we can see in everyday cognitive functioning. According to Richard Marsh (Marsh *et al.*, 1997), cryptomnesia can occur when the brain is so busy creating new ideas that it does not have enough spare resource to monitor the source of the ideas, with the result that old ideas look new.

Revision

Ideally, revision should be a continuous process throughout the module you are studying. Learning at university should largely be about understanding, analysis, application and expression, not about cramming in facts at the last moment in order to regurgitate them in an exam, with little consequent long-term learning. This ideal is not always reached, and in some areas there is a need to acquire a good deal of basic factual knowledge.

It is inevitable that your style of working and of revision is shaped by your perceptions of the assessment process. So the example we saw earlier of students shifting towards a 'surface' mode of study as an exam approached may have been a sensible one if the exam they were preparing for was mainly testing recall of factual information (however, as it was a third-year exam, typically focused on deep

understanding, it may be that some students had a nasty shock).

The point is that you do need to be strategic about your revision. Try to develop a strategy early on in the module rather than leaving revision to the last moment. The following pointers may help.

• Identify the goals of the assessment you are facing. Will you be tested on factual knowledge, on your ability to construct an argument, on deep understanding, on your ability to solve problems, or what?
• Take another look at the learning outcomes for the course to remind yourself of what it is you are meant to know. Learning outcomes may be phrased 'by the end of the course students will be able to assess . . ., describe . . ., evaluate . . .'. Take note of the verb that is being used for each outcome; these are purposively written to indicate the level and depth of knowledge required.
• Identify what you think the examiners will be looking for. This might include one or more of: factual accuracy, understanding, relevance, analytical ability, critical thinking, problem-solving, application, creativity, good structure and expression.
• Be clear about the nature of the exam. Look at old exam papers, talk to your lecturers. How much choice will you have? What different approaches are possible? For example, will you be able to focus on your strengths in analytical, creating or practical abilities (see the section on 'Assessment' below)? Read through and understand any assessment criteria that are provided by your department or module leader.
• Make a list of what you know, what you need to know and where your strengths and weaknesses lie, and use this to decide where you should concentrate your efforts.

Armed with all this information, draw up a plan. This should include the following points.

• Covering course materials, making notes and reviewing your notes.

Appendix 1
Careers and study skills

Theory map

To fully appreciate a scientific theory, you should be able to describe the theory, and you should also know the history of the theory, know evidence for and against the theory, know why the theory is important, and know whether there are any similar and competing theories.

Quick links

...to topic: development and cognition

...to textbook: pp.399–402 chart

...to class: Piaget film

...to yourself: formal operations

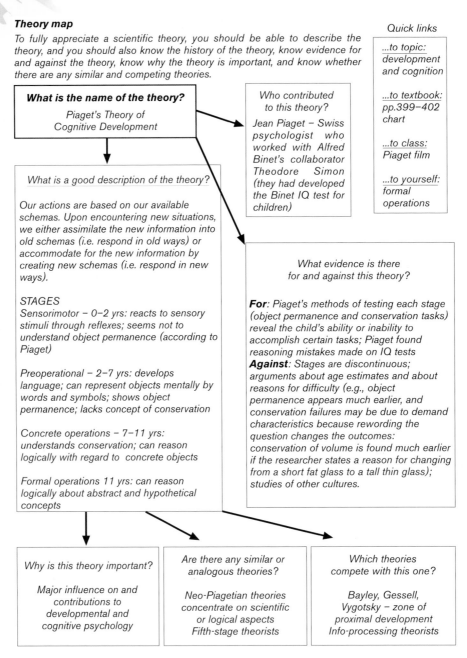

What is the name of the theory?

Piaget's Theory of Cognitive Development

Who contributed to this theory?

Jean Piaget – Swiss psychologist who worked with Alfred Binet's collaborator Theodore Simon (they had developed the Binet IQ test for children)

What is a good description of the theory?

Our actions are based on our available schemas. Upon encountering new situations, we either assimilate the new information into old schemas (i.e. respond in old ways) or accommodate for the new information by creating new schemas (i.e. respond in new ways).

STAGES
Sensorimotor – 0–2 yrs: reacts to sensory stimuli through reflexes; seems not to understand object permanence (according to Piaget)

Preoperational – 2–7 yrs: develops language; can represent objects mentally by words and symbols; shows object permanence; lacks concept of conservation

Concrete operations – 7–11 yrs: understands conservation; can reason logically with regard to concrete objects

Formal operations 11 yrs: can reason logically about abstract and hypothetical concepts

What evidence is there for and against this theory?

For: Piaget's methods of testing each stage (object permanence and conservation tasks) reveal the child's ability or inability to accomplish certain tasks; Piaget found reasoning mistakes made on IQ tests
Against: Stages are discontinuous; arguments about age estimates and about reasons for difficulty (e.g., object permanence appears much earlier, and conservation failures may be due to demand characteristics because rewording the question changes the outcomes: conservation of volume is found much earlier if the researcher states a reason for changing from a short fat glass to a tall thin glass); studies of other cultures.

Why is this theory important?

Major influence on and contributions to developmental and cognitive psychology

Are there any similar or analogous theories?

Neo-Piagetian theories concentrate on scientific or logical aspects
Fifth-stage theorists

Which theories compete with this one?

Bayley, Gessell, Vygotsky – zone of proximal development
Info-processing theorists

Figure 2 An example of an academic guide map illustrating understanding of Piaget's theory of cognitive development
Source: adapted from Motes et al., 2003

- Making summaries and overviews. It can be helpful to use a different form of representation from that used in the original learning or in your notes. Some people find spider diagrams or concept maps helpful. A similar technique is termed 'guide maps' (Motes, Bahr, Atha-Weldon and Dansereau, 2003). An example of a guide map is shown in Figure 2.
- Practising writing example essays or answers to old exam papers. (Practising writing answer plans will help if you don't have time to do the whole thing.)
- Identifying (and finding ways of practising) where you need to go beyond the course materials (e.g. in applying your knowledge to practical situations, in linking with knowledge from other modules).
- Deciding how to play to your strengths, either in terms of what to cover (but be careful not to restrict your choices too much) or in terms of the types of answer to prepare.
- Setting yourself a timetable. Aim to review all your notes well before the exam.
- Not panicking. Following the above suggestions might help!

Assessment: coursework and exams

Not all students have the skills to write good essays, nor do all students have the skills to do well in exams – although it is to be hoped that these will improve during their course of study. However, are these really the skills that are necessary to succeed in the real world?

Robert Sternberg's research (Sternberg *et al.*, 2000) has included analysing what it takes to succeed in life and has put forward the concept of successful intelligence. He defines this concept as: 'the ability to achieve success in life, given one's personal standards, within one's sociocultural context in order to adapt to, shape, and select environments via recognition of and capitalisation on strengths and remediation of or compensation for weaknesses through a balance of analytical, creative, and practical abilities.'

He argues that using the same unvarying assessment methods can result in shining the spotlight on the same students every time. Instead, he advocates the use of a variety of assessment methods so that the spotlight shines, as it were, on different students at different times.

He suggests that assessment should focus on testing memorised knowledge through creative, analytical and practical questioning (known as the CAP model of assessment). Table 5 provides illustrative examples suggested by Sternberg for each type of question. As suggested in the earlier sections on playing to your strengths and revision, do your best to identify what you feel you are good at and look for opportunities to capitalise on those strengths.

Strict rules surround what you may and may not do during the examination itself. You should make every effort to familiarise yourself with these in advance. It is a good idea, for example, to:

- know in advance what the procedure is if for some reason you are unable to attend the exam
- check whether you are allowed to have access to a dictionary
- know where and when the examination takes place
- know what you may take (e.g. water) and may not take (e.g. mobile phones, databank watches, coats) into the examination room
- check you have your examination candidate number
- listen carefully to the invigilator's instructions before the exam begins
- contact the invigilator if you feel ill during the exam
- talk to no one other than an invigilator during an examination.

Accessing resources

During your course you will be encouraged to develop the skills necessary to undertake research in psychology. In this section the focus is on the skills you need in order to access psychological resources. Typical activities include accessing journals or books from the library as determined by course reading lists, searching in library or online databases for literature reviews and project work, and searching the Internet for information.

Bibliographic databases contain information about journal articles and are an essential tool for finding

TABLE 5	EXAMPLES FROM ROBERT STERNBERG OF ASSESSMENT QUESTIONS THAT FOCUS ON THE MEMORISING, ANALYTICAL, CREATIVE AND PRACTICAL ABILITIES OF STUDENTS

Memory-based learning (verbs: who, what, where, when, why, how)
What is the fundamental attribution error?
A bias of attribution in which an individual tends to over-emphasise internal causes and personal responsibility, and to de-emphasise external causes and situational influences when observing the behaviour of other people.

Analytical thinking (verbs: analyse, compare and contrast, evaluate, explain, critique)
Explain, in terms of the structure of the eye, why we have difficulties in accurately perceiving colours in the dark.

Creative thinking (verbs: create, design, imagine, invent, suppose)
Design and describe an experiment to test whether, on average, 12-year-old children from the remote province of Shtungis have entered Piaget's cognitive-developmental stage of formal operations.

Assessing for practical thinking (verbs: use, apply, implement, employ, utilise)
Show how you might use the technique of systematic desensitisation to implement a programme to help someone combat test anxiety.

out what has already been published. They include information on the authors, title and publication, and usually an abstract or short summary. *Web of Knowledge* and *PsycLit* are particularly important. There is a variety of ways in which these can be accessed; it is important that you find out which system is used at the institution where you are studying and receive appropriate training in its use.

Searching for information on the Internet can be useful too, but it is less systematic and will not always result in the detailed and reliable information provided by the bibliographic databases. Moreover, it can waste an awful lot of your time.

The *Internet Psychologist* (http://www.vts.rdn.ac.uk/tutorial/psychologist/) is a good place to start if you want to find out how to make the best use of the Internet while you are studying psychology. It provides a list of key websites for psychology as well as helpful information on how to search effectively and to evaluate critically the material found on websites.

The SOSIG website (http://www.sosig.ac.uk/psychology/) and LTSN psychology website (www.psychology.ltsn.ac.uk) are two useful gateways to psychology resources. Both contain links that have been selected for their academic content by psychologists with researchers and students in mind.

Feedback and course evaluation
It is not uncommon for students to feel confused at the end of a module and in some ways to feel less confident of their knowledge than when they began it. This is normal and, believe it or not, can be a sign of learning – perhaps an example of the adage 'ignorance is bliss'. For example, it may be proof that you can make more sensitive observations of behaviour, recognise the complexity of a particular theory or have a better understanding of the competing theories used to explain some behaviour.

At the end of modules you may be required to fill in evaluation forms, sometimes known as 'happy sheets'. These provide you with an opportunity to reflect on different aspects of the module, such as the content of the course, the way it was taught, the ease of getting hold of resources, and so on. These are a valuable source of information for staff when they come to evaluate how successful the module was and what changes to consider next time the module runs. This means that you, as a student, have a responsibility to provide constructive comments that may benefit the next cohort of students. It is not the place to list problems that could have been addressed early on in the course. For example, 'I couldn't find the books in the library', 'We weren't given enough information about the assessment', 'I couldn't log on to the virtual learning environment' are problems that may have been solvable by seeking out help earlier, before the course ended.

If an occasion arises when there is a strong feeling in the year group that all is not well, the matter can be taken forward by the year's student representative to the appropriate committee. Why not consider standing to become the representative yourself? Remember, if one of your personal goals is to find a good job where communication and negotiation skills are important, this would be a good asset for your CV.

Conclusions

The coverage of study skills for psychologists in this chapter has been partial: we've left out more than we've put in. We've said little about easing the problems of understanding and carrying out statistical procedures, of preparing a poster or conducting a literature review. There are whole books on critical thinking and on how best to critique a research paper; and there's plenty that could be said to help support special groups, such as mature students or those with a disability.

These and other omissions are partly a consequence of space but also of a belief that study skills are not just lists of prescriptions or simply applied guidelines – they are based on an understanding about what principles underlie successful studying. We hope that the chapter has provided you with some understanding of those principles and sufficient examples of their application for you to be able to fill in some of the gaps for yourself.

Learning outcomes

When you have completed this chapter you should be able to:

- describe five key principles underlying study and key aspects of their psychological rationale
- apply the study skill methods described in the chapter to areas of your own study, such as note-taking, writing essays and revision
- reflect on some of the psychological principles underlying study skills and use these to choose study methods for situations not explicitly covered in this chapter.

Key terms

Active learner
Critical thinking skills
Declarative knowledge
Deep approach to learning
Depth of processing
Distributed practice
Elaboration
Enactment effect
Encoding specificity
Encoding variability
Essays
Generation effect
Group skills
Learning goals
Learning outcomes
Learning styles
Lectures
Metacognition
Oral and communication skills
Personal development planning (PDP)
Personal skills
Plagiarism
Procedural knowledge
Reflective practice
Retrieval schemata
Small-group work
Socratic dialogue
Total time hypothesis

Appendix 1
Careers and study skills

Further reading

Collins, S. C. and Kneale, P. E. (2001) *Study Skills for Psychology Students.* London: Arnold.

McGhee, P. (2001) *Thinking Psychologically.* Basingstoke: Palgrave.

Appendix 2

Probability values of *z*-scores from the normal distribution (values calculated by Andy Field using SPSS version 11)

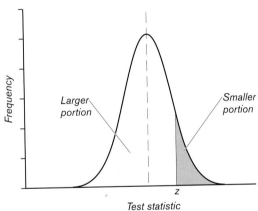

z	**Larger portion**	**Smaller portion**
.00	.50000	.50000
.01	.50399	.49601
.02	.50798	.49202
.03	.51197	.48803
.04	.51595	.48405
.05	.51994	.48006
.06	.52392	.47608
.07	.52790	.47210
.08	.53188	.46812
.09	.53586	.46414
.10	.53983	.46017
.11	.54380	.45620
.12	.54776	.45224
.13	.55172	.44828
.14	.55567	.44433
.15	.55962	.44038
.16	.56356	.43644
.17	.56749	.43251

Appendix 2

z	Larger portion	Smaller portion
.18	.57142	.42858
.19	.57535	.42465
.20	.57926	.42074
.21	.58317	.41683
.22	.58706	.41294
.23	.59095	.40905
.24	.59483	.40517
.25	.59871	.40129
.26	.60257	.39743
.27	.60642	.39358
.28	.61026	.38974
.29	.61409	.38591
.30	.61791	.38209
.31	.62172	.37828
.32	.62552	.37448
.33	.62930	.37070
.34	.63307	.36693
.35	.63683	.36317
.36	.64058	.35942
.37	.64431	.35569
.38	.64803	.35197
.39	.65173	.34827
.40	.65542	.34458
.41	.65910	.34090
.42	.66276	.33724
.43	.66640	.33360
.44	.67003	.32997
.45	.67364	.32636
.46	.67724	.32276
.47	.68082	.31918
.48	.68439	.31561
.49	.68793	.31207
.50	.69146	.30854
.51	.69497	.30503
.52	.69847	.30153
.53	.70194	.29806
.54	.70540	.29460
.55	.70884	.29116
.56	.71226	.28774
.57	.71566	.28434
.58	.71904	.28096
.59	.72240	.27760
.60	.72575	.27425
.61	.72907	.27093
.62	.73237	.26763

z	Larger portion	Smaller portion
.63	.73565	.26435
.64	.73891	.26109
.65	.74215	.25785
.66	.74537	.25463
.67	.74857	.25143
.68	.75175	.24825
.69	.75490	.24510
.70	.75804	.24196
.71	.76115	.23885
.72	.76424	.23576
.73	.76730	.23270
.74	.77035	.22965
.75	.77337	.22663
.76	.77637	.22363
.77	.77935	.22065
.78	.78230	.21770
.79	.78524	.21476
.80	.78814	.21186
.81	.79103	.20897
.82	.79389	.20611
.83	.79673	.20327
.84	.79955	.20045
.85	.80234	.19766
.86	.80511	.19489
.87	.80785	.19215
.88	.81057	.18943
.89	.81327	.18673
.90	.81594	.18406
.91	.81859	.18141
.92	.82121	.17879
.93	.82381	.17619
.94	.82639	.17361
.95	.82894	.17106
.96	.83147	.16853
.97	.83398	.16602
.98	.83646	.16354
.99	.83891	.16109
1.00	.84134	.15866
1.01	.84375	.15625
1.02	.84614	.15386
1.03	.84849	.15151
1.04	.85083	.14917
1.05	.85314	.14686
1.06	.85543	.14457
1.07	.85769	.14231

Appendix 2

z	Larger portion	Smaller portion
1.08	.85993	.14007
1.09	.86214	.13786
1.10	.86433	.13567
1.11	.86650	.13350
1.12	.86864	.13136
1.13	.87076	.12924
1.14	.87286	.12714
1.15	.87493	.12507
1.16	.87698	.12302
1.17	.87900	.12100
1.18	.88100	.11900
1.19	.88298	.11702
1.20	.88493	.11507
1.21	.88686	.11314
1.22	.88877	.11123
1.23	.89065	.10935
1.24	.89251	.10749
1.25	.89435	.10565
1.26	.89617	.10383
1.27	.89796	.10204
1.28	.89973	.10027
1.29	.90147	.09853
1.30	.90320	.09680
1.31	.90490	.09510
1.32	.90658	.09342
1.33	.90824	.09176
1.34	.90988	.09012
1.35	.91149	.08851
1.36	.91309	.08691
1.37	.91466	.08534
1.38	.91621	.08379
1.39	.91774	.08226
1.40	.91924	.08076
1.41	.92073	.07927
1.42	.92220	.07780
1.43	.92364	.07636
1.44	.92507	.07493
1.45	.92647	.07353
1.46	.92785	.07215
1.47	.92922	.07078
1.48	.93056	.06944
1.49	.93189	.06811
1.50	.93319	.06681
1.51	.93448	.06552
1.52	.93574	.06426

z	Larger portion	Smaller portion
1.53	.93699	.06301
1.54	.93822	.06178
1.55	.93943	.06057
1.56	.94062	.05938
1.57	.94179	.05821
1.58	.94295	.05705
1.59	.94408	.05592
1.60	.94520	.05480
1.61	.94630	.05370
1.62	.94738	.05262
1.63	.94845	.05155
1.64	**.94950**	**.05050**
1.65	.95053	.04947
1.66	.95154	.04846
1.67	.95254	.04746
1.68	.95352	.04648
1.69	.95449	.04551
1.70	.95543	.04457
1.71	.95637	.04363
1.72	.95728	.04272
1.73	.95818	.04182
1.74	.95907	.04093
1.75	.95994	.04006
1.76	.96080	.03920
1.77	.96164	.03836
1.78	.96246	.03754
1.79	.96327	.03673
1.80	.96407	.03593
1.81	.96485	.03515
1.82	.96562	.03438
1.83	.96638	.03362
1.84	.96712	.03288
1.85	.96784	.03216
1.86	.96856	.03144
1.87	.96926	.03074
1.88	.96995	.03005
1.89	.97062	.02938
1.90	.97128	.02872
1.91	.97193	.02807
1.92	.97257	.02743
1.93	.97320	.02680
1.94	.97381	.02619
1.95	.97441	.02559
1.96	**.97500**	**.02500**
1.97	.97558	.02442

Appendix 2

z	Larger portion	Smaller portion
1.98	.97615	.02385
1.99	.97670	.02330
2.00	.97725	.02275
2.01	.97778	.02222
2.02	.97831	.02169
2.03	.97882	.02118
2.04	.97932	.02068
2.05	.97982	.02018
2.06	.98030	.01970
2.07	.98077	.01923
2.08	.98124	.01876
2.09	.98169	.01831
2.10	.98214	.01786
2.11	.98257	.01743
2.12	.98300	.01700
2.13	.98341	.01659
2.14	.98382	.01618
2.15	.98422	.01578
2.16	.98461	.01539
2.17	.98500	.01500
2.18	.98537	.01463
2.19	.98574	.01426
2.20	.98610	.01390
2.21	.98645	.01355
2.22	.98679	.01321
2.23	.98713	.01287
2.24	.98745	.01255
2.25	.98778	.01222
2.26	.98809	.01191
2.27	.98840	.01160
2.28	.98870	.01130
2.29	.98899	.01101
2.30	.98928	.01072
2.31	.98956	.01044
2.32	.98983	.01017
2.33	.99010	.00990
2.34	.99036	.00964
2.35	.99061	.00939
2.36	.99086	.00914
2.37	.99111	.00889
2.38	.99134	.00866
2.39	.99158	.00842
2.40	.99180	.00820
2.41	.99202	.00798
2.42	.99224	.00776

z	Larger portion	Smaller portion
2.43	.99245	.00755
2.44	.99266	.00734
2.45	.99286	.00714
2.46	.99305	.00695
2.47	.99324	.00676
2.48	.99343	.00657
2.49	.99361	.00639
2.50	.99379	.00621
2.51	.99396	.00604
2.52	.99413	.00587
2.53	.99430	.00570
2.54	.99446	.00554
2.55	.99461	.00539
2.56	.99477	.00523
2.57	.99492	.00508
2.58	.99506	.00494
2.59	.99520	.00480
2.60	.99534	.00466
2.61	.99547	.00453
2.62	.99560	.00440
2.63	.99573	.00427
2.64	.99585	.00415
2.65	.99598	.00402
2.66	.99609	.00391
2.67	.99621	.00379
2.68	.99632	.00368
2.69	.99643	.00357
2.70	.99653	.00347
2.71	.99664	.00336
2.72	.99674	.00326
2.73	.99683	.00317
2.74	.99693	.00307
2.75	.99702	.00298
2.76	.99711	.00289
2.77	.99720	.00280
2.78	.99728	.00272
2.79	.99736	.00264
2.80	.99744	.00256
2.81	.99752	.00248
2.82	.99760	.00240
2.83	.99767	.00233
2.84	.99774	.00226
2.85	.99781	.00219
2.86	.99788	.00212
2.87	.99795	.00205

Appendix 2

z	Larger portion	Smaller portion
2.88	.99801	.00199
2.89	.99807	.00193
2.90	.99813	.00187
2.91	.99819	.00181
2.92	.99825	.00175
2.93	.99831	.00169
2.94	.99836	.00164
2.95	.99841	.00159
2.96	.99846	.00154
2.97	.99851	.00149
2.98	.99856	.00144
2.99	.99861	.00139
3.00	.99865	.00135
...	...	...
3.25	.99942	.00058
...	...	...
3.50	.99977	.00023
...	...	...
4.00	.99997	.00003

References

Aaronson, D. and Scarborough, H. S. (1977) Performance theories for sentence coding: some quantitative models. *Journal of Verbal Learning & Verbal Behavior*, 16(3), 277–303.

Aboud, F. (1988) *Children and Prejudice*. Oxford: Basil Blackwell.

Abrahams, F. (2002) The (un)fair usage of the 16PF (SA92) in South Africa: a response to C. H. Prinsloo and I. Ebersehn. *South African Journal of Psychology*, 29(3), 58–61.

Abrams, D. and Hogg, M. A. (1990) Social identification, self-categorisation and social influence. *European Review of Social Psychology*, 1, 195–228.

Abramson, L. Y., Metalsky, G. I. and Alloy, L. B. (1989) Hopelessness depression: a theory-based subtype of depression. *Psychological Review*, 96, 358–72.

Abramson, L. Y., Seligman, M. E. P. and Teasdale, J. D. (1978) Learned helplessness in humans: critique and reformulation. *Journal of Abnormal Psychology*, 87, 49–74.

Ackerman, P. L. and Kanfer, R. (1993) Predicting individual differences in complex skill acquisition: dynamics of ability determinants. *Journal of Applied Psychology*, 77, 598–614.

Adair, Y. and Elcock, J. (1995) Victims and pushers: police discourses of rave culture. Paper presented at BPS Annual Conference, Brighton, April.

Adams, J. (1965) Inequity in social exchange. In W. Berkowitz (ed.) *Advances in Experimental Social Psychology*, 267–99.

Adler, A. (1927) *The Practice and Theory of Individual Psychology*. New York: Harcourt Brace Jovanovich.

Adler, A. (1930) The neurotic constitution: outlines of a comparative individualistic psychology and psychotherapy (trans. B. Glueck and J. E. Lind). New York: Dodd, Mead.

Adolphs, R. and Tranel, D. (2003) Amygdala damage impairs emotion recognition from scenes only when they contain facial expressions. *Neuropsychologia*, 41, 281–9.

Adolphs, R., Tranel, D. and Damasio, A. R. (1998) The human amygdala in social judgement. *Nature*, 393, 470–4.

Adorno, T. W., Frenkel-Brunswick, E., Levinson, D. J. and Sanford, R. N. (1950) *The Authoritarian Personality*. New York: Harper.

Aiken, L. R. (1997) *Psychological Testing and Measurement*. Boston: Allyn & Bacon.

Ainsworth, M. D. S. (1967) *Infancy in Uganda: Infant Care and the Growth of Love*. Baltimore, MD: Johns Hopkins Press.

Ainsworth, M. D. S. and Bell, S. M. (1969) Exploratory behaviour of 1-year-olds in a strange situation. In B. M. Foss (ed.) *Determinants of Infant Behaviour*, Vol. 4. London: Methuen.

Ainsworth, M. D. S. and Wittig, B. A. (1969) Attachment and exploratory behaviour of one-year-olds in a strange situation. In B. M. Foss (ed.) *Determinants of Infant Behaviour*, Vol. 4. London: Methuen, 113–36.

Ainsworth, M. D. S., Blehar, M. C., Waters, E. and Wall, S. (1978) *Patterns of Attachment: a Psychological Study of the Strange Situation*. Hillsdale, NJ: Erlbaum.

Aitchison, J. (1989) *The Articulate Mammal: an Introduction to Psycholinguistics* (2nd edn). London: Hutchinson.

Ajzen, I. (1988) *Attitudes, Personality and Behavior*. Milton Keynes: Open University Press.

Ajzen, I. (1991) The theory of planned behavior. *Organizational Behavior and Human Decision Processes*, 50, 179–211.

Ajzen, I. and Madden, T. J. (1986) Prediction of goal directed behavior: attitudes, intentions and perceived behavioral control. *Journal of Experimental Social Psychology*, 22, 453–74.

Akabayashi, A., Wahlestedt, C., Alexander, J. T. and Leibowitz, S. F. (1994) Specific inhibition of endogenous neuropeptide Y synthesis in arcuate nucleus by antisense oligonucleotides suppresses feeding behavior and insulin secretion. *Brain Research: Molecular Brain Research*, 21, 55–61.

Albert, D. J., Walsh, M. L. and Jonik, R. H. (1993) Aggression in humans: what is the biological foundation? *Neuroscience and Biobehavioral Reviews*, 17, 405-4-5.

Albery, I. P. and Guppy, A. (1995) The interactionist nature of drinking and driving: a structural model. *Ergonomics*, 38, 1805–18.

Albery, I. P., Heuston, J., Ward, J., Groves, P., Durand, M., Gossop, M. and Strang, J. (2003) Measuring therapeutic attitude among drug workers. *Addictive Behaviors*, 28, 995–1005.

Alibali, M. and Goldin-Meadow, S. (1993) Gesture–speech mismatch and mechanisms of learning: what the hands reveal about a child's state of mind. *Cognitive Psychology*, 25, 468–523.

Allen, V. L. and Levine, J. M. (1971) Social support and conformity: the role of independent assessment of reality. *Journal of Experimental Social Psychology*, 7, 48–58.

Allison, P. J., Guichard, C. and Gilian, L. (2000) A prospective investigation of dispositional optimism as a predictor of health-related quality of life in head and neck cancer patients.

References

Quality of Life Research: an International Journal of Quality of Life Aspects of Treatment Care and Rehabilitation, 9(8), 951–60.

Allport, D. A., Antonis, B. and Reynolds, P. (1972) On the division of attention: a disproof of the single channel hypothesis. *The Quarterly Journal of Experimental Psychology*, 24(2), 225–35.

Allport, G. W. (1935) Attitudes. In Murchison, C. (ed.) *Handbook of Social Psychology*. Worcester, MA: Clark University Press.

Allport, G. W. (1954) *The Nature of Prejudice*. Reading, MA: Addison-Wesley.

Allport, G. W. (1961) *Pattern and Growth in Personality*. New York: Holt, Rinehart & Winston.

Altman, J., Everitt, B. J., Glautier, S., Markou, A., Nutt, D., Oretti, R., Phillips, G. D. and Robbins, T. W. (1996) The biological, social and clinical bases of drug addiction: commentary and debate. *Psychopharmacology*, 125, 285–345.

American Psychological Association (1994) *Diagnostic and Statistical Manual of Mental Disorders* (4th edn). (DSM-IV). Washington DC.

American Psychological Association (2001) *Publication Manual of the American Psychological Association* (5th edn). Washington, DC: APA Books.

Ames, C. (1992) Classroom goals, structures and student motivation. *Journal of Educational Psychology*, 84(3), 261–71.

Anand, B. K. and Brobeck, J. R. (1951) Hypothalamic control of food intake in rats and cats. *Yale Journal of Biology and Medicine*, 24, 123–40.

Anderson, J. C., Williams, S., McGee, R. and Silva, P. A. (1987) DSM-III disorders in preadolescent children. Prevalence in a large sample from a general population. *Archives of General Psychiatry*, 44 69–76.

Anderson, C. A., Anderson, K. B., Dorr, N., DeNeve, K. M. and Flanagan, M. (2000) Temperature and aggression, in M. Zanna (ed.) *Advances in Experimental Social Psychology*. New York: Academic Press.

Anderson, J. R. (1995a) *Cognitive Psychology and its Implications* (4th edn). New York: WH Freeman & Company.

Anderson, J. R. (1995b) *Learning and Memory: an Integrated Approach*. Chichester: John Wiley & Sons.

Anderson, R. C. and Pichert, J. W. (1978) Recall of previously unrecallable information following a shift in perspective. *Journal of Verbal Learning and Verbal Behaviour*, 17, 1–12.

Andreason, N.C. and Black, D. W. (1996) *Introductory Textbook of Psychiatry* (2nd edn). Washington DC: American Psychiatric Press.

Andrews, G. and Harvey, R. (1981) Does psychotherapy benefit neurotic patients? A reanalysis of the Smith, Glass and Miller data. *Archives of General Psychiatry*, 38, 1203–8.

Angrist, B., Lee, H. K. and Gershon, S. (1974) The antagonism of amphetamine-induced symptomatology by a neuroleptic. *American Journal of Psychiatry*, 131, 817–19.

Antony M. M., Brown T. A. and Barlow D. H. (1997) Heterogeneity among specific phobia types in DSM-IV. *Behaviour Research & Therapy*, 35, 1089–100.

Ardelt, M. (2000) Still stable after all these years? Personality

stability theory revisited. *Social Psychology Quarterly*. 63(4), 392–405.

Argyle, M. (1988) *Bodily Communication*. London: Methuen.

Asch, S. E. (1946) Forming impressions of personality. *Journal of Abnormal and Social Psychology*, 41, 258–90.

Asch, S. E. (1951) Effects of group pressure upon the modification and distortion of judgements. In Guetzkow, H. (ed.) *Groups, Leadership and Men*. Pittsburgh: Carnegie Press, 177–90.

Asch, S. E. (1952) *Social Psychology*. Englewood Cliffs, NJ: Prentice Hall.

Asch, S. E. (1956) Studies of independence and conformity: a minority of one against a unanimous majority. *Psychological Monographs: General and Applied*, 70, 1–70.

Aslin, R. N., Jusczyk, P. W. and Pisoni, D. B. (1998) Speech and auditory processing during infancy: constraints on and precursors to language. In W. Damon (series ed.), D. Kuhn and R. S. Siegler (vol. eds) *Handbook of Child Psychology: Vol. 2. Cognition, Perception and Language* (5th edn). New York: Wiley, 147–98.

Asmundson, G. J. G., Jacobson, S. J., Allerdings, M. D. and Norton, G. R. (1996) Social phobia in disabled workers with chronic musculoskeletal pain. *Behaviour Research & Therapy*, 34, 939–43.

Asperger, H. (1944) 'Die autistichen Psychopathen in Kindesalter', *Archiv fur Psychiatrie und Nervenkrankheiten*, 117, 76–136. Trans. U. Frith in U. Frith (ed.) (1991) *Autism and Asperger Syndrome*. Cambridge: Cambridge University Press, 37–92.

Aspinwall, L. G. and Taylor, S. E. (1990) Stress, coping and well-being: modelling a causal hypothesis. Unpublished manuscript.

Aston-Jones, G. and Bloom, F. E. (1981) Activity of norepinephrine-containing locus coeruleus neurons in behaving rats anticipates fluctuations in the sleep-waking cycle. *Journal of Neuroscience*, 1, 876–86.

Atkinson, J. W. (1981) Thematic apperceptive measurement of motivation in 1950 and 1980. In G. d'Ydewalle and W. Lens (eds) *Cognition in Human Motivation and Learning*. Hillsdale, NJ: Lawrence Erlbaum Associates, 159–98.

Atkinson, R. C. and Shiffrin, R. M. (1968) Human memory: a proposed system and its control processes. In K. W. Spence (ed.) *The Psychology of Learning and Motivation: advances in Research and Theory*, Vol. 2. New York: Academic Press, 89–195.

Augoustinos, M. and Walker, I. (1995) *Social Cognition: an Integrated Introduction*. London: Sage.

Averbach, E. and Coriell, A. S. (1961) Short-term memory in vision. *Bell System Technical Journal*, 40, 309–28.

Avina, C. and O'Donohue, W. (2002) Sexual harassment and PTSD: is sexual harassment diagnosable trauma? *Journal of Trauma & Stress*, 15, 69–75.

Ax, A. F. (1953) The physiological differentiation between fear and anger in humans. *Psychosomatic Medicine*, 15, 433–42.

Ayllon, T. and Azrin, N. H. (1968) *The Token Economy: a Motivational System for Therapy and Rehabilitation*. New York: Appleton Century Crofts.

Ayllon, T., Haughton, E. and Hughes, H. B. (1965) Interpretation of symptoms: fact or fiction. *Behaviour Research & Therapy*, 3, 1–7.

Azrin, N. H. (1976) Improvements in the community-reinforcement approach to alcoholism. *Behaviour Research & Therapy*, 14, 339–48.

Baddeley, A. D. (1986) *Working Memory*. Oxford: Oxford University Press.

Baddeley, A. D. (1995) Memory. In C. C. French and A. M. Colman (eds) *Cognitive Psychology*. London: Longman.

Baddeley, A. D. (1997) *Human Memory Theory and Practice* (revised edn). Hove: Psychology Press.

Baddeley, A. D. (1998) Recent developments in working memory. *Current Opinion in Neurobiology*, 8(2), 234–8.

Baddeley, A. D. and Hitch, G. (1974) Working memory. In G. Bower (ed.) *The Psychology of Learning and Motivation: Advances in Research and Theory and Motivation*, Vol. 8. New York: Academic Press.

Baddeley, A. D. and Hitch, G. (1977) Recency re-examined. In S. Dornic (ed.) *Attention and Performance VI*. Hillsdale, NJ: Lawrence Erlbaum Associates Inc., 647–67.

Baddeley, A. D. and Longman, D. J. A. (1978) The influence of length and frequency of training sessions on rate of learning to type. *Ergonomics*, 21, 627–35.

Baddeley, A. D. and Wilson, B. (1988) Comprehension and working memory: a single case study. *Journal of Memory and Language*, 27, 479–98.

Baddeley, A. D., Gathercole, S. and Papagno, C. (1998) The phonological loop as a language learning device. *Psychological Review*, 105(1), 158–73.

Baghdoyan, H. A., Monaco, A. P., Rodrigo-Angulo, M. L., Assens, F., McCarley, R. W. and Hobson, J. A. (1984) Microinjection of neostigmine into the pontine reticular formation of cats enhances desynchronized sleep signs. *Journal of Pharmacology and Experimental Therapeutics*, 231, 173–80.

Bahrick, H. P. (1984) Semantic memory content in permastore: fifty years of memory for Spanish learned in school. *Journal of Experimental Psychology*, 113(1), 1–29.

Bailey, A., Phillips, W. and Rutter, M. (1996) Autism: towards an integration of clinical, genetic, neuropsychological and neurobiological perspectives. *Journal of Child Psychology and Psychiatry*, 37, 89–126.

Baillargeon, R. (1987) Representing the existence and the location of hidden objects: object permanence in 6- and 8-month-old infants. *Cognition*, 23, 21–41.

Baillargeon, R., Needham, A. and DeVos, J. (1985) Object permanence in 5-month-old infants. *Cognition*, 20, 191–208.

Baker, L. E., Broadbent, J., Michael, E. K., Matthews, P. K., Metosh, C. A., Saunders, R. B., West, W. B. and Appel, J. B. (1995) Assessment of the discriminative stimulus effects of the optical isomers of ecstasy (3, 4-methylenedioxymethamphetamine; MDMA). *Behavioural Pharmacology*, 6, 263–75.

Baldwin, D. A. and Moses, L. J. (1996) The ontogeny of social information gathering. *Child Development*, 67, 1915–39.

Ball, K. and Lee, C. (2000) Relationships between psychological stress, coping and disordered eating: a review. *Psychology and Health*, 14, 1007–35.

Bandura, A. (1969) Social-learning theory of identificatory processes. In D. A. Goslin (ed.) *Handbook of Socialisation Theory and Research*. Chicago: Rand McNally.

Bandura, A. (1973) *Aggression: A Social Learning Analysis*. Oxford: Prentice-Hall.

Bandura, A. (1977a) Self-efficacy: toward a unifying theory of behavioral change. *Psychological Review*, 84, 191–215.

Bandura, A. (1977b) *Social Learning Theory*. Englewood Cliffs, NJ, Prentice-Hall.

Bandura, A. (1986) *Social Foundations of Thought and Action: a Social Cognitive Theory*. Englewood Cliffs: NJ Prentice Hall.

Bandura, A. (1997) *Self-Efficacy: The Exercise of Control*. New York: Freeman.

Bandura, A., Ross, D. and Ross, S. A. (1963) Imitation of film-mediated aggressive models. *Journal of Abnormal & Social Psychology*, 66, 3–11.

Banyard, P. (1999) *Controversies in Psychology*. London: Routledge.

Banzett, L. K., Liberman, R. P. and Moore, J. W. (1984) Long-term follow-up of the effects of behavior therapy. *Hospital & Community Psychiatry*, 35, 277–9.

Barber, N. (1995) The evolutionary psychology of physical attractiveness: sexual selection and human morphology. *Ethology and Sociobiology*, 16, 395–424.

Bargh, J. (1997) The automaticity of everyday life. In Wyer, R. S. and Srull, T. K. (eds) *Advances in Social Cognition*, Vol. 10. Mahwah, NJ: Lawrence Erlbaum, 1–61.

Bargh, J. and Chartrand, T. L. (2000) The mind in the middle: a practical guide to priming and automaticity research. In H. T Reis and C. M. Judd (eds) *Handbook of Research Methods in Social and Personality Psychology*. Cambridge: Cambridge University Press, 253–85.

Bargh, J. and Pietromonaco, P. (1982) Automatic information processing and social perception: the influence of trait information presented outside of conscious awareness on impression formation. *Journal of Personality and Social Psychology*, 43, 437–49.

Bargh, J. A., Chen, M. and Burrows, L. (1996) Automaticity of social behavior: direct effects of trait construct and stereotype activation on action. *Journal of Personality & Social Psychology*, 71, 230–44.

Barker, C., Pistrang, N. and Elliott, R. (2002) *Research Methods in Clinical Psychology: an Introduction for Students and Practitioners*. New York: Wiley.

Barker, R. (2003) Editorial. *Advances in Clinical Neuroscience and Rehabilitation*, 3, 5.

Barker, M. (2003) *Introductory Psychology: History, Themes and Perspectives*. Exeter: Crucial.

Barkley, R. A. (1997) Behavioral inhibition, sustained attention and executive function: constructing a unifying theory of ADHD. *Psychological Bulletin*, 121, 65–94.

Barkley, R. A., Fischer, M., Edelbrock, C. S. and Smallish, L. (1990)

References

The adolescent outcome of hyperactive children diagnosed by research criteria: 1. An 8-year prospective follow-up study. *Journal of the American Academy of Child & Adolescent Psychiatry*, 29 546–57.

Barlow, D. H., Blanchard, E. B., Vermilyea, J. A., Vermilyea, D. B. and DiNardo, P. A. (1986) Generalized anxiety and generalized anxiety disorder: description and reconceptualization. *American Journal of Psychiatry*, 143, 40–4.

Baron, M. S., Vitek, J. L., Bakay, R. A. E., Green, J., Kaneoke, Y., Hashimoto, T., Turner, R. S., Woodard, J. L., Cole, S. A., McDonald, W. M. and DeLong, M. R. (1996) Treatment of advanced Parkinson's disease by posterior GPi Pallidatomy: 1-year results of a pilot study. *Annals of Neurology*, 40, 355–66.

Baron, J. and Thurston, I. (1973) An analysis of the word superiority effect. *Cognitive Psychology*, 4, 207–28.

Baron, R. A. and Byrne, D. (2003) *Social Psychology* (10th edn). New York: Allyn & Bacon.

Baron, R. S., Vandello, J. A. and Brunsman, B. (1996) The forgotten variable in conformity research: impact of task importance on social influence. *Journal of Personality and Social Psychology*, 71, 915–27.

Baron-Cohen, S. (1993) From attention-goal psychology to belief-desire psychology: the development of a theory of mind and its dysfunction. In S. Baron-Cohen, H. Tager-Flusberg and D. J. Cohen (eds) *Understanding Other Minds: Perspectives From Autism*. Oxford: Oxford University Press.

Baron-Cohen, S., Leslie, A. M. and Frith, U. (1985) Does the autistic child have a 'theory of mind'? *Cognition*, 21, 37–46.

Barrett, M. (1996) Early lexical development. In P. Fletcher and B. MacWhinney (eds) *Handbook of Child Language*. Oxford: Blackwell.

Barrick, M. R. and Mount, M. K. (1992) The big five personality dimensions and job performance: a meta-analysis. *Personnel Psychology*, 44, 1–26.

Bartels, A. and Zeki, S. (2000) The neural basis of romantic love. *Neuroreport*, 11, 3829–34.

Bartlett, F. C. (1932) *Remembering*. Cambridge: Cambridge University Press.

Basbuam, A. I. and Fields, H. L. (1978) Endogenous pain control mechanisms: review and hypothesis. *Annals of Neurology*, 4, 451–62.

Bass, E. and Davis, L. (1988) *The Courage to Heal: a Guide for Women Survivors Of Child Sexual Abuse*. New York: Perennial Library/Harper & Row Publishers, Inc.

Bates, E., Camaioni, L. and Volterra, V. (1975) The acquisition of performatives prior to speech. *Merrill Palmer Quarterly*, 21, 205–26.

Bateson, G., Jackson, D. D., Haley, J. and Weakland, J. H. (1956) Toward a theory of schizophrenia. *Behavioral Science*, 1, 251–64.

Batson, C. D. (1998) Altruism and prosocial behaviour. In D. T. Gilbert, S. T. Fiske and G. Lindzey (eds) *The Handbook of Social Psychology* (4th edn). New York: McGraw-Hill.

Batson, C. D., Ahmad, N., Yin, J., Bedell, S. J., Johnson, J. W.,

Templin, C. M. and Whiteside, A. (1999) Two threats to the common good: self-interested egoism and empathy and empathy-induced altruism. *Personality and Social Psychology Bulletin*, 25, 3–16.

Batson, C. D., Duncan, B., Ackerman, P., Buckley, T. and Birch, K. (1981) Is empathic emotion a source of altruistic motivation? *Journal of Personality and Social Psychology*, 40, 290–302.

Baumeister, R. F. (1997) Esteem threat, self-regulatory breakdown and emotional distress as factors in self-defeating behaviour. *Review of General Psychology*, 1, 145–74.

Baumeister, R. F. and Leary, M. R. (1995) The need to belong: desire for interpersonal attachments as a fundamental human motivation. *Psychological Bulletin*, 117.

Beck, A. T. (1967) *Depression: Clinical, Experimental and Theoretical Aspects*. New York: Harper & Row.

Beck, A. T. (1976) *Cognitive Therapy and the Emotional Disorders*. New York: International Universities Press.

Beck, A. T. (1987) Cognitive models of depression. *Journal of Cognitive Psychotherapy: an International Quarterly*, 1, 5–37.

Becker, M. H. and Maiman, L. A. (1975) Sociobehavioral determinants of compliance with health and medical care recommendations. *Medical Care*, 13, 10–24.

Beecher, H. K. (1956) Relationship of significance of a wound to the pain experienced. *Journal of the American Medical Association*, 161, 1609–13.

Beeman, E. A. (1947) The effect of male hormone on aggressive behaviour in mice. *Physiology and Zoology*, 20, 373–405.

Bell, M. A. and Fox, N. A. (1992) The relations between frontal brain electrical activity and cognitive development during infancy. *Child Development*, 63, 1142–63.

Bell, R. Q. (1968) A reinterpretation of the direction effects in socialization. *Psychological Review*, 75, 81–95.

Bellak, L. (1993) *The TAT, CAT and SAT in Clinical Use* (5th edn). Boston: Allyn & Bacon.

Bem, D. J. (1965) An experimental analysis of self-persuasion. *Journal of Experimental Social Psychology*, 1, 199–218.

Bem, D. J. (1972) Self-perception theory. *Advances in Experimental Social Psychology*, 6, 1–62.

Bem, S. L. (1989) Genital knowledge and gender constancy in preschool children. *Child Development*, 60, 649–62.

Benjamin, R. S., Costello, E. J. and Warren, M. (1990) Anxiety disorders in a pediatric sample. *Journal of Anxiety Disorders*, 4, 293–316.

Benjamin, L. T., Jr (1997) The psychology of history and the history of psychology: a historiographical introduction. *A History of Psychology: Original Sources and Contemporary Research*. Boston, MA: McGraw-Hill, 1–21.

Bennett, C., Howe, C. and Trusswell, E. (2002) *Small Group Teaching and Learning in Psychology: a Review of Research in Small-Group Teaching and Suggestions for Good Practice*. Report and evaluation series number 1. University of York: LTSN Psychology.

Bentler, P. M. and Speckart, G. (1979) Models of attitude–behavior relations. *Psychological Review*, 86, 452–64.

Benton, D. and Cook, R. (1991) Vitamin and mineral supplements improve the intelligence scores and concentration of six-year-old children. *Personality and Individual Differences*, 12(11), 1151–8.

Berg, J. H. and McQuinn, R. D. (1986) Attraction and exchange in continuing and continuing dating relationships. *Journal of Personality and Social Psychology*, 942–52.

Berger, P. L. and Luckmann, T. (1967) *The Social Construction of Reality*. Harmondsworth: Penguin.

Berko, J. (1958) The child's learning of English morphology. *Word*, 14, 150–77.

Bernheimer, H., Birkmayer, W., Hornykiewicz, O., Jellinger, K. and Seitelberger, F. (1973) Brain dopamine and the syndromes of Parkinson and Huntington. Clinical, morphological and neurochemical correlations. *Journal Neurological Science*, 20, 415–55.

Berridge, K. C. and Robinson, T. E. (2003) Parsing reward. *Trends in Neuroscience*, 26, 507–14.

Betz, E. L. (1984) Two tests of Maslow's theory of need fulfilment. *Journal of Vocational Behaviour* 24, 204–20.

Bickerton, D. (1990) *Language and Species*. Chicago: University of Chicago Press.

Biederman, J., Rosenbaum, J. F., Chaloff, J. and Kagan, J. (1995) Behavioral inhibition as a risk factor. In J. S. March (ed.) *Anxiety Disorders in Children and Adolescents*. New York: Guildford.

Biederman, I. (1987) A theory of human image understanding. *Psychological Review*, 94, 115–47.

Biernat, M. and Billings, L. S. (2003) Standards, expectations and social comparisons. In A. Tesser and N. Schwartz (eds) *Blackwell Handbook of Social Psychology: Intraindividual Processes*. Oxford: Blackwell, 283–4.

Billig, M. (1997) Rhetorical and discursive analysis: how families talk about the royal family. In N. Hayes (ed.) *Doing Qualitative Analysis in Psychology*. Hove: Psychology Press, 39–54.

Binet, A. and Simon, T. (1905) New methods for diagnosis of the intellectual level of subnormals. *L'Année Psychologique*, 14, 1–90.

Binet, A. and Simon, T. (1916) *The development of intelligence in children (the Binet–Simon scale)* (trans. Elizabeth S. Kite). New York: Arno Press (originally published 1916).

Binet, A. and Simon, T. (1916) *The Development of Intelligence in Children*. Baltimore, Williams & Wilkins (reprinted 1973, New York: Arno Press; 1983, Salem, NH: Ayer Company).

Bishop, D. V. M., North, T. and Donlan, C. (1995) Genetic basis of specific language impairment. *Developmental Medicine & Child Neurology*, 37, 56–71.

Bisiach, E. and Luzzatti, C. (1978) Unilateral neglect of representational space. *Cortex*, 14(1), 129–33.

Blass, T. (1991) Understanding behaviour in the Milgram obedience experiment: the role of personality, situations and their interactions. *Journal of Personality and Social Psychology*, 60, 398–413.

Bliss, T. V. and Lomo, T. (1973) Long-lasting potentiation of synaptic transmission in the dentate area of the anaesthetized rabbit following stimulation of the perforant path. *Journal of Physiology*, 232, 331–56.

Bliss, T. V. P. and Gardner-Medwin, A. R. (1973) Long-lasting potentiation of synaptic transmission in the dendrite area of the unanaesthetized rabbit following stimulation of the perforant path. *Journal of Physiology* (Lond.), 232, 331–56.

Bloch, S. and Crouch, E. (1987) *Therapeutic Factors in Group Psychotherapy*. New York: Oxford University Press.

Bloom, B. S. (1974) Time and learning. *American Psychologist*, 29, 682–8.

Blundell, J. E. and Halford, J. C. G. (1998) Serotonin and appetite regulation: implications for the pharmacological treatment of obesity. *CNS Drugs*, 9, 473–95.

Bohannon, J. N. and Stanowiczz, L. (1988) The issue of negative evidence: adult responses to children's language errors. *Developmental Psychology*, 24, 684–9.

Bohannon, J. N., MacWhinney, B., Snow, C. (1990) No negative evidence revisited: beyond learnability or who has to prove what to whom. *Developmental Psychology*, 26, 221–6.

Bohner, G. and Wänke, M. (2002) *Attitudes and Attitude Change*. Hove: Psychology Press.

Bohner, G., Moskowitz, G. and Chaiken, S. (1995) The interplay of heuristic and systematic processing of social information. *European Review of Social Psychology*, 6, 33–68.

Boldero, J. and Francis, J. (2000) The relation between self-discrepancies and emotion: the moderating roles of self-guide importance, location relevance and social self-domain centrality. *Journal of Personality and Social Psychology*, 78, 38–52.

Bolton, D. and Hill, J. (1996) *Mind, Meaning and Disorder*. Oxford: Oxford University Press.

Bond, R. and Smith, P. B. (1996) Culture and conformity: a meta-analysis of studies using Asch's (1952, 1956) line judgment task. *Psychological Bulletin*, 119, 111–37.

Boneva, B. S. and Frieze, I. H. (2001) Toward a concept of a migrant personality. *Journal of Social Issues*, 57, 477–92.

Borkenau, R., Riemann, R., Angleitner, A. and Spinath, F. M. (2002) Similarity of childhood experiences and personality resemblance in monozygotic and dizygotic twins: a test of the equal environments assumption. *Personality and Individual Differences*, 33(2), 261–9.

Borkovec, T. D. and Costello, E. (1993) Efficacy of applied relaxation and cognitive-behavioral therapy in the treatment of generalized anxiety disorder. *Journal of Consulting & Clinical Psychology*, 61, 611–19.

Borkovec, T. D. and Roemer, L. (1995) Perceived functions of worry among generalized anxiety disorder subjects: distraction from more emotionally distressing topics. *Journal of Behavior Therapy & Experimental Psychiatry*, 26, 25–30.

Borucki, Z. (1985) The need for achievements as a factor modifying the relationships between organisational stress, negative job-related emotions and somatic complaints. *Polish Psychological Bulletin*, 16(3), 155–66.

References

Bouchard, T. J. Jr (1997) IQ similarity in twins reared apart: findings and responses to critics. In R. J. Sternberg and E. L. Grigorenko (eds) *Intelligence, Heredity and Environment*. New York: Cambridge University Press, 126–60.

Bouchard, T. J. Jr., Segal, N. L., Tellegen, A., McGue, M., Keyes, M. and Krueger, R. (2003) Evidence for the construct validity and heritability of the Wilson–Patterson conservatism scale: a reared-apart twins study of social attitudes. *Personality and Individual Differences*, 34(6), 959–69.

Boudewyns, P. A., Fry, T. J. and Nightengale, E. (1986) Token economy programs in VA medical centers: where are they today? *Behavior Therapist*, 6, 126–7.

Bourhis, R. Y. and Gagnon, A. (2003) Social orientations and the minimal group paradigm. In R. Brown and S. L. Gaertner (eds) *Blackwell Handbook of Social Psychology: Intergroup Processes*. Oxford: Blackwell, 89–111.

Bousfield, W. A. (1953) The occurrence of clustering of recall of randomly arranged associates. *Journal of General Psychology*, 49, 229–40.

Bouton, M. E. (1994) Conditioning, remembering and forgetting. *Journal of Experimental Psychology: animal Behaviour Processes*, 20, 219–31.

Bower, G. and Trabasso, T. (1963) Reversals prior to solution in concept identification. *Journal of Experimental Psychology*, 66(4), 409–18.

Bower, G. H., Black, J. B. and Turner, T. S. (1979) Script in memory for text. *Cognitive Psychology*, 11, 177–220.

Bower, G. H., Clark, M. C., Lesgold, A. M. and Winzenz, D. (1969) Hierarchical retrieval schemes in recall of categorized word list. *Journal of Verbal Learning & Verbal Behavior*, 8(3), 323–43.

Bower, T. G. R. and Wishart, J. G. (1972) The effects of motor skill on object permanence. *Cognition*, 1, 165–72.

Bowlby, J. (1988) *A Secure Base*. New York: Basic Books.

Bowmaker, J. (2002) The retina. In D. Roberts (ed.) *Signals and Perception: The Fundamentals of Human Sensation*. Basingstoke: Palgrave Macmillan.

Boysson-Bardies, B. de (1999) How language comes to children: from birth to two years (trans. M. DeBevoise). Cambridge, MA: MIT Press (originally published 1996).

Boysson-Bardies, B. de, Sagart, L. and Durant, C. (1984) Discernable differences in the babbling of infants according to target language. *Journal of Child Language*, 11, 1–15.

Bradley, L. and Bryant P. E. (1983) Categorizing sounds and learning to read a casual connection. *Nature*, 301, 419–21.

Bradshaw, P. W., Ley, P., Kincey, J. A. and Bradshaw, J. (1975) Recall of medical advice: comprehensibility and specificity. *British Journal of Social and Clinical Psychology*, 14, 55.

Brady, E. U. and Kendall, P. C. (1992) Comorbidity of anxiety and depression in children and adolescents. *Psychological Bulletin*, 111 244–55.

Brainerd, C. J. (1983) Working memory systems and cognitive development. In C. J. Brainerd (ed.) *Recent Advances in Cognitive Development Theory*. New York: Springer-Verlag.

Brauer, M., Judd, C. M. and Gliner, M. D. (1995) The effects of repeated attitude expressions on attitude polarizations during group discussions. *Journal of Personality and Social Psychology*, 68, 1014–29.

Breggin, P. (1997) *Brain-Disabling Treatments in Psychiatry*. New York: Springer.

Breisch, S. T., Zemlan, F. P. and Hoebel, B. G. (1976) Hyperphagia and obesity following serotonin depletion by intraventricular p-chlorphenylalanine. *Science*, 192, 382–4.

Bremner, J. G. (1999) Knowledge of the physical world in infancy. In D. Messer and W. S. Millar (eds) *Exploring Developmental Psychology*. London: Arnold.

Breslau, N., Davis, G. C., Andreski, P., Peterson, E. L. and Schultz, L. R. (1997) Sex differences in posttraumatic stress disorder. *Archives of General Psychiatry*, 54, 1044–8.

Brewer, M. B. and Gaertner, S. L. (2003) Toward reduction of prejudice: intergroup contact and social categorization. In R. Brown and S. L. Gaertner (eds) *Blackwell Handbook of Social Psychology: Intergroup Processes*. Oxford: Blackwell, 451–76.

Brewin, C. R. and Holmes, E. A. (2003) Psychological theories of posttraumatic stress disorder. *Clinical Psychology Review*, 23, 339–76.

Brewin, C. R. and Bradley, C. (1989) Patient preferences and randomized clinical trials. *British Medical Journal*, 299, 313–15.

British Psychological Society (2000) *Code of Conduct, Ethical Principles and Guidelines*. Leicester: British Psychological Society.

Britton, D. R., Koob, G. F., Rivier, J. and Vale, W. (1982) Intraventricular cortocotrophin-releasing factor enhances behavioral effects of novelty. *Life Sciences*, 31, 363–7.

Broadbent, D. (1958) *Perception and Communication*. Oxford: Pergamon Press.

Broberger, C., de Lecea, L., Sutcliffe, J. G. and Hökfelt, T. (1998) Hypocretin/orexin – and melanin concentrating hormone-expressing cells form distinct populations in the rodent lateral hypothalamus: relationship to neuropeptide Y and agouti gene-related protein systems. *Journal of Comparative Neurology*, 402, 460–74.

Brocke, B., Tasche. K. G. and Beauducel, A. (1997) Biopsychological foundations of extraversion: differential effort reactivity and state control. *Personality and Individual Differences*, 22(4), 447–58.

Bronfenbrenner, U. and Ceci, S. J. (1994) Nature–nurture reconceptualized in developmental perspective: a bioecological model. *Psychological Review*, 101, 568–86.

Brooks, L. (1978) Non-analytic concept formation and memory for instances. In E. Rosch and B. B. Lloyd (eds) *Cognition and Categorisation*. Hillsdale, NJ: Lawrence Erlbaum Associates.

Brooks, L. R., Norman, G. R. and Allen, S. W. (1991) Role of specific similarity in a medical diagnostic task. *Journal of Experimental Psychology: General*, 120(3), 278–87.

Brosnan, S. F. and de Waal, F. B. M. (2003) Monkeys reject unequal pay. *Nature*, 425, 297–99.

Brown, D., Scheflin, A. W. and Hammond, D. C. (1998) *Memory, Trauma Treatment and the Law*. New York: Norton.

Brown, G. W., Bone, M., Dalison, B. and Wing, J. K. (1966) *Schizophrenia and Social Care*. London: Oxford University Press.

Brown, H. D., Kosslyn, S. M., Breiter, H. C., Baer, L. and Jenkite, M. A. (1994) Can patients with obsessive-compulsive disorder discriminate between percepts and mental images? A signal detection analysis. *Journal of Abnormal Psychology*, 103, 445–54.

Brown R. (1986) *Social Psychology*. New York: Free Press.

Brown, J. D. and Marshall, M. A. (2001) Self-esteem and emotion: some thoughts about feelings. *Personality and Social Psychology Bulletin*, 27, 575–94.

Brown, J. R., Donelan-McCall, N. and Dunn, J. (1996) Why talk about mental states? The significance of children's conversations with friends, siblings and mothers. *Child Development*, 67, 836–49.

Brown, R. (2000a) *Prejudice: its Social Psychology* (2nd edn). Oxford: Blackwell.

Brown, R. (2000b) *Group Processes* (2nd edn). Oxford: Blackwell.

Brown, R. (2001) Intergroup relations. In M. Hewstone and W. Stroebe (eds) *Introduction to Social Psychology* (3rd edn). Oxford: Blackwell, 479–518.

Brown, R. and Gaertner, S. (eds) (2003) *Blackwell Handbook of Social Psychology: Intergroup Processes*. Oxford: Blackwell.

Brown, R. and Hanlon, C. (1970) Derivational complexity and order of acquisition in child speech. In J. R. Hayes (ed.) *Cognition and the Development of Language*. New York: Wiley, 11–53.

Brown, R. and Kulik, J. (1977) Flashbulb Memories. *Cognition*, 5, 73–99.

Brown, R. and McNeill, D. (1966) The 'tip of the tongue' phenomenon. *Journal of Verbal Learning & Verbal Behavior*, 5(4), 325–37.

Brubaker, R. and Wickersham, D. (1990) Encouraging the practice of testicular self examination: a field application of the theory of reasoned action. *Health Psychology*, 9, 154–63.

Bruce, B. and Young, A. (1998) *In the Eye of the Beholder: the Science of Face Perception*. London: Oxford University Press.

Bruce, V. and Young, A. W. (1986) Understanding face recognition. *British Journal of Psychology*, 77, 305–27.

Brune, M. (2001) Evolutionary fallacies of Nazi psychiatry. Implications for current research. *Perspectives in Biological Medicine*, 44, 426–33.

Bruner, J. S. (1957) Neural mechanisms in perception. *Psychological Review*, 64, 340–58.

Bruner, J. S., Goodnow, J. and Austin, G. A. (1956) *A Study of Thinking*. Oxford: Wiley.

Bruner, J. S. (1966) *Towards a Theory of Instruction*. Cambridge, MA: Harvard University Press.

Bruner, J. S. and Tagiuri, R. (1954) Person perception. In G. Lindzey (ed.) *Handbook of Social Psychology*. Reading, MA: Addison-Wesley, 634–54.

Buchanan, A. and Leese, M. (2001) Detention of people with dangerous severe personality disorders: a systematic review. *The Lancet*, 358 1955–9.

Bullock, M. and Lutkenhaus, P. (1990) Who am I? Self-understanding in toddlers. *Merrill-Palmer Quarterly*, 36, 217–38.

Bullock, W. A. and Gilliland, K. (1993) Eysenck's arousal theory of introversion–extraversion: a converging measures investigation. *Journal of Personality and Social Psychology*, 64, 113–23.

Bullogh, V. L. (1981) Age at menarche: a misunderstanding. *Science*, 213, 365–6.

Bunge, M. (1990) What kind of discipline is psychology; autonomous or dependent, humanistic or scientific, biological or sociological? *New Ideas in Psychology*, 8(2), 121–37.

Burger, J. M. (1981) Motivational biases in the attribution of responsibility for an accident: a meta-analysis of the defensive-attribution hypothesis. *Psychological Bulletin*, 90, 496–512.

Burkett, B. G. and Whitley, G. (1998) *Stolen Valor: How the Vietnam Generation Was Robbed of its Heroes and its History*. Dallas, TX: Verity.

Burr, V. (1995) *An Introduction to Social Constructionism*. London: Routledge.

Burt, S. A., McGue, M., Iacono, W., Comings, D. and MacMurray, J. (2002) An examination of the association between DRD4 and DRD2 polymorphisms and personality traits. *Personality and Individual Differences*, 33, 849–59.

Burton, M. J., Rolls, E. T. and Mora, F. (1976) Effects of hunger on the responses of neurons in the lateral hypothalamus to the sight and taste of food. *Experimental Neurology*, 51, 668–77.

Bushnell, I. W. R., Sai, F. and Mullin, J. T. (1989) Neonatal recognition of the mother's face. *British Journal of Developmental Psychology*, 7, 3–15.

Buss, D. M. (1994) *The Evolution of Desire: Strategies of Human Mating*. New York: Basic Books.

Buss, D. M. (1999) Human nature and individual differences. The evolution of human personality. In L. A. Pervin and O. P. John (eds) *Handbook of Personality: Theory and Research*. New York: Guildford Press.

Butler, G. (1994) Treatment of worry in GAD. In G. C. L. Davey and F. Tallis (eds) *Worry: Perspectives on Theory, Assessment and Treatment*. Wiley: Chichester.

Butterworth, G. (1974) The development of the object concept in humans infants. Unpublished DPhil thesis. University of Oxford.

Butterworth, G. (1992) Origins of self-perception in infancy. *Psychological Enquiry*, 3, 103–11.

Butzlaff, R. L. and Hooley, J. M. (1998) Expressed emotion and psychiatric relapse: a meta-analysis. *Archives of General Psychiatry*, 55 547–53.

Buysse, D. J., Barzansky, B., Dinges, D., Hogan, E., Hunt, C. E., Owens, J., Rosekind, M., Rosen, R., Simon, F., Veasey, S. and Wiest, F. (2003) Sleep, fatigue and medical training: setting an agenda for optimal learning and patient care. *Sleep*, 26, 218–25.

Byrne, D. and Glore, G. L. (1970) A reinforcement model of evaluative responses. *Personality: an International Journal*, 1, 103–28.

References

Byrne, W. (1994) The biological evidence challenged. *Scientific American*, May, 26–31.

Cacioppo, J. T., Harkins, S. G. and Petty, R. E. (1981) The nature of attitudes and cognitive responses and their relationships to behavior. In R. Petty, T. Ostrom and T. Brock (eds) *Cognitive Responses in Persuasion*. Hillsdale, NJ: Lawrence Erlbaum, 31–54.

Cahill, L., Haier, R. J., Falln, J., Alkire, M. T., Tang, C., Keator, D., Wu, J. and McGaugh, J. A. (1996) Amygdala activity at encoding correlated with long-term free recall of emotional information. *Proceedings of the National Academy of Sciences of the United States of America*, 93, 8016–21.

Calabresi, P., Centonze, D., Gubellini, P., Marfia, G. A., Pisani, A., Sancesario, G. and Bernardi, G. (2000) Synaptic transmission in the striatum: from plasticity to neurodegeneration. *Progress in Neurobiology*, 61, 231–65.

Campbell, D., Sanderson, R. E. and Laverty, S. G. (1964) Characteristics of a conditioned response in human subjects during extinction trials following a single traumatic conditioning trial. *Journal of Abnormal and Social Psychology*, 68, 627–39.

Campbell, K. H., McWhir, J., Ritchie, W. A. and Wilmut, I. (1996) Sheep cloned by nuclear transfer from a cultured cell line. *Nature*, 380, 64–6.

Campbell, N. A., Reece, J. B. and Mitchell, L. G. (1990) *Biology* (5th edn). Reading, MA: Addison-Wesley.

Cannon, W. B. (1927/1987) The James–Lange theory of emotions: a critical examination and an alternative theory. Special Issue: 100 years of the American Journal of Psychology. *American Journal of Psychology*, 100(3–4), 567–86.

Carboni, E., Acquas, E., Leone, P. and Di Chiara, G. (1989) 5HT3 receptor antagonists block morphine- and nicotine- but not amphetamine-induced reward. *Psychopharmacology*, 97, 1751–88.

Carboni, E., Imperato, A,, Perezzani, L. and Di Chiara, G. (1989) Amphetamine, cocaine, phencyclidine and nomifensine increase extracellular dopamine concentrations preferentially in the nucleus accumbens of freely moving rats. *Neuroscience*, 28, 653–61.

Cardno, A. G., Marshall, E. J., Coid, B., MacDonald, A. M., Ribchester *et al.* (1999) Heritability estimates for psychotic disorders: the Maudsley twin psychosis series. *Archives of General Psychiatry*, 56 162–70.

Carlson, N. R. (2004) *Physiology of Behaviour* (8th edn). Boston, MA: Allyn & Bacon.

Carlsson, A. and Lindqvist, M. (1963) Effects of chlorpromazine and haloperidol on formation of 3-methoxytryamine and normetanehrine in mouse brain. *Acta Pharmacolgia and Toxicologia*, 20, 140–4.

Carlsson, A., Hanson, L. O., Waters, N. and Carlsson, M. L. (1999) A glutamatergic deficiency model of schizophrenia. *British Journal of Psychiatry*, 174, 2–6.

Carpenter, M., Nagell, K. and Tomasello, M. (1998) Social cognition, joint attention and communicative competence from 9 to 15 months of age. *Monographs of the Society for Research in Child Development*, 63(4, Serial No. 255).

Carr G. D., Fibiger, H. C. and Phillips, A. G. (1989) Conditioned place preference as a measure of drug reward. In J. M. Liebman and S. J. Cooper (eds) *The Neuropharmacological Basis of Reward*. Oxford: Oxford University Press.

Carr, S. C. (2003) *Social Psychology: Context, Communication and Culture*. Milton: Wiley.

Carroll, J. B. (1993) *Human Cognitive Abilities: a Survey of Factor-analytic Studies*. New York: Cambridge University Press.

Carter, D. and Murphy, D. (1999) *Molecular Neuroscience*. Harlow: Longman.

Carter, S. J. and Cassaday, H. J. (1998) State dependent retrieval and chlorpheniramine. *Human Psychopharmacology: Clinical and Experimental*, 13, 513–23.

Case, R. (1985) *Intellectual Development from Birth to Adulthood*. New York: Academic Press.

Case, R. (1995) Capacity based explanations of working memory growth. In F. M. Weinert and W. Schneider (eds) *Memory Performance and Competencies: Issues in Growth and Development*. Mahwah, NJ: Erlbaum.

Case, R., Kurland, D. M. and Goldberg, J. (1982) Operational efficiency and growth of short term memory span. *Journal of Experimental Child Psychology*, 33, 386–404.

Casey, J. E., Rourke, B. P. and Del Dotto, J. E. (1996) Learning disabilities in children with attention deficit disorder with and without hyperactivity. *Child Neuropsychology*, 2 83–98.

Cashdan, E. (2003) Hormones and competitive aggression in women. *Aggressive Behaviour*, 29(2), 107–15.

Casper, R. C. and Lyubomirsky, S. (1997) Individual psychopathology relative to reports of unwanted sexual experiences as predictor of a bulimic eating pattern. *International Journal of Eating Disorders*, 21, 229–36.

Casscells, W., Schoenberger, A. and Graboys, T. B. (1978) Interpretation by physicians of clinical laboratory results. *New England Journal of Medicine*, 299, 999–1001.

Caterina, M. J., Schumacher, M. A., Tominaga, M., Rosen, T. A., Levine, J. D. and Julius, D. (1997) The capsaicin receptor: a heat-activated ion channel in the pain pathway. *Nature*, 389, 816–24.

Cattell, R. B. (1946) *Description and Measurement of Personality*. New York, NY: World Company Books.

Cattell, R. B. (1984) The Voyage of a laboratory, 1928–1984. *Multivariate Behavioural Research*, 19, 121–74.

Catts, H., Gillispie, M., Leonard, L., Kail, R. and Miller, C. (2002) The role of speed of processing, rapid naming and phonological awareness in reading achievement. *Journal of Learning Disabilities*, 35(6), 509–24.

Cernoch, J. M. and Porter, R. H. (1985) Recognition of maternal axillary odors by infants. *Child Development*, 56, 1593–8.

Chaiken, S. and Maheswaran, D. (1994) Heuristic processing can bias systematic processing: effects of source credibility, argument ambiguity and task performance on attitude judgement. *Journal of Personality and Social Psychology*, 66, 460–73.

Chambless, D. L. and Ollendick, T. H. (2001) Empirically supported psychological interventions: controversies and evidence. *Annual Review of Psychology*, 52, 685–716.

Chambless, D. L., Sanderson, W. C., Shoham, V., Bennett Johnson, S., Pope, K. S. *et al.* (1996) An update on empirically validated therapies. *Clinical Psychology*, 49, 5–18.

Chandler, C. J. and Stolerman, I. P. (1997) The discriminative stimulus properties of the nicotinic agonist cytisine. *Psychopharmacology*, 129, 257–64.

Chandler, C. J., Wohab, W., Starr, B. S. and Starr, M. S. (1990) Motor depression: a new role for D1 receptors? *Neuroscience*, 38, 437–45.

Chandler, C. J., Garcha, H. S. and Stolerman, I. P. (1995) Morphine and amphetamine, but not nicotine, produce conditioned place preferences in the rat. *Journal of Psychopharmacology* (suppl.), 9, A52.

Chapman, T. F. (1997) The epidemiology of fears and phobias. In G. C. L. Davey (ed.) *Phobias: A Handbook of Theory, Research and Treatment*. Wiley: Chichester.

Chartrand, T. L. and Bargh, J. A. (1996) Automatic activation of impression formation and memorisation goals: nonconscious goal priming reproduces effects of explicit task instructions. *Journal of Personality and Social Psychology*, 71, 464–78.

Chase, W. and Ericsson, K. A. (1982) Skill and working memory. In G. H. Bower (ed.) *The Psychology of Learning and Motivation*, Vol. 16. New York: Academic Press.

Chase, W. G. and Simon, H. A. (1973) The mind's eye in chess. In H. A. Chase (ed.) *Visual Information Processing*. London: Academic Press.

Cheeta, S. K and Chandler, C. J. (1998) The role motor sensitization to MDMA. *Journal of Psychopharmacology*, 12 (Suppl. A), A9.

Chemers, M. M. (2003) Leadership effectiveness: an integrative review. In M. A. Hogg and S. Tindale (eds) *Blackwell Handbook of Social Psychology: Group Processes*. Oxford: Blackwell.

Chen, S. and Chaiken, S. (1999) The heuristic-systematic model in its broader context. In Chaiken, S. and Trope, Y. *Dual Process Theories in Social Psychology*. New York: Guilford, 73–96.

Cheng, D. T., Knight, D. C., Smith, C. N., Stein, E. A. and Helmstetter, F. J. (2003) Functional MRI of human amygdala activity during Pavlovian fear conditioning: stimulus processing versus response expression. *Behavioural Neuroscience*, 117, 3–10.

Cheng, P. W. (1997) From covariation to causation: a causal power theory. *Psychological Review*, 104, 367–405.

Cherlin, A. J., Furstenberg, F. F. Jr, Chase-Lonsdale, P. L., Kiernan, K. E., Robins, P. K., Morrison, D. R. and Teitler, J. O. (1991) Longitudinal studies of effects of divorce on children in Great Britain and the United States. *Science*, 252, 1386–9.

Cherry, E. C. (1953) Some experiments on the recognition of speech, with one and two ears. *Journal of the Acoustical Society of America*, 25, 975–9.

Chi, M. T. H. (1978) Knowledge structures and memory development. In R. S. Siegler (ed.) *Children's Thinking: What develops?* Hillsdale, NJ: Erlbaum, 73–96.

Chi, M. T., Bassok, M., Lewis, M. W. and Reimann, P. *et al.* (1989) Self-explanations: how students study and use examples in learning to solve problems. *Cognitive Science*, 13(2), 145–82.

Child, I. L (1968) Personality in culture. In E. F. Borgatta and W. W. Lambert (eds) *Handbook of Personality Theory and Research*. Chicago: Rand McNally.

Choi, I. and Choi, Y. (2002) Culture and self-concept flexibility. *Personality and Social Psychology Bulletin*, 28, 1508–17.

Chomsky, N. (1957) *Syntactic Structures*. Oxford/The Hague: Mouton.

Chomsky, N. (1959) Review of B. F. Skinner's verbal behaviour. *Language*, 35, 26–129.

Chomsky, N. (1965) *Aspects of the Theory of Syntax*. Oxford: MIT Press.

Chomsky, N. (1986) *Knowledge of Language*. New York: Praeger.

Church, A. T. (2000) Culture and personality: toward an integrated cultural trait psychology. *Journal of Personality*, 68, 651–703.

Church, R. B. and Goldin-Meadow, S. (1986) The mismatch between gesture and speech as an index of transitional knowledge. *Cognition*, 23, 43–71.

Chwalisz, K., Diener, E. and Gallagher, D. (1988) Autonomic arousal feedback and emotional experience. Evidence from the spinal cord injured. *Journal of Personality and Social Psychology*, 54, 820–8.

Cialdini, R. B., Brown, S. L., Lewis, B. P., Luce, C. and Neuberg, S. L. (1997) Reinterpreting the empathy–altruism relationship: when one into one equals oneness. *Journal of Personality and Social Psychology*, 73, 481–94.

Cialdini, R. B., Schaller, M., Houlihan, D., Arps, K., Fultz, J. and Beamen, A. L. (1987) Empathy-based helping: is it selflessly or selfishly motivated? *Journal of Personality and Social Psychology*, 52, 749–58.

Clahsen, H. and Almazan, M. (1998) Syntax and morphology in Williams syndrome. *Cognition*, 68, 167–98.

Clancy, S. A., McNally, R. J., Schacter, D. L., Lenzenweger, M. F. and Pitman, R. K. (2002) Memory distortion in people reporting abduction by aliens. *Journal of Abnormal Psychology*, 111, 455–61.

Clark, D. and White, F. J. (1987) D1 Dopamine receptors – the search for a function: a critical evaluation of the D1/D2 dopamine receptor classification and its functional implications. *Synapse*, 1, 347–88.

Clark, D. M. (1986) A cognitive approach to panic. *Behaviour Research & Therapy*, 24, 461–70.

Clark, J. T., Kalra, P. S., Crowley, W. R. and Kalra, S. P. (1984) Neuropeptide Y and human pancreatic polypeptide stimulates feeding behavior in rats. *Endocrinology*, 115, 427–9.

Clarke, P. B. and Kumar, R. (1984) Effects of nicotine and d-amphetamine on intracranial self-stimulation in a shuttle box test in rats. *Psychopharmacology*, 84, 109–14.

Clemente, C. D., Sterman, M. B. (1963) Cortical synchronization and sleep patterns in acute restrained and chronic behaving cats induced by basal forebrain stimulation.

References

Electroencephalography and Clinical Neurophysiology, Suppl. 24, 172.

Codol, J. P. (1975) On the so-called 'superior conformity of the self' behaviour: twenty experimental investigations. *European Journal of Social Psychology*, 5, 457–501.

Cohen, J. (1988) Statistical power analysis for the behavioural sciences (2nd edn). New York: Academic Press.

Cohen, J. (1990) Things I have learned (so far). *American Psychologist*, 45(12), 1304–12.

Cohen, J. (1992) A power primer. *Psychological Bulletin*, 112(1), 155–9.

Cohen, J. (1994) The earth is round. *American Psychologist*, 49(12), 997–1003.

Cohen, R. L. (1984) Individual differences in event memory: a case for nonstrategic factors. *Memory and Cognition*, 12, 633–41.

Colby, A. and Kohlberg, L. (1987) The measurement of moral judgement (Vols 1 and 2). Cambridge, MA: Cambridge University Press.

Colby, A., Kohlberg, L., Gibbs, J. and Lieberman, M. (1983) A longitudinal study of moral judgement. *Monographs of the Society for Research in Child Development*, 48 (Serial No. 200), 1–124.

Cole, B. J. and Koob, G. F. (1988) Propranolol antagonizes the enhanced conditioned fear produced by cortocotrophin-releasing factor. *Journal of Pharmacology and Experimental Therapeutics*, 247, 901–10.

Coleman, J. C. (1974) *Relationships in Adolescence*. London: Routledge & Kegan Paul.

Coleman, J. C. (1980) *The Nature of Adolescence*. London: Methuen.

Coleman, J. C. and Hendry, L. B. (1999) *The Nature of Adolescence*. London: Routledge.

Collaer, M. L. and Hines, M. (1995) Human behavioural sex differences: a role for gonahal hormones in early development? *Psychological Bulletin*, 118, 55–107.

Collins, A. M. and Loftus, G. R. (1975) A spreading activation theory of semantic processing. *Psychological Review*, 82, 407–28.

Collins, S. C. and Kneale, P. E. (2001) *Study skills for psychology students*. London: Arnold.

Collis, G. M. (1977) Visual co-orientation and maternal speech. In H. R. Schaffer (ed.) *Studies in Mother–Infant Interactions*. London: Academic Press.

Coltheart, M. (1983) Iconic memory. *Philosophical Transactions of the Royal Society, London: B*, 302, 283–94.

Comings, D. E., Gade-Andavolu, R., Gonzalez, N., Wu, S., Muhleman, D., Chen, C., Koh, P., Farwell, K., Blake, H., Dietz, G., MacMurray, J. P., Lesieur, H. R., Rugle, L. J. and Rosenthal, R. J. (2001) The additive effect of neurotransmitter genes in pathological gambling. *Clinical Genetics*, 60, 107–16.

Compton, R. J., Fisher, L. R., Koenig, L. M., McKeown, R. and Munoz, K. (2003) Relationship between coping styles and perceptual asymmetry. *Journal of Personality and Social Psychology*, 84(5), 1069–78.

Connell, H. P. (1958) Amphetamine psychosis. *Maudsley Monograph No. 5*. London: Chapman & Hall.

Conner, M. and Armitage, C. J. (1998) The theory of planned behavior: a review and avenues for future research. *Journal of Applied Social Psychology*, 28, 1429–63.

Conner, M. and McMillan, B. (1999) Interaction effects in the theory of planned behaviour: studying cannabis use. *British Journal of Social Psychology*, 38, 195–222.

Conner, M. and Norman, P. (1996) *Predicting Health Behaviour*. Buckingham: Open University Press.

Conrad, R. and Hull, A. J. (1964) Information, acoustic confusion and memory span. *British Journal of Psychology*, 55, 429–32.

Conti-Ramsden, G., Crutchley, A. and Botting, N. (1997) The extent to which psychometric tests differentiate subgroups of children with SLI. *Journal of Speech, Language and Hearing Research*, 40, 765–77.

Cooley, C. H. (1902) *Human Nature and the Social Order*. New York: Scribner's.

Cooper, J., Kelly, K. A. and Weaver, K. (2003) Attitudes, norms and social groups. In M. A. Hogg and S. Tindale (eds) *Blackwell Handbook of Social Psychology: Group Processes*. Oxford: Blackwell, 259–82.

Cooper, R. P. and Aslin, R. N. (1990) Preferences for infant-directed speech in the first month after birth. *Child Development*, 61, 1584–95.

Corbett, D. and Wise, R. A. (1980) Intracranial self-stimulation in relation to ascending dopamine systems of the midbrain: a moveable electrode mapping study. *Brain Research*, 185, 1–15.

Corrigal, W. A. and Coen, K. M. (1989) Nicotine maintains robust self-administration in rats on a limited-access schedule. *Psychopharmacology*, 99, 473–8.

Corrigal, W. A., Franklin, K. B., Coen, K. M. and Clarke, P. B. (1992) The mesolimbic dopaminergic system is implicated in the reinforcing effects of nicotine. *Psychopharmacology*, 107, 285–9.

Corrigan, P. W. (1995) Use of a token economy with seriously mentally ill patients: Criticisms and misconceptions. *Psychiatric Services*, 46, 1258–63.

Corte, C. M. (2003) The impoverished self and alcoholism: content and structure of self-cognitions in alcohol dependence and recovery. Dissertation abstract international: Section B the Sciences and Engineering, Vol. 63(7-B), 3227.

Cosmides, L. and Tooby, J. (1996) Are humans good intuitive statisticians after all? Rethinking some conclusions from the literature on judgment under uncertainty. *Cognition*, 58(1), 1–73.

Costa, P. T. and McCrae, R. R. (1982) Hypochondriasis, neuroticism and ageing: when are somatic complaints unfounded? *American Psychologist*, 40, 19–28.

Cottrell, N. B. (1972) Social facilitation. In C. McClintock (ed.) *Experimental Social Psychology*. New York: Holt, Rinehart & Winston, 185–236.

Cottrell, N. B., Wack, D. L., Sekerak, G. J. and Rittle, R. H. (1968) Social facilitation of dominant responses by the presence of others. *Journal of Personality and Social Psychology*, 9, 245–50.

Court, J. H. and Raven, J. (1995) *Manual for the Raven's Progressive Matrices and Vocabulary Scales.* Oxford: Oxford Psychologists Press.

Cousins, M. (1989) *Head First: the Biology of Hope.* New York: Dutton.

Craik, F. I. M. and Lockhart, R. S. (1972) Levels of processing: a framework for memory research. *Journal of Verbal Learning and Verbal Behaviour,* 11, 671–84.

Crassini, B. and Broerse, J. (1980) Auditory–visual integration in neonates: a signal detection analysis. *Journal of Experimental Child Psychology,* 29(1), 144–55.

Crick, J. D. and Watson, F. H. C. (1953) Molecular structure of nucleic acids: a structure for deoxyribose nucleic acid. *Nature,* 171, 737.

Crick, N. R. and Dodge, K. A. (1994) A review and reformulation of social information-processing mechanisms in children's social adjustment. *Psychological Bulletin,* 115, 74–101.

Crick, N. R. and Grotpeter, J. K. (1995) Relational aggression, gender and social-psychological adjustment. *Child Development,* 67, 993–1002.

Crombez, G., Eccleston, C., Baeyens, F. and Eelen, P. (1998) When somatic information threatens, catastrophic thinking enhances attentional interference. *Pain,* 75, 187–98.

Cronbach, L. J. (1990) *Essentials of Psychological Testing.* New York: Harper & Row.

Crook, C. K. (1999) The use and significance of electronic media during development. In D. J. Messer and S. Millar (eds) *Exploring Developmental Psychology.* London: Arnold.

Crow, T. (1980) Molecular pathology of schizophrenia: more than one disease process? *British Journal of Medicine,* 280, 66–8.

Crowther, J. H., Sanftner, J., Bonifazi, D. Z. and Shepherd, K. L. (2001) The role of daily hassles in binge eating. *International Journal of Eating Disorders,* 29, 449–54.

Cryan, J. F., Bruijnzeel, A. W., Skjei, K. L. and Markou, A. (2003) Bupropion enhances brain reward function and reverses the affective and somatic aspects of nicotine withdrawal in the rat. *Psychopharmacology,* 168, 347–58.

Cunningham, J. D. and Kelley, H. H. (1975) Causal attributions for interpersonal events of varying magnitude. *Journal of Personality,* 43, 74–93.

Curran, H. V. and Travill, R. A. (1997) Mood and cognitive effects of +/-3, 4-methylenedioxymethamphetamine (MDMA, 'ecstasy'), week-end 'high' followed by mid-week low. *Addiction,* 92, 821–31.

Cutright, P. and Fernquist, R. M. (2000) Effects of societal integration, period, region and culture of suicide on male age-specific suicide rates: 20 developed countries, 1955–1989. *Social Science Research,* 29(1), 148–72, March.

D'Amico, A. and Cardaci, M. (2003) Relations among perceived self-efficacy, self-esteem and school achievement. *Psychological Reports,* 92(3), 745–54.

Dabbs, J. M. and Hargrove, M. F. (1997) Age, testosterone and behavior among female prison inmates. *Psychosomatic Medicine,* Vol. 59, Issue 5, 477–80.

Dallos, R. and Draper, R. (2002) *Introduction to Family Therapy: Systemic Theory and Practice.* Buckingham: Open University Press.

Daly, M. and Wilson, M. (1990) Is parent offspring conflict sex-linked? Freudian and Darwinian models. *Journal of Personality,* 58, 163–89.

Damasio, A. R., Grabowski, T. J., Bechara, A., Damasio, H., Ponto, L. L., Parvizi, J. and Hichwa, R. D. (2000) Subcortical and cortical brain activity during the feeling of self-generated emotions. *Nature Neuroscience,* 3, 1049–56.

Damon, W. (1977) *The Social World of the Child.* San Francisco: Jossey-Bass.

Darby, K. M., Wacker, D., Sasso, G., Steege, M., Northrup, J., Cigrand, K. and Asmus, J. (1992) Brief functional assessment techniques to evaluate aberrant behavior in an outpatient setting: a summary of 79 cases. *Journal of Applied Behavior Analysis,* 25, 713–21.

Darwin, C. (1859) *The Origin of Species* (ed. J. W. Burrows, 1982). Penguin English Library.

Darwin, C. (1859/1959) *The Origin of Species.* New York: Mentor.

Davey, A. (1983) *Learning to be Prejudiced; Growing up in Multi-ethnic Britain.* London: Edward Arnold.

Davey, G. C. L. (1994a) Pathological worrying as exacerbated problem solving. In G. C. L. Davey and F. Tallis (eds) *Worry: Perspectives on Theory, Assessment and Treatment.* Chichester: John Wiley.

Davey, G. C. L. (1994b) Self-reported fears to common indigenous animals in an adult UK population: the role of disgust sensitivity. *British Journal of Psychology,* 85, 541–54.

Davey, G. C. L. (1998) Learning theory. In C. E. Walker (ed.) *Comprehensive Clinical Psychology: Foundations of Clinical Psychology,* Vol. 1. Elsevier.

Davey, G. C. L. (2002) Smoking them out. *The Psychologist,* 15, 499.

Davey, G. C. L. (2003) Doing clinical psychology research: what is interesting isn't always useful. *The Psychologist,* 16, 412–16.

Davey, G. C. L. and Levy, S. (1998) Catastrophic worrying: personal inadequacy and a perseverative iterative style as features of the catastrophising process. *Journal of Abnormal Psychology,* 107, 576–86.

Davey, G. C. L. and McDonald, A. S. (2000) Cognitive neutralizing strategies and their use across differing stressor types. *Anxiety, Stress & Coping,* 13, 115–41.

Davey, G. C. L., Menzies, R. and Gallardo, B. (1997) Height phobia and biases in the interpretation of bodily sensations: some links between acrophobia and agoraphobia. *Behaviour Research & Therapy,* 35, 997–1001.

Davey, G. C. L., Tallis, F. and Capuzzo, N. (1996) Beliefs about the consequences of worrying. *Cognitive Therapy & Research,* 20, 499–518.

Davidson, A. R. and Jaccard, J. J. (1979) Variables that moderate the attitude-behavior relation: results of a longitudinal survey. *Journal of Personality and Social Psychology,* 37, 1364–76.

Davis, J. M. (1978) Dopamine theory of schizophrenia: a two-factor theory. In L. C.Wynne, R. L. Cromwell and S. Mattysse (eds) *The Nature of Schizophrenia.* New York: Wiley.

References

Davis, M. (1992) The role of the amygdala in fear-potentiated startle: implications for animal models of anxiety. *Trends in Pharmacological Sciences*, 13, 35–41.

Davis, E. A. (1937) The development of linguistic skill in twins, singletons and sibs and only children from 5–10. *University of Minnesota Institute of Child Welfare, Monograph*, 14.

Davis, S. F. and Palladino, J. J. (2000) *Psychology* (3rd edn). Upper Saddle River, NJ: Prentice-Hall, Inc.

Dawes, R. M. (1988) *Rational Choice in an Uncertain World*. San Diego, CA: Harcourt Brace Jovanovich.

Dawis, R. V. (1992) The individual differences in tradition in counselling psychology, *Journal of Counseling Psychology*, 39, 7–19.

De Blas, A. L., Park, D. and Friedrich, P. (1987) Endogenous benzodiazepine-like molecules in the human, rat and bovine brains studied with a monoclonal antibody to benzodiazepines. *Brain Research*, 413, 275–84.

De Casper, A. J. and Spence, M. J. (1986) Prenatal maternal speech influences newborns' perceptions of speech sounds. *Infant Behaviour and Development*, 9, 133–50.

De Renzi, E. (1986) Current issues in prosopagnosia. In H. D. Ellis, M. A. Jeeves, F. Newcombe and A. W. Young (eds) *Aspects of Face Processing*. Dordrecht: Martinus Nijhoff.

De Renzi, E., Liotti, M. and Michelli, P. (1987) Semantic amnesia with preservation of autobiographic memory: a case report. *Cortex*, 23(4), 575–97.

De Valck, E., De Groot, E. and Cluydts, R. (2003) Effects of slow-release caffeine and a nap on driving simulator performance after partial sleep deprivation. *Perception and Motor Skills*, 96, 67–78.

De Valois, K. K., De Valois, R. L. and Yund, E. W. (1979) Responses of striate cortex cells to grating and checkerboard patterns. *Journal of Physiology*, 291, 483–505.

De Valois, R. L. and De Valois, K. K. (1988) *Spatial Vision*. New York: Oxford University Press.

De Wolff, M. S. and van IJzendoorn, M. H. (1997) Sensitivity and attachment: a meta-analysis on parental antecedents of infant attachment. *Child Development*, 68, 571–92.

DeGroot, A. D. and Gobet, F. (1996) *Perception and Memory in Chess: Heuristics of the Professional Eye*. Assen: Van Gorcum.

Dejoy, D. M. and Klippel, J. A. (1984) Attributing responsibility for alcohol-related near-miss accidents. *Journal of Safety Research*, 15, 107–15.

Demetras, M. J., Post, K. N., Snow, C. E. (1986) Feedback to first language learners: the role of repetitions and clarification questions. *Journal of Child Language*, 13, 275–92.

Dennis, W. (1973) *Children of the Creche*. New York: Appleton Century Crofts.

DePaulo, B. (1994) Spotting lies: can humans learn to do better? *Current Directions in Psychological Science*, 3, 83–6.

DePaulo, B. and Friedman, H. S. (1998) Non-verbal communication. In D. T. Gilbert, S. T. Fiske and G. Lindzey (eds) *The Handbook of Social Psychology* (4th edn). New York: McGraw-Hill, 3–40.

Derrington, A. (2002) From retina to cortex. In D. Roberts (ed.) *Signals and Perception: The Fundamentals of Human Sensation*. Basingstoke: Palgrave Macmillan.

Desjarlais, R., Eisenberg, L., Good, B. and Kleinman, A. (1996) *World Mental Health: Problems and Priorities in the Low-Income Countries*. Oxford: Oxford University Press.

Desrosiers, A. and Fleurose, S. S. (2002) Treating Haitian patients: key cultural aspects. *American Journal of Psychotherapy*, 56, 508–21.

DETR (Department for the Environment, Transport and the Regions) (2000) *Road Accidents Great Britain 1999*. London: Stationery Office.

Deutsch, J. A. and Deutsch, D. (1963) Attention: some theoretical considerations. *Psychological Review*, 70(1), 51–61.

Deutsch, M. and Gerard, H. B. (1955) A study of normative and informational social influences upon individual judgements. *Journal of Abnormal and Social Psychology*, 51, 629–36.

Diamond, A. (1988) Abilities and neural mechanisms underlying AS performance. *Child Development*, 59, 523–7.

Dickinson, A. (1989) Expectancy theory in animal conditioning. In S. B. Klein and R. R. Mowrer (eds) *Contemporary Learning Theories: Pavlovian Conditioning and the States of Traditional Learning Theory*. NJ: Erlbaum, 279–308.

Dion, K., Berscheid, E. and Walster, E. (1972) What is beautiful is good. *Journal of Personality and Social Psychology*, 285–90.

Dion, K. K. and Dion, K. L. (1996) Towards understanding love. *Personal Relationships*, 3, 1–3.

Dobbing, J. (1981) Nutritional growth restriction and the nervous system. In A. N. Davison and R. H. S. Thompson (eds) *The Molecular Basis of Neuropathology*. London: Edward Arnold, 921–3.

Dockrell, J. Messer, D. and George, R. (2002) Patterns of naming objects and actions in children with word finding difficulties. *Language and Cognitive Processes*, 16, 261–86.

Dockrell. J., Messer, D., George, R. and Wilson, G. (1998) Children with word-finding difficulties – prevalence, presentation and naming problems. *International Journal of Language and Communication Disorders*, 33, 445–54.

Dogali, M., Fazzini, E., Kolodny, E., Eidelberg, D., Sterio, D., Devinsky, O. and Beric, A. (1995) Sterotactic ventral pallidotomy for Parkinson's disease. *Annals of Neurology*, 45, 753–61.

Doise, W. and Mugny, G. (1984) *The Social Development of the Intellect*. Oxford: Pergamon.

Donny, E. C., Caggiula, A. R., Knopf, S. and Brown, C. (1995) Nicotine self-administration in rats. *Psychopharmacology*, 122, 390–4.

Donny, E. C., Chaudhri, N., Caggiula, A. R,, Evans-Martin, F. F., Booth, S., Gharib, M. A., Clements, L. A. and Sved, A. F. (2003) Operant responding for a visual reinforcer in rats enhanced by noncontingent nicotine: implications for nicotine self-administration and reinforcement. *Psychopharmacology*, 169, 68–76.

Dovidio, J. F. and Penner, L. A. (2003) Helping and altruism. In G. J.

O. Fletcher and M. S. Clark (eds) *Blackwell Handbook of Social Psychology: Interpersonal Processes*. Oxford: Blackwell, 162–95.

Downer, J. L. de C. (1961) Changes in visual agnostic functions and emotional behaviour following unilateral temporal lobe damage in the 'split brain' monkey. *Nature*, 191, 50–2.

Downing, J. (1986) The psychological and physiological effects of MDMA on normal volunteers. *Journal of Psychoactive Drugs*, 18, 335–40.

Dowson, M. and McInerney, D. M. (2001) Psychological parameters of students' social and work avoidance goals: a qualitative investigation. Journal of Educational Psychology, 93(1), 35–42.

Drury, J. and Reicher, S. (2000) Collective action and psychological change: the emergence of new social identities. *British Journal of Social Psychology*, 39, 579–604.

Dryden, S., Wang, Q., Frankish, H. M., Pickavance, L. and Wilimas, G. (1995) The serotonin (5-HT) antagonist methysergide increases neuropeptide-Y (NPY) synthesis and secretion in the hypothalamus of the rat. *Brain Research*, 699, 12–18.

Dube, M. G., Kalra, S. P. and Kalra, P. S. (1999) Food intake elicited by central administration of orexins/hypocretins: Identification of hypothalamic sites of action. *Brain Research*, 842, 473–7.

Duncker, K. (1926) A qualitative (experimental and theoretical) study of productive thinking (solving of comprehensible problems). *Pedagogical Seminary*, 33, 642–708.

Duncker, K. (1945) On problem-solving. *Psychological Monographs*, 270.

Dunn, J. (1999) Mind reading and social relationships. In M. Bennett (ed.) *Developmental Psychology. Achievements and Prospects*. Philadelphia: Psychology Press.

Dunnett, S. B., Lane, D. M. and Winn, P. (1985) Ibotenic acid lesions of the lateral hypothalamus: comparison with 6-hydroxydopamine-induced sensorimotor deficits. *Neuroscience*, 14, 509-18.

Dunning, D. and Hayes, A. (1996) Evidence for egocentric comparison in social judgement. *Journal of Personality and Social Psychology*, 1(2), 213–29.

Eagly, A. H. and Chaiken, S. (1993) *The Psychology of Attitudes*. New York: Harcourt Brace.

Eagly, A. H. and Chaiken, S. (1998) Attitude structure and function. In D. Gilbert, S. Fiske and G. Lindzey (eds) *Handbook of Social Psychology* (4th edn). New York: McGraw-Hill, 269–322.

Eastridge, B. J., Hamilton, E. C., O'Keefe, G. E., Rege, R. V., Valentine, R. J., Jones, D. J., Tesfay, S. and Thal, E. R. (2003) Effect of sleep deprivation on the performance of simulated laparoscopic surgical skill. *American Journal of Surgery*, 186, 169–74.

Ebbinghaus, H. (1885) Uber das Gedachtnis. In H. Ruyer and C. E. Bussenius (eds) *Memory*. New York: Teachers College, Columbia University.

Ebbinghaus, H. (1908) *Psychology: an Elementary Textbook*. Boston, DC: Heath.

Ebstein, R. P., Novick, O., Umansky, R., Priel, B., Osher, Y., Blaine, D., Bennett, E. R., Nemanov, L., Katz, M. and Belmaker, R. H,

(1996) Dopamine D4 receptor (D4DR) exon III polymorphism associated with the human personality trait of Novelty Seeking. *Nature Genetics*, 12, 78–80.

Eccleston, C., Morley, S., Williams, A., Yorke, L. and Mastroyannopoulou, K. (2002) Systematic review of randomized controlled trials of psychological therapy for chronic pain in children and adolescents, with a subset meta-analysis of pain relief. *Pain*, 99, 157–65.

Edelmann R. J. (1992) *Anxiety: Theory, Research and Intervention in Clinical and Health Psychology*. Chichester: Wiley.

Edwards, A. L. (1957) *Techniques in Attitude Scale Construction*. New York: Appleton Century Crofts.

Ehlers, A. (1993) Interoception and panic disorder. *Advances in Behaviour Research & Therapy*, 15, 3–21.

Ehlers, A. and Clark, D. M. (2000) A cognitive model of posttraumatic stress disorder. *Behaviour Research & Therapy*, 38, 319–45.

Ehri, L. C. (1992) Reconceptualising the development of sight word reading and its relationship to recoding. In P. B. Gough, L. C. Ehri and R. Treiman (eds) *Reading Acquisition*. Hillsdale, NJ: Lawrence Erlbaum Associates, 107–43.

Ehringer, H. and Hornykiewicz, O. (1960) Verteilung von noradrenaline und dopamine (3-hydroxytyramin) in gehir des menschen und ihr verthalten bei erkrankungen de extrapyramidalen systems. *Kline Wochenschr*, 38, 1236–9.

Eimas, P. D., Siqueland, E. R., Jusczyk, P. and Vigorito, J. (1971) Speech perception in infants. *Science*, 171, 303–6.

Eisenberg, N., Fabes, R. A., Karbon, M., Murphy, B. C., Wosinski, M., Polazzi, L., Carlo, G. and Juhnke, C. (1996) The relationship of children's dispositional pro-social behaviour to emotionality, regulation and social functioning. *Child Development*, 67, 974–92.

Eisenberg, N., Guthrie, I. K. and Cumberland, A. (2002) Prosocial development in early adulthood: a longitudinal study. *Journal of Personality & Social Psychology*, 82(6), 993–1006.

Eiser, R. and van der Pligt, J. (1988) *Attitudes and Decisions*. Florence, KY: Taylor & Francis.

Ekman, P. (1999) Basic emotions. In T. Dalgleish and M. Power (eds) *Handbook of Cognition and Emotion*. Sussex: John Wiley & Sons, Ltd.

Elias, C. F., Saper, C. B., Maratos-Flier, E., Tritos, N. A., Lee, C., Kelly, J., Tatro, J. B., Hoffman, G. E., Ollmann, M. M., Barsh, G. S., Sakurai, T., Yanagisawa, M. and Elmquist, J. K. (1998) Chemically defined projections linking the mediobasal hypothalamus and the lateral hypothalamic area. *Journal of Comparative Neurology*, 402, 442–59.

Elicker, J., Englund, M. and Sroufe, L. A. (1992) Predicting peer competence and peer relationships in childhood from early parent-child relationships. In R. D. Parke and G. W. Ladd (eds) *Family–Peer Relationships: Modes of Linkage*. Hillsdale, NJ: Erlbaum, 77–106.

Ellenberger, H. F. (1970) *The Discovery of the Unconscious*. London: Allen Lane; New York: Basic Books.

Ellenbroek, B. A. and Cools, A. R. (1990) Animal models of with

References

construct validity for schizophrenia. *Behavioural Pharmacology*, 1, 469–90.

Ellinwood, E. H. and Escalante, D. O. (1977) Chronic stimulant intoxication models of psychoses. In I. Hanin and E. Usdin (eds) A*nimal Models in Psychiatry and Neurology*. Oxford: Pergamon Press.

Ellis, A. W. and Young, A. W. (1995) *A Textbook with Readings*. Hove: Psychology Press.

Emler, N. and Reicher, S. (1995) *Adolescence and Delinquency: the Collective Management of Reputation*. Oxford: Blackwell.

Epstein, A. N., Fitzsimons, J. T. and Rolls, B. J. (1970) Drinking induced by injection of angiotensin into the brain of the rat. *Journal of Physiology* (*London*), 210, 457–74.

Epstein, R., Kirshnit, C. E., Lanza, R. P. and Rubin, L. C. (1984) 'Insight' in the pigeon: antecedents and determinants of an intelligent performance. *Nature*, 308, 61–2.

Erickson, K. and Schulkin, J. (2003) Facial expressions of emotion: a cognitive neuroscience perspective. *Brain & Cognition*, 52, 52–60.

Ericsson, K. A. and Polson, P. G. (1988) An experimental analysis of the mechanisms of a memory skill. *Journal of Experimental Psychology: Learning, Memory and Cognition*, 14, 305–16.

Erikson, E. H. (1950) *Childhood and Society*. New York: WW Norton.

Erikson, E. H. (1959) Identity and the life cycle. *Psychological Issues* (Monograph 1). New York: International Universities Press.

Erikson, E. H. (1968) *Identity: Youth and Crisis*. New York: WW Norton.

Erikson, E. H. (ed.) (1978) *Adulthood*. New York: WW Norton.

Eslea, M. and Smith, P. K. (1998) The long-term effectiveness of anti-bullying work in primary schools. *Educational Research*, 40, 1–16.

Etaugh, C. A. and Bridges, J. S. (2004) *The Psychology of Women: a lifespan Perspective* (2nd edn). Boston, MA: Allyn & Bacon.

Evans, J. St B. T. (1995) Relevance and reasoning. In S. E. Newstead and J. St B. T. Evans (eds) *Perspectives on Thinking and Reasoning: Essays in Honour of Peter Wason*. Hove: Psychology Press.

Everill, J. T. and Waller, G. (1995) Reported sexual abuse and eating psychopathology: a review of the evidence for a causal link. *International Journal of Eating Disorders*, 18, 1–11.

Everson, C. A. (1993) Sustained sleep deprivation impairs host defence. *American Journal of Physiology*, 265, R1148–54.

Eysenck, H. J. (1961) The effects of psychotherapy. In H. J. Eysenck (ed.) *Handbook of Abnormal Psychology*. New York: Basic Books.

Eysenck, H. J. (1957) *Sense and Nonsense in Psychology*. Harmondsworth: Pelican.

Eysenck, H. J. (1985) *Decline and Fall of the Freudian Empire*. Harmondsworth: Penguin.

Eysenck, H. J. (1986) What is intelligence? In R. J. Sternberg and D. K. Detterman (eds) *What is Intelligence? Contemporary Viewpoints on its Nature and Definition*. Norwood, NJ: Ablex.

Eysenck, H. J. (1991) Dimensions of personality: 16, 5 or 3? Criteria for a taxonomic paradigm. *Personality and Individual Differences*, 12, 773–90.

Eysenck, H. J. (2000) *Cognitive Psychology A Student's Handbook* (4th edn). Hove: Psychology Press.

Eysenck, H. J. and Eysenck, S. B. G. (1964) *EPI Manual*. London: University of London Press.

Eysenck, M. W. and Keane, M. T. (2000) *Cognitive Psychology. A Student's Handbook* (4th edn). Hove: Psychology Press.

Fagot, B. I. (1978) The influence of sex of child on parental reactions to toddler children. *Child Development*, 49, 459–65.

Fagot, B. I. (1985) Stages in thinking about early sex role development. *Developmental Review*, 5, 83–98.

Fairburn, C. G., Cooper, Z., Doll, H. A., Norman, P. and O'Connor, M. (2000) The natural course of bulimia nervosa and binge eating disorder in young women. *Archives of General Psychiatry*, 57, 659–65.

Fairburn, C. G., Shafran, R. and Cooper, Z. (1999) Invited essay: a cognitive behavioural theory of anorexia nervosa. *Behaviour Research & Therapy*, 37, 1–13.

Fairburn, C. G., Welch, S. L., Doll, H. A., Davies, B. A. and O'Connor, M. E. (1997) Risk factors for bulimia nervosa – a community-based case-control study. *Archives of General Psychiatry*, 54, 509–17.

Falzone, T. L., Gelman, D. M., Young, J. I., Grandy, D. K., Low, M. J. and Rubinstein, M. (2002) Absence of dopamine D4 receptors results in enhanced reactivity to unconditioned, but not conditioned, fear. *European Journal of Neuroscience*, 15, 158–64.

Fantegrossi, W. E., Ullrich, T., Rice, K. C., Woods, J. H. and Winger, G. (2002) 3, 4-Methylenedioxymethamphetamine (MDMA, 'ecstasy') and its stereoisomers as reinforcers in rhesus monkeys: serotonergic involvement. *Psychopharmacology*, 161, 356–64.

Farber, E. W., Herbert, S. E. and Reviere, S. L. (1996) Childhood abuse and suicidality in obstetric patients in a hospital-based urban prenatal clinic. *General Hospital Psychiatry*, 18, 56–60.

Farrar, M. J. (1992) Negative evidence and grammatical morpheme acquisition. *Developmental Psychology*, 28, 90–8.

Fazio, R. H. (1990) Multiple processes by which attitudes guide behavior: the MODE model as an integrative framework. *Advances in Experimental Social Psychology*, 23, 75–109.

Fazio, R. H., Sanbonmatsu, D. M., Powell, M. C. and Kardes, F. R. (1986) On the automatic activation of attitudes. *Journal of Personality and Social Psychology*, 50, 229–38.

Fazio, R. H., Zanna, M. P. and Cooper, J. (1977) Dissonance and self-perception: a integrative view of each theory's proper domain of application. *Journal of Experimental Social Psychology*, 15, 70–6.

Feingold, B. F. (1973) *Introduction to Clinical Allergy*. Springfield, IL: Charles C. Thomas.

Feingold, B. F. (1975) *Why your Child is Hyperactive*. New York: Random House.

Feldman, M. P. and MacCulloch, M. J. (1965) The application of anticipatory avoidance learning to the treatment of homosexuality I: theory, technique and preliminary results. *Behaviour Research & Therapy*, 2, 165–83.

Feldman, R. S., Meyer, J. S. and Quenzer, L. F. (1997) *Principles of Neuropsychopharmacology*. Massachusetts: Sinaur Associates, Inc.

Fenson, L., Dale, P. S., Reznick, J. S., Bates, E., Thal, D. J. and Pethick, S. J. (1994) Variability in early communicative development. *Monographs of the Society for Research in Child Development*, 59 (Serial No. 242).

Ferguson, N. B. and Keesey, R. E. (1975) Effect of a quinine-adulterated diet upon body weight maintenance in male rats with ventromedial hypothalamic lesions. *Journal of Comparative and Physiological Psychology*, 89, 478–88.

Ferguson, C. A. (1964) Baby talk in six languages. *American Anthropologist*, 66, 103–13.

Ferster, C. B. (1985) Classification of behavioral pathology. In L. Krasner and L. P. Ullman (eds) *Research in Behavior Modification*. New York: Holt, Rinehart & Winston.

Festinger, L. (1950) Informal social communication. *Psychological Review*, 57, 271–82.

Festinger, L. (1957) *A Theory of Cognitive Dissonance*. Stanford, CA: Stanford University Press.

Festinger, L. and Carlsmith, J. M. (1959) Cognitive consequences of forced compliance. *Journal of Abnormal and Social Psychology*, 58, 203–10.

Fibiger, H. C., Jakubovic, A. and Phillips, A. G. (1987) The role of dopamine in intracranial self-stimulation of the ventral tegmental area. *Journal of Neuroscience*, 7, 3888–96.

Fiedler, F. E. (1965) A contingency model of leadership effectiveness. In L. Berkowitz (ed.) *Advances in Experimental Social Psychology*. New York: Academic Press, 149–90.

Fiedler, K. and Bless, H. (2001) Social cognition. In M. Hewstone and W. Stroebe (eds) *Introduction to Social Psychology* (3rd edn). Oxford: Blackwell, 115–50.

Field, A. P., Argyris, N. G., Knowles, K. A. (2001) Who's afraid of the big bad wolf: a prospective paradigm to test Rachman's indirect pathways in children. *Behaviour Research & Therapy*, 39(11), 1259–76, November.

Field, A. P. (2000) *Discovering Statistics using SPSS for Windows: Advanced Techniques for the Beginner*. London: Sage.

Field, A. P. (2001) Meta-analysis of correlation coefficients: a Monte Carlo comparison of fixed- and random-effects methods. *Psychological Methods*, 6, 161–80.

Field, A. P. (2003) *Clinical Psychology*. Exeter: Crucial.

Field, A. P. (2004) *Discovering Statistics using SPSS for Windows: Advanced Techniques for the Beginner* (2nd edn). London: Sage.

Field, A. P. and Hole, G. (2003) *How to Design and Report Experiments*. London: Sage.

Fifer, W. P. and Moon, C. (1989), Psychobiology of newborn auditory preferences. *Seminars in Perinatology*, 13, 430–3.

Filipeck, P. A., Semrud-Clikeman, M., Steingard, R. J., Renshaw, P. F., Kennedy, D. N. and Biederman, J. (1997) Volumetric MRI analysis comparing subjects having attention-deficit hyperactivity disorder with normal controls. *Neurology*, 48, 589–601.

Fincham, F. and Hewstone, M. (2001) Attribution theory and research: from basic to applied. In M. Hewstone and W. Stroebe (eds) *Introduction to Social Psychology* (3rd edn). Oxford: Blackwell, 197–238.

Fine, I., Wade, A. R., Brewer, A. A., May, M. G., Goodman, D. F., Boynton, G. M., Wandell, B. A. and MacLeod, D. I. A. (2003) Long-term deprivation affects visual perception and cortex. *Nature Neuroscience*, 6, 915–16.

Fiorillo, C. D., Tobler, P. H. and Schultz, W. (2003) Discrete coding of reward probability and uncertainty by dopamine neurons. *Science*, 299, 1898–1902.

Fischer, K. W., Shaver, P. R. and Carnochan, P. (1990) How emotions develop and how they organise development. *Cognition and Emotion*, 4, 81–127.

Fischhoff, B., Goitein, B., Shapira, Z. (1982) The experienced utility of expected utility approaches. In N. T. Feather (ed.) *Expectations and Actions: Expectancy-Value Models in Psychology*. Hillsdale, NJ: Erlbaum, 275ff.

Fischler, I. and Bloom, P. A. (1979) Automatic and attentional processes in the effect of sentence contexts on word recognition. *Journal of Verbal Learning and Verbal Behaviour*, 18, 1–20.

Fishbein, M. and Ajzen, I. (1975) *Belief, Attitude, Intention and Behavior: an Introduction to Theory and Research*. Reading, MA: Addison-Wesley.

Fisher, K. and Hardie, R. J. (2002) Goal attainment scaling in evaluating a multidisciplinary pain management programme. *Clinical Rehabilitation*, 16(8), 871–7.

Fisher, R. A. (1925/1991) *Statistical Methods, Experimental Design and Scientific Inference*. Oxford: Oxford University Press.

Fisk, A. D. and Schneider, W. (1981) Control and automatic processing during tasks requiring sustained attention: a new approach to vigilance. *Human Factors*, 23(6), 737–50.

Fiske, S. E. and Taylor, S. T. (1991) *Social Cognition* (2nd edn). New York: McGraw-Hill.

Fiske, S. T. (1980) Attention and weight on person perception. *Journal of Personality and Social Psychology*, 38, 889–906.

Flavell, J. H., Friedrichs, A. G. and Hoyt, J. D. (1970) Developmental changes in memorization process. *Cognitive Psychology*, 1, 324–40.

Flood, J. F. and Morley, J. E. (1991) Increased food intake by neuropeptide Y is due to an increased motivation to eat. *Peptides*, 12, 1329–32.

Foa, E. B. and Riggs, D. S. (1993) Post-traumatic stress disorder in rape victims. In J. Oldham, M. B. Riba, A. Tasman (eds) and *American Psychiatric Press Review of Psychiatry*, Vol. 12. Washington DC: American Psychiatric Press.

Foa, E. B., Steketee, G. and Rothbaum, B. O. (1989) Behavior/cognitive conceptualization of post-traumatic stress disorder. *Behavior Therapy*, 20, 155–76.

Fodor, J. A. (1966) How to learn to talk: some simple ways. In F. Smith and G. A. Miller (eds) *The Genesis of Language*. Cambridge, MA: MIT Press.

Fodor, J. A. (1983) *The Modularity of Mind*. Cambridge, MA: MIT Press.

References

Fonagy, P., Steele, H., Steele, M. (1991) Maternal representations of attachment during pregnancy predict the organization of infant-mother attachment at one year of age. *Child Development*, 62, 891–905.

Forbes, G. B. (2001) College students with tattoos and piercings: motives, family experiences, personality factors and perception by others. *Psychological Reports*, 89(3), 774–86.

Fordyce, W. E. (1995) *Back Pain in the Workplace: Management of Disability in Nonspecific Conditions*. Seattle: IASP Press.

Forer, B. R. (1949) The fallacy of personal validation: a classroom demonstration of gullibility. *Journal of Abnormal Psychology*, 44, 118–21.

Forgas, J. P. (1995) Mood and judgment: the affect infusion model (AIM). *Psychological Bulletin*, 117, 39–66.

Försterling, F. (2001) *Attribution: an Introduction to Theories, Research and Applications*. Hove: Psychology Press.

Fox, D. and Prilleltensky, I. (eds) (1997) *Critical Psychology: an Introduction*. London: Sage.

Foy, D. W., Resnick, H. S., Sipperelle, R. C. and Carroll, E. M. (1987) Premilitary, military and post-military factors in the development of combat-related posttraumatic stress disorder. *The Behavior Therapist*, 10, 3–9.

Frances, A., Fyer, M. and Clarkin, J. (1986) Personality and suicide. *Ann NY Academy of Sciences*, 487, 281–93.

Freedman, J. L. (2003) *Media Violence and its Effects on Aggression: Assessing the Scientific Evidence*. Toronto: University of Toronto Press.

Fremouw, W. J., Perczel, W. J. and Ellis, T. E. (1990) *Suicide Risk: Assessment and Response Guidelines*. Elmsford, NY: Pergamon.

Freud, A. (1936) *The Ego and the Mechanisms of Defence*. London: Hogarth Press.

Freud, S. (1949) *An Outline of Psychoanalysis*. London: Hogarth Press.

Frey, K. S. and Ruble, D. N. (1985) What children say when the teacher is not around: conflicting goals in social comparison and performance assessment in the classroom. *Journal of Personality and Social Psychology*, 48, 550–62.

Friedman, A. (1979) Framing pictures: the role of knowledge in automatised encoding and memory for gist. *Journal of Experimental Psychology*, 108, 316–55.

Frith, U. (1985) Beneath the surface of developmental dyslexia. In K. Patterson, M. Coltheart and J. Marshall (eds) *Surface Dyslexia: Neuropsychological and Cognitive Studies of Phonological Reading*. Hove: Lawrence Erlbaum, 301–30.

Frith, U. and Happe, F. (1994) Autism: beyond 'theory of mind'. *Cognition*, 50, 115-32.

Fromm-Reichmann, F. (1948) Notes on the development of treatment of schizophrenics by psychoanalytic psychotherapy. *Psychiatry*, 11, 263–73.

Fudala, P. J., Teoh, K. W. and Iwamoto, E. T. (1985) Pharmacological characterization of nicotine-induced place preference. *Pharmacology, Biochemistry and Behavior*, 22, 237–41.

Fung, Y. K. and Lau, Y. S. (1989) Effect of nicotine pretreatment on striatal dopaminergic system in rats. *Pharmacology, Biochemistry and Behavior*, 32(1), 221–6, January.

Furlong, M. and Oei, T. P. S. (2002) Changes to automatic thoughts and dysfunctional attitudes in group CBT for depression. *Behavioural and Cognitive Psychotherapy*, 30(3), 351–60.

Furnham, A. (1992) *Personality at Work*. London: Routledge.

Furnham, A. (1997) *The Psychology of Behaviour at Work: the Individual in the Organisation*. Sussex: Psychology Press.

Furnham, A., Reeves, E. and Bughani, S. (2002) Parents think their sons are brighter than their daughters: sex differences in parental self-estimations and estimations of their children's multiple intelligences. *Journal of Genetic Psychology*, 163, 24–39.

Furrow, D. and Nelson, K. (1986) A further look at the motherese hypothesis: a reply to Gleitman, Newport and Gleitman. *Journal of Child Language*, 13, 163–76.

Gais, S., Molle, M., Helms, K. and Born, J. (2002) Learning-dependent increases in sleep spindle density. *Journal of Neuroscience*, 22, 6830–4.

Gais, S., Plihal, W., Wagner, U. and Born, J. (2000) Early sleep triggers memory for early visual discrimination skills. *Nature Neuroscience*, 3, 1335–9.

Galambos, N. L. and Almeida, D. M. (1992) Does parent-adolescent conflict decrease in early adolescence? *Journal of Marriage and the Family*, 54, 737–47.

Gallopin, T., Fort, P., Eggermann, E., Cauli, B., Luppi, P. H., Rossier, J., Audinat, E., Muhlethaler, M. and Serafin, M. (2000) Identification of sleep-promoting neurons in vitro. *Nature*, 404, 992–5.

Galton, F. (1883). *Inquiry into Human Faculty and Its Development*. London: Macmillan.

Garcha, H. S. and Stolerman, I. P. (1989) Discrimination of a drug mixture in rats: role of training dose and specificity. *Behavioural Pharmacology*, 1, 25–31.

Gardiner, J. M. (1989) A generation effect in memory without awareness. *British Journal of Psychology*, 80, 163–8.

Gardner, F. (1991) *Self-harm: a Psychotherapeutic Approach*. New York: Brunner-Routledge.

Gardner, H. (1993) *Frames of Mind – The Theory of Multiple Intelligences* (2nd edn). New York: Basic Books.

Gardner, H. (1999) *Intelligence Reframed*. New York: Basic Books.

Gardner, H., Kornhaber, M. L. and Wake, W. K. (1996) *Intelligence, Multiple Perspectives*. New York: Harcourt Brace.

Gardner, R. A. and Gardner, B. T. (1975) Evidence for sentence constituents in the early utterances of child chimpanzee. *Journal of Experimental Psychology*, 104, 244–67.

Gardner, R. A. and Gardner, R. T. (1969) Teaching sign language to a chimpanzee. *Science*, 165, 664–72.

Garmezy, N. (1983) Stressors of childhood. In N. Garmezy and M. Rutter (eds) *Stress, Coping and Development in Children*. New York: McGraw-Hill, 43-84.

Garner, D. M., Olmsted, M. P. and Polivy, J. (1983) Development and validation of a multidimensional eating disorder inventory for anorexia nervosa and bulimia. *International Journal of Eating Disorders*, 2, 15–34.

Garrett, M. F. (1975) The analysis of sentence production. In G. Bower (ed.) *The Psychology of Learning and Motivation*, Vol. 9. New York: Academic Press, 133–77.

Garssen, B., Buikhuisen, M. and Van Dyck, R. (1996) Hyperventilation and panic attacks, *American Journal of Psychiatry*, 153(4), 513–18, April.

Gathercole, S. E. and Baddeley, A. D. (1989) Development of vocabulary in children and short term phonological memory. *Journal of Memory and Language*, 28, 200–13.

Geher, G., Warner, R. M. and Brown, A. S. (2001) Predictive validity of the emotional accuracy research scale. *Intelligence*, 19, 373–88.

Gerfen, C. R. (1995) Dopamine receptor function in the basal ganglia. *Clinical Neuropharmacology*, 18 (Suppl. 1), S162–77.

Gergen, K. (1973) Social psychology as history. *Journal of Personality and Social Psychology*, 26, 309–20.

Geshwind, N. (1970) The organisation of language and the brain. *Science*, 170, 940–4.

Gibbon, F. X. and Gerrard, M. (1989) Effects of upward and downward social comparison on mood states. *Journal of Social & Clinical Psychology*, 8, 14–31.

Gibbons, R. D., Hedeker, D., Elkin, I., Waternaux, C., Kraemer, H. C., Greenhouse, J. B., Shea, M. T., Imber, S. D., Sotsky, S. M. and Watkins, J. T. (1993) Some conceptual and statistical issues in analysis of longitudinal psychiatric data: application to the NIMH treatment of depression Collaborative Research Program dataset. *Archives of General Psychiatry*, 50, 739–50.

Gibson, J. J. (1950) *The Perception of the Visual World*. Boston: Houghton Mifflin.

Gibson, J. J. (1966) *The Senses Considered as Perceptual Systems*. Boston: Houghton Mifflin.

Gick, M. L. and Holyoak, K. J. (1980) Analogical problem solving. *Cognitive Psychology*, 12(3), 306–55.

Gick, M. L. and Holyoak, K. J. (1983) Schema induction and analogical transfer. *Cognitive Psychology*, 15(1), 1–38.

Gilbert, D. T (1998) Ordinary personology. In D. T. Gilbert, S. T. Fiske and G. Lindzey (eds) *Handbook of Social Psychology* (4th edn). New York: McGraw-Hill, 89–150.

Gilbert, D. T. (1995) Attribution and interpersonal perception. In A. Tesser (ed.) *Advanced Social Psychology*. New York: McGraw-Hill, 99–147.

Gilbert, D. T., Pelham, B. W. and Krull, D. S. (1988) On cognitive business: when person perceivers meet persons perceived. *Journal of Personality and Social Psychology*, 54, 733–40.

Gilligan, C. (1982) *In a Different Voice: Psychological Theory and Women's Development*. Cambridge, MA: Harvard University Press.

Gilovich, T., Kruger, J. and Medvec, V. H. (2002) The spotlight effect revisited: overestimating the manifest variability of our actions and appearance. *Journal of Experimental Social Psychology*, 38, 93–9.

Gleason, J. B. and A. N. Ratner (eds) (1993) *Psycholinguistics*. London: Harcourt Brace College Publishers.

Glicksohn, J. and Bozna, M. (2000) Developing a personality profile of the bomb-disposal expert: the role of sensation seeking and field dependence–independence. *Personality and Individual Differences*, 28, 85–92.

Glucksberg, S. and Cowan, G. N. J. (1970) Memory for nonattended auditory material. *Cognitive Psychology*, 1, 149–56.

Glynn, S. M. (1990) Token economy approaches for psychiatric patients: progress and pitfalls over 25 years. *Behavior Modification*, 14, 383–407.

Godden, D. and Baddeley, A. D. (1975) Context-dependent memory in two neutral environments: on land and underwater. *British Journal of Psychology*, 66, 325–32.

Goffman, E. (1959) *The Presentation of Self in Everyday Life*. Garden City, NY: Doubleday Anchor.

Gold, R. M., Jones, A. P., Sawchenko, P. E. and Kapatos, G. (1977) Paraventricular area: critical focus of a longitudinal neurocircuitry mediating food intake. *Physiology and Behavior*, 18, 1111–19.

Goldacre, B. (2002) When hospital is a prison. *Guardian*, 16 July.

Goldberg, S. R., Spealman, R. D. and Goldberg, D. M. (1981) Persistent behavior at high rates maintained by intravenous self-administration of nicotine. *Science*, 214, 573–5.

Goldin-Meadow, S. and Mylander, C. (1990) The role of parental input in the development of a morphological system. *Journal of Child Language*, 17 527–63.

Goldstein, A. J. and Chambless, D. L. (1978) A reanalysis of agoraphobic behavior. *Behavior Therapy*, 9, 47–59.

Goleman, D. (1995) *Emotional Intelligence*. New York: NY: Bantam Books.

Goodkin, K., Antoni, M. and Blaney, P. H. (1986) Stress and hopelessness in the promotion of cervical inatrpithelial neoplasia to invasive squamous cell carcenoma of the cervix. *Journal of Psychosomatic Research*, 30, 67–76.

Goodman, G. S. and Reed, R. S. (1986) Age differences in eyewitness testimony. *Law and Human Behavior*, 10, 317–32.

Goodwin, D. W., Powell, B., Bremer, D., Hoine, H. and Stern, J. (1969) Alcohol and recall: state dependent effects in man. *Science*, 163, 1358.

Gopnik, M. and Crago, M. (1991) Familial aggregation of a developmental language disorder. *Cognition*, 39, 1, 1–50.

Gorski, R. A., Gordon, J. H., Shryne, J. E. and Southam, A. M. (1978) Evidence for a morphological sex difference within the medial preoptic area of the rat brain. *Brain Research*, 148, 333–46.

Goswami, U. C. and Bryant, P. E. (1990) *Phonological Skills and Learning to Read*. Hove: Erlbaum.

Gottesman, I. I., McGuffin, P. and Farmer, A. E. (1987) Clinical genetics as clues to the 'real' genetics of schizophrenia. *Schizophrenia Bulletin*, 13, 23–47.

Goudie, A. J. (1991) Animal models of drug abuse and dependence. In P. Willner (ed.) *Behavioural Models in Psychopharmacology: Theoretical, Industrial and Clinical Perspectives*. Cambridge: Cambridge University Press.

Gough, B. and McFadden, M. (2001) *Critical Social Psychology: an Introduction*. Basingstoke: Palgrave.

Gough, D. A., Kiwan, D., Sutcliffe, S., Simpson, D. and Houghton,

References

N. (2003) A systematic map and synthesis review of the effectiveness of personal development planning for improving student learning. *LTSN Generic Centre Report* (available from: www.ltsn.ac.uk/genericcentre/).

Gould, A. and Martin, G. N. (2001) 'A good odour to breathe?' The effects of pleasant ambient odour on human visual vigilance. *Applied Cognitive Psychology*, 15, 225–32.

Gould, S. J. (1982) A nation of morons. *New Scientist*, 6 May, 349–52.

Gould, S. J. (1997) *The Mismeasure of Man*. London: Penguin.

Goyette, C. H. and Connors, C. K. (1977) Food additives and hyperkinesis. Paper presented at the 85th Annual Convention of the American Psychological Association.

Gozzo, R. A. and Dickson, M. W. (1996) Teams in organizations: recent research on performance and effectiveness. *Annual Review of Psychology*, 47, 307–38.

Grace, A. A. (1991) Phasic versus tonic dopamine release and the modulation of dopamine system responsivity: a hypothesis for the etiology of schizophrenia. *Neuroscience*, 41, 1–24.

Grady, D. L., Chi, H. C., Ding, Y. C., Smith, M., Wang, E., Schuck, S., Flodman, P., Spence, M. A., Swanson, J. M. and Moyzis, R. K. (2003) High prevalence of rare dopamine receptor D4 alleles in children diagnosed with attention-deficit hyperactivity disorder. *Molecular Psychiatry*, 8, 536–45.

Grafton, S. T., Waters, C., Sutton, J., Lew, M. F. and Couldwell, W. (1995) Pallidotomy increases activity of motor association cortex in Parkinson's disease: a positron emission tomographic study. *Annals of Neurology*, 37, 776–83.

Grasing, K., Li, N., He, S., Parrish, C., Delich, J. and Glowa, J. (2003) A new progressive ratio schedule for support of morphine self-administration in opiate dependent rats. *Psychopharmacology*, 168, 387–96.

Gratch, G., Appel, K. J., Evans, W. F., LeCompte, G. K., Wright, N. A. (1974) Piaget's stage IV object concept error: evidence of forgetting or object conception. *Child Development*, 45, 71–7.

Gray, N. S., MacCulloch, M. J., Smith, J., Morris, M. and Snowden, R. J. (2003) Violence viewed by psychopathic murderers. *Nature*, 423, 497–8.

Greenwald, A. G. (1968) Cognitive learning, cognitive response to persuasion and attitude change. In A. G. Greenwald, T. Brock and T. Ostrom (eds) *Psychological Foundations of Attitudes*. New York: Academic Press, 148–70.

Greenwald, A. G. and Banaji, M. R. (1995) Implicit social cognition: attitudes, self-esteem and stereotypes. *Psychological Review*, 102, 4–27.

Greenwald, A. G., McGhee, D. E. and Schwartz, J. L. (1998) Measuring individual differences in implicit cognition: the implicit association test. *Journal of Personality and Social Psychology*, 74, 1464–80.

Gregory, R. L. (1972) Cognitive contours. *Nature*, 238(5358), 51–2.

Gregory, R. L. (1966) *Eye and Brain: The Psychology of Seeing*. Princeton: Princeton University Press.

Gregory, R. L. (1980) Perception as hypotheses. *Philosophical Transactions of The Royal Society*, Series B, 290, 181–97.

Greisberg, S. and McKay, D. (2003) Neuropsychology of obsessive-compulsive disorder: a review and treatment implications. *Clininical Psychology Review*, 23(1), 95–117, February.

Grice, H. P. (1975) Logic and conversation. In P. Cole and J. Morgan (eds) *Syntax and Semantics* (Vol. 3: Speech Acts) New York: Academic Press, 41–58.

Griffen, C. (1991) Sex differences and gender relations: yes, but who does the washing up? Chapter in R. Cochrane and D. Carroll (eds) *Psychology and Social Issues*. London: Falmer Press.

Grosjean, F. (1980) Spoken word recognition processes and the gating paradigm. *Perception & Psychophysics*, 28, 267–83.

Gross, R. (2001) *Psychology: the Science of Mind and Behaviour* (4th edn). London: Hodder & Stoughton.

Gross, R. (2003) *Themes, Issues and Debates in Psychology*. London: Hodder Arnold.

Grossman, K. E., Grossman, K., Huber, F. and Wartner, U. (1981) German children's behaviour towards their mothers at 12 months and their fathers at 18 months in Ainsworth's 'strange situation'. *International Journal of Behavioural Development*, 4, 157–81.

Grotevant, H. D. (1998) Adolescent development in family contexts. In W. Damon (series ed.) and N. Eisenberg (vol. ed.) *Handbook of Child Psychology: Vol. 3. Social, Emotional and Personality Development* (5th edn). New York: Wiley, 1097–149.

Gruneberg, M. and Morris, M. (eds) (1978) *Aspects of Memory* (2nd edn, Vol. 1). London: Routledge.

Guarnaccia, P. J., De La Cancela, V. and Carrillo, E. (1989) The multiple meanings of ataques de nervios in the Latino community. *Medical Anthropology*, 11, 47–62.

Guerin, B. (1989) Reducing evaluation effects in mere presence. *Journal of Social Psychology*, 129, 183–90.

Guilford, J. P. (1967) *The Nature of Human Intelligence*, New York: McGraw-Hill.

Gullone, E. (1996) Developmental psychopathology and normal fear. *Behaviour Change*, 13 143–55.

Gupta, N. and Jenkins, D. G. (1984) Substance use as an employee response to the work environment. *Journal of Vocational Behaviour*, 24, 84–93.

Guzzo, R. A. and Dickson, M. W. (1996) Teams in organizations: recent research on performance and effectiveness. *Annual Review of Psychology*, 47, 307–38.

Hadlow, J. and Pitts, M. K. (1991) The understanding of common health terms by doctors, nurses and patients. *Social Science & Medicine*, 32, 193–6.

Hagerty, M. (1999) Testing Maslow's hierarchy of needs: national quality-of-life across time. *Social Indicators Research*, 46(3), 249–71.

Haier, R. J., Nuechterlein, K. H., Hazlett, E., Wu, J. C., Paek, J. (1988) Cortical glucose metabolic rate correlates of abstract reasoning and attention studied with positron emission tomography. *Intelligence*, 12, 199–217.

Hall, E. (1966) *The Hidden Dimension*. New York: Doubleday.

Hall, J. and Baker, R. (1973) Token economy systems: breakdown and control. *Behaviour Research & Therapy*, 11, 253–63.

Halpern, D. F. (1996) A process-oriented model of cognitive sex differences. *Learning and Individual Differences*, 8, 3–24.

Halstead, W. C. (1951) Biological intelligence, *Journal of Personality & Social Psychology*, 20, 118–30.

Hammersley, M. (1992) *What's Wrong with Ethnography?* London: Routledge.

Hancock, P. A. (1986) Sustained attention under thermal stress. *Psychological Bulletin*, 99, 263–81.

Haney, C., Banks, C. and Zimbardo, P. (1973) A study of prisoners and guards in a simulated prison. *Naval Research Reviews*, 30(9), 4–17.

Haney, H., Banks, C. and Zimbardo, P. (1973) Interpersonal dynamics in a simulated prison. *International Journal of Criminology and Penology*, 1, 69–97.

Hannay, D. R. (1980) The illness iceberg and trivial consultations. *Journal of the Royal College of General Practitioners*, 30, 551–4.

Happe, F. (1994) *Autism: an Introduction to Psychology Theory.* London: UCL Press Limited.

Hare, R. D. (1996) Psychopathy and antisocial personality disorder: a case of diagnostic confusion. *Psychiatric Times*, XIII Issue 2.

Haridakis, P. M. (2002) Viewer characteristics, exposure to television violence and aggression. *Media Psychology*, 4(4), 293–352.

Hariz, M. I. and Bergenheim, A.T. (2001) A 10-year follow-up review of patients who underwent Leksell's posteroventral pallidotomy for Parkinson disease. *Journal of Neurosurgery*, 94, 552–8.

Harley, T. (2001) *The Psychology of Language from Data to Theory* (2nd edn). Hove: Psychology Press.

Harlow, H. (1958) The nature of love. *American Psychologist*, 13, 673–8.

Harris, M., Clibbens, J., Chasin, J. and Tibbitts, R. (1989) The social context of early sign language development, *First Language*, 9, 81–97.

Harris, P. L. (1973) Perseverative errors in search by young infants. *Child Development*, 44, 28–33.

Harris, P. L. (1989) *Children and Emotions. The Development of Psychological Understanding.* Oxford: Blackwell.

Harris, P. L. (2000) *The Work of Imagination.* Oxford: Blackwell.

Harris, T. L. and Schwab, R. (1990) Sex-role orientation and personal adjustment. *Journal of Social Behaviour and Personality*, 5, 473–9.

Harrison, J. A., Mullen, P. D. and Green, L. (1992) A meta-analysis of studies of the health belief model with adults. *Health Education Research*, 7, 107–16.

Hart, P. (1990) *Groupthink in Government: a Study of Small Groups and Policy Failure.* Amsterdam: Swets & Zeitlinger.

Harter, S. (1999) *The Cognitive and Social Construction of the Developing Self.* New York: Guildford Press.

Hartline, H. K., Wagner, H. G. and Ratliff, F. (1956) Inhibition in the eyes of limulus. *Journal of General Physiology*, 39, 651–73.

Hasher, L. and Zacks, R. T. (1984) Automatic processing of fundamental information: The case of frequency of occurrence. *American Psychologist*, 39(12), 1372–88.

Haslam, N. (2003) The dimensional view of personality disorders: a review of the taxometric evidence. *Clinical Psychology Review*, 23, 75–93.

Hastie, R. and Park, B. (1986) The relationship between memory and judgement depends on whether the judgement task is memory based or on-line. *Psychological Review*, 93, 58–268.

Hauser, P., Zametkin, A. J., Martinez, P., Vitiello, B., Matochik, J. A., Mixson, A. J. and Weintraub, B. D. (1993) Attention deficit hyperactivity disorder in people with generalized resistance to thyroid hormone. *New England Journal of Medicine*, 328, 997–1001.

Haworth-Hoeppner, S. (2000) The critical shapes of body image: the role of culture and family in the production of eating disorders. *Journal of Marriage and the Family*, 62, 212–27.

Hay, D. F., Nash, A. and Pedersen, J. (1981) Responses of six-month-olds to the distress of their peers. *Child Development*, 52, 1071–5.

Hayduk, L. A. (1983) Personal space: where we now stand. *Psychological Bulletin*, 94, 293–335.

Hayes, N. (ed.) (1997) *Doing Qualitative Analysis in Psychology.* Hove: Psychology Press.

Haynes, R. B., Taylor, D. W. and Sackett, D. L. (1979) *Compliance in Health Care.* Baltimore, MD: Johns Hopkins University Press.

Hearnshaw, L. S. (1979) *Cyril Burt.* London: Hodder Arnold.

Heath, S. B. (1983) *Ways with Words.* Cambridge: Cambridge University Press.

Heatherington, E. M. and Stanley-Hagan, M. (1999) The adjustment of children with divorced parents: a risk and resiliency perspective. *Journal of Child Psychology & Psychiatry*, 40, 129–40.

Heatherington, E. M., Cox, M. and Cox, R. (1982) Effects of divorce on parents and children. In M. Lamb (ed.) *Nontraditional Families.* Hillsdale, NJ: Erlbaum.

Hebb, D. O. (1949) *The Organization of Behavior.* New York: Wiley.

Hebb, D. O. (1955) Drives and the CNS (conceptual nervous system). *Psychological Review*, 62, 243–59.

Heckhausen, H. (1991) *Motivation and Action.* Berlin: Springer-Verlag.

Hedges, L. V. and Nowell, A. (1995) Differences in mental test scores, variability and numbers of high-scoring individuals. *Science*, 269, 41–5.

Heider, F. (1958) *The Psychology of Interpersonal Relations.* New York: Wiley.

Heider, F. and Simmel, M. (1944) An experimental study of apparent behaviour. *American Journal of Psychology*, 57, 243–59.

Heilman, H. and Stopeck, M. H. (1985) Attractiveness and corporate success: different causal attributions for males and females. *Journal of Applied Psychology*, 70, 379-88.

Heinrichs, S. C., Pich, E. M., Miczek, K. A., Britton, K. T. and Koob, G. F. (1992) Cortocotrophin-releasing factor antagonist reduces emotionality in socially defeated rats via direct neurotropic action. *Brain Research*, 581, 190–7.

Hejmadi, A., Davidson, R. J. and Rozin, P. (2000) Exploring Hindu

References

Indian emotional expressions: evidence for accurate recognition by Americans and Indians. *Psychological Science*, 11, 183–7.

Henderson, J. M. (1992) Object identification in context: the visual processing of natural scenes. *Canadian Journal of Psychology*, 46, 319–41.

Henningfield, J. E., Miyasato, K. and Jasinski, D. R. (1983) Cigarette smokers self-administer intravenous nicotine. *Pharmacology, Biochemistry and Behavior*, 19, 887–90.

Hepburn, A. (2003) *An Introduction to Critical Social Psychology*. London: Sage.

Herbert, T. B. and Cohen, S. (1993) Stress and immunity in humans: a meta-analytic review. *Psychosomatic Medicine*, 55, 364–79.

Herrnstein, R. J. and Murray, C. (1994) *The Bell Curve: Intelligence and Class Structure in American Life*. New York: Free Press.

Herzog, D. B., Greenwood, D. N., Dorer, D. J., Flores, A. T. and Ekeblad, E. R. *et al.* (2000) Mortality in eating disorders: a descriptive study. *International Journal of Eating Disorders*, 28, 20–6.

Hetherington, A. W. and Ranson, S. W. (1940) Hypothalamic lesions and adiposity in the rat. *Anatomical Record*, 78, 149–72.

Hewitt, P. L., Flett, G. L. and Ediger, E. (1995) Perfectionism traits and perfectionistic self-presentation in eating disorder attitudes, characteristics and symptoms. *International Journal of Eating Disorders*, 18, 317–26.

Hewstone, M. (1989) *Causal Attribution: From Cognitive Processes to Collective Beliefs*. Oxford: Blackwell.

Hewstone, M. and Brown, R. (eds) (1986) *Contact and Conflict in Intergroup Encounters*. Oxford: Blackwell.

Higgins, E. T. (1999) Persons and situations: unique explanatory principles or variability in general principles? In D. Cervone and Y. Shoda (eds) *The Coherence of Personality*. New York: Guilford Press, 61–93.

Hildum, D. C. and Brown, R. W. (1956) Verbal reinforcement and interviewer bias. *Journal of Abnormal and Social Psychology*, 53, 108–11.

Hill, A. J. and Franklin, J. A. (1998) Mothers, daughters and dieting: investigating the transmission of weight control. *British Journal of Clinical Psychology*, 37, 3–13.

Hiller, M. L., Knight, K. and Simpson, D. D. (1999) Prison-based substance abuse treatment, residential aftercare and recidivism. *Addiction*, 94(6), 833–42.

Hilton, D. J. and Slugoski, B. R. (1986) Knowledge-based causal attribution: the abnormal conditions focus model. *Psychological Review*, 93, 75–88.

Hirsch, C. R., Clark, D. M., Mathews, A. and Williams, R. (2003) Self-images play a causal role in social phobia. *Behaviour Research and Therapy*, 41(8), 909–21.

Hirschfeld, R. M. and Goodwin, F. K. (1988) Mood disorders. In J. A. Talbott, R. E. Hales and S. C. Yudosfsky (eds) *The American Psychiatric Press Textbook of Psychiatry*. Vol. 7. Washington DC: American Psychiatric Press.

Hirsh-Pasek, K., Treiman, R. and Schneiderman, M. (1984) Brown and Hanlon revisited: mothers' sensitivity to ungrammatical forms. *Journal of Child Language*, 11, 81–8.

Hobson, R. P. (1993) *Autism and the Development of Mind*. Hove: Lawrence Erlbaum Associates.

Hockett, C. F. (1960) The origin of speech. *Scientific American*, 203, 89–96.

Hodgkinson, S., Mullan, M. J. and Gurling, H. M. (1990) The role of egentic factors in the etiology of the affective disorders. *Behavior Genetics*, 20, 235–50.

Hoffmeister, F. and Wuttke, W. (1975) Psychotropic drugs as negative reinforcers. *Pharmacological Review*, 27, 19–28.

Hofmeister J. F., Schneckenbach A. F. and Clayton S. H. (1979) A behavioral program for the treatment of chronic patients. *American Journal of Psychiatry*, 136, 396–400.

Hogg, M. A. and Turner, J. C. (1987) Social identity and conformity: a theory of referent informational influence. In W. Doise and S. Moskovici (eds) *Current Issues in European Social Psychology* (Vol. 2). Cambridge: Cambridge University Press, 139–82.

Hogg, M. A. and Vaughan, G. M. (1995) *Social Psychology*. London: Prentice Hall.

Hogg, M. A. and Vaughan, G. M. (2002) *Social Psychology* (3rd edn). Harlow: Prentice Hall.

Hollon, S. D., De Rubeis, R. J. and Evans, M. D. (1996) Cognitive therapy in the treatment and prevention of depression. In P. M. Salkovskis (ed.) *Frontiers of Cognitive Therapy*. New York: Guilford.

Holmes, T. H. and Rahe, R. H. (1967) The social readjustment rating scale. *Journal of Psychosomatic Research*, 11, 213–18.

Holst, V. F. and Bezdek, K. (1992) Script for typical crimes and their effects on memory for eyewitness testimony. *Applied Cognitive Psychology*, 6(7), 573–87.

Holzman, P. S. (1994) Hilgard on psychoanalysis. *Psychological Science*, 5, 190–1.

Honey, P. and Mumford, A. (1992) *The Manual of Learning Styles* (3rd edn). Maidenhead, Berkshire: Peter Honey.

Hood, B. (2003) Magic in the animal kingdom. Paper presented at the British Psychological Society Developmental Section Conference, Coventry.

Hood, B. and Williats, P. (1986) Reaching in the dark to an object's remembered position: evidence for object permanence in 5-month-old infants. *British Journal of Developmental Psychology*, 4, 57–65.

Horn, J. and Cattell, R. (1966) Refinement and test of the theory of fluid and crystalised general intelligences. *Journal of Educational Psychology*, 57(5), 253–70.

Horn, J. L. (1989) Cognitive diversity: a framework for learning. In P. L. Ackerman, R. J. Sternberg and R. Glaser (eds) *Learning and Individual Differences: Advances in Theory and Research*. New York, NY: WH Freeman & Co, 61–116.

Horne, J. A. (1988) *Why We Sleep: the Function of Sleep in Humans and Other Mammals*. Oxford: Oxford University Press.

House, R. J. (1977) A theory of charismatic leadership. In J. G. Hunt and L. L. Larson (eds) *Leadership: the Cutting Edge*. Carbondale, IL: Southern Illinois University Press.

Hovland, C. I. and Janis, I. L. (eds) (1959) *Personality and Persuasibility*. New Haven, CT: Yale University Press.

Howe, C., Tolmie, A. and Greer, K. (1995) Peer collaboration and conceptual growth in physics: task influences on children's understanding of heating and cooling. *Cognition & Instruction*, 13(4), 483–503.

Howitt, D. and Owusu-Bempah, J. (1994) *The Racism of Psychology*. London: Harvester Wheatsheaf.

Hoyenga, K. B. and Hoyenga, K. T. (1993) *Gender-Related Differences: Origins and Outcomes*. Boston, MA: Allyn & Bacon.

Hubel, D. H. and Wiesel, T. N. (1959) Receptive fields of single neurons in the cat's striate cortex. *Journal of Physiology*, 148, 574–91.

Hubel, D. H. and Wiesel, T. N. (1962) Receptive fields, binocular interaction and functional architecture in the cat's visual cortex. *Journal of Physiology*, 160, 106–54.

Hubel, D. H. and Wiesel, T. (1963) Receptive fields of cells in the striate cortex of very young, very visually inexperienced kittens. *Journal of Neurophysiology*, 26, 994–1002.

Hubel, D. H. and Wiesel, T. (1968) Receptive fields and functional architecture of monkey striate cortex. *Journal of Physiology*, 195, 215–43.

Hubel, D. H. and Wiesel, T. (1979) Brain mechanisms of vision. *Scientific American*, 241, 150–62.

Hubel, D. H., Wiesel, T. and Stryker, M. P. (1978) Anatomical demonstration of orientation columns in macaque monkey. *Journal of Comparative Neurology*, 177, 361–80.

Hugdahl, K. and Johnsen, B. H. (1989) Preparedness and electrodermal fear-conditioning – ontogenetic vs phylogenetic explanations. *Behaviour Research & Therapy*, 27(3), 269–78.

Hughes, M. and Donaldson, M. (1979) The use of hiding games for studying the coordination of viewpoints. *Educational Review*, 31, 133–40.

Hull, E. M., Lorrain, D. S. Du J., Matuszewich, L., Lumley, L. A., Putnam, S. K. and Moses, J. (1999) Hormone–neurotransmitter interactions in the control of sexual behavior. *Behaviour and Brain Research*, 105, 105–16.

Hull, C. L. (1920) Quantitative aspects of the evolution of concepts. *Psychological Monographs*, 28(1), 1–86.

Hull, C. L. (1943) *Principles of Behaviour, an Introduction to Behaviour Theory*. New York: Appleton Century.

Hume, D. (1739/40) *A Treatise of Human Nature* (ed. L. A. Selby-Bigge). Oxford: Clarendon Press (1965).

Hume, D. (1748) *An Enquiry Concerning Human Understanding*. Chicago: Open Court Publishing Co. (1927).

Humphreys, G. W. (1999) Integrative Agnosia. In G. W. Humphreys (ed.) *Case Studies in the Neuropsychology of Vision*. Hove: Psychology Press.

Hunt, E. (1983) On the nature of intelligence. *Science*, 219, 141–6.

Hunt, R. R. and Ellis, H. C. (1999) *Fundamentals of Cognitive Psychology* (6th edn). London: McGraw-Hill College Publishers.

Huston-Lyons, D. and Kornetsky, C. (1992) Effects of nicotine on the threshold for rewarding brain stimulation in rats. *Pharmacology, Biochemistry and Behavior*, 41, 755–9.

Hutchison. K. E., LaChance, H., Niaura, R., Bryan, A. and Smolen, A. (2002) The DRD4 VNTR polymorphism influences reactivity to smoking cues. *Journal of Abnormal Psychology*, 111, 134–43.

Huttunen, M. and Niskanen, P. (1978) Prenatal loss of father and psychiatric disorders. *Archives of General Psychiatry*, 35, 429–31.

Hyde, J. S., Fennema, E. and Lamon, S. J. (1990) Gender differences in mathematics performance: a meta-analysis. *Psychological Bulletin*, 107, 139–53.

Hyman, S. E. (1999) Introduction to the complex genetics of mental disorders. *Biological Psychiatry*, 45, 518–21.

Ibbotson, J. (1978) Motivation: the occupational therapist's view. *Physiotherapy*, 61, 189–91.

Imperato, A., Mulas, A. and Di Chiara, G. (1986) Nicotine preferentially stimulates dopamine release in the limbic system of freely moving rats. *European Journal of Pharmacology*, 132, 337–8.

Insko, C. A. (1965) Verbal reinforcement and attitude. *Journal of Personality and Social Psychology*, 2, 621–3.

Iriki, A., Pavlides, C., Keller, A. and Asanuma, H. (1989) Long-term potentiation in the motor cortex. *Science*, 245, 1385–7.

Isaacs, W., Thomas, J. and Goldiamond, I. (1960) Application of operant conditioning to reinstate verbal behavior in psychotics. *Journal of Speech & Hearing Disorders* 25, 8–12.

Isenberg, N., Sibersweig, D., Engelien, A., Emmerich, S., Malavade, K., Beattie, B., Leon, A. C. and Stern, E. (1999) Linguistic threat activates the human amygdala. *Proceedings of the National Academy of Sciences of the United States of America*, 96, 10456–9.

Islam, M. R. and Hewstone, M. (1993) Dimensions of contact as predictors of intergroup anxiety, perceived outgroup variability and outgroup attitude: an integrative model. *Personality and Social Psychology Bulletin*, 19, 700–10.

Isometsa, E., Henriksson, M., Marttunen, M., Heikkinen, M., Aro, H., Kuoppasalmi, K. and Lunnqvist, J. (1995) Mental disorders in young and middle aged men who commit suicide. *British Medical Journal*, 310, 1366–7.

Iwamoto, E. T. (1990) Nicotine conditions place preferences after intracerebral administration in rats. *Psychopharmacology*, 100, 251–7.

Iwata, B. A., Dorsey, M. F., Slifer, K. J., Bauman, K. E. and Richman, G. S. (1985) Toward a functional analysis of self-injury. In G. Murphy and B. Wilson (eds) *Self-injurious Behaviour*. Kidderminster: BIHM.

Izard, C. E., Libero, D. Z., Putnam, P. and Haynes, O. N. (1993) Stability of emotional experiences and their relations to traits of personality. *Journal of Personality and Social Psychology*, 64, 847–60.

Jack, S. J. and Ronan, K. R. (1998) Sensation seeking among high- and low-risk sports participants. *Personality and Individual Differences*, 25, 1063–83.

Jackson, C. (1996) *Understanding Psychological Testing*. Guildford: BPS Books.

Jacobson, N. and Weiss, R. L. (1978) Behavioral marriage therapy

III. The contents of Gurma *et al.* may be hazardous to our health. *Family Process*, 17, 149–63.

Jacobson, N. S. and Christenson, A. (1996) Studying the effectiveness of psychotherapy. *American Psychologist*, 51, 1031–9.

James, W. (1890) *Principles of Psychology* (Vol. 1). New York: Holt, Rinehart & Winston.

Janis, I. L. (1972) *Victims of Groupthink: a Psychological Study of Foreign Policy Decisions and Fiascoes*. Boston: Houghton Mifflin.

Janis, I. L. (1982) *Victims of Groupthink* (2nd edn). Boston, MA: Houghton Mifflin.

Janis, I. L. and Mann, L. (1977) *Decision Making*. New York: Free Press.

Janoff-Bulman, R. (1992) *Shattered Assumptions: Towards a New Psychology of Trauma*. New York: Free Press.

Jarrold, C. and Russell, J. (1997) Counting abilities in autism: possible implications for central coherence theory. *Journal of Autism and Development Disorders*, 27, 25–38.

Jarvella, R. J. (1971) Syntactic processing of connected speech. *Journal of Verbal Learning & Verbal Behavior*, 10(4), 409–16.

Jarvis, M. (2000) *Theoretical Approaches in Psychology*. London: Routledge.

Jarvis, M. and Russell, J. (2002) *Key Ideas in Psychology*. Cheltenham: Nelson Thornes.

Jenike M. A. (1986) Theories of etiology. In M. A. Jenke, L. Baer and W. E. Minchiello (eds) *Obsessive-Compulsive Disorders*. Littleton: MA: PSG Publishing.

Jensen, A. R. (1998) *The g Factor: the Science of Mental Ability*. Westport, CT: Praeger.

Jenson, A. (1980) *Bias in Mental Testing*. New York: Free Press.

Jewett, D. C., Cleary, J., Levine, A. S., Schaal, D. W. and Thompson, T. (1992) Effects of neuropeptide Y on food-reinforced behaviour in satiated rats. *Pharmacology, Biochemistry and Behavior*, 42, 207–12.

Jodeyr, S. (2003) Where do I belong? The experience of second generation Iranian immigrants and refugees. *Psychodynamic Practice: Individuals, Groups and Organisation*, 9(2), 205–14.

Johnson, J. G. and Sherman, M. F. (1997) Daily hassles mediate the relationship between major life events and psychiatric symptomatology: longitudinal findings from an adolescent sample. *Journal of Social & Clinical Psychology*, 16, 389–404.

Johnson, D. L., Wiebe, J. S., Gold, S. M., Andreasen, N. C., Hichwa, R. D., Watkins, G. L. and Ponto, L. L. B. (1999) Cerebral blood flow and personality: a positron emission tomography study. *American Journal of Psychiatry*, 156, 252–7.

Johnson, M. H. and Morton, J. (1991) *Biology and Cognitive Development: the Case of Face Recognition*. Oxford: Blackwell.

Johnston, T. D. and Edwards, L. (2002) Genes, interactions and the development of Behavior. *Psychological Review*, 109, 26–34.

Johnston, W. A. and Wilson, J. (1980) Perceptual processing of nontargets in an attention task. *Memory & Cognition*, 8(4), 372–7.

Johnstone, L. (2003) A shocking treatment? *The Psychologist*, 16, 236–9.

Joiner, R., Littleton, K., Faulkner, D. and Meil, D. (2000) *Rethinking Collaborative Learning*. London: Free Association Books.

Jones, C. M., Braithwaite, V. A. and Healy, S. D. (2003) The evolution of sex differences in spatial ability. *Behavioural Neuroscience*, 117, 403–11.

Jones, K. and Harrison, Y. (2001) Frontal lobe function, sleep loss and fragmented sleep. *Sleep Medicine Reviews*, 5, 463–75.

Jones, D. and Elcock, J. (2001) *History and Theories of Psychology: a Critical Perspective*. London: Arnold.

Jones, E. E. (1979) The rocky road from acts to dispositions. *American Psychologist*, 34, 107–17.

Jones, E. E. (1990) *Interpersonal Perception*. New York: Macmillan.

Jones, E. E. and Davis, K. E. (1965) From acts to dispositions: the attribution process in person perceptions. In L. Berkowitz (ed.) *Advances in Experimental Social Psychology* (Volume 2). New York: Academic Press, 219–66.

Jones, E. E. and Nisbett, R. E. (1972) The actor and the observer: divergent perceptions of the causes of behaviour. In E. E. Jones, D. E. Kanouse, H. H. Kelley, R. E. Nisbett, S. Valins and B. Weiner (eds) *Attribution: Perceiving the Causes of Behaviour*. Morristown, NJ: General Learning Press, 79–94.

Jones, E. E. and Pittman, T. S. (1982) Towards a general theory of strategic self-presentation. In Suls, J. (ed.) *Psychological Perspectives on the Self*. Hillsdale, NJ: Lawrence Erlbaum, 231–62.

Jones, E. E. and Sigall, H. (1971) The bogus pipeline: a new paradigm for measuring affect and attitude. *Psychological Bulletin*, 76, 349–64.

Jones, E. E., Goethals, G. R., Kennington, E. E. and Severance, L. J. (1972) Primacy and assimilation in the attribution process: the stable entity proposition. *Journal of Personality*, 40, 250–74.

Jones, L. W., Sinclair, R. C. and Courneya, K. S. (2003) The effects of source credibility and message framing on exercise intentions, behaviors and attitudes: an integration of the *elaboration likelihood model and prospect theory*. *Journal of Applied Social Psychology*, 33, 179–96.

Jones, R. M. (1992) Ego identity and adolescent problem behaviour. In G. R. Adams, T. P. Gulotta and R. Montemayor (eds) *Advances in Adolescent Development: Vol. 4. Adolescent Identity Formation*. Newbury Park, CA: Sage, 216–33.

Jouvet, M. (1999) Sleep and serotonin: an unfinished story. *Neuropsychopharmacology*, 21 (Suppl. 1), 24S–27S.

Jung, C. (1964) *Man and his Symbols*. Garden City, NY: Doubleday.

Just, M. A. and Carpenter, P. A. (1980) A theory of reading: from eye fixations to comprehension. *Psychological Review*, 87(4), 329–54.

Kagan, J. (1984) *The Nature of the Child*. New York: Basic Books.

Kahn, A. and McGaughey, T. A. (1977) Distance and liking: when moving close produces increased liking. *Social Psychology Quarterly*, 40, 138–44.

Kahneman, D. (1973) *Attention and Effort*. Englewood Cliffs, NJ: Prentice-Hall.

Kahneman, D. and Tversky, A. (1973) On the psychology of prediction. *Psychological Review*, 80(4), 237–51.

Kahneman, D. and Tversky, A. (1984) Choices, values and frames. *American Psychologist*, 39(4), 341–50.

Kail, R. (1990) *The Development of Memory in Children* (3rd edn). New York: Free Press.

Kalat, J. W. (2001) *Biological Psychology* (7th edn). Belmont: Wadsworth.

Kales, A. and Kales, J. (1970) Evaluation, diagnosis and treatment of clinical conditions related to sleep. *Journal of the American Medical Association*, 213, 2229–35.

Kalivas, P. W. and Weber, B. (1988) Amphetamine injection into the ventral mesencephalon sensitizes rats to peripheral amphetamine and cocaine. *Journal of Pharmacology and Experimental Therapeutics*, 245, 1095–102.

Kamin, L. (1974) *The Science and Politics of IQ*. Mahwah, NJ: Lawrence Erlbaum.

Kan, Y., Kawamura, M., Hasegawa, Y., Mochizuki, S. and Nakamura, K. (2002) Recognition of emotion from facial, prosodic and written verbal stimuli in Parkinson's disease. *Cortex*, 38(4), 623–6.

Kanfer, P. L., Ackerman, P. L., Murtha, T. and Goff, M. (1995) Personality and intelligence in industrial and organisational psychology. In D. H. Saklofske and M. Zeidner (eds) *International Handbook of Personality and Intelligence*. New York: NY: Plenum.

Kanner, A. D., Coyne, J. C., Schaefer, C. and Lazarus, R. S. (1981) Comparison of the two modes of stress management: daily hassles and uplifts versus major life events. *Journal of Behavioral Medicine*, 4, 1–39.

Kanner, L. (1943) Autistic disturbances of affective contact. *Nervous Child*, 2, 217–50.

Kapur, S. and Remington, G. (1996) Serotonin-dopamine interaction and its relevance to schizophrenia. *American Journal of Psychiatry*, 153, 466–76.

Karmiloff-Smith, A. (1992) *Beyond Modularity: a Developmental Perspective on Cognitive Science*. Cambridge, MA: MIT Press.

Karmiloff-Smith, A. and Thomas, M. S. C. (in press) *Developmental Disorders*. Unpublished manuscript.

Karmiloff-Smith, A., Grant, J., Berthoud, I., Davies, M., Howlin, P. and Udwin, O. (1997) Language and Williams syndrome: how intact is 'intact'? *Child Development*, 2, 246–62.

Katchdourian, H. (1977) *The Biology of Adolescence*. San Francisco: WH Freeman.

Katz, J. L. (1989) Drugs as reinforcers: pharmacological and behavioural factors. In J. M. Liebman and S. J. Cooper (eds) *The Neuropharmacological Basis of Reward*. Oxford: Oxford University Press.

Katz, D. (1960) The functional approach to the study of attitudes. *Public Opinion Quarterly*, 24, 163–204.

Kay, J. and Marcel, A. J. (1981) One process, not two, in reading aloud: lexical analogies do the work of non-lexical rules. *Quarterly Journal of Experimental Psychology*, 33A, 397–414.

Kaye, W. H., Nagata, T., Weltzin, T. E,, Hsu, G., Sokol, M. S., McConaha, C., Plotnivov, K. H., Weise, J. and Deep, D. (2001) Double-blind placebo-controlled administration of fluoxetine in restricting- and restricting-purging-type anorexia nervosa. *Biological Psychiatry*, 49, 644–52.

Kazdin, A. E. (1995) *Conduct Disorders in Childhood and Adolescence*. Thousand Oaks, CA: Sage.

Kazdin A. E. and Wilcoxon L. A. (1976) Systematic desensitization and non-specific treatment effects: a methodological evaluation. *Psychological Bulletin*, 83, 729–58.

Kazdin, A. E., French, N. H. and Unis, A. S. (1983) Child, mother and father evaluations of depression in psychiatric inpatient children. *Journal of Abnormal Child Psychology*, 11 167–80.

Kebabian, J. W. and Calne, D. B. (1979) Multiple receptors for dopamine. *Nature*, 277, 93–6.

Kelley, H. H. (1950) The warm–cold variable in first impressions of persons. *Journal of Personality*, 18, 431–9.

Kelley, H. H. (1952) Two functions of reference groups. In G. E. Swanson, T. M. Newcomb and E. L. Hartley (eds) *Readings in Social Psychology* (2nd edn). New York: Holt, Rinehart & Winston, 410–14.

Kelley, H. H. (1967) Attribution theory in social psychology. In D Levine (ed.) *Nebraska Symposium on Motivation* (Vol. 15). Lincoln, NE: University of Nebraska Press, 192–238.

Kelley, H. H. (1972) Causal schemata and the attribution process. In E. E. Jones, D. E. Kanouse, H. H. Kelley, R. E. Nisbett, S. Valins and Weiner, B. (eds) *Attribution: Perceiving the Causes of Behavior*. Morristown, NJ: General Learning Press, 151–74.

Kelley, H. H. (1973) The process of causal attribution. *American Psychologist*, 28, 107–28.

Kelly, G. A. (1955) *The Psychology of Personal Constructs*. New York: Norton.

Kelly, K. T. and Campbell, J. L. (1997) Attribution of responsibility for alcohol-related offenses. *Psychological Reports*, 80, 1159–65.

Kendler, K. S., Neale, M. C., Kessler, R. C., Heath, A. C. and Eaves, L. J. (1992) Generalized anxiety disorder in women: a population-based twin study. *Archives of General Psychiatry*, 49, 267–72.

Kendler, K. S., Kessler, R. C., Neale, M. C., Heath, A. C. and Eaves, L. J. (1993) The prediction of major depression in women: toward an integrated etiologic model. *American Journal of Psychiatry*, 150, 1139–48.

Kerr, J. H. (1994) *Understanding Soccer Hooliganism*. Buckingham: Open University Press.

Kerr, N. L. (1983) Motivation losses in small groups: a social dilemma analysis. *Journal of Personality and Social Psychology*, 45, 819–28.

Kerr, N. L. and Park, E. S. (2003) Group performance in collaborative and social dilemma tasks. In M. A. Hogg and S. Tindale (eds) *Blackwell Handbook of Social Psychology: Group Processes*. Oxford: Blackwell, 107–38.

Kessler, R. C., McGonagle, K. A., Zhao, S., Nelson, C. B., Hughes, M., Eshleman, S., Wittchen, H. U. and Kendler K. S. (1994) Lifetime and 12-month prevalence of DSM-III-R psychiatric disorders in the United States. Results from the National Comorbidity Survey. *Archives of General Psychiatry*, 51, 8–19.

Kiewitz, C. and Weaver, J. B. III. (2001) Trait aggressiveness, media

References

violence and perceptions of interpersonal conflict. *Personality and Individual Differences*, 31(6), 821–35.

Kilduff, T. S. and Peyron, C. (2000) The hypocretin/orexin ligand-receptor system: implications for sleep and sleep disorders. *Trends in Neuroscience*, 23, 359–65.

Kilpatrick, F. P. and Ittleson, W. H. (1953) The size-distance invariance hypothesis. *Psychological Review*, 60, 223–31.

Kimura, D. (1961) Some effects of temporal-lobe damage on auditory perception. *Canadian Journal of Psychology*, 15, 156–65.

Kimura, D. (1967) Functional asymmetry of the brain in dichotic listening. *Cortex*, 3, 163–78.

King, D. W., King, L. A., Foy, D. W. and Gudanowski, D. M. (1996) Prewar factors in combat-related post-traumatic stress disorder: structural equation modeling with a national sample of female and male Vietnam veterans. *Journal of Consulting & Clinical Psychology*, 64, 520–31.

King, N. J., Ollendick, T. H. and Gullone, E. (1991) Negative affectivity in children and adolescents: relations between anxiety and depression. *Clinical Psychology Review*, 11, 441–59.

King, N. J., Ollendick, T. H. and Mattis, S. G. (1994) Panic in children and adolescents: normative and clinical studies. *Australian Psychologist*, 29, 89–93.

King, N. J., Ollier, K., Iacune, R., Schuster, S., Bay, K., Gullone, E. and Ollendick, T. H. (1989) Fears of children and adolescents: a cross-sectional Australian study using the Revised Fear Survey Schedule for Children. *Journal of Child Psychology and Psychiatry*, 30 775–84.

Kitayama, S. and Karasawa, M. (1997) Implicit self-esteem in Japan: name letters and birthday numbers. *Personality & Social Psychology Bulletin*, 23, 736–42.

Kitayama, S., Markus, H. R., Matsumoto, H. and Norasakkunkit, V. (1997) Individual and collective processes in the construction of the self: self-enhancement, in the United States and self-criticism in Japan. *Journal of Personality and Social Psychology*, 72, 1245–67.

Kitzinger, C. (1998) Challenging gender biases: feminist psychologists at work. *Psychology Review* 4, 18–20.

Kitzinger, C. and Coyle, A. (2002) Introducing lesbian and gay psychology. *Lesbian and Gay Psychology: New Perspectives*. Oxford: BPS Blackwell.

Klein, D. F. (1993) False suffocation alarms, spontaneous panics and related conditions: an integrative hypothesis. *Archives of General Psychiatry*, 50, 306–17.

Klein, M. (1964) *Contributions to Psychoanalysis, 1921–1945*. New York: McGraw-Hill.

Kleiner, K. A. and Banks, M. S. (1987) Stimulus energy does not account for 2-month-olds' face preferences. *Journal of Experimental Psychology*, 13, 594–600.

Kline, P. (1989) Objective tests of Freud's theories. In A. M. Colman and J. G. Beaumont (eds) *Psychology Survey No. 7*. Leicester: British Psychological Society.

Kluckhorn, C. and Murray, H. (1953) *Personality in Nature, Society and Culture*, New York: Knopf.

Kluender, K. R., Diehl, R. L. and Killeen, P. R. (1987) Japanese quail can learn phonetic categories. *Science*, 237, 1195–7.

Klump, K., McGue, M. and Iacono, W. G. (2000) Age differences in genetic and environmental influences on eating attitudes and behaviors in preadolescent and adolescent female twins. *Journal of Abnormal Psychology*, 109, 239–51.

Klüver, H. and Bucy, P. C. (1938) An analysis of certain effects of bilateral temporal lobectomy in the rhesus monkey, with special reference to 'psychic blindness.' *Journal of Psychology*, 5, 33–54.

Kodama, T. and Honda, Y. (1996) Acetylcholine releases of mesopontine PGO-on cells in the lateral geniculate nucleus in sleep–waking cycle and serotonergic regulation. *Progress in Neuropsychopharmacology and Biological Psychiatry*, 20, 1213–27.

Koestner, R. and McClelland, D. C. (1990) Perspectives on competence motivation, In L. A. Pervin (ed.) *Handbook of Personality Theory and Research*. New York: Guilford Press.

Kohlberg, L. (1985) *The Psychology of Moral Development*. San Francisco: Harper.

Kohlberg, L. (1968) The child as a moral philosopher. *Psychology Today*, 2, 25–30.

Kohler, W. (1927) *The Mentality of Apes*. New York: Harcourt Brace.

Kohut, H. (1977) *The Restoration of the Self*. New York: International Universities Press.

Kolb, B. and Whishaw, I. (2003) *Fundamentals of Human Neuropsychology* (5th edn). New York: Worth.

Kolta, M. G., Shreve, P., Uretsky, N. J. (1989) Effect of pretreatment with amphetamine on the interaction between amphetamine and dopamine neurons in the nucleus accumbens. *Neuropharmacology*, 28, 9–14.

Koob, G. F. (1992) Drugs of abuse: anatomy, pharmacology and function of reward pathways. *Trends in Pharmacological Sciences*, 13, 177–84.

Koob, G. F., Vaccarino, F. J., Amalric, M. and Bloom, F. E. (1987) Positive reinforcement properties of drugs: search for neural substrates. In J. Engel and L. Oreland (eds) *Brain Reward Systems and Abuse*. New York: Raven Press.

Korabik, K. (1994) Managerial women in the People's Republic of China: the long march continues. In N. J. Adler and D. N. Israeli (eds) *Competitive Frontiers: Women Managers in Global Economy*. Cambridge, MA: Blackwell, 114–26.

Korsch, B. M., Gozzi, E. K. and Francis, V. (1968) Gaps in doctor–patient communication. *Pediatrics*, 42, 855–71.

Kosslyn, S. M. and Rosenberg, R. S. (2004) *Psychology: The Brain, The Person, The World*. Boston, MA: Pearson.

Kramer, A., Larish. J. and Strayer, D. (1995) Training for attentional control in dual task settings: a comparison of young and old adults. *Journal of Experimental Psychology: Applied*, 2, 50–76.

Krantz, S. E. and Rude, S. (1984) Depressive attributions: selection of different causes or assignment of different meanings? *Journal of Personality and Social Psychology*, 47, 193–203.

Kringlen, E. (1970) Natural history of obsessional neurosis. *Seminars in Psychiatry*, 2, 403–19.

Krueger, R. F. and Piasecki, T. M. (2002) Toward a dimensional and psychometrically-informed approach to conceptualizing psychopathology. *Behaviour Research & Therapy*, 40, 485–99.

Kucera, H. and Francis, W. N. (1967) *Computational Analysis of Present-Day American English*. Providence, RI: Brown University Press.

Kuffler, S. W. (1953) Discharge patterns and functional organization of mammalian retina. *Journal of Neurophysiology*, 16, 37–68.

Kuhl, P. K. and Padden, D. M. (1983) Enhanced discriminability at the phonetic boundaries for the place feature in the macaques. *Journal of the Acoustical Society of America*, 73, 1003–10.

Kulik, J. A. and Gump, B. B. (1997) Affective reactions to social comparison: the effects of relative performance and related attributes information about another person. *Personality and Social Psychology Bulletin*, 23, 452–68.

Kunst-Wilson, W. R. and Zajonc, R. B. (1980) Affective discrimination in stimuli that cannot be recognised. *Science*, 207, 557–8.

Kurtines, W. and Greif, E. B. (1974) The development of moral thought: review and evaluation of Kohlberg's approach. *Psychological Bulletin*, 81, 453–70.

LaBerge, D. (1983) Spatial extent of attention to letters and words. *Journal of Experimental Psychology: Human Perception & Performance*, 9(3), 371–9.

Ladouceur, R., Talbot, F. and Dugas, M. J. (1997) Behavioural expressions of intolerance of uncertainty in worry. *Behavior Modification*, 21, 355–71.

Laitinen, L. V., Bergenheim, A. T. and Hariz, M. I. (1992) Leksell's posteroventral pallidotomy in the treatment of Parkinson's disease. *Journal of Neurosurgery*, 76, 53–61.

Lam, J. N. and Steketee, G. S. (2001) Reducing obsessions and compulsions through behavior therapy. *Psychoanalytic Inquiry*, 21, 157–82.

Lamb, H. R. (1984) Deinstitutionalization and the homeless mentally ill. *Hospital Community Psychiatry*, 35, 899–907.

Lamb, R. J. and Griffiths, R. R. (1987) Self-injection of d, 1-3, 4-methylenedioxymethamphetamine (MDMA) in the baboon. *Psychopharmacology*, 91, 268–72.

Lambert, M. J., Shapiro, D. A. and Bergin, A. E. (1986) The effectiveness of psychotherapy. In S. L. Garfield and A. E. Bergin (eds) *Handbook of Psychotherapy and Behavior Change* (3rd edn). New York: Wiley.

Lamm, H. and Weismann, U. (1997) Subjective attributes of attraction: how people characterize their liking, their love and their being in love. *Personal Relationships*, 4, 271–84.

Lammers, H. B. (2000) Effects of deceptive packaging and product involvement on purchase intention: an elaboration likelihood model perspective. *Psychological Reports*, 86, 546–50.

Landers, W. F. (1971) The effect of differential experience on infants' performance in a Piagetin stage IV object concept task. *Developmental Psychology*, 5, 48–54.

Langer, E. J. (1978) Rethinking the role of thought in social interaction. In J. H. Harvey, W. J. Ickes and R. F. Kidd (eds) *New Directions in Attribution Research* (Vol. 2). Hillsdale, NJ: Lawrence Erlbaum.

Langlois, J. H. and Downs, A. C. (1980) Mothers, fathers and peers as socialization agents of sex-typed play behaviors in young children. *Child Development*, 51, 1217–47.

LaPiere, R. (1934) Attitudes versus actions. *Social Forces*, 13, 230–7.

Larner, A. J. and du Plessis, D. G. (2003) Early-onset Alzheimer's disease with presenilin-1 M139V mutation: clinical, neuropsychological and neuropathological study. *European Journal of Neurology*, 10, 319–23.

Larsen, R. and Buss, D. (2002) *Personality Psychology: Domains of Knowledge about Human Nature*. New York: McGraw-Hill.

Larson, J. R., Foster-Fishman, P. G. and Keys, C. B. (1994) Discussion of shared and unshared information in decision making groups. *Journal of Personality and Social Psychology*, 67, 446–61.

Last, J. (1963) The iceberg: completing the clinical picture of general practice. *Lancet*, ii, 28–31.

Latané, B. (1981) The psychology of social impact. *American Psychologist*, 36, 343–56.

Latané, B. and Darley, J. M. (1968) Group inhibition of bystander intervention in emergencies. *Journal of Personality & Social Psychology*, 10, 215–21.

Latané, B. and Darley, J. M. (1970) *The Unresponsive Bystander: Why Doesn't he Help?* New York: Appleton Century Crofts.

Latané, B. and Wolf, S. (1981) The social impact of majorities and minorities. *Psychological Review*, 88, 438–53.

Latané, B., Williams, K. and Harkins, S. (1979) Many hands make light the work: the causes and consequences of social loafing. *Journal of Personality and Social Psychology*, 37, 822–932.

Laurent, J., Swerdlik, M. and Ryburn, M. (1992), Review of validity research on the Stanford-Binet intelligence scale: fourth edition. *Psychological Assessment*, 4, 102–12.

Lazarus, R. S. (1991) Progress on a cognitive–motivational–relational theory of emotion. *American Psychologist*, 46, 352–67.

Lazarus, R. S. and Folkman, S. (1984) *Stress, Appraisal and Coping*. New York: Springer.

Leahey, T. H. (2001) *A History of Modern Psychology*. Upper Saddle River, NJ, Prentice-Hall.

Leana, C. R. (1985) A partial test of Janis' groupthink model: effects of group cohesiveness and leader behaviour on defective decision making. *Journal of Management*, 11, 5–17.

Leary, M. R. (1995) *Self-presentation: Impression Management and Interpersonal Behavior*. Madison, WI: Brown & Benchmark.

LeBar, K. S., Gatenby, J. C., Gore, J. C., LeDoux, J. E. and Phelps, E. A. (1998) Human amygdala activation during conditioned fear acquisition and extinction: a mixed trial fMRI study. *Neuron*, 20, 937–45.

LeBar, K. S., LeDoux, J. E., Spencer, D. D. and Phelps, E. A. (1995) Impaired fear conditioning following unilateral temporal lobectomy in humans. *Journal of Neuroscience*, 15, 6846–55.

LeBon, G. (1908) *The Crowd: a Study of the Popular Mind*. London: Urwin.

References

Lecanuet, J. P., Granier-Deferre, C. and Busnel, M. C. (1995) Human fetal auditory perception. In J. P Lecanuet, W. P. Fifer, N. A. Krasnegor and W. P. Smotherman (eds) *Fetal Development: a Psychological Perspective*. Hillsdale, NJ: Erlbaum.

LeDoux, J. (1998) *The Emotional Brain*. London: Phoenix.

LeDoux, J. E. (2000) Emotion circuits in the brain. *Annual Review of Neuroscience*, 23, 155–84.

LeDoux, J. E., Iwata, J., Cicchetti, P. and Reis, D. J. (1988) Different projections of the central amygdaloid nucleus mediate autonomic and behavioural correlates of conditioned fear. *Journal of Neuroscience*, 8, 2517–29.

Leekham, S. R. and Perner, J. (1991) Does the autistic child have a meta-representational deficit? *Cognition*, 40, 203–18.

Leibowitz, S. F., Weiss, G. F. and Suh, J. S. (1990) Medial hypothalmic nuclei mediate serotonin's inhibitory effect on feeding behavior, *Pharmacology, Biochemistry and Behavior*, 37, 735–42.

Leichtman, M. D. and Ceci, S. J. (1995) The effects of stereotypes and suggestions on preschoolers' reports. *Developmental Psychology*, 31, 568–78.

Lemere, F. and Voegtlin, W. L. (1950) An evaluation of aversive treatment of alcoholism. *Quarterly Journal of the Study of Alcoholism*, 11, 199–204.

Leon, A. C., Friedman, R. A., Sweeney, J. A., Brown, R. P. and Mann, J. J. (1990) Statistical issues in the identification of risk factors for suicidal behavior: the application of survival analysis. *Psychiatry Research*, 31, 99–108.

Leonard, L. B. (1998) *Children with Specific Language Impairment*. Cambridge, Mass.: MIT Press.

Leonard, N. H., Beauvais, L. L. and Scholl, R. W. (1995) A self concept-based model of work motivation. Paper presented at the Annual Meeting of the Academy of Management in August, USA.

Leone, P. and Di Chiara, G. (1987) Blockade by D-1 receptors by SCH 23390 antagonises morphine- and amphetamine-induced place preference conditioning. *European Journal of Pharmacology*, 135, 251–4.

Lepore, L. and Brown, R. (2002) The role of awareness: divergent automatic stereotype activation and implicit judgment correction. *Social Cognition*, 20, 321–51.

Lerner, M. J. (1980) *Belief in a Just World: a Fundamental Delusion*. New York: Plenum Press.

Lerner, M. J. and Miller, D. T. (1978) Just-world research and the attribution process: looking back and ahead. *Psychological Bulletin*, 85, 1030–51.

Leslie, A. M. (1987) Pretense and representation: the origins of 'theory of mind'. *Psychological Review*, 94, 412–26.

Leslie, A. M. and Frith, U. (1998) Autistic children's understanding of seeing, knowing and believing. *British Journal of Developmental Psychology*, 6, 315–24.

Leslie, A. M. and Thaiss, L. (1992) Domain specificity in conceptual development: neuropsychological evidence from autism. *Cognition*, 43, 225–51.

Lethem, J., Slade, P. D., Troup, J. D. G. and Bentley, G. (1983) Outline of a fear-avoidance model of exaggerated pain perception – I. *Behaviour Research & Therapy*, 21, 401–8.

LeVay, S. (1991) A difference in hypothalamic structure between heterosexual and homosexual men. *Science*, 253, 1034–7.

Levelt, W. J. M. (1989) *Speaking: from Intention to Articulation*. Cambridge, MA: MIT Press.

Levenson, R. W., Carstensen, L. L., Friesen. W. V. and Ekman, P. (1991) Emotion, physiology and expression in old age. *Psychology and Aging*, 6, 28–35.

Levenson, R. W., Ekman, P. and Friesen. W. V. (1990) Voluntary facial expression generates emotion-specific nervous system activity. *Psychophysiology*, 27, 363–84.

Levi-Montalcini, R. (1982) Developmental neurobiology and the natural history of nerve growth factor. *Annual Review of Neuroscience*, 5, 341–62.

Levine, M. P., Smolak, L., Moodey, A. F., Shuman, M. D. and Hessen, L. D. (1994) Normative developmental challenges and dieting and eating disturbances in middle school girls. *International Journal of Eating Disorders*, 15, 11–20.

Lewin, R. (1984) *Human Evolution: an Illustrated Introduction*. Boston: Blackwell Scientific Publications.

Lewis, C. and Osbourne, A. (1990) Three-year-olds' problems with false belief: conceptual deficit or linguistic artifact? *Child Development*, 61, 1514–19.

Lewis, C., Freeman, N. H., Kyriakidou, C., Maridaki-Kassotaki, K. and Berridge, D. M. (1996) Social influences on false belief access: specific sibling influences or general apprenticeship? *Child Development*, 67, 2930–47.

Lewis, M. and Brooks-Gunn, J. (1979) *Social Cognition and the Acquisition of Self*. New York: Plenum Press.

Lewis, Y. (2003) The self as a moral concept. *British Journal of Social Psychology*, 42(2), 225–37.

Lewontin, R. (2001) *The Doctrine of DNA: Biology as Ideology*. London: Penguin.

Ley, P. (1972) Primacy, rated importance and the recall of medical information. *Journal of Health and Social Behaviour*, 13, 311.

Ley, P. (1988) *Communicating with Patients*. London: Croom Helm.

Ley, P. (1989) Improving patients' understanding, recall, satisfaction and compliance. In A. Broome (ed.) *Health Psychology*. London: Chapman & Hall.

Ley, P. and Spelman, M. S. (1965) Communicating in an outpatient setting. *British Journal of Social and Clinical Psychology*, 4, 114–16.

Ley, P. and Spelman, M. S. (1967) *Communicating with the Patient*. London: Staples Press.

Ley, R. (1987) *Panic Disorder and Agoraphobia – Fear of Fear or Fear of the Symptoms Produced by Hyperventilation. Journal of Behavior Therapy & Experimental Psychiatry*, 18(4), 305–16, December.

Ley, R. and Walker, H. (1973) Effects of carbon dioxide-oxygen inhalation on heart rate, blood pressure and subjective anxiety. *Journal of Behaviour Therapy & Experimental Psychiatry*, 4, 223–8.

Li, T., Xu, K., Deng, H., Cai, G., Liu, J., Wang, R., Xiang, X., Zhao, J., Murray, R. M., Sham, P. C. and Collier, D. A. (1997) Association analysis of the dopamine D4 gene exonIII VNTR and heroin abuse in Chinese subjects. *Molecular Psychiatry*, 2, 413–16.

Libby, S., Powell, S. D., Messer, D. and Jordan, R. R. (1989) Spontaneous play in children with autism – a reappraisal. *Journal of Autism and Developmental Disorders*, 28, 6, 487–99.

Liberman, I. Y., Shankweiler, D. and Fischer, F. W. (1974) Explicit syllable and phoneme segmentation in the young child. *Journal of Experimental Child Psychology*, 18(2).

Lieberman, D. A. (2000) *Learning: Behaviour and Cognition* (3rd edn). UK: Wadsworth.

Lieberman, H. R., Tharion, W. J., Shukitt-Hale, B., Speckman, K. L. and Tulley, R. (2002) Effects of caffeine, sleep loss and stress on cognitive performance and mood during US Navy SEAL training. Sea-Air-Land. *Psychopharmacology*, 164, 250–61.

Likert, R. (1932) A technique for the measurement of attitudes. *Archives of Psychology*, 140, 1–55.

Lin, L., Faraco, J., Li, R., Kadotani, H., Rogers, W., Lin, X., Qiu, X., de Jong, P. J., Nishino, S. and Mignot, E. (1999) The sleep disorder canine narcolepsy is caused by a mutation in the hypocretin (orexin) receptor 2 gene. *Cell*, 98, 365–76.

Linaza, J. (1984) Piaget's marbles: the study of children's games and their knowledge of rules. *Oxford Review of Education*, 10, 271–4.

Linder, D. E., Cooper, J. and Jones, E. E. (1967) Decision freedom as a determinant of the role of incentive magnitude in attitude change. *Journal of Personality and Social Psychology*, 19, 1057–67.

Linehan, M. M. and Shearin, E. N. (1988) Lethal stress: a social-behavioral model of suicidal behavior. In S. Fisher and J. Reason (eds) *Handbook of Life Stress, Cognition and Health*. New York: Wiley.

Linton, M. (1975) Memory for real world events. In D. A. Norman and D. E. Rumelhart (eds) *Explorations in Cognition*. San Francisco: Freeman.

Lippitt, R. and White, R. (1943) The 'social climate' of children's groups. In R. G. Braker, J. Kounin and H. Wright (eds) *Child Behavior and Development*. New York: McGraw-Hill, 485–508.

Lisker, L. and Abramson, A. (1970) *The Voicing Dimension: Some Experiments in Comparative Phonetics*. Prague: Academia (Proceedings of the Sixth International Congress of Phonetic Sciences (1967). Prague: Academia).

Lissauer, H. (1890/1988) A case of visual agnosia with a contribution to theory. *Cognitive Neuropsychology*, 5, 157–92.

Locke, E. A. and Latham, G. P. (1985) The application of goal setting to sports. *Journal of Sports Psychology*, 7(3), 205–22.

Lockwood, P. (2002) Could it happen to you? Predicting the impact of downward comparisons on the self. *Journal of Personality and Social Psychology*, 82, 343–58.

Loehlin, J. C. (1989) Partitioning environmental and genetic contributions to behavioral development. *Am. Psychol*, 44, 1285–92.

Loftus, E. (1979) *Eyewitness Testimony*. Cambridge, MA: Harvard University Press.

Loftus, E. and Palmer, J. C. (1974) Reconstruction of automobile destruction: an example of the interaction between language and memory. *Journal of Verbal Learning and Verbal Behaviour*, 13, 585–9.

Lord, R. G., Brown, D. J. and Harvey, J. L. (2003) System constraints on leadership perceptions, behavior and influence: an example of connectionist level processes. In M. A. Hogg and S. Tindale (eds) *Blackwell Handbook of Social Psychology: Group Processes*. Oxford: Blackwell, 283–310.

Lorenz, K. (1937) The companion in the bird's world. *Auk*, 54, 245–73.

Luchins, A. S. (1942) Mechanization in problem solving – the effect of Einstellung. *Psychological Monographs*, 54(6), 95.

Luchins, A. S. (1957) Primacy–recency in impression formation. In C. Hovland (ed.) *The Order of Presentation of Persuasion*. New Haven, CT: Yale University Press.

Luchins, A. S. and Luchins, E. H. (1959) *Rigidity of Behaviour: a Variational Approach to the Effect of Einstellung*. Oxford: University of Oregon Press.

Luria, A. R. (1973) *The Working Brain*. Harmondsworth: Penguin.

Luria, A. R. (1980) *Higher Cortical Functions in Man*. New York: Basic Books.

Lusher, J. M., Chandler, C. and Ball, D. (2001) Dopamine D4 receptor gene (DRD4) is associated with novelty seeking (NS) and substance abuse: the sage continues . . . . *Molecular Psychiatry*, 6, 497–9.

Lusher, J. M., Ebersole, L. and Ball, D. (2000) Dopamine D4 receptor gene and severity of dependence. *Addiction Biology*, 5, 471–4.

Lutzker, J. R. and Martin, J. A. (1981) *Behavior Change*. Monterey, CA: Brooks.

Lynn, R. (2001) *Eugenics: a Reassessment*. Westport, CT: Praeger/Greenwood.

Lytton, H. (1980) *Parent–Child Interaction. The Socialization Process Observed in Twin and Singleton Families*. New York: Plenum.

Maccoby, E. E. (1998) *The Two Sexes: Growing Apart, Coming Together*. Cambridge, MA: Belknap Press.

Maccoby, E. E. (2000) Perspectives on gender development. *International Journal of Behavioral Development*, 24, 398–406.

MacDonald, D. A. and Friedman, H. L. (2002) Assessment of humanistic, transpersonal and spiritual constructs: state of the science. *Journal of Humanistic Psychology*, 42(4), 102–25.

MacKintosh, N. J. (ed.) (1995) *Cyril Burt: Fraud or Framed*. Oxford: Oxford University Press.

Macrae, C. N., Stangor, C. and Milne, A. B. (1994) Activating social stereotypes: a functional analysis. *Journal of Experimental Social Psychology*, 30, 370–389.

Madsen, P. L., Holm, S., Vorstrup, S., Friberg, L., Lassen, N. A. and Wildschiodtz G. (1991) Human regional cerebral blood flow during rapid-eye-movement sleep. *Journal of Cerebral Blood Flow and Metabolism*, 11, 502–507.

References

Magnusson, D., Stattin, H. and Allen, V. L. (1985) Biological maturation and social development: a longitudinal study of some adjustment processes from mid-adolescence to adulthood. *Journal of Youth and Adolescence*, 14, 267–83.

Maguire, E. A., Frackowiak, R. S. J. and Frith, C. D. (1997) Recalling the routes around London: activation of the right hippocampus in taxi drivers. *Journal of Neuroscience*, 17, 7103–7110.

Maguire, E. A., Gadian, D. G., Johnsrude, I. S., Good, J., Ashburner, R., Frackowiak, R. S. J. and Frith, C. D. (2000) Navigational-related structural change in the hippocampi of taxi drivers. *Proceedings of the National Academy of Sciences of the United States of America*, 97, 4398–4403.

Maiden, R. J., Peterson, S. A., Caya, M. and Hayslip, J. R. B. (2003) Personality changes in the old-old: a longitudinal study. *Journal of Adult Development*, 10(1), 31–9.

Main, M. and Cassidy, J. (1988) Categories of response to reunion with the parent at age 6: predictable from infant attachment classifications and stable over a 1-month period. *Developmental Psychology*, 24, 415–26.

Main, M., Kaplan, N., Cassidy, J. (1985) Security infancy, childhood and adulthood: a move to the level of representation. Monographs of the Society for Research in Child Development, 50(1–2) (Serial No. 209)

Mak, A. S., Heaven, P. C. L. and Rummery, A. (2003) The role of group identity and personality domains as indicators of self-reported delinquency. *Psychology Crime and Law*, Vol. 9(1), 9–18.

Maki, R. H. and Hasher, L. (1975) Encoding variability: a role in immediate and long term memory? *American Journal of Psychology*, 88, 217–31.

Maldonado-Irizarry, C. S., Stellar, J. R. and Kelley, A. E. (1994) Effects of cocaine and GBR-12909 on brain stimulation reward. *Pharmacology, Biochemistry and Behavior*, 48, 915–20.

Malim, T. and Birch, A. (1998) *Introductory Psychology*. London: Macmillan.

Malloy, M. H. and Berendes, H. (1998) Does breast-feeding influence intelligence quotients at 9 and 10 years of age? *Early Human Development*, Vol. 50(2), 209–217.

Mandler, G. (1967) Organisation in memory. In K. W. Spence and J. T. Spence (eds) *The Psychology of Learning and Motivation* (Vol. I, pp. 327–72) New York: Academic Press.

Maner, J. K., Luce, C. L., Neuberg, S. L., Cialdini, R. C., Brown, S. and Sagarin, B. J. (2002) The effects of perspective-taking on motivations for helping: Still no evidence for altruism. *Personality and Social Psychology Bulletin*, 28, 1601–1610.

Manetto, V., Medori, R., Cortelli, P., Montagna, P., Tinuper, P., Baruzzi, A., Rancurel, G., Hauw, J. J., Vanderhaeghen, J. J. and Mailleux, P. (1992) Fatal familial insomnia: clinical and pathologic study of five new cases. *Neurology*, 42, 312–9.

Mann, J. J., Waternaux, C., Haas, G. L. and Malone, K. M. (1999) Toward a clinical model of suicidal behavior in psychiatric patients. *American Journal of Psychiatry*, 156, 181–189.

Manstead, A. S. R. and Semin, G. R. (1980) Social facilitation effects: mere enhancement of dominant responses? *British Journal of Social and Clinical Psychology*, 19, 119–36.

Manstead, A. S. R. and Semin, G. R. (2001) Methodology in social psychology: tools to test theories. In Hewstone, M. and Stroebe, W. (eds) *Introduction to Social Psychology* (3rd edn, pp. 73–110) Oxford: Blackwell.

Maquet, P. (1999) Brain mechanisms of sleep: contribution of neuroimaging techniques. *Journal of Psychopharmacology*. 13, Supplement 1, S25–S28.

Maquet, P., Laureys, S., Peigneux, P., Fuchs, S., Petiau, C., Phillips, C., Aerts, J., Del Fiore, G., Degueldre, C., Meulemans, T., Luxen, A., Franck, G., Van Der Linden, M., Smith, C. and Cleeremans, A. (2000) Experience-dependent changes in cerebral activation during human REM sleep. *Nature Neuroscience*, 3, 831–6.

Marcia, J. E. (1966) Development and validation of ego-identity status. *Journal of Personality and Social Psychology*, 3, 551–8.

Marona-Lewicka, D., Rhee, G. S., Sprague, J. E. and Nichols, D. E. (1996) Reinforcing effects of certain serotonin-releasing amphetamine derivatives. *Pharmacology, Biochemistry and Behavior*, 53, 99–105.

Marr, D. (1982) *Vision: a Computational Investigation into the Human Representation and Processing of Visual Information*. San Francisco: WH Freeman.

Marsh, R. L., Landau, J. D. and Hicks, J. L. (1997) Contributions of inadequate source monitoring to unconscious plagiarism during idea generation. *Journal of Experimental Psychology: Learning, Memory and Cognition*, 23(4), 886–97.

Marshall, J. F., Richardson, J. S. and Teitelbaum, P. (1974) Nigrostriatal bundle damage and the lateral hypothalamic syndrome. *Journal of Comparative Physiological Psychology*, 87, 808–830.

Marshall, J. C. and Halligan, P. W. (1988) Blind sight and insight in visual-spatial neglect. *Nature*, 336(6201), 766–7.

Marshall, J. and Newcombe, F. (1973) Patterns of paralexia: a psycholinguistic approach. *Journal of Psycholinguistic Research*, 2, 175–199.

Marslen-Wilson, W. D. (1975) Sentence perception as an interactive parallel process. *Science*, 189, 226–8.

Marslen-Wilson, W. D. (1984) Spoken word recognition: a tutorial review. In H. Bouma and D. Bouwhis (eds) *Attention and Performance X: Control of Language Processes*. Hove: Lawrence Erlbaum Associates.

Marslen-Wilson, W. D. (1989) *Lexical Representation and Process*. Cambridge, MA: MIT Press.

Martin, G. N., (1996) Olfactory remediation: Current evidence and possible applications. *Social Science and Medicine*, 43, 63–70.

Martin, B. V., Holmes, D. L., Guth, M. and Kovac, P. (1979) The potential of children as eye-witnesses: a comparison of children and adults on eyewitness tasks. *Law and Human Behavior*, 3, 295–303.

Martin, P. and Bateson, P. (1993) *Measuring Behaviour: an Introductory Guide* (2nd edn). Cambridge: Cambridge University Press.

Martin, R. and Hewstone, M. (2003) Conformity and independence in groups: majorities and minorities. In M. A.

Hogg and S. Tindale (eds) *Blackwell Handbook of Social Psychology: Group Processes* (pp. 209–34) Oxford: Blackwell.

Martinez-Rodriguez, J. E., Lin, L., Iranzo, A., Genis, D., Marti, M. J., Santamaria, J. and Mignot, E. (2003) Decreased hypocretin-1 (Orexin-A) levels in the cerebrospinal fluid of patients with myotonic dystrophy and excessive daytime sleepiness. *Sleep*, 26, 287–90.

Masangkay, Z. S., McCluskey, K. A., McIntyre, C. W., Sims-Knight, J., Vaughn, B. E. and Flavell, J. H. (1974) The early development of inferences about the visual percepts of others. *Child Development*, 45, 237–46.

Maslow, A. (1954) *Motivation and Personality*. New York: Harper & Row.

Maslow, A. (1968) Toward and Psychology of being (2nd Ed.) New York: Harper & Row.

Maslow, A. (1970) Motivation and personality. New York: Harper & Row.

Masten, A., Best, K. and Garmezy, N. (1990) Resilience and development: Contributions from the study of children who overcame adversity. *Development and Psychopathology*, 2, 425–44.

Masters, M. S. and Sanders, B. (1993) Is the gender difference in mental rotation disappearing?. *Behavior Genetics*, 23, 307–41.

Matarazzo, J. D. (1980) Behavioral health and behavioral medicine. Frontiers for a new health psychology. *American Scientist* 35, 807–17.

Matas, L., Arend, R. and Sroufe, L. A. (1978) Continuity of adaptation in the second year. The relationship between the quality of attachment and later competence. *Child Development*, 49, 547–56.

Mathews, A. and MacLeod, C. (1994) Cognitive approaches to emotion and emotional disorders. *Annual Review of Psychology*, 45, 25–50.

Mathews, A. M., Bancroft, J., Whitehead, A., Hackmann, A., Julier, D., Bancroft, J., Gath, D. and Shaw, P. (1976) The behavioural treatment of sexual inadequacy: a comparative study. *Behaviour Research & Therapy*, 14, 427–36.

Matsumoto, K., Suzuki, W. and Tanaka, K. (2003) Neuronal correlates of goal-based motor selection in the prefontal cortex. *Science*, 301, 229–32.

Mayer, D. and Hanges, P. J. (2003) Understanding the stereotype threat effect with 'culture-free' tests: an examination of its mediators and measurement. *Human Performance*, Vol. 16(3), 207–30.

Mazaleski, J. L., Iwata, B. A., Vollmer, T. R., Zarcone, J. R. and Smith, R. G. (1993) Analysis of the reinforcement and extinction components in DRO contingencies with self-injury. *Journal of Applied Behavior Analysis*, 26, 143–56.

McArthur, L. A. (1972) The how and what of why: some determinants and consequences of causal attributions. *Journal of Personality and Social Psychology*, 22, 171–93.

McCain, G. and Segal, E. M. (1973) *The game of science*. Monterey, CA: Brooks/Cole.

McCall, R. B. (1979) The development of intellectual functioning in infancy and the prediction of later IQ. In J. D. Osofsky (ed.) *The handbook of infant development*. New York: Wiley, 707–41.

McCann, U. D., Ridenour, A., Shaham, Y. and Ricaurte, G. A. (1994) Serotonin neurotoxicity after $(+/-)3$, 4-methylenedioxymethamphetamine (MDMA; 'Ecstasy'), a controlled study in humans. *Neuropsychopharmacology*, 10, 129–38.

McCann, U. D., Szabo, Z., Scheffel, U., Dannals, R. F. and Ricaurte, G. A. (1998) Positron emission tomographic evidence of toxic effect of MDMA ('Ecstasy') on brain serotonin neurons in human beings. *Lancet*, 352, 433–7.

McClelland, D. C., Atkinson, J. W., Clark, R. A. and Lowell, E. L. (1953) *The achievement motive*. Englewood Cliffs: NJ: Prentice-Hall.

McCoul, M. D. and Haslam, N. (2001) Predicting high risk sexual behaviour in heterosexual and homosexual men: The roles of impulsivity and sensation seeking, *Personality and Individual Differences*, Vol. 27(8), 1303–1270.

McCracken, L. M. and Turk, D. C. (2002) Behavioral and cognitive-behavioral treatment for chronic pain – Outcome, predictors of outcome and treatment process. *Spine*, 27, 2564–73.

McCracken, L. M., Zayfert, C. and Gross, R. T. (1992) The Pain Anxiety Symptoms Scale: Development and validation of the scale to measure fear of pain. *Pain*, 50, 67–73.

McCrae, R. R. and John, O. P. (1992) An introduction to the five-factor model and its applications. *Journal of Personality*, 60, 175–215.

McDonald, C. and Murphy, K. C. (2003) *The Psychiatric clinics of North America*, 26, 41–63.

McDougall, W. (1908) An Introduction to social psychology. London: Methuen.

McGarrigle, J. and Donaldson, M. (1974) Conservation accidents. *Cognition*. 3, 341–50.

McGeogh, J. A. and McDonald, W. T. (1931) Meaningful relation and retroactive inhibition. *American Journal of Psychology*, 43, 579–88.

McGhee, P. (2001) *Thinking Psychologically*. Basingstoke: Palgrave.

McGrath, J. M. and Frueh, B. C. (2002) Fraudulent claims of combat heroics within the VA? *Psychiatric Services*, 53, 345.

McGuire, W. J. (1969) The nature of attitudes and attitude change. In Lindzey, G. and Aronson, E. (eds) *The Handbook of Social Psychology* (2nd Edition, pp. 136–314) Reading MA: Addison-Wesley.

McGurk, H. and Soriano, G. (1998) Families and social development: the 21st century. In A. Campbell and S. Muncer (eds) *The Social Child*, pp. 113–42. London: Psychology Press.

McIntosh, D. N., Zajonc, R. B., Vig, P. S. and Emerick, S. W. (1997) Facial movement, breathing, temperature and effect: implications of the vascular theory of emotional efference. *Cognition and Emotion* 11(2), 171–95.

McKenna, E. (2000) *Business Psychology and Organisational Behaviour: a Student's Handbook*. Hove: Psychology Press (Chapter 7: Groups and team building).

McNally, R. J. (1997) Atypical phobias. In G. C. L. Davey (ed.)

References

Phobias; A handbook of theory, research and treatment. Wiley: Chichester.

McNally, R. J. (2003) Progress and controversy in the study of posttraumatic stress disorder. *Annual Review of Psychology* 54 229–52.

McNeal, E. T. and Cimbolic P. (1986) Antidepressants and biochemical theories of depression. *Psychological Bulletin*, 99, 361–74.

McNeill, D. (1992) Hand and mind: What gestures reveal about thought. Chicago: University of Chicago Press.

McRae, A. L., Budney, A. J. and Brady, K. T. (2003) Treatment of marijuana dependence: a review of the literature. *Journal of Substance Abuse Treatment*, 24, 369–76.

Mead, G. H. (1934) *Mind, self and Society: From the standpoint of a Social Behaviourist* (C. W. Morris, ed.) Chicago: University of Chicago Press.

Meddis, R. (1975) On the function of sleep. *Animal Behaviour*, 23, 676–91.

Medin, D. L. and Ross, B. H. (1996) *Cognitive Psychology* (2nd ed.) London: Harcourt Brace College Publishers.

Meehan, S. M. and Schechter, M. D. (1998) LSD produces conditioned place preference in male but not female fawn hooded rats. *Pharmacology, Biochemistry and Behavior*, 59, 105–108.

Megens, A. A. and Kennis, L. E. (1996) Risperidone and related 5HT2/D2 antagonists: a new type of antipsychotic agent? *Progress in Medical Chemistry*, 33, 185–232.

Meilman, P. W. (1979) Cross-sectional age changes in ego identity status during adolescence. *Developmental Psychology*, 15, 230–1.

Meins, E., Fernyhough, C. and Wainwright, R. (2002) Maternal mind-mindedness and attachment security as predictors of theory of mind understanding. *Child Development*, 76(3), 1715–26.

Meins, E., Fernyhough, C. and Russell, J. (1998) Security of attachment as a predictor of symbolic and mentalising abilities: a longitudinal study. *Social Development*, 7(1), 1–24.

Melnick, S. M. and Hinshaw, S. P. (1996) What they want and what they get: The social goals of boys with ADHD and comparison boys. *Journal of Abnormal Child Psychology* 24 169–85.

Meltzoff, A. N. and Borton, R. W. (1979) Intermodal matching by human neonates. *Nature*, 282, 403–04.

Meltzoff, A. N. and Moore, M. K. (1977) Imitation of facial and manual gestures by human neonates. Science, 198, 75–8.

Meltzoff, A. and Gopnik, A. (1993) The role of imitation in understanding persons and developing a theory of mind. In Baron-Cohen, S. Tager-Flushberg, H. and Cohen, D. (eds) *Understanding other minds – perspective from autism*. Oxford: Oxford University Press.

Melzack, R. and Wall, P. D. (1965) Pain mechanisms: a new theory. *Science*, 150, 971–9.

Melzack, R. and Wall, P. D. (1982) The challenge of pain. New York: Basic Books.

Mendelson, W. B. (2001) Neurotransmitters and sleep. *Journal of Clinical Psychiatry*, 62 Suppl 10, 5-8.

Messer, D. (2003) Processes of Development in Early Communication. In G. Bremner and A. Slater (eds) *Theories of infant development: Essays in memory of George Butterworth*. Oxford: Blackwell.

Messer, D. and Pine, K. (2000) Is collaborative learning influenced by children's representations. In R. Joiner (ed.) *Collaborating to Learn and Learning to Collaborate*. London: Free Association Press.

Metalsky, G. I., Haberstadt, L. J. and Abramson, L. Y. (1987) Vulnerability and invulnerability to depressive mood reactions: Towards a more powerful test of the diathesis-stress and causal mediation components of the reformulated theory of depression. *Journal of Personality & Social Psychology*, 52, 386–93.

Meyer, A., Mayerhofer, A., Kovar, K. A. and Schmidt, W. J. (2002) Rewarding effects of the optical isomers of 3, 4-methylenedioxy-methylamphetamine ('Ecstasy') and 3, 4-methylenedioxy-ethylamphetamine ('Eve') measured by conditioned place preference in rats. *Neuroscience Letters*, 330, 280–4.

Meyer, D. E. and Schvaneveldt, R. W. (1971) Facilitation in recognizing pairs of words: Evidence of a dependence in retrieval operations. *Journal of Experimental Psychology*, 90, 227–35.

Michas, I. C. and Henry, L. A. (1994) The link between phonological memory and vocabulary acquisition. *British Journal of Developmental Psychology*, 12(2), 147–63.

Michaud, C., Kahn, J. P., Musse, N. *et al.* (1990) Relationships between a critical life event and eating behaviour in high school students. *Stress Medicine*, 6, 57–64.

Michener, W. and Rozin, P. (1994) Pharmacological versus sensory factors in the satiation of chocolate craving. *Physiology and Behaviour*, 56(3), 419–22.

Mifsud, J.-C., Hernadez, L. and Hoebel, B. G. (1989) Nicotine infusion infused into the nucleus accumbens increase synaptic dopamine as measured by in vivo microdialysis. *Brain Research*, 478, 365–7.

Mikhliner, M. and Solomon, Z. (1988) Attributional style and post-traumatic stress disorder. *Journal of Abnormal Psychology*, 97, 308-313.

Milberger, S., Biederman, J., Faraone, S. V. and Chen, L. (1996) Is maternal smoking during pregnancy a risk factor for attention deficit hyperactivity disorder in children? *American Journal of Psychiatry*, 153, 1138-1142.

Miles, J. (2001) *Research Methods and Statistics*. Exeter: Crucial.

Miles, T. R. (1983) Dyslexia: The pattern of difficulties. London: Granada.

Milgram, S. (1963) Behavioral study of obedience. *Journal of Abnormal and Social Psychology*, 67, 371-378.

Milgram, S. (1974) *Obedience to Authority*. London: Tavistock.

Milgram, S., Mann, L. and Harter, S. (1965) The lost-letter technique: a tool of social research. *Public Opinion Quarterly*, 29, 437-438.

Miller, R. J., Horn, A. S. and Iversen, L. L. (1974) The action of neuroleptics drugs on dopamine-stimulated adonsine cyclic 3', 5'-monophosphate production in rat neostriatum and limbic forebrain. *Molecular Pharmacology*, 10, 759-766.

Miller, D. T., Norman, S. A. and Wright, E. (1978) Distortion in perception as a consequence of the need for effective control. *Journal of Personality and Social Psychology*, 36, 598-607.

Miller, G. A. (1956) The magical number seven, plus or minus two: Some limits on our capacity for information processing. *Psychological Review*, 63, 81–97.

Miller, L. T. and Vernon, P. A. (1992) The general factor in short-term memory, intelligence and reaction time. *Intelligence*, 16–5–29.

Miller, P. M. and Plant, M. (1996) Drinking, smoking and illicit drug use among 15 and 16 year olds in the United Kingdom. *British Medical Journal*, 313, 294–7.

Milner, B. (1970) Memory and the medial temporal regions of the brain. In K. H. Pribram and E. D. Broadbent (eds) *Biology of Memory*. Academic Press, NY.

Milner, D. (1983) *Children and Race: Ten Years On*. London: Ward Lock Educational.

Minami, S., Kamegai, J., Sugihara, H., Suzuki, N., Higuchi, H. and Wakabayashi, I. (1995) Central glucoprivation evoked by administration of 2-deoxy-D-glucose induces expression of the c-fos gene in a subpopulation of neuropeptide Y neurons in the rat hypothalamus. *Brain Research: Molecular Brain Research*, 33, 305–310.

Minuchin, P. (1985) Families and individual development: Provocations from the field of family therapy. *Child Development*, 56, 289–302.

Minuchin, S., Rosman, B.L. and Baker, L. (1978) *Psychosomatic Families: anorexia Nervosa in Context*. Cambridge, MA: Harvard University Press.

Mirza, N. R., Pei, Q., Stolerman, I. P. and Zetterström, T. S. C. (1996) The nicotine receptor agonists (-)-nicotine and isoarecolone differ in their effects on dopamine release in the nucleus accumbens. *European Journal of Pharmacology*, 295, 207–10.

Mischel, W. (1983) Delay of gratification as process and as person variable in development. In D. Magnusson and V. L. Allen (eds) *Human development: an interactional perspective*. New York: Academic Press.

Mischel, W. (1984) Convergences and challenges in the search for consistency. *American Psychologist*, 39, 351–64.

Mischel, W. (1986) *An Introduction to Personality*. New York: Holt, Rinehart & Winston.

Mitchell, P. (1996) *Acquiring a Conception of Mind. A Review of Psychological Research and Theory*. Hove: Erlbaum.

Mithani, S., Martin-Iverson, M. T., Phillips, A. G. and Fibiger, H. C. (1986) The effects of haloperidol on amphetamine and methyphenidate-induced conditioned place preference and locomotor activity. *Psychopharmacology*, 90, 247–52.

Miyake, K., Chen, S. J. and Campos, J. J. (1985) Infant temperament, mother's mode of interaction and attachment in Japan: an interim report. In I. Bretherton and E. Waters (eds) Growing Points of Attachment Theory and Research.

Monographs of the Society for Research in Child Development, 50, 276–97.

Miyauchi, S., Takino, R. and Azakami, M. (1990) Evoked potentials during REM sleep reflect dreaming. *Electroencephalography and Clinical Neurophysiology*, 76, 19–28.

Mizell, C. and, Andre, C. (2003) Bullying: The consequences of interparental discord and child's self-concept. *Family Processes*, Vol. 42(2), 237–51.

Mogford, K. (1988) Oral language development in prelinguistically deaf children. In D. Bishop and K. Mogford (eds) *Language development in exceptional circumstances*. Edinburgh: Churchill Livingstone.

Mogg, K. and Bradley, B. P. (1998) A cognitive–motivational analysis of anxiety. *Behaviour Research & Therapy*, 36, 809–48.

Mogg, K., Bradley, R. B., Williams, R. and Mathews, A. (1993) Subliminal processing of emotional information in anxiety and depression. *Journal of Abnormal Psychology* 102 304–11.

Mogg, K., Millar, N. and Bradley, B. P. (2000) Biases in eye movements to threatening facial expressions in generalized anxiety disorder and depressive disorder. *Journal of Abnormal Psychology*, 109(4), 695–704, November.

Monteil, J. M. and Huguet, P. (1999) *Social Context and Cognitive Performance*. Philadelphia: Psychology Press.

Montgomery, S. A. (1995) *Selective serotonin reuptake inhibitors in the acute treatment of depression*. In F. E. Bloom and D. Kupfer (eds) *Psychopharmacology: The fourth generation of progress*. New York: Raven.

Moos, R. H. and Swindle, R. W. (1990) Stress life circumstances: Concepts and measures. *Stress Medicine*, 6, 171–8.

Mora, F., Phillips, A. G., Koolhaas, J. M. and Rolls, E. T. (1976) Prefrontal Cortex and neostriatum self-stimulation in the rat: differential effects produced by apomorphine. *Brain Research Bulletin*, 1, 421–4.

Morais, J., Alegria, J. and Content, A. (1987) The relationships between segmental analysis and alphabetic literacy: an interactive view. *Cahiers de Psychologie Cognitive/Current Psychology of Cognition*, 7(5), 415–38.

Moray, N. (1959) Attention in dichotic listening: affective cues and the influence of instructions. *The Quarterly Journal of Experimental Psychology*, 11, 56–60.

Moreland, R. L. and Beach, S, R. (1992) Exposure effects in the classroom: the development of affinity amongst students. *Journal of Experimental Social Psychology*, 28, 255–76.

Moreland, R. L. and Zajonc, R. B. (1982) Exposure effects in person perception: familiarity, similarity and attraction. *Journal of Experimental Social Psychology*, 18, 395–415.

Morris, R. G., Anderson, E., Lynch, G. S., Baudry, M. (1986) Selective impairment of learning and blockade of long-term potentiation by an N-methyl-D-aspartate receptor antagonist, AP5. *Nature*, 319, 774–76.

Morton, J. (1969) Interaction of information in word recognition. *Psychological Review*, 76, 165–78.

Morton, J. (1979) Facilitation in word recognition: Experiments causing change in the logogen model. In P. A. Kolers, M. E.

Wrolstad and M. Bouma (eds) *Processing of Visible Language* (pp. 259–68) New York: Plenum.

Moruzzi, G. (1972) The sleep–waking cycle. *Ergebbnisse der Physiologie, biologischen Chemie und Experimentellen Pharmakologie*, 64, 1–165.

Moruzzi, G. and Magoun, H. W. (1949) Brain stem reticular formation and activation of the EEG Electroencephography and Clinical Neurophysiology, 1, 455–73.

Moskovici, S. (1976) *Social Influence and Social Change*. London: Academic Press.

Moskovici, S. (1980) Towards a theory of conversion behaviour. In L. Berkowitz (ed.) *Advances in Experimental Social Psychology* (Volume 13, pp. 203–39) New York: Academic Press.

Moskovici, S. and Lage, E. (1976) Studies in social influence III: majority versus minority influence in a group. *European Journal of Social Psychology*, 6, 149–74.

Moskovici, S. and Personnaz, B. (1986) Studies on latent influence by the spectrometer method: I. The impact of psychologization in the case of conversion by a minority or a majority. *European Journal of Social Psychology*, 16, 345–60.

Moskovici, S., Lage, E. and Naffrechoux, M. (1969) Influence of a consistent minority on the responses of a majority in a color perception task. *Sociometry*, 32, 365–80.

Motes, M., Bahr, G., Atha-Weldon, C. and Dansereau, D. (2003) Academic guide maps for learning psychology. *Teaching of Psychology*, 30(3), 240–2.

Muchinsky, P. M. (1997) *Psychology Applied to Work*. Pacific Grove, CA: Brooks/Cole.

Muller, S. L., Williamson, D. A. and Martin, C. K. (2002) False consensus effect for attitudes related to body shape in normal weight women concerned with body shape. *Eating & Weight Disorders*, 7, 124–30.

Mummendey, A. and Otten, S. (1998) Positive-negative asymmetry in social discrimination. In W. Stroebe and M. Hewstone (eds) *European Review of Social Psychology* (Volume 8) Chichester: Wiley.

Murphy, C. M., Messer, D. J. (1977) Mothers, infants and pointing: a study of a gesture. In H. R. Schaffer (ed.) *Studies in mother-infant interactions*. London: Academic Press, 325–54.

Myers, R. D., Wooten, M. H., Ames, C. D. and Nyce, J. W. (1995) Anorexic action of a new potential neuropeptide Y antagonist [D-Tyr27, 36, D-Thr32]-NPY (27-36) infused into the hypothalamus of the rat. *Brain Research Bulletin*, 37, 237–45.

Myers, D. G. and Kaplan, M. F. (1976) Group-induced polarization in simulated juries. *Personality and Social Psychology Bulletin*, 2, 63–6.

Myers, D. G. and Lamm, H. (1976) The group polarization phenomenon. *Psychological Bulletin*, 83, 602–27.

Myers, L. B. (2000) Deceiving others or deceiving themselves? *The Psychologist*, 13(8), 400–403.

Navon, D. and Gopher, D. (1979) On the economy of the human information processing system. *Psychological Review*, 86, 214–55.

Neisser, U. (1964) Visual search. *Scientific American*, 210(6), 94–102.

Neisser, U. (1967) *Cognitive Psychology*. New York: Appleton Century Crofts Educational.

Neisser, U. (1982) *Memory Observed*. San Francisco: Freeman.

Neisser, U. (1984) Interpreting Harry Bahrick's discovery: What confers immunity against forgetting? *Journal of Experimental Psychology: General*, 113(1), 32–5.

Neisser, U., Novick, R. and Lazar, R. (1963) Searching for ten targets simultaneously. *Perceptual & Motor Skills*, 17(3), 955–61.

Nelson, K. (1989) Remembering: a functional developmental perspective. In R. R. Solomons, G. R. Goethals, C. M. Kelley and B. R. Stephens (eds) *Memory: Interdisciplinary Approaches* (pp. 127–50) New York: Springer.

Nemeth, C. (1986) Differential contributions of majority and minority influence. *Psychological Review*, 93, 23–32.

Neugebauer, R. (1979) Medieval and early modern theories of mental illness. *Archives of General Psychiatry*, 36, 477–83.

Newell, A. and Simon, H. A. (1961) Computer simulation of human thinking. *Science*, 134, 2011–2017.

Newstead, S. E. (2002) Examining the examiners: Why are we so bad at assessing students? *Psychology Learning and Teaching*, 2, 70–75.

Newstead, S. E. and Findlay, K. (1997) Some problems with using examination performance as a measure of teaching ability. *Psychology Teaching Review*, 6, 14–21.

Newstead, S. E. and Hoskins, S. (1999) Encouraging student motivation. In H. Fry, S. Ketteridge and S. Marshall (eds) *A Handbook of Teaching and Learning in Higher Education*. London: Kogan Page.

Nicholls, J. G., Cobb, P., Yackel, E., Wood, T., Wheatley, G. (1990) Students' theories of mathematics and their mathematical knowledge: multiple dimensions of assessment. In G. Kulm (ed) *Assessing Higher Order Thinking in Mathematics* (pp. 137–54). Washington, DC: American. Association of Advanced Science.

Nicholls, J. G., Martin, A. R., Wallace, B. G. and Fuchs, P. A. (2001) *From Neuron to Brain* (4th edn). Massachusetts: Sinauer Associates, Inc.

Nisbett, R. E. (1993) Violence and U. S. regional culture. *American Psychologist*, 48, 441–9.

Nisbett, R. E. and Borgida, E. (1975) Attribution and the psychology of prediction. *Journal of Personality and Social Psychology*, 32, 93–943.

Nisbett, R. E. and Ross, L. (1980) *Human Inference: Strategies and Shortcomings of Social Judgement*. Englewood Cliffs, NJ: Prentice Hall.

Norman, D. (1968) Towards a theory of memory and attention. *Psychological Review*, 75, 522–36.

Norman, D. and Shallice, T. (1980) Attention to action: Willed and automatic control of Behaviour. Center for Human Information Processing Report 99. LaJolla, CA: University of California, San Diego.

Northrup, J., Broussard, C., Jones, K., George, T., Vollmer, T. R. and Herring, M. (1995) The differential effects of teacher and peer attention on the disruptive classroom behavior of three children with a diagnosis of attention deficit hyperactivity disorder. *Journal of Applied Behavior Analysis*, 28, 277–88.

Noyes, R., Woodman, C., Garvey, M. J. *et al.* (1992) Generalized Anxiety Disorder vs Panic Disorder – Distinguishing Characteristics and Patterns of Comorbidity. *Journal of Nervous & Mental Disease*, 180(6), 369–79 June.

Nussbaum, D., Collins, M., Cutler, J., Zimmerman, W. and Jacques, I. (2002) Crime type and specific personality indicia: Cloninger's TCI impulsivity, empathy and attachment subscales in non-violent, violent and sexual offenders. *American Journal of Forensic Psychology*, Vol. 20(1), 23–56.

O'Brien, C. P. (1997) A range of research-based pharmacotherapies for addiction. *Science*, 278, 66–70.

O'Connor, T. G. and Croft, C. M. (2001) A twin study of attachment in preschool children. *Child Development*, 72, 1501–11.

O'Connor, T. G., Rutter, M., Beckett, C., Keaveney, L., Kreppner, J. M. and the Romanian Adoptees Study Team. (2000) The effects of global severe privation on cognitive competence: extension and longitudinal follow-up. *Child Development*, 71, 376–90.

O'Dwyer, A. M., Lucey, J. V. and Russell, G. F. 1996. Serotonin activity in anorexia nervosa after long-term weight restoration: response to D-fenfluramine challenge. *Psychological Medicine*, 26, 353–9.

O'Leary, K. D. and Wilson, G. T. (1975) *Behavior therapy: application and outcome*. Englewood Cliffs, NJ: Prentice-Hall.

O'Reilly, M. F. (1995) Functional analysis and treatment of escape-maintained aggression correlated with sleep deprivation. *Journal of Applied Behavior Analysis*, 28, 225–6.

Ochs, E. and Schieffelin, B. B. (1984) Language acquisition and socialization. In R. A. Shweder and R. A. Levine (eds) *Culture Theory*. Cambridge: Cambridge University Press.

Ogden, J. (2000) *Health Psychology: a textbook*. Buckingham PA: Open University Press.

Olds, J. and Milner, P. (1954) Positive reinforcement from electrical stimulation of septal area and other regions of the rat brain. *Journal of Comparative and Physiological Psychology*, 47, 419–27.

Olfson, M. and Klerman, G. L. (1993) Trends in the prescription of psychotropic medications: The role of physician speciality. *Medical Care*, 31, 559–64.

Olweus, D. (1991) Bully/victim problems among schoolchildren: basic facts and effects of a school based intervention program. In D. Pepler and K. Rubin (eds) *The development and treatment of childhood aggression*. Hillsdale, NJ: Erlbaum, 441–8.

Olweus, D. (1992) Victimization among schoolchildren: intervention and prevention. In G. W. Albee, L. A. Bond and T. V. Cook Monsey (eds) *Improving children's lives: global perspectives on prevention*. Newbury Park: Sage Publications.

Olweus, D. (1993) *Bullying at school: What we know and what we can do*. Oxford: Blackwell.

Oppenheim, A. N. (1992) *Questionnaire Design, Interviewing and Attitude Measurement* (new edn). London: Pinter.

Orne, M. T. (1962) On the social psychology of the psychology experiment – with particular reference to demand characteristics and their implications. *American Psychologist*, 17(11), 419–27.

Osgood, C. E., Suci, G. J. and Tannenbaum, P. H. (1957) *The Measurement of Meaning*. Urbana, IL: University of Illinois Press.

Osherson, D. N., Kosslyn, S. M. and Hollerbach, J. M. (eds) (1990) *Visual Cognition in Action: an Invitation to Cognitive Science* (Vol. 2). Cambridge, MA: MIT Press.

Ouellette, J. A. and Wood, W. (1998) Habit and intention in everyday life: the multiple processes by which past behavior predicts future behavior. *Psychological Bulletin*, 124, 54–74.

Ozonoff, S., Pennington, B. F., Rogers, S. J. (1991) Executive function deficits in high-functioning autistic individuals: relationship to theory of mind. *Journal of Child Psychology and Psychiatry*, 32, 1081–105.

Paivio, A. (1969) Mental imagery in associative learning and memory. *Psychological Review*, 76, 241–63.

Palmer, S. E. (1975) The effects of contextual scenes on the identification of objects. *Memory & Cognition*, 3(5), 519–26.

Paolini, S., Hewstone, M., Cairns, E. and Voci, A. (in press) Effects of direct and indirect cross-group friendships on judgements of Catholics and Protestants in Northern Ireland: the mediating role of anxiety-reduction. *Personality and Social Psychology Bulletin*.

Papez, J. W. (1937) A proposed mechanism of emotion. *Archives of Neurology and Psychiatry*, 38, 725–45.

Papp, L. A., Klein, D. F. and Gorman, J. M. (1993) Carbon dioxide hypersensitivity, hyperventilation and panic disorder. *American Journal of Psychiatry*, 150, 1149–1157.

Parker, L. A. (1996) LSD produces place preference and flavor avoidance but does not produce flavor aversion in rats. *Behavioral Neuroscience*, 110, 503–508.

Parker, D., Lajunen, T. and Summala, H. (2002) Anger and aggression among drivers in three European countries. *Accident Analysis and Prevention*, 34, 229–35.

Parker, D., Stradling, S. G. and Manstead, A. S. R. (1996) Modifying beliefs and attitudes to exceeding the speed limit: an intervention study based on the theory of planned behavior. *Journal of Applied Social Psychology*, 26, 1–19.

Parkes, C. M. (1993) Bereavement as a psychosocial transition: Processes of adaptation to change. In M. S. Stoebe, W. Stroebe and R. O. Hansson (eds) *Handbook of Bereavement: Theory, Research and Intervention*. New York: Cambridge University Press.

Parkin, A. J. (1996) *Explorations in Cognitive Neuropsychology*. Oxford: Blackwell.

Parrott, A. C., Lees, A., Garnham, N. J., Jones, M. and Wesnes, K. (1998) Cognitive performance in recreational users of MDMA ('ecstasy'): evidence for memory deficits. *Journal of Psychopharmacology*, 12, 79–83.

Passer, M. W. and Smith, R. E. (2001) *Psychology: Frontiers and Applications*. Boston: McGraw-Hill.

Patterson, M. L. (1983) *Nonverbal behavior: a Functional Perspective*. New York: Springer.

References

Paul, G. L. and Lentz, R. J. (1977) *Psychosocial treatment of chronic mental patients: Milieu versus social-learning programs.* Cambridge, MA: Harvard University Press.

Paul, G. L. (1966) *Insight vs desensitization in psychotherapy: an experiment in anxiety reduction.* Stanford, CA: Stanford University Press.

Paus, T., Zijdenbos, A., Worsley, K., Collins, D. L., Blumenthal, J., Giedd, J. N., Rapoport, J. L. and Evans, A. C. (1999) Structural maturation of neural pathways in children and adolescents: in vivo study. *Science*, 283, 1908–11.

Peck, B. K. and Vanderwolf, C. H. (1991) Effects of raphe stimulation on hippocampal and neocortical activity and behaviour. *Brain Research*, 568, 244–52.

Pederson, N. L. (1993) Genetic and environmental change in personality. In T. J. Bouchard and P. Proping (eds) *Twins as a tool of behavioural genetics* (pp 147–62). Sussex: Wiley.

Pederson, N. L., Plomin, R., McClearn, G. E. and Friberg, L. (1988) Neuroticism, extraversion and related traits in adult twins reared apart and reared together. *Journal of Personality and Social Psychology*. 55, 95–957.

Peeters, G. and Czapinski, J. (1990) Positive-negative asymmetry in evaluations: the distinction between affective and informational negativity effects. In W. Stroebe and M. Hewstone (eds) *European Review of Social Psychology* (Volume 1, pp. 33–60). New York: Wiley.

Pendleton, D. Schofield, T. Tate, P. and Havelock, P. (1984) *The consultation: an approach to learning and teaching.* Oxford: Oxford University Press.

Pennebaker, J. W. (1990) *The Psychology of Physical Symptoms.* New York: Springer-Verlag.

Penner, S. G. (1987) Parental responses to grammatical and ungrammatical child utterances. *Child Development*, 58, 376–84.

Pennington, D. (2000) *Social Cognition.* London: Routledge.

Pennington, D. (2003) *Essential Personality.* London: Arnold Publishers.

Perkins, K A. Grobe, J. E. Stiller, R. L. Fonte, C. and Goettler, J. E. (1992) Nasal spray nicotine replacement suppresses cigarette smoking desire and behaviour. *Clinical Pharmacology & Therapeutics*, 52, 627–34.

Perkins, K. A., DiMarco, A., Grobe, J. E., Scierka, A., Stiller, R. L. (1994) Nicotine discrimination in male and female smokers. *Psychopharmacology*, 116, 407–13.

Perls, F. (1969) *Gestalt therapy verbatim.* Lafayette CA: Real People's Press.

Peterson, C. (1992) *Personality.* New York: Harcourt Brace Jovanich.

Peterson, L. R. and Peterson, M. J. (1959) Short term retention of individual verbal items. *Journal of Experimental Psychology*, 58, 193–8.

Petitto, L. A. and Marentette, P. F. (1991) Babbling in the manual mode: Evidence for the ontogeny of language. *Science*, 251, 1493–6.

Petrides, K. V. and Furnham, A. (2001) Trait emotional intelligence: psychometric investigation with reference to established trait taxonomies. *European Journal of Personality*, 15, 425–48.

Pettigrew, T. F. (1998) Intergroup contact theory. *Annual Review of Psychology*, 49, 65–85.

Petty, R. E. and Cacioppo, J. T. (1986) The elaboration likelihood model of persuasion. *Advances in Experimental Social Psychology*, 19, 124–203.

Petty, R. E. and Cacioppo, J. T. (1996) *Attitudes and Persuasion: Classic and Contemporary Approaches.* Oxford: Westview.

Petty, R. E. and Wegener, D. (1998) Attitude change: multiple roles for persuasion variables. In D. T. Gilbert, S. T. Fiske and G. Lindzey (eds) *Handbook of Social Psychology* (4th Edition, pp. 323–90) New York: McGraw-Hill.

Petty, R. E., Cacioppo, J. T. and Goldman, R. (1981) Personal involvement as a determinant of argument-based persuasion. *Journal of Personality and Social Psychology*, 41, 847–55.

Peyron, C., Faraco, J., Rogers, W., Ripley, B., Overeem, S., Charnay, Y., Nevsimalova, S., Aldrich, M., Reynolds, D., Albin, R., Li, R., Hungs, M., Pedrazzoli, M., Padigaru, M., Kucherlapati, M., Fan, J., Maki, R., Lammers, G. J., Bouras, C., Kucherlapati, R., Nishino, S. and Mignot, E. (2000) A mutation in a case of early onset narcolepsy and a generalized absence of hypocretin peptides in human narcoleptic brains. *Nature Medicine*, 6, 991–7.

Philips, H. C. (1987) Avoidance behaviour and its role in sustaining chronic pain. *Behaviour Research & Therapy*, 325, 273–9.

Phillips, A. G. and Fibiger, H. C. (1978) The role of dopamine in maintaining intracranial self-stimulation in the ventral tegmentum, nucleus accumbens and medial prefrontal cortex. *Canadian Journal of Psychology*, 32, 58–66.

Phillips, A. G., Brooke, S. M. and Fibiger, H. C. (1975) Effects of amphetamine isomers and neuroleptics on self-stimulation from the nucleus accumbens and dorsal noradrenergic bundle. *Brain Research*, 85, 13–32.

Phillips, A. G., Carter, D. A. and Fibiger, H. C. (1976) Dopaminergic substrates of intracranial self-stimulation. *Brain Research*, 104, 221–32.

Phillips, H. (2003) The pleasure seekers. *New Scientist*, 180, 36–40.

Phillips, M. L., Young, A. W., Scott, S. K., Calder, A. J., Andrew, G, Giampietro, V., Williams, S. C. R., Bullmore, E. T., Brammer, M. and Gray, J. A. (1998) Neural responses to facial and vocal expressions of fear and disgust. *Proceedings of the Royal Society of London (B)*, 265, 1809–17.

Piaget, J. (1932) *The moral judgement of the child.* New York: Free Press.

Piaget, J. (1954) *The construction of reality in the child* (trans. M. Cook.) New York: Basic Books (originally published in French, 1936).

Piaget, J. and Inhelder, B. (1956) *The child's conception of space.* London: Routledge & Kegan Paul.

Piattelli-Palmarini, M. (1980) *Language and learning.* Cambridge, MA: Harvard University Press.

Piliavin, J. A., Dovidio, J. F., Gaertner, S. L. and Clark, R. D. (1981) *Emergency Intervention.* New York: Academic Press.

Pilkington, C. J. and Smith, K. A. (2000) Self-evaluation maintenance in a larger social context. *British Journal of Social Psychology*, 39, 213–27.

Pine, J. and Lieven, E. (1997) Lexically-based learning and early grammatical development. *Journal of Child Language*, 24, 187–219.

Pine, K. J. and Messer, D. (2000) The development of representations as children learn about balancing, *British Journal of Developmental Psychology*, 21, 2, 285–301.

Pine, K. J. and Messer, D. J. (2003) Children's changing representations of a balance beam task: a quasi-longitudinal study. Paper presented at the British Psychological Society London Conference, December 1995.

Pine, K. J., Lufkin, N. and Messer, D. (under review) More gestures than answers: Children learning about balance. *Child Development* (revision invited).

Pinel, J. P. J. (2003) *Biopsychology* (5th edn). London: Allyn & Bacon.

Pinker, S. (1994) *The Language Instinct*. New York: William Morrow & Co.

Pitts, M. K., McMaster, J. and Wilson, P. (1991) An investigation of preconditions necessary for the introduction of a campaign to promote breast self-examination amongst Zimbabwean women. *Journal of Applied Community Psychology*, 1 , 33–42.

Plaut, D. C., McCelland, J. L., Seifenberg, M. S., Patterson, K. (1996) Understanding normal and impaired word reading: computational principles in quasi-regular domains. *Psychological Review*, 103, 56–115.

Plies, K. and Florin, I. (1992) Effects of negative mood induction on the body image of restrained eaters. *Psychology and Health*, 7, 235–42.

Plomin, R. (1990) *Nature and nurture: an introduction to human behavioural genetics*. Pacific Grove, CA: Brooks/Cole Publishing.

Plomin, R. (1997) Identifying genes for cognitive abilities and disabilities. In R. J. Sternberg and E. L. Grigorenko (eds) *Intelligence, Heredity and Environment*. New York: Cambridge University Press, 89–104.

Plomin, R. (2002) Individual differences research in a postgenomic era. *Personality and Individual Differences*, 33, 909–20.

Plomin, R., DeFries, J. C., McClean, G. and McGuffin, P. (1997) *Behavioural Genetics*. New York: Freeman.

Plomin, R., DeFries, J. C., McClean, G. E. and Rutter, M. (1997) *Behavioral Genetics* (3rd edn). New York: WH Freeman & Co.

Plunkett, K. (1995) Connectionist approaches to language acquisition. In P. Fletcher, B. MacWhinney (eds) *Handbook of child language*. Oxford: Blackwell, 36–72.

Plunkett, K. and Marchman, V. (1993) From rote learning to system building. Cognition, 48, 21–69.

Plunkett, K., Karmiloff-Smith, A., Bates, E., Elman, J., Johnson, M. H. (1997) Connectionism and developmental psychology. *Journal of Child Psychology and Psychiatry*, 38, 53–80.

Plutchik, R. (1980) *A general psychoevolutionary theory of emotion. Emotion: Theory, Research and Experience*. New York: Harper & Row, pp. 3–33.

Polivy, J. and Herman, C. P. (2002) Causes of eating disorders. *Annual Review of Psychology*, 53, 187–213.

Ponomarenko, V. A., Aleshin, S. V. and Zhdan'ko, I. M. (1996) Intellectual abilities and the efficiency of flight training, *Human Physiology*, Vol. 22(4), 466–9.

Pontieri, F. E., Tanda, G., Orzi, F. and Di Chiara, G. (1996) Effects of nicotine on the nucleus accumbens and similarity to those of addictive drugs. *Nature*, 382, 255–7.

Posner, M. I. (1980) Orienting of attention. *The Quarterly Journal of Experimental Psychology*, 32(1), 3–25.

Posner, M. I. and Keele, S. W. (1970) Retention of abstract ideas. *Journal of Experimental Psychology*, 83(2,1), 304–8.

Posner, M. I., Cohen, Y. and Rafal, R. D. (1982) Neural Systems control of spatial orienting. *Philosophical Transactions of The Royal Society, B*, 298, 187–98.

Posner, M. I., Nissen, M. J. and Ogden, W. C. (1978) Attended and unattended processing modes: The role of set for spatial location. In H. L. Pick and I. J. Saltzman (eds) *Modes of Perceiving and Processing Information*. Hillsdale, NJ: Erlbaum.

Posner, M. I., Snyder, C. R. and Davidson, B. J. (1980) Attention and detection of signals. *Journal of Experimental Psychology*, 109(2), 160–74.

Posner, M. I., Walker, J. A., Friederich, F. J. and Rafal, R. D. (1984) Effects of parietal injury on covert orienting of attention. *Journal of Neuroscience*, 4, 1863–74.

Postle, B. R. and Corkin, S. (1998) Impaired word-stem completion priming but intact perceptual identification priming with novel words: Evidence from the amnesic patient H. M. *Neuropsychologia*, 39(12), 421–40.

Potter, J. (1996) Attitudes, social representations and discursive psychology. In M. Wetherell (ed.) *Identities, Groups and Social Identities*. London: Sage.

Potter, J. and Wetherell, M. (1987) *Discourse and Social Psychology: Beyond Attitudes and Behaviour*. Thousand Oaks, CA: Sage.

Poulton, R. and Menzies, R. G. (2002) Non-associative fear acquisition: a review of the evidence from retrospective and longitudinal research. *Behaviour Research & Therapy*, 40(2), 127–49.

Povinelli, D. J., Landau, K. R. and Perilloux, H. K. (1996) Self-recognition in young children using delayed versus live feedback: Evidence for a developmental asynchrony. *Child Development*, 67, 1540–54.

Pratt, J. A., Stolerman, I. P., Garcha, H. S., Giardini, V. and Feyerbend, C. (1983) Discriminative stimulus properties of nicotine: further evidence for mediation at a cholinergic receptor. *Psychopharmacology*, 81, 54–60.

Pratt, P., Tallis, F. and Eysenck, M. (1997) Information-processing, storage characteristics and worry. *Behaviour Research & Therapy*, 35, 1015–23.

Pryor, T. L., Martin, R. L. and Roach, N. 1995. Obsessive-compulsive disorder, trichotollimania and anorexia nervosa: a case report. *International Journal of Eating Disorders*, 18, 375–9.

Qu, D., Ludwig, D. S., Gammeltoft, S., Piper, M., Pelleymounter, M. A., Cullen, M. J., Mathes, W. F., Przypek, R., Kanarek, R. and Maratos-Flier, E. (1996) A role for melanin concentrating

References

hormone in the central regulation of feeding behaviour, *Nature*, 380, 243–7.

Quadrel, M. J., Fischoff, B. and Davis, W. (1993) Adolescent (in)vulnerability. *American Psychologist*, 48, 102–16.

Quine, L., Rutter, D. R. and Arnold, L. (2002) Increasing cycle helmet use in school-age cyclists: an intervention based on the theory of planned behaviour. In D. R. Rutter and L. Quine (eds) *Changing Health Behaviour* (pp. 172–92) Buckingham: Open University Press.

Rachman, S. (1998) A cognitive theory of obsessions: elaborations. *Behaviour Research & Therapy*, 36, 385–401.

Rachman, S. and Hodgson, R. T. (1968) Experimentally-induced 'sexual fetishism': replication and development. *Psychological Record*, 18, 25–7.

Rachman, S. J. and Hodgson, R. J. (1980) *Obsessions and compulsions*. Prentice Hall: Englewood Cliffs.

Rachman, S. J. and Wilson, G. T. (1980) *The effects of psychological therapy*. London: Pergamon Press.

Radford, A. (1995) *Syntactic Theory*. Cambridge: Cambridge University Press.

Radke-Yarrow, M. and Zahn-Waxler, C. (1984) Roots, motives and patterns in children's prosocial behaviour. In E. Straub, D. Bar-Tal, J. Karylowski and J. Reykowski (eds) *Development and maintenance of prosocial behaviour: International perspectives on positive behaviour* (pp. 81–99) New York: Plenum Press.

Raffi, A. R., Rondini, M., Grandi, S. and Fava, G.A. (2000) Life events and prodromal symptoms in bulimia nervosa. *Psychological Medicine*, 30, 727–31.

Ragneskog, H., Brane, G., Karlsson, I. and Kihlgren, M. (1996) Influence of dinner music on food intake and symptoms common in dementia. *Scandinavian Journal of Caring Science*, 10, 11–17.

Rahman, Q. and Wilson, G. S. (2003) Born gay? The psychobiology of human sexual orientation. *Personality and Individual Differences*, 34, 1337–82.

Raine, A., Buchsbaum, M. and LaCasse, L. (1997) Brain abnormalities in murderers indicated by positron emission tomography. *Biological Psychiatry*, 42, 495–508.

Raine, A., Meloy, J. R., Bihrle, S., Stoddard, J., LaCasse, L. and Buchsbaum, M. S. (1998) Reduced prefrontal and increased subcortical brain functioning assessed using positron emission tomography in predatory and affective murderers. *Behavioral Science and Law*, 16, 319–32.

Raisman, G. and Field, P. M. (1971) Sexual dimorphism in the preoptic area of the rat. *Science*, 173, 731–3.

Rakic, P. (1985) Mechanisms of neuronal migration in developing cerebellar cortex. In G. M. Edelman, W. N. Cowna and E. Gull (eds) *Molecular Basis of Neural Development*. Wiley, NY.

Randazzo, A. C., Muehlbach, M. J., Schweitzeer, P. K. and Walsh, J. K. (1998) Cognitive function following acute sleep restriction in children ages 10–14. *Sleep*, 21, 861–8.

Raven, B. H. (1965) Social influence and power. In I. D. Steiner and M. Fishbein (eds) *Current Studies in Social Psychology* (pp. 371–83) New York: Holt, Rinehart & Winston.

Rawlings, D. (1993) Personality correlates of liking for 'unpleasant' paintings and photographs, *Personality and Individual Differences*, Vol. 34(3), 395–410.

Read, C., Zhang, Y. and Nie, H. (1986) The ability to manipulate speech sounds depends on knowing alphabetic writing. *Cognition*, 24(1–2), 31–44.

Reason, J. (1990) *Human Error*. New York: Cambridge University Press.

Reavey, P. and Gough, B. (2000) Dis/locating blame: survivors' constructions of self and sexual abuse. *Sexualities*, 3, 325–46.

Reber, A. S. (1967) Implicit learning of artificial grammars. *Journal of Verbal Learning and Verbal Behaviour*, 6, 317–27.

Redd, A. (2000) 'Masculine Identity in the Service Class: an analysis of fight club'. *www.criticism.com*. Retrieved 25 October 2003

Ree, M. J. and Earles, J. A. (1991) Predicting training success: Not much more than g. *Personnel Psychology*, 44, 321–32.

Reed, E. and Jones, R. (eds) (1982) *Reasons for Realism: Selected Essays of James J Gibson*. Hillsdale, NJ: Erlbaum.

Reicher, G. M. (1969) Perceptual recognition as a function of meaningfulness of stimulus material. *Journal of Experimental Psychology*, 81(2), 275–80.

Reicher, S. and Haslam, A. (2002) Learning from the experiment. *The Psychologist*, 15, 344–5.

Resick, P. A. (2001) *Stress and trauma*. Psychology Press: Hove.

Rheaume, J., Ladouceur, R., Freeston, M. H. and Letarte, H. (1994) Inflated responsibility and its role in OCD. II. Psychometric studies of a semi-idiographic measure. *Journal of Psychopathology and Behavioral Assessment*, 16, 265–76.

Rhodes, W. S. and Pryor, J. B. (1982) Cognitive accessibility and causal attributions. *Journal of Personality and Social Psychology*, 8, 719–27.

Ricaurte, G. A., DeLanney, L. E., Wiener, S. G., Irwin, I., Langston, J. W. (1988) 5-Hydroxyindoleacetic acid in cerebrospinal fluid reflects serotonergic damage induced by 3, 4-methylenedioxymethamphetamine in CNS of non-human primates. *Brain Research*, 474, 359–63.

Richards, G. (1997) *Race, Racism and Psychology: towards a reflexive history*. London: Routledge.

Richards, G. (2002) *Putting Psychology in its Place*. Hove, Psychology Press.

Riddoch, J. M. and Humphreys, G. W. (1992) The smiling giraffe: an illustration of a visual memory disorder. In R. Campbell (ed.) *Mental Lives: Case Studies in Cognition* (p. 292) Malden, MA, US: Blackwell.

Ridley, A. M. and Clifford, B. R. (2002) The effects of state anxiety on the suggestibility and accuracy of child eye-witnesses. *Applied Cognitive Psychology*, 16, 547–58.

Rimm-Kaufman, S. and Kagan, J. (1996) The psychological significance of changes in skin temperature. *Motivation and Emotion*, 20, 63–70.

Ringelmann, M. (1913) Recherches sur les moteurs animés: trivail de l'homme. *Annales de l'Institut National Agronomique*, 12, 1–40.

Robbins, S. (1991) Organisational behaviour. Englewood Cliffs, NJ: Prentice Hall.

Roberts, D. C. S. and Koob, G. F. (1982) Disruption of cocaine self-administration following 6-hydroxydopamine lesions of the ventral tegmental area in rats. *Pharmacology, Biochemistry and Behavior*, 17, 901–4.

Roberts, D. C. S. and Ranaldi, R. (1995) Effect of dopaminergic drugs on cocaine reinforcement. *Clinical Neuropharmacology*, 18 (suppl. 1), S84–S95.

Roberts, D. C. S., Corcoran, M. E. and Fibiger, H. C. (1977) On the role of ascending catecholaminergic systems in intravenous self administration of cocaine. *Pharmacology, Biochemistry and Behavior*, 6, 615–20.

Robertson, J. and Robertson, J. (1967–73: films) *Young children in brief separations*. London: Tavistock Institute of Human Relations.

Robinson, L. A. Berman, J. S. and Neimeyer, R. A. (1990) Psychotherapy for the treatment of depression: a comprehensive review of controlled outcome research. *Psychological Bulletin*, 108, 30–49.

Robinson, T. E. and Berridge, K. C. (1993) The neural basis of drug-craving: an incentive-sensitization theory of addiction. *Brain Research Reviews*, 18, 247–91.

Robinson, T. E. and Berridge, K. C. (2000) The psychology and neurobiology of addiction: an incentive-sensitization view. *Addiction*, 95 (Suppl. 2), S91–S117.

Robinson, J. A. (1992) Autobiographical memory. In M. Gruneberg and P. Morris (eds) *Aspects of Memory* (Vol. 1. Practical Aspects, pp. 223–51). London: Routledge.

Rock, I. (1983) *The Logic of Perception*. Cambridge. MA: MIT Press.

Rodriguez-Manzo, G., Pellicer, F., Larsson, K. and Fernandez-Guasti, A. (2000) Stimulation of the medical preoptic area facilitates sexual behavior but does not reverse sexual satiation. *Behavioral Neuroscience*, 114, 553–60.

Rogers, C. R. (1961) *On becoming a person: a therapist's view of psychotherapy*. Boston: Houghton Mifflin.

Rogers, C. R. (1951) *Client-centred Therapy – Its Current Practices, Implications and Theory*. Boston, Houghton Mifflin.

Rogoff, B. (1990) *Apprenticeship in thinking*. New York: Oxford University Press.

Rogoff, B., Baker-Sennet, J., Lacasa, P. and Goldsmith, D. (1995) Development through participation in sociocultural activity. In J. Goodnow, P. Miller and F. Kessel (eds) Cultural Practices as Contexts for Development. *New Directions for Child Development*, 67, 45–65. (Series Ed. W. Damon)

Roid, G. H. and Miller, L. J. (1997) *Leiter international performance scale-revised*. Wood Dale, IL: Stoelting.

Roland, E. (1993) Bullying: a developing tradition of research and management. In D. E. Tattum (ed.) *Understanding and Managing Bullying*. Oxford: Heinemann Educational Books.

Rolls, B. J., Rowe, E. A. and Rolls, E. T. (1982) How sensory properties of foods affect human feeding behavior. *Physiology and Behavior*, 29, 409–17.

Rorschach, H. (1921) *Psychodiagnostik*. (Trans. Haus Huber Verlag, 1942.). Bern: Haus Huber.

Rorty, M. and Yager, J. 1996. Histories of childhood trauma and complex posttraumatic sequelae in women with eating disorders. *The Psychiatric Clinics of North America*, 19, 773–87.

Rosch, E. (1975a) Cognitive reference points. *Cognitive Psychology*, 7, 532–47.

Rosch, E. (1975b) Cognitive representations of semantic categories. *Journal of Experimental Psychology: General* 104, 192–233.

Rose, S. (1998) *Lifelines: biology, freedom, determinism*. London: Penguin.

Rose, S., Lewontin, R. and Kamin, L. (1990) *Not in our Genes: biology, ideology and human nature*. London: Penguin.

Rose, S. A. and Blank, M. (1974) The potency of context in children's cognition: an illustration through conservation. *Child Development*, 45, 499–502.

Rosenberg, M. J. and Hovland, C. I. (1960) Cognitive, affective and behavioral components of attitudes. In C. I. Hovland and M. J. Rosenberg (eds) *Attitude Organization and Change: an Analysis of Attitude Consistency among Attitude Components* (pp. 1–14) New Haven, CT: Yale University Press.

Rosenberg, S., Nelson, C. and Vivekanathan, P. S. (1968) A multidimensional approach to the structure of personality impressions. *Journal of Personality and Social Psychology*, 39, 283–94.

Rosenfarb, I. S., Goldstein, M. J., Mintz, J. and Neuchterlein, K. H. (1994) Expressed emotion and subclinical psychopathology observable within transactions between schizophrenics and their family members. *Journal of Abnormal Psychology* 104 259–67.

Rosenfeld, H. M. (1965) Effect of approval seeking induction on interpersonal proximity. *Psychological Reports*, 17, 120–2.

Rosenhan, D. L. (1973) On being sane in insane places. *Science*, 179, 250–8.

Rosenstock, I. M. (1966) Why people use health services. Millbank memorial Fund Quarterly, 44, 94.

Rosenteil, A. and Keefe, F. (1983) The use of coping strategies in chronic low back pain patients: Relationship to patient characteristics and current adjustment. *Pain*, 17, 33–44.

Rosenthal, R. and Jacobson, L. (1966) Teachers' expectancies: Determinants of pupils' IQ gains. *Psychological Reports*, 19, 115–18.

Rosenthal, R. and Jacobson, L. (1968) *Pygmalion in the Classroom: Teacher expectation and pupil's intellectual development*. New York: Holt, Rinehart & Winston.

Rosenthal, R. and Rosnow, R. (1991) *Essentials of Behavioral Research*. New York: McGraw Hill.

Rosenzweig, M. R., Breedlove, S. M. and Leiman, A. L. (2002) *Biological Psychology 3rd Edition*. Massachusetts: Sinaur Associates, Inc.

Rosnow, R. and Rosenthal, R. (2003) *Beginning Behavioral Research: a Conceptual Primer*. Englewood Cliffs, NJ: Prentice-Hall.

Ross, L. and Nisbett, R. E. (1991) *The Person and the Situation: Perspectives of Social Psychology*. New York: McGraw-Hill.

Ross, L., Amabile, T. M. and Steinmetz, J. L. (1977) Social roles,

References

social control and biases in social-perception processes. *Journal of Personality and Social Psychology*, 35, 485–94.

Ross, L., Green, D. and House, P. (1977) the 'false consensus effect': an egocentric bias in social perceptions and attribution processes. *Journal of Experimental Psychology*, 13, 279–301.

Rothbaum, F., Pott, M., Azuma, H., Miyake, K. and Weisz, J. (2000) The development of close relationships in Japan and the United States: Paths of symbiotic harmony and generative tension. *Child Development*, 71, 1121–42.

Rotter, J. B. (1966) Generalised expectancies for internal versus external control of reinforcement. *Psychological monographs* 80, 1–28.

Rowe, D. C. (1990) As the twig is bent? The myth of child-rearing influences on personality development. *Journal of Counselling and Development*, 68, 606–11.

Roy, A., Everett, D., Pickar, D. and Paul, S. M. (1987) Platelet tritiated imipramine binding and serotonin uptake in depressed patients and controls. *Archives of General psychiatry*, 44, 320–27.

Royal College of Psychiatrists (1995) The ECT handbook. London: author.

Rubin, D. C. and Kozin, M. (1984) Vivid memories. *Cognition*, 16(1), 81–95.

Rubin, D. C., Wetzler, S. C. and Nebes, R. D. (1986) Autobiographical memory across the lifespan. In D. C. Rubin (ed.) *Autobiographical Memory* (pp. 202–24) Cambridge: Cambridge University Press.

Rubin, Z. (1973) *Liking and Loving: an Invitation to Social Psychology*. New York: Holt, Rinehart & Winston.

Ruiter, R. A. C., Abraham, C. A. and Kok, G. (2001) Scary warnings and rational precautions: a review of the psychology of fear appeals. *Psychology and Health*, 16, 613–30.

Rumelhart, D. E. and McClelland, J. L. (1986) On learning the past tense of English verbs, in McClelland, Rumelhart and the PDP Research Group Parallel Distributed Processing: Exploration in the Micro Structure of Cognition. Cambridge, MA: MIT Press.

Rushton, J. (1990) 'Race differences, r/K theory and a reply to Flynn. ' *The Psychologist* 5, 195–8.

Rushton, J. P. (1998) The 'Jensen effect' and the 'Spearman-Jensen Hypothesis' of black-white IQ differences. *Intelligence*, 26, 217–25.

Russel, J. A. (1994) Is there universal recognition of emotion from facial expression? A review of the cross-cultural studies. *Psychological Bulletin*, 115, 102–41.

Russell, J., Mauthner, N., Sharpe, S. and Tidswell, T. (1991) The 'windows task' as a measure of strategic deception in preschoolers and autistic subjects. British *Journal of Developmental Psychology*, 9, 331–49.

Rutter, D. R. and Quine, L. (2002) *Changing Health Behaviour*. Buckingham: Open University Press.

Rutter, M. (1987) Psychosocial resilience and protective mechanisms. American *Journal of Orthopsychiatry* 57, 350–63.

Rutter, M. and The English and Romanian Adoptees Study Team.

(1998) Developmental catch-up and deficit, following adoption after severe global early privation. *Journal of Child Psychology and Psychiatry*, 39, 465–76.

Rutter, M., Graham, P., Chadwick, O. and Yule, W. (1976) Adolescent turmoil: fact or fiction? *Journal of Child Psychology and Psychiatry*, 17, 35–56.

Sachs, J. (1967) Recognation Memory for Syntactic and Semantic Aspects of Connected Discourse. *Perception & Psychophysics*, 2(9), 437–42.

Sachs, J. and Johnson, M. L. (1976) Language development in a hearing child of deaf parents. In von W. Raffler-Engel and Y. Lebrun (eds) *Baby talk and infant speech*. Lisse, Netherlands: Swets and Zeitlinger, 223–33.

Sahgal, A. (1993) Behavioural Neuroscience A Practical Approach Vol. 1. IRL Press, vii.

Sahu, A., Kalra, P. S. and Kalra, S. P. (1988) Food deprivation and ingestion induced reciprocal changes in neuropeptide Y concentrations of the paraventricular nucleus. *Peptide*, 9, 83–6.

Sakurai, T., Amemiya, A., Ishii, M., Matsuzki, I., Chemelli, R. M., Tanaka, H., Williams, S. C., Richardson, J. A., Kozlowski, G. P., Wilson, S., Arch, J. R., Buckingham, R. E., Haynes, A. S., Carr, S. A., Annan, R. S., McNulty, D. E., Liu, W. S., Terrett, J. A., Elshourbagy, N. A., Bergsma, D. J. and Yanagiswaw, M. (1998) Orexins and orexin receptors: a family of hypothalamic neuropeptides and G-protein coupled receptors that regulate feeding behaviour. *Cell*, 20, 573–85.

Salkovskis, P. M. (1985) Obsessional-compulsive problems: a cognitive-behavioural analysis. *Behaviour Research & Therapy*, 23, 571–83.

Salkovskis, P. M. (1999) Understanding and treating obsessive-compulsive disorder. *Behaviour Research and Therapy*, Vol. 37(Suppl 1), 29–52.

Salkovskis, P. M. and Clark, D. M. (1990) Affective responses to hyperventilation: a test of the cognitive model of panic. *Behaviour Research & Therapy*, 28, 51–62.

Saller, C. K. and Stricker, E. M. (1976) Hyperphagi and increased growth in rats after intraventricular injection of 5, 7-dihydroxytryptamine. *Science*, 192, 385–87.

Salman, E., Liebowitz, M., Guarnaccia, P. J., Jusino, C. M., and Garfinkel, R. *et al.* (1998) Subtypes of ataques de nervios: the influence of coexisting psychiatric diagnosis. *Cult. Med. Psychiatry*, 22, 231–44.

Salomon, G. (1993) *Distributed cognitions: Psychological and educational considerations*. Cambridge UK: Cambridge University Press.

Salthouse, T. A. and Prill, K. A. (1987) Inferences about age on structural and operational capacities in working memory. *Psychology and aging*, 6, 118–27.

Sanders, G. and Wenmoth, D. B. (1998) Verbal and music dichotic listening tasks reveal variations in functional cerebral asymmetry across the menstrual cycle that are phase and task dependent. *Neuropsychologia*, 36, 869–74.

Sanderson, W. C., Rapee R. M. and Barlow D. H. (1989) The

influence of an illusion of control on panic attacks induced via inhalation of 5. 5% carbon dioxide-enriched air. *Archives of General Psychiatry*, 46, 157–62.

Sanfilipo, M., Wolkin, A., Angrist, B., van Kammen, D. P., Duncan, E., Wieland, S., Cooper, T. B., Peselow, E. D. and Rotrosen, J. (1996) Amphetamine and negative symptoms of schizophrenia. *Psychopharmacology*, 123, 211–14.

Sapolsky, R. (2003) Taming stress. *Scientific American*, 289, 66–75.

Sarter, M., Hagan, J. and Dudchenko, P. (1992a) Behavioral screening for cognition enhancers: from indiscriminate to valid testing: Part I *Psychopharmacology*, 107, 144–59.

Sarter, M., Hagan, J. and Dudchenko, P. (1992b) Behavioral screening for cognition enhancers: from indiscriminate to valid testing: Part II. *Psychopharmacology* 107, 461–73.

Sastry, B. R., Goh, J. W. and Auyeung, A. (1986) Associative induction of posttetanic and log-term potentiation in CA1 neurons of rat hippocampus. *Science*, 232, 988–90.

Saxe, L. (1994) Detection of deception: Polygraph and integrity tests. *Current directions in Psychological Science*, 3, 69–73.

Saxton, M. (1997) The contrast theory of negative input. *Journal of Child Language*, 24, 139–61.

Scaife, M. and Bruner, J. S. (1975) The capacity for joint attention in the infant. *Nature*, 253, 265–6.

Scarborough, H. (1990) Very early language deficits in dyslexic children. *Child Development*, 61, 1728–43.

Scarborough, H. and Wyckoff, J. (1986) Mother, I'd still rather do it myself: some further non-effects of 'motherese'. *Journal of Child Language*, 13, 431–8.

Scarr, S. (1989) Protecting general intelligence: Constructs and consequences for interventions. In R. J. Linn (ed.) *Intelligence: Measurement, theory and public policy*. Champaign: University of Illinois Press.

Schachter, D. L. and Singer, J. E. (1962) Cognitive, social and physiological determinants of emotional state. *Psychological review*, 69, 379–99.

Schachter, D. L. and Singer, J. E (1964) The interaction of cognitive and physiological determinants of emotional state. In L. Berkowitz (ed) *Advances in Experimental Social Psychology*, (pp. 49–79). New York: Academic Press.

Schachter, D. L., Norman, K. A. and Koutstaal, W. (1998) The cognitive neuroscience of constructive memory. *Annual Review of Psychology*, 49, 289–318.

Schactel, E. (1947) On memory and childhood amnesia. *Psychiatry*, 10, 1-26.

Schaffer, H. R. and Emerson, P. E. (1964) The development of social attachments in infancy. *Monographs of the Society for Research in Child Development*, 28.

Schaie, K. W. (1989) Individual differences in rate of cognitive change in adulthood. In V. L. Bengtson and K. W. Schaie (eds) *The course of later life: Research and reflections*. New York: Springer Publishing Co.

Schaie K. W. (1996) *Intellectual development in adulthood*. Cambridge: Cambridge University Press.

Schaller, M. and Cialdini, R. B. (1988) The economics of empathic helping: Support for a mood management motive. *Journal of Experimental Social Psychology*, 24, pp. 163–81.

Schank, R. C. (1982) *Dynamic Memory*. Cambridge: Cambridge University Press.

Schank, R. C. (1986) *Explanation Patterns*. Hillsdale, NJ: Lawrence Erlbaum Associates.

Schank, R. C. and Abelson, R. P. (1977) *Scripts, Plans, Goals and Understanding*. Hillsdale, NJ: Lawrence Erlbaum Associates.

Schatz, M. (1983) On transition, continuity and coupling: an alternative approach to communicative development. In R. M. Golinkoff (ed.) *The Transition From Prelinguistic to Linguistic Communication*. Hillsdale, NJ: Erlbaum.

Scheier, M. F. and Carver, C. S. (1992) Effects of optimism on psychological and physical well-being: The influence of generalized outcome expectancies on health. *Journal of Personality*, 55, 169–210.

Schenk, S., Gittings, D., Johnstone, M. and Daniela, E. (2003) Development, maintenance and temporal pattern of self-administration maintained by ecstasy (MDMA) in rats. *Psychopharmacology*, 169, 21–7.

Schifter, D. E. and Ajzen, I. (1985) Intention, perceived control and weight loss: an application of the theory of planned behavior. *Journal of Personality and Social Psychology*, 49, 843–51.

Schildkraut, J. J., Green, A. I. and Mooney, J. J. (1985) Affective disorders: Biochemical aspects. In H. I. Kaplan and J. Sadock (eds) *Comprehensive Textbook of Psychiatry*. Baltimore: Williams & Wilkins.

Schmidt, L. A., Fox, N. A., Rubin, K. H., Hu, S. and Hamer, D. H. (2002) Molecular genetics of shyness and aggression in preschoolers. *Personality and Individual Differences*, 33, 227–38.

Schmidt, R. A. (1992) *Motor Control and Learning: a Behavioural Emphasis* (2nd ed.). Human Kinetics.

Schniering, C. A., Hudson, J. L. and Rapee, R. M. (2000) Issues in the diagnosis and assessment of anxiety disorders in children and adolescents. *Clinical Psychology Review* 20 453–78.

Schutte, N. S., Malouff, J. M., Hall, L. E., Haggerty, D. J., Cooper, J. T., Golden, C. J. and Dornheim, L. (1998) Development and validation of a measure of emotional intelligence. *Personality and Individual Differences*, 12, 351–62.

Schwartz, B. (1984) *Psychology of Learning and Behavior* (2nd ed.). Norton, London.

Schwartzman, A. E., Gold. D., Andres. D., Arbuckle. T. Y. and Chaikelson. J. (1987) Stability of intelligence: a 40-year follow up. *Canadian Journal of Psychology*, 41, 244–56.

Schwarz, N. and Bohner, G. (2003) The construction of attitudes. In A. Tesser and N. Schwarz (eds) Blackwell Handbook of Social Psychology: Intraindividual Processes (pp. 436–57) Oxford: Blackwell.

Scott, S., Deary, I. and Pelosi, A. J. (1995) General practitioners' attitudes to patients with a self diagnosis of myalgic encephalomyelitis. *British Medical Journal*, 310, 508.

Sdorow, L. M. and Rickabaugh, C. A. (2002) *Psychology* (5th ed.). London: McGraw-Hill Higher Education.

References

Searle, J. (1979) *Expression and Meaning: Studies in the Theory of Speech Acts.* Cambridge: Cambridge University Press.

Sears, D. O. (1983) The person-positivity bias. *Journal of Personality and Social Psychology*, 44, 233–50.

Sedikides, C. (1992) Changes in the valence of the self as a function of mood. In M. S. Clark (ed.) *Emotion and Social Behaviour* (pp. 271–311). Newbury Park, California: Sage.

Sedikides, C. (1993) Assessment, enhancement and verification determinants of the self-evaluation process. *Journal of Personality and Social Psychology*, 65, 317–38.

Segal, S. J. and Fusella, V. (1970) Influence of imaged pictures and sounds on detection of visual and auditory signals. *Journal of Experimental Psychology*, 83(3, *Pt.* 1), 458–64.

Seidenberg, M. S. and McClelland, J. L. (1989) A distributed developmental model of word recognition. *Psychological Review*, 96, 523–68.

Seidenberg, M. S. and Pettito, L. A. (1987) Communication, symbolic communication and language: Comment on Savage-Rumbaugh, MacDonald, Sevcik, Hopkis and Rubert (1986) *Journal of Experimental Psychology*, 116, 279–87.

Seligman, M. E. P. (1971) Phobias and preparedness. *Behavior Therapy*, 2, 307–20.

Seligman, M. E. P. (1974) Depression and learned helplessness. In R. J. Friedman and M. M. Katz (eds) *The Psychology of Depression: Contemporary Theory and Research.* New York: Winston-Wiley.

Seligman, M. E. P. (1975) *Helplessness: On depression, development and death.* San Francisco: Freeman.

Seligman, M. E. P. (1995) The effectiveness of psychotherapy. The Consumer reports study. *American Psychologist*, 50, 965–74.

Senghas, A. and Coppola, M. (2001) Children creating language: How Nicaraguan sign language acquired a spatial grammar. *Psychological Science*, 12, 323–8.

Shah, A., Frith, U. (1983) An islet of ability in autistic children: a research note. *Journal of Child Psychology and Psychiatry* 24, 613–20.

Shallice, T. (1988) From Neuropsychology to Mental Structure. Cambridge University Press.

Shallice, T. and Warrington, E. K. (1970) Independent functioning of verbal memory stores: a neuropsychological study. *The Quarterly Journal of Experimental Psychology*, 22, 261–73.

Shallice, T. and Warrington, E. K. (1975) Word recognition in a phonemic dyslexic patient. *The Quarterly Journal of Experimental Psychology*, 27, 187–99.

Sharp, S. and Smith, P. K. (1995) *Tackling bullying in your school. A practical guide for teachers.* London: Routledge.

Shatz, M. and Gelman, R. (1973) The development of communication skills: Modifications in the speech of young children as a function of listener. *Monographs of the Society for Research in Child Development*, 38, 1–37.

Shaver, K. G. (1985) *The Attribution of Blame: Causality, Responsibility and Blameworthiness.* New York: Springer-Verlag.

Shavitt, S. (1989) Operationalising functional theories of attitudes. In A. R. Pratkanis, S. J. Breckler and A. G. Greenwald (eds) *Attitude Structure and Function* (pp. 311–37) Hillsdale, NJ: Lawrence Erlbaum.

Sheeran, P. (2002) Intention-behavior relations: a conceptual and empirical review. In W. Stroebe and N. Hewstone (eds) *European Review of Social Psychology* (pp. 1–26) Hove: Wiley.

Sheeran, P., Abraham, C. and Orbell, S. (1999) Psychosocial correlates of heterosexual condom use: a meta-analysis. *Psychological Bulletin*, 125(1), 90–132.

Sher, K. J., Mann B. and Frost, R. (1984) Cognitive Dysfunction in Compulsive Checkers: Further explanations. *Behaviour Research and Therapy*, 22, 493–502.

Sherif, M, (1935) A study of some social factors in perception. *Archives of Psychology*, 27, 1–60.

Sherif, M. (1936) *The Psychology of Social Norms.* New York: Harper.

Sherif, M. (1966) *Group Conflict and Cooperation.* London: Routledge.

Shevell, M. I. and Peiffer, J. (2001) Julius Hallervorden's wartime activities: implications for science under dictatorship. *Pediatric Neurology*, 25, 162–5.

Shisslak, C. M., Crago, M. and Estes, L. S. (1995). The spectrum of eating disturbances. *International Journal of Eating Disorders*, 18, 209–19.

Shoebridge, P. and Gowers, S. G. (2000). Parental high concern and adolescent-onset anorexia nervosaa case-control study to investigate direction of causality. *British Journal of Psychiatry*, 176, 132–7.

Siegal, A., Roeling, T. A. P., Grehh, T. R. and Kruk, M. R. (1999) Neuropharmacology of brain-stimulation-evoked aggression. *Neuroscience and Biobehavioral Reviews*, 23, 359–89.

Siegel, S., Hinson, R. E., Krank, M. D. and McCully, J. (1982) Heroin 'overdose' death: contribution of drug-associated environmental cues. *Science*, 216, 436–7.

Siegler, R. S. (1996) Emerging minds: The process of change in children's thinking. New York: Oxford University Press.

Siegler, R. S. and Jenkins, E. A. (1989) How children discover new strategies. Hillsdale, NJ: Erlbaum.

Silbereisen, R. and Kracke, B. (1997) Variation in maturational timing and adjustment in adolescence. In J. Schulenberg, J. Maggs and K. Hurrelman (eds) *Health risks and developmental transitions during adolescence.* Cambridge: Cambridge University Press.

Silva, R. R., Alpert, M., Munoz, D. M., *et al.* (2000) Stress and vulnerability to posttraumatic stress disorder in children and adolescents. *American Journal of Psychiatry*, 157(8), 1229–35, August.

Simon, H. A. and Chase, W. G. (1973) Skill in chess. *American Scientist*, 61(4), 394–403.

Simpson, D. D., Joe, G. W., Rowan-Szal, G. A. (1997) Drug Abuse Treatment Retention and Process Effects on Follow-up Outcomes. *Drug Alcohol Dependency*, 47(3), 227–35.

Singer, M. T. and Lalich, J. (1995) Cults in our midst. San Francisco: Jossey-Bass.

Singh, D. (1993) Adaptive significance of female physical

attractiveness: role of waist-to-hip ratio. *Journal of Personality and Social Psychology*, 65, 293–307.

Skinner, B. K. (1971) *Beyond freedom and dignity*. Harmondsworth: Penguin.

Skinner, B. F. (1958) Teaching Machines. *Science*, 128, 969–77.

Skinner, B. S. (1957) *Verbal Behavior*. New York: Applegon Century Crofts.

Skoler, G. D., Bandura, A. and Ross, D. (1994) Aggression. In W. A. Lesko *Readings in social psychology: General, classic* and *contemporary selections* (2nd edn) (pp. 296–362). Needham Heights, MA: Allyn & Bacon.

Skowronski, J. J. and Carlston, D. E. (1989) Negativity and extremity biases in impression formation: a review of explanations. *Psychological Bulletin*, 105, 131–42.

Slade, P. (1982) Towards a functional analysis of Anorexia Nervosa and Bulimia Nervosa. *British Journal of Clinical Psychology*, 21, 167–79.

Slanger, E. and Rudestam, K. E. (1997) Motivation and Disinhibiting in High Risk Sports: Sensation Seeking and Self efficacy. *Journal of Research in Personality*, 27, 355–74.

Slater, A. M., Bremner, G., Johnson, S. P., Hayes, R. and Brown, E. (2000) Newborn infants' preference for attractive faces: The role of internal and external facial features. *Infancy*, 1, 265–74.

Slater, A. M., Von der Schulenburg, C., Brown, E., Badenoch, M., Butterworth, G., Parsons, S. and Samuels, C. (1998) Newborn infants prefer attractive faces. *Infant Behaviour and Development*, 21, 345–54.

Slater, A., Mattock, A., Brown, E. (1990) Size constancy at birth: newborn infants' responses to retinal and real sizes. *Journal of Experimental Child Psychology*, 49, 314–22.

Slobodian, P. J. and Browne, K. D. (2001) A review of car crime in England and Wales. *British Journal of Social Work*, Vol. 27(3), 465–80.

Smart, J. L. (1977) Early life malnutrition and later learning ability–critical analysis. In A. Oliverio (ed.) *Genetics, environment and intelligence* (pp. 215–35). Amsterdam: Elsevier.

Smith, M. A., McEvopy, L. K. and Gevins, A. (2002) The impact of moderate sleep loss on neuropsychologic signals during working-memory task performance. *Sleep*, 25, 784–94.

Smith, E. E., Shoben, E. J. and Rips, L. J. (1974) Structure and process in semantic memory: a featural model for semantic decisions. *Psychological Review*, 81, 214–41.

Smith, E. R. and Miller, F. D. (1983) Mediation among attributional inferences and comprehension processes: initial findings and a general method. *Journal of Personality and Social Psychology*, 44, 492–505.

Smith, M. B., Bruner, J. S. and White, R. W. (1956) *Opinions and Personality*. New York: Wiley.

Smith, P. B. and Bond, M. H. (1998) *Social Psychology Across Cultures* (2nd ed.). Hemel Hempstead: Prentice Hall Europe.

Smith, P., Nix, A., Davey, N. and Messer, D. (in press) A connectionist account of Spanish determiner production. *Journal of Child Language*.

Smith, P., Nix, A., Davey, N., Lopez-Ornat, S. and Messer, D. (2003) A connectionist account of Spanish determiner production. *Journal of Child Language*, 30(2), 305–31.

Smith, P. B. and Bond, M. H. (1998) *Social Psychology Across Cultures* (2nd ed.). London: Prentice Hall.

Snarey, J. R. (1985) Cross-cultural universality of socio-moral development: a critical review of Kohlbergian review. *Psychological Bulletin*, 97, 202–32.

Snow, C. (1977) The development of conversation between mothers and babies. *Journal of Child Language*, 4, 1–22.

Snow, C. (1995) Issues in the study of Input. In P. Fletcher and B. MacWhinney (eds) *Handbook of Child Language* (pp. 180–93). Oxford: Blackwell.

Snyder, S. H., Creese, I. and Burt, D. R. (1975) The brain's dopamine receptor: Labelling with [3H]dopamine and [3H]haloeridol. *Psychopharmacological Communications*, 1, 663–73.

Snyder, M. (1974) The self-monitoring of expressive behaviour. *Journal of Personality and Social Psychology*, 30, 526–37.

Soininen, H., Reinikainen, K. J., Puranen, M., Helkala, E. L., Paljarvi, L. and Riekkinen, P. J. (1993) Wide third ventricle correlates with low choline acetyltransferase activity of the neocortex in Alzheimer patients. *Alzheimer's Disease and Associated Disorders*, 7, 39–47.

Soler, M. J. and Ruiz, J. C. (1996) The spontaneous use of memory aids at different educational levels. *Applied Cognitive Psychology*, 10(1), 41–51.

Solso, R. L. (1998) *Cognitive Psychology* (5th ed.). London: Allyn & Bacon.

Sonnekus, I. P. (1998) Enhancing realistic academic self-actualisation: a psycho-andragogical perspective. *Dissertation Abstracts International Section A: Humanities and Social Sciences*, Vol. 58(12–A), 4557.

Spelke, E. S., Breinlinger, K., Macomber, J., Jacobson, K. (1992) Origins of knowledge. *Psychological Review*, 99, 605–32.

Spelke, E., Hirst, W. and Neisser, U. (1976) Skills of divided attention. *Cognition*, 4(3), 215–30.

Spelt, J. and Meyer, J. M. 1995. Genetics and eating disorders. In J. R. Turner, L. R. Cardon and J. K. Hewitt (eds) *Behavior Genetic Approaches in Behavioral Medicine* (pp. 167–85). New York: Plenum.

Spencer, H. (1855/1897) *The Principles of Psychology*. New York: Appleton & Co.

Sperling, G. (1960) The information available in brief visual presentation. *Psychological Monographs*, 74(11, *Whole No. 498*), 29.

Sprecher, S. (1998) Insiders' perspectives on reasons for attraction to a close other. *Social Psychology Quarterly*, 61, 287–300.

Springer, L., Stanne, M. E. and Donovan, S. S. (1997) *Effects of small-group learning on undergraduates in Science, Mathematics, Engineering and Technology: a meta analysis*. National Institute for Science Education, University of Wisconsin, Madison.

Springer, S. P. and Deutsch, G. (1998) *Left Brain, Right Brain:*

Perspectives from Cognitive Neuroscience (5th ed.). WH Freeman & Co NY.

Spyraki, C., Fibiger, H. C. and Phillips, A. G. (1982) Dopaminergic substrates of amphetamine-induced place preference conditioning. *Brain Research*, 253, 185–93.

Srivastava, S., John, O. P., Gosling, S. and Potter. J. (2003) Development of personality in early and middle adulthood: Set like plaster or persistent change? *Journal of Personality and Social Psychology*, Vol. 84(5), 1041–53.

Sroufe, L. A. (1983) Adaptation from infancy to preschool. In M. Perlmutter (ed.) *Minnesota Symposium on Child Psychology*. Hillsdale, NJ: Lawrence Erlbaum.

Srull, T. K. and Wyer, R. S. (1979) The role of category accessibility in the interpretation of information about persons: some determinants and implications. *Journal of Personality and Social Psychology*, 37, 1660–72.

St Charles, N. D. (2002) Human resource management practices, faculty morale and the impact on teaching performance and university effectiveness. *Dissertation Abstracts International Section: Humanities and Social Sciences*, Vol. 63(6–A), 2305.

Staats, A. W. (1983) Paradigmatic behaviorism: unified theory for social personality psychology. *Advances in Experimental Social Psychology*, 16, 125–79.

Stainton Rogers, R., Stenner, P., Gleeson, K. and Stainton Rogers, W. (1995) *Social Psychology: a Critical Agenda*. Cambridge: Polity.

Stainton Rogers, W. (2003) *Social Psychology: Experimental and Critical Approaches*. Buckingham: Open University Press.

Stallone, D. and Nicolaïdis, S. (1989) Increased food intake and carbohydrate preference in the rat following treatment with the serotonin antagonist metergoline, *Neuroscience Letters*, 102, 319–24.

Stanley, B. G., Magdalin, W., Seirafi, A., Thomas, W. J. and Leibowitz, S. F. (1993a) The perifornical area: major focus of patchily distributed hypothalamic neuropeptide Y-sensitive feeding systems. *Brain Research*, 604, 304–17.

Stanley, B. G., Willet, V. L., Donias, H. W., Ha, L. H. and Spears, L. C. (1993b) The lateral hypothalamus: a primary site mediating excitatory aino acid-elicited eating. *Brain Research*, 630, 41–44.

Stanley, B. G., Willet, V. L., Donias, H. W., Dee, M. G. and Duva, M. A. (1996) Lateral hypothalamic NMDA receptors and glutamate as physiological mediators of eating and weight control. *American Journal of Physiology: Regulatory, Integrative and Comparative Physiology*, 270, R443–R449.

Stanovich, K. E. (1986) Cognitive processes and the reading problems of learning disabled children: Evaluating the assumption of specificity. In J. K. Torgensen and B. Y. L. Wong (eds) *Psychological and Educational Perspectives on Learning Disabilities*. San Diego, CA: Academic Press.

Stanovich, K. E. and Siegel, L. E. (1994) Phenotypic performance profile of children with reading disabilities: a regression-based test of the phonological-core variable-difference model. *Journal of Educational Psychology*, 86, 24–53.

Stanovich, K. E. and West, R. F. (1981) The effect of sentence context on ongoing word recognition: Tests of a two-process

theory. *Journal of Experimental Psychology: Human Perception & Performance*, 7, 658–72.

Steele, C. (1997) A threat in the air: How stereotypes shape intellectual identity and performance. *American Psychologist*, 52, 613–29.

Stein, M. B., Jang, K. L. and Livesley, W. J. (2002) Heritability of social anxiety-related concerns and personality characteristics: a twin study. *Journal of Mental and Nervous Diseases*, Vol. 190(4), 219–24.

Steinberg, L., Darling, N. and Fletcher, A. C. (1995) Authoritative parenting and adolescent adjustment: an ecological journey. In P. Moen, G. H. Elder, Jr and K. Luscher (eds) *Examining lives in context: Perspectives on the ecology of human development* (pp. 423–66). Washington, DC: American Psychological Association.

Steinhausen, H. C., Seidel, R. and Metzke, C. W. (2000) Evaluation of treatment and intermediate and long-term outcome of adolescent eating disorders. *Psychological Medicine*, 30, 1089–98.

Steinman, L., Martin, R., Bernard, C., Conlon, P. and Oksenberg, J. R. (2002) Multiple sclerosis: deeper understanding of its pathogenesis reveals new targets for therapy. *Annual Review of Neuroscience*, 25, 491–505.

Stephens, D. N., Mead, A. N. and Ripley, T. L. (2002) Studying the neurobiology of stimulant and alcohol abuse and dependence in genetically manipulated mice. *Behavioural Pharmacology*, 13, 327–45.

Stern, S. E. and Faber, J. E. (1997) The lost e-mail method: Milgram's lost letter technique in the age of advertising. *Behavior Research Methods, Instruments and Computers*, 29, 260–3.

Sternberg, R. J. (1988a) *The Triangle of Love*. New York: Basic Books.

Sternberg, R. J. (1988b) *The Triarchic Mind*. New York: Cambridge Press.

Sternberg, R. J. (1999) *Cognitive Psychology* (2nd edn). London: Harcourt Brace College Publishers.

Sternberg, R. J. (2002) Successful intelligence: a new approach to leadership in R. Ronald and S. Murphy (eds) (2002) *Multiple intelligences and leadership*. LEA's organisation and management series (pp. 9–28). Mahwah, NJ, US: Lawrence Erlbaum.

Sternberg, R. J. and Ben-Zeev, T. (2001) *Complex Cognition: The Psychology of Human Thought*. Oxford: Oxford University Press.

Sternberg, R. J. and Detterman, D. K. (eds) (1986) *What Is Intelligence? Contemporary Viewpoints on Its Nature and Definition*. Norwood, NJ: ablex.

Sternberg, R. J. and Kaufman, J. C. (1998) *Human abilities, Annual Review of Psychology*, 49, 479–502.

Sternberg, R. J., Conway, B. E., Ketron, J. L., Bernstein, M. (1981) People's conceptions of intelligence. *Journal of Personality and Social Psychology*, 41, 37–55.

Sternberg, R. J., Forsythe, G. B., Hedlund, J., Horvath, J., Snook, S., Williams, W. M., Wagner, R. K. and Grigorenko, E. L. (2000) *Practical intelligence*. New York: Cambridge University Press.

Sternberg, R. J., Grigorenko, E. L. and Bundy, D. A. (2001) The predictive value of IQ. *Merrill-Palmer Quarterly*, Vol. 47(1), 1–41.

Stevenson, C. and Cooper, N. (1997) Qualitative and Quantitative Research, *The Psychologist*, April, 159–60.

Stice, E. (1998) Modeling of eating pathology and social reinforcement of the thin-ideal predict onset of bulimic symptoms. *Behaviour Research & Therapy*, 36, 931–44.

Stice, E. (2001) A prospective test of the dual-pathway model of bulimic pathology: mediating effects of dieting and negative affect. *Journal of Abnormal Psychology*, 110, 1–12.

Stokes, T. F. and Baer, D. M. (1977) An implicit technology of generalization. *Journal of Applied Behavior Analysis*, 10, 349–69.

Stokes, T. F. and Osnes, P. G. (1988) The developing applied technology of generalization and maintenance. In R. H. Horner, G. Dunlap and R. L. Koegel (eds) *Generalization and maintenance: Life style changes in applied settings*. Baltimore: Brookes.

Stolerman, I. (1992) Drugs of abuse: behavioural principles, methods and terms. *Trends in Pharmacological Sciences*, 13, 170–6.

Stolerman, I. P. (1993) Drug Discrimination. In F. van Haaren (ed.) *Methods in Behavioral Pharmacology*. Elsevier.

Stolerman, I. P. and Jarvis, M. J. (1995) The scientific case that nicotine is addictive. *Psychopharmacology*, 117, 2–10.

Stone, K. D. and Lemanek, K. L. (1990) Developmental issues in children's self-reports. In A. M. La Greca (ed.) *Through the eyes of the child: Obtaining self-reports from children and adolescents*. Boston: Allyn & Bacon.

Stoner, J. A. F. (1968) Risky and cautious shifts in the group decisions: the influence of widely held values. *Journal of Experimental Social Psychology*, 4, 442–59.

Storms, M. D. (1973) Videotape and the attribution process. *Journal of Personality and Social Psychology*, 27, 165–75.

Stratton, P. and Hayes, N. (1999) *A Student's Dictionary of Psychology*. London: Arnold.

Strauss, M. A., Sugarman, D. B. and Giles-Sims, J. (1997) Spanking by parents and subsequent antisocial behaviour of children. *Archives of Pediatrics and Adolescent Medicine*, 151, 761–7.

Striegel-Moore, R. (1997) Risk factors for eating disorders. *Ann. NY Acad. Sci.*, 817, 98–109.

Strobel, A., Spinath, F. M., Angleitner, A., Riemann, R. and Lesch, K. P. (2003) Lack of association between polymorphisms of the dopamine D4 receptor gene and personality. *Neuropsychobiology*, 47, 52–6.

Strube, G. (2000) 'Generative theories in cognitive psychology'. *Theory and Psychology*. 10(1), 117–25.

Stuart, R. B. (1967) Behavioral control of overeating. *Behaviour Research & Therapy*, 5, 357–65.

Stuart, R. B. and Davis B. (1972) *Slim chance in a fat world: Behavioral control of obesity*. Champaign, Ill.: Research Press.

Study Group Anorexia Nervosa. 1995. Anorexia nervosa: directions for future research. *International Journal of Eating Disorders*, 17, 235–41.

Stumpf, H. (1995) Gender differences in performance on tests of cognitive abilities: Experimental design issues and empirical results. *Learning and Individual Differences*, 7, 275–88.

Sutton, J. and Smith, P. K. (in press) Bullying as a group process: an adaptation of the participant role approach. *Aggressive Behaviour*.

Sutton, S. (1994) The past predicts the future: interpreting behaviour-behaviour relationships in social psychological models of health behaviours. In D. R. Rutter and L. Quine (eds) *Social Psychology and Health: European Perspectives* (pp. 71–88) Aldershot: Ashgate.

Sutton, S. (1998) Predicting and explaining intentions and behavior: how well are we doing? *Journal of Applied Social Psychology*, 28, 1317–38.

Svanborg, P. (2000) Associations between plasma glucose and DSM-III-R cluster B personality traits in psychiatric outpatients, *Neuropsychobiology*, Vol. 41(2), 79–87.

Swabb, D. F. and Fliers, E. (1985) A sexually dimorphic nucleus in the human brain. *Science*, 188, 1112–15.

Swan, D. and Goswami, U. (1997) Phonological awareness deficits in developmental dyslexia and the phonological representation hypothesis. *Journal of Experimental Child Psychology*, 66, 18–41.

Swann, W. B., Hixon, J. G. and de la Ronde, C. (1992) Embracing the bitter truth: negative self-concepts and marital commitment. *Psychological Science*, 3, 118–21.

Sylvester-Bradly, B. and Trevarthen, C. B. (1978) Baby talk as an adaptation to the infant's communication. In Waterson, N. and Snow, C. E. (eds) The development of Communication. New York: Wiley.

Tajfel, H. (1982) Social psychology of intergroup relations. *Annual Review of Social Psychology*, 33, 1–39.

Tajfel, H. and Turner, J. C. (1986a) An integrative theory of social conflict. In Worchel, S. and Austin, W. (eds) *Psychology of Intergroup Relations*. Chicago, IL: Nelson Hall.

Tajfel, H. and Turner, J. (1986b) The social identity theory of intergroup behaviour, in S. Worchel and W. G. Austin (eds) *Psychology of Intergroup Relations*. Chicago: Nelson.

Tajfel, H., Billig, M., Bundy, R. P. and Flament, C. (1971) Social categorisation and intergroup behaviour. *European Journal of Social Psychology*, 1, 149–78.

Takahashi, K. (1990) Are the key assumptions of the 'Strange Situation' procedure universal? A view from Japanese research. *Human Development*, 33, 23–30.

Talcott, J. B., Hansen, P. C. and Assoku, E. L. (2000) Visual motion sensitivity in dyslexia: Evidence for temporal and energy integration deficits. *Neuropsychologia*, 38(7), 935–43.

Tanner, J. M. (1973) Growing Up. *Scientific American*, 229 (Sept.), 35–43.

Tanskanen, A., Viinamaki, H., Hintikka, J., Koivumaa-Honkanen, H.-T. and Lehtonen, J. (1998) Smoking and suicidality among psychiatric patients. *American Journal of Psychiatry* 155, 129–30.

Tartter, V. C. (1986) *Language Processes*. NY: Holt, Rinehart & Winston.

References

Tashakkori, A. (1993) Gender, ethnicity and the structure of self-esteem: an attitude theory approach. *Journal of Social Psychology*, 4, 479–88.

Tate, P. (1994) The doctor's communication handbook. Oxford: Radcliffe Medical Press.

Taurah, L. and Chandler, C. (2003) Elevated depression scores following abstinence from MDMA. *Addiction Biology*, 8, 244–5.

Tavris, C. (1991) The Mismeasure of Women: paradoxes and perspectives in the study of gender. In J. D. Goodchilds (ed.) *Psychological Perspectives on Human Diversity in America*. Washington, DC: American Psychological Association.

Taylor, S. E. (1991) Asymmetrical effects of positive and negative events: The mobilization-minimization hypothesis. *Psychological Bulletin*, 110, 67–85.

Taylor, S. E. and Brown, J. D. (1988) Illusion and well-being: a social psychological perspective on mental health. *Psychological Bulletin*, 103, 193–210.

Taylor, S. E., Wood, J. V. and Lichtman, R. R. (1983) It could be worse: Selective evaluation as a response to victimization. *Journal of Social Issues*, 39, 19–40.

Tedeschi, J. T. (1981) *Impression Management*. New York: Academic Press.

Teitelbaum, P. and Stellar, E. (1954) Recovery from the failure to eat produced by hypothalamic lesions. *Science*, 120, 864–95.

Terrace, H. S., Petitto, L. A., Sanders, R. J. and Bever, T. G. (1979) Can an ape create a sentence? *Science*, 206(4421), 891–902.

Tesser, A. (1993) The importance of heritability in psychological research: The case of attitudes. *Psychological Review*, 100, 129–42.

Tharion, W. J., Shukitt-Hale, B. and Lieberman, H. R. (2003) Caffeine effects on marksmanship during high-stress military training with 72 hour sleep deprivation. *Aviation and Space Environmental Medicine*, 74, 309–14.

Theakston, A., Lieven, E. V. M., Pine, J. and Rowland, C. (2001) The role of performance limitations in the acquisition of verb-argument structure: an alternative account. *Journal of Child Language*, 28, 127–52.

Thomasius, R., Peterson, K., Buchert, R., Andresen, B., Zapaletalova, P., Wartberg, L., Nebling, B. and Schmoldt, A. (2003) Mood, cognition and serotonin transporter availability in current and former ecstasy (MDMA) users. *Psychopharmacology*, 167, 85–96.

Thompson, B. (1999) 'If statistical significance tests are broken/misused, what practices should supplement/replace them?' *Theory and Psychology* 9(2), 165–81.

Thompson, G. O. B., Raab, G. M., Hepburn, W. S., Hunter, R., Fulton, M. and Laxen, D. P. H. (1989) Blood-lead levels and children's behaviour: Results from the Edinburgh lead study. *Journal of Child Psychology & Psychiatry* 30 515–28.

Thompson, S. K. (1975) Gender labels and early sex-role development. *Child Development*, 46, 339–47.

Thoresen, C. E. and Mahoney, M. J. (1974) *Behavioral self-control*. New York: Holt, Rinehart & Winston.

Thorndike, E. L. (1911) *Animal Intelligence. Experimental Studies*. Oxford: Macmillan.

Thorndike, E. L. (1898) Animal intelligence: an experimental study of the association process in animals. *Psychological Review Monograph*, 2(8).

Thorndike, R. L., Hagen, E. P., Sattler, J. M. (1986), The Stanford-Binet Intelligence Scale (4th edn). Technical Manual. Chicago: Riverside.

Thorne, B. M. and Henley, T. B. (2001) *Connections in the History and Systems of Psychology*. Boston, MA, Houghton Mifflin.

Thorpe, K., Greenwood, R., Eivers, A. and Rutter, M. (2001) Prevalence and developmental course of 'secret language. *International Journal of Language & Communication Disorders*, 36(1), 43–62.

Thorpe, S. J. and Salkovskis, P. M. (1995) Phobic beliefs: do cognitive factors play a role in specific phobias? *Behaviour Research and Therapy*, 33, 805–16.

Thrasher, T. N. (1989) Role of forebrain circumventricular organs in body fluid balance. *Acta Physiologica Scandanavica*, 136 (Suppl. 583), 141–50.

Thurston, L. L. (1930) A scale for measuring attitude towards the movies. *Journal of Educational Research*, 22, 89–94.

Tice, D. M. (1992) Self-presentation and self-concept change: the looking glass self as magnifying glass. *Journal of Personality and Social Psychology*, 63, 435–51.

Tice, D. M. and Baumeister, R. F. (1990) Self-esteem, self-handicapping and self-presentation: The strategy of inadequate practice. *Journal of Personality*, 58, 443–64.

Tincoff, R. and Jusczyk, P. W. (1999) Some beginnings of word comprehension in 6-month-olds. *Psychological Science*, 10, 172–5.

Tolman, E. C. (1959) Principles of purposive behavior. In S Koch (ed.) *Psychology: a study of science* (Vol. 2 pp. 92–157). New York: McGraw-Hill.

Tolman, E. C. (1932) *Purposive behavior in animals and men*. New York: Century.

Tolman, E. C. (1948) Cognitive maps in rats and man. *The Psychological Review*, 55, 189–208.

Tomasello, M. (1992) The social base of language acquisition. *Social Development*, 1, 68–87.

Tomasello, M. (2000) Do children have adult syntactic competence? Cognition, 74, 209–53.

Tomasello, M. and Farrar, M. J. (1986) Joint attention and early language. *Child Development*, 57, 1454–63.

Tomasello, M., Akhtar, N., Dodson, K. and Rekau, L. (1997) Differential productivity in young children's use of nouns and verbs. *Journal of Child Language*, 24, 373–87.

Tomasello, M., Mannle, S. and Kruger, A. C. (1986) Linguistic environment of 1- to 2-year-old twins. *Developmental Psychology*, 22, 2, 169–76.

Tomasello, M., Strosberg, R. and Akhtar, N. (1996) Eighteen-month-old children learn words in non-ostensive contexts. *Journal of Child Language*, 23, 157–76.

Treisman, A. M. (1964) Verbal cues, language and meaning in selective attention. *American Journal of Psychology*, 77(2), 206–2119.

Treisman, A. M. (1988) Features and objects: The Fourteenth Bartlett Memorial Lecture. *Quarterly Journal of Experimental Psychology: Human Experimental Psychology*, 40*A*(2), 201–37.

Treisman, A. M. (1993) The perception of features and objects. In A. D. Baddeley and L. Weiskrantz (eds) *Attention: Selection, Awareness and Control: a Tribute to Donald Broadbent* (pp. 5–35). New York: Clarendon Press/Oxford University Press.

Treisman, A. M. and Geffen, G. (1967) Selective attention: Perception or Response? *The Quarterly Journal of Experimental Psychology*, 19(1), 1–17.

Treisman, A. M. and Gelade, G. (2000) A feature integration theory of attention. In S. Yantis (ed.) *Visual Perception: Essential Readings* (pp. 347–58) Philadelphia: Psychology Press.

Trevarthen, C. (1977) Descriptive analysis of infant communication and behaviour. In H. R. Schaffer (ed.) *Studies on mother–infant interaction*. New York: Academic.

Triandis, H. C. (1980) Values, attitudes and interpersonal behavior. In H. E. Howe Jr and H. H. Page (eds) *Nebraska Symposium on Motivation* (Vol. 27, pp. 195–259). Lincoln: University of Nebraska Press.

Triandis, H. C., McCuster, C. and Hui, C. H. (1990) Multidimensional probes of individualism and collectivism. *Journal of Personality and Social Psychology*, 59, 1006–20.

Troop, N. A. 1998. Eating disorders as coping strategies: a critique. *European Eating Disorders Review*, 6, 229–37.

Trulson, M. E. and Jacobs, B. L. (1979) Raphe unit activity in freely moving cats: correlation with level of behavioral arousal. *Brain Research*, 163, 135–50.

Tsien, J. Z., Huerta, P. T. and Tonegawa, S. (1996) The essential role of hippocampal CA1 NMDA receptor-dependent synaptic plasticity in spatial memory. *Cell*, 87, 1327–38.

Tufte, E. R. (2001) *The Visual Display of Quantitative Information* (2nd edn). Cheshire, Connecticut: Graphics Press.

Tulving, E. (1983) *Elements of Episodic Memory*. Oxford: Oxford University Press.

Tulving, E. (1985) How many memory systems are there? *American Psychologist*, 40, 385–98.

Tulving, E. and Osler, S. (1968) Effectiveness of retrieval cues in memory for words. *Journal of Experimental Psychology*, 77, 593–601.

Tulving, E. and Pearlstone, Z. (1966) Availability versus accessibility of information in memory for words. *Journal of Verbal Learning and Verbal Behaviour*, 5, 381–91.

Tulving, E. and Psotka, J. (1971) Retroactive inhibition in free recall: Inaccessibility of information available in the memory store. *Journal of Experimental Psychology*, 77, 593–601.

Tulving, E., Schachter, D. L., McLachlan, D. R. and Moscovitch, M. (1988) Priming of semantic autobiographical knowledge: a case study of retrograde amnesia. *Brain and Cognition*, 8, 3–20.

Tulving, E. and Thompson, D. M. (1973) Encoding specificity and retrieval processes in episodic memory. *Psychological Review*, 80, 352–73.

Turiel, E. (1998) The development of morality. In W. Damon (Series Ed.) and N. Eisenberg (Vol. Ed.), Handbook of child psychology. Vol. 3. *Social, Emotional and Personality Development* (pp. 863–932) New York: Wiley.

Turner, J. A. (1996) Educational and behavioral interventions for back pain in primary care. *Spine*, 21, 2851–57.

Turner, J. C. (1985) Social categorisation and the self-concept: a social cognitive theory of group behaviour. In E. J. Lawler (ed.) *Advances in Group Processes: Theory and Research* (pp. 77–122) Greenwich, CT: JAI Press.

Turner, J. C. (1991) *Social Influence*. Buckingham: Open University Press.

Turner, J. C., Hogg, M. A., Oakes, P. J., Reicher, S. D. and Wetherell, M. (eds) (1987) *Rediscovering the Social Group: a Self-Categorization Theory*. Oxford: Blackwell.

Turner, J. C., Pratkanis, A. R., Probasco, P. and Leve, C. (1992) Threat cohesion and group effectiveness: testing a social identity maintenance perspective on groupthink. *Journal of Personality and Social Psychology*, 63, 781–96.

Tversky, A. and Kahneman, D. (1974) Judgment under uncertainty: Heuristics and biases. *Science*, 185(4157), 1124–31.

Twemlow, S. W., Lerman, B. H., Twemlow, S. W. (1996) An analysis of student's reasons for studying martial arts. *Perceptual and Motor Skills*, 83, 99–103.

Uhl, G. R., Liu, Q. R. and Naiman, D. (2002) Substance abuse vulnerability loci: converging genome scanning data. *Trends in Genetics*, 18, 420–25.

Underwood, B. J. (1957) Interference and forgetting. *Psychological Review*, 64, 49–60.

Unterharnscheidt, F. (1995) A neurologist's reflections on boxing. V. Concluding remarks. *Review of Neurology*, 23, 1027–32.

Urdan, T. and Maehr, M. (1995) Beyond a two-goal theory of motivation and achievement: a case for social goals. *Review of Educational Research*, 65(3), 213–43.

Valentine, E. R. (1992) *Conceptual Issues in Psychology*. London: Routledge.

Valins, S. (1966) Cognitive affects of false heart-rate feedback. *Journal of Personality and Social Psychology*, 4, 400–408.

Van den Brink, W., Reneman, L., Booij, J., Majoie, C. B. L. M. and Den Heethen, G. J. (2003) Ecstasy: will it contribute to co-morbidity? *Addiction Biology*, 8, 233–50.

Van den Hout, M. and Kindt, M. (2003) Repeated checking causes memory distrust. *Behaviour Research & Therapy*, 41, 301–16.

Van Houdenhove, B., Neerinckx, E., Onghena, P., Vingerhoets, A., Lysens, R. and Vertommen, H. (2002) Daily hassles reported by chronic fatigue syndrome and fibromyalgia patients in tertiary care: a controlled quantitative and qualitative study. *Psychotherapy and Psychosomatics*, 71, 207–13.

Van Kammen, D. P. and Kelley, M. (1991) Dopamine and norepinephrine activity in schizophrenia; An integrated perspective. *Schizophrenia Research* 4 173–91.

Van Kammen, D. P., Bunney, W. E., Jr, Docherty, J. P., Marder, S. R., Ebert, M. H., Rosenblatt, J. E. and Rayner, J. N. (1982) d-Amphetamine-induced heterogeneous changes in psychotic behavior in schizophrenia. *American Journal of Psychiatry*, 139, 991–7.

References

Van Kammen, D. P., Docherty, J. P., Marder, S. R., Schulz, S. C., Dalton, L. and Bunney, W. E., Jr (1982) Antipsychotic effects of pimozide in schizophrenia. *Archives of General Psychiatry*, 39, 261–6.

Van Overwalle, F. (1998) Causal explanation as constraint satisfaction: a critique and a feedforward connectionist alternative. *Journal of Personality and Social Psychology*, 74, 312–28.

van IJzendoorn, M. H. (1995) Adult attachment representations, parental responsiveness and infant attachment: a meta-analysis on the predictive validity of the adult attachment interview. *Psychological Bulletin*, 117, 387–403.

van IJzendoorn, M. H., Schuengel, C. and Bakermans-Kranenburg, M. J. (1999) Disorganised attachment in early childhood: meta-analysis of precursors, concomitants and sequelae. *Development and Psychopathology*, 11, 225–49.

Vanfurth, E. F., Vanstrien, D. C., Martina, L. M. L., Vanson, M. J. M., Hendrickx, J. J. P. and vanEngeland, H. 1996. Expressed emotion and the prediction of outcome in adolescent eating disorders. *International Journal of Eating Disorders*, 20, 19–31.

VanYperen, N. W. and Van de Vliert, E. (2001) Social psychology in organizations. In M. Hewstone and W. Stroebe (eds) *Introduction to Social Psychology* (3rd Edition, pp. 259–587). Oxford: Blackwell.

Varendonck, J. (1911) Les témoignages d'enfants dans un procès retentissant. *Archives de Psychologie*, 11, 129–71.

Vasey, M. and Borkovec, T. D. (1992) A catastrophising assessment of worrisome thoughts. *Cognitive Therapy & Research*, 16, 505–20.

Vasterling, J. J., Duke, L. M., Brailey, K., Constans, J. I., Allain, A. N. and Sutker, P. B. (2002) Attention, learning and memory performances and intellectual resources in Vietnam veterans: PTSD and no disorder comparisons. *Neuropsychology*, 16, 5–14.

Vaughn, B., Egeland, B., Sroufe, L. A. and Waters, E. (1979) Individual differences in infant-mother attachment at 12 and 18 months: stability and change in families under stress. *Child Development*, 50, 971–5.

Verbrugge, L. M. (1985) Gender and health: an update on hypotheses and evidence. *Journal of Health & Social Behavior*, 26, 156–82.

Verhulst, F. C., van der Ende, J., Ferdinand, R. F. and Kasius, M. C. (1997) The prevalence of DSM-III-R diagnoses in a national sample of Dutch adolescents. *Archives of General Psychiatry*, 54, 329–36.

Vernon, P. (1950) The Structure of Human Abilities. London: Methuen.

Verrier, R. L. and Mittelman, M. A. (1996) Life-threatening cardiovascular consequences of anger in patients with coronary heart disease. *Cardiology Clinics*, 14(2), 289–67.

Vlaeyens, J., Kole-Snijders, A., Rottveel, A., Ruesnik, R. and Heuts, P. (1995) The role of fear of movement/(re)injury in pain disability. *Journal of Occupational Rehabilitation*, 5, 235–52.

Voegtlin, W. L. and Lemere, F. (1942) The treatment of alcohol addiction: a review of the literature. *Quarterly Journal of the Study of Alcohol*, 2, 717–803.

Vom Saal, F. S. (1983) Variation in infanticide and parental behavior in male mice due to prior intrauterine proximity to female fetuses: elimination by prenatal stress. *Physiology and Behavior*, 30, 675–81.

Von Neumann, J. and Morgenstern, O. (1947) *Theory of Games and Economic Behaviour* (2nd revised ed.). Princeton, NJ: Princeton University Press.

Von Wright, J. M. (1968) Selection in visual immediate memory. *The Quarterly Journal of Experimental Psychology*, 20(1), 62–8.

Voyer, D., Voyer, S. and Bryden, M. P. (1995) Magnitude of sex differences in spatial abilities: a meta-analysis and consideration of critical variables, *Psychological Bulletin*, 117, 250–70.

Vygotsky, L. S. (1962) *Thought and language*. Cambridge, MA: MIT Press.

Wacker, D. P., Steege, M. W., Northrup, J., Sasso, G., Berg, W., Reimers, T., Cooper, L., Cigrand, K. and Donn, L. (1990) A component analysis of functional communication training across three topographies of severe behavior problems. *Journal of Applied Behavior Analysis*, 23, 417–29.

Wagenaar, W. A. (1986) My Memory: a study of autobiographical memory over six years. *Cognitive Psychology*, 18, 225–52.

Wahlsten, D., Gottlieb, G. 1997. The invalid separation of effects of nature and nurture: lessons from animal, experimentation, in R. J. Sternberg and E. L. Grigorenko (1997) The cognitive costs of physical and mental health: applying the psychology of the developed world to the problems of the developing world. *Eye on Psi Chi* 2 1, 20–7, Fall Issue.

Wakefield, J. C. (1992) The concept of mental disorder: On the boundary between biological facts and social values. *American Psychologist*, 47, 373–88.

Wakeling, A. 1996. Epidemiology of anorexia nervosa. *Psychiatry Research*, 62, 3–9.

Wald, G. (1964) The receptors of human colour vision. *Science*, 145, 1007–16.

Walker, C. E. (ed.) (1998) *Comprehensive clinical psychology: Foundations of clinical psychology.* Vol. 1. Elsevier.

Walker, H. and Buckley, N. (1968) The use of positive reinforcement in conditioning attending behavior. *Journal of Applied Behavior Analysis*, 1, 242–52.

Wallach, M. A., Kogan, N. and Bem, D. J. (1962) Group influence on individual risk taking. *Journal of Abnormal and Social Psychology*, 65, 75–86.

Waller, N. G., Kojetin, B. A., Bouchard, T. J., Lykken, D. T. and Tellegen, A. (1990) Genetic and environmental influences on religious interests, attitudes and values: a study of twins reared apart and together. *Psychological Science*, 1, 138–42.

Wallerstein, J., Lewis, J. M. and Blakeslee, S. (2000) *The unexpected legacy of divorce*. New York: Hyperion.

Wallerstein, R. S. (1989) The Psychotherapy Research Project of the Menninger Foundation: an Overview. *Journal of Consulting and Clinical Psychology*, 57, 197–205.

Wallston, B. S. and Wallston, K. A. (1984) Social psychological models of health behavior. An examination and integration. In

A. Baum, S. E. Taylor and J. E. Singer (eds) *Handbook of Psychology and Health (Vol. 4) Social Psychological Aspects of Health*. Hillsdale NJ: Lawrence Erlbaum.

Wallston, B. S., Wallston, K. A., Kaplan, G. D. and Maides, S. A. (1976) Development and validation of the Health Locus of Control (HLC) Scale. *Journal of the Consulting Clinical Psychologist*, 44, 580–5.

Wallston, K. A. (1994) Cautious optimism versus cockeyed optimism. *Psychology and Health*, 9, 201–03.

Wallston, K. A. and Wallston, B. S. (1982) Who is responsible for your health? The construct of health locus of control. In G. S. Sanders and J. Suls (eds) *Social psychology of Health and illness*. Hillsdale NJ: Erlbaum.

Wallston, T. S. (1978) Three biases in the cognitive processing of diagnostic information. *Psychometric Laboratory*, University of North Carolina, Chapel Hill.

Wang, Q., Bing, C., Al-Baranzanji, K., Mossakowaska, D. E., Wang, X. M., McBay, D. L., Neville, W. A., Taddayon, M., Pickavance, L., Dryden, S., Thomas, M. E., McHae, M. Y., Gloyer, I. S., Wilson, S., Buckingham, R., Arch, J.R., Trayhurn, P. and Williams, G. (1997) Interactions between leptin and hypothalamic neuropeptide Y neurons in the control of food intake and energy homeostasis in the rat. *Diabetes*, 46, 335–41.

Ward, N. I. (1997) Assessment of chemical factors in relation to child hyperactivity. *Journal of Nutrition & Environmental Medicine* Vol. 7(4), 333–42.

Warren, R. M. and Warren, R. P. (1970) Auditory Illusions and Confusions. *Scientific American*, 223, 30–6.

Wason, P. S. (1960) On the failure to eliminate hypotheses in a conceptual task. *The Quarterly Journal of Experimental Psychology*, 12, 129–40.

Watkins, C. E., Jr, Campbell, V. L., Nieberding, R., Hallmark, R. (1996), Comparative practice of psychological assessment. *Professional Psychological Research Practice*, 27, 316–18.

Watson J. B. and Rayner R. (1920) Conditioned emotional reactions. *Journal of Experimental Psychology*, 3, 1–14.

Watson, D., Clark, L. A. and Tellegen, A. (1988) Development and validation of brief measures of positive and negative affect: The PANAS scale. *Journal of Personality and Social Psychology*, 54, 1063–70.

Watson, J. B. (1913) 'Psychology as the behaviourist views it'. *Psychological Review*, 20, 158–77.

Watson, J. B. and Rayner, R. (1920) Conditioned emotional reactions. *Journal of Experimental Psychology*, 3, 1?14.

Watson, J. B. (1930) *Behaviourism*. New York: Norton.

Watson, J. S. and Ramey, C. T. (1972) Reactions to response-contingent stimulation in early infancy. Merrill-Palmer Quarterly, 18, 219–27.

Watts F. N. (1995) An information-processing approach to compulsive checking. *Clinical Psychology & Psychotherapy*, 2, 69–77.

Wayland, S. C., Wingfield, A. and Goodglass, H. (1989) Recognition of isolated words: The dynamics of cohort reduction. *Applied Psycholinguistics*, 10(4), 475–87.

Webb, K. and Davey, G. C. L. (1993) Disgust sensitivity and fear of animals: Effect of exposure to violent or revulsive material. *Anxiety, Stress & Coping*, 5, 329–35.

Weber, E. U., Boeckenholt, U., Hilton, D. J. and Wallace, B. (1993) Determinants of diagnostic hypothesis generation: Effects of information, base rates and experience. *Journal of Experimental Psychology: Learning, Memory and Cognition*, 19(5), 1151–64.

Webster-Stratton, C. (1999) *How to Promote Children's Social and Emotional Competence*. London: Paul Chapman.

Wechsler, D. (1989), Wechsler Preschool and Primary Scale of Intelligence-Revised: Manual San Antonio, TX: Psychological Corporation.

Wechsler, D. (1991), Wechsler Intelligence Scale for Children- Third Edition: Manual San Antonio, TX: Psychological Corporation.

Wechsler, D. (1997), Wechsler Adult Intelligence Scale-Third Edition (WAIS-III), Administration and Scoring Manual San Antonio, TX: Psychological Corporation.

Weikert, D. (1996) High quality pre-school programs found to improve adult status. *Childhood*, 3, 117–20.

Weikert, D., Deloria, D., Lawser, S. and Weigerink, R. (1970) Longitudinal results of the Ypsilanti Perry preschool project. *Monographs of the High-Scope Educational Research Foundation*, No. 1.

Weinberger, M., Hiner, S. L. and Tierney, W. M. (1987) In support of hassles as a measure of stress in predicting health outcomes. *Journal of Behavioural Medicine*, 10, 19–31.

Weiner, B. (1985a) An attributional theory of achievement motivation and emotion. *Psychological Review*. 92, 548–73.

Weiner, B. (1985b) 'Spontaneous' causal thinking. *Psychological Bulletin*, 97, 74–84.

Weiner, B. (1986) *An Attributional Theory of Motivation and Emotion*. New York: Springer-Verlag.

Weiner, B. (1992) *Human Motivation: Metaphors, Theories and Research*. Newbury Park, CA: Sage.

Weiner, B. (1995) *Judgments of Responsibility: a Foundation for a Theory of Social Conduct*. London: Guilford Press.

Weingarten, H. P., Chang, P. K. and McDonald, T. J. (1985) Comparison of the metabolic and behavioral disturbances following paraventricular- and ventromedial-hypothalamic lesions. *Brain Research Bulletin*, 14, 551–9.

Weisman, A. (1997) Understanding cross-cultural prognostic variability for schizophrenia. *Cultural Diversity & Mental Health*, 3, 3–35.

Weiss, E. M., Kemmler, G., Deisenhammer, E. A., Fleischhacker, W. W. and Dalazer, M. (2003) Sex differences in cognitive functions. *Personality and Individual Differences*, 35, 863–75.

Weisz, J. R., McCarty, C. A., Eastman, K. L., Chaiyasit, W. and Suwanlert, S. (1997) Developmental psychopathology and culture: ten lessons from Thailand. In S. S. Luthar, J. A. Burack, D. Cicchetti and J. R. Weisz (eds) *Developmental Psycho-pathology: Perspectives on adjustment, risk and disorder*. Cambridge: Cambridge University Press.

Weizenbaum, J. (1966) ELIZA – A Computer Programme for the

References

Study of Natural Language Communication Between Man and Machine, *Communications of the ACM*, 9(1) pp 35–6.

Wellman, H. M. (1990) *The Child's Theory of Mind*. Cambridge, MA: MIT Press.

Wellman, H. M. and Gelman, S. A. (1998) Knowledge acquisition in foundational domains. In W. Damon (Series ed.), D. Kuhn and R. S. Siegler (Vol. eds) *Handbook of child development: Vol. 2. Cognition, perception and language* (5th ed., pp. 523–73). New York: Wiley.

Wells, A. (1995) Meta-cognition and worry: a cognitive model of generalized anxiety disorder. *Behavioural and Cognitive Psychotherapy*, 23, 301–20.

Wells, A. (1997) *Cognitive Therapy of Anxiety Disorders*. Chichester: Wiley.

Wells, A. and Papageorgiou, C. (1998) relationships between worry, obsessive-compulsive symptoms and meta-cognitive beliefs. *Behaviour Research and Therapy*, 36, 899–913.

Welsh, M. C., Pennington, B. F., Ozonoff, S., Rouse, B. and McCabe, E. R. B. (1990) Neuropsychology of early-treated phenylketonuria: specific executive function deficits. *Child Development*, 61, 1697–713.

Wenk, G. L. (2003) Neuropathologic changes in Alzheimer's disease. *Journal of Clinical Psychiatry*, 64 Suppl. 9, 7–10.

Werker, J. F. (1989) Becoming a native listener. *American Scientist*, 77, 54–69.

Werner, E. E. and Smith, R. S. (1982) *Vulnerable but Invincible: a Longitudinal Study of Resilient Children and Youth*. New York: McGraw-Hill.

Werry, J. S., Reeves, J. C. and Elkind, G. S. (1987) Attention deficit, conduct, oppositional and anxiety disorders in children: I A review of research on differing characteristics. *Journal of the American Academy of Child & Adolescent Psychiatry*, 26, 133–43.

Weston, D. (1998) The scientific legacy of Sigmund Freud: Toward a psychodynamically informed psychological science. *Psychological Bulletin*, 124, 333–71.

Wetherell, M. (1987) Social identity and group polarization. In J. C. Turner, M. A. Hogg, P. J. Oakes, S. D. Reicher and M. Wetherell (eds) *Rediscovering the Social Group: a Self-Categorization Theory*. Oxford: Blackwell.

Wetherell, M. (1997) Linguistic repertoires and literary criticism: new direction for a social psychology of gender. In M. Gergen and S. Davis (eds) *Towards a New Psychology of Gender: a Reader* (pp. 149–67). London: Routledge.

Wetherick, N. E. and Gilhooly, K. J. (1995) 'Atmosphere', matching and logic in syllogistic reasoning. *Current Psychology: Developmental, Learning, Personality, Social*, 14(3), 169–78.

Whalen, C. K. and Henker, B. (1985) The social worlds of hyperactive (ADDH) children. *Clinical Psychology Review*, 5, 447–78.

Whalen, P. J., Shin, L. M., McInerney, S. C., Fisher, H., Wright, C. I. and Rauch, S. L. (2001) A functional MRI study of human amygdala responses to facial expressions of fear versus anger. *Emotion*, 1, 70–83.

Whaley, C. P. (1978) Word non-word classification time. *Journal of Verbal Learning and Verbal Behaviour*, 17, 143–54.

Wheeler, D. (1970) Processes in word recognition. *Cognitive Psychology*, 1, 59–85.

Wickens, C. D. (1992) *Engineering Psychology and Human Performance*. New York: HarperCollins Publishers.

Wickens, C. D. and Gopher, D. (1977) Control theory measures of tracking as indices of attention allocation strategies. *Human Factors*, 19(4), 349–65.

Wickens, T. D. (2002) *Elementary Signal Detection Theory*. London: Oxford University Press.

Wicker, A. W. (1969) Attitude versus action: the relationship of verbal and overt behavioral responses to attitude objects. *Journal of Social Issues*, 25, 41–78.

Widiger, T. A. and Corbitt, E. M. (1995) Antisocial personality disorder. In W. J. Livesley (ed.) The DSM-IV personality disorders. New York: Guilford.

Wilcox, T., Nadel, L., Rosser, R. (1996) Location memory in healthy preterm and full-term infants. *Infant Behaviour and Development*, 19, 309–24.

Willerman, L., Schultz, R., Rutledge, J. N. and Bigler, E, D. (1991) In vivo brain size and intelligence. *Intelligence*, 15, 223–8.

Williams, J. M. G., Watts, F. N., MacLeod, C. and Mathews, A. (1997) *Cognitive psychology and emotional disorders*. Chichester: Wiley.

Willner, P. (1984) The validity of animal models of depression. *Psychopharmacology*, 83, 1–16.

Willner, P. (1986) Validation criteria for animal models of human mental disorders: learned helplessness as a paradigm case. *Progress in Neuropsychopharmacolology and Biological Psychiatry*, 10, 677–90.

Willner, P. (1991) Behavioural models in psychopharmacology. In P. Willner (ed.) *Behavioural Models in Psychopharmacology: Theoretical, Industrial and Clinical Perspectives*. Cambridge: Cambridge University Press.

Willner, P. and Mitchell, P. J. (2002) The validity of animal models of predisposition to depression. *Behavioural Pharmacology*, 13, 169–88.

Wills, T. A. (1985) Supportive functions of interpersonal relationships, in S. Cohen and S. L. Syme (eds) *Social support and health*. Orlando FL: Academic Press.

Wilson G. T. (1978) Aversion therapy for alcoholism: Issues, ethics and evidence. In G. A. Marlatt and P. E. Nathan (eds) *Behavioral assessment and treatment of alcoholism*. New Brunswick, NJ: Center for Alcohol Studies.

Wilson, B. and Wearing, D. (1995) Prisoner of consciousness: a state of awakening following herpes simplex encephalitis. In R. Campbell and M. Conway (eds) *Broken Memories: Case Studies in Memory Impairment* (pp. 14–30). Malden, MA, US: Blackwell.

Wilson, E. O. (2000) *Sociobiology: the new synthesis*. Cambridge, MA, Harvard University Press.

Wilson, M. S., Reschly, D. J. (1996), Assessment in school psychology training and practice. *School Psychology Review*, 25, 9–23.

Wilson, R. and Jonah, B. A. (1988) Assignment of responsibility and penalties for an impaired driving incident. *Journal of Applied Social Psychology*, 18, 564–83.

Wimmer, F., Hoffmann, R. F., Bonato, R. A. and Moffitt, A. R. (1992) The effects of sleep deprivation on divergent thinking and attention processes. *Journal of Sleep Research*, 1, 223–30.

Wimmer, H. and Goswami, U. (1994) The influence of orthographic consistency on reading development: word recognition on English and German. *Cognition*, 51, 51–103.

Wimmer, H. and Perner, J. (1983) Beliefs about beliefs: Representation and constraining function of wrong beliefs in young children's understanding of deception. *Cognition*, 13, 103–28.

Wimmer, H., Mayringer, H. and Landerl, K. (1998) Poor reading: a deficit in skill-automatization or a phonological deficit? *Scientific Studies of Reading*, 2(4), 321–40.

Wing, L. (1988) The continuum of autistic characteristics. In E. Schopler and G. Mesibov (eds) *Diagnosis and assessment in autism*. New York: Plenum Press, 91–107.

Winston, P. H. (1970) *Learning Structural Descriptions From Examples. AI Laboratory, Technical Report*. Cambridge. MA: MIT Press.

Wirth, S., Ynaike, M., Frank, L. M., Smith, A. C., Brown, E. N. and Suzuki, W. A. (2003) Single neurons in the Monkey Hippocampus and Learning of new associations. *Science*, 300, 1578–81.

Wise, R. A. and Bozarth, M. A. (1987) A psychomotor theory of addiction. *Psychological Review*, 94, 469–92.

Witte, K. (1992) Putting the fear back into fear appeals: the extended parallel process model. *Communication Monographs*, 59, 329–49.

Wolf, M. and Bowers, P. G. (1999) The double-deficit hypothesis for the Developmental Dyslexias. *Journal of Educational Psychology*, 91, 415–38.

Wolf, S. (1985) Manifest and latent influence of majorities and minorities. *Journal of Personality and Social Psychology*, 48, 899–908.

Wolfson, S. (2000) Students' estimates of the prevalence of drug use: Evidence for a false consensus effect. *Psychology of Addictive Behaviors*, 14, 295–8.

Wolke, D. (1998) Psychological development of prematurely born children. *Archives of Disease in Childhood*, 78, 567–70.

Wolke, D. and Meyer, R. (1999) Cognitive status, language attainment and prereading skills of 6-year-old very preterm children and their peers: The Bavarian Longitudinal Study. *Developmental Medicine & Child Neurology*, 41(2), 94–109.

Wolpe, J. (1958) *Psychotherapy and reciprocal inhibition*. Stanford, CA: The Stanford University Press.

Wolraich, M. L., Wilson, D. B. and White, J. W. (1995) The effect of sugar on behavior or cognition in children: a meta-analysis. *Journal of the American Medical Association*, 274, 1617–21.

Wood, D. J., Bruner, J. S. and Ross, G. (1976) The role of tutoring in problem-solving. *Journal of Child Psychology and Psychiatry*, 17, 89–100.

Wood, W., Lundgren, S., Oullette, J. A., Busceme, S. and Blackstone, T. (1994) Minority influence: a meta-analytic review of social influence processes. *Psychological Bulletin*, 106, 249–64.

Woodhead, M. M., Baddeley, A. D. and Simmonds, D. C. V. (1979) On training people to recognise faces. *Ergonomics*, 22, 333–43.

Woolverton, W. L., Goldberg, L. I. and Ginos, J. Z. (1984) Intravenous self-administration of dopamine receptor agonists by rhesus monkeys. *Journal of Pharmacology and Experimental Therapeutics*, 230, 678–83.

World Health Organization (2002) *The World Health Report, 2002: Reducing risks, promoting healthy life*.

Wortman, C. B. and Brehm, J. W. (1975) Responses to uncontrollable outcomes: an integration of the reactance theory and the learned helplessness model. In L. Berkowitz (ed.) *Advances in social psychology*. New York: Academic Press.

Yarrow, L. J. (1964) Separation from parents during early childhood. In M. L. Hoffman and L. W. Hoffman (eds) *Review of Child Development Research*. New York: Russell Sage Foundation.

Yukl, G. (1998) *Leadership in Organisations* (4th ed.). Upper Saddle River, NJ: Prentice Hall.

Zahn-Waxler, C. and Robinson, J. (1995) Empathy and guilt: Early origins of feelings and responsibility. In J. P. Tangney and K. W. Fischer (eds) *Self-conscious emotions: The psychology of shame, guilt, embarrassment and pride*. New York: Guilford Press.

Zajonc, R. B. (1965) Social facilitation. *Science*, 149, 269–74.

Zajonc, R. B. (1984) On the primacy of effect. *American Psychologist*, 39, 117–23.

Zajonc, R. B., Murphy, S. T. and Inglehart, M. (1989) Feeling and facial efference: Implications of the vascular theory of emotions. *Psychological Review*, 96, 395–416.

Zanna, M. P. and Cooper, J. (1974) Dissonance and the pill: an attribution approach to studying the arousal properties of dissonance. *Journal of Personality and Social Psychology*, 29, 703–9.

Zazzo, R. (1978) Genesis and peculiarities of the personality of twins. In W. E. Nance, G. Allen and P. Parisi (eds) *Twin Research. Progress in Clinical and Biological Research: Psychology and Methodology*. New York: Liss.

Zeldow, P. B. (1995) Psychodynamic formulations of human behaviour. In D. Wedding (ed.) *Behavior and Medicine*. St Louis, MO: Mosby Year Book.

Zillman, D. (1978) Attribution and mis-attribution of excitatory reactions. In J. H. Harvey, W. J. Ickes and R. F. Kidd (eds) *New Directions in Attribution Research Vol. 2*. Hillsdale, New, Jersey: Erlbaum.

Zillmann, D. (1988) Cognition-excitation interdependence in aggressive behaviour. *Aggressive Behavior*, 14, 51–64.

Zimbardo, P. G. and Leippe, M. R. (1991) *The psychology of attitude change and social influence*. New York: McGraw-Hill.

Zola-Morgan, S. and Squire, L. R. (1986) Memory impairment in monkeys following lesions limited to the hippocampus. *Behavioral Neuroscience*, 100, 155–60.

Zuckerman, M. (1974) The sensation seeking motive. In B. Maher (ed.) *Progress in experimental personality research* (pp. 70–148). New York: Academic Press.

References

Zuckerman, M. (1978) Sensation seeking. In H. London and J. E. Exner (eds) *Dimensions of Personality* (pp. 487–559). NY: Wiley Interscience.

Zuckerman, M. (1979) Attribution of success and failure revisited, or: the motivational bias is alive and well in attribution theory. *Journal of Personality*, 47, 245–87.

Zuckerman, M. (1990) Some dubious premises in research and theory on racial differences. *American Psychologist*, 45, 1297–303.

Zuckerman, M. (1991) Psychobiology of Personality. NY: Cambridge University Press.

Zvolensky, M. J. and Eifert G. H. (2001) A review of psychological factors/processes affecting anxious responding during voluntary hyperventilation and inhalations of carbon dioxide-enriched air. *Clinical Psychology Review*, 21, 375–400.

Name Index

A

Aaronson, D., 251
Aboud, F., 342
Abrahams, F., 504
Abrahams, L.Y., 578
Abrams, D., 433, 721
Abramson, A., 200, 201f
Ackerman, P.L., 534b
Adair, Y., 24b
Adams, J., 420
Adler, A., 16, 492, 494
Adolphs, R., 153
Adorno, T.W., 445
Aiken, L.R., 537
Ainsworth, M.D.S., 295, 345
Aitchison, J., 247, 262
Ajzen, I., 383–84, 388f, 394, 622, 623
Akabayashi, A., 146
Albert, D.J., 155
Albery, I.P., 374
Alibali, M., 314
Allen, V.L., 433
Allport, D.A., 214, 447
Allport, G.W., 376, 377b, 492, 505
Almazan, M., 327
Almeida, D.M., 357
Altman, J., 139, 149
Ames, 471
Ames, C., 473
Anderson, C.A., 459
Anderson, J.R., 207b, 215, 252f, 269, 270f, 271f, 272, 275–76, 279
Anderson, R.C., 243
Andre, C., 479
Andreasen, N.C., 598

Andrewes, D., 119
Andrews, G., 614
Angrist, B., 582
Antony, M.M., 561
Ardelt, M., 506
Argyle, M., 418, 428
Armitage, C.J., 384
Asch, S.E., 363, 370, 411–12, 413, 432
Ashworth, P., 27
Aslin, R.N., 328, 331, 437
Asmundson, G.J.G., 632
Asperger, H., 353
Aspinwall, L.G., 631
Aston-Jones, G., 157
Atkinson, J.W., 475
Atkinson, R.C., 226, 228f, 229
Augoustinos, M., 368, 408
Averback, E., 209
Avina, C., 574
Ayllon, T.T., 546, 606, 607b
Azrin, N.H., 605, 606, 607b

B

Baddeley, A.D., 22 illus, 217, 220, 222, 225, 226, 229f, 230b, 232b, 234, 245, 337, 727
Baer, D.M., 607
Baghdoyen, H.A., 157
Bailey, A., 354
Baillargeon, R., 303–4
Baker, L.E., 113b, 615
Baker, R., 607b
Baldwin, D.A., 342
Ball, K., 589
Baltes, 286
Banaji, M.R., 380, 382

Bandura, A., 16, 284, 343, 426, 427, 469, 493, 499–500, 579
Banks, M.S., 359
Banyard, P., 43, 44, 45, 46, 47t, 48b, 50, 52, 670
Banzett, L.K., 607
Barber, N., 73
Barett, M., 339
Bargh, J., 367, 382, 415–16b
Bargh, J.A., 415
Barker, K.L., 476
Barker, M., 16, 26b, 40, 44, 45, 62, 64
Barlow, D.H., 564
Baron, J., 197b
Baron, M.S., 175b
Baron, R.A., 362, 396, 437f
Baron, R.S., 433
Baron-Cohen, S., 351, 351b, 354, 356
Barrett, L., 85
Barrett, M., 325
Barrick, M.R., 535b
Bartels, A., 153
Bartlett, F.C., 14t, 231, 234, 242
Basbaum, A.I., 173
Bass, E., 491
Bates, E., 341
Bateson, G., 582, 583
Bateson, P., 670
Batson, C.D., 421, 422
Baumeister, R.F., 483, 485, 498
Beach, S.R., 419
Beck, A.T., 576–77, 610
Becker, M.H., 621
Beecher, H.K., 631
Beeman, E.A., 154

Name Index

Bell, A., 41, 64
Bell, M.A., 303
Bell, R.Q., 286
Bell, S.M., 345
Bem, D., 343, 386–87
Bem, S.L., 481
Ben-Zeev, T., 279
Benjamin, L.T., Jr., 10
Benjamin,R.S., 593
Bennett, C., 733
Bentler, P.M., 384
Benton, D., 529
Berendes, H., 528
Berg, J.H., 418
Bergenheim, A.T., 175b
Berger, P.L., 368
Berko, J., 326
Bernheimer, H., 105
Bernouilli, J., 668
Berridge, K.C., 143, 144, 149
Betz, E.L., 498
Bezdek, K.., 234
Bickerton, D., 328
Biederman, I., 192–93, 197f
Biederman, J., 591
Binet, A., 14, 284, 301, 515b, 518, 530b
Birch, A., 26b, 54, 55, 62
Bishop, D., 339
Bishop, D.V.M., 334b
Bisiach, E., 212b
Black, D.W., 598
Blank, M., 308b
Blass, T., 501b
Bless, H., 364, 365, 375
Bliss, T.V., 134
Bloch, S., 610
Bloom, B.S., 727
Bloom, F.E., 157
Bloom, P.A., 260
Blundell, J.E., 147
Bohannon, J.N., 332
Bohner, G., 378b, 380, 381, 388, 391, 393, 394
Boldero, J., 482
Bolton, D., 573
Bond, M.H., 442
Bond, R., 433
Boneva, B.S., 484
Borgida, E., 401

Borkenau, R., 510b
Borkovec, T.D., 566, 567, 614
Borton, R.W., 303
Borucki, Z., 475
Bouchard, T.J., Jr., 510b, 527
Boudewyns, P.A., 607
Bourhis, R.Y., 447
Bousfield, W.A., 230
Bouton, M.E., 124
Bower, G., 270
Bower, G.H., 230, 231f, 243
Bower, T.G.R., 302
Bowers, P.G., 338
Bowlby, J., 345, 347, 348, 497
Bowmaker, J., 162
Boysson-Bardies, B, de, 323
Bozarth, M.A., 142, 143
Bozna, M., 475
Bradley, C., 615
Bradley, L., 336, 337
Bradshaw, P.W., 232b
Brady, E.U., 593
Brainerd, C.J., 312
Brauer, M., 438
Breggin, P., 597
Brehm, J.W., 577
Breisch, S.T., 146
Bremner, G., 298, 320
Bremner, J.G., 305
Breslau, N., 572
Brewer, M.B., 447
Brewin, C.R., 572, 615
Bridges, J.S., 43, 52
Britton, D.R., 155
Broadbent, D., 206, 208f, 235
Broberger, C., 146
Broca, 13t
Brocke, B., 507
Broerse, J., 303
Bronfenbrenner, U., 527
Brooks, L., 242
Brooks-Gunn, J., 342
Brosnan, S.F., 128
Brown, D., 574
Brown, H.D., 570
Brown, J.D., 406, 482
Brown, R., 238, 254, 254b, 331, 353, 367, 429, 433, 435, 444, 445, 446f, 447, 449, 583, 627
Brown, R.W., 380

Browne, K.D., 474
Brubaker, R., 623
Bruce, V., 177, 196, 203, 418
Brune, M., 70
Bruner, J.S., 14t, 195, 269–71, 272, 313, 323, 412
Bryant, P.E., 336, 337
Buchanan, A., 587b
Bucy, P.C., 151
Bullock, W.A., 507
Bullogh, V.L., 356
Bunge, M., 512
Bunyard, P., 41
Burger, J.M., 403
Burkett, B.G., 574
Burr, V., 23
Burt, C., 36, 37
Burt, S.A., 84
Burton, M.J., 146
Bushnell, I.W.R., 345
Buss, D., 491
Buss, D.M., 465, 508
Butler, G., 565b
Butterworth, G., 298, 302, 479
Butzlaff, R.L., 583
Buysse, D.J., 159
Byrne, D., 362, 396, 418, 437f
Byrne, W., 23

C

Cacioppo, J.T., 377, 379, 388, 390
Cahill, L., 153
Calabresi, 175
Calne, G.B., 109b, 141
Campbell, D., 656–57b
Campbell, K.H., 72
Campbell, N.A., 74, 75, 78, 85
Cannon, W., 458
Carboni, E., 140, 142
Cardaci, M., 469
Carlsmith, J.M., 386, 662–63b, 708b
Carlson, N.R., 22, 23, 154
Carlsson, A., 109b, 582
Carlston, D.E., 413
Carpenter, M., 342
Carpenter, P.A., 252–53
Carr, G.D., 141
Carr, S.C., 362
Carroll. J.B., 520, 525b

Carter, D., 82
Carter, S.J., 234
Case, R., 311b, 312
Casey, J.E., 590
Cashdan, E., 508
Casper, R.C., 589
Casscells, W., 272
Cassidy, H.J., 234
Cassidy, J., 347b
Caterina, M.J., 174
Cattell, R., 520
Cattell, R.B., 492, 503
Catts, H., 338
Cave, S., 557
Ceci, S.J., 311b, 527
Cernoch, J.M., 345
Chaiken, S., 290, 378, 378b, 379,
    379b, 380, 387, 388, 389, 391,
    394
Chambless, D.L., 564, 610, 616
Chance, P., 137
Chandler, C., 113b
Chandler, C.J., 121, 142
Chandler,C.J., 113b
Chapman, T.F., 559
Chartrand, T.L., 415
Chase, W., 728
Chase, W.G., 231, 277
Cheeta, S.K., 113b
Chemers, M.M., 442
Chen, S., 290, 388
Cheng, D.T., 152
Cheng, P.W., 401
Cherlin, A.J., 348
Cherry, E.C., 206
Chi, M.T.H., 277, 311b
Child, I.L., 489
Choi. I., 484
Choi, Y., 484
Chomsky, N., 59, 246, 249, 251,
    285illus, 326–27, 329
Christenson, A., 612
Church, A.T., 501
Chwalisz, K., 458
Cialdini, R., 422
Cimbolic, P., 576
Clahsen, H., 327
Clancy, S.A., 574
Clark, D., 562–64
Clark, D.M., 561, 562, 573

Clark, J.T., 146
Clarke, P.B., 121b, 142
Clemente, C.D., 156
Clifford, B.R., 237b
Codol, J.P., 438
Coen, K.M., 142
Cohen, J., 696, 697, 729
Cohen, S., 626
Colby, A., 309
Cole, B.J., 155
Coleman, J.C., 357, 360
Collaer, M.L., 343
Collins, A.M., 239, 240f
Collins, S.C., 732, 750
Collis, G.M., 324
Colman, A.M., 219, 262, 279
Coltheart, 335
Coltheart, M., 222
Comings, D.E., 84
Compton, R.J., 511
Comte, A., 29
Connell,H.P., 108
Conner, M., 384, 393
Conners, C.K., 591
Conti-Ramsden, G., 334b
Cook, R., 529
Cooley, C.H., 481
Cools, A.R., 72
Cooper, J., 386, 432
Cooper, N., 40
Cooper, R.P., 331, 437
Cooper C., 513
Coppola, M., 328
Corbett, D., 139
Corbitt, E.M., 584
Corkin, S., 226
Corrigal, W.A., 142
Corrigan, P.W., 607
Corte, C.M., 479
Cosmides, L., 272
Costa, P.T., 492, 504
Costello, E., 614
Cottrell, N.B., 436
Court, J.H., 540
Cousins, M., 484
Cowan, G.N.J., 208
Coyle, A., 50b
Crago, M., 334b
Craik, F.I.M., 230
Crassini, B., 303

Crick, N.R., 349, 591
Croft, C.M., 347
Crombez, G., 632
Cronbach, L.J., 529, 534
Crook, C.K., 318
Crouch, E., 610
Crow, T., 108b
Crowther, J.H., 630
Cryan, J.F., 143
Curran, H.V., 113b
Cutright, P., 579
Czapinski, J., 413

D
Dabbs, J.M., 508
Dallos, R., 611, 613
Daly, M., 497
Damasio, A.R., 153
D'Amico, A., 469
Damon,W., 309
Darby, K.M., 606
Darley, J., 423, 425b
Darwin, C., 12t, 284
Das, 515b
Davey, A., 342
Davey, G.C.L., 547, 561, 565b, 567,
    568b, 572, 607, 612, 614b, 630t,
    5671
Davidson, A.R., 383
Davidson, R.J., 463
Davis, B., 607
Davis, E.A., 324b
Davis, J.M., 582
Davis, L., 491
Davison, G.C., 557, 594
Dawes, R.M., 275
Dawis, R.V., 530
Dawkins, R., 85
De Blas, A.L., 110b
De Caspar, A.J., 345
De Renzi, E., 197b, 237
De Valck, E., 159b
De Valois, K.K., 167, 193b
De Valois. R.L., 193b
de Waal, F.B.M., 128
Dejoy, D.M., 403
Demetras, M.J., 331
Dennis, W., 286
DePaulo, B., 418
Derrington, A., 166

Name Index

Descartes, R., 10, 13t, 517
Desjarlais R., 551
Detterman, D.K., 515
Deutsch, G., 93
Deutsch, M., 432
Di Chiara, G., 141
Diamond, A., 303
Dickinson, A., 134
Dion, K.K., 421
Dion, K.L., 421
Dion et al, 414
Dixon, M.W., 436
Dobbing, J., 528
Dockrell, J., 334b, 339
Dodge, K.A., 591
Dogali, M., 175b
Doise, W., 318
Dollard, J., 493
Donaldson, M., 305, 308b
Donny, E.C., 142
Dovidio, J.F., 421
Downer, J.L. de C., 152
Downing, J., 113b
Downs, A.C., 343
Draper, R., 611
Drury, J., 485
Dryden, S., 146
du Plessis, D.G., 81
Dube, M.G., 146
Duck, S., 428
Dudai, Y., 137
Duncker, K., 265
Dunn, J., 353
Dunnett, S.B., 146
Dunning, S.B., 483

E
Eagly, A.H., 378, 378b, 379, 379b, 380, 387, 389, 391, 394
Earles, J.A., 534b
Eastridge, B.J., 159
Ebbinghaus, H., 10, 13t, 235, 727
Ebstein, R.P., 84
Eccleston, C., 632
Eckensberger, L., 360
Edelmann, R.J., 563b
Edwards, A.L., 379
Edwards, L., 75
Ehlers, A., 564, 573
Ehri, L.C., 335

Ehringer, H., 105
Eifert, G.H., 562
Eimas, P.D., 321
Eisenberg, N., 349, 421
Eiser, R., 387
Ekman, P., 454
Elcock, J., 11, 24b, 27, 29, 43, 46, 46b, 52, 54
Elias, C.F., 146
Elicker, J., 347b
Ellenberger, H.F., 491
Ellenbroek, B.A., 72
Ellinwood, E.H., 72
Ellis, A.W., 196
Ellis, H.C., 245
Emerson, P.E., 284, 344
Emery, R.E., 594, 617
Emler, N., 417
Epstein, A.N., 265
Epstein, R., 148
Erickson, K., 418, 461
Ericsson, K.A., 728
Erikson, E.H., 16, 44, 51, 286, 358, 492, 494, 496
Escalante, D.O, 72
Eslea, M., 351
Etaugh, C.A., 43, 52
Evans, J., 263
Everson, C.A., 159
Eysenck, H.J., 19, 33, 38, 243, 490, 492, 493, 496, 502–3f, 522, 612
Eysenck, M.W., 22, 203, 208f, 215f, 219, 229, 245, 262, 279

F
Faber, J.E., 382
Fagot, B.I., 343
Fairburn, C.G., 571, 589
Falzone, T.L., 84
Fantegrossi, W.E., 143
Farah, M.J., 177
Farber, E.W., 579
Farrar, M.J., 324
Fazio, R.H., 384, 387
Fechner, 13t
Feingold, B.F., 591
Feldman, M.P., 605
Feldman, R.S., 119
Fenson, L., 325
Ferguson, C.A., 331

Ferguson, N.B., 146
Fernquist, R.M., 579
Ferster, C.B., 606
Festinger, L., 363, 386, 419, 420f, 662–63b, 708b
Fibiger, H.C., 140, 140f
Fiedler, K., 364, 365, 375
Fiedler 1965, F.E., 444
Field, A.P., 560, 645, 647, 651, 662, 666b, 670, 680, 688, 691, 694, 697, 698, 710
Field, P.M., 117
Fields, H.L., 173
Fifer, W.P., 345
Filipeck, P.A., 591
Fincham, F., 397, 404, 408
Fine, I., 169
Finlay, K., 733, 733f
Fiorillo, C.D., 134
Fischer,K.W., 151b
Fischler, I., 260
Fischoff, B., 472b
Fishbein, M., 383, 388f, 622
Fisher, K., 471
Fisher, R., 646–47, 649, 693, 694, 695
Fisk, A.D., 205
Fiske, S., 364
Fiske, S.E. Taylor, S.T., 375
Fiske, S.T., 413
Fiske Taylor, 368, 378, 390, 396, 406, 407, 409
Flavell, J.H., 311b
Fleurose, S.S., 545
Fliers, E., 117
Flood, J.F., 146
Foa, E.B., 573
Fodor,J.A., 327, 330b
Folkman, S., 630
Fonagy, P., 347
Forbes, G.B., 501b
Fordyce, W.E., 631
Forer, B.R., 482
Forgas, J.P., 449, 454
Fösterling, F., 396, 396b, 397, 398f, 408
Fox, D., 23
Fox, N.A., 303
Foy, D.W., 572
Frances, A., 578

Francis, J., 482
Francis, W.N., 259
Franklin, J.A., 589
Freedman, J.L., 427
Freeman, 515b
Freidman, H.L., 497
French, C.C., 219, 262, 279
Freud, A., 494
Freud, S., 13, 14t, 16–19, 44, 234, 284, 491, 492, 494–96, 547, 599
Friedman, A., 243
Friedman, H.S., 418, 428
Frieze, I.H., 484
Frith, U., 354–55b, 355
Fromm-Reichmann, F., 582
Frueh, B.C., 574
Fudala, P.J., 142
Fung, Y.K., 591
Furlong, M., 500
Furnham, A., 527, 535b
Furrow, D., 331
Fusella, V., 215, 215f, 218t

G
Gaertner, S.L., 444, 447, 449
Gage, P., 95
Gagnon, A., 447
Gais, S., 158
Galambos, N.L., 357
Galen, 506t, 507
Gallopin, T., 156
Galton, F., 12, 13t, 518
Garcha, H.S., 131
Gardiner, J.M., 729
Gardner, B.T., 247, 249
Gardner, F., 497
Gardner, H., 515b, 521, 522–24, 527, 527b
Gardner, R.A., 247, 249
Garmezy, N., 288
Garner, D.M., 590
Garrett, M.F., 254
Garssen, B., 562
Gass, R.H., 449
Gathercole, S.E., 230b
Gazzaniga, M.S., 119
Geffen, G., 208
Geher, G., 527b
Gelade, G., 210–11
Gelman, R., 331

Gerard, H.B., 432
Gerfen, C.R., 175b
Gergen, K., 368
Gerrard, M., 631
Gesell, A., 284
Geshwind, N., 93
Gibbon, F.X., 631
Gibbons, R,D., 616
Gibson, J.J., 188–89, 189f, 195, 198, 303
Gick, M.L., 267–68
Gilbert, D.T., 396, 404–5, 405, 406, 408
Gilhooley, K.J., 263
Gilian, 512
Gilligan, C., 309
Gilliland, K., 507
Gilovich, T., 480
Gleeson, S.R., 377
Glicksohn, J., 475
Glore, G.L., 418
Glucksberg, S., 208
Glynn, S.M., 607b
Godden, D., 234
Goffman, E., 480
Gold, R.M., 146
Goldberg, S.R., 142
Goldin-Meadow, S., 314, 328
Goldstein, A.J., 564
Goleman, D., 527b
Goodkin,K., 512
Goodman, G.S., 311b
Goodwin, D.W., 234
Gopher, D., 213–14, 214f, 217
Gopnik, A., 341
Gopnik, M., 334b
Gorski, R.A., 117
Goswami, U., 336, 337
Gottesman, I.I., 582, 583t
Gough, B., 363, 368, 372, 372b, 375, 396, 732
Gould, A., 170
Gould, S.J., 12, 46b, 49, 60
Gowers, S.G., 589
Goyette, C.H., 591
Grace, A.A., 109b
Grady, D.L., 84
Grafton, S.T., 175b
Gratch, G., 302
Gray, C.D., 691

Gray, J., 507
Gray, N.S., 666b
Grayson, A., 41, 670
Greenwald, A.G., 380, 382, 708b
Gregory, 185, 186, 195
Greif, E.B., 309
Gresiberg McKay, 570
Grice, 253
Griffen, C., 508b
Griffith, R.R., 113b
Grosjean, F., 256
Gross, R., 41, 51, 52, 58, 64
Grossman, K.E., 345
Grotevant, H.D., 359
Grotpeter, J.K., 349
Guarnaccia, P.J., 551b
Guerin, B., 436
Guilford, J.P., 520
Gullone, E., 593
Gump, B.B., 483
Guppy, A., 374
Gupta, N., 626
Guzzo, R.A., 436

H
Hadlow, J., 625
Hagerty, M., 498
Haier, R.J., 526
Halford, J.C.G., 147
Hall, E., 13t, 14t, 418, 419b
Hall, J., 607b
Halligan, P.W., 212
Halpern, D.F., 525b
Halstead, W.C., 526
Hammersley, M., 648, 649t
Hancock, P.A., 539
Handley, J., 722
Hanges, P.J., 525b
Hanlon, C., 331
Happe, F., 354–55b
Hardie, R.J., 471
Hare, R.D., 584
Hargrove, M.F., 508
Haridakis, P.M., 512b
Hariz, M.I., 175b
Harley, T., 243, 249, 250t, 262
Harlow, H., 284, 344
Harris, M., 298, 302, 331
Harris, P.L., 353
Harris, T.L., 508b

Name Index

Harrison, J.A., 622
Harrison, Y., 158b
Hart, P., 440
Harter, S., 342, 358
Hartline, H.K., 165
Harvey, R., 614
Hasher, L., 231, 727
Haslam, A., 372
Haslam, N., 474, 584
Hastie, R., 414
Hauser, P., 591
Haworth-Heoppner, S., 589
Hay, D.F., 349
Hayduk, L.A., 418
Hayes, N., 651
Hayes, N., 61
Haynes, R.B., 625
Hearnshaw, L.S., 37
Heath, S.B., 331
Heatherington, E.M., 348
Hebb, D.O., 467, 507–8, 526
Heckhausen, H., 469
Hedges, L.V., 525b
Heider, F., 364, 385–86, 395, 397, 398f
Heilman, H., 414
Heinrichs, S.C., 155
Hejmadi, A., 452
Henderson, J.M., 243
Hendry, L.B., 357, 360
Henker, B., 592
Henley, T.B., 35b
Henningfield, J.E., 142
Henry, L.A., 337
Hepburn, A., 40
Herbert, T.B., 626
Herman, C.P., 588, 589
Hernstein, R.J., 525b
Herzog, D.B., 587
Hetherington, A.W., 145
Hewitt, P.L., 571
Hewstone, M., 406, 408, 447
Higgins, E.T., 477
Hildum, D.C., 380
Hill, A.J., 589
Hill, J,., 573
Hiller, M.L., 471
Hilton, D.J., 401
Hines, M., 343
Hinshaw, S.P., 591

Hirsch, C.R., 479
Hirsh-Pasek, K., 331
Hitch, G., 217, 226
Hobbes, 10, 13t
Hobson, R.P., 351
Hockett, C., 246, 248t
Hodgkinson, S., 576
Hodgson, R.J., 569b
Hoffmeister, F., 143
Hofmeister, J.F., 606
Hogg, M.A., 362, 396, 421f, 428, 430, 431b, 433, 438, 443f, 449
Hole, G., 645, 647, 651, 662, 670, 680, 691, 694, 710
Hollon, S.D., 610
Holmes, E.A., 572
Holmes, T.H., 627, 628–229t
Holst, V.F., 234
Holyoak, K.J., 267–68
Honda,Y., 157
Hood, B., 302, 305
Hooley, J.M., 583
Horn, J, 520
Horne, J.A., 156f
Hornykiewicz, O., 105
Hoskins, S., 727
House, R.J., 442
Hovland, C.I., 363, 388
Howe, C., 318
Howell, D.C., 710
Hoyenga, K.B., 508
Hoyenga, K.T., 508
Hubel, D., 166, 167–68, 191, 193b, 194illus
Hughes, M., 308b
Huguet, P., 436
Hull, C., 466
Hull, C.L., 264, 269, 270f
Hull, E.M., 117
Hume, D., 645
Humphreys, G.W., 190b, 515b
Hunt, E., 522
Hunt, R.R., 245
Huston-Lyons, D., 142
Hutchison, K.E., 84
Huttunen, M., 289
Hyde, J.S., 525b
Hyman, S.E., 576

I
Ibbotson, J., 464
Insko, C.A., 380
Isenberg, N., 153
Islam, M.R., 447
Isometsa, E., 578
Ittleson, W.H., 183
Iwamoto, E.T., 142
Iwata, B.A., 606
Izard, C.E., 505

J
Jaccard, J.J., 383
Jack, S.J., 474
Jacobs, B.L., 157
Jacobson, L., 663b, 663f, 708b
Jacobson, N.S., 612
Jacobson Weiss, 603
James, W., 14t, 223, 229, 454–456
Janis, I.L., 371, 388
Janis Mann, 438, 439f
Janoff-Bulman, R., 573
Jarrold, C., 355
Jarvella, R.J., 251
Jarvis, M., 19, 20, 23, 27
Jenike, M.A., 569
Jenkins, D.G., 626
Jenkins, E.A., 313
Jensen, A.R., 526
Jenson, A., 529, 534b
Jewett, D.C., 146
Jodeyr, S., 497
John, O.P., 504
Johnson, J.G., 630
Johnson, M.H., 341
Johnson, M.L., 329
Johnston, T.D., 75
Johnston, W.A., 208
Johnstone, L., 598
Joiner, R., 318
Jonah, B.A., 403
Jones, D., 11, 20, 22, 27, 29, 43, 46, 46b, 52, 54
Jones, E.E., 382, 405, 406, 414, 416
Jones, K., 158b
Jones, L.W., 93
Jones, R., 188
Jones, R.M., 359
Jouvet, 157
Julien, R.M., 119

Jung, C., 16, 492, 494, 502
Jusczyk, P.W., 325
Just, M.A., 252–53

K
Kagan, J., 345, 456
Kahn, A., 418, 419
Kahneman, D., 208–9, 211, 213, 272, 273, 273illus, 274
Kail, R., 312
Kalat, J.W., 194f
Kalivas, P.W., 143
Kamin, L., 37
Kan, Y., 460
Kanfer, P.L., 533
Kanfer, R., 534b
Kanner, A.D., 627, 629
Kanner, L., 353
Kant, I., 517
Kaplan, M.F., 437
Kapur, S., 582
Karasawa, M., 420b
Karmiloff-Smith, A., 314, 316, 327
Katchdourian, H., 356
Katz, J.L., 141, 143, 378
Kaufman, J.C., 515
Kay, J., 335
Kaye, W.H., 147
Kazdin, A.E., 590, 604
Keane, M.T., 22, 208f, 215f, 219, 229, 245, 262, 279
Kebabian, J.W., 109b, 141
Keef, F., 632
Keele, S.W., 241
Keesey, R.E., 146
Kelley, H.H., 387, 403, 412, 430
Kelley, M., 582
Kelly, G.A., 492, 493, 499
Kendall, P.C., 593
Kendler, K.S., 565, 576
Kennis, L.E., 582
Kerr, N.L., 426, 435, 436
Kessler, R.C., 554
Kiewitz, C., 512b
Kilduff, T.S., 158
Kilpatrick, F.P., 183
Kimura, D., 93
Kindt, M., 570
King, D.W., 572
King, N.J., 590, 593

Kinnear, P.R., 691
Kitayama, S., 420b, 501b
Kitzinger, C., 44, 50b, 51
Klein, D.F.
Klein, M., 497
Kleiner, K.A., 359
Kline, P., 18
Klippel, J.A., 403
Kluckhorn, C., 489
Klump, K., 588
Klüver, H., 151
Kneale, P.E., 732
Kodama, T., 157
Koffka, 181
Kohlberg, L., 43–44b, 44, 309, 592
Kohler, W., 181, 264
Kohut, H., 497
Kolb, B., 63, 93
Kolta, M.G., 143
Koob, G.F., 13, 140, 141, 149, 155
Korabik, K., 464
Kornetsky, C., 142
Korsch, B.M., 626
Kozin, M., 238
Kracke, B., 357
Kramer, A., 528
Krantz, S.E., 404
Kringlen, E., 569
Krueger, R.F., 555
Kucera, H., 259
Kuffler, S.W., 163
Kuhl, P.K., 323
Kulik, J.A., 238, 483
Kumar, R., 142
Kunst-Wilson, W.R., 420b
Kurtines, W., 309

L
LaBerge, D., 209, 214f
Ladoucer, R., 568
Lai, Y.S., 591
Laing, R.D., 582
Laitinen, L.V., 175
Lalich, J., 486
Lam, J.N., 605
Lamanek, K.L., 593
Lamb, H.R., 597
Lamb, R.J., 113b
Lambert, M.J., 614
Laming, D., 476

Lamm, H., 421, 437
Lammers, H.B., 390
Landers, W.F., 302
Langer, C., 454–456
Langer, E.J., 404, 406
Langlois, J.H., 343
LaPiere, R., 383
Larne, A.J., 81
Larsen, R., 491
Larson, J.R., 438
Last, J.
Latané, B., 423, 425b, 435, 436
Latham, G.P., 471
Laurent, J., 538b
Lazarus, R.S., 454, 462, 630
Leahey, T.H., 11, 12
Leana, C.R., 440
Leary, M.R., 416, 498
LeBar, K.S., 152
LeBon, G., 363
Lecanuet, J.P., 291b
LeDoux, J., 96, 129, 135f, 152, 153, 170
Lee, C., 589
Leekham, S.R., 355
Leese, M., 587b
Leibowitz, S.F., 146
Leichtman, M.D., 311b
Lemere, F., 605
Lentz, R.J., 606
Leon, A.C., 579
Leonard, N.H., 334b, 472
Leone, P., 141
Lepore, L., 367
Lerner, M.J., 406, 421
Leslie, A.M., 352, 354, 355
Lethem, J., 632
LeVay, S., 117
Levelt, W.J.M., 253
Levenson, R.W., 456
Levi-Montalcini, R., 91
Levine, J.M., 433
Levine, M.P., 589
Lewin, K., 363, 363illus
Lewin, R., 74f
Lewis, C., 351b, 352
Lewis, M., 342
Lewis, Y., 478
Lewontin, R., 60, 61b, 63
Ley, P., 232b, 625, 626

Name Index

Ley, R., 561, 562, 563b
Li, T., 81
Libby, S., 354
Liberman, I.Y., 336
Lieberman, D.A., 133, 134, 137
Lieberman, H.R., 159b
Liepe, M.R., 378
Lieven, E., 332
Likert, R., 381
Lin, L., 158
Linaza, J., 307
Linder, D.E., 386
Lindqvist, M., 109b
Lineham, M.M., 579
Linton, M., 238
Lippitt, R., 443f
Lisker, L., 200, 201f
Lissauer, H., 190b
Locke, E.A., 471
Locke, J., 10, 13t, 517
Lockhart, R.S., 230
Lockwood, P., 484
Loehlin, J.C., 527
Loftus, E., 236–37b
Loftus, G.R., 239, 240f
Lomo, T., 134
Longman, D.J.A., 727
Lord, R.G., 430
Lorenz, K., 120, 344b
Luchins, A.S., 265, 266t, 268,
    413–14
Luchins, E.H., 265, 266t
Luckmann, T., 368
Luria, A.R., 95, 526
Lusher, J.M., 84
Lutkenhaus, P., 342
Lutzker, J.R., 607
Luzzatti, C., 212b
Lynn, R., 524b
Lytton, H., 324b

M
Maccoby, E.E., 344
MacCulloch, M.J., 605
MacDonald, D.A., 497
MacKintosh, N.J., 37
MacLeod, C., 567
Macrae, C.N., 367
Madden, T.J., 622
Madsen, P.L., 156

Maehr, M., 471
Magnusson, D., 357
Magoun, H.W., 156
Maguire, E.A., 97b
Maheswaran, D., 391
Mahoney, M.J., 607
Maiden, R.J., 506b
Maiman, L.A., 621
Main, M., 346, 346b, 347b
Mak, A.S., 512b
Maki, R.H., 727
Maldonado-Irizarry, C.S., 141
Malim, T., 26b, 54, 55, 62
Malloy, M.H., 528
Mandler, G., 231
Maner, J.K., 422
Manetto, V., 159
Mann, J.J., 579
Manstead, A.S.R., 375, 436
Maquet, P., 156, 158
Marcel, A.J., 335
Marchman, V., 334
Marcia, J.E., 358
Marentette, P.F., 323
Marks, D.F., 633
Marona-Lewicka, D., 113b
Marr, D., 192
Marsh, R., 745
Marshall, J., 257
Marshall, J.C., 212
Marshall, J.F., 145
Marslen-Wilson, W.D., 256–57
Martin, B.V., 311b
Martin, G.N., 170
Martin, J.A., 607
Martin, P., 670
Martin an dBateson, 665
Martin Hewstone, 431
Martinez-Rodriguez, J.E., 158
Masangkay, Z.S., 353
Maslow, A., 19, 20, 43, 471–72, 492
Masten, A., 288
Masters, M.S., 525b
Matarazzo, J.D., 618
Matas, L., 347b
Mathews, A., 567
Mathews, A.M., 603
Matsumoto, K., 134
Mayer, D., 525b
Mazaleski, J.L., 606

McArthur, L.A., 400, 401
McCain, G., 491
McCall, R.B., 528
McCann, U.D., 113b
McClelland, J.L., 337
McClelland,J.L., 334
McCoul, M.D., 474
McCracken, L.M., 632
McCrae, R.R., 492, 504
McDonald, C., 81
McDonald, W.T., 235
McDougall, W., 465
McFadden, M., 363, 368, 375, 396
McGarrigle, J., 308b
McGaughey, T.A., 418, 419
McGeogh, J.A., 235
McGhee, P., 29, 34, 368, 372, 375,
    750
McGrath, J.M., 574
McGuire, W.J., 391, 393f
McGurk, H., 287
McIlveen, R., 64
McInerney, D.M., 471
McIntosh, D.N., 457
McKenna, E., 737
McLelland, D., 475
McNally, R.J., 559, 572, 574
McNeal, E.T., 576
McNeill, D., 254, 254b
McQuinn, R.D., 418
McRae, A.L., 605
Meade, G.H., 481
Meddis, R., 157
Medin, D.L., 266t
Megens, A.A., 582
Meilman,P.W., 358
Meins, E., 352
Melnick, S.M., 591
Meltzoff, A., 341
Meltzoff, A.N., 341
Melzack, R., 173, 632
Melzoff, A.N., 303
Mendel, G., 75–76
Mendelson, W.B., 157
Menzies, R.G., 560
Messer, D., 298, 318, 324, 339, 341,
    350b
Messer, D.J., 295, 297, 314, 316,
    323
Metalsky, G.I., 578

Meyer, A., 143
Meyer, D.E., 241, 259
Meyer, J.M., 588
Meyer, R., 287b
Michas, I., 337
Michaud, C., 626
Mifsud, J.-C., 142
Mikhliner, M., 572
Miles, J., 651, 670
Miles, T.R., 338, 669
Milgram, S., 369, 372, 382, 440–42
Mill, J.S., 645, 658
Millar, N., 493
Millar, S., 298
Miller, 14t
Miller, D.T., 406, 421
Miller, F.D., 404
Miller, G.A., 223
Miller, L.J., 540
Miller, L.T., 522
Miller, P.M., 407
Miller, R., 721
Miller, R.J., 109b
Milner, B., 66
Milner, D., 342
Milner, P., 139
Minami, S., 146
Minuchin, P., 589, 612
Mirza, N.R., 141
Mischel, W., 488, 493, 500, 505, 591
Mitchell, P., 351b, 360
Mitchell, P.J., 71
Mithani, S., 141
Mittelman, M.A., 453
Miyake, K., 345
Miyauchi, S., 156
Mizell, C., 479
Mogford, K., 324b
Mogg, K., 567b
Monteil, J.M., 436
Moon, C., 345
Moore, M.K., 341
Moos, R.H., 627
Mora, F., 139
Morais, J., 336
Moray, N., 206
Moreland, R.L., 419
Morgan, 78
Morgenstern, O., 274
Morley, J.E., 146

Morris, R.G., 136
Morton, J., 260, 341
Moruzzi, G., 156, 157
Moses, L.J., 342
Moskovici, S., 363, 433
Motes, M., 746, 747
Mount, M.K., 535b
Muchinsky, P.M., 498
Mugny, G., 318
Muller, S.L., 407
Mumford, A., 735
Mummendey, A., 447
Murphy, C.M., 297, 323
Murphy, D., 82
Murphy, K.C., 81
Murray, C., 525b
Murray, H., 489
Myers, D.G., 437
Myers, L.B., 496
Mylander, C., 328

N
Navon, D., 217
Neale, J.M., 557, 594
Neisser, U., 14t, 189, 190, 191,
    191f, 195b, 234, 238
Nelson, K., 236, 331
Nemeth, C., 434
Neugebauer, R., 545
Newcombe, F., 257
Newell, A., 268
Newstead, S.E., 727, 733, 733f
Nicholls, J.G., 107f, 119, 471
Nicolaïdes, S., 146
Nicolson, R., 339
Nisbett, R.E., 364, 401, 406, 501
Niskanen, P., 289
Norman, C., 207
Norman, D., 95, 134
Norman, P., 393
Northrup, J., 606
Nowell, A., 525b
Noyes, R., 565
Nussbaum, D., 512b

O
O'Brien, C.P., 139b
Ochs, E., 331
O'Connor, T.G., 286, 347
O'Donohue, W., 574

O'Dwyer, A.M., 588
Oei, T.P.S., 500
Ogden, J., 631, 633
Olds, J., 139
O'Leary, K.D., 603
Ollendick, T.H., 616
Oltmanns, T.F., 594, 617
Olweus, D., 350
Oppenheim, A.N., 381
Orne, M.T., 35, 35b
Osbourne, A., 351b
Osgood, C.E., 381
Osler, S., 233, 234
Otten, S., 447
Ouellette, J.A., 384
Owusu-Bempah, J., 52
Ozonoff, S., 354b

P
Padden, D.M., 323
Palladino, J.J., 457
Palmer, J.C., 236–37b
Palmer, S.E., 194, 198f
Paolini, S., 447
Papagergiou, C., 568
Papp, L.A., 562
Park, B., 414
Park, E.S., 435
Parker, D., 385
Parkes, C.M., 627
Parkin, A.J., 22, 203, 219, 245, 262
Patterson, M.L., 418
Paul, G.L., 606
Paus, T., 91
Pavlov, I., 14t, 16, 120, 122–25
Pearce, J.M., 137
Pearlstone, Z., 234
Pearson, K., 699
Pearson, R., 6467
Peck, B.K., 157
Pederson, N.L., 510b
Peeters, G., 413
Peiffer, J., 70
Pendleton, D., 623, 624
Penner, L.A., 421
Penner, S.G., 331
Pennington, D., 367, 399, 497
Perkins, K.A., 133b
Perls, F., 600
Perner, J., 351b, 355

Name Index

Petersen, C., 488
Peterson, L.R., 224, 224f
Peterson, M.J., 224, 224f
Petitto, L.A., 323
Petrides, K.V., 527
Pettigrew, T.F., 447
Pettito, L.A., 249
Petty, R.E., 377, 379, 388, 390
Peyron, C., 158
Philips, H.C., 632
Phillips, A.G., 139, 140, 140f, 152
Piaget, J., 14t, 285, 285illus, 325, 329, 341
Piaget Inhalder, 306b
Piasecki, T.M., 555
Piattelli-Palmarini, M., 329
Pickles, J.R., 177
Piët, S., 476
Pietromonaco, P., 415
Piliavin, J.A., 423
Pilkington, C.J., 484
Pine, J., 332
Pine, K., 295, 314, 316, 318, 320
Pinel, 164f
Pinker, S., 327
Pittman, T.S., 416
Pitts, M. Phillipis, K., 633
Pitts, M.K., 625
Plant, M., 407
Plaut, D.C., 337
Plomin, R., 23, 66, 77f, 84, 85, 493, 527
Plunkett, K., 333, 334
Plutchik, R., 452–53
Polivy, J., 588, 589
Polson, P.G., 728
Ponomarenko, V.A., 529
Pontieri, F.E., 142
Popper, K., 29
Porter, R.H., 345
Posner, M.I., 205, 209, 210f, 211f, 212b, 213f, 241
Postle, B.R., 226
Potter, J., 363, 371, 418
Poulton, R., 560
Povinelli, D.J., 342
Powell, S., 360
Pratt, J.A., 133b
Pratt, P., 568

Prill, K.A., 528
Prilleltensky, I., 23
Pryor, J.B., 406
Pryor, T.L., 588
Psotka, J., 233

Q
Qu, D., 146
Quadrel, M.J., 621
Quine, L., 385, 390, 392–93b, 393

R
Rachman, S.J., 569b, 604
Radford, A., 325
Radke-Yarrow, M., 349
Raffi, A.R., 589
Ragneskog, H., 169
Rahe, R.H., 627, 628–229t
Rahman, Q., 117
Raine, A., 154
Raisman, G., 117
Rakic, P., 90
Ramey, C.T., 341
Randazzo, A.C., 158b
Ranson, S.W., 145
Raven, B.H., 430, 431b
Ravens, J., 540
Rawlings, D., 475
Rayner, R., 602, 666b
Read, C., 337
Reason, J., 216
Reavey, P., 372, 372b
Reber, A.S., 313
Redd, A., 18b
Ree, M.J., 534b
Reed, E., 188
Reed, R.S., 311b
Reicher, G.M., 197b
Reicher, S., 372, 417, 485
Remington, G., 582
Renaldi, R., 141
Reschly, D.J., 538b
Resick, P.A., 573
Rheaume, J., 570
Rhodes, W.S., 406
Ricaute, G.A., 113b
Richards, G., 11, 18, 38, 41, 43, 46, 47, 49, 52, 54
Rickabaugh, C.A., 184f, 185f
Riddoch, J.M., 190b

Ridley, A.M., 237b
Rimm-Kaufman, S., 456
Ringelmann, M., 436, 437b
Rivers, W.H.R., 14t
Robbins, S., 529
Robert Cloniger, C., 493
Roberts, D., 177
Roberts, D.C.S., 141
Robertson, J., 348
Robinson, J., 349349
Robinson, J.A., 236
Robinson, L.A., 614
Robinson, T.E., 143, 144, 149
Rock, I., 195
Rodriguez-Manzo, G., 117
Roemer, L., 567
Rogers, C., 14t, 19, 492, 600, 601
Rogoff, B., 318
Roid, G.H., 540
Roland, E., 350
Ronan, K.R., 474
Rorschach, H., 535
Rorty, M., 589
Rosch, E., 241, 242t
Rose, S., 23, 54, 55, 56t, 58, 60
Rose, S.A., 308b
Rosehan, D.L., 666b
Rosenberg, S., 412
Rosenberg Hovland, 379
Rosenfarb, I.S., 584
Rosenfeld, H.M., 418
Rosenteil, A., 632
Rosenthal, R., 34, 35, 35b, 36, 36f, 41, 663b, 663f, 708b
Rosenzweig, M.R., 85, 89, 90f, 147
Rosnow, R., 34, 35, 36, 36f, 41
Ross, B.H., 266t
Ross, L., 364, 406, 407
Rothbaum, F., 345
Rotter, J., 493
Rowe, D.C., 510
Rowntree, D., 691, 710
Roy, A., 576
Rubin, D.C., 224, 237–38, 238, 238f, 421
Rude, S., 404
Rudestan, K.E., 474
Ruiter, R.A., 391
Rumelhart, D.E., 334
Rushton, J., 46, 47–48b, 524b

Russel, J.A., 151b
Russell, J., 19, 354b, 355
Rutter, D.R., 393
Rutter, M., 286, 357

S
Sachs, J., 252, 329
Sahgal, A., 68b
Sahu, A., 146
Sakurai, T., 146
Salkovskis, P.M., 500, 562, 570
Saller, C.K., 146
Salman, E., 551b
Saloman, G., 521
Salthouse, T.A., 528
Sanders, B., 525b
Sanders, G., 93, 116
Sanderson, W.C., 564
Sanfilipo, M., 108b
Sanna, L.J., 476
Sapolsky, R., 155
Sarter, M., 134
Saxe, L., 460b
Saxton, M., 333b
Scaife, M., 323
Scarborough, H., 251, 331, 337
Scarr, S., 524
Schactel, E., 238
Schacter, D.L., 234, 461
Schaffer, H.R., 284, 344
Schaie, K.W., 296b, 528
Schatz, M., 353
Schenk, S., 143
Schieffelin, B.B., 331
Schifter, D.E., 623
Schildkraut, J.J., 576
Schmidt, L.A., 81
Schmidt, R.A., 277f
Schneider, W., 205
Schniering, C.A., 593
Schroeder, D.A., 428
Schulkin, J., 418, 461
Schutte, N.S., 527b
Schvaneveldt, R.W., 241, 259
Schwab, R., 508b
Schwartz, N., 380, 394
Schwartzman, A.E., 528
Scott, S., 625b
Sdorow, L.M., 184f, 185f
Searle, J., 417

Sedikides, C., 478, 484
Segal, E.M., 491
Segal, S.J., 215, 215f, 218t
Seidenberg, M.S., 249, 337
Seligman, M.E.P., 134, 552, 560, 577, 616
Semin, G. R., 375, 436
Senghas, A., 328
Serter, J.S., 449
Shah, A., 355
Shallice, T., 95, 134, 226, 257
Sharp, S., 351
Shatz, M., 331
Shaver, K.G., 403
Shavitt, S., 377
Shearin, E.N., 579
Sheeran, P., 384
Sheeran et al, 700
Sheldon, W., 493
Sher, K.J., 570
Sherif, M., 363, 431–32, 433, 445–46
Sherman, M.F., 630
Shevell, M.I., 70
Shiffrin, R.M., 226, 228f, 229
Shisslak, C.M., 587
Shoebridge, P., 589
Siegal, A., 154
Siegel, L.E., 337
Siegel, S., 125
Siegler, R.S., 311b, 312–13, 313, 320
Sigall, H., 382
Silbereisen, R., 357
Silva, R.R., 573
Simmel, M., 397, 398f
Simon, H.A., 231, 268, 277
Simon, T., 14, 284
Simpson, D.D., 471
Singer, J.E., 461
Singer, M.T., 486
Singh, D., 73b
Skinner, B.F., 14t, 16, 120, 127, 284, 285illus, 326, 493
Skinner, B.K., 137
Skoler, G.D., 426
Skowronski, J.J., 413
Slade, P., 606
Slanger, E., 474
Slater, A.M., 298, 303, 341
Slobodian, P.J., 474

Slugoski, B.R., 401
Smart, J.L., 528
Smith, E.R., 404
Smith, K.A., 484
Smith, M.A., 158b, 241
Smith, M.B., 378
Smith, P., 334
Smith, P.B., 433, 442
Smith, P.B. Bond, M.H., 42
Smith, P.K., 298, 349, 351
Smith, R.S., 287b
Snarey, J.R., 309
Snow, C., 329, 331
Snowling, M., 339
Snyder, M., 416
Snyder, S.H., 109b
Socrates, 517
Soininen, H., 87
Solomon, Z., 572
Solso, R.L., 192f, 223f, 263
Sorian, G., 287
Spearman, C., 14t, 515b, 519, 699
Speckart, G., 384
Spelke, E., 304
Spelke Hirst Neisser, 213
Spelman, M.S., 626
Spelt, J., 588
Spence, M.J., 345
Spencer, H., 12, 13t
Sperling, G., 209, 222
Spooner, Rev., 255, 256illus
Sprecher, S., 418
Springer, L., 738
Springer, S.P., 93
Spyraki, C., 141
Squire, L.R., 66
Srivastava, S., 506b
Sroufe, L.A., 347b
Srull, T.K., 415
St Charles, N.D., 469
Staats, A.W., 380
Stainton Rogers, W., 23, 25–26t, 363, 368, 371, 375, 377, 396, 430, 477
Stallone, D., 146
Stanley, B.G., 146
Stanley-Hagan, M., 348
Stanley Hall, G., 284
Stanovich, K.E., 260, 337

Name Index

Stanowiczz, L., 332
Steele, C., 525b
Steinberg, L., 525b
Steinhausen, H.C., 587
Steinman, L., 100
Steketee, G.S., 605
Stellar, E., 145
Stephens, D.N., 82
Sterman, M.B., 156
Stern, S.E., 382
Sternberg, R.J., 203, 219, 245, 265, 278, 279, 421, 515, 515b, 524, 529, 747
Stevenson, C., 40
Stice, E., 589, 590
Stokes, T.F., 607
Stolerman, I., 132b, 139
Stolerman, I.P., 131
Stone, K.D., 593
Stoner, J.A.F., 437
Stopeck, M.H., 414
Storms, M.D., 406
Stratton, P., 61
Strauss, M.A., 427
Stricker, E.M., 146
Striegel-Moore, R., 589
Strobel, A., 84
Strube, G., 20n
Stuart, R.B., 607
Stumpf, H., 525b
Sudbury, P., 85
Sutton, J., 349
Sutton, S., 382, 384
Svanborg, P., 511
Swabb, D.F., 117
Swan, D., 337
Swann, W.B., 417
Swindle, R.W., 627
Sylvester-Bradley, B., 323

T
Tagiuri, R., 412
Tajfel, H., 363, 433, 446–47, 481
Talcott, J.B., 338
Tanner, J.M., 356
Tanskanen, A., 579
Tartter, V.C., 200f
Tashakkori, A., 483
Taurah, L., 113b
Tavris, C., 44–45

Taylor, S.E., 364, 406, 631, 633
Tedeschi, J.T., 387
Teitelbaum, P., 145
Terrace, H.S., 249
Tesser, A., 418
Thaiss, L., 355
Tharion, W.J., 159b
Theakston, A., 332
Thomas, M.S.C., 327
Thomasius, R., 113b
Thompson, D.M., 233
Thompson, S.K., 51, 343
Thoresen, C.E., 607
Thorndike, E., 14t, 127, 264, 518, 538b
Thorne, B.M., 35b
Thorpe, B.M., 559
Thorpe, K., 324b
Thurston, L.L., 379, 519–20
Thurstone, I., 197b
Tice, D.M., 417, 483
Tincoff, R., 325
Tindale, S., 449
Tolman, E.C., 133–34, 468
Tomasello, M., 324, 325, 332
Tooby, J., 272
Trabasso, T., 270
Tranel, D., 153
Travill, R.A., 113b
Treisman, A.M., 207–7, 208, 208f
Trevarthen, C., 323, 341
Triandis, H.C., 384
Triandis et al, 508b
Triplett, N
Troop, N.A., 589
Trulson, M.E., 157
Tsien, J.Z., 136
Tufte, E.R., 688–90, 691
Tulving, E., 221, 233, 233illus, 234, 236, 237
Turiel, E., 309
Turk, D.C., 632
Turner, J.A., 433, 632
Turner, J.C., 438, 440, 481
Tversky, A., 272, 273, 274
Twemlow, S., 473

U
Uhl, G.R., 143
Underwood, B.J., 235

Unterharnscheidt, F., 87
Urdan, T., 471

V
Valentine, E., 34, 58, 59, 60
Valins, S., 458
Van de Vliert, E., 442
van den Hout, M., 570
van der Pligt, J., 387
Van Houdenhove, B., 630
van Ijzendoorn, M.H., 345, 347, 360
Van Kammen, D.P., 72, 108b, 582
Van Overwalle, F., 395
Vanderwolf, C.H., 157
Vanfurth, E.F., 589
VanYperen, N.W., 442
Varendonck, J., 311b
Vasey, M., 566
Vasterling et al, 572
Vaughan, G.M., 362, 396, 421f, 428, 430, 431b, 438, 443f
Vaughn, B., 347b
Verbrugge, L.M., 624
Verhulst, F.C., 593
Vernon, P., 520, 522
Verrier, R.L., 453
Vlaeyens, J., 632
Voegtlin, W.L., 605
Vom Saal, F.S., 155
Von Neumann, J., 274
Voyer, D., 525b
Vygotsky, L.S., 285, 316b, 317–19, 733

W
Wacker, D.P., 606
Wagenarr, W.A., 238, 239
Wakefield, J.C., 552
Wakeling, A., 587
Wald, G., 162
Walker, I., 368, 408
Wall, P.D., 173, 632
Wallach, M.A., 437
Waller, N.G., 380
Wallerstein, J., 497
Wallston, B.S., 620, 620b, 621, 624
Wallston, K.A., 620
Wang, Q., 146
Wänke M., 378b, 381, 394

Ward, N.I., 460
Warren, R.M., 201
Warren, R.P., 201
Warrington, E.K., 226, 257
Watkins, C.E., 535, 538b
Watson, J.B., 14t, 15–16, 55, 86b, 270, 376, 602, 666b
Watson, J.S., 341
Watts, F.N., 570
Wayland, S.C., 257
Wearing, C., 222
Weaver, J.B., 512b
Webb, K., 5671
Weber, B., 143
Weber, E.U., 273
Webster-Stratton, C., 287
Wechsler, D., 515b, 534b
Wedderburn, Z., 713
Wegener, D., 390
Weikert, D., 288b
Weinberger, M., 629
Weiner, B., 470, 475
Weingarten, H.P., 146
Weisman, A., 551
Weisman, U., 421
Weiss, E.M., 93
Weizenbaum, J., 21
Wellman, H.M., 353
Wells, A., 549, 567, 568, 610, 611b
Welsh, M.C., 355
Wenk, G.L., 92
Wenmoth, D.B., 93, 116
Werker, J.F., 323
Werner, E.E., 287b
Werry, J.S., 593
West, R.F., 260
Weston, D., 496
Wetherall, M., 371
Wetherell, M., 363, 418, 437
Wetherick, N.E., 263

Whalen, C.K., 592
Whalen, P.J., 460
Whaley, C.P., 259
Wheeler, D., 197b
Whishaw, I., 63, 93
White, R., 443f
Whitley, G., 574
Wickens, C.D., 206, 213–14, 214f, 217
Wicker, A.W., 382
Wickersham, D., 623
Widger, T.A., 584
Wiesel, T., 166, 167–68, 191, 193b, 194illus
Wilcox, T., 302
Wilcoxon, L.A., 604
Wilkinson, S., 24 illus
Willerman, L., 526
Williams, J.M., 548, 567
Williams, K.D., 449
Williams, R.L., 540
Williarts, P., 302
Willner, P., 71, 72
Wills, T.A., 626
Wilson, B., 222
Wilson, E.O., 54, 605
Wilson, G.S., 117
Wilson, G.T., 603
Wilson, J., 208
Wilson, M.S., 497, 538b
Wilson, R., 403
Wimmer, H., 158b, 336, 338, 351b
Wing, L., 353
Winston, P.H., 181f
Wirth, S., 134
Wise, R.A., 139, 142, 143
Wishart, J.G., 302
Witte, K., 391
Wittig, B.A., 295
Wlson, G.T., 604

Wolf, M., 338
Wolf, S., 435
Wolfson, S., 407, 407b
Wolke, D., 287b, 349
Wolpe, J., 602
Wolraich, M.L., 591
Wonnacott, S., 149
Wood, D., 320
Wood, D.J., 317, 433
Wood, W., 384
Woodhead, M.M., 723
Woolverton, W.L., 141
Wortman, C.B., 577
Wright, D.B., 222, 691, 710
Wundt, W., 10, 11, 12, 13, 29, 518
Wuttke, W., 143
Wycoff, J., 331
Wyer, R.S., 415

Y
Yager, J., 589
Yarrow, L.J., 345
Yerkes, R., 46b
Young, A.W., 196, 418
Yukl, G., 442

Z
Zacks, R.T., 231
Zahn-Waxler, C., 349, 349349
Zajonc, R.B., 419, 420b, 435–36, 457, 462
Zanna, M.P., 386
Zazzo, R., 324b
Zeki, S., 153
Zeldow, P.B., 19
Zillman, D., 425, 458, 459
Zimbardo, P.G., 373, 373b, 378
Zola-Mogan, S., 66
Zuckerman, M., 406, 474, 507–8
Zvolensky, M.J., 562

Subject Index

A

a-Ketoglutarate, 104
abducens cranial nerve, 90f
abnormal psychology, 544
    behaviourist model, 548
    cognitive model, 548–49
    definition of, 544
    medical model, 545–47
    normal behaviour, 547
    psychoanalytic model, 547
abnormality, definitions of
    maladaptive behaviour, 551–52
    social norms, 550–51
    statistical norms, 549–50
    stress and impairment, 552
acetylcholine (ACh), 101f, 104, 104t, 141, 157, 176
ACTH *see* adrenocorticotrophic hormone
adaptational psychology, 12
ADD *see* attention deficit disorder
adenine, 80f
ADHD *see* attention deficit hyperactivity disorder
adipsia, 145
adolescence
    biological changes, 356
    cultural roles, 357
    focal theory, 357
    generation gap, 357
    identify formation, 358–59
    puberty, 356–57
    sexual relationships, 356
    storm and stress, 357
adolescent disorders, 590–93
adoption studies, 510–11b, 521b
    see also twin studies

adrenal cortex, 114f
adrenal glands, 89f, 114f
adrenal medulla, 114f
adrenaline, 101f, 102, 103, 155
adrenocorticotrophic hormone (ACTH), 116f, 155
affecting the environment (Bell), 285–86
afferent neurons, 86, 121, 122f
ageing, and personality, 506b
aggression, 487b
    amygdala, 154, 154f
    bio-social approach, 425–26
    Bobo doll experiment, 427
    excitation-transfer approach, 425–26
    hormones, 154–55
    modelling, 426–27
    neural mechanisms, 154
    operant conditioning, 426–27
    road rage, 424–25, 426b
    social learning theory, 426–27
agonist drugs, 109, 110b, 121b, 141
alcoholism
    foetal alcohol syndrome, 288–89
    pharmacological treatment of, 126, 127b
aldosterone, 148
alexithymia, 527b
alleles
    chromosomes, 77
    dominant and recessive, 76f
    Huntington's disease, 76, 77f
    mutant (polymorphisms), 80
    phenylketonuria (PKU), 77, 77f
altruism, 422–23

Alzheimers's disease, 87, 92, 112, 134
amacrine cells, 162f
American Psychological Association (APA)
    classification of psychological disorders, 553
    founding of, 14t
    homosexuality as disorder, 14t, 50
    reporting conventions, 684
amino acids, 78–79, 80–81, 101f, 104
amnesia, 220, 238
AMPA receptors, 135f, 136
amphetamines
    cocaine, 140–41
    psychosis, 108b, 112, 582
ampullae, 174f
amygdala, 171f
    aggression, 154, 154f
    connections of, 153f
    emotional experience, 460
    fear, 152–53
    hypothalamic nuclei, and eating, 145f
    limbic system, 96, 96f, 97
    mesolimbic pathway, 140f
    nuclei of, 152f
    stress, 155
analysis of variance *see* ANOVA
anatomy, 56t
androcentrism, 42–45
    moral development theory, 43–44b
androgens, 117, 154–55
angiotensin, 148

Subject Index

animal cognition
    behaviourist view, 133
    cognitive/associative learning, 120, 134
    expectancy, 134
    latent learning, 133
    learned helplessness, 134
    spatial learning, 131b, 134
animal research
    ethical issues, 70
    licensing procedure, 70–71
    use of animals, 132–33b
    validity, 71–72
anorexia nervosa (AN), 147, 586–87
    see also eating disorders
ANOVA (analysis of variance)
    covariation, 400, 400f
    Friedman's, 705, 705f
    one-way independent, 703–4
    one-way related, 704–5, 705f
    three-way repeated measures, 706
    two-way independent, 706
    two-way mixed, 705–6, 706f
antagonists (drugs), 109, 141
anterior brain region, 94f
anterior pituitary, 114f
anterior thalamus, 151, 151f, 152f
anti-dementia drugs, 112
anti-depressant drugs, 109, 143, 596t, 597
anti-psychotic drugs, 108b
anti-schizophrenia drugs, 108b
anti-social behaviour, 552
antivivisection movement, 70
anxiety, 558–59
anxiety disorders
    Ataque de Nervious, 551
    benzodiazepines, 110b, 157, 596t, 597
    classical conditioning, 559–60
    definition of, 559
    evolutionary account, 560
    inverse agonist drugs, 110b
    multiple pathways, 560–61
    situational phobias, 561
    specific phobias, 559–61
    treatments, 597–98

see also generalised anxiety disorder
anxiolytic drugs, 110b
APA *see* American Psychological Association
aphagia, 145
aphasia, 93
apperceptive agnosia, 2fp
apraxia, 93
archival research, 371
arcuate nucleus, 145f
Army Alpha and Beta tests, 46b
arousability theory, 507
Articulate Mammal, The (Aitcheson), 247
Artificial Intelligence, 20–22b
Asch's line experiments, 432
assessment (competencies), 532–33
assessment (coursework and exams)
    CAP model, 747, 748t
    exam procedures, 747
    successful intelligence concept, 747
associative learning
    versus cognitive learning, 120, 134
    concept learning, 269
    sensitisation of incentive salience, 143–44
Ataque de Nervious (anxiety-disorder), 551
attachment
    adult attachment interview (AAI), 249, 346, 347, 347b
    attachment type, 345, 346, 347, 349
    Bowlby's theory, 345
    ethology, 345
    Freudian theory, 344
    imprinting, 344b
    learning theory, 344
    longitudinal studies of, 347b
    maternal behaviour, 345–46
    parental, 284
    security of attachment, 347, 349
    separation, 345, 348
    strange situation, 345, 346b, 347

    unresolved, 347b
attention
    controlled/automatic processes, 204–5
    definition of, 204
    divided attention, 211–17
    focused auditory attention, 206–9
    focused visual attention, 209–11
    human error, 216
    vigilance, 205–6
attention deficit disorder (ADD)
    biological theories, 591
    psychological theories, 591–92
    specific learning disabilities, 590–91
attention deficit hyperactivity disorder (ADHD), 458–59, 590, 591b, 592t
attitude-behaviour correlation
    correspondence hypothesis, 383
    dual-process model, 384
    theory of planned behaviour (TPB), 383–84, 383f
    theory of reasoned action (TRA), 383–84
attitude change
    behavioural change, 384–85
    Bem's self-perception theory, 386–87
    consistency theories, 385–86
    impression management theory, 387
attitude formation
    classical conditioning, 380–81
    operant conditioning, 380
attitude measurement
    direct measurement, 381–82
    indirect measurement, 382
attitude scales, 25t
attitudes
    attitude objects, 377
    definitions of, 377, 378b
    functions of, 377–79
    implicit attitudes, 380
    importance of, 376, 377b
    knowledge function, 378
    maintaining self-esteem, 378

multidimensional approach, 379–80
social constructionism, 25–26t
social identity function, 378–79
unidimensional approach, 379
utilitarian function, 378
attraction
cost-reward ratio, 418–19
equity theory, 420–21, 421f
familiarity, 419
mere exposure effect, 419, 420f
proximity, 419–20
reinforcement-affect model, 418
social exchange theory, 418–19
triangular model of love, 421, 422f
attribution
causal attribution, 395
cognitive approach, 396
'common-sense' approach, 397, 398f
correspondence inference theory, 397–99
covariation and configuration models, 399–402
definitions of, 396b
depression, 577f, 578
events, causes of, 395–96
motivation, 402–4
perceived causes, 396
spontaneous/deliberative attributions, 404–5
three-stage model for, 404–5, 405f
attributional bias
actor-observer differences, 406
correspondence bias, 405–6
false consensus effect (FCE), 407
fundamental attribution error (FAE), 405–6
self-serving biases, 406–7
atypical drugs, 109b
audition
auditory nerve and cortex, 169–70
ear, components of, 169, 170f
auditory cortex, 169–70, 170f
autism, 351

characteristics of, 354
executive functioning and central coherence, 354–55b
mindblindness, 354
triad of impairments, 354b
autobiographical memory (AM)
childhood amnesia, 238
distribution over life span, 237–38, 238f
eyewitness testimony, 236b
flashbulb memories, 238, 239b
forgetting, 238–39
knowledge/episodes, 236, 237
reminiscence bump, 238
repisodes, 238
retention function, 238
autonomic nervous system (ANS), 86, 89
autoreceptors (presynaptic receptors), 107, 108f, 112
axon, 88, 91, 100
axon hillock, 88, 91f, 99, 100
Ax's emotional experiment, 455

B
B-endorphin, 101f
baby talk, 330–31, 331f, 332b
bar charts, 684, 685, 685f
barbiturates, 157
Barnum effect, 482
baroreceptors, 148
basal forebrain nuclei, 152f
basal ganglia
connections of, 106
globus pallidus, 97, 105b, 175b
motor control, 174–75
striatum, 97, 105b, 139, 140f
substantia nigra, 97, 105b, 175b
Beck's cognitive theory, 576–77
Beck's cognitive therapy, 610
Behaviour of Organisms (Skinner), 14t
behaviour therapies
classical conditioning
anxiety hierarchy, 603–4b
aversion therapy, 605
counterconditioning, 602, 603
exposure therapies, 602

extinction, 602
fear hierarchy, 603, 603b
flooding, 602, 603
graduated exposure, 604
reciprocal inhibition, 602–3
systematic desensitisation, 602, 603–4
faulty learning, 602
operant conditioning
behavioural self-control, 606–9
functional analysis, 605–6
group therapy, 606
response shaping, 606
token economy schemes, 606, 607b
uses of, 605
behavioural genetics, 23, 68f
as controversial area, 294–95
evolutionary theory (Darwin), 72–75
Mendelian genetics, 75–78
personality, 509–11
and psychology, 81–82
see also DNA
behavioural neuroscience *see* psychobiology
behavioural psychologist, 3t
behaviourism
animal cognition, 133
behavioural therapies, 16
classical conditioning, 16
criticisms of, 16, 19
environment, interaction with, 16
forms of explanation, 15b
learning theory, 284
methodology, effect on, 16
operant conditioning, 16, 128
social control, 16
teaching techniques, 16
theory development, effect on, 16
Bem's self-perception theory, 386–87
benzodiazepines (BZs), 110b, 157, 596t, 597
between-group design *see* independent measures design

Subject Index

bias
androcentrism, 42–44
cross-cultural psychology, 51
cultural, 539–41
Cyril Burt case, 37
ethnocentrism, 42–43
feminist psychology, 51–52
heterosexism, 50–51b
methodology, 48–49, 51
objectivity
adoption of group as norm, 50
causality, ascribing, 50
constituency interests, 49
fixed differences, belief in, 50
generalisation from samples, 49
between group differences, emphasis on, 49
hypothetical averages, 49
minority groups, ignoring of, 50
reductionism, 58
social constructionism, 24
social issues, engagement with, 52
social policy, 51
see also attributional bias; racism
bibliographic databases, 747–48
Binet's mental tests, 14t, 284, 516b, 530b, 538b
binocular vision, 165
biochemistry, 56t
biogeography, 74
biological psychology *see* psychobiology
biomedical model, 618
biopsychology *see* psychobiology
biotechnology, 81
bipolar cells, 162f, 163, 164, 164f
Black Intelligence Test of Cultural Homogeneity (BITCH), 540
bladder, 89f
blind spot, 161f, 162, 162b
blood-brain barrier (BBB), 87
blood sugar levels, 511
bobo doll experiment, 427
bodily fluid theory, 506t

body shape, and desirability, 73b
'bogus pipeline technique,' 382
boxplots (box-whisker diagrams), 686–87, 686f, 689f
brain
autopsy, 13t
cortex, 96, 106, 145f
forebrain, 96
functional lateralisation, 92–94b, 96
hindbrain, 97f, 98
limbic system, 96, 96f, 151
midbrain, 97–98
protection of, 87–88
see also basal ganglia
brain communication
action potential, 99–100
electrical communication, 98
ion channel, 99
ion concentration, 98–99
membrane potential, 98, 100f
neuron polarisation, 99
postsynaptic potentials, 99, 107
resting potential, 98–99
sodium-potassium pump, 99
synaptic regulation, 107–8
synaptic transmission, 100–105, 107
see also psychopharmacology
brain development
cellular proliferation, 90–91, 92, 92f
over lifespan, 91–92
synaptogenesis, 91
brain lobes, 95b, 96
brain orientations, 92, 94f
brain regions, 94
brain reward mechanisms
drinking, and thirst, 147–48
eating, 144–47
substance misuse, 138–44
British Psychological Society (BPS)
accreditation, 6–7
career prospects, 721
Chartered Psychologist status, 713
Divisions and Special Groups within, 2–3, 50b, 715
ethical guidelines, 39, 70, 652,

654, 655, 657, 670 (*see also* ethical issues)
founding of, 14t
psychological tests, definition of, 532b
Broadbent's filter model of selective attention, 206
Broca's area (brain), 93
Brown-Peterson experiment, 224
bulimia nervosa (BN), 147, 586–87
see also eating disorders
bullying, 349–51, 350b
bystander intervention
bystander-calculus model, 423
bystander effect, 423
cognitive stage model of decision-making, 423, 425b
diffusion of responsibility, 423
Kitty Genovese murder case, 423, 424b
pluralistic ignorance, 423

C

carbon monoxide, 101f
careers, in psychology, 712–22
Carroll's hierarchical model of intelligence, 520
Cartesian dualism, 10
catastrophic misrepresentation of bodily sensations, 561, 562–64, 632
catatonic schizophrenia, 581t
catecho-o-methyltransferase (COMT), 103
catecholamines, 101f
categorical data, 707–8
causes, *versus* correlations, 644–45
central nervous system (CNS), 86, 87–88, 88f, 161
central sulcus, 96f
CER *see* conditioned emotional response
cerebellum, 96f, 175
cerebral commisures, 96
cerebrospinal fluid (CSF), 87, 147
cerveau isole, 156
chemistry, 56t
Chi-square χ^2, 705, 705f
Chi-square test (Pearson), 707–8

child development, 282b
child psychology, 282b
childhood amnesia, 238
childhood anxiety, 592–93
childhood disorders, 590–93
children's apperception test (CAT),
    535–36, 535f
chlorpromazine, 109b
choline, 104
chromosomes
    alleles, 77
    autosomes, 78
    crossover, 78, 79f
    linkage, 78
    meiosis, 78
    mitosis, 78, 79f
    pre-natal development, 290
    X and Y, 77–78, 116
    see also DNA
ciliary muscle, 161f
cingulate cortex, 96f, 151, 151f,
    153
cingulate gyrus, 152f
Clark's psychological model (panic
    disorder), 562–64
classical conditioning
    alcoholism, treatment of, 126,
        127b
    attitude formation, 380–81
    behaviour therapies, 602–5
    behaviourism, 16
    conditioned emotional
        response (CER), 124, 152
    conditioned place preference
        (CPP), 139, 140, 141, 141b,
        141f, 142, 143
    conditioned response (CR)
        as identical to UCR,
            124–26
        measurement of, 123–24
        response amplitude, 123
        response latency, 123
        response probability, 123
    conditioned stimulus (CS)
        association with UCS, 123f,
            124, 125f, 126
        contiguity, 126, 134
        differential contingency,
            126
        extinction, 123f, 124

spontaneous recovery,
    123f, 124
countercondtioning, 127b
development of, 123f
drug tolerance, 125b
fetishes, 126b
first findings published, 14t
'Little Albert' study, 559–60
neutral stimulus, and reflex,
    122
Pavlov's dog experiments,
    122–25
stimulus
    generalisation/discriminati
        on, 124
    unconditioned response
        (UCR), 123
    unconditioned stimulus
        (UCS), 123
Client-Centred Therapy (Rogers),
    14
clinical psychology, 570–71b
    analogue studies, 572
    as a career, 713–14
    correlational relationships, 571
    experimental
        psychopathology, 571
    information processing biases,
        571
    phenomenology of disorders,
        571
    prospective studies, 571
    qualitative methods, 571
    questionnaire studies, 571
    survey studies, 571
Clinical Psychology Division
    (BPS), 3
clitoris, 117f
CoA, 104
cocaine, 288–89
cochlea, 169, 170f
cochlear duct, 174f
cochlear nerve, 170f
cochlear nucleus, 170f
cognitive approach
    cognitive neuropsychology,
        20
    cognitivism, 20
    computer modelling, 20–22, 55
    controlled experiment, 20

impact of, 22
cognitive behaviour therapy, 549
    (CBT)
cognitive development
    social process (Vygotsky)
        cultural psychology, 318–19
        guided participation, 318
        modelling, 317–18
        peer interaction, 318
        private speech, 317
        scaffolding, 317–18
        social/cultural
            participation, 317
        thought/language/conscio
            usness relationship, 317
        zone of proximal
            development (ZPD),
                317, 317f
    see also information
        processing theories; moral
        development; Piaget's
        theory of cognitive
        development;
        representations
cognitive interviewing, 4t
Cognitive Learning and Student
    Strategies Project (CLaSS),
    735
cognitive neuropsychology, 20
cognitive neuroscience, 68f
cognitive psychology
    beginnings of, 14t
    forms of explanation, 15b
    in hierarchy of sciences, 56t
Cognitive Psychology (Neisser), 14t
cognitive tests, 531, 533–34
cognitive therapy, 577
    Beck's cognitive therapy, 610
    contemporary cognitive
        therapies, 610, 611b
    Ellis's rational-emotive
        therapy, 609–10
cognitive x value theory, 468, 469
cohort studies, 521b
cohorts, 296b
'common sense psychology,' 364,
    395
comparative psychology, 12, 68f
compliance, 430, 625–26, 626f
computer modelling

Subject Index

language acquisition, 20–22, 55, 333–35, 334b
object recognition, 191–92
concha, 170f
conditioned emotional response (CER), 124, 152
  see also classical conditioning
conditioned place preference (CPP), 139, 140, 141, 141b, 141f, 142, 143
  see also classical conditioning
conditioned response (CR), 123–26
  see also classical conditioning
conditioned stimulus (CS), 123, 123f, 124, 125f, 126, 134
  see also classical conditioning
cone receptors, 162f
confidence intervals, 647, 684, 685, 693
conformity, 430, 432, 433, 501b
confounding variables, 370, 645
conspecifics, 75
construct validity, 72, 537t
content validity, 643
continuous reinforcement schedules (CRF), 129, 142
  see also reinforcement
control group design
  post-test only, 660–61, 660f
  pre-test/post-test, 661, 661f
conversion (minority group influence), 433–34
cornea, 161f
corpus callosum, 96
correlation
  cause and effect, 644–45
  child directed speech (CDS), 331, 332b
  clinical psychology, 571
  coefficient of determination R^2, 699
  confounding variables, 645
  contiguous events, 645
  cross-sectional design, 644, 665
  linear relationships, 698–99
  partial and semi-partial correlations, 699–700, 700f
  Pearson's correlation coefficient r, 696, 697, 699

regression, 700
social psychology, 369
Spearmans's ρ, 699
tertium quid, 645
correspondence inference theory, 397–99
cortex, 96, 106, 145f
corticotrophin-releasing hormone (CRH), 155
cortisol, 155
counselling psychology, career in, 714–15
Counselling Psychology Division (BPS), 3
counsellor, definition of, 550
covariation and configuration models (Kelley)
  configuration account
    augmentation principle, 402
    causal schemata, 401–2
    discounting principle, 402
    multiple necessary cause schema, 402
    multiple sufficient causal schema, 401–2
  covariation account
    ANOVA approach, 400, 400f
    consensus, 400f, 401
    consistency, 400f, 401
    distinctiveness, 400–401, 400f
    evaluation of, 400f, 401
    internal/external causes, 400
cranial nerves, 87, 90f, 173
criboform plate, 171f
criterion-referenced tests, 532–33
criterion validity, 643
Cronbach's alpha, 643
cross-cultural studies, 51, 309, 521b
cross-sectional studies, 296b, 700
  see also correlation
crowd behaviour dynamics, 3t
cryptomnesia, 745
cultural psychology, 318–19
culture-specific disorders, 551
cytosine, 80f

D

DA *see* dopamine
data collection methods
  ethnographic observations, 297
  interviews/questionnaires, 297
  laboratory settings, 295, 296–97, 297b
  naturalistic settings, 295–96, 297
  observational studies, 295, 297
  parental descriptions, 297
  techniques, 297
Data Protection Act, 655
deductive reasoning, 29, 275
  see also hypothetico-deductive method
demonic possession, 545
dendrites, 88, 91, 91f
denial, 17
Deoxyribonucleic Acid *see* DNA
depression, 573
  anti-depressants, 596t, 597
  bipolar disorder, 575–76
  hypermania, 575b
  major depression (unipolar)
    attributional theories, 577f, 578
    Beck's cognitive theory, 576–77
    biological causes, 576
    learned helplessness theory, 577–78
  mania, 575b, 576
  monoamine oxidase inhibitors (MAOIs), 596t, 597
  seasonal affective disorder (SAD), 573
  serotonin reuptake inhibitors (SSRIs), 596t, 597
  suicide and parasuicide, 578–79
  tricyclic anti-depressants, 596t, 597
dermis, 172f
determinism, 30
  see also free will, and determinism
Deutsch and Deutsch response selection model, 207–8, 208f

developmental psychology, 282b
  birth difficulties, 287b
  continuity/discontinuity, 283
  data collection methods, 295–97
  development, causes of, 283–86
  disadvantage, 287–88
  environmental effects, 286–89
  extreme deprivation, 286–87
  founding father of (G. Stanley Hall), 284
  genetic effects, 289–95
  growth, 283
  predictability, 283
  research methods, 295–97
  study designs, 295, 296b
  see also cognitive development
developmental science, 282b
diazepam (Valium), 110b
diencephalon, 96
diet, 619f
disclaiming, 24b
discourse analysis
  qualitative methods, 571, 648–49
  social constructionism, 23–24b, 369
  social psychology, 371–72, 372b
discursive practices, 23–24b
disease model see medical model
disgust, 453t, 560–61, 571
disorganized schizophrenia, 581t
displacement, 17
displaying data, 671–90
dissociation of function, 226, 227b
Disulfiram, 127b
divided attention
  attentional capacity, 211, 213
  central/multiple resources, 217
  dual task paradigm, 213–14, 215, 217, 218t, 227b
  practice and automaticity, 213–15
  unilateral visual neglect, 212–13b, 213f
  see also attention
divorce, 348

DNA (Deoxyribonucleic Acid), 72, 74
  definition of, 79, 80f
  disorders, genetics of, 81
  double helix structure, 79, 80f, 81f
  Human Genome Project, 83
  molecular biotechnology techniques, 82–83
  mutations, 80
  nucleotides, 79, 80, 80f, 81f
  personality traits, study of, 81, 84b
  protein synthesis, 80–81
  proteins, 78–79
  replication, 79–80
Dolly, the cloned sheep, 72
dominant hemisphere (brain), 93
DOPAC (metabolite), 103
dopamine (DA), 54, 84, 101f, 102, 103, 104t, 105b, 108–9b, 121b, 139–43, 582
dorsal lateral tegmental nucleus, 153f
dorsal motor nucleus of vagus, 153f
dorsal striatum, 140f
double dissociation methodology, 193b
double helix structure, 79, 80f, 81f
DOVAC (metabolite), 142, 142f
Down's syndrome, 60, 291, 354
dream analysis, 600
drinking, and thirst, 147–48
drive theory (Zajonc), 435–36
drug-based treatments
  anxiety
    anxiolytics (tranquillisers), 596t, 597
    benzodiazepines, 596t, 597
  depression
    anti-depressants, 596t, 597
    monoamine oxidase inhibitors (MAOIs), 596t, 597
    serotonin reuptake inhibitors (SSRIs), 596t, 597
    tricyclic anti-depressants, 596t, 597

schizophrenia
    antipsychotics, 596–97, 596t
    dopamine levels, reduction in, 597
drug self-administration, 139, 140, 141, 143
drug tolerance, and overdose, 125b
drugs see psychopharmacology
DSM-IV classifications, 50b, 580, 584, 585t, 586
dynorphin, 101f
dyslexia
  acquired phonological dyslexia, 257b, 258
  acquired surface dyslexia, 257b, 258
  differences across languages, 337–38
  double deficit model, 338
  phonological core hypothesis, 337
  and visual system, 338

E
ear, components of, 169, 170f
  see also audition
eardrum, 169, 170f
eating
  arcuate nucleus, 146
  glucoreceptors, 145
  hunger and satiety centres, 145
  insulin, 146
  lateral hypothalamus, 145–46, 145f
  neuropeptides, 146
  nigrostriatal pathway, 145–46
  paraventricular nucleus, 146
  ventromedial hypothalamus, 145–46, 145f
eating disorders
  anorexia nervosa (AN), 586
  biopsychosocial model of
    body dissatisfaction, 590
    familial influences, 589
    life experience factors, 589589
    media/peer pressure, 589

Subject Index

psychological factors, 589–90
bulimia nervosa (AN), 586
diagnosis of, 586–87
DSM-IV criteria for, 586
neuroendocrine dysfunction, 588
serotonin levels, 588–89
echolalia, 354
ecological validity, 644
ecstasy (drug) *see* MDMA
Educational and Child Psychology Division (BPS), 3
educational psychology, career in, 715–16
effect size
Cohen's *d*, 696
Pearson's correlation coefficient *r*, 696, 697
statistical power, 697
statistical significance, 51, 694–95
efferent neurons, 86, 122, 122f
electro-dermal activity, 455
electroconvulsive therapy (ECT), 598
electroencephalogram (EEG), 155–56
electrooculogram (EOG), 156
Elements of Psychophysics (Fechner), 13t
Ellis's rational-emotive therapy, 609–10
embryology, 74
emotions
aggression, 154–55
amygdala brain activity, 460
anger, 453t
arousal, 453–54, 458–59, 461
autonomic nervous system (ANS) activity, 456
Ax's emotional experiment, 455
categories of, 150f, 151b
characteristics of, 452–63
cognitive appraisal theories, 461–62
components of, 150
definition of, 453–54
disgust, 453t

emotional brain, 151
facial expressions, 454
facial feedback hypothesis, 457b
fear, beyond, 153
fight or flight response, 150, 155
functions of, 454
hippocampus, and fear, 153, 154f
measurement of, 462b
mental evaluations, 461
Papez circuit, 151
positive/negative, 453t
self-report questionnaires, 462b
situation, relevance of, 461–62
somatic theory of, 454–58
stress, 155
two-factor theory of, 461–62
vascular theory of emotional feedback, 457b
see also amygdala
empathy, 422
empiricism, 30
endocrine feedback, 115
endocrine glands, 112, 114f
hypothalamic-pituitary portal system, 115
hypothalamus, 114–15, 117
pituitary gland, 114, 116f
endocrinology, 112
see also hormones
endorphins, 101f, 104t
environmental psychology, 4–5t
enzymes, 80
epidermis, 172f
epistemology, 28
error bars, 684–85, 684f
essay writing, 738–42
essential goodness of children (Rousseau), 284
estradiol, 117
ethical issues
advice, 657
animal research, 70–71
BPS code of conduct, 39, 70, 652, 654, 655, 657, 670
children/adults with impairments, 654

confidentiality, 655
consent forms, 653–54, 653f, 655
debriefing, 374, 654–55
deception, 374, 654
freedom to withdraw, 655
human research, 70
identification of (activity), 656–57b
informed consent, 374, 652–54
obedience to authority study (Milgram), 373, 653
observational methods, 665
participant protection, 374, 655, 657
payment of participants, 654
privacy, 374
Stanford prison experiment (Zimbardo), 373, 373b, 374illus
ethnocentrism, 42–43
ethology, 54
eugenics, 60, 70, 509
Eustachian tube, 170f
evolutionary theory
anxiety disorders, 560
Darwin, 72–75
environment, role of, 75
eugenics, 60, 70
evidence in support of, 74
natural selection, 12, 73, 73b
personality, 508–9
pet behaviour, 4t
exam procedures, 747
excitatory postsynaptic potentials (EPSP), 99, 107
exocytosis, 105f
experimental designs
boredom effects, 660
compatible/incompatible trials, 654b
control condition, 658
control groups, 658
counterbalancing, 660
extraneous variables, 659
independent measures design, 659–60
matched design, 659
mixed design, 661
post-test only control group

design, 660–61, 660f
cognitive dissonance:
    Festinger and
    Carlsmith, 662–63b,
    663f
independent t-test, 701
one-way independent
    ANOVA, 703
post-test only two-condition
    repeated measures design,
    661, 662f
implicit attitudes:
    Greenwald et al,
    663–64b, 664f
related t-test, 702
pre-test/post-test control
    group design, 661, 661f
blame the teachers:
    Rosenthal and
    Jacobson, 663b, 663f
pre-test/post-test two
    condition repeated
    measures design, 662, 662f
random sampling, 658–59, 660
repeated measures design,
    659–60
    one-way related ANOVA,
    704
Soloman four-group design,
    661, 662f
systematic/unsystematic
    variation, 659
variables, levels of, 658
experimental psychology
laboratory, first, 13t, 14t
experiments,
    experimental control, 31–32,
    38b
    experimenter artifacts
        expectancy, 36
        intentional errors, 36, 37
        interpretation errors, 36
        observation errors, 36
    measurement, 32–33, 38, 38b
        of hypothetical constructs,
        38
        multiple measures for
            same construct, 38
        reification, 38
        specific context of, 38

operationism, 32–33
participant artifacts, 35, 36f
    demand characteristics, 35,
    36f
    good subject effect, 35
pure and quasi-experiments,
    32
validity, 32
expertise
    as 'fuzzy' concept, 277
    problem solving methods, 278
    problems, representation of,
    277
    recall patterns, 277–78
    schemata, use of, 277
explanation, forms of, 15b
Expression of Emotions in Man
    and Animals (Darwin), 13t
external auditory canal (meatus),
    170f
extinction (conditioning), 123f,
    124, 130f, 132, 602
extracelluar fluid, 147
extraneous variables, 659
extrapyramidal system, 174–75
extreme case formulation, 23–24b
extroversion
    measurement of, 32–33
    trait theory, 502–3
eye, 89f, 161f
    see also vision
eyewitness testimony
    autobiographical memory
    (AM), 236b
    children, 4t, 311b
    misleading questions, 2b
Eysenck Personality Inventory
    (EPI), 33

F
F-scale, 445
F statistic, 703, 705, 706
5-HIAA, 103
5-HT *see* serotonin
5-HTP, 103
face recognition
    context, 195, 198f
    face recognition units, 193b
    name of person, 193–94b
    perceptual processes, 193b

person identity units, 193b
face validity, 72, 537t
facial cranial nerve, 90f
faculty psychology, 11
false consensus effect (FCE), 407
false memory effects, 2fp
falsifiability, 19, 29
family therapy, 611–12, 613b
fear, 453t
    amygdala, 152–53
    hippocampus, 153, 154f
    multiple pathways, 560
fear hierarchy, 603, 603b
feminist psychology, 51–52
field experiments, 370
field studies, 371
fissures (brain), 96
fixed interval (FI) schedules, 130f,
    131
    see also reinforcement
fixed ratio (FR) schedules, 130,
    130f, 133b, 140b, 142
    see also reinforcement
flashbulb memories, 238, 239b
Fluoxetine (Proxac), 147
focused auditory attention
    attentional filter, 206, 208f
    attenuation, 206, 208
    Broadbent's filter model of
        selective attention, 206
    Deutsch and Deutsch response
        selection model, 207–8,
        208f
    dichotic listening task, 206,
        207b
    Kahneman's capacity model of
        attention, 208–9
    shadowing, 206, 207b, 208
    Treisman's attenuator model of
        selective attention, 206–7,
        208f
focused visual attention
    assembling a project, 210–11
    covert attention
        impairment of, 212b, 213f
        versus overt attention, 209
    sensory memory, 209–11
    shifting and the spotlight
        analogy, 209, 210f, 211f
    iconic memory, 209

Subject Index

sensory memory, 209–11
Triesman's feature integration model, 210–11
zoom lens analogy, 209–10, 214f
foetal alcohol syndrome, 288–89, 289
follicle stimulating hormone (FSH), 116f
forebrain, 96, 156
forensic psychology, career in, 716–17
Forensic Psychology Division (BPS), 3
form perception
brightness constancy, 184
closure principle, 181, 182f
colour constancy, 184
constancies, 182–84, 189
continuity principle, 181, 182f
figure-ground separation, 181, 182f
laws of pragnanz, 181, 182f, 189
proximity principle, 181, 182f
retinal size, 183, 183f
shape constancy, 182, 183b
similarity principle, 181, 182f
size constancy, 183–84, 184f
size-distance invariance hypothesis, 183–84
visual illusions, 184–86, 189
fornix, 96f, 151, 151f, 152f
fossil records, 74
fovea, 161f, 162
free association, 599
free-riding, 436
free will, and determinism
behaviourism, 58, 59
choice, 58
neurogenetic determinism, 58
phenomena, 59–60
scientific approach, 58
soft determinism, 59
uncaused behaviour, 58
voluntary behaviour, 59
frequency distributions see histograms
Friedman's ANOVA, 705, 705f
frontal cortex, 303

frontal lobes, 95b, 96
functional lateralisation (left brain/right brain), 92–94b, 96
functionalism, 12
fundamental attribution error (FAE), 405–6
funding, for postgraduate training, 715

G
GABA (3-aminobuytyric acid), 101f, 104t, 104, 105b, 110b, 157
GAD see generalised anxiety disorder
gallbladder, 89f
gametes, 78
gender
bias, 23
biological influences, 343
brain lateralisation differences, 93
gender constancy, 343
identity, 343
intelligence, 525b
sex versus gender differences, 343
social learning/reinforcement, 343–44
gene cloning, 82
general paresis, 545
generalised anxiety disorder (GAD), 547
biological theories, 565
chronic/non-chronic worriers, 564–65, 566
dispositional characteristics, 568
dysfunctional beliefs, 567–68, 568b
information processing biases, 567
nature of, 564
pathological worry, 564, 565b
Stroop procedure, 567
genetic development
genetic disorders, 291–92
genotype/phenotype, 61–63, 76, 291
inheritance, 291–92
intelligence, 292–95

mutations, 291
pre-natal development, 289–91
genetic engineering, 70
genetic fingerprinting, 290
genetics
alleles, dominant/recessive, 76, 76f, 77, 77f
biotechnology, 81
chromosomes, and inheritance, 77–78
dichotomous traits, 75, 76
dominant/recessive traits, 76
psychology, 81
see also behavioural genetics; chromosomes; genetic development
Gestalt theories, 13
direct perception, 198
phi phenomenon, 14t
problem-solving, 264–65
Gilbert et al.'s three-stage model for attribution, 404–5
glial cells, 88, 90
global assessment of functioning (GAF) scale, 554t, 555–57
globus pallidus, 97, 105b, 106, 175b
glossopharyngeal cranial nerve, 90f
glucogen, 146
glucorticoids, 155
glucose, 146
glutamate, 101f, 102, 104, 104t, 105b, 135f, 136, 162–63, 164
glycogen, 146
goal theories, 470, 472b
gonads, 114f
graphs
chartjunk, 690f
features of good and bad, 688–90
means, 684–86
medians, 686–87, 686f
misrepresentation of data, 690, 690f
relationships, 687–88
website on, 691
Greek philosophers, 10
group decision-making
group polarisation, 437–38

groupthink, 438–40
persuasive arguments, 438
self-categorisation, 438
social comparison, 438
group therapies, 610–11
group types, 430
group working, 737–38
checklist of good practice, 739b
critical thinking skills, 737
different perspectives, 738
groups skills, 738
oral communication skills, 737
oral presentations, 737, 738b
personal skills, 738
seminars and tutorial, 737
groups
differences between, 12
group norms, 431–32, 438
group size, 436
in- and out-groups, 438
see also intergroup conflict; leadership; obedience to authority; social influence
growth hormone, 116f
guanine, 80f
Guilford's structure of intellect model, 520, 520f
gustatory system
brain, and cranial nerves, 173
heat-sensitive receptors, 174
taste buds, 173
Guttman scale, 381
gynaecology, 116
gyri (brain), 96

H
H statistic, 704f
hair follicle, 172f
Head Start programme (USA), 288
health, psychological, 554t, 555–57
health psychology
biomedical model of health/illness, 618
as career, 717
definition of, 618–19
diet, 619f
disease prevention, 619
doctor-patient

communication, 624–25, 625b
health belief model (HBM), 621–22, 622f
health promotion, 619
healthy behaviour prediction, 620–21
illness, psychology of, 626–32
individual responsibility, 618
lifestyle factors, 619
patient compliance, 625–26
personality tests, use of, 535b
professional advice, seeking, 623–24
stress, and coping styles, 619
theory of planned behaviour (TPB), 622–23, 623f
Health Psychology Division (BPS), 3
heart, 89f
Heckhausen's expectancy-value model, 469
Heider's balance theory, 385–86, 385f
Heider's 'common-sense' approach, 397, 398f
Hereditary Genius (Galton), 13t
heredity-environment debate *see* nature-nurture debate
heritability, 510b
heteroreceptors, 108f
heterosexism, 50b
heuristics, 273–74
hierarchy of needs (Maslow), 471
hindbrain, 97f, 98
hippocampus, 96, 96f, 97b, 134, 151f, 152f, 153, 154f
histograms
drawing of, 672b
properties of, 671–74
history, of psychology, 10–14, 54
History of Experimental Psychology, A (Boring), 14t
holistic approach, 13, 19, 600
homeostasis, 125b, 465, 466b
homogeneity of variance, 697
homosexuality
brain structure, 117
not a disorder (APA), 14t
horizontal cells, 162f

horizontal plane (brain), 94f
hormones, 508
activational effects, 116
aggression, 154–55
amine hormones, 114
maternal stress, 288–89
neurotransmitters, 112, 113
organisational effects, 116, 117
protein hormones, 114
sexual differentiation
androgens, 117
aromatisation hypothesis, 117
genital development, 116–17, 117f
Wolffian and Mullerian systems, 116
X and Y chromosomes, and H-Y antigen, 116
sexual motivation, 473–74
steroid hormones, 114, 115f
targets, 114f
types of, 114
Horn and Cattell's fluid and crystallised intelligence, 520
human error
active failures, 216
cognitive processes underlying, 216
knowledge-based processes, 216
latent conditions, 216
person approach, 216
rule-based processes, 216
skilled processes, 216
systems approach, 216
Human Genome Project, 72, 83
humanistic theory, 15b, 492
clinical and counselling psychology, 19
evaluation of, 19–20
hierarchy of needs, 498
motivation, 471–72
positive aspects of personality, 497
self-actualisation, 19, 498
subjectivity, 19
humanistic therapies
client-centred therapy, 600, 601–2

Subject Index

Gestalt therapy, 600
holistic therapies, 600
hunger, 468b
   see also eating
Huntington's disease, 76, 77f, 97, 175
HVA (DA metabolite), 103, 142, 142f
hyperaphagia, 145
hypnotics, 157
hypoglossal cranial nerve, 90f
hypothalamus, 96
   eating, 145–46
   emotion, 151, 151f, 154
   endocrine glands, 114–15, 117
hypotheses
   confirmation bias, 270–72
   experimental (alternative), 638–39
   formation, 269–72
   generating from theories, 636–38, 642b
   null, 638–39
   one- and two-tailed, 639
   resolution, 272
   scientific and non-scientific statements, 638
   testing, 269–72
   see also probability
hypothetical constructs, 32–33, 33b, 38
hypothetico-deductive method, 30–31, 31f, 48–49
hypovolemic thirst, 147, 148

I

iconic memory, 209, 221, 222–23
identity
   adolescence, 358–59
   attitudes, 378–79
   collectivist/individual, 484–85
   culture, role of, 484–85
   gender, 342–44, 343
   self-esteem, 482–83
   self-handicapping hurdles, 483
   self-image, 484
   self-perception, 482
   self-presentation, 479–80
   self-schema, 480–81
   self-serving bias, 483

selfhood, functions of, 478–79
   social identity theory, 481
   social influence, 433
   social norms, 485, 485b
   see also self; self-concept; self-knowledge
identity crises, 485–86
illness, psychology of
   pain, 631–32
   psychosomatic illness, 626
   see also health psychology; stress
implicit association test, 382
implicit attitudes test (IAT), 663–64b
impression formation
   first impressions, 409
      central and peripheral traits, 411–12, 411f, 412t
      context-dependence, 412–13
      halo effect, 411
      implicit personality theory, 412
   levels of processing
      scrambled sentence priming, 415–16b
      subliminal priming techniques, 415, 415b, 416b
   physical appearance, 414
   primacy/recency effects, 413–14
   stereotypes, 414
impression management, 387, 411
   public/private behaviour, 416–17
   self-concept, 417
   self-esteem, 417
   self-presentation strategies, 416–17
   validity, 382
incus, 170f
independent/dependent (predictor/outcome) variables, 400, 400f, 642–43, 700
independent measures design, 659–60
individual differences, 12, 43

indolamines, 101f
inductive method, and positivism, 29
inductive reasoning
   concept learning, 269–72
   decision making, 274–75
   definition of, 269
   judgements, 272–74
infants, 282b
inferior colliculus, 169, 170f
information processing theories
   children's memory, 311b, 312
   encoding limitations, 312
   information processing capacity, 312
   microgenetic study, 313
   'neo-Piagetian' approach, 312
   overlapping waves theory, 312–13
   Siegler's balancing rules experiments, 312, 315b
   speed of processing, 312
inhibitory postsynaptic potentials (IPSP), 99, 107
insanity, 544
insomnia, 158
intelligence
   across life span, 528
   biological perspective, 525–28
   brain structure and size, 526
   Carroll's hierarchical model of intelligence, 520
   cognitive-contextual theories, 522–25
   constituency interests, 49
   contemporary issues, 528–29
   as context-specific, 524b
   definitions of, 514–16
   diet and IQ, 528–29
   emotional intelligence, 527b
   evaluation of, 520–21
   Gardner's theory of multiple intelligences, 522–24
      bodily-kinesthetic intelligence, 523t
      interpersonal intelligence, 523t
      intrapersonal intelligence, 523t
      linguistic intelligence, 523t

logical-mathematical intelligence, 523t
musical intelligence, 523t
natural intelligence, 523t
savant syndrome, 523
spatial intelligence, 523t
gender, 525b
gender and race differences, 525b
genetic development, 292–95
Guilford's structure of intellect model, 520, 520f
heritability, 527–28
Horn and Cattell's fluid and crystallised intelligence, 520
intelligence acquisition, 526–28
leading individuals, focus on, 517–18
nature-nurture debate, 292–95
neurological effort, and intelligence, 526b
research methods, 521b
single/multiple, 518, 519, 519b
as socially constructed, 515
Spearman's two-factor theory, 14t, 519
Sternberg's triarchic theory, 524
analytic intelligence, 524
creative intelligence, 524
practical intelligence, 524
Thurstone's factor analytic theory, 519–20
Vernon's hierarchical model of, 520
in the workplace, 529
see also IQ
intelligence quotient see IQ
intelligence tests
Binet's mental tests, 14t, 284, 516b, 530b, 538b
first, 14t
limitations of, 523t
psychometric tests, 519–21, 534b, 538b
see also IQ
interaction effect, 707
interaction graph, 707f

intercranial self-stimulation (ICSS), 139–40, 141, 142
intergroup conflict
contact hypothesis, 447
environmental factors, 445
group membership, 446–47
in- versus out-group favouritism, 446–47
minimal group paradigm, 446
prejudice and discrimination, 444–45
self-esteem, 447
Sherif's realistic conflict theory, 445–46
social identity theory, 447
internal consistency reliability, 536
Internet searching, 748
interneurons, 121–22, 122f
Interpretation of Dreams (Freud), 14t
interstitial fluid, 147
interval data, 641–42
intestines, 89f
intracellular fluid, 147
intravascular fluid (blood plasma), 147
ionotropic receptors, 107f
ions, 98–99
IQ (intelligence quotient)
abnormality, definitions of, 550
Army Alpha and Beta tests, 46b
definition of, 519
and diet, 528–29
post-traumatic stress disorder, 572–73
Stanford-Binet IQ test, development of, 14t
test score development, 288b
Wechsler IQ scores, 532, 533t, 534b
iris, 161f
islets of Langerhans (pancreas), 89f, 114f

J
James-Lange theory of physiological arousal, 454–58
Journal of Criminal Psychology, 4t

Journal of Cross-cultural Psychology, 14t
journals, submitting manuscripts to, 683–84
judgements
base rate information, 272–73, 274
gambler's fallacy (law of averages), 274
heuristics, 273–74
probabilistic judgements, 272

K
Kahneman's capacity model of attention, 208–9
Kanizsa's triangle, 48f
Karmiloff-Smith representational-redescription (RR) model, 314, 316
Klüver-Bucy syndrome, 151
Kohlberg's theory (moral development), 43–44b, 309–10
Kruskal-Wallis test, 704, 704f
kurtosis, 672–73

L
labia majora, 117f
labia minora, 117f
laboratory-based studies, 370
Langerhans, islets of (pancreas), 89f, 114f
language, 248t
arbitrariness, 247
creativity, 247
cultural transmission, 247
displacement, 247
duality of patterning, 247
human-specific, 246–49
power relations, 24b
semanticity, 247
spontaneous usage, 247
structure dependence, 247
teaching to primates
apes and children, comparative achievements of, 249, 250t
methodological problems, 249
symbol systems, 247

Subject Index

language acquisition
  caregiver-infant interaction
    body games, 323
    joint attention, 324–25, 324b
    word games, 323–24
  child directed speech (CDS), 330–31, 331f, 332b
  Chomsky and Skinner, 284
  communication *versus* language, 325–26
  connectionist networks
    backpropagation, 333
    computer models, 333–35
    general learning processes, 333
    past tense, modelling, 334b
  constructivist views
    grammar acquisition, 332–33
    verb-island hypothesis, 332
  dual-route model, 329–30
  error correction, adult expansions, 331–32, 333b
  hearing and vocalising
    babbling, 323
    conditioned head turning, 323
    cooing, 323
    habituation/dishabituation, 321–23
    phoneme identification, 321–23
    social interaction, words and attention, 323–25
  holophrases, 325
  imitation, 330, 330b
  language acquisition device (LAD), 326, 327f, 330b
  linguistic rules, 325, 326
  nature-nurture, 322b
  principles and parameters theory
    modular view of language, 327
    parameter setting process, 328–29
    sign language,
    spontaneous development of, 328
  reinforcement, 326
  specific language impairment (SLI), 334b
  telegraphic speech, 325
  universal grammar, 326, 327f, 332
  vocabulary development, 325
  word production, 325
  see also non-verbal communication
language acquisition device (LAD), 326, 327f, 330b
language comprehension
  constituents, psychological reality of, 250, 251–53
  Eliza computer model, 20–22
  garden path sentences, 252–53
  grammar, 250
  immediacy principle, 252
  parsing, 250–51, 252
  phrase structure, 250
  syntax, 250
  word order, 250
  wrap-up, 251–53
language production
  conceptualisation, 253
  formulation, 253–55
  lexicalisation
    lemma, 253
    lexical selection, 253
    malapropisms, 253–54, 254t
    semantic errors, 253, 254t
    tip of the tongue phenomenon, 254, 254b
  phonological specification, 255
  syntactic planning, 254–55
language recognition
  cohort model, 256–57
  gating, 256
  mental lexicon, 256
  phonemes, 256
  shadowing, 256, 256b
  word recognition
    lexical decision task, 259, 259b
    logogen model, 260, 260f
    priming task, 259–60, 259b
    word frequency, 258–60
    see also reading; speech perception
lateral geniculate nucleus (LGN), 165–66, 166f
lateral hypothalamus (LH), 145f, 153f
leadership
  leadership style, 442–44
  trait approach, 442
learned helplessness theory, 134, 577–78
learning
  cognitive/associative, 120, 134
  concept learning, 269–72
  effective, 725–35
  evolution, 120
  habituation, 120–21, 121b, 122b
  imprinting, 120
  long-term potentiation, 134–36
  preparedness, 120
  reflexes, 121–22
  sensitisation of incentive salience, 143–44
  and traumatic experiences (activity), 656–57b
  see also classical conditioning; operant conditioning; reinforcement
learning theory, 284–85, 344, 548
  see also social learning theory
lectures and note-taking, 736–37
left brain/right brain, 92–94b, 96
Leiter International Performance Scale-Revised test, 540
lens, 161f
leptin, 468b
leptokurtic distribution, 673, 673f
leu-enkephalin, 101f
leuteinizing hormone (LH), 116f
lexicon, mental, 335
Ley's model of patient compliance, 625–26, 626f
licensing procedure, 70–71
lie detector (polygraph), 69, 460b, 462b

life span development theory, 50b, 282b, 286, 494, 496
ligament, 161f
Likert scale, 25t, 381, 381b
liking *see* attraction
limbic cortex, 140f
limbic system, 96, 96f, 151, 171f
    amygdala, 96, 97
    cingulate cortex, 96
    fornix, 96
    hippocampus, 96, 97b, 134
    mamillary bodies, 96
    septum, 96
line charts, 684, 685, 685f
line of best fit (regression line), 688
lipids, 88
literacy, 335–38
    dyslexia, 337–38
    and language, 335b
    see also reading
litigation mania, 551
'Little Albert' study, 559–60
liver, 89f
locus coeruleus, 153f
logical positivism, 29
long-term memory (LTM)
    encoding, 230–33
    forgetting, 234–35
        interference, 235, 235f
        repression, 234–35
        trace decay, 235
    long-term memory systems, 221
    mnemonics, 232–33
        acronyms, 232
        elaboration mnemonics, 232, 233f
        loci, 232
        reduction mnemonics, 232
    organisation, 230–32
        automatic processing, 231
        effortful processing, 231
        incidental learning, 231
        memory improvement, 232b
        schema, 231–32
        structure, 230–31
    retrieval, 233–34
        availability/accessibility of memories, 233–34

constructive memory, 234
context-dependent memory, 234
encoding specificity principle, 234
mood-dependent memory, 234
retrieval cues, 233–34
state-dependent memory, 234
see also memory
long-term potentiation (LTP)
    AMPA receptors, 135f, 136
    glutamate receptors, role of, 135f, 136
    hippocampal activity, 134, 135f, 136
    NMDA receptors, 135f, 136
    pre- and postsynaptic neurons, activation of, 136
    synaptic transmission, facilitation of, 134
longitudinal studies, 521b
    attachment, 347b
    moral development, 309
    research methods, 296b, 521b
longitudinal study, 296b
lost-letter technique, 382
loving *see* attraction
lungs, 89f

M
madness, 544
magic number (Miller), 14t
magnocellular pathway, 166f
malleus, 170f
mammillary bodies, 96f, 151, 151f, 152f
mammillothalamic tract, 151f, 152f
mania, 575b, 576
Mann-Whitney test, 701–2, 701f
matched design, 659
McGuire's inverted U-shaped curve hypothesis, 391, 393, 393f
MDMA (ecstasy), 112, 113b, 143
mean, 532, 675–76, 675b, 677, 678–79, 678t, 684
    see also graphs

measurement (of variables)
    demand characteristic, 644
    interval data, 641–42
    level of, 640
    measurement error, 640, 644
    nominal data, 640
    ordinal data, 641
    ratio data, 642
    reliability, 643
    validity, 643
    variables, 639–40
measures of central tendency (mode/median/mean)
    reporting conventions for, 683–84
    see also mean; median; mode
medial dorsal nucleus, 171f
medial geniculate nucleus (MGN), 170, 170f
medial prefrontal cortex (mPFC), 134
median, 674–75, 675b, 683
    see also graphs
median preoptic nucleus (MPN), 148
medical model
    biological *versus* psychological causes, 545–46, 546b
    dysfunction, concept of, 547
    medication/surgical treatment, 546
    normal behaviour, extreme forms of, 547
    pathology model, 547
    reductionism, 545–47
    somatogenic hypothesis, 545
    stigmatisation, 547, 548b, 549illus
meiosis, 78
Meissner's corpuscle, 172f
melanin-concentrating hormone (MCH), 146
memory
    amnesia, 220
    echoic memory, 221
    episodic memory, 221, 222
    explicit/implicit memory processes, 221–22
    iconic memory, 221, 222–23
    memory duration, 221

Subject Index

memory systems, 220–21
metamemory, 311b
neuropsychological evidence, 222
procedural memory, 221, 222
sensual memory, 221
verbal memory systems, 221
see also autobiographical memory; long-term memory; semantic memory; short-term memory
Memory (Ebbinghaus), 13t
Mendelian genetics *see* genetics
meninges, 87, 90f
menstrual cycle, 93–94, 116
Merkel's disk, 172f
mesencephalon
    colliculi, inferior and superior, 97–98
    red nucleus, 98
    reticular formation, 98
    substantia nigra, 98
    tectum, 97–98
    tegmentum, 97–98
mesolimbic pathway, 139–40, 140f, 142, 143
mesolimibic system, 109b
messenger Ribonucleic Acid (mRNA), 78–79, 82f, 83f
met-enkephalin, 101f
metabotropic reactors, 107f
metamemory, 311b
metencephalon, 97f, 98
MHPG, 103
midbrain, 97–98
Milgram's experiments (obedience to authority), 39, 39b, 373, 440–42, 653
mind, theory of *see* theory of mind
mind-body dualism, 10–11
Mind (journal), 13t
mitochondria, 88, 91f
mitosis
    brain development, 90–91, 92, 92f
    chromosomes, 78, 79f
mixed design (mixed-plot design), 674

bimodal distribution, 674
    multimodal distribution, 674
MODE model, 384
molecular biology, 74, 82–83, 84
molecular genetics, 511
monoamine oxidase inhibitors (MAOIs), 112, 596t, 597
monoamine oxidase (MAO), 103
monoamines, 101f
monozygotic/dizygotic twins, 81, 293
    see also twin studies
Mood Adjective Checklist (MACL), 462b
mood disorders, 573, 575–79
moral development
    children's rules, 307
    cross-cultural studies, 309
    heteronomous/ autonomous morality, 307
    Kohlberg's theory, 43–44b, 309–10
    moral dilemma stories, 309
    moral realism, 308
    moral subjectivism, 308
    Piaget's investigations, 307–9
    stages of, 309, 310
morphemes, 326b
morphosyntax, 326b
Moskovici's dual process model, 434
Moskovici's genetic model of minority influence, 433–34
motherese, 330–31, 331f, 332b
motivation
    achievement motivation, 475
    arousal theory, 467
    cross-dressing and transvestism, 474
    definition of, 464
    drive theory, 465–66
    expectancy theory, 468, 469, 472b
    goal theories, 470, 472b
        ego-involved goals, 470
        goal-attainment scaling (GAS), 470
        goal-setting theory, 470
        mastery goals, 470
        performance goals, 470

        social goals, 470
        task-involved goals, 470
    incentive theory, 467–71
    instincts, 465
    locus of control, 470, 470t, 472–73, 473b
    and money, 465
    persuasion processes, 390–91
    self-development, 471–72
    self-efficacy theory, 469–70, 472b
    sensation-seeking, 474–75
    sexual motivation, 473–74
    see also brain reward mechanisms; Weiner's attribution model
motor control
    brain regions, 174–75
    information, passage of, 175–76
MRI scans, 22, 68, 69b, 97b, 152
Mullarian-inhibiting factor, 116
Muller-Lyer illusion, 184–86, 185f
multi-item scales, 381
multiple sclerosis (MS), 100
murderers, 552
myelencephalon, 97f, 98
myelin, 88, 91f, 100, 100f
myelin sheath, 100

N

narcolepsy, 158–59
nasal hemiretina, 165, 166f
nasopharynx, 171f
natural science, psychology as, 12
natural selection, 12, 73, 73b
nature-nurture debate
    biological explanations, popularity of, 60–63, 62b
    empiricists and nativists, 284
    genes and environment, relationship between, 60, 61b
    genotype/phenotype, 61–62, 62f
    hereditarian explanations, 60
    intelligence
        environment, 293, 294–95
        genetic factors, 292–94
        heritability, 294–95

siblings, 293, 294t
twin studies, 293
learning theory, 284
see also language acquisition
needs, hierarchy of (Maslow), 19
negatively skewed distribution, 673, 673f
neotony, 47–48b
Nerve Growth Factor (NGF), 91
nervous system
afferent nerves, 86
autonomic nervous system (ANS), 86, 89
blood-brain barrier (BBB), 88
brain ventricles, 87
cells of, 86
neurons, 88, 91f, 92f
support cells, 88, 90
central nervous system (CNS), 86, 87–88, 88f, 161
cranial nerves, 87, 90f
efferent nerves, 86
parasympathetic nervous system, 86–87, 89
peripheral nervous system (PNS), 86, 87, 88f
somatic nervous system (SNS), 86, 155
spinal cord, 87, 88f, 89f
subdivisions of, 86–87
sympathetic nervous system, 86–87, 89
neurogenetic determinism, 54
neuromuscular junction (NMI), 175f
neurons, 88, 91f, 92f
components of, 91f
long-term potentiation (LTP), 136
reflexes, 121–22, 122f
synaptic regulation, 107
synaptic transmission, 102
see also brain communication
Neuropeptide Y (NPY), 146
neuropsychology, 68f, 718
as a career, 717–19
Neuropsychology Division (BPS), 3
neurosecretery cells, 115
neurotransmission

modification by drugs
autoreceptor stimulation and antagonism, 112
drug action, multiple sites of, 112
drugs that block reuptake, 112
enhance neurotransmitter release, 112
metabolism, inhibition of, 112
postsynaptic antagonism, 112
postsynaptic stimulation, 112
precursor drugs, 110
storage prevention, 112
synthesis inhibition, 110
see also brain communication
neurotransmitters, 88
categories of, 101f
competitive/non-competitive drugs, 109, 110f
hormones, 112, 113
particular, 102
receptors, 102, 104t, 105
release of, 102, 105f
synthesis of, 102, 102–3f
see also brain communication
nicotine
action at ACh receptors, 141
addictive properties of, 141, 142
dopamine (DA), 141–42
ICSS, effect on, 142
nicotine receptors, 141
nicotine self-administration, 142
reinforcement schedules, 142
in vivo microdialysis, 141–42
nigrostriatal pathway, 105b, 145–46
nitric oxide, 101f
NMDA receptors, 135f, 136
nociception
anterior lateral system, 173
pain control, 173
nodes of ranvier, 88, 91f, 100, 100f
nominal data, 640

non-experimental designs, 664–67
case studies, 665, 666b, 667
cross-sectional design, 665
ideographic *versus* nomothetic approaches, 665
observational methods, 665, 666b
quasi-experimental designs, 664–65, 666b
single-subject designs, 665
non-verbal communication
interpersonal distance (proxemics), 418, 419b
meaning types, 417–18
non-verbal cues, 418
reasons for, 418
noradrenaline (NA), 101f, 102, 103, 104t, 157
norm-referenced tests, 532, 533t
normal behaviour, extreme forms of, 547
normal distribution, 532, 532f, 672, 673f
see also histograms
nose, components of, 171f
nostril, 171f
nucleus accumbens (NAcc), 139–40, 140f, 141, 142, 142f
nucleus basalis, 153f
nucleus (neuron), 88
nucleus reticularis pontis caudalis, 153f
nucleus (solitary tract), 148
null hypothesis, 72, 638–39, 695

O
obedience to authority
group pressure, 441b
immediacy of authority figure, 441b
immediacy of victim, 441b
Milgram's experiments, 39, 373, 440–42, 653
persuasion, 441b
obesity, 146–47, 146b
object recognition
3-D world, computer simulation of, 191–92
geons, and feature theory, 192–93, 197f

Subject Index

recognition-by-components theory, 192–93
observational learning, 284
obsessive-compulsive disorder
  compulsive checking, 569
  compulsive washing, 569
  contamination, fear of, 569b
  executive deficits, 570
  neurophysiological deficits, 569–70
  obsessions, 568–69
  psychological factors, 570
  unwanted thoughts, 569
occipital lobe, 96, 96f
occupational psychology, as a career, 718–19
Occupational Psychology Division (BPS), 3
oculomotor cranial nerve, 90f
Oedipus complex, 17
oestrogen, 117
offender profiling, 3t
olfaction
  nasal membrane, 170–71
  nose, components of, 171f
  olfactory cortex, 170–71, 171f
  olfactory epithelium, 170, 171f
olfactory bulb, 96f, 152f, 171f
olfactory cranial nerve, 90f
olfactory epithelium, 171f
olfactory mucus, 171f
olfactory tract, 171f
olfactory tubercle, 140f
one-way independent ANOVA, 703–4
  cognitive dissonance: Festinger and Carlsmith, 662–63b, 663f, 708b
one-way related ANOVA, 704–5, 705f
operant conditioning
  aggression, 426–27
  attitude formation, 380
  behaviour therapies, 605–9
  behaviourism, 16, 128
  drug self-administration, 139, 140
  law of effect, 126f, 127
  ner box, 128, 129illus, 32–33b

see also classical conditioning; reinforcement
opsins, 162
optic chiasm, 145f, 166f
optic cranial nerve, 90f
optic nerve, 161f, 162, 162f, 165, 166f
optic radiation, 166f
optic tract, 166f
optimistic bias, 2fp
orbitofrontal cortex, 171f
ordinal data, 641
orexin, 146, 158–59
orienting response, 121
Origin of Intelligence in the Child (Piaget), 14t
Origin of Species (Darwin), 12t, 72
osmoreceptors, 147–48
osmotic thirst, 147, 466
ossicles, 169
outer
outer/middle/inner ear, 169, 170f
outliers, 675, 677
oval window, 170f
ovaries, 114f
oxytocin, 116f

P
Pacinian corpuscle, 172f
pain
  gate control model, 173, 631–32, 632f
  pain anxiety, 632
  pain perception, 631
  pain symptoms, catastrophising of, 632
  phantom limb phenomenon, 631
pallidotomy, 175b
pancreas (islets of Langerhans), 89f, 114f
panic disorder (PD), 551b, 611b
  biological theories, 562
  hyperventilation model, 562, 563b
  nature of, 561
  panic attacks, 561, 562b
parabrachial nucleus, 153f
parafasicular nucleus, 172f
parahippocampal gyrus, 152f

parametric tests
  homogeneity of variance, 697
  independence, 698
  interval data, 697
  normally distributed data, 697
paranoid schizophrenia, 581t
parasympathetic nervous system, 86–87, 89
paraventricular nucleus (PVN), 145f, 153f
parental attachment, 284
parietal lobe, 96, 96f, 212
Parkinson's disease, 97
  basal ganglia, 106, 175
  inibitory/excitatory pathways, 105b
  pallidotomy, 175b
parvocelluar pathway, 166f
pattern recognition
  face recognition, 195, 193–94b, 198f
  feature detectors, 190, 194f, 195b, 195t
  template matching, 189–90, 191f, 192f, 193f, 195b, 198
  visual object agnosia, 189, 190b
  visual search experiments, 192, 195b, 195f
Pavlov's experiments, 122–25
  see also classical conditioning
peers, 282b
penis, 89f, 117f
perception
  context effects, 198f
    constructive perception, 199
    letter recognition, 195, 194b
    word recognition, 194b, 199t
  depth perception
    binocular cues, 186b, 186f, 187, 187b
    direct perception, 196–98
    monocular cues, 187–88
    motion cues, 187–88
  direct/constructive processes, 195, 196–98

distal *versus* proximal stimulus, 180
psychophysics, 180–81
versus sensation, 180
sensory thresholds, 181
see also form perception; object recognition; speech perception
periaqueductal gray matter (PAG), 153f, 173
peripheral nervous system (PNS), 86, 87, 88f
personal constructs, 499
personal development planning (PDP), 730–33
personal growth, 1, 3
personality
  academic psychology, 490–91
  applications
    criminal behaviour, 512b
    health, 512b
    television violence, 512–13b
  attributes of, 488–89
  clinical psychology, 489–90
  conformity and obedience, 501b
  cultural influences, 501b
  definitions of, 487–89
  descriptions, 2b
  idiographic approach, 490
  nomothetic approach, 490
  observation, 489b
  personality traits, and quantitative methods, 490
personality disorders (PDs)
  anti-social personality disorder (ASPD), 584–86
  criminal activity, 584, 585–86
  dangerous people with severe personality disorders (DSPD), 585, 587b
  DSM-IV general diagnostic criteria for, 584, 585t
personality research, 489–91
personality tests, 534–36, 535b
personality theories, 491
  behavioural, 493
  biological, 493, 505–13

cognitive-behavioural, 493, 497, 498–500
humanistic, 492, 497–98
psychodynamic, 491, 494–97
trait theory, 492, 501–5
persuasion processes
  cognitive processes involved in, 388
  elaboration likelihood model (ELM), 388, 389, 390, 392–93b
  fear appeals, 391, 393, 393f
  heuristic systematic model (HSM), 388, 390–91
  subjection to in everyday life, 387–88
  Yale model of persuasive communication, 388, 388f
PET scans, 68, 69b, 97b, 153, 511–12, 526
pharmacodynamics, 109
pharmacokinetics, 109
pharmacotherapies *see* drug-based treatments
phenylketunoria (PKU), 60
  DNA mutations, 80
  impaired executive functioning, 355
  inheritance of, 291–92, 292f
  recessive allele in, 77, 77f
philosophy, 10, 11, 28
phobias, 479, 559–61, 603–4b
phonemes, 200, 201, 256, 321–23
photoreceptors, 161–63
phrenology, 11
physics, 55, 56t
physiological approach, 11, 56t, 68f
  biological processes, 22
  brain function, 22, 23
  determinism, 22
  evolutionary explanations, limitations of, 23
  forms of explanation, 15b
  heredity, study of, 23
  reductionism, 22, 23
  techniques, 22
Piaget's theory of cognitive development
  abstract tasks, 305, 308b

concrete operations stage, 306b, 307f
conservation tasks, 305, 308b
discovery play, 305
formal operations stage, 306b
moral development, 307–9
pre-operational stage, 306b, 307f
sensorimotor stage, 299–305
  accommodation, 300b, 311
  adaptation, 300b
  assimilation, 300b, 311
  cross-modal integration, 303
  direct perception, 303
  equilibration, 300b
  object permanence, 301–3
  object properties, 303–5
  schema, 300b
  size constancy, 303
  specific heredity, 300b
  stage theory, 301, 302f
  substages of, 301b
social processes, 305
pictograms, 336–37
pineal gland, 114f
pinna, 170f
pituitary gland, 114f
  anterior and posterior, 114, 116f
  hypothalamus, 114–15
PKU *see* phenylketunoria
placebo effect, 614
plagiarism, 745
platykurtic distribution, 673, 673f
polygraph (lie detector), 69, 460b, 462b
polymerase chain reaction (PCR), 82
polymorphisms, 80
polypeptides, 80
pons, 156–58
Ponzo illusion, 184–85, 185f
populations
  confidence intervals, 693
  standard error
    effect in the population, 692
    sampling distribution, 692
    sampling variation, 692

Subject Index

standard error of the mean (SE), 693
see also sampling
Positive and negative Affect Schedule (PANAS), 462b
positively skewed distribution, 672–73, 673f
positivism, 368
see also logical positivism
positron emission tomography *see* PET scans
post-test only control gout design, 660–61, 660f, 662–63b, 663f
post-test only two-condition repeated measures design, 661, 662f, 663–64b, 664f
post-traumatic stress disorder (PTSD)
  'conceptual bracket creep,' 574
  controversies in study of, 574
  emotional processing theory, 573
  faked symptoms, 574
  'mental defeat,' 573
  nature of, 572
  recovered memories of trauma, 574
  stress, 574
  theory of shattered assumptions, 573
  vulnerability factors, 572–73
postcentral gyrus, 96f
posterior (brain region), 94f
posterior pituitary, 114f
postgraduate training
  counselling psychology, 714
  educational psychology, 715–16
  forensic psychology, 716–17
  health psychology, 717
  neuropsychology, 718
  research, 720
pre-natal development
  cell differentiation, 290
  cell division, 290
  cell migration, 290
  chromosomes, 290
  environmental influences, 290
  ...us, 290
  ...s, 290

habituation, 290, 291b
zygote formation, 290
pre-test/post-test control group design, 661, 661f, 663b, 663f
pre-test/post-test two condition repeated measures design, 662, 662f
precentral gyrus, 96f
predictive validity, 71–72, 537t
prefrontal cortex, 134, 139, 140f, 154
prefrontal neocortex, 140f
prejudice
  attitude formation, 380–81
  discrimination, 444–45
presynaptic terminal, 91f
primacy effect, 251
primary motor cortex, 174
primary olfactory cortex, 171f
priming paradigms, 382
Principles of Physiological Psychology (Wundt), 13t
Principles of Psychology (James), 14t
Principles of Psychology (Spencer), 13t
prisoners and guards experiment (Zimbardo), 39
pro-social behaviour, 349
  altruism, 422–23
  bystander intervention, 423–24
  empathy, 422
  helping, 421
  negative state relief theory, 422–23
probability, and hypotheses
  errors, Types I and II, 696
  one- and two-tailed tests, 695–96
  statistical models, 693
  statistical significance
    effect size, 694–95
    null hypothesis, 'rejection' of, 695
    p-value, of test statistic, 695
  test statistics, 694–95
problem-solving,
  analogies, 267–68
  barriers to success, 265–66

behaviourist theories, 264
general problem solver model
  algorithms, 268, 268b
  heuristics, 268–69, 268b
  initial state, 268
  intermediate states, 268
  means-end analysis, 269
  operations, 268
  subgoals, 269
Gestalt theories, 264–65
well- *versus* ill-defined problems, 264
progressive ratio (PR) schedules, 140b
see also reinforcement
prolactin, 116f
prosopagnosia, 193
proteins
  amino acids, 78–79
  codons, 80
  DNA transcription, 80, 82f
  messenger Ribonucleic Acid (mRNA), 78–79, 82f, 83f
  ribosomes, 80
  transfer Ribonucleic Acid (tRNA), 80, 82f
proxemics, 418, 419b
Prozac, 23, 596t, 597
psychoanalytic theory
  abnormal psychology, 547
  cultural impact, 18, 18b
  developmental stages, 17, 494, 495
  early school, 13, 15b
  ego-psychologists, 494
  Erikson's life-span theory, 494, 496
  evaluation of, 18–19
  methodology, 17–18, 19
  mind, structure of, 17, 17f
  neo-Freudians, 494
  personality, structure of, 17
  preconscious processes, 491
  unconscious/conscious processes, 491, 494, 494f, 497
psychobiology
  applications of, 69b
  definition of, 66
  genetic research tools, 66

multidisciplinary, 66–69
reductionism, 66, 67f
subdisciplines of, 66–69
psychological disorders, 558–93
Psychological Society of Great
    Britain, 13t
psychologists
    activities of, 3–6
    versus psychiatrists, 550t
    see also careers, in psychology
psychology
    applications of, 2–3
    forerunners of, 11–12
    skills of, 1, 712–13
    subject matter of, 1–2
psychology curriculum, 6–7
psychometric tests
    acquiescence/social
        desirability, 538–39
    versus assessment, 531
    categories of, 532–33
    cognitive tests, 531, 533–34
    criterion-referenced tests, 532
    cultural bias, 539–41
    definition of, 530
    ecological validity, 539
    employee selection, 533
    ideographic tests, 533
    intelligence tests, 519–21,
        534b, 538b
    mood/environmental
        influences, 539
    normative tests, 532, 533t
        mean score, 532
        normal distribution curve,
            532, 532f
        range, 532
        standard deviation, 532
        Wechsler IQ scores, 532,
            533t
    objectivity, 531
    personality tests, 534–36
    psychological tests, BPS
        definition of, 532b
    questionnaire design, 71
    standardisation, 531, 536
    test, definition of, 531
    test reliability, 536–37
    test validity, 537, 537t
    uses of, 531

psychopathology *see* abnormal
    psychology
psychopharmacology, 68f
    DA hypothesis of
        schizophrenia, 108–9b
    drug action, 109
        agonists, 109, 110b
        antagonists, 109
        competitive and non-
            competitive, 109, 110f
        inverse agonists, 109, 110b
        partial agonists, 109
    drug classification, 108
    drug research, as inconclusive,
        109
    habituation, 121b
    neurotransmission,
        modification by drugs,
        110–12
psychophysiology, 68f
psychostimulants, 140–41
psychotherapies
    defence mechanisms, 599
    libido, 599
    methods of, 598
    stages of development, 599
    techniques of, 599–600
psychotherapists, 550t
psychotherapy, 497
punishment, 129f
    features of, 128–29
    positive and negative, 128
    problems with, 129
    see also reinforcement
pupil, 161f
Pygmalion effect, 36
pyramidal motor system, 174

Q
qualitative methods
    discourse analysis, 571,
        648–49
    grounded theory, 649
    versus quantitative methods,
        648, 649t
    social constructionism, 369
quantitative methods
    confidence levels, 647
    fit, of statistical models, 648
    report writing, 742–43

research process, summary of,
    647, 647f
statistical models, 647–48
statistics, use of, 646–48
quasi-experiments, 32, 50, 664–65
questionnaires, 13t, 297, 462b, 571

R
racism, scientific
    biological assumptions of,
        45–46
    evaluation of, 47–48b
    evidence of, 24b
    problems with, 46–47
    racial difference studies, 46,
        47t
    racist theories, 45, 46b
random sampling, 658–59, 660
range
    interquartile range, 677–78
    lower quartile, 677–78
    normative tests, 532
    upper quartile, 677–78
raphe nucleus, 157
ratio data, 642
rational-emotive therapy, 609–10
Ravens Progressive Matrices,
    540–41
reaction formation, 17, 19
reading
    acquired dyslexias, 257b, 258
    cognitive skills development,
        336–37
    connectionist modelling, 337
    dual-route model, 257–58,
        258t, 335
    Frith's stage theory, 335–36,
        336b
    letter/sound correspondences,
        336
    orthography, 257
    phonological skills, 257–58,
        335–37
    short-term memory (STM),
        337
    visual/phonological routes,
        257–58
    vocabulary development, 336,
        337
recency effect, 251

Subject Index

receptors
   autoreceptors, 107, 108f
   DA receptors (D1 and D2),
      140–41
   heteroreceptors, 107, 108t
   ionotropic receptors, 106, 107,
      107f
   metabotropic receptors, 106,
      107, 107f
   photoreceptors, 161–63
reductionism
   abnormal psychology, 545–47
   bias, 58
   biological, 54
   determinism, 58, 59
   experimental, 55
   levels of explanation, 55–58,
      55t
   machine reductionism, 55
   neurogenetic explanations, 57
   physiological, 22, 23, 54
   psychobiology, 66, 67f
   rejection of by Gestalt school,
      13
reflexes
   afferent neurons, 121, 122f
   efferent neurons, 122, 122f
   interneurons, 121–22, 122f
   motor neurons, 122f
   reflex, 121, 122f
reflexive discourse, 11
reformist delusions, 551
reinforcement, 129f
   acquisition, 131
   discriminative stimuli (SD),
      132–33b
   extinction, 130f, 132
   generalisation, 132
   interoceptive/exteroceptive
      stimuli, 132
   positive/negative, 128, 129f
   primary/secondary, 128
   punishment, 128–29
   schedules of, 130b
      continuous reinforcement
         schedules (CRF), 129,
         142
      cumulative chart of, 130f
      fixed interval (FI)
         schedules, 130f, 131

   fixed ratio (FR) schedules,
      130, 130f, 133b, 140b,
      142
   partial reinforcement, 129,
      130f
   progressive ratio (PR)
      schedules, 140b
   variable interval (VI)
      schedules, 130f, 131,
      133b
   variable ratio (VR)
      schedules, 130–31
   shaping of successive
      approximations, 131–32
   spontaneous recovery, 132
   see also operant conditioning
reinforcement sensitivity theory,
   507
REM sleep, 156–58
Remembering (Bartlett), 14t
renin, 148
repeated measures design, 659–60,
   704
   post-test only two-condition,
      661, 662f
   pre-test/post-test two
      condition, 662, 662f
repisodes, 238
report writing, 683–84, 742–47
representations, 316
   enactive, 313
   iconic, 313
   implicit/explicit knowledge,
      313
   representational-redescription
      (RR) model
      abstraction level, 314, 316
      E2 level, 314, 316
      explicit level, 316
      implicit level, 314, 316
      language abilities, 316
      microgenetic study in
         support of, 316
      stage-theory, rejection of,
         316
   speech and gestures, 313–14
   symbolic representations, 313
repression
   childhood amnesia, 238
   forgetting, 234–35

   unconscious processes, 17
research, as a career, 719
residual schizophrenia, 581t
resources, accessing, 747–48
reticular formation, 98, 156, 172f
retina,
   binocular vision, 165
   bipolar cells, 162f, 163, 164,
      164f
   blind spot, 161f, 162, 162b
   complex cells, 167, 167f
   fovea, 161f, 162
   hypercomplex cells, 195b
   lateral geniculate nucleus
      (LGN), 165–66, 166f
   lateral inhibition, 164–65, 165f
   nasal hemiretina, 165, 166f
   optic nerve, 161f, 162, 162f,
      165, 166f
   photoreceptors, 161–63
   receptive fields, 162f, 163,
      163b, 166, 167, 195b
   retinal ganglion cells, 163, 164f
   rhodopsin, 162
   rods and cones, 161–62,
      163–64
   simple and complex cells, 166,
      167f, 195b
   temporal hemiretina, 165, 166f
   visual cortex, 166
   see also vision
retinal ganglion cells, 162f
retrospective questionnaire
   studies, 571
revision, 745–47
rhodopsin, 162
Ringelmann effect, 436, 437b
road rage, 424–25, 426b
rod receptors, 162f
rods and cones, 161–62, 163–64
Rogerian therapist, computer
   emulation of, 22
Rorschach inkblot test, 535
round window, 170f
Ruffin's ending, 172f

S
saccule, 174f
sadness, 453t
sagittal plane (brain), 94f

salt, 147
salutatory conduction, 100
sampling
    cluster sampling, 668
    opportunity sampling, 668–69
    quota sampling, 668
    random sampling, 668
    representativeness, 51
    snowball sampling, 669
    systematic sampling, 668
    variation, 676
    volunteer sampling, 669
    see also populations
satellite cells, 88
satiety, 468b
scaffolding, 317–18
scatterplots, 686f, 687–88
schemata
    associative networks, 365, 366f
    categories, 364–65
    cultural knowledge, 242
    event schemata, 366b
    person schemata, 366b
    role schemata, 366b
    scenes, 243
    schema, 366b, 367
    scripts, 242–43, 243b
    self-schemata, 366b
    uses and abuses of, 243
schizophrenia, 54, 112
    biochemical factors, 582
    biological/psychological causes, 545–46, 546b
    catatonic schizophrenia, 581t
    concordance studies, 581–82, 583t
    cultural definitions, 550–51
    DA hypothesis of, 108–9b
    diagnosis of, 580
    diathesis-stress mode, 580–81
    disorganized, 581t
    drug-based treatments, 596–97
    DSM-IV description of, 580
    experience of, 579–80
    expressed emotion (EE), 583–84
    inherited disposition, 581–82
    maladaptive behaviour, 552
    neo-analytic perspectives, 582–83
    operant reinforcement methods, 546
    paranoid schizophrenia, 581t
    prevalence of, 580
    residual schizophrenia, 581t
    subtypes of, 580, 581t
    vulnerability factors, 582
schools, of psychology, 12–13
science
    aims of, 30, 33
    appeal of, 28–29
    assumptions of, 30, 33
    development of, 29
    epistemology, 28
    new paradigm research, 40
    psychology as, 28, 33, 39–40
Science and Human Behaviour (Skinner), 14t
science of mind, development of, 11–12
scientific method
    hypothetico-deductive method, 30–31, 31f, 48–49
    see also hypotheses; theories
Scientific Procedures Act (1986), 70
sclera, 161f
seasonal affective disorder (SAD), 573
secondary motor cortex, 174
selective serotonin reuptake inhibitors (SSRIs), 112, 596t, 597
self
    definition of, 477, 478
    development of, 471–72, 478t, 479
    executive/categorical, 340, 341–42
    ideal/ought, 19, 477
    personal/relational, 477
    see also adolescence; attachment; identity; theory of mind
self-concept
    adult imitation, 341
    ethnic identity, 342
    ethnocentrism, 43
    self-description, 342
    self-other distinction, 340–42
    spontaneous, 477b
self-efficacy theory, 469–70, 472b, 500
self-esteem, 378, 417, 447, 453, 482–83
self-fulfilling prophecies, 576, 577f
self-knowledge
    egocentricity, 481
    explicit feedback, 481–82
    reflected appraisal, 481
    social identity theory, 481
    socialisation/group membership, 480–81
self-serving biases, 406–7
semantic differential scales, 381–82, 381b, 411
semantic memory, 221, 222
    attribute model of, 241
    concepts, 239
    individual-specific, 241
    prototype model of, 241–42, 242t
    semantic priming, 241
    spreading activation model, 239, 240f, 241
    typicality effect, 239, 240f
    see also schemata
semicircular canals, 174, 174f
sensation-seeking, 507–8
sensitisation of incentive salience, 143–44
sensory cortex, 154f
sensory nuclei (thalamus), 154f
separation anxiety disorder (SAD), 593
septum, 140f
sequential research design studies, 296b
serotonin (5-HT), 23, 101f, 102, 103, 104t, 112, 113b, 143, 146, 157, 576
sex chromosomes, 77–78, 116
sex differences, 343, 508–9, 508b
    see also gender
shadowing, 206, 207b, 208
Sherif's realistic conflict theory, 445–46
short-term memory (STM)
    levels of processing, 230
    and LTM, distinction between

Subject Index

capacity, 223, 223b, 224b
duration, 223–25
encoding, 225, 225b
neuropsychology, 226, 227b
serial position effect, 225f, 226
modal model of memory
connected memory stores, 227–28
rehearsal, 227, 228, 228f
retrieval, 227, 228f
purpose of, 228–29
short-term memory systems, 221
working memory, 229–30
see also memory
siblings, 282b
Siegler's balancing rules experiments, 312, 315b
signal detection theory (SDT), 205–6
skewness, 672–73
skill acquisition (Anderson)
associative stage, 276
automatic actions, 276
autonomous stage, 276, 277f
cognitive stage, 275–76
declarative knowledge, 275–76
procedural knowledge, 276
Stroop effect, 276–77
skin, 89f, 172f
Skinner box, 128, 129illus, 132–33b
skull, 87, 90f
sleep, psychobiology of
alpha activity, 155
beta activity, 155
delta waves, 155–56
dreams, 156
need for, 157–58
neural mechanisms of, 156–57
and neurotransmitters, 157
PGO waves, 157
REM sleep, 156–58
sleep deprivation, 158b, 159, 159b
sleep spindles, 155, 158
slow wave sleep, 156
stages of, 155–56
sorders, 158–59
g pills, 157

smoking, effects of on unborn child, 288–89
Social Attitude Inventory (Eysenck), 38
social constructionism, 368–69
antiscientific, 25
assumptions of, 23
attitudes, 25–26t
core processes, 368
discourse analysis, 23–24b, 369
forms of explanation, 15b
intelligence, 515
language, as central, 369
positivism, 23, 368
qualitative methods, 369
subjectivity, 25
uses of, 24–25
Social Darwinism, 12
social drive theory, 435
social influence
Asch's line experiments, 432
compliance, 430
conformity, 430, 431, 433
conversion, 433–34
free-riding, 436
informational and normative, 432–33
majority influence, 431, 432
power and influence, 430–31, 431b
prototype person, 438
Ringelmann effect, 436, 437b
Sherif's autokinetic effect experiment, 431–32, 433
single process account, 435
social compensation, 436
social facilitation/inhibition, 435–36
social identity, 433
social loafing, 436
social interaction
attraction, 418–21
culture, and learning (Vygotsky), 285
language acquisition, 323–25
non-verbal communication, 417–18
personality, 498–99
social learning theory

aggression, 426–27
behaviourism, 16
personality, 499–500
social phobia, 479
social psychology
categorisation and schema, 364–67
concerns of, 362–63
correlational research, 369
definitions of, 362, 362b
descriptive research, 369
discourse analysis, 371–72, 372b
ethics in, 373–74
experimental methods, 369–70
in hierarchy of sciences, 56t
history of, 363
non-experimental methods, 370–71
social cognition, 364
stereotyping, 367–68
social readjustment rating scale (SRRS), 627, 628–29t
social worker specialist, definition of, 550
sociobiology, 54
sociology, 56t
Soloman four-group design, 661, 662f
soluble gases, 101f
soma, 8, 91f
somatic nervous system (SNS), 86, 155
somatogenic hypothesis, 545
somatosensation, 171–72
somatosensory cortex, 172f
spatial frequency theory, 167–68
Spearman's two-factor theory, 519
specific language impairment (SLI), 334b
speech perception
categorical perception, 201, 201f
invariance of, 199–200
phoneme restoration effect, 201
segmentation problem, 200, 200f
top-down processing, 201
Sperling's experiment, 222

spinal accessory cranial nerve, 90f
spinal cord, 87, 88f, 89f
spinoreticular tract, 172f, 173
spinotectal tract, 172f, 173
spinothalamic tract, 172f, 173
split-half reliability, 536, 643
sports psychology, 4t
standard deviation
    abbreviation for, 684
    calculation of, 680–81, 680b
    normative tests, 532
    and shape of distribution,
        680f, 681
    and Z-scores, 683
standard error, 684, 692–93
Stanford-Binet IQ test, 14t, 538b
stapes, 170f
statistical models of difference,
    700–707
statistical significance, 694–95
stem cell research, 91
stereotyping, 367–68
    automaticity, 367
    generalisations, 367
stigmatisation, 547, 548b, 549illus
stomach, 89f
strange situation, 345, 346b, 347
    see also attachment
stress
    adrenaline, 155
    chronic stressors, 627
    coping styles, 619, 630–31
    daily hassles, 627, 629–30
    definition of, 626–27
    impairment, 552
    social readjustment rating
        scale (SRRS), 627, 628–29t
striatum, 97, 105b, 106, 139, 140f,
    175, 175b
Stroop effect, 95, 215, 276–77, 567
structuralism, 12
study designs, 295, 296b
Study of Thinking, A (Bruner,
    Goodnow and Austin), 14t
study skills
    application of, 735–49
    definition of, 723–24
    effective learning, 725–35
    essay writing, 738–42
    exam procedures, 747

feedback and course
        evaluation, 748–49
    graduate skills, 724, 724b
    lectures and note-taking,
        736–37
    metacognition, 735–36
    plagiarism, avoiding, 743–45
    prerequisite skills, 724, 724b
    report writing, 742–47
    resources, accessing, 747–48
    revision, 745–47
subarachnoid space, 87, 90f
subfornical organ, 148
substance misuse
    addiction, 139
    amphetamine and cocaine,
        140–41
    drug-taking motivations, 138b
    giving up, 139b, 142–44
    immunological treatments,
        139b
    nicotine, 141–42
    reward pathways, 139–40
    theories of addiction, 143–44
substantia nigra, 97, 105b, 106,
    140f, 175b
subthalamic nucleus (STN)
    (brain), 105, 106
successful intelligence concept,
    747
suicide and parasuicide
    attempters and completers,
        characteristics of, 579t
    risk factors, 578–79
sulci (brain), 96
sum of squares, 679–80, 679t
superior olivary nuclei, 169, 170f
supplementary motor area (SMA),
    174
surprise, 453t
survey studies, 370, 571
survival of the fittest, 73
sweat glands, 89f
sylvian fissure (brain), 96f
symbolic play, 325
sympathetic nervous system,
    86–87, 89
synapse, 88, 91f, 102, 105f
synaptic regulation
    autoreceptors, 107, 108f

enzymatic metabolism, 108
    heteroreceptors, 107, 108t
    metabolites, 102–3f, 108
    presynaptic neuron, 107
    reuptake, 108
synaptic transmission
    excitatory and inhibitory
        pathways, 102, 105b
    neurotransmitters, 101–5
    postsynaptic neurons, 102
    receptors, 105, 107, 107f
syntax, 326b

T
T statistic, 702f, 703
t-test, independent, 701, 701f
    cognitive dissonance:
        Festinger and Carlsmith,
        662–63b, 663f
    degrees of freedom (df), 701
    t-distributions, 701
t-test, related, 702–3, 702f
    implicit attitudes: Greenwald
        et al., 663–64b, 664f, 708b
    t-distributions, 702
3-aminobuytyric acid (GABA),
    101f, 104, 104t, 105b, 110b, 157
tabula rasa concept (Locke), 13t,
    284
taste see gustatory system
Teachers and Researchers in
    Psychology Division (BPS), 3
teaching psychology, as a career,
    719–21
tectum, 172f
telencephalon, 96
temporal hemiretina, 165, 166f
temporal lobe, 96, 96f
teratogens, effects of on unborn
    child, 288–89
test development (Gesell), 284
test reliability, 536–37, 643
test-retest reliability, 537, 643
test validity, 537, 537t
testes, 114f
testosterone, 117, 154
thalamus, 96, 96f, 106
thalidomide, 289
thematic apperception test (TAT),
    535–36, 535f

Subject Index

theology/medicine/education, and psychology, 11
theoretical approaches, evaluating, 26b
theories, 638–39, 650b
   see also hypotheses; qualitative methods; quantitative methods
theory of mind
   autism, 351, 353–56
   child's 'desire' theory, 353
   counterfactual reasoning, 353
   decoupler, 352
   eye direction detector (EDD), 351–52
   false belief task, 351b
   metarepresentations, 352
   mindmindedness, 352
   origins of, 351–53
   peer interaction, 353
   pretend play, 352
   'simulation,' 353
   triadic relationships, 351–52
theory of planned behaviour (TPB), 383–84, 383f
theory of reasoned action (TRA), 383–84
therapies *see* treatments/therapies
thirst, 147–48
   angiotensis, 466
   extracellular/intracellular, 466
   homeostasis, 466b
   osmosis, 147, 466
three-way repeated measures ANOVA, 706
Thurston scale, 381
Thurstone's factor analytic theory, 519–20
thymine, 80f
thyroid, 114f
thyroid-stimulating hormone (TSH), 116f
time-series design, 705
tolerance, drug, 125b, 144f
touch
   anterior lateral system, 171–172
   al column, 171–72
   ceptive messages, 171–72
   components of, 171, 172

somatosensory cortex, 172, 173f
tactile stimuli, transmission of, 171–172
trait theory (personality), 492
   Cattell's sixteen-trait theory, 503–4
   extroversion/psychoticism/neuroticism (Eysenck), 502–3f
   factor analysis, 504
   five-trait theories (Big Five), 504, 506b
   heritability, 503
   introversion-extroversion/thinking-feeling/sensation-intuition (Jung), 502
   Sixteen Personality Factor (16PF) test, 504
   three-trait theories, 502–3
   traits, definition of, 502b, 505
transfer Ribonucleic Acid (tRNA), 80, 82f
transference, 599–600
transverse plane (brain), 94f
treatments/therapies
   behaviour therapies, 602–9
   biological treatments, 595–98
   cognitive therapy, 609–10
   effectiveness of
      criteria for, 612, 614b
      evidence in support of, 616
      internal validity, 614–15
      placebo effect, 614
      randomised controlled trials (RCT), 614–15
      spontaneous remission, 612
   family therapy, 611–12, 613b
   group therapies, 610–11
   humanistic therapies, 600–602
   psychotherapies, 598–600
Treisman's attenuator model of selective attention, 206–7, 208f
Treisman's feature integration model, 210–11
tricyclic anti-depressants, 596t, 597
trigeminal cranial nerve, 90f

trigeminal facial motor nuclei, 153f
trochlear cranial nerve, 90f
tryptophan, 103
twin studies
   behavioural genetics, 81, 510–11b
   intelligence, 293, 527
   language development, 324, 324b
   monozygotic/dizygotic twins, 81, 293
   research methods, 521b
two-way independent ANOVA, 706
two-way mixed ANOVA, 705–6, 706f
   blame the teachers: Rosenthal and Jacobson, 663b, 663f, 708b
tympanic membrane, 169, 170f
tyrosine, 103

U
U statistic, 702
UK National Child Development Study, 348
unconditioned response (UCR), 123, 124–26
   see also classical conditioning
unconditioned stimulus (UCS), 123, 123f, 124, 125f, 126
   see also classical conditioning
unconscious processes, 13, 17, 491, 494, 494f, 497, 547
undifferentiated schizophrenia, 581t
universal grammar, 326, 327f, 332
utricle, 174f

V
vagus nerve, 90f, 146
validity
   animal models of behaviour, 71–72
   concurrent validity, 537t
   construct validity, 72, 537t
   content validity, 643
   criterion validity, 643
   ecological validity, 539, 644
   experiments, 32

external validity, 34
face validity, 72, 537t
impression management, 382
internal validity, 34, 614–15
predictive validity, 71–72, 537t
Valium, 596t, 597
variability, 676–77
variable interval (VI) schedules, 130f, 131, 133b
see also reinforcement
variable ratio (VR) schedules, 130–31
see also reinforcement
variables, 639–40
cause and effect, 644–45
confounding, 370
direct and indirect measurement, 639–40
discrete/continuous, 642–43
extraneous, 659
independent/dependent (predictor/outcome), 400, 400f, 642–43, 700
levels of, 658
variance, 678–81
variance measure, 680
variation, 659
vasopressin, 116f, 148
ventral posterior nucleus, 172f
ventral tegmental area (VTA), 139, 140f, 141, 153f
ventromedial hypothalamus, 145f
Vernon's hierarchical model of intelligence, 520

vestibular nerve, 170f
vestibular system, 174, 174f
vestibulocochlear cranial nerve, 90f
'Viennese Circle,' of philosophers, 29
vision
experience, 168–69
the eye, 161f
hypercolumns, 168
spatial frequency theory, 167–68
see also retina
vivisection, 70
VMA, 103
Völkpsychologie (folk psychologists), 363
vomoronasal organ, 171f

W
Wallace, Glenda, 714
website, for this book!, 7
Wechsler Adult Intelligence Scale (WAIS-R), 223b, 526, 534b, 538b
Weiner's attribution model (motivation)
controllability, 402
defensive attributional bias, 403b
locus of control, 402, 470–71, 472b
outcome-dependent affects, 402–3

responsibility and blame, 403–4, 403b
stability, 402
Wernike's area, 93
Wilcoxon signed-rank test, 702f, 703
Williams syndrome, 327
withdrawal symptoms, 143
within-subjects design *see* repeated measures design
Wolffian and Mullerian systems (hormones), 116
working memory, 22, 217
central executive, 229, 229f
phonological loop, 229–30, 229f
visuospatial scratchpad, 229–30, 229f
and vocabulary learning, 230b
see also memory
World Health Organization (WHO), 553, 619

Y
Yale model of persuasive communication, 388, 388f

Z
Z-scores, 682–83, 751–58
Zimbardo experiment, 39
zone of proximal development (ZPD), 317, 317f
Zyban (bupropion), 143
zygotes, 78, 290